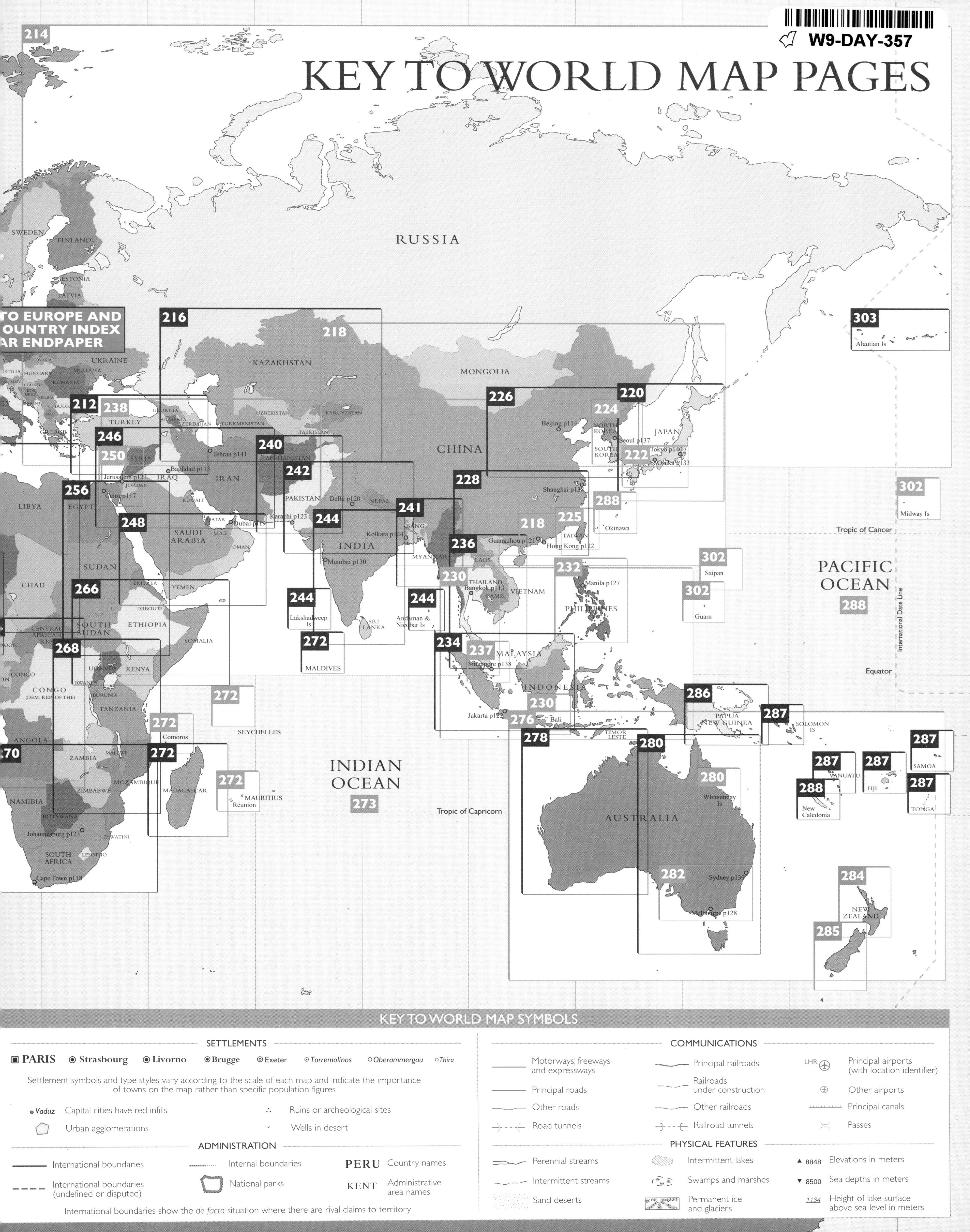
KEY TO WORLD MAP PAGES
214
TO EUROPE AND
COUNTRY INDEX
AR ENDPAPER
RUSSIA
SWEDEN
FINLAND
ESTONIA
LATVIA
UKRAINE
MOLDOVA
HUNGARY
ROMANIA
BULG.
GREECE
TURKEY
GEORGIA
ARMENIA
AZERBAIJAN
TURKMENISTAN
UZBEKISTAN
KYRGYZSTAN
TAJIKISTAN
KAZAKHSTAN
MONGOLIA
CHINA
AFGHANISTAN
PAKISTAN
NEPAL
INDIA
IRAN
IRAQ
SYRIA
JORDAN
KUWAIT
QATAR
U.A.E.
OMAN
SAUDI ARABIA
YEMEN
LIBYA
EGYPT
SUDAN
CHAD
ERITREA
DJIBOUTI
ETHIOPIA
SOUTH SUDAN
CENTRAL AFRICAN REP.
SOMALIA
UGANDA
KENYA
RWANDA
BURUNDI
CONGO
CONGO (DEM. REP. OF THE)
TANZANIA
ANGOLA
ZAMBIA
MALAWI
MOZAMBIQUE
ZIMBABWE
NAMIBIA
BOTSWANA
SOUTH AFRICA
LESOTHO
ESWATINI
MADAGASCAR
MAURITIUS
Réunion
Comoros
SEYCHELLES
INDIAN OCEAN
MALDIVES
Lakshadweep Is
SRI LANKA
Andaman & Nicobar Is
BANG.
MYANMAR
LAOS
THAILAND
CAMB.
VIETNAM
PHILIPPINES
MALAYSIA
INDONESIA
Bali
TIMOR-LESTE
PAPUA NEW GUINEA
SOLOMON IS
AUSTRALIA
Whitsunday Is
NEW ZEALAND
New Caledonia
VANUATU
FIJI
SAMOA
TONGA
NORTH KOREA
SOUTH KOREA
JAPAN
TAIWAN
Okinawa
Saipan
Guam
Midway Is
Aleutian Is
PACIFIC OCEAN
Tropic of Cancer
Tropic of Capricorn
Equator
International Date Line
Tehran p141
Baghdad p115
Jerusalem p123
Cairo p117
Dubai p119
Karachi p123
Delhi p120
Kolkata p124
Mumbai p130
Beijing p114
Seoul p137
Tokyo p140
Osaka p133
Shanghai p135
Guangzhou p121
Hong Kong p122
Manila p127
Bangkok p113
Singapore p138
Jakarta p122
Sydney p139
Melbourne p128
Johannesburg p123
Cape Town p118
216
218
212
238
246
250
256
248
240
242
244
241
236
226
220
224
222
228
288
225
232
230
234
237
266
268
272
273
276
278
280
282
284
285
286
287
302
303
KEY TO WORLD MAP SYMBOLS
SETTLEMENTS
PARIS
Strasbourg
Livorno
Brugge
Exeter
Torremolinos
Oberammergau
Thira
Settlement symbols and type styles vary according to the scale of each map and indicate the importance of towns on the map rather than specific population figures
Vaduz
Capital cities have red infills
Urban agglomerations
Ruins or archeological sites
Wells in desert
ADMINISTRATION
International boundaries
International boundaries (undefined or disputed)
Internal boundaries
National parks
PERU
Country names
KENT
Administrative area names
International boundaries show the de facto situation where there are rival claims to territory
COMMUNICATIONS
Motorways, freeways and expressways
Principal roads
Other roads
Road tunnels
Principal railroads
Railroads under construction
Other railroads
Railroad tunnels
LHR
Principal airports (with location identifier)
Other airports
Principal canals
Passes
PHYSICAL FEATURES
Perennial streams
Intermittent streams
Sand deserts
Intermittent lakes
Swamps and marshes
Permanent ice and glaciers
8848
Elevations in meters
8500
Sea depths in meters
1134
Height of lake surface above sea level in meters

OXFORD

ATLAS

OF THE

WORLD

TWENTY-SIXTH EDITION

FOREWORD

An authoritative and serious reference work, the Oxford *Atlas of the World* is one of the finest atlases available anywhere in the world. The atlas incorporates computer-derived maps that have been produced using the very latest in digital cartographic techniques. Country names are shown in conventional English form and are those that are in common usage. They are the forms used by publications such as *Newsweek* and *The Washington Post*, and by the BBC and the British Foreign Office. Alternative country names appear in parentheses on the maps where space permits – for example, Myanmar (Burma) – and are cross-referenced in the index, for example, Ivory Coast = Côte d'Ivoire.

How to use the Atlas

The atlas is divided into a number of sections which are explained below.

World Statistics and "A Divided World: Land and Maritime Boundaries"

World statistics on topics such as area and population for every country in the world. Also included in this section is a listing of the world's largest cities by population, arranged in country alphabetical order. This section is followed by the highly topical "*A Divided World*" feature, which examines some of the major issues concerning land and maritime boundaries.

Images of Earth

A beautifully illustrated satellite imagery section showing 17 of the world's major cities and regions in the Americas, Europe, Africa, Asia, and Australasia.

Gazetteer of Nations

A comprehensive A–Z reference providing concise profiles of every country's geography, climate, history, politics, and economy, together with ready-reference tables, and illustrated with flags and locator maps.

World Geography

A richly informative section comprising 42 pages of maps, charts, graphs, and diagrams that explain key themes about the world in which we live. The topics covered include the Solar System, climate, the natural world, population, energy, and trade. Explanatory text on each spread describes the patterns shown by the data.

World Cities

A detailed selection of maps for 70 urban areas around the world. These are useful for planning trips abroad as well as for comparative studies of cities worldwide.

World Maps

An outstanding collection of 179 pages of distinctive Philip's cartography. The highly acclaimed physical world maps combine relief shading with layer-colored contours to give a striking visual picture of the Earth's surface. Roads, railroads, canals, and airports are accurately depicted on the maps, and towns and cities are clearly marked. More information on the key features employed in the construction and presentation of the maps is given on the facing page.

Geographical Glossary and Index

The 86,000-name index to the world maps includes geographical features as well as towns and cities, with both latitude/longitude and letter/figure grid references. Preceding the index is a list of geographical terms from various foreign languages that may be found in the place names on the maps and also in the index, together with their meanings.

Specialist Geography Consultants

The editors are grateful to the following for their contributions to the '*World Geography*' section in this atlas:

Dr Dibyesh Anand, John Burden, Peter Grego, Keith Lye, Garrett Nagle, Ross Reynolds, Robin Scagell, John Woodruff

The editors would also like to thank **Richard Chiles** and the staff at **NPA Satellite Mapping, CGG Services (UK) Ltd, Edenbridge, Kent, UK** (www.npa.cgg.com) for sourcing and processing the satellite imagery that appears in the atlas.

Gazetteer of Nations
Text Keith Lye/Philip's

Photographic Acknowledgements
Alamy /*AlamyCelebrity* 82, /*Jon Arnold Images Ltd* 91, /*B.A.E. Inc.* 79, /*Jens Benninghofen* 11 (center), /*Chessocampo* 8, 9, /*Mark Conlin* 85 (bottom), /*David R. Frazier Photolibrary, Inc.* 98, /*Søren Lund Hviid* 101, /*Images and Stories* 94, /*Galen Rowell/Mountain Light* 11 (bottom), /*Kevin Schafer* 85 (top), /*Travel Pix* 13 (top), /*Xinhua* 107 /*ZUMA Press Inc.* 93 (left & right);
Copernicus Sentinel data 2017 / NPA Satellite Mapping, CGG Services (UK) Ltd 11 (top);
Corbis /*Jay Dickman* 109 (top), /*Gideon Mendel* 89 (top), /*Liba Taylor* 104, /*David Turnley* 109 (bottom);
© Crown copyright 2007. Published by the Met Office, UK 80;
Galaxy Picture Library /*Robin Scagell* 73;
Getty Images /*Alexis Huguet/AFP* 94, /*Hannele Lahti* 85 (center);
Garrett Nagle 87;
NASA 13 (bottom), /ESA, HFF team (STScl) 68, /GSFC 81 (bottom);
NSIDC courtesy J. Maslanik and M. Tschudi, University of Colorado 81 (top);
NPA Satellite Mapping, CGG Services (UK) Ltd 14–33, 66-67, 110–111, 144–145, 156–157, 208–209, 252–253, 274–275, 290–291, 324–325;
Science Photo Library /*Sputnik* 97.

Star Charts (page 69)
Wil Tirion

Cartography by Philip's

World Cities

Page 121, Edinburgh, and page 125, London:
This product includes mapping data licensed from Ordnance Survey® with the permission of the Controller of Her Majesty's Stationery Office. © Crown copyright 2019. All rights reserved. Licence number 100011710.

www.philips-maps.co.uk

Philip's, a division of Octopus Publishing Group Limited (www.octopusbooks.co.uk)
Carmelite House, 50 Victoria Embankment, London EC4Y 0DZ
An Hachette UK Company (www.hachette.co.uk)

Published in North America by
Oxford University Press USA
198 Madison Avenue
New York, NY 10016

www.oup.com/us

OXFORD UNIVERSITY PRESS — Oxford is a registered trademark of Oxford University Press

Library of Congress Cataloging-in-Publication Data available

ISBN 978-0-19-006581-2

Printing (last digit): 9 8 7 6 5 4 3 2 1

Printed in Malaysia

USER GUIDE

The reference maps which form the main body of this atlas have been prepared in accordance with the highest standards of international cartography to provide an accurate and detailed representation of the Earth. The scales and projections used have been carefully chosen to give balanced coverage of the world, while emphasizing the most densely populated and economically significant regions. A hallmark of Philip's mapping is the use of hill shading and relief coloring to create a graphic impression of landforms: this makes the maps exceptionally easy to read. However, knowledge of the key features employed in the construction and presentation of the maps will enable the reader to derive the fullest benefit from the atlas.

Map Sequence

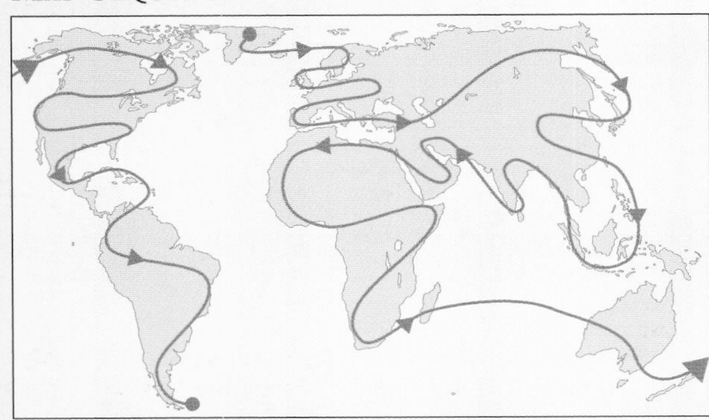

The atlas covers the Earth continent by continent: first Europe; then its land neighbor Asia (mapped north before south, in a clockwise sequence), then Africa, Australia and Oceania, North America, and South America. This is the classic arrangement adopted by most cartographers since the 16th century. For each continent, there are maps at a variety of scales. First, physical relief and political maps of the whole continent; then a series of larger-scale maps of the regions within the continent, each followed, where required, by still larger-scale maps of the most important or densely populated areas. The governing principle is that by turning the pages of the atlas, the reader moves steadily from north to south through each continent, with each map overlapping its neighbors.

Map Presentation

With very few exceptions (for example, for the Arctic and Antarctica), the maps are drawn with north at the top, regardless of whether they are presented upright or sideways on the page. In the borders will be found the map title; a locator diagram showing the area covered; continuation arrows showing the page numbers for maps of adjacent areas; the scale; the projection used; the degrees of latitude and longitude; and the letters and figures used in the index for locating place names and geographical features. Physical relief maps also have a height reference panel identifying the colors used for each layer of contouring.

Map Symbols

Each map contains a vast amount of detail which can only be conveyed clearly and accurately by the use of symbols. Points and circles of varying sizes locate and identify the relative importance of towns and cities; different styles of type are employed for administrative, geographical, and regional place names to aid identification. A variety of pictorial symbols denote landforms such as glaciers, marshes, and coral reefs, and man-made structures including roads, railroads, airports, and canals. International borders are shown by red lines. Where neighboring countries are in dispute, for example in parts of the Middle East, the maps show the *de facto* boundary between nations, regardless of the legal or historical situation.

The symbols are explained on the front endpapers of the atlas.

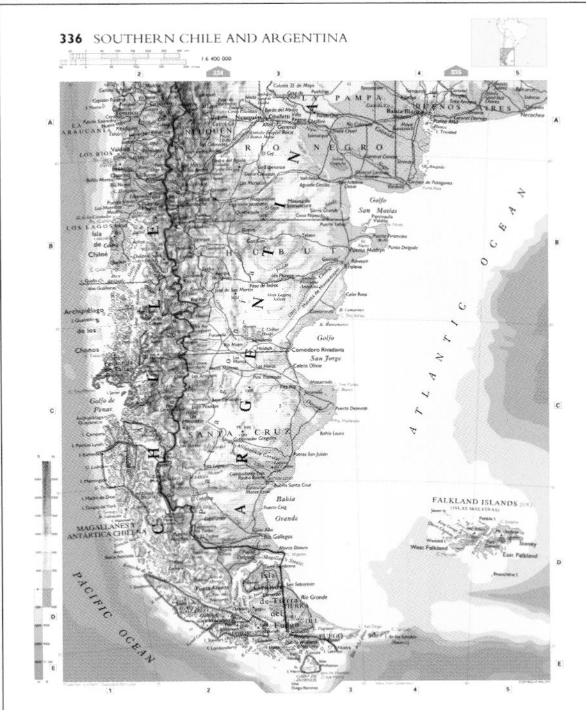

Map Scales

1:16 000 000
1 inch = 252 statute miles

The scale of each map is given in the numerical form known as the "representative fraction." The first figure is always one, signifying one unit of distance on the map; the second figure, usually in millions, is the number by which the map unit must be multiplied to give the equivalent distance on the Earth's surface. Calculations can easily be made in centimeters and kilometers, by dividing the Earth units figure by 100 000 (i.e. deleting the last five 0s). Thus 1:1 000 000 means 1 cm = 10 km. The calculation for inches and miles is more laborious, but 1 000 000 divided by 63 360 (the number of inches in a mile) shows that 1:1 000 000 means approximately 1 inch = 16 miles. The table below provides distance equivalents for scales down to 1:50 000 000.

LARGE SCALE

1:1 000 000	1 cm = 10 km	1 inch = 16 miles
1:2 500 000	1 cm = 25 km	1 inch = 39.5 miles
1:5 000 000	1 cm = 50 km	1 inch = 79 miles
1:6 000 000	1 cm = 60 km	1 inch = 95 miles
1:8 000 000	1 cm = 80 km	1 inch = 126 miles
1:10 000 000	1 cm = 100 km	1 inch = 158 miles
1:15 000 000	1 cm = 150 km	1 inch = 237 miles
1:20 000 000	1 cm = 200 km	1 inch = 316 miles
1:50 000 000	1 cm = 500 km	1 inch = 790 miles

SMALL SCALE

Measuring Distances

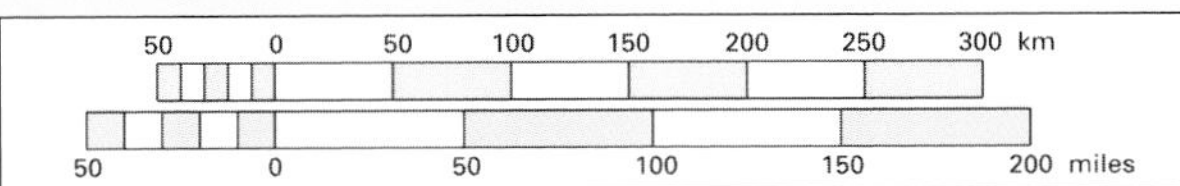

Although each map is accompanied by a scale bar, distances cannot always be measured with confidence because of the distortions involved in portraying the curved surface of the Earth on a flat page. As a general rule, the larger the map scale, the more accurate and reliable will be the distance measured. On small-scale maps such as those of the world and of entire continents, measurement may only be accurate along the "standard parallels," or central axes, and should not be attempted without considering the map projection.

Map Projections

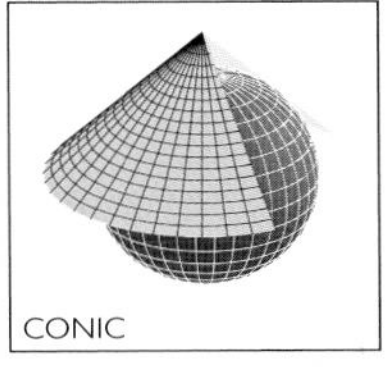

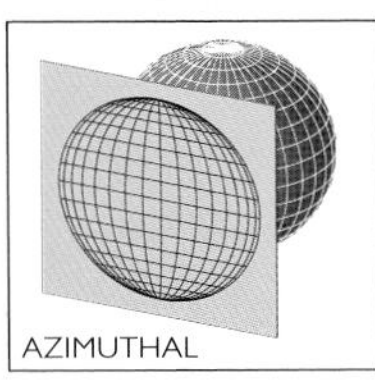

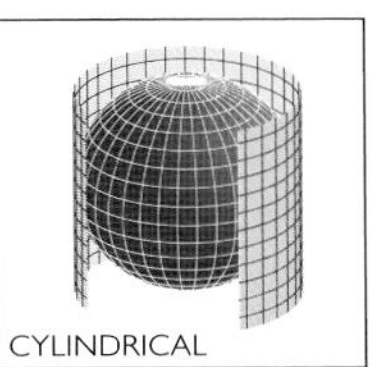

Unlike a globe, no flat map can give a true scale representation of the world in terms of area, shape, and position of every region. Each of the numerous systems that have been devised for projecting the curved surface of the Earth on to a flat page involves the sacrifice of accuracy in one or more of these elements. The variations in shape and position of land masses such as Alaska, Greenland, and Australia, for example, can be quite dramatic when different projections are compared.

For this atlas, the guiding principle has been to select projections that involve the least distortion of size and distance. The projection used for each map is noted in the border. Most fall into one of three categories – conic, azimuthal, or cylindrical – whose basic concepts are shown above. Each involves plotting the forms of the Earth's surface on a grid of latitude and longitude lines, which may be shown as parallels, curves, or radiating spokes.

Latitude and Longitude

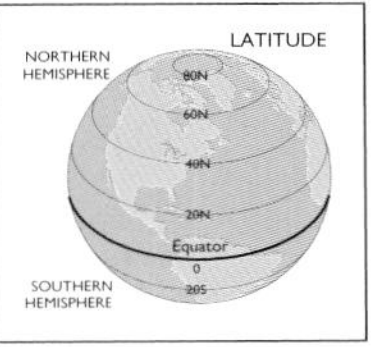

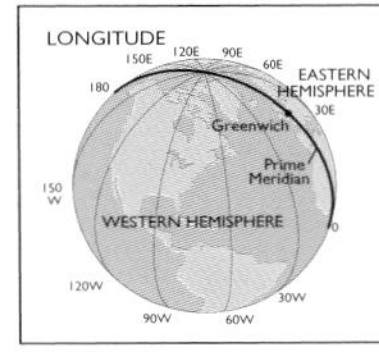

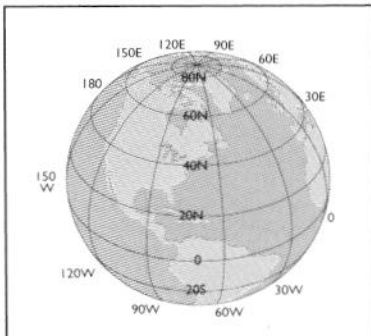

Accurate positioning of individual points on the Earth's surface is made possible by reference to the geometrical system of latitude and longitude. Latitude *parallels* are drawn west–east around the Earth and numbered by degrees north and south of the Equator, which is designated 0° of latitude. Longitude *meridians* are drawn north–south and numbered by degrees east and west of the *prime meridian*, 0° of longitude, which passes through Greenwich in England. By referring to these coordinates and their subdivisions of minutes (1/60th of a degree) and seconds (1/60th of a minute), any place on Earth can be located to within a few hundred meters. Latitude and longitude are indicated by blue lines on the maps; they are straight or curved according to the projection employed. Reference to these lines is the easiest way of determining the relative positions of places on different maps, and for plotting compass directions.

Name Forms

For ease of reference, both English and local name forms appear in the atlas. Oceans, seas, and countries are shown in English throughout the atlas; country names may be abbreviated to their commonly accepted form (for example, Germany, not The Federal Republic of Germany). Conventional English forms are also used for place names on the smaller-scale maps of the continents. However, local name forms are used on all large-scale and regional maps, with the English form given in brackets only for important cities – the large-scale map of Russia and Northern Asia thus shows Moskva (Moscow). For countries which do not use a Roman script, place names have been transcribed according to the systems adopted by the British and US Geographic Names Authorities. For China, the Pin Yin system has been used, with some more widely known forms appearing in brackets, as with Beijing (Peking). Both English and local names appear in the index, the English form being cross-referenced to the local form.

CONTENTS

World Statistics

Countries 6
Cities 7

A Divided World

Land Boundaries 10–11
Maritime Boundaries 12–13

Images of Earth

Oslo, Norway 16
Marseilles, France 17
Vienna, Austria 18
Gibraltar, UK 19
Tehran, Iran 20
Naypyidaw, Myanmar 21
Tunis, Tunisia 22
Tombouctou (Timbuktu), Mali 23
Canberra, Australia 24
Niagara Falls, USA 25
Philadelphia, USA 26
Oklahoma, USA 27
Kingston, Jamaica 28
Quito, Ecuador 29
Salar de Uyuni, Bolivia 30
Cape Horn, Chile 31

Gazetteer of Nations

An A–Z Gazetteer of Countries 34–65

World Geography

The Universe 68–69
The Solar System 70–71
Seasons, Time and Motion 72–73
Geology of the Earth 74–75
The Atmosphere 76–77
Climate 78–79
Climate Change and Global Warming 80–81
Water and Vegetation 82–83
Oceans and Seas 84–85
Biodiversity and the Natural World 86–87
Population 88–89
Cities 90–91
Migrants and Refugees 92–93
Conflict and Co-operation 94–95
Energy 96–97
Minerals 98–99
Employment, Trade, and Industry 100–101
Tourism and Travel 102–103
Health 104–105
Wealth 106–107
Standards of Living 108–109

World Cities

Amsterdam 112
Athens 112
Atlanta 113
Baghdad 113
Bangkok 113
Barcelona 114
Beijing 114
Berlin 115
Boston 116
Brussels 116
Budapest 117
Buenos Aires 117
Cairo 117
Cape Town 118
Copenhagen 118
Chicago 119
Dubai 119
Dallas-Fort Worth 120
Delhi 120
Edinburgh 121
Guangzhou 121
Helsinki 121
Hong Kong 122
Istanbul 122
Jakarta 122
Jerusalem 123
Johannesburg 123
Karachi 123
Kolkata 124
Lagos 124
Las Vegas 124
Lima 124
London 125
Lisbon 126
Los Angeles 126
Madrid 127
Manila 127
Melbourne 128
México City 128
Milan 128
Miami 129
Moscow 129
Montréal 130
Mumbai 130
Munich 131
New Orleans 131
New York 132
Orlando 133
Osaka 133
Oslo 133
Paris 134
Prague 135
Rio de Janeiro 135
Rome 136
San Francisco 136
St Petersburg 137
Santiago 137
São Paulo 137
Seoul 137
Shanghai 138
Singapore 138
Stockholm 139
Sydney 139
Tokyo 140
Tehran 141
Toronto 141
Venice 142
Vienna 142
Warsaw 143
Washington 143

World Maps

The World

Map Symbols Front Endpaper

The World: Physical 146–147
1:76 000 000

The World: Political 148–149
1:76 000 000

Arctic Ocean 150
1:28 000 000

Antarctica 151
1:28 000 000

Atlantic Ocean 152
1:41 000 000

Islands of the Atlantic 153
Bermuda 1:400 000
New Providence Island 1:400 000
Madeira 1:800 000
Azores 1:1 600 000
Canary Islands 1:1 600 000
Falkland Islands 1:6 400 000
Ascension Island 1:400 000
St Helena 1:400 000
Cape Verde Islands 1:8 000 000

Greenland 154
1:10 000 000

Iceland 155
1:2 000 000

Europe

Europe: Physical 158
1:16 000 000

Europe: Political 159
1:16 000 000

Scandinavia 160–161
1:4 800 000
Iceland 1:4 800 000
Færoe islands 1:4 800 000

Denmark and Southern Sweden 162–163
1:2 000 000

Southern Norway 164
1:2 000 000

British Isles 165
1:4 000 000

Ireland 166
1:1 600 000

Scotland 167
1:1 600 000

England and Wales 168–169
1:1 600 000

Netherlands, Belgium and Luxembourg 170
1:2 000 000

France 171
1:4 000 000

Northern France 172–173
1:2 000 000

Southern France 174–175
1:2 000 000

Central Europe 176–177
1:4 000 000

Germany and Switzerland 178–179
1:2 000 000

Austria, Czechia and Slovakia 180–181
1:2 000 000

Hungary, Romania and the Lower Danube 182–183
1:2 000 000

Poland and the Southern Baltic 184–185
1:2 000 000

Eastern Europe 186–187
1:8 000 000

Baltic States, Belarus and Ukraine 188–189
1:4 000 000

The Volga Basin and the Caucasus 190–191
1:4 000 000

Southern Europe 192–193
1:8 000 000

Western Spain and Portugal 194–195
1:2 000 000

Eastern Spain 196–197
1:2 000 000

Northern Italy, Slovenia and Croatia 198–199
1:2 000 000

Southern Italy 200–201
1:2 000 000

The Balkans 202–203
1:2 000 000

Southern Greece and Western Turkey 204–205
1:2 000 000

Mediterranean Islands 206–207
Ibiza, Majorca, Minorca 1:800 000
Malta 1:400 000
Corfu 1:800 000
Rhodes 1:800 000
Levkas, Zante, Cephalonia 1:800 000
Crete 1:1 000 000
Cyprus 1:1 000 000

Asia

Asia: Physical 210
1:40 000 000

Asia: Political 211
1:40 000 000

Turkey and Transcaucasia 212–213
1:4 000 000

Russia and Northern Asia 214–215
1:16 000 000

CONTENTS

Kazakhstan and Central Asia 216–127
1:8 000 000

China and the Far East 218–219
1:12 000 000
Hong Kong, Macau and Shenzhen 1:800 000

Japan 220–221
1:4 000 000
Ryukyu Islands 1:4 000 000

Southern Japan 222–223
1:2 000 000

Korea 224
1:3 100 000
Jeju-do 1:3 100 000

Taiwan 225
1:1 400 000
Chinmen 1:1 400 000
Matsu 1:1 400 000

Northern China and Korea 226–227
1:4 800 000

Southern China and Taiwan 228–229
1:4 800 000
Hainan 1:4 800 000

South-east Asia 230–231
1:10 000 000
Java and Madura 1:6 000 000
Bali 1:1 600 000

Philippines 232–233
1:3 200 000

Western Indonesia and Malaysia 234–235
1:5 600 000

Mainland South-east Asia 236–237
1:4 800 000
Ko Phuket 1:800 000
Ko Samui 1:800 000
Pinang 1:800 000
Singapore 1:800 000

Southern Asia and the Middle East 238–239
1:14 000 000

Afghanistan and Pakistan 240
1:5 600 000

Bangladesh, North-east India and Myanmar 241
1:4 800 000

Northern India, Pakistan and Nepal 242–243
1:4 800 000
Jammu and Kashmir 1:4 800 000

Southern India and Sri Lanka 244–245
1:4 800 000
Lakshadweep Islands 1:4 800 000
Andaman and Nicobar Islands 1:4 800 000

The Middle East 246–247
1:5 600 000

Southern Arabian Peninsula 248–249
1:5 600 000
Emirates of the U.A.E. 1:5 600 000

Eastern Mediterranean 250–251
1:2 000 000

Africa

Africa: Physical 254
1:33 600 000

Africa: Political 255
1:33 600 000

The Nile Valley 256–257
1:6 400 000
The Nile Delta 1:3 200 000

Central North Africa 258–259
1:6 400 000

North-west Africa 260–261
1:6 400 000

West Africa 262–263
1:6 400 000

Central Africa 264–265
1:6 400 000
São Tomé and Príncipe 1:6 400 000

Ethiopia and the Horn of Africa 266–267
1:6 400 000

East Africa 268–269
1:6 400 000

Southern Africa 270–271
1:6 400 000

Madagascar 272
1:6 400 000
Comoros 1:2 000 000
Mayotte 1:800 000
Seychelles 1:2 000 000
Réunion 1:800 000
Mauritius 1:800 000
Maldives 1:6 400 000

Indian Ocean 273
1:40 000 000

Australia and Oceania

Australia and Oceania: Physical and Political 276–277
1:16 000 000

Western Australia 278–279
1:6 400 000

Eastern Australia 280–281
1:6 400 000
Whitsunday Group 1:2 000 000
Tasmania 1:6 400 000
Torres Strait 1:6 400 000

South-eastern Australia 282–283
1:3 200 000

New Zealand – North Island 284
1:2 800 000

New Zealand – South Island 285
1:2 800 000
Chatham Islands 1:2 800 000

Papua New Guinea 286
1:5 200 000

Islands of the South-west Pacific 287
Fiji 1:4 000 000
Vanuatu 1:4 000 000
Solomon Islands 1:4 000 000
Tonga 1:4 000 000
Yap 1:830 000
Chuuk 1:830 000
Samoan Islands 1:4 000 000

Pacific Ocean 288–289
1:43 200 000
Okinawa 1:1 550 000
Iwo-Jima 1:200 000
Palau 1:1 550 000
New Caledonia 1:5 750 000
Tahiti 1:1 150 000
French Polynesia 1:26 000 000
Niue 1:830 000
Rarotonga 1:415 000

North America

North America: Physical 292
1:28 000 000

North America: Political 293
1:28 000 000

Canada 294–295
1:12 000 000
Northern Canada 1:12 000 000

Western Canada 296–297
1:5 600 000

Eastern Canada 298–299
1:5 600 000

United States 300–301
1:12 000 000
Alaska 1:12 000 000
Hawai‘i 1:12 000 000

Hawai‘i and the U.S. Pacific Islands 302
1:2 500 000
Hawaiian Islands 1:21 000 000
O‘ahu 1:500 000
Northern Marianas 1:17 500 000
Wake Island 1:200 000
Midway Islands 1:200 000
Guam 1:800 000
Saipan and Tinian 1:800 000
Tutuila 1:640 000
Manu‘a Islands 1:640 000

Alaska 303
1:8 000 000

United States – West 304–305
1:5 360 000

Central and Southern California and Western Washington 306–307
1:2 000 000

United States – Midwest and North-east 308–309
1:5 360 000

Chicago and the Midwest 310–311
1:2 000 000

North-eastern United States 312–313
1:2 000 000

United States – South 314–315
1:5 360 000

South-eastern United States 316–317
1:2 000 000

Mexico 318–319
1:6 400 000

Central America and the West Indies 320–321
1:6 400 000
Puerto Rico and the Virgin Islands 1:1 600 000
Jamaica 1:1 600 000
Panama Canal 1:800 000

Lesser Antilles 322–323
Northern Leewards 1:600 000
Antigua and Barbuda 1:600 000
St Kitts and Nevis 1:600 000
Guadeloupe 1:600 000
ABC Islands 1:600 000
Martinique 1:600 000
Dominica 1:600 000
St Lucia 1:600 000
St Vincent and the Grenadines 1:600 000
Montserrat 1:600 000
Grenada 1:600 000
Barbados 1:600 000
Trinidad and Tobago 1:600 000

South America

South America: Physical 326
1:28 000 000

South America: Political 327
1:28 000 000

South America – North-west 328–329
1:6 400 000
Margarita 1:600 000

South America – West 330–331
1:6 400 000
Galapagos Islands 1:3 200 000
Easter Island 1:400 000
Robinson Crusoe Island 1:400 000

Eastern Brazil 332–333
1:6 400 000

Central South America 334–335
1:6 400 000

Southern Chile and Argentina 336
1:6 400 000

Geographical Glossary 337–338

Index to World Maps 339–448

WORLD STATISTICS: COUNTRIES

This alphabetical list includes the principal countries and territories of the world. If a territory is not completely independent, the country it is associated with is named. The area figures give the total area of land, inland water, and ice. The population figures are 2018 estimates where available. The annual income is the Gross Domestic Product per capita (PPP) in US dollars; the figures are the latest available, usually 2018 estimates.

Country/Territory	Area km² Thousands	Area miles² Thousands	Population Thousands	Capital	Annual Income US $
Afghanistan	652	252	34,941	Kabul	2,000
Albania	28.7	11.1	3,057	Tirana	13.300
Algeria	2,382	920	41,657	Algiers	15,400
American Samoa (US)	0.20	0.08	51	Pago Pago	13,000
Andorra	0.47	0.18	86	Andorra La Vella	49,900
Angola	1,247	481	30,356	Luanda	6,800
Anguilla (UK)	0.10	0.04	17	The Valley	12,200
Antigua & Barbuda	0.44	0.17	96	St John's	28,000
Argentina	2,780	1,074	44,694	Buenos Aires	20,500
Armenia	29.8	11.5	3,038	Yerevan	10,200
Aruba (Netherlands)	0.19	0.07	117	Oranjestad	25,300
Australia	7,741	2,989	23,470	Canberra	52,400
Austria	83.9	32.4	8,793	Vienna	52,100
Azerbaijan	86.6	33.4	10.047	Baku	18,100
Azores (Portugal)	2.2	0.86	246	Ponta Delgada	15,200
Bahamas, The	13.9	5.4	333	Nassau	33,500
Bahrain	0.69	0.27	1,443	Manama	50,100
Bangladesh	144	55.6	159,453	Dhaka	5.000
Barbados	0.43	0.17	293	Bridgetown	18,600
Belarus	208	80.2	9,528	Minsk	20,000
Belgium	30.5	11.8	11,571	Brussels	48,200
Belize	23.0	8.9	386	Belmopan	8,500
Benin	113	43.5	11,341	Porto-Novo	2,400
Bermuda (UK)	0.05	0.02	71	Hamilton	85,700
Bhutan	47.0	18.1	766	Thimphu	9,500
Bolivia	1,099	424	11,306	La Paz/Sucre	7,500
Bosnia-Herzegovina	51.2	19.8	3,850	Sarajevo	13.500
Botswana	582	225	2,249	Gaborone	18,000
Brazil	8,514	3,287	208,847	Brasilia	16,200
Brunei	5.8	2.2	451	Bandar Seri Begawan	80,000
Bulgaria	111	42.8	7,058	Sofia	23,200
Burkina Faso	274	106	19,743	Ouagadougou	2,000
Burundi	27.8	10.7	11,845	Bujumbura	700
Cabo Verde	4.0	1.6	568	Praia	7,3000
Cambodia	181	69.9	16,450	Phnom Penh	4,300
Cameroon	475	184	25,641	Yaoundé	3,800
Canada	9,971	3,850	35,882	Ottawa	49,700
Canary Is. (Spain)	7.2	2.8	2,105	Las Palmas/Santa Cruz	19,900
Cayman Is. (UK)	0.26	0.10	60	George Town	43,800
Central African Republic	623	241	5,745	Bangui	700
Chad	1,284	496	15,833	Ndjaména	2,400
Chile	757	292	17,925	Santiago	26,000
China	9,597	3,705	1,384,689	Beijing	18,100
Colombia	1,139	440	48,169	Bogotá	14,900
Comoros	2.2	0.86	821	Moroni	1,600
Congo	342	132	4,955	Brazzaville	6,800
Congo (Dem. Rep. of the)	2,345	905	85,281	Kinshasa	800
Cook Is. (NZ)	0.24	0.09	9	Avarua	12,300
Costa Rica	51.1	19.7	4,997	San José	17,600
Côte d'Ivoire (Ivory Coast)	322	125	26,261	Yamoussoukro	4,200
Croatia	56.5	21.8	4,270	Zagreb	26,200
Cuba	111	42.8	11,116	Havana	11,900
Curaçao (Netherlands)	0.44	0.17	150	Willemstad	15,000
Cyprus	9.3	3.6	1,237	Nicosia	40,000
Czechia	78.9	30.5	10,686	Prague	37,400
Denmark	43.1	16.6	5,810	Copenhagen	52,100
Djibouti	23.2	9.0	884	Djibouti	3,800
Dominica	0.75	0.29	74	Roseau	9,900
Dominican Republic	48.5	18.7	10,299	Santo Domingo	18,400
Ecuador	284	109	16,499	Quito	11,700
Egypt	1,001	387	99,413	Cairo	13,400
El Salvador	21.0	8.1	6,187	San Salvador	8,000
Equatorial Guinea	28.1	10.8	797	Malabo	22,700
Eritrea	118	45.4	5,971	Asmara	1,700
Estonia	45.1	17.4	1,244	Tallinn	34,100
Eswatini (Swaziland)	17.4	6.7	1,087	Mbabane	11,000
Ethiopia	1,104	426	108,386	Addis Ababa	2,300
Falkland Is. (UK)	12.2	4.7	3	Stanley	96,200
Faroe Is. (Denmark)	1.4	0.54	51	Tórshavn	40,000
Fiji	18.3	7.1	926	Suva	10,200
Finland	338	131	5,537	Helsinki	46,400
France	552	213	67,364	Paris	45,800
French Guiana (France)	90.0	34.7	250	Cayenne	8,300
French Polynesia (France)	4.0	1.5	290	Papeete	17,000
Gabon	268	103	2,119	Libreville	18,500
Gambia, The	11.3	4.4	2,093	Banjul	2,800
Georgia	69.7	26.9	4,926	Tbilisi	11,500
Germany	357	138	80,458	Berlin	52,600
Ghana	239	92.1	28,102	Accra	6,500
Gibraltar (UK)	0.006	0.002	29	Gibraltar Town	61,700
Greece	132	50.9	10,762	Athens	29,100
Greenland (Denmark)	2,176	840	58	Nuuk	37,600
Grenada	0.34	0.13	112	St George's	16,200
Guadeloupe (France)	1.7	0.66	402	Basse-Terre	7,900
Guam (US)	0.55	0.21	168	Agana	30,500
Guatemala	109	42.0	16,581	Guatemala City	8,400
Guinea	246	94.9	11,855	Conakry	2,300
Guinea-Bissau	36.1	13.9	1,833	Bissau	1,900
Guyana	215	83.0	741	Georgetown	8,500
Haiti	27.8	10.7	10,788	Port-au-Prince	1,900
Honduras	112	43.3	9,183	Tegucigalpa	5,200
Hungary	93.0	35.9	9,826	Budapest	31,900
Iceland	103	39.8	344	Reykjavik	55,900
India	3,287	1,269	1,296,834	New Delhi	7,900
Indonesia	1,905	735	262,787	Jakarta	13,200
Iran	1,648	636	83,025	Tehran	19,600
Iraq	438	169	40,194	Baghdad	17,700
Ireland	70.3	27.1	5,068	Dublin	78,800
Israel	20.6	8.0	8,425	Jerusalem	38,000
Italy	301	116	62,247	Rome	39,600
Jamaica	11.0	4.2	2,812	Kingston	9,400
Japan	378	146	126,168	Tokyo	44,200
Jordan	89.3	34.5	10,458	Amman	9,400
Kazakhstan	2,725	1,052	18,745	Astana	27,600
Kenya	580	224	48,398	Nairobi	3,700
Kiribati	0.73	0.28	109	Tarawa	2,100
Korea, North	121	46.5	25,381	Pyŏngyang	1,700
Korea, South	99.3	38.3	51,418	Seoul	41,400
Kosovo	10.9	4.2	1,908	Pristina	11,600
Kuwait	17.8	6.9	2,916	Kuwait City	67,000
Kyrgyzstan	200	77.2	5,849	Bishkek	3,800
Laos	237	91.4	7,234	Vientiane	8,000
Latvia	64.6	24.9	1,924	Riga	30,000
Lebanon	10.4	4.0	6,100	Beirut	14,700
Lesotho	30.4	11.7	1,962	Maseru	3,500
Liberia	111	43.0	4,810	Monrovia	1,400
Libya	1,760	679	6,755	Tripoli	11,500
Liechtenstein	0.16	0.06	39	Vaduz	139,100
Lithuania	65.2	25.2	2,793	Vilnius	34,800
Luxembourg	2.6	1.0	606	Luxembourg	106,700
Macedonia, North	25.7	9.9	2,119	Skopje	15,700
Madagascar	587	227	25,684	Antananarivo	1,600
Madeira (Portugal)	0.78	0.30	289	Funchal	25,800
Malawi	118	45.7	19,843	Lilongwe	1,200
Malaysia	330	127	31,810	Kuala Lumpur/Putrajaya	30,900
Maldives	0.30	0.12	392	Malé	21,800
Mali	1,240	479	18,430	Bamako	2,400
Malta	0.32	0.12	449	Valletta	45,600
Marshall Is.	0.18	0.07	76	Majuro	3,700
Martinique (France)	1.1	0.43	386	Fort-de-France	14,400
Mauritania	1,026	396	3,840	Nouakchott	4,000
Mauritius	2.0	0.79	1,364	Port Louis	23,700
Mayotte (France)	0.37	0.14	213	Mamoudzou	4,900
Mexico	1,958	756	125,959	Mexico City	20,600
Micronesia, Fed. States of	0.70	0.27	104	Palikir	3,500
Moldova	33.9	13.1	3,438	Kishinev	7,300
Monaco	0.002	0.0008	31	Monaco	115,700
Mongolia	1,567	605	3,103	Ulan Bator	13,400
Montenegro	14.0	5.4	614	Podgorica	19,000
Montserrat (UK)	0.10	0.39	5	Brades	8,500
Morocco	447	172	34,314	Rabat	8,900
Mozambique	802	309	27,234	Maputo	1,300
Myanmar (Burma)	677	261	55,623	Yangôn/Naypyidaw	6,500
Namibia	824	318	2,533	Windhoek	11,200
Nauru	0.02	0.008	10	Yaren	12,300
Nepal	147	56.8	29,718	Katmandu	2,900
Netherlands	41.5	16.0	17,151	Amsterdam/The Hague	56,400
New Caledonia (France)	18.6	7.2	283	Nouméa	31,100
New Zealand	271	104	4,546	Wellington	40,100
Nicaragua	130	50.2	6,085	Managua	5,700
Niger	1,267	489	19,866	Niamey	1,200
Nigeria	924	357	203,453	Abuja	6,000
Northern Mariana Is. (US)	0.46	0.18	52	Saipan	13,300
Norway	324	125	5,372	Oslo	74,400
Oman	310	119	4,613	Muscat	46,600
Pakistan	796	307	207,863	Islamabad	5,700
Palau	0.46	0.18	22	Melekeok	15,000
Panama	75.5	29.2	3,801	Panamá	25,700
Papua New Guinea	463	179	7.027	Port Moresby	3,700
Paraguay	407	157	7,026	Asunción	13,400
Peru	1,285	496	31,331	Lima	14,200
Philippines	300	116	105,893	Manila	8,900
Poland	323	125	38,421	Warsaw	32,000
Portugal	88.8	34.3	10,355	Lisbon	32,000
Puerto Rico (US)	8.9	3.4	3,295	San Juan	39,700
Qatar	11.0	4.2	2,364	Doha	130,500
Réunion (France)	2.5	0.97	846	St-Denis	6,200
Romania	238	92.0	21,457	Bucharest	26,400
Russia	17,075	6,593	142,123	Moscow	29,300
Rwanda	26.3	10.2	12,187	Kigali	2,300
St Kitts & Nevis	0.26	0.10	53	Basseterre	29,800
St Lucia	0.54	0.21	166	Castries	14,400
St Vincent & Grenadines	0.39	0.15	102	Kingstown	12,000
Samoa	2.8	1.1	201	Apia	5,900
San Marino	0.06	0.02	34	San Marino	60,300
São Tomé & Príncipe	0.96	0.37	204	São Tomé	3,200
Saudi Arabia	2,150	830	33,091	Riyadh	55,900
Senegal	197	76.0	15,021	Dakar	3,700
Serbia	77.5	29.9	7,078	Belgrade	17,600
Seychelles	0.46	0.18	95	Victoria	30,500
Sierra Leone	71.7	27.7	6,312	Freetown	1,600
Singapore	0.68	0.26	5,996	Singapore City	100,300
Slovakia	49.0	18.9	5,446	Bratislava	35,100
Slovenia	20.3	7.8	2,102	Ljubljana	36,700
Solomon Is.	28.9	11.2	660	Honiara	2,200
Somalia	638	246	11,259	Mogadishu	400
South Africa	1,221	471	55,380	Cape Town/Pretoria	13,700
Spain	498	192	49,331	Madrid	40,100
Sri Lanka	65.6	25.3	22,577	Colombo	13,400
Sudan	1,886	728	43,121	Khartoum	4,200
Sudan, South	620	239	10,205	Juba	1,500
Suriname	163	63.0	598	Paramaribo	15,100
Sweden	450	174	10,041	Stockholm	53,000
Switzerland	41.3	15.9	8,293	Bern	64,700
Syria	185	71.5	19,454	Damascus	-
Taiwan	36.0	13.9	23,546	Taipei	53,000
Tajikistan	143	55.3	8,605	Dushanbe	3,400
Tanzania	945	365	55,451	Dodoma	3,400
Thailand	513	198	68,616	Bangkok	19,500
Timor-Leste (East Timor)	14.9	5.7	1,322	Dili	5,200
Togo	56.8	21.9	8,176	Lomé	1,700
Tonga	0.65	0.25	106	Nuku'alofa	6,100
Trinidad & Tobago	5.1	2.0	1,216	Port of Spain	32,300
Tunisia	164	63.2	11,516	Tunis	12,400
Turkey	775	299	81,257	Ankara	28,000
Turkmenistan	488	188	5,411	Ashkhabad	19,500
Turks & Caicos Is. (UK)	0.43	0.17	54	Cockburn Town	29,100
Tuvalu	0.03	0.01	11	Fongafale	4,100
Uganda	241	93.1	40,854	Kampala	2,500
Ukraine	604	233	43,952	Kiev	9,300
United Arab Emirates	83.6	32.3	9,701	Abu Dhabi	69,400
United Kingdom	242	93.4	65,105	London	45,700
United States of America	9,629	3,718	329,256	Washington, DC	62,600
Uruguay	175	67.6	3,369	Montevideo	23,300
Uzbekistan	447	173	30,024	Tashkent	7,700
Vanuatu	12.2	4.7	288	Port-Vila	2,900
Vatican City	0.0004	0.0002	1	Vatican City	-
Venezuela	912	352	31,689	Caracas	12,400
Vietnam	332	128	97,040	Hanoi	7,500
Virgin Is. (UK)	0.15	0.06	36	Road Town	42,300
Virgin Is. (US)	0.35	0.13	107	Charlotte Amalie	36,100
Yemen	528	204	28,667	Sana'	2,400
Zambia	753	291	16,445	Lusaka	4,100
Zimbabwe	391	151	14,030	Harare	2,800

This list shows the principal cities with more than 900,000 inhabitants. The figures are taken from the most recent census or estimate available and as far as possible are the population of the metropolitan area or urban agglomeration. The list includes Metropolitan Statistical Areas from the United States Census Bureau. All the figures are in thousands. Local name forms have been used for the smaller cities (for example, Antwerpen).

AFGHANISTAN	
Kabul	4,012
ALGERIA	
Algiers	2,694
ANGOLA	
Luanda	7,774
ARGENTINA	
Buenos Aires	14,967
Córdoba	1,548
Rosario	1,488
Mendoza	1,133
San Miguel de Tucumán	956
ARMENIA	
Yerevan	1,080
AUSTRALIA	
Sydney	4,792
Melbourne	4,771
Brisbane	2,338
Perth	1,991
Adelaide	1,320
AUSTRIA	
Vienna	1,901
AZERBAIJAN	
Baku	2,286
BANGLADESH	
Dhaka	19,578
Chittagong	4,861
Khulna	975
BELARUS	
Minsk	2,005
BENIN	
Abomey-Calavi	928
BELGIUM	
Brussels	2,050
Antwerpen	1,032
BOLIVIA	
La Paz	1,814
Santa Cruz	1,641
Cochabamba	1,237
BRAZIL	
São Paulo	21,650
Rio de Janeiro	13,293
Belo Horizonte	5,972
Brasília	4,470
Recife	4,028
Pôrto Alegre	4,094
Fortaleza	3,977
Salvador	3,752
Curitiba	3,579
Campinas	3,210
Goiânia	2,565
Belém	2,280
Manaus	2,171
Vitória	2,003
Santos	1,853
São Luís	1,460
Natal	1,395
João Pessoa	1,347
Maceió	1,294
Joinville	1,270
Florianópolis	1,197
Teresina	1,001
Aracaju	973
BULGARIA	
Sofia	1,272
BURKINA FASO	
Ouagadougou	2,531
CAMBODIA	
Phnom Penh	1,952
CAMEROON	
Yaoundé	3,656
Douala	3,412
CANADA	
Toronto	6,082
Montréal	4,172
Vancouver	2,531
Calgary	1,477
Edmonton	1,397
Ottawa	1,363
CHAD	
Ndjamena	1,323
CHILE	
Santiago	6,680
Valparaiso	967
CHINA	
Shanghai	25,582
Beijing	19,618
Chongqing	14,838
Tianjin	13,215
Guangzhou, Guangdong	12,638
Shenzhen	11,908
Chengdu	8,813
Nanjing, Jiangsu	8,245
Wuhan	8,176
Xi'an, Shaanxi	7,444
Hong Kong	7,429
Dongguan, Guangdong	7,360
Hangzhou	7,236
Foshan	7,196
Shenyang	6,921
Suzhou, Jiangsu	6,339
Harbin	6,115
Qingdao	5,381
Dalian	5,300
Jinan, Shandong	5,052
Zhengzhou	4,940
Changsha	4,345
Kunming	4,230
Changchun	4,241
Shantou	4,174
Ürümqi	4,011
Hefei	3,980
Shijiazhuang	3,950
Ningbo	3,815
Taiyuan, Shanxi	3,725
Nanning	3,628
Xiamen	3,585
Fuzhou, Fujian	3,532
Wenzhou	3,419
Nanchang	3,373
Changzhou, Jiangsu	3,372
Tangshan	3,145
Wuxi, Jiangsu	3,144
Lanzhou	2,936
Zhongshan	2,872
Zibo	2,555
Handan	2,528
Weifang	2,466
Huizhou	2,360
Yantai	2,359
Shaoxing	2,350
Huai'an	2,420
Luoyang	2,236
Guiyang	2,136
Nantong	2,123
Baotou	2,096
Xuzhou	2,054
Liuzhou	2,042
Hohhot	2,009
Yangzhou	1,901
Baoding	1,889
Linyi	1,843
Taizhou, Zhejiang	1,818
Haikou	1,805
Yancheng	1,779
Daqing	1,763
Putian	1,712
Lianyungang	1,703
Zhuhai	1,671
Jaingmen	1,640
Datong	1,659
Anshan	1,600
Xiangyang	1,607
Wuhu	1,685
Jilin	1,569
Quanzhou	1,568
Qiqihar	1,515
Yinchuan	1,483
Cixi	1,480
Xining	1,452
Jining, Shandong	1,450
Hengyang	1,433
Yichang	1,432
Qinhuangdao	1,432
Huainan	1,393
Chaozhou	1,389
Zhangjiakou	1,367
Anyang	1,328
Tai'an	1,290
Fushun	1,288
Taizhou, Jiangsu	1,282
Suqian	1,276
Zhanjiang	1,231
Mianyang	1,228
Yiwu	1,227
Dongying	1,205
Rizhao	1,186
Nanchong	1,173
Shiyan	1,162
Ganzhou	1,158
Zhuzhou	1,145
Yingkou	1,138
Zhenjiang	1,124
Benxi	1,122
Chifeng	1,105
Jiaxing	1,140
Jingzhou	1,101
Jinzhou	1,101
Baoji	1,098
Guilin	1,096
Puning	1,095
Tengzhou	1,094
Pingdingshan	1,093
Ruian	1,089
Xiangtan	1,089
Nanyang	1,088
Huaibei	1,076
Suzhou	1,068
Liuan	1,063
Zaozhuang	1,063
Jieyang	1,049
Xinxiang	1,044
Jinhua	1,024
Liuyang	1,020
Yueyang	990
Yueqing	983
Fuyang	978
Wenling	971
COLOMBIA	
Bogotá	10,574
Medellín	3,934
Cali	2,726
Barranquilla	2,218
Bucaramanga	1,295
Cartagena	1,047
CONGO	
Brazzaville	2,230
Pointe-Noire	1,138
CONGO (DEM. REP. OF THE)	
Kinshasa	13,171
Mbuji-Mayi	2,305
Lubumbashi	2,281
Kananga	1,335
Kisangani	1,167
COSTA RICA	
San José	1,358
CÔTE D'IVOIRE (IVORY COAST)	
Abidjan	4.921
CUBA	
Havana	2,136
CZECHIA	
Prague	1,292
DENMARK	
Copenhagen	1,321
DOMINICAN REPUBLIC	
Santo Domingo	3,172
ECUADOR	
Guayaquil	2,899
Quito	1,822
EGYPT	
Cairo	20,076
Alexandria	5,086
EL SALVADOR	
San Salvador	1,107
ETHIOPIA	
Addis Ababa	4,400
FINLAND	
Helsinki	1,279
FRANCE	
Paris	10.901
Lyon	1,690
Marseilles	1,599
Lille	1,054
Toulouse	997
Bordeaux	945
Nice	942
GEORGIA	
Tbilisi	1,077
GERMANY	
Berlin	3,552
Hamburg	1,793
Munich	1,504
Cologne	1,096
GHANA	
Kumasi	3,065
Accra	2,439
GREECE	
Athens	3,156
GUATEMALA	
Guatemala City	2,851
GUINEA	
Conakry	1,843
HAITI	
Port-au-Prince	2,637
HONDURAS	
Tegucigalpa	1,363
HUNGARY	
Budapest	1,759
INDIA	
Delhi	28,514
Mumbai	19,980
Kolkata	14,681
Bengaluru	11,440
Chennai	10,456
Hyderabad	9,428
Ahmedabad	7,681
Surat	6,564
Pune	6,276
Jaipur	3,717
Lucknow	3,505
Calicut	3,175
Kanpur	3,081
Malappuram	2,950
Kochi	2,858
Indore	2,822
Nagpur	2,808
Thrissur	2,774
Coimbatore	2,641
Patna	2,352
Thiruvananthapuram	2,369
Bhopal	2,278
Agra	2,110
Vadodara	2,110
Vishakhapatnam	2,076
Kannur	2,048
Nashik	1,952
Vijayawada	1,911
Ludhiana	1,806
Rajkot	1,767
Madurai	1,676
Kollam	1,670
Meerut	1,636
Varanasi	1,615
Jamshedpur	1,543
Raipur	1,521
Srinagar	1,515
Aurangabad	1,476
Jabalpur	1,411
Jodhpur	1,397
Asansol	1,391
Ranchi	1,370
Tiruppur	1,369
Allahabad	1,355
Amritsar	1,335
Gwalior	1,317
Dhanbad	1,302
Kota	1,299
Bareilly	1,195
Bhilainagar-Durg	1,177
Aligarh	1,143
Tiruchchirapalli	1,143
Moradabad	1,127
Mysore	1,126
Chandigarh	1,110
Bhubaneswar	1,100
Guwahati	1,083
Hubli-Dharwad	1,079
Salem	1,062
Solapur	1,014
Jalandhar	1,014
Saharanpur	972
INDONESIA	
Jakarta	10,517
Bekasi	3,159
Surabaya	2,903
Bandung	2,538
Depok	2,503
Medan	2,285
Tangerang	2,222
Semarang	1,800
Palembang	1,665
Makassar	1,530
Batam	1,401
Pekanbaru	1,138
Bogor	1,115
Bandar Lampung	1,047
Padang	949
Denpasar	944
Samarinda	943
IRAN	
Tehran	8,896
Mashhad	3,097
Esfahan	2,041
Shiraz	1,605
Karaj	1,585
Tabriz	1,582
Qom	1,241
Ahvaz	1,212
IRAQ	
Baghdad	6,812
Mosul	1,527
Basra	1,299
Kirkuk	981
IRELAND	
Dublin	1,201
ISRAEL	
Tel Aviv-Yafo	4,011
Haifa	1,135
ITALY	
Rome	4,210
Milan	3,132
Naples	2,198
Turin	1,786
JAPAN	
Tokyo–Yokohama	37,468
Osaka–Kobe	19,281
Nagoya	9,507
Fukuoka–Kitakyushu	5,551
Shizuoka–Hamamatsu	2,899
Sapporo	2,665
Sendai	2,306
Hiroshima	2,095
Kyoto	1,459
JORDAN	
Amman	2,065
KAZAKHSTAN	
Almaty	1,829
Astana	1,068
KENYA	
Nairobi	4,386
Mombasa	1,214
KOREA, NORTH	
Pyŏngyang	3,038
KOREA, SOUTH	
Seoul	9,963
Busan	3,467
Incheon	2,763
Daegu	2,221
Daejeon	1,558
Gwangju	1,518
Yongin	1,039
Suwon	1,265
Changwon	1,060
Goyang	1,039
Seognam	948
Ulsan	910
KUWAIT	
Kuwait City	2,989
LEBANON	
Beirut	2,385
LIBERIA	
Monrovia	1,418
LIBYA	
Tripoli	1,158
MADAGASCAR	
Antananarivo	3,058
MALAWI	
Lilongwe	1,030
MALAYSIA	
Kuala Lumpur	7,564
Johor Bahru	983
MALI	
Bamako	2,447
MAURITANIA	
Nouakchott	1,205
MEXICO	
Mexico City	21,581
Guadalajara	5,023
Monterrey	4,712
Puebla	3,097
Toluca	2,354
Tijuana	2,058
León	1,780
Torreón	1,497
La Laguna	1,490
Ciudad Juárez	1,480
Querétaro	1,288
San Luis Potosí	1,179
Mérida	1,122
Mexicali	1,082
Aguascalientes	1,070
Cuernavaca	1,043
Chihuahua	1,012
Tampico	971
Acapulco	955
Saltillo	950
Morelia	924
MONGOLIA	
Ulan Bator	1,520
MOROCCO	
Casablanca	3,684
Rabat	1,847
Fès	1,184
Tangier	1,116
Marrakesh	976
MOZAMBIQUE	
Matola	1,635
Maputo	1,102
MYANMAR (BURMA)	
Rangoon	5,157
Mandalay	1,374
Naypyidaw	925
NEPAL	
Katmandu	1,330
NETHERLANDS	
Amsterdam	1,132
Rotterdam	1,008
NEW ZEALAND	
Auckland	1,557
NICARAGUA	
Managua	1,048
NIGER	
Niamey	1,214
NIGERIA	
Lagos	13,463
Kano	3,820
Ibadan	3,383
Abuja	2,919
Port Harcourt	2,731
Benin City	1,628
Onitsha	1,285
Kaduna	1,083
Aba	1,023
Uyo	1,012
Nnewi	930
NORWAY	
Oslo	1,012
PAKISTAN	
Karachi	15,400
Lahore	11,738
Faisalabad	3,311
Rawalpindi	2,156
Gujranwala	2,110
Peshawar	2,065
Multan	1,931
Hyderabad	1,782
Islamabad	1,061
Quetta	1,042
PANAMA	
Panamá	1,783
PARAGUAY	
Asunción	3,222
PERU	
Lima	10,391
PHILIPPINES	
Manila	13,482
Davao	1,745
Cebu	956
POLAND	
Warsaw	1,768
PORTUGAL	
Lisbon	2,927
Porto	1,307
PUERTO RICO	
San Juan	2,454
ROMANIA	
Bucharest	1,821
RUSSIA	
Moscow	12,410
St Petersburg	5,383
Novosibirsk	1,636
Yekaterinburg	1,482
Nizhniy Novgorod	1,264
Kazan	1,254
Chelyabinsk	1,216
Omsk	1,184
Samara	1,171
Rostov	1,134
Ufa	1,129
Krasnoyarsk	1,111
Perm	1,062
Voronezh	1,056
Volgograd	1,014
RWANDA	
Kigali	1,058
SAUDI ARABIA	
Riyadh	6,907
Jedda	4,433
Mecca	1,967
Medina	1,430
Dammam	1,197
SENEGAL	
Dakar	2,978
SERBIA	
Belgrade	1,389
SIERRA LEONE	
Freetown	1,136
SINGAPORE	
Singapore City	5,792
SOMALIA	
Mogadishu	2,082
SOUTH AFRICA	
Johannesburg	5,486
Cape Town	4,430
Ekurhuleni	3,741
Durban	3,134
Pretoria	2,378
Port Elizabeth	1,231
SPAIN	
Madrid	6,497
Barcelona	5,494
SUDAN	
Khartoum	5,534
SWEDEN	
Stockholm	1,583
SWITZERLAND	
Zürich	1,371
SYRIA	
Damascus	2,320
Aleppo	1,754
Homs	1,295
TAIWAN	
Xinbei	4,325
Taipei	2,706
Taoyuan	2,190
Kaohsiung	1,532
T'aichung	1,283
TANZANIA	
Dar es Salaam	6,084
Mwanza	1,003
THAILAND	
Bangkok	10,156
Chon Buri	1,361
Samut Prakan	1,272
TOGO	
Lomé	1,746
TUNISIA	
Tunis	2,291
TURKEY	
Istanbul	14,751
Ankara	4,919
Izmir	2,937
Bursa	1,916
Adana	1,730
Gaziantep	1,632
Konya	1,271
Antalya	1,184
Diyarbakir	999
Mersin	978
UGANDA	
Kampala	2,986
UKRAINE	
Kiev	2,957
Kharkov	1,436
Odessa	1,011
Dnepropetrovsk	969
Donetsk	919
UNITED ARAB EMIRATES	
Dubai	2,785
Sharjah	1,571
Abu Dhabi	1,420
UNITED KINGDOM	
London	9,046
Manchester	2,690
Birmingham	2,570
Glasgow	1,661
UNITED STATES OF AMERICA	
New York	18,819
Los Angeles	12,458
Chicago	8,864
Houston	6,115
Dallas–Fort Worth	6,066
Miami	6,036
Philadelphia	5,659
Atlanta	5,572
Washington, DC	5,207
Phoenix–Mesa	4,359
Boston	4,308
Detroit	3,600
Seattle	3,397
San Francisco	3,325
San Diego	3,212
Minneapolis–St Paul	2,889
Tampa–St Petersburg	2,807
Denver	2,753
Las Vegas	2,541
Riverside-San Bernardino	2,374
Baltimore	2,315
San Antonio	2,217
St Louis	2,213
Portland	2,104
Sacramento	2,054
Austin	1,915
Charlotte	1,886
Orlando	1,882
Cleveland	1,776
San Jose	1,776
Indianapolis	1,753
Cincinnati	1,733
Pittsburgh	1,718
Kansas City	1,663
Columbus	1,598
Virginia Beach–Norfolk	1,478
Milwaukee	1,435
Raleigh	1,327
Jacksonville	1,244
Providence	1,205
Nashville	1,199
Salt Lake City	1,147
Memphis	1,139
Richmond	1,081
Louisville	1,073
Hartford	990
New Orleans	979
Oklahoma	969
Tucson	960
URUGUAY	
Montevideo	1,737
UZBEKISTAN	
Tashkent	2,464
VENEZUELA	
Caracas	2,935
Maracaibo	2,179
Valencia	1,860
Barquisimeto	1,189
Maracay	1,178
VIETNAM	
Ho Chi Minh City	8,145
Hanoi	4,283
Can Tho	1,444
Haiphong	1,219
Da Nang	1,064
YEMEN	
Sana'	2,779
Aden	922
ZAMBIA	
Lusaka	2,524
ZIMBABWE	
Harare	1,515

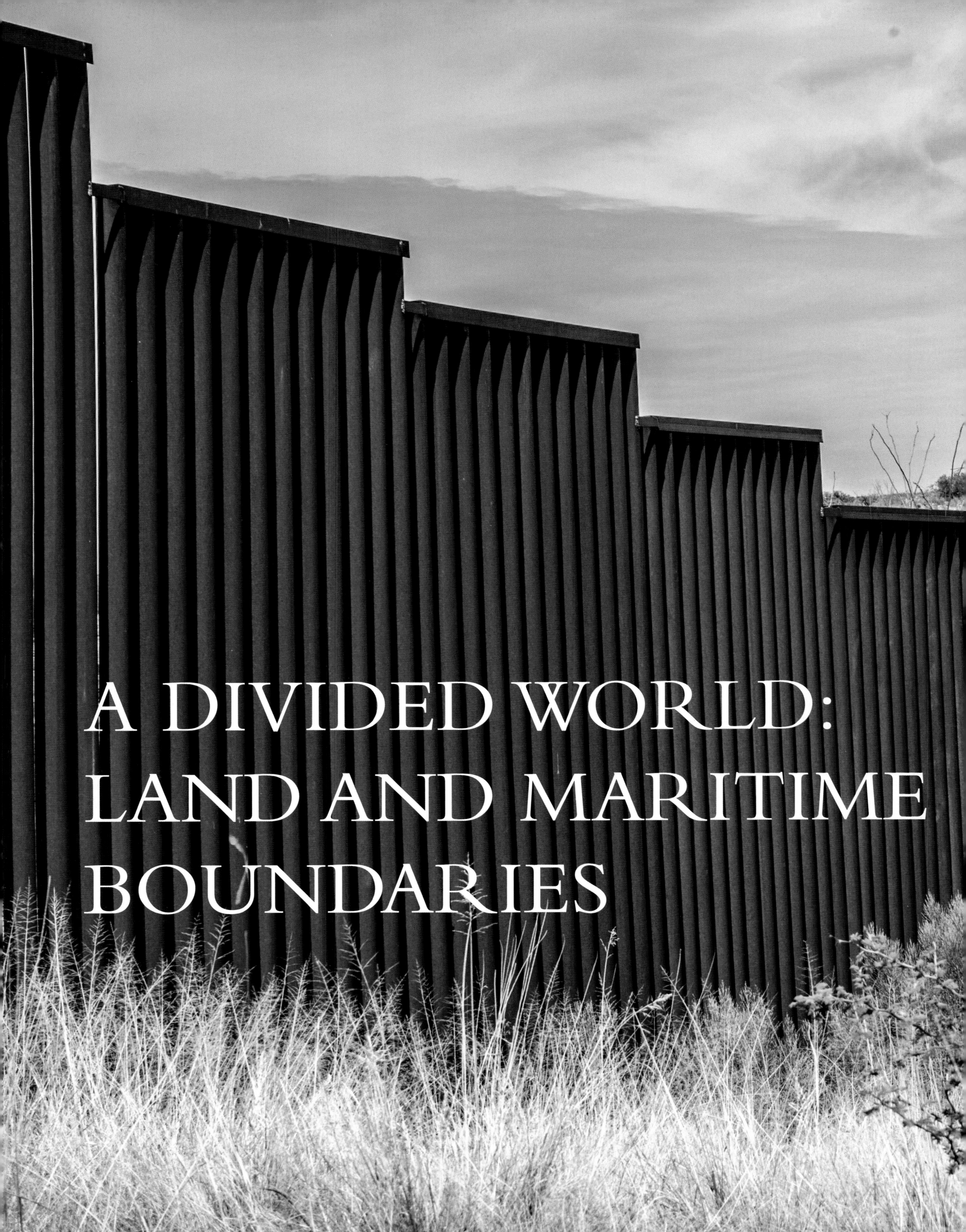

A DIVIDED WORLD: LAND AND MARITIME BOUNDARIES

"Good fences make good neighbors." Many people, in many languages, have expressed this sentiment as they contemplate their neighbors across a boundary line. The established political map of the world in the 21st century shows a mosaic of political units that fit together with no space unoccupied. The defined areas of nation states create boundaries that can be a focus for either cooperation or conflict. In areas where conflict is in the past and people on both sides of the fence can benefit from the free flow of goods and people, a boundary marker may be no more than a ceremonial sign. In more contentious areas, where it is seen necessary to control movement, formidable and physical barriers may be erected. The fence shown in this image marks the division between the United States and Mexico.

For more information:
148 World Political Map
151 Antarctica

In order to establish order, and impose control over territory, humans have long wanted to divide land and sea into areas that are exclusively owned and ruled – that are "sovereign." The great, early empires exerted their control through conquest, and later by imposing their form of civilization over a territory. In the era of European exploration, colonies were established on the coasts of the southern continents and, from these trading posts, influence was extended inland. Boundaries were often ill-defined and large areas of land were beyond the effective control of colonial outposts.

It was from the 17th century that the concept of sovereignty and territory became linked. From this concept evolved the notion of nation-states being the building blocks of the world political map as we now see it. However, even in the 21st century, we know not to look at a map of the world with political boundaries and think that it is static and unchanging.

The majority of boundaries in Africa were imposed by European powers (see feature below). Boundaries were often drawn with scant regard for the needs of the indigenous population. The 20th century saw many new states emerging after World War I with the breakup of the Ottoman and Austro-Hungarian empires. This creation of new, and smaller, states continued into the 1980s and 1990s with the fragmentation of Yugoslavia, followed by the breakup of the USSR. Since the year 2000, five new countries have gained independence (East Timor, Montenegro, Serbia, Kosovo, and South Sudan).

Boundaries can change, sometimes gradually, and peacefully, by agreement; sometimes cataclysmically through war or invasion. The purpose and function of boundaries also varies. Boundaries can be used to control immigration, and to mark divisions between religions, language, and culture. Very "closed" boundaries, such as that between North Korea and its neighbors, severely restrict the movement of people and goods. The more open boundaries between many countries in the European Union promote freer movement. Looking beyond the confines of single nation-states, some countries are willing to surrender a degree of individual sovereignty in exchange for greater collective economic or military power.

BREAKDOWN OF EMPIRES SINCE 1945

In 1939, large areas of the world were still under colonial rule, although in India and Africa especially, the colonial powers depended on indigenous political rulers to administer at the local level. Immediately after the end of World War I, the League of Nations had established mandates. Countries that were victorious in the war, such as Great Britain and France, undertook to administer regions that had previously been colonies of Germany or of the Ottoman Empire. Eventual independence was the goal. Japan was the only country to expand its empire during the inter-war period.

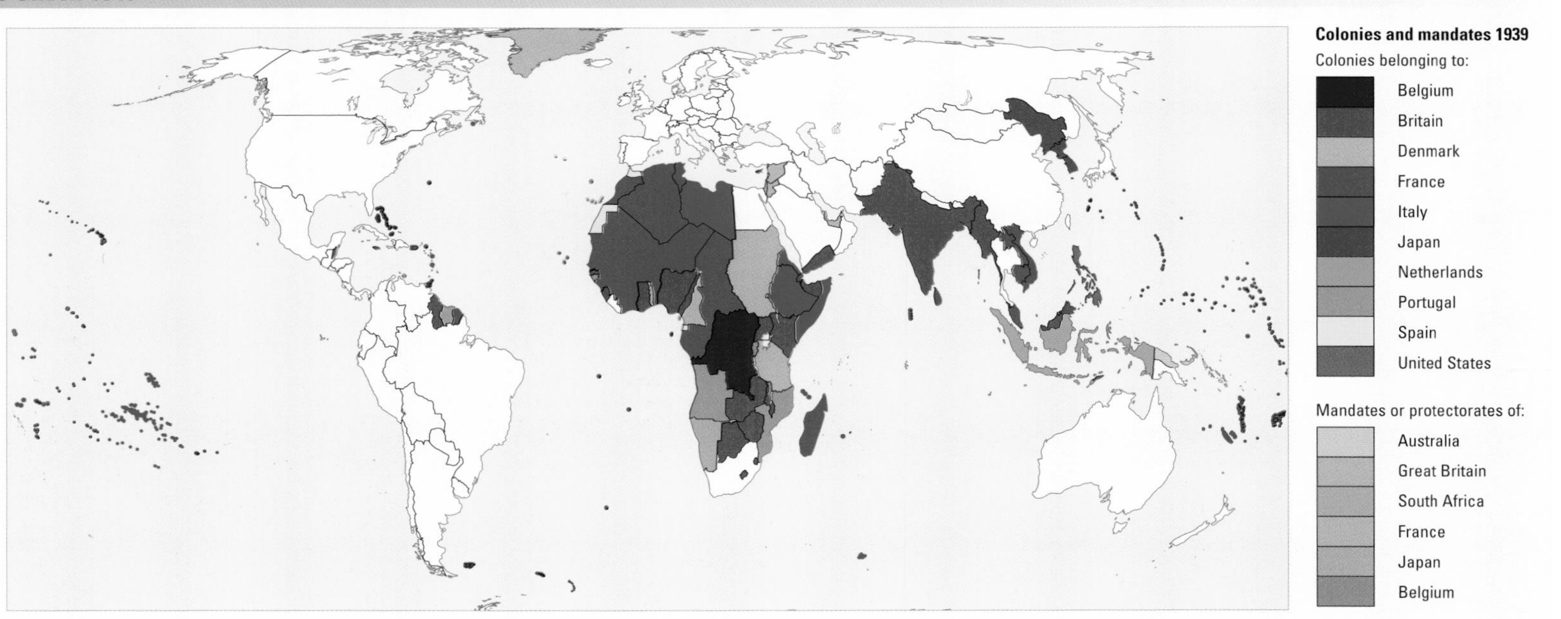

INDEPENDENT AFRICA

Africa is where the profound effects that boundaries can have on people, society, and economic development are most evident. It retains the legacy of its colonial past: over 80% of its boundaries were created by European powers. First came contact through trade along the coasts followed, in the mid-19th century, by exploration of the interior. The often-forceful acquisition of territory by European colonizers was based on establishing trade links to exploit natural resources. From the early coastal settlements, spheres of influence were established. The independence granted to India, and other countries in Asia, in the 1940s, encouraged African nationalists to press for similar political freedoms in their own continent. Gradually, throughout the 20th century, states gained independence from their former colonial powers.

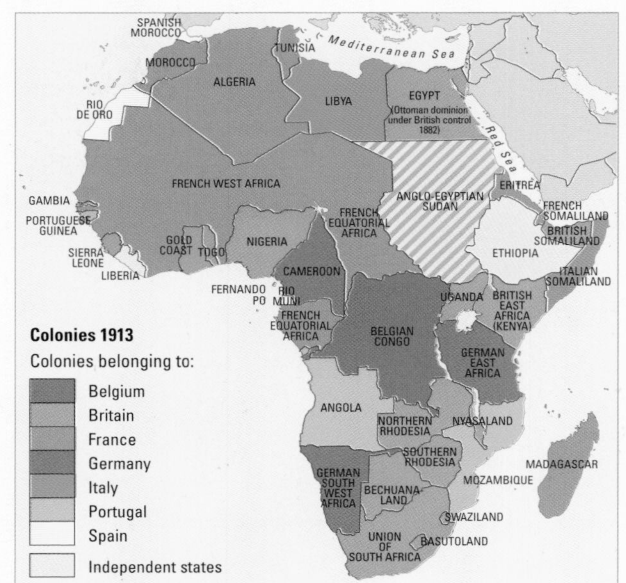

◄ The boundaries of the African continent were mainly of European construction. France and Great Britain were the dominant colonial powers, and their influence lingers in their former territories with the use of French and English as official languages.

► In the main, the boundaries of colonial Africa, quickly drawn during the "scramble for Africa" between 1881 and 1914, survived into modern times as the boundaries of the new independent countries. In more recent times, Eritrea and South Sudan have broken away as separate states. The final status of Western Sahara is yet to be resolved.

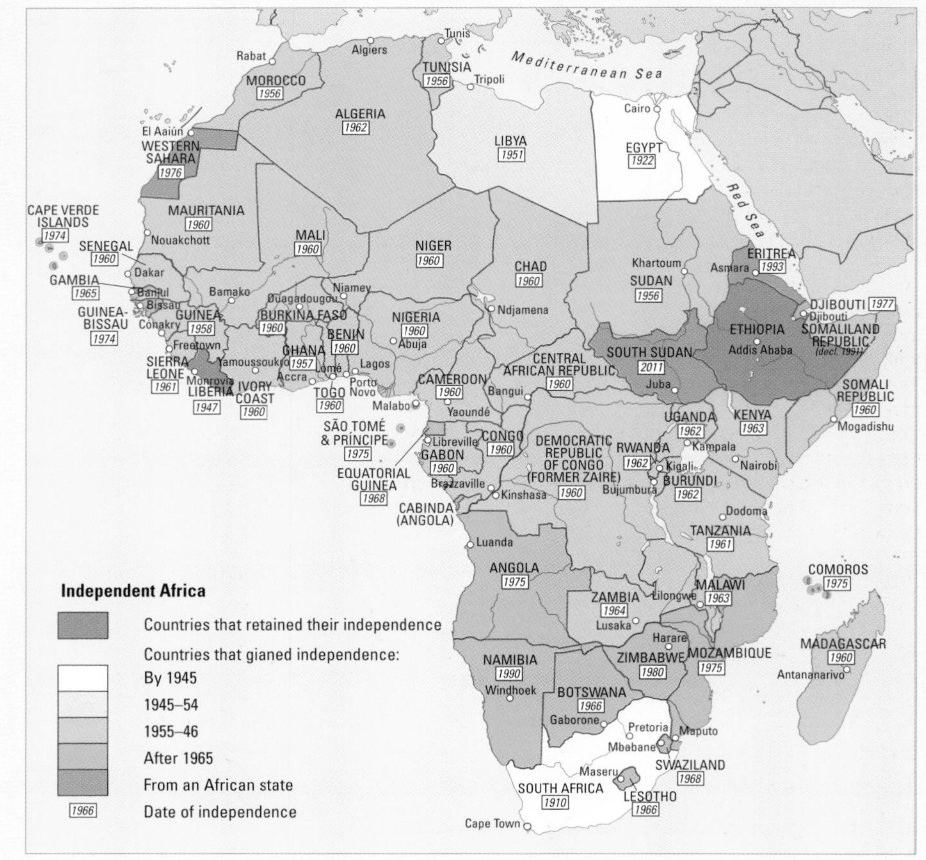

HARD AND SOFT BOUNDARIES

The conventional way of showing an international boundary on an atlas map is to draw a solid line. However, this symbol can conceal myriad differences in the strength and function of a boundary. A "hard" boundary may physically prevent the free movement of people with solid barriers and armed guards. A "soft" boundary may have little effect on people and vehicles as they cross from one country to another. An example of where international boundaries can be considered soft, are those between the European countries that have joined the Schengen Area. The Schengen Agreement aims to reduce border checks, and to ease the movement of goods, and people, between the participating nations. In many places, the only indication that you have crossed a boundary will be a small sign by the side of a road. However, restrictions can be reintroduced, as was the case in 2016, when seven countries put in place border controls in response to the flood of migrants entering southern Europe. In contrast, where a nation wants to control movement, a boundary may be formed of a physically impermeable barrier. The Berlin Wall (1961-89) that divided the city is an example of a hard border. Many people risked their lives to cross this boundary. In the 21st century, some countries, such as Israel and the United States, are extending existing barriers in response to perceived threats from other nations.

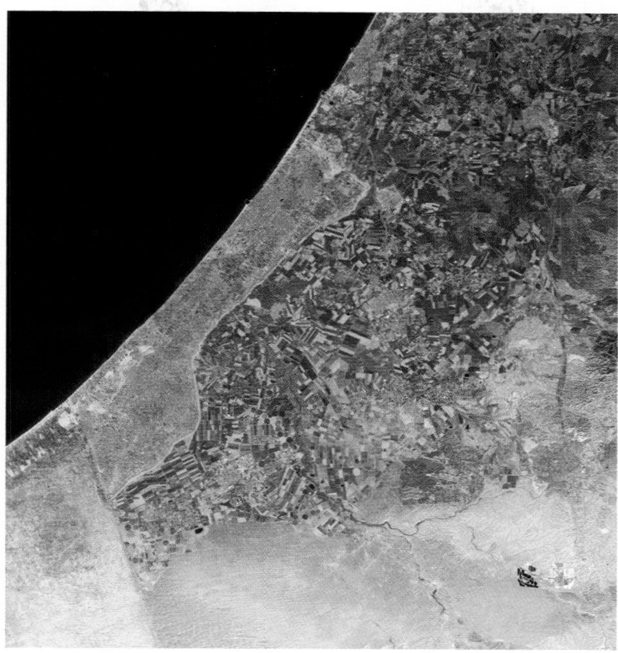

▲ On this satellite image of the Mediterranean coast of Israel, the shape of the Gaza Strip is clearly visible. A security barrier stretches along the entire boundary and all cross-border movements are strictly controlled. The barrier is reinforced by a buffer zone.

► Boundary crossing points can provide an opportunity for elaborate ceremonies. Every evening at sunset since 1959, the gates at the crossing point at Wagah, between India and Pakistan, are closed with a colorful military display.

◄ There are 26 countries in Europe are party to the Schengen agreement. This means that, in most cases, border controls have been removed and no checks are made on passengers traveling by road, rail, and air once they are within the Schengen area.

Schengen states

- Existing Schengen states
- Existing Schengen states not part of the EU
- Non-Schengen EU states

DRAWING THE LINE

Where to draw the line? Historically, physical features presented themselves as an obvious place to establish a boundary. They were seen as self-evident and natural. Boundaries could follow rivers and mountain ranges. France can be seen as a good example of this – it is bounded by coasts, the Pyrenees, the river Rhine, and the Alps. Physical features can also act as a line of defense and, theoretically, can be easily described in treaties. However, they can have drawbacks. Where does the boundary lie in a river – in the middle, or following just one bank? River courses are not static and will migrate across the landscape. So it has to be decided if the boundary will remain with the original line of the river, or follow any new course. Around one-quarter of all boundaries follow mountain ranges. Conflict can arise from imprecise definitions in treaties over whether the border is to follow the line of the highest peaks, or the watershed. Allied to this are difficulties of surveying in mountainous terrain.

The world political map also displays boundaries that appear to have been drawn with a ruler, as indeed they were. Straight-line boundaries were often hastily drawn and imposed in Africa and the Middle East without much concern over cutting across existing tribal and linguistic barriers.

All political boundaries are artifical constructions in some way. Divisions following language and ethnic divides were attempted in eastern Europe in the postwar era in the 20th century, but this still led to conflict. There is no perfect solution.

ANTARCTIC TREATY

Most maps of Antarctica in atlases will omit the boundary lines shown on the map to the right. However, these claims to the continent are still valid—although now "frozen." Antarctica has been protected for 50 years by a unique international agreement: the Antarctic Treaty. In 1959, 12 nations signed the original treaty, and this number has now risen to 52 signatories. Prior to the Treaty, disputes over sovereignty were escalating. The seven nations shown here have formal claims to the territory. The United States and Russian Federation have reserved their rights to submit similar claims. The basis of the claims is discovery, geographical proximity, and occupation. The Treaty effectively puts all territorial claims on hold and no new claims can be made. The main purpose of the Treaty is to ensure that the continent is used for peaceful purposes with freedom for scientific investigation and cooperation. There are also agreements on environmental safeguards, management of fishing, and conservation of wildlife. Commercial exploitation of minerals is not allowed. More than 40 permanent, year-round scientific research stations are maintained by 28 of the Treaty nations, with more operating in the Antarctic summer. The Treaty is considered to be one of the most successful international agreements.

▲ The flags of the Antarctic Treaty nations around the ceremonial South Pole.

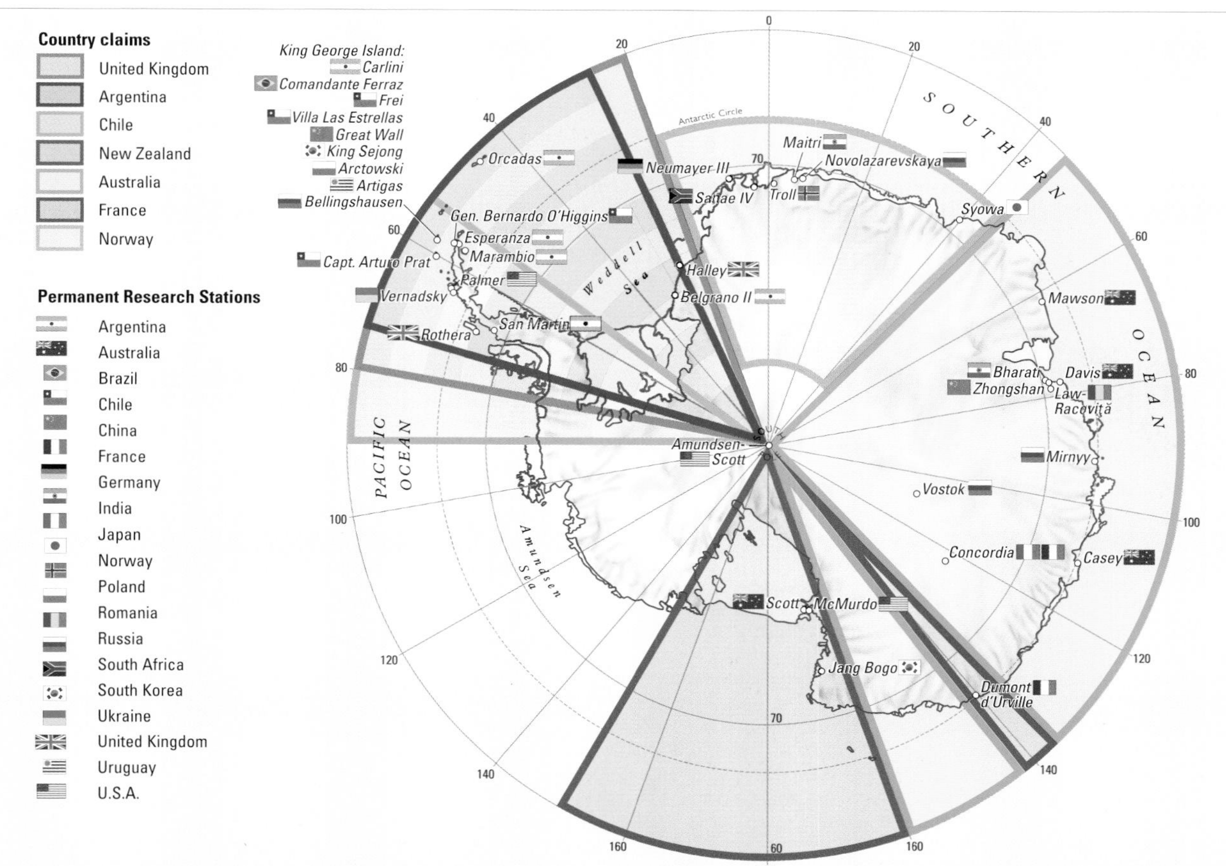

For more information:
84 Oceans and Seas
150 Arctic Ocean

As on land, the seas and oceans can be subject to territorial claims. On most atlas maps, maritime boundaries are rarely shown in anything other than a simplified form. Any boundary lines on the maps may just be indicating which offshore islands belong to a particular state. However, because nations want to be able to harvest and exploit the valuable natural resources of the seas and ocean beds, there needs to be a plan to establish sovereignty.

For coastal states, sovereignty does not end at the coastline, but it graduates and changes, moving through a series of zones outward to the high seas. From early times, control of waters close to the coast, or access through narrow straits, was largely dependent on having a strong naval power. Over time, the acceptance of international customary law codified acceptable limits to maritime sovereignty, especially in regard to territorial seas. However, it was the coming into force, in 1994, of the United Nations Convention on the Law of the Sea (UNCLOS) that has provided an internationally accepted program for making and approving national claims to maritime territory. In addition to providing a framework for defining maritime boundaries, UNCLOS has established obligations for protecting the marine environment and controlling the exploitation of mineral resources in the deep seabed, and ocean floor, lying beyond national jurisdiction. This relies on the principle of international law of the "common heritage of mankind" that holds that certain defined territorial areas should be held in trust for future generations.

COASTAL STATE WATERS

Coastal states can claim jurisdiction over a series of maritime zones. Internal waters lie landward of the territorial sea baseline (an officially agreed low-water line). The width of the territorial sea has been set by UNCLOS at 12 nautical miles (nm) from the baseline. The contiguous zone acts as a buffer to the territorial sea and stretches out to 24 nm from the coast. Beyond that, states can claim up to 200 nm as an exclusive economic zone (EEZ). This allows states sovereign rights for exploring, exploiting, conserving, and managing natural resources. The high seas are open to all states, both coastal and landlocked.

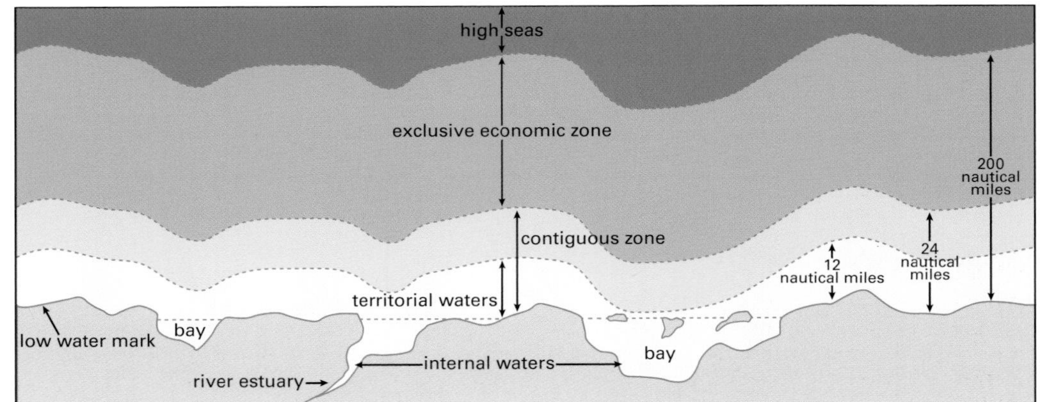

TERRITORIAL SEA

UNCLOS states that "every state has the right to establish the breadth of its territorial sea up to a limit not exceeding 12 nautical miles (nm)." Traditionally, most states had claimed a territorial sea of 3 nm. This program was known as "the canon shot" rule, because it was about the limit of the area that could be controlled from the shore by firepower. However, because UNCLOS allows claims of up to 12 nm, many states now claim this—or more. To help mitigate the need for excessive claims for territorial seas, other zones, such as the exclusive economic zone (EEZ), have been developed within UNCLOS to provide some protection for national economic interests farther out from the coast.

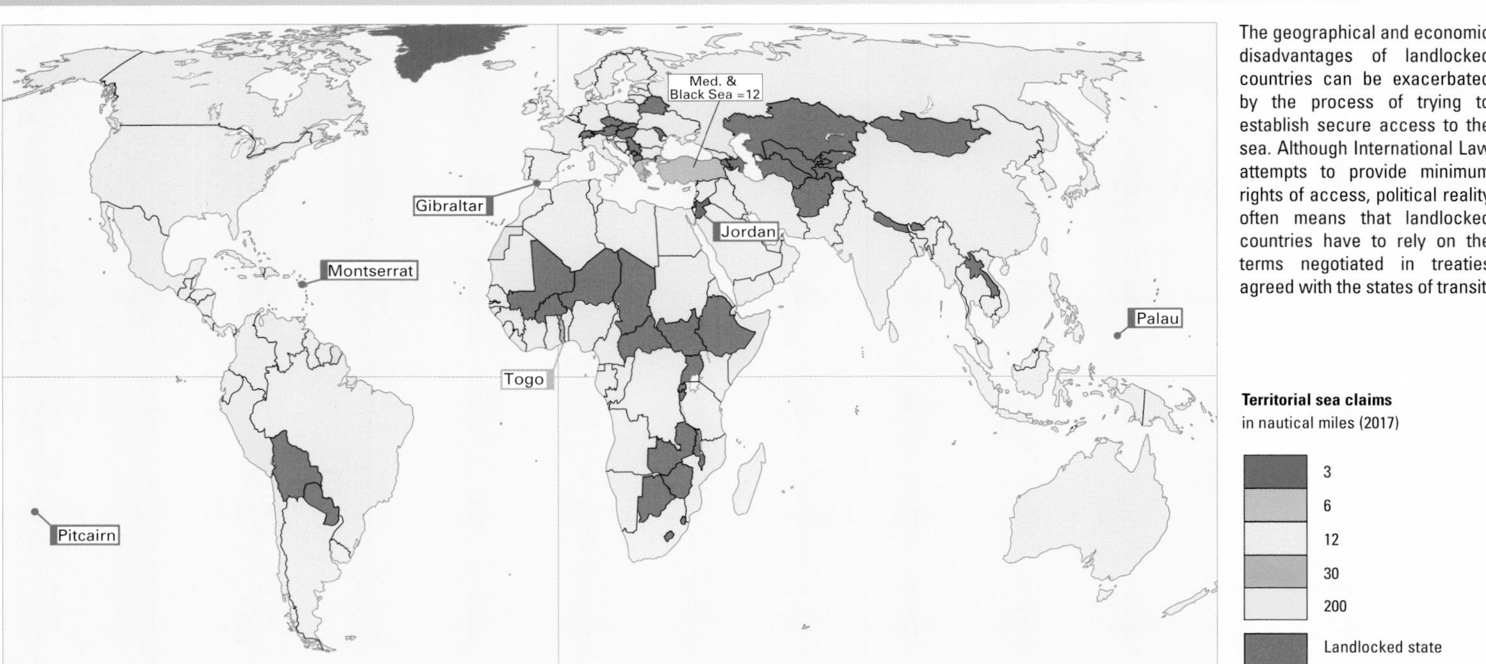

The geographical and economic disadvantages of landlocked countries can be exacerbated by the process of trying to establish secure access to the sea. Although International Law attempts to provide minimum rights of access, political reality often means that landlocked countries have to rely on the terms negotiated in treaties agreed with the states of transit.

SOUTH CHINA SEA

UNCLOS establishes clear guidelines on the limits of the maritime boundaries that states may claim. Complications arise when applying the theory in the real world. The twists and turns of coastlines, the relative importance of offshore islands, and the distance between opposite states all need to be taken into account. Boundaries need to be agreed between adjacent, and neighboring, states. Because having the rights to exploit natural resources in zones controlled by a state are so economically important, nations are willing to go to great lengths to press their claims to maritime territory. One highly contested area lies in the South China Sea around the Spratly Islands. This territorial dispute involves Brunei, China, Malaysia, the Philippines, Taiwan, and Vietnam. At stake are potentially significant oil and gas reserves, rich fishing grounds, and strategic control of shipping lanes. China's ambitious, but ill-defined, claims in the South China Sea are depicted on the map by what China calls the "Nine-dash line." This assertion of sovereignty clashes with the claims for EEZs by the neighboring states. Although the Spratly Islands are far from China's coast, China claims them on the basis of historic occupation. In recent years, China has been artificially strengthening and extending more than half a dozen reefs, including building an airfield on Fiery Cross Reef. The other parties in this dispute have also undertaken reclamation work, but it is the scale of China's efforts that is causing concern. The United States wants to preserve the right of free passage through the South China Sea and deploys aircraft and ships in this area despite objections from China.

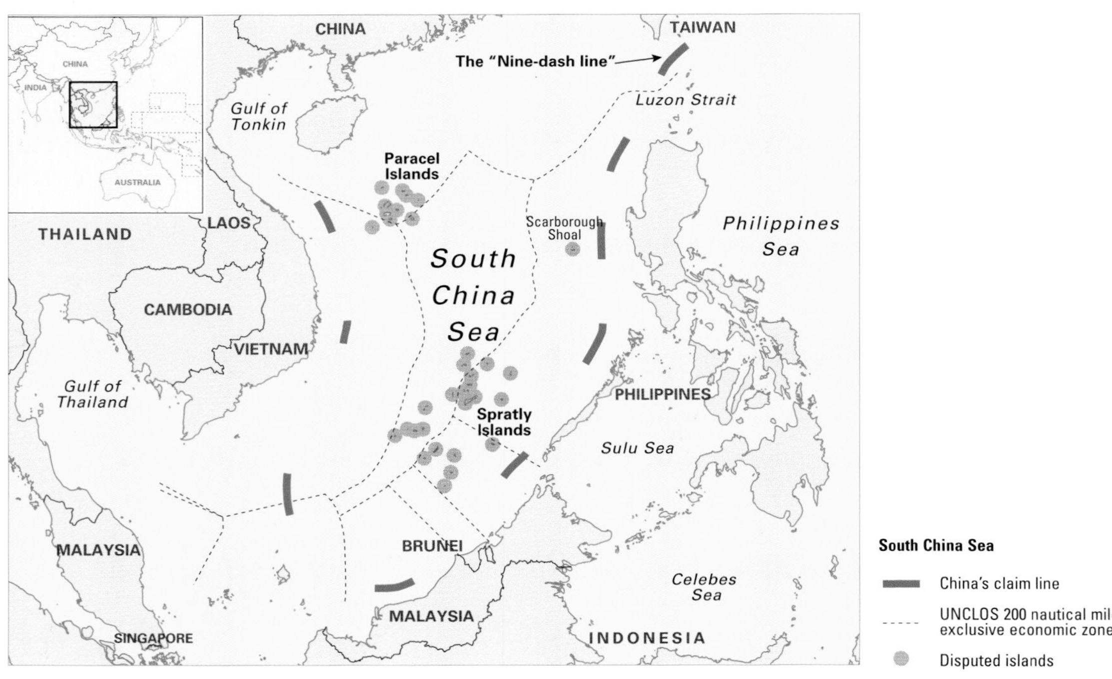

CONTINENTAL MARGIN

In addition to the zones that can be claimed up to 200 nautical miles from a state's coastline (see page 12), nations can claim certain rights over their continental shelf. The continental shelf is defined as the natural prolongation of a state's land territory into, and under, the sea. Establishing the legally acceptable outer edge of this geographical feature is technically complex and expensive to research. However, it can be worth the investment, because it allows a state to exploit minerals and nonliving material in the subsoil of the seabed. It does not, however, confer exclusive fishing rights.

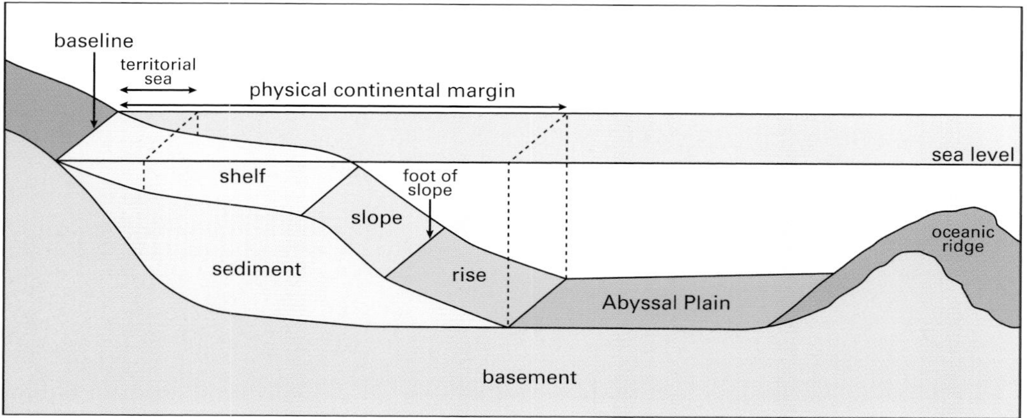

DISPUTED ISLANDS

Islands, large or small, can allow a state to claim significant areas of ocean and the seabed. Islands, as defined by UNCLOS, must be clearly capable of inhabitation and of economic life. If it can be established that an island satisfies this criteria, and is part of the territory of a state, the state may claim all the maritime zones, as outlined on page 12, radiating out from the island's coastline. There are approximately half a million pieces of land that might be considered islands, and 27 states that are entirely insular in nature. If states satisfy farther criteria, they can be considered an "archipelagic sovereign state" under the terms of UNCLOS. This confers the right to construct the baselines that are the starting point for their maritime zones, as joining the outermost points of their outermost islands.

In the quest to establish maritime territory, conflict can arise out of the disputed sovereignty of islands, and over the definition of what legally constitutes an island. Some of the geographic criteria to be evaluated are that islands should be permanent features, above water at high tide, and not reliant on ice cover to be above water. In order to try to strengthen the case of a geographical feature that might not satisfy the conditions to be a legitimate island under the regime of UNCLOS, countries may artificially augment what land is available. This has happened in the Spratly Islands in the South China Sea (see page 12). If an "island" fails to satisfy the criteria, it might be categorized as a rock. One case is Rockall, lying 290 miles (460 km) west of Great Britain in the Atlantic Ocean. It lies within the UK's EEZ, but does not generate its own EEZ or continental shelf claim.

▲ Rock or island? Known as Tok-do to South Korea, and Takeshima to Japan (and internationally as the Liancourt Rocks), these sharp rocks lying in the Sea of Japan are at the root of a long-running dispute between the two countries.

ARCTIC REGION

The map, below, produced by IBRU, the Centre for Borders Research at Durham University in the UK, shows some of the complexity involved in establishing areas of maritime jurisdiction in the Arctic region. Although there are a number of disagreements, all of the Arctic states have followed the rules and procedures for defining their areas of the seabed as set out in UNCLOS. The states involved are Russia, Norway, and Denmark (who have formally submitted their claims), plus Canada and the United States who are continuing to gather data in preparation to submit their claims.

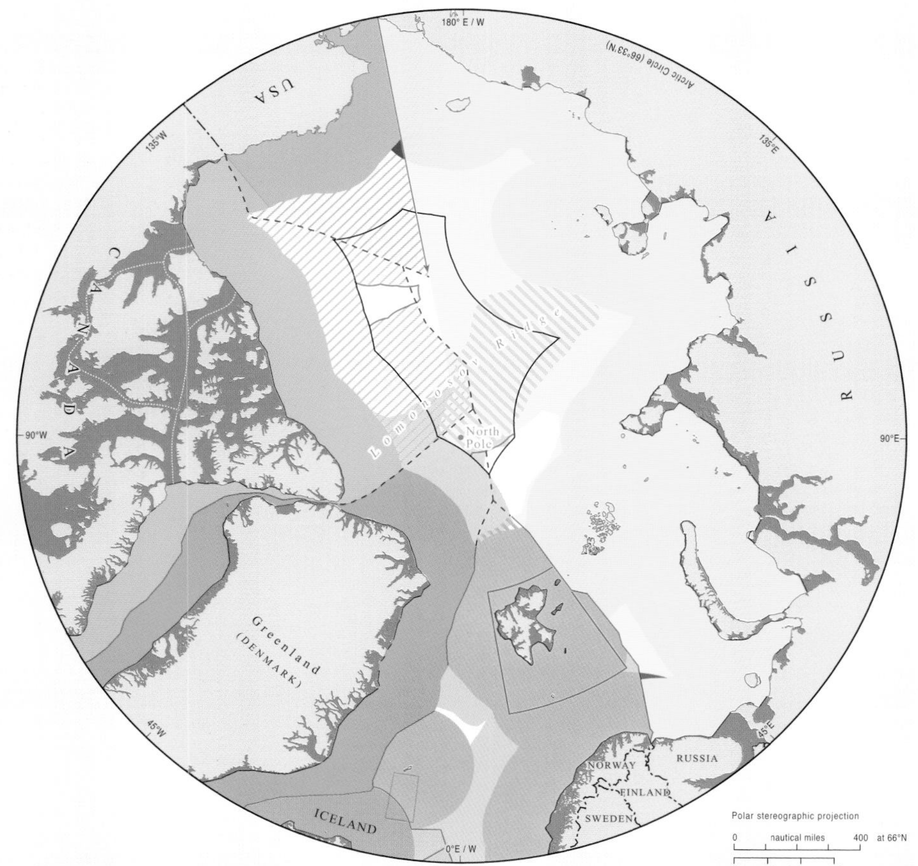

Source: IBRU, Durham University, UK
For explanation of notes: www.durham.ac.uk/ibru/resources/arctic

OUTER SPACE

Who owns the Moon? By being the first to step on the Moon's surface in the 1960s does this confer any rights? Where does the boundary lie between air space and outer space—and does it matter? International law recognizes the rights of states to control their own air space and to exclude, or even attack, unauthorized aircraft. The Outer Space Treaty of 1967, and the 1979 Moon Treaty, tried to address some of these issues by recognizing the freedom of using outer space for peaceful purposes. The development of the law in this context owes much to the doctrine of the common heritage of mankind, as embodied in the concept of the "high seas" in UNCLOS, and in the Antarctic Treaty. The Outer Space Treaty states that "Outer space, including the Moon and other celestial bodies, is not subject to national appropriation by claim of sovereignty, by means of use or occupation, or by any other means."

▲ Commander Eugene Cernan from the Apollo 17 mission stands by the U.S. flag on the surface of the Moon in 1972. Commander Cernann said that the astronauts were leaving as they came, "with peace and hope for all mankind."

One of the great natural wonders of the world, the Grand Canyon was carved by the Colorado River, which winds across this high plateau region of northwest Arizona for more than 277 miles (446 km). The steep sides of the canyon reveal hundreds of millions of years of geological history, and tourists come from all over the world to admire the magnificent multicolored rock formations. At its deepest point, the canyon plunges down for more than a mile (1.6 km), and at its widest it spans 18 miles (29 km). The most spectacular section of the canyon, the backward "C" shape toward the bottom right in this image, is contained within the Grand Canyon National Park.
[Map page 305] *NPA Satellite Mapping, CGG Services (UK) Ltd*

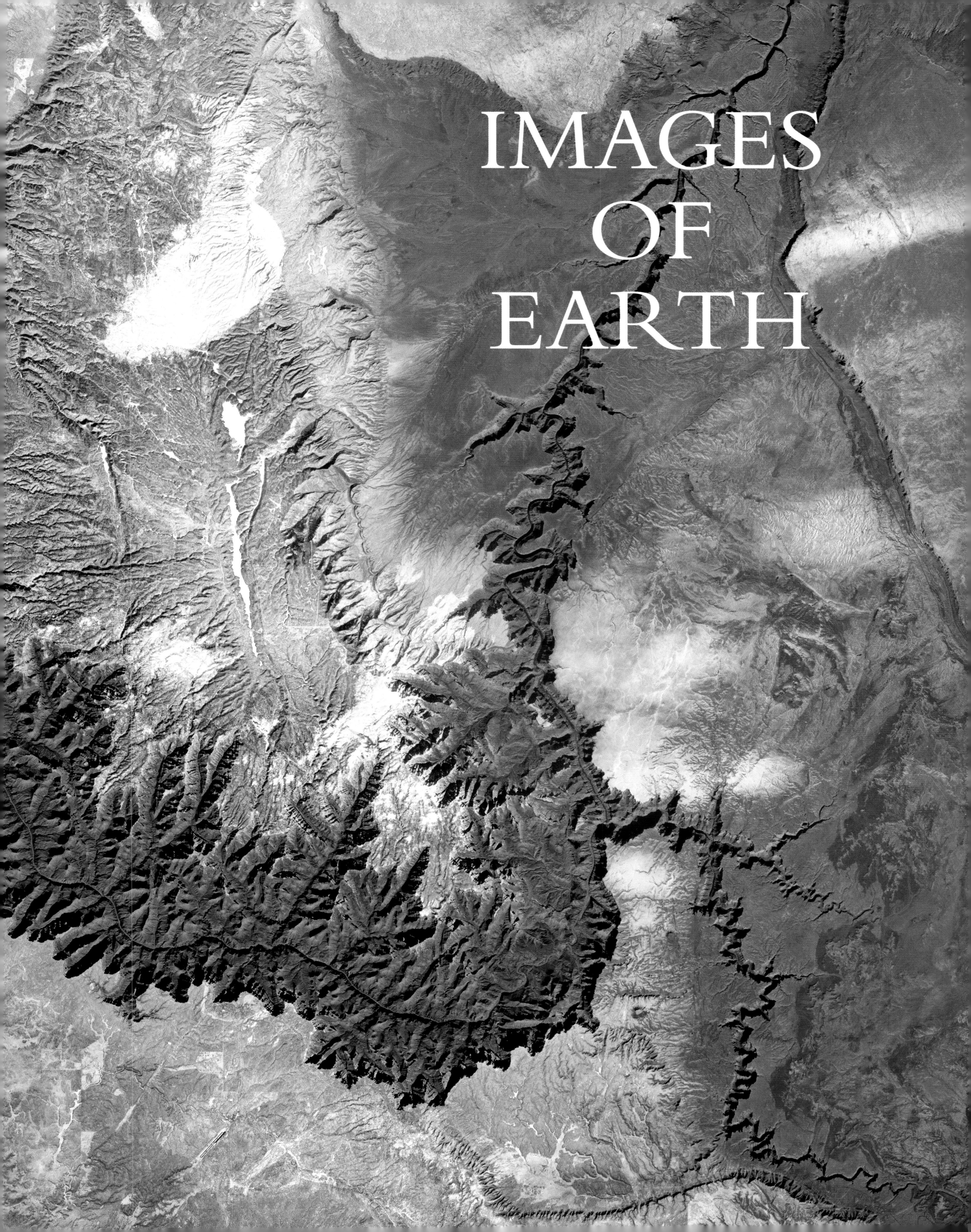
IMAGES
OF
EARTH

16 OSLO, NORWAY

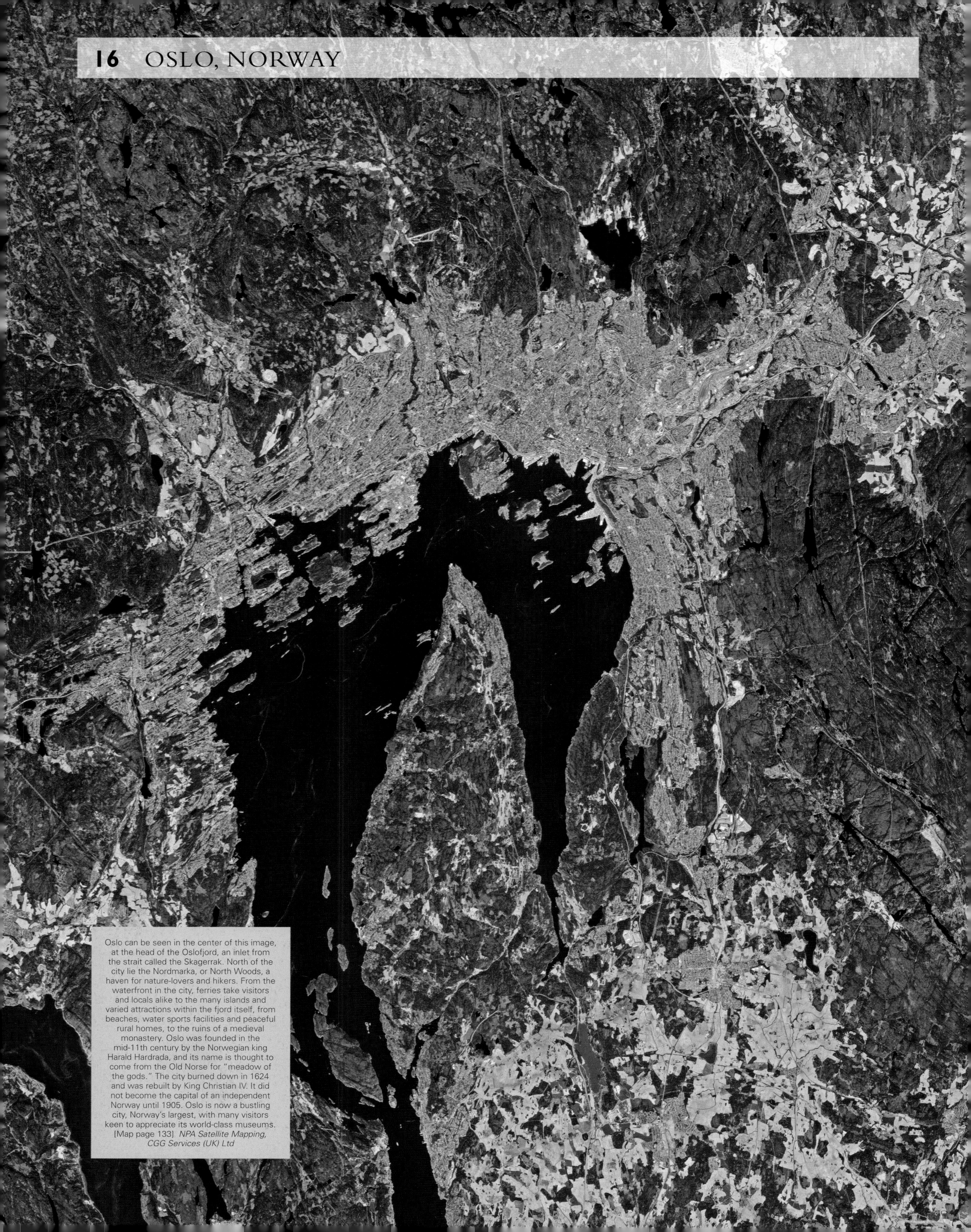

Oslo can be seen in the center of this image, at the head of the Oslofjord, an inlet from the strait called the Skagerrak. North of the city lie the Nordmarka, or North Woods, a haven for nature-lovers and hikers. From the waterfront in the city, ferries take visitors and locals alike to the many islands and varied attractions within the fjord itself, from beaches, water sports facilities and peaceful rural homes, to the ruins of a medieval monastery. Oslo was founded in the mid-11th century by the Norwegian king Harald Hardrada, and its name is thought to come from the Old Norse for "meadow of the gods." The city burned down in 1624 and was rebuilt by King Christian IV. It did not become the capital of an independent Norway until 1905. Oslo is now a bustling city, Norway's largest, with many visitors keen to appreciate its world-class museums. [Map page 133] *NPA Satellite Mapping, CGG Services (UK) Ltd*

Marseilles, the second largest city in France, is the capital of both the Bouche-du-Rhone department and the Provence-Alpes-Côte d'Azur region. Although there is evidence of human habitation in the region dating back some 30,000 years, the site itself was founded as the Greek colony of Massalia in *c.*600 BCE and was an important trading post for both them and the Romans, and later was the main point of entry for goods arriving from French colonies in North Africa. It is still France's largest Mediterranean port dealing in over 80 million tons of freight a year. The city's economy and manufacturing industries are closely linked to the port, with petroleum refining and ship building the city's chief industries. The tiny island to the right of the archipelago in the bay is the site of the Chateau d'If, in which Alexandre Dumas's Count of Monte Cristo was imprisoned. [Map page 175] *NPA Satellite Mapping, CGG Services (UK) Ltd*

18 VIENNA, AUSTRIA

Vienna, Austria's capital city, lies on the Danube River in the northeast corner of the country. It has a generally temperate climate, protected from the Alps in the west by the Vienna Woods, which can be seen to the left in this image. Just visible in the center, southwest of the Danube, is an elongated green patch called the Prater, a vast amusement park with a famous Ferris wheel. Vienna has long been an important and powerful center of trade and culture, being situated on the ancient "Amber Road," a north–south trade route between the Baltic and the Mediterranean. It was the seat of the Holy Roman empire from 1558 to 1806 and then the capital of Austria–Hungary until the end of World War I in 1918. Its architecture reflects its position as a wealthy center of power, with magnificent concert halls, palaces, museums, and opera houses. [Map page 142] *NPA Satellite Mapping, CGG Services (UK) Ltd*

The British overseas territory of Gibraltar occupies the tip of the peninsula on the eastern side of the Bay of Gibraltar, on the southern Mediterranean coast of Spain. It can be seen here on the right of the image, with the famous "Rock of Gibraltar" clearly visible as an elongated green patch. The Spanish city on the opposite side of the bay, to the left in this picture, is Algeciras. Gibraltar's strategic position at the entrance to the Mediterranean Sea from the Atlantic Ocean has long made it a desirable territory. It was captured from the Spanish by an Anglo–Dutch fleet in 1704 and formally ceded to Britain by the Treaty of Utrecht in 1713. Gibraltar has been a source of tension with Spain ever since; the population, however, has voted overwhelmingly to remain under British control.

[Map page 195] *NPA Satellite Mapping, CGG Services (UK) Ltd*

The city of Tehran, in north central Iran, stretches from the center to the left of this image. It lies between the snow-covered Elburz Mountains in the north and the Dasht-e Kavir desert to the south. The Elburz Mountains contain Iran's highest peak, Damavand, and its three major ski resorts. Tehran's climate is hot and dry, with the mountains keeping the humidity of the Caspian Sea away from the city. They also, however, along with the low rainfall, serve to trap air pollution, which has become an increasing problem. From the 13th century Tehran was a wealthy trading center, famous for its pomegranates. It expanded under the Safavid dynasty in the 16th century, but did not replace Esfahan as capital of Persia, as it was then known, until the late 18th century. It is now a major metropolis, by far the most populous city in Iran, and contains one-tenth of the country's population. [Map page 141] *NPA Satellite Mapping, CGG Services (UK) Ltd*

Naypyidaw has been the capital of Myanmar only since 2005, when the military government moved to a greenfield site near the middle of the country from the old capital, Yangôn, some 200 miles (320 km) to the south. Construction was begun in 2002 and was mostly completed in about ten years. The reason given for the move by the government was that Yangôn was too crowded for expansion. The city is divided into zones, including residential, military, hotels, and ministry. The large structure visible in the middle of the picture is the ministry zone, which includes the 31 parliamentary buildings and the presidential palace. The group of structures to its west is the Zabu Thiri Sports Complex. The city is low-rise, with apartment buildings not exceeding four storeys. Yangôn remains the commercial, cultural, and financial hub of the country. [Map page 241] *NPA Satellite Mapping, CGG Services (UK) Ltd*

22 TUNIS, TUNISIA

Tunis lies on the Mediterranean north coast of Tunisia. It is the country's largest city and its capital. Just above center in this image is Carthage, now an affluent suburb of Tunis. Carthage is bordered to the north by the shallow saline lake Sebkhet Arina, and to the south by Lake Tunis; in the east it narrows to a point stretching into the Gulf of Tunis. Carthage was founded by the Phoenicians in the 9th century BC. Its strategically important location – close to Sicily and protected by the Gulf of Tunis – was ideal for trade with Europe and it became a great commercial center and imperial power. It was destroyed by the Romans, along with Tunis, in 146 BC but soon grew powerful and prosperous again as a Roman colony. Carthage was finally eclipsed in power by neighboring Tunis when the Arabs took control in the 8th century AD. [Map page 258] *NPA Satellite Mapping, CGG Services (UK) Ltd*

Tombouctou lies on the southern edge of the Sahara Desert, approximately 8 miles (13 km) north of the River Niger. In this image, it looks like an irregular brown smudge in the middle of the orange Saharan sands. A road can be seen leading south from Tombouctou to Kabara, which is connected to the River Niger by a canal. Tombouctou developed as a trading center on the trans-Saharan caravan routes. From the 14th to the 16th centuries, it flourished as a major intellectual center for Islamic culture, attracting thousands of scholars from the wider Islamic world. Its three great mosques date from this time. European explorers did not visit Tombouctou until the early 19th century, although rumors of its great wealth had reached Europe many centuries before. Today, it is on the UNESCO list of World Heritage Sites in Danger.

[Map page 262] *USGS / NPA Satellite Mapping, CGG Services (UK) Ltd*

Canberra lies in the northeastern corner of the Australian Capital Territory, an enclave completely surrounded by New South Wales, in the southeast of the country. It was chosen to be Australia's capital city in 1909, after rivalry between Sydney and Melbourne – Australia's two largest cities – made a compromise choice necessary. The American architects Walter Burley Griffin and Marion Mahony Griffin won an international competition to design the new city, and their geometrical motifs of circles, triangles and hexagons can be seen in this satellite image. Canberra lies north and south of Lake Burley Griffin, an ornamental lake created by a dam across the Molonglo River. The National Museum of Australia sits on Acton peninsula, which protrudes into the lake. The prominent hill to the west of Canberra is the Black Mountains Nature Reserve; to the east is the Mount Ainslie Nature Reserve. Both contain significant Aboriginal heritage sites. [Map page 283] *©KARI 2019, Distribution SI Imaging Services, Republic of Korea, all rights reserved / NPA Satellite Mapping, CGG Services (UK) Ltd*

The Niagara River and the North American Great Lakes were created about 10,000 years ago at the end of the last ice age. The Niagara River drains Lake Erie into Lake Ontario, and it was the uneven erosion of different rock strata on the river's course that eventually carved out the spectacular waterfalls. The Niagara Falls have long been a popular tourist destination, and were well known in the past for such daredevil exploits as going over them in a barrel, or crossing on a tightrope. Goat Island separates the two main waterfalls, with the slightly larger Horseshoe (or Canadian) Falls lying to the east, and the American Falls to the west. The Falls are constantly being eroded, but the rate of erosion has been considerably reduced by the diversion of water above the Falls to hydroelectric power generating facilities.

[Map page 312] *USDA/NPA Satellite Mapping, CGG Services (UK) Ltd*

26 PHILADELPHIA, USA

Bordered to the east by the Delaware River, Philadelphia was founded in 1682 by Quaker William as the capital of the colony he led, Pennsylvania. From the start, the streets were laid out on a grid system for ease of transport, with wide streets to act as fire breaks. The city was the location of both the First and Second Continental Congresses, at the second of which the Declaration of Independence was debated and signed, and of the Constitutional Congress, at which the US Constitution was drawn up and signed. The small town grew to become America's first great industrialized city and port. Manufacturing has largely been replaced by services and information technology in importance to the city's economy. The skyscrapers of the city center business district can be seen towards the top of the image.
[Map page 313] *NPA Satellite Mapping, CGG Services (UK) Ltd*

Oklahoma City is bisected by the North Canadian River (also known as the Oklahoma River). It has three major man-made lakes – a common feature of the state – which can be seen in this image: lower right is the flame-shaped Lake Stanley Draper; center left is Lake Overholser; and above center is Lake Hefner. These reservoirs provide recreational opportunities, as well as City was founded in the "Land Run" of April 22, 1889, when previously unassigned lands were opened up for settlement. Within hours of the official noon start, around 10,000 settlers had claimed land around Oklahoma Station, a stop on the Atchison, Topeka and Santa Fe Railroad. The city grew rapidly, becoming a major distribution point for livestock and crops, and expanded still further with the discovery of oil in the late 1920s. It was a major stop on the famous highway Route 66.

[Map page 314] *NPA Satellite Mapping, CGG Services (UK) Ltd*

KINGSTON, JAMAICA

The city of Kingston lies on the southeast coast of Jamaica, backed by the Blue Mountains. The narrow Palisadoes peninsula protects the fine natural harbor and is the location of the Norman Manley airport, named for the prime minister who negotiated Jamaica's full independence in 1962. Kingston itself was founded in 1692 after an earthquake destroyed Port Royal, which was situated at the tip of the peninsula. It became a trading center for raw cane sugar, bananas and rum. The mountains form a verdant backdrop to the city, rising steeply from the coastal plain. The famous Blue Mountain Coffee is grown on the lower slopes, while the higher slopes are preserved as forest. In the 1970s Kingston was a significant force in popular culture, when Bob Marley became the first reggae artist to gain international success.

[Map page 320] *NPA Satellite Mapping, CGG Services (UK) Ltd*

The capital of Ecuador, Quito lies just south of the equator in a valley of the Andes, at an altitude of 9,350 ft (2,850 m). It is surrounded by a circle of volcanoes. Pichincha, seen to the left in this image, is the closest volcano to Quito, at a distance of only 5 miles (8 km). An active stratovolcano, Pichincha has had three major explosive eruptions in the last 2,000 years, with the most recent occurring in 1660. Were a similar event to happen today, the city would be under dire threat. Quito was a market center even before the establishment of an Inca settlement. It was occupied by the Spanish in 1534, who used the native population to build many churches and convents. Historic buildings in the well-preserved old town contain distinctive religious sculptures and carvings dating from this time. [Map page 328] *NPA Satellite Mapping, CGG Services (UK) Ltd*

30 SALAR DE UYUNI, BOLIVIA

The largest salt flat in the world, the Salar de Uyuni lies high up in the Andes (11,995 ft, 3,656 m) in the southwest of Bolivia. It covers an area of 4,086 square miles (10,582 square km), dwarfing the Bonneville Salt Flats in Utah by a factor of 100. Salt has been extracted from the flats by locals for many years. During the 20th century, it was discovered that here, among the other minerals, there are substantial amounts of lithium chloride – about 40% of the world's resources of lithium, a metal that is in high demand for batteries. The Bolivian government has set up a small-scale corporation to extract lithium from the brine that underlies the salt. The sparse wildlife in this harsh landscape includes vicuñas and three species of flamingo, which breed in November.

[Map page 330] *NPA Satellite Mapping, CGG Services (UK) Ltd*

Cape Horn is the rocky headland at the southern end of Hornos Island, the southernmost part of the Tierra del Fuego archipelago in South America. It marks the meeting point between the Atlantic and Pacific oceans. Cape Horn was discovered by the Dutch explorer Willem Schouten, who, with the Amsterdam merchant Isaac Le Maire, set out to find a new route between Europe and the 'East Indies' after the Dutch East India Company was granted a monopoly over trade through the Magellan Strait. In 1616 Schouten rounded the cape, naming it Cape Horn for his birthplace of Hoorn in the Netherlands. The new route, which was longer but much wider than that through the Magellan Strait, soon became popular. From the 18th to the 20th centuries, when the Panama Canal opened, it was a major shipping route for trade between Australia and the Far East and Europe. [Map page 336] *NPA Satellite Mapping, CGG Services (UK) Ltd*

GAZETTEER OF NATIONS

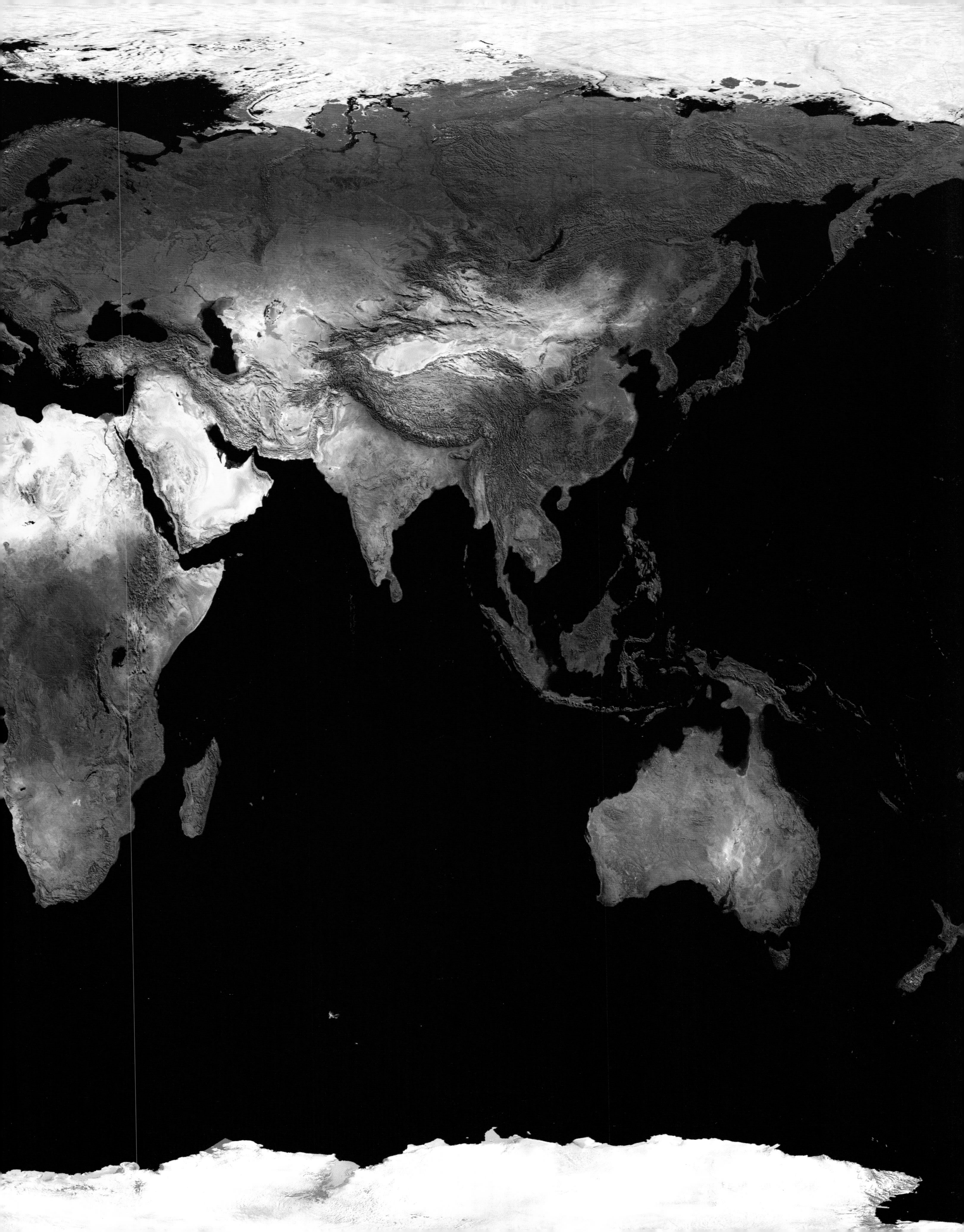

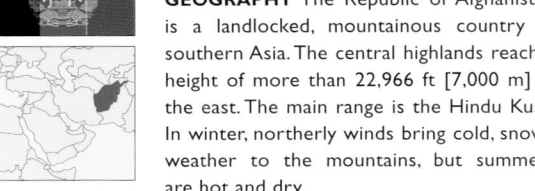

AFGHANISTAN

GEOGRAPHY The Republic of Afghanistan is a landlocked, mountainous country in southern Asia. The central highlands reach a height of more than 22,966 ft [7,000 m] in the east. The main range is the Hindu Kush. In winter, northerly winds bring cold, snowy weather to the mountains, but summers are hot and dry.

POLITICS & ECONOMY The modern history of Afghanistan began in 1747, with the unification of local tribes. In the 19th century, Russia and Britain struggled for control of the country. Following Britain's withdrawal in 1919, Afghanistan became fully independent. Soviet troops invaded in 1979 to support a socialist regime in Kabul, but they withdrew in 1989. By 2001, a group called the Taliban ("Islamic students") controlled 90% of the country. In 2001 an international force invaded Afghanistan. This NATO-led military force failed to defeat the extremists and its combat troops were withdrawn in 2014. Presidential elections in the same year saw Ashraf Ghani elected president. In 2015 Islamic State emerged in the east, while the Taliban insurgency grew in strength. By 2019 the Taliban controlled large parts of some provinces, and many areas remained under constant threat of attack. The UN recorded over 3,800 civilian deaths in 2018. Despite President Ghani's offer of peace talks in February 2018, the Taliban refused to negotiate with his administration, although US–Taliban peace talks took place in early 2019.

AREA 251,772 sq mi [652,090 sq km] **POPULATION** 34,941,000
CAPITAL Kabul **GOVERNMENT** Islamic Republic
ETHNIC GROUPS Pashtun (Pathan) 42%, Tajik 27%, Hazara 9%, Uzbek 9%, others 13%
LANGUAGES Pashtu, Dari/Persian (both official), Uzbek
RELIGIONS Islam (Sunni Muslim 80%, Shi'ite Muslim 19%), others 1%
CURRENCY Afghani = 100 puls

ALBANIA

GEOGRAPHY The Republic of Albania lies in the Balkan peninsula, facing the Adriatic Sea. About 70% of the land is mountainous, with most Albanians living on the western coastal lowlands.

The coastal areas of Albania experience a typical Mediterranean climate, with fairly dry, sunny summers and cool, moist winters. The mountains have a severe climate, with heavy winter snowfalls.

POLITICS & ECONOMY Albania is one of Europe's poorest nations. A former Communist country, ruled for nearly 50 years by the Stalinist dictator Enver Hoxha, Albania adopted a multiparty system in the early 1990s. The transition to democracy has been hindered by poor infrastructure and widespread corruption. A center-right government was defeated in 2013 by a Socialist-led coalition, which has pledged to fight organised crime and crack down on the trafficking and production of illegal drugs.

Albania has been a member of NATO since 2009 and was granted EU candidate status in 2014. In 2017, agriculture employed about 42% of the people. Albania has some oil, gas, and minerals: chromite, copper, and nickel are exported.

AREA 11,100 sq mi [28,748 sq km] **POPULATION** 3,057,000
CAPITAL Tirana **GOVERNMENT** Multiparty republic
ETHNIC GROUPS Albanian 83%, Greek 1%, Macedonian, Vlach, Roma
LANGUAGES Albanian (official)
RELIGIONS Islam 57%, Christianity 17% (Roman Catholic 10%, Orthodox 7%)
CURRENCY Lek = 100 qindars

ALGERIA

GEOGRAPHY The People's Democratic Republic of Algeria is Africa's largest country. Most Algerians live in the north, on the fertile coastal plains and hill country bordering the Mediterranean Sea. Four-fifths of Algeria is in the Sahara, the world's largest desert. The coast has a Mediterranean climate but the arid Sahara is hot by day and cold at night.

POLITICS & ECONOMY France ruled Algeria from 1830 until 1962, when the socialist FLN (National Liberation Front) formed a one-party government. Following the recognition of opposition parties in 1989, a Muslim group, the FIS (Islamic Salvation Front), won an election in 1991. The FLN canceled the elections and civil conflict broke out. About 100,000 people were killed in the 1990s. Abdelaziz Bouteflika has been elected president four times: the last being in 2014. Constitutional changes introduced in 2016 limited presidents to two terms, but Bouteflika, despite ill-health, nevertheless announced that he would stand in 2019 elections. Widespread street protests led him to resign the presidency in April 2019.

Algeria is a developing country. Its chief resources, oil and natural gas, account for about 97% of export revenue. Its gas reserves are the largest in Africa. The challenge for the future is to diversify the economy. Cement, iron and steel, textiles, and vehicles are manufactured.

AREA 919,590 sq mi [2,381,741 sq km] **POPULATION** 41,657,000
CAPITAL Algiers **GOVERNMENT** Socialist republic
ETHNIC GROUPS Arab-Berber 99%
LANGUAGES Arabic and Berber (official), French **RELIGIONS** Sunni Muslim 99% **CURRENCY** Algerian dinar = 100 santeem

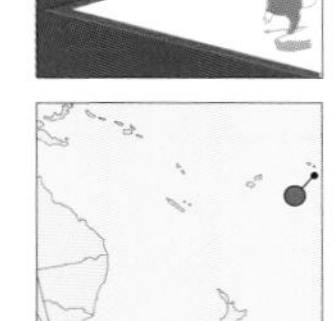

AMERICAN SAMOA

An "unincorporated territory" of the United States, American Samoa lies in the south-central Pacific Ocean.

AREA 77 sq mi [199 sq km]
POPULATION 51,000 **CAPITAL** Pago Pago

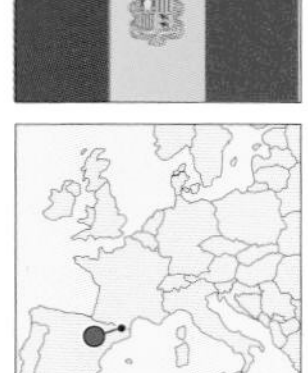

ANDORRA

In this prosperous mini-state, situated in the Pyrenees Mountains, tourism (especially winter sports) accounts for almost 80% of GDP. Most Andorrans live in the six valleys (the Valls) that drain into the River Valira.

AREA 181 sq mi [468 sq km]
POPULATION 86,000 **CAPITAL** Andorra La Vella

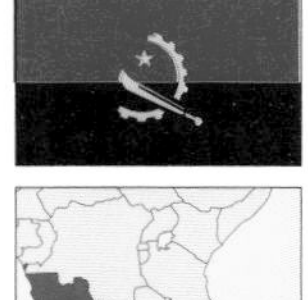

ANGOLA

GEOGRAPHY Situated in southwestern Africa, the Republic of Angola is the seventh largest country on the continent. Much of Angola lies on the South African plateau, with only a narrow coastal plain in the west.

Angola has a tropical climate, with temperatures of over 68°F [20°C] throughout the year, though the highest areas are cooler. The coast is dry, but the rainfall increases to the north and east.

POLITICS & ECONOMY Portugal controlled the coastal slave trade from the 17th century and extended its control inland in the 19th century. Independence, gained in 1975, was followed by 27 years of civil war which only finally ended when the rebel leader, Jonas Savimbi, was killed in 2002. Elections in 2008 began a transition toward a more democratic system. In 2017, after 38 years in power, Jose Eduardo dos Santos stood down as president and was replaced by former defence minister, Joao Lourenco.

Angola is a developing country, where 85% of the people are poor farmers. The main food crops are cassava and maize with coffee being exported. Angola has important oil reserves. Angola also mines diamonds and has reserves of copper, manganese, and phosphates. From 2005, foreign loans and oil revenue fueled a building boom, although growth slowed with lower oil prices worldwide.

AREA 481,351 sq mi [1,246,700 sq km] **POPULATION** 30,356,000
CAPITAL Luanda **GOVERNMENT** Multiparty republic
ETHNIC GROUPS Ovimbundu 37%, Kimbundu 25%, Bakongo 13%, others 25%
LANGUAGES Portuguese (official), many others
RELIGIONS Roman Catholic 41%, Protestant 38%, others 9%, none 12%
CURRENCY Kwanza = 100 cêntimos

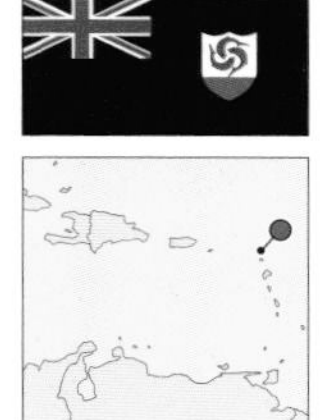

ANGUILLA

Formerly part of St Kitts and Nevis, Anguilla, the most northerly of the Leeward Islands, became a British dependency (now a British overseas territory) in 1980. The main sources of revenue are tourism and offshore banking, with lobster accounting for half of exports.

AREA 37 sq mi [96 sq km]
POPULATION 17,000 **CAPITAL** The Valley

ANTIGUA & BARBUDA

This former British dependency became independent in 1981. Tourism and offshore banking are vital to its service-based economy. In 2017 Hurricane Irma devastated Barbuda.

AREA 171 sq mi [442 sq km]
POPULATION 96,000 **CAPITAL** St John's

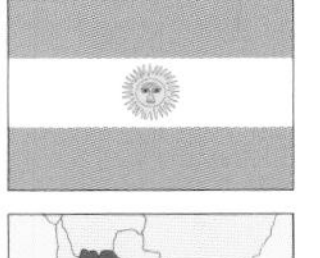

ARGENTINA

GEOGRAPHY The Argentine Republic is South America's second largest and the world's eighth largest country. In the west, the high Andes range contains Mount Aconcagua, the highest peak in the Americas. In southern Argentina, the Andes Mountains overlook Patagonia, a plateau region. The fertile plain of the Pampas occupies the east-central area.

The climate varies from subtropical in the north to temperate in the south. Rainfall is abundant in the north-east but lower to the west and south. Patagonia is largely desert.

POLITICS & ECONOMY The earliest people were American Indians, but 86% of the people are now of European ancestry. After Spanish rule ended in 1816, Argentina experienced periods of regional instability and military rule. In 1982, Argentina's military regime invaded the Falkland (Malvinas) Islands, but Britain regained the islands later that year. In 1983 civilian rule was restored. The ongoing dispute with Britain over the sovereignty of the Falkland Islands continues to cloud diplomatic relations.

The World Bank classifies Argentina as a "high-income" economy. Manufactures include food products, cars, electrical equipment, and textiles. Oil is the main resource and the chief farm products are beef, maize, and wheat. Exports include oil, meat, wheat, maize, vegetable oils, hides and skins, and wool. In 1991, Argentina was a founding member of Mercosur, an alliance of South American countries aimed at creating a common market. Following the economic, social, and political crisis of 2001, government policies barely allowed fitful recovery, with the country defaulting on repayment of its international debt in 2002 and 2014. Major market reforms have followed the election of Conservative Mauricio Macri in 2015.

AREA 1,073,512 sq mi [2,780,400 sq km] **POPULATION** 44,694,000
CAPITAL Buenos Aires **GOVERNMENT** Federal republic
ETHNIC GROUPS European 97%, Mestizo, Amerindian
LANGUAGES Spanish (official)
RELIGIONS Roman Catholic 92%, Protestant 2%, Jewish 2%, others
CURRENCY Argentine peso = 100 centavos

ARMENIA

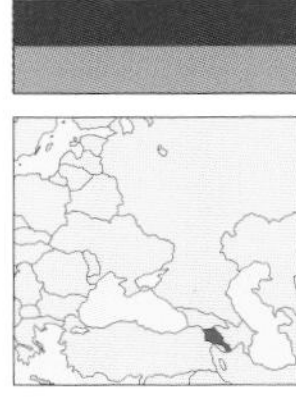

GEOGRAPHY The Republic of Armenia is a landlocked country in southwestern Asia. Most of Armenia consists of a rugged plateau, crisscrossed by long faultlines which make the area prone to earthquakes. The highest point is Mount Aragats, at 13,419 ft [4,090 m] above sea level. The height of the land gives rise to severe winters and cool summers. The highest peaks are snow-capped, but the total yearly rainfall is generally low.

POLITICS & ECONOMY In 1920, Armenia became a Communist republic and, in 1922, it became, with Azerbaijan and Georgia, part of the Transcaucasian Republic within the Soviet Union. But the three territories became separate Soviet Socialist Republics in 1936. After the breakup of the Soviet Union in 1991, Armenia became an independent republic. The ongoing dispute over Nagorno-Karabakh, an area enclosed by Azerbaijan where most people are Armenians, has been a major cause of conflict and instability which has hampered the economic development of both countries. The issue also sours relations with Turkey.

Armenia's economy has suffered because of its former dependency on a centrally planned Soviet system. In 2015, the country joined the Russian-led Eurasian Customs Union, and in 2017 it signed a Comprehensive and Enhanced Partnership Agreement (CEPA) with the EU. In April 2018 unprecedented street protests led to the resignation of the prime minister.

AREA 11,506 sq mi [29,800 sq km] **POPULATION** 3,038,000
CAPITAL Yerevan **GOVERNMENT** Multiparty republic
ETHNIC GROUPS Armenian 98%, Yezidi 1%
LANGUAGES Armenian (official)
RELIGIONS Armenian Apostolic 95%
CURRENCY Dram = 100 luma

NOTE: This alphabetical list includes the principal countries and territories of the world. The area figures give the total area of land, inland water, and ice. The population figures are 2018 estimates where available.

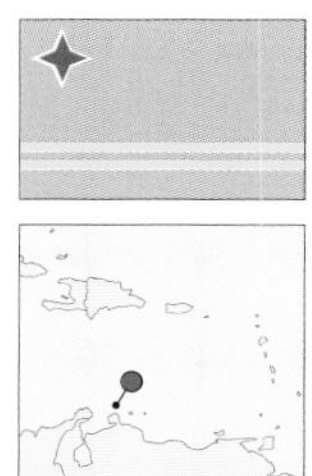

ARUBA

Formerly part of the Netherlands Antilles, Aruba (the most westerly of the Lesser Antilles) became a separate self-governing Dutch territory in 1986.

AREA 75 sq mi [193 sq km]
POPULATION 117,000 **CAPITAL** Oranjestad

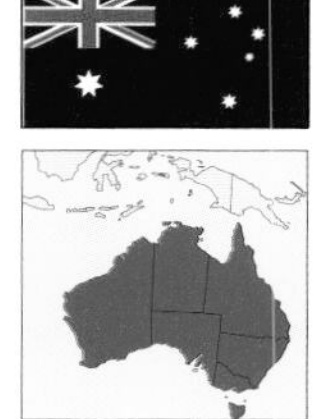

AUSTRALIA

GEOGRAPHY The Commonwealth of Australia, the world's sixth largest country, is also a continent. Australia is the flattest of the continents with its main highlands lying in the east. Here the Great Dividing Range separates the eastern coastal plains from the Central Plains. This range extends from Cape York Peninsula to Victoria in the far south. The longest rivers, the Murray and Darling, drain the southeastern part of the Central Plains. The Western Plateau makes up two-thirds of Australia. A few mountain ranges break the monotony of the generally flat landscape. Only 10% of Australia, notably the tropical north, the northeast coast and the southeast, has an average annual rainfall of more than 39 inches [1,000 mm]. But extreme weather events, including a prolonged drought in the Murray–Darling basin in the early 21st century and severe flooding in Queensland in 2010–12, cause periodic problems.

POLITICS & ECONOMY The Aboriginal people of Australia entered the continent from Southeast Asia more than 50,000 years ago. The first European explorers were Dutch in the 17th century, but they did not settle. In 1770, the British Captain Cook explored the east coast and, in 1788, the first British settlement was established for convicts on the site of what is now Sydney. Whilst maintaining links with the British Isles, the last 50 years has seen people from other parts of Europe and, most recently, from Asia settling in the country. Ties with Britain were also weakened by Britain's membership of the European Union, and Australia has now forged stronger links with the nations of eastern Asia, especially China, Indonesia, and Japan. The issue of retaining the monarch of the UK as the head of state is a recurring theme but, in a referendum in 1999, the majority of Australians voted to remain a constitutional monarchy. The conservative Liberal–National coalition swept into power in 2013, ending six years of Labor Party rule. They won again in 2016, by a very narrow margin. Elections are due in 2019.

Australia is a prosperous country. Crops can be grown on only 6% of the land, with dry pasture covering another 58%. Yet the country remains a major producer and exporter of farm products, particularly cattle, wheat, and wool. Grapes grown for wine-making are also important. The country is rich in a wide range of minerals, and Australia also produces oil and natural gas. Metals, minerals and farm products account for the bulk of exports. Australia's imports are mostly manufactured goods, though its own manufacturing industry is growing. The service sector contributes over 70% of total GDP.

AREA 2,988,885 sq mi [7,741,220 sq km] **POPULATION** 23,470,000
CAPITAL Canberra **GOVERNMENT** Federal constitutional monarchy
ETHNIC GROUPS Caucasian 92%, Asian 7%, Aboriginal 1%
LANGUAGES English (official) **RELIGIONS** Non-Christian 30%, Roman Catholic 23%, Protestant 23%, other Christian 6%
CURRENCY Australian dollar = 100 cents

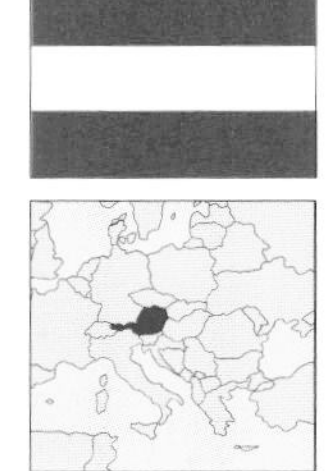

AUSTRIA

GEOGRAPHY Austria is a landlocked country at the heart of Europe. The River Danube flows across northern Austria on its way from Germany to the Black Sea. Southern Austria contains ranges of the Alps, reaching their highest point at Grossglockner, 12,457 ft [3,797 m] above sea level.

The climate is temperate in the west and more continental in the east. Winters are cold and snowy. Summers are warm and dry in the east.

POLITICS & ECONOMY Formerly part of the Austro-Hungarian Empire, Austria was annexed by Germany in 1938. In 1955, Austria became a neutral federal republic later joining the European Union in 1995. In recent years, Austria has been governed by coalitions. Presidential elections in 2016 resulted in victory for Alexander Van der Bellen of the Austrian Greens. In 2017 new Chancellor Sebastian Kurz of the right-wing Austrian People's Party dissolved the coalition with the Social Democrats and called early elections, later forming a coalition with the far-right Freedom Party.

Austria has a highly developed economy, with plenty of hydroelectric power and some oil, gas, and coal reserves. Although manufacturing, metals, and metal products are important to the economy, banking, insurance services, and tourism predominate. Dairy and livestock farming are the leading agricultural activities. Major crops include barley, potatoes, rye, sugar beet, and wheat.

AREA 32,378 sq mi [83,859 sq km] **POPULATION** 8,793,000
CAPITAL Vienna **GOVERNMENT** Federal republic
ETHNIC GROUPS Austrian 91%, Croatian, Slovene, others
LANGUAGES German (official) **RELIGIONS** Roman Catholic 74%, Protestant 5%, Islam and others 21% **CURRENCY** Euro = 100 cents

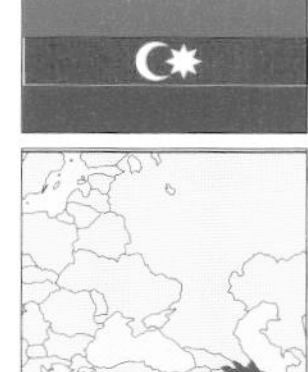

AZERBAIJAN

GEOGRAPHY The Azerbaijani Republic is a country in the southwest of Asia, facing the Caspian Sea to the east. It includes the area of the Naxçivan Autonomous Republic, which is completely cut off from the rest of Azerbaijan by Armenian territory. The Caucasus Mountains border Russia in the north.

Azerbaijan has hot summers and cool winters. The plains are fairly dry, but the mountains are rainy.

POLITICS & ECONOMY For a short period after the Russian Revolution of 1917, Azerbaijanis set up an independent state before the area was occupied by Russian forces in 1920. In 1922, the Communists set up a Transcaucasian Republic consisting of Armenia, Azerbaijan, and Georgia under Russian control. In 1936, the three areas became separate Soviet Socialist Republics within the Soviet Union. In 1991, following the breakup of the Soviet Union, Azerbaijan became an independent nation again. After independence, Azerbaijan clashed with Armenia over the enclave of Nagorno-Karabakh. A ceasefire in 1994 left Armenia in control of 20% of Azerbaijan's area, including Nagorno-Karabakh.

Azerbaijan has huge oil reserves. Oil extraction and manufacturing, including oil refining, and the production of chemicals, are vital for the export earnings which are funding investment in the country's infrastructure. Problems remain with corruption, and the government, which has been led by members of the Aliyev family since 1993, has been accused of authoritarianism.

AREA 33,436 sq mi [86,600 sq km] **POPULATION** 10,047,000
CAPITAL Baku **GOVERNMENT** Federal multiparty republic
ETHNIC GROUPS Azeri 91%, Dagestani 2%, Russian 2%, Armenian, others **LANGUAGES** Azerbaijani (official), Lezgi, Russian, Armenian
RELIGIONS Islam 93%, Russian Orthodox 2%, Armenian Orthodox 2%
CURRENCY Azerbaijani manat = 100 qapik

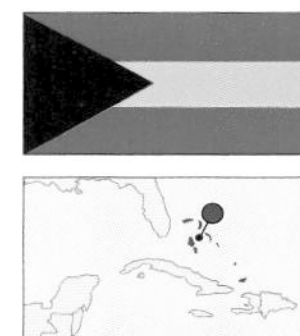

BAHAMAS, THE

A coral-limestone archipelago off the coast of Florida, The Bahamas became independent from Britain in 1973, and has since developed strong ties with the United States. Tourism and banking are major activities.

AREA 5,358 sq mi [13,878 sq km]
POPULATION 333,000 **CAPITAL** Nassau

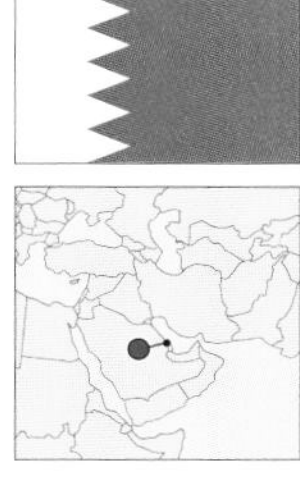

BAHRAIN

The Kingdom of Bahrain, an island nation in the Persian Gulf, became independent from the UK in 1971. An important financial services center, it is less dependent on oil than other Gulf states. Oil accounts for 60% of its exports.

In 2017, Bahrain joined Saudi Arabia, the UAE, and Egypt in imposing a blockade on neighboring Qatar.

AREA 268 sq mi [694 sq km]
POPULATION 1,443,000 **CAPITAL** Manama

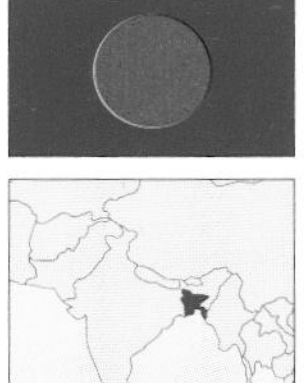

BANGLADESH

GEOGRAPHY The People's Republic of Bangladesh is one of the world's most densely populated countries. Apart from hilly regions in the far northeast and southeast, most of the land is flat and covered by fertile alluvium spread over the land by the Ganges, Brahmaputra, and Meghna rivers. These rivers overflow when they are swollen by the annual monsoon rains. Dry northerly winds blow in winter, but moist southerly winds bring heavy rain in summer.

POLITICS & ECONOMY In 1947, British India was partitioned between the mainly Hindu India and the Muslim Pakistan. Pakistan consisted of two parts, West and East Pakistan, which were separated by about 1,000 mi [1,600 km] of Indian territory. Differences developed between West and East Pakistan and after a nine-month civil war, East Pakistan declared itself to be the new nation of Bangladesh in 1971. A famine in 1974 and a coup in 1975 were followed by political upheavals. The army took control in 2007, but elections in 2008 returned Sheikh Hasina's Awami League to power. Hasina was re-elected for a third term in 2014, and the Awami League won a convincing victory in 2018 parliamentary elections. Since 2017 more than 1,000,000 Muslim Rohingya have fled to Bangladesh from Myanmar.

Bangladesh is one of the world's poorest countries. Its economy depends mainly on agriculture, and garment production.

AREA 55,598 sq mi [143,998 sq km] **POPULATION** 159,453,000
CAPITAL Dhaka **GOVERNMENT** Multiparty republic
ETHNIC GROUPS Bengali 98%, tribal groups
LANGUAGES Bengali (official), English **RELIGIONS** Islam 89%, Hinduism 10% **CURRENCY** Taka = 100 paisas

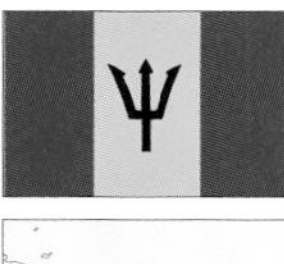

BARBADOS

The most easterly Caribbean country, Barbados became independent from the UK in 1966. A densely populated island, Barbados is prosperous by comparison with most Caribbean countries.

AREA 166 sq mi [430 sq km]
POPULATION 293,000 **CAPITAL** Bridgetown

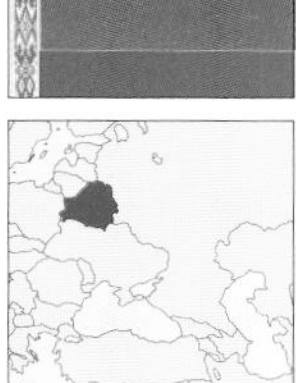

BELARUS

GEOGRAPHY The Republic of Belarus is a landlocked country in Eastern Europe. The land is low-lying and mostly flat. In the south, much of it is marshy and this area contains Europe's largest marsh and peat bog, the Pripet Marshes. The climate is affected by both the moderating influence of the Baltic Sea and continental conditions to the east. The winters are cold and the summers warm.

POLITICS & ECONOMY In 1918, Belarus (White Russia) became an independent republic, but Russia invaded the country and, in 1919, a Communist state was set up. In 1922, Belarus became a founder republic of the Soviet Union. In 1991, Belarus again became an independent republic, and though Belarus continued to support reunification with Russia, any surrender of sovereignty was not expected. President Alexander Lukashenko, who has been re-elected five times between 1994 and 2015, has been criticized for his autocratic rule, his poor record on human rights, and his disregard for freedom of speech.

According to the World Bank, Belarus has an "upper-middle-income" economy. Most economic activities remain under government control. From the 1990s, the economy stagnated, but 2017 onwards saw signs of modest economic recovery. Mining and manufacturing are the most valuable activities.

AREA 80,154 sq mi [207,600 sq km] **POPULATION** 9,528,000
CAPITAL Minsk **GOVERNMENT** Multiparty republic
ETHNIC GROUPS Belarusian 84%, Russian 8%, Polish, Ukrainian, others
LANGUAGES Belarusian, Russian (both official)
RELIGIONS Eastern Orthodox 80%, others 20%
CURRENCY Belarusian ruble = 100 kapyeyka

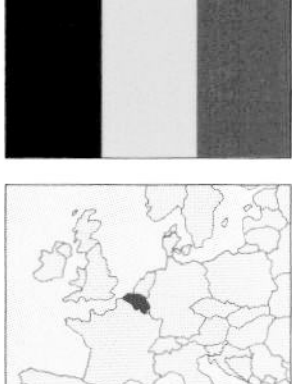

BELGIUM

GEOGRAPHY The Kingdom of Belgium is a densely populated country in Western Europe. Behind the coastline on the North Sea, which is 39 mi [63 km] long, lie its coastal plains. Central Belgium consists of low plateaux and the only highland region is the Ardennes in the southeast.

Belgium has a cool, temperate climate. Moist winds from the Atlantic Ocean bring fairly heavy rain, especially in the Ardennes.

POLITICS & ECONOMY In 1815, Belgium and the Netherlands united as the "low countries," but Belgium became independent in 1830. Belgium's economy was weakened by the two World Wars, but, from 1945, the country recovered quickly, first through collaboration with the Netherlands and Luxembourg, which formed a customs union called Benelux, and later through its membership of the European Union.

Tension between the Dutch-speaking Flemings in the north and the French-speaking Walloons in the south is an ongoing political problem. In the 1970s, the government divided the country into three economic regions: Flanders, Wallonia, and bilingual Brussels. In 1993, Belgium adopted a federal constitution, giving each region its own parliament. However, in 2010, differences between the parties led to the collapse of the coalition government. Since 2014, Charles Michel has led a four-party coalition. King Philippe succeeded to the throne in 2013. In March 2016, Islamic State terrorists targeted Brussels' Zaventem Airport and Maalbeek station.

Belgium is a major trading nation, though, with few natural resources, most materials used in manufacturing are imported. Major products include chemicals, processed food, and steel. Flanders has a long history of textile production. Agriculture employs less than 2% of the people, but farmers produce most of the country's food. Barley and wheat are major crops, followed by flax, hops, potatoes, and sugar beet. But the most valuable agricultural activities are dairy farming and livestock rearing. Brussels is a major centre for diplomacy.

AREA 11,787 SQ MI [30,528 SQ KM] **POPULATION** 11,571,000
CAPITAL BRUSSELS **GOVERNMENT** FEDERAL CONSTITUTIONAL MONARCHY
ETHNIC GROUPS BELGIAN 89% (FLEMING 58%, WALLOON 31%), OTHERS 11%
LANGUAGES DUTCH, FRENCH, GERMAN (ALL OFFICIAL)
RELIGIONS ROMAN CATHOLIC 75%, OTHERS 25%
CURRENCY EURO = 100 CENTS

BELIZE

GEOGRAPHY Behind the southern coastal plain, the land rises to the Maya Mountains, which reach 3,674 ft [1,120 m] at Victoria Peak. The north is mostly low-lying and swampy. Temperatures are high all year round, while the average annual rainfall ranges from 51 inches [1,300 mm] in the north to over 150 inches [3,800 mm] in the south. Hurricanes caused much damage in the 1990s and 2000s, but tourist numbers have continued to increase.

POLITICS & ECONOMY From 1862, Belize (then called British Honduras) was a British colony. Full independence was achieved in 1981, but Guatemala, which had claimed the area since the early 19th century, opposed this. Relations improved in the 1990s, when Guatemala recognized Belize's independence although there are still tensions over a boundary dispute. In 2011, the United States added Belize and El Salvador to its list of illegal drug producers.

The World Bank classifies Belize as an "upper-middle-income" developing country. Its economy is based on agriculture, and sugarcane is the chief commercial crop. Other crops include bananas, citrus fruits, maize, and rice. Forestry, fishing, and tourism are other important economic activities, with the last being Belize's chief foreign earner.

AREA 8,867 SQ MI [22,966 SQ KM] **POPULATION** 386,000
CAPITAL BELMOPAN **GOVERNMENT** CONSTITUTIONAL MONARCHY
ETHNIC GROUPS MESTIZO 49%, CREOLE 25%, MAYAN INDIAN 11%, GARIFUNA 6%, OTHERS 9%
LANGUAGES ENGLISH (OFFICIAL), SPANISH, CREOLE, MAYA
RELIGIONS ROMAN CATHOLIC 39%, PROTESTANT 27%, OTHERS
CURRENCY BELIZEAN DOLLAR = 100 CENTS

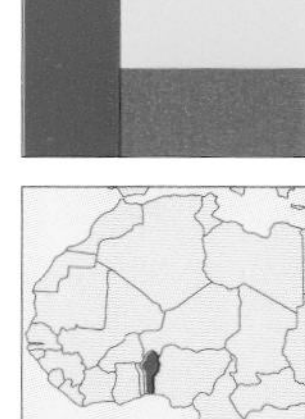

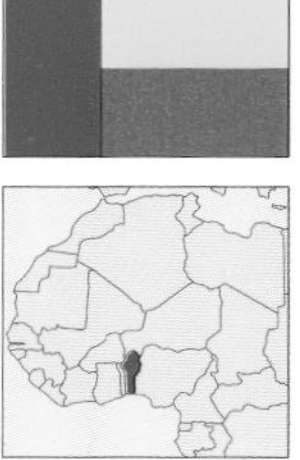

BENIN

GEOGRAPHY The Republic of Benin is one of Africa's smallest countries. It extends north–south for about 390 mi [620 km]. Lagoons line the short coastline, and the country has no natural harbors.

Benin has a hot, wet climate. The average annual temperature on the coast is about 77°F [25°C], and the average rainfall is around 52 inches [1,330 mm]. The inland plains are wetter than the coast.

POLITICS & ECONOMY After slavery was ended in the 19th century, the French gained influence in the area. Benin became self-governing in 1958 and fully independent as Dahomey in 1960. After much instability and many changes of government, a military group took over in 1972. The country, renamed Benin in 1975, became a one-party socialist state. Socialism was abandoned in 1989 and former coup leader Mathieu Kérékou served as president until 2006, when a former banker, Thomas Yayi Boni, was elected president. In 2016 elections, businessman Patrice Talon defeated the ruling party candidate.

Benin is a poor developing country. About half of the people live by subsistence farming. Exports include cotton, petroleum, and palm products. Cocoa, coffee, groundnuts (peanuts), tobacco, and shea nuts are also grown for export.

AREA 43,483 SQ MI [112,622 SQ KM] **POPULATION** 11,341,000
CAPITAL PORTO-NOVO **GOVERNMENT** MULTIPARTY REPUBLIC
ETHNIC GROUPS FON, ADJA, BARIBA, YORUBA, FULANI
LANGUAGES FRENCH (OFFICIAL), FON, ADJA, YORUBA
RELIGIONS CHRISTIANITY 43%, TRADITIONAL BELIEFS 30%, ISLAM 27%
CURRENCY CFA FRANC = 100 CENTIMES

BERMUDA

A group of about 150 small islands situated 570 mi [920 km] east of the USA. Its main sources of revenue are tourism, international business, and offshore finance.

AREA 21 SQ MI [53 SQ KM]
POPULATION 71,000 **CAPITAL** HAMILTON

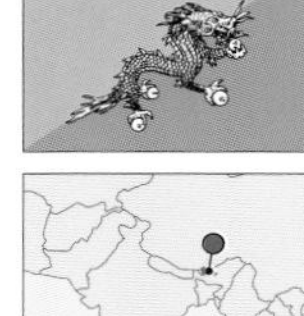

BHUTAN

GEOGRAPHY A mountainous, isolated Himalayan country located between India and Tibet. The climate is similar to that of Nepal, being dependent on altitude and affected by monsoonal winds.

POLITICS & ECONOMY The monarch of Bhutan is head of both state and government, and this predominantly Buddhist country remains, even in the Asian context, both conservative and poor, with an economy based mainly on hydropower. In 2008, Bhutan held its first ever democratic elections, turning it into a constitutional monarchy.

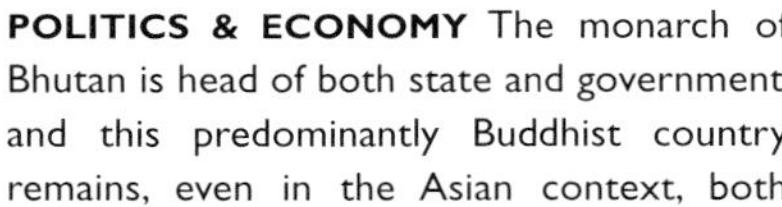

AREA 18,147 SQ MI [47,000 SQ KM] **POPULATION** 766,000
CAPITAL THIMPHU **GOVERNMENT** CONSTITUTIONAL MONARCHY
ETHNIC GROUPS BHUTANESE 50%, NEPALESE 35%
LANGUAGES DZONGKHA (OFFICIAL) **RELIGIONS** BUDDHISM 75%, HINDUISM 25% **CURRENCY** NGULTRUM = 100 CHHERTUM

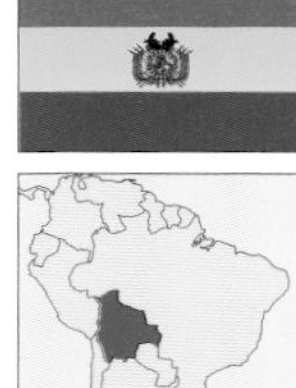

BOLIVIA

GEOGRAPHY The Plurinational State of Bolivia, as the country is officially called, is an isolated and landlocked South American country which straddles the Andes Mountains. The highest point is 21,391 ft [6,520 m] at Nevado Sajama in the west. About 40% of Bolivians live on the Altiplano, a high plateau in the Andes. The sparsely populated east consists of a vast lowland plain.

The Bolivian climate is greatly affected by altitude, with the Andean peaks permanently snow-covered and the eastern plains remaining hot and humid.

POLITICS & ECONOMY American Indians have lived in Bolivia for at least 10,000 years. The main groups today are the Aymara and Quechua people.

In the last 50 years, Bolivia has been ruled by a succession of civilian and military governments. Economic problems have led to a widening of the gap between rich and poor and, in 2005, Evo Morales, an Aymara farmer, was elected president. His policies of nationalization and redistributing wealth to peasants aroused opposition. Re-elected in 2009 and 2014, Morales was a keen advocate of state control and nationalized energy production. In 2017 Bolivia's highest court overruled the constitution, allowing Morales to stand again for president in 2019.

Although one of South America's poorest countries, it has its second largest reserves of natural gas. Other resources include silver, tin, zinc, and lithium, but the main activity is agriculture.

AREA 424,162 SQ MI [1,098,581 SQ KM] **POPULATION** 11,306,000
CAPITAL LA PAZ (SEAT OF GOVERNMENT); SUCRE (LEGAL CAPITAL/SEAT OF JUDICIARY) **GOVERNMENT** MULTIPARTY REPUBLIC
ETHNIC GROUPS MESTIZO 30%, QUECHUA 30%, AYMARA 25%, WHITE 15%
LANGUAGES SPANISH, AYMARA, QUECHUA (ALL OFFICIAL)
RELIGIONS ROMAN CATHOLIC 95%
CURRENCY BOLIVIANO = 100 CENTAVOS

BOSNIA-HERZEGOVINA

GEOGRAPHY The Republic of Bosnia-Herzegovina is one of the seven republics to emerge from the former Federal People's Republic of Yugoslavia. Much of the country is mountainous or hilly, with an arid limestone plateau in the southwest. The River Sava, which forms most of the northern border with Croatia, is a tributary of the River Danube. Because of the country's odd shape, the coastline is limited to a short stretch of 13 mi [20 km] on the Adriatic coast. A Mediterranean climate, with dry, sunny summers and moist, mild winters, prevails only near the coast. Inland, the weather is more severe, with hot, dry summers and bitterly cold, snowy winters.

POLITICS & ECONOMY In 1918, Bosnia-Herzegovina became part of the Kingdom of the Serbs, Croats, and Slovenes, which was renamed Yugoslavia in 1929. Germany occupied the area during World War II (1939–45). From 1945, Communist governments ruled Yugoslavia as a federation containing six republics, one of which was Bosnia-Herzegovina. In the 1980s, the country faced problems as Communist policies proved unsuccessful.

In 1990, free elections were held in Bosnia-Herzegovina and the non-Communists won a majority. A Muslim, Alija Izetbegovic, was elected president. In 1991, Croatia and Slovenia, other parts of the former Yugoslavia, declared themselves independent. In 1992, Bosnia-Herzegovina held a vote on independence. Most Bosnian Serbs boycotted the vote, while the Muslims and Bosnian Croats voted in favor. Many Bosnian Serbs, opposed to independence, started a war against the non-Serbs. They soon occupied more than two-thirds of the land. The war spread when Croat forces seized other parts of the country.

In 1995, the country retained its external boundaries, but it was divided into two self-governing provinces – one Bosnian Serb and the other Muslim Croat. Stability was restored with the help of NATO, but the country remained divided. In December 2011, after 14 months of political crisis, Muslim Croat and Serb leaders agreed on the formation of a central government, with a federal presidency that rotates between a Serb, a Muslim, and a Croat. In 2016, the country formally requested membership of the European Union.

The infrastructure and economy were shattered by the war in the early 1990s. Although some stability has been regained it is still considered one of the most corrupt European states. The economy relies on exporting metals and receiving foreign aid. Farm products include fruits, maize, tobacco, vegetables, and wheat, but food has to be imported.

AREA 19,767 SQ MI [51,197 SQ KM] **POPULATION** 3,850,000
CAPITAL SARAJEVO **GOVERNMENT** FEDERAL REPUBLIC
ETHNIC GROUPS BOSNIAN 48%, SERB 37%, CROAT 14%
LANGUAGES BOSNIAN, SERBIAN, CROATIAN
RELIGIONS ISLAM 40%, SERBIAN ORTHODOX 31%, ROMAN CATHOLIC 15%, OTHERS 14% **CURRENCY** CONVERTIBLE MARKA = 100 CONVERTIBLE PFENNIGA

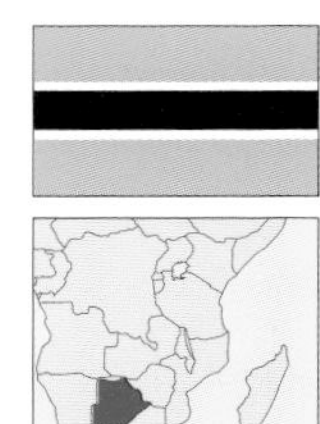

BOTSWANA

GEOGRAPHY The Republic of Botswana is a landlocked country in southern Africa. The Kalahari, a semidesert area covered mostly by grasses and thorn scrub, covers much of the country. Most of the south has no permanent streams but large depressions in the north form inland drainage basins. In one of them, the Okavango River, which rises in Angola, forms a large, swampy delta.

Temperatures are high in the summer months (October to April), but the winter months are much cooler. In winter, nighttime temperatures sometimes drop below freezing point. The average annual rainfall ranges from over 16 inches [400 mm] in the east to less than 8 inches [200 mm] in the southwest.

POLITICS & ECONOMY The earliest inhabitants of the region were the San, sometimes known as Bushmen. They had a nomadic way of life, hunting wild animals and collecting wild plant foods.

Britain ruled the area as the Bechuanaland Protectorate between 1885 and 1966. When the country became independent, it was renamed Botswana. Since then, the country has been a stable, multiparty democracy. In March 2018 Mokgweetsi Masisi was elected as the fifth president since independence. However, in a setback to development, the UN has said that around 25% of the adult population are infected with HIV/AIDS.

In 1966, Botswana was extremely poor, but since then per capita income has grown quickly. The discovery of minerals has boosted the economy. About 25% of the people depend on agriculture. Safari-based tourism, often upmarket, is important.

AREA 224,606 sq mi [581,730 sq km] **POPULATION** 2,249,000
CAPITAL Gaborone **GOVERNMENT** Multiparty republic
ETHNIC GROUPS Tswana (or Setswana) 79%, Kalanga 11%, Basarwa 3%, others **LANGUAGES** English (official), Setswana
RELIGIONS Christianity 72%, Badimo 6%, others 2%
CURRENCY Pula = 100 thebe

BRAZIL

GEOGRAPHY The Federative Republic of Brazil is the world's fifth largest country. It contains three main regions. The Amazon basin in the north covers more than half of Brazil. The Amazon, the world's second longest river, has a far greater volume than any other river. The second region, the north-east, consists of a coastal plain and the sertão, which is the name for the inland plateaux and hill country. The main river in this region is the São Francisco.

The third region is made up of the plateaux in the southeast. This area, which covers about a quarter of the country, is the most developed and densely populated part of Brazil. Its main river is the Paraná, which flows south through Argentina.

Manaus, on the Amazon, has high temperatures all through the year. Rainfall is heavy, though the period from June to September is drier than the rest of the year. The capital, Brasília, and the city Rio de Janeiro in the south also have tropical climates, with much more marked dry seasons than Manaus. The far south has a temperate climate. The northeastern interior is the driest region, with an average annual rainfall of only 10 inches [250 mm] in places. Rainfall is also unreliable and severe droughts are common in this region.

POLITICS & ECONOMY The Portuguese explorer Pedro Alvarez Cabral claimed Brazil for Portugal in 1500. The Portuguese developed their colony by enslaving many local Amerindian people and introducing about 4 million African slaves. Brazil declared itself an independent empire in 1822 and a republic in 1889. From the 1930s, Brazil faced periods of military rule and widespread corruption. However, civilian rule was restored in 1985.

After two unpopular presidencies, financial stability was established under President Itamar Franco. One of the "BRICS" nations (Brazil, Russia, India, China, and South Africa), Brazil has a rapidly industrializing economy. But many people, including poor farmers and residents of the favelas (city slums), do not share in the country's economic boom. Poverty led to the election of President Luíz Inácio Lula da Silva (generally called "Lula") in 2002. In 2010, he was succeeded by Dilma Roussef. She was re-elected for a second term in 2014, but was impeached in 2016 over financial irregularities and convicted of fraud in early 2018. In October 2018 Jair Bolsonaro, a polarizing figure from the far-right of Brazilian politics, was elected president.

Brazil is Latin America's leading economy, with industry as the most important economic sector. It is among the world's top producers of bauxite, chrome, diamonds, gold, iron ore, manganese, and tin. It is also a major manufacturing country, and it is self-sufficient in oil.

Brazil is a major farming nation and agriculture employs 16% of the work force. Coffee is a leading export. Other products include bananas, citrus fruits, cocoa, maize, rice, soybeans, and sugarcane. Brazil is also South America's top producer of eggs, meat, and milk. The rate of deforestation, whilst remaining a global concern as it may accelerate global warming, has been reduced in recent years.

AREA 3,287,338 sq mi [8,514,215 sq km] **POPULATION** 208,847,000
CAPITAL Brasília **GOVERNMENT** Federal republic
ETHNIC GROUPS White 54%, Mixed 38%, Black 6%, others 2%
LANGUAGES Portuguese (official)
RELIGIONS Roman Catholic 80%
CURRENCY Real = 100 centavos

BRUNEI

The Islamic Sultanate of Brunei, a British protectorate until 1984, lies on the north coast of Borneo. The climate is tropical and rain forests cover large areas. Brunei is a prosperous country because of its oil and natural gas production, and the Sultan is said to be among the world's richest men.

AREA 2,226 sq mi [5,765 sq km]
POPULATION 451,000 **CAPITAL** Bandar Seri Begawan

BULGARIA

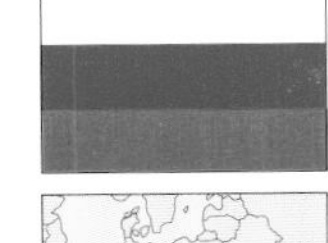

GEOGRAPHY The Republic of Bulgaria is a country in the Balkan peninsula, facing the Black Sea in the east. The heart of Bulgaria is mountainous. The main ranges are the Balkan Mountains in the center and the Rhodope (or Rhodopi) Mountains in the south.

Summers are hot and winters are cold, though seldom severe. The rainfall is moderate.

POLITICS & ECONOMY Ottoman Turks ruled Bulgaria from 1396 and ethnic Turks still form a sizable minority in the country. In 1879, Bulgaria became a monarchy, and in 1908 it became fully independent. Bulgaria was an ally of Germany in World War I (1914–18) and again in World War II (1939–45). In 1944, Soviet troops invaded Bulgaria and, after the war, the monarchy was abolished and the country became a Communist ally of the Soviet Union. Reforms in the Soviet Union in the late 1980s led Bulgaria's government to introduce a multi-party system in 1990. A non-Communist government was elected in 1991, in the first free elections in 44 years. Throughout the 1990s, Bulgaria faced many problems and it sought to become aligned to the West. Bulgaria became a member of NATO in 2004 and a member of the European Union in 2007. Presidential elections in 2016 were won by Socialist-backed independent Ruman Radev, prompting early parliamentary elections and a coalition government.

Bulgaria has some mineral deposits, including brown coal, manganese, gold, and iron ore. Manufacturing is the leading activity, with principal products including chemicals, processed foods, metal products, machinery, and textiles. Corruption and the prevalence of organized crime still hinder economic growth.

AREA 42,823 sq mi [110,912 sq km] **POPULATION** 7,058,000
CAPITAL Sofia **GOVERNMENT** Multiparty republic
ETHNIC GROUPS Bulgarian 77%, Turkish 8%, Roma 4%, Macedonian, Armenian, others **LANGUAGES** Bulgarian (official), Turkish
RELIGIONS Eastern Orthodox 59%, Islam 8%, others
CURRENCY Lev = 100 stotinki

BURKINA FASO

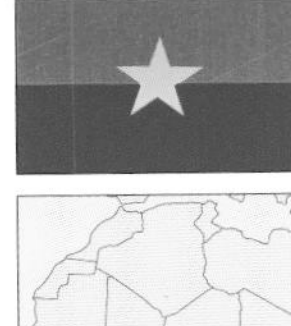

GEOGRAPHY The Democratic People's Republic of Burkina Faso is a landlocked country, a little larger than the United Kingdom, in West Africa. However, Burkina Faso has only a quarter of the population of the UK. The country consists of a plateau, between about 650 ft and 2,300 ft [200 m to 700 m] above sea level. The plateau is cut by several, mainly seasonal, rivers.

The capital city, Ouagadougou, in central Burkina Faso, has high temperatures throughout the year. Most of the rain falls between May and September, but the rainfall is erratic and droughts are common.

POLITICS & ECONOMY The people of Burkina Faso are divided into two main groups: the Voltaic group which includes the Mossi, who form the largest single group, and the Bobo. The French conquered the Mossi capital of Ouagadougou in 1897 and they made the area a protectorate. In 1919, the area became a French colony called Upper Volta. After independence in 1960, Upper Volta became a, sometimes violent and unstable, one-party state. Following a coup in 1983, Thomas Sankara took power and, in 1984, renamed the country Burkina Faso. Long-term president Blaise Compaoré was ousted in 2014. Former PM Marc Kabore won the ensuing election. Terrorism is an increasing problem.

Burkina Faso is one of the world's poorest countries and has become very dependent on foreign aid. Most of the land is dry with thin soils. The country's main food crops are beans, maize, millet, rice, and sorghum. Cotton, groundnuts (peanuts), and shea nuts, whose seeds produce a fat used to make cooking oil and soap, are grown for sale abroad.

The country has few resources and manufacturing is on a small scale. There are deposits of gold, manganese, zinc, lead, and nickel, but lack of infrastructure hinders development. The country's key exports are cotton, gold and livestock. Many young men seek jobs abroad in Ghana and Côte d'Ivoire and the money they send home to their families is important to the country's economy.

AREA 105,791 sq mi [274,000 sq km] **POPULATION** 19,743,000
CAPITAL Ouagadougou **GOVERNMENT** Multiparty republic
ETHNIC GROUPS Mossi 40%, Gurunsi, Senufo, Lobi, Bobo, Mande, Fulani
LANGUAGES French (official), Mossi, Fulani
RELIGIONS Islam 61%, Christianity 23%, traditional beliefs 16%
CURRENCY CFA franc = 100 centimes

BURUNDI

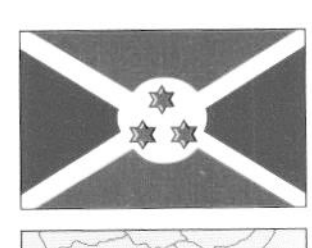

GEOGRAPHY The Republic of Burundi is the fifth smallest country in mainland Africa. It is also the second most densely populated after its northern neighbor, Rwanda. Part of the Great African Rift Valley, which runs throughout eastern Africa into southwestern Asia, lies in western Burundi. It includes part of Lake Tanganyika. Bujumbura, the capital city, lies on the shore of Lake Tanganyika and has a warm climate. A dry season occurs from June to September, but the other months are fairly rainy. The mountains and plateaux to the east are cooler and wetter.

POLITICS & ECONOMY The Twa, a pygmy people, were the first known inhabitants of Burundi. About 1,000 years ago, the Hutu, a people who speak a Bantu language, gradually began to settle the area, pushing the Twa into remote areas.

From the 15th century, the Tutsi, a cattle-owning people from the northeast, gradually took over the country. The Hutu, though greatly outnumbering the Tutsi, were forced to serve the Tutsi overlords.

Germany conquered the area that is now Burundi and Rwanda in the late 1890s. This was followed by Belgian control during World War I (1914–18). Full independence was achieved in 1962. Since this time rivalry between the Hutu and Tutsi has led to periodic outbreaks of appalling violence, most notably in 1972 and 1993. Many thousands of civilians have been massacred. A cease-fire and power-sharing agreement was reached in 2001, which was followed, in 2005, by parliamentary elections. Pierre Nkurunziza, a Hutu, has led Burundi since then, although political unrest followed his election to a third term in 2015. A referendum in 2018 backed constitutional reforms that could allow Nkurunziza to continue in power until 2034. In 2017 the International Criminal Court opened an investigation into human rights abuses in the country.

Burundi is one of the world's poorest countries. About 94% of the people live by farming, mostly at subsistence level. Livestock are raised and fishing is important. A lack of basic infrastructure and a poorly educated population are hindering development.

AREA 10,747 sq mi [27,834 sq km] **POPULATION** 11,845,000
CAPITAL Bujumbura **GOVERNMENT** Republic **ETHNIC GROUPS** Hutu 85%, Tutsi 14%, Twa (Pygmy) 1% **LANGUAGES** French and Kirundi (both official) **RELIGIONS** Roman Catholic 62%, traditional beliefs 23%, Islam 10%, Protestant 5% **CURRENCY** Burundi franc = 100 centimes

CABO VERDE

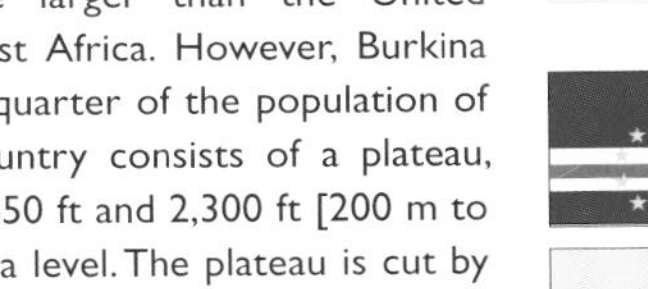

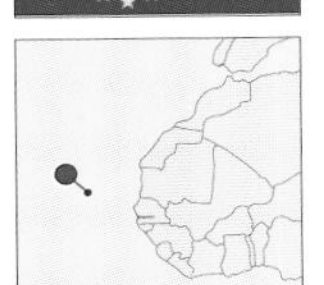

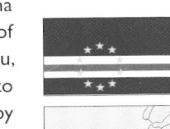

Cabo Verde consists of ten large and five small islands, and is situated 350 mi [560 km] west of Dakar in Senegal. The islands have a tropical climate, with high temperatures all year round. Cabo Verde became independent from Portugal in 1975 and is rated as a "lower-middle-income" country by the World Bank.

AREA 1,557 sq mi [4,033 sq km]
POPULATION 568,000 **CAPITAL** Praia

CAMBODIA

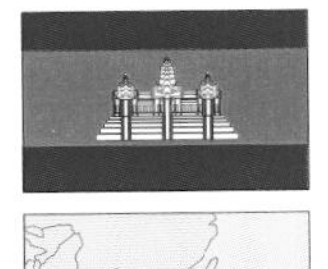

GEOGRAPHY The Kingdom of Cambodia is a country in Southeast Asia. Low mountains border the country except in the south-east. Most of Cambodia consists of plains drained by the River Mekong, which enters Cambodia from Laos in the north and exits through Vietnam in the southeast. The north-west contains Tonlé Sap (or Great Lake). In the dry season, this lake drains into the River Mekong. But in the wet season, the level of the Mekong rises and water flows in the opposite direction from the river into Tonlé Sap – the lake then becomes the largest freshwater lake in Asia.

Cambodia has a tropical monsoon climate, with high temperatures throughout the year. The dry season, when winds blow from the north or northeast, runs from November to April. During the rainy season (May to October), moist winds blow from the south or southeast. The high humidity and heat often make conditions unpleasant. Rainfall is heaviest near the coast, and rather lower inland.

POLITICS & ECONOMY From 802 to 1432, the Khmer people ruled a great empire, which reached its peak in the 12th century. The Khmer capital was at Angkor. The Hindu stone temples built there and at nearby Angkor Wat form the world's largest group of religious buildings. France ruled the country between 1863 and 1954, when the country became an independent monarchy. The monarchy was abolished in 1970 and Cambodia became a republic.

In 1970, the Communists under Prime Minister Lon Nol staged a military coup and proclaimed the Khmer Republic, which plunged the country into a civil war. The Khmer Rouge under Pol Pot took control in 1975, renaming the country Kampuchea, and launched a reign of terror in which between 1 million and 2.5 million people were killed. In 1979, Vietnamese and Cambodian troops overthrew the Khmer Rouge government. Vietnam withdrew in 1989, and in 1991 Prince Sihanouk was recognized as head of state. In 1993 the monarchy was restored. In 2004, King Sihanouk abdicated and his son, Prince Norodom Sihamoni, became king. Hun Sen's Cambodian People's Party has been in power since 1998, and he has been prime minister since 1985. In 2017, the Supreme Court dissolved the only credible opposition party, leading to a predictable but controversial victory for Hun Sen's party in 2018 parliamentary elections.

Cambodia is a poor country whose economy, although devastated by war, has now had over 20 years of relative stability and growth. Garment manufacture is the main activity. In 2005 offshore oil reserves were discovered and there is potential to mine bauxite, iron, and gold. Tourism is growing rapidly. However, there are still many obstacles to development.

AREA 69,898 SQ MI [181,035 SQ KM] **POPULATION** 16,450,000
CAPITAL PHNOM PENH **GOVERNMENT** CONSTITUTIONAL MONARCHY
ETHNIC GROUPS KHMER 90%, VIETNAMESE 5%, CHINESE 1%, OTHERS
LANGUAGES KHMER (OFFICIAL), FRENCH, ENGLISH
RELIGIONS BUDDHISM 96%, OTHERS 4% **CURRENCY** RIEL = 100 SEN

CAMEROON

GEOGRAPHY The Republic of Cameroon in West Africa derived its name from the Portuguese word camarões, or prawns. This name was used by Portuguese explorers who fished for prawns along the coast.

Behind the narrow coastal plains on the Gulf of Guinea, the land rises to a series of plateaux, with a mountainous region in the southwest where the volcano Mount Cameroun is situated.

The rainfall is heavy, especially in the highlands, but it becomes drier to the north. Temperatures are high on the coast, while the inland plateaux are cooler.

POLITICS & ECONOMY Germany lost Cameroon after World War I (1914–18). The country was then divided into two parts, one ruled by Britain and the other by France. In 1960, French Cameroon became the independent Cameroon Republic. In 1961, after a vote in British Cameroon, part of the territory joined the Cameroon Republic to become the Federal Republic of Cameroon – the other part joined Nigeria. It adopted the name Republic of Cameroon in 1984, but the country had two official languages. In 1995, partly to placate the English-speaking people, Cameroon became the 52nd member of the Commonwealth. A controversial amendment passed by parliament in 2008 has enabled President Paul Biya to run successfully for third and fourth terms in office in 2011 and 2018 respectively. The country has faced insurgency from Boko Haram since 2014, and increased unrest in the English-speaking provinces.

Cameroon's economy is based on agriculture, which employs 70% of the work force. The chief food crops include cassava, maize, millet, sweet potatoes, and yams. Cocoa and coffee are exported, along with oil and bauxite. In 2002, Cameroon's claim over the disputed oil-rich Bakassi peninsula was upheld and the handover by Nigeria completed in 2008. Cameroon has few manufacturing industries, but it is self-sufficient in food. Despite a high literacy rate, economic development is marred by endemic corruption.

AREA 183,568 SQ MI [475,442 SQ KM] **POPULATION** 25,641,000
CAPITAL YAOUNDÉ **GOVERNMENT** MULTIPARTY REPUBLIC
ETHNIC GROUPS CAMEROON HIGHLANDERS 31%, BANTU 27%, KIRDI 11%, FULANI 10%, OTHERS **LANGUAGES** FRENCH AND ENGLISH (BOTH OFFICIAL)
RELIGIONS CHRISTIANITY 40%, TRADITIONAL BELIEFS 40%, ISLAM 20%
CURRENCY CFA FRANC = 100 CENTIMES

CANADA

GEOGRAPHY Canada is the world's second largest country after Russia but with only 15% of its population. Much of the land is too cold or too mountainous for human settlement. Around 90% of Canadians live within 124 mi [200 km] of the southern border.

Western Canada is rugged: it includes the Pacific ranges and the mighty Rocky Mountains. East of the Rockies are the interior plains. In the north lie the bleak Arctic islands, while to the south lie the densely populated lowlands around lakes Erie and Ontario and in the St Lawrence River valley. The melting of Arctic ice, attributed to global warming, has led to concern about international rights over the Arctic waters off northern Canada.

Canada has a cold climate. In winter, temperatures fall below freezing point throughout most of Canada. But the southwestern coast has a relatively mild climate. Along the Arctic Circle, mean temperatures are below freezing for seven months a year. The west and southeast have high rainfall, but the prairies are dry with 10 inches to 20 inches [250 mm to 500 mm] of rain every year.

POLITICS & ECONOMY Canada's first people, the ancestors of the Native Americans, or Indians, arrived in North America from Asia around 40,000 years ago. The Inuit (Eskimos) were later arrivals from Asia. Europeans first reached Canada in 1497 and soon Britain and France began to compete for control.

France gained an initial advantage, and the French founded Québec in 1608. The British later occupied eastern Canada and, in 1867, they passed the British North America Act, which set up the Dominion of Canada, which was made up of Québec, Ontario, Nova Scotia, and New Brunswick. Other areas were added, the last being Newfoundland in 1949. Canada is a constitutional monarchy, and the British monarch is Canada's head of state. The provinces have a high level of autonomy.

In 1995, the people of Québec voted narrowly against a move to make Québec a sovereign state. In 2006, the national parliament voted to recognize Québec as a nation within a united Canada – a symbolic act of reconciliation. Another major issue concerns the rights of Aboriginal minorities. In 1999, Canada created the territory of Nunavut for the Inuit population. Nunavut covers 64% of what was formerly the eastern part of the Northwest Territories. Nine years of Conservative party rule was ended in late 2015 with an emphatic election victory by the Liberal Party under Justin Trudeau.

Canada is a highly developed and prosperous country. Although farmland covers only 8% of the country, high levels of productivity mean that Canada is one of the world's leading producers of barley, wheat, meat, and milk. Forestry and fishing are also important. Canada is rich in natural resources, especially oil and natural gas, and is a major exporter of minerals. The country also produces copper, gold, iron ore, uranium, and zinc. Manufacturing is important in the urban areas, where over 80% of the people live. Manufactures include processed mineral and farm products, cars, chemicals, electronic goods, paper, and timber products. Although the USA is Canada's largest trading partner, increased levels of business involve Asian countries.

AREA 3,849,653 SQ MI [9,970,610 SQ KM] **POPULATION** 35,882,000
CAPITAL OTTAWA **GOVERNMENT** FEDERAL MULTIPARTY CONSTITUTIONAL MONARCHY **ETHNIC GROUPS** BRITISH ORIGIN 28%, FRENCH ORIGIN 23%, OTHER EUROPEAN 15%, AMERINDIAN/INUIT 2%, OTHERS
LANGUAGES ENGLISH AND FRENCH (BOTH OFFICIAL)
RELIGIONS ROMAN CATHOLIC 43%, PROTESTANT 23%, JUDAISM, ISLAM, HINDUISM
CURRENCY CANADIAN DOLLAR = 100 CENTS

CAYMAN ISLANDS

The Cayman Islands are an overseas territory of the UK, consisting of three low-lying islands. Financial services are the main economic activity and the islands offer a secret tax haven to many companies and banks.

AREA 102 SQ MI [264 SQ KM]
POPULATION 60,000 **CAPITAL** GEORGE TOWN

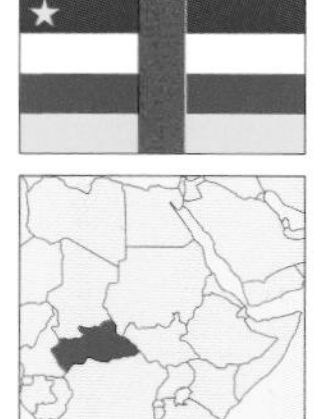

CENTRAL AFRICAN REPUBLIC

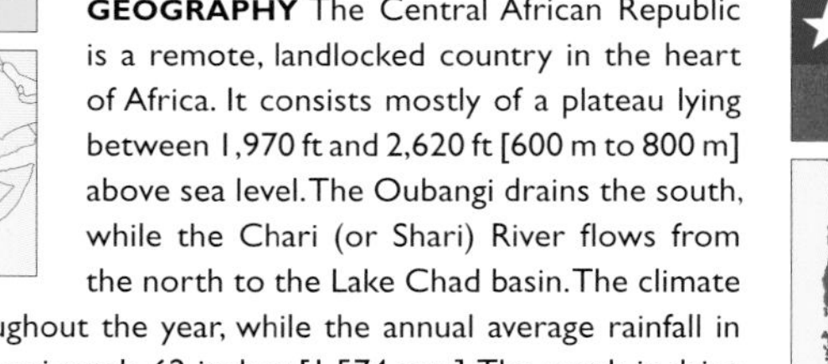

GEOGRAPHY The Central African Republic is a remote, landlocked country in the heart of Africa. It consists mostly of a plateau lying between 1,970 ft and 2,620 ft [600 m to 800 m] above sea level. The Oubangi drains the south, while the Chari (or Shari) River flows from the north to the Lake Chad basin. The climate is warm throughout the year, while the annual average rainfall in the capital Bangui totals 62 inches [1,574 mm]. The north is drier, with an average annual rainfall of about 31 inches [800 mm].

POLITICS & ECONOMY France set up an outpost at Bangui in 1889 and ruled the country as a colony from 1894. Known as Ubangi-Shari, the country was ruled by France as part of French Equatorial Africa until it gained independence in 1960.

Central African Republic became a one-party state in 1962, but army officers seized power in 1966. The head of the army, Jean-Bedel Bokassa, made himself emperor in 1976. The country was renamed the Central African Empire, but Bokassa was removed in 1979. The country again became a republic.

The election in 1993 ended 12 years of military rule. In 2003 General François Bozizé seized power and served as president from 2005 until he was deposed in 2013 by rebel leader Michel Djotodia. Djotodia resigned in 2014 following international pressure. After an interim period, Faustin-Archange Touadera, a former prime minister, was elected president in February 2016 in largely peaceful elections. After the withdrawal of some foreign peacekeeping forces in early 2017 there was an upsurge in violence, prompting a fresh refugee crisis.

The World Bank classifies Central African Republic as a "low-income" developing country. Over 80% of the people are farmers. The main crops are bananas, maize, manioc, millet, and yams. Coffee, cotton, timber, and tobacco are produced for export. The country has significant natural resources including uranium and diamonds. Development has been impeded by the country's remote position, its poor transport system, and its untrained work force. The country depends heavily on aid.

AREA 240,534 SQ MI [622,984 SQ KM] **POPULATION** 5,745,000
CAPITAL BANGUI **GOVERNMENT** MULTIPARTY REPUBLIC
ETHNIC GROUPS BAYA 33%, BANDA 27%, MANDJIA 13%, SARA 10%, MBOUM 7%, MBAKA 4%, OTHERS **LANGUAGES** FRENCH (OFFICIAL), SANGHO
RELIGIONS TRADITIONAL BELIEFS 35%, PROTESTANT 25%, ROMAN CATHOLIC 25%, ISLAM 15% **CURRENCY** CFA FRANC = 100 CENTIMES

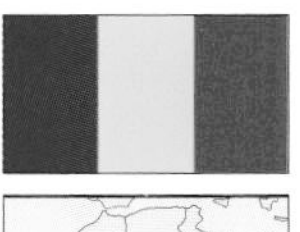

CHAD

GEOGRAPHY The Republic of Chad is a landlocked country in north-central Africa. It is Africa's fifth largest country and is over twice the size of France, the country which once ruled it as a colony.

Ndjamena in central Chad has a hot, tropical climate, with a marked dry season from November to April. The south of the country is wetter, with an average yearly rainfall of around 39 inches [1,000 mm]. The burning-hot desert in the north has an average yearly rainfall of less than 5 inches [130 mm].

POLITICS & ECONOMY Chad straddles two worlds. The north is populated by Muslim Arab and Berber peoples, while black Africans live in the south. Chad became independent from France in 1960, but the 1970s were marked by ethnic strife that led to conflict with Libya. Chad and Libya agreed a truce in 1987, and in 1994 the International Court of Justice ruled against Libya's claim to the Aozou Strip. From 2004, Chad forces clashed with pro-Sudanese militias as the conflict in Sudan's Darfur province spilled over the border. In 2010 a settlement was agreed with Sudan, and Chad held elections in 2011 when Idriss Deby retained the presidency. He won a fifth term in 2016. In 2018 the parliament approved a new constitution that expands Deby's powers. The militant Islamist group Boko Haram has mounted attacks in Chad.

One of the world's poorest countries, Chad has a large refugee population. Farming and fishing employ 83% of the people. Cotton is the chief export crop. Chad has few manufacturing industries, but it has had a recent economic boost from oil exports via a pipeline connecting its oilfields to the coast in Cameroon.

AREA 495,752 SQ MI [1,284,000 SQ KM] **POPULATION** 15,833,000
CAPITAL NDJAMENA **GOVERNMENT** MULTIPARTY REPUBLIC
ETHNIC GROUPS 200 DISTINCT GROUPS: MOSTLY MUSLIM IN THE NORTH AND CENTER; MOSTLY CHRISTIAN OR ANIMIST IN THE SOUTH
LANGUAGES FRENCH AND ARABIC (BOTH OFFICIAL), MANY OTHERS
RELIGIONS ISLAM 53%, CHRISTIANITY 34%, ANIMIST 7%
CURRENCY CFA FRANC = 100 CENTIMES

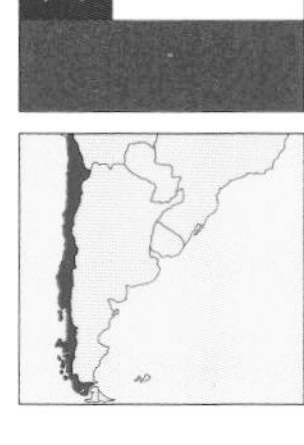

CHILE

GEOGRAPHY The Republic of Chile stretches about 2,650 mi [4,260 km] from north to south, although the maximum east–west distance is only about 267 mi [430 km]. The high Andes Mountains form Chile's eastern borders with Argentina and Bolivia. To the west are basins and valleys, with coastal uplands overlooking the shore. Most people live in the central valley, where the capital, Santiago, is situated. Earthquakes are common. In February 2010, an earthquake with a magnitude of 8.8 (the biggest in 50 years) struck central Chile, killing more than 400 people.

Santiago has a Mediterranean climate with hot, dry summers and mild, moist winters. The Atacama Desert in the north is extremely arid, while the south is cold and stormy.

POLITICS & ECONOMY Amerindian people reached the southern tip of South America 8,000 years ago. In 1520, Portuguese navigator Ferdinand Magellan was the first European to sight Chile and the country became a Spanish colony in the 1540s. Independent from 1818, Chile won mineral-rich areas from Peru and Bolivia during the War of the Pacific (1879–83).

In 1970, Salvador Allende became the first Communist leader to be elected democratically. He was overthrown in 1973 by army officers, who were supported by the CIA. General Augusto Pinochet then ruled as a dictator until 1989. Since then, government leaders have been democratically elected which has contributed to the country's prosperity and stability. Presidential elections in late 2017 saw a return to office for Sebastian Pinera.

According to the World Bank classifications, Chile has a "high-income" economy, one of the strongest in Latin America. Mining, especially copper, is important and minerals dominate exports. But manufacturing is the most valuable activity. Products include processed foods, metals, iron and steel, transport equipment, and textiles. The chief crop is wheat, while beans, fruits, maize, and livestock products are also important. Chile's fishing industry is one of the world's largest.

AREA 292,133 SQ MI [756,626 SQ KM] **POPULATION** 17,925,000
CAPITAL SANTIAGO **GOVERNMENT** MULTIPARTY REPUBLIC
ETHNIC GROUPS MESTIZO 95%, AMERINDIAN 4%
LANGUAGES SPANISH (OFFICIAL), ENGLISH, OTHERS **RELIGIONS** ROMAN CATHOLIC 70%, PROTESTANT 17% **CURRENCY** CHILEAN PESO = 100 CENTAVOS

CHINA

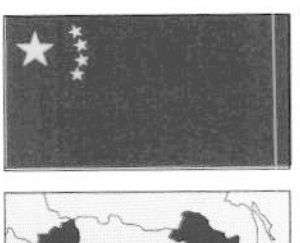

GEOGRAPHY The People's Republic of China is the world's third largest country. Most people live in the east – on the coastal plains or in the fertile valleys of the Huang He (Hwang Ho or Yellow River), the Chang Jiang (Yangtse Kiang), which is Asia's longest river at 3,960 mi [6,380 km], and the Xi Jiang (Si Kiang). Western China is thinly populated. It includes the bleak Tibetan plateau, which is bounded by the Himalaya, the world's highest mountain range. Deserts include the Gobi along the Mongolian border and the Takla Makan in the far west. Earthquakes are common. Beijing has cold winters and warm summers with moderate rainfall. To the south, Shanghai has milder winters and more rain. The southeast has a wet, subtropical climate, but the west has a severe climate. Lhasa has very cold winters and a low rainfall.

POLITICS & ECONOMY China is one of the world's oldest civilizations, going back 3,500 years. Mongols conquered China in the 13th century, but Chinese rule was restored in 1368. The Manchu people of Mongolia ruled the country from 1644 to 1912, when the country became a republic.

War with Japan (1937–45) was followed by civil war between the nationalists and the Communists. The Communists triumphed in 1949, setting up the People's Republic of China. In the 1980s, following the death of the revolutionary leader Mao Zedong (Mao Tse-tung) in 1976, China encouraged formerly forbidden policies, namely private enterprise and foreign investment. But the Communist leaders have not permitted political freedom. Opponents are still harshly treated, while attempts to negotiate some degree of autonomy for Tibet have been rejected and central control over Hong Kong has been increased. There remain tensions between China and its neighbours over territorial disputes in the East and South China seas. In 2018 the Communist Party abolished the two-term presidential limit, opening the way for Xi Jinping, who became president in 2013, to remain in power indefinitely.

China's economy has expanded greatly since the 1970s and many new industries have been set up in the east. Between 1989 and 2011, the economy grew by over 9% per year. China has benefited from its admission to the World Trade Organization. The global financial crisis in 2008 slowed the economic growth rate, though China's grew faster than any other major economy. In 2014 it became the world's largest economy. Since then, however, the economic growth rate has fallen to its lowest level since the 1990s and a looming trade war with the US is a threat to recovery.

China remains a poor country. Agriculture employs around 35% of the work force, although only 10% of the land is farmed. Around 50% of the population lives in urban areas. Farm products include rice, sweet potatoes, tea, and wheat. Livestock farming is important, and China has more than a third of the world's pigs. Resources include coal, iron ore, and other metals. Manufactures include cement, chemicals, fertilizers, machinery, telecommunications equipment, ships, and textiles. China is now a major producer of consumer goods, including cameras, computer products, refrigerators, and television sets, but problems remain such as pollution, inequality, and an inefficient state sector.

AREA 3,705,387 SQ MI [9,596,961 SQ KM] **POPULATION** 1,384,689,000
CAPITAL BEIJING **GOVERNMENT** SINGLE-PARTY COMMUNIST REPUBLIC
ETHNIC GROUPS HAN CHINESE 92%, MANY OTHERS
LANGUAGES MANDARIN CHINESE (OFFICIAL) **RELIGIONS** ATHEIST (OFFICIAL)
CURRENCY RENMINBI YUAN = 10 JIAO = 100 FEN

COLOMBIA

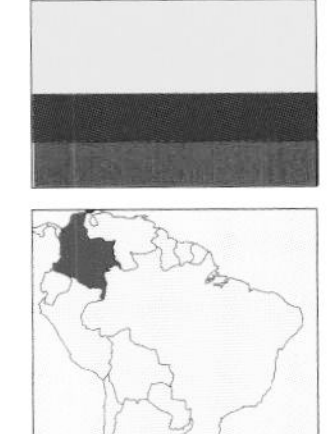

GEOGRAPHY The Republic of Colombia, in northeastern South America, is the only country in the continent to have coastlines on both the Pacific Ocean and the Caribbean Sea. Colombia also contains the northernmost ranges of the Andes Mountains.

There is a tropical climate in the lowlands, but the altitude greatly affects the climate in the Andes. The capital, Bogotá, which stands on a plateau in the eastern Andes at about 9,200 ft [2,800 m] above sea level, has mild temperatures throughout the year. Rainfall is heavy, especially on the Pacific coast.

POLITICS & ECONOMY Amerindian people have lived in Colombia for thousands of years. But today, only a small proportion of the people are of unmixed Amerindian ancestry. Colombia emerged as a republic in 1886.

Although there have been some attempts to quell the violent conflict involving drug cartels, Colombia still faces economic and security problems. Andrés Pastrana, president in 1998–2002, tried to end the guerrilla war, but peace talks collapsed and conflict resumed. His successors, Alvaro Uribe and Juan Manuel Santos, pursued tough policies against the rebels. In 2016 the government and FARC (Revolutionary Armed Forces of Colombia) signed a peace agreement and in 2017 FARC formally dissolved itself as an armed group. In 2018 Ivan Duque was elected president, promising to make changes to the peace accord.

Steps have been taken to develop the country's infrastructure to boost employment, and the economy was improving strongly until 2015 when the growth of GDP fell back to 2.5% from a high of nearly 5%. Petroleum, coffee, coal, gold, emeralds, cut flowers, and chemicals are exported.

AREA 439,735 SQ MI [1,138,914 SQ KM] **POPULATION** 48,169,000
CAPITAL BOGOTÁ **GOVERNMENT** MULTIPARTY REPUBLIC
ETHNIC GROUPS MESTIZO 58%, WHITE 20%, MIXED 14%, BLACK 4%
LANGUAGES SPANISH (OFFICIAL) **RELIGIONS** ROMAN CATHOLIC 90%
CURRENCY COLOMBIAN PESO = 100 CENTAVOS

COMOROS

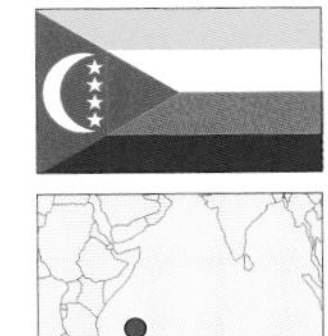

The Union of the Comoros consists of three large volcanic islands and some smaller ones lying at the north end of the Mozambique Channel in the Indian Ocean. France took over one of the islands, Mayotte, in 1843, and in 1886 the other islands came under French protection. They became independent in 1974, but Mayotte has remained French. Relations between the three remaining islands have been rocky. The constitution of 2001 granted greater autonomy to each island, with a rotating presidency. President Assoumani's attempts to undermine this system led to further unrest in 2018. Very dependent on foreign aid, Comoros is one of Africa's poorest nations. Exports include cloves, perfume oil, copra, and vanilla.

AREA 863 SQ MI [2,235 SQ KM]
POPULATION 821,000 **CAPITAL** MORONI

CONGO

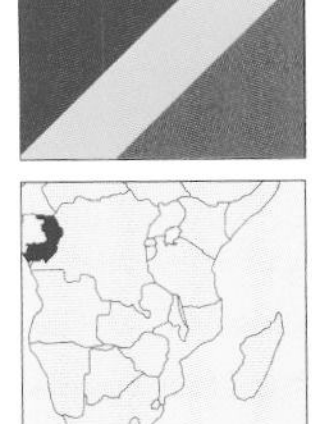

GEOGRAPHY The Republic of the Congo is a country on the River Congo in west-central Africa. The equator runs through the center of the country. Congo has a narrow coastal plain on which its main port, Pointe Noire, stands. Behind the plain are uplands through which the River Kouilou-Niari has carved a fertile valley. Central Congo consists of high plains with the north comprising large swampy areas in the valleys of the tributaries of the River Congo.

Congo has a hot, wet equatorial climate. Brazzaville has a dry season between June and September. The coast is drier and cooler because of the cold offshore Benguela ocean current.

POLITICS & ECONOMY Part of the huge Kongo kingdom between the 15th and 18th centuries, the coast of the Congo later became a center of the European slave trade. The area came under French protection in 1880 and it was later governed as part of the larger region of French Equatorial Africa. The country remained under French control until 1960.

Congo became a one-party state in 1964 and a military group took over the government in 1968. In 1970, Congo declared itself a Communist country, though it continued to seek aid from Western countries. Multiparty elections were held in 1992, but the elected president, Pascal Lissouba, was overthrown in 1997 by former president Denis Sassou-Nguesso. Civil war broke out with a fragile peace being restored in 2002. Sassou-Nguesso, president for over 30 years, despite accusations of corruption and unfair elections, is one of Africa's longest serving leaders.

Despite being one of Africa's largest petroleum producers, around 70% of the population live in poverty. Agriculture is an important activity, employing about 32% of the people, but many farmers produce little more than they need to feed their families. Major food crops include bananas, cassava, maize, and rice, while the leading cash crops are coffee and cocoa. Congo's main exports are oil (making up more than 90% of the total), timber, sugar, and diamonds. Manufacturing is still relatively unimportant, hampered by poor transport links, but it is gradually being developed.

AREA 132,046 SQ MI [342,000 SQ KM] **POPULATION** 4,955,000
CAPITAL BRAZZAVILLE **GOVERNMENT** REPUBLIC
ETHNIC GROUPS KONGO 48%, SANGHA 20%, TEKE 17%, M'BOCHI 12%
LANGUAGES FRENCH (OFFICIAL), MANY OTHERS **RELIGIONS** CHRISTIANITY 50%, ANIMIST 48%, ISLAM 2% **CURRENCY** CFA FRANC = 100 CENTIMES

CONGO (DEMOCRATIC REPUBLIC OF THE)

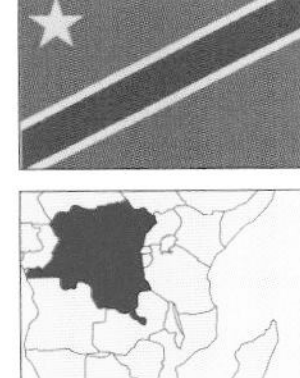

GEOGRAPHY The Democratic Republic of the Congo, formerly known as Zaïre, is the world's 11th largest country. Much of the country lies within the drainage basin of the huge River Congo. The river reaches the sea at the country's short coastline, which is only 25 mi [40 km] long. Mountains rise in the east, where the country's borders run through lakes Tanganyika, Kivu, Edward, and Albert.

POLITICS & ECONOMY Portuguese navigators reached the coast in 1482, but the interior was not explored until the late 19th century. In 1885, the country, known as the Congo Free State, became the personal property of King Léopold II of Belgium and was then administered as a Belgian colony from 1908 until 1960.

The country, riven by ethnic rivalries, became a one-party state after a coup by President Mobutu in 1965. He renamed it Zaïre and held on to power for over 30 years. He was ousted in 1997 by Laurent Kabila, a rebel leader backed by Rwanda and Uganda, who gave the country its present name. Further rifts and violence continued until Kabila was assassinated in 2001. The presidency was taken over by his son Joseph, who negotiated the Pretoria Accord with Rwanda which called for an end to fighting and the establishment of a unity government. The country remains beset by violence. According to aid agencies more than 1.5 million people were internally displaced during 2017. Elections at the end of Kabila's term as president were twice delayed, but in 2019 opposition candidate Felix Tshisekedi became president.

The Democratic Republic of the Congo is one of the world's poorest countries. Decades of insurrection and instability have devastated what was once a relatively industrialized economy. It has a vast wealth of natural resources, much of it still to be exploited and, with foreign help, some reform is under way. The economy relies on mining: the country is the world's largest producer of cobalt and a major producer of copper and diamonds. However, the industry is plagued by financial irregularities. Agriculture, at subsistence level, employs 60% of the work force.

AREA 905,350 SQ MI [2,344,858 SQ KM] **POPULATION** 85,281,000
CAPITAL KINSHASA **GOVERNMENT** REPUBLIC
ETHNIC GROUPS OVER 200; THE LARGEST ARE MONGO, LUBA, KONGO, MANGBETU-AZANDE **LANGUAGES** FRENCH (OFFICIAL), TRIBAL LANGUAGES
RELIGIONS ROMAN CATHOLIC 50%, PROTESTANT 20%, ISLAM 10%, OTHERS
CURRENCY CONGOLESE FRANC = 100 CENTIMES

COSTA RICA

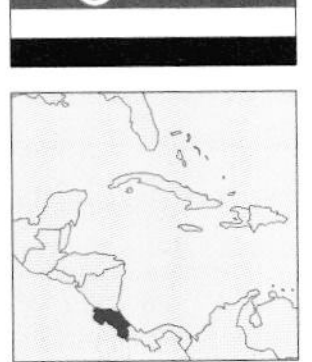

GEOGRAPHY The Republic of Costa Rica in Central America has coastlines on both the Pacific Ocean and the Caribbean Sea. Central Costa Rica consists of mountain ranges and plateaux with many volcanoes.

The coolest months of the year are December and January. The northeast trade winds bring heavy rain to the Caribbean coast, while there are lower amounts of rainfall in the highlands and on the Pacific coastlands.

POLITICS & ECONOMY Christopher Columbus reached the Caribbean coast in 1502 and was followed by Spanish settlers. Spain ruled the country until 1821, when the Central American colonies broke away to join Mexico. In 1823, these states then split from Mexico and set up the Central American Federation. Later, this union broke up and Costa Rica became independent in 1838.

From the late 19th century onward, Costa Rica experienced a number of revolutions, with periods of dictatorship alternating with spells of democracy. In 1948, following a revolt, the armed forces were completely abolished and it remains without a standing army today. Since that year, Costa Rica has enjoyed a long period of consistent stable democracy. Center-left candidate and former Minister of Labor and Social Security, Louis Solis, won the presidential elections of March 2018.

Costa Rica is one of the most prosperous countries in Central America. There are high educational standards, a high average life expectancy (about 76 years for men and 81 years for women), and the most developed welfare system in Central America. Agriculture employs 14% of the people. Costa Rica's natural resources include its forests, but it lacks minerals apart from some bauxite and manganese. Manufacturing is increasing, with the USA being Costa Rica's main trading partner. Tourism is a fast-growing industry. There are concerns, however, that it is acting as a conduit for drugs and associated corruption.

AREA 19,730 sq mi [51,100 sq km] **POPULATION** 4,987,000
CAPITAL San José **GOVERNMENT** Multiparty republic
ETHNIC GROUPS White (including Mestizo) 94%, Black 3%, Amerindian 1%, Chinese 1%, others **LANGUAGES** Spanish (official), English **RELIGIONS** Roman Catholic 76%, Evangelical Protestant 14%
CURRENCY Costa Rican colón = 100 céntimos

CÔTE D'IVOIRE (IVORY COAST)

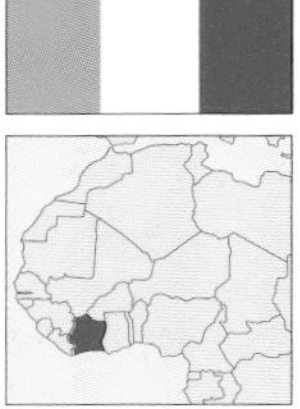

GEOGRAPHY The Republic of Côte d'Ivoire, in West Africa, was more commonly known as the Ivory Coast. The southeast coast is bordered by sand bars that enclose lagoons. The southwest coast is lined by rocky cliffs.

Côte d'Ivoire has a hot and humid tropical climate, with high temperatures all year. The south has two rainy seasons: between May and July, and from October to November. Inland, the rainfall decreases and the north has one dry and one rainy season.

POLITICS & ECONOMY From 1895, the Ivory Coast, as it was known, was governed as part of French West Africa.

Côte d'Ivoire became fully independent in 1960. Its first president, Félix Houphouët-Boigny, became the longest serving head of state in Africa with an uninterrupted period in office which ended with his death in 1993. Houphouët-Boigny, a pro-Western leader, made Côte d'Ivoire a one-party state. In 1983, the National Assembly voted to make Yamoussoukro, the president's birthplace, the new capital. In 1999, a military coup occurred, but civilian rule was restored in 2000, when Laurent Gbagbo was elected president. By 2004, after an army rebellion, the government held the south, while mainly Muslim rebels held the north. Elections in 2010 were won by Alassane Outtara, but Gbagbo refused to stand down and was finally deposed in 2011. Outtara won an overwhelming 84% of the vote in 2015's elections.

Agriculture employs 68% of the population and the country is the world's largest producer of cocoa beans. Coffee and palm oil are also important exports. Political instability and the lack of modern infrastructure are impeding economic growth.

AREA 124,503 sq mi [322,463 sq km] **POPULATION** 26,261,000
CAPITAL Yamoussoukro **GOVERNMENT** Multiparty republic
ETHNIC GROUPS Akan 42%, Voltaiques 18%, Northern Mandes 16%, Krous 11%, Southern Mandes 10% **LANGUAGES** French (official), many native dialects **RELIGIONS** Islam 39%, Christianity 33%, traditional beliefs 12% **CURRENCY** CFA franc = 100 centimes

CROATIA

GEOGRAPHY The Republic of Croatia was one of the six republics that made up the former Communist country of Yugoslavia until it became independent in 1991. The region of Dalmatia borders the Adriatic Sea and here are found the coastal ranges of mountains, comprising large tracts of bare limestone. Most of the rest of the country consists of the fertile Pannonian plains.

The coastal area has a typical Mediterranean climate, with hot, dry summers and mild, moist winters. Inland, the climate becomes more continental. Winters are cold, while temperatures often soar to 100°F [38°C] in the summer months.

POLITICS & ECONOMY Once part of the Holy Roman empire, Croatia was an independent kingdom in the 10th and 11th centuries. In 1102, the crowns of Hungary and Croatia were joined, creating a union that lasted 800 years. In 1526, part of Croatia came under the Turkish Ottoman empire, while the rest fell under the control of the Austrian Habsburgs.

After Austria–Hungary was defeated in World War I (1914–18), Croatia became part of the new Kingdom of the Serbs, Croats, and Slovenes. This kingdom was renamed Yugoslavia in 1929. Germany occupied Yugoslavia during World War II (1939–45).

After the war, Communists took power with Josip Broz Tito as the country's leader. Despite ethnic differences between the people, Tito held Yugoslavia together until his death in 1980. In the 1980s, economic and ethnic problems, including a deterioration in relations with Serbia, threatened stability. In the 1990s, Yugoslavia split into five nations, one of which was Croatia, which declared itself independent in 1991.

After Serbia supplied arms to Serbs living in Croatia, war broke out between the two republics, causing great damage. Croatia lost more than 30% of its territory. But in 1992, the United Nations sent a peacekeeping force to Croatia, which effectively ended the war with Serbia. In the same year, when war broke out in Bosnia-Herzegovina, Bosnian Croats occupied parts of the country. But in 1994, Croatia helped to end Croat–Muslim conflict in Bosnia-Herzegovina and, in 1995, after retaking some areas occupied by Serbs, it helped to draw up the Dayton Peace Accord, ending the civil war.

The conflict in the early 1990s badly disrupted the economy. Slow but steady economic growth in the early 2000s was thwarted by the recession of 2008. Various obstacles were overcome and Croatia acceded to membership of the EU in 2013. Problems remain with high unemployment and uneven regional development. Its intricate coastline and islands on the Adriatic Sea are a gift to the tourist industry. Croatia's main exports are manufactures, especially shipbuilding.

AREA 21,829 sq mi [56,538 sq km] **POPULATION** 4,270,000
CAPITAL Zagreb **GOVERNMENT** Multiparty republic
ETHNIC GROUPS Croat 90%, Serb 5%, others
LANGUAGES Croatian 96% **RELIGIONS** Roman Catholic 88%, Orthodox 4%, Islam 1%, others **CURRENCY** Kuna = 100 lipas

CUBA

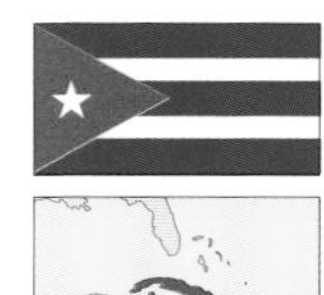

GEOGRAPHY The Republic of Cuba is the largest island country in the Caribbean Sea. It consists of one large island, Cuba, the Isle of Youth (Isla de la Juventud), and about 1,600 small islets. Mountains and hills cover about a quarter of Cuba. The highest mountain range, the Sierra Maestra in the southeast, reaches 6,562 ft [2,000 m]. The rest of the land consists of gently rolling country or coastal plains, crossed by fertile valleys carved by the short, mostly shallow and narrow rivers.

POLITICS & ECONOMY Christopher Columbus discovered the island in 1492 and Spaniards began to settle there from 1511. Spanish rule ended in 1898, when the United States defeated Spain in the Spanish–American War. American influence in Cuba remained strong until 1959, when revolutionary forces under the leadership of Fidel Castro overthrew the dictatorship of Fulgencio Batista.

The United States opposed Castro's policies, when he turned to the Soviet Union for assistance. In 1962, a world crisis was averted when, under intense US pressure, the Soviet Union withdrew missile sites that could have been used to launch nuclear strikes against the United States. The breakup of the Soviet Union in 1991 damaged Cuba's economy and it worked to increase its trade with Latin America and China. Fidel Castro's brother, Raul, took over the leadership in 2008. He introduced reforms in 2009–12. In 2011, a new law allowed people to buy and sell private property. December 2014 saw the start of moves to normalize relations between Cuba and the US. During 2015, banking and diplomatic ties were re-established. The following year, some trade ties with the US were opened, as were diplomatic links with the EU. Fidel Castro died in April 2016. In 2017, the US government introduced new sanctions and travel restrictions. In April 2018 Raul Castro stood down and Miguel Díaz-Canel was named as president.

Sugar cane accounts for more than 60% of the country's exports. The other main crop is tobacco, and citrus fruits, rice, cattle, and milk production all make a contribution to the economy. Nickel oxide is exported and tourism is also important. Cuba has signed an agreement with Russia to exploit off-shore oil deposits.

AREA 42,803 sq mi [110,861 sq km] **POPULATION** 11,147,000
CAPITAL Havana **GOVERNMENT** Socialist republic
ETHNIC GROUPS White 65%, Mestizo 25%, Black 10%
LANGUAGES Spanish (official) **RELIGIONS** Roman Catholic 27%, Santeria 13% **CURRENCY** Cuban peso = 100 centavos

CURAÇAO

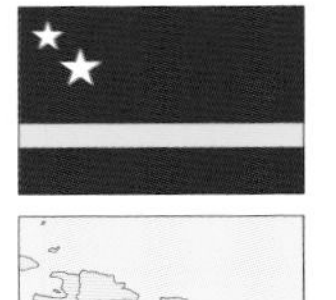

Part of the Netherlands Antilles until 2010, Curaçao is a self-governing territory within the Kingdom of the Netherlands. Oil refining, tourism and trade are important.

AREA 171 sq mi [444 sq km]
POPULATION 150,000 **CAPITAL** Willemstad

CYPRUS

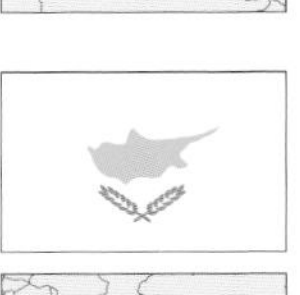

GEOGRAPHY The Republic of Cyprus is an island nation in the northeastern Mediterranean Sea. Geographers regard it as part of Asia, but it resembles southern Europe in many ways. Its scenic mountain ranges include the southern Troodos Mountains, which reach 6,401 ft [1,951 m] at Mount Olympus, and the Kyrenia range in the north. Between them lies the Mesaoria plain. The climate is Mediterranean, with hot, dry summers and mild, moist winters.

POLITICS & ECONOMY Greeks settled on Cyprus around 3,200 years ago. From AD 330, the island was part of the Byzantine empire until, in the 1570s, Cyprus became part of the Turkish Ottoman empire. Turkish rule continued until 1878 when Cyprus was leased to Britain then went on to be proclaimed a colony in 1925. In the 1950s, Greek Cypriots, who made up four-fifths of the population, began a campaign for enosis (union) with Greece. Their leader was the Greek Orthodox Archbishop Makarios. A secret guerrilla force called EOKA attacked the British, who exiled Makarios in 1956; he returned to Cyprus in 1959.

Cyprus became an independent country in 1960, although Britain retained two military bases. Independent Cyprus had a constitution which provided for power-sharing between the Greek and Turkish Cypriots. But the constitution proved unworkable and fighting broke out between the two communities.

In 1974, Makarios was overthrown by Greek officers and Turkey invaded northern Cyprus. In 1979, the north was proclaimed the Turkish Republic of Northern Cyprus. The only country to recognize this state remains Turkey. In 2002, the European Union invited Cyprus to become a member in 2004. In 2004, the people voted on a UN plan to reunify Cyprus. The Turkish-Cypriots voted in favor, but the Greek-Cypriots voted against, unhappy at limits on their right to return to property located in the north. As a result, only the south was admitted to EU membership on May 1, 2004. Talks on reunification continue, but progress is slow.

Cyprus got its name from the Greek word kypros, meaning copper. But little copper remains and the chief minerals today are asbestos and chromium. However, the most valuable activity in Cyprus is tourism. Manufactures include cement, clothes, footwear, tiles, and wine. Only around 8% of the population are involved in agriculture but 70% are involved in the service industry.

Problems due to the global financial crisis, and the south joining the euro in 2008, resulted in a contraction of the economy and a bailout from the EU at the beginning of 2013. Cypriot banks' substantial exposure to Greek debt is a cause for concern.

AREA 3,572 sq mi [9,251 sq km] **POPULATION** 1,237,000
CAPITAL Nicosia **GOVERNMENT** Multiparty republic
ETHNIC GROUPS Greek Cypriot 77%, Turkish Cypriot 18%, others
LANGUAGES Greek and Turkish (both official), English
RELIGIONS Greek Orthodox 78%, Islam 18%
CURRENCY Euro = 100 cents

CZECHIA

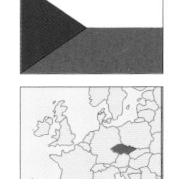

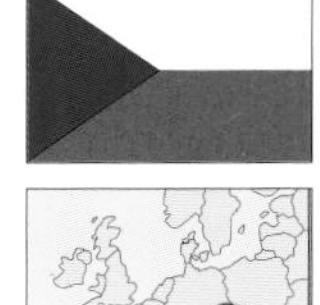

GEOGRAPHY Until recently known as the Czech Republic, Czechia is the western three-fifths of the former country of Czechoslovakia. It contains two regions: Bohemia in the west and Moravia in the east. Mountains border much of the country in the west. The Bohemian basin in the north-center is a fertile lowland region, with Prague, the capital city, at its heart. Highlands cover much of the center of the country, with lowlands in the southeast.

The climate is influenced by the country's landlocked position in east-central Europe. Summers are warm and winters cold.

POLITICS & ECONOMY Czechoslovakia was born out of World War I (1914–18) and then occupied by Germany during World War II (1939–45). In 1948, Communist leaders took power and Czechoslovakia was allied to the Soviet Union. In the late 1980s, when democratic reforms were introduced in the Soviet Union, the Czechs also demanded change. Free elections were held in 1990, but differences between the Czechs and Slovaks led to the partitioning of the country (the "velvet divorce") on January 1, 1993. A former dissident, Vaclav Havel, became the first president. Czechia became a member of NATO in 1999 and a member of the European Union in 2004. In 2016, Parliament approved a new short form for the country's name, and the Czech Republic became Czechia. Milos Zeman won a second term as president in January 2018, campaigning on an anti-immigration stance.

Under Communist rule, Czechia became one of the most industrialized parts of Eastern Europe. Today, it is relatively prosperous although it is still emerging from the recession of 2011–2013. The country has deposits of coal, uranium, iron ore, magnesite, tin, and zinc. Manufacturing employs about 27% of Czechia's work force.

AREA 30,450 sq mi [78,866 sq km] **POPULATION** 10,686,000
CAPITAL Prague **GOVERNMENT** Multiparty republic
ETHNIC GROUPS Czech 64%, Moravian 5%, Slovak 1%, Polish, German, Silesian, Gypsy, Hungarian, Ukrainian
LANGUAGES Czech (official)
RELIGIONS Atheist 40%, Roman Catholic 39%, Protestant 4%, Orthodox 3%, others **CURRENCY** Czech koruna = 100 haler

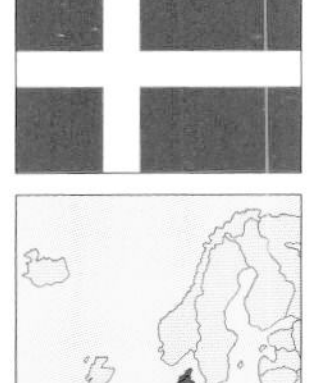

DENMARK

GEOGRAPHY The Kingdom of Denmark is the smallest country in Scandinavia. It consists of a peninsula, called Jutland (or Jylland), which is joined to Germany, and more than 400 islands, 89 of which are inhabited. The land is flat and mostly covered by rocks deposited by huge ice sheets during the last Ice Age. The highest point in Denmark is on Jutland. It is only 561 ft [171 m] above sea level. Denmark has a mild, moist climate, except during cold spells in winter when the Sound (Øresund) between Sjælland and Sweden may freeze over.

POLITICS & ECONOMY Once a Viking stronghold, Denmark formed a union with Norway and Sweden (which included Finland) in the 14th century. Sweden broke away in 1523, while Denmark lost Norway to Sweden in 1814. After 1945, Denmark joined NATO and became a member of the European Economic Community (now the European Union) in 1973. However, the country decided not to join the eurozone in a referendum in 2000. In 2009, Greenland joined the Færoe Islands in becoming a self-governing territory within the Danish realm.

Despite being affected by the global recession of the late 2000s, Denmark is a prosperous country with a generous welfare system. Resources include oil and gas. Manufacturing employs around 12% of the work force. Products include furniture, processed food, machinery, and wind turbines. Meat and dairy farming, using intensively scientific methods, employs 3% of the people.

AREA 16,639 sq mi [43,094 sq km] **POPULATION** 5,810,000
CAPITAL Copenhagen **GOVERNMENT** Parliamentary monarchy
ETHNIC GROUPS Scandinavian, Inuit, Færoese **LANGUAGES** Danish (official), Greenlandic, English, Færoese **RELIGIONS** Evangelical Lutheran 95% **CURRENCY** Danish krone = 100 øre

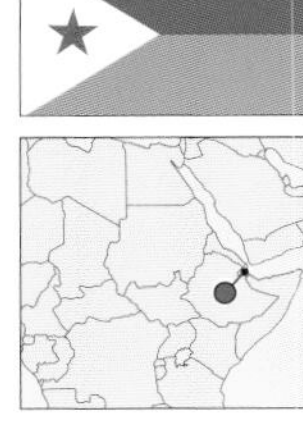

DJIBOUTI

GEOGRAPHY The Republic of Djibouti in eastern Africa occupies a strategic position where the Red Sea meets the Gulf of Aden. Djibouti has one of the world's hottest and driest climates.

POLITICS & ECONOMY Known as the French Territory of the Afars and Issas until 1977, Djibouti owes much of its importance to its rail link to Addis Ababa which allows it to function as a port for Ethiopia and other landlocked African states. It also acts as a regional military base for both France and the USA. The current president, Ismail Omar Guelleh, has been in office since 1999. Djibouti is dominated by one political party, the People's Rally for Progress, with opposition parties having only limited freedom.

Djibouti is a poor country with few natural resources and the climate is unable to support much agriculture. Its economy is based largely on the revenue it gets from its port facilities and it relies heavily on foreign assistance. Unemployment is high at 60%.

AREA 8,958 sq mi [23,200 sq km] **POPULATION** 884,000
CAPITAL Djibouti **GOVERNMENT** Multiparty republic
ETHNIC GROUPS Somali 60%, Afar 35% **LANGUAGES** Arabic and French (both official) **RELIGIONS** Islam 94%, Christianity 6%
CURRENCY Djiboutian franc = 100 centimes

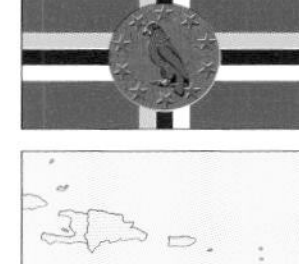

DOMINICA

The Commonwealth of Dominica, a former British colony, became independent in 1978. The island has a mountainous spine and, although less than 10% of the land is cultivated, agriculture employs 40% of the population. The economy has been over-reliant on growing bananas and Dominica is trying to develop its ecotourism business.

AREA 290 sq mi [751 sq km] **POPULATION** 74,000 **CAPITAL** Roseau

DOMINICAN REPUBLIC

GEOGRAPHY Second largest of the Caribbean nations in both area and population, the Dominican Republic shares the island of Hispaniola with Haiti, with the Dominican Republic occupying the eastern two-thirds. The country is mountainous, and the hot and humid climate eases with altitude.

POLITICS & ECONOMY In 1492, Christopher Columbus landed on Hispaniola and Spaniards soon settled the island, followed by the French, who occupied the western third of the island (which is now Haiti). Civil war broke out in 1966 but US intervention ended the conflict. Since 1966, the young democracy has survived violent elections under the continued watchful eye of the United States.

The Dominican Republic is a developing country and recently tourism and the service industry have overtaken agriculture as the mainstays of the economy. Sugarcane, coffee, rice, bananas, and cocoa are leading crops. Food processing is also important and some ferronickel is produced.

AREA 18,730 sq mi [48,511 sq km] **POPULATION** 10,299,000
CAPITAL Santo Domingo **GOVERNMENT** Multiparty republic
ETHNIC GROUPS Mulatto 73%, White 16%, Black 11%
LANGUAGES Spanish (official) **RELIGIONS** Roman Catholic 95%
CURRENCY Dominican peso = 100 centavos

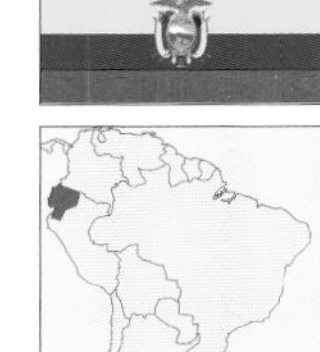

ECUADOR

GEOGRAPHY The Republic of Ecuador straddles the equator on the west coast of South America. Three ranges of the high Andes Mountains form the backbone of the country. Between the towering, snow-capped peaks of the mountains, some of which are volcanoes, lie a series of high plateaux, or basins. Nearly half of Ecuador's population live on these plateaux. The coast has a warm tropical climate, despite the cold offshore Peruvian Current. Inland, the altitude gives the plateaux spring-like weather throughout the year.

POLITICS & ECONOMY The Inca people of Peru conquered much of what is now Ecuador in the late 15th century and their language, Quechua, is still widely spoken today. Spanish forces defeated the Incas in 1533 and took control of Ecuador until 1822.

In the 19th and 20th centuries, Ecuador suffered from political instability, while successive governments failed to tackle the country's social and economic problems. A war with Peru in 1941 led to a loss of territory. Economic crises in the early 21st century led to the adoption of the US dollar as the official currency. In 2011, voters approved sweeping reforms and Rafael Correa won a third term in 2013. In 2017, Socialist Lenin Moreno became president. In early 2018, a referendum vote reinstated the two-term presidential limit that Correa had abolished.

The World Bank classifies Ecuador as an "upper-middle-income" developing country. Much dependent on its oil resources and the fluctuating world price of petrol, Ecuador has tried to diversify its economy. There is a wide disparity in the degree to which some stratas of society benefit from oil revenue: many live in poverty. Agriculture employs 28% of the people, and bananas, cocoa, and coffee are all important crops. Fishing, forestry, mining, and manufacturing play a significant part in the economy.

AREA 109,483 sq mi [283,561 sq km] **POPULATION** 16,499,000
CAPITAL Quito **GOVERNMENT** Multiparty republic
ETHNIC GROUPS Mestizo (mixed White/Amerindian) 72%, Montubio 7%, Afroecuadorian 7%, Amerindian 7%, White 6%
LANGUAGES Spanish (official), Quechua, Shuar
RELIGIONS Roman Catholic 95% **CURRENCY** US dollar = 100 cents

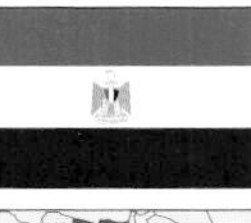

EGYPT

GEOGRAPHY The Arab Republic of Egypt is Africa's third largest country by population after Nigeria and Ethiopia, though it ranks 12th in area. Most of Egypt is desert. Almost all the people live either in the Nile Valley and its fertile delta or along the Suez Canal. This waterway, between the Mediterranean and Red seas, shortens the sea journey between the United Kingdom and India by 6,027 mi [9,700 km]. Recent attempts have been made to irrigate parts of the western desert.

Apart from the Nile Valley, Egypt can be divided into three other main regions. The Western and Eastern deserts are parts of the Sahara. The Sinai peninsula (Es Sina), to the east of the Suez Canal, is a mountainous desert region, falling geographically within Asia. It contains Egypt's highest peak, Gebel Katherîna (8,650 ft [2,637 m]); few people live in this area.

Egypt is a dry country. The low rainfall occurs, if at all, in winter and the country is one of the sunniest places on Earth.

POLITICS & ECONOMY Ancient Egypt, dating from around 5,000 years ago, was one of the great early civilizations. Throughout the country, pyramids, temples, and richly decorated tombs are memorials to its great achievements.

After Ancient Egypt declined, the country came under successive foreign rulers. The Arabs, who first occupied Egypt in the 7th century introducing their language and Islam, had a profound and lasting effect. Their influence was so great that most Egyptians now regard themselves as Arabs.

Egypt came under British rule in 1882, but it gained partial independence in 1922, becoming a monarchy. The monarchy was abolished in 1952, when Egypt became a republic. The creation of Israel in 1948 led Egypt into a series of wars in 1948–9, 1956, 1967, and 1973. In 1979, Egypt signed a peace treaty with Israel and regained the Sinai region, which it had lost in a war in 1967. Extremists opposed contacts with Israel and, in 1981, President Sadat, who had signed the treaty, was assassinated.

While Egypt plays a major part in Arab affairs, most of its people are poor. In February 2011, Hosni Mubarak, Egypt's president since 1981, was ousted following huge popular demonstrations. A Supreme Military Council took power and organized elections in 2011–12. President Muhammed Mursi from the formerly banned Muslim Brotherhood was elected in June 2012. Mursi was removed from power by the military in July 2013 and Abdel Fattah al-Sisi was elected in 2014. He was re-elected in March 2018, after credible opposing candidates withdrew or were arrested. In 2017, Egypt joined Saudi Arabia, the UAE, and Bahrain in imposing a blockade on Qatar.

Egypt is Africa's second most industrialized country after South Africa, but most people are poor. Oil and textiles are the country's main exports with tourism vitally important to the economy. The country is struggling to support its rapidly growing population.

AREA 386,659 sq mi [1,001,449 sq km] **POPULATION** 99,413,000
CAPITAL Cairo **GOVERNMENT** Republic
ETHNIC GROUPS Egyptians/Bedouins/Berbers 99%
LANGUAGES Arabic (official), French, English **RELIGIONS** Islam (mainly Sunni Muslim) 90%, Christianity (mainly Coptic Christian) and others 10% **CURRENCY** Egyptian pound = 100 piastres

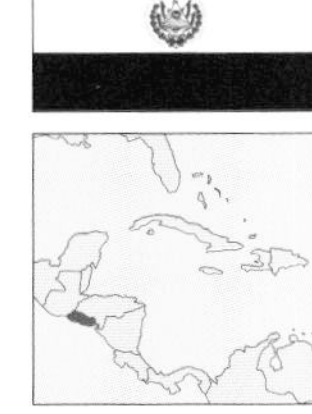

EL SALVADOR

GEOGRAPHY The Republic of El Salvador is the only country in Central America not to have a coast on the Caribbean Sea. El Salvador has a narrow coastal plain along the Pacific Ocean. Behind the coastal plain, the coastal range is a zone of rugged mountains, including volcanoes, which overlooks a densely populated inland plateau. Beyond the plateau, the land rises to the sparsely populated interior highlands. The coast has a hot tropical climate, but inland this is moderated by the altitude. Rain is heavy between May and October.

POLITICS & ECONOMY Amerindians have lived in El Salvador for thousands of years. The ruins of Mayan pyramids, built between AD 100 and 1000, are still found in the western part of the country. Spain first conquered the area in 1524, and ruled until 1821.

In 1823, all the Central American countries, except for Panama, set up the Central American Federation, with El Salvador withdrawing in 1840 and declaring its independence in 1841. Suffering from instability throughout the 19th century, the 20th century saw more stable government, although from 1931 military dictatorships alternated with elected governments.

The country remained poor and in the 1970s protesters demanded that the government introduce reforms. Kidnappings and murders committed by left- and right-wing groups were common. A civil war broke out in 1979 between the US-backed government forces and left-wing guerrillas. A ceasefire was agreed in 1992. In 2011, the United States added El Salvador and Belize to its list of countries considered to be major producers or transit routes of illegal drugs. Its murder rate is one of the world's highest.

The World Bank classifies El Salvador as a "lower-middle-income" economy. Often hit by natural disasters, the country relies heavily on remittances from abroad, especially the USA. About three-quarters of the country is farmed. Coffee, grown in the highlands, is the main export, followed by sugar and cotton, which grow on the coastal lowlands. Fishing for lobsters and shrimps is important, but manufacturing is on a small scale.

AREA 8,124 sq mi [21,041 sq km] **POPULATION** 6,187,000
CAPITAL San Salvador **GOVERNMENT** Republic
ETHNIC GROUPS Mestizo (mixed White and Amerindian) 86%, White 13%, Amerindian 1% **LANGUAGES** Spanish (official) **RELIGIONS** Roman Catholic 57%, Protestant 21% **CURRENCY** US dollar = 100 cents

EQUATORIAL GUINEA

GEOGRAPHY The Republic of Equatorial Guinea is a small republic in west-central Africa. It consists of a mainland territory which makes up 90% of the land area, called Rio Muni, between Cameroon and Gabon, and five offshore islands in the Bight of Bonny, the largest of which is Bioko. The island of Annobon lies 350 mi [560 km] southwest of Rio Muni. Rio Muni consists mainly of hills and plateaux behind the coastal plains.

The climate is hot and humid. Bioko is mountainous, with the land rising to 9,869 ft [3,008 m], and hence it is particularly rainy. However, there is a marked dry season between the months of December and February. Mainland Rio Muni has a similar climate, though the rainfall diminishes inland.

POLITICS & ECONOMY Portuguese navigators reached the area in 1471. In 1778, Portugal granted Bioko, together with rights over Rio Muni, to Spain. In 1959, Spain made Bioko and Rio Muni provinces of overseas Spain and, in 1963, it gave them a degree of self-government. Equatorial Guinea became independent in 1968.

The first president of Equatorial Guinea, Francisco Macias Nguema, proved to be a tyrant. Overthrown in 1979, a Supreme Military Council then took control, led by Obiang Nguema. In 1991, a nominally democratic system was restored, with Obiang as president. He has been re-elected several times, most recently in 2016, in a series of flawed elections. Equatorial Guinea is widely recognized as one of Africa's worst abusers of human rights.

Agriculture employs two-thirds of the people. The most valuable crop is coffee. Oil, which has been produced since 1966, accounts for most of the export revenue and has fueled recent rapid economic growth. The country is one of the largest oil producers in sub-Saharan Africa.

AREA 10,830 sq mi [28,051 sq km] **POPULATION** 797,000
CAPITAL Malabo **GOVERNMENT** Republic
ETHNIC GROUPS Bubi (on Bioko), Fang (in Rio Muni)
LANGUAGES Spanish and French (both official)
RELIGIONS Christianity **CURRENCY** CFA franc = 100 centimes

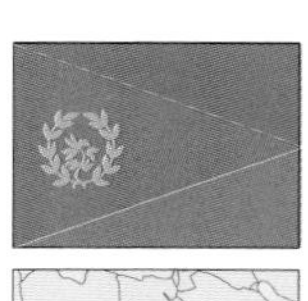

ERITREA

GEOGRAPHY The State of Eritrea consists of a hot, dry coastal plain facing the Red Sea, with a fairly mountainous area in the center. Most people live in the cooler highland area.

POLITICS & ECONOMY From the 1st century AD, Eritrea was part of the ancient Kingdom of Axum. The Ottoman Turks took over the area in the 16th century and it became an Italian colony in the 1880s. The Italians were driven out in 1941 and, in 1952, it became part of Ethiopia. A guerrilla struggle launched in 1961 ended in 1993, when Eritrea became independent. Economic recovery was hampered by conflict first with Yemen, over three islands in the Red Sea, and then with Ethiopia. A fragile peace has been negotiated and the country faces the huge task of reconstruction. The UN has repeatedly accused the country's leaders of human rights violations and hundreds of thousands of people have fled the country.

The main economic activities are farming and livestock rearing with some manufacturing based around Asmara. Exploitation of the country's copper and gold resources may drive future economic growth, if very real social problems can be overcome.

AREA 45,405 sq mi [117,600 sq km] **POPULATION** 5,971,000
CAPITAL Asmara **GOVERNMENT** Transitional government
ETHNIC GROUPS Tigrinya 55%, Tigre 30%, Saho 4%, Kunama 2%, others 9% **LANGUAGES** Tigrinya, Arabic, English (all official), others
RELIGIONS Islam, Coptic Christian, Roman Catholic
CURRENCY Nakfa = 100 cents

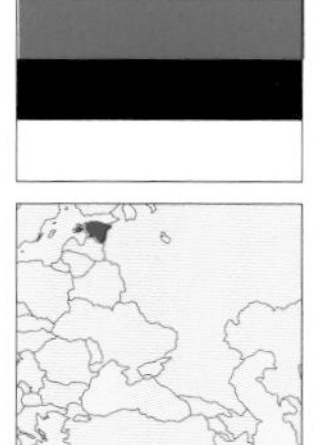

ESTONIA

GEOGRAPHY The Republic of Estonia is the smallest of the three states on the Baltic Sea, which were formerly part of the Soviet Union, but became independent in the early 1990s. Estonia consists of a generally flat plain which was covered by ice sheets during the Ice Age. The land is strewn with moraine (rocks deposited by the ice).

The country is dotted with more than 1,500 small lakes. The large Lake Peipus (Ozero Chudskoye) and the River Narva together make up much of Estonia's eastern border with Russia. The largest of the islands is Saaremaa (Ösel). The climate is fairly mild because of the moderating effects of the sea.

POLITICS & ECONOMY The ancestors of the Estonians, who are related to the Finns, settled in the area several thousand years ago. German crusaders, known as the Teutonic Knights, introduced Christianity in the early 13th century. By the 16th century, German noblemen owned much of the land in Estonia. In 1561, Sweden took the northern part of the country and Poland the south. From 1625, Sweden controlled the entire country until handing it over to Russia in 1721. Estonian nationalists campaigned for their independence from around the mid-19th century. Finally, Estonia was proclaimed independent in 1918.

In 1939, Germany and the Soviet Union agreed to take over parts of Eastern Europe. In 1940, Soviet forces occupied Estonia, but they were driven out by the Germans in 1941. Soviet troops returned in 1944 and Estonia became one of the 15 Soviet Socialist Republics of the Soviet Union. The Estonians strongly opposed Soviet rule and many of them were deported to Siberia.

Political changes in the Soviet Union in the late 1980s led to renewed demands for freedom. In 1990, the Estonian government declared the country independent and, finally, the Soviet Union recognized this act in September 1991. In January 2011, Estonia became the 17th member of the eurozone.

Under Soviet rule, Estonia was the most prosperous of the three Baltic states. Turning increasingly to the West, it became a member of both the North Atlantic Treaty Organization and the European Union in 2004. From March 2017 NATO made a major deployment of armed forces to Estonia amid reports of a Russian troop build-up across the border. Estonia's resources include oil shale and its forests. Industries produce fertilizers, processed food, machinery, petrochemical products, wood products, and textiles. Agriculture and fishing are also important activities. Around a quarter of the population are of Russian origin and, due to official language requirements, they can be subject to discrimination.

AREA 17,413 sq mi [45,100 sq km] **POPULATION** 1,244,000
CAPITAL Tallinn **GOVERNMENT** Multiparty republic
ETHNIC GROUPS Estonian 69%, Russian 26%, Ukrainian 2%, Belarusian 1%, Finnish 1% **LANGUAGES** Estonian (official), Russian
RELIGIONS Lutheran, Russian and Estonian Orthodox, Methodist, Baptist, Roman Catholic **CURRENCY** Euro = 100 cents

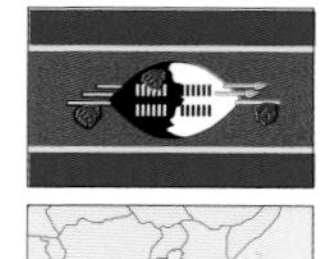

ESWATINI

GEOGRAPHY Offically renamed in 2018 as the Kingdom of Eswatini, this is a small, landlocked country in southern Africa. The country has four regions which run north–south. In the west, the Highveld, with an average height of 3,950 ft [1,200 m], makes up 30% of Eswatini. The Middleveld, between 1,150 ft and 3,280 ft [350 m to 1,000 m], covers 28% of the country. The Lowveld, with an average height of 886 ft [270 m], covers another 33%. Finally, the Lebombo Mountains reach 2,600 ft [800 m] along the eastern border. The Lowveld is almost tropical, with average temperatures of 72°F [22°C] and low rainfall.

POLITICS & ECONOMY In 1894, Britain and the Boers of South Africa agreed to put Swaziland, as it was then known, under the control of the South African Republic (the Transvaal). But at the end of the Anglo–Boer War (1899–1902), Britain took control of the country. In 1968, when it became fully independent as a constitutional monarchy, the head of state was King Sobhuza II. Sobhuza died in 1982 and was succeeded by his son, who, in 1986, became King Mswati III. Political parties were banned in elections in 1993 and 1998 and Mswati ruled by decree. In 2005, Mswati signed a new constitution, but Eswatini remains an absolute monarchy.

This is a developing country. Farm products and processed food and drink, sugar, wood pulp, citrus fruits, and canned fruit are the leading exports. It is heavily dependent on South Africa and it shares two problems with its large neighbor – widespread poverty and the world's highest incidence of HIV/AIDS.

AREA 6,704 sq mi [17,364 sq km] **POPULATION** 1,087,000
CAPITAL Mbabane **GOVERNMENT** Monarchy
ETHNIC GROUPS African 97%, European 3%
LANGUAGES Siswati and English (both official)
RELIGIONS Zionist (a mix of Christianity and traditional beliefs) 40%, Roman Catholic 20%, Islam 10% **CURRENCY** Lilangeni = 100 cents

ETHIOPIA

GEOGRAPHY Ethiopia is a landlocked country in northeastern Africa. The land is mainly mountainous, though there are extensive plains in the east, bordering southern Eritrea, and in the south, bordering Somalia. The highlands are divided into two blocks by an arm of the Great Rift Valley which runs throughout eastern Africa. North of the Rift Valley, the land is especially rugged, rising to 14,872 ft [4,533 m] at Ras Dashen. Southeast of Ras Dashen is Lake Tana, source of the River Abay (Blue Nile). The climate is affected by the altitude. The rainfall in the highlands is generally more than 39 inches [1,000 mm]. The lowlands are hot and arid.

POLITICS & ECONOMY Ethiopia was the home of an ancient monarchy, which became Christian in the 4th century. In the 7th century, Muslims gained control of the lowlands, but Christianity survived in the highlands. Ethiopia resisted attempts to colonize it, until Italy invaded the country in 1935. With help from the UK, the Italians were driven out in 1941 and the Emperor Haile Selassie was put back on the throne.

In 1952, Eritrea was federated with Ethiopia. But in 1961, Eritrean nationalists demanded their freedom and began a struggle that ended in their independence in 1993. Devastation caused by drought, famine, and war led to the overthrow of Haile Selassie in 1974. In 1995, because of Ethiopia's great ethnic diversity, the country was divided into nine provinces. In 1998, boundary disputes with Eritrea led to conflict. A peace agreement was reached in 2001, but border incursions by both sides continued. In 2016, human rights protests broke out across the country, leading to the resignation of PM Hailemariam Desalegn and his replacement by Abiy Ahmed in 2018. In July 2018 he signed a peace agreement with Eritrea and reopened the border.

Ethiopia's agriculture-based economy is at the mercy of a fickle climate. Coffee and the drug "khat" are leading exports. Although still heavily dependent on foreign aid, Ethiopia has one of the fastest growing non-oil economies in Africa.

AREA 426,370 sq mi [1,104,300 sq km] **POPULATION** 108,386,000
CAPITAL Addis Ababa **GOVERNMENT** Federation of nine provinces
ETHNIC GROUPS Oromo 34%, Amhara 27%, Somali 6%, Tigraway 6%, Sidama 4%
LANGUAGES Amharic (official), Oromo, many others
RELIGIONS Ethiopian Orthodox 43%, Islam 34%, Protestant 19%
CURRENCY Birr = 100 santim

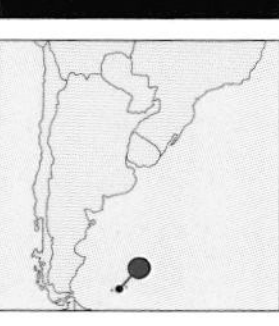

FALKLAND ISLANDS

Comprising two main islands and over 200 small ones, the Falkland Islands lie 300 mi [480 km] from South America. Sheep farming and fishing are the main activities, though oil and diamonds are being sought. Argentina disputes Britain's sovereignty of the islands, but a referendum in 2013 resulted in an overwhelming vote to stay British.

AREA 4,700 sq mi [12,173 sq km]
POPULATION 3,000 **CAPITAL** Stanley

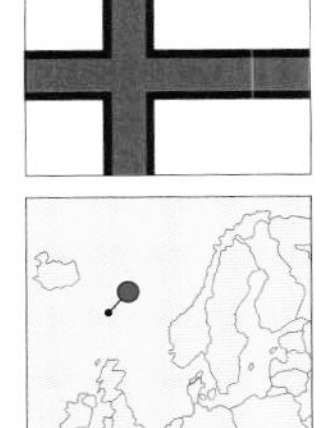

FÆROE ISLANDS

The Færoe Islands are a group of 18 volcanic islands and some reefs in the North Atlantic Ocean. The islands have been Danish since the 1380s, but they became largely self-governing in 1948. The islands are heavily reliant on fishing although the discovery of some oil may allow diversification in the future. Denmark still provides a subsidy.

AREA 540 SQ MI [1,399 SQ KM]
POPULATION 51,000 **CAPITAL** TÓRSHAVN

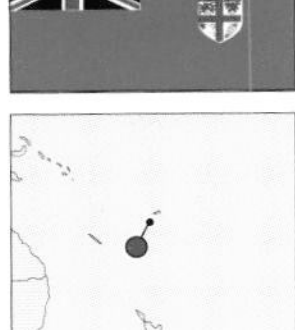

FIJI

The Republic of Fiji (the official name of Fiji since February 2011) consists of more than 800 Melanesian islands, the biggest being Viti Levu and Vanua Levu. The climate is tropical. A former British colony, Fiji became independent in 1970. Its recent history has been marred by efforts of indigenous Fijians to impose their rule, stopping members of the ethnic Indian community from holding senior cabinet posts. Such political instability has harmed the economy.

AREA 7,056 SQ MI [18,274 SQ KM] **POPULATION** 926,000 **CAPITAL** SUVA

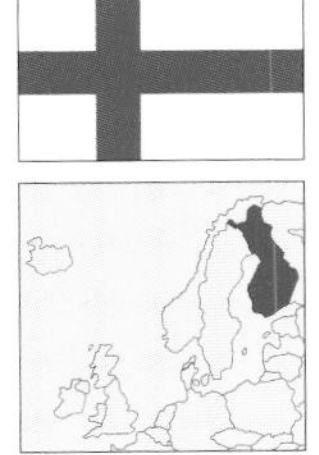

FINLAND

GEOGRAPHY The Republic of Finland is a beautiful country in northern Europe. In the south, behind the coastal lowlands where most Finns live, lies a region of sparkling lakes carved out by ice sheets in the Ice Age. The thinly populated northern uplands cover about two-fifths of the country.

Helsinki, the capital city, has warm summers, but the average temperatures between the months of December and March are below freezing. Snow covers the land in winter. The north has less precipitation than the south, but it is much colder.

POLITICS & ECONOMY Between 1150 and 1809, Finland was under Swedish rule and close links between the countries continue today. Swedish remains an official language in Finland and many towns have Swedish as well as Finnish names.

In 1809, Finland became a grand duchy of the Russian empire. It finally declared itself independent in 1917, following the Russian Revolution. But during World War II (1939–45), the Soviet Union declared war on Finland and took part of Finland's territory. Finland allied itself with Germany, but it lost more land to the Soviet Union at the end of the war.

After World War II, Finland became a neutral country and negotiated peace treaties with the Soviet Union. Finland also strengthened its relations with other northern European countries and became an associate member of the European Free Trade Association (EFTA) in 1961 and a full member in 1986. It then joined the European Union on January 1, 1995, adopting the euro as its currency in 2002.

Forests are the chief resource and wood, wood products, and paper once dominated the economy. They still make up about a quarter of exports, but, since World War II, Finland has set up many new industries, which employ around a quarter of the people. One of Finland's main advantages is a well-qualified work force who enjoy one of the highest rates of per capita income in Western Europe. Major exports include telecommunications equipment, paper products, and iron and steel. However, dealing with a growing aging population is a challenge to be met.

AREA 130,558 SQ MI [338,145 SQ KM] **POPULATION** 5,537,000
CAPITAL HELSINKI **GOVERNMENT** MULTIPARTY REPUBLIC
ETHNIC GROUPS FINNISH 93%, SWEDISH 6%
LANGUAGES FINNISH AND SWEDISH (BOTH OFFICIAL)
RELIGIONS EVANGELICAL LUTHERAN 71% **CURRENCY** EURO = 100 CENTS

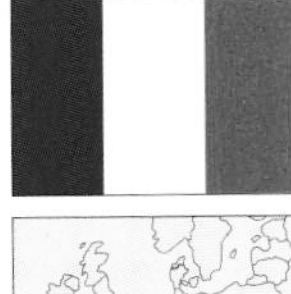

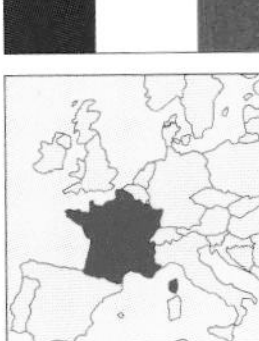

FRANCE

GEOGRAPHY The Republic of France is the largest country in Western Europe. The scenery is extremely varied. The Vosges Mountains overlook the Rhine valley in the northeast, the Jura Mountains and the Alps form the borders with Switzerland and Italy in the southeast, while the Pyrenees straddle France's border with Spain. The only large highland area entirely within France is the Massif Central between the Rhône–Saône valley and the basin of Aquitaine in southern France.

Brittany (Bretagne) and Normandy (Normande) form a scenic region. Fertile lowlands cover most of northern France, including the densely populated Paris basin. Another major lowland area, the Aquitanian basin, is in the southwest, while the Rhône–Saône valley and the Mediterranean lowlands are in the southeast.

The climate of France varies from west to east and from north to south. The west comes under the moderating influence of the Atlantic Ocean, giving generally mild weather. To the east, summers are warmer and winters colder. The climate also becomes warmer as one travels from north to south. The Mediterranean Sea coast has hot, dry summers and mild, moist winters. The Alps, Jura, and Pyrenees mountains have snowy winters. Winter sports centers are found in all three areas.

POLITICS & ECONOMY The Romans conquered France (then called Gaul) in the 50s BC. Roman rule began to decline in the 5th century AD and, in 486, the Frankish realm (as France was known) became independent under a Christian king, Clovis. In 800, Charlemagne, who had been king since 768, became emperor of the Romans. He extended France's boundaries, but in 843 his empire was divided into three parts and the area of France contracted. After the Norman invasion of England in 1066, large areas of France came under English rule, but this was all but ended in 1453.

France later became a powerful monarchy. But the French Revolution (1789–99) ended absolute rule by French kings. In 1799, Napoleon Bonaparte took power and fought a series of brilliant military campaigns before his final defeat in 1815. The monarchy was restored until 1848, when the Second Republic was founded. In 1852, Napoleon's nephew became Napoleon III, but the Third Republic was established in 1875. France was the scene of much fighting during World War I (1914–18) and World War II (1939–45), causing great loss of life and much damage to the economy.

In 1946, France adopted a new constitution, establishing the Fourth Republic. But political instability and costly colonial wars slowed France's post-war recovery. In 1958, Charles de Gaulle was elected president and he introduced a new constitution, giving the president extra powers and inaugurating the Fifth Republic.

Since the 1960s, France has made rapid economic progress, becoming one of the most prosperous nations in the European Union. But France's government faced a number of problems, including unemployment, pollution, and the growing number of elderly people. France is still facing economic challenges due to low growth and high public spending. A social issue concerns the large numbers of immigrants, including Muslims from North Africa, and in 2005, France was rocked by inter-ethnic violence. It has suffered several terrorist attacks since 2015.

In 2002, the euro replaced the franc as France's currency. In 2009, the right-wing president Nicolas Sarkozy announced that France would rejoin NATO. Presidential elections in 2017 were won by Emmanuel Macron. His proposed labor reforms sparked strikes in 2018, and price increases introduced to reduce the use of fossil fuels prompted violent street demonstrations by the "yellow shirts," which continued into 2019.

France is one of the world's most developed countries. Its natural resources include its fertile soil, together with deposits of bauxite, coal, iron ore, oil and natural gas, and potash. France is also one of the world's top manufacturing nations, and it has often innovated in bold and imaginative ways. The TGV and hypermarkets are typical examples. Paris is a world center of fashion industries. Manufactures include aircraft, cars, chemicals, electronic and metal products, machinery, processed food, steel, and textiles.

Agriculture employs about 4% of the people, but France is the largest producer of farm products in Western Europe, producing most of the food it needs. Wheat is the leading crop and livestock farming is of major importance. Fishing and forestry are leading industries, while tourism is a major activity.

AREA 212,934 SQ MI [551,500 SQ KM] **POPULATION** 67,364,000
CAPITAL PARIS **GOVERNMENT** MULTIPARTY REPUBLIC
ETHNIC GROUPS CELTIC, LATIN, ARAB, TEUTONIC, SLAVIC
LANGUAGES FRENCH (OFFICIAL) **RELIGIONS** ROMAN CATHOLIC 85%, ISLAM 8%, OTHERS **CURRENCY** EURO = 100 CENTS

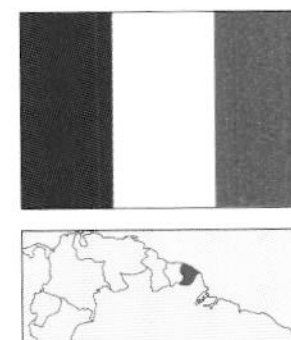

FRENCH GUIANA

GEOGRAPHY French Guiana is the smallest country in mainland South America. The coastal plain is swampy in places, but some dry areas are cultivated. Inland lies a plateau, with the low Serra Tumucumaque in the south. Most of the rivers run north toward the Atlantic Ocean.

French Guiana has a hot, equatorial climate, with high temperatures throughout the year. The rainfall is heavy, especially between December and June, but the climate is dry between August and October. The northeast trade winds blow constantly across the country.

POLITICS & ECONOMY The first people to live in what is now French Guiana were Amerindians. Today, only a few of them survive in the interior. The first Europeans to explore the coast arrived in 1500, and they were followed by adventurers seeking El Dorado, the mythical city of gold. Cayenne was founded in 1637 by a group of French merchants and the area became a French colony in the late 17th century.

France used the colony as a penal settlement for political prisoners from the times of the French Revolution in the 1790s. From the 1850s to 1945, the country became notorious as a place where prisoners were harshly treated. Many of them died, unable to survive in the tropical conditions.

In 1946, French Guiana became an overseas department of France, and in 1974 it also became an administrative region. An independence movement developed in the 1980s, but most people want to retain their links with France. In 2010, the people voted in a referendum to reject plans for increased autonomy.

Although it has rich forest and mineral resources, such as bauxite (aluminum ore), French Guiana is a developing country. It depends greatly on France for money to run its services and the government is the country's biggest employer. Since 1968, Kourou in French Guiana, the European Space Agency's rocket-launching site, has earned money for France by sending communications satellites into space.

AREA 34,749 SQ MI [90,000 SQ KM] **POPULATION** 250,000
CAPITAL CAYENNE **GOVERNMENT** OVERSEAS DEPARTMENT OF FRANCE
ETHNIC GROUPS BLACK OR MIXED 66%, EAST INDIAN/CHINESE AND AMERINDIAN 12%, WHITE 12%, OTHERS 10%
LANGUAGES FRENCH (OFFICIAL) **RELIGIONS** ROMAN CATHOLIC
CURRENCY EURO = 100 CENTS

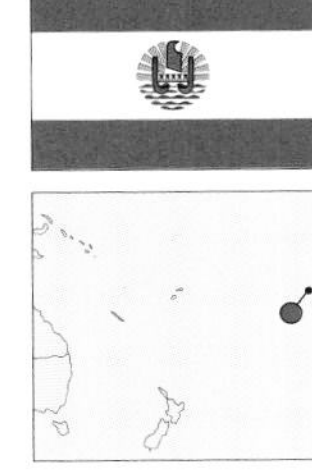

FRENCH POLYNESIA

French Polynesia consists of 130 islands, of which Tahiti is the most densely populated. A French protectorate since 1843, France has tested nuclear weapons on the uninhabited atolls. French Polynesia gained increased autonomy in 1984, but the links with France ensure a high standard of living.

AREA 1,544 SQ MI [4,000 SQ KM]
POPULATION 290,000 **CAPITAL** PAPEETE

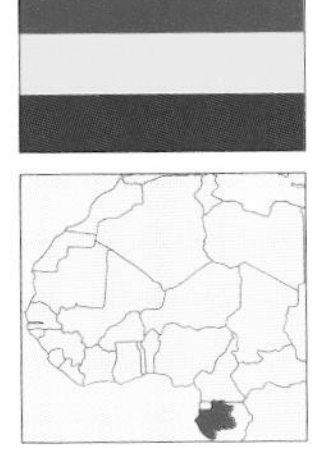

GABON

GEOGRAPHY The Gabonese Republic lies on the equator in west-central Africa. In area, it is a little larger than the United Kingdom, with a coastline 500 mi [800 km] long. Behind the narrow, partly lagoon-lined coastal plain, the land rises to hills, plateaux, and mountains divided by deep valleys carved by the River Ogooué and its tributaries.

Most of Gabon has an equatorial climate, with high temperatures and humidity throughout the year.

POLITICS & ECONOMY Gabon became a French colony in the 1880s, but it achieved full independence in 1960. In 1964, an attempted coup was put down when French troops intervened and crushed the revolt. In 1967, Bernard-Albert Bongo, who later renamed himself El Hadj Omar Bongo, became president and remained in power until his death in 2009, when he was succeeded by his son, Ali Ben Bongo Ondimba. In 2016 presidential elections, marred by violence and accusations of fraud, Ali Bongo won a second term. After a mystery illness in late 2018, question marks remained over Ali Bongo's ability to hold power.

Gabon's natural resources include its forests, oil and gas deposits, manganese, and uranium. Its mineral deposits make it one of Africa's better-off countries. But agriculture still employs about 30% of the people and many farmers produce little more than they need to support their families. Falling oil revenue means that the economy has to diversify and one growth sector is eco-tourism.

AREA 103,347 SQ MI [267,668 SQ KM] **POPULATION** 2,119,000
CAPITAL LIBREVILLE **GOVERNMENT** MULTIPARTY REPUBLIC
ETHNIC GROUPS FOUR MAJOR BANTU TRIBES: FANG, BAPOUNOU, NZEBI AND OBAMBA **LANGUAGES** FRENCH (OFFICIAL), FANG, MYENE, NZEBI, BAPOUNOU/ESCHIRA, BANDJABI
RELIGIONS CHRISTIANITY 65%, ANIMIST, ISLAM
CURRENCY CFA FRANC = 100 CENTIMES

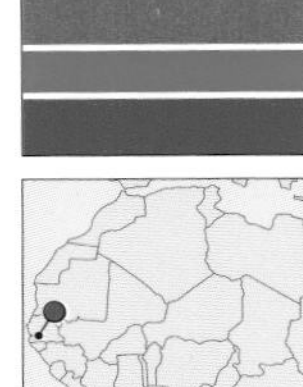

GAMBIA, THE

GEOGRAPHY The Republic of The Gambia is the smallest country in mainland Africa. It consists of a narrow strip of land bordering the River Gambia. The Gambia is almost entirely enclosed by Senegal, except along the short Atlantic coastline.

The Gambia has hot and humid summers, but winter temperatures (November to May) drop to around 61°F [16°C]. In the summer, moist southwesterlies bring rain, which is heaviest on the coast.

POLITICS & ECONOMY English traders established themselves on the River Gambia in the late 16th century and the country was a British colony from 1888 until independence in 1965.

In 1981, an attempted coup in The Gambia was put down with the help of Senegalese troops. Following this, in 1982, The Gambia and Senegal set up a defense alliance, called the Confederation of Senegambia, which was dissolved in 1989. In 1994, a military group led by Captain Yahya Jammeh overthrew the government of Sir Dawda Jawara. Jammeh remained in power until 2016, when he was defeated by Adama Barrow. Jammeh refused to accept the result and left only after neighboring countries undertook mediation and threatened armed intervention. Barrow's United Democratic Party won a landslide victory at parliamentary elections in 2017.

Agriculture is the chief activity, employing three-quarters of the population and accounting for around 30% of GDP. Food crops include cassava, millet, and sorghum, but groundnuts (peanuts) and groundnut products are the main exports. About one-third of the population live below the poverty line. Tourism is important to the economy, as are remittances sent back from overseas workers. Offshore oilfields were discovered in 2004 but this resource has yet to be developed.

AREA 4,361 SQ MI [11,295 SQ KM] **POPULATION** 2,093,000
CAPITAL BANJUL **GOVERNMENT** REPUBLIC
ETHNIC GROUPS MANDINKA 42%, FULA 18%, WOLOF 16%, JOLA 10%, SERAHULI 9%, OTHERS
LANGUAGES ENGLISH (OFFICIAL), MANDINKA, WOLOF, FULA
RELIGIONS ISLAM 90%, CHRISTIANITY 8%, TRADITIONAL BELIEFS 2%
CURRENCY DALASI = 100 BUTUTS

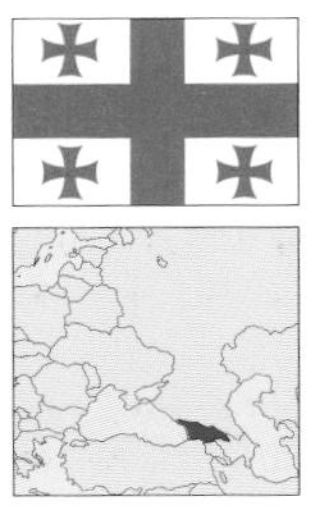

GEORGIA

GEOGRAPHY Georgia is a country on the borders of Europe and Asia, facing the Black Sea. The land is rugged with the Caucasus Mountains forming its northern border.

The highest mountain in this range, Mount Elbrus (18,510 ft [5,642 m]), lies over the border in Russia. The Black Sea plains have hot summers and mild winters. The rainfall is heavy, though inland areas are drier.

POLITICS & ECONOMY The first Georgian state was set up nearly 2,500 years ago but has been overrun by a variety of conquering armies. From the 16th to the 18th centuries, Persia and the Turkish Ottoman empire struggled for control of the area, and in the late 18th century Georgia sought the protection of Russia. By the early 19th century, it was part of the Russian empire. After the Russian Revolution of 1917, Georgia declared its independence, but Russia invaded, making it part of the Soviet regime. Georgia declared itself independent in 1991 and it became a separate country when the Soviet Union was dissolved in 1991.

Georgia contains three regions populated by minority peoples: Abkhazia in the northwest, South Ossetia in north-central Georgia, and Ajaria in the southwest. Civil war broke out in South Ossetia in the early 1990s, while fierce fighting continued in Abkhazia until the late 1990s. In 2000, Georgia agreed to recognize Ajaria's autonomy in the country's constitution. In 2003, the pro-Western Mikhail Saakashvili was elected president following the "Rose Revolution." Following Saakashvili's re-election in 2008, relations with Russia deteriorated. In August 2008, Georgia tried to retake South Ossetia by force. Russian troops counterattacked and drove Georgian troops out of South Ossetia and Abkhazia. After parliamentary elections in 2012 were won by the opposition Georgian Dream coalition, Saakashvili resigned and was replaced by Giorgi Margvelashvili. Georgian Dream changed the presidency to a mainly ceremonial role and won a majority in 2016 elections. In 2018 Mamuka Bakhtadze became prime minister.

Georgia is a developing country. Agriculture, food processing, and perfume-making are important activities. Products include barley, citrus fruits, grapes for wine-making, maize, tea, tobacco, and vegetables. Sheep and cattle are reared. Hydroelectricity provides most of Georgia's power needs but gas and oil have to be imported. Unemployment remains high.

AREA 26,911 SQ MI [69,700 SQ KM] **POPULATION** 4,926,000
CAPITAL TBILISI **GOVERNMENT** MULTIPARTY REPUBLIC
ETHNIC GROUPS GEORGIAN 84%, AZERI 7%, ARMENIAN 6%, RUSSIAN 1%, OTHERS 2%
LANGUAGES GEORGIAN (OFFICIAL), RUSSIAN, ARMENIAN, AZERI; ABKHAZ (OFFICIAL IN ABKHAZIA) **RELIGIONS** GEORGIAN ORTHODOX 84%, ISLAM 10%, ARMENIAN GREGORIAN 4% **CURRENCY** LARI = 100 TETRI

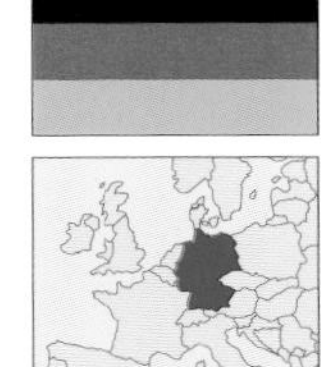

GERMANY

GEOGRAPHY The Federal Republic of Germany is the fourth largest country in Western Europe, after France, Spain, and Sweden. The North German Plain borders the North Sea in the northwest and the Baltic Sea in the northeast. Major rivers draining the plain include the Weser, Elbe, and Oder.

The central highlands include the Harz Mountains, the Thuringian Forest (Thüringer Wald), the Ore Mountains (Erzgebirge), and the Bohemian Forest (Böhmerwald) on the Czech border. The Bavarian Alps in the south contain Germany's highest peak, Zugspitze, at 9,718 ft [2,962 m] above sea level. The Black Forest (Schwarzwald) in the southwest overlooks the River Rhine. Northwestern Germany has a mild climate, but the Baltic coasts are cooler. To the south, the climate becomes more continental, especially in the highlands.

POLITICS & ECONOMY Germany and its allies were defeated in World War I (1914–18) and the country became a republic. Adolf Hitler came to power in 1933 and ruled as a dictator. His order to invade Poland led to the start of World War II (1939–45), which ended with Germany in ruins.

In 1945, Germany was divided into four military zones. In 1949, the American, British, and French zones were amalgamated to form the Federal Republic of Germany (West Germany), while the Soviet zone became the German Democratic Republic (East Germany), a Communist state. Berlin, which had also been partitioned, became a divided city. West Berlin was part of West Germany, while East Berlin became the capital of East Germany. Bonn was the capital of West Germany.

Tension between East and West mounted during the Cold War, but West Germany rebuilt its economy quickly. In East Germany, the recovery was less rapid. In the late 1980s, reforms in the Soviet Union led to unrest in East Germany. Free elections were held in East Germany in 1990 and, on October 3, 1990, Germany was reunited.

In the 1990s, the government faced many problems, especially those arising from reunification. In 1999, the parliament moved from Bonn to the reconstructed Reichstag building in Berlin. In 2005, Angela Merkel became Germany's first female Chancellor. Merkel's unpopular policy of welcoming asylum seekers adversely affected her party's showing in 2017 elections and boosted the vote of the far-right.

West Germany's "economic miracle" after World War II was greatly helped by foreign aid. Today, Germany is one of the world's major economic powers. It is a leading member of the European Union and the 19-member eurozone. Since 2011, it has helped to maintain the eurozone by supporting debt-ridden countries, such as Greece. The mainstay of its export-led economy is manufacturing. Exports include machinery, metals, chemicals, and vehicles. Germany has some coal, potash, and rock salt deposits, but it imports many industrial raw materials. Germany also imports food. Leading agricultural products include fruits, grapes for wine-making, potatoes, sugar beet, and vegetables. Livestock include beef cattle and pigs.

AREA 137,846 SQ MI [357,022 SQ KM] **POPULATION** 80,458,000
CAPITAL BERLIN **GOVERNMENT** FEDERAL MULTIPARTY REPUBLIC
ETHNIC GROUPS GERMAN 92%, TURKISH 2%, SERBO-CROATIAN, ITALIAN, GREEK, POLISH, SPANISH **LANGUAGES** GERMAN (OFFICIAL)
RELIGIONS PROTESTANT (MAINLY LUTHERAN) 34%, ROMAN CATHOLIC 34%, ISLAM 4%, OTHERS **CURRENCY** EURO = 100 CENTS

GHANA

GEOGRAPHY The Republic of Ghana faces the Gulf of Guinea in West Africa. This hot country, just north of the equator, was formerly known as the Gold Coast. In the southwest, behind the thickly populated southern coastal plains, which are lined with lagoons, lies a plateau region.

Accra has a hot, tropical climate. Rain occurs all through the year, though Accra is drier than areas inland.

POLITICS & ECONOMY Portuguese explorers reached the area in 1471 and named it the Gold Coast. The area became a center of the slave trade in the 17th century until it was ended in the 1860s and, gradually, the British took control of the area. After independence in 1957, attempts were made to develop the economy by creating large state-owned manufacturing industries. But debt and corruption, together with falls in the price of cocoa, the chief export, caused economic problems. This led to instability and frequent coups. In 1981, power was invested in a Provisional National Defense Council, led by Flight-Lieutenant Jerry Rawlings. The government steadied the economy and introduced reforms. Incumbent John Dramani Mahama lost to human rights lawyer Nana Akufo-Addo in the 2016 presidential elections.

The World Bank classifies Ghana as a "lower-middle-income" developing country. Although the majority of the people are poor and farming employs 56% of the population, Ghana has one of Africa's fastest growing economies. Now exploiting recently discovered offshore oil reserves, the country is benefiting from years of stable government and efficient administration.

AREA 92,098 SQ MI [238,533 SQ KM] **POPULATION** 28,102,000
CAPITAL ACCRA **GOVERNMENT** REPUBLIC
ETHNIC GROUPS AKAN 47%, MOLE-DAGBON 17%, EWE 14%, GA-DANGME 7%, GURMA 6% **LANGUAGES** ENGLISH (OFFICIAL), ASANTE, EWE, FANTE, BORON, DAGOMBA **RELIGIONS** CHRISTIANITY 71%, ISLAM 18%, TRADITIONAL BELIEFS 5% **CURRENCY** CEDI = 100 PESEWAS

GIBRALTAR

Gibraltar occupies a strategic position on the south coast of Spain where the Mediterranean meets the Atlantic. It was recognized as a British possession in 1713 and, despite Spanish claims, its population has consistently voted to retain its contacts with Britain.

AREA 2.3 SQ MI [6 SQ KM]
POPULATION 29,000 **CAPITAL** GIBRALTAR TOWN

GREECE

GEOGRAPHY The Hellenic Republic, as Greece is officially called, is a rugged country situated at the southern end of the Balkan peninsula. Olympus, at 9,570 ft [2,917 m], is the highest peak. Islands make up about a fifth of the land area. Low-lying areas in Greece have mild, moist winters and hot, dry summers. The east coast has more than 2,700 hours of sunshine a year and only about half of the rainfall of the west. The mountains have a much more severe climate, with snow on the higher slopes in winter.

POLITICS & ECONOMY Around 2,500 years ago, Greece became the birthplace of Western civilization, and Ancient Greek ruins and art still attract millions of tourists to the country. The first civilization, the Minoan, was centered on Crete. It flourished between about 3000 and 1400 BC. Following the end of the related Mycaenean period on the mainland (1580–1100 BC), a "dark age" lasted until about 800 BC. But from 750 BC, Greeks became rich traders and the city-state of Athens reached its peak in 461–431 BC. Greece became a Roman province in 146 BC and, in 365, it became part of the Byzantine empire.

The Byzantine empire fell to the Turks in 1453. But Greece became an independent monarchy in 1830. After World War II (1939–45), when Germany ruled Greece, a civil war broke out between Greek Communists and nationalists. It ended in 1949 and a military dictatorship seized power in 1967. The monarchy was abolished in 1973 and democracy was restored in 1974. Greece joined the European Community (now the European Union) in 1981 and, on January 1, 2002, the euro became the sole unit of currency. Greece suffered hugely following the international financial crisis of 2008, entering into three international bailout agreements. From 2018 there were signs of economic recovery.

Greece is one of the EU's less economically developed members. Manufactured products include processed food, cement, chemicals, metal products, textiles, and tobacco. Greece also mines lignite (brown coal), bauxite, and chromite. Crops include barley, grapes, dried fruits, olives, potatoes, sugar beet, and wheat. Livestock farming is important and tourism is a major industry.

AREA 50,949 SQ MI [131,957 SQ KM] **POPULATION** 10,762,000
CAPITAL ATHENS **GOVERNMENT** MULTIPARTY REPUBLIC
ETHNIC GROUPS GREEK 93% **LANGUAGES** GREEK (OFFICIAL)
RELIGIONS GREEK ORTHODOX 98%
CURRENCY EURO = 100 CENTS

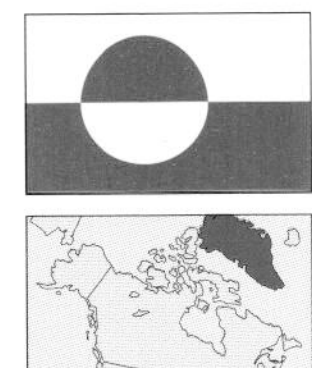

GREENLAND

Greenland is the world's largest island. With an ice sheet covering four-fifths of the land, settlements are confined to the coast. Greenland became a Danish possession in 1380. Full internal self-government was granted in 1981 and, in 2009, Greenland became a self-governing territory, though it remains dependent on Danish subsidies.

AREA 838,999 SQ MI [2,175,600 SQ KM]
POPULATION 58,000 **CAPITAL** NUUK

GRENADA

The most southerly of the Windward Islands in the Caribbean Sea, Grenada became independent from the UK in 1974. A military group seized power in 1983, when the prime minister was killed. US troops intervened and restored order and constitutional government.

AREA 133 SQ MI [344 SQ KM]
POPULATION 112,000 **CAPITAL** ST GEORGE'S

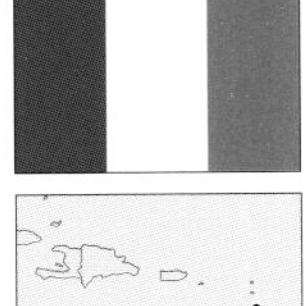

GUADELOUPE

Guadeloupe is a French overseas department which includes seven Caribbean islands, the largest of which is Basse-Terre. French aid has helped to maintain a reasonable standard of living for the people.

AREA 658 SQ MI [1,705 SQ KM]
POPULATION 402,000 **CAPITAL** BASSE-TERRE

GUAM

Guam, a strategically important "unincorporated territory" of the USA, is the largest of the Mariana Islands in the Pacific Ocean. Its economy depends on US military spending.

AREA 212 SQ MI [549 SQ KM]
POPULATION 168,000 **CAPITAL** HAGATNA

GUATEMALA

GEOGRAPHY The Republic of Guatemala in Central America contains a densely populated mountain region, with fertile soils. There are many volcanoes, some active. South of the mountains lie the thinly populated Pacific coastlands, while a large inland plain occupies the north. The lowlands of Guatemala are hot and rainy, but the central highlands are cooler and drier. Guatemala City has a pleasant, warm climate with a dry season between November and April.

POLITICS & ECONOMY Much of what is now Guatemala was part of the Maya empire which thrived between AD 300 and 900. Spain ruled the area from the 1520s until 1821, with Guatemala achieving full independence in 1839. Instability and periodic violence have marred its progress. Guatemala has a long-standing claim over Belize, but this was reduced in 1983 to the southern fifth of the country. Between 1960 and 1996, civil war occurred between left-wing groups, including many Amerindians, and government forces. In 2015, Jimmy Morales was elected president following the arrest of the previous incumbent for corruption.

Guatemala is ranked as an "upper-middle-income" economy with agriculture employing 38% of the population. Coffee, sugar, bananas, and beef are exported, and the spice cardamom and cotton are also important. Maize is the main food crop. Poverty is endemic in the countryside and problems of malnutrition, infant mortality, and illiteracy are yet to be overcome. In 2018 Guatemalans voted to take their territorial dispute with Belize to the International Court of Justice.

AREA 42,042 SQ MI [108,889 SQ KM] **POPULATION** 16,581,000
CAPITAL GUATEMALA CITY **GOVERNMENT** REPUBLIC
ETHNIC GROUPS LADINO (MIXED HISPANIC AND AMERINDIAN) 55%, AMERINDIAN 43%, OTHERS 2%
LANGUAGES SPANISH (OFFICIAL), AMERINDIAN LANGUAGES
RELIGIONS ROMAN CATHOLIC, INDIGENOUS MAYAN BELIEFS
CURRENCY US DOLLAR; QUETZAL = 100 CENTAVOS

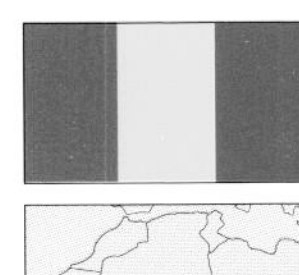

GUINEA

GEOGRAPHY The Republic of Guinea faces the Atlantic Ocean in West Africa. A flat, swampy plain borders the coast. Behind this plain, the land rises to a plateau region called Fouta Djallon. The Upper Niger Plains in the northeast are where the Niger, one of Africa's longest rivers, rises.

Guinea has a tropical climate and Conakry has its rainy period between May and November, the coolest season. In the dry season, hot harmattan winds blow from the Sahara.

POLITICS & ECONOMY Guinea came under the influence of several medieval African states, including Ancient Ghana and Ancient Mali. France began to control the area in the late 19th century with Guinea becoming independent in 1958. Its leaders pursued socialist policies but resorted to repressive measures to hold on to power. A military regime under Lansana Conté took over in 1984, but a multiparty system was restored in 1992. Following Conté's death in 2008, an army group led by Captain Mousa Dadis Camara seized power. But in 2010, Alpha Condé was elected president in Guinea's first democratic election since independence. He was re-elected in 2015.

Guinea is a "low-income" developing country. Its resources include bauxite (aluminum ore), diamonds, gold, iron ore, and uranium. Bauxite and alumina (processed bauxite) account for more than half of the country's exports. Agriculture employs more than 75% of the people, but most farmers are poor. Manufactures include alumina, processed food, and textiles.

AREA 94,925 SQ MI [245,857 SQ KM] **POPULATION** 11,855,000
CAPITAL CONAKRY **GOVERNMENT** MULTIPARTY REPUBLIC
ETHNIC GROUPS PEUHL 40%, MALINKE 30%, SOUSSOU 20%, OTHERS 10%
LANGUAGES FRENCH (OFFICIAL)
RELIGIONS ISLAM 85%, CHRISTIANITY 8%, TRADITIONAL BELIEFS 7%
CURRENCY GUINEAN FRANC = 100 CAURIS

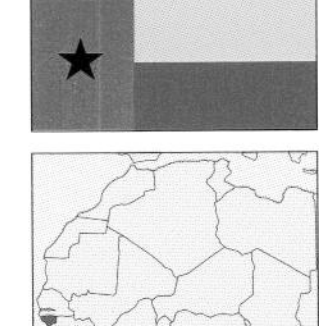

GUINEA-BISSAU

GEOGRAPHY The Republic of Guinea-Bissau, formerly known as Portuguese Guinea, is a small country in West Africa. The land is mostly low-lying, with a broad, swampy coastal plain and many flat offshore islands. The country has a tropical climate, with a dry season (December to May) and a wet season (June to November).

POLITICS & ECONOMY Portuguese explorers reached Guinea-Bissau in 1446 and the area became a center of the slave trade. From 1836, Portugal administered Guinea-Bissau with the Cape Verde Islands, but in 1879 the territories were separated.

In 1956, African nationalists in Portuguese Guinea (as Guinea-Bissau was then known) and Cape Verde founded the African Party for the Independence of Guinea and Cape Verde (PAIGC). The PAIGC began a guerrilla war in 1963 and, by 1968, it held two-thirds of the country. In 1972, a rebel National Assembly, elected by the people in the PAIGC-controlled area, voted to make the country independent as Guinea-Bissau.

The newly independent Guinea-Bissau faced many problems arising from its underdeveloped economy and its lack of trained people to work in the administration. One objective of the leaders of Guinea-Bissau was to unite their country with Cape Verde. But, in 1980, army leaders overthrew Guinea-Bissau's government. The Revolutionary Council, which took over, opposed unification with Cape Verde. Guinea-Bissau ceased to be a one-party state in 1991 and multiparty elections were held in 1994. Civil war and military coups followed until a civilian government was restored in 2004. Following another military coup in 2012, after the death of President Bacai Sanha, a government by Transitional National Council was established. Jose Mario Vaz was elected president in 2014, but political infighting meant that a consensus prime minister was not appointed until 2018.

The economy is massively in debt and relies on foreign aid: Guinea-Bissau is one of the world's poorest countries. Agriculture employs 82% of the people. Crops include cashew nuts, coconuts, groundnuts (peanuts), maize, and rice. The country is a major hub for drug trafficking between Latin America and Europe.

AREA 13,948 SQ MI [36,125 SQ KM] **POPULATION** 1,833,000
CAPITAL BISSAU **GOVERNMENT** REPUBLIC
ETHNIC GROUPS BALANTA 30%, FULA 20%, MANJACA 14%, MANDINGA 13%, PAPEL 7% **LANGUAGES** PORTUGUESE (OFFICIAL), CRIOULO
RELIGIONS ISLAM 50%, TRADITIONAL BELIEFS 40%, CHRISTIANITY 10%
CURRENCY CFA FRANC = 100 CENTIMES

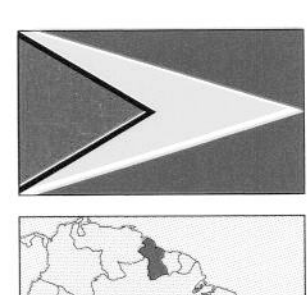

GUYANA

GEOGRAPHY The Cooperative Republic of Guyana faces the Atlantic Ocean in north-eastern South America. The coastal plain is flat and much of it is below sea level. The climate is hot and humid, though the interior highlands are cooler than the coast. Rainfall is heavy, occurring on more than 200 days a year.

POLITICS & ECONOMY Britain gained control of the area in 1814 and ruled British Guiana until it became independent as Guyana in 1966. A black lawyer, Forbes Burnham, was the first prime minister. Under a new constitution adopted in 1980, the president's powers were increased. Burnham became president and served in this post until he died in 1985. The current president is David Granger, who was elected in 2015.

Ethnic tensions, and political rivalries, persist between the descendants of African slaves and those descended from Indians brought in by the British. The discovery of substantial oil deposits offshore has led to political upheaval and disputes with Venezuela.

Guyana is a poor country. Its resources include gold, bauxite (aluminum ore) and other minerals, forests, and fertile soils. Sugarcane and rice are leading crops. Guyana has potential for producing hydroelectricity from its many rivers.

AREA 83,000 SQ MI [214,969 SQ KM] **POPULATION** 741,000
CAPITAL GEORGETOWN **GOVERNMENT** MULTIPARTY REPUBLIC
ETHNIC GROUPS EAST INDIAN 43%, BLACK 30%, AMERINDIAN 9%, OTHERS 18%
LANGUAGES ENGLISH (OFFICIAL), CREOLE, HINDI, URDU
RELIGIONS CHRISTIANITY 57%, HINDUISM 28%, ISLAM 7%, OTHERS 8%
CURRENCY GUYANESE DOLLAR = 100 CENTS

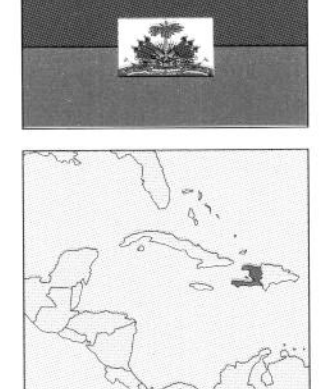

HAITI

GEOGRAPHY The Republic of Haiti occupies the western third of Hispaniola in the Caribbean. The land is mainly mountainous. The climate is hot and humid, though the northern highlands have more than twice as much rainfall as the southern coast.

POLITICS & ECONOMY Visited by Christopher Columbus in 1492, Haiti was later developed by the French. The country became independent in 1804. Haiti subsequently suffered from instability, violence, and dictatorial rule. Elections in 1990 returned Jean-Bertrand Aristide as president, but he was overthrown in 1991. In 1995, René Préval was elected president, but Aristide was again elected in 2000. In 2004, rebel activity forced Aristide to flee. Elections in 2016 were won by Jovenel Moise, but the political situation remained unstable with violent rioting in 2019.

In January 2010, an earthquake hit Port-au-Prince, killing up to 230,000 people and devastating the economy. As many as 80% of the people live below the poverty line.

AREA 10,714 SQ MI [27,750 SQ KM] **POPULATION** 10,788,000
CAPITAL PORT-AU-PRINCE **GOVERNMENT** MULTIPARTY REPUBLIC
ETHNIC GROUPS BLACK 95%, MIXED/WHITE 5%
LANGUAGES FRENCH AND CREOLE (BOTH OFFICIAL)
RELIGIONS ROMAN CATHOLIC 80%, PROTESTANT 16%, VOODOO
CURRENCY GOURDE = 100 CENTIMES

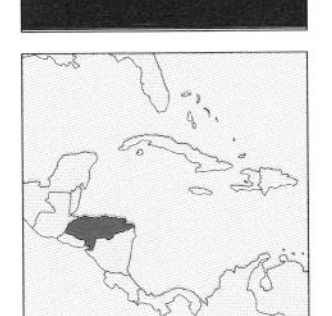

HONDURAS

GEOGRAPHY The Republic of Honduras is the second largest country in Central America. The northern coast, on the Caribbean Sea, extends for more than 373 mi [600 km], but the Pacific coast in the southeast is only about 50 mi [80 km] long. Honduras has a tropical climate, but the highlands are cooler. The rainiest months are between May and November. Hurricanes often hit the north coast. Hurricane Mitch in 1998 caused the worst destruction in modern times.

POLITICS & ECONOMY Once part of the Maya empire, the area was claimed for Spain by Christopher Columbus in 1502, and Spain ruled from 1625 until 1821. Honduras became part of the Central American Federation but withdrew in 1838.

In the 1890s, American companies developed plantations to grow bananas. But instability slowed economic progress. Since 1980, civilian governments friendly toward the United States have ruled Honduras, but in 2008 it joined the "Bolivarian Alternative to the Americas," a left-wing alliance then headed by Venezuelan President Chavez. A military coup in 2009 removed President Manuel Zelaya. In January 2014 Juan Orlando Hernández became president and was re-elected in a disputed election in 2017.

Honduras is one of Central America's least industrialized countries with around 50% of its economy linked to the USA. Its few resources include silver, lead, and zinc. Agriculture is the main activity. Bananas and coffee are exported and maize is the chief food crop. Products include processed food and textiles.

Violent crime (Honduras has the world's highest murder rate) makes the country one of the least secure in Central America.

AREA 43,277 SQ MI [112,088 SQ KM] **POPULATION** 9,183,000
CAPITAL Tegucigalpa **GOVERNMENT** Republic
ETHNIC GROUPS Mestizo 90%, Amerindian 7%, Black (including Black Carib) 2%, White 1%
LANGUAGES Spanish (official), Amerindian dialects
RELIGIONS Roman Catholic 97%
CURRENCY Honduran lempira = 100 centavos

HUNGARY

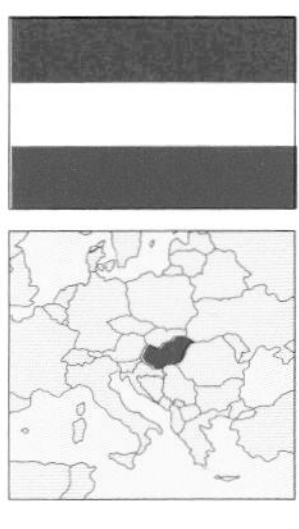

GEOGRAPHY Hungary is a landlocked country in central Europe. The land is mostly low-lying and drained by the Danube (Duna) and its tributary, the Tisza. Most of the land east of the Danube belongs to the region of the Great Plain (Nagy Alföld), which covers about half of Hungary.

Hungary lies far from the moderating influence of the sea, but it does contain Lake Balaton, the largest lake in central Europe. As a result of its position in the European landmass, summers are warmer and sunnier, and the winters colder than in Western Europe.

POLITICS & ECONOMY Following first an alliance, then occupation by Germany during World War II, Hungary was gradually taken over by a Communist government. From 1949, Hungary was an ally of the Soviet Union with Soviet troops crushing an anti-Communist revolt in 1956. But in the 1980s, reforms in the Soviet Union led to the growth of anti-Communist groups and, in 1989, Hungary adopted a new constitution making it a multiparty state and made moves toward a more free market economy. In 2004, Hungary became a member of both the North Atlantic Treaty Organization and the European Union. Right-wing prime minister Viktor Orban won a third term in power in April 2018 campaigning on an anti-immigrant, anti-Muslim ticket. Widespread protests followed.

Before World War II, Hungary's economy was based mainly on agriculture but the Communist era saw the introduction of many manufacturing industries. From the late 1980s, the increase in private ownership of businesses caused problems, including high rates of unemployment and inflation. High levels of government borrowing left the country vulnerable to the recession of 2008 when the country had to ask for outside financial help. Leading manufactures include aluminum, chemicals, electrical and electronic goods, and telecommunications equipment.

AREA 35,920 SQ MI [93,032 SQ KM] **POPULATION** 9,826,000
CAPITAL Budapest **GOVERNMENT** Multiparty republic
ETHNIC GROUPS Magyar 92%, Roma, German, Serb, Romanian, Slovak
LANGUAGES Hungarian (official)
RELIGIONS Roman Catholic 52%, Calvinist 16%, Lutheran 3%, others
CURRENCY Forint = 100 fillér

ICELAND

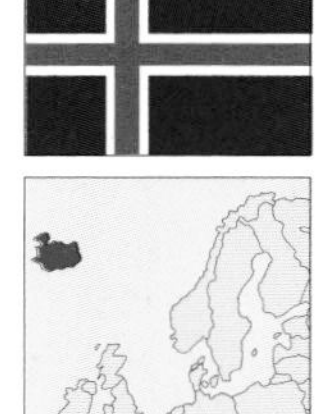
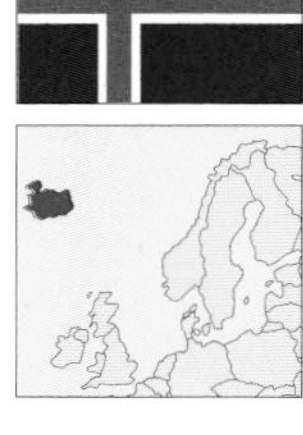

GEOGRAPHY The Republic of Iceland, in the North Atlantic Ocean, is closer to Greenland than Scotland. Iceland sits astride the Mid-Atlantic Ridge and it is slowly getting wider as the ocean is being stretched apart by continental drift.

Iceland has around 200 volcanoes, and eruptions are frequent. An eruption under the Vatnajökull ice cap in 1996 created a subglacial lake which subsequently burst, causing severe flooding. Geysers and hot springs are common, and in 2010 a volcanic eruption and its resulting ash cloud disrupted international air services. Ice caps and glaciers cover about an eighth of the land. The only habitable regions are the coastal lowlands. Despite its northerly position, Iceland's climate is moderated by the warm waters of the North Atlantic Drift. The port of Reykjavik is ice-free all year round.

POLITICS & ECONOMY Norwegian Vikings colonized Iceland in AD 874, and in 930 the settlers founded the world's oldest parliament, the Althing.

Iceland joined forces with Norway in 1262. But when Norway united with Denmark in 1380, Iceland came under Danish rule. Iceland became a self-governing kingdom, still with links to Denmark, in 1918, and a fully independent republic in 1944. Iceland has played a leading part in European affairs. Iceland has few resources besides its fishing grounds, and fishing and fish processing dominate overseas trade. To protect this vital part of its economy, it has been involved in several fishing and whaling disputes. Iceland applied to join the EU in 2009 but in 2013 suspended its application citing potential difficulties over fishing agreements as one reason. Elections in the fall of 2017, after the collapse of the previous government, led to Katrin Jakobsdottir of the Left-Green movement heading a broad coalition.

Barely 1% of the land is used to grow crops, but 23% of the country can be used for grazing sheep and cattle. Vegetables and fruit are grown in greenhouses, heated by water from the hot springs. Iceland's economy was badly hit by the global financial crisis of 2008–9, but it is steadily recovering.

AREA 39,768 SQ MI [103,000 SQ KM] **POPULATION** 344,000
CAPITAL Reykjavik **GOVERNMENT** Multiparty republic
ETHNIC GROUPS Icelandic 97%, Danish 1%
LANGUAGES Icelandic (official) **RELIGIONS** Evangelical Lutheran 87%, other Protestant 4%, Roman Catholic 2%, others
CURRENCY Icelandic króna = 100 aurar

INDIA

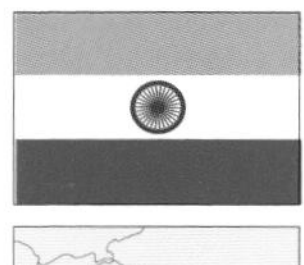

GEOGRAPHY The Republic of India is the world's seventh largest country. In population, it ranks second only to China. The north is mountainous, with mountains and foothills of the Himalayan range. Rivers, such as the Brahmaputra and Ganges (Ganga), rise in the Himalaya and flow across the fertile northern plains. Southern India consists of the Deccan, an extensive plateau. The Deccan is bordered by two mountain ranges, the Western Ghats and the Eastern Ghats.

India has three main seasons. The cool season runs from October to February. The hot season runs from March to June. The rainy monsoon season starts in the middle of June and continues into September. Delhi has moderate rainfall, with about 25 inches [640 mm] a year. The southwestern coast and the northeast have far more rain. Darjeeling in the northeast has an average annual rainfall of 120 inches [3,040 mm]. But parts of the Thar Desert in the northwest have only 2 inches [50 mm] of rain.

POLITICS & ECONOMY In southern India, most of the people are descendants of the dark-skinned Dravidians, who were among India's earliest people. Most northerners are descendants of lighter-skinned Aryans who arrived around 3,500 years ago.

India was the birthplace of several major religions, including Hinduism, Buddhism, and Sikhism. Islam was introduced from about AD 1000. The Muslim Mughal empire was founded in 1526. From the 17th century, Britain began to gain influence and, from 1858 to 1947, India was ruled as part of the British empire. An independence movement began after the Sepoy Rebellion (1857–9), and in 1885 the Indian National Congress was formed. In 1920, Mohandas K. Gandhi became its leader. When independence was finally achieved in 1947, British India was divided into modern India and Muslim Pakistan. Partition was marred by mass slaughter as Hindus and Sikhs fled from Pakistan, and Indian Muslims poured into Pakistan. In the ensuing disputes, some 1 million people were killed.

India has 15 major languages and hundreds of minor ones, together with many religions. The country remains the world's largest democracy. It has faced many problems, especially with Pakistan, over the disputed territory of Jammu and Kashmir. Two wars in 1965 and 1972 failed to alter greatly the 1948 cease-fire lines. In the late 1980s, Kashmiri nationalists in the Indian-controlled area waged a campaign, demanding either integration into Pakistan or independence. India sent in troops and accused Pakistan of intervention. In the 1990s, Pakistani-backed guerrillas fought to break India's hold on the Srinagar valley, Kashmir's most populous region. Tension mounted following the testing of nuclear devices by both countries in 1998. Relations improved, but an attack on buildings in Mumbai in 2008, allegedly by Pakistanis, caused further tension. In 2009–11, the dispute with Maoists in central and eastern India flared up again.

Classified by the World Bank as a "lower-middle-income" economy, India's economy grew rapidly after 2004 under a government led by the United Progressive Alliance. By 2010–11, India's economy was the world's second fastest growing after China, but growth then slowed. In May 2014, a landslide election was won by the Hindu nationalist Bharatiya Janata Party, led by Narendra Modi, who promised to revitalize the economy. Elections are due to be held in 2019.

Agriculture employs about 53% of the people, and services 31%. Crops include rice, wheat, millet, sorghum, peas, and beans. India has more cattle than any other country. Resources include coal, iron ore, and oil. Manufacturing has expanded greatly since 1947. Iron and steel, machinery, refined petroleum, textiles, and transport equipment are major products.

AREA 1,269,212 SQ MI [3,287,263 SQ KM] **POPULATION** 1,296,834,000
CAPITAL New Delhi **GOVERNMENT** Multiparty federal republic
ETHNIC GROUPS Indo-Aryan (Caucasoid) 72%, Dravidian 25%, others (mainly Mongoloid) 3%
LANGUAGES Hindi, English, Telugu, Bengali, Marathi, Tamil, Urdu, Gujarati, Malayalam, Kannada, Oriya, Punjabi, Assamese, Kashmiri, Sindhi, and Sanskrit are all official languages
RELIGIONS Hinduism 80%, Islam 13%, Christianity 2%, Sikhism 2%, Buddhism, and others **CURRENCY** Indian rupee = 100 paise

INDONESIA

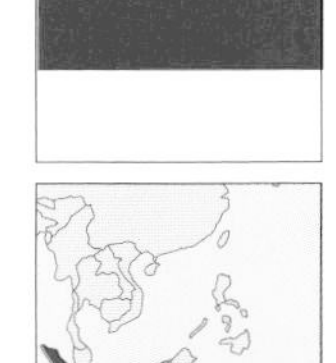

GEOGRAPHY The Republic of Indonesia is an island nation in Southeast Asia. In all, Indonesia contains about 13,600 islands, fewer than 6,000 of which are inhabited. Three-quarters of the country is made up of five main areas: the islands of Sumatra, Java and Sulawesi (Celebes), together with Kalimantan (southern Borneo), and western New Guinea. The islands are generally mountainous and volcanic. The larger islands have extensive coastal lowlands. The climate is hot and humid, with a high rainfall. Only Java and the Sunda Islands have relatively dry seasons.

POLITICS & ECONOMY Indonesia is the world's most populous Muslim nation, though Islam was introduced as recently as the 15th century. It became a Dutch colony in 1799. After a long struggle, the Netherlands recognized Indonesia's independence in 1949. The economy has expanded, but ethnic and religious conflict has slowed down economic progress.

In the early 21st century, Indonesia was facing many problems, arising from widespread corruption in the government and the army. Separatists were operating in Aceh province in northern Sumatra and in West Papua, Christian–Muslim clashes led to loss of life in the Moluccas, and East (formerly Portuguese) Timor became an independent country. In December 2004, a tsunami killed more than 100,000 people. Aceh province was granted autonomy in 2006, but separatists in the Papua region continue to agitate for independence. Indonesia has suffered terrorist attacks from Islamist groups in recent years.

Indonesia, a developing country, has a growing industrial sector hampered by inadequate infrastructure. It exports oil and natural gas, and mines tin and other minerals. Timber, textiles, rubber, coffee, and tea are also exported. Rice is the main food crop.

AREA 735,354 SQ MI [1,904,569 SQ KM] **POPULATION** 262,787,000
CAPITAL Jakarta **GOVERNMENT** Multiparty republic
ETHNIC GROUPS Javanese 41%, Sundanese 15%, Madurese 3%, Minangkabau 3%, Betawi 2%, Bugis 2%, Banten 2%, others 32%
LANGUAGES Bahasa Indonesian (official), many others
RELIGIONS Islam 86%, Protestant 6%, Roman Catholic 3%, Hinduism 2%, Buddhism 1%
CURRENCY Indonesian rupiah

IRAN

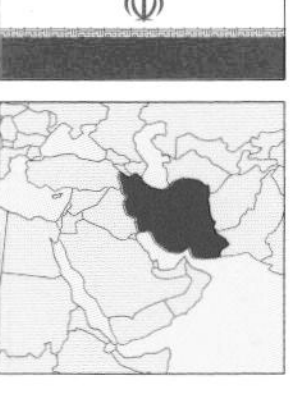

GEOGRAPHY The Republic of Iran contains a barren central plateau which covers about half of the country. It includes the Dasht-e Kavir (Great Salt Desert) and the Dasht-e Lut (Great Sand Desert). The Elburz Mountains north of the plateau contain Iran's highest peak, Damavand, while narrow lowlands lie between the mountains and the Caspian Sea. West of the plateau are the Zagros Mountains, beyond which the land descends to the plains bordering the Persian Gulf.

Much of Iran has a severe, dry climate, with hot summers and cold winters. In Tehran, rain falls on only about 30 days in the year and the annual temperature range is more than 45°F [25°C]. The climate in the lowlands, however, is generally milder.

POLITICS & ECONOMY Iran was called Persia until 1935. The empire of Ancient Persia flourished between 550 and 350 BC. Islam was introduced in AD 641.

Britain and Russia competed for influence in the area in the 19th century, and in the early 20th century the British began to develop the country's oil resources. In 1925, the Pahlavi family took power. Reza Khan became shah (king) and worked to modernize the country. The Pahlavi dynasty ended in 1979 when a religious leader, Ayatollah Ruhollah Khomeini, made Iran an Islamic republic. In 1980–8, Iran and Iraq fought a war over disputed borders. Khomeini died in 1989. In 2005, a hardliner, Mahmoud Ahmadinejad, was elected president. Iran's nuclear policies led to the application of international sanctions against it in 2009–12. The more moderate Hassan Rouhani was elected president in 2013 and re-elected in 2017. In 2015, after years of negotiations, a deal was agreed allowing for some economic sanctions to be lifted if Iran limited its nuclear activity. The following year UN inspectors reported satisfactory progress. In 2018, however, the US administration accused Iran of non-compliance and withdrew from the deal and renewed sanctions.

Iran's prosperity is based on its oil production and oil accounts for more than 80% of the country's exports. Agriculture is important and the main crops are wheat and barley. Livestock farming and fishing are other important activities, although Iran has to import much of the food it needs.

AREA 636,368 sq mi [1,648,195 sq km] **POPULATION** 83,025,000
CAPITAL Tehran **GOVERNMENT** Islamic republic
ETHNIC GROUPS Persian 53%, Azeri 16%, Kurd 10%, Lur 6%, Arab 2%, Baloch 2%, Turkmen 2% **LANGUAGES** Persian, Turkic, Kurdish
RELIGIONS Islam 98% (Shi'ite Muslim 89%)
CURRENCY Iranian rial = 100 dinars

IRAQ

GEOGRAPHY The Republic of Iraq lies at the head of the Persian Gulf. Rolling deserts cover western and southwestern Iraq, with part of the Zagros Mountains in the northeast. The northern plains, across which flow the rivers Euphrates (Nahr al Furat) and Tigris (Nahr Dijlah), are dry. But the southern plains, including Mesopotamia and the delta of the Shatt al Arab, contain irrigated farmland, together with marshland.

The climate of Iraq ranges from temperate in the north to subtropical in the south. Baghdad, in central Iraq, has cool winters, with occasional frosts, and hot summers. The rainfall is generally low.

POLITICS & ECONOMY Mesopotamia was the home of several great civilizations, including Sumer, Babylon, and Assyria. It later became part of the Persian empire. Islam was introduced in AD 637 and Baghdad became the brilliant capital of the powerful Arab empire. But Mesopotamia declined after the Mongols invaded it in 1258. From 1534, Mesopotamia became part of the Turkish Ottoman empire. Britain invaded the area in 1916 and, in 1921, renamed the country Iraq and set up an Arab monarchy. Iraq finally became independent in 1932.

By the 1950s, oil dominated Iraq's economy. In 1952, Iraq agreed to take 50% of the profits of the foreign oil companies. This revenue enabled the government to pay for welfare services and development projects. Since 1958, when army officers killed the king and made Iraq a republic, Iraq has undergone turbulent times. In the 1960s, the Kurds, who live in northern Iraq and also in Iran, Turkey, Syria, and Armenia, pressed for self-rule. The government rejected their demands and war broke out. A peace treaty was signed in 1975, but conflict has continued.

In 1979, Saddam Hussein became Iraq's president. Under his leadership, Iraq invaded Iran in 1980, starting an eight-year war. Iraqi Kurds supported Iran and the Iraqi government attacked Kurdish villages with poison gas. In 1990, Iraqi troops occupied Kuwait, but an international force drove them out in 1991. From 1991, Iraqi troops attacked Shi'ite Marsh Arabs and Kurds. In 1998, Iraq's failure to permit UN inspectors, charged with disposing of Iraq's deadliest weapons, access to suspect sites led to the Western bombardment of Iraqi military sites. Another major offensive occurred in 2001. In March–April 2003, a coalition force headed by the United States invaded Iraq, overthrowing Saddam Hussein's regime. Despite ongoing violence, elections were held in 2005, and again in 2010. Following a period of deadlock, Nouri al-Maliki continued as prime minister. He was replaced in 2014 by Haider al-Abadi, and in 2018 by Adil Abd Al-Mahdi. From 2013 Islamic State militants increased their attacks and seized control of large parts of the country, with the loss of thousands of lives. By late 2017 they had been restricted to a few strongholds. The government continues to block any Kurdish ambitions towards independence.

Civil war, war damage, mismanagement, and UN sanctions have damaged the economy. Oil remains the main resource. Farmland covers about a fifth of the land. Products include barley, cotton, dates, fruit, livestock, wheat, and wool. But Iraq still has to import food. Manufactures include refined oil, petrochemicals, and consumer goods.

AREA 169,235 sq mi [438,317 sq km] **POPULATION** 40,194,000
CAPITAL Baghdad **GOVERNMENT** Parliamentary Democracy
ETHNIC GROUPS Arab 77%, Kurdish 19%, Assyrian and others
LANGUAGES Arabic (official), Kurdish (official in Kurdish areas), Assyrian, Armenian **RELIGIONS** Islam 97% (Shi'ite Muslim 63%)
CURRENCY Iraqi dinar = 1,000 fils

IRELAND

GEOGRAPHY Ireland occupies five-sixths of the island which is also called Ireland. The country consists of a large lowland region surrounded by a broken rim of low mountains. The uplands include the Mountains of Kerry where Carrauntoohill, Ireland's highest peak at 3,415 ft [1,041 m], is situated. The River Shannon is the longest in Ireland, flowing through three large lakes, loughs Allen, Ree, and Derg.

Ireland has a mild, rainy climate influenced by the warm North Atlantic Drift, whose effects are greatest in the west. However, Dublin in the east is cooler than places on the west coast.

POLITICS & ECONOMY In 1801, the Act of Union created the United Kingdom of Great Britain and Ireland. But Irish discontent intensified in the 1840s when a potato blight caused a famine in which a million people died and nearly a million emigrated. Britain was blamed for not having done enough to help. In 1916, an uprising in Dublin was crushed, but between 1919 and 1922 civil war broke out. In 1922, the Irish Free State was created as a Dominion in the British Commonwealth, but Northern Ireland remained part of the UK.

Ireland became a republic in 1949. In 1973, it became a member of the European Community (now the European Union) and, until the global financial crisis of 2008–9, it prospered. In 1998, Ireland took part in the negotiations to produce a constitutional settlement in Northern Ireland. Ireland agreed to give up its claim on Northern Ireland and, in 2007, a power-sharing government was set up in the north. Following elections in 2016, Enda Kenny's Fine Gael formed a minority government. He was succeeded in 2017 by Leo Varadkar.

Major farm products include barley, cattle and dairy products, pigs, potatoes, poultry, sheep, sugar beet, and wheat. Fishing is important. Manufacturing is the main activity. In 2010, the economy shrank, but by 2013 austerity measures had borne fruit.

AREA 27,132 sq mi [70,273 sq km] **POPULATION** 5,068,000
CAPITAL Dublin **GOVERNMENT** Multiparty republic
ETHNIC GROUPS Irish 94% **LANGUAGES** Irish (Gaelic) and English (both official) **RELIGIONS** Roman Catholic 92%, Protestant 3%
CURRENCY Euro = 100 cents

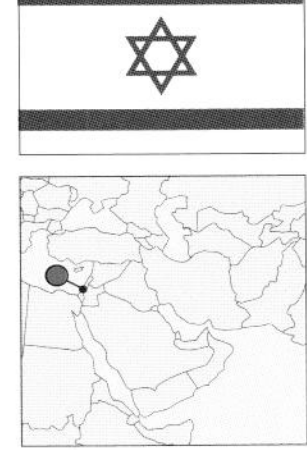

ISRAEL

GEOGRAPHY The State of Israel is a small country in the eastern Mediterranean. It includes a fertile coastal plain, where Israel's main industrial cities, Haifa (Hefa) and Tel Aviv-Jaffa, are situated. Inland lie the Judaeo-Galilean highlands, which run from northern Israel to the northern tip of the Negev Desert. To the east lies part of the Great Rift Valley, which contains the River Jordan, the Sea of Galilee, and the Dead Sea. Summers are hot and dry. Winters on the coast are mild and moist, but rainfall decreases from west to east and from north to south.

POLITICS & ECONOMY Israel is part of a region called Palestine. Some Jews have always lived in the area, though most modern Israelis are descendants of immigrants who began to settle there from the 1880s. Britain ruled Palestine from 1917. Large numbers of Jews escaping Nazi persecution arrived in the 1930s, provoking an Arab uprising against British rule. In 1947, the UN agreed to partition Palestine into an Arab and a Jewish state with the State of Israel coming into being in May 1948. Other Arab–Israeli wars in 1956, 1967, and 1973 led to land gains for Israel.

In 1978, Israel signed a treaty with Egypt which led to the return of the occupied Sinai peninsula to Egypt in 1979. But conflict continued between Israel and the PLO (Palestine Liberation Organization). In 1993, the PLO and Israel agreed to establish Palestinian self-rule in two areas: the occupied Gaza Strip, and in the town of Jericho in the occupied West Bank. The agreement was extended in 1995 to include more than 30% of the West Bank. Israel's prime minister, Yitzhak Rabin, was assassinated in 1995. In 1996, Benjamin Netanyahu was elected prime minister. The peace process stalled until Ehud Barak defeated Netanyahu in 1999. In 2001, Ariel Sharon became prime minister and, in 2005, he handed over the Gaza Strip to the Palestinian Authority. Israeli forces clashed with Palestinians in Gaza and southern Lebanon in 2005–9. Talks in 2010 and 2013 between Israel and the Palestinian Authority collapsed. Further violence along the Gaza border in 2018 led to attempts by the UN and Egypt to broker a long-term ceasefire. Benjamin Netanyahu was re-elected for a record-breaking fifth time in 2019.

Israel has developed a very diverse economy. Manufactures include chemicals, electronic equipment, plastics, processed food, scientific instruments, and textiles. Fruit and vegetables are major exports. Lacking natural resources, Israel has to import raw materials, crude oil, and grain. Offshore gas fields are being exploited.

AREA 7,954 sq mi [20,600 sq km] **POPULATION** 8,425,000
CAPITAL Jerusalem **GOVERNMENT** Multiparty republic
ETHNIC GROUPS Jewish 76%, Arab and others 24%
LANGUAGES Hebrew and Arabic (both official)
RELIGIONS Judaism 76%, Islam (mostly Sunni) 17%, Christianity 2%, Druze and others 5% **CURRENCY** New Israeli shekel = 100 agorot

ITALY

GEOGRAPHY The Republic of Italy is famous for its history and traditions, its art and culture, and its beautiful scenery. Northern Italy is bordered in the north by the high Alps, with their many climbing and skiing resorts. The Alps overlook the northern plains – Italy's most fertile and densely populated region – drained by the River Po. The rugged Apennines form the backbone of southern Italy. Bordering the range are scenic hilly areas and coastal plains. Southern Italy contains a string of volcanoes, stretching from Vesuvius, through the Lipari Islands, to Etna on Sicily, the largest Mediterranean island. Northern Italy has cold, often snowy, winters, but the summer months are warm and sunny, with brief summer thunderstorms. Rainfall is abundant. The south has mild, moist winters and warm, dry summers.

POLITICS & ECONOMY Magnificent ruins throughout Italy testify to the glories of the ancient Roman empire, which was founded, according to legend, in 753 BC. Reaching its peak in the AD 100s, it finally collapsed in the 400s, although the Eastern Roman empire, also called the Byzantine empire, survived for another 1,000 years.

In the Middle Ages, Italy was split into many tiny states. These states made a great contribution to the Renaissance, the revival of art and learning, in the 14th to 16th centuries. Beautiful cities, such as Florence (Firenze) and Venice (Venézia), testify to the artistic achievements of this period.

Italy finally became a united kingdom in 1861, although the Papal Territories (a large area ruled by the Roman Catholic Church) were not added until 1870. The Pope and his successors disputed this takeover and it was not finally resolved until 1929, when the Vatican City was set up in Rome as a fully independent state.

Italy fought in World War I (1914–18) alongside the Allies – Britain, France, and Russia. In 1922, the dictator Benito Mussolini, leader of the Fascist Party, took power. Under Mussolini, Italy conquered Ethiopia. During World War II (1939–45), Italy at first fought on Germany's side against the Allies until late in 1943 it declared war on Germany. Italy became a republic in 1946. Playing an important part in European affairs, it was a founder member of the North Atlantic Treaty Organization (NATO) in 1949 and also, in 1958, of what has since become the European Union.

After the setting up of the European Union, Italy's economy developed quickly, despite problems such as greater prosperity in the north compared to the south. The greater economic development in the north forced many people to leave the poor south to find jobs in the north or abroad. Social problems, corruption at high levels of society, and a succession of weak coalition governments all contributed to instability. Between 1998 and 2011, power shifted between center-left and center-right coalitions. In 2016, constitutional changes aimed at creating more stable governments were rejected in a referendum, leading to prime minister Matteo Renzi's resignation. A populist coalition government took office in 2018.

Only 50 years ago, Italy was a mainly agricultural society, but it is now a leading industrial power. It lacks mineral resources, and imports most of the raw materials used in industry. Manufactures include textiles and clothing, processed food, machinery, cars, and chemicals. The chief industrial region is in the northwest.

Farmland covers around 42% of the land, pasture 17%, and forest and woodland 22%. Major crops include citrus fruits, grapes which are used to make wine, olive oil, sugar beet, and vegetables. Livestock farming is important, though meat is imported.

AREA 116,339 sq mi [301,318 sq km] **POPULATION** 62,247,000
CAPITAL Rome **GOVERNMENT** Multiparty republic
ETHNIC GROUPS Italian 94%, German, French, Albanian, Slovene, Greek
LANGUAGES Italian (official), German, French, Slovene
RELIGIONS Predominantly Roman Catholic
CURRENCY Euro = 100 cents

JAMAICA

GEOGRAPHY Jamaica is the third largest of the Caribbean islands. Half the country lies above 1,000 ft [300 m] and moist southeast trade winds bring rain to the central mountain range.

The "cockpit country" in the northwest of the island is an inaccessible limestone area of steep broken ridges and isolated basins.

POLITICS & ECONOMY Jamaica gained independence from Britain in 1962. Since then, power has alternated between the People's National Party and the Jamaica Labor Party and, despite some violence, there has been relative political stability. There is some support for becoming a republic. Problems arise from the marked polarization of society between rich and poor, and the murder rate is high. Tourism and sugarcane farming are important, with alumina and bauxite being exported.

AREA 4,244 sq mi [10,991 sq km] **POPULATION** 2,812,000
CAPITAL Kingston **GOVERNMENT** Constitutional monarchy
ETHNIC GROUPS Black 91%, Mixed 7%, East Indian 1%
LANGUAGES English (official), patois English
RELIGIONS Protestant 65%, Roman Catholic 3%
CURRENCY Jamaican dollar = 100 cents

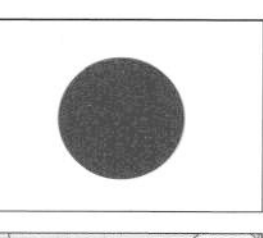

JAPAN

GEOGRAPHY Japan's four largest islands – Honshu, Hokkaido, Kyushu, and Shikoku – make up 98% of the country. But Japan contains thousands of small islands. The four largest islands are mainly mountainous, while many of the small islands are the tips of volcanoes. Japan has more than 150 volcanoes, about 60 of which are active. Volcanic eruptions, earthquakes and tsunamis (powerful sea waves) are common. In March 2011, a massive earthquake, the most powerful recorded in Japan (magnitude 9.0), struck Honshu in the northeast. The tremors and a tsunami caused great loss of life and severe damage to nuclear reactors at Fukushima, shutting down all nuclear power generation at that time.

The climate of Japan varies greatly from north to south. Hokkaido in the north has cold, snowy winters. At Sapporo, temperatures below 4°F [–20°C] have been recorded between December and March. But summers are warm, with temperatures sometimes exceeding 86°F [30°C]. Rain falls throughout the year, though Hokkaido is one of the driest parts of Japan. Tokyo has higher rainfall and temperatures, while the southern islands of Shikoku and Kyushu have warm temperate climates. Summers are long and hot; winters are cold.

POLITICS & ECONOMY In the late 19th century, Japan began a program of modernization. Under its new imperial leaders, it began to look for lands to conquer. In 1894–5, it fought a war with China and, in 1904–5, it defeated Russia. Soon its overseas empire included Korea and Taiwan. In 1930, Japan invaded Manchuria (northeast China), and in 1937 it began a war against China. In 1941, Japan launched an attack on the US base at Pearl Harbor in Hawai'i. This drew both Japan and the United States into World War II.

Japan surrendered in 1945 when the Americans dropped atomic bombs on two cities, Hiroshima and Nagasaki. The United States occupied Japan until 1952, during which time Japan adopted a democratic constitution. The emperor, who had previously been regarded as a god, became a constitutional monarch. In 2017, parliament passed a bill allowing the emperor to abdicate. Akihito stood down in favour of his son, Naruhito, in 2019.

From the 1960s, Japan experienced many changes as the country rapidly built up new industries, becoming the world's second richest economic power after the United States. But economic success has brought problems. For example, the rapid growth of cities has led to housing shortages and pollution. Other problems arise from an aging population.

The leading activity is manufacturing. Lacking natural resources, Japan imports most of the materials and fuels it needs, and its success has been based on its use of the latest technology, its skilled work force, its vigorous export policies, and the relatively low expenditure on defense. Exports include machinery, electrical and electronic equipment, iron and steel, chemicals, textiles, and ships. Japan's economy suffered a stagnation in the 1990s. Signs of recovery from 2005 were shattered by the global financial crisis in 2008–9, when exports greatly declined. The economy went back into recession following the 2011 earthquake and tsunami, and the consequent extensive reconstruction work that was required. However, since then the economy has largely recovered with Prime Minister Shinzo Abe pursuing proactive policies to stimulate the economy. The Japanese economy is the world's third largest.

Japan is one of the world's top fishing nations and fish is an important source of protein for the Japanese. Because the land is so rugged, only 15% of the country can be farmed. Yet Japan produces about 70% of the food it needs. Rice is the chief crop, taking up about half of the total farmland.

AREA 145,880 sq mi [377,829 sq km] **POPULATION** 126,168,000
CAPITAL Tokyo **GOVERNMENT** Constitutional monarchy
ETHNIC GROUPS Japanese 99%, Chinese, Korean, Brazilian, and others
LANGUAGES Japanese (official)
RELIGIONS Shintoism and Buddhism 84% (most Japanese consider themselves to be both Shinto and Buddhist), others
CURRENCY Yen = 100 sen

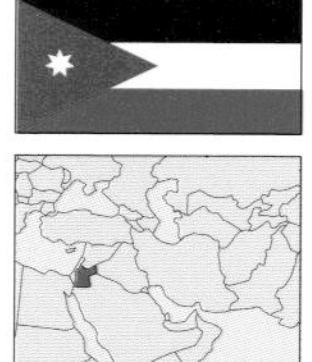

JORDAN

GEOGRAPHY The Hashemite Kingdom of Jordan is an Arab country in southwestern Asia. The Great Rift Valley in the west contains the River Jordan and the Dead Sea, which Jordan shares with Israel. East of the Rift Valley is the Transjordan plateau, where most Jordanians live. To the east and south lie vast areas of desert.

Amman has a much lower rainfall and longer dry season than the Mediterranean lands to the west. The Transjordan plateau, on which Amman stands, is a transition zone between the Mediterranean climate zone and the desert climate to the east.

POLITICS & ECONOMY In 1921, Britain created the territory of Transjordan east of the River Jordan. In 1923, Transjordan became self-governing, but Britain retained control of its defenses, finances, and foreign affairs. This territory became fully independent as Jordan in 1946. Jordan has suffered from instability arising from the Arab–Israeli conflict since the creation of the State of Israel in 1948. After the first Arab–Israeli War in 1948–9, Jordan acquired East Jerusalem and the fertile area of the West Bank. In 1967, Israel occupied this area. In Jordan, the presence of Palestinian refugees led to civil war in 1970–1.

In 1974, Arab leaders declared that the PLO (Palestine Liberation Organization) was the sole representative of the Palestinian people. In 1988, King Hussein of Jordan renounced Jordan's claims to the West Bank and passed responsibility for it to the PLO. Opposition parties were legalized in 1991 and elections were held in 1993. In October 1994, Jordan and Israel signed a peace treaty, ending a state of war that had lasted more than 40 years. Jordan's King Hussein commanded respect for his role in Middle Eastern affairs until his death in 1999. He was succeeded by his eldest son, who became Abdullah II. In 2005, suicide bombings on hotels in Amman damaged Jordan's reputation as a stable country. The king has the power to dissolve parliament and appoint governments. Prime Minister Hani Al-Mulki resigned in 2018 after street protests over his economic reforms, and was replaced by Omar al-Razzaz.

Jordan has an "upper-middle-income" economy. It lacks natural resources, apart from phosphates and potash, and depends on substantial aid. The country is currently having to absorb high numbers of refugees from neighboring Syria.

AREA 34,495 sq mi [89,342 sq km] **POPULATION** 10,458,000
CAPITAL Amman **GOVERNMENT** Constitutional monarchy
ETHNIC GROUPS Arab 98%, of which Palestinians make up roughly half
LANGUAGES Arabic (official)
RELIGIONS Islam (mostly Sunni) 92%, Christianity (mostly Greek Orthodox) 6%
CURRENCY Jordanian dinar = 100 piastre

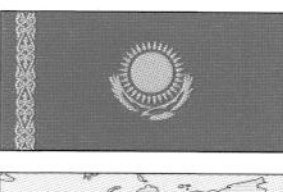

KAZAKHSTAN

GEOGRAPHY Kazakhstan is a large country in west-central Asia. In the west, the Caspian Sea lowlands include the Karagiye depression, which reaches 433 ft [132 m] below sea level. The lowlands extend eastward through the Aral Sea area. The north contains high plains, but the highest land is along the eastern and southern borders. These areas include parts of the Altai and Tian Shan mountain ranges. Eastern Kazakhstan contains several freshwater lakes, the largest of which is Lake Balkhash. The water in the rivers has been used for irrigation, causing ecological problems. For example, the Aral Sea, deprived of water, shrank from 25,830 sq mi [66,900 sq km] in 1960 to 6,630 sq mi [17,160 sq km] in 2004. Large areas are now barren desert.

Kazakhstan has an extreme climate. Winters are cold and snowy. The rainfall is generally low.

POLITICS & ECONOMY After the Russian Revolution of 1917, many Kazakhs wanted to make their country independent. But the Communists prevailed and in 1936 Kazakhstan became a republic of the Soviet Union, called the Kazakh Soviet Socialist Republic. During World War II and also after the war, the Soviet government moved many people from the west into Kazakhstan. From the 1950s, people were encouraged to work on a "Virgin Lands" project, which involved bringing large areas of grassland under cultivation.

Reforms in the Soviet Union in the 1980s led to its breakup in December 1991. Kazakhstan maintained contacts with Russia through the Commonwealth of Independent States (CIS). In 1997, the government moved its capital from Almaty to Aqmola (later renamed Astana), a town in the north. By the mid-2000s, the economy was in better shape than the other ex-Soviet republics in Central Asia, although President Nazarbayev, first elected in 1991, was criticized for his authoritarian rule. In 2007, constitutional changes enabled Nazarbayev to stand for the presidency as many times as he wished, and he was re-elected, virtually unopposed, in 2011 and 2015. Constitutional reforms approved by parliament in 2017 handed some of his powers to the cabinet.

The World Bank classifies Kazakhstan as an "upper-middle-income" developing country. Livestock farming, especially sheep and cattle, is an important activity, and major crops include barley, cotton, rice, and wheat. The country is rich in mineral resources, including coal and oil reserves, together with uranium, bauxite, copper, lead, tungsten, and zinc. Manufactures include chemicals, food products, machinery, and textiles. Oil is exported via a pipeline through Russia. However, to reduce the country's dependence on Russia, another pipeline to China was inaugurated in 2009.

AREA 1,052,084 sq mi [2,724,900 sq km] **POPULATION** 18,745,000
CAPITAL Astana **GOVERNMENT** Multiparty republic
ETHNIC GROUPS Kazakh 63%, Russian 24%, Uzbek 3%, Ukrainian 2%, others 8%
LANGUAGES Kazakh (official); Russian, the former official language, is widely spoken
RELIGIONS Islam 70%, Russian Orthodox 24%
CURRENCY Tenge = 100 tiyn

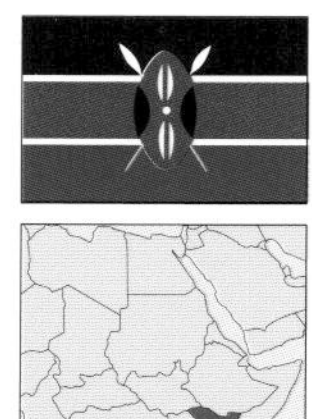

KENYA

GEOGRAPHY The Republic of Kenya is a country in East Africa which straddles the equator. Behind the narrow coastal plain on the Indian Ocean, the land rises to high plains and highlands, broken by volcanic mountains, including Mount Kenya, the country's highest peak at 17,057 ft [5,199 m]. Crossing the country is an arm of the Great Rift Valley, on the floor of which are several lakes, including Baringo, Magadi, Naivasha, Nakuru, and, on the northern frontier, Lake Turkana (formerly Lake Rudolf). Nairobi, in the southwestern highlands, has summer temperatures which are about 10°F [18°C] lower than humid Mombasa. Only about 15% of Kenya has a reliable annual rainfall of 31 inches [800 mm].

POLITICS & ECONOMY The Kenyan coast has been a trading center for more than 2,000 years. Britain took over the coast in 1895 and soon extended its influence inland. In the 1950s, a secret movement, called Mau Mau, launched an armed struggle against British rule. Although Mau Mau was eventually defeated, Kenya became independent in 1963.

Kenya was a one-party state for much of the time after 1963, with democracy restored in 1992. Elections in 2007 led to inter-ethnic violence when the opposition refused to accept the declared results. A deal was agreed by President Mwai Kibaki and Raila Odinga, who became prime minister. In 2011, Somali attacks and kidnappings in northern Kenya provoked Kenya to send forces into Somalia to combat the Islamist al-Shabab group. Elections in August 2017 were declared void because of irregularities. The opposition boycotted the re-run and Uhuru Kenyatta won.

Many Kenyans are subsistence farmers. The chief food crop is maize. The main cash crops and the leading exports are coffee and tea. Manufactures include chemicals, leather and footwear, petroleum products, and textiles. Oil was discovered in 2012.

AREA 224,080 SQ MI [580,367 SQ KM] POPULATION 48,398,000
CAPITAL Nairobi GOVERNMENT Multiparty republic
ETHNIC GROUPS Kikuyu 22%, Luhya 14%, Luo 13%, Kalenjin 12%, Kamba 11%, others
LANGUAGES Kiswahili and English (both official)
RELIGIONS Protestant 47%, Roman Catholic 23%, Islam 11%, others 19%
CURRENCY Kenyan shilling = 100 cents

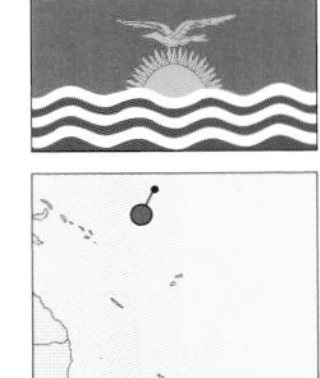

KIRIBATI

The Republic of Kiribati comprises three groups of coral atolls scattered over about 2 million sq mi [5 million sq km]. Kiribati straddles the equator and temperatures are high and the rainfall is abundant.

Formerly part of the British Gilbert and Ellice Islands, Kiribati became independent in 1979. The main export is copra and the country depends heavily on foreign aid.

AREA 280 SQ MI [726 SQ KM] POPULATION 109,000 CAPITAL Tarawa

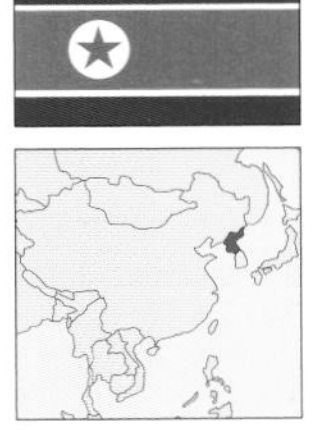

KOREA, NORTH

GEOGRAPHY The Democratic People's Republic of Korea occupies the northern part of the Korean peninsula. Mountains form the heart of the country, with the highest peak, Paektu-san, reaching 9,003 ft [2,744 m]. North Korea has a severe climate, with cold, snowy winters. In summer, winds from the oceans bring rain.

POLITICS & ECONOMY North Korea was created in 1945, when the peninsula, which had been a Japanese colony since 1910, was divided into two parts. Soviet forces occupied the north, with US forces in the south. Soviet occupation led to a Communist government being established in 1948 under the leadership of Kim Il Sung, who effectively became a dictator.

The Korean War began in June 1950 when North Korean troops invaded the South. North Korea, aided by China and the Soviet Union, fought with South Korea, which was supported by troops from the United States and other UN members. The war ended in July 1953. An armistice was signed but no permanent peace treaty was agreed. The end of the Cold War in the late 1990s eased the situation. North and South Korea joined the United Nations in 1991, though North Korea remained isolated from most other countries. In 1993, North Korea withdrew from the Nuclear Non-Proliferation Treaty, arousing suspicions that it was developing nuclear weapons. Kim Il Sung died in 1994 and was succeeded by his son, Kim Jong Il. From 2003, the United States accused North Korea of developing nuclear weapons, and it has since then carried out several tests, resulting in increased international isolation and tension. Kim Jong Il died in 2011, and his son, Kim Jong-Un, succeeded him. He expanded the nuclear program, but also appeared willing to negotiate with the US, meeting President Trump in 2018 and 2019, although with no concrete results. In 2018 he became the first North Korean leader to enter South Korea.

North Korea's resources include coal, copper, iron ore, lead, tin, tungsten, and zinc. Manufactures include chemicals, iron and steel, machinery, processed food, and textiles. Rice is the chief food crop, but food shortages have occurred in recent years.

AREA 46,540 SQ MI [120,538 SQ KM] POPULATION 25,381,000
CAPITAL Pyŏngyang GOVERNMENT Single-party people's republic
ETHNIC GROUPS Korean 99%
LANGUAGES Korean (official)
RELIGIONS Buddhism and Confucianism
CURRENCY North Korean won = 100 chon

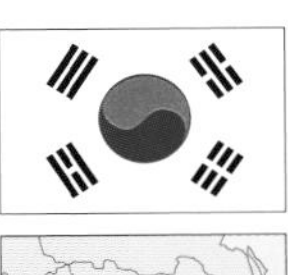

KOREA, SOUTH

GEOGRAPHY The Republic of Korea, as South Korea is officially known, occupies the southern part of the Korean peninsula. Mountains cover much of the country.

The southern and western coasts are major farming regions. Many islands are found along the west and south coasts. The largest of these is Jeju-do, which contains South Korea's highest peak, Hallasan, which rises to 6,398 ft [1,950 m].

Like North Korea, South Korea is chilled in winter by cold, dry winds from central Asia. Summers are hot and wet, especially in July and August.

POLITICS & ECONOMY After Japan's defeat in World War II (1939–45), North Korea was occupied by troops from the Soviet Union, while South Korea was occupied by United States forces. A National Assembly elected in 1948 in South Korea created the Republic of Korea, while North Korea became a Communist state. North Korea invaded the South in June 1950, sparking off the Korean War (1950–3). Despite the destruction caused by the war, South Korea under a series of rather authoritarian governments began to industrialize the economy between the 1960s and 1980s. In 1987, a new constitution permitted the election of presidents every five years. Tensions between South and North Korea continue, but at an historic meeting in 2018, South Korea's President Moon and North Korea's Kim Jon-Un agreed to work towards peace and reducing nuclear arms on the Korean peninsula.

Until the onset of the global financial crisis in 2008, South Korea had one of the world's fastest growing economies. Heavy industries produce chemicals, fertilizers, iron and steel, and ships, together with a wide range of consumer products, such as mobile phones, computers, cars, and television sets. The economy relies heavily on exports. Farming and fishing remain important. Rice is the chief crop, together with fruits, grains, and vegetables.

AREA 38,327 SQ MI [99,268 SQ KM] POPULATION 51,418,000
CAPITAL Seoul GOVERNMENT Multiparty republic
ETHNIC GROUPS Korean 99%
LANGUAGES Korean (official) RELIGIONS No affiliation 43%, Christianity 32%, Buddhism 24%, others 1%
CURRENCY South Korean won = 100 jeon

KOSOVO

GEOGRAPHY The Republic of Kosovo in the central Balkans, formerly part of Serbia, declared its independence in February 2008. Its independence was recognized by the United States and major EU countries, but Serbia, and its ally Russia, refused recognition. It is a landlocked country, consisting of a river basin bounded by uplands in the north and southwest. It has cold, snowy winters and hot, dry summers.

POLITICS & ECONOMY Most people are Albanian-speakers who are Muslims, but there is an important Christian Serb minority. In the early 13th century, Kosovo was part of the Serbian empire but, after 1389, it came under Muslim Turkish Ottoman rule.

Serbia regained control of Kosovo in 1912 and, in 1918, it became part of the Kingdom of Serbia. In 1946, it became part of the Socialist Federal Republic of Yugoslavia, becoming an autonomous province within the Republic of Serbia. In 1989, Serbia curtailed Kosovo's autonomy, while Albanian speakers declared their province independent. In 1995, the Albanian speakers set up the Kosovo Liberation Army, which launched an uprising against Serbia. In 1998, Serbia began repressive measures against Kosovo, resulting in massacres and ethnic cleansing of Albanian-speaking Kosovars. In 1999, NATO forces bombed Serbia and placed Kosovo under a temporary administration. Finally, the Kosovo Assembly declared its independence on February 17, 2008. Whilst Serbia still does not recognize Kosovo as an independent state, the two countries are engaged in diplomatic talks.

Kosovo is a poor country, with one of the lowest per capita incomes in Europe. Many people are subsistence farmers and its industries have declined because of lack of investment. The economy is highly dependent on international aid.

AREA 4,203 SQ MI [10,887 SQ KM] POPULATION 1,908,000
CAPITAL Pristina GOVERNMENT Republic
ETHNIC GROUPS Albanian 92%, others 8%
LANGUAGES Albanian and Serbian (both official), Turkish
RELIGIONS Islam, Serbian Orthodox, Roman Catholic
CURRENCY Euro = 100 cents

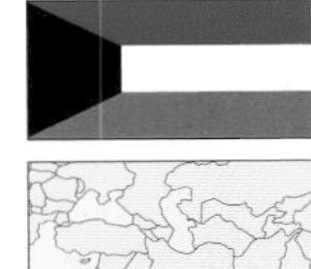

KUWAIT

GEOGRAPHY The State of Kuwait, at the northern end of the Persian Gulf, is an emirate. The land is low-lying and largely desert in nature. Summer temperatures are high but winters are cooler. Rainfall is low.

POLITICS & ECONOMY British influence began in 1775 and, in 1899, the local ruler concluded a treaty with Britain, agreeing to support British interests in return for protection. Kuwait became independent in 1961. Prosperity came from oil exports. Iraq invaded Kuwait in 1990, but it was liberated in 1991 by a coalition force. In 2004, the government announced legislation for women to vote and stand for parliament. In recent years there has been increasing unrest caused by militant Islamists, as well as tension between parliament and the ruling Al-Sabah family.

AREA 6,880 SQ MI [17,818 SQ KM]
POPULATION 2,916,000 CAPITAL Kuwait City

KYRGYZSTAN

GEOGRAPHY The Republic of Kyrgyzstan is a landlocked country between China, Tajikistan, Uzbekistan, and Kazakhstan. The country is mountainous, with spectacular scenery. The highest mountain, Pik Pobedy in the Tian Shan range, reaches 24,406 ft [7,439 m] in the east. The lowlands have warm summers and cold winters. But January temperatures in the mountains plummet to –18°F [–28°C]. Kyrgyzstan has a low annual rainfall.

POLITICS & ECONOMY In 1876, Kyrgyzstan became a province of Russia. In 1916, Russia crushed a rebellion among the Kyrgyz, and many subsequently fled to China. In 1922, the area became an autonomous oblast (self-governing region) of the newly formed Soviet Union, but in 1936 it became one of the Soviet Socialist Republics. Under Communist rule, local customs and religious worship were suppressed, but education and health services were greatly improved.

In 1991, Kyrgyzstan became an independent country following the breakup of the Soviet Union. The Communist Party was dissolved, but the country maintained links with Russia. The first two elections as an independent state produced unpopular presidents who were swept from power and had to flee the country. Sooronbay Jeenbekov won more than 54% of votes in the presidential elections of October 2017.

As one of the poorest countries of the former Soviet Union, Kyrgyzstan sought to reform its Soviet-style economy in the 1990s. Classified as a "lower-middle income" economy by the World Bank, agriculture is the main activity. Major products include cotton, eggs, fruits, grain, tobacco, vegetables, and wool, but food is imported. Attracting foreign investment and legitimizing business practices will be vital to economic growth.

AREA 77,181 SQ MI [199,900 SQ KM] POPULATION 5,849,000
CAPITAL Bishkek GOVERNMENT Multiparty republic
ETHNIC GROUPS Kyrgyz 65%, Uzbek 14%, Russian 13%
LANGUAGES Kyrgyz and Russian (both official)
RELIGIONS Islam 75%, Russian Orthodox 20%
CURRENCY Kyrgyzstani som = 100 tyiyn

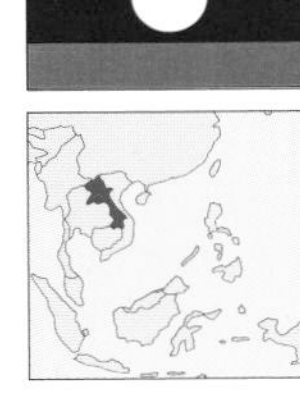

LAOS

GEOGRAPHY The Lao People's Democratic Republic is a landlocked country in Southeast Asia. Mountains and plateaux cover much of the country. Most people live on the plains bordering the River Mekong and its tributaries. This river, one of Asia's longest, forms much of the country's northwestern and southwestern borders.

Laos has a tropical monsoon climate. Winters are dry and sunny with winds blowing from the northeast. From April, the monsoon season starts with the arrival of moist southwesterly winds.

POLITICS & ECONOMY France made Laos a protectorate in the late 19th century and ruled it, with Cambodia and Vietnam, as part of French Indochina. Laos became an independent kingdom in 1954. After independence, a power struggle between royalist government forces and a pro-Communist group called Pathet Lao caused instability. A civil war broke out and continued into the 1970s. The Pathet Lao took control in 1975 and the king abdicated. In the 1990s, Laos started to open to the world and began tentative reforms. In 2011, a stock exchange was opened in Vientiane, as part of a gradual move toward capitalism.

Laos relies heavily on foreign aid. Agriculture employs nearly 73% of the population and accounts for 26% of the gross domestic product. Rice is the main crop. Timber and coffee are exported. But the most valuable export is electricity, which is produced at hydroelectric power stations on the River Mekong and is exported to Thailand. Laos also produces opium.

AREA 91,428 SQ MI [236,800 SQ KM] POPULATION 7,234,000
CAPITAL Vientiane GOVERNMENT Single-party republic
ETHNIC GROUPS Lao 55%, Khmou 11%, Hmong 8%, others 26%
LANGUAGES Lao (official), French, English RELIGIONS Buddhism 67%, traditional beliefs and others 33% CURRENCY Kip = 100 att

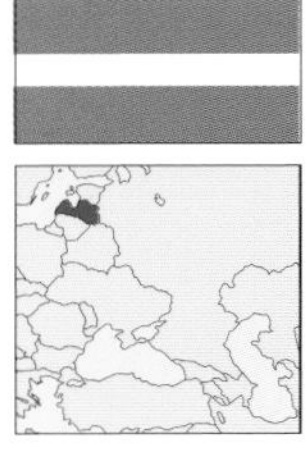

LATVIA

GEOGRAPHY The Republic of Latvia is one of three states on the southeastern corner of the Baltic Sea which were ruled as parts of the Soviet Union between 1940 and 1991. Latvia consists mainly of flat plains separated by low hills, composed of glacial moraine.

Riga has warm summers, but the winter months are sub-zero. The rainfall is moderate.

POLITICS & ECONOMY In 1800, Russia was in control of Latvia, but Latvians declared their independence after World War I. In 1940, under a German–Soviet pact, Soviet troops occupied Latvia, but they were driven out by the Germans in 1941. Soviet troops returned in 1944 and Latvia became part of the Soviet Union. Under Soviet rule, many Russian immigrants settled in Latvia and many Latvians feared that the Russians would become the dominant ethnic group.

In the late 1980s, when reforms were being introduced in the Soviet Union, Latvia's government ended absolute Communist rule and made Latvian the official language. In 1990, it declared the country to be independent, an act which was finally recognized by the Soviet Union in September 1991.

Latvia held the first free elections to its parliament (the Saeima) in 1993. Voting was limited only to citizens of Latvia on June 17, 1940, and their descendants. This meant that about 34% of Latvian residents were unable to vote. In 1994, Latvia restricted the naturalization of non-Latvians, including many Russian settlers, who were not allowed to vote or own land. However, in 1998, the government agreed that all children born since independence should have automatic citizenship. In 2004, Latvia became a member of the North Atlantic Treaty Organization and the European Union. Latvia was hit hard by the global financial crisis in 2009. It adopted the euro in January 2014.

The World Bank classifies Latvia as a "high-income" country. Manufactures include electronic goods, farm machinery, fertilizers, processed food, plastics, radios, and vehicles. Latvia produces only about a tenth of the electricity it needs; it imports the rest from Belarus, Russia, and Ukraine.

AREA 24,942 sq mi [64,600 sq km] **POPULATION** 1,924,000
CAPITAL Riga **GOVERNMENT** Multiparty republic
ETHNIC GROUPS Latvian 59%, Russian 28%, Belarusian, Ukrainian, Polish, Lithuanian **LANGUAGES** Latvian (official), Russian, Lithuanian **RELIGIONS** Lutheran, Russian Orthodox, Roman Catholic
CURRENCY Euro = 100 cents

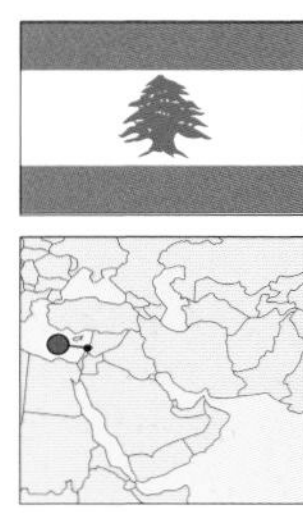

LEBANON

GEOGRAPHY The Republic of Lebanon is a country on the eastern shores of the Mediterranean Sea. Behind the coastal plain are the rugged Lebanon Mountains (Jabal Lubnan), which rise to 10,131 ft [3,088 m]. Another range, the Anti-Lebanon Mountains (Al Jabal Ash Sharqi), forms the eastern border with Syria. Between the two ranges is the Bekaa (Biqa) Valley, a fertile farming region. The coast has hot, dry summers and mild, wet winters. Heavy rain falls on the mountains, with snow at high altitudes.

POLITICS & ECONOMY Lebanon was ruled by Turkey from 1516 until World War I. France then took control from 1923 until independence in 1946. Muslims and Christians then agreed to share power, and Lebanon made rapid economic progress until the late 1950s, when development was slowed by periodic conflict between Sunni and Shia Muslims, Druze, and Christians. The situation was further complicated by the presence of Palestinian refugees, who used bases in Lebanon to attack Israel.

In 1975, civil war broke out as private armies representing the many factions struggled for power. This led to intervention by Israel in the south and Syria in the north. UN peacekeeping forces arrived in 1978, but violence continued in the 1980s. Peace was restored in the 1990s, but, in 2005, the assassination of Rafik Hariri, former prime minister, was blamed on Syria. Under pressure, Syria withdrew its forces from Lebanon. In 2006, a 34-day conflict between Israeli troops and Hezbollah guerrillas caused devastation in southern Lebanon. The civil war in neighboring Syria has had a major destabilizing effect on Lebanon. Refugees from Syria now make up one-third of the population.

Lebanon's civil war almost destroyed the valuable trade and financial services that had been Lebanon's chief source of income, together with tourism and manufacturing. The years 2011–7 were marked by slow economic growth. In 2018 Lebanon announced plans to explore potential offshore gas and oil reserves.

AREA 4,015 sq mi [10,400 sq km] **POPULATION** 6,100,000
CAPITAL Beirut **GOVERNMENT** Multiparty republic
ETHNIC GROUPS Arab 95%, Armenian 4%, others
LANGUAGES Arabic (official), French, English, Armenian
RELIGIONS Islam 60%, Christianity 39%
CURRENCY Lebanese pound = 100 piastres

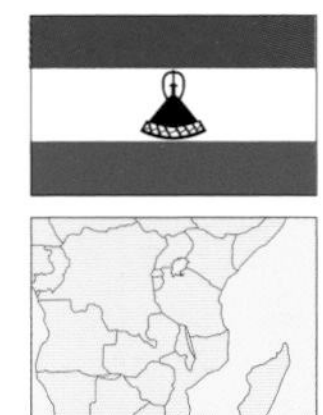

LESOTHO

GEOGRAPHY The Kingdom of Lesotho is a landlocked country, completely enclosed by South Africa. The land is mountainous, rising to 11,424 ft [3,482 m] on the northeastern border. The Drakensberg range covers most of the country.

The climate of Lesotho is greatly affected by the altitude, because most of the country lies above 4,920 ft [1,500 m]. Summers are warm but winters are cold. The rainfall averages about 28 inches [700 mm].

POLITICS & ECONOMY The political entity that eventually became Lesotho coalesced under King Moshoeshoe I in the 1820s who united various groups fleeing from tribal wars in southern Africa. Britain made the area a protectorate in 1868 and, in 1871, placed it under the British Cape Colony in South Africa. In 1884, Basutoland, as the area was called, was reconstituted as a British protectorate, where whites were not allowed to own land.

The country became independent in 1966 as the Kingdom of Lesotho, with Moshoeshoe II, great-grandson of Moshoeshoe I, as its king. Since independence, times have been turbulent with various factions, including the military, vying for power. Since 2012, a coalition government has been in place, under Thomas Thabane (2012–15) and then Pakalitha Mosisili (2015–17). Thabane returned to power in 2017 after Mosisili lost a vote of no confidence.

Lesotho faces many problems: agriculture is vulnerable to vagaries of the weather and the population has one of the highest rates of HIV-Aids infection in the world. The UN has classified 40% of the people as "ultra-poor."

Lesotho lacks natural resources with agriculture employing 86% of the people, mostly at subsistence level. Remittances sent home by Basotho working abroad, mainly in South Africa, are important to the economy. The textile industry has been a significant employer of women but this has suffered due to competition from Asia.

AREA 11,720 sq mi [30,355 sq km] **POPULATION** 1,962,000
CAPITAL Maseru **GOVERNMENT** Constitutional monarchy
ETHNIC GROUPS Sotho 99% **LANGUAGES** Sesotho and English (both official) **RELIGIONS** Christianity 80%, traditional beliefs 20%
CURRENCY Loti = 100 lisente

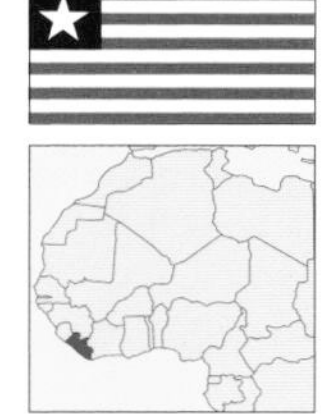

LIBERIA

GEOGRAPHY The Republic of Liberia is a country in West Africa. Behind the coastline, 311 mi [500 km] long, lies a narrow coastal plain. Beyond, the land rises to a plateau region, with the highest land along the border with Guinea. Liberia has a tropical climate with high temperatures and high humidity all through the year. Rainfall is abundant all year round, but there is a particularly wet period from June to November. Rainfall generally increases from east to west.

POLITICS & ECONOMY In the late 18th century, some white Americans in the United States wanted to help freed black slaves return to Africa. In 1816, they set up the American Colonization Society, which bought land in what is now Liberia.

In 1822, the Society landed former slaves at a settlement which they named Monrovia after US president Monroe. In 1847, Liberia became a fully independent republic with a constitution much like that of the United States. For many years, Americo-Liberians controlled the country's government with the American Firestone Company, which ran the rubber plantations, being especially influential. Other foreign companies readily exploited Liberia's mineral resources, including its huge iron-ore deposits.

In 1980, a military group composed of people from the local population killed the Americo-Liberian president, William R. Tolbert. An army sergeant, Samuel K. Doe, was made president. Elections held in 1985 resulted in victory for Doe. From 1989, the country was plunged into civil war between various ethnic groups. Doe was assassinated in 1990 and the struggle with rebel groups continued. West African peacekeeping forces arrived in Liberia and, in 1995, a ceasefire was agreed. A council of state was set up in 1997 and Charles Taylor became president. Taylor fled the country in 2003, and in 2006 he was extradited and faced war crimes charges, on several of which he was convicted in 2012. Following elections in 2005, Ellen Johnson-Sirleaf became Africa's first woman president. She was re-elected in 2011. Elections in 2017 were won by former soccer player George Weah.

Liberia's economy was devastated by the civil war and, more recently, by the outbreak of Ebola in the region. Agriculture is important, but most farmers live at subsistence level. Food crops include cassava, rice, and sugarcane, while rubber, cocoa, and coffee are exported. The most valuable exports are rubber and iron ore.

Liberia also obtains revenue from its "flag of convenience" which is used by about one-sixth of the world's commercial shipping.

AREA 43,000 sq mi [111,369 sq km] **POPULATION** 4,810,000
CAPITAL Monrovia **GOVERNMENT** Multiparty republic
ETHNIC GROUPS Indigenous African tribes 95% (including Kpelle, Bassa, Grebo, Gio, Kru, Mano)
LANGUAGES English (official), ethnic languages
RELIGIONS Christianity 86%, Islam 12%, traditional beliefs and others 2% **CURRENCY** Liberian dollar = 100 cents

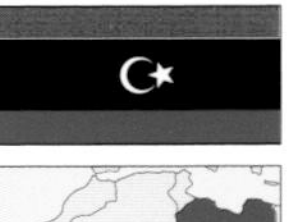

LIBYA

GEOGRAPHY Bordering the Mediterranean Sea, the State of Libya is the fourth largest country in Africa. Most people live on the coastal plains in the northeast and northwest. The Sahara, the world's largest desert, which occupies 95% of Libya, reaches the Mediterranean coast along the Gulf of Sidra (Khalij Surt).

The coastal plains in the northeast and northwest have Mediterranean climates, with hot, dry summers and mild, sometimes wet winters. Hot desert conditions prevail inland.

POLITICS & ECONOMY Italy took possession of Libya in 1911, but lost it during World War II. Britain and France jointly ruled Libya until 1951, when the country became independent.

In 1969, a military group headed by Colonel Muammar Gaddafi deposed the king and set up a military government. Under Gaddafi, the government took control of the economy and used money from oil exports to finance welfare services and development projects. Gaddafi was criticized for supporting terrorist groups around the world, and Libya became isolated from the mid-1980s.

From 2004, relations with the West improved and diplomatic links were restored with many nations, including the United States. However, in February 2011, the arrest of a human rights campaigner sparked off protests in Benghazi which rapidly spread. In October of that year, Gaddafi was killed and a National Transition Council was set up as the de facto government. Libya has struggled to find political stability and the elections held in 2014 produced rival governments, backed by secular and Islamist militias, which are fighting for control. Libya is a major route for migrants from Africa to Europe.

The discovery of oil and natural gas in 1959 led to a transformation of Libya's economy. This formerly poor country soon became Africa's richest in terms of its per capita income. But it remains a developing country, because oil accounts for nearly all of its export revenues. Agriculture is important, although Libya imports about 80% of its food. Crops include barley, citrus fruits, dates, olives, potatoes, and wheat, while cattle, sheep, and poultry are raised. Libya has oil refineries and petrochemical plants. Development and foreign investment await political stability.

AREA 679,358 sq mi [1,759,540 sq km] **POPULATION** 6,755,000
CAPITAL Tripoli **GOVERNMENT** Transitional
ETHNIC GROUPS Libyan Arab and Berber 97% **LANGUAGES** Arabic (official), Berber **RELIGIONS** Islam (Sunni Muslim) 97%
CURRENCY Libyan dinar = 1,000 dirhams

LIECHTENSTEIN

The tiny Principality of Liechtenstein is sandwiched between Switzerland and Austria. The River Rhine flows along its western border, while Alpine peaks rise in the east and south. The climate is relatively mild. Since 1924, Liechtenstein has been in a customs union with Switzerland. Taxation is low and the country is a haven for foreign companies. In 2004, the head of state Prince Hans-Adam II handed over the running of the country to his son, Prince Alois, though he remains titular head of state. In 2009, Liechtenstein agreed to share tax information with a number of countries in order to improve its reputation as a legitimate financial center.

AREA 62 sq mi [160 sq km] **POPULATION** 39,000 **CAPITAL** Vaduz

LITHUANIA

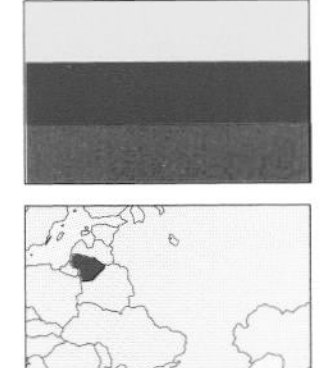

GEOGRAPHY The Republic of Lithuania is the southernmost of the three Baltic states which were ruled as part of the Soviet Union between 1940 and 1991. Much of the land is flat or gently rolling, with the highest land in the southeast.

Winters are cold and summers warm. The annual rainfall in the west is about 25 in [630 mm]. Eastern areas are drier.

POLITICS & ECONOMY The Lithuanian people were united into a single nation in the 12th century, and later joined a union with Poland. In 1795, Lithuania came under Russian rule. After World War I (1914–18), Lithuania declared itself independent, and in 1920 it signed a peace treaty with the Russians. In 1940, the Soviet Union occupied Lithuania, but was ousted by Germany a year later. After Soviet forces returned in 1944, Lithuania was integrated into the Soviet Union. However, Lithuanians resisted attempts to suppress their culture and steadfastly clung on to their language and staunch Catholic faith. In 1988, when the Soviet Union was introducing reforms, the Lithuanians demanded independence which was recognized by the Soviet Union in 1991.

Since 1991, Lithuania has sought to reform its economy and introduce a private enterprise system. Lithuania has also drawn closer to the West and, in 2004, it became a member of both the North Atlantic Treaty Organization and the European Union. Its first attempt to join the eurozone in 2007 was rejected due to high inflation but it adopted the euro in 2015.

The World Bank now classifies Lithuania as a "high-income" economy and it is growing faster than most other EU economies. Lithuania lacks natural resources, but manufacturing, based on imported materials, is the most valuable activity.

Area 25,174 sq mi [65,200 sq km] **Population** 2,824,000
Capital Vilnius **Government** Multiparty republic
Ethnic groups Lithuanian 84%, Polish 6%, Russian 5%, Belarusian 1% **Languages** Lithuanian (official), Russian, Polish
Religions Mainly Roman Catholic **Currency** Euro = 100 cents

LUXEMBOURG

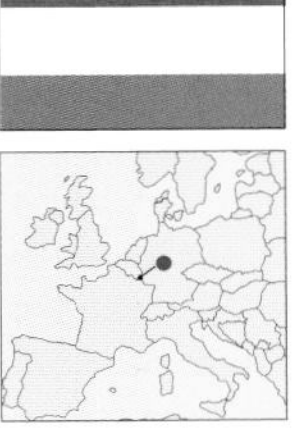

GEOGRAPHY The Grand Duchy of Luxembourg is one of the smallest and oldest countries in Europe. Luxembourg has a temperate climate. The south has warm summers and falls, when grapes ripen in sheltered southeastern valleys. Winters are sometimes severe, especially in upland areas.

POLITICS & ECONOMY Germany occupied Luxembourg in World Wars I and II. In 1944–5, northern Luxembourg was the scene of the Battle of the Bulge. In 1948, Luxembourg joined Belgium and the Netherlands in "Benelux," a customs union, and in the 1950s, it was one of the six founders of what is now the European Union. Its capital is a major financial center and contains several international agencies. In 2008, parliament restricted the monarch to a ceremonial role following the grand duke's refusal to sign a law allowing euthanasia.

Luxembourg has iron-ore reserves and is a major steel producer. It also has many high-technology industries, producing electronic goods and computers. Steel and other manufactures, including chemicals, rubber products, glass, and aluminum, dominate the country's exports. Other major activities include financial services, although the "LuxLeaks" scandal in 2009, revealing advantageous tax arrangements for several multi-national companies, temporarily damaged Luxembourg's reputation.

Area 998 sq mi [2,586 sq km] **Population** 606,000
Capital Luxembourg **Government** Constitutional monarchy (Grand Duchy) **Ethnic groups** Luxembourger 63%, Portuguese 13%, Italian, French, Belgian, Slavs **Languages** Luxembourgish (official), Portuguese, French, German **Religions** Roman Catholic 87%, others 13% **Currency** Euro = 100 cents

MACEDONIA, NORTH

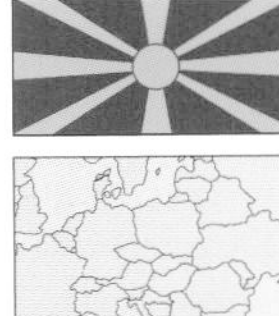

GEOGRAPHY The Republic of North Macedonia is a country in southeastern Europe, which was once one of the six republics that made up the former Yugoslavia. This landlocked country is largely mountainous or hilly. North Macedonia has hot summers, though highland areas are cooler. Winters are cold and snowfalls are often heavy. The climate is fairly continental in character and rain occurs throughout the year.

POLITICS & ECONOMY Until the 20th century, North Macedonia's history was closely tied to the larger area of Macedonia, which included parts of northern Greece and south-western Bulgaria. This region reached its peak in power at the time of Philip II (382–336 BC) and his son Alexander the Great (336–323 BC). After Alexander's death, his empire was split up and it gradually declined. The area became a Roman province in the 140s BC and part of the Byzantine empire from AD 395. In the 6th century, Slavs from eastern Europe settled in the area, followed by Bulgars from central Asia in the 9th century. The Byzantine empire regained control in 1018, but Serbia took Macedonia in the early 14th century. In 1371, the Ottoman Turks conquered the area and ruled it for more than 500 years.

In 1913, at the end of the Balkan Wars, the area was divided between Serbia, Bulgaria, and Greece. At the end of World War I, Serbian Macedonia became part of the Kingdom of the Serbs, Croats, and Slovenes, which was renamed Yugoslavia in 1929.

In the early 1990s, the country broke up into five separate republics with Macedonia declaring its independence in 1991. Greece objected to the use of the name Macedonia, which it considered to be a Greek name. It also objected to a symbol on Macedonia's flag and a reference in the constitution to the desire to reunite the three parts of the old Macedonia.

Macedonia adopted a new clause in its constitution rejecting any Macedonian claims on Greek territory and, in 1993, the United Nations accepted the new republic as a member under the name of the Former Yugoslav Republic of Macedonia (FYROM). By the end of 1993, all the countries of the EU, except Greece, were establishing diplomatic relations with the FYROM. In 1995, Greece lifted its trade ban when Macedonia agreed to redesign its flag. The issue over its name remained unresolved until 2018, when Macedonia and Greece agreed on the new name of the Republic of North Macedonia, paving the way for North Macedonia to apply for membership of the EU and NATO.

The World Bank describes North Macedonia as an "upper-middle-income" economy showing steady growth since independence due to conservative government financial policies working toward a more open economy. Manufactures dominate the country's exports. Coal is mined, but oil and natural gas are imported. The country is self-sufficient in its basic food needs and has a low rate of inflation, although it remains one of Europe's poorest economies and unemployment is high.

Area 9,928 sq mi [25,713 sq km] **Population** 2,119,000
Capital Skopje **Government** Multiparty republic
Ethnic groups Macedonian 64%, Albanian 25%, Turkish 4%, Romanian 3%, Serb 2% **Languages** Macedonian and Albanian (official) **Religions** Macedonian Orthodox 65%, Islam 33%
Currency Macedonian denar = 100 deni

MADAGASCAR

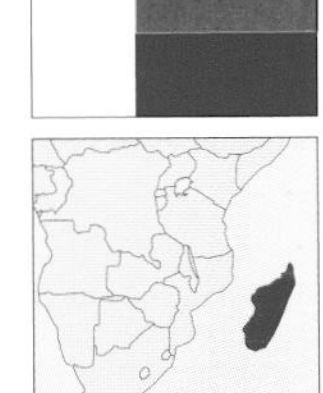

GEOGRAPHY The Democratic Republic of Madagascar, in southeastern Africa, is an island nation, which has an area larger than France. Behind the narrow coastal plains in the east lies a highland zone, mostly between 2,000 ft and 4,000 ft [610 m to 1,220 m] above sea level. Broad plains border the Mozambique Channel in the west.

Temperatures in the highlands are moderated by the altitude. The winters (from April to September) are dry, but heavy rains occur in summer. The eastern coastlands are warm and humid. The west is drier, and the south and southwest are hot and dry. It has a unique fauna and flora.

POLITICS & ECONOMY People from Southeast Asia began to settle on Madagascar around 2,000 years ago. Subsequent influxes from Africa and Arabia added to the island's diverse heritage, culture, and language.

The island was a French colony from 1895 until it achieved independence as the Malagasy Republic in 1960. In 1972, army officers seized control and, in 1975, under the leadership of Lieutenant-Commander Didier Ratsiraka, the country was renamed Madagascar. In 2002, the country came close to civil war when Ratsiraka and his opponent, Marc Ravalomanana, both claimed victory in presidential elections. Ravalomanana became president, but he was deposed in 2009, in a move backed by the military and condemned internationally. Elections in 2013 returned Hery Rajaonarimampiana as president. In late 2018 Andry Rajoelina was elected president, narrowly defeating Ravalomanana.

Madagascar is a poor country. Poverty and population growth impose pressure on the dwindling forests and the unique wildlife, as well as causing severe soil erosion. Farming, fishing, and forestry employ about 80% of the people. Food crops include bananas, cassava, rice, and sweet potatoes. Coffee and vanilla are exported.

Area 226,657 sq mi [587,041 sq km] **Population** 25,684,000
Capital Antananarivo **Government** Republic
Ethnic groups Merina, Betsimisaraka, Betsileo, Tsimihety, Sakalava and others
Languages Malagasy and French (both official)
Religions Traditional beliefs 52%, Christianity 41%, Islam 7%
Currency Malagasy ariary = 5 iraimbilanja

MALAWI

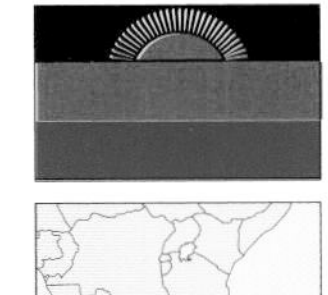

GEOGRAPHY The Republic of Malawi includes part of Lake Malawi, which is drained by the River Shire, a tributary of the River Zambezi. The land is mostly mountainous. The highest peak, Mulanje, reaches 9,849 ft [3,002 m] in the southeast.

While the low-lying areas of Malawi are hot and humid all year round, the uplands have more pleasant weather. Lilongwe has a warm and sunny climate. Frosts sometimes occur in July and August, in the middle of the long dry season.

POLITICS & ECONOMY Malawi, then called Nyasaland, became a British protectorate in 1891. In 1953, Britain established the Federation of Rhodesia and Nyasaland, which also included what are now Zambia and Zimbabwe. Black African opposition, led in Nyasaland by Dr Hastings Kamuzu Banda, led to the dissolution of the federation in 1963. In 1964, Nyasaland became independent as Malawi, with Banda as prime minister. Banda was an autocrat who maintained his control of the country by operating a one-party system and being made "president for life" in 1971 until he retired after elections in 1994. Bakili Muluzi became the first president after Banda and, despite Malawi aspiring toward more open government, subsequent administrations have been mired in accusations of corruption and treason.

Malawi is one of the world's poorest countries with more than half the population living below the poverty line. More than 90% of the people are farmers, but many grow little more than they need to feed their families. Some progress has been made in recent years to grow the economy and Malawi is starting to exploit its uranium deposits, but development is hampered by lack of infrastructure.

Area 45,747 sq mi [118,484 sq km] **Population** 19,843,000
Capital Lilongwe **Government** Multiparty republic
Ethnic groups Chewa, Lomwe, Yao, Ngoni, Tumbuka, Nyanja, Sena, Tonga, Ngonde and others
Languages Chichewa and English (both official)
Religions Christianity 68%, Islam 25%
Currency Malawian kwacha = 100 tambala

MALAYSIA

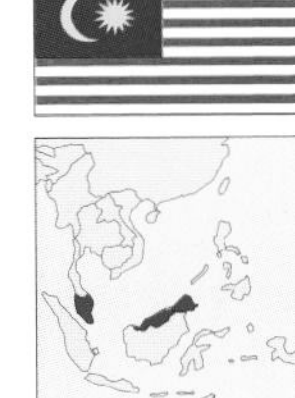

GEOGRAPHY The Federation of Malaysia consists of two main parts. Peninsular Malaysia, which is joined to mainland Asia, contains about 80% of the population. The other main regions, Sabah, and Sarawak, are in northern Borneo, an island which Malaysia shares with Indonesia. Behind the coastal lowlands, the interior is mountainous.

Malaysia has a hot equatorial climate. The temperatures are high all through the year, though the mountains are much cooler than the lowland areas. Rainfall is heavy throughout the year.

POLITICS & ECONOMY Around 1,200 years ago, Indian traders introduced Hinduism and Buddhism into the Malay peninsula, while Arabs introduced Islam in the 15th century. Portuguese traders reached Melaka in 1509, but the Dutch took over in 1641. Britain became established in this region in 1786.

Japan occupied the area during World War II (1939–45), but it reverted to British rule in 1945. Malaya (Peninsular Malaysia) became independent in 1957. Malaysia was created in 1963, when Malaya, Singapore, Sabah, and Sarawak agreed to unite, but Singapore withdrew in 1965.

From 1981, Malaysia experienced rapid economic progress under the 22-year term of Prime Minister Mahathir bin Mohamad. Although not unaffected by global financial crises, the succeeding governments continued to develop a broad-based economy with an emphasis on manufacturing, tourism, and the service industry. In 2018 Mahathir was again elected prime minister, at the age of 92.

The World Bank classifies Malaysia as an "upper-middle-income" developing country. Palm oil, rubber, and tin are major products. Manufactures include cars, chemicals, a wide range of electronic goods, plastics, textiles, rubber, and wood products.

AREA 127,320 sq mi [329,758 sq km] **POPULATION** 31,810,000
CAPITAL Kuala Lumpur; Putrajaya (administrative capital)
GOVERNMENT Federal constitutional monarchy
ETHNIC GROUPS Malay and other indigenous groups 61%, Chinese 24%, Indian 7%, others
LANGUAGES Malay (official), Chinese, English
RELIGIONS Islam, Buddhism, Daoism, Hinduism, Christianity, Sikhism
CURRENCY Ringgit = 100 sen

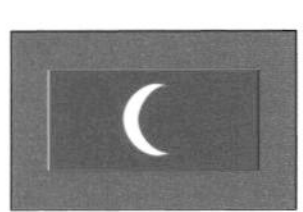

MALDIVES

The Republic of the Maldives consists of about 1,200 low-lying coral islands, south of India. The highest point is 79 ft [24 m], but most of the land is only 6 ft [1.8 m] above sea level. It became a British territory in 1887 and independent in 1965. It left the Commonwealth of Nations in 2016. Tourism and fishing are the main industries.

AREA 115 sq mi [298 sq km] **POPULATION** 392,000 **CAPITAL** Malé

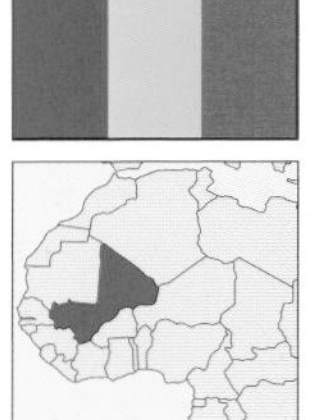

MALI

GEOGRAPHY The Republic of Mali is a landlocked country in northwestern Africa. The land is generally flat, with the highest land in the north. Northern Mali is hot and practically rainless. The south has enough rain for farming.

POLITICS & ECONOMY Between the 4th and 16th centuries, Mali was part of three African empires – Ancient Ghana, Ancient Mali and Songhay. However, after 1591, when Songhay was defeated by Morocco, the area was divided into small kingdoms. France ruled the area, then known as French Sudan, from 1893 until the country became independent as Mali in 1960.

The first socialist government was overthrown in 1968 by an army group led by Moussa Traoré, but he was ousted in 1991. Multiparty democracy was restored in 1992 and Alpha Oumar Konaré was elected president. Konaré stood down in 2002 and Ahmadou Touré, who had restored democracy in 1992, was elected president. In 2012, an army coup overthrew Touré; three successive "unity cabinets" followed. The coup leaders said that the government was failing to give them enough arms to tackle a rebellion by ethnic Tuaregs in northern Mali. A fragile peace prevails, although there has been an increase in Islamist extremist groups in the country in recent years.

Mali is a very poor country and 70% of the land is desert or semi-desert. Only about 2% of the land is used for growing crops, while 25% is used for grazing animals. Agriculture employs more than one-third of the people, many of whom subsist by nomadic livestock rearing. Mali's chief exports are cotton and gold.

AREA 478,838 sq mi [1,240,192 sq km] **POPULATION** 18,430,000
CAPITAL Bamako **GOVERNMENT** Multiparty republic
ETHNIC GROUPS Mande 50% (Bambara, Malinke, Soninke), Peul 17%, Voltaic 12%, Songhai 6%, Tuareg and Moor 10%, others
LANGUAGES French (official), many African languages
RELIGIONS Islam 95%, traditional beliefs 3%, Christianity 2%
CURRENCY CFA franc = 100 centimes

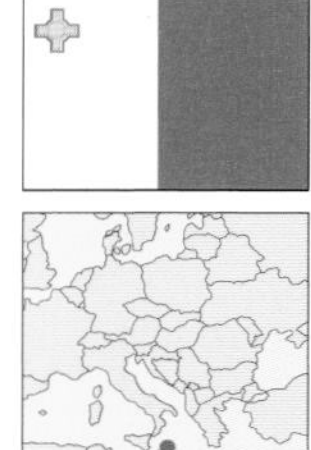

MALTA

GEOGRAPHY The Republic of Malta consists of two main islands, Malta and Gozo, with a third, much smaller island called Comino lying between the two large islands and two islets. The climate is typically Mediterranean, with hot, dry summers and mild, moist winters.

POLITICS & ECONOMY Malta has fascinating Stone Age and Bronze Age remains. The islands later came under Phoenician, Greek, Carthaginian, Roman, and Arab rule. In about 1090, Malta fell under the Norman kings of Sicily and, from 1530, the Knights Hospitallers (also called the Knights of St John of Jerusalem). France took the islands in 1798, but the British drove them out in 1800. British rule was officially recognized in 1815.

During World War I (1914–18), Malta was an important naval base. In World War II (1939–45), Italian and German aircraft bombed the islands. In recognition of the islanders' bravery, the British King George VI awarded the George Cross to Malta in 1942: the emblem is incorporated into its flag. Malta became independent in 1964 and a republic in 1974. Since the 1980s Malta has pursued a policy of neutrality whilst maintaining links with Europe and the United States. It became a member of the European Union in May 2004, and adopted the euro as its official currency in 2008.

The World Bank classifies Malta as a "high-income" developing country. It lacks natural resources, and most people work in the former naval dockyards, which are now used for commercial shipbuilding and repair, in manufacturing industries, notably electronics, and in the tourist industry.

Manufactures include processed food and chemicals. Farming is difficult, because of the rocky soils. Crops include barley, fruits, potatoes, and wheat. Malta also has a small fishing industry.

AREA 122 sq mi [316 sq km] **POPULATION** 449,000
CAPITAL Valletta **GOVERNMENT** Multiparty republic
ETHNIC GROUPS Maltese 96%, British 2%
LANGUAGES Maltese and English (both official)
RELIGIONS Roman Catholic 98%
CURRENCY Euro = 100 cents

MARSHALL ISLANDS

The Republic of the Marshall Islands, a former US territory, became fully independent in 1991. This island nation, lying north of Kiribati in a region known as Micronesia, is heavily dependent on US aid. The main activities are agriculture and tourism.

AREA 70 sq mi [181 sq km]
POPULATION 76,000 **CAPITAL** Majuro

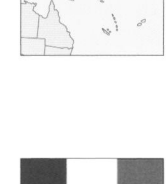

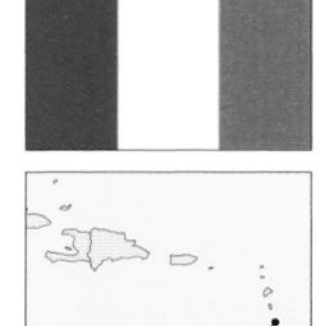

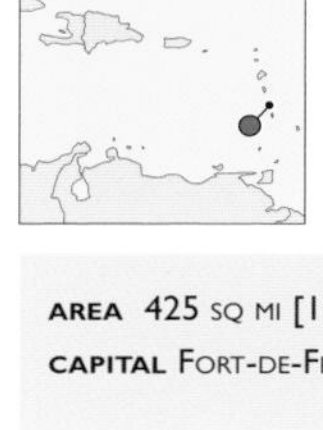

MARTINIQUE

Martinique, a volcanic island nation in the Caribbean, was colonized by France in 1635. It became a French overseas department in 1946. Tourism and agriculture are major activities. About 70% of Martinique's gross domestic product is provided by the French government, allowing for a good standard of living.

AREA 425 sq mi [1,102 sq km] **POPULATION** 386,000
CAPITAL Fort-de-France

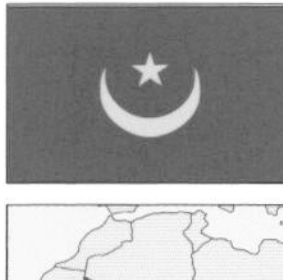

MAURITANIA

GEOGRAPHY The Islamic Republic of Mauritania in northwestern Africa is nearly twice the size of France. But France has almost 20 times as many people. Part of the world's largest desert, the Sahara, covers northern Mauritania and most Mauritanians live in the southwest. The amount of rainfall and the length of the rainy season increase from north to south. Much of the land is desert, but southwesterly winds bring summer rain to the south.

POLITICS & ECONOMY Originally part of the great African empires of Ghana and Mali, Mauritania became a French protectorate in 1903. In 1920, the country became a territory of French West Africa and a French colony. Mauritania finally became independent in 1960.

In 1976, Spain withdrew from Spanish (now Western) Sahara, a territory bordering Mauritania to the north. Morocco occupied the northern two-thirds of this territory, while Mauritania took the rest. Following this, Saharan guerrillas belonging to POLISARIO (the Popular Front for the Liberation of Saharan Territories) began an armed struggle for independence. In 1979, Mauritania withdrew from the southern part of Western Sahara, which was then occupied by Morocco. Democracy was restored after a new constitution was adopted in 1991. A military group seized power in 2005, but democratic elections were held in 2007. The military again seized control in 2008, and in 2009 its leader, Mohamad Ould Abdel Aziz, was elected president. He was re-elected in 2014. In 2010–11, al Qaeda militants committed terrorist acts in Mauritania and their presence in the country is having a serious destabilizing effect.

Mauritania is a "lower-middle-income" developing country. Nearly half of the population are engaged in agriculture and at the mercy of frequent droughts. The coastal waters provide good fishing grounds. In 2006, Mauritania became Africa's newest oil producer, when an offshore platform came online for the first time. Mauritania has extensive mineral deposits.

AREA 395,953 sq mi [1,025,520 sq km] **POPULATION** 3,840,000
CAPITAL Nouakchott **GOVERNMENT** Multiparty Islamic republic
ETHNIC GROUPS Mixed Moor/Black 40%, Moor 30%, Black 30%
LANGUAGES Arabic (official), Pulaar, Soninke, Wolof, French
RELIGIONS Islam **CURRENCY** Ouguiya = 5 khoums

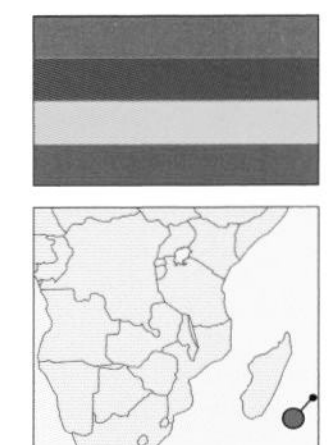

MAURITIUS

The Republic of Mauritius lies in the Indian Ocean east of Madagascar. It was previously ruled by France and Britain until it achieved independence in 1968. It became a republic in 1992. Sugar production is in decline with tourism and textiles vital to the economy. It has few natural resources.

AREA 788 sq mi [2,040 sq km]
POPULATION 1,364,000 **CAPITAL** Port Louis

MEXICO

GEOGRAPHY The United Mexican States, as Mexico is officially named, is the world's most populous Spanish-speaking country. Much of the land is mountainous, although most people live on the central plateau. Mexico contains two large peninsulas: Lower (or Baja) California in the northwest, and the flat Yucatán peninsula in the southeast.

The climate varies according to the altitude. The resort of Acapulco on the southwest coast has a dry and sunny climate. Mexico City, at about 7,546 ft [2,300 m] above sea level, is much cooler. Most rain occurs between June and September.

POLITICS & ECONOMY In the mid-19th century, Mexico lost land to the United States, and between 1910 and 1921 violent revolutions created chaos. Reforms were introduced in the 1920s and, in 1929, the Institutional Revolutionary Party (PRI) was formed. The PRI ruled Mexico effectively as a one-party state until 2001. The new president, Vicente Fox, faced many problems. He was succeeded by Felipe Calderón in 2006, who in 2012 was succeeded by Enrique Peña Nieto. The left-winger Andres Manuel López Obrado was elected president in 2018.

The World Bank classifies Mexico as an "upper-middle-income" developing country. Agriculture is important. Food crops include beans, maize, rice, and wheat, while cash crops include coffee, cotton, fruits, and vegetables. However, oil and oil products are the chief exports, while manufacturing is the most valuable activity. Mexico is the world's leading silver producer, and it also mines copper, gold, lead, zinc, and other minerals. Factories near the northern border assemble goods, such as car parts and electrical products, for US companies.

Hopes for the future lie in increasing cooperation with the US and Canada. The election of Donald Trump as US President in 2016 led to the renegotiation of the North American Free-Trade Agreement (NAFTA). In October 2018 a new trade deal – United States-Mexico-Canada Agreement (USMCA) – was reached but has not yet been ratified.

AREA 756,061 sq mi [1,958,201 sq km] **POPULATION** 125,959,000
CAPITAL Mexico City **GOVERNMENT** Federal republic
ETHNIC GROUPS Mestizo 60%, Amerindian 30%, White 9%
LANGUAGES Spanish (official) **RELIGIONS** Roman Catholic 83%, Protestant 2%, others 15% **CURRENCY** Mexican peso = 100 centavos

MICRONESIA

The Federated States of Micronesia, a former US territory in the western Pacific Ocean, became fully independent in 1991. The main exports are fish and agricultural products. Tourism is important.

AREA 271 sq mi [702 sq km]
POPULATION 104,000 **CAPITAL** Palikir

MOLDOVA

GEOGRAPHY The Republic of Moldova is a small country sandwiched between Ukraine and Romania. It was formerly one of the 15 republics that made up the Soviet Union.

Much of the land is hilly and the highest areas are located near the center of the country.

Moldova has a moderately continental climate, with warm summers and fairly cold winters when temperatures dip below freezing point. Most of the rain comes in the warmer months.

POLITICS & ECONOMY In the 14th century, the Moldavian people formed a state that comprised part of Romania and the historic region of Bessarabia. Following rule by the Ottoman Turks, Russia took control of Bessarabia in 1812. After World War I (1914–18), Bessarabia declared independence and voted to unite with Romania. This move was not recognized by Russia and in 1940 the area was annexed by the USSR. From 1944, the Moldovan Soviet Socialist Republic became part of the Soviet Union.

In 1989, the Moldovans asserted their independence and ethnicity by making Romanian the official language and, at the end of 1991, Moldova became an independent nation. But Trans-Dniester, an area east of the River Dniester inhabited by mainly Russian and Ukrainian speakers, has sought autonomy. In 2006, its people voted for independence and union with Russia, but this vote was not recognized internationally.

In 2001, Moldovans returned the Communist Party to power. Under President Vladimir Voronin, Moldova enjoyed a period of economic growth. The Communist Party was re-elected in 2005 and 2009. Following allegations of fraud, further elections were held in 2010. In 2014, Moldova signed its Association Agreement with the EU. Russia restricted some agricultural imports in response. In 2016, in the first direct presidential elections in some years, pro-Russian Igor Dodon was elected with 55% of the vote.

In terms of its GNP per capita, Moldova is one of Europe's poorest countries. Agriculture is the leading activity and products include fruits, maize, tobacco, and wine. Moldova has few natural resources and it imports materials and fuels for its industries.

AREA 13,070 sq mi [33,851 sq km] **POPULATION** 3,438,000
CAPITAL Kishinev **GOVERNMENT** Multiparty republic
ETHNIC GROUPS Moldovan/Romanian 78%, Ukrainian 8%, Russian 6%, Gagauz 4%, others **LANGUAGES** Moldovan/Romanian (official), Gagauz, Russian **RELIGIONS** Eastern Orthodox 98%
CURRENCY Moldovan leu = 100 bani

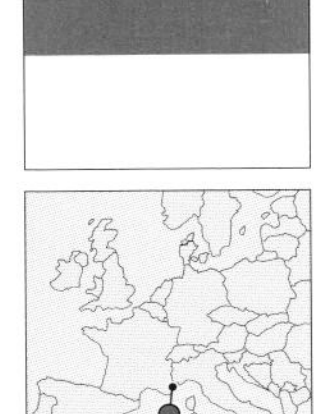

MONACO

The tiny Principality of Monaco consists of a narrow strip of coastline and a rocky peninsula on the French Riviera. Its considerable wealth is derived largely from banking, finance, gambling, recreation, and tourism. Monaco's citizens do not pay any income tax. The Grimaldi family have ruled the country for over 720 years with Prince Albert II as the current reigning monarch.

AREA 0.8 sq mi [2 sq km] **POPULATION** 31,000 **CAPITAL** Monaco

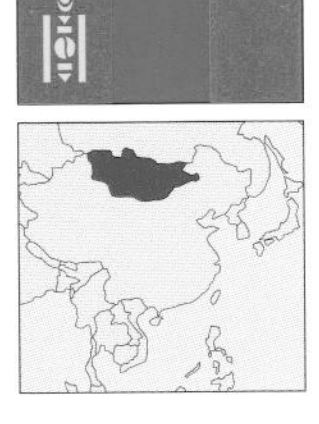

MONGOLIA

GEOGRAPHY The State of Mongolia is the world's largest landlocked country. It consists mainly of high plateaux, with a cold desert, the Gobi, in the southeast.

Ulan Bator lies on the northern edge of the desert plateau. It has bitterly cold winters. Summer temperatures are moderated by the altitude.

POLITICS & ECONOMY In the 13th century, Genghis Khan united the Mongolian peoples and built up a great empire. Under his grandson, Kublai Khan, the Mongol empire extended from Korea and China to eastern Europe and present-day Iraq.

The Mongol empire broke up in the late 14th century. In the early 17th century, Inner Mongolia came under Chinese control, and by the late 17th century Outer Mongolia had become a Chinese province. In 1911, the Mongolians drove the Chinese out of Outer Mongolia and made the area a Buddhist kingdom. But in 1924, under Russian influence, the Communist Mongolian People's Republic was set up. In 1990, the people demonstrated for more freedom, and free elections in June 1990 were won by the Communist Mongolian People's Revolutionary Party (MPRP). The Democratic Party coalition won in 1996, but the MPRP regained control in 2000. In 2009, the Democratic Party candidate, Tsakhiagiin Elbegdorj, was elected president. He was re-elected in 2013. In 2016 parliamentary elections, the Mongolian People's Party won a landslide. Presidential elections in 2017 were won by former martial arts star Khaltmaa Battulga of the Democratic Party.

The majority of the population were once nomads but, under Communist rule, most people were moved into permanent homes on government-owned farms. Livestock and animal products remain important, but minerals and fuels now account for more than three-fifths of Mongolia's exports. There is much mineral wealth yet to be exploited.

AREA 604,826 sq mi [1,566,500 sq km] **POPULATION** 3,103,000
CAPITAL Ulan Bator **GOVERNMENT** Multiparty republic
ETHNIC GROUPS Khalkha Mongol 95%, Kazakh 5%
LANGUAGES Khalkha Mongolian (official), Turkic, Russian
RELIGIONS Tibetan Buddhist Lamaism 53%
CURRENCY Mongolian tögrög = 100 möngös

MONTENEGRO

The Republic of Montenegro, on the shores of the Adriatic Sea, became independent in 2006.

The coastal region has a Mediterranean climate. However, inland, the Dinaric Alps, which reach a height of 8,274 ft [2,522 m], have a more severe climate.

Serbia fell under Turkish rule in the 14th century, but Montenegro remained Christian. Montenegro was absorbed into Serbia in 1918 and it later became part of the Kingdom of the Serbs, Croats, and Slovenes, renamed as Yugoslavia in 1929. After World War II, Montenegro was recognized as one of the six republics of Yugoslavia.

In 2016, long-term prime minister Milo Djukanovich was replaced by Dusko Markovic. Incumbent Filip Vuljanovic won the 2013 presidential election. Montenegro is a candidate for EU membership and joined NATO in 2017. The pro-European Djukanovich was elected president in April 2018.

Manufacturing is the main activity, and steel and aluminum are major products. Farming also remains important. Montenegro became a member of the World Trade Organization in 2012.

AREA 5,415 sq mi [14,026 sq km] **POPULATION** 614,000
CAPITAL Podgorica **GOVERNMENT** Republic
ETHNIC GROUPS Montenegrin 43%, Serb 32%, Bosnian 8%, Albanian 5%, others **LANGUAGES** Serbian and Montenegrin (both official), Bosnian, Albanian **RELIGIONS** Orthodox, Islam, Roman Catholic **CURRENCY** Euro = 100 cents

MONTSERRAT

Montserrat is a British overseas territory in the Caribbean Sea. The climate is tropical and hurricanes often cause much damage. Intermittent eruptions of the Soufrière Hills volcano between 1995 and 1998, and again in 2003, led to the emigration of many people and the virtual destruction of Plymouth, the then capital. A new airport was opened in 2005.

AREA 39 sq mi [102 sq km] **POPULATION** 5,000 **CAPITAL** Brades

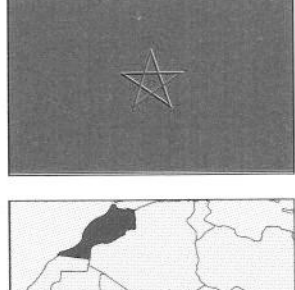

MOROCCO

GEOGRAPHY The Kingdom of Morocco lies in northwestern Africa. Behind the western coastal plain the land rises to a broad plateau and ranges of the Atlas Mountains. The High (Haut) Atlas contains the highest peak, Djebel Toubkal, at 13,665 ft [4,165 m]. East of the mountains, the land descends to the Sahara. The Canaries Current cools the Atlantic coast. Inland, summers are hot and dry. Winters are mild, with moderate rainfall. Snow often falls on the High Atlas Mountains.

POLITICS & ECONOMY The original people of Morocco were the Berbers, but, in the 680s, Arab invaders introduced Islam and the Arabic language. By the early 20th century, France and Spain controlled Morocco, which became an independent kingdom in 1956. Although Morocco is a constitutional monarchy, King Hassan II ruled the country in a generally authoritarian way, from his accession in 1961 to his death in 1999. His successor, Mohamed VI, faced several problems, including that of Western Sahara, which he claimed for Morocco (partly for its phosphate reserves), and the activities of Islamist extremists. After pro-democracy protests in 2011, a new constitution was introduced, granting the prime minister more power. A moderate Islamist party won a majority in parliamentary elections in 2011 and 2017.

Morocco is classified as a "lower-middle-income" developing country. It is the world's third largest producer of phosphate rock, which is used to make fertilizer. Farming employs about 45% of Moroccans. Chief crops include barley, beans, citrus fruits, maize, olives, sugar beet, and wheat. Processed phosphates are exported, but most of Morocco's manufactures are for home consumption. Fishing and tourism are also important.

AREA 172,413 sq mi [446,550 sq km] **POPULATION** 34,314,000
CAPITAL Rabat **GOVERNMENT** Constitutional monarchy
ETHNIC GROUPS Arab-Berber 99% **LANGUAGES** Arabic (official), Berber dialects, French **RELIGIONS** Islam 99%
CURRENCY Moroccan dirham = 100 santeem

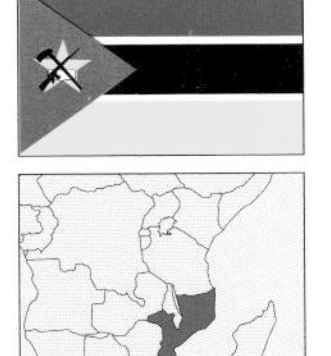

MOZAMBIQUE

GEOGRAPHY The Republic of Mozambique borders the Indian Ocean in southeastern Africa. The coastal plains are narrow in the north but broaden in the south. Inland lie plateaux and hills, which make up another two-fifths of the country. Mozambique has a mostly tropical climate. The capital Maputo, which lies outside the tropics, has hot and humid summers, though the winters are mild and fairly dry.

POLITICS & ECONOMY In 1885, when the European powers divided Africa, Mozambique was recognized as a Portuguese colony. But black African opposition to European rule gradually increased. In 1961, the Front for the Liberation of Mozambique (FRELIMO) was founded to oppose Portuguese rule. In 1964, FRELIMO launched a guerrilla war, which continued for ten years, until Mozambique became independent in 1975.

After independence, Mozambique became a one-party state. Its government aided African nationalists in Rhodesia (now Zimbabwe) and South Africa. But the white governments of these countries helped an opposition group, the Mozambique National Resistance Movement (RENAMO), to lead an armed struggle against Mozambique's government. Civil war, combined with droughts, caused much suffering in the 1980s. In 1989, FRELIMO ended one-party rule and multiparty elections were held in 1994. In 1995 Mozambique became the 53rd member of the Commonwealth. In January 2015, Filipe Nyusi became the country's 4th president.

In the early 1990s, the UN rated Mozambique as one of the world's poorest countries, but from the second half of the 1990s there has been economic growth, although hampered by cycles of drought and flood, most recently the hugely destructive Cyclone Idai in 2019. About 80% of the people are poor farmers. Mozambique is becoming a major exporter of coal and gas.

AREA 309,494 sq mi [801,590 sq km] **POPULATION** 27,234,000
CAPITAL Maputo **GOVERNMENT** Multiparty republic
ETHNIC GROUPS Indigenous tribal groups (Shangaan, Chokwe, Manyika, Sena, Makua, others) 99% **LANGUAGES** Portuguese (official), many others **RELIGIONS** Roman Catholic 28%, Protestant 28%, Islam 18% **CURRENCY** Metical = 100 centavos

MYANMAR (BURMA)

GEOGRAPHY The Union of Burma has been officially known as the Union of Myanmar since 1989. Mountains border the country in the east and west, with the highest mountains in the north. Myanmar's highest mountain is Hkakabo Razi, which is 19,294 ft [5,881 m] high. Between these ranges are the fertile valleys of the Irrawaddy and Sittang rivers. The Irrawaddy delta is a leading rice-growing area.

Myanmar has a tropical monsoon climate with three seasons. The rainy season runs from late May to mid-October. A cool, dry season follows, between late October and the middle part of February. The hot season lasts from late February to mid-May. In May 2008, cyclone Nargis devastated the south, including the Irrawaddy delta, killing more than 80,000 people.

POLITICS & ECONOMY The ancestors of the country's main ethnic group today, the Burmese, arrived in the 9th century AD. They encroached on areas occupied since ancient times by a variety of indigenous tribes. Britain conquered Burma in the 19th century making it a province of British India until, in 1937, they granted Burma limited self-government. Japan then invaded and occupied Burma from 1942 until the end of World War II in 1945. Burma became a fully independent country in 1948.

Revolts by Communists and various hill people led to instability in the 1950s. In 1962, Burma became a military dictatorship and, in 1974, a one-party state. The National League for Democracy led by Aung San Suu Kyi won the elections in 1990, but the military continued their repressive rule by ignoring the results.

In 2010, Aung San Suu Kyi was released from house arrest. A military-backed party was victorious in elections in 2010, and in 2011 a civilian government, backed by the military, took power. In 2012, Aung San Suu Kyi won a parliamentary seat, while her party, the National League for Democracy (NLD), won 43 of the 44 contested seats. The general elections held in 2015 were a victory for the NLD, although constitutional rules have barred Aung San Suu Kyi from becoming president. Violent confrontations have continued between the Buddhist majority and minority ethnic groups, notably the Muslim Rohingya, more than a million of whom have fled to Bangladesh to escape a military crackdown that the UN has termed ethnic cleansing.

Agriculture is the main activity, employing 70% of the people. The chief crop is rice with maize, pulses, oilseeds, and sugarcane also important. Myanmar's chief exports are natural gas, wood products and rice. Myanmar has many mineral resources including oil and gas. Tourism is set to become increasingly important.

AREA 261,227 sq mi [676,578 sq km] **POPULATION** 55,623,000
CAPITAL Rangoon (Yangon); Naypyidaw (administrative capital)
GOVERNMENT Multiparty Republic **ETHNIC GROUPS** Burman 68%, Shan 9%, Karen 7%, Rakhine 4%, Chinese, Indian, Mon
LANGUAGES Burmese (official); minority ethnic groups have their own languages **RELIGIONS** Buddhism 89%, Christianity, Islam
CURRENCY Kyat = 100 pyas

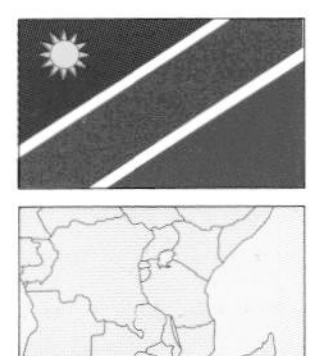

NAMIBIA

GEOGRAPHY When it was ruled by South Africa, the Republic of Namibia was known as South West Africa. The coastal region contains the arid Namib Desert, which is virtually uninhabited. Inland is a central plateau, bordered by a rugged spine of mountains stretching north–south. Eastern Namibia contains part of the Kalahari, a semi-desert area extending into Botswana. Namibia has a warm and arid climate. Windhoek has an average annual rainfall of 15 inches [370 mm], which often occurs in thunderstorms during the hot summer.

POLITICS & ECONOMY During World War I, South African troops defeated the Germans who ruled what is now Namibia. After World War II, many people challenged South Africa's right to govern the territory, and a civil war began in the 1960s between African guerrillas and South African troops. A ceasefire was agreed in 1989 and Namibia became independent in 1990. In the 1990s, the government pursued a policy of "national reconciliation." An enclave on the coast, Walvis Bay (Walvisbaai), remained part of South Africa until 1994, when it was transferred to Namibia. In 2004, the nationalist leader, Sam Nujoma, president since 1990, retired. He was succeeded by Hifikepunye Pohamba, who in turn was followed by Hage Geingob after elections in 2014.

Namibia has reserves of diamonds, uranium, zinc, and copper. Agriculture employs 16% of the people and much is at subsistence level. Fishing is important. Namibia has few industries and unemployment is high at around 34%. Potential offshore oil reserves are being explored. Tourism is expanding.

AREA 318,259 sq mi [824,292 sq km] **POPULATION** 2,533,000
CAPITAL Windhoek **GOVERNMENT** Multiparty republic
ETHNIC GROUPS Ovambo 50%, Kavango 9%, Herero 7%, Damara 7%, White 6%, Nama 5%
LANGUAGES English (official), Afrikaans, German, indigenous dialects
RELIGIONS Christianity 90% (Lutheran 51%)
CURRENCY Namibian dollar = 100 cents

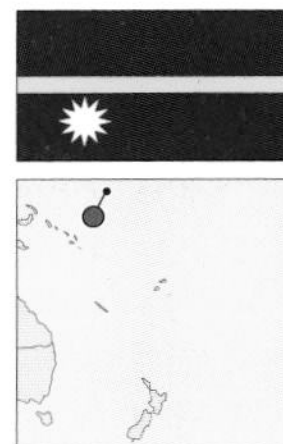

NAURU

Nauru is the world's smallest republic, located in the western Pacific Ocean. Independent since 1968, Nauru's prosperity is based on phosphate mining. Since 2013, Australia has detained asylum-seekers on the island.

AREA 8 sq mi [21 sq km]
POPULATION 10,000 **CAPITAL** Yaren

NEPAL

GEOGRAPHY Over three-quarters of Nepal lies in the Himalayan region, culminating in the world's highest peak (Mount Everest, or Chomolongma in Nepali) at 29,035 ft [8,850 m]. As a result, climatic conditions vary widely according to the altitude.

POLITICS & ECONOMY Nepal was united in the late 18th century, although it remains a diverse patchwork of peoples. From the mid-19th century to 1951, power was held by the royal Rana family. The first democratic elections in 32 years were held in 1991, but, by the early 21st century, Nepal faced many problems, including an uprising of Maoist guerrillas. In 2005, King Gyanendra seized power but failed to stop the conflict. In 2006, the Maoists joined a provisional coalition government. In elections in April 2008, the Maoists became the largest single party. In May, Nepal became a republic after the abolition of the monarchy. A new constitution was adopted in 2015. Parliamentary elections in 2017 were won by a coalition of Communist and Maoist parties, and Khadga Prasad Sharma Oli became prime minister in 2018.

Agriculture is the main activity and poverty is rife in this overwhelmingly rural country. Nepal is heavily dependent on aid and remittances sent from abroad. Tourism is growing in importance. There are also ambitious plans to exploit the hydroelectric potential offered by the ferocious Himalayan rivers.

AREA 56,827 sq mi [147,181 sq km] **POPULATION** 29,718,000
CAPITAL Katmandu **GOVERNMENT** Multiparty republic
ETHNIC GROUPS Brahman, Chhetri, Newar, Gurung, Magar, Tamang, Sherpa, and others
LANGUAGES Nepali (official), local languages
RELIGIONS Hinduism 81%, Buddhism 11%, Islam 4%
CURRENCY Nepalese rupee = 100 paisa

NETHERLANDS

GEOGRAPHY The Netherlands lies at the western end of the North European Plain, which extends to the Ural Mountains in Russia. Except for the far southeastern corner, the Netherlands is flat and about 40% lies below sea level at high tide. To prevent flooding, the Dutch have built dykes (sea walls) to hold back the waves. Large areas which were once under the sea, but which have been reclaimed, are known as polders. Because of its position on the North Sea, the Netherlands has a temperate climate, with mild, rainy winters.

POLITICS & ECONOMY Before the 16th century, the area that is now the Netherlands was under a succession of foreign rulers; including the Romans, the Germanic Franks, the French, and the Spanish. The Dutch declared their independence from Spain in 1581 and their status was finally recognized by Spain in 1648. In the 17th century, the Dutch built up a great overseas empire, especially in Southeast Asia. But in the early 18th century, the Dutch lost control of the seas to England.

France controlled the Netherlands from 1795 to 1813. In 1815, the Netherlands, then containing Belgium and Luxembourg, became an independent kingdom. Belgium broke away in 1830 and Luxembourg followed in 1890.

The Netherlands was neutral in World War I (1914–18), but was occupied by Germany in World War II (1939–45). After the war, the Netherlands Indies became independent as Indonesia. The Netherlands became active in West European affairs and, with Belgium and Luxembourg, it formed the customs union of Benelux in 1948. In 1949, it joined NATO (the North Atlantic Treaty Organization), and the European Coal and Steel Community (ECSC) in 1953. In 1957, it became a founder member of the European Economic Community (now the European Union), and, in 2002, it adopted the euro as its sole unit of currency. After a series of short-lived governments, Mark Rutte's VVD has led a stable coalition since 2012, and remained the largest party after elections in 2017. The right-wing Freedom Party did not make the expected gains. In 2013, after a 33-year reign, Queen Beatrix abdicated in favor of her son, Prince Willem Alexander.

2010 saw the dissolution of the Netherlands Antilles, an island territory in the Caribbean. Curaçao and St Maarten became nations in the Kingdom of the Netherlands. The small islands of Bonaire, St Eustatius, and Saba became special municipalities.

The Netherlands is a highly industrialized country, and industry and commerce are the most valuable activities. Its resources include natural gas, some oil, salt, and china clay. But the Netherlands imports many of the materials needed by its industries and it is, therefore, a major trading country. Industrial products are wide-ranging, including aircraft, chemicals, electronic equipment, machinery, textiles, and vehicles. Farming is scientific and yields are high. Dairy farming is the leading farming activity. Major products include barley, flowers and bulbs, potatoes, sugar beet, and wheat.

AREA 16,033 sq mi [41,526 sq km] **POPULATION** 17,151,000
CAPITAL Amsterdam; The Hague (seat of government)
GOVERNMENT Constitutional monarchy
ETHNIC GROUPS Dutch 81%, Indonesian, Turkish, Moroccan, and others **LANGUAGES** Dutch and Frisian (both official)
RELIGIONS Roman Catholic 30%, Protestant 20%, Islam 6%, others
CURRENCY Euro = 100 cents

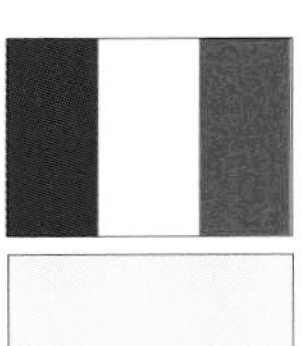

NEW CALEDONIA

New Caledonia is the most southerly of the Melanesian countries in the Pacific. It has been a French possession since 1853 and an Overseas Territory since 1958. In a referendum in 2018 the population voted against becoming independent. The country is rich in mineral resources, especially nickel.

AREA 7,172 sq mi [18,575 sq km] **POPULATION** 283,000 **CAPITAL** Nouméa

NEW ZEALAND

GEOGRAPHY New Zealand lies about 994 mi [1,600 km] southeast of Australia. It consists of two main islands and several other small ones. Much of North Island is volcanic. Active volcanoes include Ngauruhoe and Ruapehu. Hot springs and geysers are common, and steam from the ground is used to produce electricity. The Southern Alps, which contain the country's highest peak, Aoraki Mount Cook, at 12,217 ft [3,724 m], form the backbone of South Island. This island also has some large, fertile plains.

New Zealand lies on the geologically active "Pacific ring of fire." Most of the 14,000 earthquakes that occur every year have a magnitude of less than 5.0. But, in 2010 and 2011, two earthquakes, with magnitudes of 7.0 and 6.3 respectively, struck Christchurch on South Island, causing great damage. The 2011 earthquake resulted in a death toll of more than 180.

Auckland in the north has a warm, humid climate throughout the year. Wellington has cooler summers, while in Dunedin, in the southeast, temperatures sometimes dip below freezing in winter. The rainfall is heaviest on the western highlands.

POLITICS & ECONOMY Evidence suggests that early Maori settlers arrived in New Zealand more than 1,000 years ago. The Dutch navigator Abel Tasman reached New Zealand in 1642, but his discovery was not followed up. In 1769, the British Captain James Cook rediscovered the islands. During the early 19th century, British settlers arrived and, in 1840, under the Treaty of Waitangi, Britain took possession of the islands. From the 1870s, the Maoris were slowly integrated into colonial society.

In 1907, New Zealand became a self-governing dominion in the British Commonwealth. The country's economy developed quickly and the people became increasingly prosperous. However, after Britain joined the European Economic Community in 1973, New Zealand's exports to Britain shrank and the country had to reassess its economic and defense strategies and seek new markets. The world recession led the government to cut back on welfare spending in the 1990s. The preservation of Maori culture and rights are major issues as the Maoris, a Polynesian people, make up about 15% of the population. Other mainly Polynesian Pacific people make up another 7%. Ties with Britain have been reduced. In November 2008, the center-right National Party defeated the Labor Party in elections. John Key was Prime Minister from 2008–16, when he resigned and was replaced by the socially conservative Bill English. Elections in 2017 resulted in a coalition between Jacinda Adern's National Party, the Greens and New Zealand First. In 2019 the country was shocked by an anti-Islamic terrorist attack in Christchurch.

The economy once depended on agriculture, but manufacturing now employs twice as many people as farming. Meat and dairy products are leading commodities. Sheep rearing has declined as the area under cattle, deer, and vines has expanded. In 2008–9, New Zealand's economy entered a period of recession. The economy is now growing but is still fragile.

AREA 104,453 sq mi [270,534 sq km] **POPULATION** 4,546,000
CAPITAL Wellington **GOVERNMENT** Constitutional monarchy
ETHNIC GROUPS European 68%, Maori 15%, Asian 9%, Polynesian 7%
LANGUAGES English and Maori (both official)
RELIGIONS Anglican 24%, Presbyterian 18%, Roman Catholic 15%, others **CURRENCY** New Zealand dollar = 100 cents

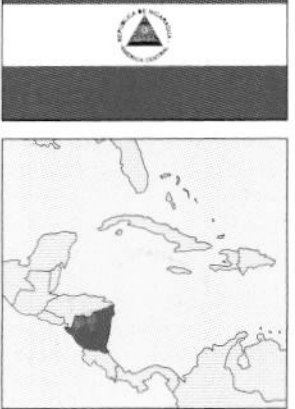

NICARAGUA

GEOGRAPHY The Republic of Nicaragua is a large country in Central America. In the east is a broad plain bordering the Caribbean Sea. The plain is drained by rivers that flow from the Central Highlands. The fertile western Pacific region contains about 40 volcanoes, many of which are active, and earthquakes are common.

Nicaragua has a tropical climate. Managua is hot throughout the year and there is a marked rainy season from May to October. In October 1998, Hurricane Mitch caused great devastation in Nicaragua. The Central Highlands and Caribbean region are cooler and wetter. The wettest region is the humid Caribbean plain.

POLITICS & ECONOMY In 1502, Christopher Columbus claimed the area for Spain, which ruled Nicaragua until 1821. By the early 20th century, the United States had considerable influence in the country and, in 1912, US forces entered Nicaragua. From 1927 to 1933, rebels under General Augusto César Sandino tried to drive US forces out of the country. In 1933, US marines set up a Nicaraguan army, the National Guard, to help to defeat the rebels. Its leader, Anastasio Somoza Garcia, had Sandino murdered in 1934, and from 1937 Somoza ruled as a dictator.

In the mid-1970s, many people began to protest against Somoza's rule and joined a guerrilla force, called the Sandinista National Liberation Front, named after General Sandino. The rebels defeated the Somoza regime in 1979. In the 1980s, US-supported forces, called the "Contras," launched a campaign against the Sandinista government. The US government opposed the Sandinista regime, under Daniel José Ortega Saavedra, claiming that it was a Communist dictatorship. A coalition, the National Opposition Union, defeated the Sandinistas in 1990. In 2001, the Sandinista candidate, Ortega, was defeated in presidential elections, but he was re-elected in 2006, 2011, and 2016. In 2018 he backed down from proposed reforms to the social security system after widespread and violent protests.

In the early 1990s, Nicaragua faced many problems in rebuilding its shattered economy. Agriculture employs about 28% of the people with coffee, cotton, sugar and bananas being grown for export, while rice is the main food crop. Attempts are being made to develop the tourist industry.

AREA 50,193 sq mi [130,000 sq km] **POPULATION** 6,085,000
CAPITAL Managua **GOVERNMENT** Multiparty republic
ETHNIC GROUPS Mestizo 69%, White 17%, Black 9%, Amerindian 5%
LANGUAGES Spanish (official)
RELIGIONS Roman Catholic 59%, Protestant 23%, others
CURRENCY Nicaraguan córdoba = 100 centavos

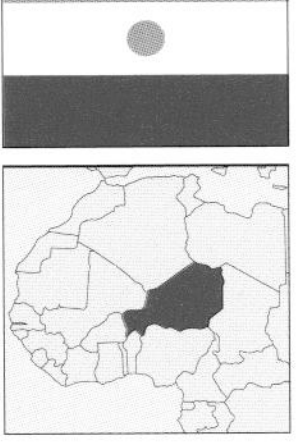

NIGER

GEOGRAPHY The Republic of Niger is a landlocked nation in north-central Africa. The northern plateaux lie in the desert area of the Sahara, while central Niger contains the rugged Aïr Mountains. The most fertile, densely populated region is the Niger valley.

Niger has a tropical climate and the south has a rainy season between June and September. The north is practically rainless.

POLITICS & ECONOMY Since independence in 1960, Niger, a French territory from 1900, has suffered severe droughts. Food shortages and the collapse of the traditional nomadic way of life of some of Niger's people have caused political instability. After a period of military rule, a multiparty constitution was adopted in 1992, but the military again seized power in 1996. Later that year, the coup leader, Colonel Ibrahim Barre Mainassara, was elected president. He was assassinated in 1999, but parliamentary rule was restored. After a coup in 2010, Mahamadou Issoufou was elected president in 2011. He gained a second term in a largely uncontested election in 2016. Islamist militants are an increasing problem.

Niger's chief resource is uranium and the country is one of the world's largest producers. The export of minerals accounts for 40% of total exports although there is much more to be exploited. Despite its considerable resources, Niger remains one of the world's poorest countries. Only 3% of the land can be used for growing crops but agriculture supports around 90% of the people.

AREA 489,189 sq mi [1,267,000 sq km] **POPULATION** 19,866,000
CAPITAL Niamey **GOVERNMENT** Multiparty republic
ETHNIC GROUPS Hausa 55%, Djerma 21%, Tuareg 9%, Fula 8%, others **LANGUAGES** French (official), Hausa, Djerma
RELIGIONS Islam 80%, indigenous beliefs, Christianity
CURRENCY CFA franc = 100 centimes

NIGERIA

GEOGRAPHY The Federal Republic of Nigeria is the most populous nation in Africa. The country's main rivers are the Niger and Benue, which meet in central Nigeria. North of the two river valleys are high plains and plateaux. The Lake Chad basin is in the northeast, with the Sokoto plains in the northwest. The south contains hilly uplands and plains. The south has a hot, rainy climate. The north is drier and often hotter than the south.

POLITICS & ECONOMY Nigeria has a long artistic tradition. Major cultures include the Nok (500 BC to AD 200), the Ife, a major Yoruba culture which developed about 1,000 years ago, and the Benin (15th to 17th centuries). Britain gradually extended its influence over the area in the second half of the 19th century.

Nigeria became an independent nation in 1960 and a federal republic in 1963. A federal constitution dividing the country into regions was necessary because Nigeria contains more than 250 ethnic and linguistic groups, as well as several religious ones. Local rivalries have long been a threat to national unity, and six new states were created in 1996 in an attempt to overcome this. Civil war occurred between 1967 and 1970, when the people of the southeast attempted unsuccessfully to secede during the Biafran War. Between 1960 and 1998, Nigeria had only nine years of civilian government.

In 1998–9, civilian rule was restored but Nigeria faced many problems, including violence in the Niger delta region and religious conflict. From 2009 onwards, northern Nigeria has been hit by violent attacks from the Islamist organization, Boko Haram. 2015 saw the first ever democratic change of power in Nigeria when Muhammadu Buhari was elected president.

Nigeria is a developing country with great potential although most of the population currently live in poverty. Its chief natural resource is oil, which accounts for most of its exports. Agriculture employs 70% of the people and the country is a major producer of cocoa, palm oil and palm kernels, groundnuts (peanuts), and rubber. Industry is increasing and manufactures include cement, chemicals, fertilizers, textiles, and timber.

AREA 356,667 sq mi [923,768 sq km] **POPULATION** 203,453,000
CAPITAL Abuja **GOVERNMENT** Federal multiparty republic
ETHNIC GROUPS Hausa and Fulani 29%, Yoruba 21%, Ibo (or Igbo) 18%, Ijaw 10%, Kanuri 4%, many others
LANGUAGES English (official), Hausa, Yoruba, Ibo
RELIGIONS Islam 50%, Christianity 40%, traditional beliefs 10%
CURRENCY Naira = 100 kobo

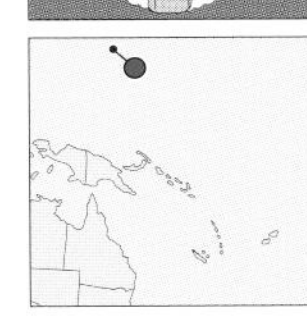

NORTHERN MARIANA ISLANDS

The Commonwealth of the Northern Mariana Islands contains 16 mountainous islands north of Guam in the western Pacific Ocean. In a 1975 plebiscite, the islanders voted for Commonwealth status in union with the United States, and in 1986 they were granted US citizenship.

AREA 179 sq mi [464 sq km] **POPULATION** 52,000 **CAPITAL** Saipan

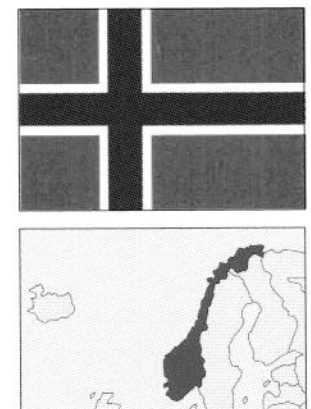

NORWAY

GEOGRAPHY The Kingdom of Norway forms the western part of the rugged Scandinavian peninsula. The deep inlets along the highly indented coastline were gouged out by glaciers during the Ice Age. The warm North Atlantic Drift off the coast of Norway moderates the climate, with mild winters and cool summers. Nearly all the ports are ice-free throughout the year. Inland, winters are colder and snow cover lasts for at least three months a year.

POLITICS & ECONOMY Norway was united with Denmark for over 400 years from the 14th century until 1814 when Denmark handed Norway over to Sweden. Denmark retained control of Norway's colonies – Greenland, Iceland and the Færoe Islands. The union with Sweden ended in 1903 and Norway became independent. Although Germany occupied Norway during World War II (1939–45), the country recovered quickly afterward and it now has one of the world's highest standards of living. In 1960, Norway and six other countries formed the European Free Trade Association (EFTA), but, in 1994, it voted against joining the European Union. In 2013, a center-right coalition government was elected with Erna Solberg as prime minister. She was returned to power in 2017.

Norway's chief resources and exports are offshore oil and natural gas, which are exploited via tightly regulated companies. To guard against the future decline of oil and gas production, a large sovereign wealth fund has been built up. Farmland covers only 3% of the land. Dairy farming, meat production, and fishing are important, but Norway has to import food. Norway has many industries powered by cheap hydroelectricity.

AREA 125,049 sq mi [323,877 sq km] **POPULATION** 5,372,000
CAPITAL Oslo **GOVERNMENT** Constitutional monarchy
ETHNIC GROUPS Norwegian 94% **LANGUAGES** Norwegian (official)
RELIGIONS Evangelical Lutheran 86%
CURRENCY Norwegian krone = 100 øre

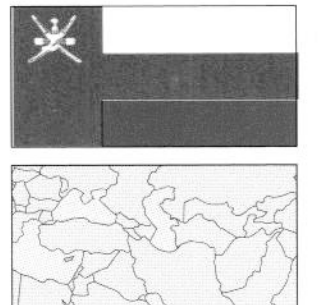

OMAN

GEOGRAPHY The Sultanate of Oman occupies the southeastern corner of the Arabian peninsula. It also includes the tip of the Musandam peninsula, overlooking the strategic Strait of Hormuz. Oman has a hot tropical climate. In Muscat, temperatures may reach 117°F [47°C] in the summer months.

POLITICS & ECONOMY Although strongly influenced by Britain since the end of the 18th century, Oman never became a colony. Since 1970 when Qaboos ibn Said, the absolute ruler, overthrew his father in a bloodless coup, Oman has followed a path of modernization. In 2000, Oman held elections to its consultative parliament and, in 2004, the Sultan appointed Oman's first woman minister. In 2011, following anti-government demonstrations, Sultan Qaboos promised more reforms.

Oil and natural gas make up about 80% of Oman's exports; reserves are declining, and Oman is actively seeking to diversify its economy. Agriculture and fishing remain important. Crops include alfalfa, bananas, coconuts, dates, limes, tobacco, vegetables, and wheat, but Oman still has to import food. The tourist industry has grown rapidly in recent years.

AREA 119,498 sq mi [309,500 sq km] **POPULATION** 4,613,000
CAPITAL Muscat **GOVERNMENT** Monarchy with consultative council
ETHNIC GROUPS Arab, Baluchi, Indian, Pakistani
LANGUAGES Arabic (official), Baluchi, English **RELIGIONS** Islam (mainly Ibadhi), Christian 5%, Hinduism 5% **CURRENCY** Omani rial = 1,000 baisa

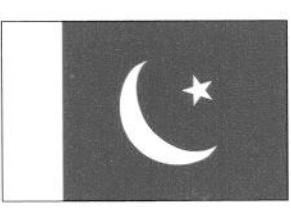

PAKISTAN

GEOGRAPHY The Islamic Republic of Pakistan contains high mountains, fertile plains, and rocky deserts. The Karakoram range, which contains K2, the world's second highest peak, lies in the northern part of Jammu and Kashmir, which is occupied by Pakistan but claimed by India. Other mountains rise in the west. Plains, drained by the River Indus and its tributaries, occupy much of eastern Pakistan. Arid areas include the Thar Desert and the Baluchistan plateau. Most of Pakistan has hot summers and mild winters, though the mountains are cold in winter. The rainfall is generally sparse.

POLITICS & ECONOMY Pakistan was the site of the Indus Valley civilization which developed about 4,500 years ago. However, Pakistan's modern history dates from 1947, when British India was divided into India and Pakistan. Muslim Pakistan was divided into two parts: East and West Pakistan, but East Pakistan broke away in 1971 to become Bangladesh. In 1948–9, 1965, and 1971, Pakistan and India clashed over Kashmir. In 1998, Pakistan responded in kind to India's nuclear weapons tests, but, in 2003–7, Pakistan and India launched a series of initiatives aimed at achieving peace.

Pakistan has been subject to alternating periods of military and civilian rule: the latter often characterized by inefficiency and corruption. The country's leaders have experienced turbulent times: Benazir Bhutto (daughter of the hanged prime minister, Zulfiqar Ali Bhutto) was twice dismissed as prime minister on charges of corruption in 1990 and 1996, and subsequently assassinated during an election campaign in 2007. Nawaz Sharif, prime minister from 2013 to 2017, resigned after corruption charges, and in 2018 former international cricketer Imran Khan became prime minister.

Both government and military struggle to control the Afghan border region where Taliban-linked extremists are active. Terrorist activity emanating from this region has hit targets elsewhere in the country. The Christian minority has also been targeted.

Lack of political stability has hindered economic development and discouraged foreign investment. The economy is agrarian, employing nearly half the population. Textiles are the main export and remittances from overseas workers are crucial.

AREA 307,372 sq mi [796,095 sq km] **POPULATION** 207,863,000
CAPITAL Islamabad **GOVERNMENT** Federal republic **ETHNIC GROUPS** Punjabi, Sindhi, Pashtun (Pathan), Baluchi, Muhajir
LANGUAGES English and Urdu (both official), many others
RELIGIONS Islam 97%, Christianity, Hinduism
CURRENCY Pakistani rupee = 100 paisa

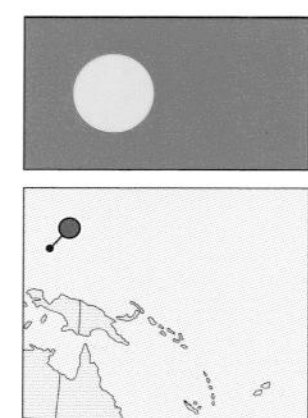

PALAU

The Republic of Palau became independent in 1994, after 47 years as a US-administered UN Trust Territory. The economy relies heavily on aid from the USA and Taiwan, tourism, fishing, and subsistence agriculture. The main crops include cassava, coconuts, and copra. Palau's low-lying islands are vulnerable to rising sea levels.

AREA 177 sq mi [459 sq km] **POPULATION** 22,000 **CAPITAL** Melekeok

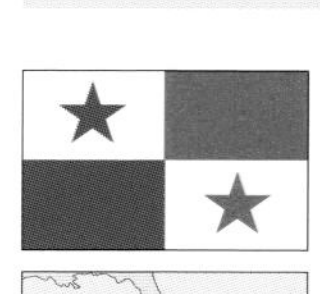

PANAMA

GEOGRAPHY The Republic of Panama forms an isthmus linking Central America to South America. The Panama Canal, which is 50.7 mi [81.6 km] long, cuts across the isthmus. It has made the country a major transport hub.

Panama has a tropical climate. Temperatures are high, though the mountains are much cooler than the coastal plains. The main rainy season is between May and December.

POLITICS & ECONOMY Christopher Columbus landed in Panama in 1502 and Spain soon took the area. In 1821, Panama became independent from Spain and a province of Colombia.

In 1903, Colombia refused a request by the United States to build a canal. Panama revolted against Colombian rule, and became an independent state. The United States then began to build the canal, which was opened in 1914. The United States administered the Panama Canal Zone, a strip of land along the canal. But many Panamanians resented US influence and, in 1979, the Canal Zone was returned to Panama. Control of the canal itself was handed over by the USA to Panama on December 31, 1999.

Panama's government has changed many times since independence, and there have been periods of military dictatorships, including that of General Manuel Antonio Noriega in the 1980s. He was finally convicted of drug offences in the United States in 1992. In May 2014, Juan Carlos Varela of the Panameñista party was elected president. In 2011, the US Congress approved a long-stalled free-trade agreement with Panama.

The Panama Canal is an important source of revenue and, since 2016, new locks and channels have increased capacity and the size of ships that can be accommodated. Away from the canal, the main activity is agriculture, which employs 17% of the work force. The service industry accounts for nearly 80% of GDP.

AREA 29,157 sq mi [75,517 sq km] **POPULATION** 3,801,000
CAPITAL Panamá City **GOVERNMENT** Multiparty republic
ETHNIC GROUPS Mestizo 70%, Black and Mixed 14%, White 10%, Amerindian 6% **LANGUAGES** Spanish (official), English
RELIGIONS Roman Catholic 85%, Protestant 15%
CURRENCY US dollar; Balboa = 100 centésimos

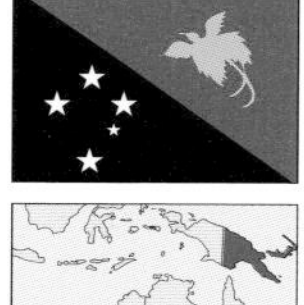

PAPUA NEW GUINEA

GEOGRAPHY Papua New Guinea is an independent country in the Pacific Ocean, north of Australia. Papua New Guinea includes the eastern part of New Guinea, the Bismarck Archipelago, the northern Solomon Islands, the D'Entrecasteaux Islands, and the Louisiade Archipelago. The land is largely mountainous.

Papua New Guinea has a tropical climate, with high temperatures. Most of the rain occurs during the monsoon season (December–April). In the dry season, winds blow from the southeast.

POLITICS & ECONOMY The Dutch colonized western New Guinea (now part of Indonesia) in 1828, but it was not until 1884 that Germany appropriated northeastern New Guinea and Britain took the southeast. In 1906, Britain handed the southeast over to Australia when it became known as the Territory of Papua. When World War I broke out in 1914, Australia took German New Guinea, and in 1921 the League of Nations gave Australia a mandate to rule the area, which was named the Territory of New Guinea. In 1949, Papua and New Guinea were combined as one entity, becoming fully independent in 1975.

In the 1990s there was a secessionist revolt on the island of Bougainville, lying at the eastern end of the territory. A peace agreement signed in 2001 granted a degree of autonomy, and paved the way for a referendum on independence, which has been scheduled for late 2019.

There was political turmoil in 2011–12, when Prime Minister Michael Somare was replaced by Peter O'Neill, who was formally elected prime minister in August 2012. He was re-elected in 2017.

Agriculture employs 85% of the people, mostly at subsistence level. Mining is important with copper a major export. There are large reserves of natural gas and the development of production facilities to convert this to liquefied form for export could have a profound effect on the economy.

AREA 178,703 sq mi [462,840 sq km] **POPULATION** 7,027,000
CAPITAL Port Moresby **GOVERNMENT** Constitutional monarchy
ETHNIC GROUPS Papuan, Melanesian, Micronesian
LANGUAGES English, Tok Pisin, Hiri Motu (all official); more than 800 indigenous languages **RELIGIONS** Traditional beliefs 34%, Roman Catholic 22%, Lutheran 16% **CURRENCY** Kina = 100 toea

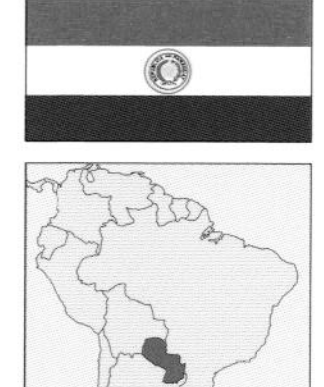

PARAGUAY

GEOGRAPHY The Republic of Paraguay is a landlocked country, and rivers, notably the Paraná, Pilcomayo (Brazo Sur), and Paraguay, form most of its borders. The flat region of the Gran Chaco lies in the northwest, while the southeast contains plains, hills and plateaux. Northern Paraguay lies in the tropics, while the south is subtropical. Most of the country has a warm, humid climate.

POLITICS & ECONOMY Paraguayans achieved independence in 1811 after being part of a wider Spanish colonial possession since 1776. For many years, Paraguay was torn by internal strife and conflict with its neighbors. A war against Brazil, Argentina, and Uruguay (1865–70) led to the deaths of more than half of Paraguay's population, and a great loss of territory.

General Alfredo Stroessner took power in 1954 and ruled as a dictator until he was overthrown in 1989 (he died in exile in Brazil in 2006). However, the return of democracy in the years that followed often seemed precarious, because of rivalries between politicians and army leaders, together with economic problems arising partly from the financial crises experienced in neighboring Argentina and Brazil in 1999. In 2008, a former Roman Catholic bishop, Fernando Lugo, who was regarded as a champion of the poor, was elected president, ending more than six decades of rule by the Colorado Party. They returned to power, however, in the 2013 presidential election, which was won by Horacio Cartes, and in 2017, with the election of Mario Abdo Benítez.

Agriculture and forestry, employing about a third of the population, are important. Paraguay produces hydroelectricity and exports power to its neighbors although it has few other natural resources. Paraguay remains a conduit for smuggling drugs.

AREA 157,047 sq mi [406,752 sq km] **POPULATION** 7,026,000
CAPITAL Asunción **GOVERNMENT** Multiparty republic
ETHNIC GROUPS Mestizo 95% **LANGUAGES** Spanish and Guaraní (both official) **RELIGIONS** Roman Catholic 90%, Protestant 6%
CURRENCY Guaraní = 100 céntimos

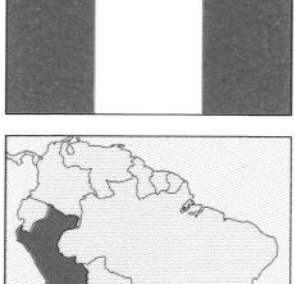

PERU

GEOGRAPHY The Republic of Peru lies in the tropics in western South America. A narrow coastal plain borders the Pacific Ocean in the west. Inland are ranges of the Andes Mountains, which rise to 22,205 ft [6,768 m] at Nevado Huascarán, an extinct volcano. East of the Andes lies the Amazon basin.

Lima, on the coastal plain, has an arid climate. The coastal region is chilled by the cold, offshore Humboldt Current. Rainfall increases inland and many mountains in the high Andes are snow-capped.

POLITICS & ECONOMY Spanish conquistadores conquered the Inca empire in Peru in the 1530s. In1820, an Argentinian, José de San Martín, led an army into Peru and declared it independent although Spain still held large areas. In 1823, the Venezuelan Simon Bolívar led another army into Peru which resulted in surrender by the Spanish in 1826. Peru suffered much instability throughout the 19th century.

Political turmoil continued in the 20th century. In 1980, when civilian rule was restored, a left-wing group called the Sendero Luminoso, or the "Shining Path," instigated guerrilla warfare against the government. From 1990 to 2000 Alberto Fujimori was president. His increasingly authoritarian rule saw, in 1992, the suspension of the constitution and dismissal of the legislature. Fujimori left Peru in 2000, but was later extradited, and in 2009 he was found guilty of ordering killings and kidnappings and was sentenced to 25 years in jail. President Padro Pablo Kuczynski resigned over allegations of corruption in 2018 and was replaced by Vice-President Martin Vizcarra.

Peru's economy benefits from a wide range of mineral resources: lead, silver, zinc, and iron ore, with copper being the most valuable export. Fish products are exported. Although recent economic growth has been strong, lack of basic infrastructure prevents the spread of prosperity away from the coastal areas.

AREA 496,222 sq mi [1,285,216 sq km] **POPULATION** 31,331,000
CAPITAL Lima **GOVERNMENT** Constitutional republic
ETHNIC GROUPS Amerindian 45%, Mestizo 37%, White 15%
LANGUAGES Spanish and Quechua (both official), Aymara, other Amazonian languages **RELIGIONS** Roman Catholic 81%
CURRENCY Nuevo sol = 100 céntimos

PHILIPPINES

GEOGRAPHY The Republic of the Philippines is an island nation in southeastern Asia. It includes about 7,100 islands, of which 2,770 are named and about 1,000 are inhabited. Luzon and Mindanao, the two largest islands, make up more than two-thirds of the country. The land is mainly mountainous.

The country has a hot tropical climate. The dry season runs from December to April. The rest of the year is wet. Much of the rainfall comes from the typhoons which periodically strike the east coast with devastating effect. In November 2013, Typhoon Haiyan, one of the strongest typhoons ever recorded, resulted in the deaths of over 6,000 people.

POLITICS & ECONOMY The first European to reach the Philippines was the Portuguese navigator Ferdinand Magellan in 1521. Spanish explorers claimed the region in 1565 when they established a settlement on Cebu. The Spaniards ruled the country until 1898, when the United States took over at the end of the Spanish–American War. Japan invaded the Philippines in 1941, but US forces returned in 1944. The country became fully independent as the Republic of the Philippines in 1946.

Since independence, the country's problems have included armed uprisings by left-wing guerrillas demanding land reform, Muslim separatist groups, crime, corruption, and unemployment. The dominant figure in recent times was Ferdinand Marcos, who ruled in a dictatorial manner from 1965 to 1986. His most recent successor, elected in 2016, is the populist Rodrigo Duterte, whose harsh crackdown on drug dealers and users is popular domestically but has led internationally to accusations of human rights abuses. Fighting, killings and kidnappings continued throughout the 2000s, but an outline peace plan was signed in 2012 although not all rebel groups have committed to it. Islamic insurgency is a problem in the south.

The Philippines is a developing country and is recovering steadily from the 2008 global financial crisis. Agriculture employs around one-third of the population. The main foods are rice and maize, while bananas, cocoa, coffee, sugarcane, and tobacco are grown commercially. Shellfish and sea fishing are also important, while manufacturing plays an increasingly significant part in the economy. Remittances from overseas workers make a large contribution and attempts are being made to encourage foreign investment.

AREA 115,830 sq mi [300,000 sq km] **POPULATION** 105,893,000
CAPITAL Manila **GOVERNMENT** Multiparty republic
ETHNIC GROUPS Tagalog 28%, Cebuano 13%, Ilocano 9%, Bisaya 8%, and others **LANGUAGES** Filipino (Tagalog) and English (both official), and eight major dialects
RELIGIONS Roman Catholic 83%, Protestant 9%, Islam 5%
CURRENCY Philippine peso = 100 centavos

PITCAIRN

Pitcairn Island is a British overseas territory in the Pacific Ocean. Its inhabitants are descendants of the original settlers – nine mutineers from HMS Bounty and 18 Tahitians who arrived in 1790.

AREA 21 sq mi [55 sq km]
POPULATION 54 **CAPITAL** Adamstown

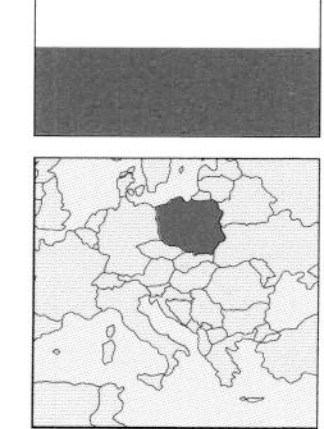

POLAND

GEOGRAPHY The Republic of Poland faces the Baltic Sea and behind its lagoon-fringed coast lies a broad plain. A plateau lies in the southeast, while the Sudeten Highlands straddle part of the border with Czechia. Part of the Carpathian Range (the Tatra) lies in the southeast.

Poland's climate is influenced by its position in Europe. Warm, moist air masses come from the west, while cold air masses come from the north and east. Summers are warm, but winters are cold and snowy.

POLITICS & ECONOMY Poland's boundaries have changed several times in the last 200 years, partly as a result of its geographical location between the powers of Germany and Russia. It disappeared from the map in the late 18th century, when the Polish state of the Grand Duchy of Warsaw was established. But in 1815, the country was partitioned between Austria, Prussia, and Russia. Poland became independent in 1918, but in 1939 it was divided between Germany and the Soviet Union. The country again became independent in 1945, when it lost land to Russia but gained some from Germany. Communists took power in 1948, but opposition mounted and eventually became focused through an organization called Solidarity.

A coalition government was formed between Solidarity and the Communists in 1989. In 1990, the Communist Party was dissolved and Lech Walesa, a trade unionist, became president. Facing many problems in developing a market economy, he was defeated in presidential elections in 1995. Poland joined NATO in 1999 and the European Union in 2004. Beata Maria Szydlo was elected prime minister in November 2015, but was replaced two years later by Mateusz Morawiecki. That year saw demonstrations over new laws that would have given the government power over the judiciary.

Poland's economy has grown strongly since the fall of Communism and especially since accession to the EU. It has large reserves of coal. Manufactures include chemicals, food, machinery, ships, steel, and textiles. Farming, although important, lacks investment and needs modernization.

AREA 124,807 SQ MI [323,250 SQ KM] **POPULATION** 38,421,000
CAPITAL WARSAW **GOVERNMENT** MULTIPARTY REPUBLIC
ETHNIC GROUPS POLISH 97%, GERMAN, BELARUSIAN, UKRAINIAN
LANGUAGES POLISH (OFFICIAL) **RELIGIONS** ROMAN CATHOLIC 90%, EASTERN ORTHODOX **CURRENCY** ZLOTY = 100 GROSZY

PORTUGAL

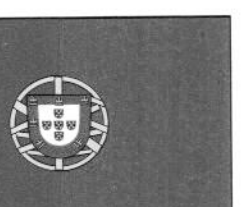

GEOGRAPHY The Republic of Portugal is the most westerly of Europe's mainland countries. The land rises from the coastal plains on the Atlantic Ocean to the western edge of the huge plateau, or Meseta, which occupies most of the Iberian peninsula. The climate is moderated by winds blowing from the Atlantic. Summers are cooler and winters are milder than in other Mediterranean lands. Portugal also contains two autonomous regions: the Azores and Madeira island groups.

POLITICS & ECONOMY Portugal became a separate country, independent of Spain, in 1143. In the 15th century, Portugal led the "Age of European Exploration" resulting in the growth of a large Portuguese empire. Portuguese power began to decline in the 16th century and, between 1580 and 1640, Portugal was ruled by Spain. In 1910 Portugal became a republic. Instability hampered progress and army officers seized power in 1926. In 1928, they chose Antonio de Salazar to be minister of finance.

Salazar became prime minister in 1932 and ruled as a dictator from 1933 until 1968. In 1974, army officers mounted a coup which led to free elections in 1978. Portugal joined the European Community (now the European Union) in 1986, and in 2002 joined the eurozone. In 2011–12, there was public unrest when the government introduced austerity measures in order to obtain an international financial bailout to help its weak economy. In 2014 Portugal was able to exit the international bailout, and from 2015 the center-left government has relaxed some of the measures.

Agriculture and fishing were the economic mainstays until the mid-20th century, when the economy started to diversify and manufacturing became the most valuable activity. Lagging behind the economies of other Western European countries, Portugal faces increasing competition from central Europe and Asia.

AREA 34,285 SQ MI [88,797 SQ KM] **POPULATION** 10,355,000
CAPITAL LISBON **GOVERNMENT** MULTIPARTY REPUBLIC
ETHNIC GROUPS PORTUGUESE 99% **LANGUAGES** PORTUGUESE (OFFICIAL)
RELIGIONS ROMAN CATHOLIC 85%, PROTESTANT
CURRENCY EURO = 100 CENTS

PUERTO RICO

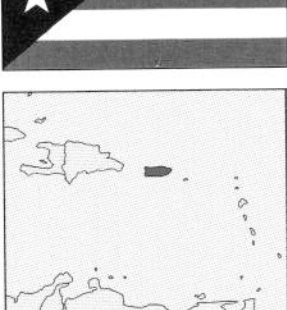

The Commonwealth of Puerto Rico, a mainly mountainous island, is the easternmost of the Greater Antilles chain. The climate is hot and wet. Puerto Rico is a dependent territory of the United States and the people are US citizens. 2017's non-binding referendum resulted in a vote to become a US state, but the turnout was only 23%. Puerto Rico is the most industrialized country in the Caribbean. Tax exemptions attract US companies to the island and manufacturing is expanding. The chief exports are chemicals, machinery, and food.

AREA 3,427 SQ MI [8,875 SQ KM]
POPULATION 3,295,000 **CAPITAL** SAN JUAN

QATAR

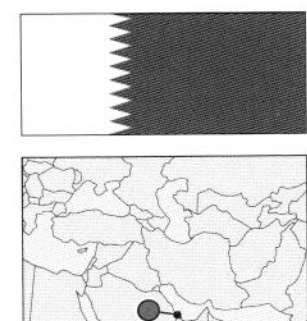

The prosperous State of Qatar occupies a low, barren peninsula on the Persian Gulf. A British protectorate from 1916, Qatar became independent in 1971. Oil, first discovered in 1939, is the mainstay of the economy. In 2017 Saudi Arabia, the UAE, Egypt, and Bahrain implemented a blockade on Qatar. In 2019 Qatar withdrew from OPEC.

AREA 4,247 SQ MI [11,000 SQ KM] **POPULATION** 2,364,000 **CAPITAL** DOHA

RÉUNION

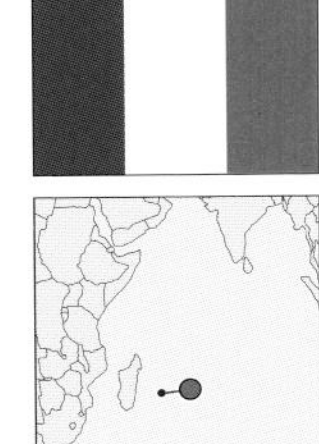

Réunion is a French overseas department in the Indian Ocean. The land is mainly mountainous, though the lowlands are intensely cultivated. Sugar and sugar products are the main exports, but French aid, given to the island in return for its use as a military base, is important to the economy.

AREA 969 SQ MI [2,510 SQ KM]
POPULATION 846,000 **CAPITAL** ST-DENIS

ROMANIA

GEOGRAPHY Romania is a country on the Black Sea in Eastern Europe. Eastern and southern Romania form part of the Danube river basin. The delta region, near the mouth of the Danube, where the river flows into the Black Sea, is one of Europe's finest wetlands. The southern part of the coast contains several resorts. At the heart of the country is the region of Transylvania, ringed in the east, south, and west by scenic mountains which are part of the Carpathian mountain system. Romania has hot summers and cold winters. Rainfall is heaviest in spring and early summer.

POLITICS & ECONOMY The entity that eventually coalesced into modern Romania was born out of the breakup of the Turkish empire in the late 18th century. In 1862 the regions of Wallachia and Moldavia were united under the new heading of Romania. After World War I (1914–18), Romania, which had fought on the side of the Allies, gained territory, including Transylvania, where most people were Romanians. This almost doubled the country's size and population. In 1939, Romania lost territory to Hungary, Bulgaria, and the Soviet Union. Occupied by Soviet troops in 1944, Romania regained northern Transylvania from Hungary in 1945. In 1947, Romania officially became a Communist country. It was ruled for decades by the dictator Ceausescu.

In 1990, Romania held its first free elections since the end of World War II. Initially the government was dominated by former Communists, led by Ion Iliescu, but there was a move toward the center-right at the elections in 1996. Iliescu again served as president from 2000 until 2004. Romania joined NATO in 2004 and the European Union in 2007. Klaus Iohannis of the center-right became president in December 2014.

Romania has an "upper-middle-income" economy but growth has been hindered by political instability, lack of reform, corruption, and the international financial crisis of 2008. Following the global downturn, the government was forced to implement austerity measures which led to civil unrest. Exports are increasing and include cars, industrial machinery, metals, textiles, and chemicals. Trade is mainly with other EU states especially Germany and Italy.

AREA 92,043 SQ MI [238,391 SQ KM] **POPULATION** 21,457,000
CAPITAL BUCHAREST **GOVERNMENT** MULTIPARTY REPUBLIC
ETHNIC GROUPS ROMANIAN 89%, HUNGARIAN 7%, ROMA 2%, UKRAINIAN **LANGUAGES** ROMANIAN (OFFICIAL), HUNGARIAN, ROMANY **RELIGIONS** EASTERN ORTHODOX 87%, PROTESTANT 7%, ROMAN CATHOLIC 5% **CURRENCY** LEU = 100 BANI

RUSSIA

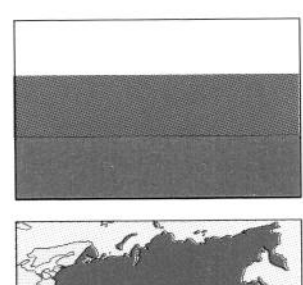

GEOGRAPHY Russia is the world's largest country. About 25% lies west of the Ural Mountains in European Russia, where 80% of the population lives. It is mostly flat or undulating, but the land rises to the Caucasus Mountains in the south, where Russia's highest peak, Elbrus, at 18,510 ft [5,642 m], is found. Asian Russia, or Siberia, contains vast plains and plateaux, with mountains in the east and south. The Kamchatka peninsula in the far east has many active volcanoes. Russia contains several of the world's longest rivers. It also includes part of the world's largest inland body of water, the Caspian Sea, and Lake Baikal, the world's deepest lake.

Moscow has a continental climate, with cold, snowy winters and hot summers. Siberia has a harsher, drier climate.

POLITICS & ECONOMY In the 9th century AD, a state called Kievan Rus was founded by people known as the East Slavs. Kiev, now capital of Ukraine, became a major trading center, but, in 1237, Mongol armies conquered Russia and destroyed Kiev. Russia was part of the Mongol empire until the late 15th century with Moscow becoming the most important Russian city.

In the 16th century, Moscow's grand prince was retitled "tsar," and the first one, Ivan the Terrible, expanded the Russian territory. In 1613, Michael Romanov became tsar, founding a dynasty which ruled until 1917. In the 18th century, Tsar Peter the Great began to westernize Russia and, by 1812, when Napoleon failed to conquer the country, Russia was a major European power. However, in the 19th century demands for reform were growing.

In World War I (1914–18), the Russian people suffered great hardships and, in 1917, Tsar Nicholas II was forced to abdicate. In November 1917, the Bolsheviks seized power under Vladimir Lenin and set up the Union of Soviet Socialist Republics (also called the USSR or the Soviet Union).

From 1924, Joseph Stalin introduced a socialist economic program, suppressing all opposition. In 1939, the Soviet Union and Germany signed a non-aggression pact, but Germany invaded the Soviet Union in 1941. Soviet forces pushed the Germans back, occupying Eastern Europe. They reached Berlin in May 1945. From the late 1940s, tension between the Soviet Union and its allies and Western nations developed into a "Cold War." This continued until 1991, when the Soviet Union was dissolved.

The Soviet Union collapsed due to the failure of its economic policies. From 1991, Boris Yeltsin, as president of the newly independent Russia, introduced democratic and economic reforms. Yeltsin retired in 1999 and, in 2000, was succeeded by Vladimir Putin. Putin, who was re-elected in 2004, sought to develop contacts with the West. Russia's size and diversity make national unity hard to achieve with secessionist movements instigating violent, sometimes fatal, incidents in Chechenia, Dagestan, Ingushetia, and Kabardino-Balkaria. From 2006, relations with the West appeared to deteriorate, with Russia criticizing the expansion of NATO in Eastern Europe.

In 2008, Putin, was replaced by Dmitry Medvedev, but was again re-elected in 2012 and 2018. In August 2008, Russia fought a short war against Georgia, which had attacked the secessionist region of South Ossetia. In early 2014, political unrest in Ukraine allowed pro-Russian forces to bring Crimea under Russian control. Further tensions with the West have arisen over Russia's support for the regime of Syria's President Assad and accusations that Russia interfered in the 2016 US presidential election.

Russia's economy was thrown into disarray after the collapse of the Soviet Union, but is now classified as an "upper-middle-income" economy. Russia was admitted to the Council of Europe in 1997 and was also invited to join the G7 group of industrialized countries in 1997.

The Russian economy is underpinned by a wealth of natural resources; in particular, natural gas and coal. Gazprom, the state-run gas corporation, is a major supplier to Europe. Reliance on exporting such commodities makes the economy vulnerable to fluctuations in global prices. Future prosperity needs economic reform and investment in infrastructure.

Russia is a major producer of farm products, though it imports grains. Major crops include barley, flax, fruits, oats, rye, potatoes, sugar beet, sunflower seeds, vegetables, and wheat.

AREA 6,592,812 SQ MI [17,075,400 SQ KM] **POPULATION** 142,123,000
CAPITAL MOSCOW **GOVERNMENT** FEDERAL MULTIPARTY REPUBLIC
ETHNIC GROUPS RUSSIAN 80%, TATAR 4%, UKRAINIAN 2%, CHUVASH 1%, MORE THAN 100 OTHERS
LANGUAGES RUSSIAN (OFFICIAL), MANY OTHERS
RELIGIONS MAINLY RUSSIAN ORTHODOX, ISLAM, JUDAISM
CURRENCY RUSSIAN RUBLE = 100 KOPEKS

RWANDA

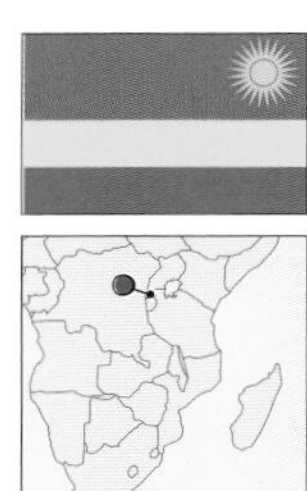

GEOGRAPHY The Republic of Rwanda is a small, landlocked country in east-central Africa. Lake Kivu and the River Ruzizi in the Great African Rift Valley form the country's western border.

Kigali stands on the central plateau of Rwanda. Here, temperatures are moderated by the altitude. Rainfall is abundant, but much heavier rain falls on the western uplands, while the Rift Valley floor is drier and warmer than the rest of Rwanda.

POLITICS & ECONOMY Germany conquered the area, called Ruanda-Urundi, in the 1890s. However, Belgium occupied the region during World War I (1914–18) and ruled it until 1961 when it became independent as a republic. This decision followed a rebellion by the majority Hutu people against the Tutsi monarchy which resulted in about 150,000 deaths. Many Tutsis fled to Uganda, where they formed a rebel army. Relations between Hutus and Tutsis deteriorated and, in 1994, between 500,000 and 800,000 people were massacred in Rwanda. After the Tutsis had restored order, Hutu rebels fled into the Democratic Republic of the Congo. In 2009, Rwanda became the 54th member of the Commonwealth. Paul Kagame has been president since 2000.

According to the World Bank, Rwanda is a "low-income" developing country with economic growth driven by exporting tea and coffee. Most people are poor farmers. Food crops include bananas, beans, cassava, and sorghum. Some cattle are raised.

AREA 10,169 sq mi [26,338 sq km] **POPULATION** 12,187,000
CAPITAL Kigali **GOVERNMENT** Republic
ETHNIC GROUPS Hutu 84%, Tutsi 15%, Twa 1%
LANGUAGES French, English and Kinyarwanda (all official)
RELIGIONS Roman Catholic 57%, Protestant 26%, Adventist 11%, Islam 5% **CURRENCY** Rwandan franc = 100 centimes

ST HELENA

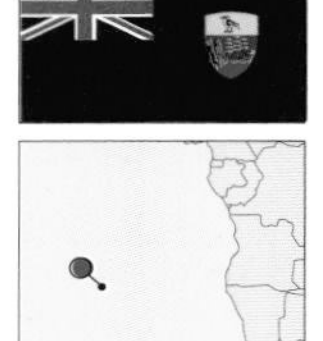

St Helena, which became a British colony in 1834, is an isolated volcanic island in the South Atlantic Ocean. Now a British overseas territory, it is also the administrative center of Ascension and Tristan da Cunha.

AREA 47 sq mi [122 sq km]
POPULATION 5,000 **CAPITAL** Jamestown

ST KITTS AND NEVIS

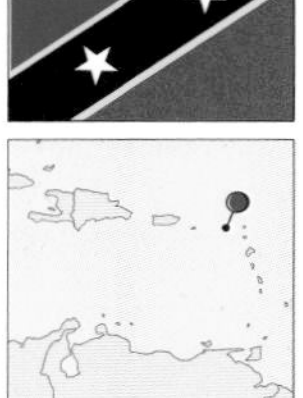

The Federation of St Kitts and Nevis comprises two well-watered volcanic islands, whose highest mountain rises to 3,793 ft [1,156 m]. The islands were the first in the Caribbean to be colonized by Britain (in 1623 and 1628), and they became an independent country in 1983. In 1998, a vote for the secession of Nevis fell short of the two-thirds majority required. Tourism, offshore finance, and service industries have replaced sugar as the principal earner.

AREA 101 sq mi [261 sq km]
POPULATION 53,000 **CAPITAL** Basseterre

ST LUCIA

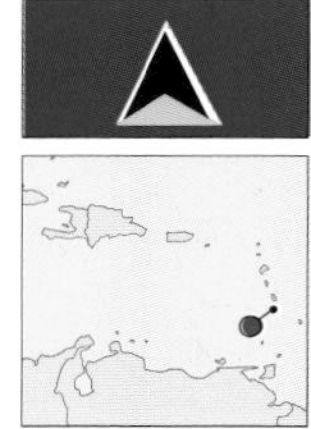

St Lucia, which became independent from Britain in 1979, is a mountainous, forested island of extinct volcanoes. It exports bananas and coconuts, and now attracts many tourists.

AREA 208 sq mi [539 sq km]
POPULATION 166,000 **CAPITAL** Castries

ST MAARTEN

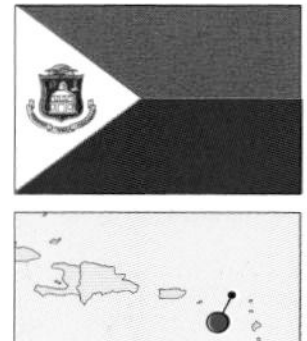

Part of the Netherlands Antilles until 2010, the southern part of the island of St Maarten is a self-governing territory within the Kingdom of the Netherlands. In 2017, Hurricane Irma caused extensive damage.

AREA 13 sq mi [34 sq km]
POPULATION 43,000 **CAPITAL** Philipsburg

ST VINCENT AND THE GRENADINES

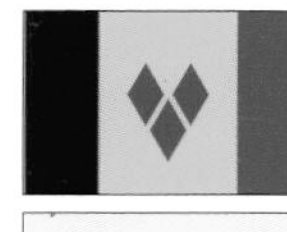

St Vincent and the Grenadines achieved its independence from Britain in 1979. Tourism is growing, but the territory is less prosperous than its neighbors.

AREA 150 sq mi [388 sq km]
POPULATION 102,000 **CAPITAL** Kingstown

SAMOA

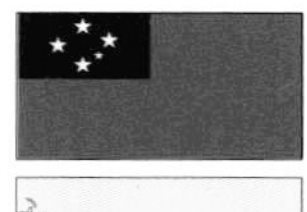

The Independent State of Samoa (formerly Western Samoa) comprises two islands in the south Pacific Ocean. Governed by New Zealand from 1920, the terrtory became independent in 1962. Exports include coconut cream and beer.

AREA 1,093 sq mi [2,831 sq km]
POPULATION 201,000 **CAPITAL** Apia

SAN MARINO

San Marino in northern Italy has been independent since 885 and a republic since the 14th century. It is the world's oldest republic. It has a friendship and cooperation treaty with Italy dating back to 1862. The state is governed by an elected council and has its own legal system. It has no armed forces and the police are "hired" from the Italian constabulary. The chief occupations are tourism, limestone quarrying, textiles, and wine-making.

AREA 24 sq mi [61 sq km] **POPULATION** 34,000 **CAPITAL** San Marino

SÃO TOMÉ AND PRÍNCIPE

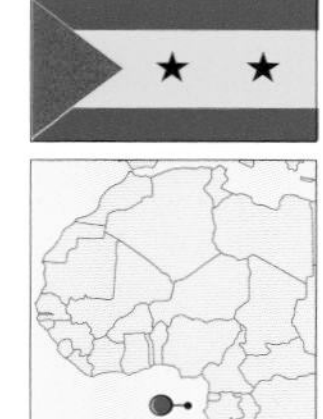

The Democratic Republic of São Tomé and Príncipe, a mountainous island territory west of Gabon, became a colony of Portugal in 1522. Independent since 1975, the economy has relied heavily on cocoa and foreign aid. Future growth depends on offshore oil.

AREA 372 sq mi [964 sq km] **POPULATION** 204,000 **CAPITAL** São Tomé

SAUDI ARABIA

GEOGRAPHY The Kingdom of Saudi Arabia occupies about three-quarters of the Arabian peninsula in southwest Asia. Deserts cover most of the land with mountains bordering the Red Sea plains in the west. In the north is the sandy Nafud Desert (An Nafud). In the south is the Rub' al Khali (the "Empty Quarter"), one of the world's bleakest deserts. Saudi Arabia has a hot dry climate. Summer temperatures in Riyadh often exceed 104°F [40°C].

POLITICS & ECONOMY Saudi Arabia contains the two holiest places in Islam – Mecca (or Makka), the birthplace of the Prophet Muhammad in AD 570, and Medina (Al Madinah), where he died in 632. These places are visited by huge numbers of pilgrims.

The monarch, who, since 2015, has been King Salman, has supreme authority in this ultra-conservative country. In March 2015 Saudi Arabia began its controversial military involvement in Yemen, launching airstrikes against Houthi rebels. In 2017, Saudi Arabia, the UAE, Bahrain, and Egypt imposed a blockade on Qatar. The Crown Prince Muhammad bin Salman has introduced a few small reforms.

Since 1933, oil has been the mainstay of the economy: the country has more than 25% of the world's known reserves. Oil products make up about 90% of exports. Irrigation and desalination projects have increased crop production. Problems have arisen from increasing unemployment, especially among the young, and moves are being made to diversify the economy.

AREA 829,995 sq mi [2,149,690 sq km] **POPULATION** 33,091,000
CAPITAL Riyadh **GOVERNMENT** Absolute monarchy with consultative assembly **ETHNIC GROUPS** Arab 90%, Afro-Asian 10%
LANGUAGES Arabic (official)
RELIGIONS Islam 100%
CURRENCY Saudi riyal = 100 halalas

SENEGAL

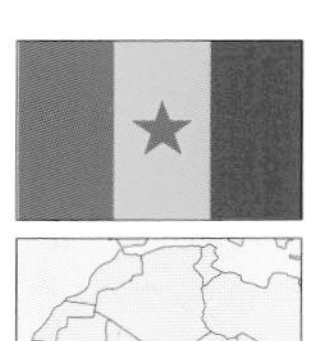

GEOGRAPHY The Republic of Senegal is on the west coast of Africa. The volcanic Cape Verde (Cap Vert), on which Dakar stands, is the most westerly point in Africa. Plains cover most of Senegal, though the land rises gently in the southeast.

Dakar has a tropical climate, with a short rainy season between July and October.

POLITICS & ECONOMY In 1882, Senegal became a French colony, and from 1895 it was ruled as part of French West Africa, the capital of which, Dakar, developed as a major port and city.

In 1959, Senegal joined French Sudan (now Mali) to form the Federation of Mali. But Senegal withdrew in 1960 and became the separate Republic of Senegal. Its first president, Léopold Sédar Senghor, served until 1981, when he was succeeded by Abdou Diouf. However, in 2000, Diouf was defeated in elections by Abdoulaye Wade which peacefully ended the 40-year rule of the Socialist Party. The current president is Macky Sall.

According to the World Bank, Senegal is a "low-income" country much dependent on foreign aid. It was badly hit in the 1960s and 1970s by droughts. Agriculture still employs 77% of the population, though many farmers produce little more than they need to feed their families. Food crops include groundnuts (peanuts), millet, and rice. Phosphates are the country's chief resource, but Senegal also refines oil, which it imports from Gabon and Nigeria. Dakar is a busy port. Tourism is growing. Economic growth will depend on modernizing infrastructure and guaranteeing reliable power supplies.

AREA 75,954 sq mi [196,722 sq km] **POPULATION** 15,021,000
CAPITAL Dakar **GOVERNMENT** Multiparty republic
ETHNIC GROUPS Wolof 43%, Pular 24%, Serer 15%
LANGUAGES French (official), tribal languages
RELIGIONS Islam 94%, Christianity (mainly Roman Catholic) 5%, traditional beliefs 1%
CURRENCY CFA franc = 100 centimes

SERBIA

GEOGRAPHY The Republic of Serbia lies in the central Balkan peninsula. A landlocked country, it contains large, fertile lowlands drained by the River Danube and its tributaries, with uplands in the south. Most of Serbia has a continental climate, with cold, snowy winters and hot, dry summers. Heavy rains occur in the spring and the fall.

POLITICS & ECONOMY Around 1,500 years ago, South Slavs moved into the Balkan peninsula, and each group founded its own state. Serbia came under the Turkish Ottoman empire in the 15th century. In 1918, the South Slavs united as the Kingdom of the Serbs, Croats, and Slovenes, which was renamed Yugoslavia in 1929. Germany invaded in 1941, but Communist partisans, led by Josip Broz Tito, took power in 1945.

From 1945, the country became the Federal People's Republic of Yugoslavia. In 1991–2, the country split apart, with Bosnia-Herzegovina, Croatia, Macedonia and Slovenia proclaiming their independence. The remaining republics, Serbia and Montenegro, retained the name Yugoslavia. In 2003, these two republics agreed to form the loose Union of Serbia and Montenegro. In 2006, the Montenegrins voted for full independence, and Serbia and Montenegro became separate republics. In 2008, the province of Kosovo declared itself independent, an act which Serbia refused to recognize. In 2011, the European Commission recommended Serbia for European Union candidate status, but said talks could start only after it normalized ties with Kosovo. Accession talks started in January 2014 although Serbia still falls short of acknowledging Kosovo as fully independent.

Serbia's resources include bauxite, coal, copper, and other metals, together with oil and natural gas. The country relies on exports and manufacturing, with aluminum, machinery, plastics, steel, textiles, and vehicles being important. Agriculture employs around one-fifth of the work force with crops including fruits, maize, potatoes, tobacco, and wheat. There are serious challenges to development including unemployment and an aging population.

AREA 29,913 sq mi [77,474 sq km] **POPULATION** 7,078,000
CAPITAL Belgrade **GOVERNMENT** Republic
ETHNIC GROUPS Serb 83%, Hungarian 4%, others
LANGUAGES Serbian (official), Hungarian
RELIGIONS Serbian Orthodox, Roman Catholic, Islam, Protestant
CURRENCY New dinar = 100 paras

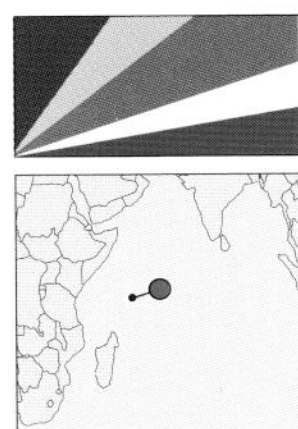

SEYCHELLES

The Republic of Seychelles in the western Indian Ocean achieved independence from Britain in 1976. Coconuts are the main cash crop, and fishing and tourism are important to the country's economy.

AREA 176 sq mi [455 sq km]
POPULATION 95,000 **CAPITAL** Victoria

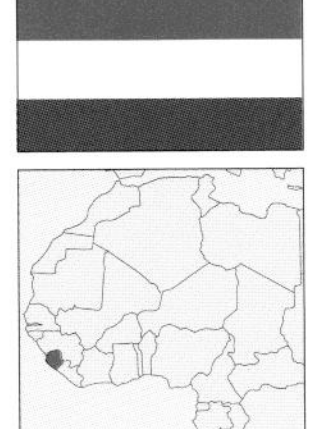

SIERRA LEONE

GEOGRAPHY The Republic of Sierra Leone in West Africa is about the same size as the country of Ireland. The coast contains several estuaries in the north, and extensive mangrove swamps. The most prominent feature is the mountainous Freetown (or Sierra Leone) peninsula.

Sierra Leone has a tropical climate, with heavy rainfall between April and November.

POLITICS & ECONOMY A former British territory, Sierra Leone became independent in 1961 and a republic in 1971. The military seized power in 1992 and the following 11 years of civil war resulted in tens of thousands of deaths and mutilations. The war was only brought to an end in 2002 with the intervention of the UK and a UN peacekeeping force. The last of the UN troops left the country in 2005, and national elections were held in 2007. In 2010, the UN Security Council lifted the last remaining sanctions against Sierra Leone. Ernest Bai Koroma was elected president in 2012 for a second term. Julius Maada Bio of the People's Party won the 2018 election.

Sierra Leone has a "low-income" economy and, although it is showing signs of reasonable growth, the legacy of destruction left by the war has still to be overcome. About 59% of the people live by farming, mainly at subsistence level. The leading exports are minerals, including bauxite and rutile (titanium ore), and diamonds. The trade in the latter as "blood diamonds" helped perpetuate the civil war and much diamond mining is still unlicensed.

AREA 27,699 sq mi [71,740 sq km] **POPULATION** 6,312,000
CAPITAL Freetown **GOVERNMENT** Multiparty republic
ETHNIC GROUPS Native African tribes 90% **LANGUAGES** English (official), Mende, Temne, Limba **RELIGIONS** Islam 60%, traditional beliefs 30%, Christianity 10% **CURRENCY** Leone = 100 cents

SINGAPORE

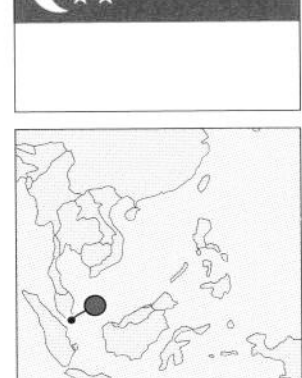

GEOGRAPHY The Republic of Singapore is an island country at the southern tip of the Malay peninsula. It consists of the large Singapore Island and 58 small islands, 20 of which are inhabited. The climate is hot and humid. Temperatures are high and rainfall is heavy throughout the year.

POLITICS & ECONOMY In 1819, Sir Thomas Stamford Raffles, agent of the British East India Company, made a treaty with the Sultan of Johor allowing the British to build a settlement on Singapore Island. Singapore soon became the leading British trading center in Southeast Asia and it later became a naval base. Japanese forces seized the island in 1942, but British rule was restored in 1945.

In 1963, Singapore became part of the Federation of Malaysia, which also included Malaya and the territories of Sabah and Sarawak on Borneo. In 1965, Singapore broke away and became independent.

The People's Action Party (PAP) has ruled Singapore since 1959. Its leader, Lee Kuan Yew, served as prime minister from 1959 until 1990, when he was succeeded by Goh Chok Tong. In 2004, Lee Hsien Loong, son of Lee Kuan Yew, became prime minister and has since been re-elected three times, in 2006, 2011, and 2015.

The World Bank classifies Singapore as a "high-income" economy, where a skilled work force has created a fast-growing economy. Trade and finance are major activities. The global financial crisis in 2008–9 caused great concern, but recovery was rapid. Manufactures include electronic products, machinery, scientific instruments, textiles, and ships. Petroleum products and manufactures are the main exports.

AREA 264 sq mi [683 sq km] **POPULATION** 5,996,000
CAPITAL Singapore City **GOVERNMENT** Multiparty republic
ETHNIC GROUPS Chinese 77%, Malay 14%, Indian 8%
LANGUAGES Chinese, Malay, Tamil and English (all official)
RELIGIONS Buddhism, Islam, Christianity, Hinduism
CURRENCY Singapore dollar = 100 cents

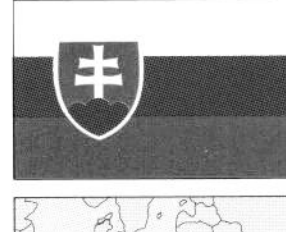

SLOVAKIA

GEOGRAPHY Slovakia is a predominantly mountainous country, consisting of part of the Carpathian range. The highest peak is Gerlachovsky in the Tatra Mountains, which reaches 8,711 ft [2,655 m]. The south is comprised of a fertile lowland. Slovakia has cold winters and warm summers. Kosice, in the east, has average temperatures ranging from 27°F [–3°C] in January to 68°F [20°C] in July. The highland areas are much colder. Snow or rain falls throughout the year. Kosice has an average annual rainfall of 24 inches [600 mm], the wettest months being July and August.

POLITICS & ECONOMY Slavic peoples settled here in the 5th century AD. They were subsequently conquered by Hungary, beginning a millennium of Hungarian rule and suppression of Slovak culture.

In 1867, Hungary and Austria united to form Austria–Hungary, of which the present-day Slovakia was a part. Austria–Hungary collapsed at the end of World War I (1914–18) and the Czech and Slovak people then united to form a new nation, Czechoslovakia. But Czech domination led to resentment by many Slovaks. In 1939, Slovakia declared itself independent, before Germany occupied the country. At the end of World War II, Slovakia again became part of Czechoslovakia.

The Communist Party took control in 1948 and although many people sought reform in the 1960s, they were crushed by the Russians. In the late 1980s, demands for democracy mounted and a non-Communist government took office in 1990. Elections in 1992 led to victory for the Movement for a Democratic Slovakia headed by a former Communist and nationalist, Vladimir Meciar, and Slovakia became independent in 1993.

Independence raised national aspirations among Slovakia's Magyar-speaking community which makes up about 10% of the population. Issues about the status of this minority group have soured relations with Hungary, and were not helped by the government making Slovak the only official language. Slovakia became a member of NATO and the European Union in 2004. On January 1, 2009, it became the 16th country to adopt the euro. In 2012, the opposition party Smer, led by former Prime Minister Robert Fico, won a landslide election. Fico stood down in the aftermath of the murder of an investigative journalist. He was replaced by Peter Pellegrini.

Before 1948, Slovakia's economy was based on farming, but Communist governments developed manufacturing industries. Economic and social reform, following membership of the eurozone, has resulted in strong economic growth, driven by the export of cars and electronic goods. Since the late 1980s, many state-run businesses have been handed over to private owners.

AREA 18,924 sq mi [49,012 sq km] **POPULATION** 5,446,000
CAPITAL Bratislava **GOVERNMENT** Multiparty republic
ETHNIC GROUPS Slovak 86%, Hungarian 10%
LANGUAGES Slovak (official), Hungarian
RELIGIONS Roman Catholic 69%, Protestant 11%, others
CURRENCY Euro = 100 cents

SLOVENIA

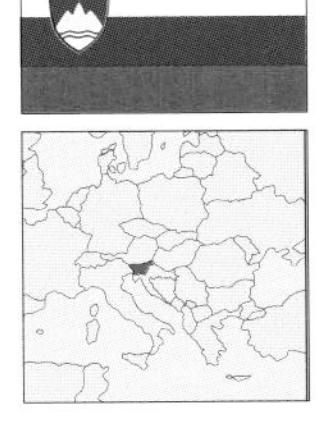

GEOGRAPHY The Republic of Slovenia was one of the six republics which made up the former Yugoslavia. Much of the land is mountainous, rising to 9,396 ft [2,864 m] at Mount Triglav in the Julian Alps (Julijske Alpe) in the northwest. Central Slovenia contains the limestone Karst region. The Postojna caves near Ljubljana are among the largest in Europe.

The coast has a mild Mediterranean climate, but inland the climate is more continental.

POLITICS & ECONOMY In the last 2,000 years, the Slovene people have been independent as a nation for less than 50 years. The Austrian Habsburgs ruled over the region from the 13th century until World War I when, in 1918, Slovenia became part of the Kingdom of the Serbs, Croats, and Slovenes (later called Yugoslavia). During World War II, Slovenia was invaded and partitioned between Italy, Germany, and Hungary, but, after the war, Slovenia again became part of Yugoslavia.

From the late 1960s, some Slovenes demanded independence, but the central government opposed the breakup of the country. In 1990, when Communist governments had collapsed throughout Eastern Europe, elections were held and a non-Communist coalition government was set up. Slovenia then declared itself independent. This led to fighting between Slovenes and the federal army, but Slovenia did not become a battlefield. Slovenia's independence was recognized in 1992 and a coalition led by the Liberal Democrats was elected. In 2004, Slovenia became a member of the North Atlantic Treaty Organization and the European Union. In 2013, the coalition government of Janez Jansa collapsed amidst criticisms over its austerity measures and allegations of corruption. Marjan Sarec succeeded Miro Cerar as prime minister in 2018; he heads a center-left minority government.

The reform of the formerly state-run economy caused problems for Slovenia. However, since 1993, the country has made considerable economic progress although this stumbled in the European financial crisis of 2012 when tough austerity measures were unpopular.

Manufacturing is the strongest part of the economy and exports include chemicals, machinery and transport equipment, metal goods, and textiles. Slovenia mines some iron ore, lead, lignite, and mercury. Fruits, maize, potatoes, and wheat are major crops, and livestock are also raised.

AREA 7,821 sq mi [20,256 sq km] **POPULATION** 2,102,000
CAPITAL Ljubljana **GOVERNMENT** Multiparty republic
ETHNIC GROUPS Slovene 83%, Croat 2%, Serb 2%, Hungarian, Bosnian **LANGUAGES** Slovenian (official), Serbo-Croatian
RELIGIONS Roman Catholic 58%
CURRENCY Euro = 100 cents

SOLOMON ISLANDS

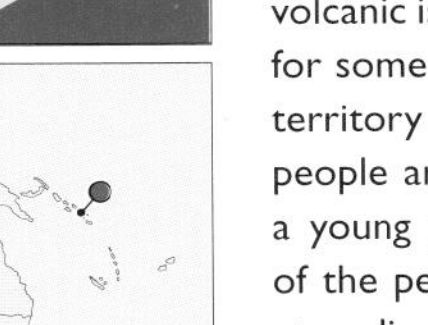

The Solomon Islands, a chain of mainly volcanic islands in the Pacific Ocean extending for some 1,400 mi [2,250 km], were a British territory between 1893 and 1978. Most people are Melanesians, and the islands have a young population profile, with about 35% of the people aged under 15. The country is struggling to recover from five years of civil conflict and poverty is rife. Fish, coconuts, cocoa, and forestry products underpin the economy.

AREA 11,157 sq mi [28,896 sq km]
POPULATION 660,000 **CAPITAL** Honiara

SOMALIA

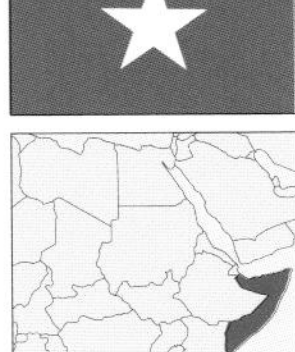

GEOGRAPHY The Federal Republic of Somalia is in a region known as the "Horn of Africa." It is more than twice the size of Italy, the country which once ruled the southern part of Somalia. The most mountainous part of the country is in the north, behind the narrow coastal plains that border the Gulf of Aden. Rainfall is sparse, with the wettest regions in the south and northern mountains. Droughts are common and temperatures are generally high.

POLITICS & ECONOMY European powers became interested in the Horn of Africa in the 19th century. In 1884, Britain made the northern part of what is now Somalia a protectorate, while Italy took the south in 1905. The new boundaries divided the Somalis into five areas: the two Somalilands, Djibouti (which was taken by France in the 1880s), Ethiopia, and Kenya. Since then, many Somalis have wanted to create a Greater Somalia. Italy invaded British Somaliland in 1940, but was defeated in 1941. Britain ruled both Somalilands until 1950, when the United Nations asked Italy to take over the former Italian Somaliland for ten years. In 1960, the two Somalilands united to become Somalia.

Somalia has faced many problems. Economic difficulties led a military group to seize power in 1969. In the 1970s, Somalia supported an uprising of Somali-speaking people in the Ogaden region of Ethiopia. But, in 1988, Somalia and Ethiopia signed a peace treaty. In the 1990s, Somalia gradually broke apart. In 1991, the people in what was once British Somaliland set up the "Somaliland Republic," but it failed to get international recognition. The northeast, called Puntland, also seceded, while the south was riven by clan warfare. In 2004–5, a Somali parliament was set up in Kenya, moving to Baidoa, in Somalia, in 2006 (Mogadishu was regarded as unsafe). In 2006, Mogadishu was taken over by the Islamist Union of Islamic Courts, but government forces backed by Ethiopian troops defeated the Islamists. Ethiopia finally withdrew all its troops in January 2009. In 2012, the militant group al-Shabab was driven out of central Somalia, but continues to carry out attacks. President Mohamed Abdullahi Mohamed, elected in 2017, has indicated that he is willing to talk to the militants.

Somalia's economy has been shattered by war, droughts, and periodic floods. Many Somalis are nomads, who raise livestock.

Live animals, meat, and hides and skins are exported. Crops include bananas, citrus fruits, cotton, maize, and sugarcane.

AREA 246,199 sq mi [637,657 sq km] **POPULATION** 11,259,000
CAPITAL Mogadishu **GOVERNMENT** Single-party republic, military dominated **ETHNIC GROUPS** Somali 85%, Bantu, Arab
LANGUAGES Somali (official), Arabic **RELIGIONS** Islam (Sunni Muslim)
CURRENCY Somali shilling = 100 cents

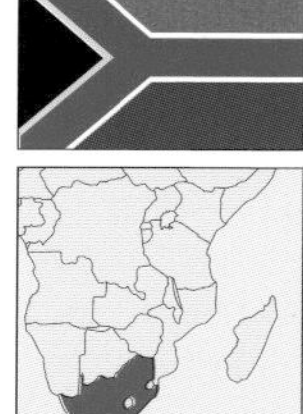

SOUTH AFRICA

GEOGRAPHY The Republic of South Africa comprises mainly of the southern part of the huge plateau which makes up most of southern Africa. The highest peaks are in the Drakensberg range. Part of the Namib Desert lies in the northwest. The area around Cape Town has a sunny climate with mild, rainy winters. Inland, large areas of the plateau are arid.

POLITICS & ECONOMY Early inhabitants in South Africa were the Khoisa, followed in the last 2,000 years by Bantu-speaking people. Their descendants include the Zulu, Xhosa, Sotho, and Tswana. The Dutch founded a settlement at the Cape in 1652, but Britain colonized the area in the early 19th century. The Dutch, called Boers or Afrikaners, resented British rule and moved inland. Rivalry between the groups led to Anglo–Boer Wars in 1880–1 and 1899–1902.

In 1910, the country was united as the Union of South Africa. In 1948, the National Party won power and introduced the policy of apartheid, under which non-whites could not vote and their human rights were strictly limited. Multiracial elections were held in 1994 and Nelson Mandela, leader of the African National Congress (ANC), became president following 27 years in prison. After Mandela retired, the ANC won elections in 1999 and 2004, led by Thabo Mbeki, and in 2009 when Jacob Zuma became president. Zuma resigned in 2018 over allegations of corruption, which he denies. He was replaced by Cyril Ramaphosa.

South Africa is Africa's most developed country and is one of the "BRICS" group of emerging global economic powers. However, most of the black people are poor, with farms still white-owned. Unemployment is high at 26% and it has nurtured an associated high crime rate. Natural resources include diamonds and gold; mining and manufacturing are the most valuable activities.

AREA 471,442 sq mi [1,221,037 sq km] **POPULATION** 55,380,000
CAPITAL Cape Town (legislative); Pretoria/Tshwane (administrative); Bloemfontein (judiciary) **GOVERNMENT** Multiparty republic
ETHNIC GROUPS Black 79%, White 10%, Colored 9%, Asian 2%
LANGUAGES Afrikaans, English, Ndebele, Pedi, Sotho, Swazi, Tsonga, Tswana, Venda, Xhosa and Zulu (all official)
RELIGIONS Christianity 68%, Islam 2%, Hinduism 1%
CURRENCY Rand = 100 cents

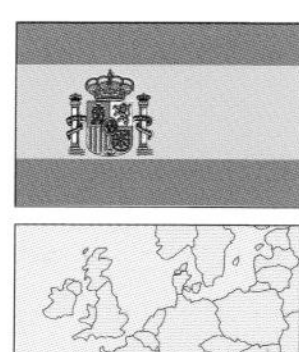

SPAIN

GEOGRAPHY The Kingdom of Spain is the second largest country in Western Europe after France. It shares the Iberian peninsula with the much smaller Portugal. The Meseta, an extensive plateau, covers most of Spain. It is mainly flat, but is crossed by the sierras, a series of mountain ranges.

The northern highlands include the Cantabrian Mountains (Cordillera Cantabrica) and the high Pyrenees, which form Spain's border with France. But Mulhacén, the highest peak on the Spanish mainland, is in the Sierra Nevada in the southeast. Spain also has fertile coastal plains. Other major lowlands include the Ebro river basin in the northeast and the Guadalquivir river basin in the southwest. Spain also encompasses the Balearic Islands in the Mediterranean Sea and the Canary Islands off the northwest coast of Africa.

The Meseta has a continental climate, with hot summers and cold winters, when temperatures often fall below freezing point. Snow frequently covers the mountain ranges on the Meseta. The Mediterranean coasts have hot, dry summers and mild winters.

POLITICS & ECONOMY In the early 16th century, Spain rose to be a world power. At its peak, it controlled much of Central and South America, parts of Africa, and the Philippines in Asia. Spain's influence began to decline in the late 16th century. Its sea power was destroyed by a British fleet in the Battle of Trafalgar (1805), and by the 20th century it was a poor country.

Spain became a republic in 1931, but the republicans were defeated in the Spanish Civil War (1936–9). General Francisco Franco became the country's dictator, though technically Spain remained a monarchy. On Franco's death in 1975, there was a peaceful transition to democracy, with Juan Carlos as king. In 2014 he abdicated in favor of his son Felipe.

Within Spain there are several groups, with their own languages and cultures, who have been vocal in their aim to run their own affairs. In the northern Basque region, the separatist group, ETA, waged a long-running terrorist campaign, finally announcing its complete disarmament in 2017.

Spain's regional makeup is complicated and the powers devolved to the regional parliaments since the 1970s are unevenly distributed. There are 17 regions, with Catalonia, the Basque Country, and Galicia having gained special status. A referendum in Catalonia in October 2017 led the regional government to declare independence. The central government swiftly cracked down and imposed direct rule.

Spain has been badly affected by the global recession of 2008. An unemployment rate of 23% and sluggish economic growth has forced the country to undertake drastic austerity measures. Agriculture employs only 4% of the population, as compared with 19% in industry and 76% in the service sector. Farmland occupies two-thirds of the land area. Manufactures include cars, chemicals, electronic goods, food, metal goods, and textiles. Spain lacks natural resources apart from some iron ore.

AREA 192,103 sq mi [497,548 sq km] **POPULATION** 49,331,000
CAPITAL Madrid **GOVERNMENT** Constitutional monarchy
ETHNIC GROUPS Composite of Mediterranean and Nordic types
LANGUAGES Castilian Spanish (official) 74%, Catalan 17%, Galician 7%, Basque 2% **RELIGIONS** Roman Catholic 94%, others 6% **CURRENCY** Euro = 100 cents

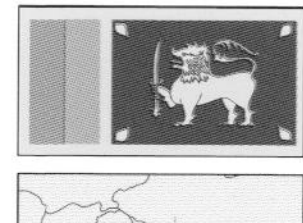

SRI LANKA

GEOGRAPHY The Democratic Socialist Republic of Sri Lanka is an island nation, separated from the southeast coast of India by the Palk Strait. The land is mostly low-lying, but a mountain region dominates the south-central part of the country.

The western part of Sri Lanka has a wet equatorial climate. Temperatures are high and the rainfall is heavy.

POLITICS & ECONOMY From the early 16th century, Ceylon (as Sri Lanka was then known) was ruled successively by the Portuguese, Dutch, and British. Independence was achieved in 1948 and the country was renamed Sri Lanka in 1972.

After independence, rivalries between the two main ethnic groups, the Buddhist Sinhalese and the minority Hindu Tamils, marred progress. In 1956 Solomon Bandaranaike was elected prime minister on a wave of Sinhalese nationalism, but he was assassinated in 1959 by an extremist Buddhist monk. He was succeeded by his wife. Sirimavo Bandaranaike, the world's first woman prime minister.

Conflict between Tamils and Sinhalese continued in the 1970s and 1980s. In 1987, India helped to engineer a cease-fire but withdrew its troops in 1990 after failing to subdue the main guerrilla group, the Tamil Tigers, who wanted to set up an independent Tamil homeland in the northeast. The Tamil Tigers were finally defeated in May 2009. In 2019, Islamist terrorists killed several hundred people in a series of suicide bombings.

In late 2004, a tsunami, caused by a sudden movement of the plates underlying the eastern Indian Ocean, struck parts of the coast of Sri Lanka, killing more than 30,000 people.

Sri Lanka is classed as a "lower-middle-income" economy and growth has been strong since the end of the conflict with the Tamil Tigers. Agriculture employs about 30% of the people. Coconuts, rubber, and tea are exported, but rice is the main food crop. Factories process farm products and manufacture textiles.

AREA 25,332 sq mi [65,610 sq km] **POPULATION** 22,577,000
CAPITAL Colombo **GOVERNMENT** Multiparty republic
ETHNIC GROUPS Sinhalese 74%, Tamil 9%, Moor 7%
LANGUAGES Sinhala and Tamil (both official)
RELIGIONS Buddhism 69%, Islam 8%, Hinduism 7%, Christianity 6%
CURRENCY Sri Lankan rupee = 100 cents

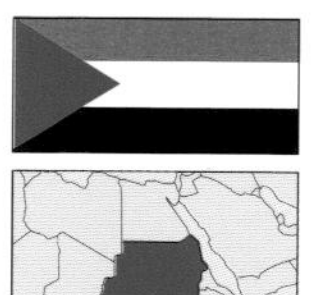

SUDAN

GEOGRAPHY The Republic of Sudan was Africa's largest country until 2011, when the people in the south voted to secede and form the new nation of South Sudan. Sudan is mainly arid, with part of the vast Sahara in the north. The main feature is the fertile River Nile valley, where most people live.

POLITICS & ECONOMY In the 19th century, Egypt gradually took control of Sudan. In 1881, a Muslim religious teacher, the Mahdi ("divinely appointed guide"), led a rebellion which was quashed, in 1898, by Britain and Egypt. In 1899, these two countries agreed to rule Sudan jointly as a condominium. After independence in 1952, the black Africans in the south feared domination by the Muslim north. They objected to Arabic becoming the sole official language and, in 1964, civil war broke out. The war ended in 1972, when the south was granted regional self-government.

In 1983, the announcement that Islamic law would apply throughout Sudan sparked off further resistance from the rebel Sudan People's Liberation Army (SPLA) in the south. In 1998, Sudan's government announced that it accepted the idea of a referendum. In 2005, a peace agreement was signed, and the referendum took place in 2011, when around 99% of the people in the south voted to set up their own country, South Sudan.

Since 2003, another conflict has raged in the western province of Darfur, where government-backed militias battled with local rebel forces. In 2008, the International Criminal Court charged President al-Bashir with war crimes. Re-elected in 2010 and 2015, Bashir was ousted and arrested by the military in April 2019.

The majority of the population are poor and live by subsistence agriculture. Cotton (the main crop), gum arabic, and sesame seeds are exported, but the most valuable exports are gold and oil products. More than 80% of the oil is produced in South Sudan, but Sudan has the infrastructure to exploit and export it.

AREA 728,222 sq mi [1,886,086 sq km] **POPULATION** 43,121,000
CAPITAL Khartoum **GOVERNMENT** Federal presidential democratic republic **ETHNIC GROUPS** Arab, Black, Beja, others
LANGUAGES Arabic and English (both official), Nubian, Beja
RELIGIONS Islam, traditional beliefs
CURRENCY Sudanese pound = 100 piastres

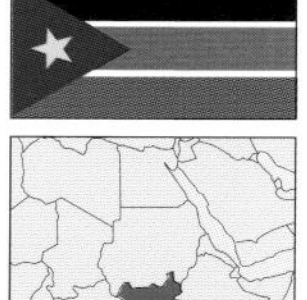

SUDAN, SOUTH

GEOGRAPHY The Republic of South Sudan is a landlocked country in east-central Africa. Much of the land is low-lying and drained by the White Nile and its tributaries. Mountains lie in the far south. The country has a wet tropical climate. Forests, swamps, and grasslands cover large areas.

POLITICS & ECONOMY South Sudan has about 200 ethnic groups. The South's deep cultural differences with the mainly Arab-Muslim north led to civil war (1964–1972 and 1983–2005). In January 2011, as part of the peace agreement, a referendum was held in which the vast majority of the people in the south voted for independence. Civil war broke out in 2013, displacing millions. Fighting was reduced after the president signed a power-sharing agreement in 2018 but disputes remain. In early 2017, famine was declared in parts of the country.

Most people depend on agriculture and forestry, but South Sudan has many mineral resources, including oil.

AREA 239,285 sq mi [619,745 sq km] **POPULATION** 10,205,000
CAPITAL Juba **GOVERNMENT** Republic
ETHNIC GROUPS Dinka, Kakwa, Bari, Azande, Shilluk, others
LANGUAGES English and Arabic (both official), local languages
RELIGIONS Traditional beliefs, Christianity
CURRENCY South Sudanese pound = 100 piastres

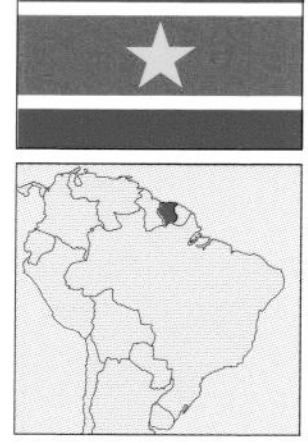

SURINAME

GEOGRAPHY The Republic of Suriname is sandwiched between French Guiana and Guyana in northeastern South America. The narrow coastal plain was once swampy, but it has been drained and now consists mainly of farmland. Inland lie hills and low mountains, which rise to 4,035 ft [1,230 m].

Suriname has a hot, wet and humid climate. Temperatures are high throughout the year.

POLITICS & ECONOMY In 1667, the British handed Suriname to the Dutch in return for New Amsterdam, an area that is now the state of New York. Slave revolts and Dutch neglect hampered development. In the early 19th century, Britain and the Netherlands disputed the ownership of the area with Britain relinquishing its claim in 1813. Slavery was abolished in 1863 and Indian and Indonesian laborers were introduced to work on the plantations.

Suriname became fully independent in 1975, but the economy was weakened when thousands of skilled people emigrated from Suriname to the Netherlands. Following a coup in 1980, Suriname was ruled by a military dictator, Desiré ("Dési") Bouterse. The adoption of a new constitution led to the restoration of democracy in 1988. Ronald Venetiaan was elected president in 2000. The guilder was replaced by the Surinamese dollar in 2004. In 2010, the Mega Combination coalition, led by Bouterse, won parliamentary elections and Bouterse became president. His party won a slim majority in 2015.

Suriname's economy is based on mining and metal processing. Offshore oil reserves are ripe for exploitation and gold reserves are attracting foreign investment. Tourism also has potential. Suriname was a leading producer of bauxite, but this has declined.

AREA 63,037 SQ MI [163,265 SQ KM] **POPULATION** 598,000
CAPITAL PARAMARIBO **GOVERNMENT** MULTIPARTY REPUBLIC
ETHNIC GROUPS HINDUSTANI/EAST INDIAN 37%, CREOLE (MIXED WHITE AND BLACK) 31%, JAVANESE 15%, BLACK 10%, AMERINDIAN 2%, CHINESE 2%, OTHERS
LANGUAGES DUTCH (OFFICIAL), SRANANG TONGO
RELIGIONS HINDUISM 27%, PROTESTANT 25%, ROMAN CATHOLIC 23%, ISLAM 20% **CURRENCY** SURINAMESE DOLLAR= 100 CENTS

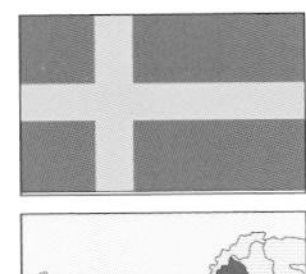

SWEDEN

GEOGRAPHY The Kingdom of Sweden is the largest of the countries of Scandinavia in both area and population. It shares the Scandinavian peninsula with Norway. The western part of the country, along the border with Norway, is mountainous. The highest point is Kebnekaise, which reaches 6,936 ft [2,114 m] in the northwest. The climate becomes increasingly severe from south to north.

POLITICS & ECONOMY Swedish Vikings plundered areas to the south and east between the 9th and 11th centuries. Sweden, Denmark, and Norway were united in 1397, but Sweden regained its independence in 1523. In 1809, Sweden lost Finland to Russia, but, in 1814, it gained Norway from Denmark. The union between Sweden and Norway was dissolved in 1905. Sweden remained neutral in World Wars I and II. Since 1945, Sweden has become a prosperous country and, in 1995, it joined the European Union. However, it did not adopt the euro, nor has it joined NATO.

Sweden has wide-ranging welfare provision but it comes at a high cost to the taxpayer. In 2006, a center-right alliance defeated the Social Democrats, who had governed for 65 of the previous 74 years. The current prime minister, elected in 2014, is Stefan Löfven.

Sweden is a highly developed industrial country: the economy is strong and unemployment low. Major products include steel and steel goods. Steel is used in the country's engineering industry to manufacture aircraft, cars, machinery, and ships. Sweden has some of the world's richest iron ore deposits which are found near Kiruna in the far north. Most of this ore is exported, and Sweden has to import most of the materials needed by its own industries. Forestry is also important and hydroelectricity is a major source of energy. In 1996, Sweden announced the decommissioning of its nuclear power stations with the first reactor closing in 1999, followed by a second in 2005. But in 2009, the government, under pressure to diversify from fossil fuels, reversed this policy.

AREA 173,731 SQ MI [449,964 SQ KM] **POPULATION** 10,041,000
CAPITAL STOCKHOLM **GOVERNMENT** CONSTITUTIONAL MONARCHY
ETHNIC GROUPS SWEDISH 91%, FINNISH, SAMI **LANGUAGES** SWEDISH (OFFICIAL), FINNISH, SAMI
RELIGIONS LUTHERAN 87%, ROMAN CATHOLIC, ORTHODOX
CURRENCY SWEDISH KRONA = 100 ÖRE

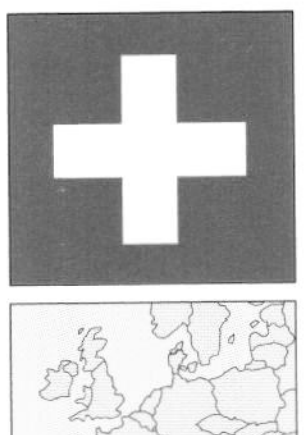

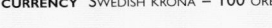

SWITZERLAND

GEOGRAPHY The Swiss Confederation is a landlocked country in Western Europe. Much of the land is mountainous. The Jura Mountains lie along Switzerland's western border with France, while the Swiss Alps make up about 60% of the country in the south and east. Four-fifths of the population live on the fertile Swiss plateau, which contains most of Switzerland's large cities.

The climate of Switzerland is generally temperate but varies greatly according to the altitude. The plateau has warm summers and cold, snowy winters. Rain occurs throughout the year.

POLITICS & ECONOMY In 1291, three small cantons (states) united to defend their freedom against the Habsburg rulers of the Holy Roman empire. They were Schwyz, Uri, and Unterwalden, and they called the confederation they formed "Switzerland." Switzerland expanded and, in the 14th century, defeated Austria in three wars of independence. After a defeat by the French in 1515, the Swiss adopted a policy of neutrality, which they still follow. In 1815, the Congress of Vienna expanded Switzerland to 22 cantons and guaranteed its neutrality. Switzerland's 23rd canton, Jura, was created in 1979 from part of Bern.

Neutrality combined with the vigour and independence of its people have made Switzerland prosperous. In 2002, Switzerland became a member of the United Nations, although it has remained outside the EU.

Although lacking in natural resources, Switzerland is a wealthy, industrialized country. Products include chemicals, electrical equipment, machinery and machine tools, precision instruments, processed food, watches, and textiles. Farmers produce about three-fifths of the country's food – the rest is imported. Crops include fruits, potatoes, and wheat. Tourism and banking are also important. Swiss banks attract investors from all over the world.

AREA 15,940 SQ MI [41,284 SQ KM] **POPULATION** 8,293,000
CAPITAL BERN **GOVERNMENT** FEDERAL REPUBLIC
ETHNIC GROUPS GERMAN 65%, FRENCH 18%, ITALIAN 10%, ROMANSCH 1%, OTHERS **LANGUAGES** GERMAN, FRENCH, ITALIAN AND ROMANSCH (ALL OFFICIAL) **RELIGIONS** ROMAN CATHOLIC 42%, PROTESTANT 35% **CURRENCY** SWISS FRANC = 100 CENTIMES

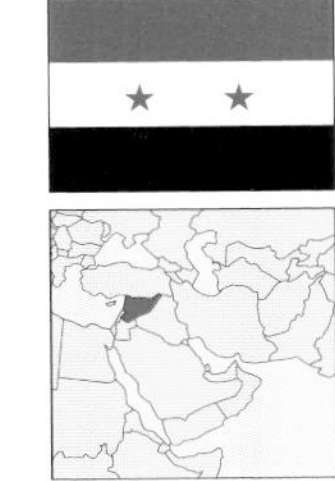

SYRIA

GEOGRAPHY The Syrian Arab Republic has a narrow coastal plain and is overlooked by a low mountain range which runs north–south. Another range, the Jabal ash Sharqi, runs along the border with Lebanon.

The coast has a Mediterranean climate, with dry, warm summers and wet, mild winters. The low mountains cut off Damascus from the sea. It has less rainfall than the coastal areas. To the east, the land becomes drier.

POLITICS & ECONOMY After the collapse of the Turkish Ottoman empire in World War I, Syria was governed by France until independence in 1946. In 1967 Syria lost the strategic Golan Heights, to Israel. In 1970, Lieutenant-General Hafez al-Assad took power, establishing a stable but repressive regime. Hafez al-Assad died in 2000 and was succeeded by his son, Bashar al-Assad. From 2011, civil war, and the occupation of Syrian territory by jihadist militants, devastated the country with the number of deaths of civilians, rebels and government forces estimated at over half a million. Millions of people were internally displaced or sought refuge elsewhere. With the help of Russian forces, the government had regained control of most of Syria's biggest cities by 2019, but parts of the countryside remained under the control of rebels and Kurds, with the Islamic State reduced to a small enclave on the Iraqi border. The Syrian government has repeatedly been accused of using chemical warfare on its own citizens.

Syria's main resources are oil, hydroelectricity, and fertile land. However, the economy has been crippled by the civil war.

AREA 71,498 SQ MI [185,180 SQ KM] **POPULATION** 19,454,000
CAPITAL DAMASCUS **GOVERNMENT** MULTIPARTY REPUBLIC
ETHNIC GROUPS ARAB 90%, KURDISH, ARMENIAN, OTHERS
LANGUAGES ARABIC (OFFICIAL), KURDISH, ARMENIAN
RELIGIONS SUNNI MUSLIM 74%, OTHER ISLAM 16%
CURRENCY SYRIAN POUND = 100 PIASTRES

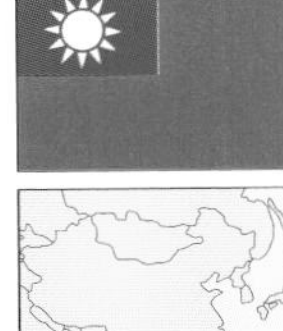

TAIWAN

GEOGRAPHY High mountain ranges run down the length of the island, with dense forest in many areas. The climate is warm, moist, and suitable for agriculture.

POLITICS & ECONOMY Chinese settlers occupied Taiwan from the 7th century. In 1895, Japan seized the territory from the Portuguese, who had named it Isla Formosa, or "beautiful island." China regained the island after World War II and, in 1949, it became the refuge of the Nationalists who had been driven out of China by the Communists. They set up the Republic of China, which, with US help, began to widen its economic base and develop manufacturing industries.

In the early 21st century, the Taiwanese declared full nationhood; however, China has never relinquished its claim of sovereignty over the island. Relations have improved since Taiwan and China signed a free-trade pact in 2010 although tensions still surface periodically. China is now Taiwan's main export market. Its major exports are electronic goods and petrochemicals.

AREA 13,900 SQ MI [36,000 SQ KM] **POPULATION** 23,546,000
CAPITAL TAIPEI **GOVERNMENT** UNITARY MULTIPARTY REPUBLIC
ETHNIC GROUPS TAIWANESE 84%, MAINLAND CHINESE 14%
LANGUAGES MANDARIN CHINESE (OFFICIAL), MIN, HAKKA
RELIGIONS BUDDHISM, TAOISM, CHRISTIANITY
CURRENCY NEW TAIWAN DOLLAR = 100 CENTS

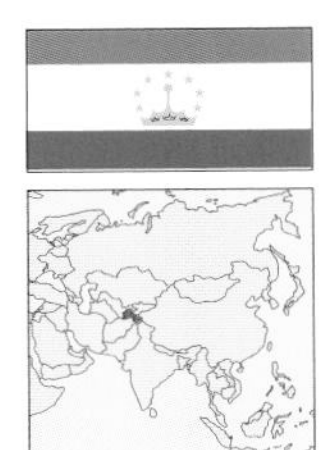

TAJIKISTAN

GEOGRAPHY The Republic of Tajikistan is one of the five central Asian republics that formed part of the former Soviet Union. Only 7% of the land is below 3,280 ft [1,000 m], while almost all of eastern Tajikistan is above 9,840 ft [3,000 m]. The highest point is Pik Imeni Ismail Samani (formerly known as Communism Peak or Pik Kommunizma), which reaches 24,590 ft [7,495 m]. The main ranges are the westward extension of the Tian Shan Range in the north and the snow-capped Pamirs in the southeast. Earthquakes are common throughout the country. The climate is continental, with hot, dry summers in the lower valleys and bitterly cold winters, especially in the mountains.

POLITICS & ECONOMY Russia conquered parts of Tajikistan in the late 19th century, and by 1920 Russia took complete control. In 1924, Tajikistan became part of the Uzbek Soviet Socialist Republic, but, in 1929, it was expanded, taking in some areas populated by Uzbeks, becoming the Tajik Soviet Socialist Republic.

While the Soviet Union began to introduce reforms during the 1980s, many Tajiks demanded freedom. In 1989, the Tajik government made Tajik the official language instead of Russian and, in 1990, it stated that its local laws overruled Soviet ones. Tajikistan became fully independent in 1991, following the breakup of the Soviet Union. In 1992, civil war broke out between the government, which was run by former Communists, and an alliance of democrats and Islamic forces. A ceasefire was agreed in 1996. In 2013, Emomali Rahmon, president since 1994, was re-elected for a 4th term. However, his parliamentary elections have been tainted by accusations of fraud.

Tajikistan is the poorest country in Central Asia and many people have left to find work in Russia. Economic hardship is fueling interest in radical Islam, especially amongst the young. Agriculture, mainly on irrigated land, is the main activity and cotton is the chief product. Other crops include fruits, grains, and vegetables. The country has large hydroelectric resources and it produces aluminum. Economic ties are being fostered with China.

AREA 55,521 SQ MI [143,100 SQ KM] **POPULATION** 8,605,000
CAPITAL DUSHANBE **GOVERNMENT** REPUBLIC
ETHNIC GROUPS TAJIK 80%, UZBEK 15%, RUSSIAN 1%, KYRGYZ 1%
LANGUAGES TAJIK (OFFICIAL), RUSSIAN
RELIGIONS ISLAM (SUNNI MUSLIM 95%, SHIA MUSLIM 3%)
CURRENCY SOMONI = 100 DIRAMS

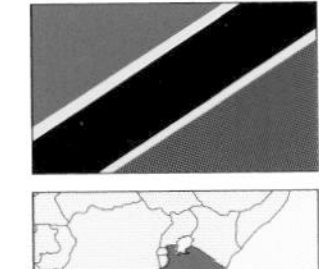

TANZANIA

GEOGRAPHY The United Republic of Tanzania consists of the former mainland country of Tanganyika and the island nation of Zanzibar, which also includes the island of Pemba. Behind a narrow coastal plain, most of Tanzania is a plateau, which is broken by arms of the Great African Rift Valley. In the west, this valley contains lakes Nyasa and Tanganyika. The highest peak is Kilimanjaro, Africa's highest mountain at 19,340 ft [5,895 m].

The coast has a hot and humid climate, with the greatest rainfall in April and May. The inland plateaux and mountains are cooler and less humid.

POLITICS & ECONOMY Mainland Tanganyika became a German territory in the 1880s, while Zanzibar and Pemba became a British protectorate in 1890. Following Germany's defeat in World War I, Britain took over Tanganyika, which remained a British territory until its independence in 1961. In 1964, Tanganyika and Zanzibar united to form the United Republic of Tanzania. The country's president, Julius Nyerere, pursued socialist policies of self-help (ujamaa) and egalitarianism. Many of his social reforms were successful, though the country failed to make economic progress. Nyerere resigned as president in 1985. His successors followed more liberal economic policies.

Tanzania is a poor country in terms of per capita income, but the overall economic growth rate is high, at around 7%, due to gold mining and tourism. Crops are grown on only 4% of the land, yet agriculture employs about 80% of the people and provides 85% of exports. Food crops include bananas, cassava, maize, millet, and rice. Minerals, including gold, as well as cashews, tobacco, coffee, and tea are exported. Offshore gas fields have been discovered.

AREA 364,899 sq mi [945,090 sq km] **POPULATION** 55,451,000
CAPITAL Dodoma **GOVERNMENT** Multiparty republic
ETHNIC GROUPS Native African 99% (of which 95% are Bantu consisting of more than 130 tribes)
LANGUAGES Swahili (Kiswahili) and English (both official)
RELIGIONS Islam 35% (99% in Zanzibar), traditional beliefs 35%, Christianity 30%
CURRENCY Tanzanian shilling = 100 cents

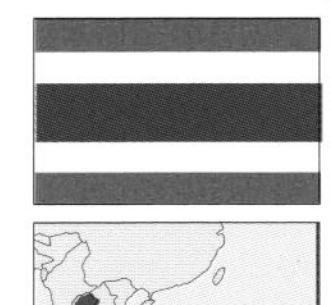

THAILAND

GEOGRAPHY The Kingdom of Thailand is one of the ten countries in Southeast Asia. The highest land is in the north, where Doi Inthanon, the highest peak, reaches 8,415 ft [2,565 m]. The Khorat plateau, in the north-east, makes up about 30% of the country and is the most heavily populated part of Thailand. In the south, Thailand shares the finger-like Malay peninsula with Burma and Malaysia.

Thailand has a tropical climate. Monsoon winds from the south-west bring heavy rains in May to October. Mountains shelter the central plains from the rain-bearing winds.

POLITICS & ECONOMY The first Thai state was set up in the 13th century and, by 1350, it included most of what is now Thailand. European contact began in the early 16th century, but their interference was unwelcome and, by the late 17th century, all Europeans were forced to leave. In 1782, a Thai General, Chao Phraya Chakkri, became king, founding a dynasty which continues today. The country became known as Siam. From the mid-19th century, contacts with the West were restored. In World War I, Siam supported the Allies against Germany and Austria–Hungary although in 1941 it was aligned with Japan against the UK and US.

After 1967, when Thailand became a member of ASEAN (Association of Southeast Asian Nations), its economy expanded rapidly. In 1997, with other eastern Asian economies, it suffered an economic recession. Thailand has also faced conflict in the south, where the government has clashed with minority Muslim groups. In 2001, Thaksin Shinawatra, a businessman, became prime minister. In 2006, his party won a majority, the result of a boycott of opposition parties. Following mass protests, a military junta took power until civilian rule was restored in 2007. In 2011, Thaksin's sister, Yingluck Shinawatra, was elected prime minister. Elections held in early 2014 were later declared invalid and the military took control. General Prayuth Chan-ocha was appointed prime minister. Elections are taking place in 2019.

Classified as an "upper-middle income country," Thailand has a well-developed infrastructure and an export-led economy. Agriculture employs 32% of the people and rice is the chief crop. Cassava, cotton, maize, rubber, sugarcane, and tobacco are also grown. Tin is mined, but the chief exports are manufactures and food products. Tourism plays a significant part in the economy.

AREA 198,114 sq mi [513,115 sq km] **POPULATION** 68,616,000
CAPITAL Bangkok **GOVERNMENT** Constitutional monarchy
ETHNIC GROUPS Thai 75%, Chinese 14%, others 11%
LANGUAGES Thai (official), English, ethnic and regional dialects
RELIGIONS Buddhism 95%, Islam, Christianity
CURRENCY Thai baht = 100 satang

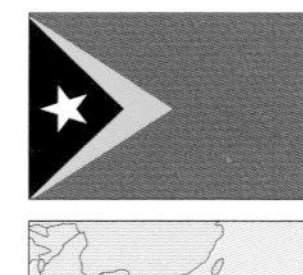

TIMOR-LESTE

The Republic of Timor-Leste (East Timor) is mainly rugged. Temperatures are generally high and the rainfall is moderate. Portugal, the ruling colonial power, withdrew in 1975 and Indonesia seized control. Brutal suppression by Indonesia led to a vote for independence in 1999, which came into force in 2002. Support from the UN and Australia was crucial in bringing stability and allowing reconstruction. Agriculture is the main activity, employing 64% of the work force. In 2006, Timor-Leste and Australia signed a deal to share the revenue from the oil and natural gas deposits under the Timor Sea. The economy is now growing steadily at around 5% per annum.

AREA 5,743 sq mi [14,874 sq km] **POPULATION** 1,322,000 **CAPITAL** Dili

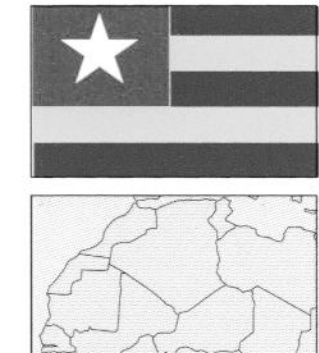

TOGO

GEOGRAPHY The Republic of Togo is a long, narrow country in West Africa. From north to south, it extends about 311 mi [500 km]. Its coastline on the Gulf of Guinea is only 40 mi [64 km] long and it is only 90 mi [145 km] at its widest point.

Togo's climate is generally tropical, and it has high temperatures all through the year. The main wet season is from March to July, with a minor wet season in October and November.

POLITICS & ECONOMY Togo became a German protectorate in 1884, but, in 1919, Britain took over the western third of the territory, while France took over the eastern two-thirds. In 1956, the people of British Togoland voted to join Ghana, while French Togoland became an independent republic in 1960.

A military regime took power in 1963. In 1967, General Gnassingbé Eyadéma became head of state, a position he maintained until his death in 2005. Elections held during this period were deemed unfair and were boycotted by opposition parties. His son, Faure Gnassingbé, took over as president, but international pressure forced him to step down. He was, however, re-elected in 2005, 2010 and 2015. Serious challenges to the stranglehold of this family will have to await future elections.

Togo is a poor, developing country dependent on agriculture. Major food crops include cassava, maize, millet, and yams. Togo is one of the world's largest producers and exporters of phosphates. Economic growth will depend on reforms and foreign assistance.

AREA 21,925 sq mi [56,785 sq km] **POPULATION** 8,176,000
CAPITAL Lomé **GOVERNMENT** Multiparty republic
ETHNIC GROUPS Native African 99% (largest tribes are Ewe, Mina and Kabre) **LANGUAGES** French (official), African languages
RELIGIONS Traditional beliefs 51%, Christianity 29%, Islam 20%
CURRENCY CFA franc = 100 centimes

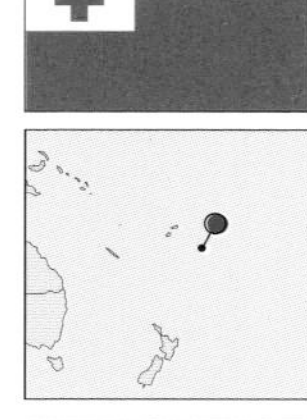

TONGA

The Kingdom of Tonga, a former British protectorate, became independent in 1970. Situated in the south Pacific Ocean, it contains more than 170 islands, 36 of which are inhabited. In 2010, Tonga held its first election for a popularly elected parliament. Agriculture is the main activity and unemployment is high.

AREA 251 sq mi [650 sq km] **POPULATION** 106,000 **CAPITAL** Nuku'alofa

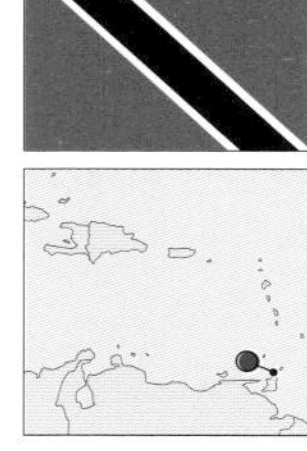

TRINIDAD AND TOBAGO

The Republic of Trinidad and Tobago became independent from Britain in 1962. These tropical islands, populated by people of African, Asian (mainly Indian) and European origin, are hilly and forested, though there are some fertile plains. Oil production is the mainstay of the economy.

AREA 1,981 sq mi [5,130 sq km]
POPULATION 1,216,000 **CAPITAL** Port of Spain

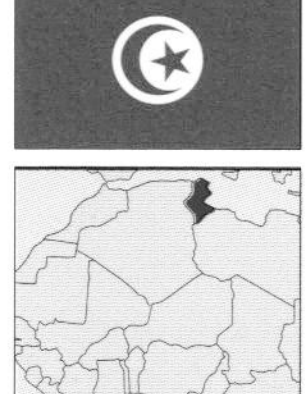

TUNISIA

GEOGRAPHY The Republic of Tunisia is the smallest country in North Africa. The mountains in the north are an eastward and comparatively low extension of the Atlas Mountains. To the north and east of the mountains lie fertile plains, especially between Sfax, Tunis, and Bizerte. In the south, low-lying regions contain the Chott Djerid, a vast salt pan, part of the Sahara.

Northern Tunisia has a Mediterranean climate, with dry, sunny summers, and mild winters with a moderate rainfall. The average yearly rainfall decreases toward the south.

POLITICS & ECONOMY In 1881, France established a protectorate over Tunisia and ruled the country until 1956. The new parliament abolished the monarchy and declared Tunisia to be a republic in 1957, with the nationalist leader, Habib Bourguiba, as president. His government introduced many reforms, including votes for women, but there were problems including unemployment among the middle class and fears that the ideas of Western visitors might undermine Muslim values. In 1987, the prime minister, Zine el Abidine Ben Ali, removed Bourguiba, and became president. He was re-elected five times until, in 2011, anti-government demonstrations forced him to flee the country. Mohamed Béji Caid Essebsi assumed the presidency in 2014.

The World Bank classifies Tunisia as an "upper-middle-income" developing country and it is one of the more prosperous in North Africa. The main resources and chief exports are phosphates and oil. Most industries are concerned with food processing. Fishing is important. The flourishing tourism industry has been hit hard by the fallout from terrorist attacks in 2015.

AREA 63,170 sq mi [163,610 sq km] **POPULATION** 11,516,000
CAPITAL Tunis **GOVERNMENT** Multiparty republic
ETHNIC GROUPS Arab 98%, European 1% **LANGUAGES** Arabic (official), French **RELIGIONS** Islam 98%, Christianity 1%, others
CURRENCY Tunisian dinar = 1,000 millimes

TURKEY

GEOGRAPHY The Republic of Turkey lies in two continents. European Turkey, also called Thrace, lies west of a waterway linking the Mediterranean and Black seas. Most of Asian Turkey consists of plateaux and mountains, which rise to 16,945 ft [5,165 m] at Mount Ararat, near the border with Armenia. Earthquakes are common. Central Turkey has a dry climate, with hot, sunny summers and cold winters. The west has a Mediterranean climate, but the Black Sea coast has cooler summers.

POLITICS & ECONOMY In AD 330, the Roman empire moved its capital to Byzantium, which it renamed Constantinople. Muslim Seljuk Turks from central Asia invaded Anatolia (Asian Turkey) in the 11th century. In the 14th century, another group of Turks, the Ottomans, conquered the area and, in 1453, they took Constantinople, renaming it Istanbul. The Ottomans built up a vast empire which collapsed during World War I (1914–18). Turkey became a republic in 1923 and Mustafa Kemal, or Atatürk ("father of the Turks"), began to modernize and secularize the country.

Since the 1940s, Turkey has sought to strengthen its ties with Western powers. It joined NATO (North Atlantic Treaty Organization) in 1951 and it applied to join the European Economic Community in 1987. But Turkey's conflict with Greece, together with its invasion of northern Cyprus in 1974, have led many Europeans to treat Turkey's aspirations to full EU membership with caution. Political instability, military coups, conflict with Kurdish nationalists in eastern Turkey, and concern about the country's record on human rights are problems still to be solved.

Turkey has enjoyed democracy since 1983. In 1999, the Muslim Virtue Party (successor to the Islamist Welfare Party) lost ground. The largest numbers of parliamentary seats were won by the ruling Democratic Left Party and the far-right National Action Party. However, in the elections in 2002, the moderate Islamic Justice and Development Party (AKP) won 362 of the 500 seats in parliament. Despite concerns about its Islamist roots, the AKP was re-elected in 2007 and 2011. In 2014, Recep Tayyip Erdogan was elected president after serving as prime minister since 2003. The conflict in Syria has increased tensions along the border, and Turkey has carried out several attacks on Kurdish areas of Syria and Iraq. A failed coup in 2016 was followed in 2017 by a referendum on giving the president more powers. The result was a disputed narrow victory for Erdogan, who went on to win a further term as president in 2018.

Turkey came close to economic collapse in 2002, but its recovery enabled it to withstand the global financial crisis in 2008, and bounce back by 2010–11. However, the economy is vulnerable to political instability in the region and investor confidence. Agriculture employs 26% of the people, with barley, cotton, fruits, nuts, maize, tobacco, and wheat being the major crops.

AREA 299,156 sq mi [774,815 sq km] **POPULATION** 81,257,000
CAPITAL Ankara **GOVERNMENT** Multiparty republic
ETHNIC GROUPS Turkish 73%, Kurdish 18%
LANGUAGES Turkish (official), Kurdish, Arabic
RELIGIONS Islam (mainly Sunni Muslim) 99%
CURRENCY Turkish lira = 100 kurus

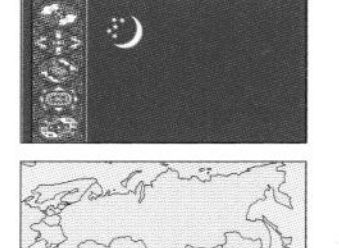

TURKMENISTAN

GEOGRAPHY The Republic of Turkmenistan is one of the five central Asian republics which once formed part of the former Soviet Union. Most of the land is low-lying, with mountains stretching along the southern and south-western borders. In the west lies the salty Caspian Sea. Most of Turkmenistan is arid and the Garagum (Kara Kum), Asia's largest sand desert, covers about 80% of the country. Turkmenistan has a continental climate, with average annual rainfall varying from 3 inches [80 mm] in the desert to 12 inches [300 mm] in the mountains. Summer months are hot, but winter temperatures drop well below freezing point.

POLITICS & ECONOMY Just over 1,000 years ago, Turkic people settled in the lands east of the Caspian Sea and the name "Turkmen" dates from this time. Mongol armies conquered the area in the 13th century and Islam was introduced in the 14th century. Russia took over the area in the 1870s and 1880s. The area came under Communist rule in 1917 and, in 1924, it became the Turkmen Soviet Socialist Republic.

In the 1980s, when the Soviet Union began to introduce reforms, the Turkmen began to demand more freedom and, in 1991, asserted that their own laws held sway over those of Soviet Russia. In late 1991, Turkmenistan became fully independent although the country maintained ties with Russia through the Commonwealth of Independent States (CIS).

In 1992, Turkmenistan adopted a new constitution, allowing for the setting up of political parties, providing that they were not ethnic or religious in character. But, effectively, Turkmenistan remained a one-party state and, in 1992, Saparmurad Niyazov, the former Communist and at that time Democratic Party leader, was the only presidential candidate. In 1999, parliament declared Niyazov president for life. Niyazov died in 2006 and was succeeded by Gurbanguly Berdymukhamedov. He was returned to power in undemocratic elections in 2012 and 2017.

Faced with many economic problems, Turkmenistan began to look south rather than to the CIS for support. As part of this policy, it joined the Economic Cooperation Organization, which had been set up in 1985 by Iran, Pakistan, and Turkey. In 1996, the completion of a rail link from Turkmenistan to the Iranian coast was an important step in the development of Central Asia. Oil and natural gas are the chief resources, and gas pipelines to China and Iran were opened in 2009 and 2010. Agriculture remains the main activity, with cotton as the most important commercial crop. Manufactures include cement, glass, petrochemicals, and textiles.

AREA 188,455 sq mi [488,100 sq km] **POPULATION** 5,411,000
CAPITAL Ashkhabad **GOVERNMENT** Single-party republic
ETHNIC GROUPS Turkmen 85%, Uzbek 5%, Russian 4%
LANGUAGES Turkmen (official), Russian, Uzbek
RELIGIONS Islam 89%, Eastern Orthodox 9%
CURRENCY Turkmen manat = 100 tenge

TURKS AND CAICOS ISLANDS

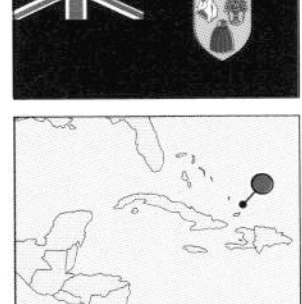

The Turks and Caicos Islands, a British territory since 1776, are a group of about 30 islands. Fishing, tourism, and offshore finance are the major economic activities.

AREA 166 sq mi [430 sq km]
POPULATION 54,000 **CAPITAL** Cockburn Town

TUVALU

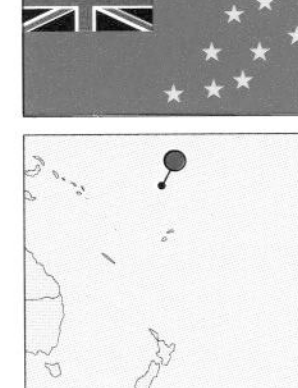

Tuvalu, formerly called the Ellice Islands, was a British territory from the 1890s until it became independent in 1978. It consists of nine low-lying coral atolls in the southern Pacific Ocean. Copra is the only significant export.

AREA 10 sq mi [26 sq km]
POPULATION 11,000 **CAPITAL** Funafuti

UGANDA

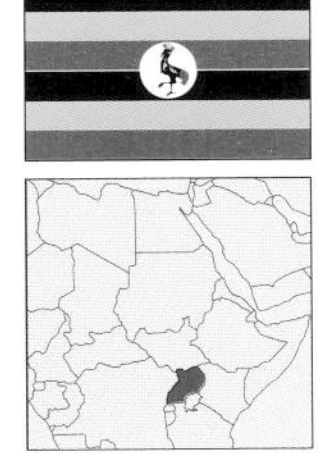

GEOGRAPHY The Republic of Uganda is a landlocked country on the East African plateau. It contains part of Lake Victoria, Africa's largest lake and a source of the River Nile, which occupies a shallow depression in the plateau. The equator runs through Uganda, and the country is warm throughout the year, though the high altitude moderates the temperature. The wettest regions are the lands to the north of Lake Victoria, where the capital, Kampala, is situated, and the western mountains, especially the high Ruwenzori range.

POLITICS & ECONOMY Little is known of the early history of Uganda. When Europeans first reached the area in the 19th century, many of the people were organized in kingdoms, the most powerful of which was Buganda, the home of the Baganda people. Britain took control of the country between 1894 and 1914, and administered it until independence in 1962.

In 1967, Uganda became a republic and Buganda's Kabaka (king), Sir Edward Mutesa II, was made president. But tensions between the Kabaka and the prime minister, Apollo Milton Obote, led to the dismissal of the Kabaka in 1966. Obote also abolished the traditional kingdoms, including Buganda. Obote was overthrown in 1971 by an army group led by General Idi Amin Dada. Amin ruled as adictator: he forced most of the Asians who lived in Uganda to leave the country and had many of his opponents killed.

In 1978, a border dispute between Uganda and Tanzania led Tanzanian troops to enter Uganda. With help from Ugandan opponents of Amin, they overthrew Amin's government. In 1980, Obote led his party to victory in the elections, but following charges of fraud, Obote's opponents instigated a guerrilla war. A military group overthrew Obote in 1985, though strife continued until 1986, when Yoweri Museveni's National Resistance Movement seized power. In 1993, Museveni restored the traditional kingdoms. Elections were held in 1994, but political parties were forbidden. Museveni was re-elected five times between 1996 and 2016. In recent years, Uganda has faced the rebel Lord's Resistance Army (LRA) in the north. The LRA extended its activities into the Central African Republic, the Democratic Republic of the Congo, and Sudan. By 2017, more than a million South Sudanese had sought refuge in Uganda.

Agriculture dominates the economy, employing over 80% of the work force. The chief exports are coffee and gold. Economic reforms and some investment in infrastructure have resulted in a strengthening of the economy. Newly discovered oil will be a valuable asset.

AREA 93,065 sq mi [241,038 sq km] **POPULATION** 40,854,000
CAPITAL Kampala **GOVERNMENT** Republic
ETHNIC GROUPS Baganda 17%, Ankole 8%, Basogo 8%, Iteso 8%, Bakiga 7%, Langi 6%, Rwanda 6%, Bagisu 5%, Acholi 4%, Lugbara 4%, and others
LANGUAGES English and Swahili (both official), Ganda
RELIGIONS Roman Catholic 42%, Protestant 42%, Islam 12%, traditional beliefs 4%
CURRENCY Ugandan shilling = 100 cents

UKRAINE

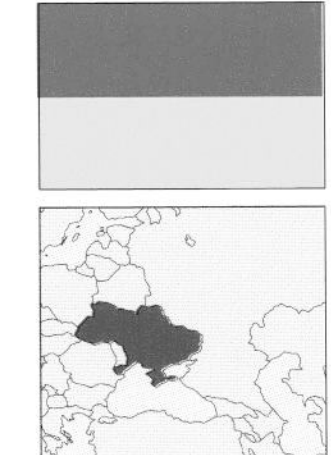

GEOGRAPHY Ukraine is the second largest country in Europe after Russia. It was formerly part of the Soviet Union, which split apart in 1991. This mostly flat country faces the Black Sea in the south. The Crimean peninsula includes a highland region overlooking Yalta. Ukraine has warm summers, but the winters are cold, becoming more severe from west to east. In the summer, the east is often warmer than the west. Most rain falls in the summer months.

POLITICS & ECONOMY Kiev was the original capital of the early Slavic civilization known as Kievan Rus. In the 17th and 18th centuries, parts of Ukraine came under Polish and Russian rule, but, by the late 18th century, Russia had gained most of Ukraine. In 1918, Ukraine gained independence, but only until 1922 when it became part of the Soviet Union.

In the 1980s, Ukrainian people demanded more say over their affairs and regained their independence in 1991. In the early 21st century, Ukraine has been pulled in two directions – either closer integration with Russia or with the EU. In 2005, the pro-Western leader Viktor Yushchenko was elected president. Economic problems, and political infighting, led to a Russian-leaning party, led by Viktor Yanukovych, winning most seats in parliament in 2006. An election in 2007 resulted in a pro-Western coalition government led by Yulia Tymoshenko. In 2010, the pro-Russian Viktor Yanukovych was declared winner of the presidential election, but in 2013–14 mass protests over his backtracking on a cooperation agreement with the EU forced him from power. Russia invaded and seized Crimea, and sent troops into other parts of eastern Ukraine, where unrest continues. The annexation of Crimea has not been recognized by Ukraine or the wider world. The pro-West Petro Poroshenko was elected president in 2014.

Manufacturing is the chief economic activity including iron and steel, machinery, and vehicles. Ukraine has large coalfields and its own hydroelectric and nuclear power plants, but the country imports oil and natural gas (much of it from Russia). Agriculture contributes 13% of GDP and wheat and sugar are exported.

AREA 233,089 sq mi [603,700 sq km] **POPULATION** 43,952,000
CAPITAL Kiev **GOVERNMENT** Multiparty republic
ETHNIC GROUPS Ukrainian 78%, Russian 17%, Belarusian, Moldovan, Bulgarian, Hungarian, Polish
LANGUAGES Ukrainian (official), Russian
RELIGIONS Mostly Ukrainian Orthodox
CURRENCY Hryvnia = 100 kopiykas

UNITED ARAB EMIRATES

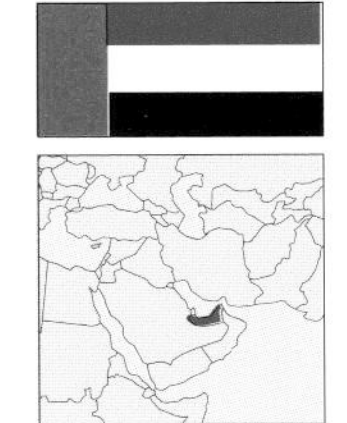

The United Arab Emirates (UAE) were formed in 1971 when the seven Trucial States of the Persian Gulf (Abu Dhabi, Dubai, Sharjah, Ajman, Umm al Qawayn, Ra's al Khaymah, and Al Fujayrah) joined together. The economy of this hot and dry state depends on oil production, and the resulting revenues give the UAE one of the highest per capita GDPs in Asia. Tourism and finance are important sources of revenue.

AREA 32,278 sq mi [83,600 sq km]
POPULATION 9,701,000 **CAPITAL** Abu Dhabi

UNITED KINGDOM

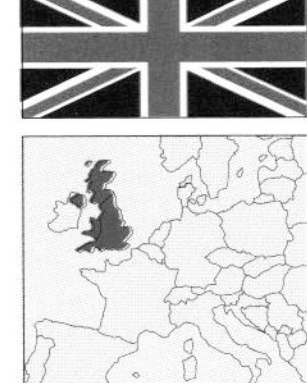

GEOGRAPHY The United Kingdom (or UK) is a union of four countries. Three of them – England, Scotland, and Wales – make up Great Britain. The fourth country is Northern Ireland. The Isle of Man and the Channel Islands are not part of the UK. They are self-governing British dependencies.

The land is highly varied. Much of Scotland and Wales is mountainous, and the highest peak is Scotland's Ben Nevis at 4,411 ft [1,345 m]. England has some highland areas, including the Cumbrian Mountains (or Lake District) and the Pennine range in the north, but it also has extensive areas of fertile lowland. Northern Ireland is also a mixture of lowlands and uplands and it contains the UK's largest lake, Lough Neagh.

The UK has a mild climate, influenced by the warm North Atlantic Drift which is a continuation of the Gulf Stream originating from the Gulf of Mexico. Moist winds from the southwest bring rain, but the rainfall decreases from west to east. Winds from the east and north bring cold weather in winter.

POLITICS & ECONOMY In ancient times, Britain was invaded by many peoples, including Iberians, Celts, Romans, Angles, Saxons, Jutes, Norsemen, Danes, and the Normans, who arrived in 1066. King Edward I annexed Wales in 1282 and united it with England. Union with Scotland was achieved in 1707 and this created a country known as the United Kingdom of Great Britain.

Ireland came under Norman rule in the 11th century, and much of its later history was concerned with a struggle against English domination. In 1801, Ireland became part of the United Kingdom of Great Britain and Ireland. But in 1921, southern Ireland, where most of the people were Roman Catholics, broke away to become the Irish Free State. In Northern Ireland, where the majority of the people were Protestants, most people wanted to remain citizens of the United Kingdom. The country now became the United Kingdom of Great Britain and Northern Ireland.

The modern history of the UK began in the 18th century with the expansion of the British empire, despite the loss in 1783 of its 13 North American colonies. The other significant milestone occurred in the late 18th century, when the UK became the first country to industrialize its economy.

The British empire broke up after World War II (1939–45), though the UK still administers many small, mainly island, territories around the world. The empire was transformed into the Commonwealth of Nations, a free association of independent countries which numbered 53 in 2019.

The UK has retained an important world role. In 2001, it played a prominent role in creating a broad alliance to counter international terrorism following attacks on the United States. It was also a member of the coalition force which invaded Iraq in 2003. It became a member of the European Economic Community (now the European Union) in 1973. Membership of the EU has been important to the British economy, but some have feared a loss of British sovereignty and identity. A referendum in June 2016 on the UK's future in the EU resulted in a narrow vote to leave. The process of leaving was triggered in March 2017 and the following month, a snap general election resulted in the Conservative government losing its overall majority. Despite problems getting a departure deal approved by parliament, the UK is due to leave the EU in 2019.

Since the late 1990s some powers have been devolved to Scotland, Wales, and Northern Ireland. The Northern Ireland Assembly has followed a fitful path since its establishment in 1998. The National Assembly for Wales and the Scottish Parliament both opened in 1999. In a referendum on Scottish independence held in 2014, 55% of voters elected to stay within the UK.

The UK is a major industrial and trading nation. It lacks natural resources apart from coal, iron ore, oil, and natural gas, and has to import most of the materials for its industries. The UK also has to import food, because it produces only about two-thirds of the food it needs. In the first half of the 20th century, Britain was a major exporter of cars, ships, steel, and textiles. But many industries have suffered from competition from other countries, with lower labor costs. From 2008, Britain's economy was hit by a global financial crisis, which led the country into recession. Severe austerity measures were introduced.

The UK is one of the world's most urbanized countries, and agriculture employs only 1% of the work force. Production is high because of the use of scientific methods and modern machinery. However, in the early 21st century, especially following the outbreak of foot-and-mouth disease in 2001, questions were raised about the future of rural industries. Major crops include barley, potatoes, sugar beet, and wheat. Sheep are the leading livestock, but beef and dairy cattle, pigs, and poultry are also important. Fishing is another major activity and the UK is one of the largest fishing countries in the EU.

Service industries play a major part in the UK's economy. Financial and insurance services bring in much-needed foreign exchange, while tourism has become a major earner.

AREA 93,381 SQ MI [241,857 SQ KM] **POPULATION** 65,105,000
CAPITAL LONDON **GOVERNMENT** CONSTITUTIONAL MONARCHY
ETHNIC GROUPS ENGLISH 84%, SCOTTISH 9%, WELSH 5%, N. IRISH 3%, WEST INDIAN, INDIAN, PAKISTANI AND OTHERS
LANGUAGES ENGLISH (OFFICIAL), WELSH, GAELIC
RELIGIONS CHRISTIANITY (ANGLICAN, ROMAN CATHOLIC, PRESBYTERIAN, METHODIST), ISLAM, SIKHISM, HINDUISM, JUDAISM
CURRENCY POUND STERLING = 100 PENCE

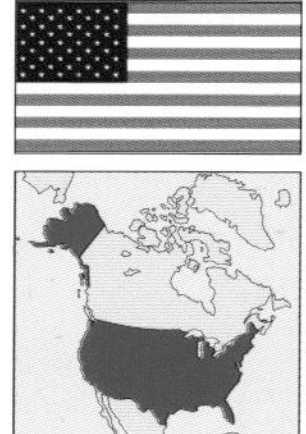

UNITED STATES OF AMERICA

GEOGRAPHY The United States of America is the world's fourth largest country in area and the third largest in population. It contains 50 states, 48 of which lie between Canada and Mexico, plus Alaska in northwestern North America, and Hawai'i, a group of volcanic islands in the north Pacific Ocean. Densely populated coastal plains lie to the east and south of the Appalachian Mountains. The central lowlands, drained by the Mississippi–Missouri rivers, stretch from the Appalachians to the Rocky Mountains in the west. The Pacific region contains fertile valleys, separated by mountain ranges.

The climate varies greatly, ranging from the Arctic cold of Alaska to the intense heat of Death Valley, a bleak desert in California. Of the 48 states between Canada and Mexico, winters are cold and snowy in the north, but mild in the south.

POLITICS & ECONOMY The first people in North America, the ancestors of the Native Americans (or American Indians), arrived perhaps 40,000 years ago from Asia. Although Vikings probably reached North America 1,000 years ago, European exploration proper did not begin until the late 15th century.

The first Europeans to settle in large numbers were the British, who founded settlements on the eastern coast in the early 17th century. British rule ended in the War of Independence (1775–83). The country expanded in 1803 when a vast territory in the south and west was acquired through the Louisiana Purchase, while the border with Mexico was fixed in the mid-19th century. The Civil War (1861–5) ended slavery and the serious threat that the nation might split into two parts. In the late 19th century, the West was opened up, while immigrants flooded in from Europe and elsewhere.

During the late 19th and early 20th centuries, industrialization led to the United States becoming the world's leading economic superpower and a pioneer in science and technology. It took on the mantle of the champion of Western democracy and, following the breakup of the former Soviet Union, it became the world's only superpower. But the attacks on the country on September 11, 2001, revealed its vulnerability to terrorists and rogue states. The response was vigorous. In 2001, it attacked the Taliban government in Afghanistan, which was protecting al Qaeda terrorists. Then, in 2003, it led a coalition force to invade Iraq and overthrow Saddam Hussein.

From 2008–16, Democrat Barack Obama was president. Bitterly fought elections in 2016 resulted in a win for businessman Donald Trump, on a ticket of protectionism, removing Obama's changes to health care and a crackdown on immigration. Policy announcements included major tax cuts, and the imposition of high import tariffs on such products as steel. Some of his more controversial plans, such as those to cut immigration, have been blocked by the courts and became harder to achieve after the Democrats gained a majority in the House of Representatives in November 2018.

The US economy has long been considered to be the world's largest, but some authorities now see it being challenged by China. Recovery from the global financial crisis of 2008 has been slow. There remains a wide disparity between rich and poor in the US and as many as 30 million Americans live below the poverty line.

Natural resources include oil, natural gas, coal, a wide range of metal ores, and timber. Manufacturing is the single most valuable activity, employing around 10% of the working population. Major products include vehicles, food products, chemicals, machinery, printed goods, metal products, and scientific instruments. California, with its many high-tech electronics industries, is the top manufacturing state.

AREA 3,717,792 SQ MI [9,629,091 SQ KM] **POPULATION** 329,256,000
CAPITAL WASHINGTON, DC **GOVERNMENT** FEDERAL REPUBLIC
ETHNIC GROUPS WHITE 80%, AFRICAN AMERICAN 13%, ASIAN 4%, AMERINDIAN 1%, OTHERS
LANGUAGES ENGLISH, SPANISH, MORE THAN 30 OTHERS
RELIGIONS PROTESTANT 51%, ROMAN CATHOLIC 24%, JUDAISM 2%, MORMON 2%, ISLAM 1%
CURRENCY US DOLLAR = 100 CENTS

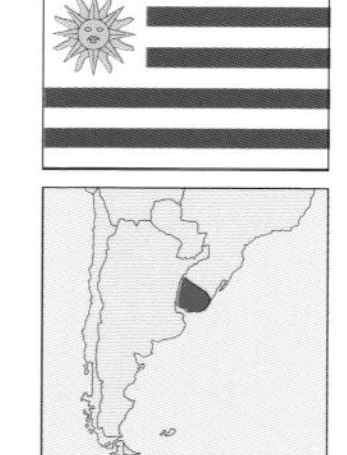

URUGUAY

GEOGRAPHY Uruguay is South America's second smallest independent country after Suriname. The land consists mainly of flat plains and hills. The River Uruguay, which forms the country's western border, flows into the Río de la Plata, a large estuary which leads into the South Atlantic Ocean.

Uruguay has a mild climate, with rain in every month, though droughts sometimes can occur. Summers are pleasantly warm and winters relatively mild.

POLITICS & ECONOMY In 1726, Spanish settlers founded Montevideo in order to halt the Portuguese gaining influence in the area. By the late 18th century, Spaniards had settled in most of the country and Uruguay became part of a colony called the Viceroyalty of La Plata, which also included Argentina, Paraguay, and parts of Bolivia, Brazil, and Chile. In 1820 Brazil annexed Uruguay, ending Spanish rule. In 1825, Uruguayans, supported by Argentina, began a struggle for independence.

Finally, in 1828, Brazil and Argentina recognized Uruguay as an independent republic. Social and economic developments were slow, but, from 1903, Uruguay became stable and democratic.

From the 1950s, economic problems incited unrest from terrorist groups, notably the Tupumaros, until the army took over the government in 1973. Military rule continued until elections were held in 1984. In the early 21st century, Uruguay faced many economic problems, many of which were the result of the economic crisis in Argentina. Tabaré Vázquez replaced Jose Mujica as president in March 2015. Vázquez had previously been president in 2005–10.

The World Bank now classifies Uruguay as a "high-income" economy but, although it is one of the more prosperous countries in South America, there is still a minority underclass living in poverty. Agriculture employs 13% of the work force, and farm products, notably hides and leather goods, beef, and wool, are the main exports, while many manufacturing industries process farm products. Crops include maize, potatoes, wheat, and sugar beet. Uruguay depends largely on renewable power for energy, notably hydropower, wind and solar. In 2008, Uruguay announced the discovery of an offshore natural gas field, which is being explored.

AREA 67,574 SQ MI [175,016 SQ KM] **POPULATION** 3,369,000
CAPITAL MONTEVIDEO **GOVERNMENT** MULTIPARTY REPUBLIC
ETHNIC GROUPS WHITE 88%, MESTIZO 8%, MULATTO OR BLACK 4%
LANGUAGES SPANISH (OFFICIAL)
RELIGIONS CHRISTIANITY 58% (ROMAN CATHOLIC 47%), OTHERS
CURRENCY URUGUAYAN PESO = 100 CENTÉSIMOS

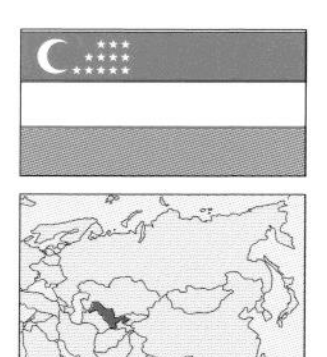

UZBEKISTAN

GEOGRAPHY The Republic of Uzbekistan is one of the five republics in Central Asia which were once part of the Soviet Union. Plains cover most of western Uzbekistan, with highlands in the east. The main rivers, the Amudarya and Syrdarya, drain into the Aral Sea. So much water has been taken from these rivers to irrigate the land to grow cotton that the Aral Sea has now shrunk to about a quarter of its size in 1960. The former lake area is now desert. Uzbekistan has cold winters and hot summers. The largely uninhabited Kyzyl Kum desert lies in central Uzbekistan.

POLITICS & ECONOMY Russia took the area in the 19th century. After the Russian Revolution of 1917, the Communists took over and, in 1924, they set up the Uzbek Soviet Socialist Republic. Under Communism, all aspects of Uzbek life were controlled and religious worship was discouraged, but education, health, housing, and transport were improved. In the late 1980s, the people demanded more autonomy, leading to independence in 1991 with the breakup of the Soviet Union.

Islam Karimov, leader of the People's Democratic Party (formerly the Communist Party), was first elected president in December 1991. Dissent was not tolerated and opposition leaders were arrested and accused of threatening national stability. Initially, Karimov's government allowed the US to use Uzbekistan as a base for its military campaign in Afghanistan, but relations cooled in 2005 and the US was asked to remove its troops. In an about-face in 2009, ties with Russia deteriorated and those with the US improved and they were again able to transport supplies through Uzbekistan to their troops. The United Nations has condemned the country's human rights record. Karimov remained in power until his death in 2016, when Prime Minister Shavjat Mirziyoyev was elected to replace him. Mirziyoyev has improved relations with neighbouring countries and made moves to open up the economy.

The World Bank classifies Uzbekistan as a "lower-middle-income" developing country. Uzbekistan is one of the world's largest cotton exporters, although this has declined in recent years. The country produces coal, copper, gold, oil, and natural gas.

AREA 172,741 SQ MI [447,400 SQ KM] **POPULATION** 30,024,000
CAPITAL TASHKENT **GOVERNMENT** SOCIALIST REPUBLIC
ETHNIC GROUPS UZBEK 80%, RUSSIAN 5%, TAJIK 5%, KAZAKH 3%, TATAR 2%, KARA-KALPAK 2%
LANGUAGES UZBEK (OFFICIAL), RUSSIAN **RELIGIONS** ISLAM 88%, EASTERN ORTHODOX 9% **CURRENCY** UZBEKISTANI SUM = 100 TYIYN

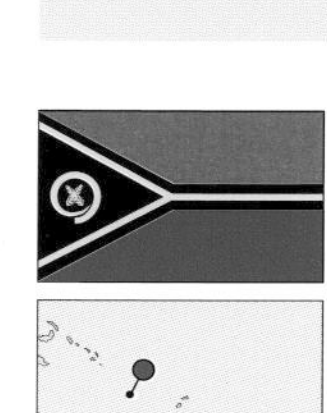

VANUATU

The Republic of Vanuatu, formerly the Anglo-French Condominium of the New Hebrides, became independent in 1980. It consists of a chain of 80 islands in the south Pacific Ocean. Its economy is based on agriculture, and it exports copra, beef and veal, timber, and cocoa.

AREA 4,706 SQ MI [12,189 SQ KM]
POPULATION 288,000 **CAPITAL** PORT-VILA

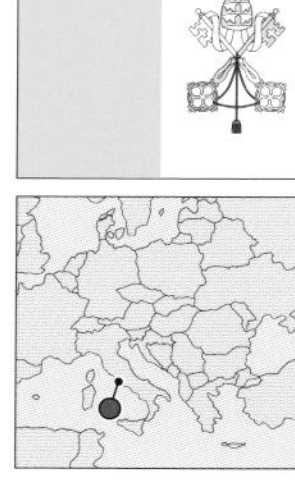

VATICAN CITY

Vatican City State, the world's smallest independent nation, is an enclave on the west bank of the River Tiber in Rome. It forms an independent base for the Holy See, the governing body of the Roman Catholic Church.

AREA 0.17 SQ MI [0.44 SQ KM]
POPULATION 1,000

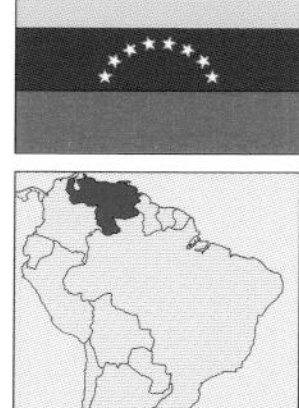

VENEZUELA

GEOGRAPHY The Bolivarian Republic of Venezuela, in northern South America, contains the Maracaibo lowlands around the oil-rich Lake Maracaibo in the west. Andean ranges enclose the lowlands and extend across most of the northern part of the country. The Orinoco river basin, containing tropical grasslands called llanos, lies between the northern highlands and the Guiana Highlands in the southeast. The Orinoco is Venezuela's longest river. Venezuela has a tropical climate. Rainfall is heaviest in the mountains, but much of the country has a dry season between December and April.

POLITICS & ECONOMY In the early 19th century, Venezuelans such as Simón Bolívar and Francisco de Miranda rebeled against Spanish colonial rule, leading to full independence in 1821.

The country has greatly benefited from its oil resources (first exploited in 1917) which are some of the world's largest In 1960, Venezuela helped to form OPEC (the Organization of Petroleum Exporting Countries) and, in 1976, the government of Venezuela took control of the country's oil industry. In 1999, Hugo Chavez, who had staged an unsuccessful coup in 1992, was elected president. Chavez remained in office until his death in 2013 when he was succeeded by the socialist Nicolás Maduro. A severe economic downturn followed and Maduro's rule became increasingly autocratic. In 2018 he was re-elected to a second term, but the election was widely regarded as fraudulent. The result was declared invalid by the National Assembly, whose leader, Juan Guaidó, declared himself interim president in 2019. Maduro refused to step down. The ongoing crisis has led to hyperinflation and widespread shortages of food, medicines and electricity.

The political crisis has devastated Venezuela's economy, which has long been dependent on oil exports. The majority of the people live in poverty and unemployment is high. Other exports include bauxite and aluminum, iron ore, and farm products. Beef cattle, dairy cattle, and poultry are raised. Crops include bananas, citrus fruits, coffee, and rice. The main industry is petroleum refining. Cement, steel, and textiles are also produced.

AREA 352,143 SQ MI [912,050 SQ KM] **POPULATION** 31,689,000
CAPITAL CARACAS **GOVERNMENT** FEDERAL REPUBLIC
ETHNIC GROUPS SPANISH, ITALIAN, PORTUGUESE, ARAB, GERMAN, AFRICAN, INDIGENOUS PEOPLE **LANGUAGES** SPANISH (OFFICIAL), INDIGENOUS DIALECTS **RELIGIONS** ROMAN CATHOLIC 96%
CURRENCY BOLÍVAR = 100 CÉNTIMOS

VIETNAM

GEOGRAPHY The Socialist Republic of Vietnam occupies an S-shaped strip of land facing the South China Sea in Southeast Asia. The coastal plains include two densely populated, fertile delta regions: the Red (Hong) delta facing the Gulf of Tonkin in the north, and the Mekong delta in the south.

Vietnam has a tropical climate, though the driest months of January to March are a little cooler than the wet, hot summer months, when monsoon winds blow from the southwest. Typhoons (cyclones or hurricanes) sometimes hit the coast, causing extensive flooding and much damage.

POLITICS & ECONOMY China dominated Vietnam for a thousand years before AD 939, when a Vietnamese state was founded. The French took over the area between the 1850s and 1880s, and they ruled Vietnam as part of French Indochina, which also included Cambodia and Laos.

Japan conquered Vietnam during World War II (1939–45). In 1946, war broke out between the Vietminh, a nationalist group, and the French colonial government. France withdrew in 1954 and Vietnam was divided into a Communist North Vietnam, led by the Vietminh leader, Ho Chi Minh, and a non-Communist South.

In 1957, a Communist insurgency, led by the Viet Cong, rebeled against South Vietnam's government provoking a war that gradually escalated. The United States aided the South, but after it withdrew in 1975, South Vietnam surrendered. In 1976, the united Vietnam became a socialist republic. From the mid-1990s, diplomatic and trade relations were restored between the US and Vietnam, and the US is now its main trading partner. In 2007, Vietnam became a member of the World Trade Organization after 12 years of negotiations. The benefits of moves to modernize the economy have not been enjoyed by all groups in society: there is poverty in rural areas. Human rights issues remain a concern. Political power remains entirely in the hands of the ruling Communist Party.

Agriculture is the main activity although its share of economic output is diminishing. Rice and coffee are the main crops. Vietnam produces electronic goods, textiles, chromium, tin, and phosphates.

AREA 128,065 SQ MI [331,689 SQ KM] **POPULATION** 97,040,000
CAPITAL HANOI **GOVERNMENT** SOCIALIST REPUBLIC
ETHNIC GROUPS VIETNAMESE 87%, CHINESE, HMONG, THAI, KHMER, CHAM, MOUNTAIN GROUPS
LANGUAGES VIETNAMESE (OFFICIAL), ENGLISH, CHINESE
RELIGIONS BUDDHISM, CHRISTIANITY, INDIGENOUS BELIEFS
CURRENCY DONG = 10 HAO = 100 XU

VIRGIN ISLANDS, BRITISH

The British Virgin Islands, the most northerly of the Lesser Antilles, are a British overseas territory, with a substantial measure of self-government.

AREA 58 SQ MI [151 SQ KM]
POPULATION 35,000 **CAPITAL** ROAD TOWN

VIRGIN ISLANDS, US

The Virgin Islands of the United States, a group of three islands and 65 small islets, are a self-governing US territory, which was purchased from Denmark in 1917. Its residents are US citizens and they elect a non-voting delegate to the US House of Representatives.

AREA 134 SQ MI [347 SQ KM]
POPULATION 107,000 **CAPITAL** CHARLOTTE AMALIE

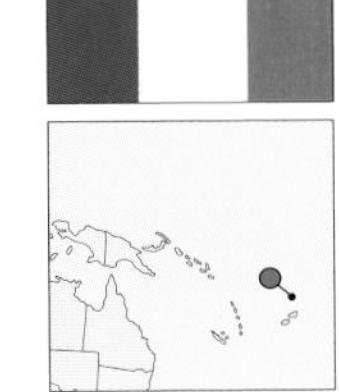

WALLIS AND FUTUNA

Wallis and Futuna, in the south Pacific Ocean, is the smallest and the poorest of France's overseas "collectivities." French aid is vital to an economy based on subsistence agriculture.

AREA 77 SQ MI [200 SQ KM]
POPULATION 16,000 **CAPITAL** MATA-UTU

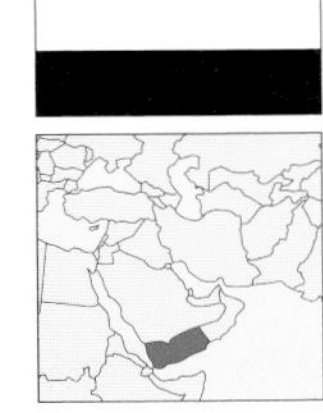

YEMEN

GEOGRAPHY The Republic of Yemen faces the Red Sea and the Gulf of Aden in the southwestern corner of the Arabian peninsula. Behind the narrow coastal plain along the Red Sea, the land rises to the mountains of the High Yemen. The climate ranges from hot and often humid conditions on the coast to the cooler highlands. Most of the country is arid. The south coasts are particularly hot and humid.

POLITICS & ECONOMY After World War I, northern Yemen, which had been ruled by Turkey, began to evolve into a separate state from the south, where Britain was in control. Britain withdrew in 1967 and a left-wing government took power in the south. In North Yemen, the monarchy was abolished in 1962 and the country became a republic.

Clashes occurred between the two factions but, in 1990, the two Yemens merged to form a single country. In the 2000s, the government faced conflict with Shi'ite northern rebels, called Houthis, al Qaeda supporters, and southern separatists. In 2011, protesters in the cities called on President Ali Abdullah Saleh to resign. He pledged not to run at the next election and to introduce constitutional reforms, including the introduction of a parliamentary system, but the violent protests continued. Rebel activity in the north turned into civil war in 2014, with the Houthi occupying Sana' in 2014, and declaring a new government. A Saudi-led coalition is combating the Houthi, while US drone strikes target Islamic State and al-Qaeda bases. UN-brokered peace talks began in 2018. There is a growing refugee crisis, famine, and a major cholera outbreak.

Yemen is the poorest country in the Middle East, and its economy has been devastated by the civil war. Sheep are reared and crops such as barley, fruits, wheat, and vegetables are grown. Cash crops include coffee and cotton. Petroleum extraction is important to the economy. Remittances from Yemenis abroad are a major source of revenue.

AREA 203,848 SQ MI [527,968 SQ KM] **POPULATION** 28,667,000
CAPITAL SANA' **GOVERNMENT** MULTIPARTY REPUBLIC
ETHNIC GROUPS PREDOMINANTLY ARAB **LANGUAGES** ARABIC (OFFICIAL)
RELIGIONS ISLAM **CURRENCY** YEMENI RIAL = 100 FILS

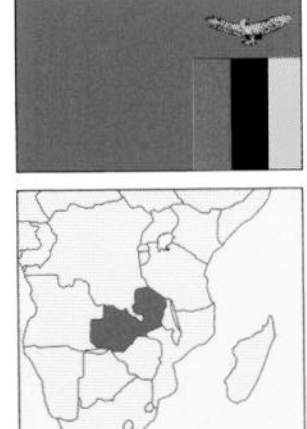

ZAMBIA

GEOGRAPHY The Republic of Zambia is a landlocked country in southern Africa. Zambia lies on the plateau that makes up most of the southern part of the continent. Much of the land is between 2,950 ft and 4,920 ft [900 m to 1,500 m] above sea level. The Muchinga Mountains in the northeast rise above this flat land. Lakes include Bangweulu, which is entirely within Zambia, together with parts of lakes Mweru and Tanganyika in the north. Zambia lies in the tropics, but temperatures are moderated by the altitude.

POLITICS & ECONOMY European contact with Zambia began in the 19th century, when the explorer David Livingstone crossed the River Zambezi. In the 1890s, the British South Africa Company, set up by Cecil Rhodes, the British financier and statesman, made treaties with local chiefs and gradually took over the area. In 1911, the Company named the area Northern Rhodesia and, in 1924, Britain took control of the country.

In 1953, Britain formed a federation of Northern Rhodesia, Southern Rhodesia (now Zimbabwe), and Nyasaland (now Malawi). Due to African opposition, the federation was dissolved in 1963 and Northern Rhodesia gained independence as Zambia in 1964. Kenneth Kaunda became president and remained in office for 27 years until Frederick Chiluba was elected in 1996. The current president, Edgar Lungu, took office in 2015.

At nearly 7% per annum, Zambia's economy grew strongly in the early years of this century, until copper prices began to fall in 2015. Copper, however, remains the main resource, and accounts for about 60% of the country's exports. Zambia also produces cobalt, lead, zinc, and gemstones. Agriculture employs about 55% of the people, as compared with around 10% in industry and mining. Food crops include cassava, fruits and vegetables, maize, millet, and sorghum. Cash crops include coffee, sugarcane, and tobacco.

AREA 290,586 SQ MI [752,618 SQ KM] **POPULATION** 16,445,000
CAPITAL LUSAKA **GOVERNMENT** MULTIPARTY REPUBLIC
ETHNIC GROUPS NATIVE AFRICAN (BEMBA, TONGA, MARAVI/NYANJA)
LANGUAGES ENGLISH, BEMBA, KAONDA, NYANJA AND ABOUT 70 OTHERS
RELIGIONS CHRISTIANITY 62%, ISLAM, HINDUISM
CURRENCY ZAMBIAN KWACHA = 100 NGWEE

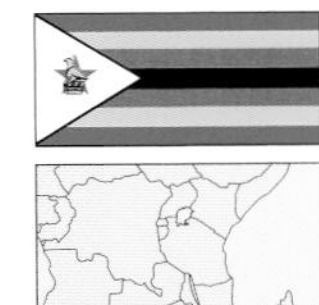

ZIMBABWE

GEOGRAPHY The Republic of Zimbabwe is a landlocked country in southern Africa. Most of the country lies on a high plateau between the Zambezi and Limpopo rivers, ranging from 2,950 ft to 4,920 ft [900 m to 1,500 m] above sea level. From October to March, the weather is hot and wet, but in the winter, daily temperatures can vary greatly.

POLITICS & ECONOMY The Shona people became dominant in the region about 1,000 years ago. The British South Africa Company, under the statesman Cecil Rhodes, occupied the area in the 1890s, after obtaining mineral rights from local chiefs. The area was named Rhodesia, and later Southern Rhodesia, becoming a self-governing British colony in 1923. Between 1953 and 1963, Southern and Northern Rhodesia (now Zambia) were united with Nyasaland (Malawi) in the Central African Federation.

In 1965, the European government of Southern Rhodesia (then called Rhodesia) declared their country independent, but Britain refused to accept this. After a civil war, the country became legally independent in 1980. Order was restored when the Shona prime minister, Robert Mugabe, brought his Ndebele rivals into his government. In 1987, Mugabe became the country's executive president.

From the late 1990s, Mugabe's government supported a violent campaign of land redistribution, seizing white-owned farms to be occupied by landless "war veterans." In elections in 2008, Mugabe lost to Morgan Tsvangirai, but intimidation of opposition supporters led Tsvangirai to withdraw from a run-off. In September 2008, a power-sharing government was set up, with Mugabe as president and Tsvangirai as prime minister. The election in 2013 saw Mugabe returned as president for the seventh time. He was finally forced out by military intervention in late 2017 and replaced by his former vice-president Emmerson Mnangagwa, who went on to win a narrow victory in presidential elections in 2018.

In the 2000s, the economy collapsed and many people starved as a result of food shortages. The breakdown of public services led to a cholera epidemic. In 2009 the government allowed the use of foreign currencies in an effort to stem hyperinflation. The economy now appears to be stabilizing. Zimbabwe has valuable mineral reserves. Agriculture employs 66% of the work force. Maize is the main food crop. Cash crops include cotton, sugar, and tobacco. Cattle ranching is also important.

AREA 150,871 SQ MI [390,757 SQ KM] **POPULATION** 14,030,000
CAPITAL HARARE **GOVERNMENT** MULTIPARTY REPUBLIC
ETHNIC GROUPS SHONA 82%, NDEBELE 14%, OTHER AFRICAN GROUPS 2%, MIXED AND ASIAN 1% **LANGUAGES** ENGLISH, SHONA, NDEBELE
RELIGIONS CHRISTIANITY, TRADITIONAL BELIEFS
CURRENCY MULTIPLE CURRENCIES

The shallow waters around the islands of The Bahamas can be seen clearly in this image, showing up as a brighter, paler blue than the deeper waters of the Caribbean Sea. The Bahamas is made up of approximately 700 coral and limestone islands, of which only about 30 are inhabited, and 2,000 cays, stretching from southeast of Florida to just north of Cuba, the large island visible towards the bottom of the image. The islands are low-lying and flat, reaching a high point of only 206 ft (63 m) at Mount Alvernia on Cat Island. The history of The Bahamas is informed by its strategic location at the gateway between the Caribbean Sea and the Gulf of Mexico. In the 17th and 18th centuries the islands became a haven for pirates, who took advantage of their proximity to well-traveled shipping lanes and even founded a short-lived "pirate republic" at Nassau on New Providence. [Map page 320] *NPA Satellite Mapping, CGG Services (UK) Ltd*

WORLD GEOGRAPHY

For more information:
70 Orbits of the planets
Planetary data

About 13.8 billion years ago, time and space began with the most colossal explosion in cosmic history: the so-called Big Bang that is believed to have initiated the Universe. According to current theory, in the first millionth of a second of its existence it expanded from a dimensionless point of infinite mass and density into a fireball about the size of our present Solar System – and it has been expanding ever since.

It took about 380,000 years for the primal fireball to cool enough for atoms to form. They were mostly hydrogen which is still the most abundant material in the Universe. The radiation from this era still pervades the Universe, though its subsequent expansion means that we see it at about 3° above absolute zero instead of its original 3,000°C. Observations of this faint background glow reveal slight fluctuations. It is these which appear to have become, over the next billion years or so, the large-scale structures in the present Universe. As well as the matter which we can see, there is evidence of a much greater quantity of dark matter whose nature remains unknown. Within knots of this dark matter, the first stars and galaxies formed, probably within the first billion years of the life of the Universe. Our own Galaxy was among them.

There were several generations of stars, each feeding on the wreckage of its extinct predecessors as well as the original galactic gas swirls. With each new generation, progressively larger atoms were forged in stellar furnaces, and the Galaxy's range of elements, once restricted to hydrogen and helium, grew larger. About 9 billion years after the Big Bang, a star formed on the outskirts of our Galaxy with enough matter left over to create a retinue of planets. Nearly 5 billion years after that, human beings evolved.

The Sun is one of more than 100 billion stars in the home galaxy alone. Our Galaxy, in turn, forms part of a local group consisting of approximately 50 similar structures, mostly small "dwarf" galaxies but a few large ones, and one – the Andromeda Galaxy – similar in size to our own. There are at least 100 billion galaxies in the Universe, many of which are members of huge galaxy clusters.

LIFE OF A STAR

For most of its existence, a star produces energy by the nuclear fusion of hydrogen into helium at its core. The duration of this hydrogen-burning period – known as the *main sequence* – depends on the star's mass; the greater the mass, the higher the core temperatures and the sooner the star's supply of hydrogen is exhausted. Dim, dwarf stars consume their hydrogen slowly, eking it out over billions of years. The Sun, like other stars of its mass, should spend about 10 billion years on the main sequence; since it was formed less than 5 billion years ago, it still has half its life left.

Once all of a star's core hydrogen has been fused into helium, nuclear activity moves outward into layers of unconsumed hydrogen. For a time, energy production sharply increases: the star grows hotter and expands enormously, turning into a so-called red giant. Its energy output will increase a thousandfold, and it will swell to a hundred times its former diameter.

After a few hundred million years, helium in the core will become sufficiently compressed to initiate a new cycle of nuclear fusion: from helium to carbon. The star will contract somewhat, before beginning its last expansion, in the Sun's case engulfing the Earth and perhaps Mars. In this bloated condition, the Sun's outer layers will break off into space, leaving a tiny inner core, mainly of carbon, that shrinks progressively under its own gravity. The white dwarf star thus formed can attain a density more than 10,000 times that of normal matter, with crushing surface gravity to match. Gradually, the nuclear fires will die down, and the Sun will reach its terminal stage: a black dwarf, emitting insignificant amounts of energy.

Black holes

However, stars more massive than the Sun may undergo a different transformation. The additional mass allows gravitational collapse to continue indefinitely: eventually, all the star's remaining matter shrinks to a point, and its density approaches infinity – a state that will not permit even subatomic structures to survive.

The star has become a *black hole*: an anomalous "singularity" in the fabric of space and time. Although vast coruscations of radiation will be emitted by any matter falling into its grasp, the singularity itself has an escape velocity that exceeds the speed of light, and nothing can ever be released from it. Within the boundaries of the black hole, the laws of physics are suspended.

GALACTIC STRUCTURES

▲ The galaxy cluster Abell 2744, nicknamed Pandora's Cluster for the wide range of galaxy phenomena within it. The brightest galaxies are ellipticals of various shapes, but spiral and barred spiral galaxies are also visible. The cross-shaped features on the star images are optical effects in the Hubble Space Telescope.

Many of the Universe's 100 billion galaxies show clear structural patterns, originally classified by the American astronomer Edwin Hubble in 1925. Spiral galaxies like our own have a central, almost spherical bulge and a surrounding disk composed of spiral arms. Barred spirals have a central bar of stars across the nucleus, with spiral arms trailing from the ends of the bar. Elliptical galaxies have a more uniform appearance, ranging from a flattened disk to a near sphere.

Most galaxies, however, have no obvious structure at all. Galaxies also vary enormously in size, from dwarf galaxies only 2,000 light years across to great assemblies of stars 80 or more times larger.

THE HOME GALAXY

The Sun and its planets are located in one of the spiral arms of the Galaxy, about 26,000 light years from the galactic center and orbiting around it in a period of about 220 million years. The center is invisible from the Earth, masked by vast, light-absorbing clouds of interstellar dust.

The Galaxy is probably around 12 billion years old and, like other spiral galaxies, has three distinct regions. The central bulge is about 30,000 light years in diameter. The disk in which the Sun is located is not much more than 1,000 light years thick, but approximately 130,000 light years from end to end. Around the Galaxy is the halo, a spherical zone 300,000 light years across, studded with globular star clusters and sprinkled with individual suns.

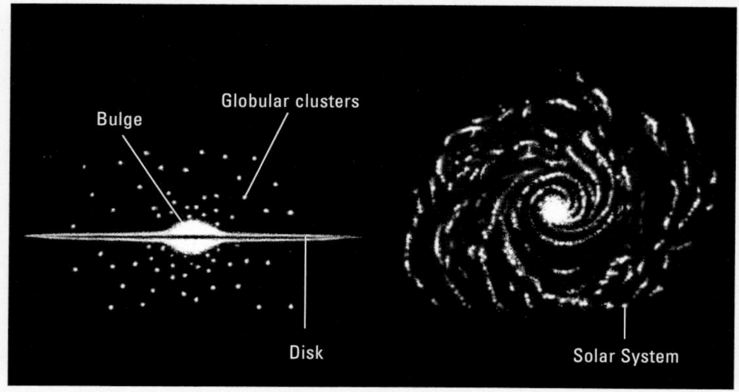

THE END OF THE UNIVERSE

The likely fate of the Universe is disputed. According to one theory (*top of diagram, below*), the expansion begun at the time of the Big Bang will continue "indefinitely," with aging galaxies moving farther and farther apart in an immense, dark graveyard.

Alternatively, gravity may overcome the expansion (*bottom of diagram*). Galaxies will fall back together until everything is again concentrated at a single point, followed by a new Big Bang and a new expansion, in an endlessly repeated cycle.

Observations of distant galaxies suggest that the expansion of the Universe is accelerating. This is attributed to a hypothetical dark energy filling the Universe, so continued expansion is considered likely.

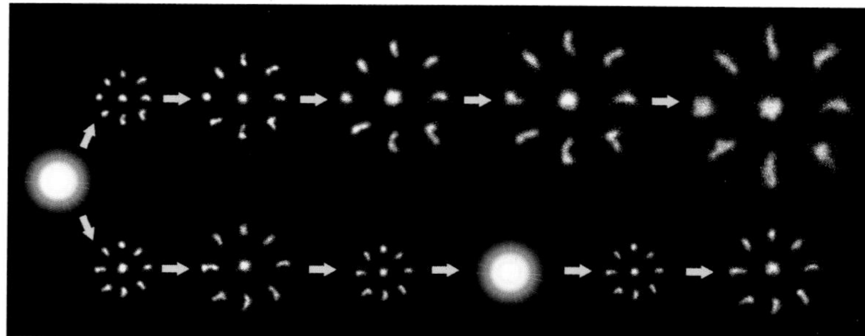

THE NEAREST STARS

The nearest stars, excluding the Sun, with their distance from Earth in light years*

Proxima Centauri	4.2	UV Ceti A & B	8.8	61 Cygni A & B	11.4
Alpha Centauri A & B	4.4	Ross 154	9.7	Procyon A & B	11.4
Barnard's Star	6.0	Ross 248	10.3	Struve 2398 A & B	11.5
Luhman 16 A & B	6.5	Epsilon Eridani	10.4	Groombridge 34 A & B	11.6
WISE 0855-0714	7.3	HD 217987	10.7	DX Cancri	11.7
Wolf 359	7.9	Ross 128	11.0	Tau Ceti	11.8
Lalande 21185	8.3	WISE 1506+7027	11.1		
Sirius A & B	8.7	L789-6 A, B & C	11.1		

* A light year is about 5,900 billion miles [9,500 billion km]

Many of the nearest stars, like Alpha Centauri A and B, are double stars, orbiting about their common center of gravity and to all intents and purposes equidistant from Earth. Many of them are dim objects including brown dwarfs: self-luminous objects which are intermediate in mass between planets and stars.

However, they include Sirius, the brightest star in the sky, and Procyon, the seventh brightest. Both are larger than the Sun; of the nearest stars, only Epsilon Eridani is similar in size and luminosity. Most of the other bright stars in the sky are within 500 light years of the Sun – a small fraction of the diameter of our Galaxy.

STAR CHARTS

NORTHERN HEMISPHERE SKY

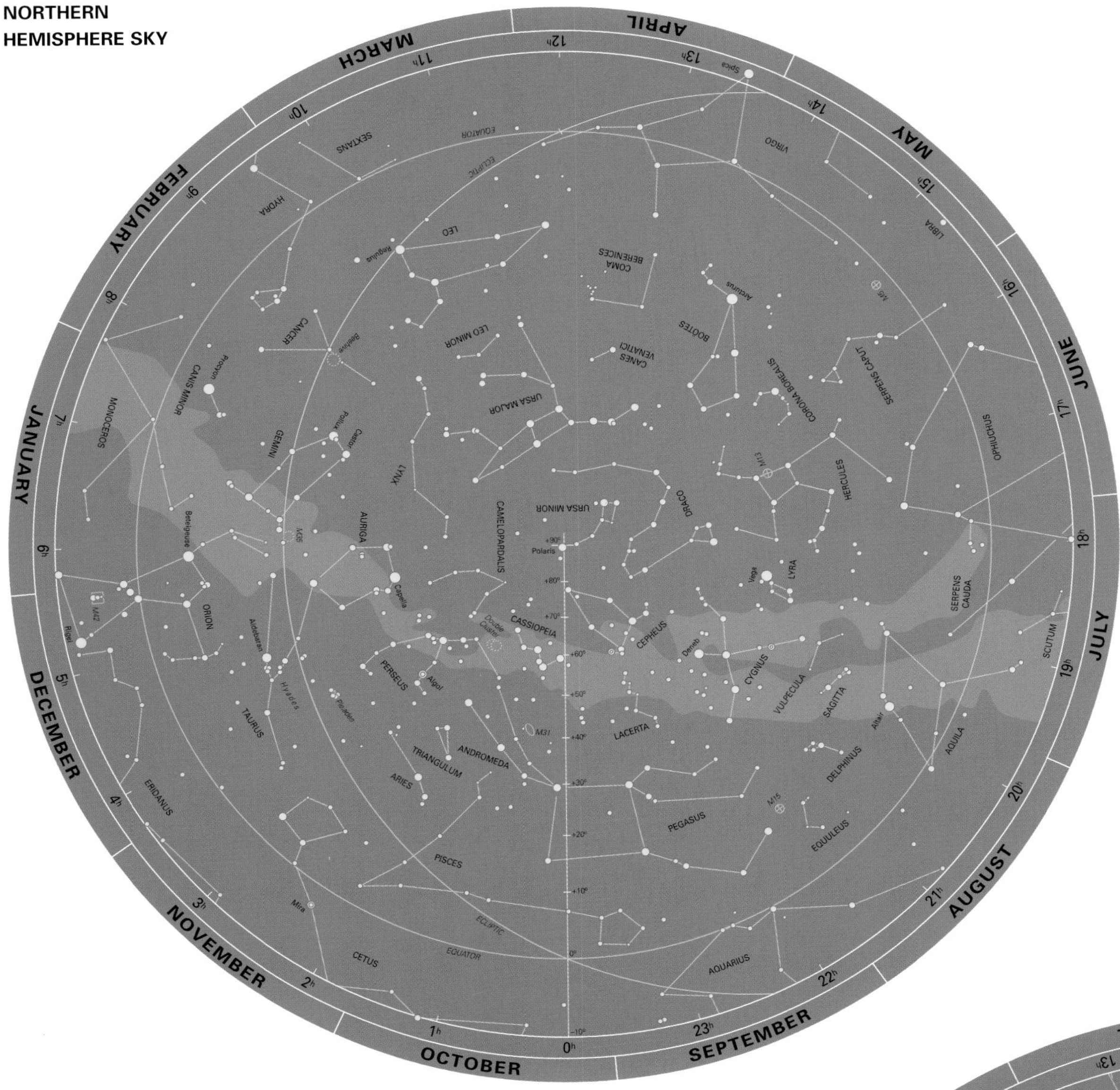

THE CONSTELLATIONS

The constellations and their English names

Andromeda	Andromeda	Lacerta	Lizard
Antlia	Air Pump	Leo	Lion
Apus	Bird of Paradise	Leo Minor	Little Lion
Aquarius	Water Carrier	Lepus	Hare
Aquila	Eagle	Libra	Scales
Ara	Altar	Lupus	Wolf
Aries	Ram	Lynx	Lynx
Auriga	Charioteer	Lyra	Lyre
Boötes	Herdsman	Mensa	Table Mountain
Caelum	Chisel	Microscopium	Microscope
Camelopardalis	Giraffe	Monoceros	Unicorn
Cancer	Crab	Musca	Fly
Canes Venatici	Hunting Dogs	Norma	Level
Canis Major	Great Dog	Octans	Octant
Canis Minor	Little Dog	Ophiuchus	Serpent Bearer
Capricornus	Sea Goat	Orion	Orion
Carina	Ship's Keel	Pavo	Peacock
Cassiopeia	Cassiopeia	Pegasus	Winged Horse
Centaurus	Centaur	Perseus	Perseus
Cepheus	Cepheus	Phoenix	Phoenix
Cetus	Whale	Pictor	Easel
Chamaeleon	Chameleon	Pisces	Fishes
Circinus	Compasses	Piscis Austrinus	Southern Fish
Columba	Dove	Puppis	Ship's Stern
Coma Berenices	Berenice's Hair	Pyxis	Mariner's Compass
Corona Australis	Southern Crown	Reticulum	Net
Corona Borealis	Northern Crown	Sagitta	Arrow
Corvus	Crow	Sagittarius	Archer
Crater	Cup	Scorpius	Scorpion
Crux	Southern Cross	Sculptor	Sculptor
Cygnus	Swan	Scutum	Shield
Delphinus	Dolphin	Serpens	Serpent
Dorado	Swordfish	Sextans	Sextant
Draco	Dragon	Taurus	Bull
Equuleus	Little Horse	Telescopium	Telescope
Eridanus	River Eridanus	Triangulum	Triangle
Fornax	Furnace	Triangulum Australe	Southern Triangle
Gemini	Twins	Tucana	Toucan
Grus	Crane	Ursa Major	Great Bear
Hercules	Hercules	Ursa Minor	Little Bear
Horologium	Clock	Vela	Ship's Sails
Hydra	Water Snake	Virgo	Virgin
Hydrus	Sea Serpent	Volans	Flying Fish
Indus	Indian	Vulpecula	Fox

SOUTHERN HEMISPHERE SKY

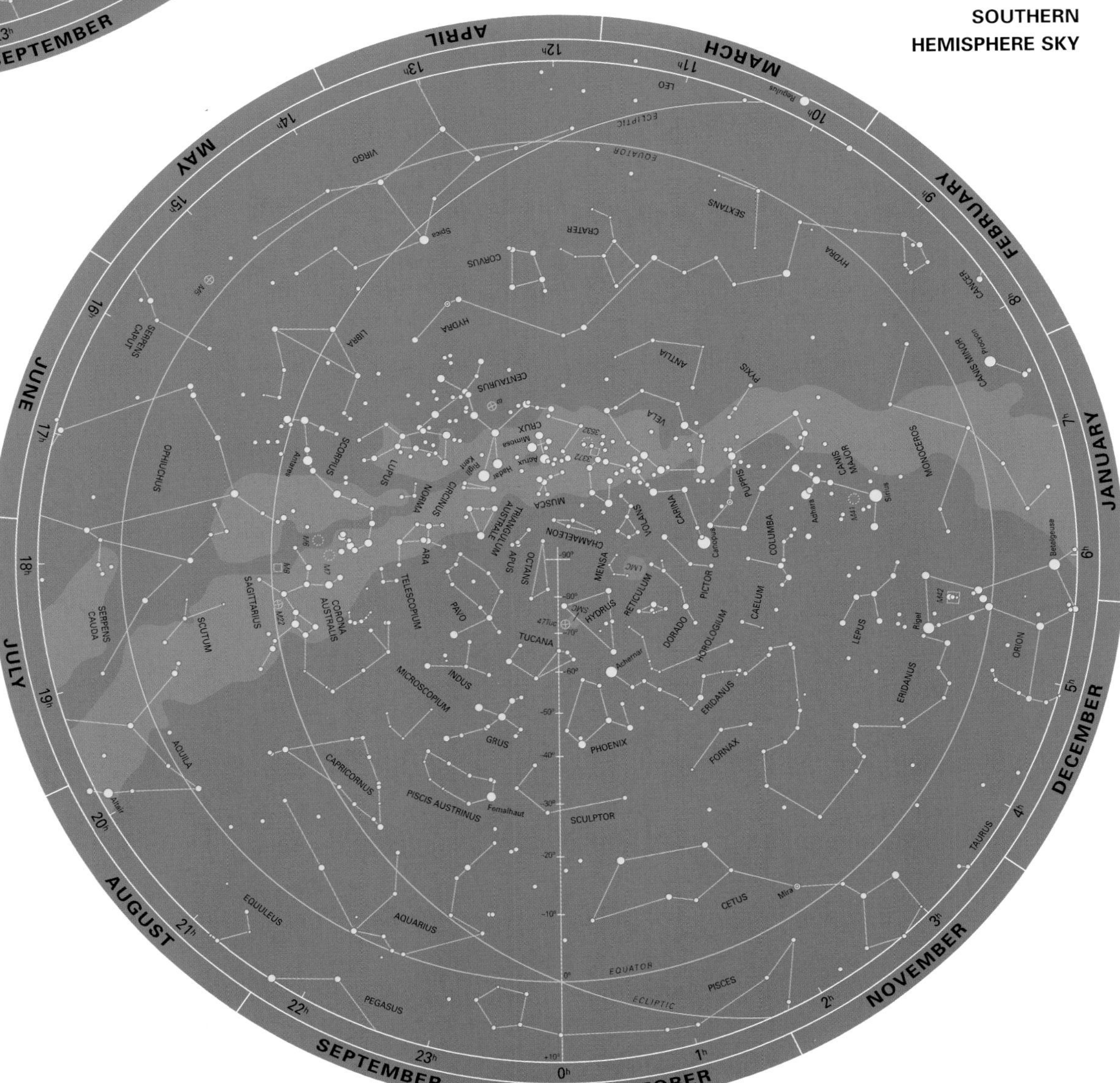

The charts on this page show the entire heavens divided into northern and southern hemispheres, with 10° of overlap between them around the perimeter of each one. However, the view from any particular location on Earth will be different, and will change both hourly as the Earth turns, and throughout the year as the Earth goes around the Sun.

The Sun's annual path through the heavens is known as the "ecliptic," and is shown here by an orange line. When the Sun is in the sky its light drowns out our view of the stars, so only that part of the heavens opposite the Sun is visible at a particular time. The sky's equivalent of longitude is known as "right ascension." As the stars appear to rotate around the Earth once every 24 hours, right ascension is measured eastward in hours and minutes, and is marked around the edge of the maps. The equivalent of latitude is "declination," measured in degrees north or south of the celestial equator, and shown by the vertical line on each chart.

Using the charts

At any place and time you can see half of the whole sky, assuming a flat horizon. If you were at one of the poles your view would be shown as a circle centered on the middle of the map for the appropriate hemisphere, with the horizon marked by the celestial equator. From all other locations the center of your view (your overhead point) will be at some other point on the map whose location changes with time. The closer you are to Earth's equator, the closer the center will be to the edge of the map and more stars in the opposite hemisphere will be visible.

So first choose the appropriate chart for your hemisphere and hold it with the month at the bottom. At 11 p.m., not allowing for Daylight Saving Time (Summer Time), your overhead point will be at the same declination as your geographical latitude and stars lower on the map will be due south (or north in the southern hemisphere). From latitude 50° in mid August, for example, your overhead point will be close to the star Deneb in the constellation of Cygnus. Stars on the opposite side of the map will be below your northern horizon, while stars below Deneb will be due south.

STAR MAGNITUDES

Apparent visual magnitudes

The magnitude scale of star brightnesses is developed from the system used by the Ancient Greeks in which the brightest stars were first magnitude and the faintest visible to the naked eye were sixth. Today the scale has a mathematical basis and extends, at the brightest end, through to negative magnitudes.

The Milky Way is shown in light blue on these charts.

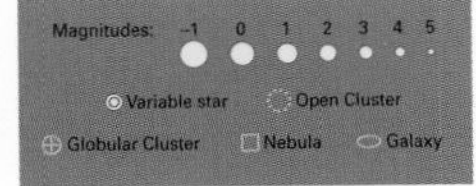

For more information:
68 The Home Galaxy
72 The seasons
Day and night
73 The Moon

Lying about halfway from the center of one of billions of galaxies that populate the observable Universe, our Solar System contains eight planets and their moons, at least five dwarf planets, innumerable asteroids, comets and other icy bodies, and a miscellany of dust and gas, all tethered by the immense gravitational field of the Sun, the star whose thermonuclear furnaces provide them all with heat and light.

The Solar System was formed about 5 billion years ago, when a spinning cloud of gas, mostly hydrogen but seeded with other heavier elements, condensed enough to ignite a nuclear reaction and create a star. The Sun still accounts for almost 99.9% of the system's total mass.

By composition as well as distance, the planetary array divides quite neatly in two: an inner system of four small, solid planets, including the Earth, and an outer system, from Jupiter to Neptune, of four much larger planets composed of lighter materials, such as gas, liquid, and ice. Lying mostly between the two groups is a scattering of rocky asteroids, numbering perhaps a million or more. They may be debris left over from the formation of the inner Solar System. In 2006, Pluto was demoted from its former status as a planet and is now regarded as a member of the Kuiper Belt of icy bodies at the fringes of the Solar System.

Much of the early history of science is the story of people trying to make sense of the wandering points of light that were all they knew of the planets. Now, men have stood on the Earth's Moon, space probes have landed on several bodies, and distant landscapes have been mapped with astonishing accuracy, transforming our knowledge of our celestial environment.

In the 1980s, the Voyager space probes skimmed all four major planets of the outer Solar System, bringing new revelations with each close approach. The Magellan (Venus), Galileo (Jupiter) and Cassini–Huygens (Saturn) missions have transformed our knowledge of those planets and the giants' moons, and a host of orbiters and landers have shown us Mars in a new light. A spacecraft also reached Pluto in 2015.

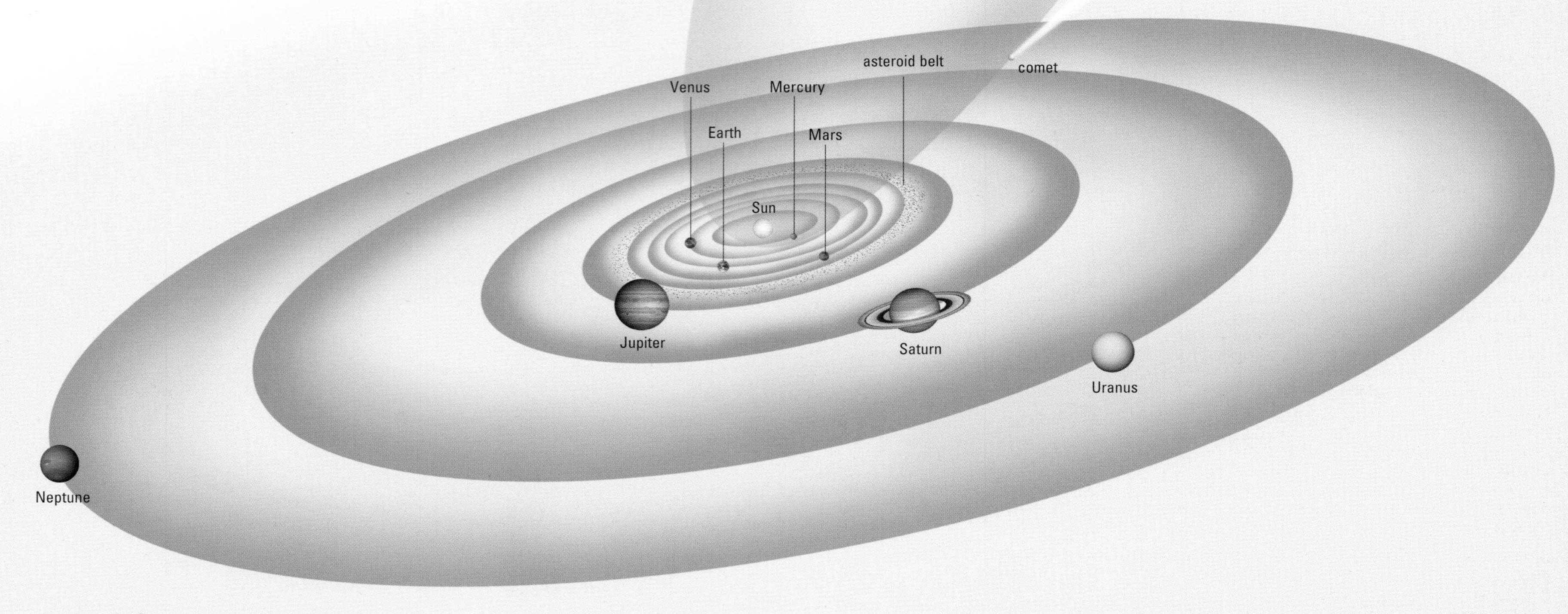

Diagram not drawn to scale

ORBITS OF THE PLANETS

The diagram above shows the Solar System as it might appear to an observer a few light-hours away in the direction of the constellation Hercules. Seen from such a position, above the plane of the ecliptic, all the planets revolve about the Sun in a counterclockwise direction. The perspective view exaggerates the elliptical form of all the planetary orbits: only Mercury follows a path that deviates noticeably from circularity.

The diagram also portrays the main asteroid belt between Mars and Jupiter, and the orbit of a comet. Comets reside in a vast spherical halo beyond the Solar System, and are occasionally diverted toward the Sun on highly elliptical orbits which may take many thousands of years to complete. Most, therefore, still await discovery, though there are a number of shorter-period comets which return regularly, such as Halley's Comet.

PLANETARY DATA

	Mean distance from Sun (million miles)	Mass (Earth = 1)	Period of orbit (Earth days/years)	Period of rotation (Earth days)	Equatorial diameter (miles)	Average density (water = 1)	Surface gravity (Earth = 1)	Number of known satellites*
Sun	–	*332,946*	–	*25.38*	*865,000*	*1.41*	*27.9*	–
Mercury	36.0	0.06	87.97d	58.65	3,032	5.43	0.38	0
Venus	67.2	0.82	224.7d	243.02	7,521	5.24	0.91	0
Earth	93.0	1.00	365.3d	1.00	7,926	5.51	1.00	1
Mars	141.6	0.11	687.0d	1.029	4,220	3.94	0.38	2
Jupiter	484.0	317.8	11.86y	0.411	88,848	1.33	2.36	79
Saturn	891.0	95.2	29.45y	0.428	74,900	0.69	0.91	62
Uranus	1,785.2	14.5	84.02y	0.720	31,764	1.27	0.89	27
Neptune	2,793.1	17.2	164.8y	0.673	30,776	1.64	1.13	14

Planetary days are given in sidereal days – that is, with respect to the stars rather than the Sun. The difference is caused by the movement of the planet in its orbit, so the interval between successive noons is slightly different from that between the rising of a particular star. The Earth's own sidereal day is 23h 56m in solar time. The equatorial diameters of most planets differ from their polar diameters as a consequence of their rotation, which is most marked in the case of Jupiter and Saturn, which are very noticeably flattened at the poles. Strictly speaking, the figures for surface gravity apply to the four inner planets only, as the outer planets have no solid surfaces. In their case, the figure is given for an arbitrary point in the atmosphere where the pressure is 1 bar.

** Number of known satellites at mid-2019*

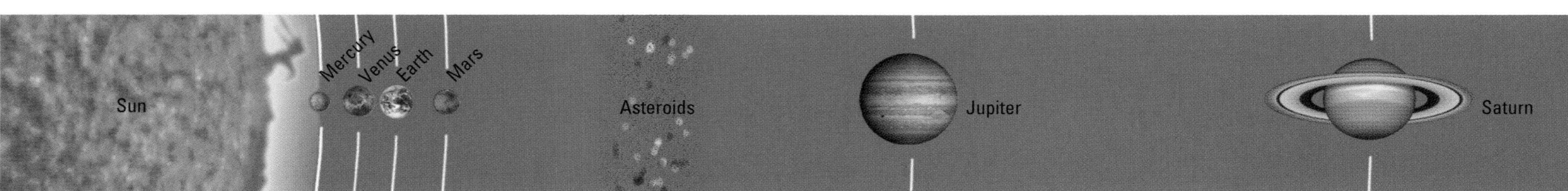

THE PLANETS

Mercury is the closest planet to the Sun and hence the fastest-moving. It is very hot, with a cratered, wrinkled surface very similar to that of Earth's Moon. It is small and has low gravity, so there is no significant atmosphere.

Venus has much the same physical dimensions as Earth. Its dense atmosphere is composed of 97% carbon dioxide resulting in a runaway greenhouse effect that makes the surface, at 890°F, the hottest of all the planets in the Solar System. Radar mapping revealed a terrain consisting of highland regions and vast, rolling plains crossed by volcanic flows and dotted with craters. Discharges from volcanic regions could explain the sulfuric-acid rain detected by spacecraft. Soft-landers last less than an hour in Venus's fierce climate.

Earth seen from space is easily the most beautiful of the inner planets; it is also, and more objectively, the largest, as well as the only known home of life. Living things are the main reason why the Earth is able to retain a substantial proportion of reactive oxygen in its atmosphere; the oxygen in turn supports the life that constantly regenerates it. The Earth's natural satellite, the Moon, is believed to have been created when an asteroid struck our planet in its infancy.

Mars, smaller and cooler than the Earth, is nevertheless the most likely planet other than Earth where life may have formed. The planet was, at some stage in the distant past, a geologically active world with water on its surface: rivers, lakes, and even an ocean. Liquid water may well exist today, but trapped beneath its dusty, boulder-strewn surface. The Martian landscape features huge extinct volcanoes, a giant canyon system, craters, and sand dunes. Its thin atmosphere is mostly carbon dioxide, and its polar caps are of frozen carbon dioxide and water ice. It has two tiny moons, probably captured asteroids.

Jupiter has about three times the mass of all the other planets combined. The planet is mostly gas, under intense pressure in the lower atmosphere above a core of fiercely compressed hydrogen and helium. The upper layers form strikingly colored rotating belts, the outward sign of the intense storms created by Jupiter's rapid rotation. The Great Red Spot is a storm feature that has persisted for at least 130 years. Jupiter has at least 79 moons. Most are very small, but the four largest – Io, Europa, Ganymede, and Callisto – are fascinating worlds in their own right. Io is the most volcanically active world known, and Europa possesses an ocean deep below its icy surface. The planet also has a system of rings, though nowhere near as prominent as Saturn's.

Saturn is structurally similar to Jupiter, rotating fast enough to produce an obvious bulge at its equator. It is composed of 89% hydrogen and 11% helium, and has wind velocities in the outer atmosphere of 1,600 ft/sec. Ever since the invention of the telescope, Saturn's rings have been the feature that has most attracted observers. The rings consist of thousands of individual ringlets, composed of icy particles ranging in size from 30 feet down to microscopic. Titan, the largest of Saturn's 62 known moons, has a dense atmosphere.

Uranus was unknown to the ancients. Although it is faintly visible to the naked eye, it was not established as a planet until 1781. In its interior is probably a rocky core surrounded by frozen methane, water, and ammonia; the atmosphere is of hydrogen, helium, and some methane, which gives the planet its greenish-blue color. There is a system of thin, dark rings and a retinue of 27 moons, all but five of which are small.

Neptune is always more than 2.5 billion miles from Earth, and despite its diameter of over 31,000 miles, it can only be seen by telescope. Its discovery in 1846 was the result of mathematical predictions by astronomers seeking to explain irregularities in the orbit of Uranus. Like Uranus, it has a ring system; recent observations have revealed a total of 14 moons.

In 2006, following an increasing number of discoveries of objects orbiting the Sun of similar size to Pluto but at a greater distance, the International Astronomical Union issued for the first time a definition of a planet. A planet is defined as "a body orbiting the Sun, which is essentially round as a consequence of its gravity, and which does not share its orbital neighborhood with similar bodies." On this definition, Pluto is no longer classified as a planet, but is instead a member of a new category of "dwarf planet," which relaxes the last criterion but excludes bodies in orbit around another one.

Mean distance from the Sun in millions of miles

Mercury — 36.0 Mercury

Venus — 67.2 Venus

Earth — 93.0 Earth

Mars — 141.6 Mars

Jupiter — 483.7 Jupiter

Saturn — 886.6 Saturn

Uranus — 1,784.0 Uranus

Neptune — 2,795.2 Neptune

Diagrams not drawn to scale

Uranus

Neptune

For more information:

70 Orbits of the planets
76 Circulation of the air
78 Climate
84 Ocean currents

The basic units of time measurement are the day and the year. The day is one rotation of the Earth on its axis. Our present calendar is based on the solar year of 365.24 days, the time taken by the Earth to orbit the Sun. Calendars based on the movements of the Sun and Moon have been used since ancient times. The length of the year, reckoned by the Julian Calendar introduced by Julius Caesar, was about 11 minutes too long. The cumulative error was rectified in 1582 by the Gregorian Calendar, when Pope Gregory XIII decreed that the day following October 4 was October 15, and that century years did not count as leap years unless they were divisible by 400. England finally adopted the reformed calendar in 1752, when it was 11 days behind the European mainland.

The rotation of the Earth on its axis causes day and night. The Earth rotates through 360° every 24 hours, and the world is divided into 24 time zones centered on lines of longitude at 15° intervals.

The tilt of the Earth's axis, which is also called the "obliquity of the ecliptic," accounts for the seasons which are so familiar in the middle latitudes. However, geological evidence shows that, over long periods of time, climates change, and the advances and retreats of the ice during the Pleistocene Ice Age may have been caused by regular variations in the Earth's tilt, its orbit around the Sun, and changes in the season when it is closest to the Sun (perihelion).

THE SEASONS

Seasons occur because the Earth's axis is tilted at an angle of approximately 23½°. When the northern hemisphere is tilted to a maximum extent toward the Sun, on June 20 or 21, the Sun is overhead at the Tropic of Cancer (latitude 23½° North). This is midsummer, or the summer solstice, in the northern hemisphere.

On September 22 or 23, the Sun is overhead at the equator, and day and night are of equal length throughout the world. This is the autumnal equinox in the northern hemisphere.

On December 21 or 22, the Sun is overhead at the Tropic of Capricorn (23½° South), the winter solstice in the northern hemisphere. The overhead Sun then tracks north until, on March 20 or 21, it is overhead at the equator. This is the spring (vernal) equinox in the northern hemisphere.

In the southern hemisphere, the seasons are the reverse of those in the north.

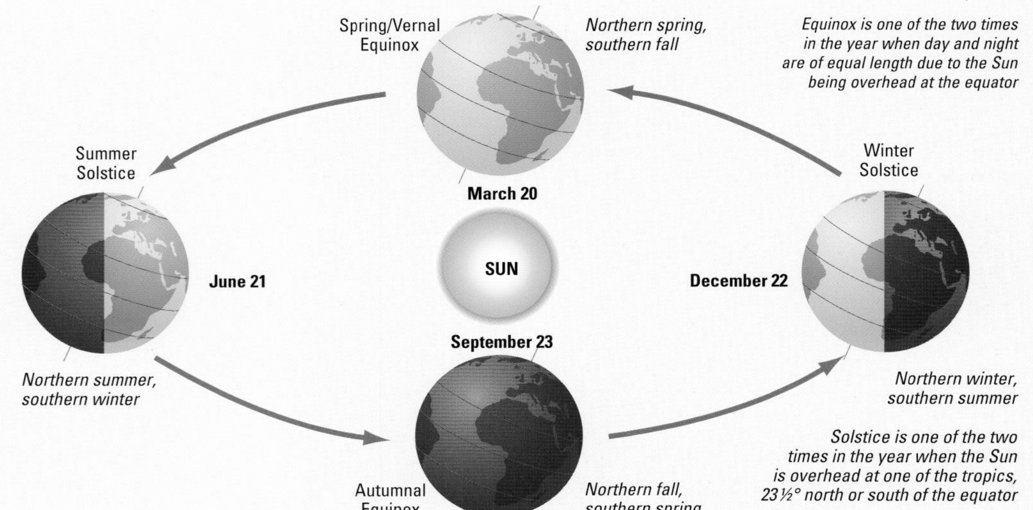

DAY AND NIGHT

The Sun appears to rise in the east, reach its highest point at noon, and then set in the west, to be followed by night. In reality, it is not the Sun that is moving but the Earth rotating from west to east. The moment when the Sun's upper limb first appears above the horizon is termed sunrise; the moment when the Sun's upper limb disappears below the horizon is sunset.

At the summer solstice in the northern hemisphere (June 21), the Arctic has total daylight and the Antarctic total darkness. The opposite occurs at the winter solstice (December 21 or 22). At the equator, the length of day and night are almost equal all year.

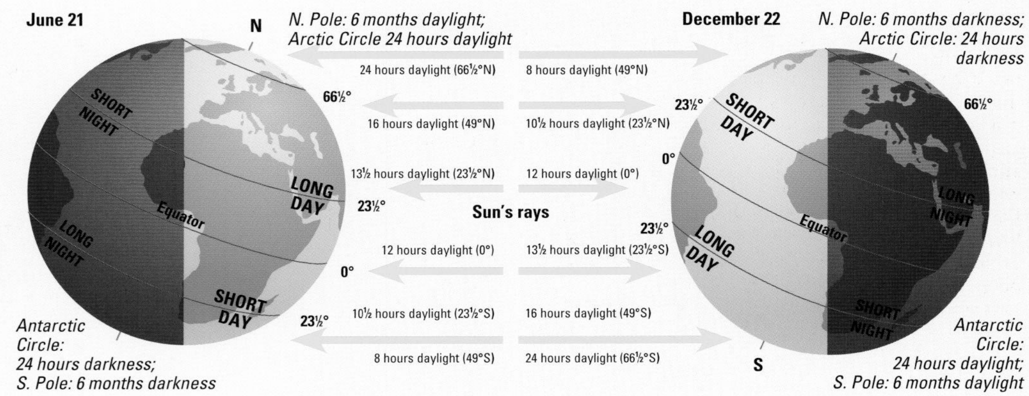

EARTH DATA

Aphelion (maximum distance from Sun):	94,500,000 miles	**Length of year:**	365 days, 5 hours, 48 minutes, 45 seconds of mean solar time	**Polar circumference:**	24,860 miles
Perihelion (minimum distance from Sun):	91,400,000 miles	**Superficial area:**	197,000,000 sq miles	**Equatorial diameter:**	7,926 miles
Angle of tilt (obliquity of the ecliptic):	23° 26′	**Land surface:**	57,500,000 sq miles (29.2%)	**Polar diameter:**	7,900 miles
Length of year – solar tropical (equinox to equinox):	365.24 days	**Water surface:**	139,500,000 sq miles (70.8%)	**Equatorial radius:**	3,963 miles
		Equatorial circumference:	24,901 miles	**Polar radius:**	3,950 miles
				Volume of the Earth:	259,880 × 10^6 cu miles
				Mass of the Earth:	5.97 × 10^{24} kg

SUNRISE AND SUNSET

The term "equinox" comes from the Latin for "equal night." At the spring and autumnal equinoxes, the Sun is vertically overhead at midday at the equator and all places on Earth have 12 hours of darkness and 12 hours of daylight. The graphs of sunrise and sunset show that these occasions occur on March 21 and on September 22 or 23. The graphs also show that, because the Sun remains high in the sky at the equator throughout the year, the length of day and night there remains roughly the same throughout the year, with sunrise around 6 a.m. and sunset around 6 p.m.

The further north or south one travels, the greater the difference between the number of hours of daylight and darkness. For example, the graph (*right*) shows that at latitude 60°N sunrise varies from just after 9 a.m. in midwinter (on December 22 or 23) to about 2.30 a.m. in midsummer (around the summer solstice on June 21). By contrast, the second graph (*far right*) shows that sunset at latitude 60°N occurs at about 2.45 p.m. in midwinter and 9.20 p.m. in midsummer.

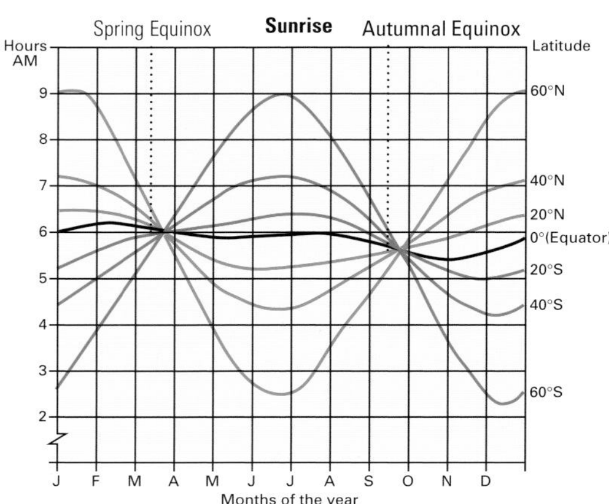

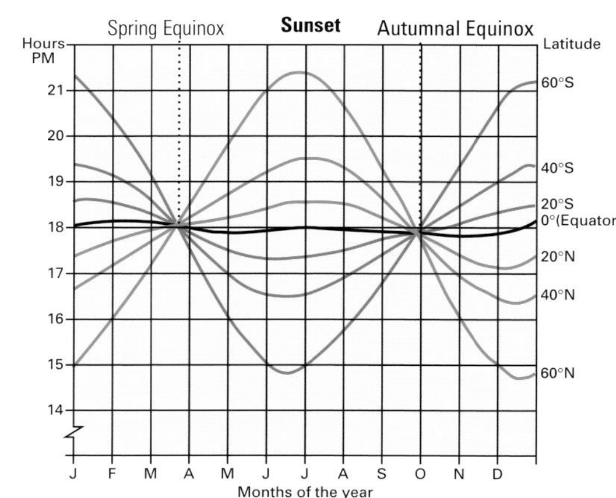

THE MOON

The Moon rotates more slowly than the Earth, taking just over 27 days to make one complete rotation on its axis. This corresponds to the Moon's orbital period around the Earth, and therefore the Moon always presents the same hemisphere toward us; some 41% of the Moon's far side is never visible from the Earth. The interval between one New Moon and the next is 29½ days – this is called a lunation, or lunar month. The Moon shines only by reflected sunlight, and emits no light of its own. During each lunation the Moon displays a complete cycle of phases, caused by the changing angle of illumination from the Sun.

PHASES OF THE MOON

Mean distance from Earth: 238,856 miles; Mean diameter: 2,159 miles;
Mass: approximately 1/80 that of Earth; Surface gravity: one-sixth of Earth's;
Daily range of temperature at lunar equator: 504°F; Average orbital speed: 2,287 mph

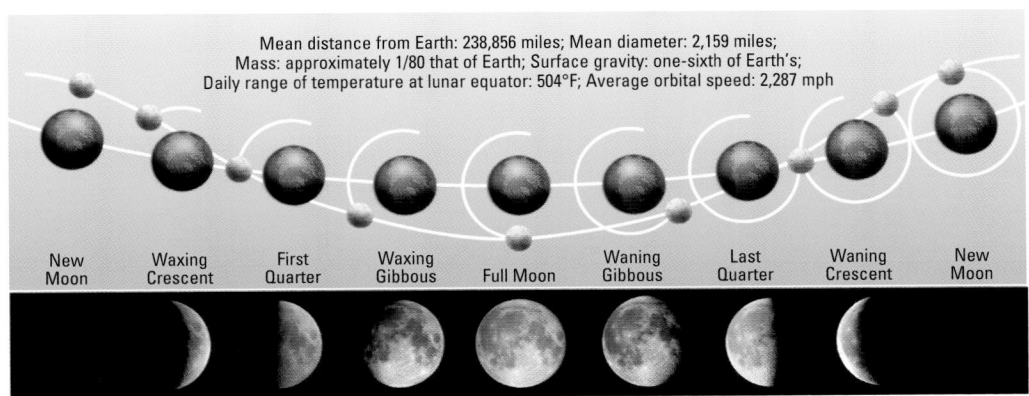

New Moon | Waxing Crescent | First Quarter | Waxing Gibbous | Full Moon | Waning Gibbous | Last Quarter | Waning Crescent | New Moon

MOON DATA

Distance from Earth

The Moon orbits at a mean distance of 238,856 miles, at an average speed of 2,287 mph in relation to the Earth.

Size and mass

The average diameter of the Moon is 2,159 miles. It is 400 times smaller than the Sun but is about 400 times closer to the Earth, so we see them as the same size. The Moon has a mass of 7.35×10^{22} kg, with a density 3.344 times that of water.

Visibility

Only 59% of the Moon's surface is visible from the Earth over time. Sunlight reflected from the Moon takes 1.3 seconds to reach the Earth (the Sun itself is around 8½ light-minutes away).

Temperature

With the Sun overhead, the temperature on the lunar equator can reach 243°F [117°C]. At night it can sink to −261°F [−163°C].

ECLIPSES

When the Moon passes between the Sun and the Earth, the Sun becomes partially eclipsed (1). A partial eclipse becomes a total eclipse if the Moon proceeds to cover the Sun completely (2) and the dark central part of the lunar shadow touches the Earth. The broad geographical zone covered by the Moon's outer shadow (P) has only a very small central area (often less than 62 miles wide) that experiences totality. Totality can never last for more than 7½ minutes at maximum, but is usually much briefer than this. Lunar eclipses take place when the Moon moves through the shadow of the Earth, and can be partial or total. Any single location on Earth can experience a maximum of four solar and three lunar eclipses in any single year, while a total solar eclipse occurs an average of once every 360 years for any given location.

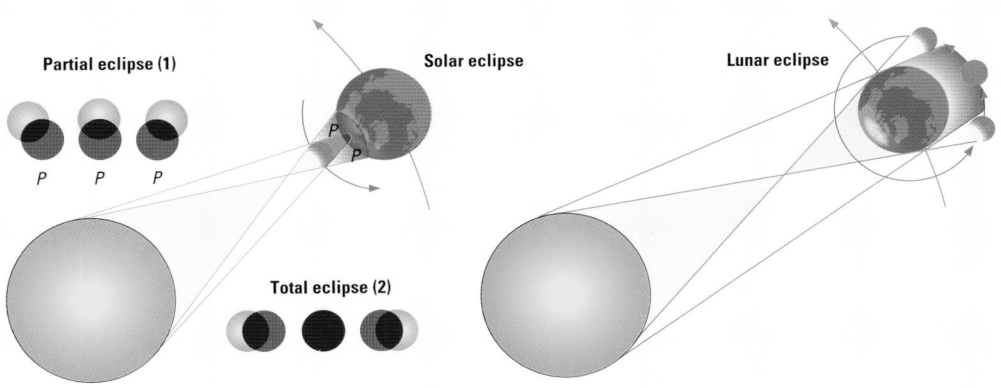

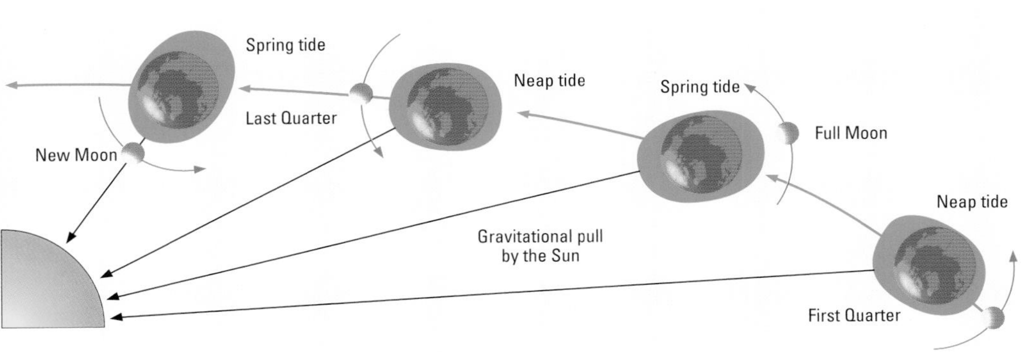

TIDES

The daily rise and fall of the ocean's tides are the result of the gravitational pull of the Moon and that of the Sun, though the effect of the latter is not as strong as that of the Moon. This effect is greatest on the hemisphere facing the Moon and causes a tidal "bulge." Spring tides occur when the Sun, Earth, and Moon are aligned; high tides are at their highest, and low tides fall to their lowest. When the Moon and Sun are farthest out of line (near the Moon's First and Last Quarters), neap tides occur, producing the smallest range between high and low tides.

Spring tide
Last Quarter
New Moon
Neap tide
Spring tide
Full Moon
Neap tide
Gravitational pull by the Sun
First Quarter

TIME ZONES

The Earth rotates through 360° in 24 hours, and so moves 15° every hour. The world is divided into 24 standard time zones, each centered on lines of longitude at 15° intervals. At the center of the first zone is the prime meridian, or Greenwich meridian. All places to the west of Greenwich are one hour behind for every 15° of longitude; places to the east are ahead by one hour for every 15°.

International Date Line

When it is 12 noon on the Greenwich meridian, 180° east it is midnight of the same day – while 180° west the day is just beginning. To overcome this, the International Date Line was established, approximately following the 180° meridian. Thus, if you were to travel eastward from Japan (140°E) to Hawai'i (160°W), you would pass from Sunday night into Sunday morning.

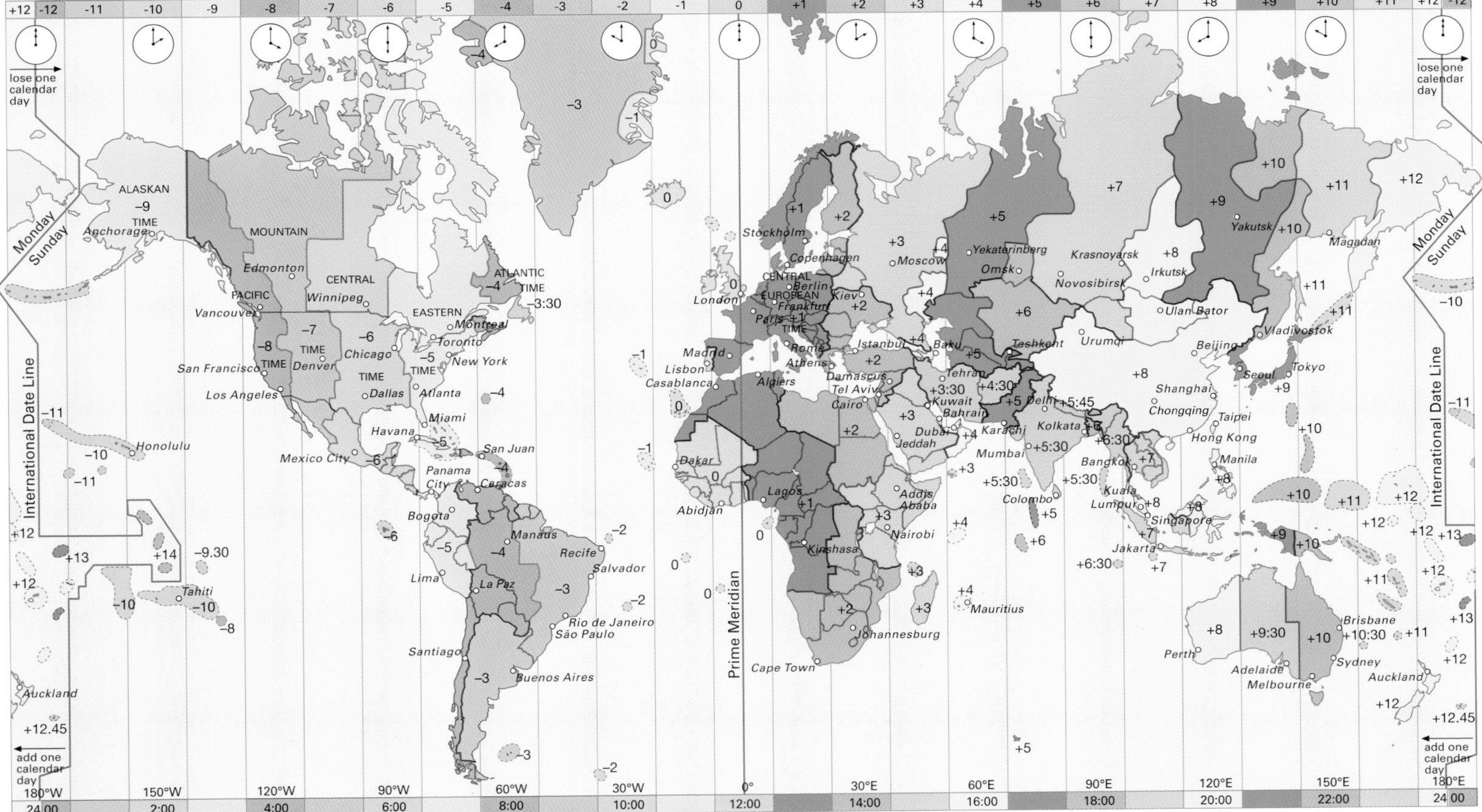

Projection: *Mercator*

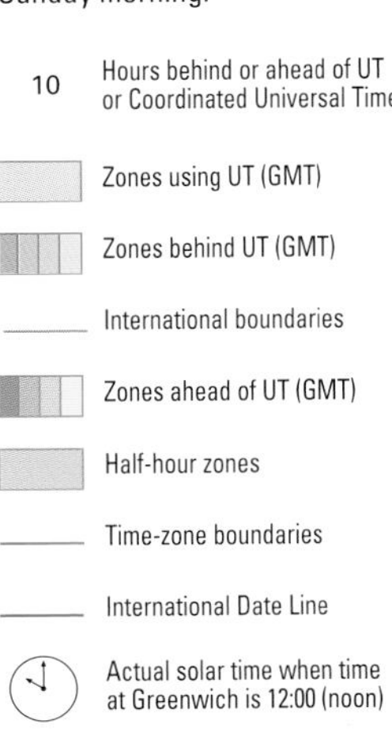

Note: Some of the above time zones are affected by the incidence of Daylight Saving Time in countries where it is adopted.

For more information:
98 Minerals

Every year, earthquakes and volcanic eruptions cause much destruction throughout the world. Such phenomena were once thought to be unconnected, but since the late 1960s, scientists have understood that these events are surface manifestations of the tremendous forces operating in the Earth's interior that are slowly but constantly changing the face of our planet.

The Earth is divided into three zones. The crust, a brittle, low-density zone, overlies the dense mantle. Separating the crust from the mantle is a distinct boundary called the Mohorovičić (or Moho) discontinuity. Enclosed by the mantle is the Earth's core, which consists mainly of iron and nickel.

Temperatures inside the Earth range from about 1,600°F in the upper mantle to perhaps 9,000°F in the core. Heat creates convection currents in a semimolten part of the mantle called the asthenosphere. Above the asthenosphere is the lithosphere, a solid layer about 40 miles thick, consisting of the crust and part of the mantle. The lithosphere is divided into rigid plates, moved around by the currents in the asthenosphere, a process named plate tectonics.

The Earth was formed around 4.6 billion years ago. Lighter elements floated toward the surface, where they formed crustal rocks. The oldest rocks so far discovered are about 4 billion years old, while the oldest fossils occur in rocks formed around 3.5 billion years ago. An explosion of life occurred at the start of the Cambrian period, 570 million years ago. The fossil record since the start of the Cambrian has enabled scientists to piece together the story of life on Earth.

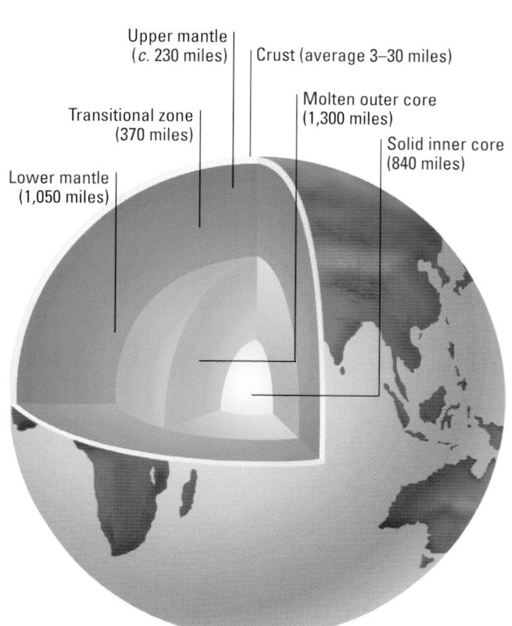

CONTINENTAL DRIFT

Trench
Rift
New ocean floor
Zones of slippage

In 1915, Alfred Wegener produced a series of world maps proposing that, around 200 million years ago, the continents had been joined together in a supercontinent that he called Pangaea. This land mass started to break up about 180 million years ago and the parts drifted to their present positions. In the 1950s and 1960s, evidence from studies of the ocean floor suggested that the low-density continents rest on huge slow-moving plates. The arrows on the present-day world map (*below*) show that the continents are still on the move.

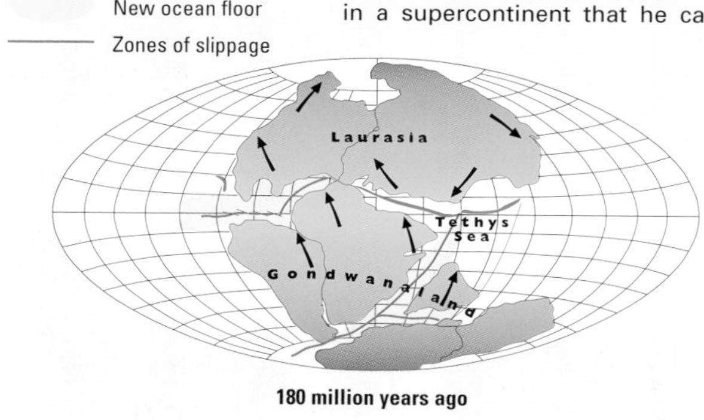

180 million years ago

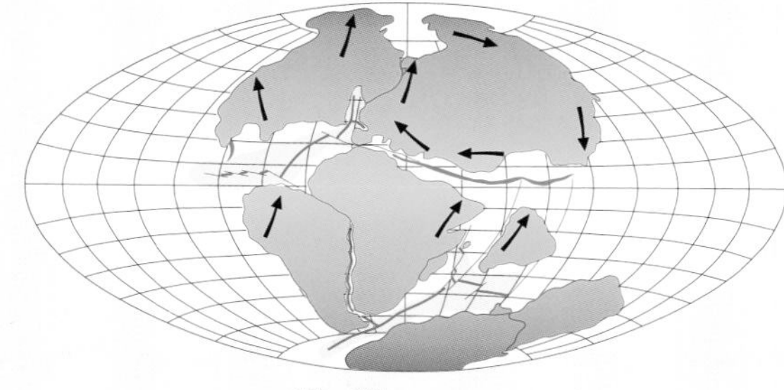

135 million years ago

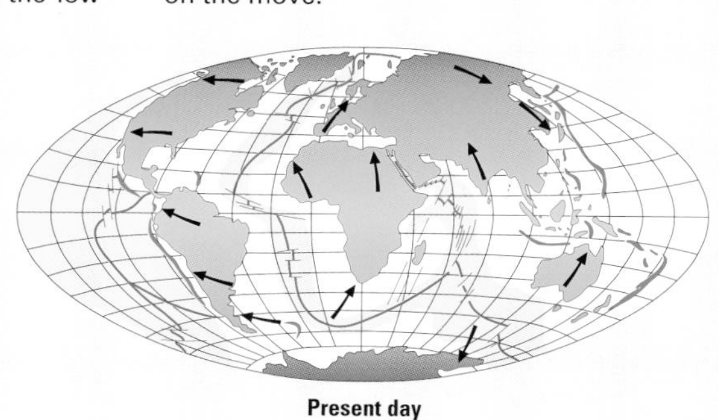

Present day

DISTRIBUTION OF VOLCANOES

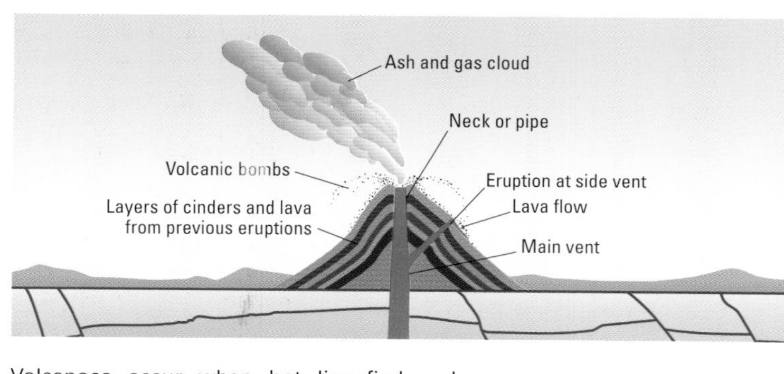

Volcanoes occur when hot liquefied rock beneath the Earth's crust is pushed up by pressure to the surface as molten lava. There are some 550 known active volcanoes, around 20 of which are erupting at any one time.

Submarine volcanoes
▲ Land volcanoes active since 1700
— Boundaries of tectonic plates

PLATE TECTONICS

The huge ridges that run through the oceans represent boundaries between plates. Here plates are diverging and molten magma from the mantle rises along a central rift valley to form new crustal rock. These ocean ridges, which are active zones where earthquakes and volcanic eruptions are common, are called constructive plate margins. Destructive plate margins, which occur when two contrasting plates converge, are marked by deep-ocean trenches as one plate is forced under the other. The descending plate is melted to produce the magma that fuels volcanoes alongside the trenches. Movements of descending plates are often sudden, triggering earthquakes in overlying continental areas.

Sea-floor spreading in the Atlantic Ocean and plate collision

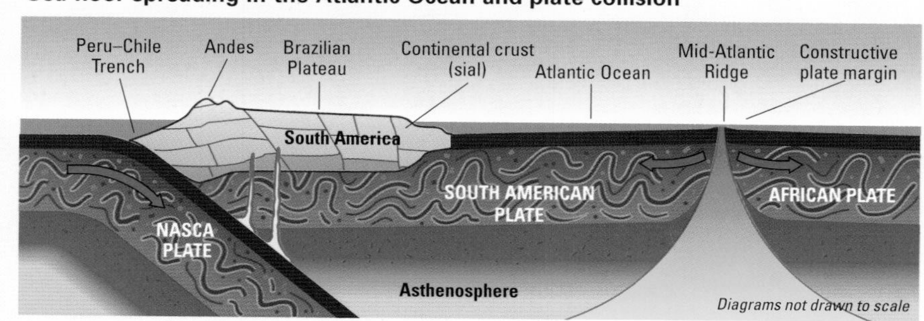

Sea-floor spreading in the Indian Ocean and continental plate collision

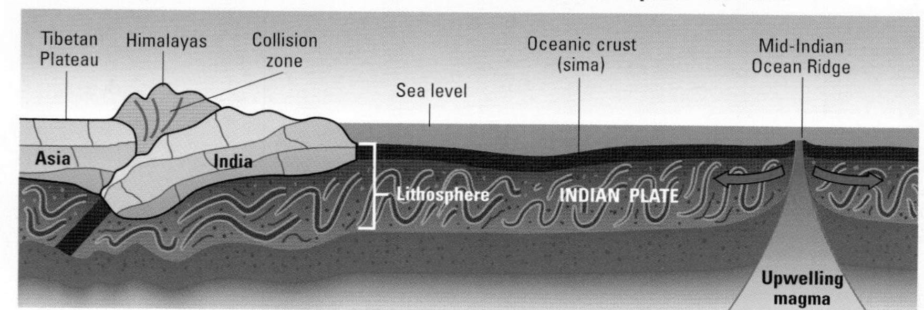

GEOLOGICAL TIME

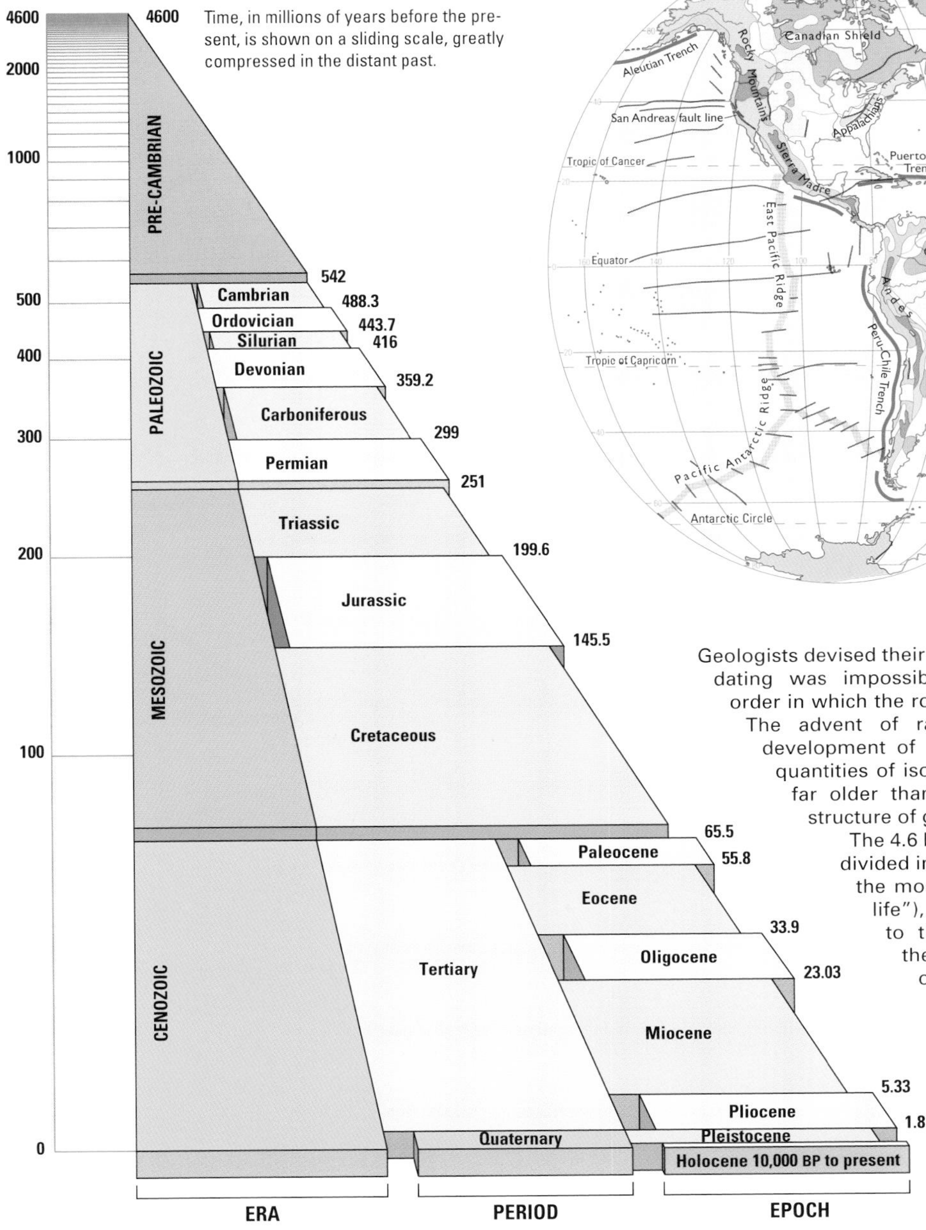

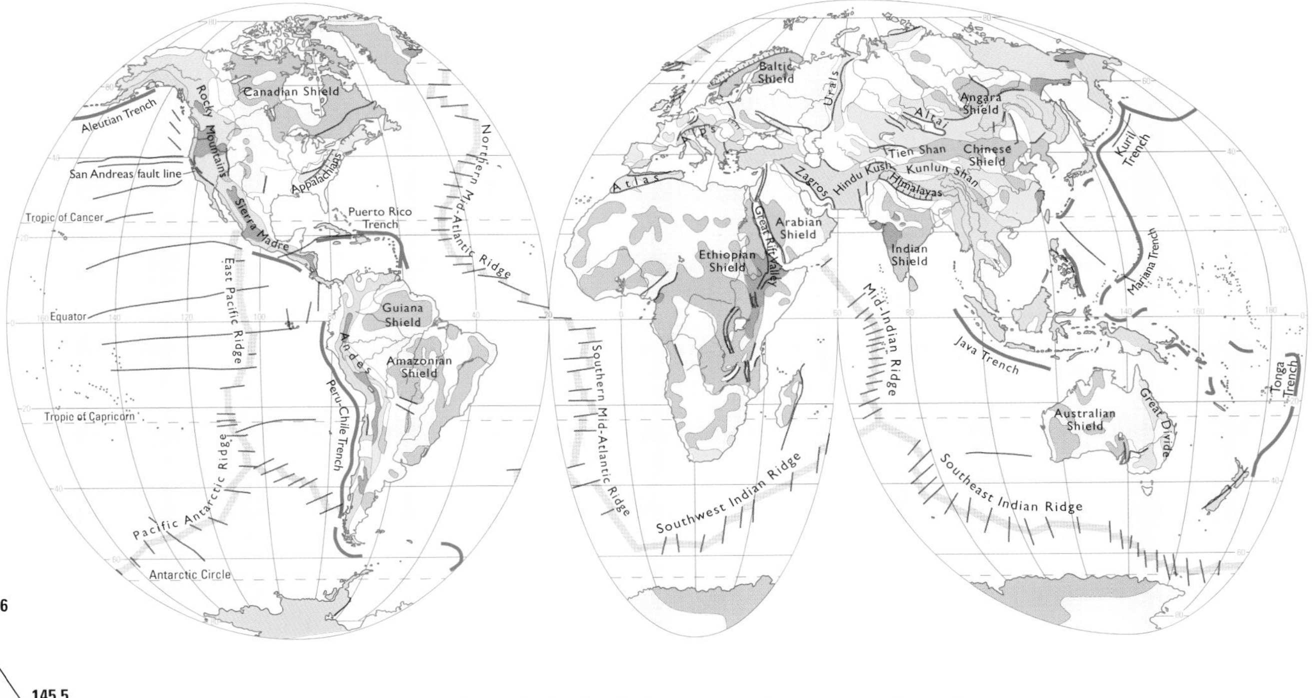

Time, in millions of years before the present, is shown on a sliding scale, greatly compressed in the distant past.

ERA	PERIOD	EPOCH	Millions of years
PRE-CAMBRIAN			4600–542
PALEOZOIC	Cambrian		542–488.3
	Ordovician		488.3–443.7
	Silurian		443.7–416
	Devonian		416–359.2
	Carboniferous		359.2–299
	Permian		299–251
MESOZOIC	Triassic		251–199.6
	Jurassic		199.6–145.5
	Cretaceous		145.5–65.5
CENOZOIC	Tertiary	Paleocene	65.5–55.8
		Eocene	55.8–33.9
		Oligocene	33.9–23.03
		Miocene	23.03–5.33
		Pliocene	5.33–1.81
	Quaternary	Pleistocene	1.81
		Holocene 10,000 BP to present	

Pre-Cambrian shields
Sedimentary cover on Pre-Cambrian shields
Paleozoic (Caledonian and Hercynian) folding
Sedimentary cover on Paleozoic folding
Mesozoic folding
Sedimentary cover on Mesozoic folding
Cenozoic (Alpine) folding
Sedimentary cover on Cenozoic folding
Intensive Mesozoic and Cenozoic vulcanism
Principal faults
Oceanic marginal troughs
Mid-oceanic ridges
Overthrust faults

Geologists devised their timescale on the basis of relative, not calendar, ages. Accurate dating was impossible and estimates were often bitterly disputed, but the order in which the rocks were formed could be deduced from careful observation. The advent of radioactive dating – culminating in the 1950s with the development of a mass spectrometer capable of accurately measuring tiny quantities of isotopes – appears to have settled the arguments. The Earth is far older than geologists first imagined, but their painstakingly-created structure of geological time has withstood the advent of high technology.

The 4.6 billion (4,600 million) years since the formation of the Earth are divided into four great eras, further split into periods and, in the case of the most recent era, epochs. The present era is the Cenozoic ("new life"), extending backward through "middle life" and "ancient life" to the Pre-Cambrian, named after the Latin word for Wales, the location of some of the earliest known fossils. Most of the Earth's geological history is encompassed by the Pre-Cambrian: though traces of ancient life have since been found, it was largely the proliferation of fossils from the beginning of the Paleozoic era onward, some 570 million years ago, which first allowed precise subdivisions to be made.

Like the Cambrian, most are named after regions exemplifying a period's geology. Others – such as the Carboniferous ("coal-bearing") or the Cretaceous ("chalk-bearing") – are more directly descriptive.

EARTHQUAKES

Earthquake magnitude is usually rated according to either the Richter scale or the Modified Mercalli scale, both devised by seismologists in the 1930s. The Richter scale measures absolute earthquake power with mathematical precision: each step upward represents a tenfold increase in the amplitude of the shockwave. Theoretically, there is no upper limit, but most of the largest earthquakes measured have been rated at between 8.8 and 8.9. The 12-point Mercalli scale, based on observed effects, is often more meaningful, ranging from I (earthquakes noticed only by seismographs) to XII (total destruction); intermediate points include V (people awakened at night; unstable objects overturned), VII (collapse of ordinary buildings; chimneys and monuments fall), and IX (conspicuous cracks in ground; serious damage to reservoirs).

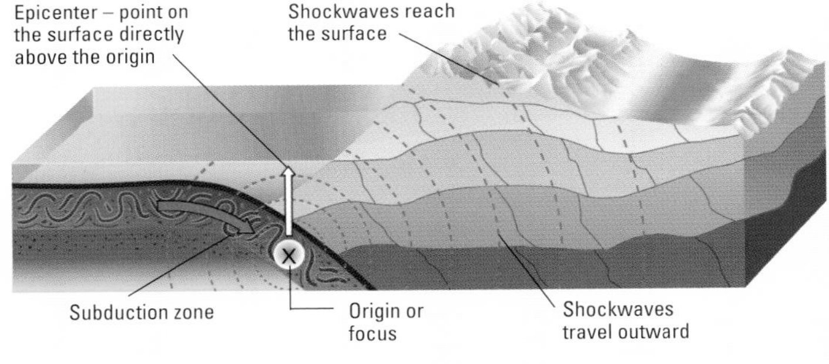

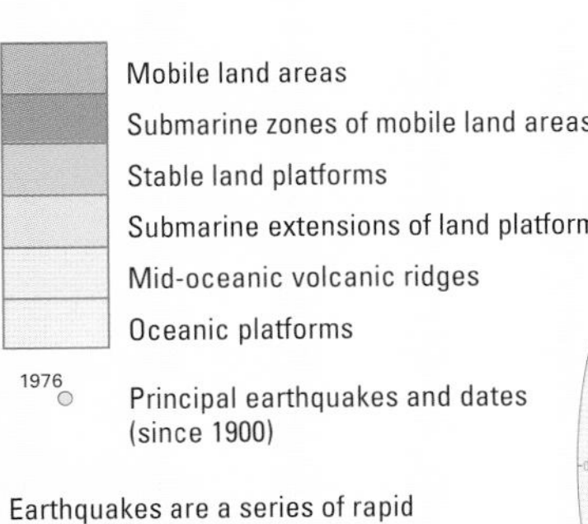

Earthquakes are a series of rapid vibrations originating from the slipping or faulting of parts of the Earth's crust when stresses within build up to breaking point. They usually happen at depths varying from 5 to 20 miles. Severe earthquakes cause extensive damage when they take place in populated areas, destroying structures and severing communications. Most initial loss of life occurs due to secondary causes such as falling masonry, fires, and flooding.

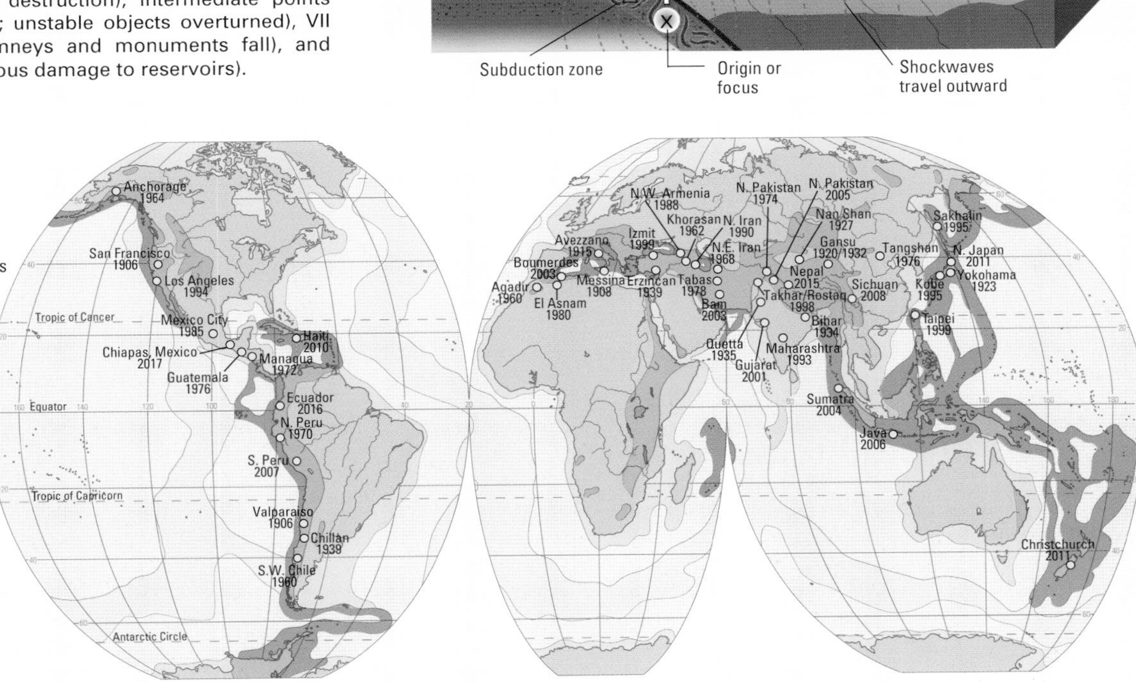

Notable Earthquakes Since 1900

Year	Location	Mag.	Deaths
1906	San Francisco, USA	8.3	3,000
1906	Valparaiso, Chile	8.6	22,000
1908	Messina, Italy	7.5	83,000
1915	Avezzano, Italy	7.5	30,000
1920	Gansu (Kansu), China	8.6	180,000
1923	Yokohama, Japan	8.3	143,000
1927	Nan Shan, China	8.3	200,000
1932	Gansu (Kansu), China	7.6	70,000
1934	Bihar, India/Nepal	8.4	10,700
1935	Quetta, India*	7.5	60,000
1939	Chillan, Chile	8.3	28,000
1939	Erzincan, Turkey	7.9	30,000
1960	S. W. Chile	9.5	2,200
1960	Agadir, Morocco	5.8	12,000
1962	Khorasan, Iran	7.1	12,230
1964	Anchorage, USA	9.2	125
1968	N. E. Iran	7.4	12,000
1970	N. Peru	7.8	70,000
1972	Managua, Nicaragua	6.2	5,000
1974	N. Pakistan	6.3	5,200
1976	Guatemala	7.5	22,500
1976	Tangshan, China	8.2	255,000
1978	Tabas, Iran	7.7	25,000
1980	El Asnam, Algeria	7.3	20,000
1985	Mexico City, Mexico	8.1	4,200
1988	N.W. Armenia	6.8	55,000
1990	N. Iran	7.7	36,000
1993	Maharashtra, India	6.4	30,000
1994	Los Angeles, USA	6.6	51
1995	Kobe, Japan	7.2	5,000
1995	Sakhalin, Russia	7.5	2,000
1998	Takhar, Afghanistan	6.1	4,200
1998	Rostaq, Afghanistan	7.0	5,000
1999	Izmit, Turkey	7.4	15,000
2001	Gujarat, India	7.7	14,000
2003	Bam, Iran	6.6	30,000
2004	Sumatra, Indonesia	9.0	250,000
2005	N. Pakistan	7.6	74,000
2006	Java, Indonesia	6.4	6,200
2007	S. Peru	8.0	600
2008	Sichuan, China	7.9	70,000
2010	Haiti	7.0	230,000
2011	Christchurch, NZ	6.3	182
2011	N. Japan	9.0	20,000
2015	Nepal	7.8	8,500
2016	Ecuador	7.8	668
2017	Chiapas, Mexico	8.2	98

* now Pakistan

For more information:
79 Beaufort wind scale
Monsoon
80 Climate change
Global warming
84 Ocean currents

The atmosphere is a meteor shield, a radiation deflector, a thermal blanket, and a source of chemical energy for the Earth's diverse life forms. Five-sixths of its mass is in the lowest layer, the troposphere, which ranges in thickness from 11–6 miles between the equator and the poles. Powered by the Sun, the air is always on the move, flowing generally from high- to low-pressure areas. The troposphere is the layer where virtually all weather phenomena, including clouds, precipitation, and winds, occur. Above the troposphere is the stratosphere, which contains the important ozone layer and extends to about 30 miles above the Earth's surface. Beyond 60 miles, atmospheric density is lower than most laboratory vacuums.

STRUCTURE OF THE ATMOSPHERE

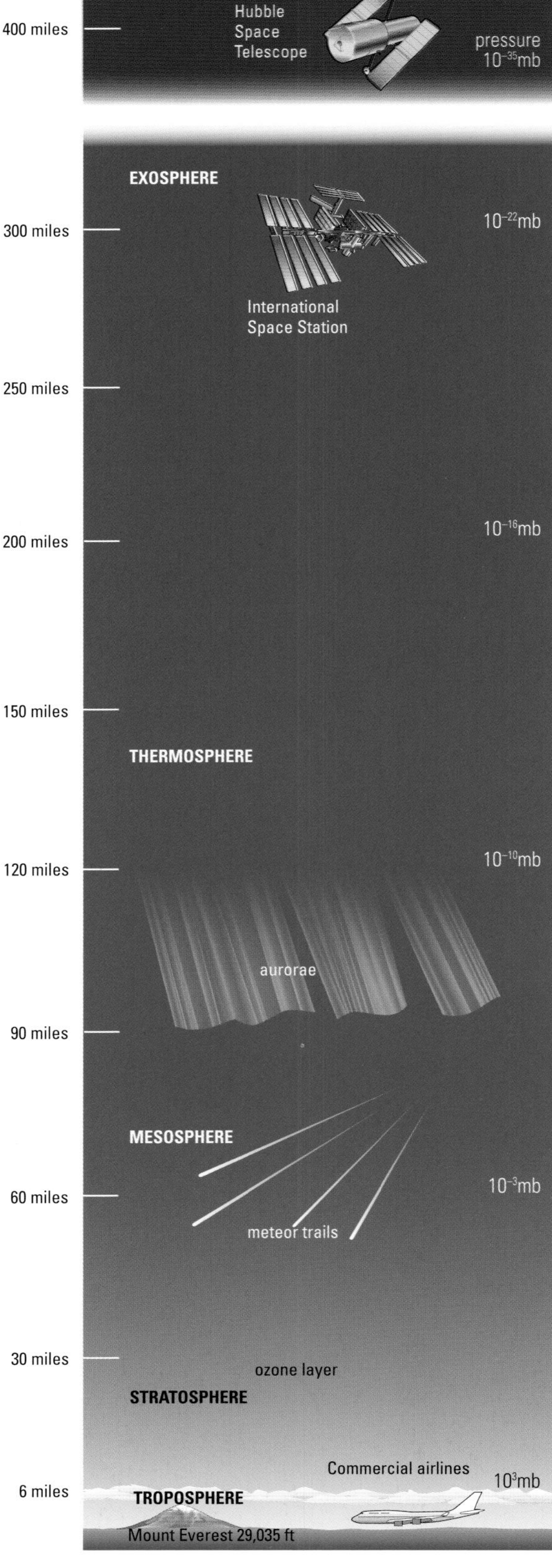

CIRCULATION OF THE AIR

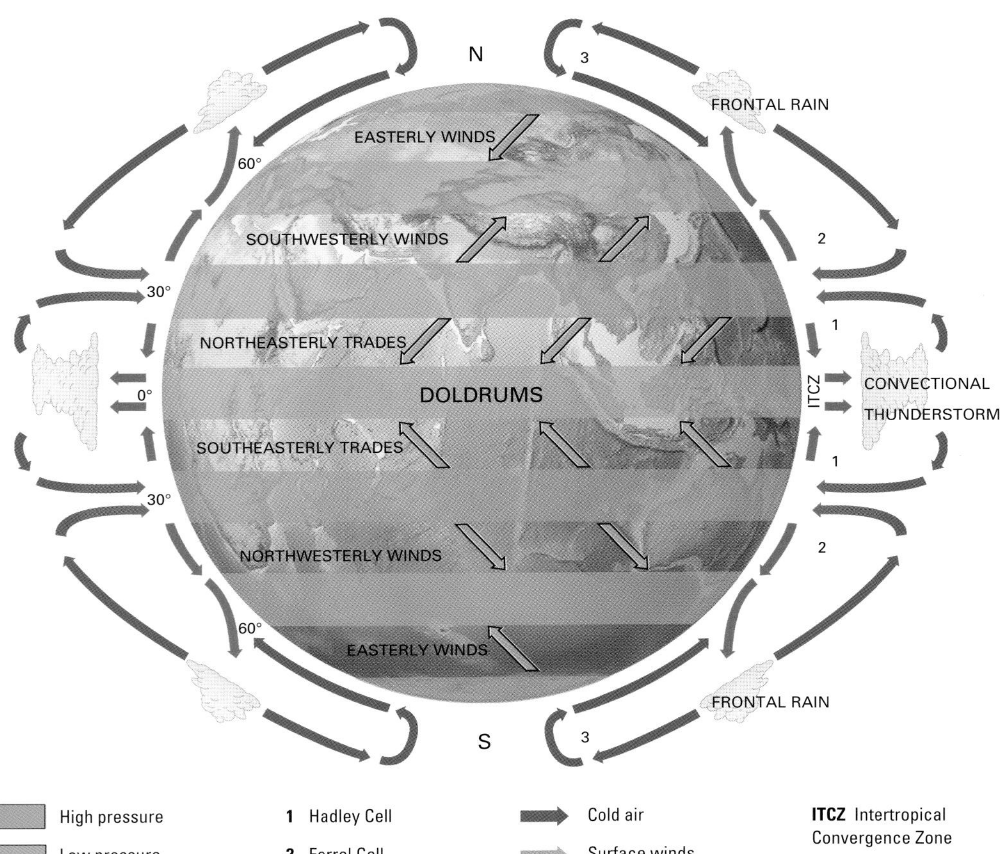

FRONTAL SYSTEMS

Depressions, also known as cyclones or lows, form on the polar front where relatively cold and dry polar air flows alongside warmer, moister subtropical air. They occur when the flow high above the polar front generates a surface inward-swirling circulation that moves along the polar front as a wave.

The warm front is the leading edge of the subtropical air that glides up and over the cooler air ahead of it. This gently ascending flow produces a characteristic sequence of clouds ahead of the warm front and a band of precipitation a few hundred miles wide immediately in advance it. Conditions within the warm sector are often overcast with layer cloud and generally light rain or drizzle. The cloud sometimes breaks up downwind of hills.

Another band of precipitation often occurs just ahead of the cold front that is the leading edge of the cooler polar air. Cumulus clouds tend to occur in the air behind the cold front, producing scattered showers. The changes of temperature, wind direction, and cloud, etc, are illustrated by the diagram below.

CHEMICAL COMPOSITION

Gaseous composition of the principal atmospheric layers

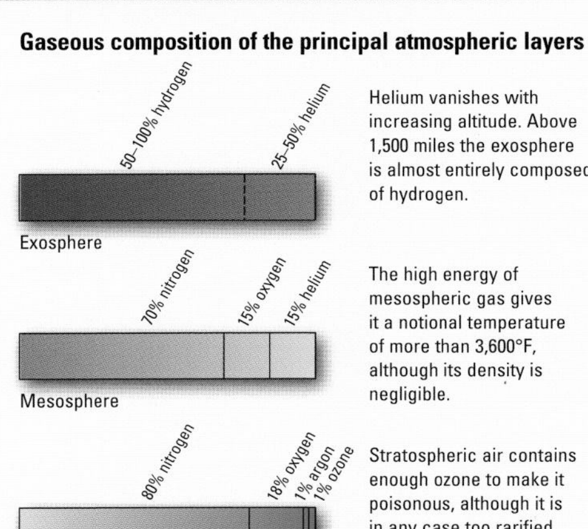

Helium vanishes with increasing altitude. Above 1,500 miles the exosphere is almost entirely composed of hydrogen.

The high energy of mesospheric gas gives it a notional temperature of more than 3,600°F, although its density is negligible.

Stratospheric air contains enough ozone to make it poisonous, although it is in any case too rarified to breathe.

The narrowest of all the layers, this thin region contains about 85% of the atmosphere's total mass and almost all of its water vapor. It is also the realm of the Earth's weather.

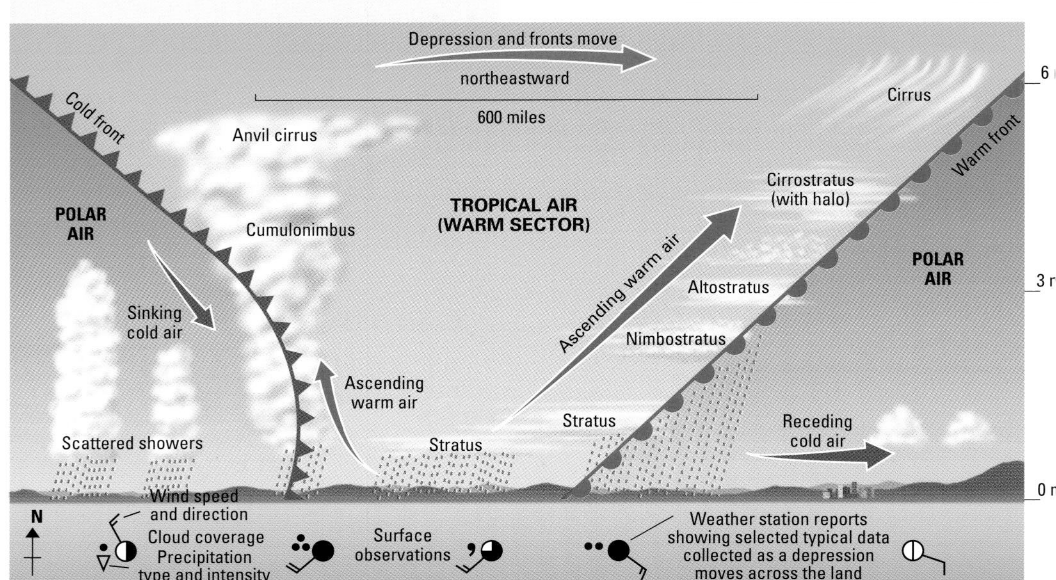

AIR MASSES

Air masses are large bodies of air where the variations of the main physical properties (that is, temperature and humidity) are relatively gentle. The term is generally applied only to the lower layers of the atmosphere, although air masses can cover areas of tens of thousands of square miles.

Air masses derive their temperature and humidity from the regions over which they lie. These regions are known as "source regions." The principal ones are:

- areas of relative calm, such as semipermanent high-pressure areas;
- areas where the surface is relatively uniform, including deserts, oceans, and ice-fields.

These are the "highs" marked on the map below.

As air masses move from their source regions, they may be changed due to the effects of the surface over which they move. These changes create "secondary air masses." For example, a warm air mass that travels over a cold surface is cooled and becomes more stable. Hence, it may form low cloud or fog, but is unlikely to produce much rain. By contrast, a cold air mass that passes over a warm surface is warmed and becomes less stable. The rising air is likely to produce more rain.

When two contrasting air masses meet, they form a "front." As warm air is lighter than cold, dense air, it begins to rise over it, condensing as it rises to form cloud and rain.

CLASSIFICATION OF CLOUDS

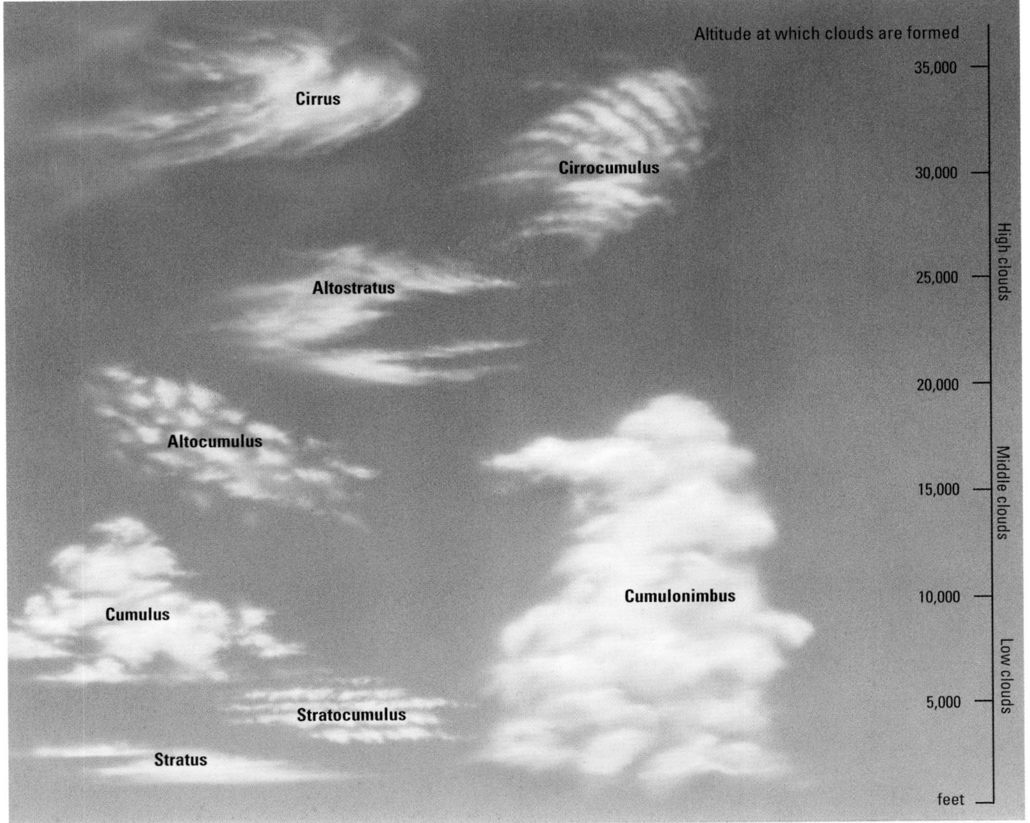

Clouds form when damp, usually rising, air is cooled. Thus they form when a wind rises to cross hills or mountains; when a mass of air rises over, or is pushed up by, another mass of denser air; or when local heating of the ground causes convection currents.

The first classification of clouds was developed by a London chemist, Luke Howard, in 1803, and it was later modified by the World Meteorological Organization. The types of clouds are classified according to altitude as high, middle, or low. The high ones, composed of ice crystals, are cirrus, cirrostratus, and cirrocumulus.

The middle clouds are altostratus – a gray or bluish striated, fibrous or uniform sheet producing light drizzle – and altocumulus, a thicker and fluffier version of cirrocumulus.

Low clouds include nimbostratus, a dark gray layer that brings rain or snow; cumulus, a detached heap, dark at the base; stratus, which forms dull, overcast skies at low levels; and stratocumulus, which consists of fluffy grayish-white layers.

Cumulonimbus, associated with storms and rains, heavy and dense with a flat base and a high, fluffy outline, can be tall enough to occupy middle as well as low altitudes.

PRESSURE AND SURFACE WINDS

WEATHER RECORDS

Pressure and winds

Highest barometric pressure:
Agata, Siberia, 1,083.8 mb at altitude 862 ft [262 m], December 31, 1968.

Lowest barometric pressure:
Typhoon Tip, 300 mi [480 km] west of Guam, Pacific Ocean, 870 mb, October 12, 1979.

Highest recorded wind speed:
Bridge Creek, Oklahoma, USA, 318 mph [512 km/h], May 3, 1999. Measured by Doppler radar monitoring a tornado.

Windiest place:
Port Martin, Antarctica, where winds of more than 40 mph [64 km/h] occur for not less than 100 days a year.

Worst recorded storm:
Bangladesh (then East Pakistan) cyclone, November 13, 1970 – over 300,000 dead or missing. The 1991 cyclone, Bangladesh's and the world's second worst in terms of loss of life, killed an estimated 138,000 people.

Worst recorded tornado:
Tri-state tornado – Missouri/Illinois/Indiana, USA, March 18, 1925 – 695 deaths, lasted 3 hours with 219 mi [352 km] path length. A suspected tornado in Bangladesh on April 26, 1989, killed approximately 1,300 people.

For more information:
76 Circulation of the air
77 Classification of clouds
Pressure and winds
80 Climate change
Global warming
82 Hydrological cycle
83 Natural vegetation
84 Ocean currents

Weather is the day-to-day or hour-to-hour condition of the air, while climate is weather in the long term – the seasonal pattern of hot and cold, wet and dry, averaged over a long period.

Most classifications of climate are based on a system developed in the early 19th century by Vladimir Köppen, a Russian meteorologist. Using a code based on letters and a classification centered on two main features, temperature and precipitation, he identified five main climatic types: tropical (A), dry (B), warm temperate (C), cold temperate (D), and polar (E). A highland mountain climate (H) was added later to account for the variety of altitudinal climatic zones on high mountains. Each of these main regions was then further subdivided.

Latitude is a major factor in determining climate, but other factors add to the complexity. These include the differential heating of land and sea, the distance from the sea, the effect of mountains on winds, and the influence of ocean currents. For example, New York City, Naples, and the Gobi Desert share almost the same latitude, but their climates are very different.

During the last Ice Age, the Earth underwent alternating cold periods, called glacials, separated by warm interglacials. The Milankovich theory suggests such cycles may be caused by variations in the Earth's path around the Sun, changing from almost circular to elliptical every 95,000 years, and variations in the Earth's tilt from 21.5° to 24.5° every 42,000 years. Another factor is that the Earth is now closest to the Sun in the middle of winter in the northern hemisphere and furthest away in summer. But 12,000 years ago, at the height of the last glacial period, the northern winter fell with the Sun at its most distant.

Studies of these cycles suggest that we are now in an interglacial with a new glacial period on the way. However, scientists believe that global warming, largely a result of burning fossil fuels and deforestation, may be occurring much faster than the great, slow cycles of the Solar System.

Tropical rainy climates
All mean monthly temperatures above 64°F [18°C].

- **Af** Rain forest climate
- **Am** Monsoon climate
- **Aw** Savanna climate

Dry climates
Low rainfall combined with a wide range of temperatures.

- **BS** Steppe climate
- **BW** Desert climate

Warm temperate rainy climates
The mean temperature is below 64°F [18°C] but above 26°F [–3°C] and that of the warmest month is over 50°F [10°C].

- **Cw** Dry winter climate
- **Cs** Dry summer climate
- **Cf** Climate with no dry season

Cold temperate rainy climates
The mean temperature of the coldest month is below 26°F [–3°C] but that of the warmest month is still over 50°F [10°C].

- **Dw** Dry winter climate
- **Df** Climate with no dry season

Polar climates
The mean temperature of the warmest month is below 50°F [10°C], giving permanently frozen subsoil.

- **ET** Tundra climate

The mean temperature of the warmest month is below 32°F [0°C], giving permanent ice and snow.

- **EF** Polar climate

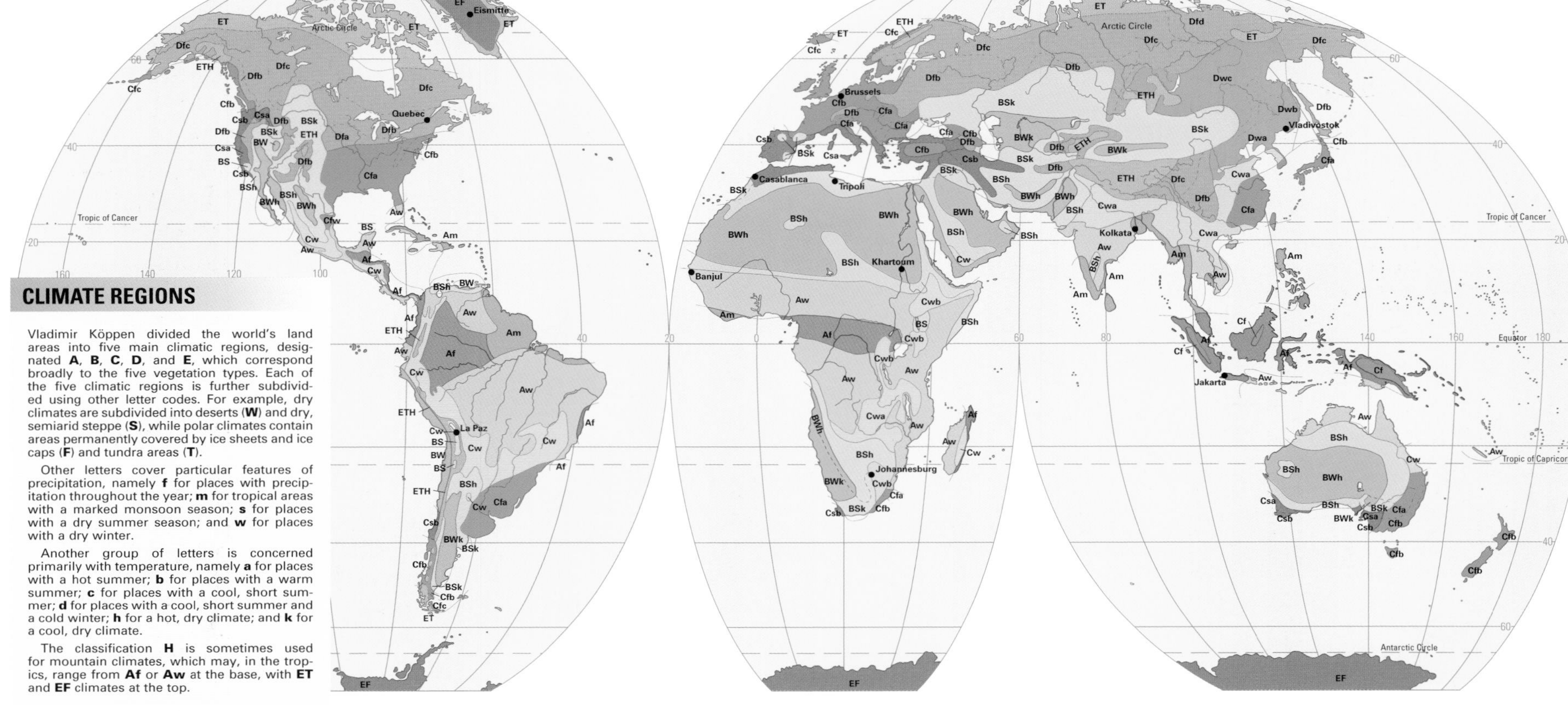

CLIMATE REGIONS

Vladimir Köppen divided the world's land areas into five main climatic regions, designated **A**, **B**, **C**, **D**, and **E**, which correspond broadly to the five vegetation types. Each of the five climatic regions is further subdivided using other letter codes. For example, dry climates are subdivided into deserts (**W**) and dry, semiarid steppe (**S**), while polar climates contain areas permanently covered by ice sheets and ice caps (**F**) and tundra areas (**T**).

Other letters cover particular features of precipitation, namely **f** for places with precipitation throughout the year; **m** for tropical areas with a marked monsoon season; **s** for places with a dry summer season; and **w** for places with a dry winter.

Another group of letters is concerned primarily with temperature, namely **a** for places with a hot summer; **b** for places with a warm summer; **c** for places with a cool, short summer; **d** for places with a cool, short summer and a cold winter; **h** for a hot, dry climate; and **k** for a cool, dry climate.

The classification **H** is sometimes used for mountain climates, which may, in the tropics, range from **Af** or **Aw** at the base, with **ET** and **EF** climates at the top.

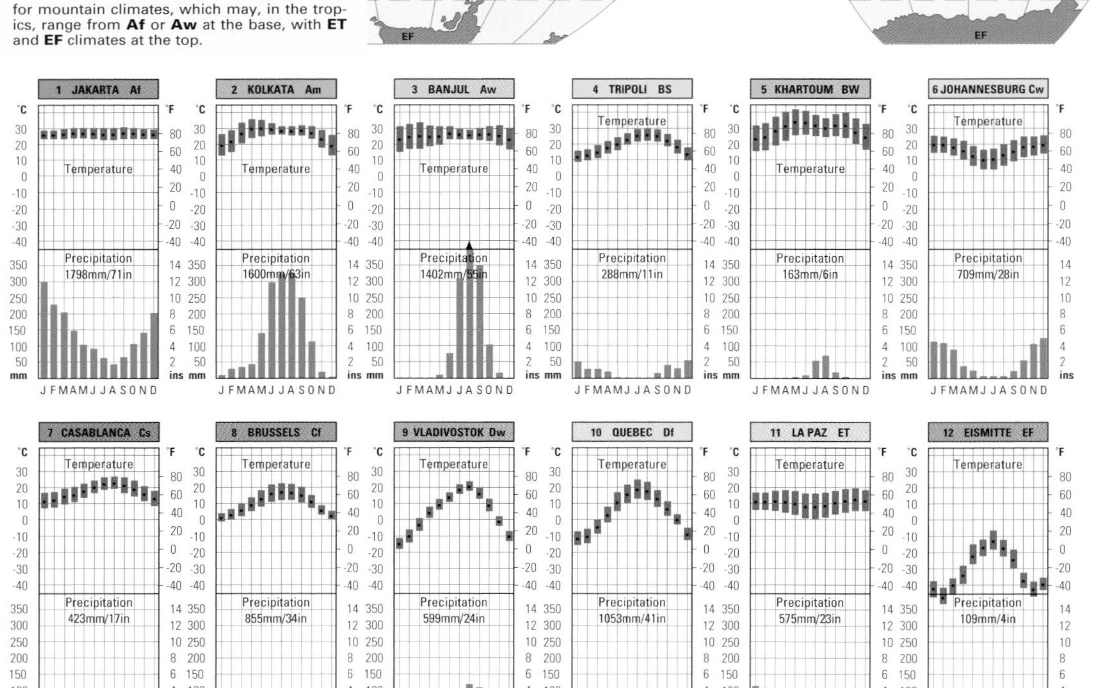

CLIMATE AND WEATHER TERMS

Anticyclone: area of high pressure with light winds and generally quiet weather.
Absolute humidity: mass of water vapor contained in a given volume of air.
Cloud cover: amount of cloud in the sky; measured in oktas (from 0–9), with 0 clear, and 9 "sky obscured."
Condensation: the conversion of water vapor into liquid.
Cyclone: violent storm resulting from counterclockwise rotation of winds in the northern hemisphere and clockwise in the southern: called hurricane in North America, typhoon in the Far East.
Depression: large area of low barometric pressure, a few thousand miles across.
Dew: deposition of small water droplets on the Earth's surface by direct condensation of water vapor.
Dew point: the temperature at which air becomes saturated by cooling at constant barometric pressure and absolute humidity
Drizzle: precipitation drops between 0.01–0.02 inches [0.2 and 0.5 mm] in diameter.
Evaporation: conversion of water from liquid into vapor or moisture in the air.
Front: the dividing line between two air masses.
Frost: the surface deposition of water vapor as minute ice crystals, when temperature reaches the frost point.
Hail: variably-sized pieces of ice that fall in downdrafts from cumulonimbus clouds.
Humidity: amount of water vapor in the air.
Isobar: line joining places with the same barometric pressure.
Isotherm: line connecting places of equal temperature.
Lightning: massive electrical discharge released in thunderstorm from cloud to cloud or cloud to ground, the result of the top becoming positively charged and the bottom negatively charged.
Precipitation: measurable rain, snow, sleet, or hail.
Prevailing wind: most common direction of wind at a given location.
Rain: precipitation of liquid particles with diameter larger than 0.02 inches [0.5 mm].
Relative humidity: observed quantity of water vapor in a mass of air over the saturation value at a given temperature (as a percentage).
Snow: flake-like coagulations of ice crystals that fall from clouds in subzero temperatures.
Thunder: sound produced by the rapid expansion of air heated by lightning.
Tornado: rapidly-rotating funnel-shaped cloud or debris column that must reach the surface and be attached to a parent cumulonimbus cloud.

BEAUFORT WIND SCALE

Named after Admiral Sir Francis Beaufort, the 19th-century British naval officer who devised it, the Beaufort Scale assesses wind speed according to its effects. It was originally designed as an aid for sailors, but has since been adapted for use on the land. It is used internationally.

Scale	Wind speed mph	km/h	Effect
0	0–1	0–1	**Calm** Smoke rises vertically
1	1–3	1–5	**Light air** Wind direction shown only by smoke drift
2	4–7	6–11	**Light breeze** Wind felt on face; leaves rustle; vanes moved by wind
3	8–12	12–19	**Gentle breeze** Leaves and small twigs in constant motion; wind extends small flag
4	13–18	20–28	**Moderate** Raises dust and loose paper; small branches move
5	19–24	29–38	**Fresh** Small trees in leaf sway; crested wavelets on inland waters
6	25–31	39–49	**Strong** Large branches move; difficult to use umbrellas; overhead wires whistle
7	32–38	50–61	**Near gale** Whole trees in motion; difficult to walk against wind
8	39–46	62–74	**Gale** Twigs break from trees; walking very difficult
9	47–54	75–88	**Strong gale** Slight structural damage
10	55–63	89–102	**Storm** Trees uprooted; serious structural damage
11	64–72	103–117	**Violent storm** Widespread damage
12	73+	118+	**Hurricane**

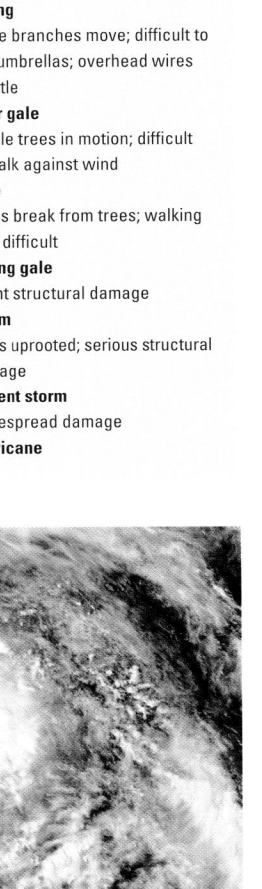

▲ In the Pacific Ocean, off south-east Asia, Typhoon Haiyan developed into a Category 5 storm during November 2013. Moving westwards, wind speeds of 170 mph (275 km/h) were recorded before it hit the Philippines. This makes it the strongest typhoon to make landfall, and over 6,000 people lost their lives.

THE MONSOON

Monsoon is the term given to the seasonal reversal of wind direction, most noticeably in Southeast Asia. It results from a combination of factors: the extreme heating and cooling of large land masses in relation to the less marked changes in temperature of the adjacent seas; the northward movement of the Intertropical Convergence Zone (ITCZ); and the effect of the Himalayas on the circulation of the air.

In March, winds blow outward from the mainland. But as the Sun and the ITCZ move northward, the land is intensely heated, and a low-pressure system develops. The southeast trade winds change direction and are sucked into the interior to become southwesterlies, bringing heavy rain. By November, the Sun and the ITCZ have again moved south and the wind directions are again reversed. Cool winds blow from the Asian interior to the sea, losing any moisture on the Himalayas before descending to the coast.

TEMPERATURE

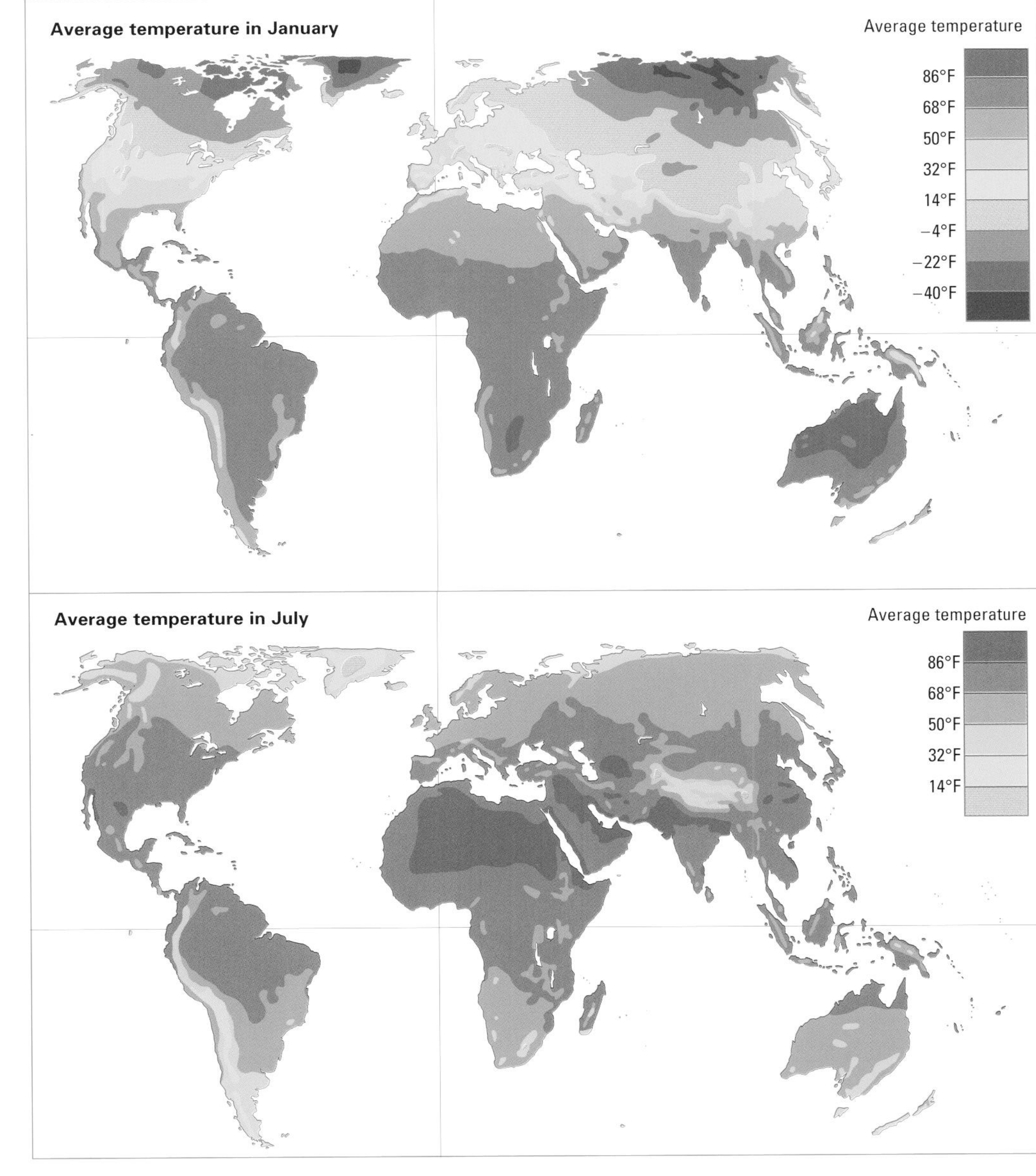

PRECIPITATION (RAINFALL AND SNOW)

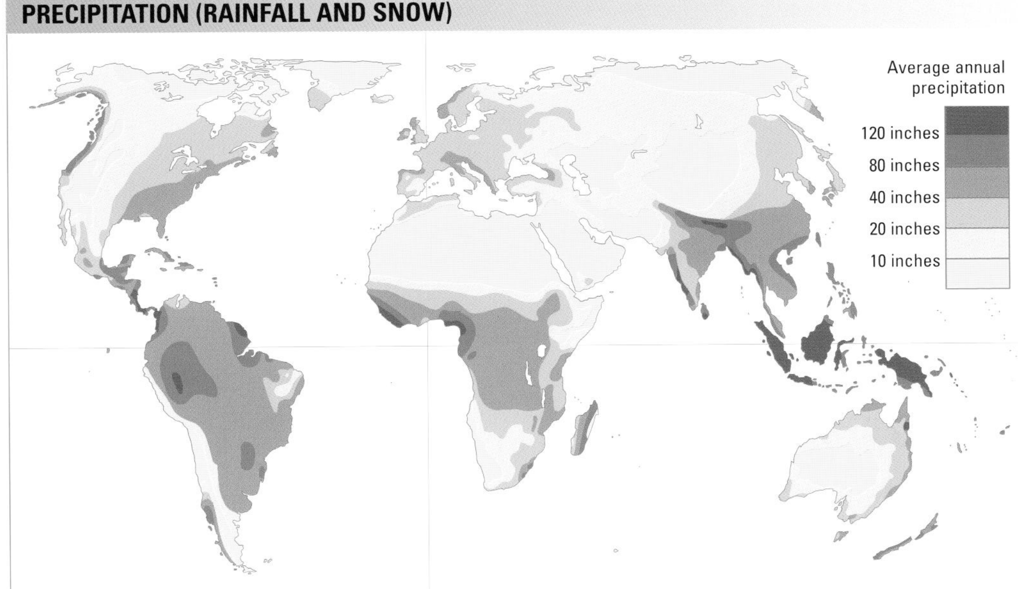

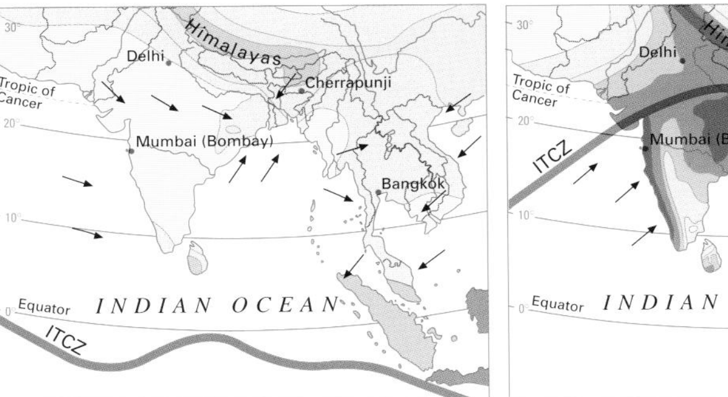

March – Start of the hot, dry season. The ITCZ is over the southern Indian Ocean.

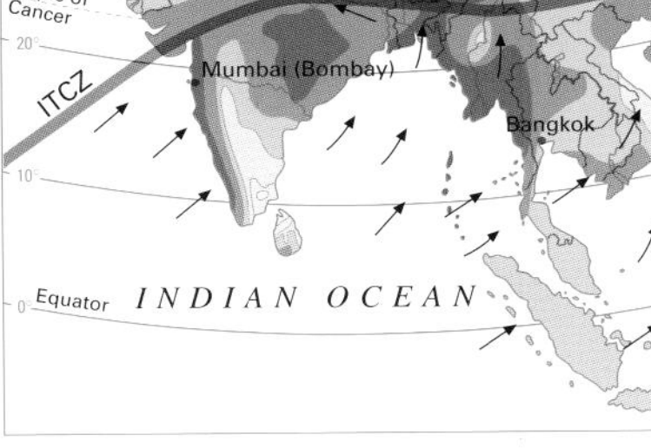

July – The rainy season. The ITCZ has migrated northward; winds blow onshore.

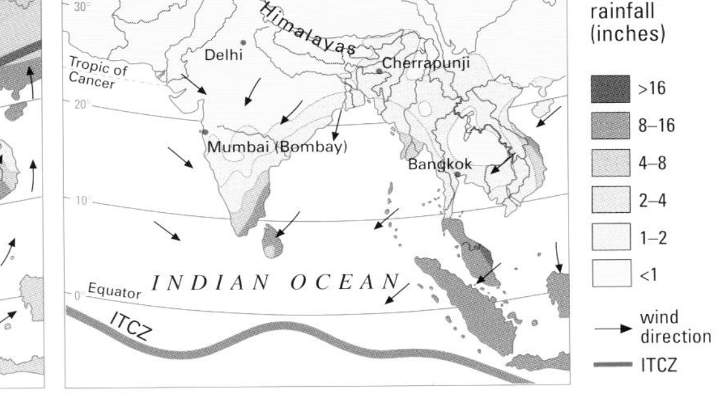

November – The ITCZ has returned south. The offshore winds are cool and dry.

CLIMATE RECORDS

TEMPERATURE

Highest recorded temperature:
Death Valley, California, USA, 134°F [56.7°C], 10 July 1913.

Highest mean annual temperature:
Dallol, Ethiopia, 94°F [34.4°C], 1960–6.

Longest heatwave:
Marble Bar, W. Australia, 162 days over 100°F [38°C], October 23, 1923, to April 7, 1924.

Lowest recorded temperature (outside poles):
Verkhoyansk, Siberia, −93.6°F [−69.8°C], February 7, 1982. Verkhoyansk also registered the greatest annual range of temperature: −90°F to 98°F [−68°C to 37°C].

Lowest mean annual temperature:
Polus Nedostupnosti, Pole of Cold, Antarctica, −72°F [−57.8°C].

PRECIPITATION

Driest place:
Quillagua, N. Chile, mean annual rainfall 0.02 inches [0.5 mm], 1964–2001.

Wettest place (average):
Mt Wai'ale'ale, Hawai'i, USA, mean annual rainfall 459.8 inches [11,680 mm].

Wettest place (12 months):
Cherrapunji, Meghalaya, N.E. India, 1,042 inches [26,461 mm], August 1860 to August 1861. Cherrapunji also holds the record for rainfall in one month: 115 inches [2,930 mm], July 1861. (*See Monsoon maps below.*)

Wettest place (24 hours):
Fac Fac, Réunion, Indian Ocean, 71.9 inches [1,825 mm], March 15–16, 1952.

Heaviest hailstones:
Gopalganj, Bangladesh, up to 2.25 lb [1.02 kg], April 14, 1986 (killed 92 people).

Heaviest snowfall (continuous):
Bessans, Savoie, France, 68 inches [1,730 mm] in 19 hours, April 5–6, 1969.

Heaviest snowfall (season/year):
Mt Baker, Washington, USA, 1,140 inches [28,956 mm], June 1998 to June 1999.

For more information:
76 Atmosphere
78 Climate
84 Ocean currents

Ever since the Industrial Revolution began, the amount of carbon dioxide in the atmosphere has steadily increased. It is the result of burning fossil fuels, and the destruction of forests which absorb carbon dioxide. In the late 18th century, carbon dioxide made up about 280 parts per million by volume (ppmv). It has risen to over 400 ppmv in 2019.

Carbon dioxide is one of the "greenhouse gases" which also include CFCs (which also cause ozone depletion in the upper atmosphere), methane, and nitrous oxides. Another greenhouse gas is water vapor. The quantity of vapor in the atmosphere has increased during recent decades as an expression of increased evaporation. This enhances the greenhouse effect as a positive feedback.

Greenhouse gases are so-called because they absorb part of the Earth's radiation going out to space and re-radiate a proportion of it back down. This critically important natural process acts to insulate the Earth and is essential to life. Without it, our planet would be some 54°F [30°C] colder than it is. But the increase in the volume of carbon dioxide in particular has caused global temperatures to rise. These changes were detailed by the Intergovernmental Panel on Climate Change (IPCC) report in 2013. While computer projections are difficult to make, the IPCC report concluded that a rise in temperatures of between 2.7°F [1.5°C] (compared to the 1850–1900 global mean) and at least 3.6°F [2.0°C] is likely by 2100. Global warming will almost certainly alter weather patterns, causing food and water shortages in vulnerable parts of the world, massive floods, and a rise in sea levels of between 1.71 ft [0.52 m] and 3.22 ft [0.98 m].

While an international ban has been imposed on some greenhouse gases, their residence time in the atmosphere may have long-lasting consequences.

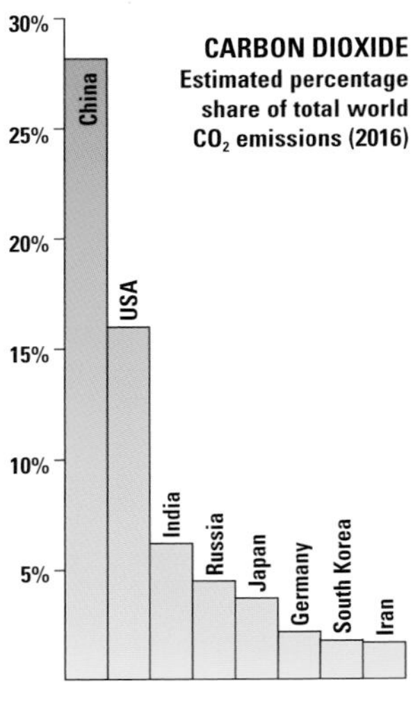

In 2010 it was estimated that China was generating almost 80% of its electricity from coal-fired power stations to support its economic boom. It has since overtaken the USA to become the world's biggest producer of carbon dioxide.

GLOBAL WARMING

High atmospheric concentrations of heat-absorbing gases are a major cause in the rise of average surface temperatures worldwide – up by 1.78°F [0.99°C] between 1880 and 2016. Global warming is also likely to bring about a rise in sea levels that may flood some of the world's densely populated coastal areas (see panel at foot of page 81).

Evidence of global warming is attributed mainly to the "greenhouse effect," caused by the emission of certain gases, notably carbon dioxide, into the atmosphere. Despite international action to control emissions of some greenhouse gases, carbon dioxide levels are still rising.

Carbon dioxide emissions in tonnes per capita (2016)

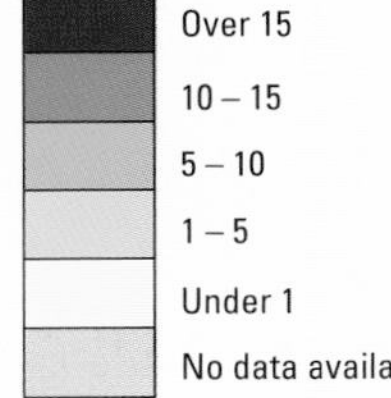

CLIMATE CHANGE

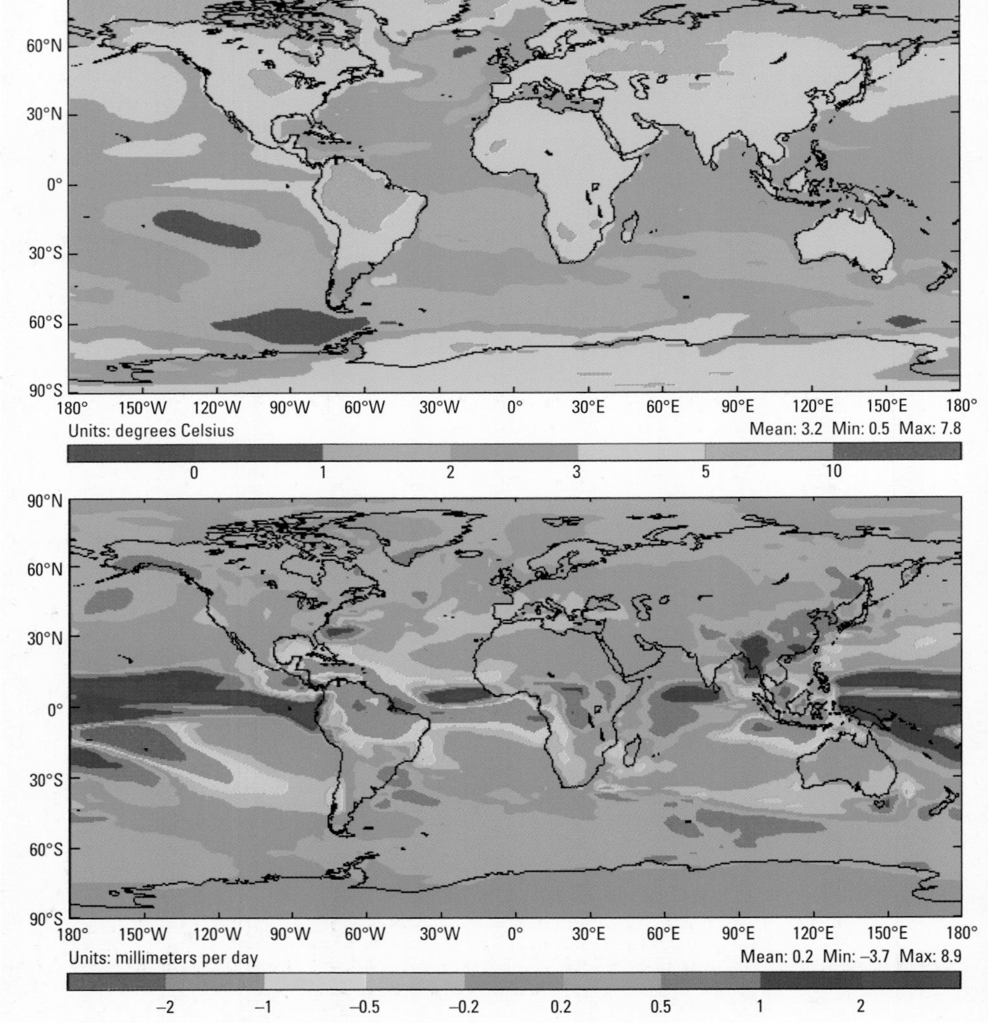

Annual average surface air temperature

The map summarizes the change in long-term mean values between the predicted average for the period from 2070 to 2100, and the observed average for 1960 to 1990. The predictions are from a long-term "run" of a "coupled" atmosphere-ocean computer model that represents the complex processes in the Earth's climate system. It assumes that the atmospheric concentration of carbon dioxide will increase more than twofold during the 21st century, assuming "medium growth" of the global economy, and that no measures to combat the emission of greenhouse gases are taken. Note that the predicted increase in average surface temperature suggests a warming across Britain and Ireland of between 2°C [3.6°F] in the north and west to possibly 4°C [7.2°F] in the southeast. Very broadly, the oceans and some adjacent continental areas are likely to see the smaller increases.

Annual average precipitation

Predictions from climate models always involve some degree of uncertainty. This is because our understanding of the climate system and its complex workings are imperfect, as are the model representations of the physical system. Additionally, we are unsure quite how the world will evolve economically and politically over the coming decades – although different scenarios are used in this regard. The map of predicted precipitation change indicates broadly, for example, an increase across Britain and Ireland. The largest increases of some 0.01–0.02 inches [0.2–0.5 mm] a day are anticipated to be over northern and western areas. This equates to some 3–7 inches [75–180 mm] a year.

It should be noted that both these maps mask quite significant seasonal detail, which is also predicted by the models.

ARCTIC SEA ICE

The fact that the Arctic sea ice is disappearing has been known for decades. The underlying cause is believed by all but a handful of climatologists to be global warming, brought about by greenhouse-gas emissions. At current rates of shrinkage, this looks likely to happen some time between 2020 and 2050.

The reason is that Arctic air is warming twice as fast as the atmosphere as a whole. While some of the causes of this are understood, others are not. The darkness of land and water compared to the reflectiveness of snow and ice means that when the snow and ice melt to reveal land or water, the area exposed absorbs more heat from the Sun and reflects less of it back into space. The result is a feedback loop that accelerates local warming.

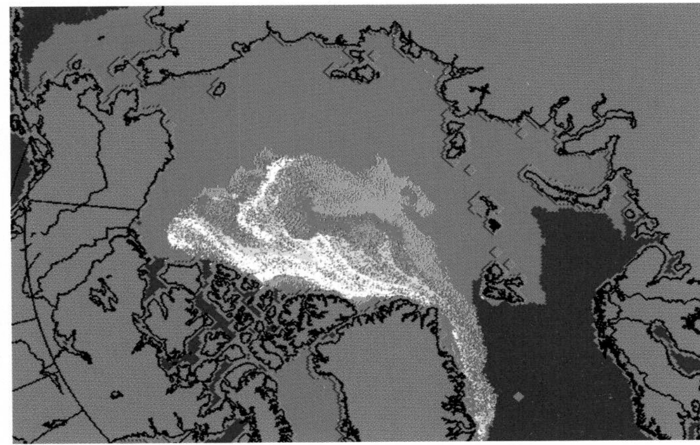

The diagram and map show that ice older than 1 year, which used to cover up to 60% of the Arctic Ocean, now covers only 30%. The oldest ice, over 4 years old, now comprises only 5% of the ice in the Arctic Ocean, whereas during the 1980s it covered roughly 25% of the region.

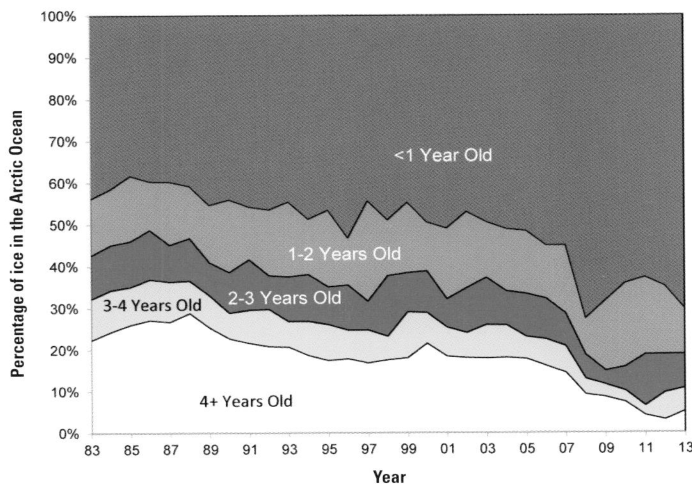

NSIDC courtesy J. Maslanik and M. Tschudi, University of Colorado

REGIONAL CLIMATE CHANGE

Climate modelers have produced simulations of global and continental surface temperature changes over the last century. This is done using only "natural forcing" by modeling the impact on atmospheric temperatures from known solar variability and volcanic eruptions. In addition, the same period of time is simulated by adding to natural forcing the impact of anthropogenic (human) influence due to measured changes in the concentration of greenhouse gases, particulate matter, etc.

The separate model "runs" are then compared with the observed temperature changes to illustrate which of the simulations matches the observations best.

This is a powerful means of verifying the relative roles of natural and human induced changes in atmospheric composition, and known solar output fluctuations on climate change.

► Climate model simulations for 1906 to 2009 using "natural forcings only" (blue bands) and "natural plus anthropogenic forcings" (pink bands). Regional decadal averages of observed temperature (black lines) are plotted as anomalies with respect to the 1880 to 1919 average. Blue and pink bands define the 5% to 95% range of possibilities for multiple runs for just natural forcings and natural plus anthropogenic forcings of the Coupled Model Intercomparison Project Phase 5.

Models using only natural forcings

Models using both natural and anthropogenic forcings

Observations
(dashed when spatial coverage is less than 50%)

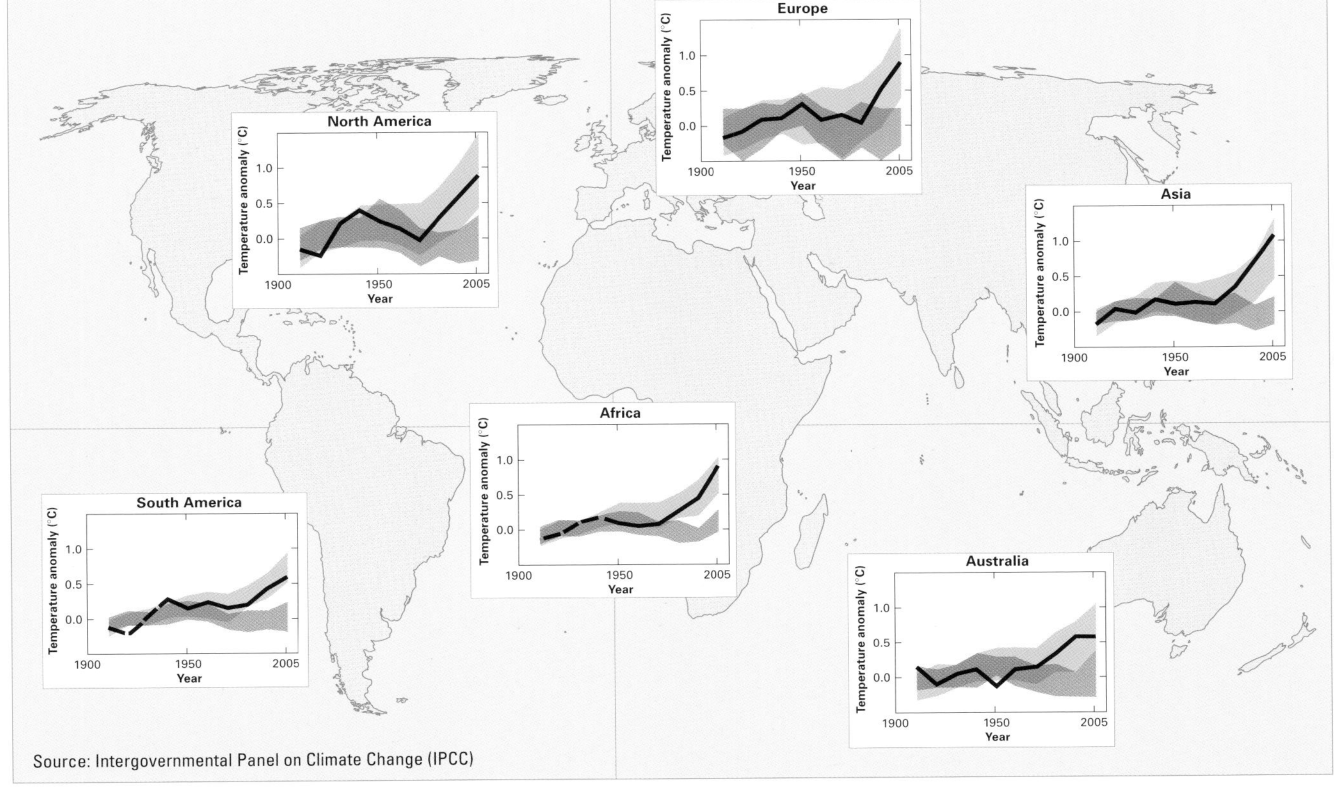

Source: Intergovernmental Panel on Climate Change (IPCC)

PROJECTED CHANGE IN GLOBAL WARMING

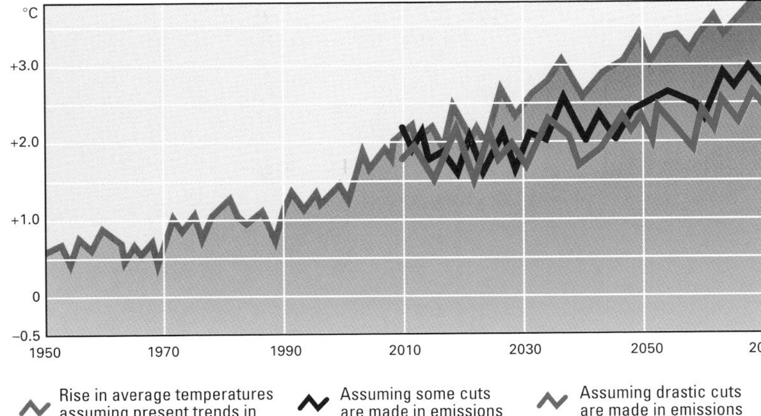

Rise in average temperatures assuming present trends in CO_2 emissions continue

Assuming some cuts are made in emissions

Assuming drastic cuts are made in emissions

Climate models are used to provide the best scientifically-based estimates of the future global climate. A typical method is to run the models for some decades ahead and then to compare the predicted average with a past 30-year period. A range of climate models are used, run with different scenarios that express the breadth of possibilities of, for example, industrial development and the degree of atmospheric pollution "clean-up" by industrial nations.

The diagram above shows global observed and predicted surface mean temperature change from 1950 to 2070 with three prediction scenarios. The first (red) assumes rapid economic growth and continued population increases. The second (blue) assumes some attempts are made to cut greenhouse gas emissions, while the green line involves the greater use of cleaner technologies, with global population peaking mid-century then declining.

REGIONAL CLIMATE CHANGE

The rate at which global sea level has increased since about the middle of the 19th century exceeds the increase estimated over the last two thousand years. The recent change is one expression of the impact of global warming through a combination of glacier melt and thermal expansion of the ocean; it is estimated that these count for 75% of the total observed rise since the 1970s. A combination of tide-gauge records and, more recently, altimeter observations from satellites, indicate that the global average increase of sea-level from 1901 to 2010 was 7.5 inches [190 mm] with an averaged global annual rise of 0.07 inches [1.7 mm] per year. This value has increased in recent periods from 0.08 inches [2.0 mm] per year (1971–2010) to 0.13 inches [3.2 mm] per year (1993–2010).

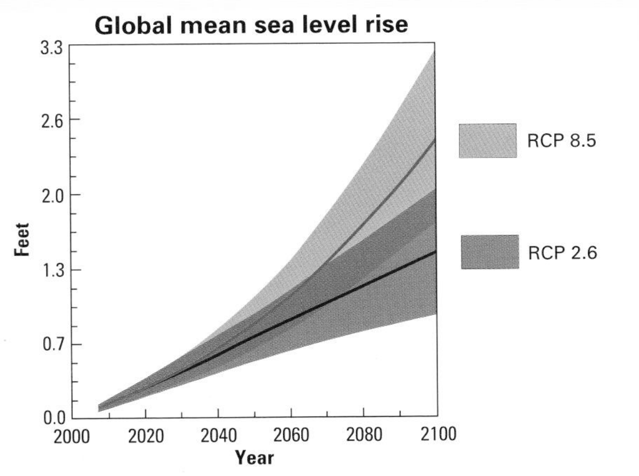

Source: Intergovernmental Panel on Climate Change (IPCC)

A combination of advanced global climate prediction models run through to 2100 produce an averaged forecast of the likely range of global mean sea level increase for two extreme CO_2, and other greenhouse gas, scenarios. The values on the graph are relative to the global mean conditions for the period 1986–2005. These "Representative Concentration Scenarios" (RCPs) vary from the lowest impact future (RCP 2.6) for which CO_2 concentration reaches 421 ppm by 2100, to the strongest impact (RCP 8.5) for which CO_2 increases to 936 ppm by 2100.

The upper and lower boundaries of the two bands of color on the graph show the predicted upper and lower possibilities of future sea level increase. The solid colored line is the median value that has 50% of estimates above it and 50% below. The low impact future indicates a median value of a 1.31 ft [0.4 m] increase by 2100 while the highest impact future is about double that at 2.46 ft [0.75 m].

For more information:
78 Climate regions
79 Precipitation
86 Biodiversity

Without the hydrological cycle, by which water is constantly recycled between the oceans, the atmosphere and the land, the continents would be barren. Precipitation enables plants to grow and soils to form, creating the world's natural vegetation regions and the ecosystems that support animal life.

Running water also plays a major role in shaping landforms. Yet in many parts of the world, people do not have safe water to drink and suffer from diseases caused by water-borne organisms and pollution. It is estimated that 770 million people lack access to safe water and more people have a mobile phone than a toilet.

Experts argue that world demand for water is increasing at about twice the rate of population growth. It is predicted that, by 2025, half the world's population will face water shortages. This could lead to conflict and even boundary wars – 300 major rivers cross national frontiers and access to their water is likely to be disputed.

THE HYDROLOGICAL CYCLE

The world's water balance is regulated by the constant recycling of water between the oceans, the atmosphere and the land. The movement of water between these three reservoirs is known as the "hydrological cycle." The oceans play a vital role in the hydrological cycle: 74% of the total precipitation falls over the oceans and 84% of the total evaporation comes from the oceans. Water vapor in the atmosphere circulates around the planet, transporting energy as well as the water itself. When the vapor cools, it falls as rain or snow. The whole cycle is driven by the Sun.

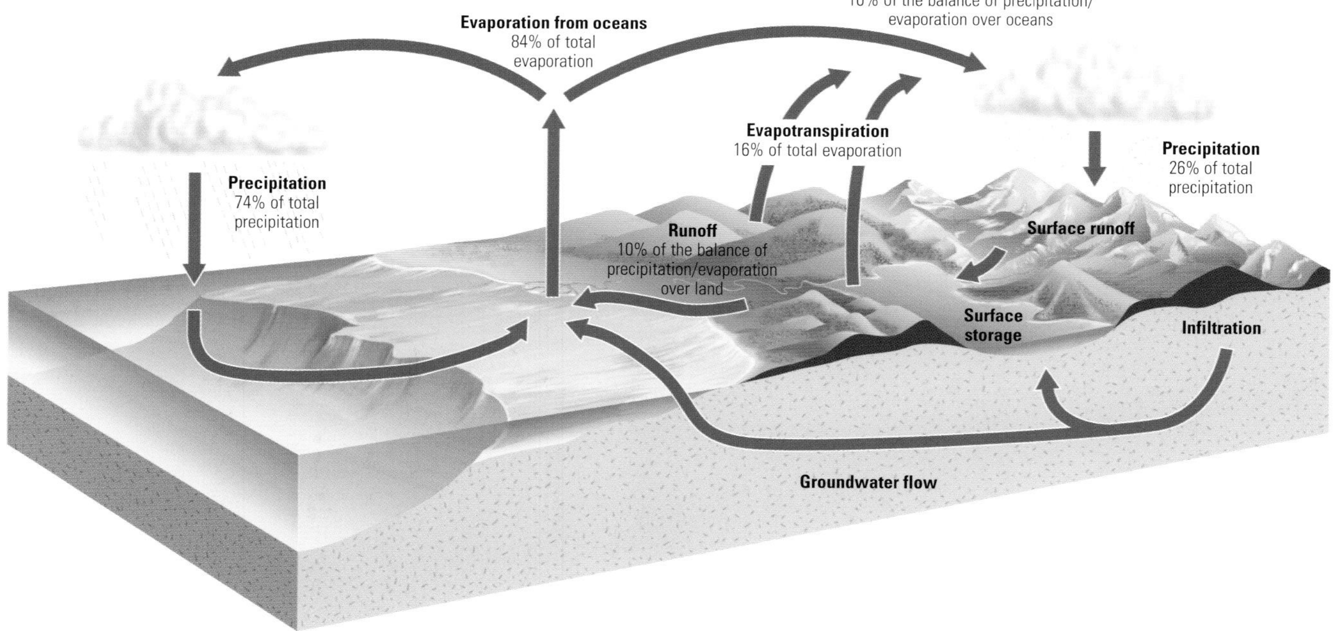

WATER DISTRIBUTION

The distribution of planetary water is shown by percentage. Oceans and ice caps together account for more than 99% of the total; the breakdown of the remainder is estimated.

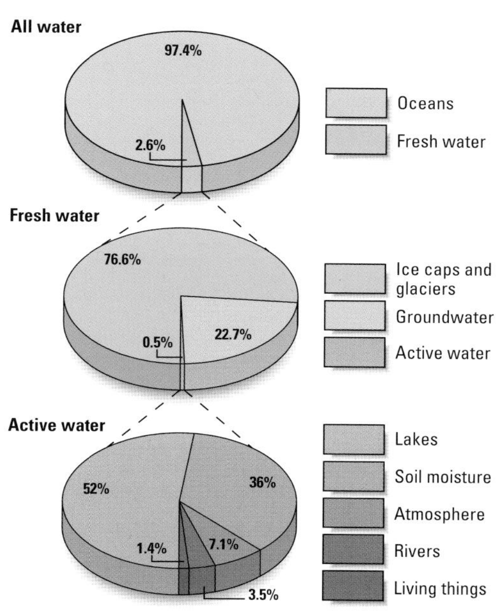

Almost all the world's water is 3,000 million years old, and all of it cycles endlessly through the hydrosphere, though at different rates. Water vapor circulates over days, even hours; deep-ocean water circulates over millennia; and ice-cap water remains solid for millions of years.

ANNUAL SEDIMENT YIELD

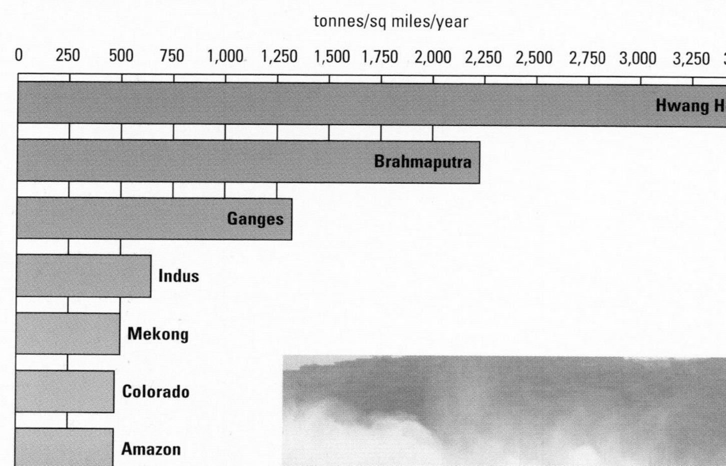

Around 20% of all land-derived sediment is carried by three Asian rivers: the Hwang Ho (Yellow River), the Brahmaputra, and the Ganges. Together, these three rivers carry around 3,000 million tonnes of sediment each year into the oceans. Sediment yield is affected by runoff and vegetation cover, and is steadily increasing due to large-scale deforestation, most notably in South-east Asia and the Amazon basin. In these regions, deforesting the slopes allows the heavy tropical rains to wash away whatever thin and fragile soil there is, leading to severe erosion of the land.

▼ To prevent as excess of sediment building up and slowing the flow of the Hwang Ho (Yellow River), the river's mud, silt and sand is blasted downstream at an annual event at the Xiaolangdi Reservoir, near Jiyuan, in Henan province.

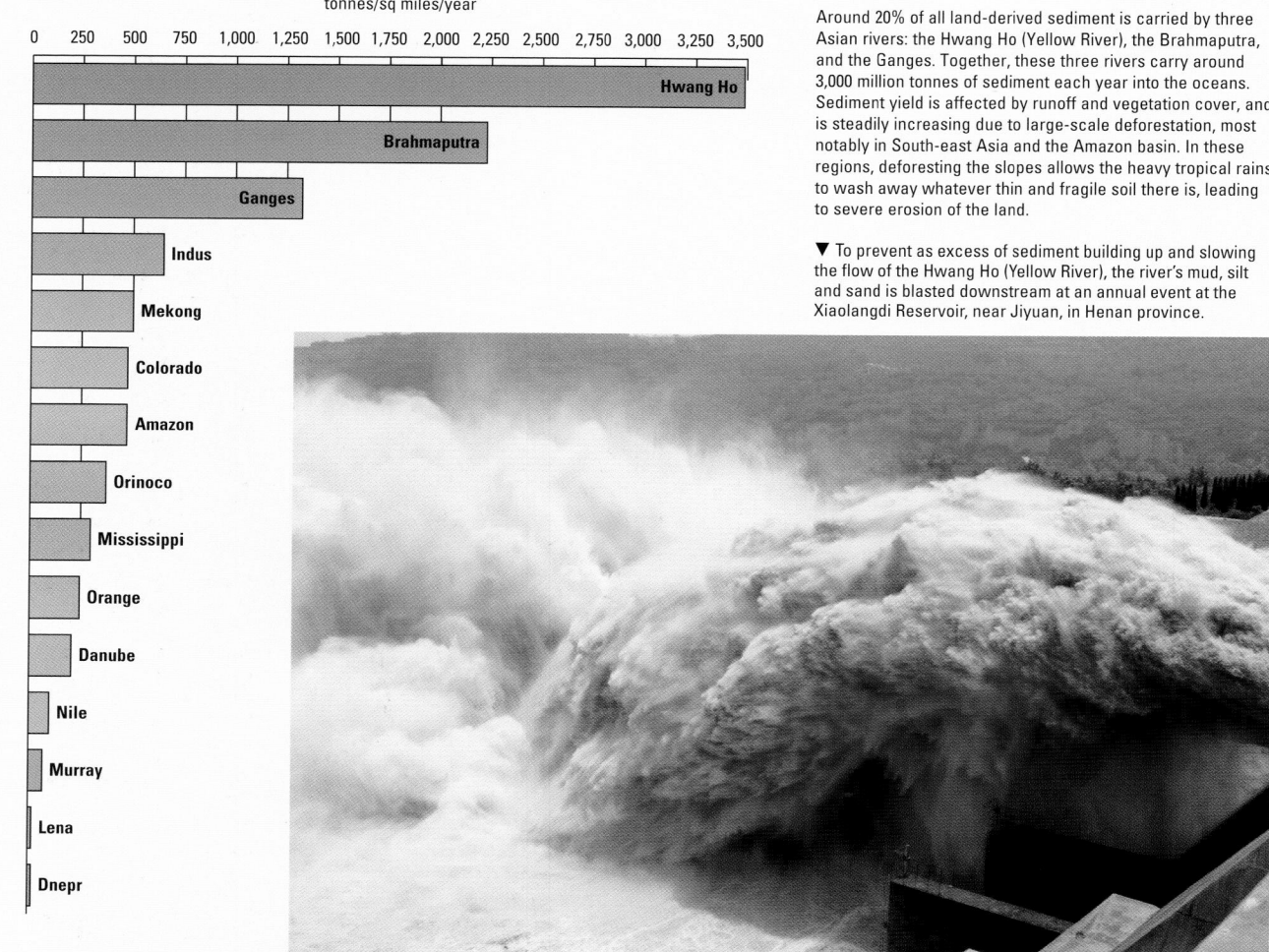

LONGEST RIVERS

		miles	km
Nile	Africa	4,160	6,695
Amazon	South America	4,010	6,450
Yangtse	Asia	3,960	6,380
Mississippi-Missouri	North America	3,710	5,971
Yenisey-Angara	Asia	3,445	5,550
Hwang Ho	Asia	3,395	5,464
Ob-Irtysh	Asia	3,360	5,410
Congo	Africa	2,900	4,670
Paraná-Plate	South America	2,796	4,500
Mekong	Asia	2,796	4,500
Amur	Asia	2,760	4,442
Lena	Asia	2,735	4,402
Irtysh	Asia	2,640	4,250
Mackenzie	North America	2,630	4,240
Niger	Africa	2,595	4,180
Yenisey	Asia	2,540	4,090
Missouri	North America	2,540	4,088
Mississippi	North America	2,350	3,782
Murray-Darling	Australia	2,330	3,750
Volga	Europe	2,300	3,700
Ob	Asia	2,285	3,680
Zambezi	Africa	2,200	3,540
Purus	South America	2,080	3,350
Madeira	South America	1,990	3,200
Yukon	North America	1,980	3,185
Indus	Asia	1,925	3,100
Darling	Australia	1,905	3,070
Rio Grande	North America	1,880	3,030
Brahmaputra	Asia	1,800	2,900
São Francisco	South America	1,800	2,900
Syrdarya	Asia	1,775	2,860
Danube	Europe	1,770	2,850
Salween	Asia	1,740	2,800
Paraná	South America	1,740	1,740
Tocantins	South America	1,710	2,750
Orinoco	South America	1,700	2,740
Euphrates	Asia	1,675	2,700
Murray	Australia	1,600	2,575
Paraguay	South America	1,580	2,550
Amudarya	Asia	1,575	2,540

WATER SCARCITY

Human populations require fresh water for many purposes – drinking, cooking, washing, farming, industry, recreation and energy production. Given population growth and rising standards of living in some areas, there will inevitably be increased pressure on this resource in certain places. Water scarcity can be physical and/or economic.

- Areas with little or no water scarcity – less than 25% of water from rivers is withdrawn for agriculture, industry and domestic purposes
- Areas with physical water scarcity – more than 75% of water from rivers is withdrawn for agriculture, industry and domestic purposes
- Areas approaching physical water scarcity – more than 60% of water from rivers is withdrawn and scarcity is expected in the near future
- Areas with economic water scarcity – less than 25% of water from rivers is withdrawn but human, institutional and financial problems limit access to water
- No data available

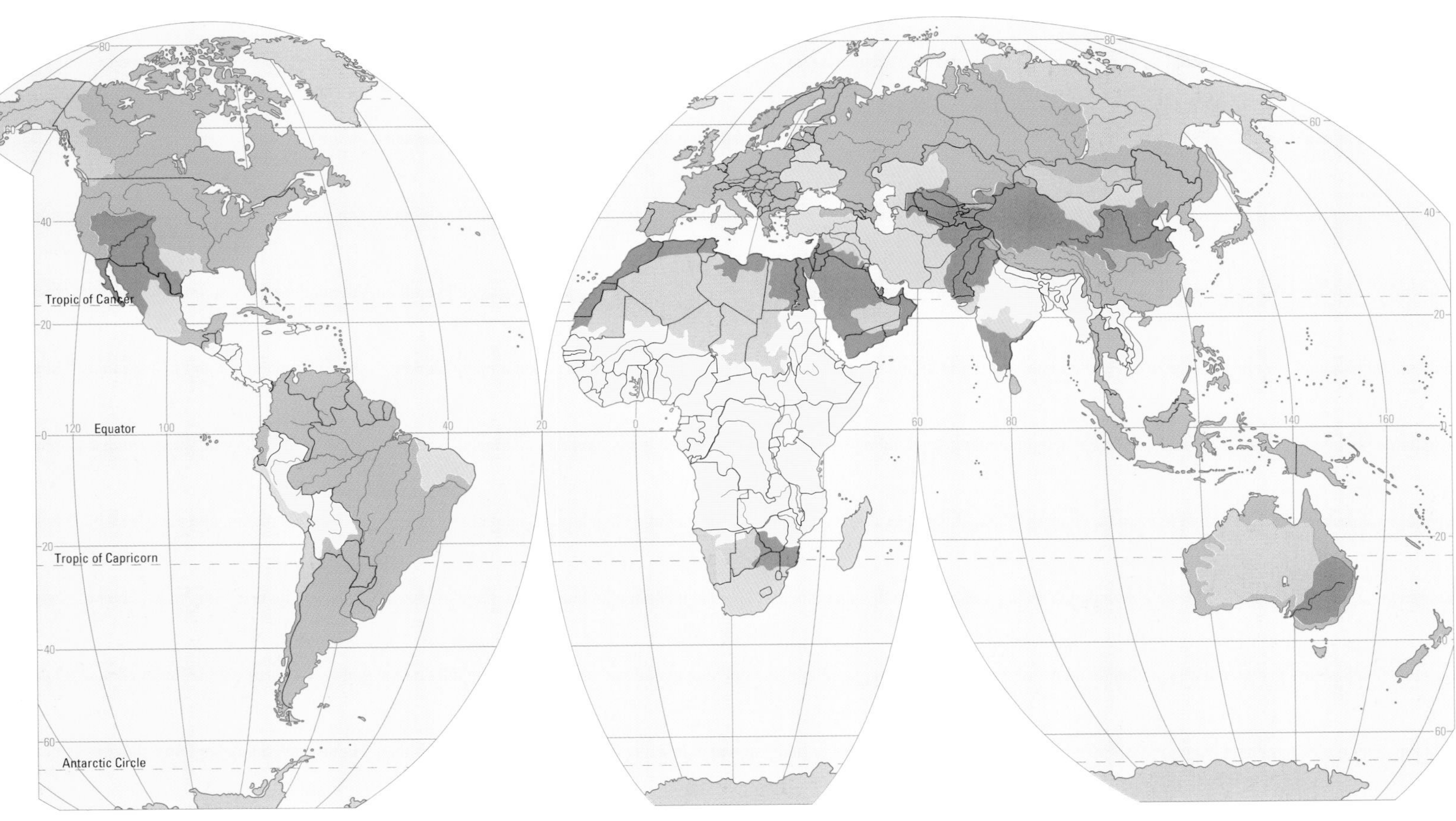

NATURAL VEGETATION

The map below illustrates the natural "climax vegetation" of a region, as dictated by its climate and topography. In most cases, human agricultural activity has drastically altered the pattern of the vegetation. The various vegetation regions support different kinds of animals and wildlife, and, in an undisturbed state, they are highly developed biological communities, or "biomes."

The blue line on the map represents the northern limit of tree growth, and the red lines indicate the northern and southern limits of palm growth. The majority of the numerous species are tropical or subtropical. Some, such as the coconut, date, sago, and oil palms, are important economically.

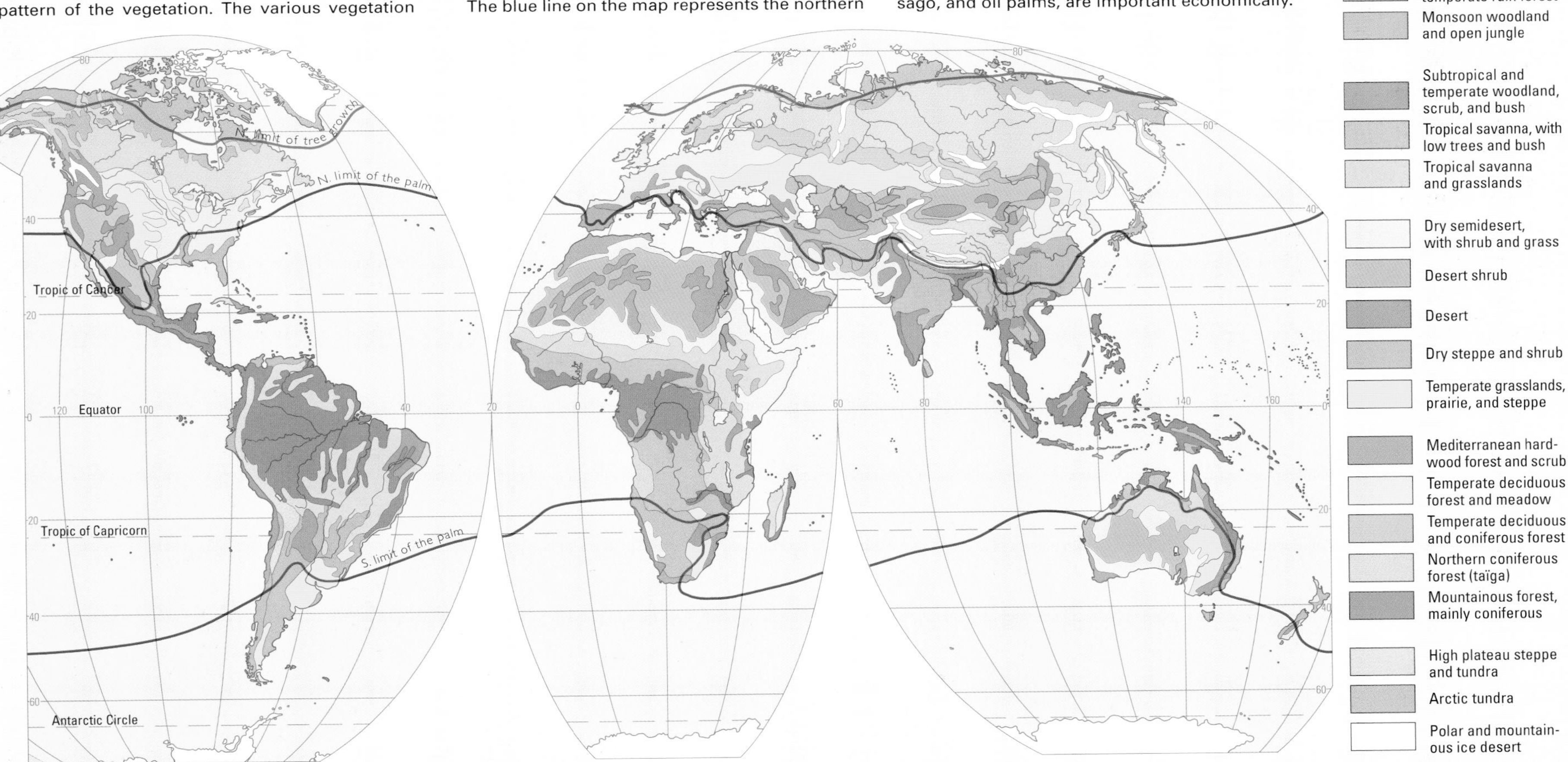

- Tropical rain forest
- Subtropical and temperate rain forest
- Monsoon woodland and open jungle
- Subtropical and temperate woodland, scrub, and bush
- Tropical savanna, with low trees and bush
- Tropical savanna and grasslands
- Dry semidesert, with shrub and grass
- Desert shrub
- Desert
- Dry steppe and shrub
- Temperate grasslands, prairie, and steppe
- Mediterranean hardwood forest and scrub
- Temperate deciduous forest and meadow
- Temperate deciduous and coniferous forest
- Northern coniferous forest (taïga)
- Mountainous forest, mainly coniferous
- High plateau steppe and tundra
- Arctic tundra
- Polar and mountainous ice desert

For more information:
79 Temperature and precipitation
80 Climate change and global warming
82 Water distribution
86 Population
98 Minerals

Oceans cover about 70% of the Earth's surface and are of great importance to humans in a number of ways. These include regulating global climates and providing a source of economic materials, such as food resources. In addition, oceans are important for leisure and recreation. They have also been described as the "highways in the globalized world." However, anthropogenic (man-made) stresses are changing the oceans faster than at almost any time in our planet's history.

Increasingly larger fishing fleets are now catching fewer large predatory fish but greater quantities of the smaller fish that are further down the food chain. The most prized food fish, such as cod and salmon, which tend to be top-level predators, are declining in numbers, leaving smaller, less desirable fish to be caught. Not only does this affect the type of fish available for human consumption, but it could also change marine ecosystems forever.

There are a number of possible strategies for the future, but there are clearly no simple solutions to the problems associated with such a politically, economically, and environmentally sensitive global industry. Fish resources could be conserved in a number of ways – for example, the protection of juveniles as well as policies to encourage breeding and discourage the marketing of illegal catches would help boost stocks. Catches could be restricted in order to match supply with demand and to protect sensitive species.

OCEANIC CONVEYOR BELTS

Oceanic convection occurs where cold, salty water from polar regions sinks into the depths and makes its way toward the Equator. The densest water is found in the Antarctic area. This cold, dense water sweeps round Antarctica at a depth of about 2.5 miles [4 km]. It then spreads into the deep basins of the Atlantic Ocean, the Pacific Ocean, and the Indian Ocean. Surface currents bring warm water to the North Atlantic from the Indian and Pacific Oceans. These waters give up their heat to cold winds, which blow from Canada across the North Atlantic. This water then sinks and starts the reverse convection of the deep ocean current. The amount of heat given up is about a third of the energy that is received from the Sun. Because the conveyor operates in this way, the North Atlantic is warmer than the North Pacific, so there is proportionally more evaporation there. The water left behind by evaporation contains more salt and it is therefore much denser, which causes it to sink. Eventually, this water is transported into the Pacific Ocean where it picks up more warm water, and thus its salinity and therefore its density is reduced.

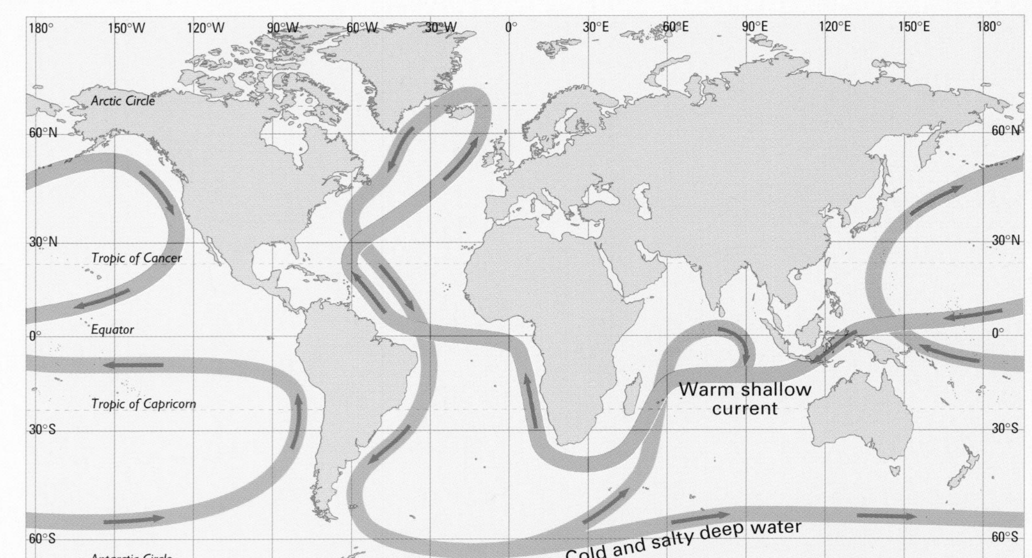

OCEAN CURRENTS

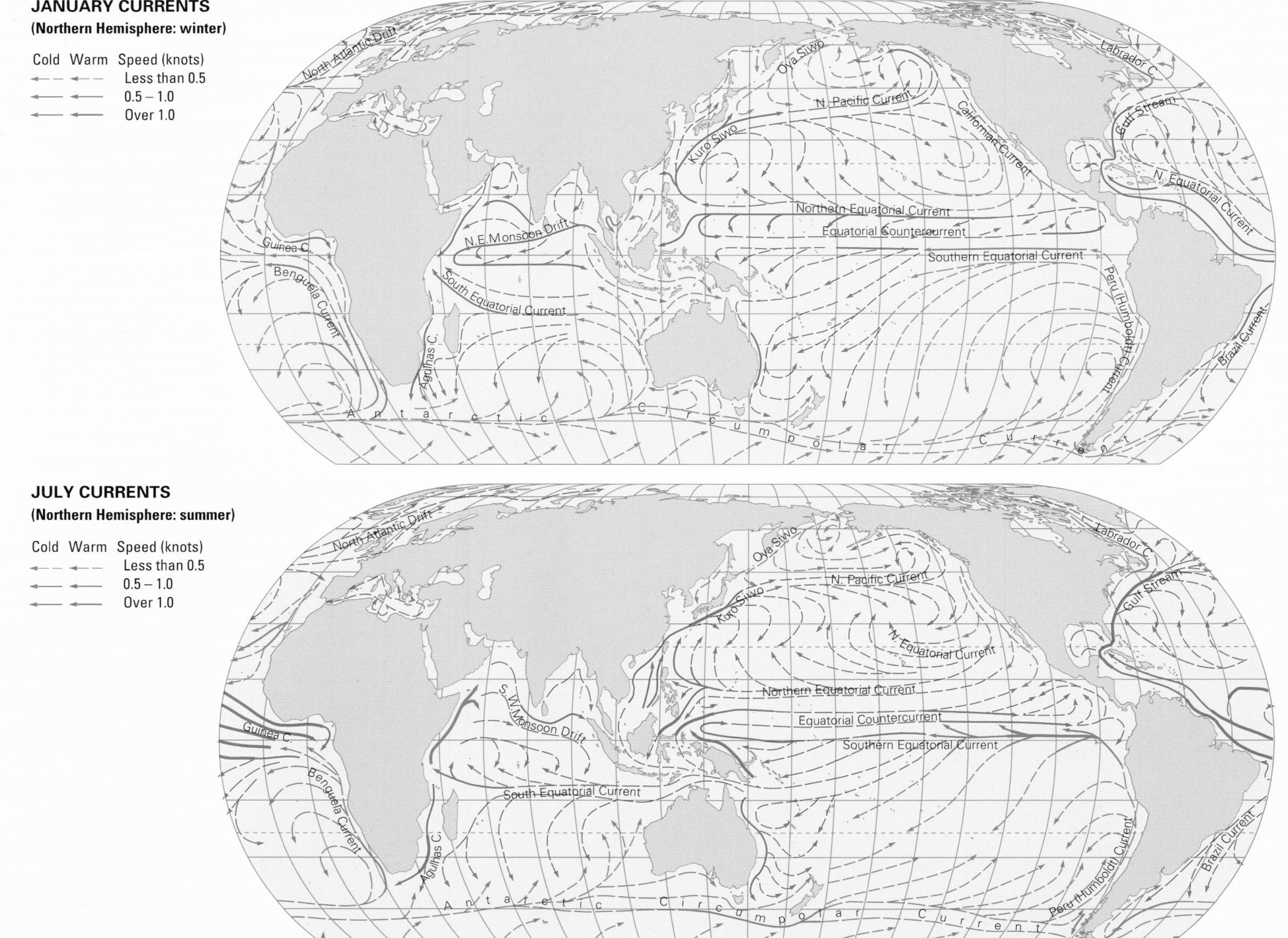

Moving immense quantities of energy as well as billions of tonnes of water every hour, the ocean currents are a vital part of the great heat engine that drives the Earth's climate. They themselves are produced by a twofold mechanism. At the surface, winds push huge masses of water before them; in the deep ocean below, an abrupt temperature gradient separates the churning surface waters from the still depths (*see the ocean conveyor belt diagram above*).

Coriolis effect
The pattern of circulation of the great surface currents is determined by the displacement known as the "Coriolis effect." As the Earth turns, the vast mass of ocean water is deflected to one side. The deflection is most obvious near the Equator, where the Earth's surface is spinning eastward at 1,000 mph; currents moving poleward are curved clockwise in the northern hemisphere and counterclockwise in the southern hemisphere.

Ocean currents
The result is a system of spinning circles known as "gyres." Warm currents move constantly from the Equator toward the poles, while cold water moves in the reverse direction. In this way, ocean currents act like a thermostat, helping to regulate temperatures around the world.

Depending on the annual movements of the prevailing wind belts, some currents on or near the Equator may reverse their direction in the course of the year, a variation on which Asia's monsoon rains depend and whose occasional failure has brought disaster to millions of people.

FISHING

As stocks are overfished and dwindle, it is important to manage them carefully so that there are sufficient resources for future generations. The Marine Stewardship Council (MSC) is an international, nonprofit organization set up to help make the seafood market sustainable. It oversees and manages the distinctive blue labeling system that tells consumers which species of fish they can buy without destroying stocks. This system is popular with large food retailers who wish to be seen supporting sustainable fish catches. It is estimated that over 30% of shoppers worldwide recognize the MSC ecolabel. However, only 8% of the world's fisheries are MSC certified.

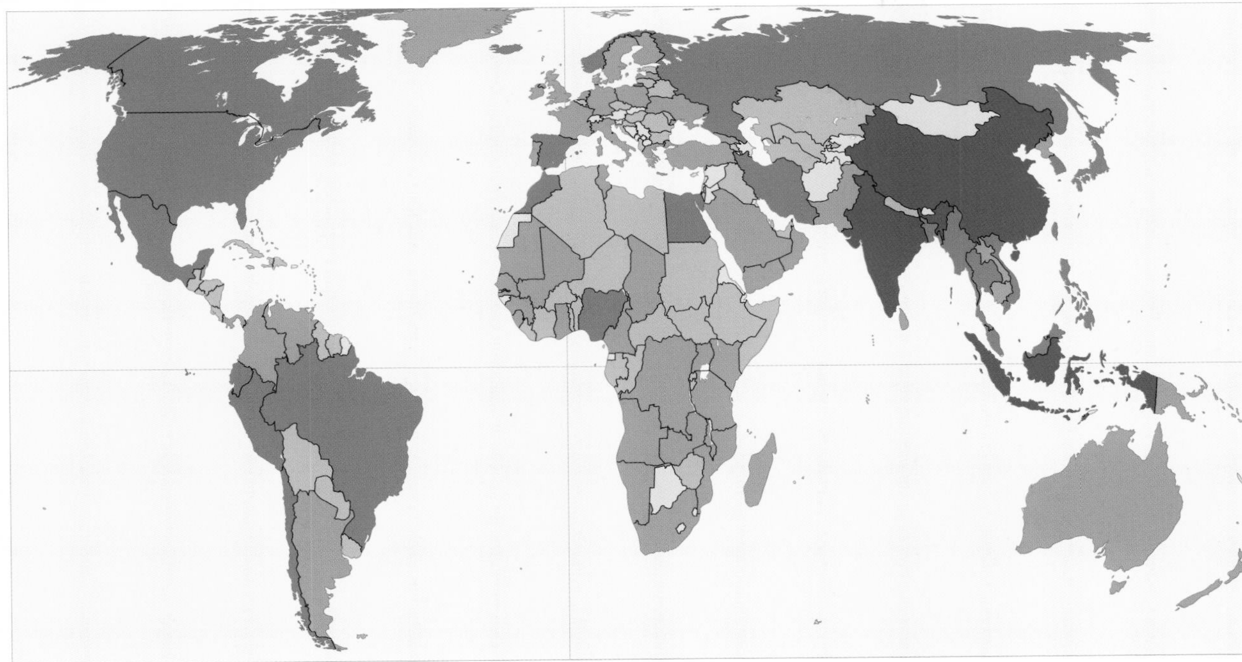

There has been a dramatic rise in world wild fish catches, from under 20 million tonnes in 1950 to an estimated 94.5 million tonnes in 2014, but this is now leveling off as the stocks become depleted and protection of fish stocks increases. Farmed fish totals rose from almost nothing in 1950 to 2019 where farmed fish will overtake the wild catch. Currently, about 3 billion people get 20% of their animal protein from fishery products.

Total world fish catch in metric tonnes, inland and marine fishing (2017)

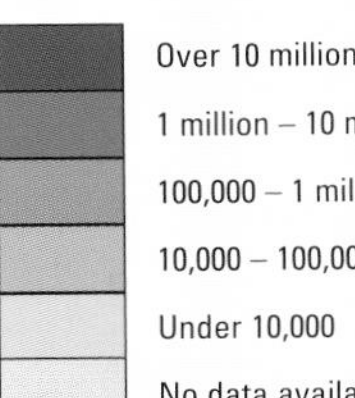

AQUACULTURE

▲ This aerial photo shows shrimp farms, near Mahajanga, in northwestern Madagascar. Shrimp farming is being used to stimulate the country's economy.

Aquaculture involves raising fish commercially, usually for food. In contrast, a fish hatchery releases juvenile fish into the wild for recreational fishing or to supplement a species' natural numbers. The most important fish species raised by fish farms are salmon, carp, tilapia, catfish, and cod. Salmon makes up 85% of the total sale of Norwegian fish farming. Farming was introduced when populations of wild Atlantic salmon in the North Atlantic and Baltic Sea crashed due to overfishing.

Technological costs are high, and include using drugs, such as antibiotics to keep fish healthy and steroids to improve growth. Breeding programs are also expensive. Outputs are high per hectare and per farmer, and efficiency is high also. However, environmental effects can be damaging. Salmon are carnivores and so need to be fed pellets made from other fish. It is possible that farmed salmon actually represent a net loss of protein in the global food supply, as it takes between 4–11 lbs [2–5 kg] of wild fish to grow 2 lbs [1 kg] of salmon. In contrast, most global aquaculture production (*c.* 85%) uses non-carnivorous fish species, such as tilapia and catfish, for domestic markets. Fish like herring, mackerel, sardine, and anchovy are used to produce the feed for farmed salmon, and so the production of salmon leads to the depletion of other fish species on a global scale.

Other environmental costs include the sea lice and disease that spread from farmed salmon into wild stocks, and pollution (created by uneaten food, faeces, and chemicals used to treat them) contaminating surrounding waters. Organic debris of this type, with steroids and other chemical waste, can contaminate coastal waters. In addition, the accidental escape of fish can affect local wild fish gene pools, when escaped fish interbreed with wild populations, reducing their genetic diversity, and potentially introducing non-natural genetic variation. In some parts of the world, escapees of farmed fish threaten native wild fish, as salmon is an alien species (for example, the salmon farming industry in British Columbia, Canada, has inadvertently introduced a non-native species – Atlantic salmon – into the Pacific Ocean).

However, the positive environmental benefits of not removing fish from wild stocks, but of growing them in farms, are great. Wild populations are allowed to breed and maintain stocks, whilst the farmed variety provides food.

▲ These floating aquaculture pens contain northern bluefin tuna in Baja California, Mexico. Small tuna are caught off-shore and moved to large enclosures.

PLASTIC

Yet more alarming for the health of the oceans and their wildlife is the plague of plastic. The UN Environment Program estimated in 2006 that every square kilometer of sea held nearly 18,000 pieces of floating plastic. Much of it was, and is, in the central Pacific, where scientists believe as much as 100 million tonnes of plastic jetsam are suspended in two separate "gyres" of garbage over an area twice the size of the USA. This has been referred to as the Great Pacific Garbage Patch – about 90% of the plastic in the sea has been carried there by wind or water from land. It takes decades to sink or decompose.

▲ In the main, the plastic in the oceans comes from food and drink packaging. The larger pieces can be mistakenly eaten by animals such as seals, and turtles, which can choke them. Smaller pieces are swallowed by fish which can then work their way up through the food chain to humans. Harm is also caused by the chemicals contained within plastics.

RESPONSES TO THE THREATS

In the case of the oceans, a conservative estimate of the cost of climate change is that by the year 2100 it will amount to nearly US $2 trillion annually, or about 0.4% of global GDP. Economists at the Stockholm Environment Institute arrived at the figure by looking at five measures: how much fisheries and tourism stood to lose, and what the economic impact would be of rising sea levels, more storms, and less carbon being absorbed by the oceans.

If the world continues to warm at its present rate and temperatures rise by 7.2°F [4°C] by 2100, the total will come to US $1.98 trillion. However, if drastic measures are taken to cut emissions and they rise by only 4°F [2.2°C], this figure will be US $612 billion. Governments worldwide were urged by the 1972 Stockholm Convention to control the dumping of waste in their oceans by implementing new laws. The United Nations met in London after this recommendation to begin the Convention on the Prevention of Marine Pollution by Dumping of Wastes and Other Matter, which was implemented in 1975. The International Maritime Organization was given responsibility for this convention and a Protocol was finally adopted in 1996, a major step in the regulation of ocean dumping.

The United Nations Convention on the Law of the Sea, signed in 1982 but only entering into force in 1994, established a framework of law for the oceans, including rules for deep-sea mining and economic exclusion zones extending 200 nautical miles around nation states.

For more information:
78 Climate
80 Climate change
Global warming
83 Natural vegetation

Biodiversity refers to the variety of living material. It includes the variety of species, the variety within the same species, and the variety of ecosystems within which species operate. Estimates of the number of species in the world vary from between 7 million and 80 million. The currently accepted total is about 14 million, yet only 2 million species have been formally identified.

Biodiversity is vital for human survival. It remains the basis for our food and most of our medicine. In less economically developed countries (LEDCs), over 20% of the food consumed is gathered from natural sources. At a global level, over 15% of animal protein consumed is from sea fish. More than 60% of the world's population rely on traditional medicines for their health care. In Mexico, the Popoluca Indians "farm" over 250 species of plant. Many medicines come from natural sources. Aspirin, for example, comes from an acid taken from the bark of willow trees. The anti-cancer drug "taxol" originates from the wild Pacific yew tree. It is estimated that the pharmaceuticals industry gains US $32 billion per year in profits from traditional remedies.

However, the loss of biodiversity is increasing at an accelerating rate. Up to 27,000 species a year may be lost, and the United Nations Environment Programme (UNEP) suggests that the current rate of extinction is 50–100 times greater than "normal", and believes that up to 25% of all the world's species may be lost by 2025. The main reasons for the decline are the introduction of alien species and habitat destruction. Human impact on biodiversity has brought about more extinctions than any other single factor since the extinction of the dinosaurs (65 million years ago).

Since 1600, 39% of animal extinctions have been due to the introduction of alien species, 36% from habitat destruction, and 23% from hunting or deliberate extermination. The introduction of rats, cats and other species has led to the extinction of many flightless birds in Polynesia. Plantation crops, such as rubber, often thrive best when taken away from their natural homes, since in the new lands there may not be the pests to control them. One noted example of extinction was caused by the introduction of the Nile perch into Lake Victoria, East Africa: introduced in the 1960s, it led to the extinction of some 50 species of cichlid fish within 20 years.

In 2019, over 27,000 species out of approximately 71,000 species on the IUCN (International Union for Conservation of Nature and Natural Resources) Red List of Threatened Species, were in danger of extinction. This included one in four mammals, two in five amphibians, one in three coral and one in eight birds.

THREATENED SPECIES
Total number of threatened species for selected countries in each continent

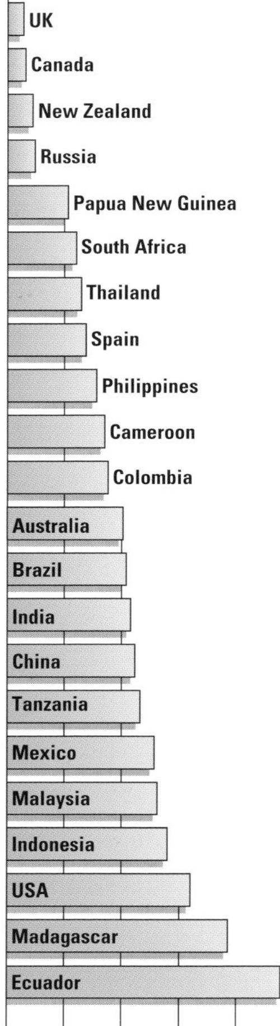

Source: IUCN Red List 2019

THREATENED MAMMAL SPECIES

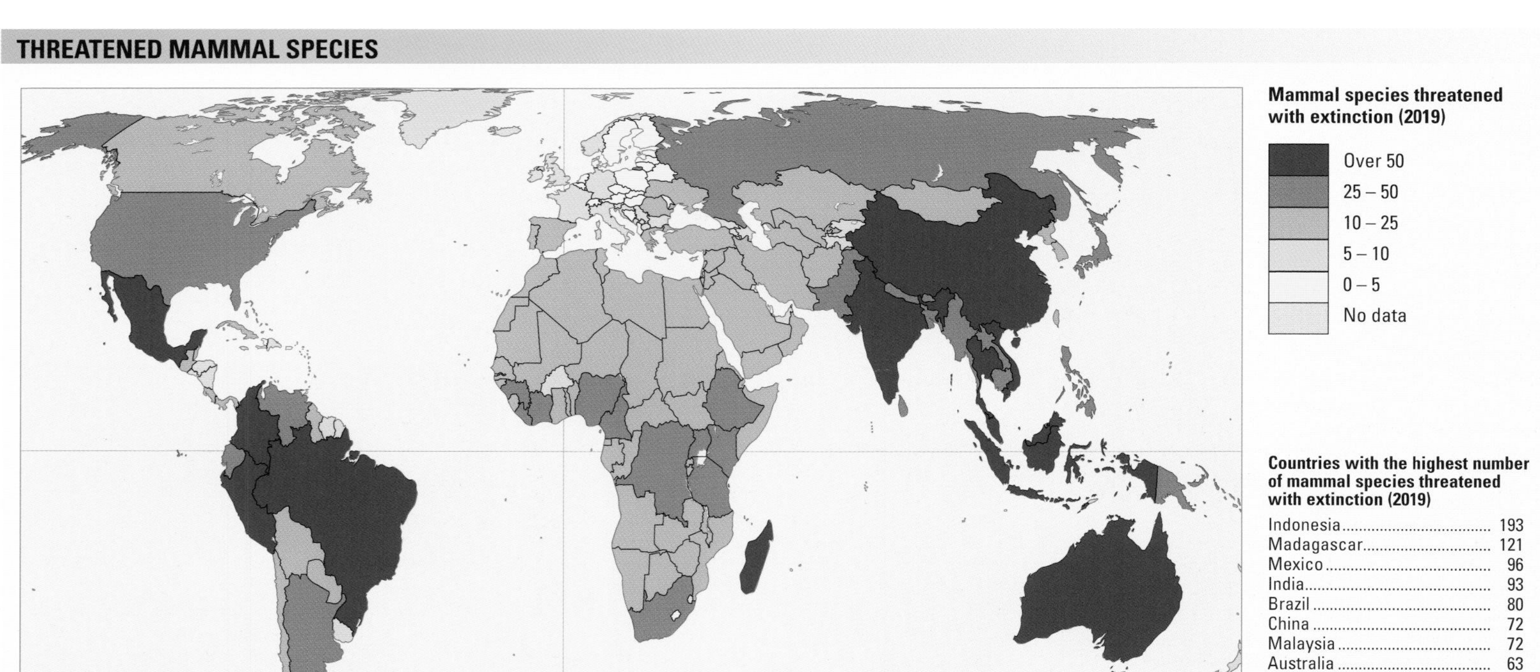

Countries with the highest number of mammal species threatened with extinction (2019)

Indonesia	193
Madagascar	121
Mexico	96
India	93
Brazil	80
China	72
Malaysia	72
Australia	63
Thailand	59
Vietnam	57
Colombia	57
Peru	52

BIODIVERSITY HOTSPOTS

Up to 75% of the world's most threatened mammals, birds and amphibians live in an area covering just 2.3% of the Earth's surface, and roughly half of all flowering plant species and 42% of land-based vertebrates exist in 36 biological hotspots.

Scientists argue that, with limited financial resources, governments and conservationists should prioritize by protecting the small total land areas that account for a very high percentage of global biodiversity. In 1999, scientists identified 25 such areas, mostly in the tropics, which were the centre of global biodiversity.

The number of hotspots has risen to 36. These include the mountains of central Asia, the whole of Japan, the Horn of Africa including the Ethiopian highlands, and the Himalayas region. The hotspots once covered 15.7% of the Earth's surface, an area roughly the size of Russia and Australia combined – now they cover only 2.3% of the Earth's surface, an area slightly larger than India.

Over 70% of all mammals, 86% of all birds, and 92% of all amphibians are crammed into this small area of the world's total land mass. Madagascar and the Indian Ocean Islands hotspot was found to have very high concentrations of plant and vertebrate families that are found nowhere else on the globe.

Global warming could have a devastating effect on biodiversity hotspots such as the Amazonian and Indonesian rainforests. By 2100, between 12% and 39% of the land surface of the Earth will have a new climate. There are numerous species that will be unable to move in order to stay within their preferred climate range. These species will either have to evolve rapidly or die out.

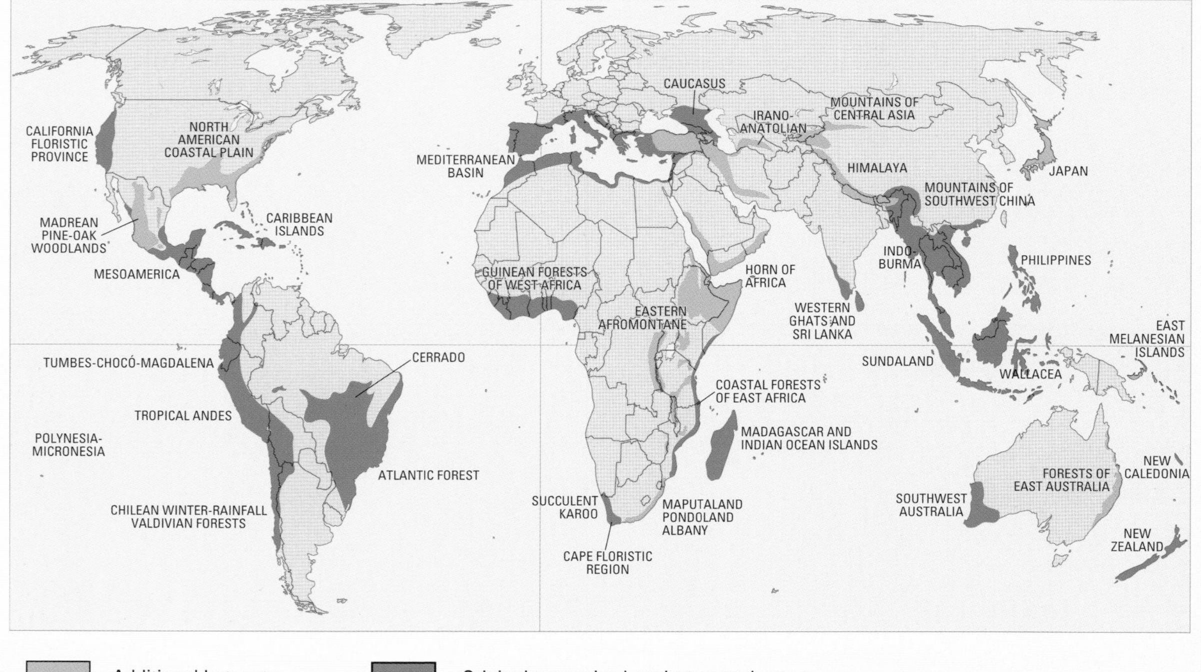

AUSTRALIA'S INTRODUCED SPECIES

Australia's native plants and animals adapted to life on an isolated continent over millions of years. Since European settlement in the 18th century they have had to compete with a range of species introduced by the settlers, which impact on the native species by predation, competition for food and shelter, destroying habitat, and by spreading diseases. Introduced species typically have few predators or fatal diseases, and some have very high reproductive rates.

Management and the prevention of the introduction of new invasive species are key environmental and agricultural policy issues for the Australian federal and state governments.

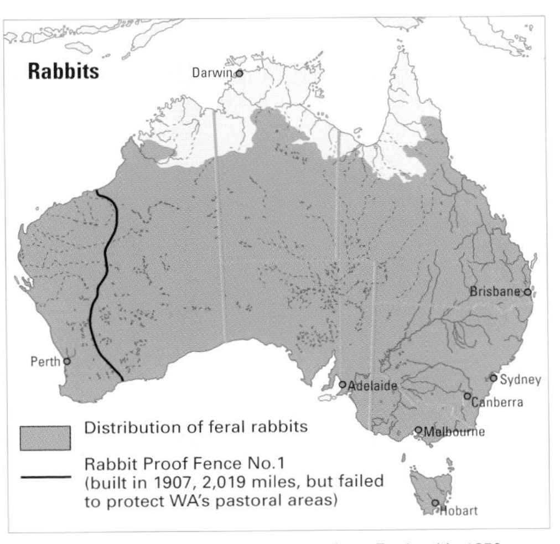

▲ Rabbits were introduced to Australia from England in 1859 for hunting, and quickly spread throughout the country. They are one of the most destructive introduced species in Australia, competing with native wildlife, damaging vegetation, and degrading the land.

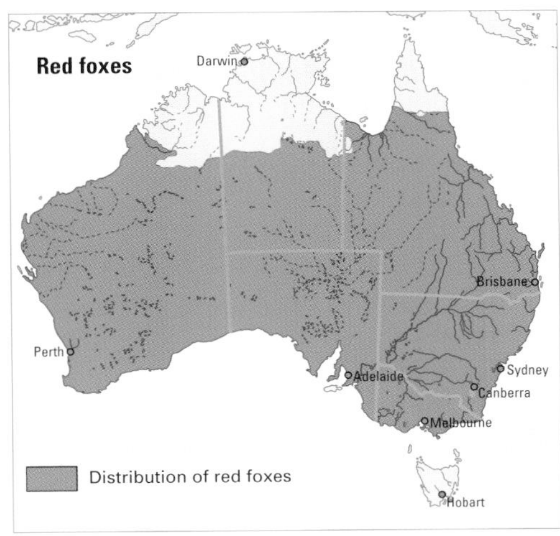

▲ The red fox was introduced from Europe for recreational hunting in 1855 and populations became established in the wild within 15 years. They prey on newborn lambs and have also been responsible for the decline of a number of native species.

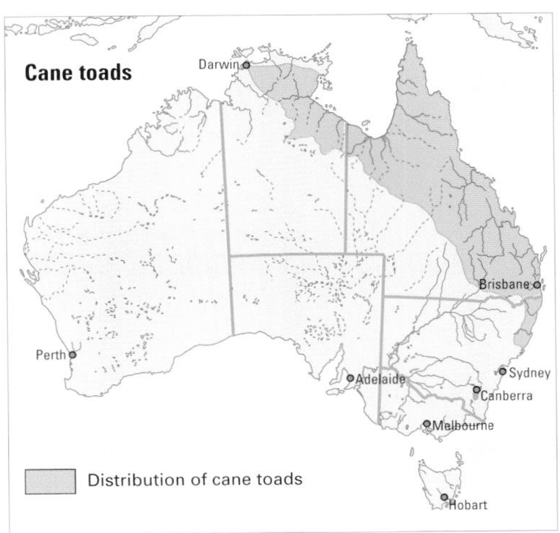

▲ Cane toads were introduced in 1935 to control beetles which were threatening the sugar-cane industry. However, this failed as both the toad and the beetle are still thriving. They adapted well to the Australian environment and with no natural predators they quickly spread. They eat small native wildlife and poison any predators.

THE VALUE OF NATURE

According to the National Ecosystem Assessment (NEA), lakes, forests, parks, and wildlife are a huge financial asset. Moreover, it is claimed that the natural world is vital for human existence, not only in providing food, water, and air, but also for the cultural and spiritual benefits that it provides.

Economic benefits include food production, which utilizes insects for pollination, earthworms for mixing the soil, and soil microbes for recycling nutrients. In the UK, for example, the value of pollinating insects has been calculated to be $727 million, and the value of wetlands, which help to provide clean water, at $2.5 billion. Globally, bees are believed to provide $368 billion worth of services, or about 9.5% of the total economic value of agriculture. One third of the food the world produces is dependent on bees for pollination.

Although the natural world provides many benefits including food supply, water supply, climate regulation, and breakdown of waste products, these are under-valued. Some of the benefits are non-quantifiable but include recreation and long-term health. Moreover, the way in which ecosystems have been used has changed over the last sixty years or so. Population increase and rising standards of living have contributed to a huge growth in agricultural production. It has also, however, contributed to the decline in ecosystem services, such as air, water, and soil quality.

Although some ecosystems are delivering services well, there are others which are showing long-term decline. Those that are in decline include marine fisheries, wild species diversity, and soil quality.

Ecosystems, and ecosystems services, constantly change as a result of demographic, economic, social, and cultural factors. For example, since the 1940s there has been intensification of agriculture at the expense of many habitats, including wetlands, forests, and grasslands.

Types of ecosystem service

Provisioning services

These are the services obtained from ecosystems such as food, fibre, fuel, and water from aquifers, rivers, and lakes. Goods can come from heavily managed ecosystems (intensive farms and fish farms) or from semi-natural ones (such as by hunting and fishing). Most of these food producing ecosystems are land-based but some are water-based (aquaculture). Ecosystems also provide a variety of materials for construction and fuel including wood, charcoal, biofuels, and plant oils. They are also an important source of raw materials for the pharmaceuticals industry.

Supporting services

These are the essentials for life and include primary productivity, soil formation, and the cycling of nutrients. Ecosystems provide the conditions for growing food. Habitats provide all that an individual plant or animal needs to survive: food; water; nutrients; and shelter. Every habitat provides a variety of niches that can be essential for a species' lifecycle. For example, migratory birds depend on different habitats at different times of the year.

Ecosystems also help maintain genetic diversity (biodiversity) which is the variety of genetic materials between ecosystems, niches, and populations.

Regulating services

These are a diverse set of services and include pollination, regulation of pests and diseases, and production of goods. Other services include climate and climatic hazard regulation, and water quality regulation. For example, trees provide shade and influence water availability and, by removing air pollutants from the atmosphere, they improve air quality. Ecosystems influence global climate by storing and sequestering greenhouse gases such as carbon dioxide. As vegetation grows, it removes carbon dioxide and locks it in its tissue.

Ecosystems moderate extreme events: they act as buffers against natural disasters. Mangrove forests can help protect a shoreline against hurricane damage, and wetlands can absorb flood waters. Vegetation can help reduce soil erosion.

Insects and the wind help pollinate plants. Around 90 out of 115 leading food crops, such as cocoa and coffee, depend upon animal pollination.

Ecosystems are also important for the control of pests and vector borne diseases. Birds, bats, wasps, frogs, and fungi are all examples of natural controls.

Cultural services

These occur when people interact with the environment and this provides cultural goods and benefits. Open spaces provide the opportunity for outdoor recreation, learning, and spiritual well-being. Recreation can lead to major improvements in physical and mental health. Also, tourism provides a major source of income to many countries.

▲ The wide variety of provisions on display in this Malaysian market are testament to the value of ecosystems for the supply of food.

▲ The destruction of large areas of vegetation can lessen the value of ecosystems. The deforested and drowned rain forest at Batang Ai, Sarawak, Malaysia, above, is the result of land being cleared for a hydroelectric power station.

	Mountains, moorlands, and heaths	Woodlands
Provisioning	Food*	Timber*
	Fibre*	Species diversity*
	Fuel*	Fuelwood*
	Freshwater*	Freshwater*
Regulating	Climate regulation†	Climate regulation†
	Flood regulation†	Flood regulation†
	Wildfire regulation†	Erosion control†
	Water quality regulation†	Disease and pest control†
	Erosion control†	Wildfire regulation†
		Air and water quality regulation†
		Soil quality regulation†
		Noise regulation†
Cultural	Recreation and tourism*	Recreation and tourism*
	Aesthetic values*	Aesthetic values*
	Cultural heritage*	Cultural heritage*
	Spiritual values*	Employment*
	Education*	Education*
	Sense of place*	Sense of place*
	Health benefits*	Health benefits*

The goods and services derived from mountains, moorlands, and heaths, and those from woodlands are shown in the table.

Key
Items marked * denote goods
Items marked † denote services

For more information:

90 Urbanization of the Earth
Urban population
91 Largest cities

LARGEST NATIONS

The world's most populous nations, in millions (2018)

1. China	1,385
2. India	1,282
3. USA	329
4. Indonesia	263
5. Brazil	209
6. Pakistan	208
7. Nigeria	204
8. Bangladesh	160
9. Russia	142
10. Japan	126
11. Mexico	126
12. Ethiopia	108
13. Philippines	106
14. Egypt	99
15. Vietnam	97
16. Congo (Dem. Rep.)	85
17. Iran	83
18. Turkey	81
19. Germany	81
20. Thailand	69
21. France	67
22. UK	65
23. Italy	62
24. Myanmar (Burma)	56
25. Tanzania	56

MOST CROWDED NATIONS

Population per square mile (2018)

1. Monaco	39,394
2. Singapore	23,062
3. Bahrain	5,343
4. Vatican City	5,000
5. Malta	3,742
6. Maldives	3,271
7. Bangladesh	2,868
8. Mauritius	1,727
9. Barbados	1,704
10. San Marino	1,689

LEAST CROWDED

Population per square mile (2018)

1. Mongolia	5.1
2. Australia	7.9
3. Namibia	8.0
4. Iceland	8.6
5. Guyana	8.9
6. Canada	9.3
7. Suriname	9.5
8. Mauritania	9.7
9. Libya	9.9
10. Botswana	10.0

In 8000 BC, following the development of agriculture, the world had an estimated population of 8 million and by AD 1000 it was about 300 million. The onset of the Industrial Revolution in the late 18th century led to a population explosion. The 1,000 million mark was passed by 1850, it doubled by the 1920s, and doubled again to 4,000 million by 1975.

In the 1990s, demographers estimated that the world's population, which passed the 7 billion mark in 2012, would reach 9.3 billion by 2050 and only level out in 2200, at a peak of around 11 billion. However, in the early 21st century, after the rate of population growth had shown signs of decline, the Institute for Applied Systems Analysis suggested that the world's population might peak at about 9 billion in 2070. Whatever the global projections, everyone agreed that the greatest population growth would be in the developing countries.

The developing world includes what the World Bank (2019) describes as low-income economies (per capita GNI of US $995 or less), lower-middle-income economies (per capita GNI of US $996 to US $3,895), and upper-middle-income economies (per capita GNI of US $3,956 to US $12,055). Most developing countries are in Africa, Asia, and Latin America. The developed world, made up of high-income, industrialized economies (per capita GNI of US $12,056 or more), contains Australasia, most of Europe and North America, and Japan.

In developing countries, a high proportion of the population is young and so these countries face high expenditure on health and education. In developed countries, the population pyramids are becoming top-heavy, with increasingly aging populations.

POPULATION DENSITY

The places marked on the map reflect the size of the urban agglomerations and conurbations, rather than the actual city limits. San Francisco itself, for example, has an official population of less than a million people. All cities with more than 5 million inhabitants are named on the map.

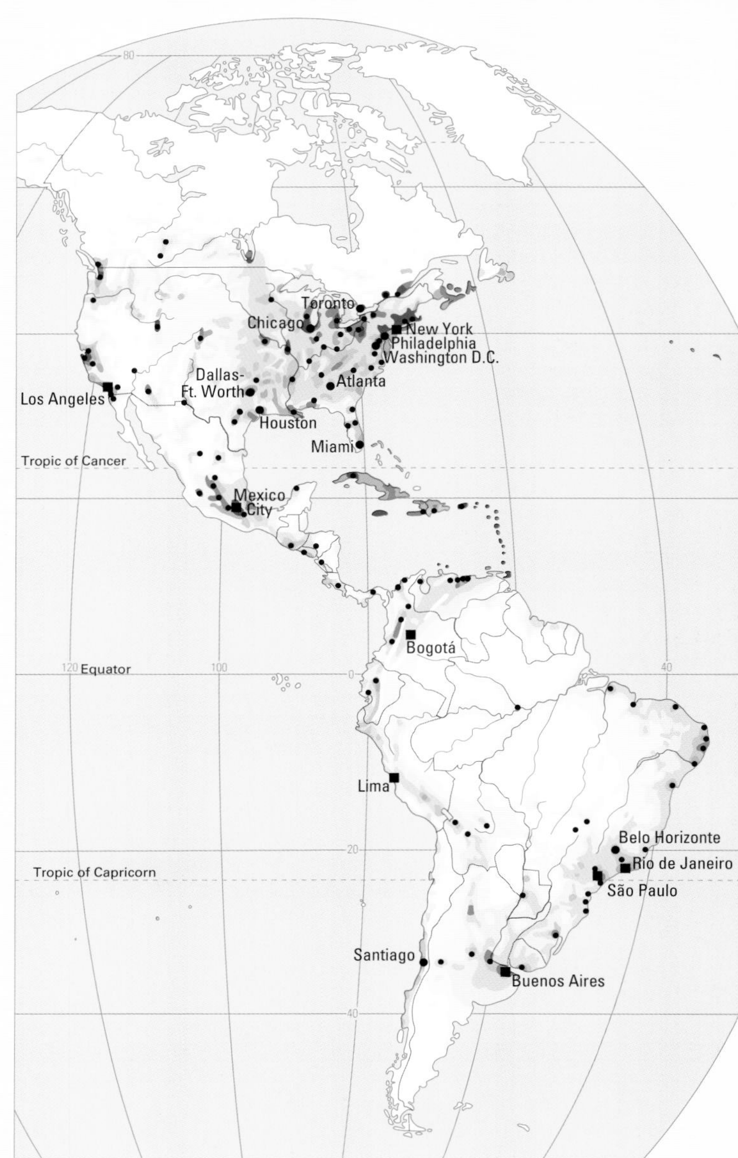

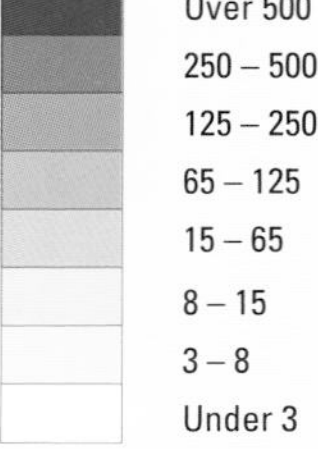

POPULATION CHANGE

The projected population change for the years 2004–2050

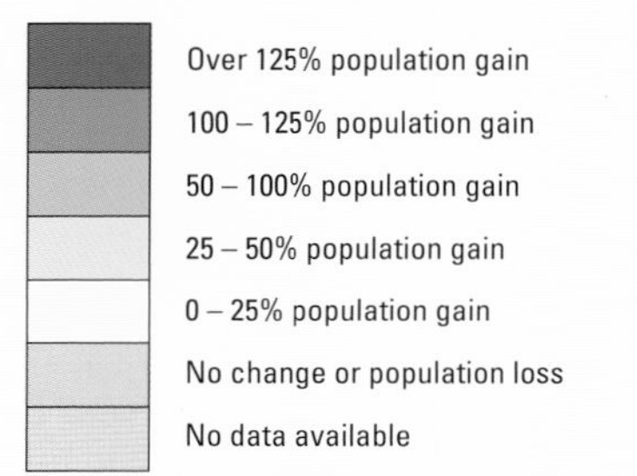

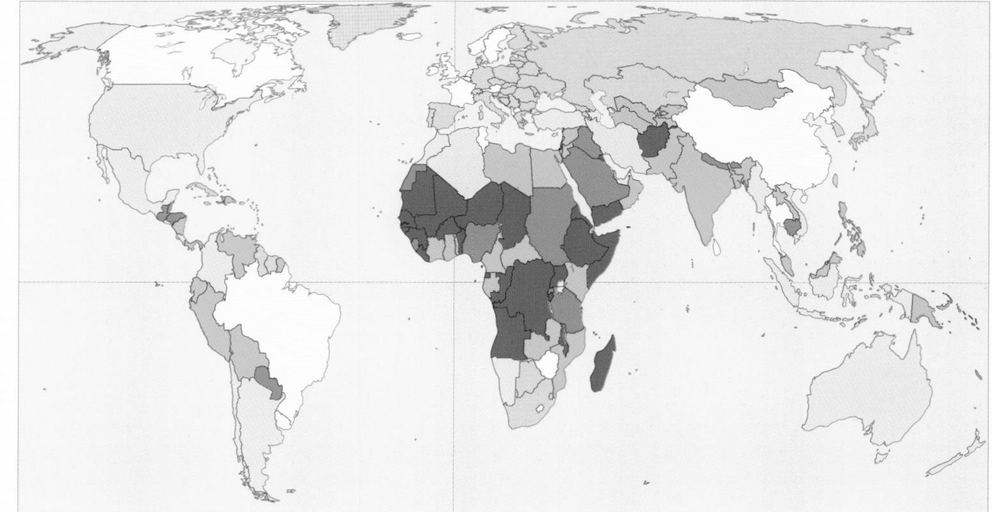

Based on estimates for the year 2050, below are listed the ten most populous nations in the world, in millions:

1. India	1,628	6. Pakistan	295
2. China	1,437	7. Bangladesh	280
3. USA	420	8. Brazil	221
4. Indonesia	308	9. Congo (Dem. Rep.)	181
5. Nigeria	307	10. Ethiopia	173

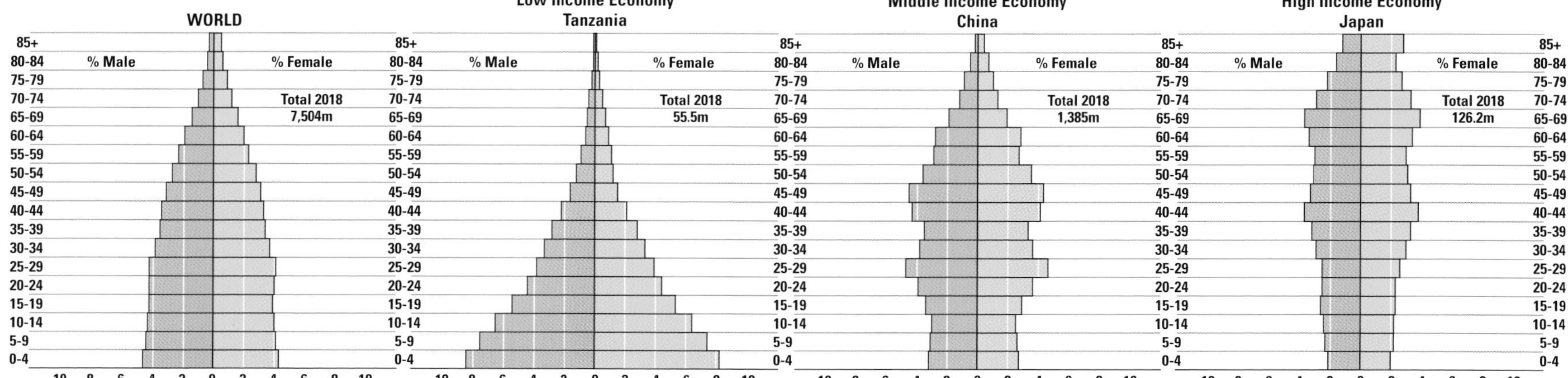

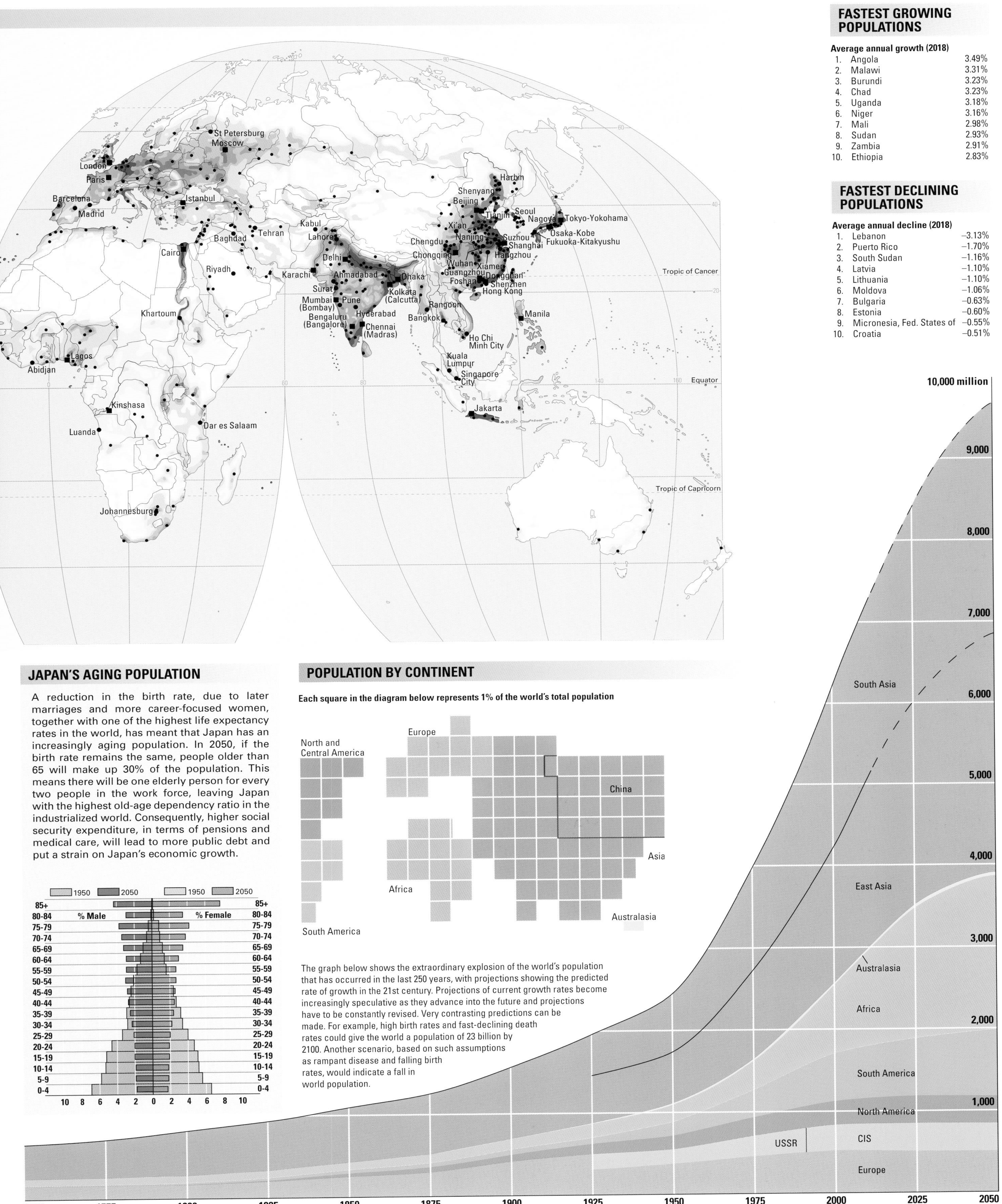

FASTEST GROWING POPULATIONS

Average annual growth (2018)

1.	Angola	3.49%
2.	Malawi	3.31%
3.	Burundi	3.23%
4.	Chad	3.23%
5.	Uganda	3.18%
6.	Niger	3.16%
7.	Mali	2.98%
8.	Sudan	2.93%
9.	Zambia	2.91%
10.	Ethiopia	2.83%

FASTEST DECLINING POPULATIONS

Average annual decline (2018)

1.	Lebanon	–3.13%
2.	Puerto Rico	–1.70%
3.	South Sudan	–1.16%
4.	Latvia	–1.10%
5.	Lithuania	–1.10%
6.	Moldova	–1.06%
7.	Bulgaria	–0.63%
8.	Estonia	–0.60%
9.	Micronesia, Fed. States of	–0.55%
10.	Croatia	–0.51%

JAPAN'S AGING POPULATION

A reduction in the birth rate, due to later marriages and more career-focused women, together with one of the highest life expectancy rates in the world, has meant that Japan has an increasingly aging population. In 2050, if the birth rate remains the same, people older than 65 will make up 30% of the population. This means there will be one elderly person for every two people in the work force, leaving Japan with the highest old-age dependency ratio in the industrialized world. Consequently, higher social security expenditure, in terms of pensions and medical care, will lead to more public debt and put a strain on Japan's economic growth.

POPULATION BY CONTINENT

Each square in the diagram below represents 1% of the world's total population

The graph below shows the extraordinary explosion of the world's population that has occurred in the last 250 years, with projections showing the predicted rate of growth in the 21st century. Projections of current growth rates become increasingly speculative as they advance into the future and projections have to be constantly revised. Very contrasting predictions can be made. For example, high birth rates and fast-declining death rates could give the world a population of 23 billion by 2100. Another scenario, based on such assumptions as rampant disease and falling birth rates, would indicate a fall in world population.

For more information:

80 Greenhouse gases
82 Water distribution
88 Population density
102 World trade

In 2008, for the first time in history, more than half of the world's population lived in urban areas. By 2050, it is thought that 5.3 billion people in the developing world will be living in an urban environment, with Asia having over 60% of the world's urban population and Africa almost 25%.

Urbanization is greatest in industrialized countries. For example, in 2010, 82% of the people in the US lived in urban areas; but in low-income countries, which had nearly 40% of the world's population in the early 21st century, only 31% lived in urban areas.

A typical city in a developing country contains millions of people living, often illegally, in shanty towns (or "informal settlements"), while thousands live on the streets. Yet many of these shanty towns are healthier than the industrial cities of 19th-century Europe and North America. Indeed, surveys have shown that migrants to cities in developing countries are less likely to face poverty than they are in rural areas, while benefiting from greater access to healthcare services and education.

Modern cities face many problems today, including pollution, unemployment, and crime. Yet, with competent government, they are capable of generating the wealth they need to solve them, as well as making a major contribution to the nation's economy.

Megacities are cities with a population of over 10 million people. Megacities grow as a result of economic growth, rural to urban migration, and high rates of natural increase. As the cities grow, they swallow up rural areas and nearby towns. Some of these cities have populations that are bigger than those of entire countries – Mumbai, for example, has more people than Sweden and Norway combined.

Nevertheless, megacities contain between 4% and 7% of the world's total population, and grow at relatively slow rates, perhaps 1.5% per year. The first megacity was Tokyo, which now has a population of about 37 million (larger than Canada's population). By 2019, other megacities will include Mumbai, Delhi, Mexico City, São Paulo, New York, Dhaka, Karachi, and Lagos. Lagos has been growing at a very fast rate of 5% per annum and is expected to increase at this rate until after 2020. Usually, very large cities grow more slowly than medium-sized cities.

By 2020, all but four of the world's megacities will be in developing regions, 12 of them in Asia alone. The impact of megacities on their region is huge. For example, rapid economic growth and urbanization in China has had a negative impact on the urban environment. China contains 16 of the 20 most polluted cities in the world and is the largest producer of greenhouse gases.

Megacities are important for the generation of wealth – in more economically developed countries (MEDCs) urban areas generate over 80% of national economic output, while in less economically developed countries (LEDCs) it is over 40%. However, there are some aspects of megacities, such as crime and environmental issues, where they are less than attractive.

URBAN POPULATION

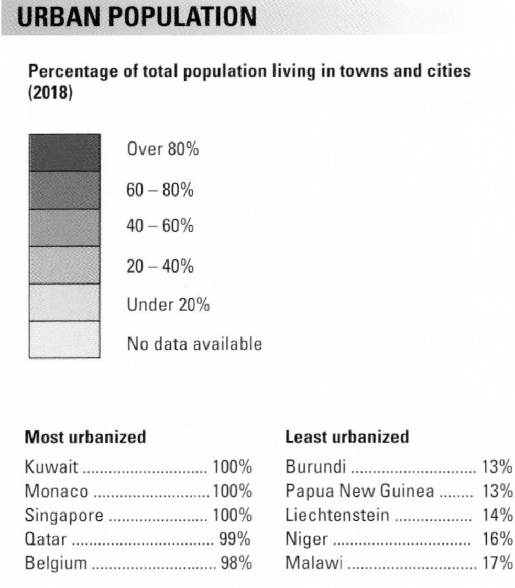

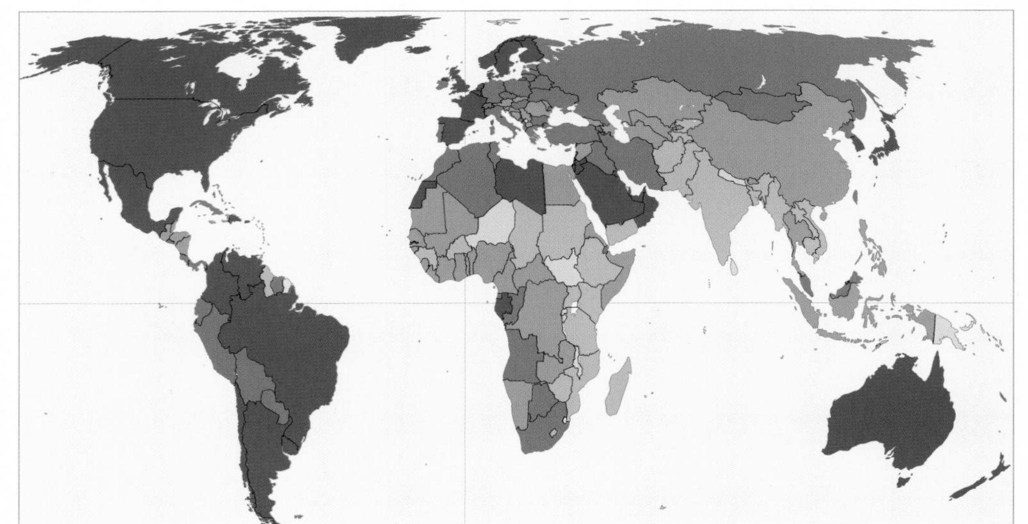

Most urbanized		Least urbanized	
Kuwait	100%	Burundi	13%
Monaco	100%	Papua New Guinea	13%
Singapore	100%	Liechtenstein	14%
Qatar	99%	Niger	16%
Belgium	98%	Malawi	17%

THE URBANIZATION OF THE EARTH

City-building, 1900–2005; each white spot represents a city of at least 1 million inhabitants

1900

1950

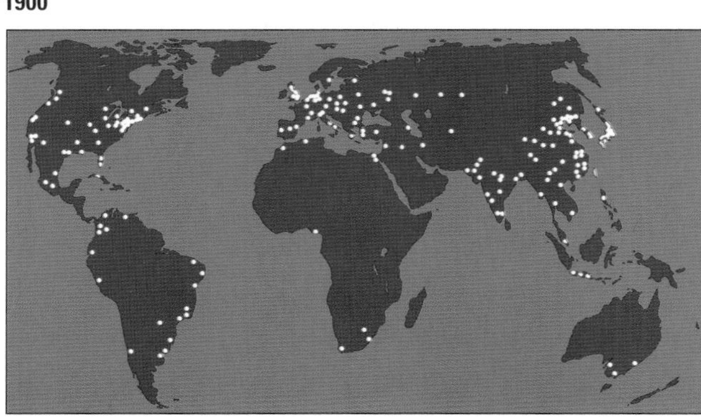

1975

2005

URBANIZATION

The urban population of 3.7 billion people in 2012 was larger than the entire global population in 1947, 65 years earlier. Cities and urban areas are gaining an estimated 60 million people per year – over 1 million every week.

Urbanization rates vary across the world; the US and UK have far lower rates of urbanization compared to less developed countries. This is because a high proportion of their populations already live in cities. The largest percentage increases in the urban population in the next decade will be in Africa and Asia. For example, Lagos in Nigeria increased from 675,000 inhabitants in 1960 to 13,463,000 in 2018.

Rapid urban growth reflects three factors:

1. Migration to cities from rural areas.
2. Natural population increases (births minus deaths).
3. Reclassification of previously rural areas as urban as they become built up and engulfed by urban sprawl.

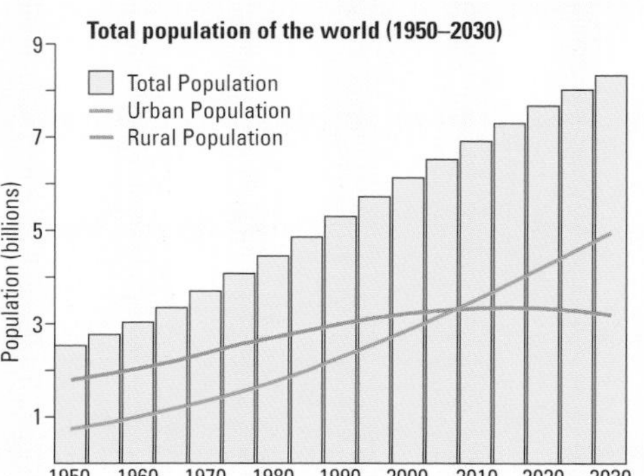

SLUM CITIES

The total number of slum dwellers in the world reached 1 billion in 2007, with one in every three city residents living in inadequate housing, with no or few basic services.

Urbanization in most developing countries has been proceeding so rapidly that local governments have been unable to provide the necessary services and housing to meet demand.

In some cities, many people make their homes in squatter settlements, or slums, which are frequently without basic services such as power, water, and sanitation. They are often on hazardous, dangerous or polluted land, and the building structures are inadequate and sometimes unsafe. Slum dwellers have limited access to credit and formal job markets due to stigmatization, discrimination, and geographical isolation.

Slums have a high concentration of poverty and social and economic deprivation, which may include broken families, unemployment, and economic, physical, and social exclusion. Yet these communities are often a dynamic part of the city's economy, keeping the wheels of the city turning in many different ways. Their inhabitants often take the initiative in setting up their own local government and self-help associations.

Some of the world's richest cities also have a homeless underclass, although calculating the numbers of people involved is problematic. Yet it is the case that homelessness and unemployment are currently affecting an increasing number of people in the developed world.

The locus of poverty is moving from the countryside to cities, in a process now recognized as the "urbanization of poverty."

Efforts to improve the living conditions of slum dwellers peaked during the 1980s. However, renewed concern about poverty has recently led governments to adopt specific targets on slums in the United Nations Millennium Declaration, which aims to improve the lives of at least 100 million slum dwellers by the year 2020.

SLUM FACTBOX

- A slum is defined by the UN as "a dilapidated area of a city characterized by substandard housing, squalor, and lacking in tenure security."
- 78% of the urban population in developing countries live in slums.
- More than 41% of Kolkata's slum households have lived there for more than 30 years.
- In most African cities between 40% and 70% of the city's population live in slums or squatter settlements.
- Slum populations in some parts of the world often include university lecturers, students, civil servants, and formal private-sector employees.
- The majority of slum households in Bangkok have a color television.
- Singapore is one of the few countries that successfully practises comprehensive public-sector housing development.
- Slums are the fastest growing human habitat in the world.

SUSTAINABLE CITIES

Large sprawling cities are often considered unsustainable because they consume huge amounts of resources and produce vast amounts of waste. The concept of "Sustainable Urban Development" is designed to meet the needs of the present generation without compromising the needs of future generations.

In the "compact" sustainable city, inputs are smaller and there is more recycling. Compact cities minimize the amount of distance traveled, use less space, require less infrastructure (pipes, cables, roads, etc), reduce urban sprawl, and the provision of public transport is easier. But if the compact city covers too large an area, it becomes congested, overcrowded, overpriced, and polluted. As a result, it then becomes unsustainable.

In order to achieve sustainability, a number of options are available:

- reducing the use of fossil fuels, e.g. by promoting public transport;
- keeping waste production to within levels that can be treated locally;
- providing sufficient green spaces;
- reusing and reclaiming land, e.g. brownfield sites;
- active involvement of the local community;
- conservation of non-renewable resources;
- using renewable resources.

CITY GROWTH

The growth of some of the world's largest cities in millions, 1950–2015

Comparisons of city populations over time are problematic due to changes in the definition of the city limits. These figures attempt to take such changes into consideration.

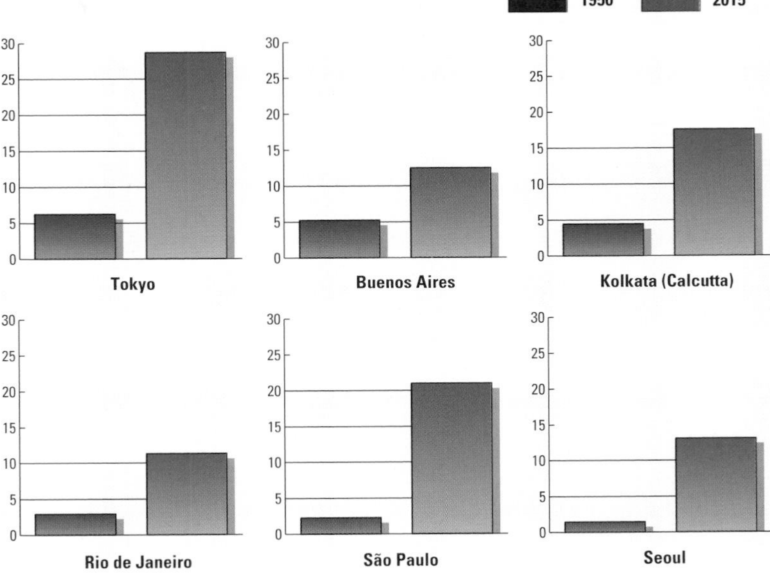

LARGEST CITIES

◀ Mt. Fuji stands sentinel over the futuristic skyline of the Shinjuku area of Tokyo, the world's most populous city. Originally a fishing village called Edo, the greater metropolitan area of Tokyo-Yokohama is now home to over 38 million people and is the capital of Japan.

In 2008, for the first time in history, the majority of the world's population lived in cities. Below is a list of the urban areas in the world with over 10 million inhabitants in 2018.

1. Tokyo–Yokohama	37.5
2. Delhi	28.5
3. Shanghai	25.6
4. São Paulo	21.7
5. Mexico City	21.6
6. Cairo	20.1
7. Mumbai	20.0
8. Beijing	19.6
9. Dhaka	19.6
10. Osaka-Kobe	19.3
11. New York	18.8
12. Karachi	15.4
13. Buenos Aires	15.0
14. Chongqing	14.8
15. Istanbul	14.8
16. Kolkata	14.7
17. Manila	13.5
18. Lagos	13.5
19. Rio de Janeiro	13.3
20. Tianjin	13.2
21. Kinshasa	13.2
22. Guangzhou	12.6
23. Los Angeles	12.5
24. Moscow	12.4
25. Shenzhen	11.9
26. Lahore	11.7
27. Bengaluru	11.4
28. Paris	10.9
29. Bogotá	10.6
30. Jakarta	10.5
31. Chennai	10.5
32. Lima	10.4
33. Bangkok	10.2

The population figures above are based on urban agglomerations rather than legal city limits. In some cases, where two adjacent cities have merged into one concentration, such as Tokyo–Yokohama, they have been regarded as a single unit.

URBAN ADVANTAGES

RELATIVE MORTALITY

Infant deaths (under 1 year old) per 1,000 live births in rural and urban areas of selected countries

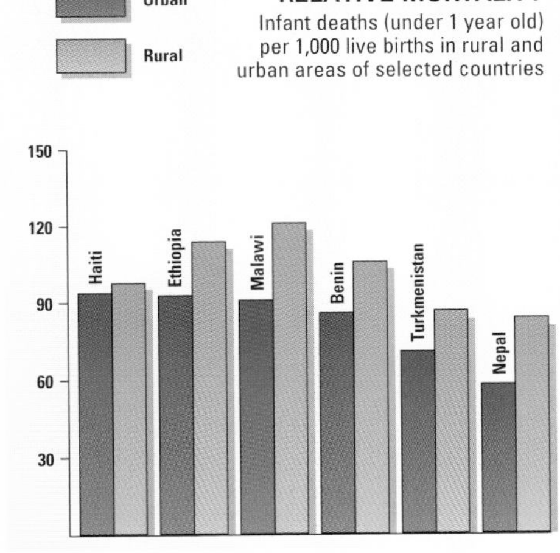

RELATIVE LITERACY

Adult literacy rates (%) in rural and urban areas of selected countries

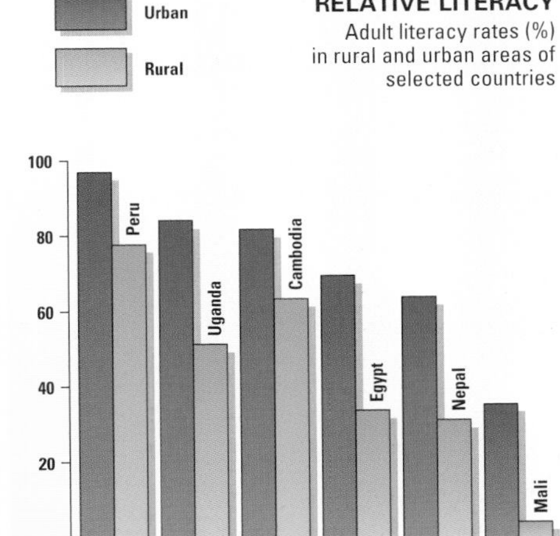

Despite overcrowding and poor housing, living standards in the developing world's cities are almost invariably better than in the surrounding countryside. Resources – financial, material, and administrative – are concentrated in the towns, which are usually also the centers of political activity and pressure. Governments – frequently unstable, and rarely established on a solid democratic base – are usually more responsive to urban discontent than to rural misery.

In many developing countries, especially in Africa, food prices are kept artificially low, thus appeasing the underemployed urban masses at the expense of agricultural development.

This imbalance encourages further cityward migration, helping to account for the astonishing rate of post-1950 urbanization and putting great strain on the ability of many nations to provide even modest improvements for their people.

For more information:
88 Population density
94 Conflict
95 United Nations
95 International organizations

Migration is the permanent or semi-permanent change in residence. Migration can be voluntary or forced, international or internal, long- or short-distance. Most voluntary migrants are moving for work (especially for young people), to retire, or for educational or health reasons. In contrast, forced migrations may be due to civil conflict, environmental damage, or persecution.

According to the United Nations, the number of international migrants, as a percentage of the total world population, is continuing to grow. They represented 2.8% of the total population in 2000 growing to 3.4% in 2017, a total of 258 million people. Six out of every 10 international migrants live in Asia (80 million) or Europe (78 million). The fastest growth in migrant numbers has been in Africa, with many migrants heading north hoping to reach Europe. There has been substantial growth in the number of people displaced by force, up to 68.5 million at the end of 2017. It has been estimated that, on average, some 44,000 people are forced to flee their homes every day. In terms of numbers, the United States remains, by far, the top destination country for international migrants. The Mexico–United States migration corridor is the largest in the world. Mexico has been establishing a new role for itself as a country of transmigration and also of settlement. In recent years there has been a huge influx of people from Central America trying to access the United States via Mexico.

Migrants sending money home to their families, remittances, constitute a vital flow of financial aid to some economies. According to the World Bank, worldwide remittances are expected to grow to US $715 billion in 2019, with three-quarters of this total destined for developing nations. The true size, including unrecorded flows through formal and informal channels, is believed to be significantly larger. Recorded remittances are more than twice as large as official aid and nearly two-thirds of foreign direct investment.

The definition of a refugee is someone who has been forced to flee their own country, as to remain there would be unsafe. Refugees are a sub-group of international migrants, numbering about 10% of the total in 2017, around 26 million people. The vast majority of refugees (who may also apply for the status of asylum seeker in the host country) stay in developing countries rather than richer countries. Lebanon, with 1 in 6 of its population being a refugee, has the world's highest ratio of refugees in relation to its national population. The ten leading countries of asylum took in 62% of the worldwide refugee population in 2017. The largest numbers are in Turkey (3.1 million) and Jordan (2.9 million).

DESTINATIONS AND ORIGINS OF MIGRANTS

Top destination countries for international migrants, in millions (2017)

1.	USA	49.8
2.	Saudi Arabia	12.2
3.	Germany	12.2
4.	Russia	11.7
5.	UK	8.8
6.	UAE	8.3
7.	France	7.9
8.	Canada	7.9
9.	Australia	7.0
10.	Spain	5.9

Top countries of origin of international migrants, in millions (2017)

1.	India	16.6
2.	Mexico	13.0
3.	Russia	10.6
4.	China	10.0
5.	Bangladesh	7.5
6.	Syria	6.9
7.	Pakistan	6.0
8.	Ukraine	5.9
9.	Philippines	5.7
10.	UK	4.9

MIGRANTS

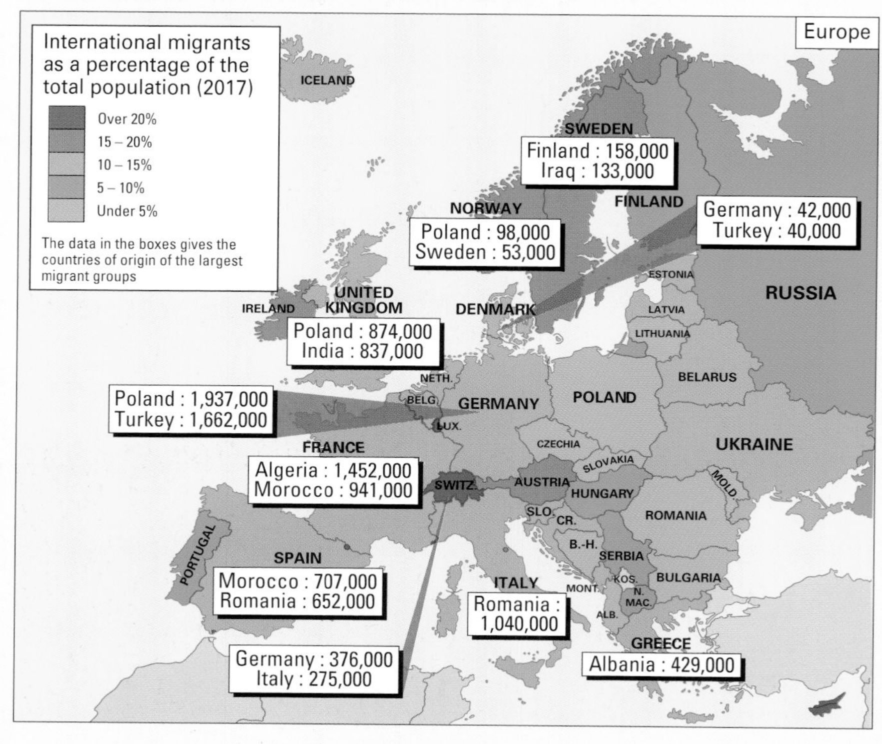

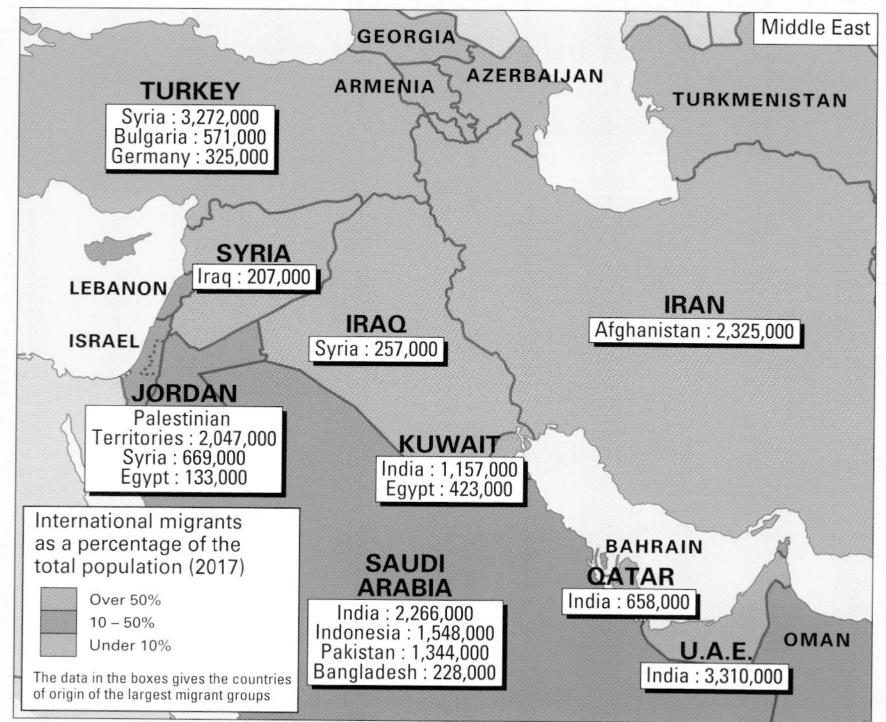

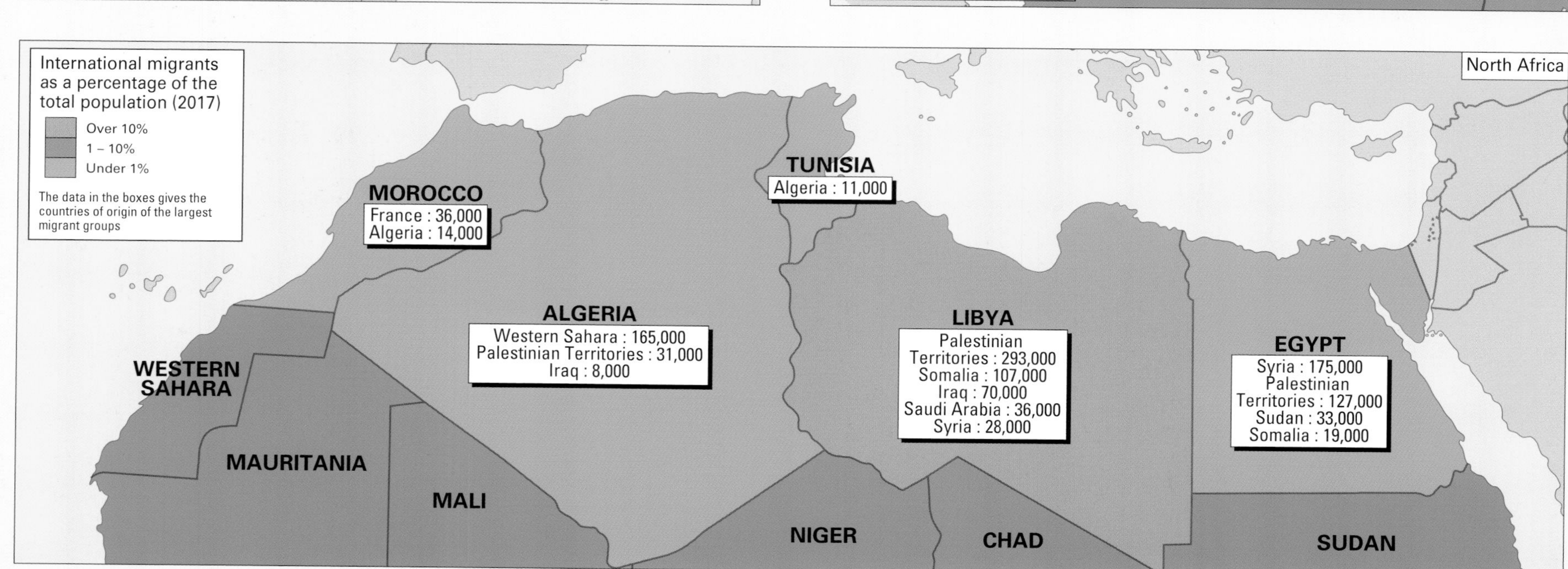

REMITTANCES

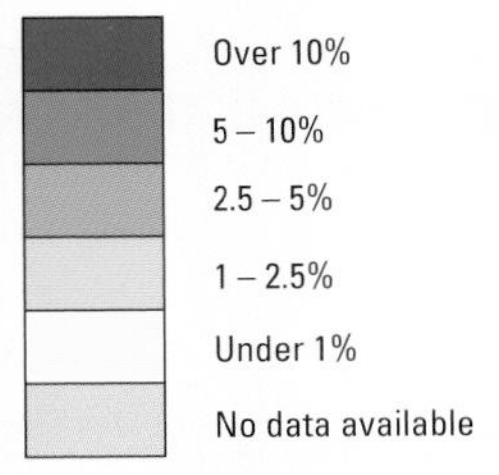

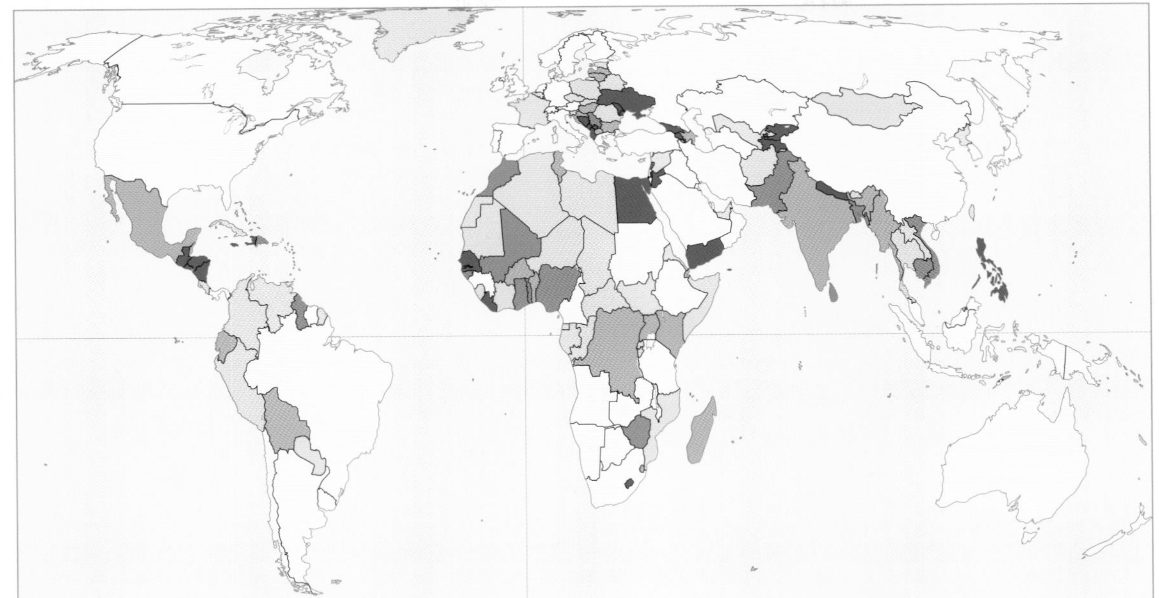

Money sent home by migrants as a percentage share of total GDP (2017)

1. Tonga 37.1%
2. Kyrgyzstan 32.9%
3. Haiti 32.4%
4. Tajikistan 31.3%
5. Nepal 27.8%
6. El Salvador 20.4%
7. Moldova 20.2%
8. Honduras 18.8%
9. Jamaica 16.6%
10. Samoa 16.4%

REFUGEES

◀ Since August 2017, over 700,000 Rohingya people, from the northern Rakhine province in Myanmar, have fled to refugee camps in neighbouring Bangladesh. Fleeing persecution and the destruction of their homes in Myanmar, they are now living in difficult conditions in camps such as this one at Cox's Bazar. The United Nations have called the Rohingya's situation the "world's fastest growing refugee crisis".

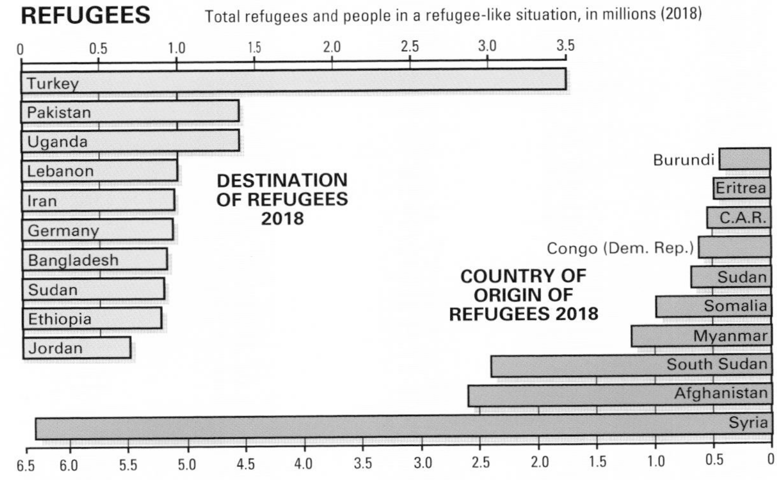

Refugee population by region (2017)

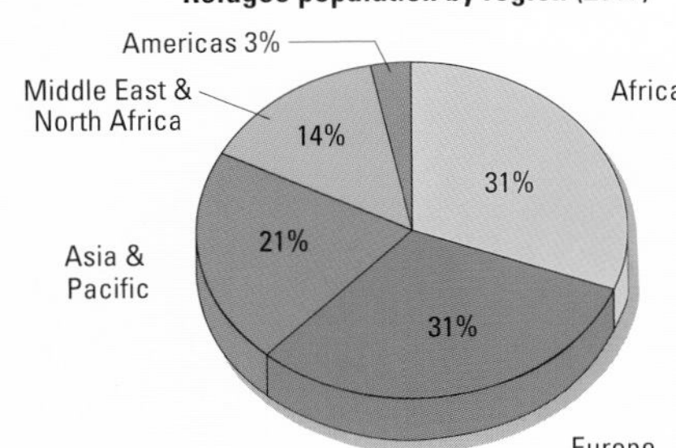

Internally Displaced Persons, in millions (2017)

At the end of 2017, an estimated 40 million people were displaced within their own countries due to armed conflict, generalized violence, or human rights violations. The top ten countries with internally displaced people are (in millions):

1. Colombia 7.7
2. Syria 6.2
3. Congo, Dem. Rep 4.4
4. Iraq 2.6
5. Somalia 2.1
6. Yemen 2.0
7. Sudan 2.0
8. South Sudan 1.9
9. Afghanistan 1.8
10. Ukraine 1.8

▲ It is estimated that some 40 million people worldwide have been internally displaced. Although not legally classified as refugees, they can find themselves living in similar situations whilst remaining within their own country's borders. Make shift shelters, such as this in eastern Ghouta in Syria, have become home to families fleeing fighting between rebel groups and the Syrian regime.

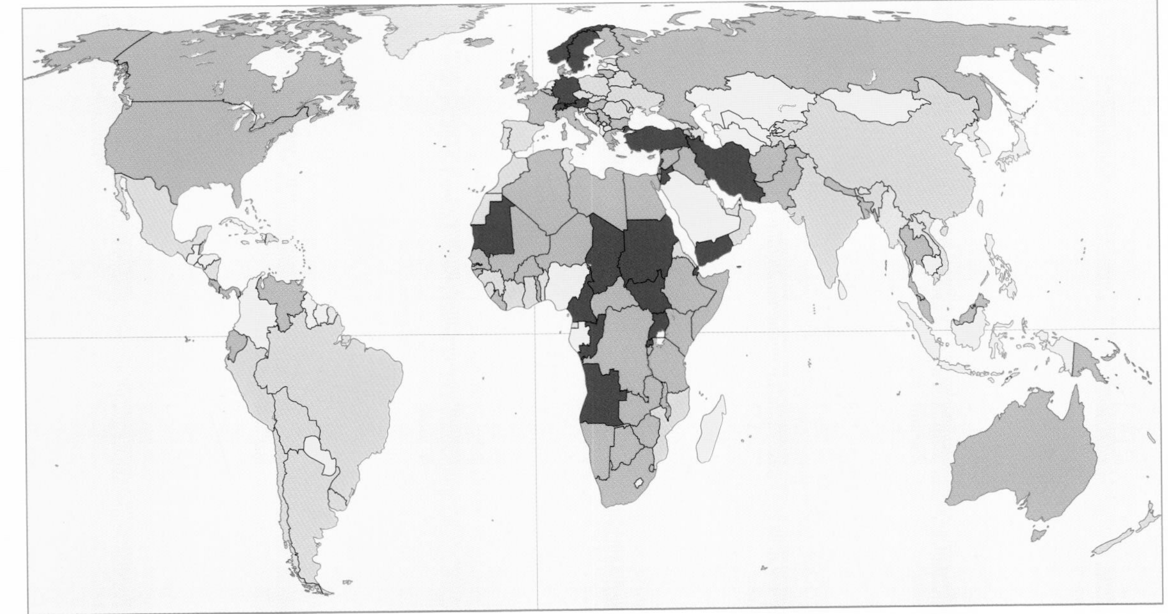

Total refugees* as a percentage of the population (2018)

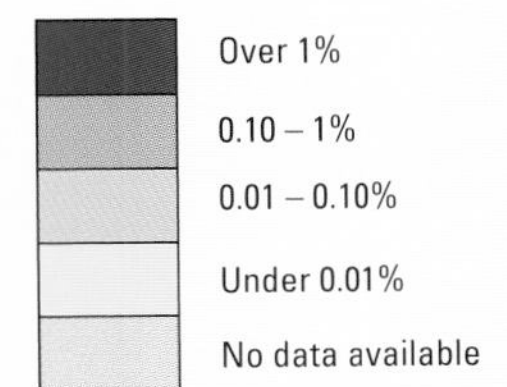

*includes people in a refugee-like situation

For more information:
92 Migration

In the late 1980s, many people hoped that the end of the Cold War, following the collapse of Communist regimes in the former Soviet Union and Eastern Europe, would herald a new era of international stability. Instead, ethnic and religious antagonisms surfaced in many areas. Nationalist rivalries, suppressed under Communist rule, replaced ideological factors as the major cause of conflict. Since, 2010, there has been accelerated political change, especially across North Africa and the Middle East.

Some countries are more likely to fail than others. Demographic stress is a major factor. Where there are large numbers of unemployed youths concentrated in large cities and a lack of growth, the chances of conflict escalate.

The causes of state failure and civil disintegration are multiple, but certain characteristics increase vulnerability. Extreme income and gender inequality increase the risk of discord. Corrupt governments that are widely regarded as illegitimate and ineffective are "at risk." Democracy, especially with a strong parliament, lowers the risk of state failure; autocracy increases it. Population pressure, exacerbated by internally displaced people, refugees, and food scarcity, contribute to state failure and civil unrest. Governments that fail to protect human rights are especially prone to fail.

The Arab Spring, a term given to the Arab Revolution, is a wave of demonstrations, protests, and wars that began in December 2010. A number of rulers have been forced from power in Tunisia, Egypt, Libya, and Yemen. In addition, there have been civil uprisings in Bahrain, Syria, and Ukraine. However, the major oil-rich nations (Saudi Arabia, UAE, Qatar, Kuwait, and Oman) have managed to keep their ruling families in power.

The protests have shared techniques of civil resistance in sustained campaigns involving strikes, demonstrations, marches, and rallies, but were also noticeable for their use of social media to organize and raise awareness of the situation.

Despite the words of John F. Kennedy, US President 1961–3, that "Mankind must put an end to war or war will put an end to mankind," in 2019 military conflicts are taking place around the world in countries such as Afghanistan, Somalia, Yemen, Pakistan, Mexico (the "drugs war"), South Sudan, Nigeria, Syria, Iraq, Libya, and Ukraine.

▲ UN peacekeepers in the Democratic Republic of the Congo, April 2019. The UN is currently involved in 14 operations worldwide.

ARMED CONFLICTS

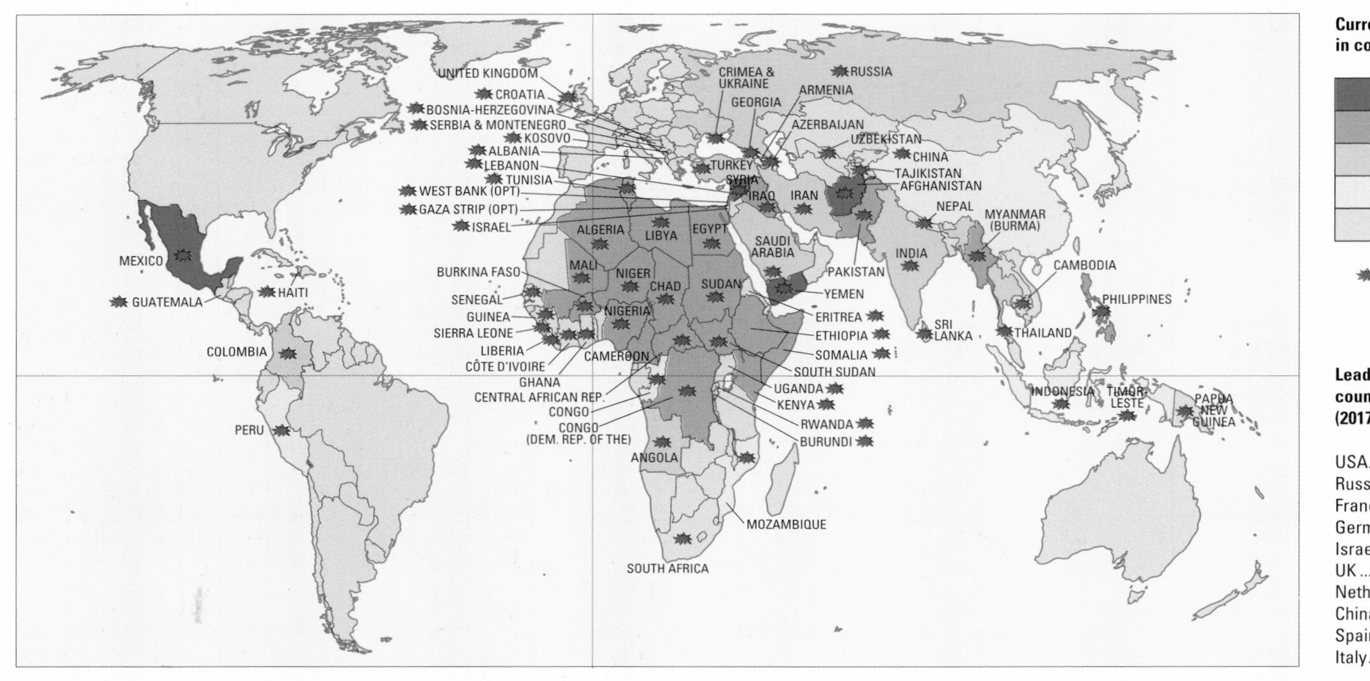

Current military and civilian deaths in countries with conflict, per year (2018)

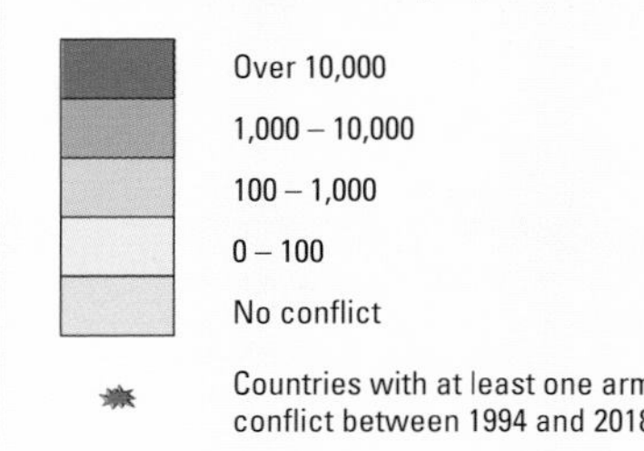

Leading arms exporting countries (US $ million) (2017)

USA	$12,394
Russia	$6,148
France	$2,163
Germany	$1,653
Israel	$1,263
UK	$1,214
Netherlands	$1,167
China	$1,131
Spain	$814
Italy	$660

Leading recipients of arms deliveries (US $ million) (2017)

Saudi Arabia	$4,111
India	$3,358
Egypt	$2,355
Australia	$1,806
China	$1,117
South Korea	$918
Algeria	$905
UK	$899
UAE	$848
Italy	$794

GLOBAL PEACE INDEX

The Global Peace Index (GPI) is an attempt to measure the relative position of nations' peacefulness. It quantifies: levels of security and safety; domestic and international conflict; and degree of militarization. Syria remains the least peaceful country with Libya and Ukraine showing the most deterioration.

Global Peace Index (2018)

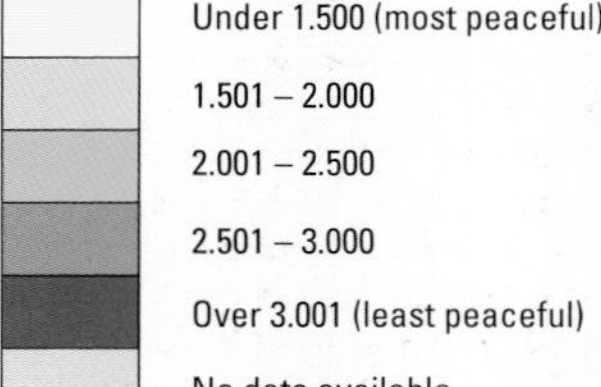

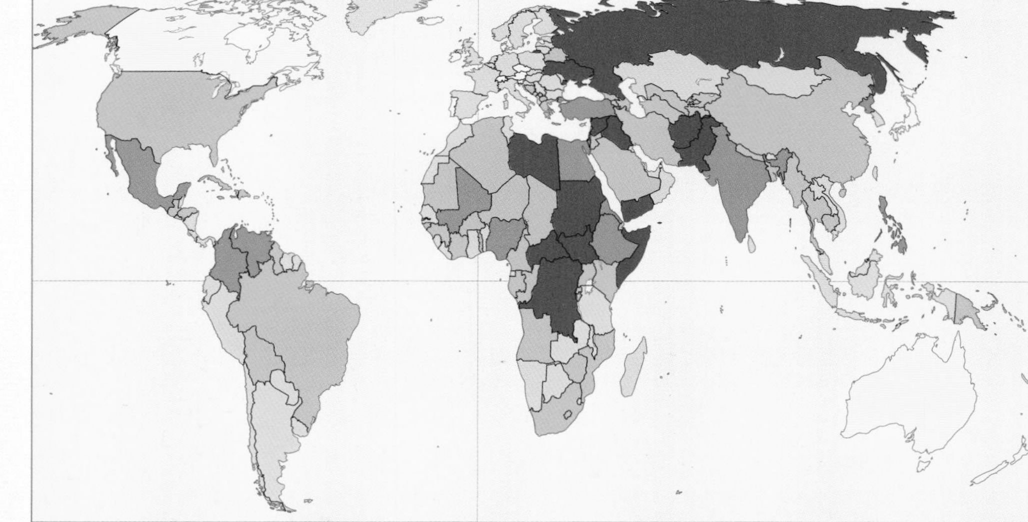

Five most peaceful countries

Country	GPI
Iceland	1.096
New Zealand	1.192
Austria	1.274
Portugal	1.318
Denmark	1.353

Five least peaceful countries

Country	GPI
Syria	3.600
Afghanistan	3.585
South Sudan	3.508
Iraq	3.425
C.A.R.	3.326

INTERNATIONAL ORGANIZATIONS

UN

Year of joining

1940s
1950s
1960s
1970s
1980s
1990s
2000s
Non-members

★ 1% – 10% contribution to funding

☆ Over 10% contribution to funding

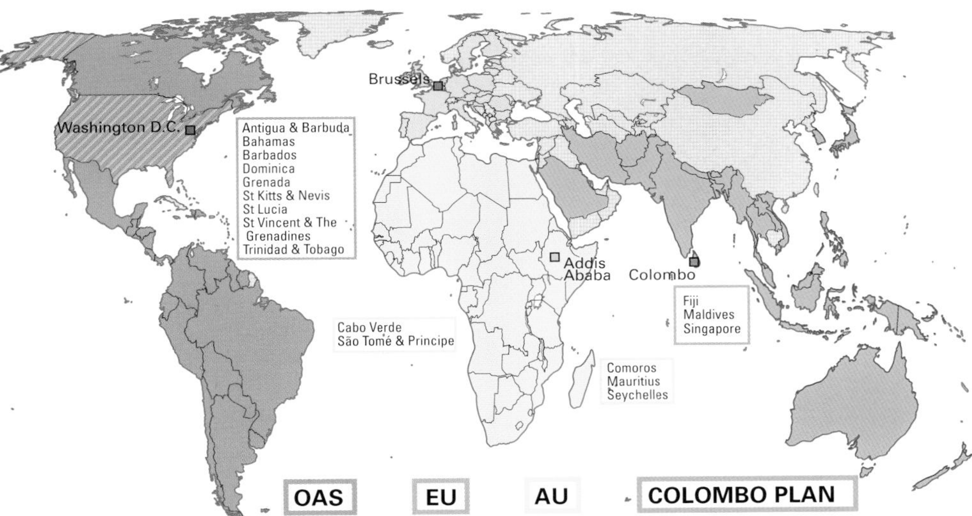

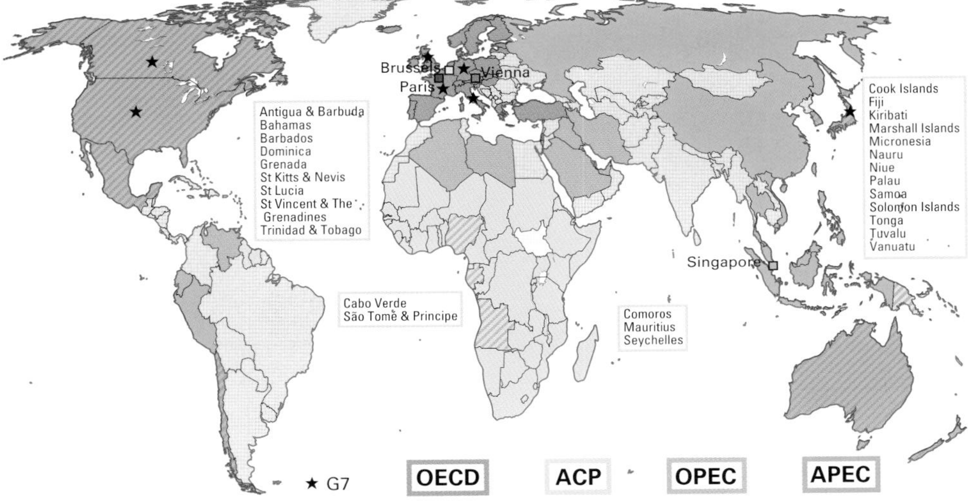

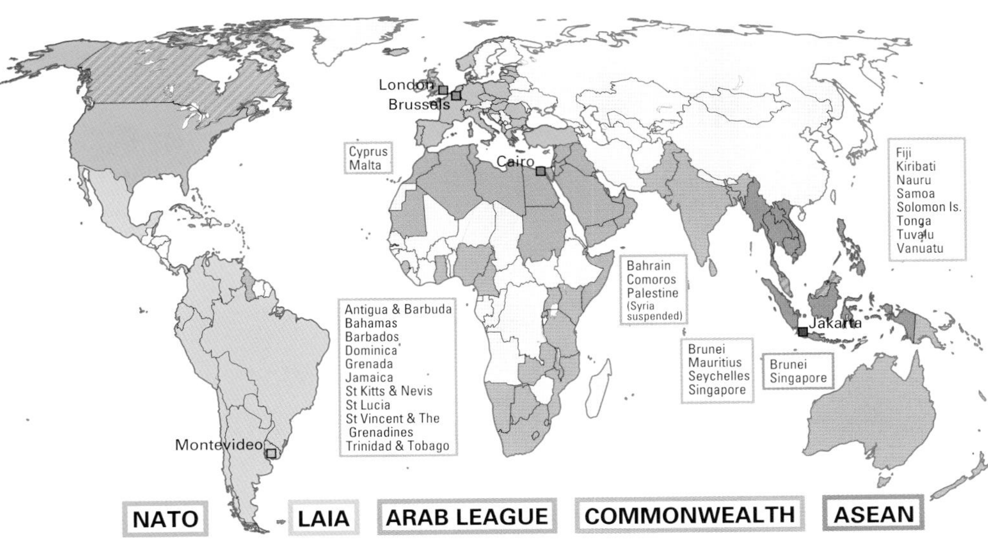

UNITED NATIONS

The creation of the United Nations in 1945 held out hope that the world's nations, tired of war, would have the means to control humanity's aggressive instincts. Although the UN lacks the power to halt conflicts, it has often helped to achieve negotiation. Economic pressures have led to another kind of cooperation, resulting in the creation of common markets and economic unions, such as ASEAN in Southeast Asia, the European Union, and NAFTA in North America.

The United Nations Organization was born as World War II drew to its conclusion. That body would replace the League of Nations, which, since its inception in 1920, had failed to curb the aggression of some of its member nations. At the United Nations Conference on International Organization held in San Francisco, the United Nations Charter was drawn up. Ratified by the Security Council and signed by the 51 original members, it came into effect on October 24, 1945.

The Charter set out the aims of the organization: to maintain peace and security, and to develop friendly relations between nations; to achieve international cooperation in solving economic, social, cultural, and humanitarian problems; to promote respect for human rights and fundamental freedoms; and to harmonize the activities of nations in order to achieve these common goals.

Membership From the original 51, membership of the UN has now grown to 193. There are only two independent states that are not members – Taiwan and the Vatican City. Official languages are Chinese, English, French, Russian, Spanish, and Arabic.

Funding The UN budget for 2018–19 was US $5.4 billion. Contributions are assessed by the members' ability to pay, with the maximum 22% of the total (the USA's share), and the minimum 0.001%. The 28-member EU pays approximately 35% of the budget.

Peacekeeping The UN has been involved in 67 peacekeeping operations worldwide since 1948. They are involved in 14 operations in mid 2019.

OAS The **Organization of American States** was formed in 1948. It aims to promote social and economic cooperation between countries in the developed North America and developing Latin America.

EU The **European Union** evolved from the European Community in 1993. Cyprus, Czechia, Estonia, Hungary, Latvia, Lithuania, Malta, Poland, Slovakia, and Slovenia joined the EU in May 2004; Bulgaria and Romania joined in 2007; Croatia joinded in 2013. The other 15 members of the EU are Austria, Belgium, Denmark, Finland, France, Germany, Greece, Ireland, Italy, Luxembourg, Netherlands, Portugal, Spain, Sweden, and the UK. Together, the 28 members aim to integrate economies, coordinate social developments, and bring about political union. The UK plans to leave the EU in 2019.

AU The **African Union** was set up in 2002, taking over from the Organization of African Unity (1963). It has 55 members. The main objectives of the OAU were, *inter alia*, to rid the continent of the remaining vestiges of colonization and apartheid; to promote unity and solidarity among African states; to coordinate and intensify cooperation for development; to safeguard the sovereignty and territorial integrity of member states; and to promote international cooperation within the framework of the United Nations.

COLOMBO PLAN Formed in 1951, its 27 members aim to promote economic and social development in Asia and the Pacific. Saudi Arabia joined in 2012.

G7 Group of seven leading industrialized nations, comprising Canada, France, Germany, Italy, Japan, the UK, and the USA. Periodic meetings are held to discuss major world issues, such as world recessions. The EU is also represented at meetings. Russian membership was suspended in 2014.

OECD The **Organization for Economic Cooperation and Development** (formed in 1961) comprises 36 major free-market economies. The "G7" is its "inner group" of leading industrial nations, comprising Canada, France, Germany, Italy, Japan, the UK, and the USA. The mission of the OECD is to promote policies that will improve the economic and social well-being of people around the world.

ACP The **African, Caribbean and Pacific Group of States** was formed in 1963. Members enjoy economic ties with the EU. The ACP Group's main objectives are sustainable development of its member states and their gradual integration into the global economy, which entails making poverty reduction a matter of priority; coordination of the activities of the ACP Group in the framework of the implementation of ACP–EU Partnership Agreements; establishment and consolidation of peace and stability in a free and democratic society.

OPEC The **Organization of Petroleum Exporting Countries** was formed in 1960. It controls about three-quarters of the world's oil supply. Its mission is to coordinate and unify the petroleum policies of its member countries, and to ensure the stabilization of oil markets in order to secure an efficient, economic, and regular supply of petroleum to consumers, a steady income to producers, and a fair return on capital for those investing in the petroleum industry. Qatar left in January 2019.

APEC Formed in 1989, the **Asia–Pacific Economic Cooperation** aims to enhance economic growth and prosperity for the region and to strengthen the Asia–Pacific community. APEC is the only intergovernmental grouping in the world operating on the basis of non-binding commitments, open dialog, and equal respect for the views of all participants. There are 21 member economies.

NATO The **North Atlantic Treaty Organization** (formed in 1949) continues despite the winding-up of the Warsaw Pact in 1991. Bulgaria, Estonia, Latvia, Lithuania, Romania, Slovakia, and Slovenia became members in 2004, and Albania and Croatia in 2009. Montenegro joined in 2017. Its main aim is to provide peace and security to its North Atlantic members through collective defense – an attack on one country is seen as an attack on all of NATO.

LAIA The **Latin American Integration Association** (formed in 1980) superceded the Latin American Free Trade Association formed in 1961. Its aim is to promote freer regional trade.

ARAB LEAGUE Formed in 1945, the Arab League aims to promote economic, social, political, and military cooperation. There are 22 member nations. Syria's membership was suspended in 2011.

COMMONWEALTH The **Commonwealth of Nations** evolved from the British Empire. Pakistan was suspended in 1999, but reinstated in 2004. Zimbabwe was suspended in 2002 and, in response to its continued suspension, Zimbabwe left the Commonwealth in 2003. Fiji was suspended in 2006 following a military coup. Rwanda joined the Commonwealth in 2009, as the 54th member state, becoming only the second country that was not formerly a British colony to be admitted to the group. The Gambia left between 2013 and 2018. Their objective is to build stronger democratic institutions and processes across the Commonwealth and to support economic growth in their member countries. There are currently 53 members.

ASEAN The **Association of Southeast Asian Nations** was formed in 1967. Cambodia joined in 1999. The aims of ASEAN include: to accelerate the economic growth, social progress, and cultural development in the region; to promote regional peace and stability; and to collaborate more effectively for the greater utilization of their agriculture and industries, the expansion of their trade, including the study of the problems of international commodity trade, the improvement of their transportation and communications facilities, and the raising of the living standards of their peoples.

For more information:
80 Global warming
Carbon dioxide
98 Minerals

Every year, the world's energy consumption is about the equivalent of what would come from burning 12,000 million tonnes of oil (12,000 MtOe) – a 20-fold increase since 1850. Two-fifths of this total actually comes from burning oil and most of the rest comes from coal and natural gas.

The oil crises in the 1970s precipitated concern over dependence on finite fossil fuels as the primary source of energy, and growing environmental awareness has added impetus to the search for alternative energy resources. Fossil fuel combustion damages the environment through the release of gases and particulate matter, but two other major sources of energy, hydroelectricity and nuclear power, are also controversial. Hydroelectricity production involves flooding large areas to create reservoirs, while nuclear power stations generate dangerous radioactive wastes and can cause major disasters. Nuclear power has been a growing source of energy, but the 2011 Japanese earthquake, with the consequent serious damage to the Fukushima nuclear power station, has caused many countries to rethink their energy strategies.

Alternative energy resources may soon provide a much larger proportion of the world's energy consumption. Solar and wind energy may become important in such countries as China and India, while tidal, wave, and geothermal energy all have potential in appropriate areas. Experts calculate that solar power could, in theory, supply between five and ten times the present electricity supply of developing countries.

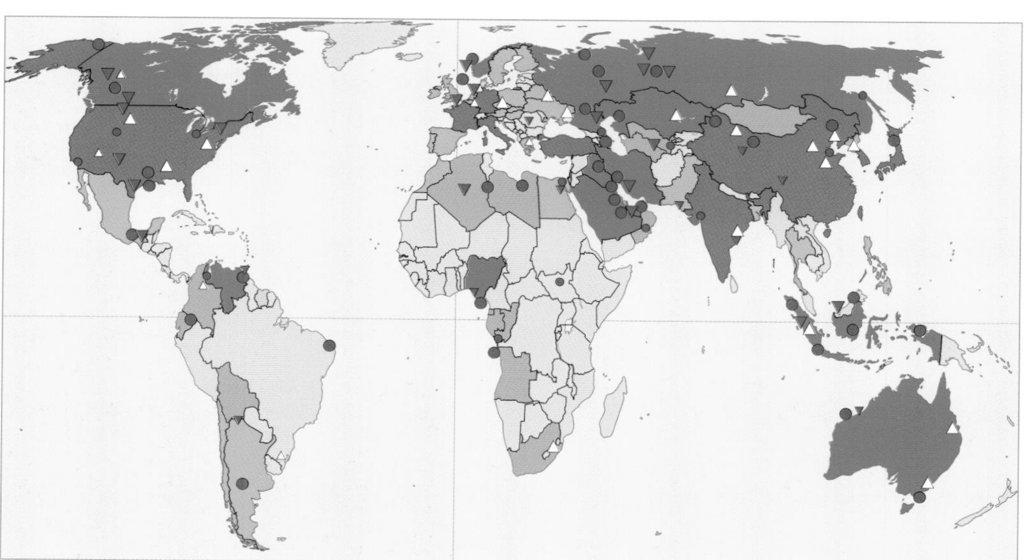

ENERGY BALANCE

Difference between energy production and consumption in millions of tonnes of oil equivalent (MtOe) (2017)

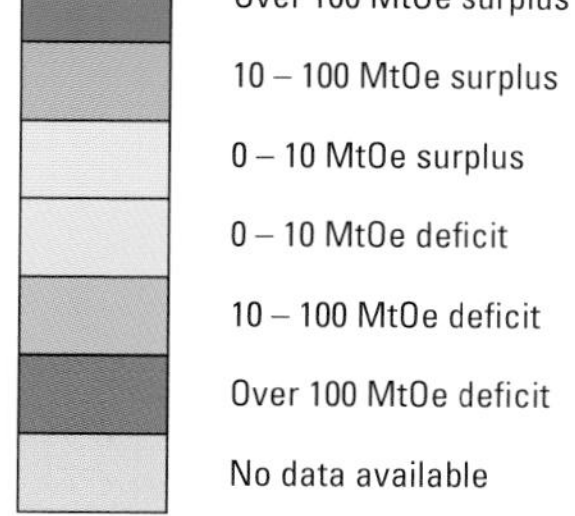

● Principal oilfields • Secondary oilfields
▼ Principal gasfields ▾ Secondary gasfields
△ Principal coalfields △ Secondary coalfields

ENERGY CONSUMPTION

Energy consumed by world regions, measured in million tonnes of oil equivalent in 2017. Total world consumption was 13,513 MtOe. Energy from commercially traded fuels, and modern renewables used to generate electricity, are included. Excluded are biomass fuels such as wood, peat and animal waste which, though important locally in some countries, are not always reliably documented statistically.

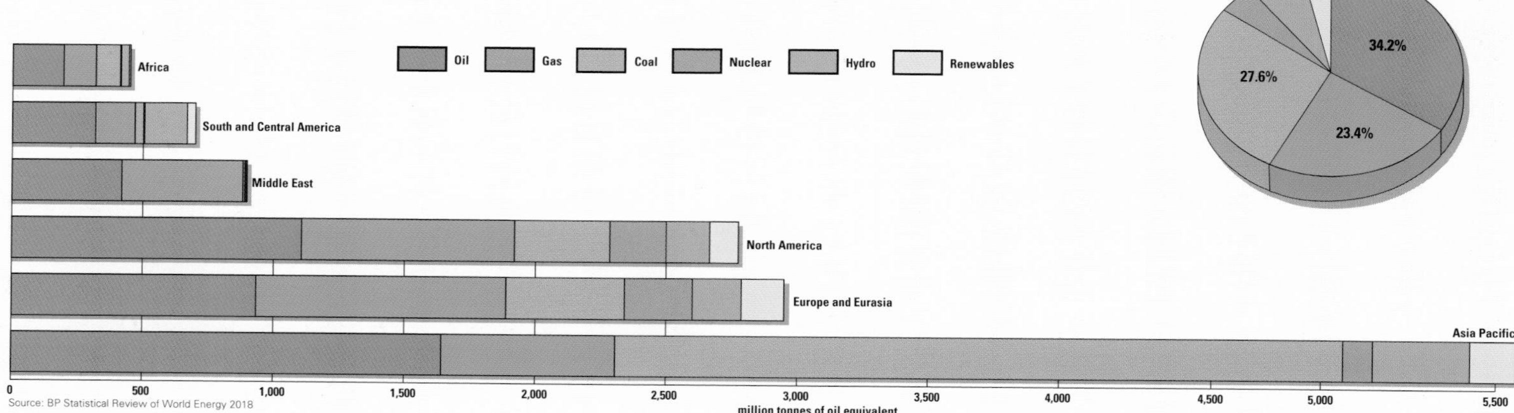

Source: BP Statistical Review of World Energy 2018

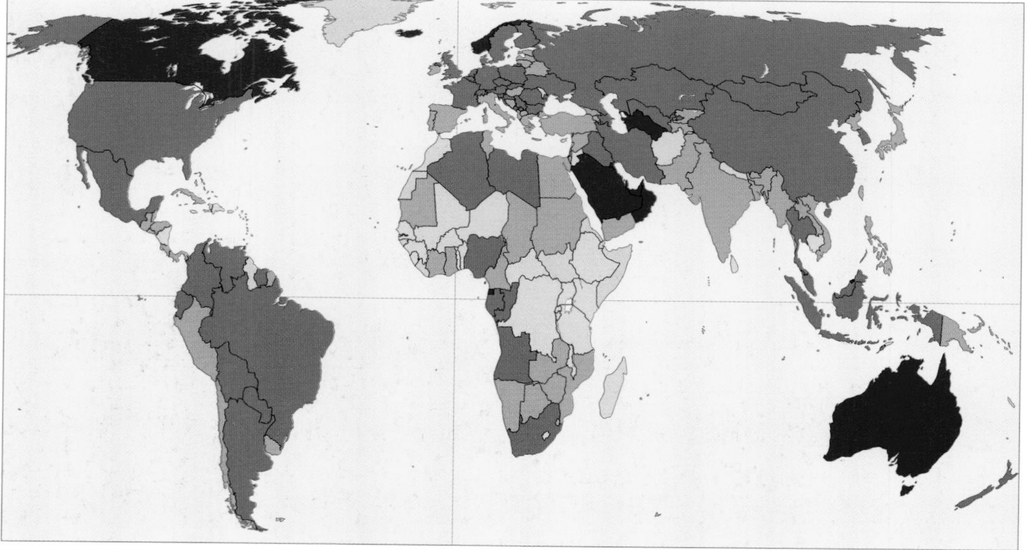

ENERGY PRODUCTION

Energy production in tonnes of oil equivalent per capita (2017)

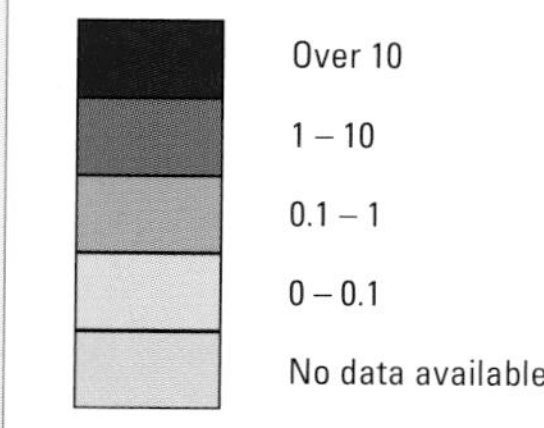

Highest energy producers, tonnes of oil equivalent per capita (2017)

Qatar	113.6
Kuwait	58.4
Brunei	42.5
Norway	40.6
United Arab Emirates	38.6

OIL MOVEMENTS

Major oil exporting regions

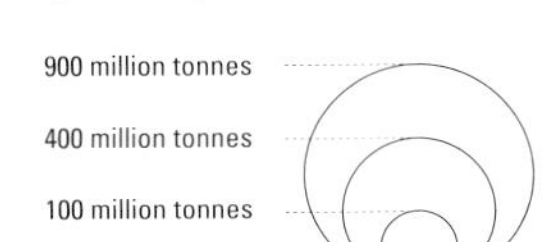

Major global oil movements (percentage of total world trade)

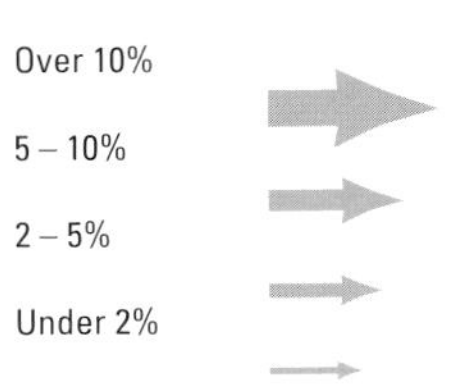

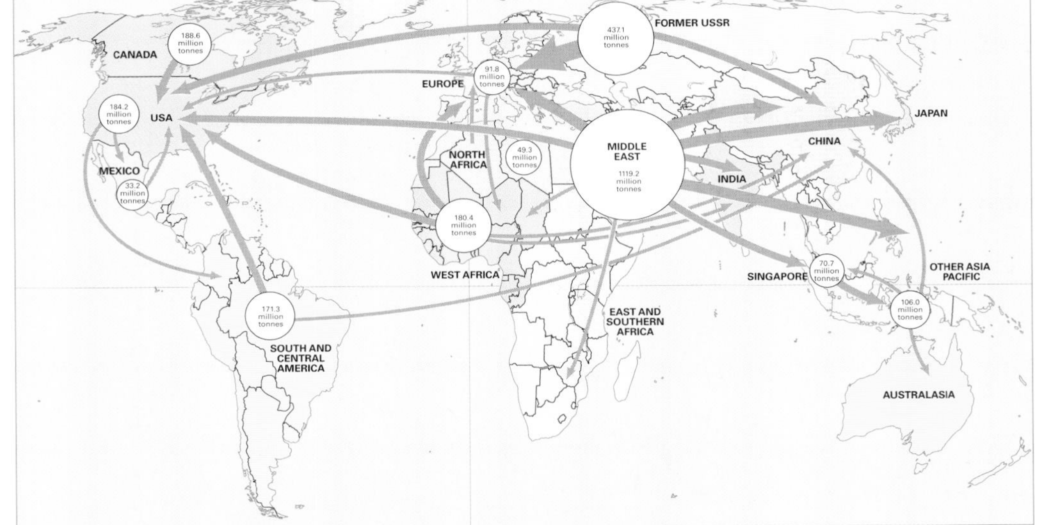

▲ A view over the tanks of the Liquefied Natural Gas (LNG) tanker Grand Aniva. LNG is natural gas that has been filtered and purified then cooled to -260°F (-162°C), which turns it into a liquid, 1/600th of its original volume, allowing it to be transported in special highly-insulated tanks on ships to markets around the world.

ENERGY RESERVES

WORLD OIL RESERVES

World oil reserves by region and country, billion tonnes (2017)

World total: 239 billion tonnes

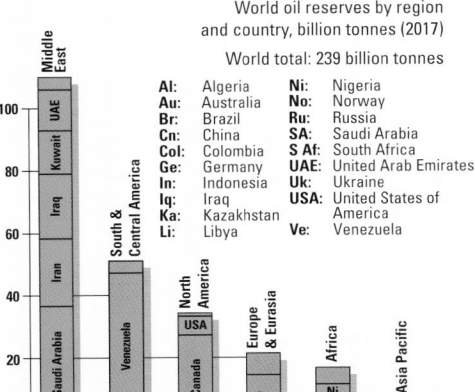

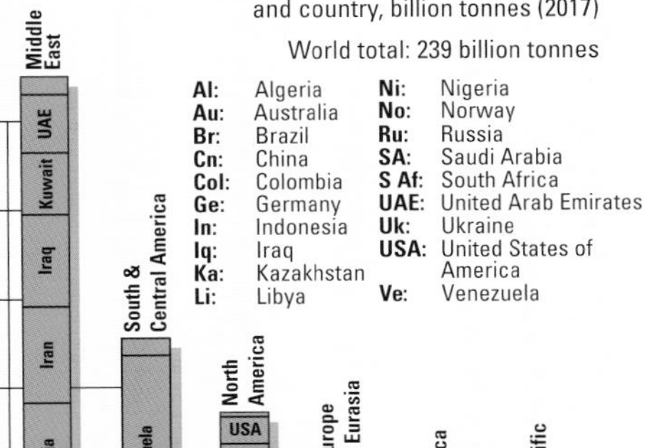

WORLD GAS RESERVES

World natural gas reserves by region and country, billion tonnes of oil equivalent (2017)

World total: 174 billion tonnes of oil equivalent

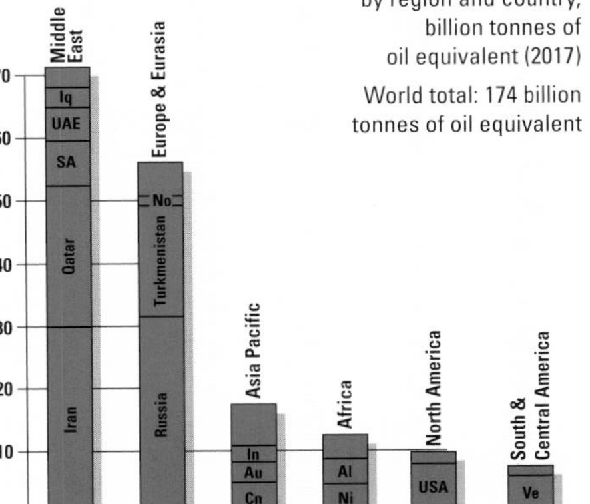

WORLD COAL RESERVES

World coal reserves (including lignite) by region and country, billion tonnes (2017)

World total: 1,139 billion tonnes

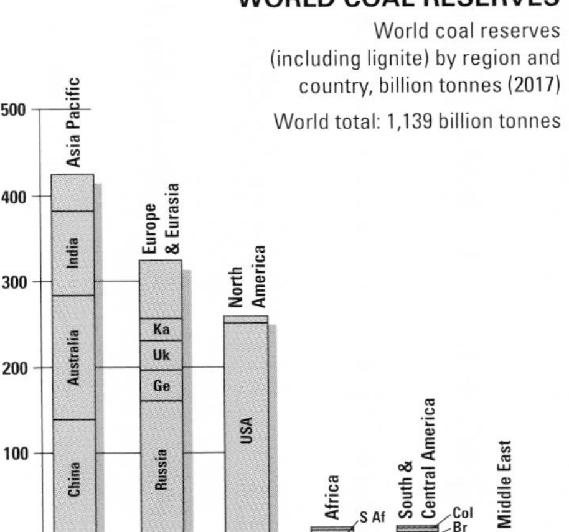

NUCLEAR POWER

Major producers by percentage of domestic electricity generation (2017)

Country	% of nuclear as proportion of domestic electricity	Country	% of nuclear as proportion of domestic electricity
1. France	72	11. Armenia	33
2. Ukraine	55	12. Czechia	33
3. Slovakia	54	13. South Korea	27
4. Belgium	50	14. Spain	21
5. Hungary	50	15. USA	20
6. Sweden	40	16. UK	19
7. Slovenia	39	17. Romania	18
8. Bulgaria	34	18. Russia	18
9. Switzerland	33	19. Canada	15
10. Finland	33	20. Taiwan	13

Although the 1980s were a bad time for the nuclear power industry, the industry picked up in the early 1990s. Despite this, growth has recently been curtailed whilst countries review their energy mix, in light of the March 2011 Japanese earthquake and tsunami that seriously damaged the Fukushima nuclear power station. Germany, for example, is phasing out its nuclear power production.

PEAK OIL

"Peak oil" refers to the peak of oil production. We depend on oil for many things: we use it for fuel, transport and heating, as a raw material in the plastics industry, and for fertilizer in food production. But as oil production decreases after peak oil, so will all of these, unless we can find new materials and alternatives.

Peak oil varies by country. The peak of oil discovery occurred in the 1960s, and by the 1980s the world was using more oil than was being discovered. Since then, the gap between use and discovery has been increasing, and many countries have now passed their peak oil production.

The International Energy Agency suggests that global peak oil will occur between 2013 and 2037. In contrast, the US Geological Survey suggests it will not occur until 2059. M. King Hubbert, who popularized the theory of peak oil, predicted that it would occur in 1995. It is claimed that in 1950 the world consumed 4 billion barrels of oil per annum, while the average discovery was 30 billion barrels per annum. Now, however, research suggests the figures are reversed: new discoveries are around 4 billion barrels per year, with an annual consumption of 30 billion barrels.

FRACKING

Hydraulic fracturing, commonly known as "fracking," releases natural gas or oil that is trapped in shale rock and is unobtainable by conventional techniques. This is accomplished by boring holes into the rock and injecting a liquid mix of chemicals under pressure, thus fracturing the rock and forcing the trapped oil or gas to the surface.

Just as nuclear scientists in the 1950s and 1960s believed that nuclear energy was going to be the answer to the world's energy needs, oil and gas producers believe that gas derived from shale could provide a plentiful supply of low-cost energy. As a result, shale gas could transform the pattern of energy trade in the world. Nevertheless, fracking has its critics and there may be problems related to the extraction of shale gas.

Shale is one of the most common forms of sedimentary rock on Earth. Significant reserves have been found in China, Argentina, the USA, and South Africa, and these are therefore having a new geopolitical influence. The world's gas trade has long been dominated by Russia, Qatar, and Algeria, but shale gas development has since taken off in the USA. In 2010, the USA replaced Russia as the world's largest gas producer and a new wave of gas producers may soon emerge.

However, as with the nuclear dawn, there are potential drawbacks with fracking. It may pollute soil and ground water, release methane, produce toxic byproducts that have to be disposed of, and it may also trigger earthquakes.

HYDROELECTRICITY

Major producers by percentage of world total and by percentage of domestic electricity generation (2018)

Country	% of world total production	Country	% of hydroelectric as proportion of domestic electricity
1. China	26.9	1. Albania	100.0
2. United States	8.1	2. Paraguay	100.0
3. Brazil	7.9	3. Nepal	99.8
4. Canada	6.4	4. Congo, Dem. Rep.	99.7
5. Japan	3.9	5. Namibia	99.1
6. India	3.9	6. Tajikistan	98.5
7. Russia	3.8	7. Zambia	97.0
8. Norway	2.5	8. Norway	96.0
9. Turkey	2.1	9. Ethiopia	92.7
10. France	2.0	10. Kyrgyzstan	91.3

Countries heavily reliant on hydroelectricity are usually small and non-industrial: a high proportion of hydroelectric power more often reflects a modest energy budget than vast hydroelectric resources. The USA, for instance, produces only 6% of its domestic power requirements from hydroelectricity; yet that 6% amounts to almost half the hydropower generated by the whole of Africa.

ALTERNATIVE ENERGY RESOURCES

Solar: Each year the Sun bestows upon the Earth almost a million times as much energy as is locked up in all the planet's oil reserves, but only an insignificant fraction is trapped and used commercially. In a few installations around the world, mirrors focus the Sun's rays on to boilers, whose steam generates electricity by spinning turbines, and the use of photovoltaic panels in sunny climates has also started to become established.

Wind: Caused by uneven heating of the Earth, winds are themselves a form of solar energy. Windmills have been long used for wind power; recent models are often arranged in banks on wind-swept high ground or situated off coastlines. Wind-power figures are given in the table (*right*). Wind power contributes over 30% of all electricity generated in Denmark.

Tidal: The energy from tides is potentially enormous, although only a few installations have so far been built to exploit it. In theory, at least, waves and currents could also provide almost unimaginable power, and the thermal differences in the ocean depths are another huge well of potential energy. But work on extracting it is still at the experimental stage.

Geothermal: The Earth's temperature rises by 1°F for every 50 feet descent, with much steeper temperature gradients in geologically active areas. El Salvador, for example, produces 25% of its electricity from geothermal power stations, whilst the USA is the world's leading producer. Some of the oldest and most successful applications are in Iceland, where 87% of all households are heated by geothermal energy.

Biomass: The oldest of human fuels ranges from animal dung, still burned in cooking fires in much of North Africa and elsewhere, to sugarcane plantations feeding high-technology distilleries to produce ethanol for motor-vehicle engines. In Brazil and South Africa, plant ethanol provides up to 25% of motor fuel. Throughout the developing world, most biomass energy comes from firewood: although accurate figures are impossible to obtain, it may yield as much as 10% of the world's total energy consumption.

WIND POWER

World wind energy generating capacity, in megawatts

Year	Megawatts
1994	3,710
1996	6,115
1998	9,600
2000	17,800
2002	31,000
2003	39,300
2004	47,671
2005	58,982
2006	74,151
2007	93,927
2008	121,188
2009	157,899
2010	196,653
2011	238,035
2012	282,482
2013	318,105
2014	370,000
2015	434,856
2016	486,661
2017	540,000

For more information:
74 Geology
101 Globalization

The use of metals played a vital part in the evolving technologies of early peoples. Copper first came into use around 10,000 years ago, bronze about 5,000 years ago, and iron 3,300 years ago. In the early stages of the Industrial Revolution, the location of coal, iron ore, and water power usually determined the location of new industries. But due to continuing improvements in transport, including oil pipelines, industries can now be located almost anywhere.

Minerals are distributed unevenly and some industrial countries, lacking their own mineral resources, import most of the raw materials they need. Some imports come from mineral-rich countries, such as Australia, but others come from developing countries, especially in Africa and South America. Most developing countries export unprocessed ores, losing out on the higher revenues gained from exporting metals.

Most minerals come from land deposits, because undersea deposits, with the exception of oil reserves under the continental shelves, have been inaccessible. But shortages of terrestrial minerals may one day encourage exploitation of the ocean floor.

URANIUM

Uranium was first discovered by the German chemist Martin Klaproth in 1789. In its pure state, uranium is an immensely heavy, white metal. Its main use is as a fuel in nuclear reactors and in nuclear weaponry, although depleted uranium is employed as a projectile in anti-missile cannons, where its mass ensures a lethal punch.

Uranium is very scarce: the main source is the rare ore pitchblende, which itself contains only 0.2% uranium oxide. This blackish, lustrous ore occurs in quartz veins. Only a minute fraction of that is the radioactive U^{235} isotope, though so-called breeder reactors can transmute the more common U^{238} into highly radioactive plutonium.

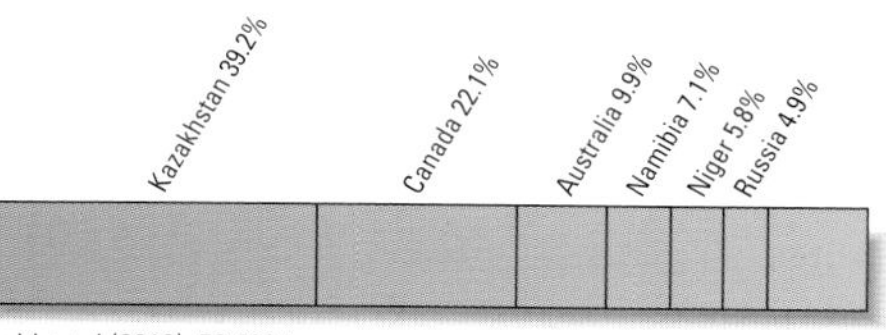

World total (2018): 59,462 tonnes

► Bingham Canyon Mine in Utah, USA, is one of the largest open-pit mines in the world. It measures over 2.5 miles [4 km] wide and 3,900 ft [1,200 m] deep. Copper-containing rocks are excavated from the surface downward in terraces. These terraces are 50–80 ft [15–25 m] high and provide access for equipment to work the rock face whilst maintaining stability of the sloping pit walls.

Today's copper market is booming due to global demands from construction, telecommunications, and electronics companies. Over 17 million tonnes of copper have been mined from Bingham Canyon Mine to date, as well as gold, silver and other minerals.

DIAMOND

Most of the world's diamond is found in kimberlite, or "blue ground," a basic igneous rock; erosion may wash the diamond from its kimberlite matrix and deposit it with sand or gravel on river beds. Only a small proportion of the world's diamond, the most flawless, is cut into gemstones – "diamonds"; most are used in industry, where the material's remarkable hardness and abrasion resistance finds a use in cutting tools, drills, and dies. In 2018, the world's major producers were Russia (30.2%), Australia (27.0%), the Democratic Republic of the Congo (23.8%), Botswana (11.1%), South Africa (3.2%), and Zimbabwe (3.2%). Natural diamonds now account for about 3% of all industrial diamond output. Synthetic diamond production in centers such as China, Ireland, Japan, Russia, and the USA far exceeds it.

BLOOD DIAMONDS

Blood Diamonds, or "Conflict Diamonds," are stones that are produced in areas controlled by rebel forces that are opposed to internationally recognized governments. The rebels sell these diamonds, using the money to purchase arms or to fund their military actions. These diamonds are often the main source of funding for the rebels – however, arms merchants, smugglers, and dishonest diamond traders facilitate their actions.

The flow of Blood Diamonds originated mainly from Sierra Leone, Angola, Democratic Republic of Congo, Liberia, and Côte d'Ivoire. In 2003, the United Nations and other groups introduced a certification procedure known as the "Kimberley Process," to try to eradicate this practice. This procedure requires each nation to certify that all rough diamond exports are produced through legitimate mining and sales activity.

Over 80 countries participate in the agreement.

Aluminum: Produced mainly from its oxide, bauxite, which yields 25% of its weight in aluminum. The cost of refining and production is often too high for producer-countries to bear, so bauxite is largely exported. Lightweight and corrosion resistant, aluminum alloys are widely used in aircraft, vehicles, cans, and packaging.

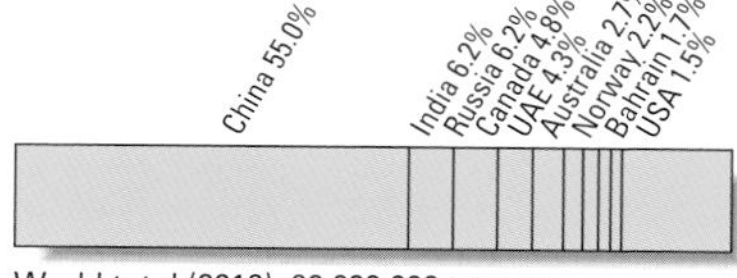

World total (2018): 60,000,000 tonnes

Lead: A soft metal, obtained mainly from galena (lead sulfide), which occurs in veins associated with iron, zinc, and silver sulfides. Its use in vehicle batteries accounts for the USA's prime consumer status; lead is also made into sheeting and piping. Its use as an additive to paints and petrol is decreasing.

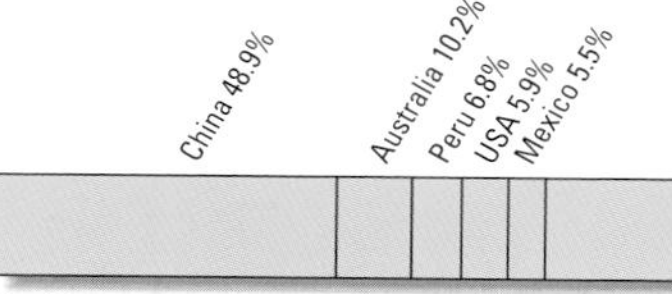

World total (2018): 4,400,000 tonnes

Tin: Soft, pliable and non-toxic, used to coat "tin" (tin-plated steel) cans, in the manufacture of foils and in alloys. The principal tin-bearing mineral is cassiterite (SnO_2), found in ore formed from molten rock.

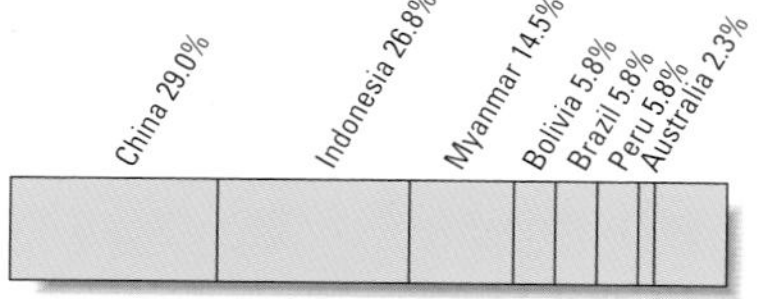

World total (2018): 310,000 tonnes

Gold: Regarded for centuries as the most valuable metal in the world and used to make coins, gold is still recognized as the monetary standard. A soft metal, it is alloyed to make jewelry; the electronics industry values its corrosion resistance and conductivity.

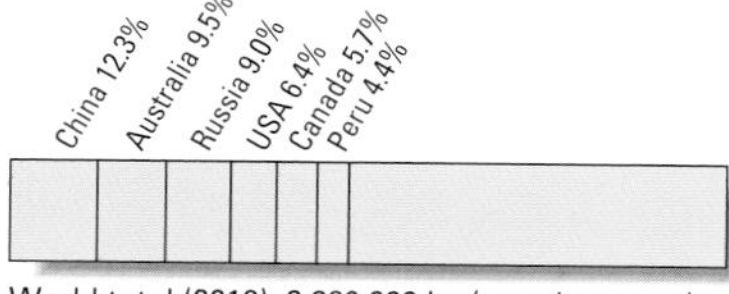

World total (2018): 3,260,000 kg (metal content)

Copper: Derived from low-yielding sulfide ores, copper is an important export for several developing countries. An excellent conductor of heat and electricity, it forms part of most electrical items, and is used in the manufacture of brass and bronze. Major importers include Japan and Germany.

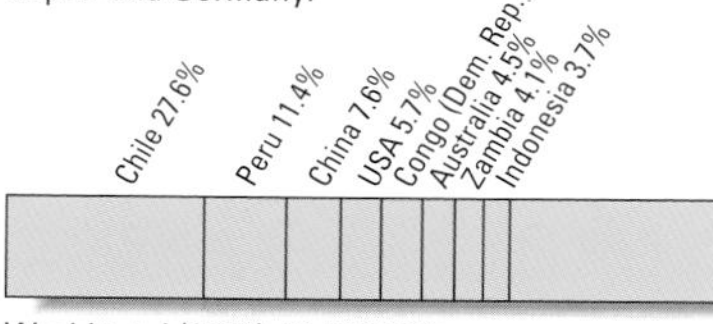

World total (2018): 21,000,000 tonnes

Mercury: The only metal that is liquid at normal temperatures, most is derived from its sulfide, cinnabar, found only in small quantities in volcanic areas. Apart from its value in thermometers and other instruments, most mercury production is used in anti-fungal and anti-fouling preparations, and to make detonators.

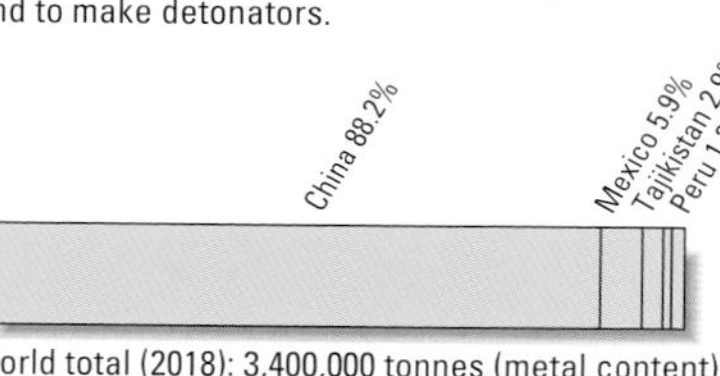

World total (2018): 3,400,000 tonnes (metal content)

Zinc: Often found in association with lead ores, zinc is highly resistant to corrosion, and about 40% of the refined metal is used to plate sheet steel, particularly vehicle bodies – a process known as galvanizing. Zinc is also used in dry batteries, paints, and dyes.

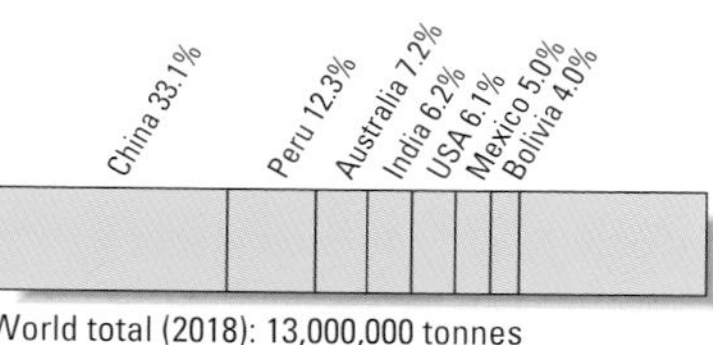

World total (2018): 13,000,000 tonnes

Silver: Most silver comes from ores mined and processed for other metals (including lead and copper). Pure or alloyed with harder metals, it is used for jewelry and ornaments. Industrial use includes dentistry, electronics, photography, and as a chemical catalyst.

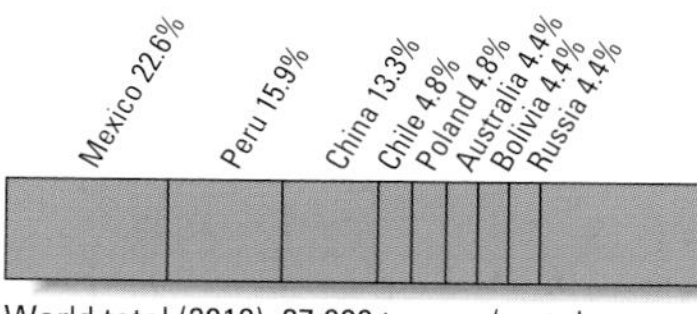

World total (2018): 27,000 tonnes (metal content)

DISTRIBUTION OF MINERALS

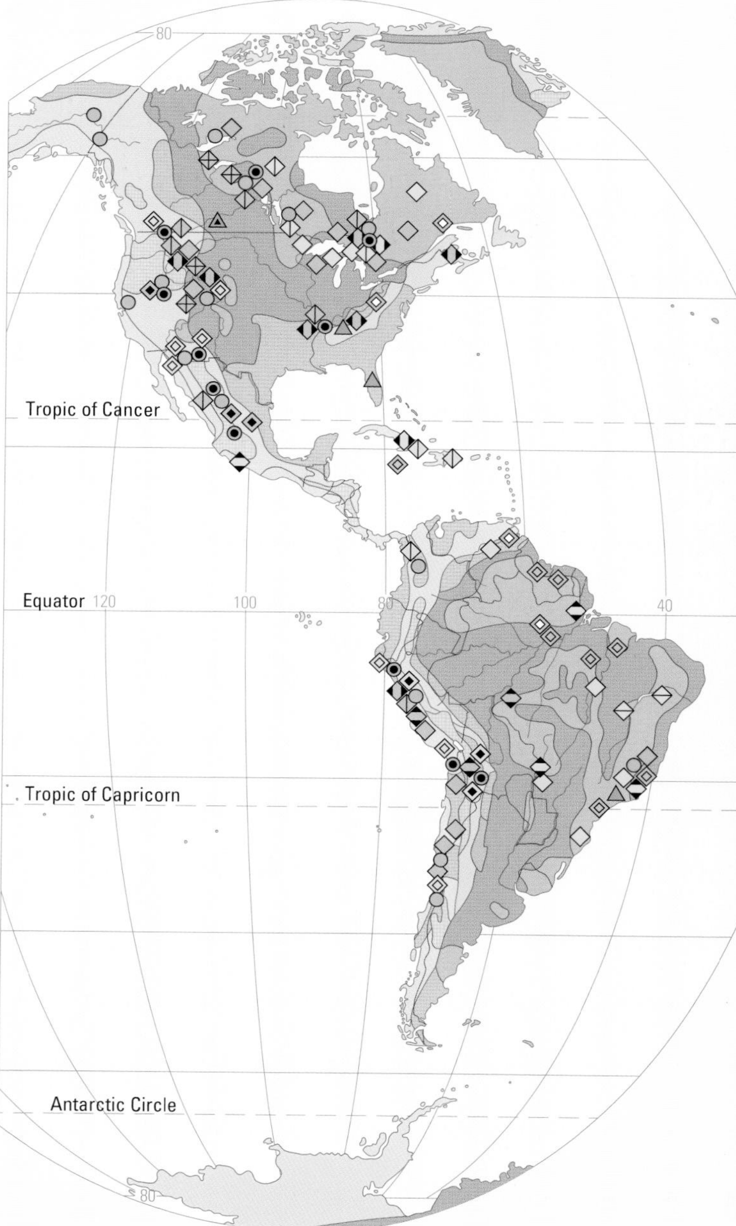

IRON ORE

Ever since the art of high-temperature smelting was discovered, some time in the second millennium BC, iron has been by far the most important metal known to man. The earliest iron plows transformed primitive agriculture and led to the first human population explosion, while iron weapons – or the lack of them – ensured the rise or fall of entire cultures.

Widely distributed around the world, iron ores usually contain 25–60% iron; blast furnaces process the raw product into pig-iron, which is then alloyed with carbon and other minerals to produce steels of various qualities. From the time of the Industrial Revolution, steel has been almost literally the backbone of modern civilization, the prime structural material on which all else is built.

Iron smelting usually developed close to the sources of ore and, later, to the coalfields that fueled the furnaces. Today, most ore comes from a few richly-endowed locations where large-scale mining is possible.

Iron and steel plants are generally built at coastal sites so that giant ore carriers, which account for a sizable proportion of the world's merchant fleet, can more easily discharge their cargoes.

World production of pig-iron (2018)

Total world production: 1,200 million tonnes

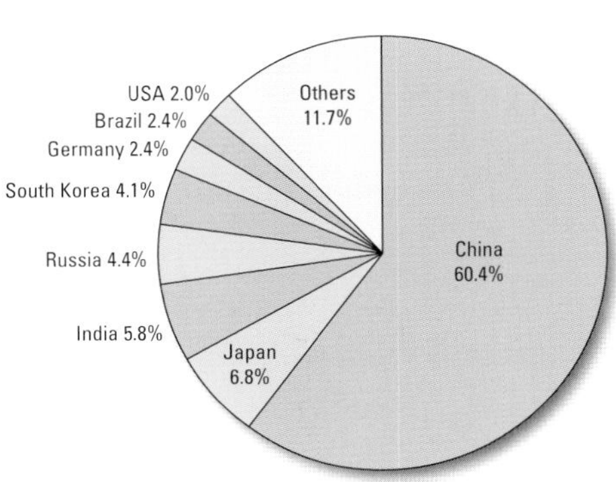

Iron ore

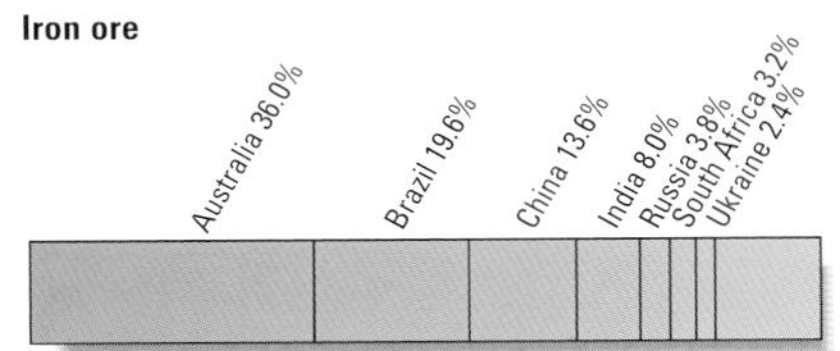

World total (2018): 2,500,000 tonnes

RARE EARTHS

Rare earth elements, or rare earth metals, are a set of 17 chemical elements, specifically the 15 lanthanides plus scandium and yttrium. Despite their name, rare earth elements are relatively plentiful, but are typically dispersed and not often found concentrated in economically exploitable ore deposits.

Until 1948, most of the world's rare earths were sourced from sand deposits in India and Brazil. Between the 1960s and the 1980s, the leading producer was California, USA. Today, China produces over 90% of the world's rare earth supply, although it only has less than 23% of proven reserves. The US Geological Survey is currently actively surveying southern Afghanistan for rare earth deposits under the protection of US military forces.

New demand has recently strained supply, and there is a growing concern that the world may soon face a shortage of the rare earths. In recent years, China has reduced its export quotas and halted production in some of its mines in order to conserve scarce resources and protect the environment.

A recently developed source of rare earths is electronic waste, and other wastes have rare earth components. Advances in recycling technology have made extraction of rare earths from these materials more feasible.

Rare earths are used as follows:

- **Neodymium** To make powerful magnets in loudspeakers and computer hard drives; also used in wind turbines and hybrid cars.
- **Lanthanum** In camera and telescope lenses.
- **Cerium** In catalytic converters in cars, and in the refining of oil.
- **Praseodymium** As an alloy, to create strong metals in aircraft engines.
- **Gadolinium** For X-ray machines, MRI scanning systems, and television screens.
- **Yttrium, terbium, europium** For television and computer screens, and for visual display units.

SCRAP METAL

Scrap metal has been an important source material for the manufacturing industry in domestic markets for decades, its value fluctuating according to the state of the local economy. Recently, however, with growing concern for the global environment and the rapid development of the economies in the Far East, the industry has become far more globalized. Container loads of processed-metal scrap from time-expired machinery in the Western world are now being exported to the Far East to be recycled. Processed-steel scrap accounts for almost half of the requirements for "furnace feed" for the world's steelmakers, and 40% of the world's copper requirements are derived from scrap.

Two major advantages of using scrap rather than refining mined ore are the energy and raw material savings that can be made. If 1 tonne of steel scrap is recycled, it saves 120 lb [54 kg] of limestone, 2,500 lb [1,130 kg] of iron ore and 1,400 lb [635 kg] of coal, with a consequent 86% reduction in air pollution, 40% saving in water use, and 76% reduction in water pollution. Huge energy savings, with consequent cuts in greenhouse-gas emissions, can also be made by using scrap.

As well as bulk minerals, such as those quoted above, alloys using nickel, chromium, tungsten, molybdenum, cobalt, and titanium, which are often only available in limited supplies and are expensive to produce, can also be recycled. The techniques involved to do this work are often very sophisticated, involving X-ray spectrometry and other computer-controlled methods, in order to recover high-value but low-volume metals from devices such as computers and televisions.

With companies having to take increased responsibility for their products, from manufacturing to sale and thence to their ultimate disposal at the end of their useful life, recycling scrap metals will become a much more important method of conserving the world's raw materials and preserving the environment in the future.

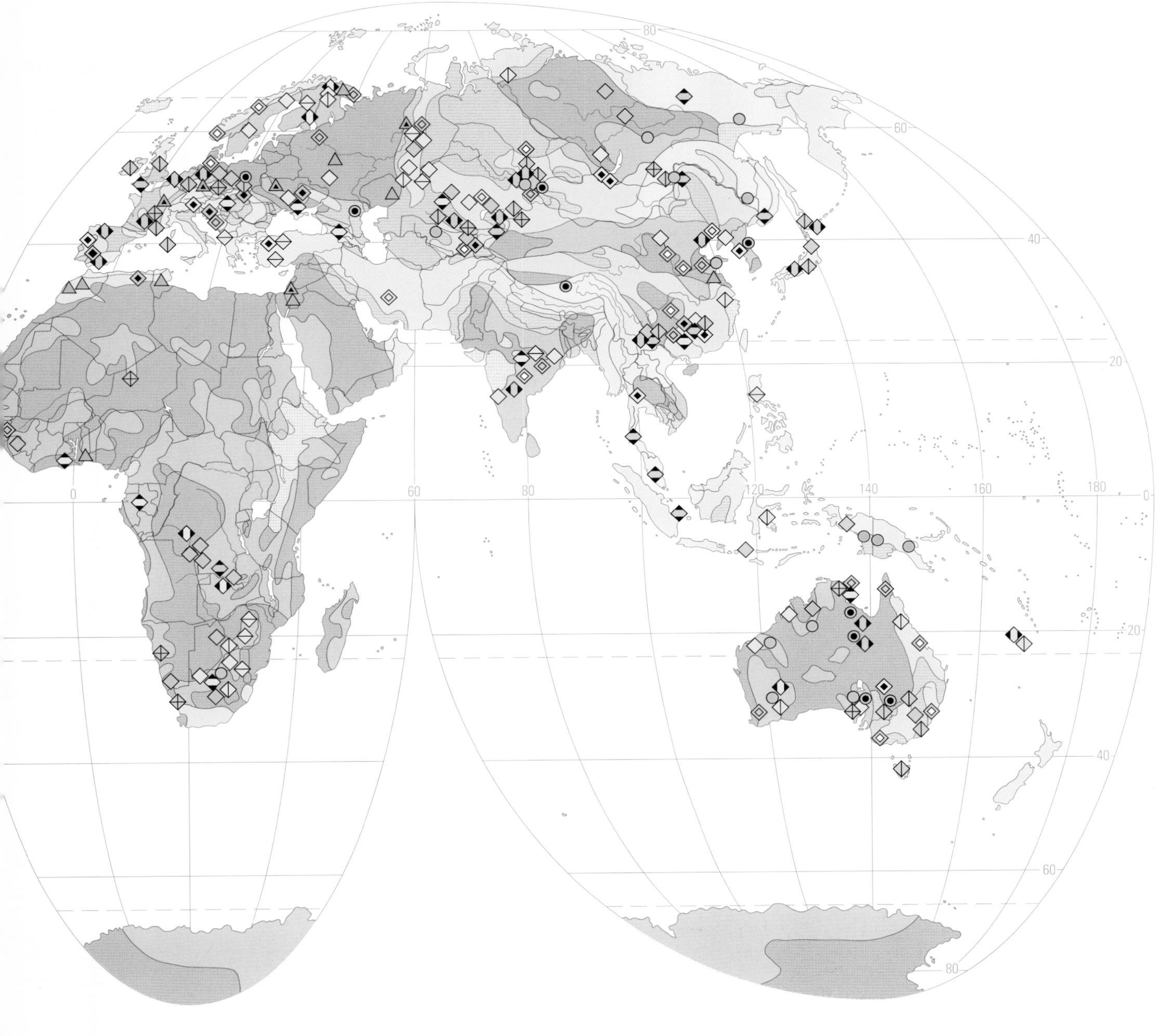

STRUCTURAL REGIONS

- Pre-Cambrian shields
- Sedimentary cover on Pre-Cambrian shields
- Paleozoic (Caledonian and Hercynian) folding
- Sedimentary cover on Paleozoic folding
- Mesozoic folding
- Sedimentary cover on Mesozoic folding
- Cenozoic (Alpine) folding
- Sedimentary cover on Cenozoic folding
- Intensive Mesozoic and Cenozoic vulcanism

DISTRIBUTION

Iron and ferro-alloys

- Chromium
- Cobalt
- Iron ore
- Manganese
- Molybdenum
- Nickel ore
- Tungsten

Non-ferrous metals

- Bauxite (Aluminum)
- Copper
- Lead
- Mercury
- Tin
- Zinc
- Uranium

Precious metals and stones

- Diamonds
- Gold
- Silver

Fertilizers

- Phosphates
- Potash

For more information:
97 Oil movements
98 Minerals
106 Levels of income

The Industrial Revolution, which began in Britain in the late 18th century, represented a major technological advance in the evolution of human society. It enabled a group of countries to become prosperous by replacing expensive human labor with increasingly sophisticated machinery. In economic terms, manufacturing is the transformation of raw materials, energy, labor, and machines into finished goods, which have a higher value than the various elements used in production.

The economies of countries can be compared by reference to their per capita Gross Domestic Products (GDPs), namely, the total value of goods and services produced within a country in a year, divided by the population. If this is calculated using Purchasing Power Parity (PPP) exchange rates, it better reflects the real state of the economy by taking into account differences in price levels in each country. The industrialized, or developed, countries accounted for 15% of the world's population in 2015 with an average per capita GDP of over US $43,000. On the other hand, low-income developing countries, with small industrial sectors, accounted for 77% of the world's population. Their per capita GDPs can be as low as $400.

Tanzania, with its low-income economy, had a per capita GDP in 2018 of US $3,400. Agriculture employs 80% of the people, while light industry together with services employs 20%. By contrast, Germany had a per capita GDP in 2018 of $52,600. Agriculture employs only 2% of the population, with 25% in industry and 74% in services. Germany's industrial sector differs greatly from Tanzania's, with its emphasis on vehicles, machinery, chemicals, and electronics.

Since the 1970s, some former developing countries in eastern Asia achieved rapid economic growth through industrialization. Despite setbacks in the late 1990s, they demonstrated that a developing industrial sector can transform an economy, which starts off with certain advantages, such as low labor costs. But economic success also depends on such factors as education to provide skills, and regulations that attract foreign investors. China, whose economy grew by more than 10% per year between 2002 and 2012, satisfies many of these criteria, though its record on human rights leaves much to be desired.

EMPLOYMENT

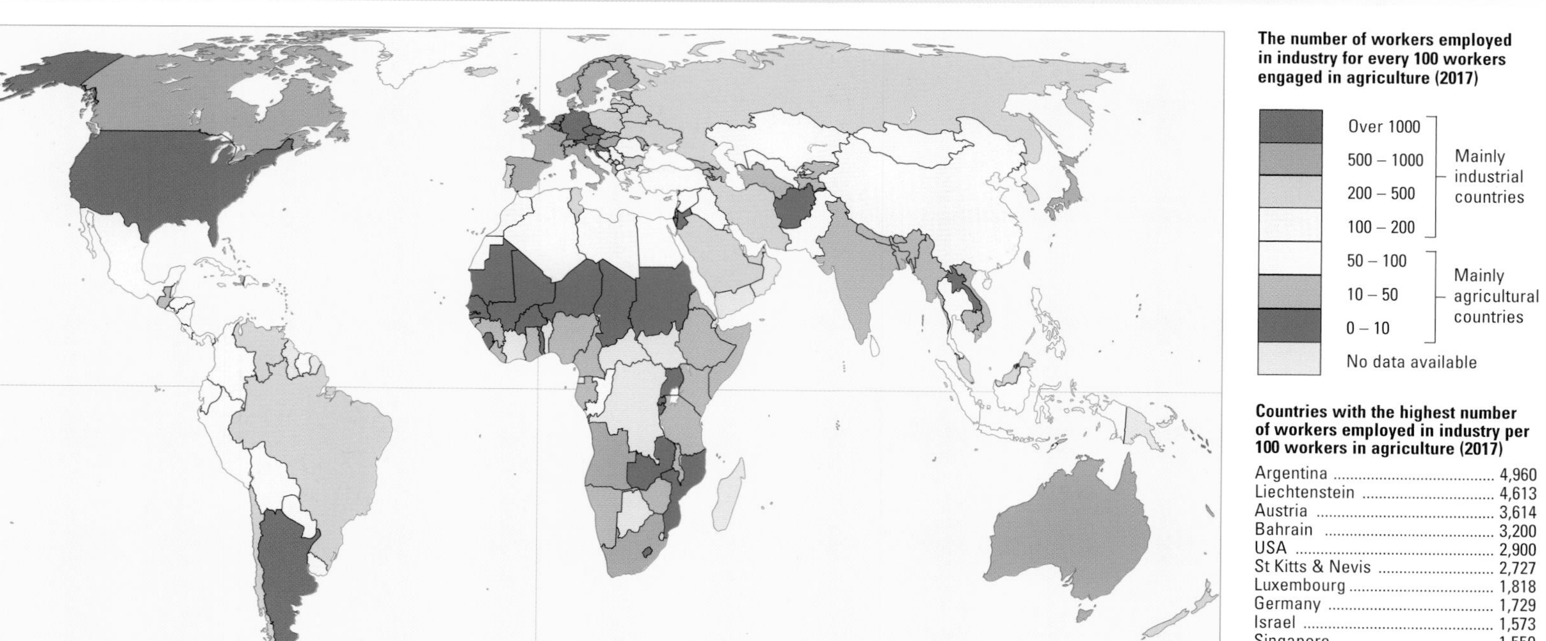

DIVISION OF EMPLOYMENT

Distribution of workers between agriculture, industry and services, selected countries

The six countries selected illustrate the usual stages of economic development, from dependence on agriculture through industrial growth to the expansion of the service sector.

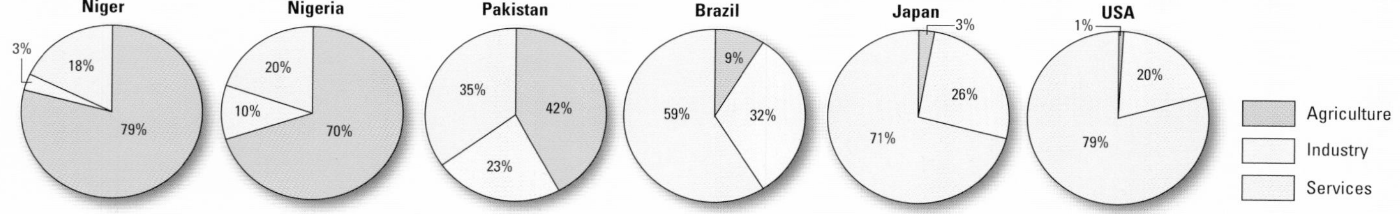

WORLD TRADE

Percentage share of total world exports by value (2019)

International trade is dominated by a handful of powerful maritime nations: the members of "G7" (Canada, France, Germany, Italy, Japan, UK and USA) and the "BRICS" nations (Brazil, Russia, India, China, and South Africa).

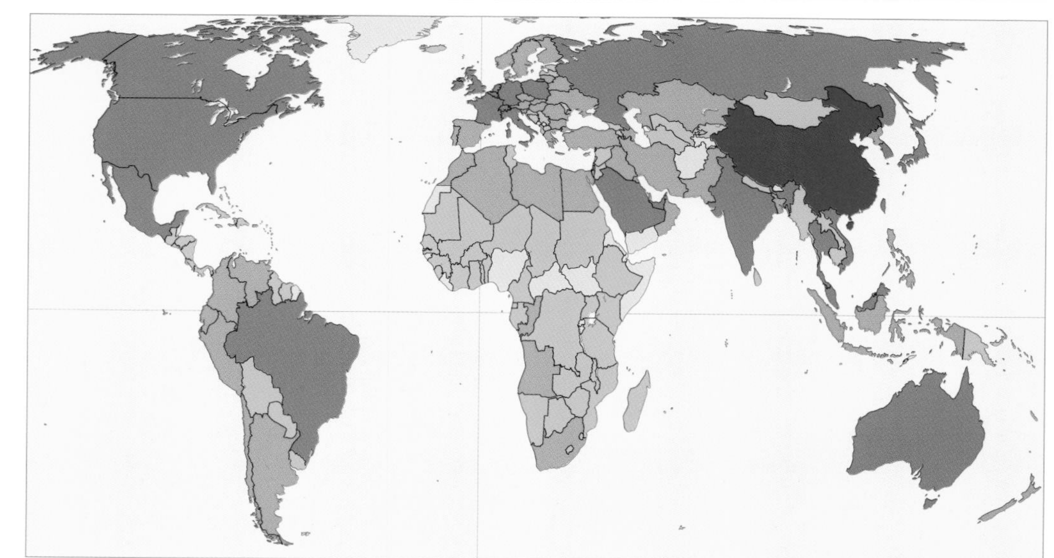

INDUSTRY AND TRADE

Manufactured goods (including machinery and transport) as a percentage of total exports (2017)

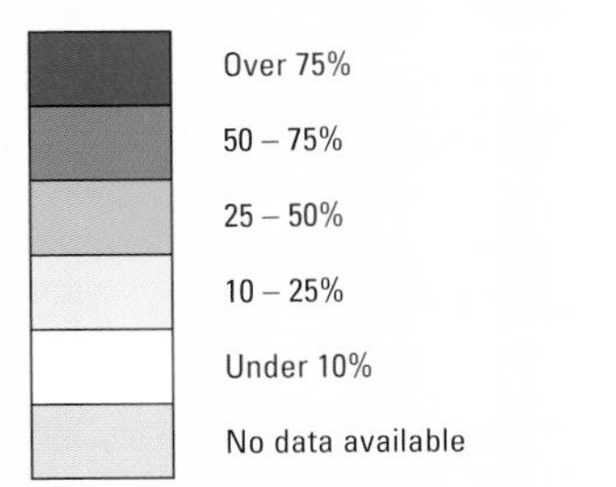

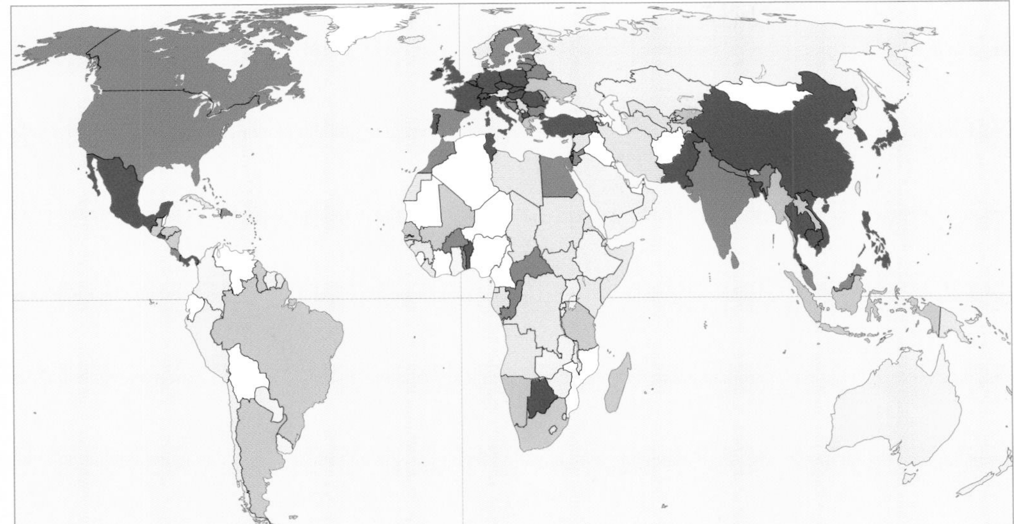

Countries most dependent on the export of manufactured goods (2017)

Bangladesh	96%
Benin	96%
Botswana	95%
China	94%
Cambodia	93%
Israel	92%

UNEMPLOYMENT

Highest rates of unemployment, percentage of the labor force (2018)

1. Zimbabwe 95%
2. Burkina Faso 77%
3. Syria 50%
4. Senegal 48%
5. Haiti 41%
6. Kenya 40%
7. Congo 36%
8. Afghanistan 35%
9. Kosovo 35%
10. Libya 34%
11. Lesotho 28%
12. Namibia 28%
13. Gabon 28%
14. Eswatini 28%
15. South Africa 28%
16. Yemen 27%
17. Venezuela 26%
18. North Korea 26%
19. North Macedonia 23%
20. Mozambique 22%

IMPORTANCE OF SERVICE SECTOR

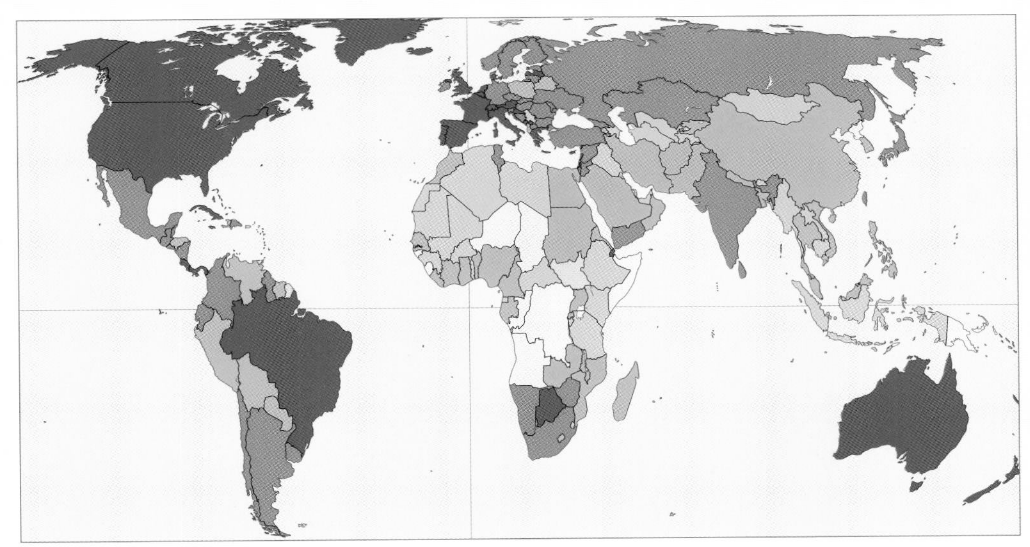

Percentage of total GDP from service sector (2018)

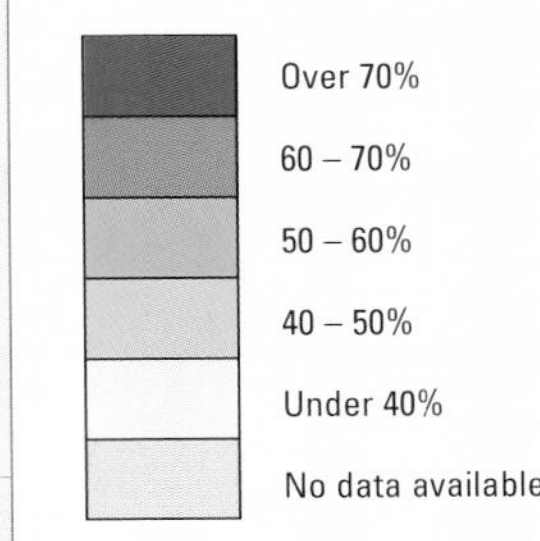

The service sector involves those parts of business such as accountancy, advertising, financial services, tourism, etc. No actual goods are produced, but high levels of income may be generated.

GLOBALIZATION

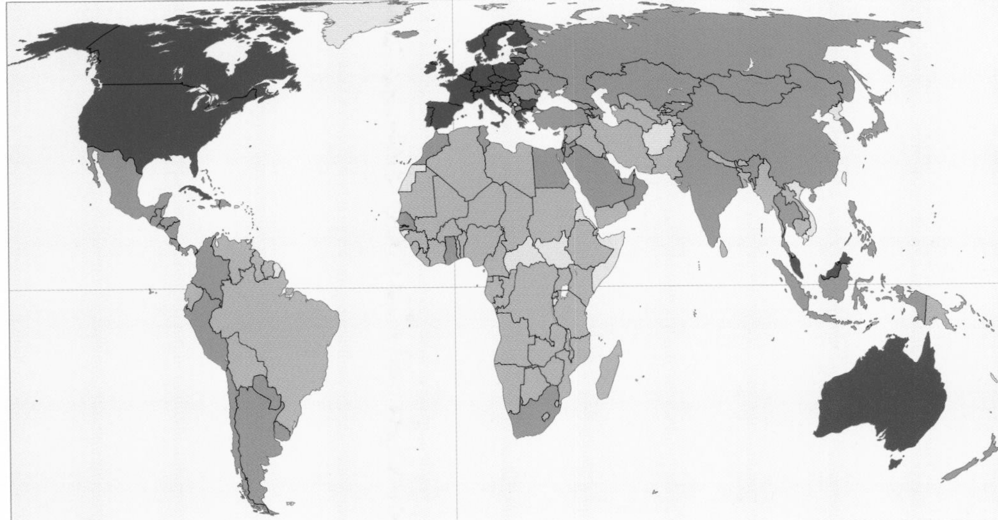

GLOBALIZATION INDEX
2018 KOF Globalization Index
(Rankings for 2016)

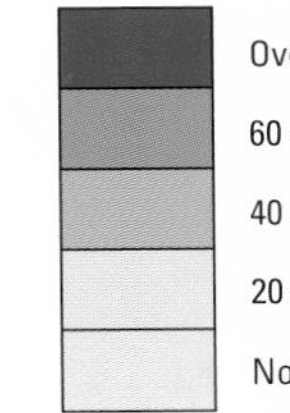

The KOF index of globalization is named after the Swiss Federal Institute of Technology in Zürich, Switzerland, which devised it. Countries are scored on each of the three criteria below:

- **economic globalization**, characterized as long-distance flows of goods, capital and services, as well as information and perceptions that accompany market exchanges (this accounts for 38% of the globalization index);
- **political globalization**, characterized by a diffusion of government policies (this accounts for 23% of the globalization index);
- **social globalization**, expressed as the spread of ideas, information, images, and people (this accounts for the remaining 39% of the globalization index).

The higher values denote a greater level of globalization.

The concept of globalization developed in the 1960s after the Canadian academic Marshall McLuhan used the term "global village" to describe the breakdown of spatial barriers around the world. He argued that the similarities between places were greater than the differences between them, and that much of the world had been caught up in the same economic and social processes. He suggested that economic activities operated at a global scale and that other scales were becoming less important.

Today, globalization is defined by the International Monetary Fund (IMF) as "the growing interdependence of countries worldwide through the increasing volume and variety of cross-border transactions in goods and services and of international capital flows, and through the more rapid and widespread diffusion of technology." Essentially, it means that all countries, with the possible exception of North Korea, are increasingly bound in a global network of migration, trade, products and services, investment, and the diffusion of ideas and culture.

Globalization has occurred as a result of many factors, such as:

- improvements in transport and ICT, leading to a "shrinking" world;
- the desire to reach new markets;
- the attempt to tap cheap sources of labor;
- the expansion of economic activity to use resources from a wide range of locations;
- the rise of free-market economies and the spread of democratic governments;
- the role of trading blocs, free trade, and the impact of the World Trade Organization;
- the importance of multinational companies.

For more information:
73 Time zones
78 Climate

Tourism and travel is one of the world's largest economic sectors in terms of revenue generated. It has the potential to create prosperity in all parts of the world. Small economies in attractive areas are often completely dominated by tourism: in some Caribbean islands, for example, tourist spending provides over 90% of the total income and is the biggest foreign-exchange earner.

In 2018, the World Trade and Tourism Council reported that this sector, directly and indirectly, provided over 319 million jobs. This equates to 1 in 10 jobs around the world and this is predicted to grow in the coming years. In terms of the economic impact, the industry contributed 10.4% to global GDP in 2018 (US$8.8 trillion).

Increasingly, attention is being paid to the development potential of tourism in less developed countries. The United Nations General Assembly declared 2017 as the International Year of Sustainable Tourism for Development. This has the aim of raising awareness of the potential for economic growth, social inclusion and the preservation of culture and the environment. It is also seen as a contributing factor towards ensuring that tourism is fundamental to the implementation of the 17 UN Sustainable Development Goals (see page 107).

Even with new initiatives, challenges lie ahead. International financial assistance remains at a modest level.

AIR TRAVEL

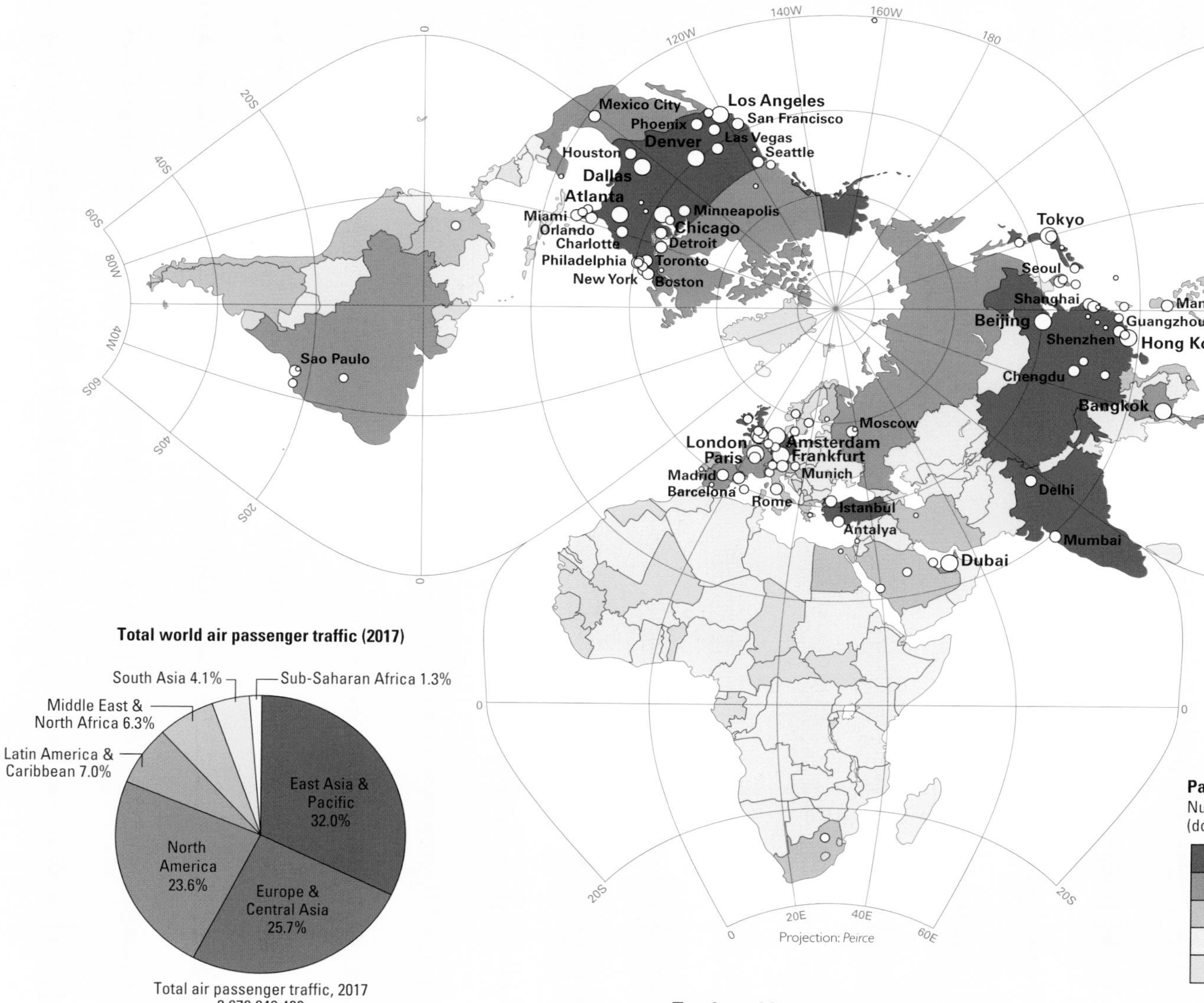

Total world air passenger traffic (2017)

South Asia 4.1%
Sub-Saharan Africa 1.3%
Middle East & North Africa 6.3%
Latin America & Caribbean 7.0%
East Asia & Pacific 32.0%
North America 23.6%
Europe & Central Asia 25.7%

Total air passenger traffic, 2017
3,978,849,400

Projection: Peirce

Passenger traffic
Number of passengers carried (domestic and international, 2017)

Over 100 million
50 – 100 million
10 – 50 million
Under 10 million
No data available

Major airports
Number of passengers (international and domestic)

Over 50 million
25 – 50 million
15 – 25 million
10 – 15 million

Air freight accounts for 35% of all international freight handled by value.

Total world passenger traffic (2017)

MAJOR AIRPORTS

WORLD'S BUSIEST AIRPORTS
Total passengers in millions (2018)

1. Atlanta Hartsfield Intl. (ATL) 107.4
2. Beijing Capital Intl. (PEK) 101.0
3. Dubai Intl. (DXB) 89.1
4. Los Angeles Intl. (LAX) 87.5
5. Tokyo Haneda (HND) 87.1
6. Chicago O'Hare Intl. (ORD) 83.3
7. London Heathrow (LHR) 80.1
8. Hong Kong Intl. (HKG) 74.5
9. Shanghai Pudong Intl. (PVG) 74.0
10. Paris Charles de Gaulle (CDG) 72.2
11. Amsterdam Schiphol (AMS) 71.1
12. Delhi Indira Gandhi Intl. (DEL) 69.9
13. Guangzhou Baiyun (CAN) 69.8
14. Frankfurt (FRA) 69.5
15. Dallas/Fort Worth (DFW) 69.1

Dubai International handles the most international passengers (88.9 million in 2018), followed by London's Heathrow (75.3 million).

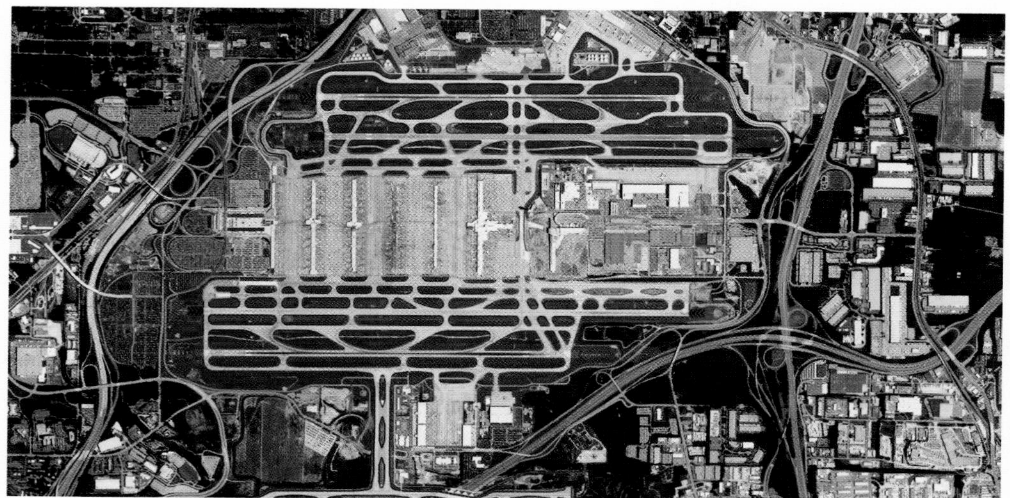

▲ Hartsfield-Jackson Atlanta International Airport, Georgia, USA, is the world's busiest airport.

IMPORTANCE OF TOURISM

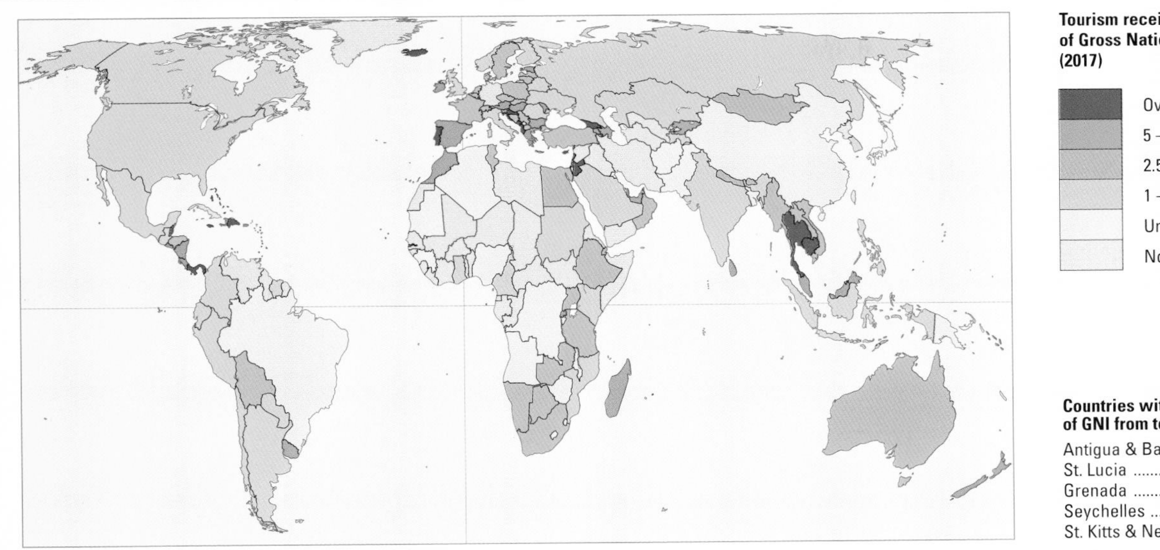

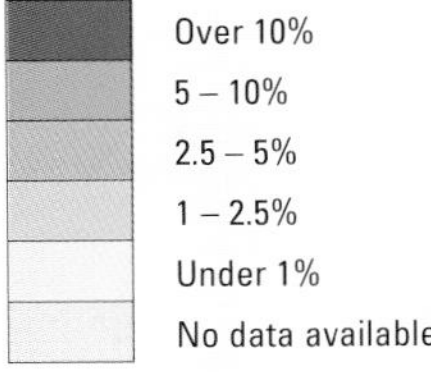

Countries with highest percentage of GNI from tourism receipts (2017)

Antigua & Barbuda	54.9%
St. Lucia	50.7%
Grenada	50.4%
Seychelles	43.1%
St. Kitts & Nevis	39.4%

TOURIST DESTINATIONS

UNESCO WORLD HERITAGE SITES 2018

Total sites = 1,092 (845 cultural, 209 natural and 38 mixed)

Region	Cultural sites	Natural sites	Mixed sites
Africa	52	38	5
Arab States	76	5	3
Asia & Pacific	181	65	23
Europe & North America	440	63	22
Latin America & Caribbean	96	38	7

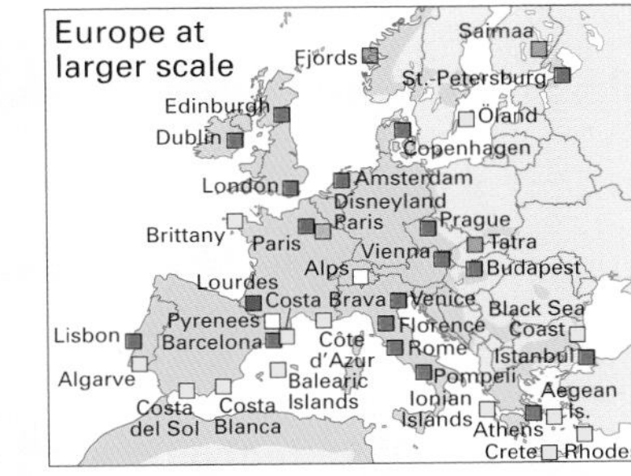

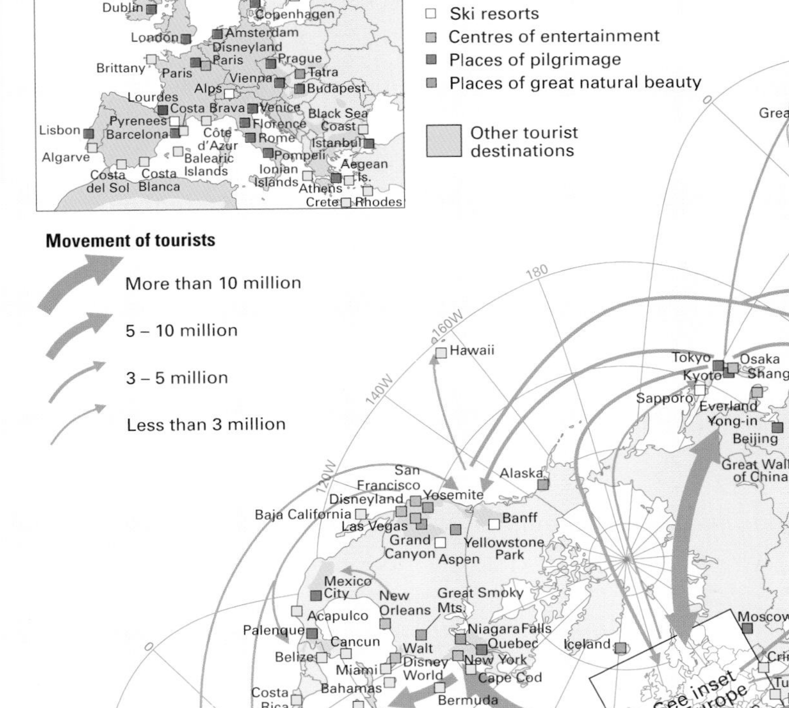

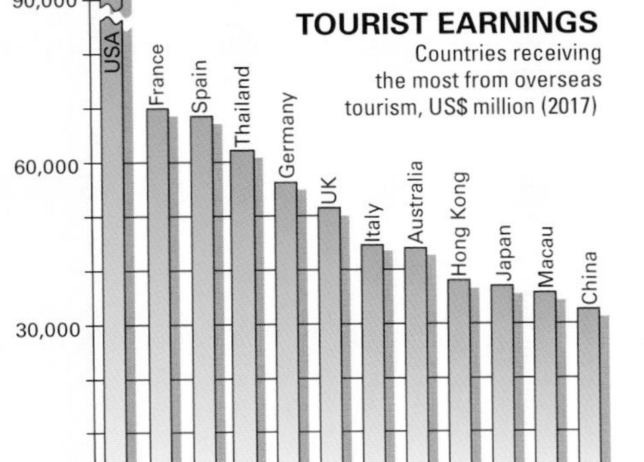

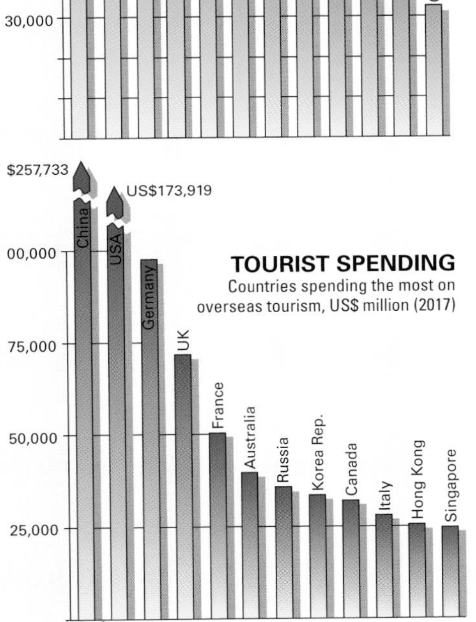

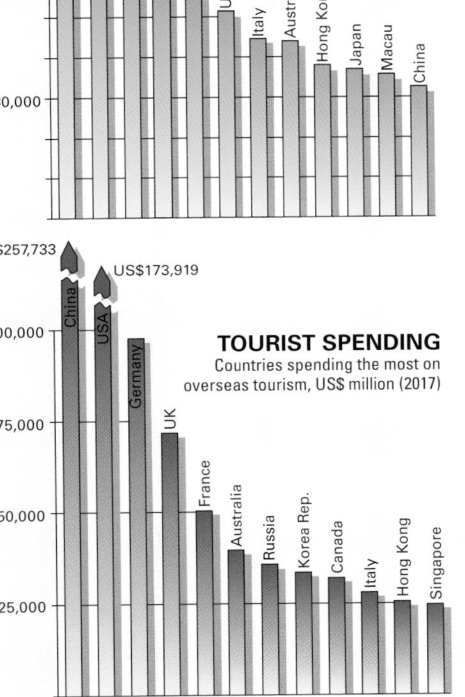

World's top tourism destinations

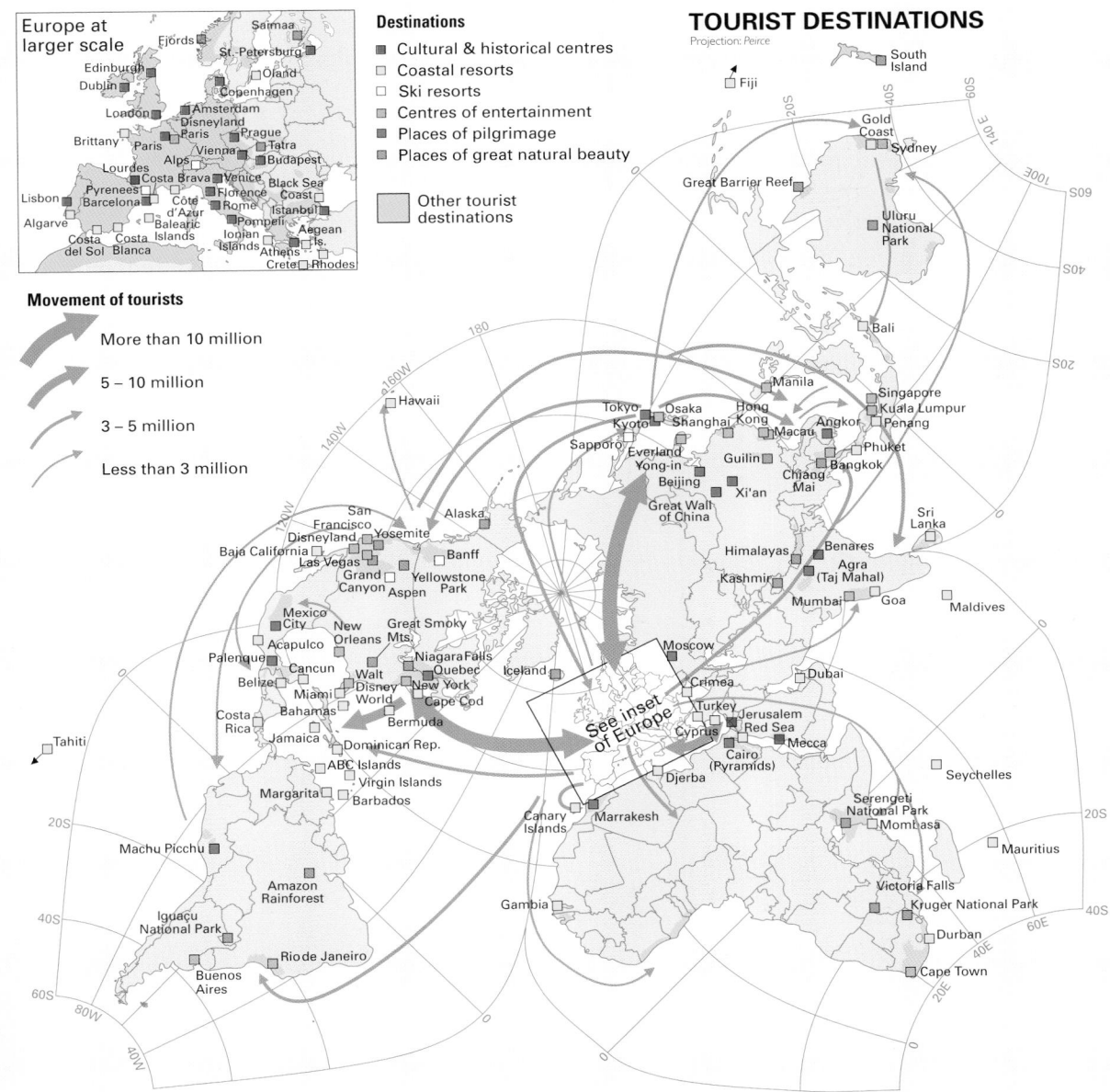

The UNWTO (United Nations World Tourism Organization) ranks countries by international tourism receipts (see top bar chart above) and international tourist arrivals (see table right). The USA continues to top the international tourism receipts ranking (210,700 million US$ in 2017) with Spain in second place. France has remained at the top of the list of main destinations for several years, with Spain rising to second place in 2017. In 2017, France recorded 87 million visitors and it is ranked third in terms of tourism earnings.

International tourist arrivals

	Country	millions (2017)
1.	France	86.9
2.	Spain	81.8
3.	United States of America	76.9
4.	China	60.7
5.	Italy	58.3
6.	Mexico	39.3
7.	United Kingdom	37.7
8.	Turkey	37.6
9.	Germany	37.5
10.	Thailand	35.4

Visitors to the USA

	Country	thousands (2017)
1.	Canada	20,200
2.	Mexico	17,800
3.	United Kingdom	4,500
4.	Japan	3,600
5.	China	3,200
6.	South Korea	2,300
7.	Germany	2,100
8.	Brazil	1,900
9.	France	1,700
10.	Australia	1,300

For more information:
82 Water distribution
91 Slum cities
Urban advantages
109 Distribution of spending

Until the late 1990s, when the full extent of the AIDS crisis emerged, average life expectancies at birth were rising almost everywhere. By 2011, they ranged from 81 years in high-income economies to 56 in sub-Saharan Africa. These figures represented an enormous advance on the situation in 1880, when citizens of Berlin had an estimated life expectancy of 30 years.

The ravages of AIDS have been greatest in southern Africa. One of the worst affected countries is Swaziland, where over 25% of the adult population were thought to be infected in 2009. Life expectancy fell from 61 years in 2000, to 32 years in 2009, but recovered to 52 years in 2016. In much of the world, average life expectancies are still increasing. The rises are attributed to improvements in agriculture and, hence, nutrition, as well as health education, improved sanitation and the quality of drinking water, together with advances in medicine.

Besides AIDS, the people of the developing world are subject to another affliction – malnutrition. The map below shows that in most of Africa, Asia, and Latin America, the average daily calorie supply per person is so low as to cause malnutrition. Malnutrition is a serious condition – among pregnant women it causes high rates of child mortality.

Deficiency diseases occur when people do not have a balanced diet. Protein deficiency causes stunting and kwashiorkor, which can be fatal, especially among young children, while vitamin deficiencies cause such illnesses as beri beri, pellagra, scurvy, and rickets. Iron deficiency causes anemia, while a lack of iodine causes mental retardation.

Infectious diseases, in association with deficient diets, continue to affect people in developing countries. Around the turn of the century, a WHO report stated that infectious diseases cause over 16 million deaths a year. Most of the victims are young and otherwise fit people in developing countries. The major killers are AIDS, cholera, dysentery, malaria, measles, pneumonia, respiratory infections, tuberculosis, and typhoid.

Infectious diseases are much less important as causes of death in developed countries, where cancer and circulatory diseases, such as atherosclerosis and hypertension, which cause strokes and heart attacks, are the most common causes of fatality. Because these diseases tend to kill older people, they are relatively less important in the developing countries where people have shorter lifespans.

Harmful habits are also generally practiced more by the rich than the poor. For example, smoking is an important cause of death in developed countries, while poor diet and high alcohol consumption can badly affect health.

▲ Almost 10% of the world's population does not have access to safe water (the diagram at the bottom left-hand corner of page 105 shows how this breaks down by region). This places a huge strain on the millions of mainly women and children who have to walk, collect, and carry drinkable water in order to survive. UNICEF is dedicated to help improve this situation and to react swiftly in the case of emergencies such as civil war, as with the case of this man in Liberia.

MALNUTRITION

Prevalence of undernourishment as a percentage of the population (2016)

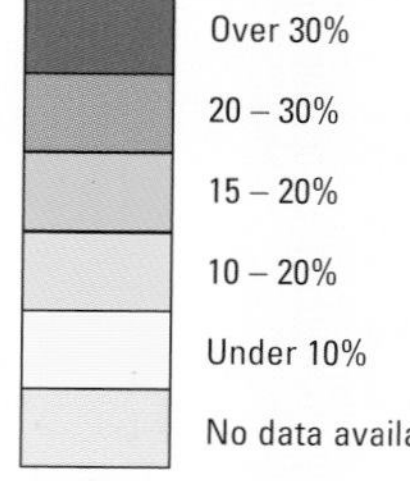

This map highlights the countries where, for a large part of the population, the food intake is insufficient to meet dietary energy requirements.

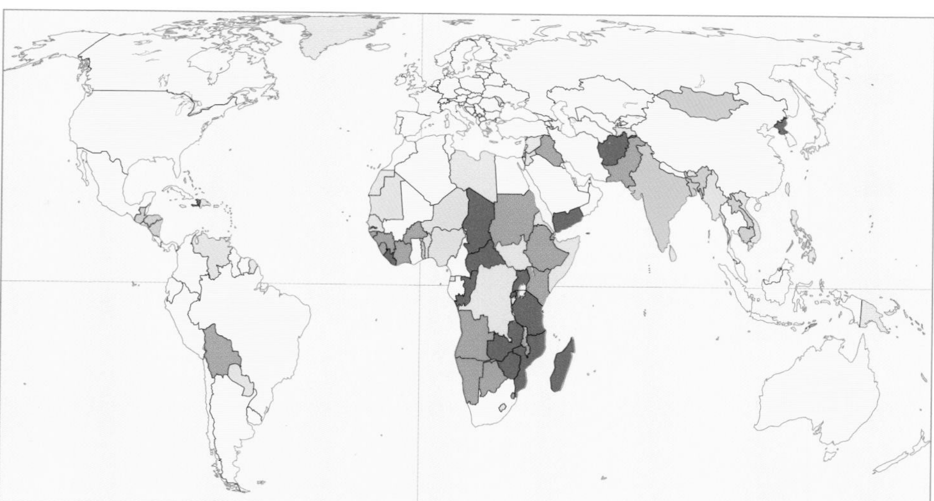

MATERNAL MORTALITY RATE

The number of mothers who died during pregnancy or childbirth per 100,000 live births

Countries with highest maternal mortality rate	
Sierra Leone	1,360
Central African Republic	882
Chad	856
Nigeria	814
South Sudan	789
Somalia	732
Liberia	725
Burundi	712
Gambia	706
Congo, Dem. Rep.	693

The maternal mortality rate is the annual number of female deaths per 100,000 live births from any cause related to or aggravated by pregnancy or its management (excluding accidental or incidental causes).

LEVEL OF OBESITY

Percentage of total adult population considered to be obese (2016)*

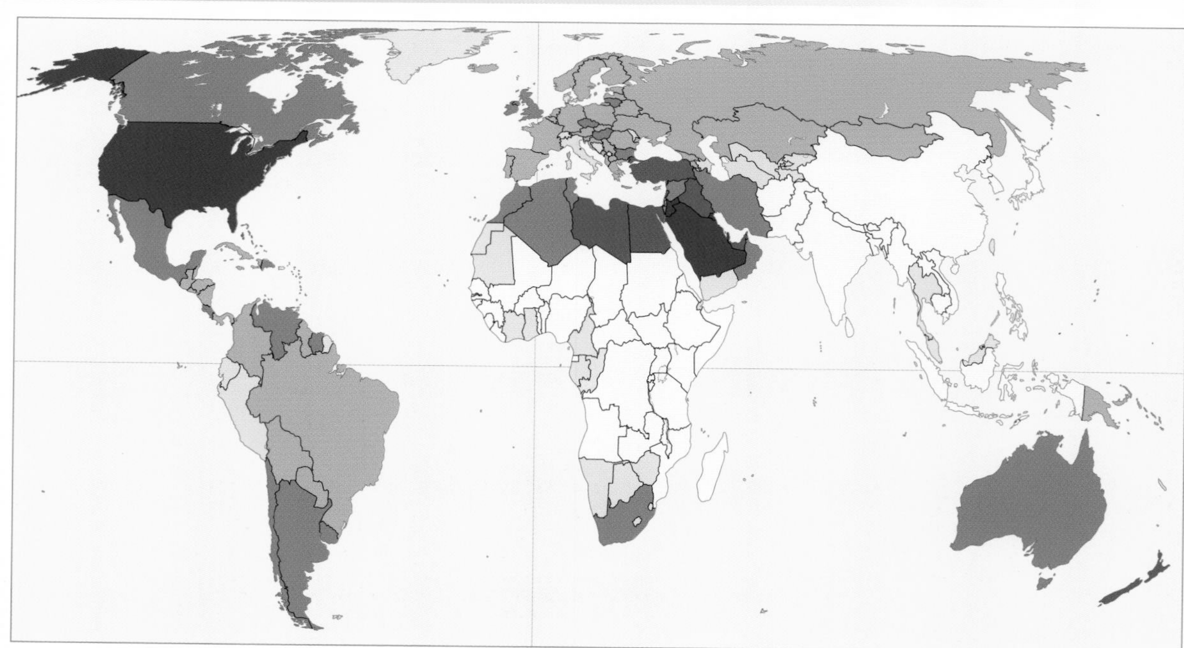

*Obesity is defined as an adult having a Body Mass Index (BMI) greater than 30.0

INFANT MORTALITY

Number of babies who died under the age of one, per 1,000 live births (2018)

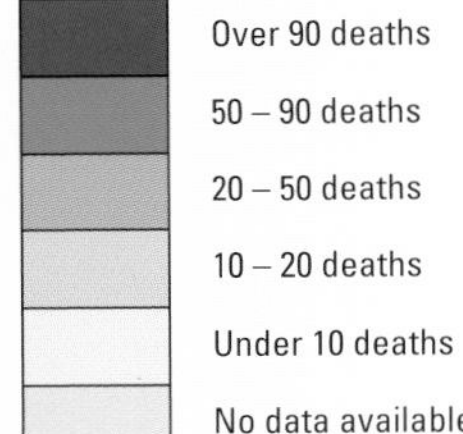

Highest infant mortality

Afghanistan	108.5 deaths
Somalia	93.0 deaths
South Sudan	90.4 deaths

Lowest infant mortality

Slovenia	1.6 deaths
Monaco	1.8 deaths
Japan	2.0 deaths

THE AIDS CRISIS

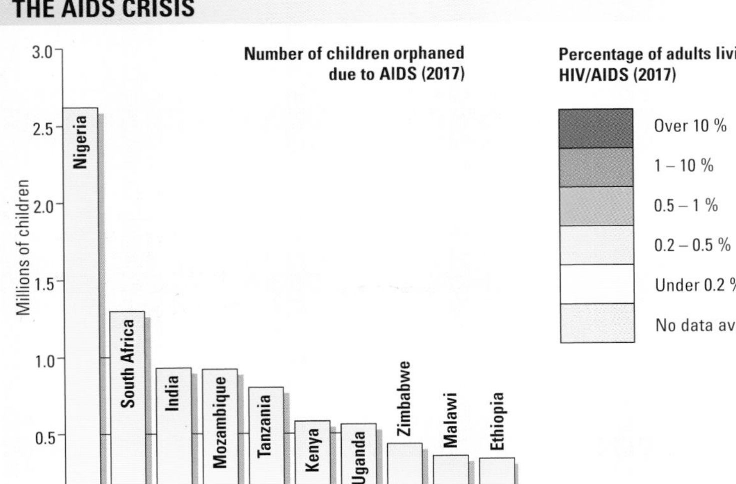

Percentage of adults living with HIV/AIDS (2017)

Over 10 %
1 – 10 %
0.5 – 1 %
0.2 – 0.5 %
Under 0.2 %
No data available

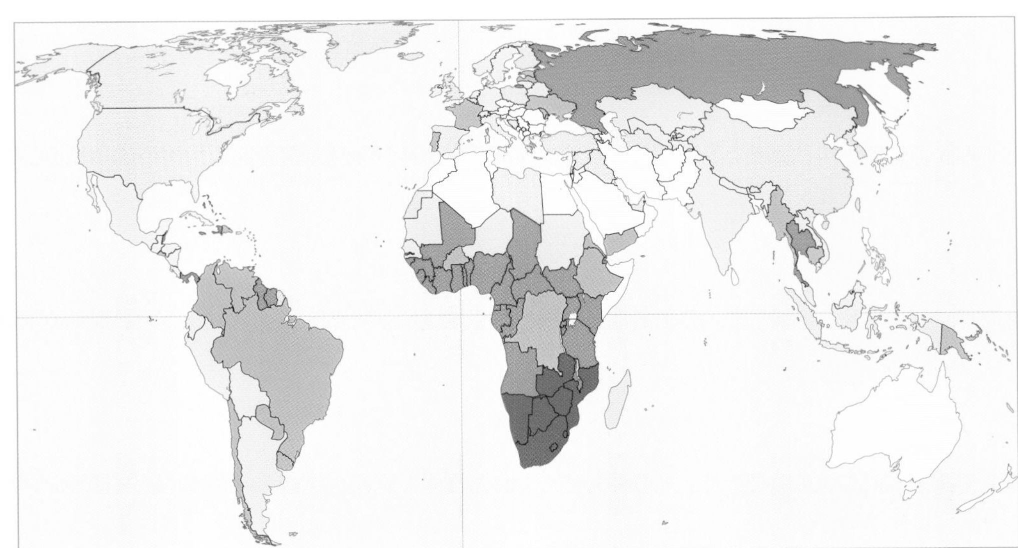

EXPENDITURE ON HEALTH

Public health expenditure per capita, in US $ PPP

Countries with the highest spending		Countries with the lowest spending	
Luxembourg	$5,356	Myanmar	$6
Monaco	$5,337	Eritrea	$8
Norway	$5,080	Afghanistan	$10
Netherlands	$4,298	Congo (Democratic Republic)	$12
United States	$4,126	South Sudan	$13
Denmark	$4,037	Central African Republic	$16
Austria	$3,826	Niger	$18
Switzerland	$3,739	Haiti	$19
Germany	$3,522	Ethiopia	$21
Sweden	$3,397	Bangladesh	$23

The allocation of limited funds for health care in developing countries is rarely evenly spread – for example, the quality of treatment can vary enormously from place to place within the same country. Urban dwellers tend to have much better access to health provisions than those living in rural areas.

CAUSES OF DEATH

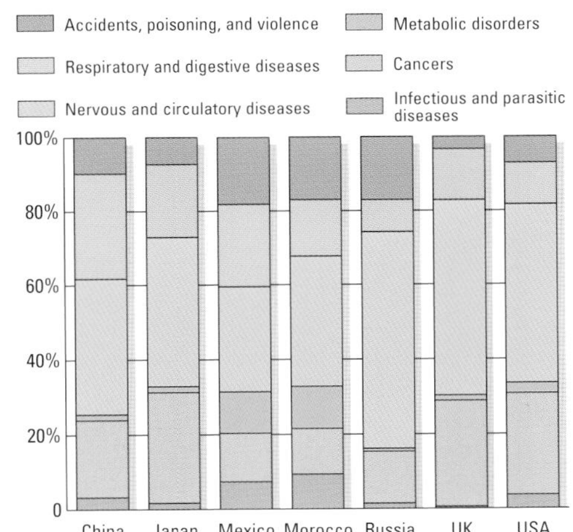

MEDICAL PROVISION

Doctors per 100,000 population, selected countries

Although the ratio of people to doctors gives a good approximation of a country's health provision, it is not an absolute indicator. Raw numbers may mask inefficiency and other weaknesses. The definition of a doctor also varies from nation to nation.

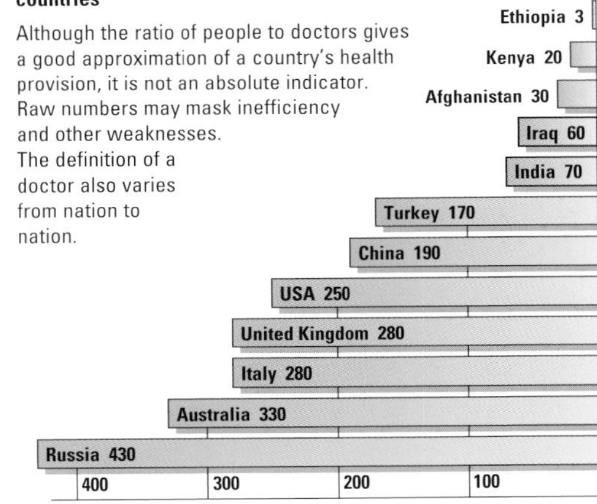

ACCESS TO SAFE WATER

Percentage of urban and rural population with access to safe water, by region

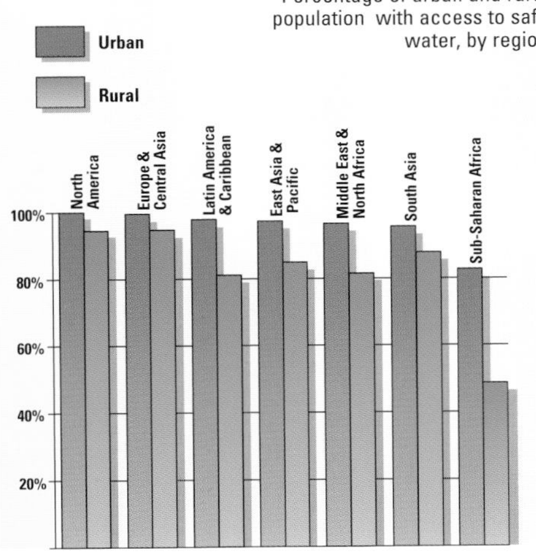

SANITATION

Percentage of population with access to sanitation services, selected countries

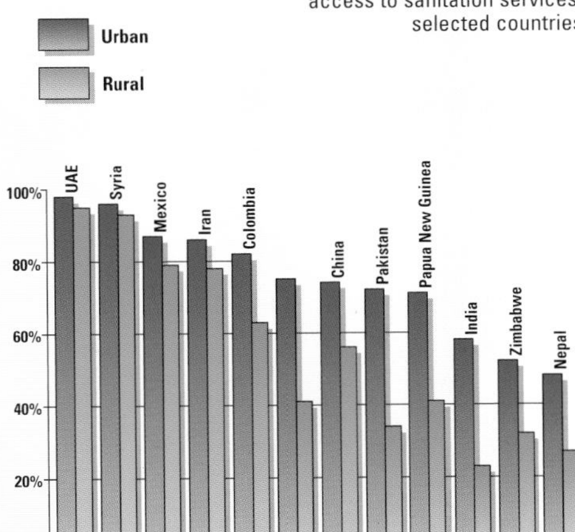

MALARIA

Cases of malaria per 100,000 people exposed to malaria-infected environments

40,000
30,000
20,000
10,000
Malawi
Uganda
Gambia
Burkina Faso
Zambia
Liberia
Burundi
Kenya
Papua New Guinea
Mozambique
Solomon Islands

For more information:
100 Industrial output
100 World trade
109 Distribution of spending

Perhaps the most glaring differences in the world today are those between the rich and the poor. The World Bank divides countries into three main groups based on average economic production expressed in terms of per capita GNI (Gross National Income). They are the low-income economies (most African countries and much of Asia), the middle-income economies (most of Latin America and most of the former USSR), and the high-income economies of Canada, the United States, Western Europe, Japan, and Australia.

Per capita GNIs are a measure of the total goods and services produced by a country divided by the population, and then converted into US dollars at official exchange rates. They are useful indicators of a country's prosperity, though, like all statistics, they must be treated with care. For example, the prices for goods and services in China are far cheaper than they are in the United States. China's per capita GNI in 2017 was $8,690 (as compared with $58,270 in the US), but the PPP (Purchasing Power Parity, which adjusts the figure for cost-of-living differences) estimate of China's per capita GNI was considerably higher at $16,800. Another problem with per capita GNIs is that they are averages, which often conceal wide internal variations.

The pattern of poverty varies from region to region. In Latin America, much progress has been made through industrialization, though startling inequalities still exist between rich and poor. China and other countries in eastern Asia, including South Korea and Taiwan, have followed Japan's example in pursuing export-led industrial policies. The success of China's Special Economic Zones, where foreign investment is encouraged, has led to a huge rise in China's per capita GNI.

In contrast to the dynamism of Asia, Africa lags behind as an impoverished continent. Corrupt governments, wasteful expenditures, civil wars, natural disasters, faulty national and international policy environments, high population growth, and the failure to break away from the neocolonial trading patterns – all these contribute to keeping the majority of Africans impoverished. An initiative in some African countries has been to improve the infrastructure and develop tourism, creating employment and providing much-needed foreign currency. But the social and environmental cost of mass tourism needs to be taken seriously too.

The International Monetary Fund and the World Bank argue that real economic progress in Africa will be achieved only when African countries create market-friendly economies that encourage trade through export-led manufacturing, while at the same time strictly controlling public spending.

CONTINENTAL SHARES

Shares of population and of wealth (GNI) by continent

These generalized continental figures show the startling difference between rich and poor, but mask the successes or failures of individual countries. Japan, for example, with just over 3% of Asia's population, produces almost 19% of the continent's output. Within countries, the difference between rich and poor can also be startling. In Brazil, for example, the richest 20% of the population own 60% of the wealth.

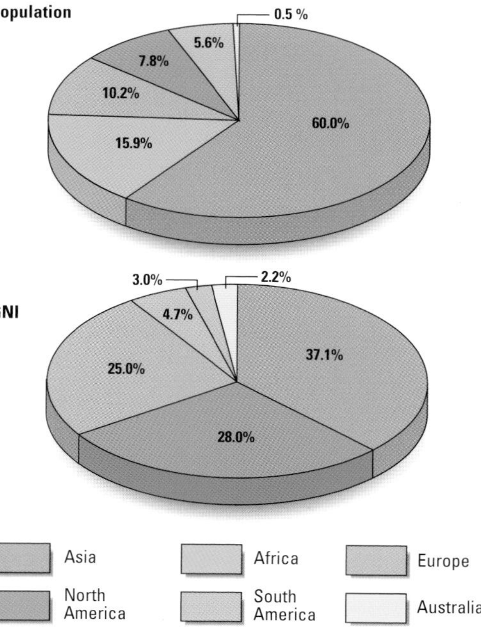

LEVELS OF INCOME

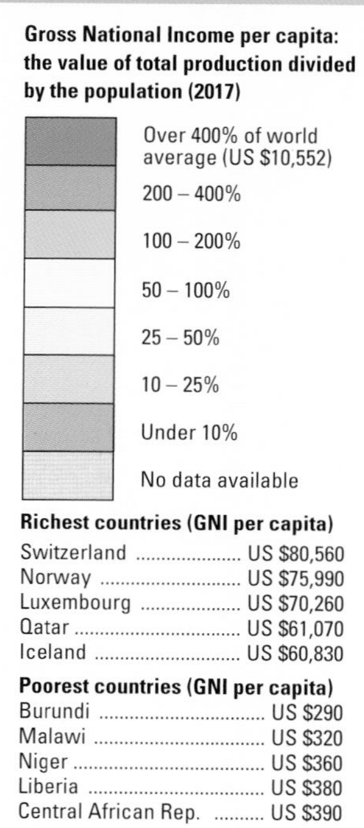

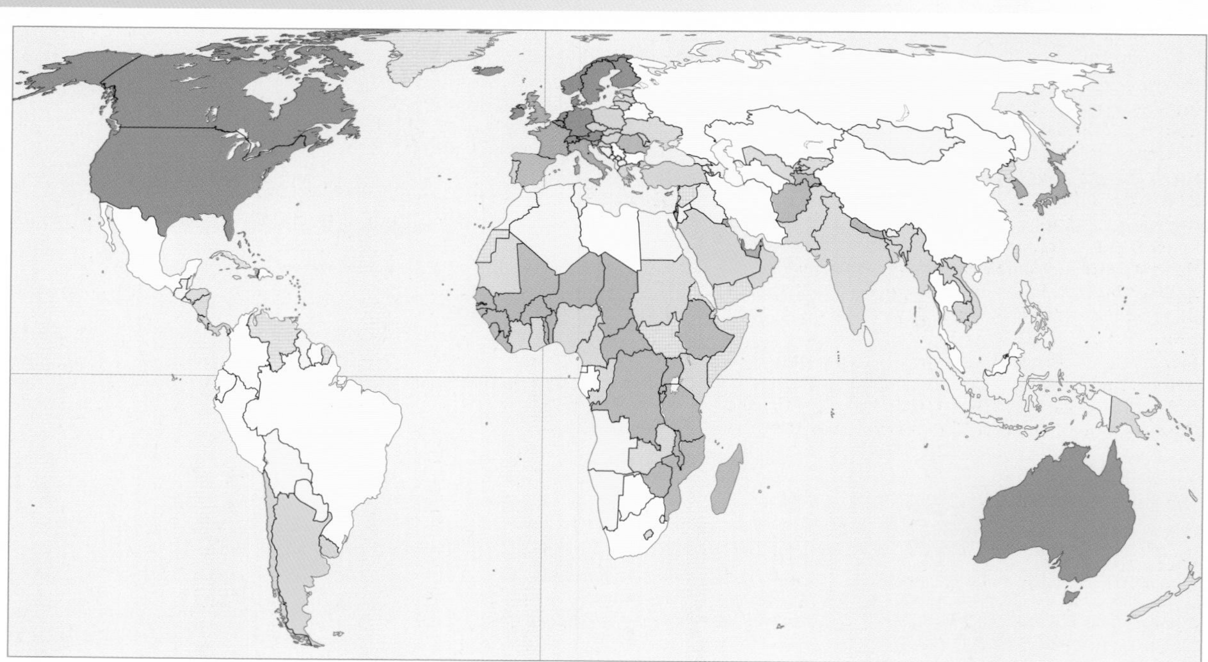

INDICATORS

The gap between the world's rich and poor is now so great that it is difficult to illustrate on a single graph. Within each income group (as defined by the World Bank), however, comparisons have some meaning. The wealth gap in many developing countries, though, is wide, with a small, rich class and a large, impoverished majority, while many high-income countries contain an underclass of unemployed and homeless people.

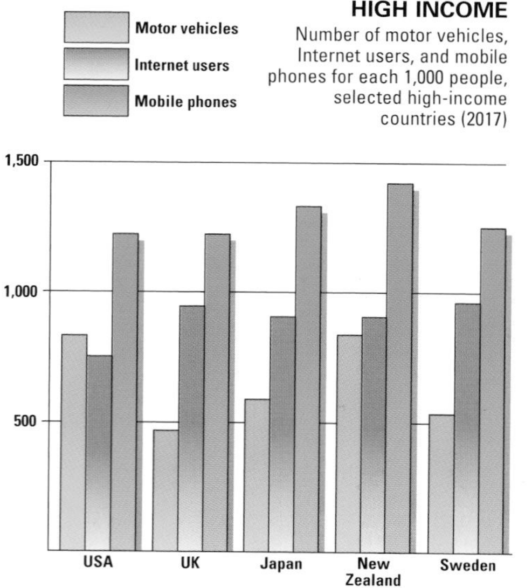

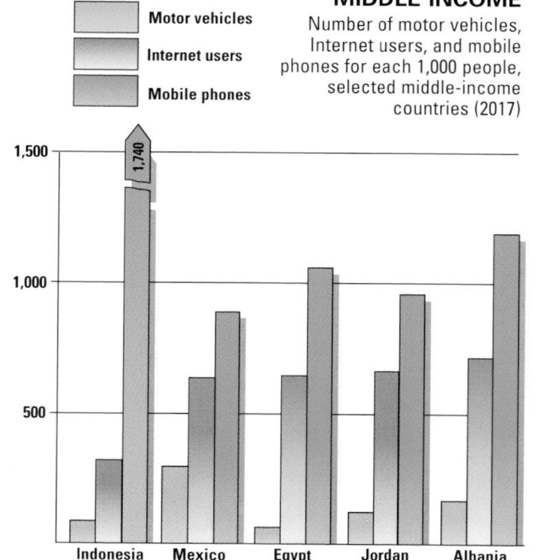

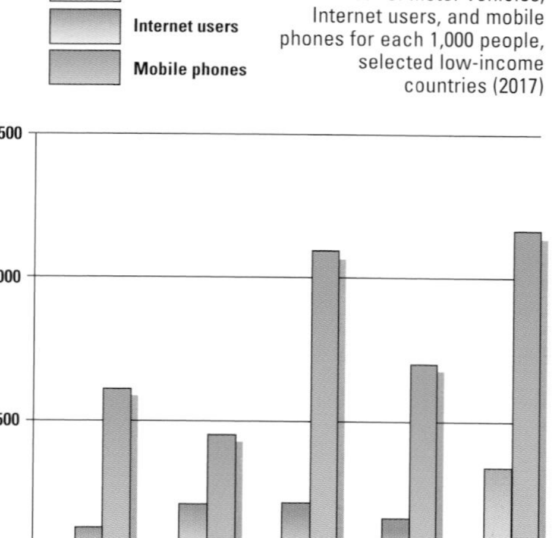

STATE FINANCE

Inflation rates (*shown on the map, right*) are an indication of a country's financial stability and, usually, of its prosperity. Annual inflation rates above 20% are usually marked by slow or even negative growth of the GNI. Above 50%, it becomes hyperinflation and an economy is left reeling.

In the late 1980s and early 1990s, many high-income countries had to contend with annual inflation rates of 10% or more, while Japan, the growth leader, had an average inflation rate of just 1.3% between 1985 and 1994.

Market-friendly policies, including low taxes and state spending, liberal trade policies, and a warm welcome for foreign investors, are major factors in countries that have enjoyed rapid economic growth in the decades since 1980. For example, the setting-up of Special Economic Zones in eastern China has led to a spectacular rise in that country's per capita GNI. However, an effective government remains a crucial factor in economic growth in most countries.

Other successful countries include South Korea and Singapore, although an Asian market crash in 1997 temporarily halted the dramatic economic expansion of these countries.

INFLATION

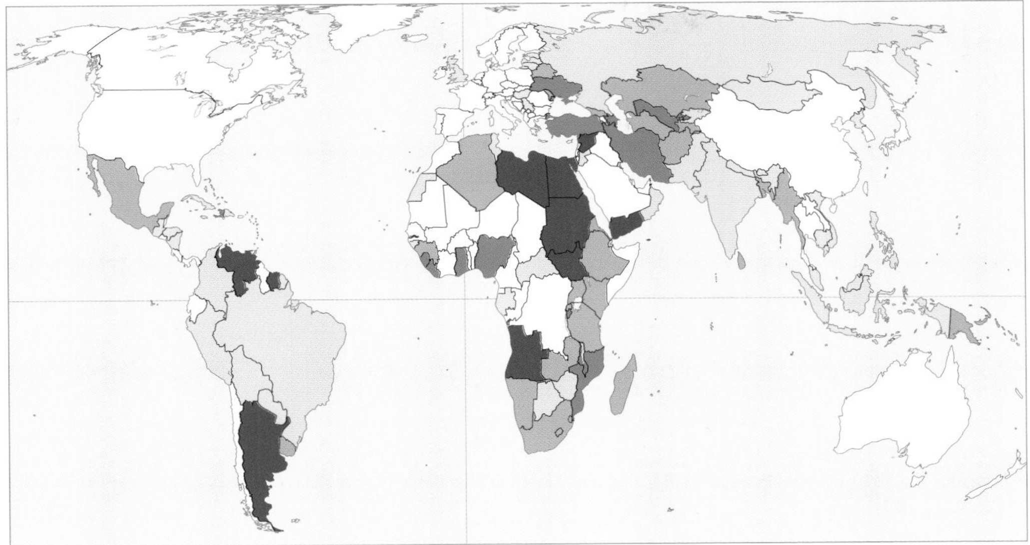

Average annual rate of inflation (2017)

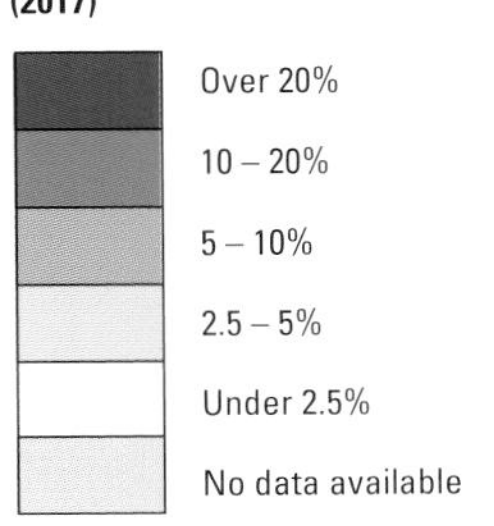

Highest average inflation

Venezuela	652%
South Sudan	182%
Libya	33%

Lowest average inflation

Andorra	-0.9%
Solomon Islands	-0.5%
Liechtenstein	-0.4%

UNITED NATIONS SUSTAINABLE DEVELOPMENT GOALS

In 2000, the United Nations set out 8 Millennium Development Goals (MDGs) that were to be achieved by 2015. The goals were:

1. To eradicate extreme poverty and hunger.
2. To achieve universal primary education.
3. To promote gender equality and empower women.
4. To reduce child mortality.
5. To improve maternal health.
6. To combat HIV/AIDS, malaria, and other diseases.
7. To ensure environmental sustainability.
8. To develop a global partnership for development.

Progress towards achieving these goals has been uneven: some countries achieved many of the goals, whereas others achieved few, if any. However, some targets have been met such as the MDG for poverty reduction. According to the 2015 MDG Report, the poverty rates and the number of people living in extreme poverty fell in every developing region – including in Sub-Saharan Africa, where rates were highest. In the developing regions, the proportion of people living on less than $1.25 a day fell from 47% in 1990 to 14% in 2015. In 2015, about 900 million fewer people than in 1990 lived in conditions of extreme poverty.

To follow on from the MDG, the Sustainable Development Goals (SDGs) were adopted by all the world's governments at the United Nations in September 2015. The aim is that they will guide global development for the 15 years until 2030. There are 17 goals - as illustrated by the official United Nations icons below. Although the SDGs are not legally binding, governments are expected to establish national frameworks in order to achieve them.

The ultimate aim is to go further than the MDGs and end all forms of poverty. It has been recognized that defeating poverty has to be coupled with strategies to encourage economic growth, and to address a range of social needs including education, health, social protection, and job opportunites, while tackling climate change and protecting the environment.

Progress will be monitored by using a set of global indicators, and annual reports will be published. There is, of course, a cost to achieving these goals. The more developed countries will have to provide development assistance to help the countries most in need.

It is acknowledged that climate change has affected public health, food and water security, migration, peace, and security. Collective action will have to be taken to mitigate the worst effects of climate change. Goal 13 (Climate Action) reflects the importance of this issue, and the hope is that it will be possible to limit the increases in global mean temperature to no more than 3.6°F [2.0°C] above pre-industrial levels.

▲ To mark the 70th anniversary of the United Nations, and ahead of the United Nations Sustainable Development Summit in September 2015, massive projections of the icons for the 17 goals are seen on the façade of the General Assembly building in New York, United States. The aim was to raise awareness of the 2030 Agenda for Sustainable Development.

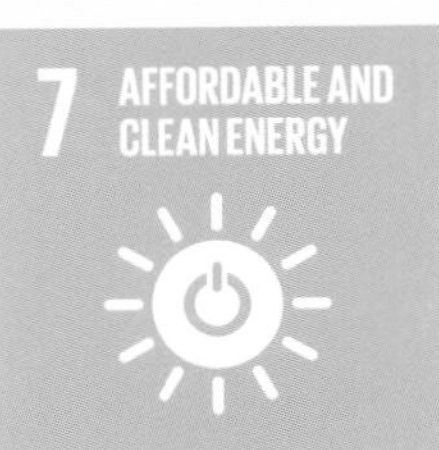

12 RESPONSIBLE CONSUMPTION AND PRODUCTION

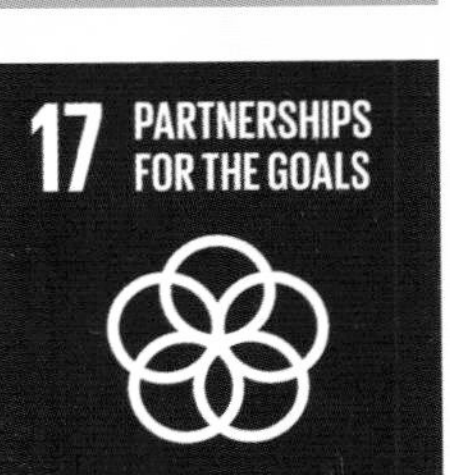

Philip's supports the Sustainable Development Goals

For more information:
82 Water supply
88 Population density
90 Urban population
91 Urban advantages
92 World's refugees
100 Employment
The work force
105 Infant mortality
106 Wealth

Wealth is a basic factor in determining standards of living. Everywhere, the rich have more of everything, including higher average life expectancies, while the poor have to spend most of their income on basic human needs, such as food and clothing. Yet poverty and wealth are relative terms: slum dwellers living on social security in an industrial society feel their poverty acutely, but have far more resources than an average African living in a rural area.

In 1990 the United Nations Development Program published its first Human Development Index (HDI), an attempt to construct a comparative scale by which a simplified form of well-being might be measured. The HDI, expressed as a value between 0 and 0.999, combines figures for life expectancy and literacy with a wealth scale, based on Purchasing Power Parity.

The world's countries are divided into three groups: those with a high HDI (0.8 and above); those with a medium HDI (0.5 to 0.799); and those with a low HDI (below 0.5). In 2018, Norway and Australia were top in the world rankings and Niger was bottom. In fact, 34 of the 41 countries with a low HDI were from Africa. Besides having low per capita GNIs, the average life expectancy in these countries was 59 years, while the adult literacy rate was 36%. By comparison, the average life expectancy at birth in countries in the high HDI group was 79 years, while the literacy rate was 94%.

Comparisons between countries with similar per capita GNIs reveal the effects of government actions. For example, the World Bank classifies both India and China as low-income economies, but India's HDI at 0.640 is much lower than that of China, at 0.752. This reflects not only China's economic progress in the 1980s and 1990s, but also differences in average life expectancies (69 years in India and 76 years in China), and adult literacy rates (71% in India and 96% in China).

Disparities in standards of living exist not only between countries but also between individuals, groups, and regions within countries. For example, income distribution figures show that, in the United States, the poorest 10% of households receive less than 2% of the income.

Other contrasts exist in developing countries between rural communities, where incomes are low and basic services are often in short supply, and urban areas, where even those living in slums are generally better off than their rural neighbors. Other striking differences exist between men and women. For example, while adult literacy rates for men and women living in developed countries are more or less the same, large differences exist in many developing countries. In countries in the lowest HDI category, only 36% of women were literate, as compared with 58% of men.

Female education is a factor in population control, especially as women's fertility rates appear to fall in direct proportion to the amount of secondary education they receive. This point was acknowledged in 2004 by the UN Population Fund, which defined four main objectives relating to women and population control: the reduction of maternal, infant, and child mortality; better education, especially for girls; universal access to reproductive health services; and gender equality.

Statistical analysis presents many problems of interpretation, especially when trying to define such intangible factors as a sense of well-being. For example, education helps create wealth; but are rich countries wealthy because their people are well educated, or are they well educated because they are rich?

HUMAN DEVELOPMENT INDEX

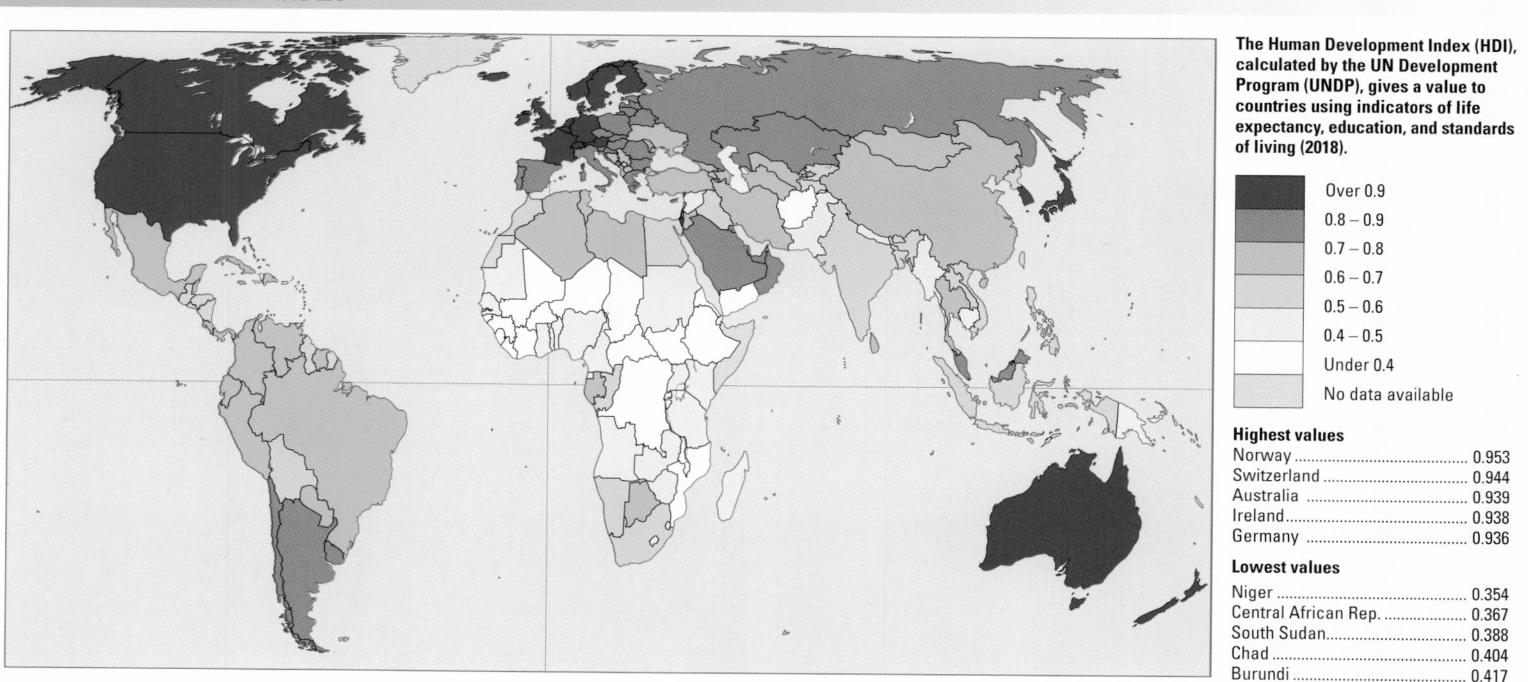

EDUCATION

The developing countries made great efforts in the 1970s and 1980s to bring at least a basic education to their people. In all but the poorest nations, primary school enrolments rose above 60%. However, figures often include teenagers or young adults, and there are still 300 million children worldwide who receive no schooling at all. A lack of resources has restricted the development of secondary and higher education. Most primary school education is free in the poorer countries, but fees are often paid for secondary and higher education, thus heightening the differences between rich and poor.

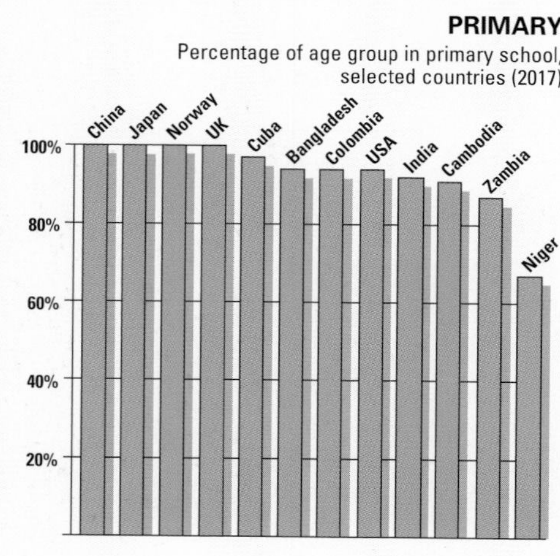

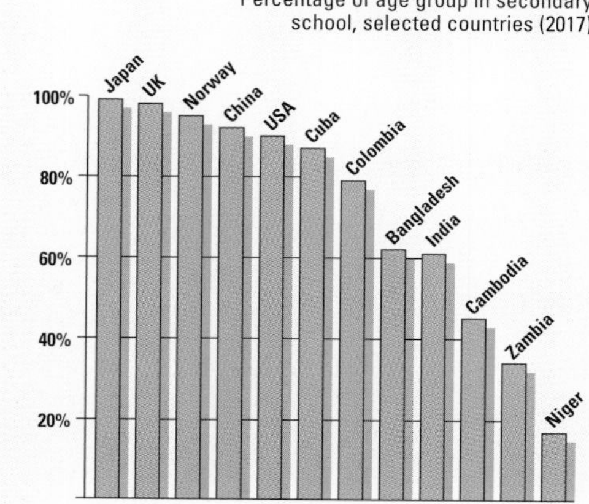

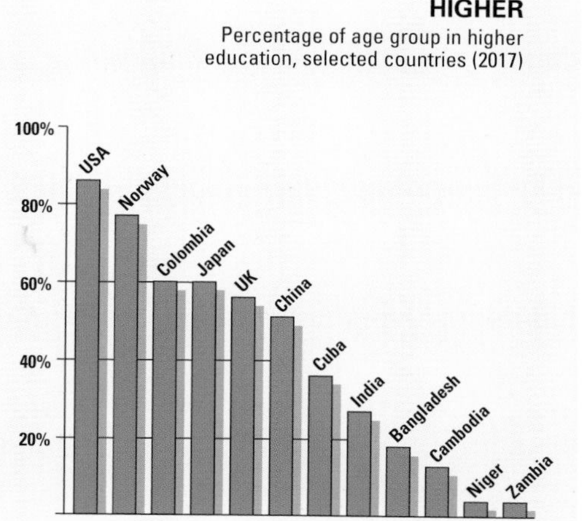

DISTRIBUTION OF SPENDING

Percentage share of household spending

A high proportion of the average income of households in developing nations is spent on basic needs such as food and clothing. In most Western countries food and clothing account for less than 25% of expenditure.

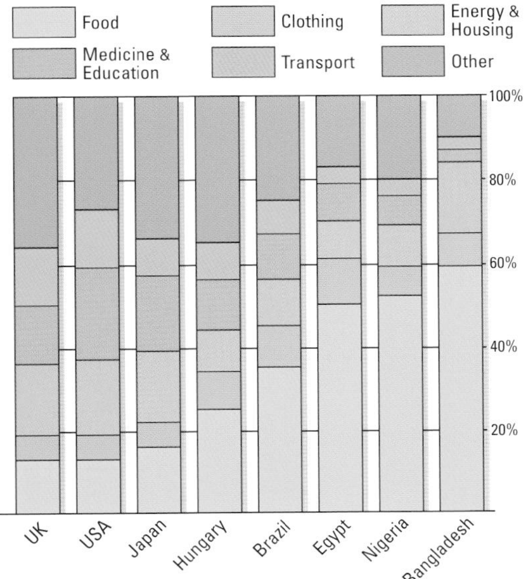

▲ These two images illustrate the reality of suburban life for people at either end of the economic scale. At the top is part of a huge area of "tract housing" in California, where large houses of a similar design are laid out by a developer, complete with gardens, drives, and swimming pools. Below, is a much more haphazard arrangement of home-built, rudimentary shelters, many without sanitation and most with no electricity, in Crossroads Township, outside Cape Town in South Africa.

FERTILITY AND EDUCATION

Fertility rates compared with female education, selected countries

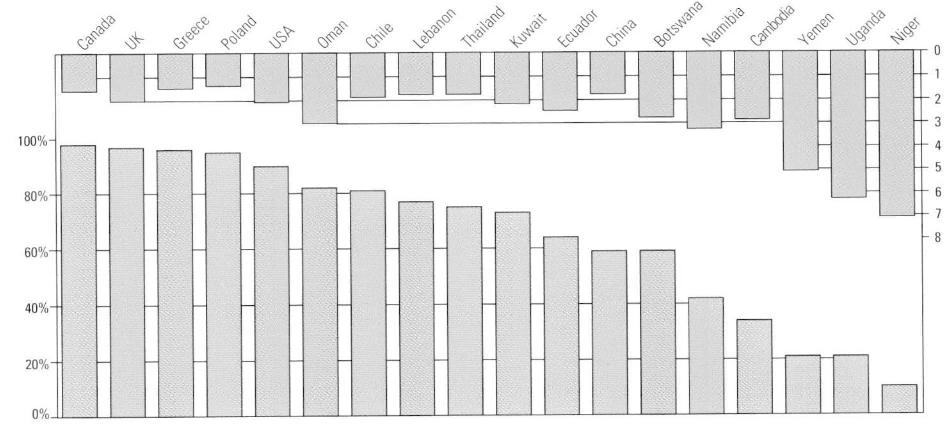

There seems to be a strong link between access to secondary education and the fertility rate. In developed countries, young girls have a high access to education and a low fertility rate. In contrast, in many developing countries women have a high fertility rate but lack access to education. This can be for a complex mix of social, economic, and cultural reasons. Despite a few high-profile examples of female politicians in different parts of the world, all evidence points to the continuing marginalization of women from the political and economic processes of decision-making. Female wages are, on average, only two-thirds of those of men.

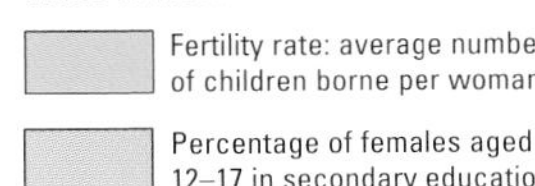

GENDER INEQUALITY INDEX

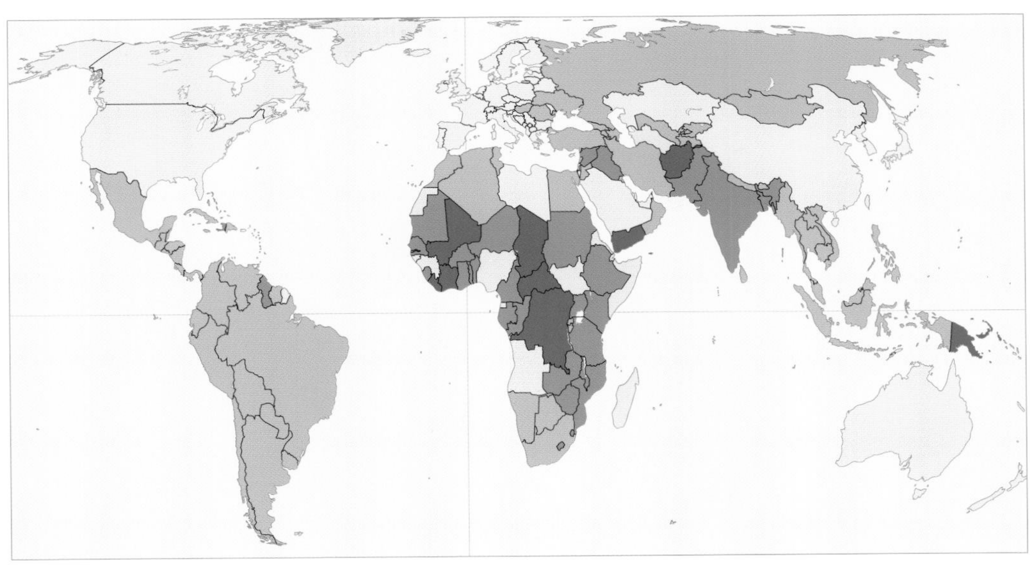

The Gender Inequality Index is a composite measure reflecting inequality in achievements between women and men in three categories: reproductive health, empowerment, and the labor market. It varies between 0, when women and men fare equally, and 1, when women or men fare poorly compared to the other in all categories (2017).

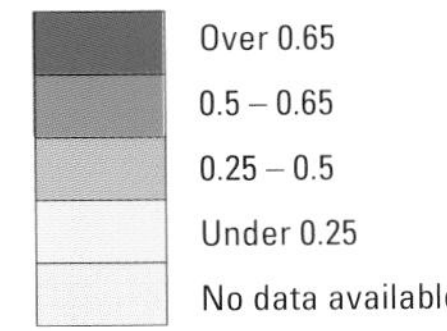

Most equal

Switzerland	0.039
Denmark	0.040
Netherlands	0.044

Least equal

Yemen	0.834
Papua New Guinea	0.741
Chad	0.708

GENDER EQUALITY

The UN's Millennium Development Goal 3 was to *"Eliminate gender disparity in primary and secondary education"* in all levels of education no later than 2015. According to the 2015 Millennium Development Goal Report, achieving parity in education is an important step toward equal opportunity for men and women in the social, political, and economic domains. The Gender Parity Index (GPI) shows the ratio between the enrolment rate of girls and that of boys. The GPI grew from 91% in 1999 to 98% in 2015 for the developing regions as a whole – falling within the +/– 3-point margin of 100% that is the accepted measure for parity.

While most of the developing world had reached a GPI of at least 99% at the primary level by 2015, the Index was still lagging behind in Western Asia and sub-Saharan Africa. These two regions, however, have recorded the greatest progress. Between 1999 and 2015, girls' participation in primary education increased from 72% to 96% in sub-Saharan Africa, and from 87% to 97% in Western Asia.

Girls have shown the greatest progress at the secondary level of education. The GPI for secondary education in the developing world as a whole has risen from 78% in 1990 to 98% in 2015.

It is in tertiary education where the greatest disparities are to be found. Only one developing region, Western Asia, has achieved the target. The most extreme disparities at the expense of women are in sub-Saharan Africa and Southern Asia.

In general, countries with lower levels of national wealth tend to have more men enrolled in tertiary education than women, while the opposite occurs in countries with higher average incomes.

The GPI measures the rate of girls' school enrolment as a percentage of boys' enrolment in primary, secondary and tertiary education.

GENDER PARITY INDEX (GPI)

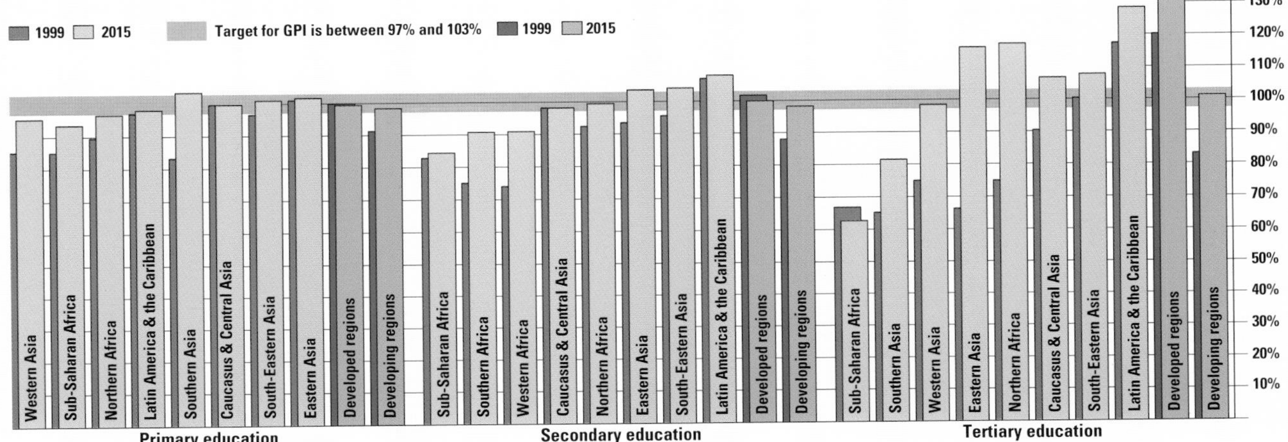

WORLD CITIES

The island city state of Singapore, which lies just 1° north of the equator, guards the Strait of Singapore, part of an important short-cut between the South China Sea and the Indian Ocean and one of the busiest shipping routes on the planet. Singapore's colonial and post-colonial history has been dominated by its strategic location; Sir Stamford Raffles set up a major trading post for the British East India Company here in 1820 and it was seen as a vital base for the Japanese in the Second World War. Since independence in 1963, much of Singapore's economic wealth has depended on its role in the trans-shipment of cargo. The Singapore's international airport, Changi, situated at the eastern tip of the island is also a major transport hub. It was built partly on reclaimed land.
[Map page 138] *NPA Satellite Mapping, CGG Services (UK) Ltd*

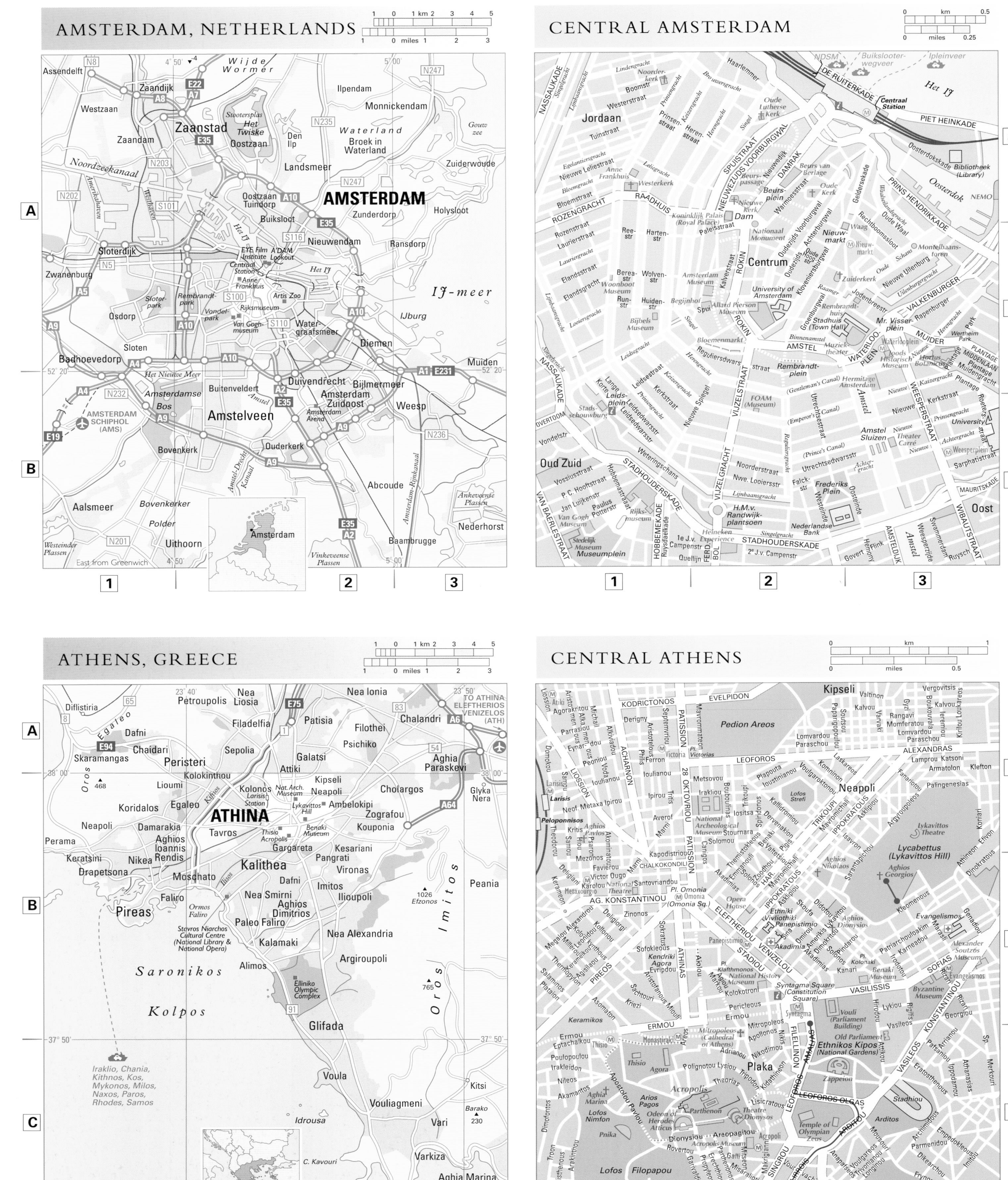
AMSTERDAM, NETHERLANDS
1 0 1 km 2 3 4 5
1 0 miles 1 2 3
Assendelft
Zaandijk
Westzaan
Zaanstad
Zaandam
Het Twiske
Oostzaan
Den Ilp
Ilpendam
Monnickendam
Waterland
Broek in Waterland
Noordzeekanaal
Landsmeer
Zuiderwoude
AMSTERDAM
Oostzaan Tuindorp
Buiksloot
Zunderdorp
Holysloot
Sloterdijk
Nieuwendam
Ransdorp
Zwanenburg
Het IJ
IJ-meer
Osdorp
Sloterpark
Rembrandtpark
Vondelpark
Rijksmuseum
Van Gogh-museum
Artis Zoo
Watergraafsmeer
IJburg
Sloten
Diemen
Badhoevedorp
Het Nieuwe Meer
Muiden
Amsterdamse Bos
Buitenveldert
Duivendrecht
Bijlmermeer
Amsterdam Zuidoost
Amsterdam Arena
Weesp
AMSTERDAM SCHIPHOL (AMS)
Amstelveen
Bovenkerk
Ouderkerk
Abcoude
Aalsmeer
Bovenkerker Polder
Uithoorn
Baambrugge
Nederhorst
Amsterdam
East from Greenwich
1 2 3
A B
CENTRAL AMSTERDAM
0 km 0.5
0 miles 0.25
Centraal Station
Het IJ
PIET HEINKADE
DE RUITERKADE
Jordaan
Westerkerk
Anne Frankhuis
Dam
Koninklijk Palais (Royal Palace)
Nationaal Monument
Nieuwmarkt
Centrum
University of Amsterdam
Amsterdam Museum
Rembrandthuis
Stadhuis (Town Hall)
Oosterdok
Bibliotheek (Library)
NEMO
Rembrandtplein
AMSTEL
Hermitage Amsterdam
Hortus Botanicus
Leidseplein
Stadsschouwburg
FOAM (Museum)
Amstel Sluizen
Theater Carré
Oud Zuid
Frederiks Plein
Nederlandsche Bank
Van Gogh Museum
Stedelijk Museum
Museumplein
Rijksmuseum
Heineken Experience
Oost
STADHOUDERSKADE
1 2 3
ATHENS, GREECE
1 0 1 km 2 3 4 5
1 0 miles 1 2 3
Nea Liosia
Petroupolis
Nea Ionia
Diflistiria
Dafni
Filadelfia
Patisia
Filothei
Chalandri
TO ATHINA ELEFTHERIOS VENIZELOS (ATH)
Chaidari
Skaramangas
Sepolia
Psichiko
Peristeri
Galatsi
Aghia Paraskevi
Kolokinthou
Liouni
Attiki
Kipseli
Neapoli
Cholargos
Glyka Nera
Koridalos
Egaleo
Kolonos
ATHINA
Ambelokipi
Zografou
Neapoli
Damarakia
Tavros
Kouponia
Perama
Aghios Ioannis Rendis
Gargareta
Kesariani
Keratsini
Nikea
Kalithea
Pangrati
Drapetsona
Moschato
Vironas
Peania
Faliro
Dafni
Imitos
Pireas
Nea Smirni
Ilioupoli
Aghios Dimitrios
Paleo Faliro
Nea Alexandria
Stavros Niarchos Cultural Centre (National Library & National Opera)
Kalamaki
Argiroupoli
Saronikos Kolpos
Alimos
Elliniko Olympic Complex
Oros Imitos
Glifada
Iraklio, Chania, Kithnos, Kos, Mykonos, Milos, Naxos, Paros, Rhodes, Samos
Voula
Kitsi
Vouliagmeni
Idrousa
Vari
Varkiza
Aghia Marina
Athens
East from Greenwich
1 2 3
A B C
CENTRAL ATHENS
0 km 1
0 miles 0.5
Kipseli
Pedion Areos
LEOFOROS ALEXANDRAS
Neapoli
Larisis
National Archaeological Museum
Lycabettus (Lykavittos Hill)
Aghios Georgios
Pl. Omonia (Omonia Sq.)
AG. KONSTANTINOU
PIREOS
ATHINAS
STADIOU
VASILISSIS SOFIAS
Syntagma Square (Constitution Square)
Vouli (Parliament Building)
Benaki Museum
Byzantine Museum
ERMOU
Mitropoleos (Cathedral of Athens)
Monastiraki
Thisio
Agora
Plaka
Ethnikos Kipos (National Gardens)
Zappeion
Acropolis
Parthenon
Theatre of Dionysos
Temple of Olympian Zeus
LEOFOROS OLGAS
Stadhiou
Lofos Filopapou
Greek Dance Theatre
1 2 3
Tram Route

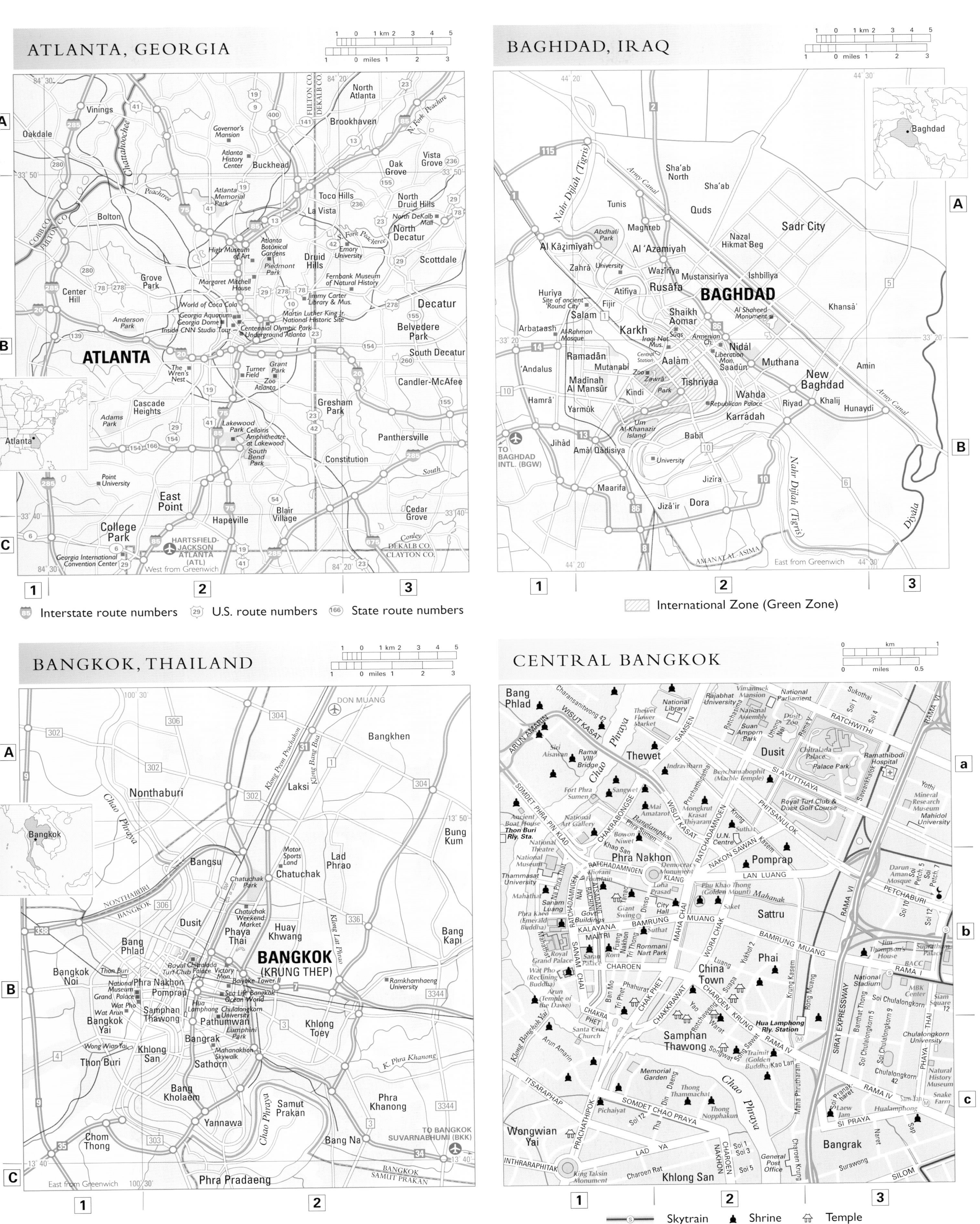

ATLANTA, GEORGIA
1 0 1 km 2 3 4 5
1 0 miles 1 2 3
Vinings
Oakdale
Chattahoochee
Governor's Mansion
Atlanta History Center
Buckhead
North Atlanta
Brookhaven
FULTON CO.
DEKALB CO.
Oak Grove
Vista Grove
Peachtree
Atlanta Memorial Park
Toco Hills
La Vista
North Druid Hills
North DeKalb Mall
Bolton
COBB CO.
FULTON CO.
High Museum of Art
Atlanta Botanical Gardens
Piedmont Park
Druid Hills
Emory University
North Decatur
Scottdale
Center Hill
Grove Park
Margaret Mitchell House
Fernbank Museum of Natural History
Jimmy Carter Library & Mus.
World of Coca Cola
Georgia Aquarium
Georgia Dome
Inside CNN Studio Tour
Centennial Olympic Park
Underground Atlanta
Martin Luther King Jr. National Historic Site
Decatur
Anderson Park
Belvedere Park
South Decatur
ATLANTA
The Wren's Nest
Turner Field
Grant Park
Zoo Atlanta
Candler-McAfee
Cascade Heights
Adams Park
Gresham Park
Lakewood Park
Cellairis Amphitheatre at Lakewood
South Bend Park
Panthersville
Constitution
Point University
East Point
Blair Village
Cedar Grove
Hapeville
College Park
HARTSFIELD-JACKSON ATLANTA (ATL)
Georgia International Convention Center
DEKALB CO.
CLAYTON CO.
West from Greenwich
Atlanta
Interstate route numbers
U.S. route numbers
State route numbers
BAGHDAD, IRAQ
1 0 1 km 2 3 4 5
1 0 miles 1 2 3
Baghdad
Nahr Dijlah (Tigris)
Army Canal
Sha'ab North
Sha'ab
Tunis
Quds
Maghreb
Sadr City
Abdhati Park
Al Kāzimīyah
Al 'Azamīyah
Nazal Hikmat Beg
Zahrā
University
Wazīrīya
Mustansirīya
Ishbīlīya
Huriya
Site of ancient 'Round City'
Atifiya
Rusāfa
BAGHDAD
Fijir
Salam
Shaikh Aomar
Al Shaheed Monument
Khansā'
Arbataash
Al-Rahman Mosque
Karkh
Sūqs
Iraqi Nat. Mus.
Armenian Ch.
Nidāl
'Andalus
Ramadān
Mutanabi
Central Station
Aalām
Liberation Mon.
Saadūn
Muthana
Amin
Zoo
Zawrā' Park
Tishriyaa
New Baghdad
Madīnah Al Mansūr
Kindi
Wahda
Hamrā'
Yarmūk
Republican Palace
Riyad
Khalij
Hunaydi
Um Al-Khanazir Island
Karrādah
TO BAGHDAD INTL. (BGW)
Jihād
Amāl Qādisiya
Babil
University
Maarifa
Jizīra
Jizā'ir
Dora
Diyāla
AMANAT AL-ASIMA
East from Greenwich
International Zone (Green Zone)
BANGKOK, THAILAND
1 0 1 km 2 3 4 5
1 0 miles 1 2 3
DON MUANG
Bangkhen
Klong Prem Prachakon
Klong Bang Bua
Laksi
Nonthaburi
Chao Phraya
Bung Kum
Bangkok
Bangsu
Motor Sports Land
Chatuchak
Lad Phrao
Chatuchak Park
NONTHABURI
BANGKOK
Chatuchak Weekend Market
Dusit
Phaya Thai
Huay Khwang
Klong Lat Phrao
Bang Kapi
Bang Phlad
Chitralada Palace
BANGKOK (KRUNG THEP)
Royal Turf Club
Victory Mon.
Baiyoke Tower II
Ramkhamhaeng University
Bangkok Noi
Thon Buri
National Museum
Phra Nakhon
Pomprap
Grand Palace
Wat Pho
Wat Arun
Sea Life Bangkok Ocean World
Hua Lamphong
Chulalongkorn University
Samphan Thawong
Pathumwan
Bangkok Yai
Lumphini Park
Khlong Toey
Wong Wian Yai
Khlong San
Bangrak
Mahanakhon Skywalk
Thon Buri
Sathorn
K. Phra Khanong
Bang Kholaem
Samut Prakan
Phra Khanong
Yannawa
Chom Thong
Bang Na
TO BANGKOK SUVARNABHUMI (BKK)
BANGKOK
SAMUT PRAKAN
East from Greenwich
Phra Pradaeng
CENTRAL BANGKOK
0 km 1
0 miles 0.5
Bang Phlad
National Library
Rajabhat University
Vimanmek Mansion
National Parliament
Sukothai
WISUT KASAT
ARUN AMARIN
Thewet Flower Market
SAMSEN
National Assembly
Suan Amporn Park
Dusit Zoo
RATCHWITHI
Siri Aisawan
Rama VIII Bridge
Thewet
Dusit
Chitralada Palace
Palace Park
Ramathibodi Hospital
Indravihārn
Benchamabophit (Marble Temple)
SI AYUTTHAYA
Fort Phra Sumen
Sangwet
Mai Amatarot
Prachathipatai
Mongkrut Krasat Thiyaram
Royal Turf Club & Dusit Golf Course
Mineral Research Museum
Mahidol University
Ancient Boat House
National Art Gallery
Thon Buri Rly. Sta.
Bowon Niwet
U.N. Centre
National Theatre
Khao San
Phra Nakhon
Pomprap
National Museum
RATCHADAMNOEN
Democracy Monument
KLANG
LAN LUANG
Thammasat University
Mahathat
Loha Prasad
Phu Khao Thong (Golden Mount)
Mahanak
PETCHABURI
Darun Aman Mosque
Giant Swing
City Hall
Saket
Sattru
Phra Kaeo (Emerald Buddha)
Sanam Luang
Govt. Buildings
KALAYANA
BAMRUNG MUANG
Suthat
MAITRI
Rommani Nart Park
Phai
Jim Thompson's House
Royal Grand Palace
Saranrom Palace
CHAROEN
China Town
BACC
RAMA I
Wat Pho (Reclining Buddha)
National Stadium
MBK Centre
Siam Square
Arun (Temple of the Dawn)
Phahurat
CHAK PHET
Soi Chulalongkorn
Hua Lamphong Rly. Station
Santa Cruz Church
Samphan Thawong
Chulalongkorn University
SIRAT EXPRESSWAY
RAMA IV
Traimit (Golden Buddha)
Kao Lan
Klong Bangkok Yai
Arun Amarin
Memorial Garden
Chao Phraya
Natural History Museum
Snake Farm
ITSARAPHAP
Thong Thammachat
Thong Nopphakun
Pichaiyat
SOMDET CHAO PRAYA
SI PRAYA
Wongwian Yai
Bangrak
LAD YA
INTHRARAPHITAK
King Taksin Monument
Charoen Rat
Khlong San
General Post Office
Surawong
SILOM
Skytrain
Shrine
Temple

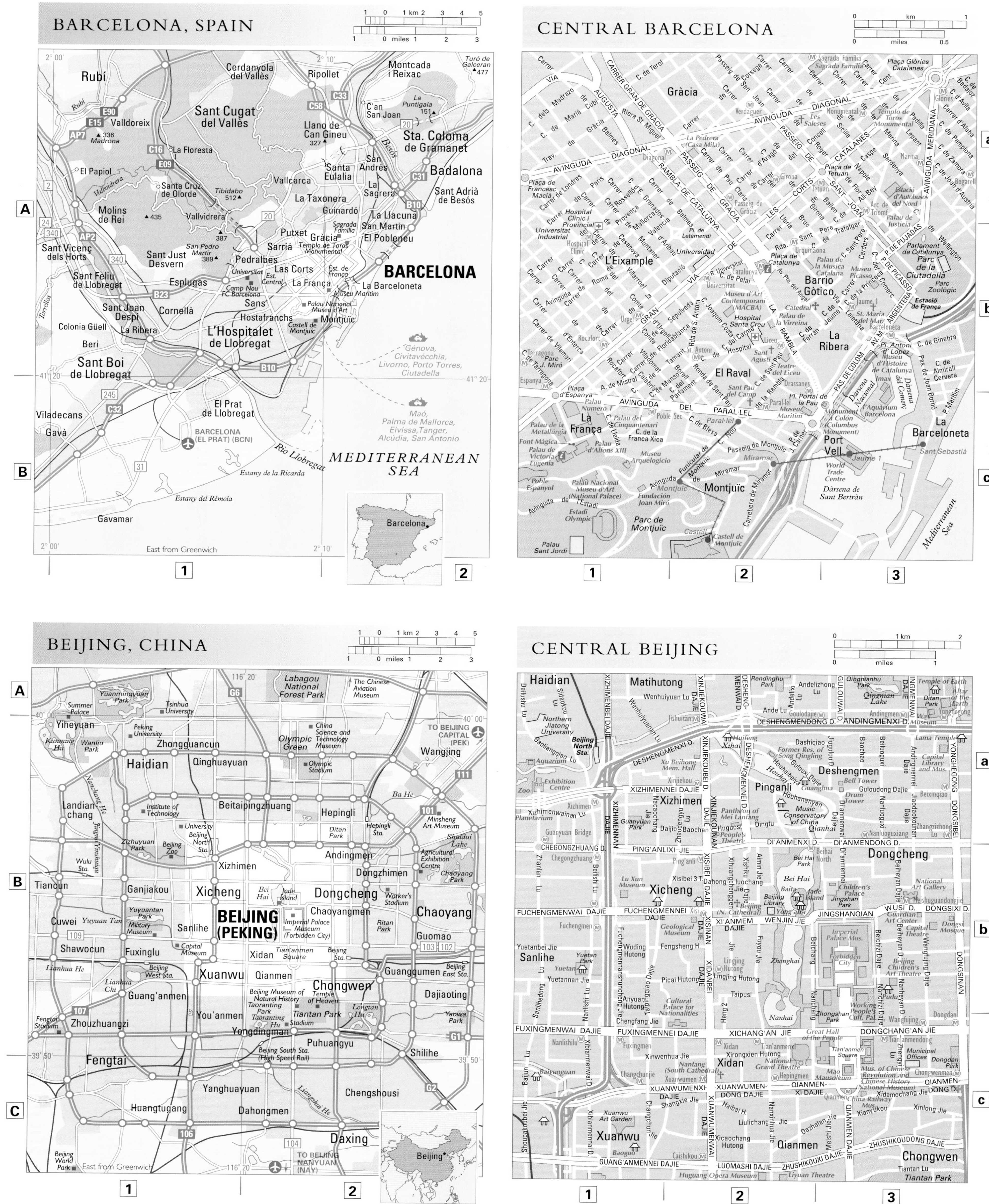
BARCELONA, SPAIN
Rubí
Cerdanyola del Vallès
Ripollet
Montcada i Reixac
Sant Cugat del Vallès
Valldoreix
Llano de Can Gineu
Sta. Coloma de Gramanet
La Floresta
El Papiol
Santa Cruz de Olorde
Tibidabo
Santa Eulalia
San Andrés
Badalona
Vallcarca
La Sagrera
Sant Adrià de Besós
Molins de Rei
Vallvidrera
La Taxonera
Guinardó
La Llacuna
San Martin
El Poblenou
Putxet
Gràcia
Sagrada Familia
Templo de Toros Monumental
Sant Vicenç dels Horts
Sant Just Desvern
Sarriá
Pedralbes
Las Corts
BARCELONA
Sant Feliu de Llobregat
Esplugas
La França
La Barceloneta
Museu Maritim
Sant Joan Despí
Cornellà
Sans
Hostafranchs
Montjuïc
Colonia Güell
La Ribera
L'Hospitalet de Llobregat
Beri
Sant Boi de Llobregat
Gènova, Civitavècchia, Livorno, Porto Torres, Ciutadella
Viladecans
El Prat de Llobregat
Maó, Palma de Mallorca, Eivissa, Tanger, Alcúdia, San Antonio
Gavà
BARCELONA (EL PRAT) (BCN)
Rio Llobregat
MEDITERRANEAN SEA
Estany de la Ricarda
Estany del Rèmola
Gavamar
East from Greenwich
CENTRAL BARCELONA
Gràcia
Sagrada Familia
Plaça Glòries Catalanes
AVINGUDA DIAGONAL
La Pedrera (Casa Milà)
RAMBLA DE CATALUNYA
PASSEIG DE GRÀCIA
Plaça de Francesc Macià
Hospital Clínic i Provincial
Universitat Industrial
L'Eixample
Universidad
Plaça de Catalunya
Barrio Gòtico
Parc de la Ciutadella
Parc Zoològic
Estació de França
Museu d'Art Contemporani (MACBA)
Hospital Santa Creu
Catedral
La Ribera
El Raval
Plaça d'Espanya
AVINGUDA DEL PARAL·LEL
La França
Palau Nacional Museu d'Art (National Palace)
Montjuïc
Port Vell
La Barceloneta
World Trade Centre
Dàrsena de Sant Bertràn
Parc de Montjuïc
Castell de Montjuïc
Palau Sant Jordi
Estadi Olympic
Mediterranean Sea
BEIJING, CHINA
Yuanmingyuan Park
Summer Palace
Tsinghua University
Labagou National Forest Park
The Chinese Aviation Museum
Yiheyuan
Peking University
China Science and Technology Museum
TO BEIJING CAPITAL (PEK)
Zhongguancun
Olympic Green
Wangjing
Haidian
Qinghuayuan
Olympic Stadium
Beitaipingzhuang
Hepingli
Landianchang
Institute of Technology
Minsheng Art Museum
Beijing Zoo
Andingmen
Xizhimen
Dongzhimen
Tiancun
Ganjiakou
Xicheng
Dongcheng
Chaoyangmen
Cuiwei
BEIJING (PEKING)
Imperial Palace Museum (Forbidden City)
Chaoyang
Sanlihe
Shawocun
Fuxinglu
Xidan
Guomao
Xuanwu
Qianmen
Guangqumen
Guang'anmen
Chongwen
Temple of Heaven
Tiantan Park
Dajiaoting
Zhouzhuangzi
You'anmen
Yongdingmen
Fengtai
Puhuangyu
Shilihe
Beijing South Sta. (High Speed Rail)
Yanghuayuan
Chengshousi
Huangtugang
Dahongmen
Daxing
TO BEIJING NANYUAN (NAY)
East from Greenwich
CENTRAL BEIJING
Haidian
Matihutong
Beijing North Sta.
Deshengmen
Pinganli
Xizhimen
Dongcheng
Xicheng
Imperial Palace Mus.
Forbidden City
Sanlihe
Zhonghai
Nanhai
Xidan
Tian'anmen Square
Xuanwu
Qianmen
Chongwen
Tiantan Park
Temple

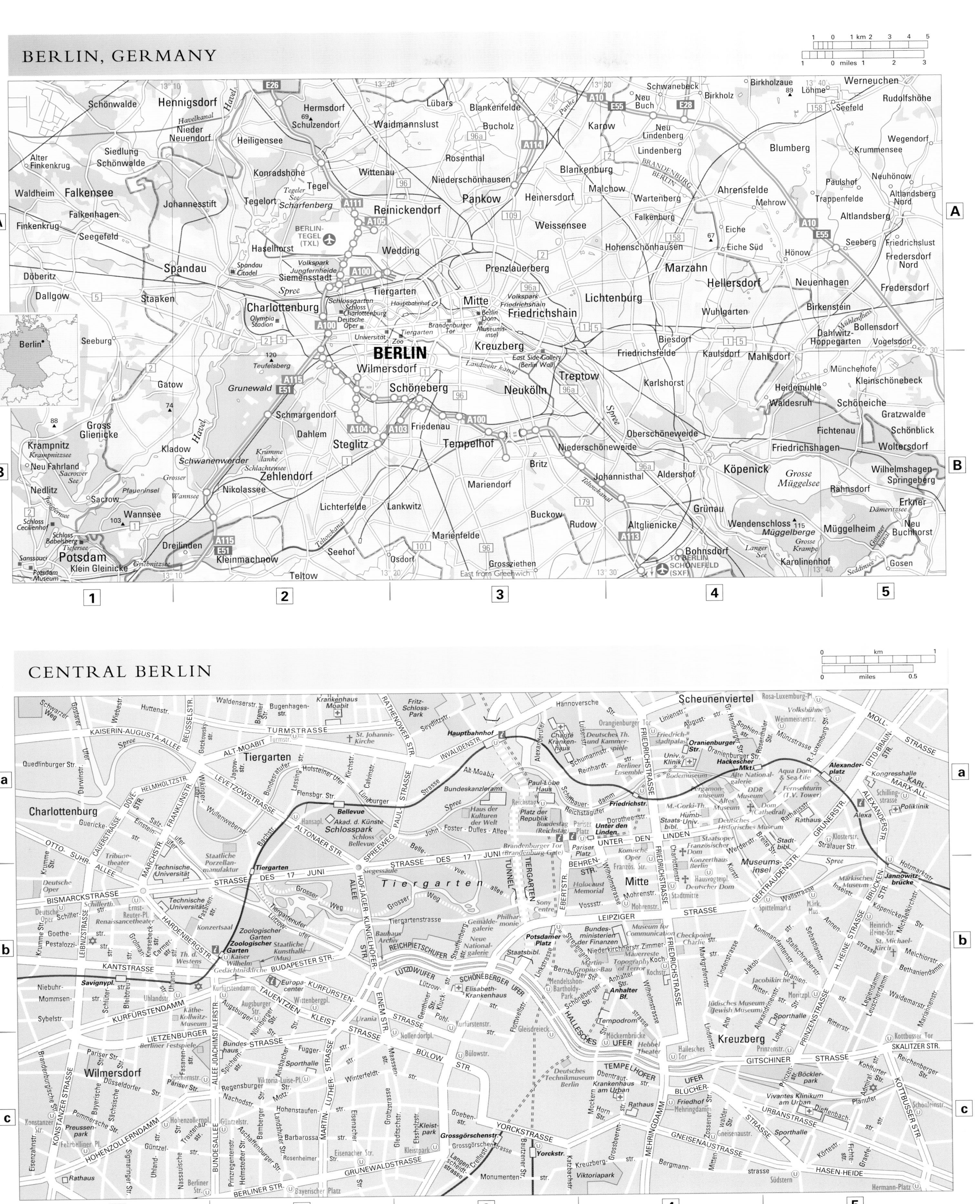
BERLIN, GERMANY
km
miles
Schönwalde
Hennigsdorf
Havelkanal
Nieder Neuendorf
Hermsdorf
Schulzendorf
Lübars
Waidmannslust
Blankenfelde
Bucholz
Karow
Neu Buch
Schwanebeck
Birkholz
Birkholzaue
Löhme
Werneuchen
Rudolfshöhe
Seefeld
Heiligensee
Rosenthal
Neu Lindenberg
Lindenberg
Blumberg
Krummensee
Wegendorf
Alter Finkenkrug
Siedlung Schönwalde
Konradshöhe
Tegel
Wittenau
Niederschönhausen
Blankenburg
BRANDENBURG
BERLIN
Paulshof
Neuhönow
Waldheim
Falkensee
Johannestift
Tegelort
Tegeler See
Scharfenberg
Reinickendorf
Pankow
Heinersdorf
Malchow
Wartenberg
Ahrensfelde
Mehrow
Trappenfelde
Altlandsberg Nord
Falkenhagen
Altlandsberg
Finkenkrug
Seegefeld
BERLIN-TEGEL (TXL)
Weissensee
Falkenburg
Eiche
Eiche Süd
Seeberg
Friedrichslust
Haselhorst
Wedding
Hohenschönhausen
Hönow
Fredersdorf Nord
Spandau
Spandau Citadel
Volkspark Jungfernheide
Siemensstadt
Prenzlauerberg
Marzahn
Hellersdorf
Neuenhagen
Fredersdorf
Döberitz
Spree
Tiergarten
Dallgow
Staaken
Charlottenburg
Schlossgarten
Schloss Charlottenburg
Hauptbahnhof
Mitte
Volkspark Friedrichshain
Friedrichshain
Lichtenburg
Wuhlgarten
Birkenstein
Olympia Stadion
Deutsche Oper
Berlin Dom
Brandenburger Tor
Museums-insel
Universität
Tiergarten
Zoo
Bollensdorf
Dahlwitz-Hoppegarten
Vogelsdorf
Seeburg
BERLIN
Kreuzberg
East Side Gallery (Berlin Wall)
Biesdorf
Friedrichsfelde
Kaulsdorf
Mahlsdorf
Teufelsberg
Wilmersdorf
Landwehr kanal
Treptow
Münchehofe
Gatow
Grunewald
Schöneberg
Neukölln
Karlshorst
Heidemühle
Kleinschönebeck
Waldesruh
Schöneiche
Schmargendorf
Gratzwalde
Gross Glienicke
Friedenau
Tempelhof
Dahlem
Steglitz
Oberschöneweide
Fichtenau
Schönblick
Krampnitz
Krampnitzsee
Kladow
Havel
Krumme Lanke
Schlachtensee
Niederschöneweide
Friedrichshagen
Woltersdorf
Neu Fahrland
Sacrower See
Schwanenwerder
Britz
Köpenick
Grosse Müggelsee
Wilhelmshagen
Springeberg
Zehlendorf
Johannisthal
Aldershof
Nedlitz
Grosser Wannsee
Nikolassee
Pfaueninsel
Mariendorf
Teltowkanal
Rahnsdorf
Sacrow
Lichterfelde
Lankwitz
Erkner
Dämeritzsee
Wannsee
Buckow
Rudow
Grünau
Altglienicke
Wendenschloss
Müggelberge
Müggelheim
Neu Buchhorst
Schloss Cecilienhof
Schloss Babelsberg
Tiefersee
Dreilinden
Marienfelde
Grosse Krampe
Langer See
Gosener Kanal
Bohnsdorf
Sanssouci
Potsdam
Klein Gleinicke
Griebnitzsee
Kleinmachnow
Seehof
Osdorf
Grossziethen
TO BERLIN SCHÖNEFELD (SXF)
Karolinenhof
Gosen
Seddinsee
Potsdam Museum
Teltow
East from Greenwich
Berlin
CENTRAL BERLIN
km
miles
Scheunenviertel
Hauptbahnhof
Tiergarten
Charlottenburg
Bellevue
Schloss Bellevue
Bundeskanzleramt
Haus der Kulturen der Welt
Paul-Löbe Haus
Platz der Republik
Bundestag (Reichstag)
Friedrichstr.
Oranienburger Str.
Hackescher Mkt.
Alexanderplatz
Fernsehturm (T.V. Tower)
Dom (Cathedral)
Alte National-galerie
Pergamon-museum
Bodemuseum
Unter den Linden
Museums-insel
Tiergarten
Siegessäule
Technische Universität
Zoologischer Garten
Kaiser Wilhelm Gedächtniskirche
Europa-center
Potsdamer Platz
Sony Centre
Philhar-monie
Holocaust Memorial
Mitte
Checkpoint Charlie
Jüdisches Museum (Jewish Museum)
Anhalter Bf.
Kreuzberg
Deutsches Technikmuseum Berlin
Jannowitz-brücke
Savignypl.
Kurfürstendamm
Wilmersdorf
Grossgörschenstr.
Yorckstr.
Viktoriapark
Hermann-Platz

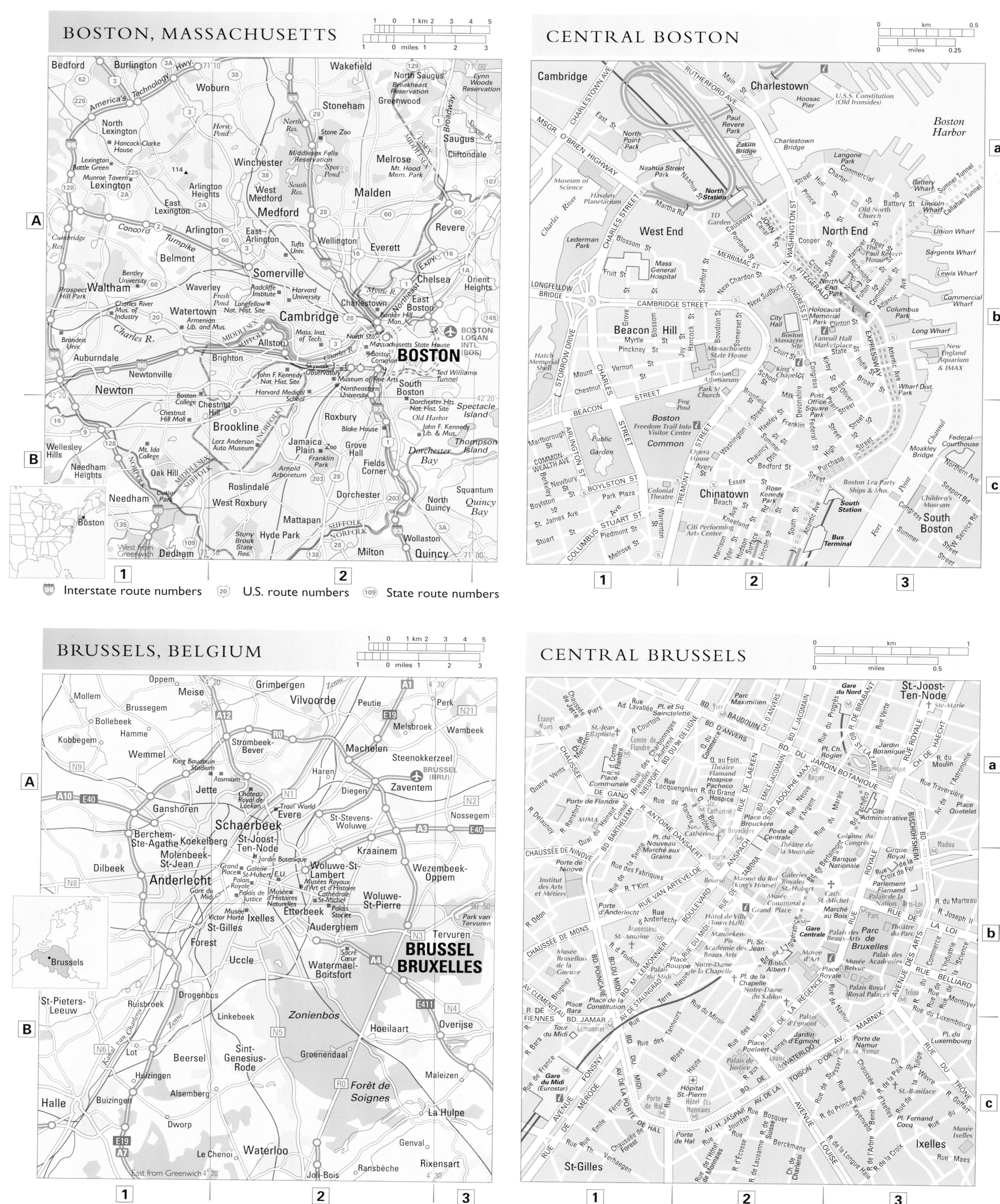

BOSTON, MASSACHUSETTS
Interstate route numbers
U.S. route numbers
State route numbers
Bedford
Burlington
Wakefield
Woburn
Stoneham
Winchester
Medford
Malden
Melrose
Saugus
Lexington
Arlington
Belmont
Somerville
Everett
Revere
Chelsea
Waltham
Watertown
Cambridge
BOSTON
Newton
Brookline
Roxbury
Dorchester
Jamaica Plain
Needham
Dedham
Hyde Park
Mattapan
Milton
Quincy
Wollaston
North Quincy
Quincy Bay
Dorchester Bay
BOSTON LOGAN INTL. (BOS)
CENTRAL BOSTON
Cambridge
Charlestown
Boston Harbor
West End
North End
Beacon Hill
Boston Common
Public Garden
Chinatown
South Boston
South Station
North Station
BRUSSELS, BELGIUM
Grimbergen
Vilvoorde
Meise
Machelen
Zaventem
BRUSSEL (BRU)
Jette
Ganshoren
Schaerbeek
Evere
St-Joost-Ten-Node
Koekelberg
Molenbeek-St-Jean
Anderlecht
Ixelles
Etterbeek
St-Gilles
Forest
Uccle
Auderghem
Watermael-Boitsfort
BRUSSEL BRUXELLES
Zonienbos
Forêt de Soignes
Waterloo
Halle
La Hulpe
Tervuren
Overijse
CENTRAL BRUSSELS
Gare du Nord
St-Joost-Ten-Node
Gare Centrale
Gare du Midi (Eurostar)
Grand Place
Parc de Bruxelles
Palais Royal (Royal Palace)
Ixelles
St-Gilles

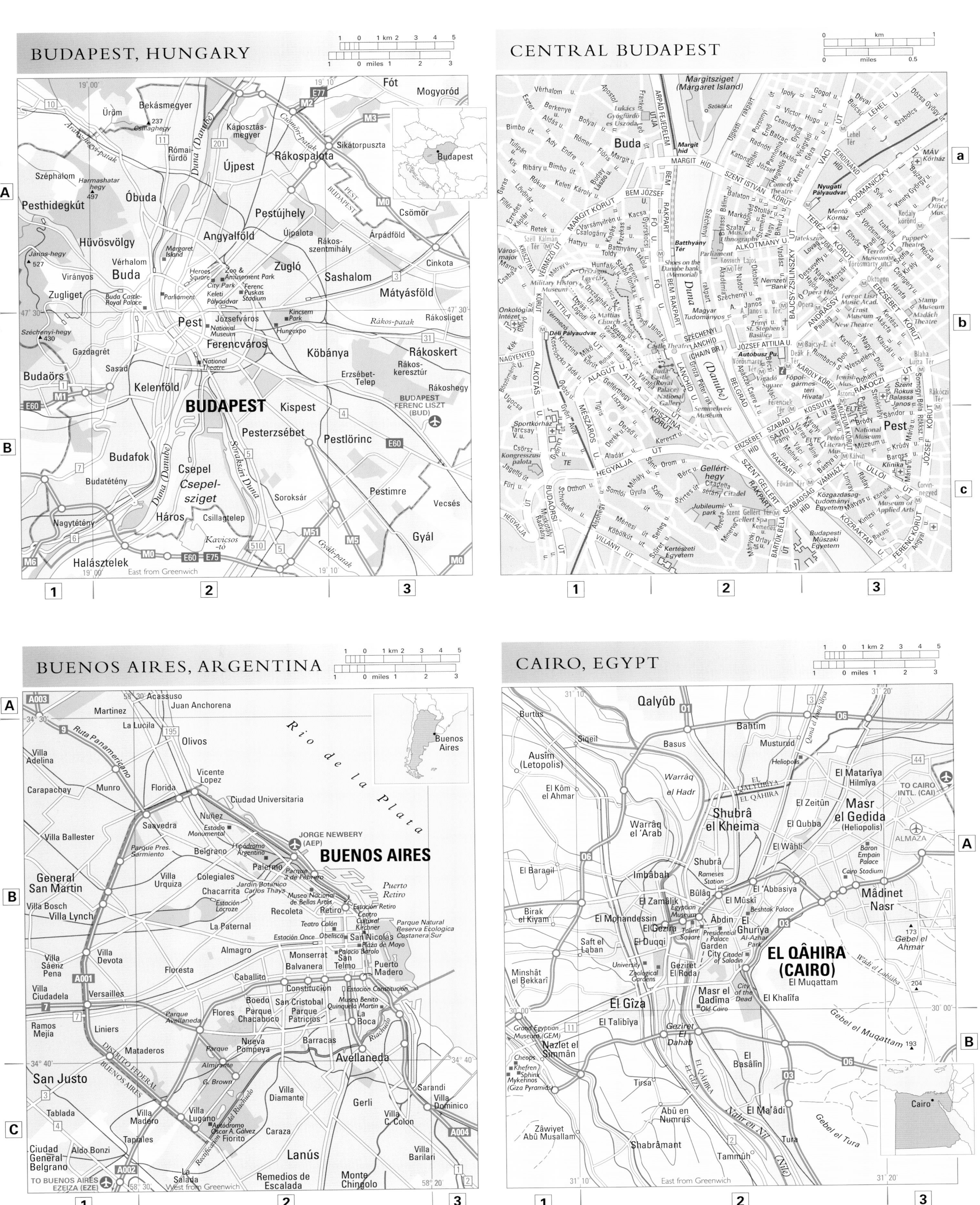
BUDAPEST, HUNGARY
km
miles
East from Greenwich
Budapest
BUDAPEST
Buda
Pest
Óbuda
Újpest
Rákospalota
Pestújhely
Angyalföld
Zugló
Sashalom
Mátyásföld
Kőbánya
Rákoskert
Ferencváros
Józsefváros
Kelenföld
Budaörs
Budafok
Csepel
Csepel-sziget
Pesterzsébet
Kispest
Pestlőrinc
Soroksár
Pestimre
Vecsés
Gyál
Háros
Csillagtelep
Nagytétény
Halásztelek
Hűvösvölgy
Pesthidegkút
Fót
Mogyoród
Csömör
Árpádföld
Cinkota
Rákosliget
Rákoshegy
BUDAPEST FERENC LISZT (BUD)
Duna (Danube)
Ráckevei (Soroksári) Duna
CENTRAL BUDAPEST
Margitsziget (Margaret Island)
MARGIT HÍD
SZÉCHENYI LÁNCHÍD (CHAIN BR.)
ERZSÉBET HÍD
SZABADSÁG HÍD
Duna (Danube)
Gellért-hegy
Citadella
Buda Castle (Royal Palace)
Parliament
Déli Pályaudvar
Nyugati Pályaudvar
Magyar Tudományos Akadémia
St. Stephen's Basilica
Opera House
National Museum
Budapesti Műszaki Egyetem
Közgazdasági tudományi Egyetem
BUENOS AIRES, ARGENTINA
Río de la Plata
Buenos Aires
BUENOS AIRES
Olivos
Martínez
Acassuso
Florida
Vicente Lopez
Munro
Carapachay
Villa Adelina
Villa Ballester
General San Martín
Saavedra
Belgrano
Palermo
Colegiales
Chacarita
Recoleta
Retiro
Puerto Retiro
JORGE NEWBERY (AEP)
La Paternal
Almagro
Balvanera
Monserrat
San Nicolás
San Telmo
Puerto Madero
Constitución
La Boca
Barracas
Avellaneda
Flores
Floresta
Caballito
Boedo
Versailles
Liniers
Mataderos
Nueva Pompeya
San Justo
Ramos Mejía
Villa Lugano
Villa Madero
Tapiales
Lanús
Gerli
Sarandí
Villa Domínico
Remedios de Escalada
Monte Chingolo
Ciudad General Belgrano
Aldo Bonzi
TO BUENOS AIRES EZEIZA (EZE)
CAIRO, EGYPT
Cairo
EL QÂHIRA (CAIRO)
Qalyûb
Bahtîm
Shubrâ el Kheima
Shubrâ
Masr el Gedida (Heliopolis)
El Matarîya
El Zeitûn
El Qubba
Mâdinet Nasr
TO CAIRO INTL. (CAI)
ALMAZA
Imbâbah
El Zamâlik
El Mohandessin
El Gezîra
El Duqqi
Bûlâq
Âbdîn
El Ghurîya
El Muqattam
Masr el Qadîma
Old Cairo
El Khalîfa
El Gîza
El Talibîya
Gezîret el Dahab
Nazlet el Simmân
Giza Pyramids
El Basâtîn
El Ma'âdi
Tura
Tirsa
Abû en Numrus
Shabrâmant
Tammûh
Nahr en Nîl (Nile)
Gebel el Muqattam
Gebel el Tura

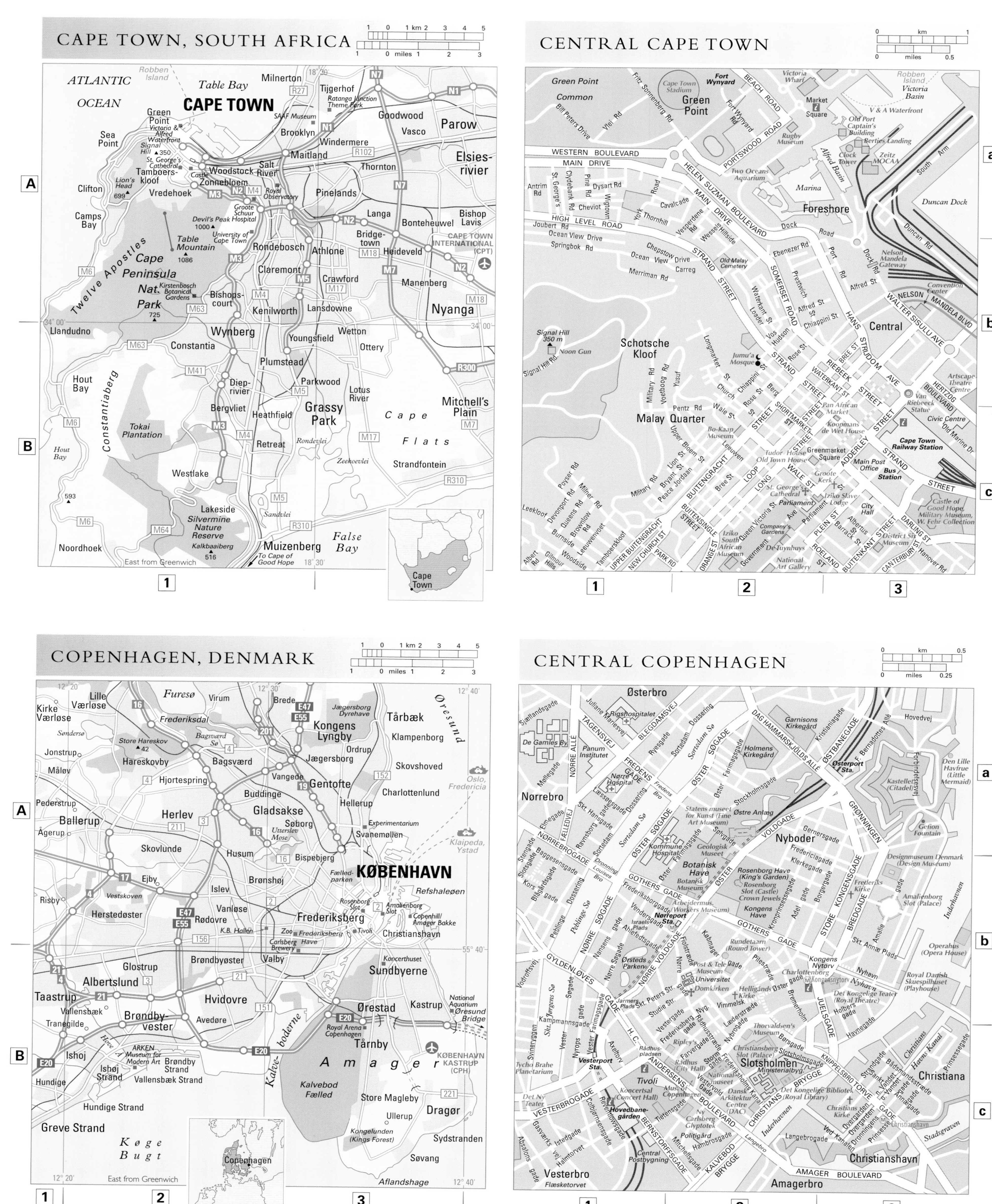
CAPE TOWN, SOUTH AFRICA
CENTRAL CAPE TOWN
COPENHAGEN, DENMARK
CENTRAL COPENHAGEN

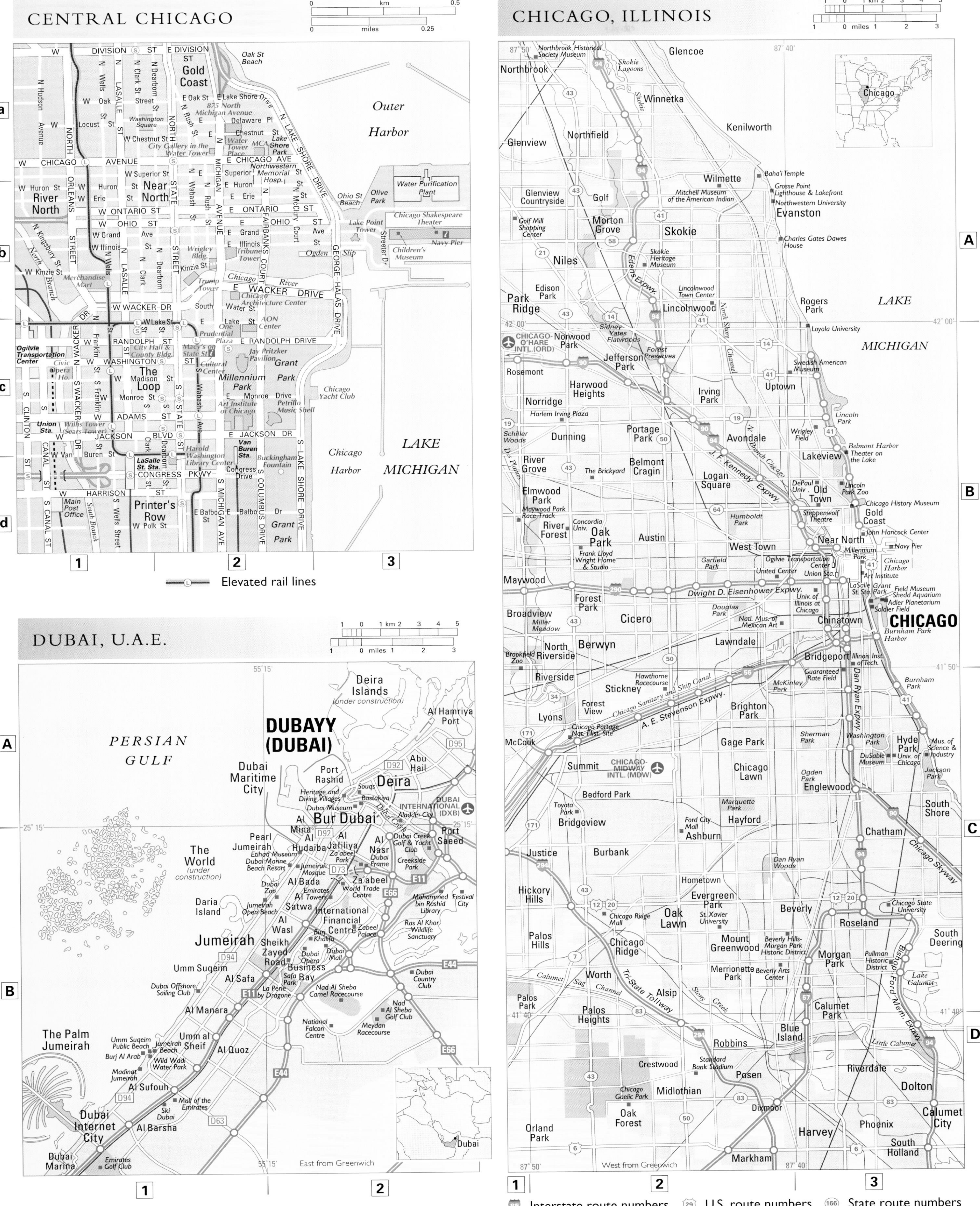
CENTRAL CHICAGO
0 km 0.5
0 miles 0.25
a
b
c
d
1
2
3
DIVISION ST
E DIVISION ST
Oak St Beach
Gold Coast
E Oak St
E Lake Shore Drive
875 North Michigan Avenue
Delaware Pl
Outer Harbor
N Hudson Avenue
W Oak St
W Locust St
Washington Square
W Chestnut St
City Gallery in the Water Tower
Chestnut St
Water Tower Place
MCA
Lake Shore Park
N LAKE SHORE DRIVE
W CHICAGO AVENUE
E CHICAGO AVE
Northwestern Memorial Hosp.
Water Purification Plant
W Huron St
River North
W Superior St
Huron St
Near North
Erie St
E Huron
E Erie
Ohio St Beach
Olive Park
W ONTARIO ST
E ONTARIO ST
Chicago Shakespeare Theater
W OHIO ST
E OHIO ST
Lake Point Tower
W Grand Ave
E Grand Ave
W Illinois St
E Illinois St
Wrigley Bldg.
Tribune Tower
Navy Pier
Ogden Slip
Children's Museum
Streeter Dr
N Kingsbury St
North Branch
W Kinzie St
Kinzie St
Merchandise Mart
Trump Tower
Chicago River
E WACKER DRIVE
Chicago Architecture Center
GEORGE HALAS DRIVE
W WACKER DR
South Water St
W Lake St
Lake St
One Prudential Plaza
AON Center
RANDOLPH ST
E RANDOLPH DRIVE
Ogilvie Transportation Center
City Hall & County Bldg.
Macy's on State St
Jay Pritzker Pavilion
Civic Opera Ho.
W WASHINGTON ST
Cultural Center
Grant Park
The Loop
W Madison St
Millennium Park
Monroe St
E Monroe Drive
Art Institute of Chicago
Petrillo Music Shell
Chicago Yacht Club
ADAMS ST
Union Sta.
Willis Tower (Sears Tower)
JACKSON BLVD
E JACKSON DR
Harold Washington Library Center
Van Buren Sta.
Buckingham Fountain
W Van Buren St
LaSalle St. Sta.
CONGRESS PKWY
Congress Drive
Chicago Harbor
LAKE MICHIGAN
HARRISON ST
Main Post Office
South Branch
Printer's Row
W Polk St
E Balbo St
Balbo Dr
Grant Park
S CANAL ST
S CLINTON ST
S WACKER DR
S Franklin St
S Wells Street
S LAKE SHORE DRIVE
S COLUMBUS DRIVE
S MICHIGAN AVE.
Wabash Ave
Elevated rail lines
DUBAI, U.A.E.
1 0 1 km 2 3 4 5
1 0 miles 1 2 3
55°15'
25°15'
A
B
1
2
Deira Islands (under construction)
Al Hamriya Port
PERSIAN GULF
DUBAYY (DUBAI)
D95
Abu Hail
Dubai Maritime City
Port Rashid
D92
Deira
Heritage and Diving Villages
Souqs
Bastakiya
Dubai Museum
DUBAI INTERNATIONAL (DXB)
Aladdin City
Bur Dubai
Dubai Creek
Port Saeed
Al Mina
D92
Al Jafiliya
Al Hudaiba
Al Nasr
Dubai Creek Golf & Yacht Club
Pearl Jumeirah
Etihad Museum
Za'abeel Park
Dubai Frame
Creekside Park
The World (under construction)
Dubai Marine Beach Resort
Jumeirah Mosque
D73
Za'abeel
Dubai Zoo
Al Bada
World Trade Centre
E11
Emirates Al Towers
E66
Mohammed bin Rashid Library
Festival City
Daria Island
Jumeirah Open Beach
Satwa
International Financial Centre
Al Wasl
Zabeel Palace
Ras Al Khor Wildlife Sanctuary
Jumeirah
Burj Khalifa
Sheikh Zayed Road
Dubai Mall
D94
Dubai Opera
Umm Sugeim
Business Bay
Al Safa
E44
Dubai Country Club
Dubai Offshore Sailing Club
E11
Safa Park
La Perle by Dragone
Nad Al Sheba Camel Racecourse
Al Manara
Nad Al Sheba Golf Club
National Falcon Centre
Meydan Racecourse
The Palm Jumeirah
Umm Sugeim Public Beach
Jumeirah Beach
Umm al Sheif
Al Quoz
Burj Al Arab
Wild Wadi Water Park
E66
Madinat Jumeirah
E44
Al Sufouh
D94
Mall of the Emirates
Ski Dubai
Dubai Internet City
Al Barsha
D63
Dubai Marina
Emirates Golf Club
East from Greenwich
Dubai
CHICAGO, ILLINOIS
1 0 1 km 2 3 4 5
1 0 miles 1 2 3
87°50'
87°40'
42°00'
41°50'
41°40'
A
B
C
D
1
2
3
Northbrook Historical Society Museum
Glencoe
Northbrook
Skokie Lagoons
Chicago
Winnetka
Kenilworth
Northfield
Glenview
Baha'i Temple
Wilmette
Grosse Point Lighthouse & Lakefront
Mitchell Museum of the American Indian
Northwestern University
Glenview Countryside
Golf
Evanston
Golf Mill Shopping Center
Morton Grove
Skokie
Charles Gates Dawes House
Niles
Skokie Heritage Museum
Edens Expwy.
Edison Park
Lincolnwood Town Center
Park Ridge
Lincolnwood
Rogers Park
LAKE
Sidney Yates Flatwoods
Loyola University
CHICAGO-O'HARE INTL. (ORD)
Norwood Park
Forest Preserves
MICHIGAN
Jefferson Park
Swedish American Museum
Rosemont
Harwood Heights
Irving Park
Uptown
Norridge
Lincoln Park
Harlem Irving Plaza
Schiller Woods
Dunning
Portage Park
Avondale
Wrigley Field
Belmont Harbor
Theater on the Lake
River Grove
Belmont Cragin
Lakeview
The Brickyard
J. F. Kennedy Expwy.
Des Plaines
Logan Square
Elmwood Park
DePaul Univ.
Old Town
Lincoln Park Zoo
Chicago History Museum
Maywood Park Race Track
Humboldt Park
Steppenwolf Theatre
Gold Coast
River Forest
Concordia Univ.
Oak Park
Austin
John Hancock Center
Near North
Navy Pier
Frank Lloyd Wright Home & Studio
West Town
Millennium Park
Garfield Park
Ogilvie Transportation Center
Chicago Harbor
Maywood
United Center
Union Sta.
Art Institute
Dwight D. Eisenhower Expwy.
LaSalle St. Sta.
Grant Park
Field Museum
Shedd Aquarium
Forest Park
Univ. of Illinois at Chicago
Adler Planetarium
Soldier Field
Broadview
Douglas Park
Miller Meadow
Natl. Mus. of Mexican Art
Cicero
Chinatown
CHICAGO
Burnham Park Harbor
North Riverside
Berwyn
Lawndale
Brookfield Zoo
Bridgeport
Illinois Inst. of Tech.
Hawthorne Racecourse
Guaranteed Rate Field
Riverside
Stickney
McKinley Park
Burnham Park
Chicago Sanitary and Ship Canal
Forest View
Brighton Park
Dan Ryan Expwy.
A. E. Stevenson Expwy.
Lyons
Chicago Portage Natl. Hist. Site
Sherman Park
Washington Park
Hyde Park
Mus. of Science & Industry
McCook
Gage Park
DuSable Museum
Univ. of Chicago
Summit
CHICAGO-MIDWAY INTL. (MDW)
Chicago Lawn
Ogden Park
Jackson Park
Englewood
Bedford Park
Marquette Park
South Shore
Toyota Park
Bridgeview
Ford City Mall
Hayford
Ashburn
Chatham
Chicago Skyway
Justice
Burbank
Dan Ryan Woods
Hometown
Hickory Hills
Evergreen Park
Chicago State University
Chicago Ridge Mall
Oak Lawn
St. Xavier University
Beverly
Roseland
South Deering
Palos Hills
Mount Greenwood
Beverly Hills-Morgan Park Historic District
Chicago Ridge
Morgan Park
Pullman Historic District
Merrionette Park
Beverly Arts Center
Bishop Ford Mem. Expwy.
Calumet Sag Channel
Worth
Tri-State Tollway
Alsip
Stony Creek
Lake Calumet
Palos Park
Palos Heights
Calumet Park
Blue Island
Little Calumet
Robbins
Crestwood
Standard Bank Stadium
Riverdale
Posen
Dolton
Chicago Gaelic Park
Midlothian
Oak Forest
Dixmoor
Calumet City
Orland Park
Harvey
Phoenix
South Holland
Markham
West from Greenwich
Interstate route numbers
U.S. route numbers
State route numbers
COPYRIGHT PHILIP'S

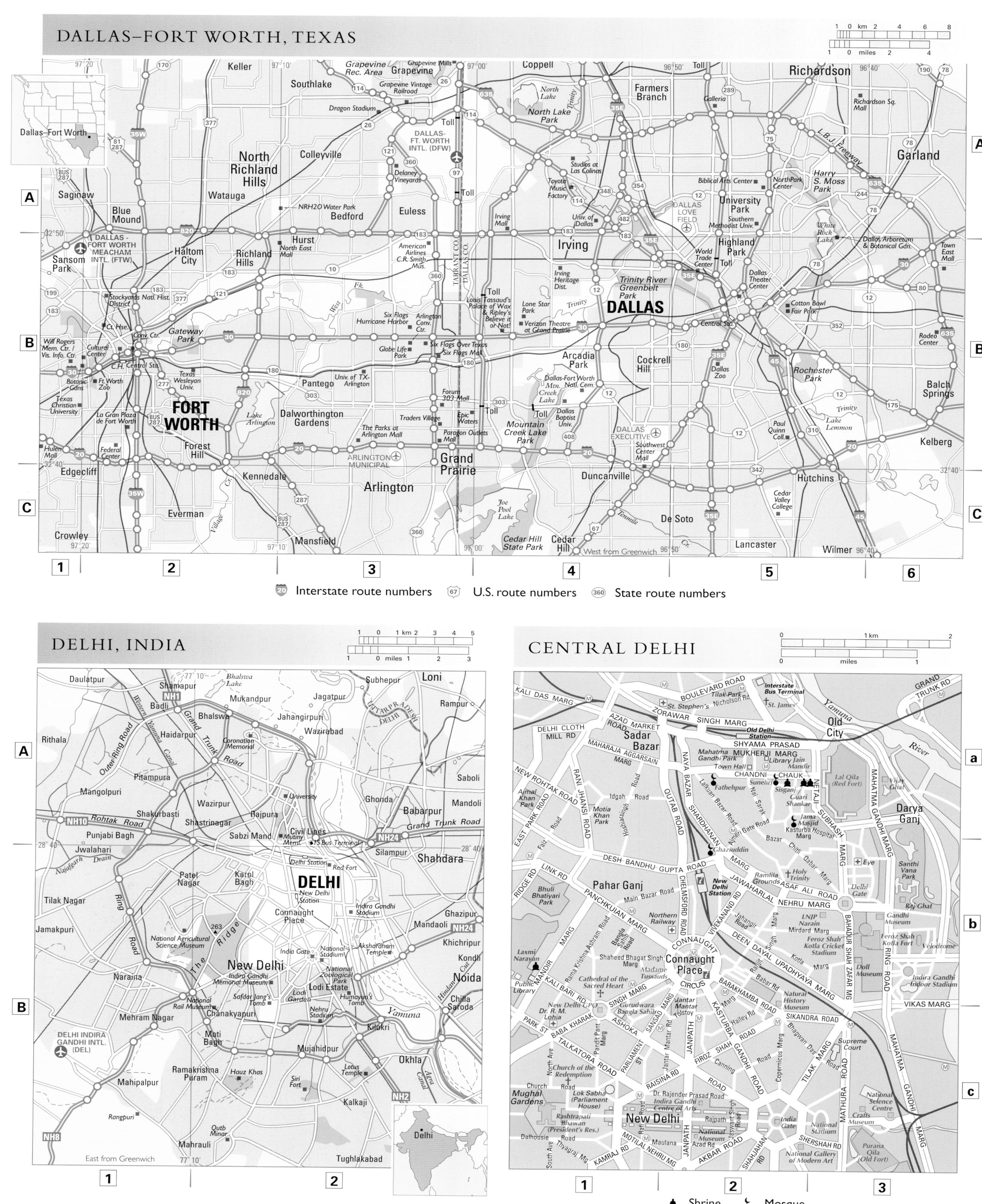

DALLAS–FORT WORTH, TEXAS
0 km 2 4 6 8
0 miles 2 4
Dallas–Fort Worth
Keller
Grapevine Rec. Area
Grapevine
Grapevine Mills
Coppell
Toll
Richardson
Southlake
Grapevine Vintage Railroad
North Lake
Farmers Branch
Galleria
Richardson Sq. Mall
Dragon Stadium
North Lake Park
DALLAS-FT. WORTH INTL. (DFW)
L.B.J. Freeway
Garland
North Richland Hills
Colleyville
Studios at Las Colinas
Delaney Vineyards
Toyota Music Factory
Biblical Arts Center
NorthPark Center
Harry S. Moss Park
Saginaw
Watauga
DALLAS LOVE FIELD
University Park
Blue Mound
NRH2O Water Park
Bedford
Euless
Irving Mall
Univ. of Dallas
Southern Methodist Univ.
White Rock Lake
DALLAS - FORT WORTH MEACHAM INTL. (FTW)
Hurst
North East Mall
American Airlines C.R. Smith Mus.
Irving
Highland Park
World Trade Center
Dallas Arboretum & Botanical Gdn.
Town East Mall
Sansom Park
Haltom City
Richland Hills
Irving Heritage Dist.
Trinity River Greenbelt Park
Dallas Theater Center
Stockyards Natl. Hist. District
Louis Tussaud's Palace of Wax & Ripley's Believe it or Not!
Lone Star Park
DALLAS
Cotton Bowl
Fair Park
Ct. Hse.
Conv. Ctr.
Gateway Park
Six Flags Hurricane Harbor
Arlington Conv. Ctr.
Verizon Theatre at Grand Prairie
Central Sta.
Will Rogers Mem. Ctr. / Vis. Info. Ctr.
Cultural Center
Globe Life Park
Six Flags Over Texas
Six Flags Mall
Arcadia Park
Cockrell Hill
Rodeo Center
Central Sta.
C.H.
Botanic Gdns
Ft. Worth Zoo
Texas Wesleyan Univ.
Univ. of TX-Arlington
Pantego
Dallas-Fort Worth Natl. Cem.
Dallas Zoo
Rochester Park
Balch Springs
Texas Christian University
FORT WORTH
La Gran Plaza de Fort Worth
Lake Arlington
Dalworthington Gardens
Traders Village
Forum 303 Mall
Epic Waters
Mountain Creek Lake
Mountain Creek Lake Park
Dallas Baptist Univ.
Paul Quinn Coll.
Lake Lemmon
Kelberg
The Parks at Arlington Mall
Paragon Outlets Mall
DALLAS EXECUTIVE
Southwest Center Mall
Hulen Mall
Federal Center
Forest Hill
ARLINGTON MUNICIPAL
Grand Prairie
Edgecliff
Kennedale
Duncanville
Hutchins
Arlington
Cedar Valley College
Everman
Joe Pool Lake
De Soto
Crowley
Mansfield
Cedar Hill State Park
Cedar Hill
Lancaster
Wilmer
TARRANT CO.
DALLAS CO.
West from Greenwich
Interstate route numbers
U.S. route numbers
State route numbers
DELHI, INDIA
0 1 km 2 3 4 5
0 miles 1 2 3
Daulatpur
Shamapur
Bhalswa Lake
Subhepur
Loni
Badli
Mukandpur
Jagatpur
Rampur
Bhalswa
Jahangirpuri
UTTAR PRADESH
DELHI
Rithala
Haidarpur
Coronation Memorial
Wazirabad
Outer Ring Road
Grand Trunk Road
Western Yamuna Canal
Pitampura
Saboli
Mangolpuri
University
Ghonda
Mandoli
Wazirpur
Babarpur
Shakurbasti
Rajpura
Rohtak Road
Shastrinagar
Punjabi Bagh
Sabzi Mand
Civil Lines
Mutiny Meml.
IS Bus Terminal
Jwalahari
Najafgarh Drain
Silampur
Shahdara
Delhi Station
Red Fort
Patel Nagar
Karol Bagh
DELHI
Tilak Nagar
New Delhi Station
Indira Gandhi Stadium
Ghazipur
Connaught Place
Mandaoli
Jamakpuri
Ring Road
National Agricultural Science Museum
The Ridge
Khichripur
India Gate
National Stadium
Akshardham Temple
Kondli
New Delhi
National Zoological Park
Noida
Indira Gandhi Memorial Museum
Lodi Estate
Hindan Cut
Chilla Saroda
Naraina
Safdar Jang's Tomb
Lodi Garden
Humayun's Tomb
National Rail Museum
Nehru Stadium
Yamuna
Mehram Nagar
Chanakyapuri
Kilokri
DELHI INDIRA GANDHI INTL. (DEL)
Moti Bagh
Mujahidpur
Okhla
Agra Canal
Lotus Temple
Ramakrishna Puram
Hauz Khas
Siri Fort
Mahipalpur
Kalkaji
Rangpuri
Qutb Minar
Mahrauli
Tughlakabad
East from Greenwich
Delhi
CENTRAL DELHI
0 1 km 2
0 miles 1
KALI DAS MARG
BOULEVARD ROAD
Tilak Park
Interstate Bus Terminal
GRAND TRUNK RD
St. Stephen's
Nicholson Rd
St. James
AZAD MARKET ROAD
ZORAWAR SINGH MARG
Yamuna
DELHI CLOTH MILL RD
Sadar Bazar
Old Delhi Station
Old City
River
SHYAMA PRASAD MUKHERJI MARG
MAHARAJA AGGARSAIN MARG
Mahatma Gandhi Park
Library
Jain Mandir
Town Hall
NEW ROHTAK ROAD
CHANDNI CHAUK
Lal Qila (Red Fort)
Fatehpur
Sunehri
Sisganj
Gauri Shankar
NETAJI SUBHASH MARG
MAHATMA GANDHI MARG
Vijay Ghat
Ajmal Khan Park
Motia Khan Park
Idgah Road
Jama Masjid
Darya Ganj
Kasturba Hospital
Ajmeri Gate Road
EAST PARK ROAD
Ghaziuddin
DESH BANDHU GUPTA ROAD
Eye
Santhi Vana Park
LINK RD
Ramlila Grounds
Holy Trinity
Pahar Ganj
New Delhi Station
ASAF ALI ROAD
Delhi Gate
RIDGE RD
Bhuli Bhatiyari Park
Main Bazar Road
JAWAHARLAL NEHRU MARG
Raj Ghat
PANCHKUIAN MARG
Northern Railway
LNJP Narain
Gandhi Museum
Mirdard Marg
Feroz Shah Kotla Fort
Feroz Shah Kotla Cricket Stadium
Velodrome
DEEN DAYAL UPADHYAYA MARG
Laxmi Narayan
Shaheed Bhagat Singh Marg
CONNAUGHT CIRCUS
Connaught Place
Madame Tussauds
Doll Museum
Indira Gandhi Indoor Stadium
Public Library
MANDIR MARG
Cathedral of the Sacred Heart
BARAKHAMBA ROAD
Natural History Museum
VIKAS MARG
KALI BARI MARG
SINGH MARG
New Delhi GPO
Gurudwara Bangla Sahib
Jantar Mantar
Tolstoy
Dr. R. M. Lohia
BABA KHARAK
ASHOKA
SIKANDRA ROAD
PARK ST
TALKATORA ROAD
JANPATH
KASTURBA GANDHI MARG
FIROZ SHAH ROAD
Supreme Court
BAHADUR SHAH ZAFAR MG
RING ROAD
Church of the Redemption
PARLIAMENT ST
RAISINA RD
Canning
Copernicus Marg
TILAK MARG
Bhagwan Das Road
MATHURA ROAD
Mughal Gardens
Lok Sabha (Parliament House)
Dr. Rajender Prasad Road
Indira Gandhi Centre of Arts
National Science Centre
Crafts Museum
Rashtrapati Bhawan (President's Res.)
New Delhi
India Gate
National Stadium
Dalhousie Road
National Museum
Rajpath
SHERSHAH RD
Purana Qila (Old Fort)
South Ave
Thyagaraj Mg
KAMRAJ RD
MOTILAL NEHRU MG
Maulana Azad Rd
AKBAR ROAD
SHAHJAHAN RD
National Gallery of Modern Art
Shrine
Mosque

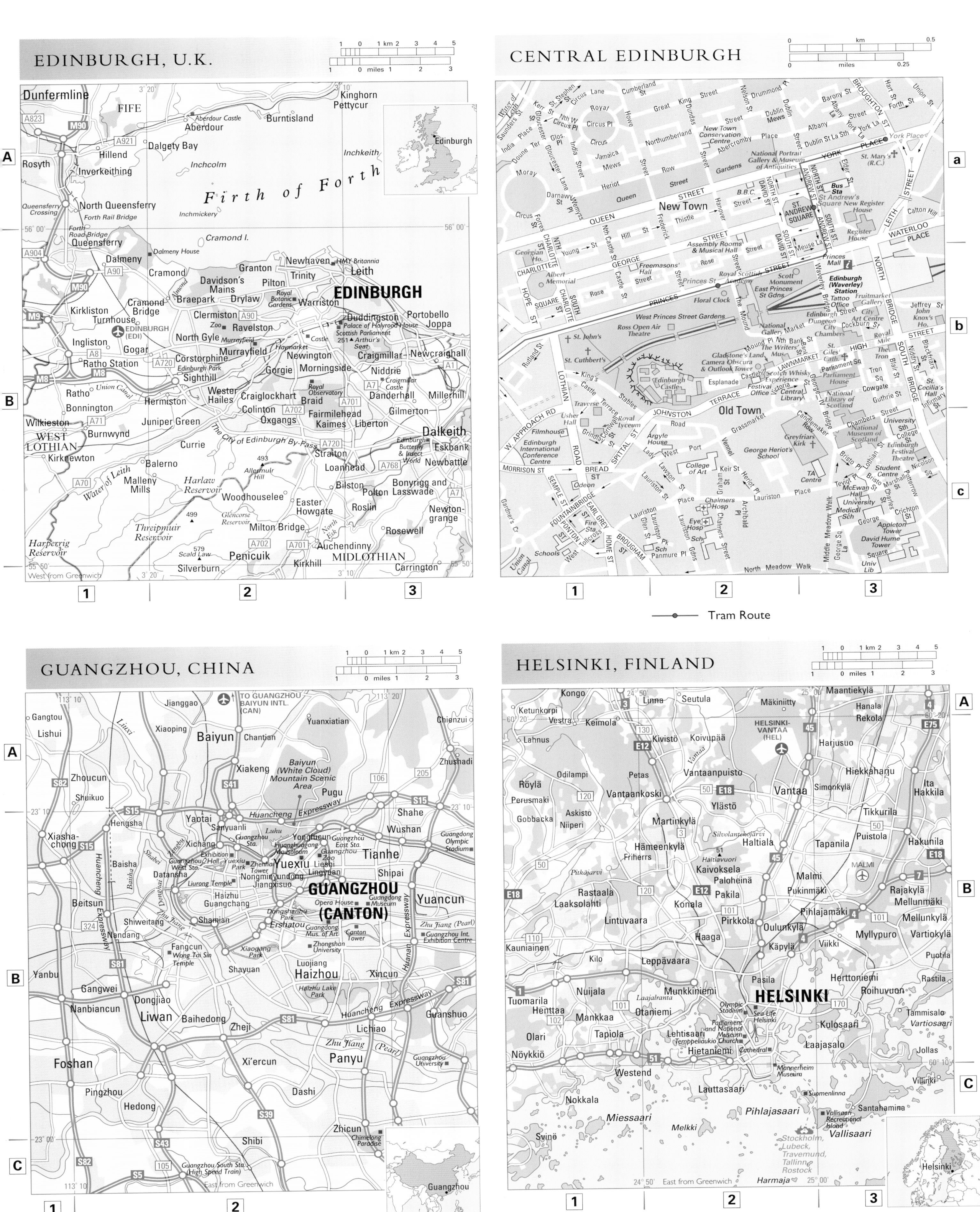
EDINBURGH, U.K.
West from Greenwich
Dunfermline
FIFE
Kinghorn
Pettycur
Aberdour
Burntisland
Dalgety Bay
Hillend
Rosyth
Inverkeithing
Inchkeith
Inchcolm
Firth of Forth
Queensferry Crossing
North Queensferry
Forth Rail Bridge
Inchmickery
Forth Road Bridge
Queensferry
Cramond I.
Dalmeny
Dalmeny House
Cramond
Granton
Newhaven
HMY Britannia
Leith
Trinity
Davidson's Mains
Pilton
EDINBURGH
Kirkliston
Cramond Bridge
Braepark
Drylaw
Royal Botanic Gardens
Warriston
Turnhouse
Clermiston
Duddingston
Portobello
Joppa
EDINBURGH (EDI)
Ravelston
Palace of Holyrood House
Scottish Parliament
Arthur's Seat
Ingliston
North Gyle
Murrayfield
Haymarket
Castle
Gogar
Corstorphine
Newington
Craigmillar
Newcraighall
Ratho Station
Edinburgh Park
Morningside
Niddrie
Sighthill
Gorgie
Ratho
Union Canal
Royal Observatory
Craigmillar Castle
Bonnington
Hermiston
Wester Hailes
Craiglockhart
Braid
Danderhall
Millerhill
Wilkieston
Juniper Green
Colinton
Oxgangs
Fairmilehead
Gilmerton
WEST LOTHIAN
Burnwynd
Kaimes
Liberton
Dalkeith
Kirknewton
Currie
The City of Edinburgh By-Pass
Edinburgh Butterfly & Insect World
Eskbank
Straiton
Balerno
Allermuir Hill
Loanhead
Newbattle
Water of Leith
Malleny Mills
Harlaw Reservoir
Bilston
Polton
Bonyrigg and Lasswade
Woodhouselee
Easter Howgate
Roslin
Newtongrange
Glencorse Reservoir
Threipmuir Reservoir
Milton Bridge
North Esk
Rosewell
Harperrig Reservoir
Scald Law
Penicuik
Auchendinny
MIDLOTHIAN
Silverburn
Kirkhill
Carrington
Edinburgh
CENTRAL EDINBURGH
Tram Route
New Town
Queen Street
George Street
Princes Street
Rose Street
St. Andrew Square
Edinburgh (Waverley) Station
Bus Sta
Princes Mall
National Portrait Gallery & Museum of Antiquities
New Register House
Register House
Calton Hill
Waterloo Place
York Place
Scott Monument
East Princes St Gdns
West Princes Street Gardens
Floral Clock
Royal Scottish Academy
National Gallery
The Mound
Ross Open Air Theatre
St. John's
St. Cuthbert's
Edinburgh Castle
Esplanade
Castlehill
Lawnmarket
High Street
St. Giles Cath.
Parliament Sq
Royal Mile
Old Town
Camera Obscura & Outlook Tower
Gladstone's Land
The Writers' Mus.
Scotch Whisky Experience
Festival Office
Central Library
National Library of Scotland
Victoria St
George IV Bridge
Grassmarket
Greyfriars Kirk
Johnston Terrace
Usher Hall
Royal Lyceum
Traverse Theatre
Filmhouse
Edinburgh International Conference Centre
Lothian Road
Argyle House
Lady Lawson St
George Heriot's School
College of Art
Lauriston Place
Chalmers Hosp
Eye Hosp
Sch
Candlemaker Row
Chambers Street
National Museum of Scotland
University
Festival Theatre
Student Centre
McEwan Hall
University Medical Sch
George Square
Appleton Tower
David Hume Tower
Middle Meadow Walk
North Meadow Walk
Union Canal
Schools
Fountainbridge
Morrison St
Bread St
Odeon
North Bridge
South Bridge
Waverley Bridge
Fruitmarket Gallery
City Art Centre
Edinburgh Dungeon
City Chambers
John Knox's Ho.
Tron
The Tron
St. Cecilia's Hall
St. Mary's (R.C.)
Jeffrey St
Cowgate
Charlotte Square
Georgian Ho.
Albert Memorial
Heriot Row
Moray Place
Circus Pl
Royal Circus
Drummond Pl
Dublin St
Leith Street
Broughton St
New Town Conservation Centre
Assembly Rooms & Musical Hall
Freemasons' Hall
GUANGZHOU, CHINA
East from Greenwich
TO GUANGZHOU BAIYUN INTL. (CAN)
Jianggao
Gangtou
Lishui
Xiaoping
Baiyun
Chantian
Yuanxiatian
Chienzui
Zhushadi
Zhoucun
Xiakeng
Baiyun (White Cloud) Mountain Scenic Area
Pugu
Shuikuo
Huancheng Expressway
Shahe
Hengsha
Yaotai
Sanyuanli
Wushan
Xiasha-chong
Xichang
Guangzhou Sta.
Yongfuun
Tianhe
Guangdong Olympic Stadium
Baisha
Yuexiu
Liesi
Shipai
Datansha
Nongminyundong
Jiangxisuo
GUANGZHOU (CANTON)
Yuancun
Beitsun
Haizhu
Guangchang
Opera House
Guangdong Museum
Shiweitang
Shamian
Ershatou
Canton Tower
Nandang
Zhu Jiang (Pearl)
Fangcun
Wong Tai Sin Temple
Xiaogang Park
Zhongshan University
Yanbu
Shayuan
Luojiang
Haizhou
Xincun
Gangwei
Dongjiao
Haizhu Lake Park
Nanbiancun
Liwan
Baihedong
Guanshuo
Zheji
Lichiao
Foshan
Xi'ercun
Panyu
Guangzhou University
Pingzhou
Dashi
Hedong
Zhicun
Chimelong Paradise
Shibi
Guangzhou South Sta. (High Speed Train)
Guangzhou
HELSINKI, FINLAND
East from Greenwich
Kongo
Linna
Seutula
Mäkiniitty
Maantiekylä
Ketunkorpi
Vestra
Keimola
Hanala
Rekola
HELSINKI-VANTAA (HEL)
Lahnus
Kivistö
Koivupää
Harjusuo
Odilampi
Petas
Vantaanpuisto
Hiekkaharju
Röylä
Vantaankoski
Ylästö
Vantaa
Simonkylä
Ita Hakkila
Perusmaki
Askisto
Tikkurila
Gobbacka
Niiperi
Martinkylä
Puistola
Haltiala
Tapanila
Hakunila
Hämeenkylä
Friherrs
Kaivoksela
Malmi
Paloheinä
Rastaala
Pakila
Pukinmäki
Rajakylä
Laaksolahti
Konala
Mellunmäki
Pihlajamäki
Lintuvaara
Pirkkola
Oulunkylä
Myllypuro
Vartiokylä
Kauniainen
Haaga
Käpylä
Viikki
Puotila
Kilo
Leppävaara
Pasila
Herttoniemi
Rastila
Tuomarila
Nuijala
Munkkiniemi
HELSINKI
Roihuvuori
Henttaa
Mankkaa
Otaniemi
Olympic Stadium
Sea Life Helsinki
Tammisalo
Vartiosaari
Olari
Tapiola
Lehtisaari
Kulosaari
Nöykkiö
Hietaniemi
Cathedral
Laajasalo
Jollas
Westend
Mannerheim Museum
Villinki
Lauttasaari
Suomenlinna
Nokkala
Santahamina
Miessaari
Pihlajasaari
Vallisaari
Melkki
Svinö
Stockholm, Lubeck, Travemund, Tallinn, Rostock
Harmaja
Helsinki

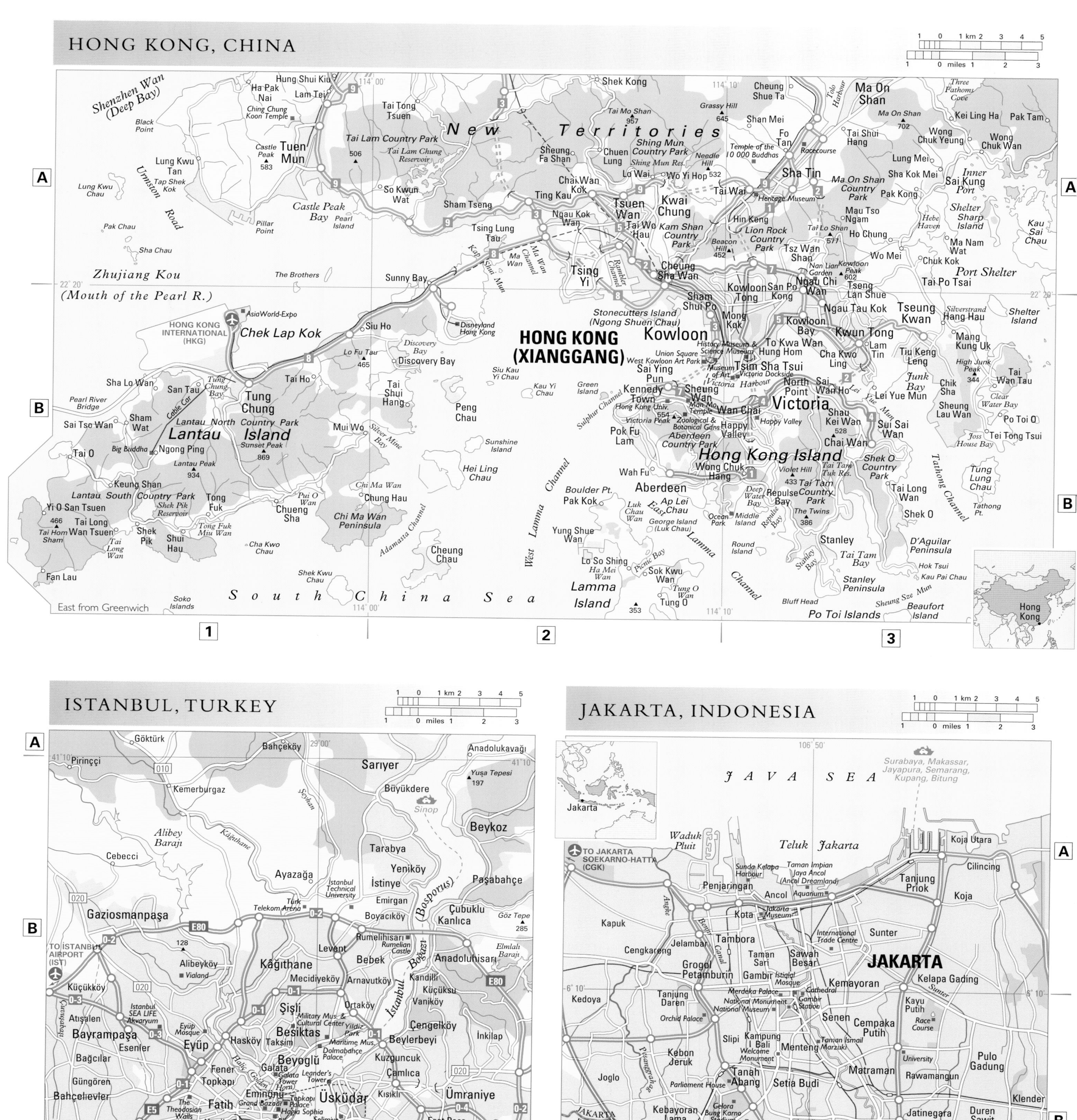
HONG KONG, CHINA
Shenzhen Wan (Deep Bay)
New Territories
Tai Mo Shan 957
Tuen Mun
Tai Lam Country Park
Tsuen Wan
Kwai Chung
Sha Tin
Ma On Shan
Tsing Yi
Zhujiang Kou
(Mouth of the Pearl R.)
HONG KONG INTERNATIONAL (HKG)
Chek Lap Kok
Tung Chung
Lantau Island
Lantau North Country Park
Lantau South Country Park
Lantau Peak 934
Sunset Peak 869
Discovery Bay
Disneyland Hong Kong
Peng Chau
HONG KONG (XIANGGANG)
Kowloon
Tsim Sha Tsui
Victoria Harbour
Victoria
Hong Kong Island
Victoria Peak 554
Aberdeen
Lamma Island
West Lamma Channel
East Lamma Channel
Stanley
Sai Kung
Port Shelter
Tseung Kwan
Cheung Chau
Po Toi Islands
South China Sea
East from Greenwich
ISTANBUL, TURKEY
Sarıyer
Beykoz
İstanbul Boğazı (Bosporus)
Gaziosmanpaşa
Kağıthane
Şişli
Beşiktaş
Beyoğlu
Eyüp
Fatih
Üsküdar
İSTANBUL
Kadıköy
Ümraniye
Bakırköy
Zeytinburnu
Marmara Denizi (Sea of Marmara)
TO ISTANBUL AIRPORT (IST)
TO ISTANBUL SABIHA GÖKCEN (SAW)
Istanbul
East from Greenwich
JAKARTA, INDONESIA
JAVA SEA
Teluk Jakarta
Surabaya, Makassar, Jayapura, Semarang, Kupang, Bitung
TO JAKARTA SOEKARNO-HATTA (CGK)
Tanjung Priok
Kota
JAKARTA
Kemayoran
Menteng
Tanah Abang
Kebayoran Baru
Jatinegara
Kelapa Gading
JAKARTA HALIM PERDANAKUSUMA (HLP)
Jakarta
East from Greenwich

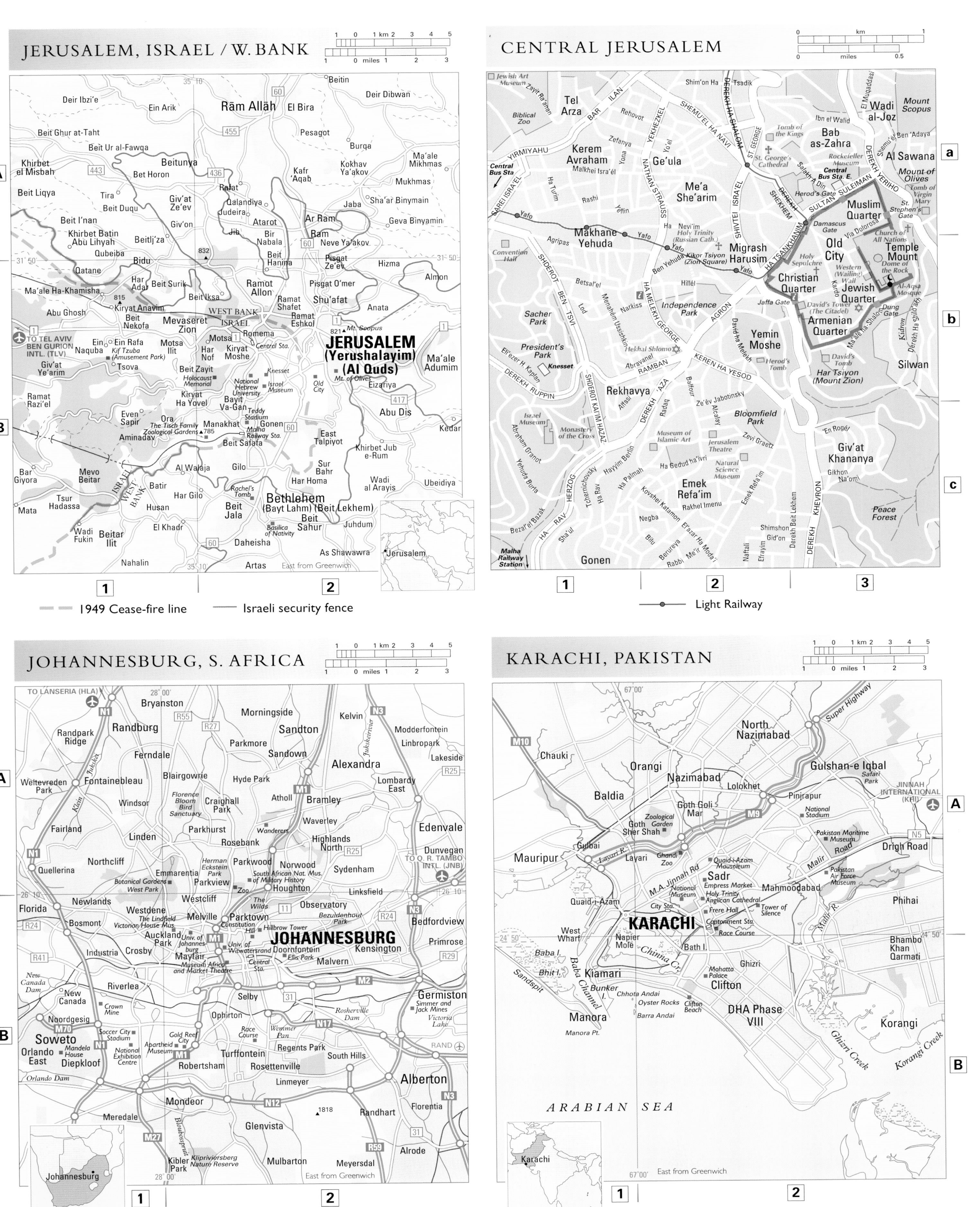
JERUSALEM, ISRAEL / W. BANK
km
miles
Beitin
Deir Dibwan
Deir Ibzi'e
Ein Arik
Rām Allāh
El Bira
Beit Ghur at-Taht
Pesagot
Burqa
Beit Ur al-Fawqa
Beitunya
Kafr 'Aqab
Kokhav Ya'akov
Ma'ale Mikhmas
Khirbet el Misbah
Bet Horon
Mukhmas
Beit Liqya
Tira
Giv'at Ze'ev
Qalandiya
Sha'ar Binyamin
Beit Duqu
Rafat
Jaba
Beit I'nan
Judeira
Ar Ram
Geva Binyamin
Khirbet Batin Abu Lihyah
Giv'on
Atarot
Ram
Beitlj'za
Jib
Bir Nabala
Neve Ya'akov
Qubeiba
Beit Hanina
Pisgat Ze'ev
Hizma
Bidu
Qatane
Almon
Har Adar
Beit Surik
Ramot Allon
Pisgat O'mer
Ma'ale Ha-Khamisha
Beit Iksa
Ramat Shafet
Shu'afat
Abu Ghosh
Kiryat Anavim
WEST BANK
ISRAEL
Ramat Eshkol
Anata
Beit Nekofa
Mevaseret Zion
Mt. Scopus
TO TEL AVIV BEN GURION INTL. (TLV)
Ein Naquba
Ein Rafa
Motsa Ilit
Motsa
Romema
Central Sta.
JERUSALEM
(Yerushalayim)
(Al Quds)
Kif Tzuba (Amusement Park)
Har Nof
Kiryat Moshe
Giv'at Ye'arim
Tsova
Beit Zayit
Knesset
Ma'ale Adumim
Holocaust Memorial
National Hebrew University
Israel Museum
Old City
Mt. of Olives
Eizariya
Ramat Razi'el
Kiryat Ha Yovel
Bayit Va-Gan
Abu Dis
Even Sapir
Ora
Teddy Stadium
The Tisch Family Zoological Gardens
Manakhat
Malha Railway Sta.
Gonen
Kedar
Aminadav
Beit Safafa
East Talpiyot
Khirbet Jub e-Rum
Bar Giyora
Mevo Beitar
Al Walaja
Gilo
Sur Bahr
Har Homa
Wadi al Arayis
Ubeidiya
ISRAEL
WEST BANK
Batir
Tsur Hadassa
Har Gilo
Rachel's Tomb
Bethlehem
(Bayt Lahm) (Beit Lekhem)
Mata
Husan
Beit Jala
Beit Sahur
Juhdum
El Khadr
Basilica of Nativity
Wadi Fukin
Beitar Ilit
Daheisha
As Shawawra
Nahalin
Artas
East from Greenwich
Jerusalem
1949 Cease-fire line
Israeli security fence
CENTRAL JERUSALEM
km
miles
Jewish Art Museum
Tel Arza
Shim'on Ha Tsadik
Wadi al-Joz
Mount Scopus
Biblical Zoo
Tomb of the Kings
Ibn el Walid
Bab as-Zahra
Kerem Avraham
Ge'ula
St. George's Cathedral
Rockefeller Museum
Al Sawana
Central Bus Sta
Central Bus Sta. E.
Mount of Olives
Me'a She'arim
Herod's Gate
Tomb of the Virgin Mary
Muslim Quarter
St. Stephen's Gate
Damascus Gate
Makhane Yehuda
Church of All Nations
Old City
Temple Mount
Convention Hall
Migrash Harusim
Holy Sepulchre
Dome of the Rock
Christian Quarter
Western (Wailing) Wall
Jewish Quarter
Al-Aqsa Mosque
Jaffa Gate
David's Tower (The Citadel)
Dung Gate
Sacher Park
Independence Park
Armenian Quarter
Yemin Moshe
President's Park
Knesset
Herod's Tomb
David's Tomb
Silwan
Har Tsiyon (Mount Zion)
Rekhavya
Israel Museum
Monastery of the Cross
Bloomfield Park
Museum of Islamic Art
Jerusalem Theatre
Giv'at Khananya
Natural Science Museum
Emek Refa'im
Peace Forest
Gonen
Malha Railway Station
Light Railway
JOHANNESBURG, S. AFRICA
km
miles
TO LANSERIA (HLA)
Bryanston
Morningside
Kelvin
Randburg
Randpark Ridge
Sandton
Modderfontein
Parkmore
Linbropark
Ferndale
Sandown
Lakeside
Alexandra
Blairgowrie
Weltevreden Park
Fontainebleau
Hyde Park
Lombardy East
Florence Bloom Bird Sanctuary
Craighall Park
Windsor
Atholl
Bramley
Waverley
Fairland
Parkhurst
Wanderers
Highlands North
Edenvale
Linden
Rosebank
Dunvegan
Northcliff
Herman Eckstein Park
Parkwood
Norwood
TO O. R. TAMBO INTL. (JNB)
Quellerina
Emmarentia
South African Nat. Mus. of Military History
Sydenham
Botanical Gardens West Park
Parkview
Zoo
Houghton
Linksfield
Newlands
Westcliff
The Wilds
Observatory
Florida
Westdene
The Lindfield Victorian House Mus.
Melville
Parktown
Bezuidenhout Park
Bosmont
Constitution Hill
Hillbrow Tower
Bedfordview
Auckland Park
Univ. of Johannesburg
Univ. of Witwatersrand
JOHANNESBURG
Primrose
Industria
Crosby
Doornfontein
Kensington
Mayfair
Ellis Park
Museum Africa and Market Theatre
Central Sta.
Malvern
New Canada Dam
Riverlea
New Canada
Selby
Germiston
Crown Mine
Simmer and Jack Mines
Noordgesig
Ophirton
Rosherville Dam
Victoria Lake
Soweto
Soccer City Stadium
Gold Reef City
Race Course
Wemmer Pan
Orlando East
Mandela House
National Exhibition Centre
Apartheid Museum
Regents Park
South Hills
Diepkloof
Turffontein
RAND
Robertsham
Rosettenville
Orlando Dam
Alberton
Linmeyer
Mondeor
Florentia
Meredale
Glenvista
Randhart
Johannesburg
Kibler Park
Klipriviersberg Nature Reserve
Mulbarton
Meyersdal
Alrode
East from Greenwich
KARACHI, PAKISTAN
km
miles
Super Highway
North Nazimabad
Chauki
Orangi
Gulshan-e Iqbal
Safari Park
Nazimabad
Lolokhet
JINNAH INTERNATIONAL (KHI)
Baldia
Pinjirpur
Goth Goli Mar
National Stadium
Zoological Garden
Goth Sher Shah
Pakistan Maritime Museum
Mauripur
Gulbai
Lyari R.
Drigh Road
Layari
Ghandi Zoo
Quaid-i-Azam Mausoleum
Malir
Sadr
Pakistan Air Force Museum
M.A. Jinnah Rd
Empress Market
Mahmoodabad
National Museum
Holy Trinity Anglican Cathedral
Quaid-i-Azam
City Sta.
Frere Hall
Tower of Silence
Phihai
KARACHI
Cantonment Sta.
West Wharf
Race Course
Napier Mole
Bath I.
Bhambo Khan Qarmati
Chinna Cr.
Baba I.
Bhit I.
Ghizri
Sandspit
Baba Channel
Kiamari
Mohatta Palace
Clifton
Bunker I.
Chhota Andai
Oyster Rocks
Clifton Beach
DHA Phase VIII
Barra Andai
Manora
Korangi
Manora Pt.
Ghizri Creek
Korangi Creek
ARABIAN SEA
Karachi
East from Greenwich

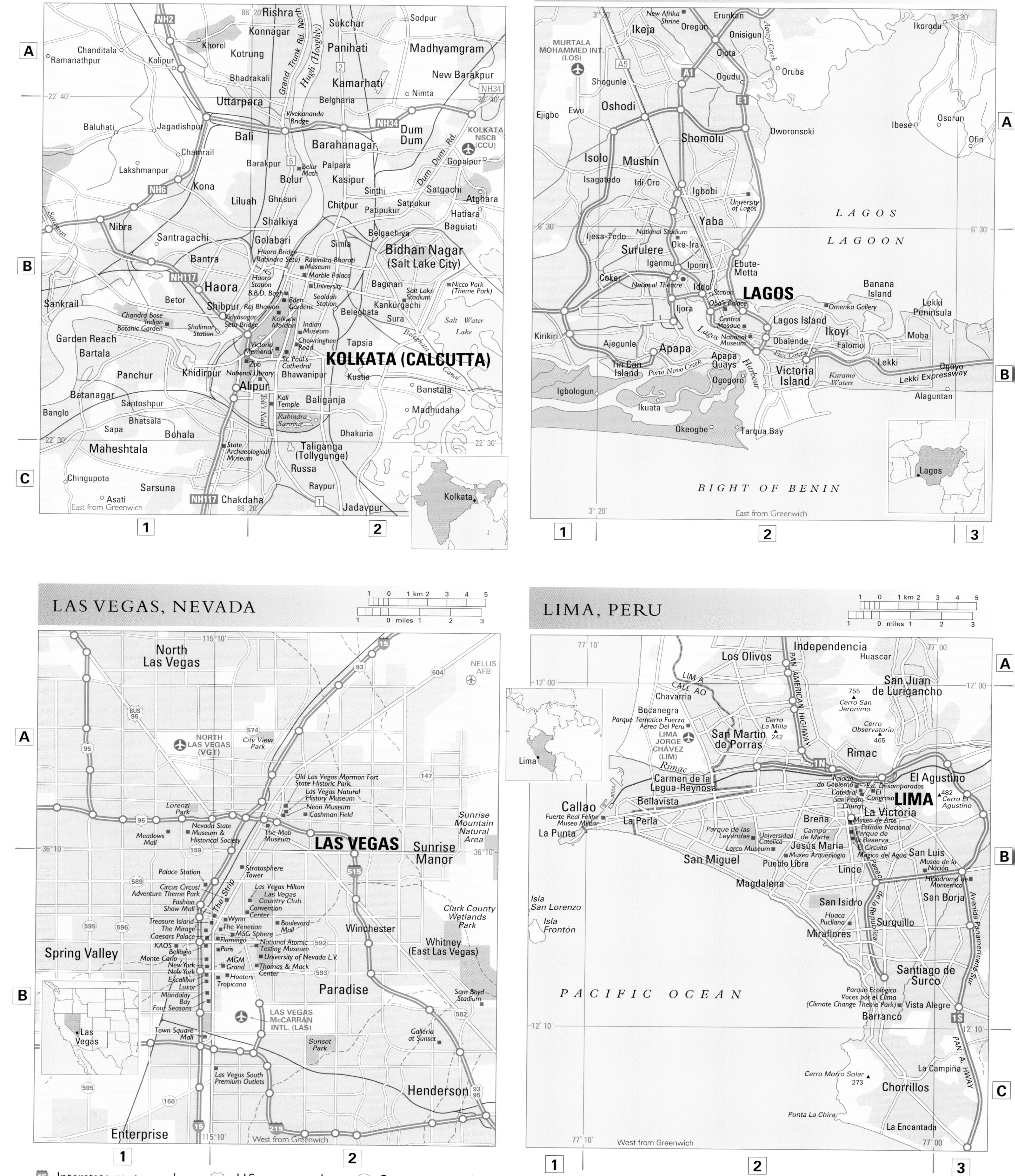

Interstate route numbers U.S. route numbers State route numbers

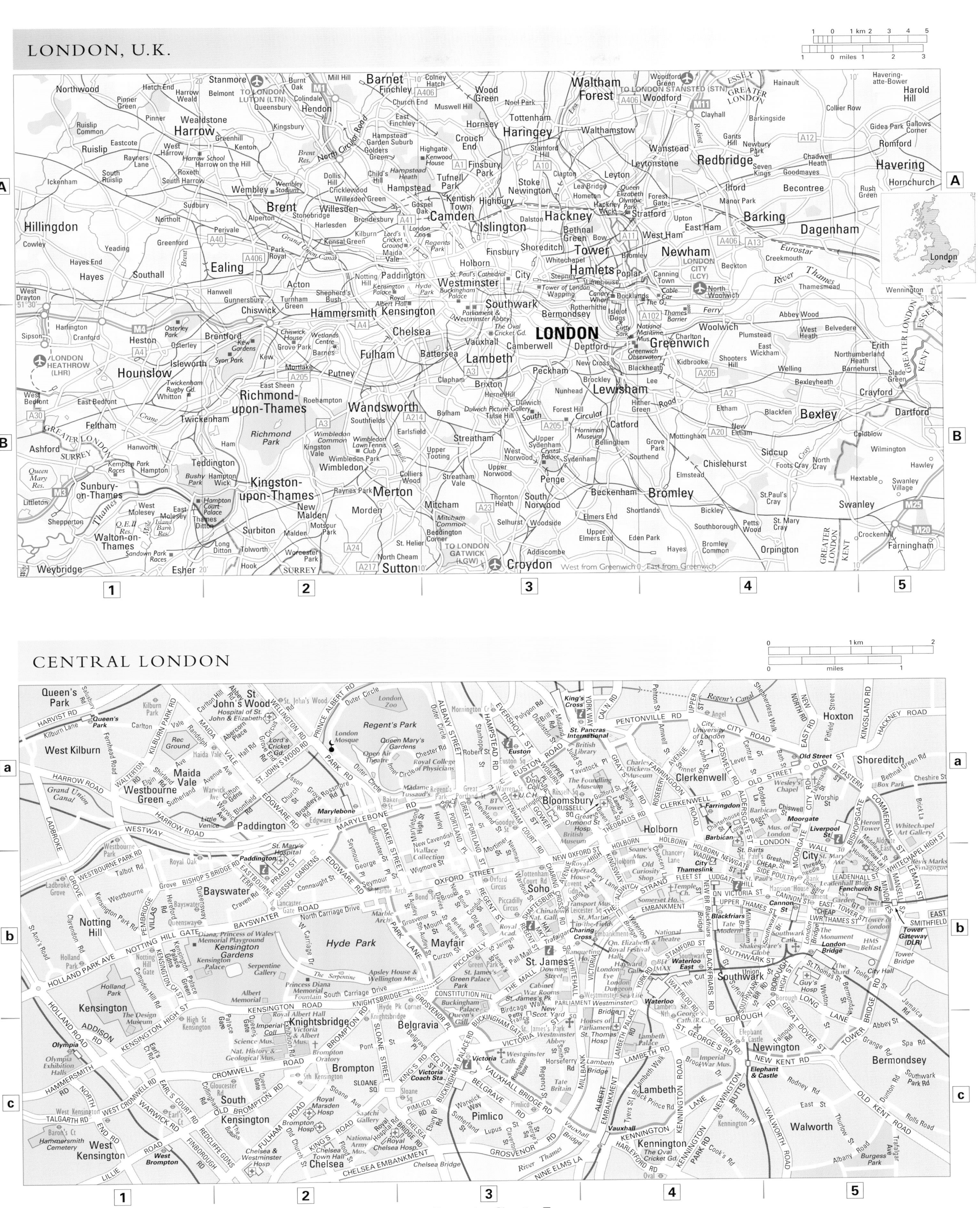
LONDON, U.K.
1 0 1 km 2 3 4 5
1 0 miles 1 2 3
Northwood
Stanmore
Barnet
Waltham Forest
Woodford
Harold Hill
Harrow
Hendon
Finchley
Wood Green
Tottenham
Haringey
Walthamstow
Redbridge
Romford
Havering
Ruislip
Wembley
Hampstead
Hornsey
Wanstead
Ilford
Hillingdon
Brent
Camden
Islington
Hackney
Leyton
Stratford
Barking
Dagenham
Ealing
Paddington
Westminster
City
Tower Hamlets
Newham
Acton
Hammersmith
Kensington
Southwark
Bermondsey
Docklands
Hayes
Southall
Chiswick
Chelsea
LONDON
Deptford
Greenwich
Woolwich
Brentford
Fulham
Battersea
Lambeth
Camberwell
Erith
Hounslow
LONDON HEATHROW (LHR)
Richmond-upon-Thames
Putney
Wandsworth
Brixton
Peckham
Lewisham
Bexley
Crayford
Dartford
Feltham
Twickenham
Richmond Park
Streatham
Catford
Sidcup
Teddington
Kingston-upon-Thames
Wimbledon
Merton
Mitcham
Norwood
Penge
Beckenham
Bromley
Chislehurst
Swanley
Sunbury-on-Thames
Walton-on-Thames
Surbiton
Morden
Sutton
Croydon
Orpington
Weybridge
Esher
TO LONDON GATWICK (LGW)
TO LONDON LUTON (LTN)
TO LONDON STANSTED (STN)
LONDON CITY (LCY)
GREATER LONDON
KENT
SURREY
ESSEX
West from Greenwich 0 East from Greenwich
A B 1 2 3 4 5
CENTRAL LONDON
0 1 km 2
0 miles 1
Queen's Park
St. John's Wood
Regent's Park
King's Cross
Hoxton
Shoreditch
West Kilburn
Maida Vale
Euston
St. Pancras International
Clerkenwell
Westbourne Green
Marylebone
Bloomsbury
Paddington
Holborn
Barbican
City
Whitechapel
Bayswater
Soho
Notting Hill
Hyde Park
Mayfair
Kensington Gardens
St. James
Southwark
Tower Bridge
Kensington
Knightsbridge
Belgravia
Westminster
Waterloo
Lambeth
Newington
Bermondsey
Olympia
Brompton
South Kensington
Pimlico
Vauxhall
Kennington
Walworth
West Kensington
Chelsea
River Thames
a b c 1 2 3 4 5
Congestion Charging Zone
COPYRIGHT PHILIP'S

LISBON, PORTUGAL

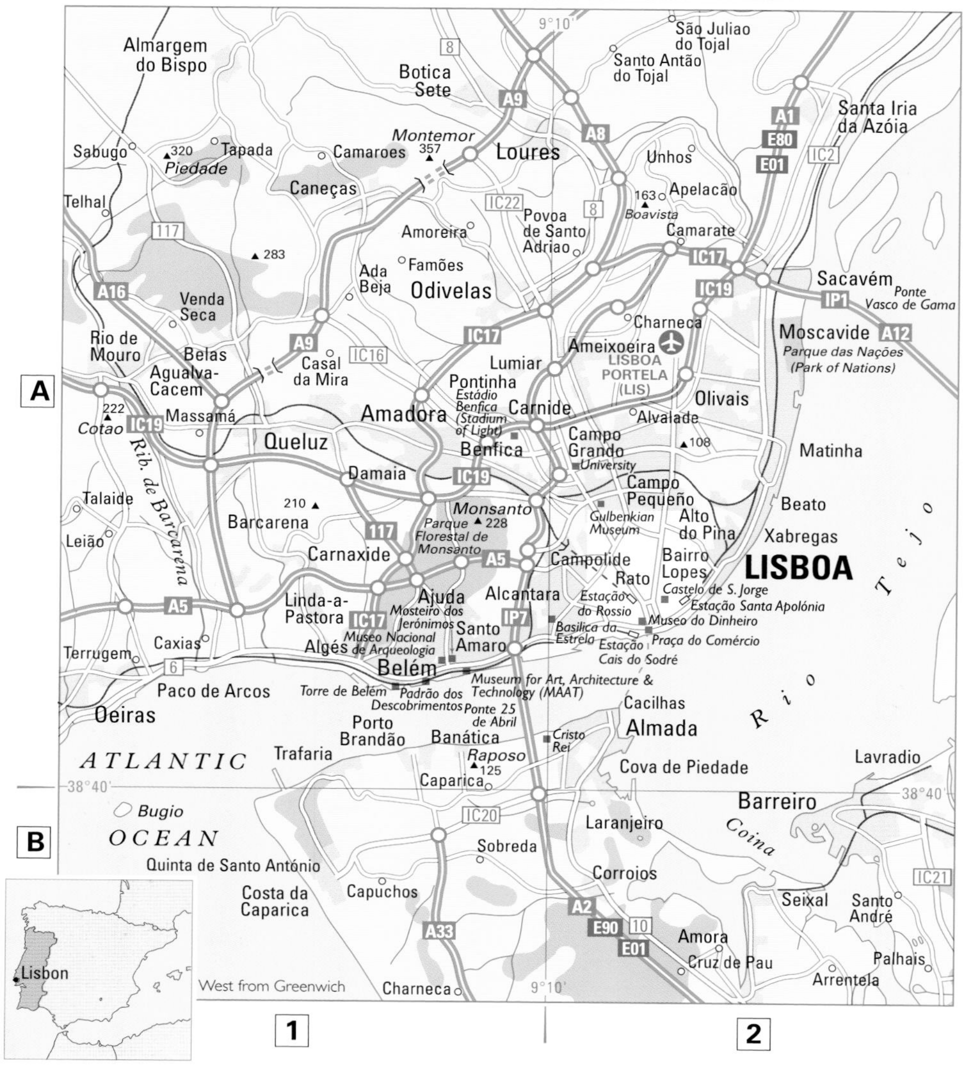

1 0 1 km 2 3 4 5
1 0 miles 1 2 3

Almargem do Bispo
Botica Sete
São Julião do Tojal
Santo Antão do Tojal
Santa Iria da Azóia
Sabugo
Tapada
Piedade
Camaroes
Montemor
Loures
Unhos
Telhal
Caneças
Apelação
Povoa de Santo Adrião
Camarate
Amoreira
Famões
Ada Beja
Odivelas
Sacavém
Ponte Vasco de Gama
Venda Seca
Charneca
Moscavide
Parque das Nações (Park of Nations)
Rio de Mouro
Belas
Casal da Mira
Lumiar
Ameixoeira
LISBOA PORTELA (LIS)
Agualva-Cacem
Pontinha
Estádio Benfica (Stadium of Light)
Carnide
Olivais
Cotao
Massamá
Amadora
Alvalade
Queluz
Benfica
Campo Grande
University
Matinha
Talaide
Damaia
Campo Pequeno
Rib. de Barcarena
Monsanto
Gulbenkian Museum
Beato
Leião
Barcarena
Parque Florestal de Monsanto
Alto do Pina
Xabregas
Carnaxide
Campolide
Rato
Bairro Lopes
LISBOA
Linda-a-Pastora
Ajuda
Alcantara
Estação do Rossio
Castelo de S. Jorge
Estação Santa Apolónia
Caxias
Mosteiro dos Jerónimos
Santo Amaro
Basílica da Estrela
Museu do Dinheiro
Praça do Comércio
Terrugem
Museu Nacional de Arqueologia
Algés
Estação Cais do Sodré
Belém
Museum for Art, Architecture & Technology (MAAT)
Paco de Arcos
Torre de Belém
Padrão dos Descobrimentos
Ponte 25 de Abril
Cacilhas
Rio Tejo
Oeiras
Porto Brandão
Cristo Rei
Almada
ATLANTIC
Trafaria
Banática
Raposo
Lavradio
Cova de Piedade
Caparica
Barreiro
Bugio
OCEAN
Sobreda
Laranjeiro
Coina
Quinta de Santo António
Corroios
Costa da Caparica
Capuchos
Seixal
Santo André
Amora
Cruz de Pau
Palhais
Arrentela
Charneca
Lisbon
West from Greenwich
9°10′
38°40′

CENTRAL LISBON

0 km 1
0 miles 0.5

Palácio de Justiça
Penitenciária
Hosp. Infantil
Maternidade
Praça Duque Saldanha
Instituto Superior Técnico
Av. Casal Ribeiro
Parque Eduardo VII
Pavilhão Carlos Lopes
Praça Marquês de Pombal
Estefânia
Rua Pascoal de Melo
Hospital Estefânia
Praça do Chile
Amoreiras
Penha de França
Anjos
Hospital M. Bombarda
Hospital de Santa Marta
Hospital dos Capuchos
Rato
Museu Nacional de História Natural e de Ciência
Jardim Botanico
Avenida da Liberdade
Hosp. do Desterro
Instituto de Medicina Legal
Bairro Lopes
Graça
Palácio de Assembleia Nacional
Hospital de S. José
Restauradores
Praça dos Restauradores
Teatro Nacional
Estação do Rossio
Bairro Alto
Hospital de Jesus
Praça Rossio
Museu do Arqueológico do Carmo
Castelo de São Jorge (St. George's Castle)
Museu de Arte Decorativas
Estação Santa Apolónia
Teatro Nac. de São Carlos
Elevador de Santa Justa
Baixa-Chiado
Biblioteca Nacional
Museu do Dinheiro
Alfama
Museu Antoniano (St. Anthony Mus.)
Sé Catedral
Military Museum
Praça de Dom Luís I
Rua do Arsenal
Praça do Comércio
Baixa
Dom José I
Av. Ribeira das Naus
Estação Cais do Sodré
Estação Fluvial
Terreiro do Paço
Rio Tejo (Tagus)
Seixal
Montijo, Barreiro

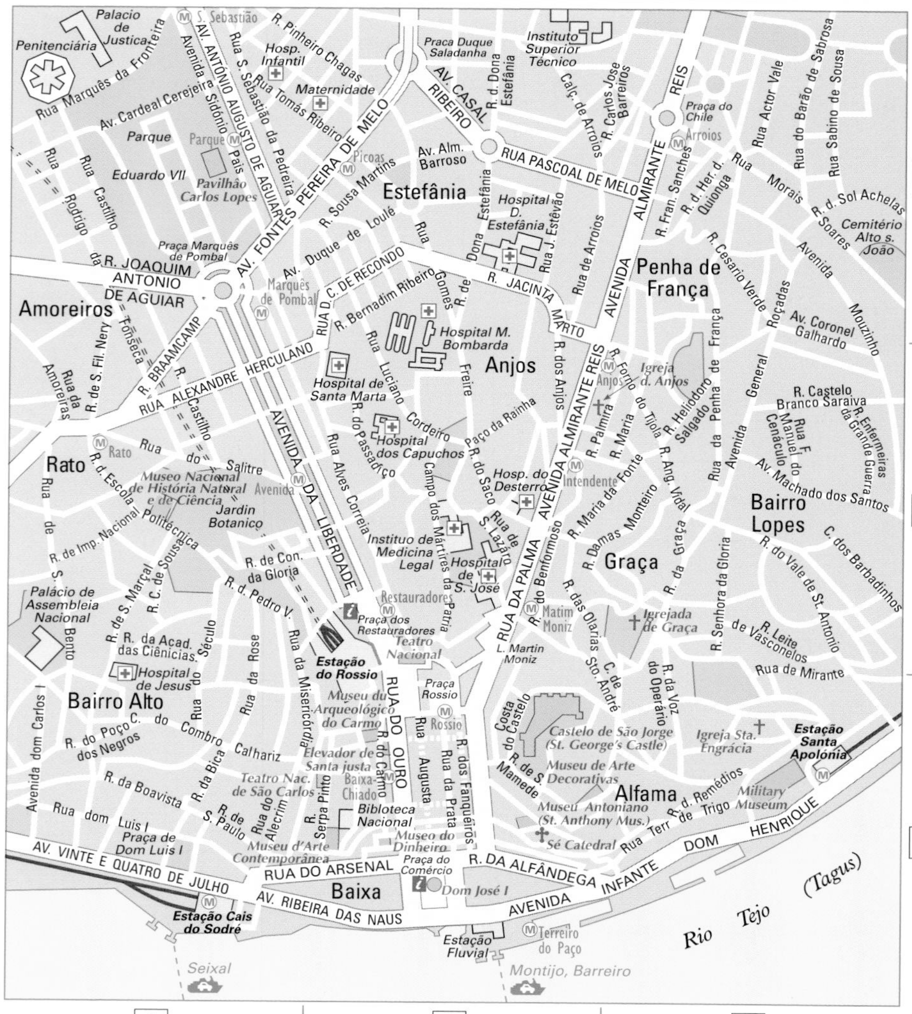

LOS ANGELES, CALIFORNIA

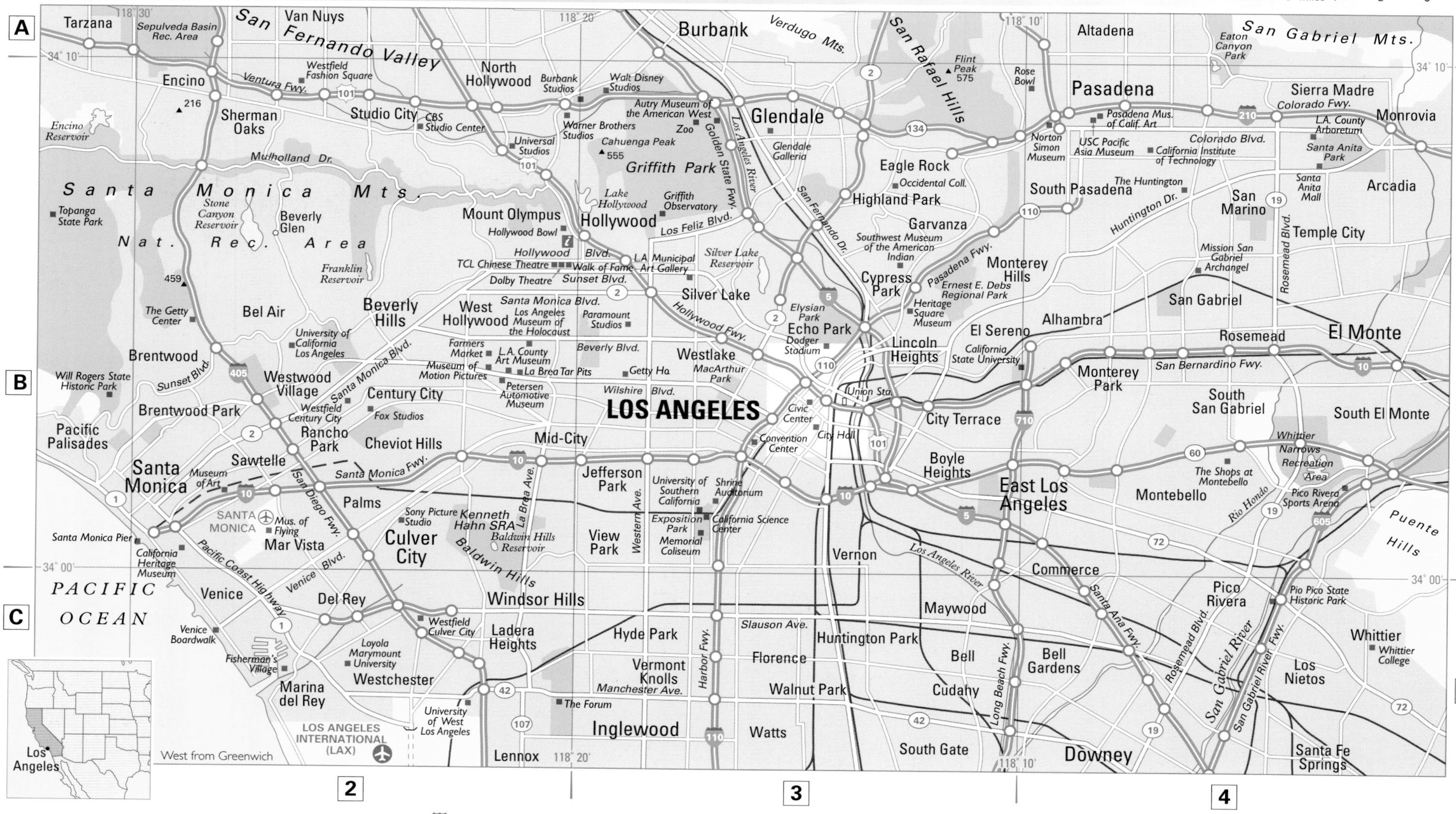

1 0 1 km 2 3 4 5
1 0 miles 1 2 3

Tarzana
Sepulveda Basin Rec. Area
San Fernando Valley
Van Nuys
Burbank
Verdugo Mts.
San Rafael Hills
Altadena
San Gabriel Mts.
Westfield Fashion Square
North Hollywood
Walt Disney Studios
Flint Peak 575
Rose Bowl
Eaton Canyon Park
Encino
Ventura Fwy.
Burbank Studios
Autry Museum of the American West
Pasadena
Sierra Madre
Sherman Oaks
Studio City
CBS Studio Center
Warner Brothers Studios
Zoo
Glendale
Pasadena Mus. of Calif. Art
Colorado Fwy.
Monrovia
Encino Reservoir
Universal Studios
Cahuenga Peak 555
Glendale Galleria
Norton Simon Museum
USC Pacific Asia Museum
California Institute of Technology
Colorado Blvd.
L.A. County Arboretum
Santa Anita Park
Mulholland Dr.
Griffith Park
Eagle Rock
Occidental Coll.
South Pasadena
The Huntington
Arcadia
Santa Monica Mts.
Topanga State Park
Stone Canyon Reservoir
Beverly Glen
Lake Hollywood
Griffith Observatory
Highland Park
San Marino
Santa Anita Mall
Mount Olympus
Hollywood
Hollywood Bowl
Los Feliz Blvd.
Garvanza
Huntington Dr.
Temple City
Nat. Rec. Area
Hollywood Blvd.
TCL Chinese Theatre
Walk of Fame
L.A. Municipal Art Gallery
Silver Lake Reservoir
Southwest Museum of the American Indian
Monterey Hills
Mission San Gabriel Archangel
Franklin Reservoir
Dolby Theatre
Sunset Blvd.
Cypress Park
Ernest E. Debs Regional Park
The Getty Center
Bel Air
Beverly Hills
West Hollywood
Santa Monica Blvd.
Los Angeles Museum of the Holocaust
Paramount Studios
Silver Lake
Heritage Square Museum
San Gabriel
Elysian Park
Echo Park
Dodger Stadium
El Sereno
Alhambra
Rosemead
El Monte
Brentwood
University of California Los Angeles
Farmers Market
L.A. County Art Museum
Beverly Blvd.
Westlake
MacArthur Park
Lincoln Heights
California State University
Will Rogers State Historic Park
Sunset Blvd.
Westwood Village
Museum of Motion Pictures
La Brea Tar Pits
Getty Ho
Monterey Park
San Bernardino Fwy.
Brentwood Park
Westfield Century City
Century City
Fox Studios
Petersen Automotive Museum
Wilshire Blvd.
LOS ANGELES
Civic Center
Union Sta.
City Terrace
South San Gabriel
South El Monte
Pacific Palisades
Rancho Park
Cheviot Hills
Mid-City
City Hall
Convention Center
Whittier Narrows Recreation Area
Santa Monica
Museum of Art
Sawtelle
Santa Monica Fwy.
Jefferson Park
University of Southern California
Shrine Auditorium
Boyle Heights
East Los Angeles
The Shops at Montebello
Montebello
SANTA MONICA
Mus. of Flying
Palms
Sony Picture Studio
Kenneth Hahn SRA
Exposition Park
California Science Center
Pico Rivera Sports Arena
Rio Hondo
Puente Hills
Santa Monica Pier
Mar Vista
Culver City
Baldwin Hills Reservoir
View Park
Memorial Coliseum
Western Ave.
California Heritage Museum
Pacific Coast Highway
San Diego Fwy.
Vernon
Los Angeles River
Commerce
PACIFIC
Venice
Venice Blvd.
Del Rey
Baldwin Hills
Windsor Hills
Pico Rivera
Pio Pico State Historic Park
OCEAN
Maywood
Venice Boardwalk
Westfield Culver City
Ladera Heights
Hyde Park
Slauson Ave.
Huntington Park
Whittier
Whittier College
Loyola Marymount University
Fisherman's Village
Bell
Bell Gardens
Santa Ana Fwy.
Rosemead Blvd.
San Gabriel River
San Gabriel River Fwy.
Marina del Rey
Westchester
Vermont Knolls
Manchester Ave.
Florence
Walnut Park
Cudahy
Los Nietos
Harbor Fwy.
Long Beach Fwy.
University of West Los Angeles
The Forum
LOS ANGELES INTERNATIONAL (LAX)
Inglewood
Watts
South Gate
Downey
Santa Fe Springs
Lennox
Los Angeles
West from Greenwich
118°30′ 118°20′ 118°10′
34°10′ 34°00′

Interstate route numbers U.S. route numbers State route numbers

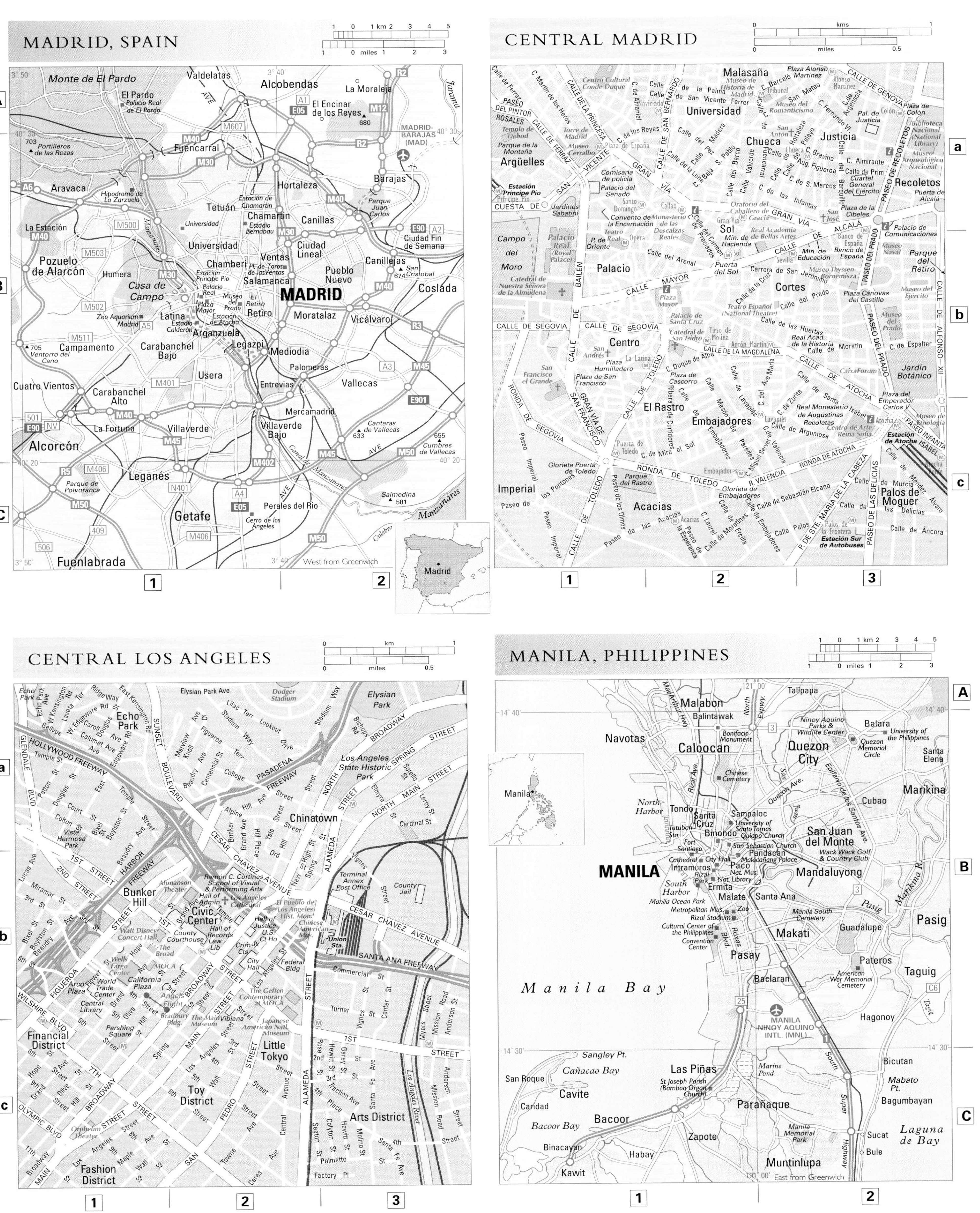
MADRID, SPAIN
West from Greenwich
Monte de El Pardo
Valdelatas
Alcobendas
La Moraleja
El Pardo
Palacio Real de El Pardo
El Encinar de los Reyes
MADRID-BARAJAS (MAD)
Portilleros de las Rozas
Fuencarral
Aravaca
Hipódromo de La Zarzuela
Hortaleza
Barajas
Tetuán
Estación de Chamartín
Chamartín
Estadio Bernabéu
Canillas
Parque Juan Carlos
La Estación
Universidad
Ciudad Lineal
Ciudad Fin de Semana
Pozuelo de Alarcón
Chamberí
Ventas
Canillejas
San Cristobal
Humera
Casa de Campo
Salamanca
Pueblo Nuevo
Coslada
MADRID
Zoo Aquarium Madrid
Latina
Retiro
Moratalaz
Vicálvaro
Arganzuela
Campamento
Carabanchel Bajo
Legazpi
Mediodia
Ventorro del Cano
Usera
Palomeras
Vallecas
Cuatro Vientos
Carabanchel Alto
Entrevias
Mercamadrid
La Fortuna
Villaverde
Villaverde Bajo
Canteras de Vallecas
Cumbres de Vallecas
Alcorcón
Leganés
Parque de Polvoranca
Canal de Manzanares
Salmedina
Getafe
Perales del Rio
Cerro de los Angeles
Manzanares
Fuenlabrada
Madrid
CENTRAL MADRID
Malasaña
Plaza Alonso Martinez
Universidad
Chueca
Justicia
Argüelles
Recoletos
Estación Principe Pio
Palacio Real (Royal Palace)
Sol
Puerta del Sol
Palacio
Campo del Moro
Catedral de Nuestra Señora de la Almudena
Plaza Mayor
Cortes
Parque del Retiro
Centro
Museo del Prado
Jardín Botánico
El Rastro
Embajadores
San Francisco el Grande
Estación de Atocha
Imperial
Acacias
Palos de Moguer
Estación Sur de Autobuses
Parque del Rastro
CALLE MAYOR
GRAN VIA
CALLE DE ALCALÁ
PASEO DEL PRADO
CALLE DE SEGOVIA
CALLE DE ATOCHA
RONDA DE TOLEDO
RONDA DE ATOCHA
CENTRAL LOS ANGELES
Dodger Stadium
Elysian Park
Echo Park
HOLLYWOOD FREEWAY
Los Angeles State Historic Park
Chinatown
Vista Hermosa Park
HARBOR FREEWAY
Bunker Hill
Civic Center
Walt Disney Concert Hall
Union Sta
SANTA ANA FREEWAY
CESAR CHAVEZ AVENUE
County Jail
Terminal Annex Post Office
California Plaza
The Broad
MOCA
Angels Flight
Bradbury Bldg.
Pershing Square
Central Library
Financial District
Little Tokyo
Toy District
Arts District
Fashion District
Los Angeles River
ALAMEDA STREET
MANILA, PHILIPPINES
East from Greenwich
Malabon
Balintawak
Talipapa
Navotas
Caloocan
Quezon City
Balara
University of the Philippines
Quezon Memorial Circle
Santa Elena
Marikina
North Harbor
Tondo
Santa Cruz
Sampaloc
Cubao
San Juan del Monte
Binondo
University of Santo Tomas
MANILA
Intramuros
Paco
Pandacan
Malacañang Palace
Mandaluyong
South Harbor
Ermita
Malate
Santa Ana
Pasig
Manila Bay
Makati
Guadalupe
Pasay
Pateros
Taguig
Baclaran
MANILA NINOY AQUINO INTL. (MNL)
Hagonoy
Sangley Pt.
Cañacao Bay
Las Piñas
Marine Pond
Bicutan
San Roque
Cavite
Caridad
Bacoor Bay
Bacoor
Parañaque
Mabato Pt.
Bagumbayan
Zapote
Manila Memorial Park
Sucat
Laguna de Bay
Binacayan
Habay
Bule
Kawit
Muntinlupa

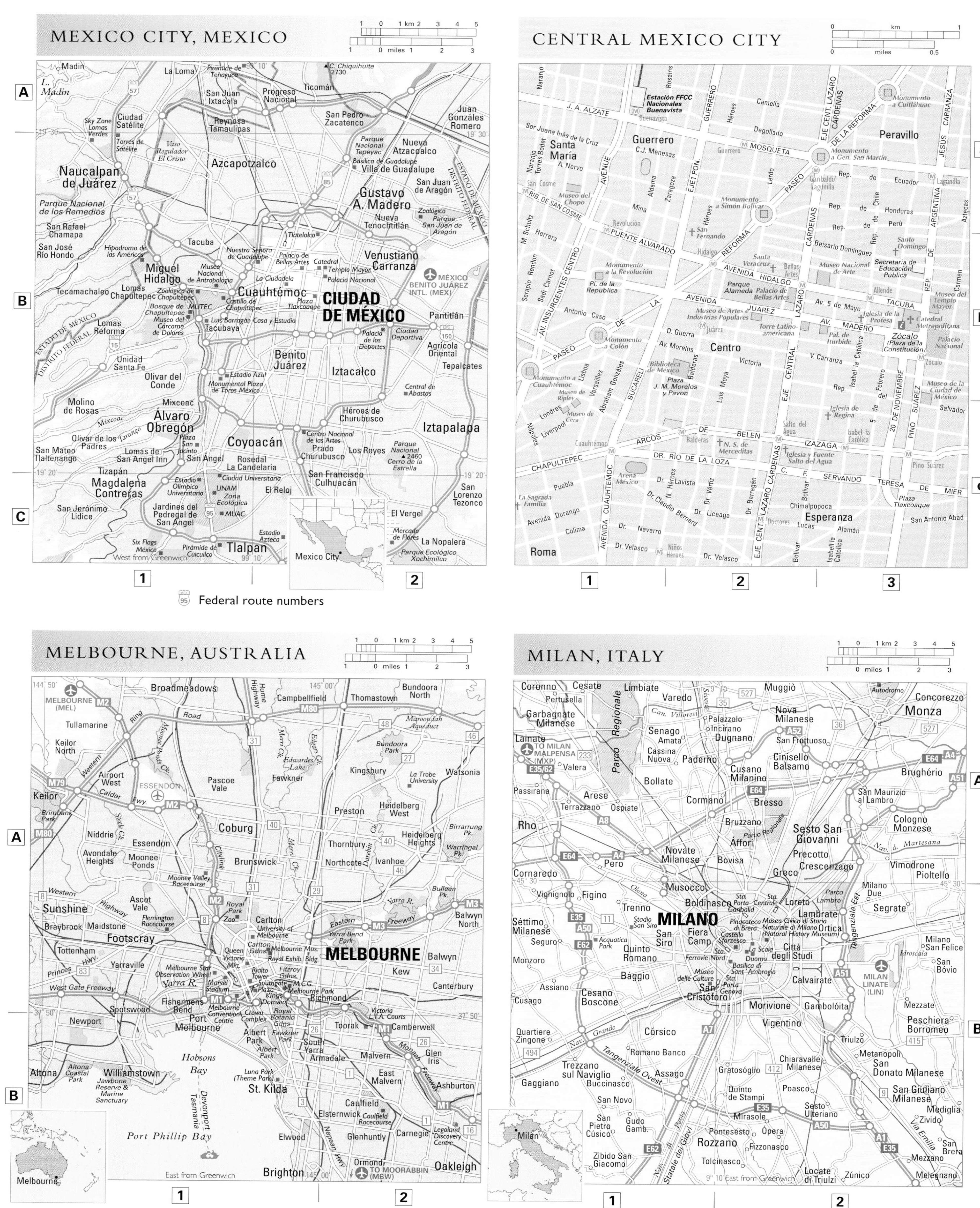
MEXICO CITY, MEXICO
CENTRAL MEXICO CITY
MELBOURNE, AUSTRALIA
MILAN, ITALY
Federal route numbers
CIUDAD DE MÉXICO
Naucalpan de Juárez
Azcapotzalco
Gustavo A. Madero
Venustiano Carranza
Cuauhtémoc
Miguel Hidalgo
Benito Juárez
Iztacalco
Álvaro Obregón
Coyoacán
Iztapalapa
Magdalena Contreras
Tlalpan
MÉXICO BENITO JUÁREZ INTL. (MEX)
Mexico City
Guerrero
Santa María
Peravillo
Centro
Esperanza
Roma
Zócalo (Plaza de la Constitución)
Palacio Nacional
Catedral Metropolitana
MELBOURNE
Broadmeadows
Coburg
Brunswick
Footscray
Sunshine
Williamstown
Port Melbourne
St. Kilda
Richmond
Kew
Camberwell
Caulfield
Brighton
Oakleigh
Hobsons Bay
Port Phillip Bay
MELBOURNE (MEL)
Melbourne
MILANO
Monza
Sesto San Giovanni
Rho
Cinisello Balsamo
Bollate
Cormano
Bresso
Corsico
Rozzano
San Donato Milanese
Trezzano sul Naviglio
MILAN LINATE (LIN)
TO MILAN MALPENSA (MXP)
Milan
East from Greenwich
West from Greenwich

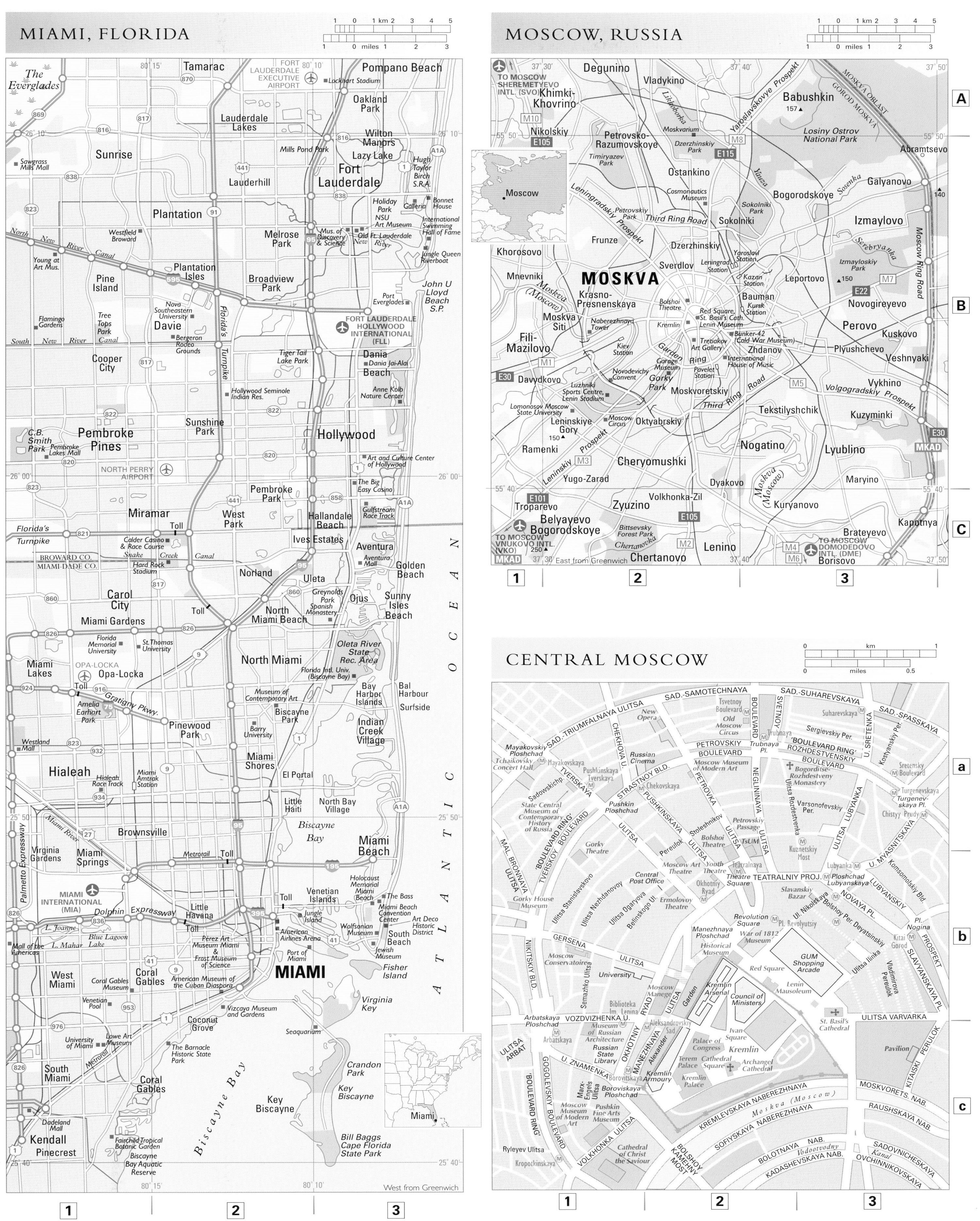
MIAMI, FLORIDA
km
miles
The Everglades
Tamarac
FORT LAUDERDALE EXECUTIVE AIRPORT
Lockhart Stadium
Pompano Beach
Oakland Park
Lauderdale Lakes
Wilton Manors
Sunrise
Sawgrass Mills Mall
Mills Pond Park
Lazy Lake
Hugh Taylor Birch S.R.A.
Lauderhill
Fort Lauderdale
Holiday Park
Galleria
Bonnet House
NSU Art Museum
International Swimming Hall of Fame
Plantation
Westfield Broward
Melrose Park
Mus. of Discovery & Science
Old Ft. Lauderdale
Jungle Queen Riverboat
North New River Canal
Young at Art Mus.
Plantation Isles
Pine Island
Broadview Park
John U Lloyd Beach S.P.
Port Everglades
Nova Southeastern University
Flamingo Gardens
Tree Tops Park
Davie
FORT LAUDERDALE HOLLYWOOD INTERNATIONAL (FLL)
Bergeron Rodeo Grounds
South New River Canal
Florida's Turnpike
Tiger Tail Lake Park
Dania Beach
Dania Jai-Alai
Cooper City
Anne Kolb Nature Center
Hollywood Seminole Indian Res.
C.B. Smith Park
Pembroke Pines
Pembroke Lakes Mall
Sunshine Park
Hollywood
Art and Culture Center of Hollywood
NORTH PERRY AIRPORT
The Big Easy Casino
Pembroke Park
Miramar
West Park
Hallandale Beach
Gulfstream Race Track
Florida's Turnpike
Toll
Calder Casino & Race Course
Snake Creek Canal
Ives Estates
Aventura
Aventura Mall
BROWARD CO.
MIAMI-DADE CO.
Hard Rock Stadium
Golden Beach
Norland
Uleta
Carol City
Greynolds Park
Spanish Monastery
Ojus
Sunny Isles Beach
North Miami Beach
Miami Gardens
Florida Memorial University
St. Thomas University
Oleta River State Rec. Area
OPA-LOCKA
Opa-Locka
North Miami
Florida Intl. Univ. (Biscayne Bay)
Miami Lakes
Amelia Earhart Park
Gratigny Pkwy.
Museum of Contemporary Art
Bay Harbor Islands
Bal Harbour
Surfside
Biscayne Park
Pinewood Park
Barry University
Indian Creek Village
Westland Mall
Hialeah
Hialeah Race Track
Miami Amtrak Station
Miami Shores
El Portal
Little Haiti
North Bay Village
Miami River
Brownsville
Biscayne Bay
Palmetto Expressway
Virginia Gardens
Miami Springs
Metrorail
Miami Beach
Holocaust Memorial Miami Beach
The Bass
MIAMI INTERNATIONAL (MIA)
Dolphin Expressway
Little Havana
Venetian Islands
Jungle Island
Miami Beach Convention Center
Art Deco Historic District
L. Joanne
Wolfsonian Museum
American Airlines Arena
South Beach
Blue Lagoon Lake
L. Mahar
Mall of the Americas
Perez Art Museum Miami & Frost Museum of Science
Jewish Museum
Port of Miami
Fisher Island
West Miami
Coral Gables Museum
Coral Gables
American Museum of the Cuban Diaspora
MIAMI
Venetian Pool
Vizcaya Museum and Gardens
Virginia Key
Coconut Grove
Seaquarium
University of Miami
Lowe Art Museum
The Barnacle Historic State Park
South Miami
Metrorail
Crandon Park
Coral Gables
Key Biscayne
Biscayne Bay
Key Biscayne
Dadeland Mall
Kendall
Fairchild Tropical Botanic Garden
Bill Baggs Cape Florida State Park
Pinecrest
Biscayne Bay Aquatic Reserve
ATLANTIC OCEAN
Miami
West from Greenwich
MOSCOW, RUSSIA
km
miles
TO MOSCOW SHEREMETYEVO INTL. (SVO)
Degunino
Vladykino
Yaroslavskoye Prospekt
MOSKVA OBLAST
GOROD MOSKVA
Khimki-Khovrino
Likhoborka
Babushkin
Nikolskiy
Petrovsko-Razumovskoye
Moskvarium
Dzerzhinskiy Park
Losiny Ostrov National Park
Abramtsevo
Timiryazev Park
Moscow
Ostankino
Yauza
Galyanovo
Leningradskiy Prospekt
Cosmonautics Museum
Sokolniki Park
Bogorodskoye
Sosenka
Petrovsky Park
Third Ring Road
Sokolniki
Izmaylovo
Frunze
Dzerzhinskiy
Yaroslavl Station
Serebryanka
Moscow Ring Road
Khorosovo
Sverdlov
Leningrad Station
Kazan Station
Izmaylovskiy Park
Mnevniki
MOSKVA
Leportovo
Moskva (Moscow)
Krasno-Presnenskaya
Bolshoi Theatre
Bauman
Kursk Station
Novogireyevo
Red Square, St. Basil's Cath., Lenin Museum
Moskva Siti
Naberezhnaya Tower
Kremlin
Perovo
Fili-Mazilovo
Bunker-42 (Cold War Museum)
Kuskovo
Tretiakov Art Gallery
Kiev Station
Zhdanov
Plyushchevo
Garden Ring
International House of Music
Veshnyaki
Garage Museum
Davydkovo
Pavelet Station
Novodevichy Convent
Gorky Park
Vykhino
Luzhniki Sports Centre, Lenin Stadium
Moskvoretskiy
Volgogradskiy Prospekt
Lomonosov Moscow State University
Third Ring Road
Tekstilyshchik
Leninskiye Gory
Moscow Circus
Oktyabrskiy
Kuzyminki
Ramenki
Leninskiy Prospekt
Nogatino
Lyublino
Cheryomushki
Yugo-Zarad
Dyakovo
Maryino
Moskva (Moscow)
Troparevo
Volkhonka-Zil
Zyuzino
Kuryanovo
Belyayevo Bogorodskoye
Kapotnya
TO MOSCOW VNUKOVO INTL. (VKO)
Bittsevsky Forest Park
Chertanovka
Brateyevo
Lenino
TO MOSCOW DOMODEDOVO INTL. (DME)
Chertanovo
Borisovo
MKAD
East from Greenwich
CENTRAL MOSCOW
km
miles
SAD.-SAMOTECHNAYA
SAD.-SUHAREVSKAYA
Tsvetnoy Boulevard
Suharevskaya
SAD.-SPASSKAYA
SAD.-TRIUMFALNAYA ULITSA
New Opera
Old Moscow Circus
Sergievskiy Per.
Kostyanskiy Per.
Trubnaya
Trubnaya Pl.
'BOULEVARD RING' ROZHDESTVENSKIY BOULEVARD
Mayakovskiy Ploshchad
PETROVSKIY BOULEVARD
Tchaikovsky Concert Hall
Mayakovskaya
Russian Cinema
Moscow Museum of Modern Art
Bogorditse-Rozhdestvenskiy Monastery
Sretensky Boulevard
Pushkinskaya
Tverskaya
STRASTNOY BLD.
Chekovskaya
Turgenevskaya
Turgenevskaya Pl.
Sadovskichp.
State Central Museum of Contemporary History of Russia
Pushkin Ploshchad
Varsonofevskiy Per.
Chistyy Prudy
Stoleshnikov
Petrovsky Passage
Gorky Theatre
Bolshoi Theatre
TsUM
Kuznetsky Most
Pereulok
Moscow Art Theatre
Youth Theatre
Teatralnaya
Lubyanka
TEATRALNIY PROJ.
Ploshchad Lubyanskaya
Central Post Office
Okhotniy Ryad
Theatre Square
Slavanskiy Bazar
NOVAYA PL.
Gorky House Museum
Ulitsa Stanislavskovo
Ulitsa Nezhdanovoy
Ulitsa Ogaryova
Belinskogo Ul.
Ermolovoy Theatre
Revolution Square
Pl. Revolyutsiy
Ul. Nikolskaya
Bolshoy Per. Deyatsinskiy
Pl. Nogina
Kitai Gorod
Manezhnaya Ploshchad
War of 1812 Museum
Historical Museum
GUM Shopping Arcade
GERSENA
ULITSA
Moscow Conservatoire
University
Red Square
Ulitsa Ilinka
Vladimirova Pereulok
SLAVYANSKAYA PL.
NIKITSKY BLD.
Semazhko Ulitsa
Moscow Manege
Garden
Kremlin Arsenal
Council of Ministers
Lenin Mausoleum
Biblioteka Im. Lenina
ULITSA VARVARKA
Arbatskaya Ploshchad
VOZDVIZHENKA U.
Aleksandrovsky Sad
St. Basil's Cathedral
Arbatskaya
Museum of Russian Architecture
Palace of Congress
Ivan Square
Kremlin
Pavilion
KITAISKI PERULOK
ULITSA ARBAT
Russian State Library
Terem Palace
Cathedral Square
Archangel Cathedral
U. ZNAMENKA
Borovitskaya
Kremlin Armoury
Kremlin Palace
Marx-Engels Ulitsa
Boroviskaya Ploshchad
MOSKVORETS. NAB.
RAUSHSKAYA NAB.
'BOULEVARD RING' GOGOLEVSKIY BOULEVARD
Moscow Museum of Modern Art
Pushkin Fine Arts Museum
KREMLEVSKAYA NABEREZHNAYA
Moskva (Moscow)
SOFIYSKAYA NABEREZHNAYA
VOLKHONKA ULITSA
Cathedral of Christ the Saviour
BOLSHOY KAMENNY MOST
BOLOTNAYA NAB.
Vodootvodny Kanal
SADOVNICHESKAYA
OVCHINNIKOVSKAYA
KADASHEVSKAYA NAB.
Ryleyev Ulitsa
Kropotkinskaya
Interstate route numbers
U.S. route numbers
State route numbers

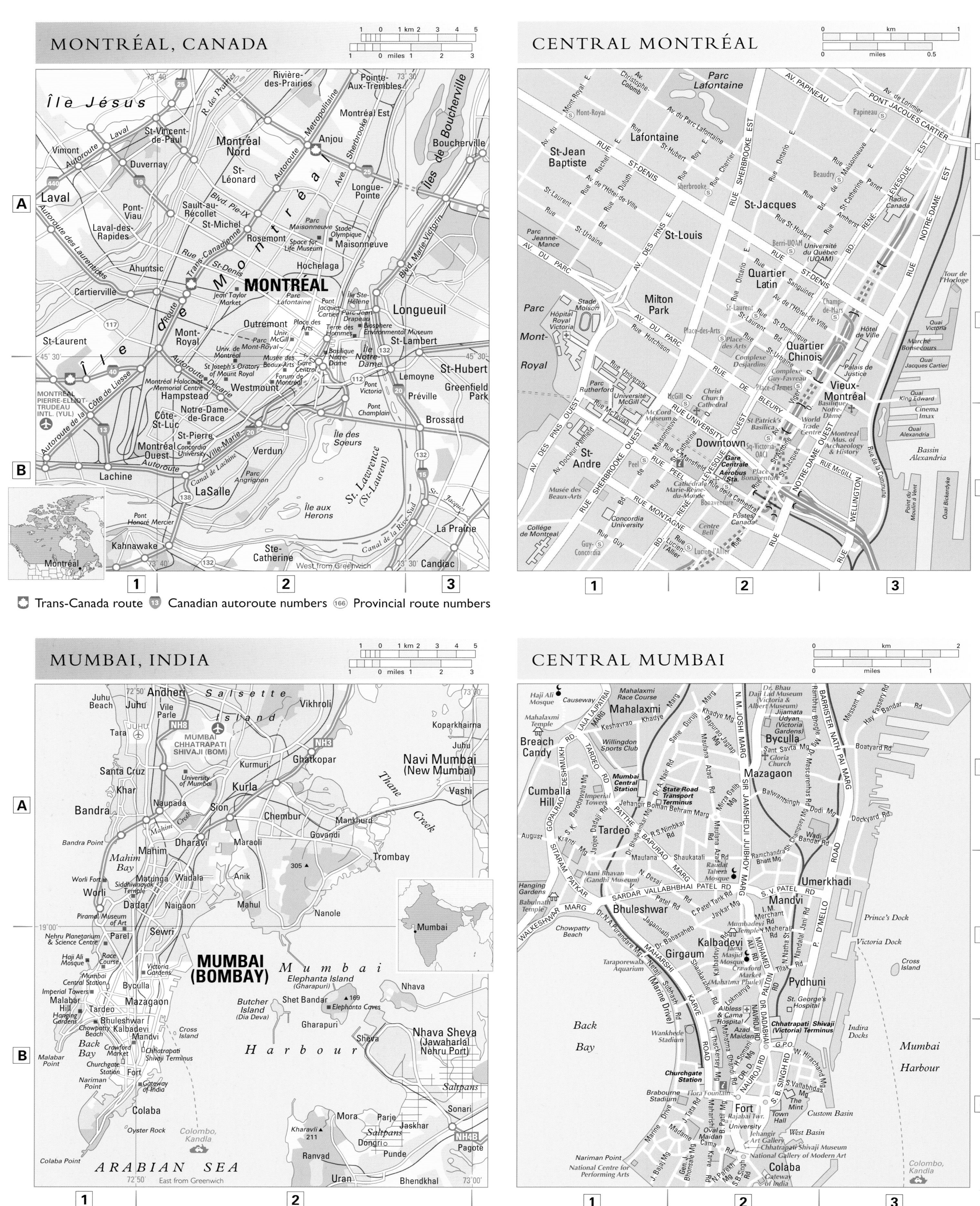
MONTRÉAL, CANADA
km
miles
Île Jésus
Rivière-des-Prairies
Pointe-Aux-Trembles
Montréal Est
Anjou
Montréal Nord
St-Vincent-de-Paul
Duvernay
Vimont
Laval
St-Léonard
Boucherville
Îles de Boucherville
Longue-Pointe
Pont-Viau
Sault-au-Récollet
St-Michel
Laval-des-Rapides
Rosemont
Maisonneuve
Hochelaga
Ahuntsic
Cartierville
MONTRÉAL
Longueuil
Outremont
Mont-Royal
St-Laurent
St-Lambert
St-Hubert
Lemoyne
Préville
Greenfield Park
Westmount
Hampstead
Côte-St-Luc
Notre-Dame-de-Grace
Montréal Ouest
St-Pierre
Verdun
Brossard
Lachine
LaSalle
Île des Soeurs
Île aux Herons
St. Lawrence (St-Laurent)
La Prairie
Kahnawake
Ste-Catherine
Candiac
MONTREAL PIERRE-ELLIOT-TRUDEAU INTL. (YUL)
Montréal
West from Greenwich
Trans-Canada route
Canadian autoroute numbers
Provincial route numbers
CENTRAL MONTRÉAL
km
miles
Parc Lafontaine
Lafontaine
St-Jean Baptiste
St-Jacques
St-Louis
Quartier Latin
Milton Park
Parc Mont-Royal
Quartier Chinois
Vieux-Montréal
Downtown
St-Andre
Bassin Alexandria
MUMBAI, INDIA
km
miles
Salsette Island
Andheri
Juhu
Vikhroli
Ghatkopar
Kurla
Navi Mumbai (New Mumbai)
Vashi
Thane Creek
Bandra
Chembur
Trombay
Dharavi
Mahim
Worli
Dadar
Sewri
MUMBAI (BOMBAY)
Mumbai Harbour
Elephanta Island (Gharapuri)
Butcher Island (Dia Deva)
Nhava Sheva (Jawaharlal Nehru Port)
Colaba
ARABIAN SEA
Uran
Mumbai
East from Greenwich
CENTRAL MUMBAI
km
miles
Mahalaxmi
Breach Candy
Byculla
Mazagaon
Cumballa Hill
Tardeo
Umerkhadi
Mandvi
Bhuleshwar
Kalbadevi
Girgaum
Pydhuni
Back Bay
Mumbai Harbour
Fort
Colaba
Chhatrapati Shivaji (Victoria) Terminus
Churchgate Station
Prince's Dock
Victoria Dock
Indira Docks

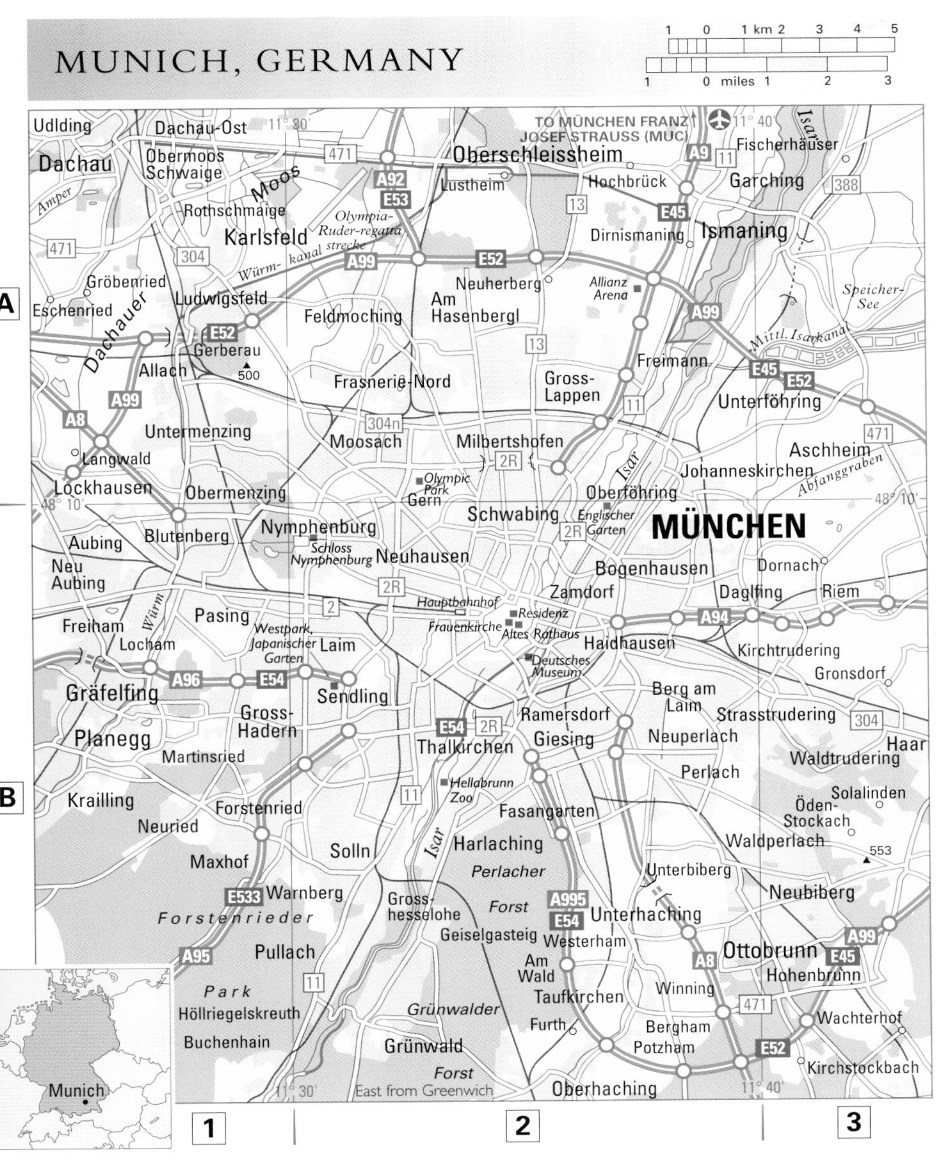

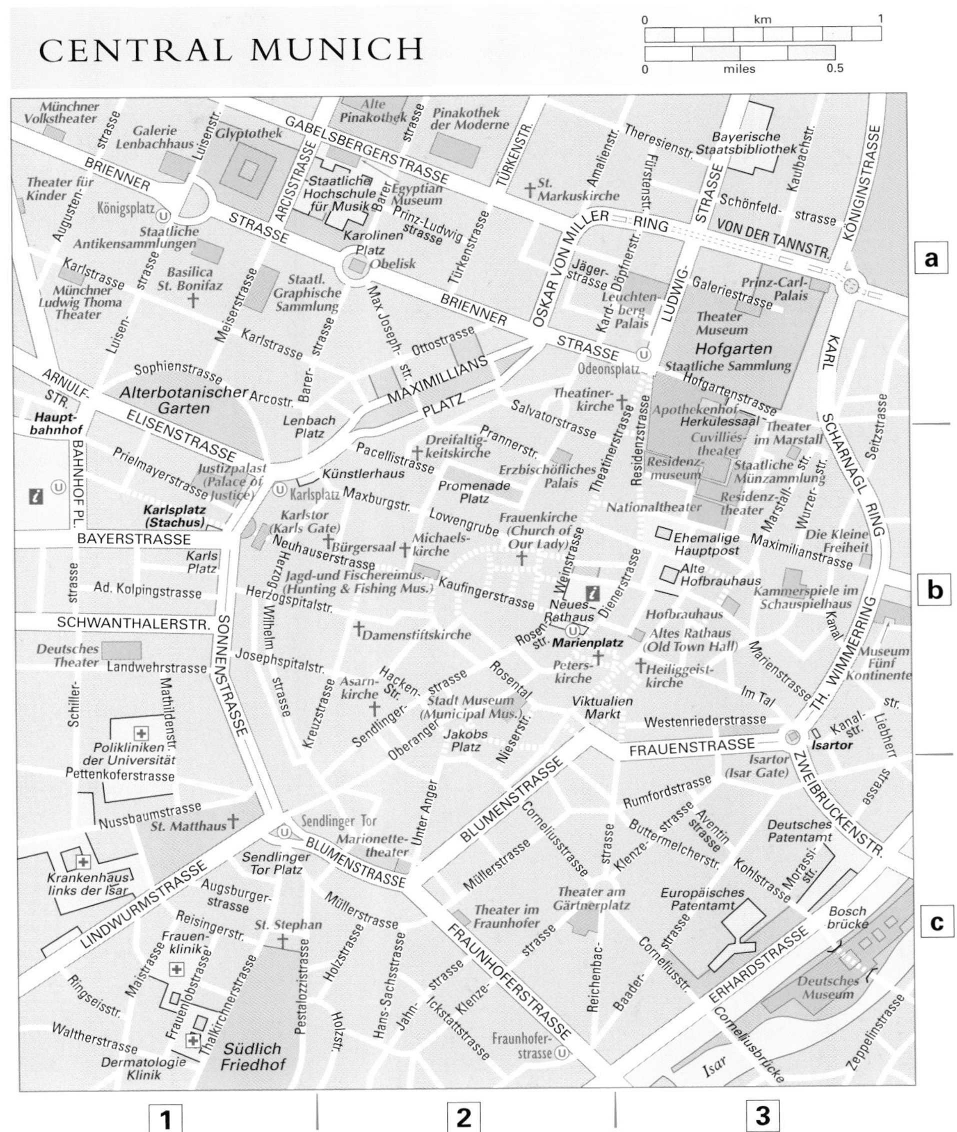

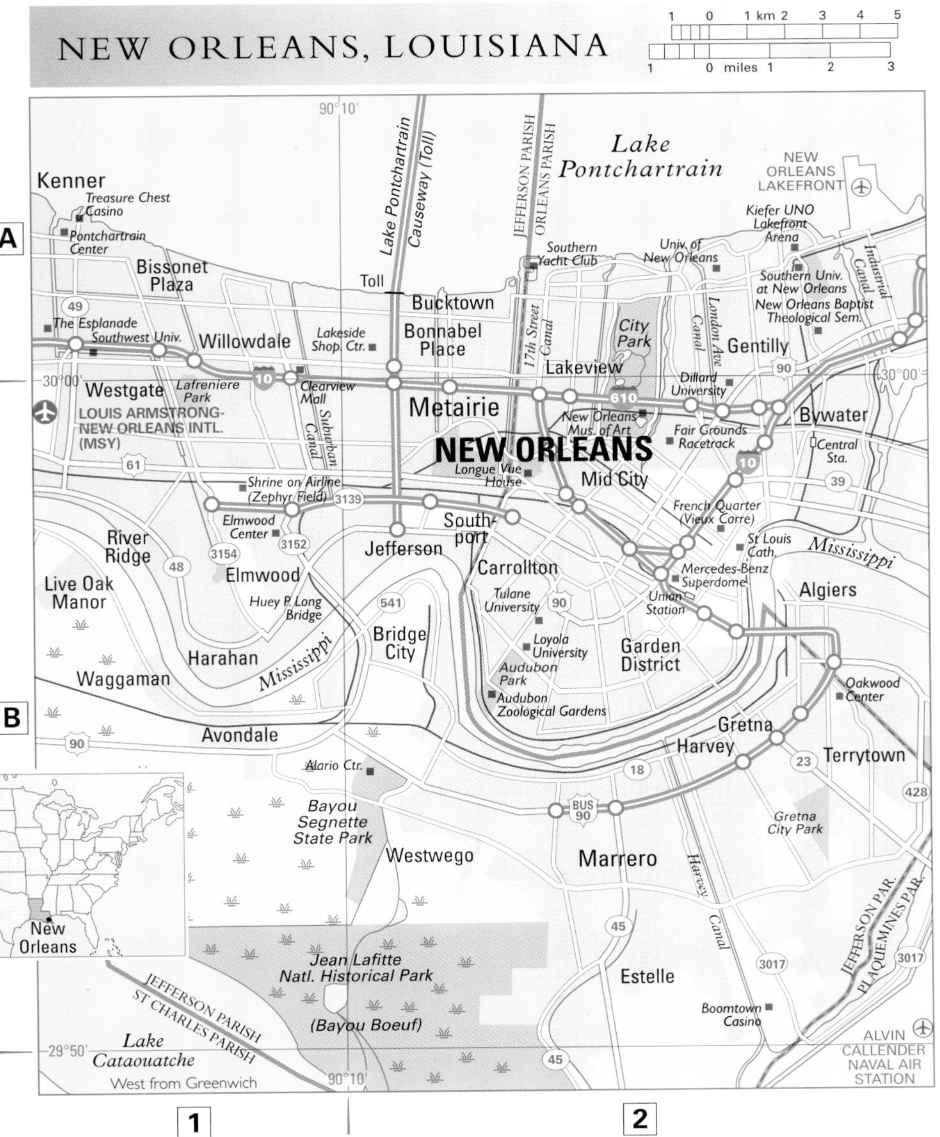

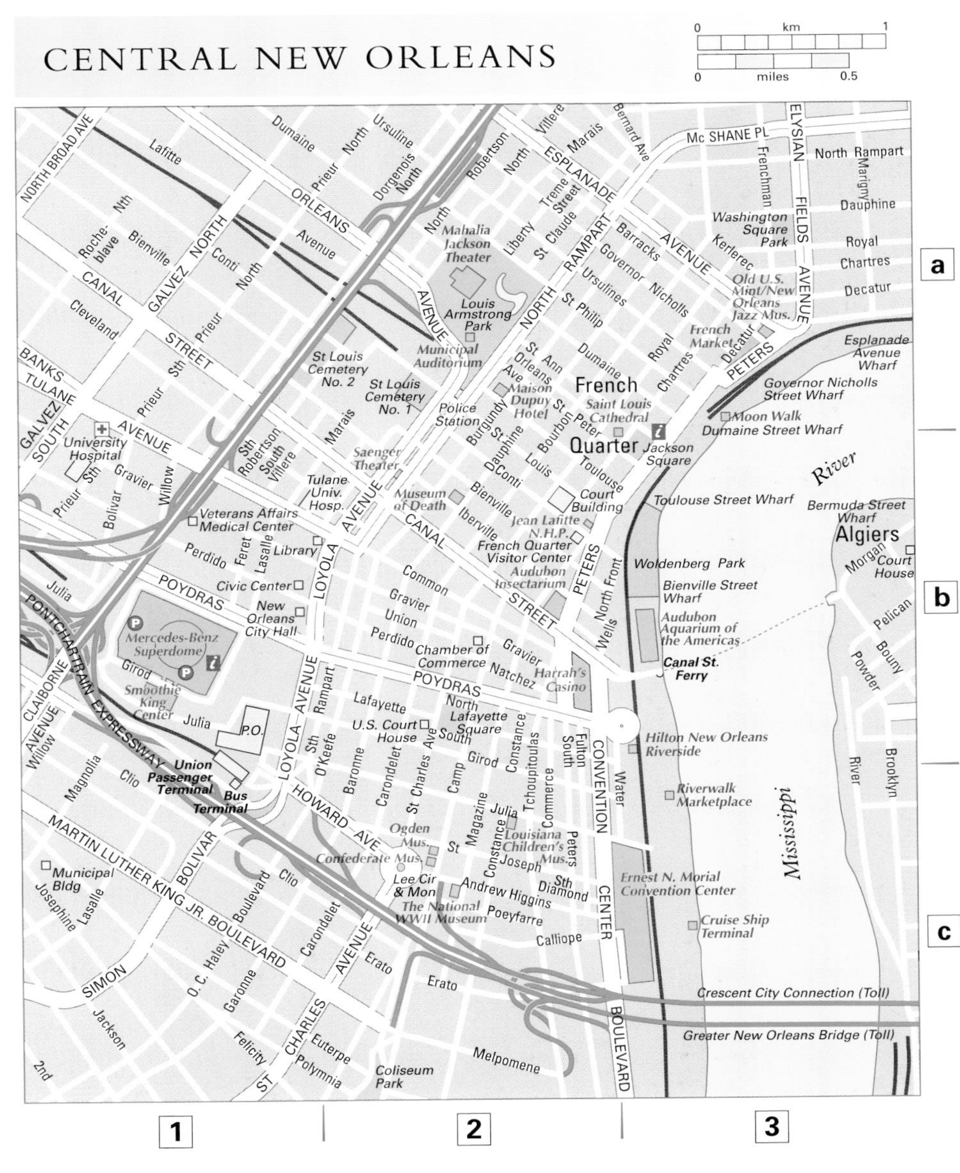

Interstate route numbers
U.S. route numbers
State route numbers

NEW YORK, NEW YORK

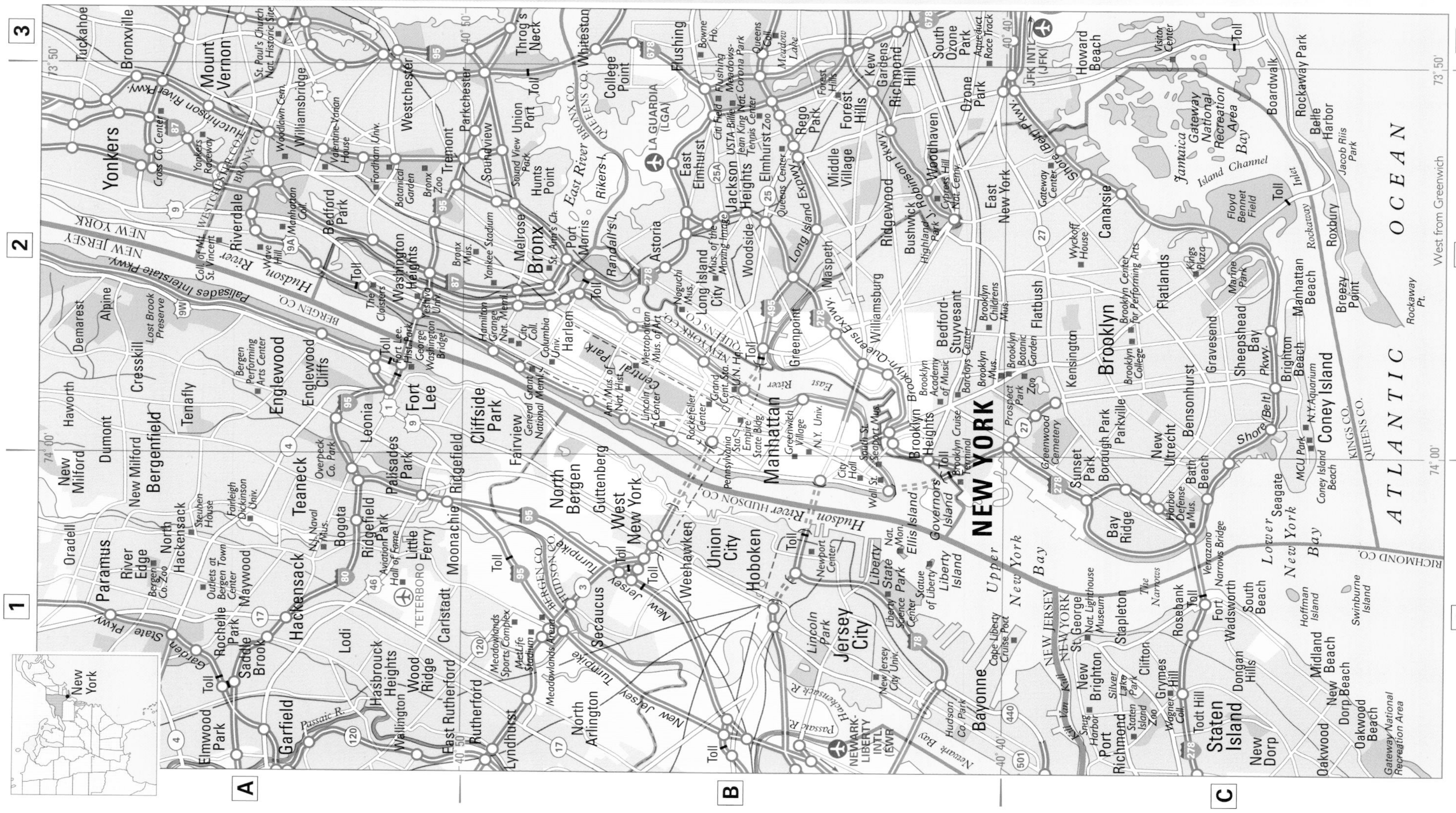

0 1 km 2 3 4 5

0 miles 1 2 3

CENTRAL NEW YORK

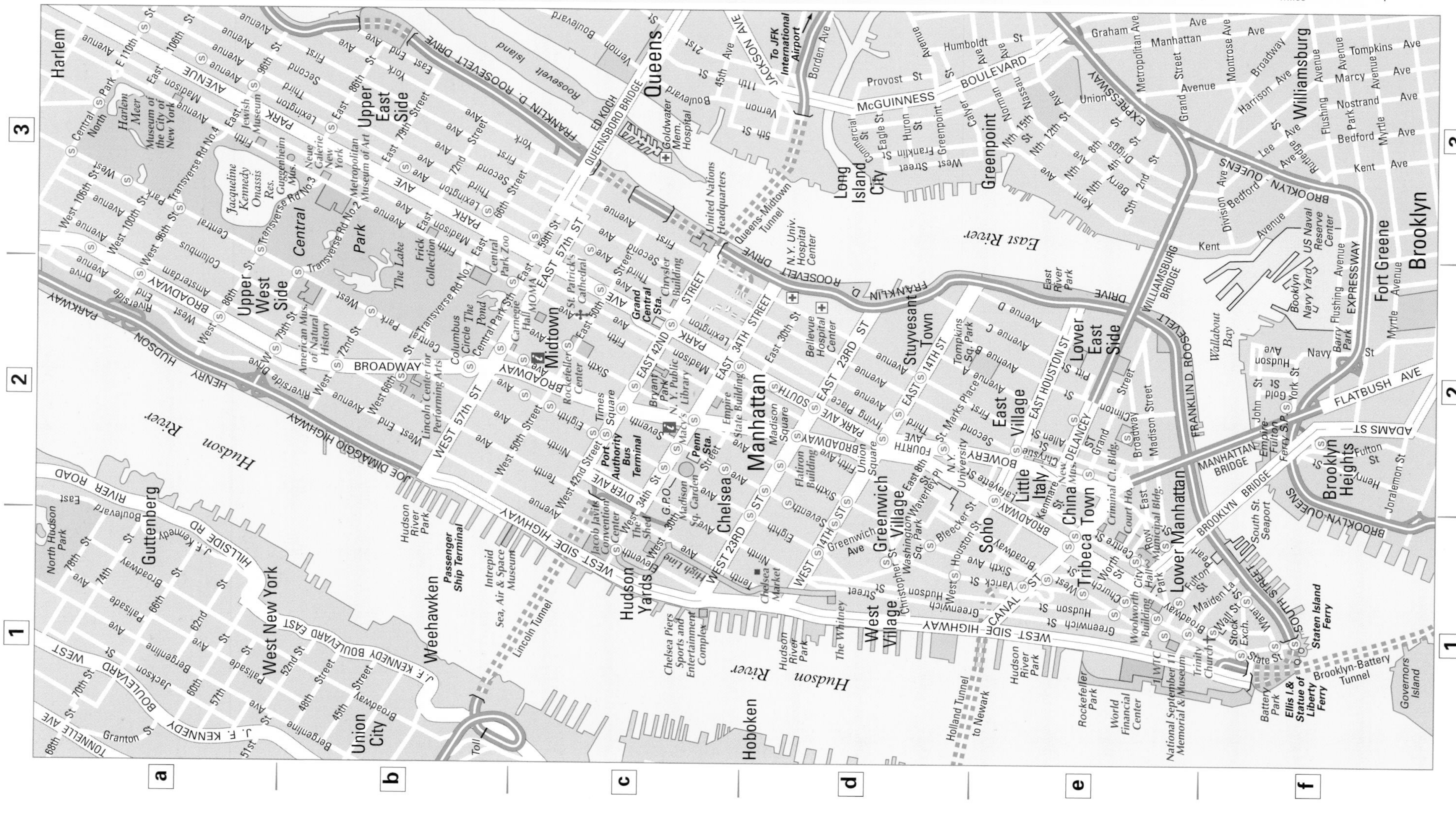

0 1 km 2

0 miles 1

ORLANDO, FLORIDA

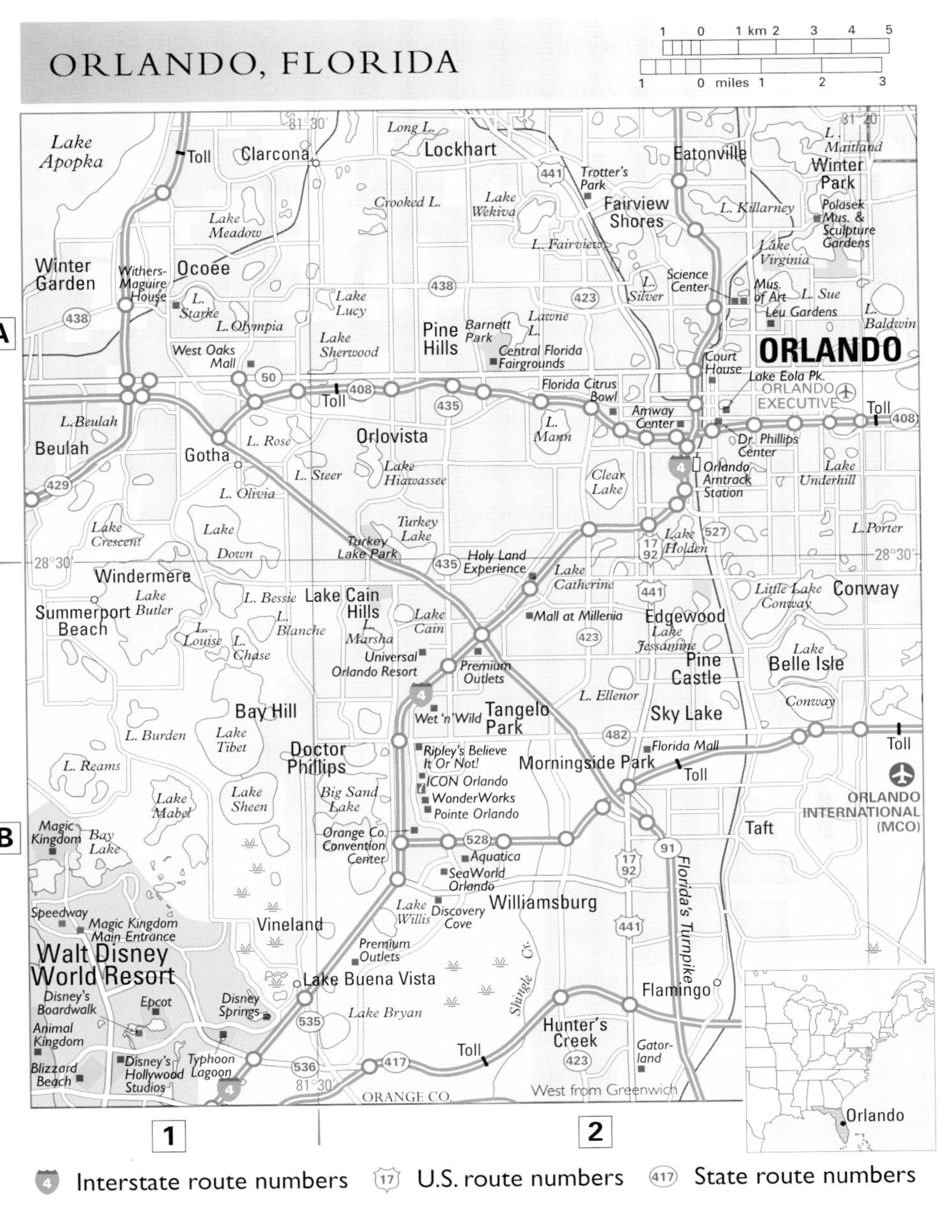

OSAKA, JAPAN

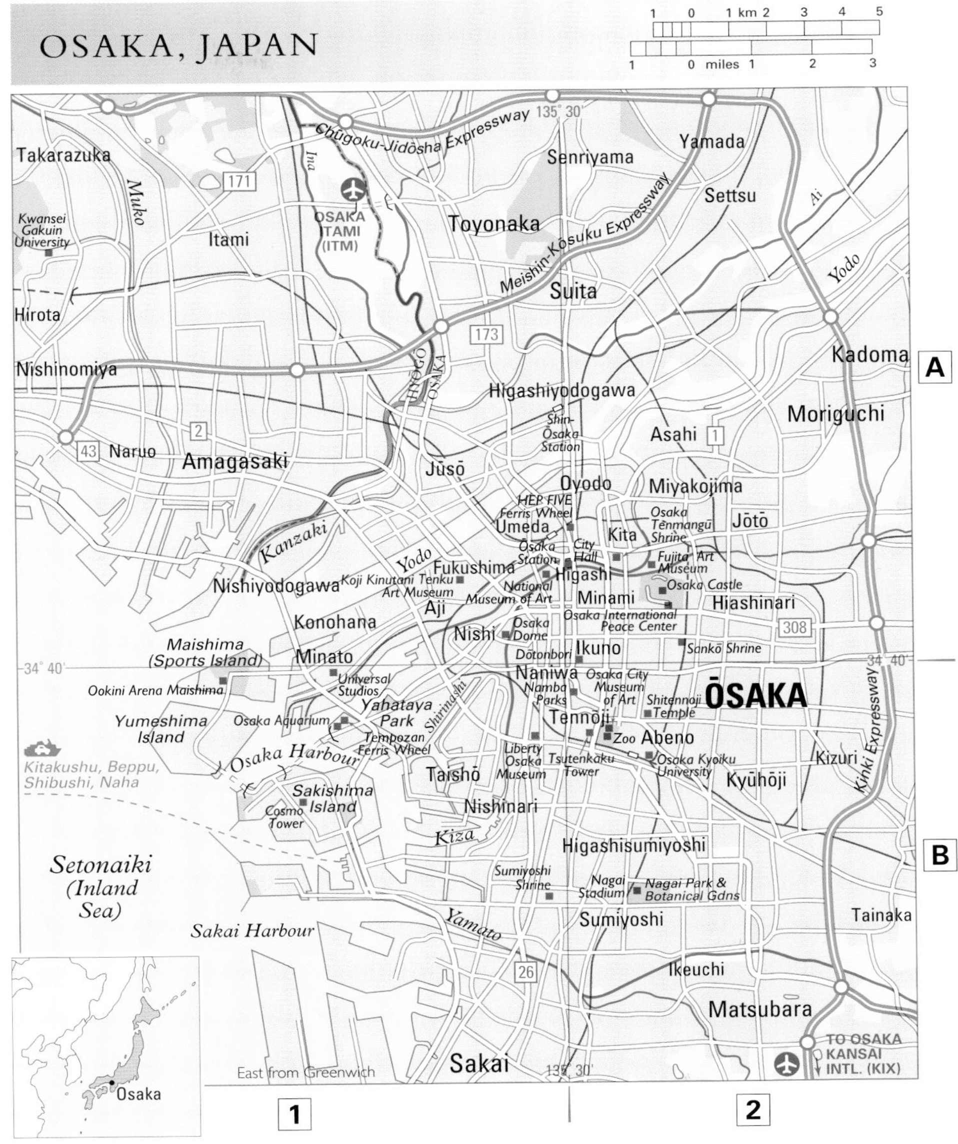

OSLO, NORWAY

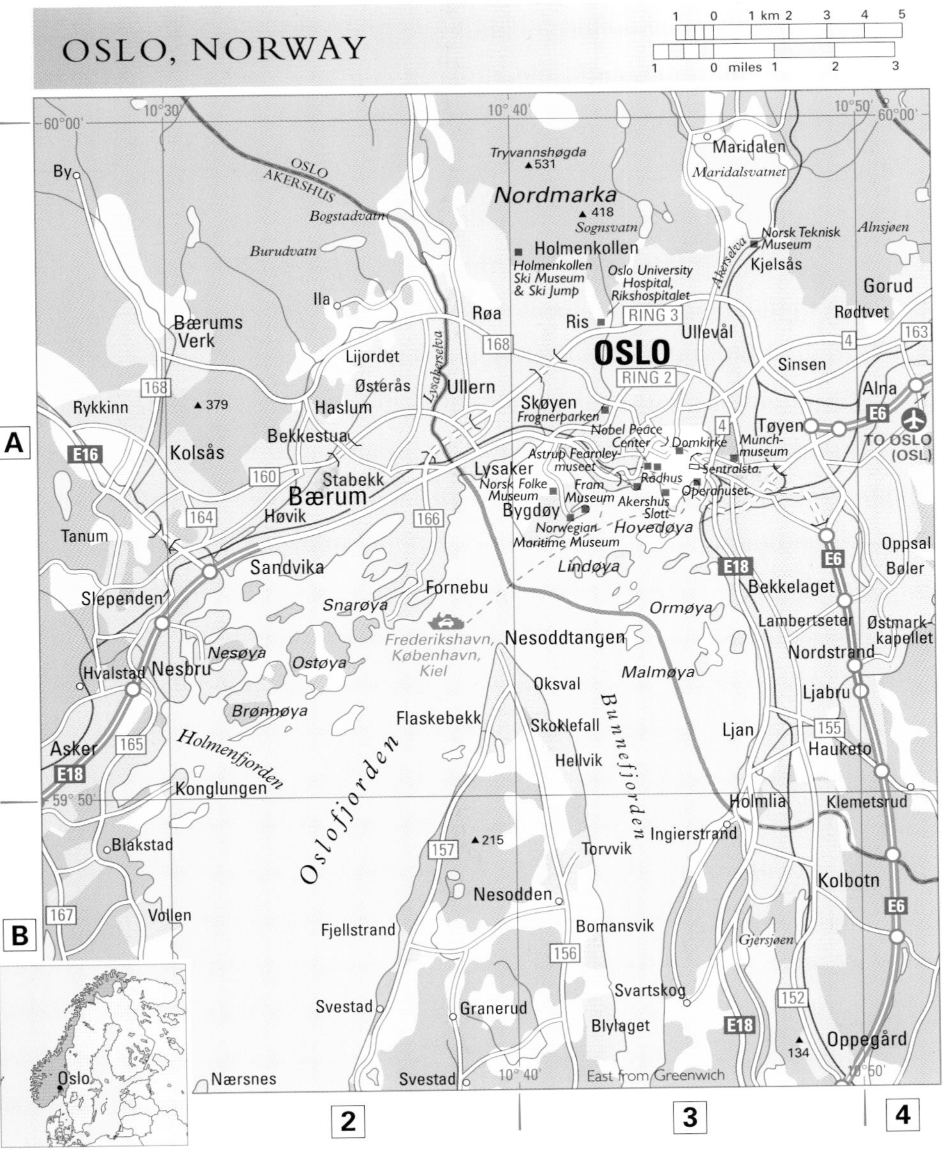

CENTRAL OSLO

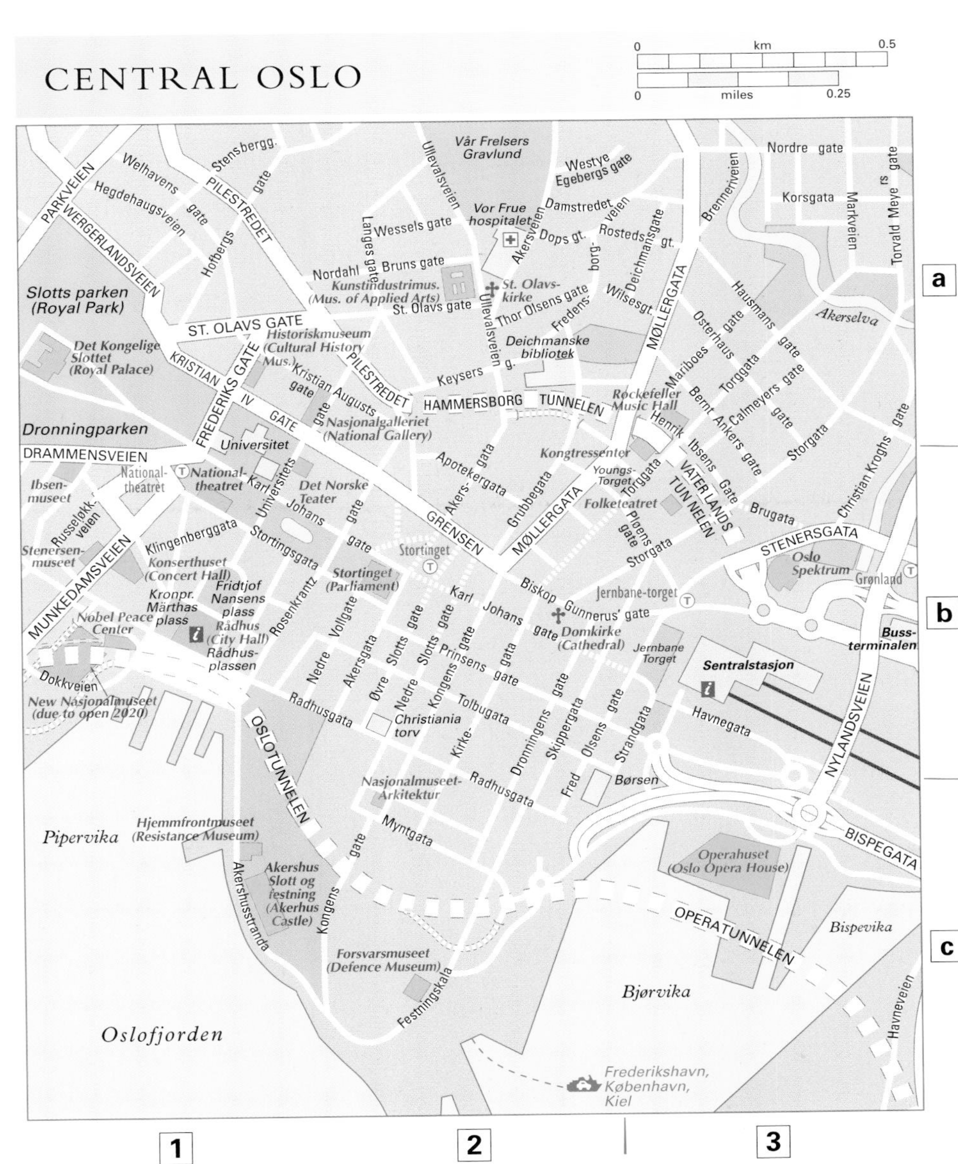

PARIS, FRANCE

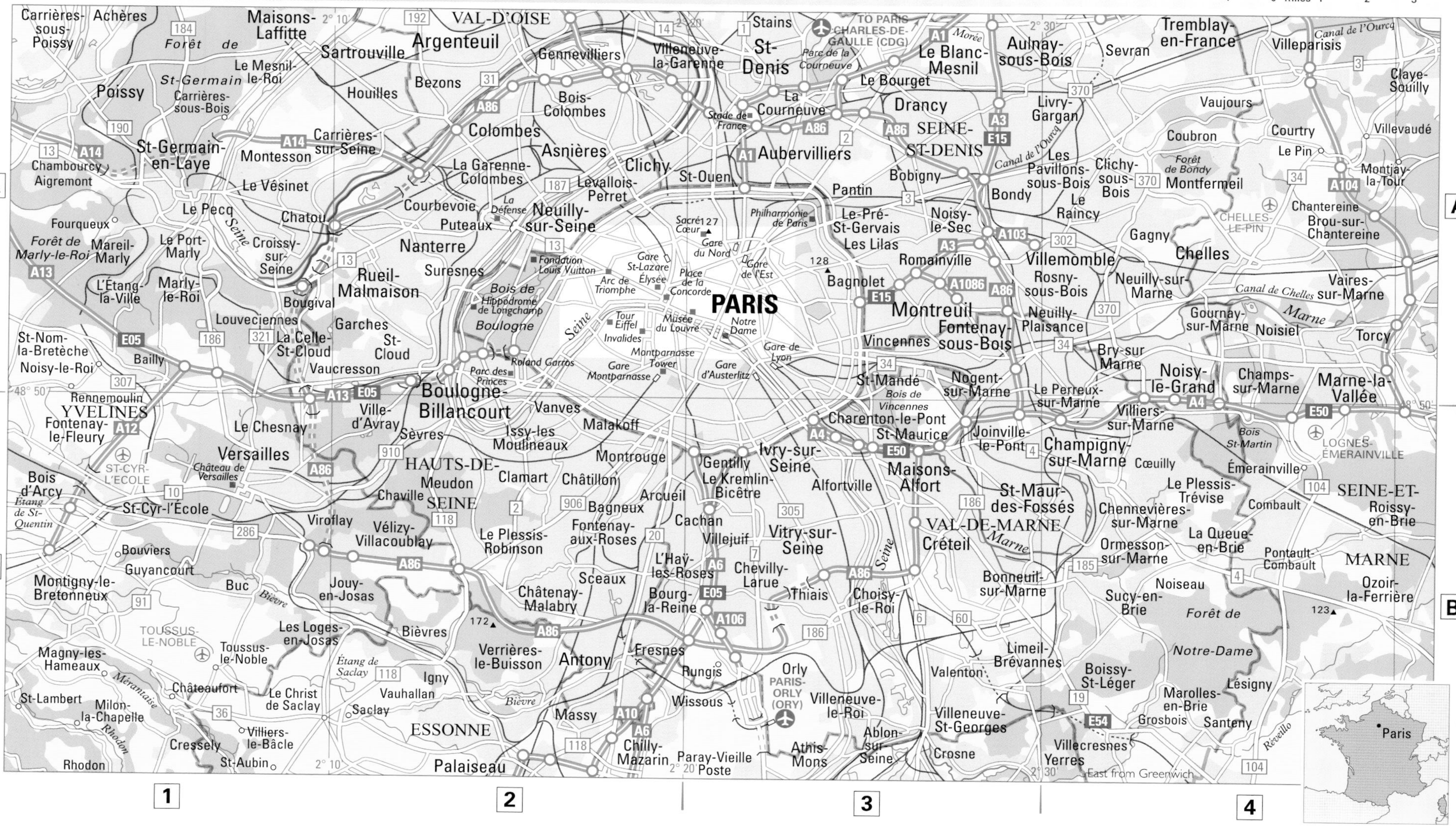

1 0 1 km 2 3 4 5

1 0 miles 1 2 3

East from Greenwich

CENTRAL PARIS

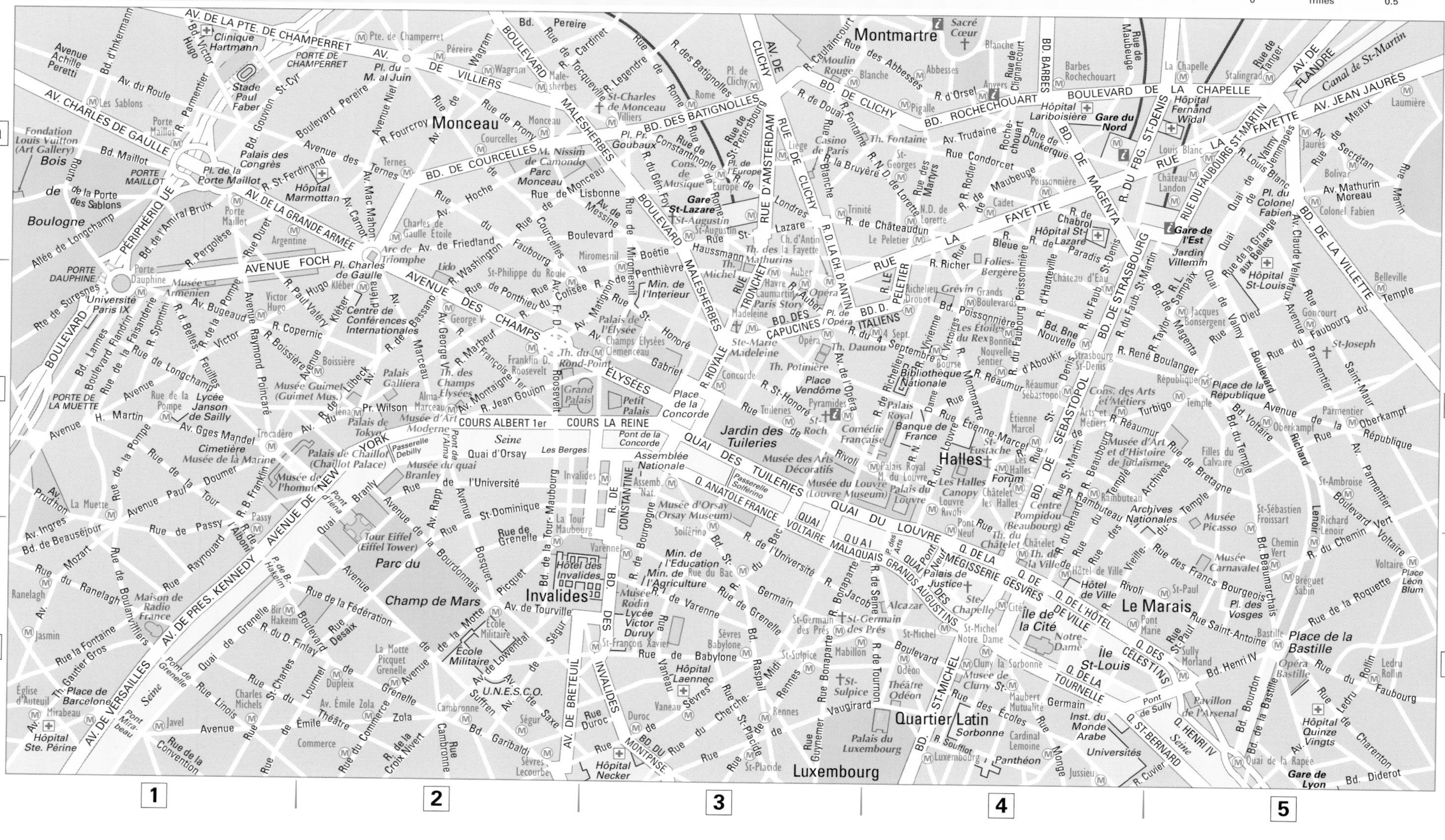

0 km 1

0 miles 0.5

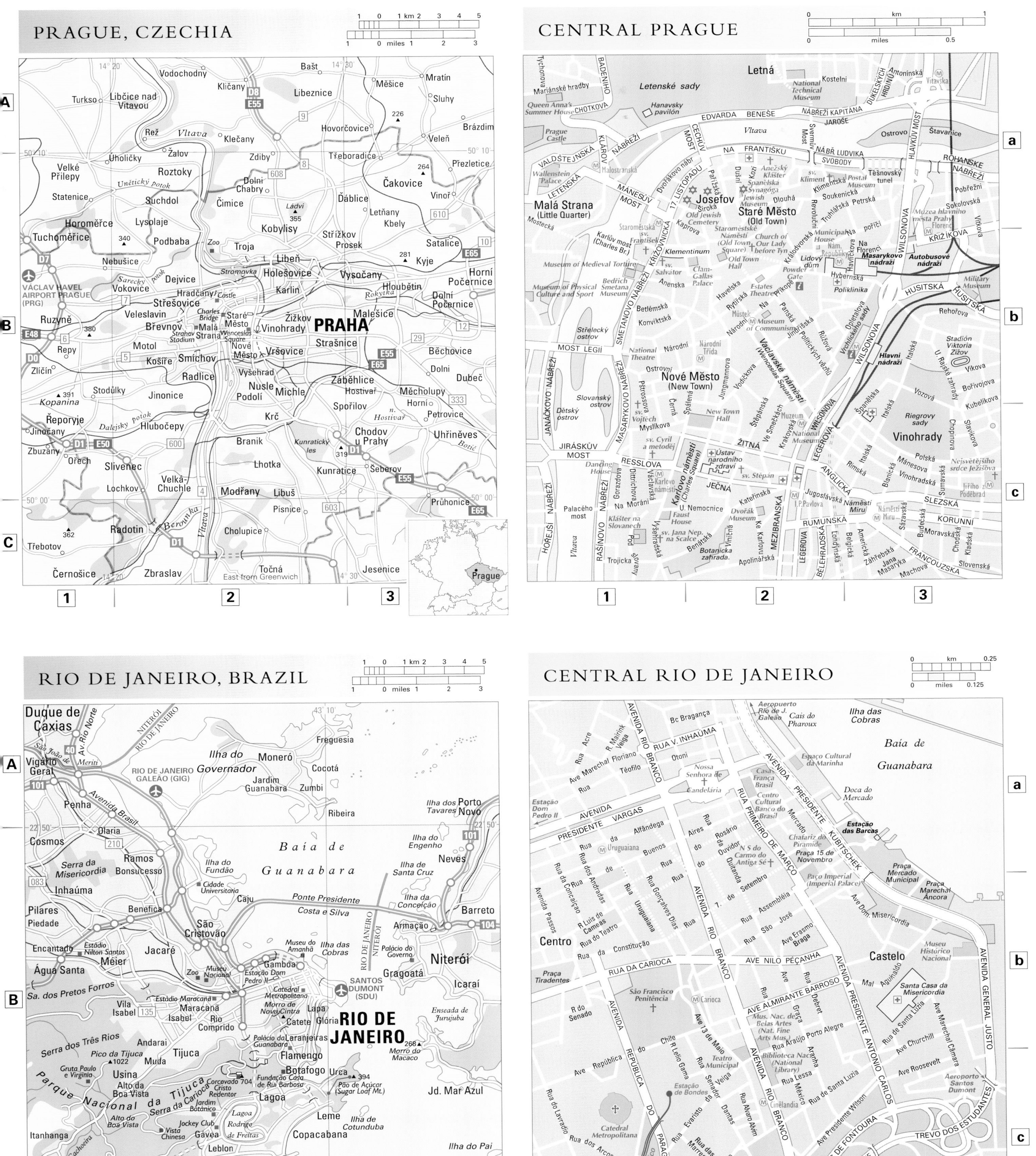
PRAGUE, CZECHIA
PRAHA
Vltava
Holešovice
Karlín
Vysočany
Žižkov
Vinohrady
Smíchov
Břevnov
Střešovice
Dejvice
Libeň
Nusle
Vršovice
Strašnice
Michle
Krč
Braník
Modřany
Zbraslav
Radotín
Ruzyně
Kobylisy
Troja
Suchdol
Roztoky
Čakovice
Letňany
Kbely
Prosek
Satalice
Horní Počernice
Chodov u Prahy
Jesenice
VÁCLAV HAVEL AIRPORT PRAGUE (PRG)
East from Greenwich
CENTRAL PRAGUE
Letná
Letenské sady
Prague Castle
Malá Strana (Little Quarter)
Josefov
Staré Město (Old Town)
Nové Město (New Town)
Vinohrady
Václavské náměstí (Wenceslas Square)
Karlovo náměstí (Charles Square)
Karlův most (Charles Br.)
Masarykovo nádraží
Hlavní nádraží
Autobusové nádraží
National Theatre
Vltava
RIO DE JANEIRO, BRAZIL
RIO DE JANEIRO
Duque de Caxias
Ilha do Governador
RIO DE JANEIRO GALEÃO (GIG)
Baía de Guanabara
Niterói
Ponte Presidente Costa e Silva
SANTOS DUMONT (SDU)
Parque Nacional da Tijuca
Tijuca
Botafogo
Flamengo
Lagoa
Copacabana
Ipanema
Leblon
Gávea
São Cristóvão
Méier
Pão de Açúcar (Sugar Loaf Mt.)
Corcovado
Cristo Redentor
ATLANTIC OCEAN
West from Greenwich
CENTRAL RIO DE JANEIRO
Baía de Guanabara
Ilha das Cobras
Centro
Castelo
AVENIDA RIO BRANCO
AVENIDA PRESIDENTE VARGAS
AVENIDA PRESIDENTE ANTÔNIO CARLOS
Praça Tiradentes
Catedral Metropolitana
Passeio Publico
Paço Imperial (Imperial Palace)
Estação das Barcas
Museu de Arte Moderna (Museum of Modern Art)
Aeroporto Santos Dumont
Enseada da Glória

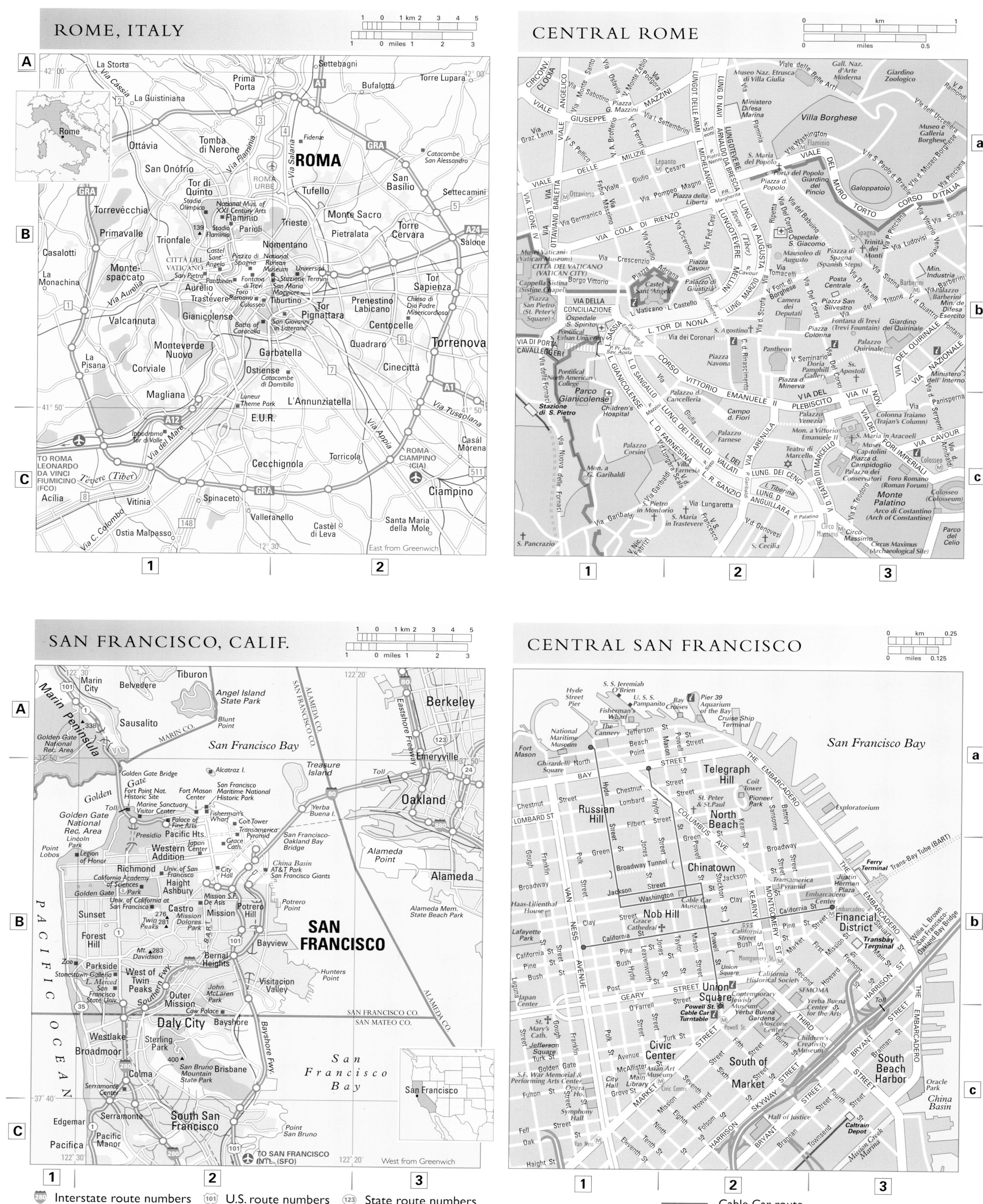
ROME, ITALY
1 0 1 km 2 3 4 5
1 0 miles 1 2 3
A
B
C
1
2
La Storta
Settebagni
Prima Porta
Torre Lupara
Bufalotta
La Giustiniana
Via Cassia
Rome
Ottávia
Tomba di Nerone
Via Flaminia
Via Salaria
ROMA
Fidene
GRA
Catacombe San Alessandro
San Onófrio
Tor di Quinto
San Basílio
Settecamini
Torrevécchia
Stadio Olimpico
National Mus. of XXI Century Arts
Flaminio
Tufello
Monte Sacro
Trieste
Pietralata
Torre Cervara
Primavalle
Parioli
Salone
Casalotti
Trionfale
Nomentano
La Monachina
Monte-spaccato
CITTÀ DEL VATICANO
Castel Sant' Angelo
Piazza di Spagna
National Roman Museum
Università
Stazione Termini
Tor Sapienza
San Pietro
Pantheon
Fontana di Trevi
San Maria Maggiore
Via Aurelia
Aurelio
Trastevere
Foro Romano
Colosseo
Tiburtino
Tor Pignattara
Prenestino Labicano
Chiesa di Dio Padre Misericordioso
Valcannuta
Gianicolense
San Giovanni in Laterano
Baths of Caracalla
Centocelle
La Pisana
Monteverde Nuovo
Garbatella
Quadraro
Torrenova
Corviale
Ostiense
Catacombe di Domitilla
Cinecittà
Magliana
Luneur Theme Park
L'Annunziatella
A12
A1
E.U.R.
Via Appia
Via Tuscolana
Ippodromo Tor di Valle
Via del Mare
Casál Morena
TO ROMA LEONARDO DA VINCI FIUMICINO (FCO)
Tevere (Tiber)
Cecchignola
Torricola
ROMA CIAMPINO (CIA)
Acília
Vitínia
Spinaceto
Ciampino
Valleranello
Castèl di Leva
Santa Maria della Mole
Via C. Colombo
Ostia Malpasso
East from Greenwich
CENTRAL ROME
0 km 1
0 miles 0.5
a
b
c
1
2
3
Villa Borghese
Giardino Zoologico
Gall. Naz. d'Arte Moderna
Museo Naz. Etrusco di Villa Giulia
Museo e Galleria Borghese
Piazza del Popolo
Galoppatoio
Musei Vaticani (Vatican Museum)
CITTÀ DEL VATICANO (VATICAN CITY)
Cappella Sistina (Sistine Chapel)
Piazza San Pietro (St. Peter's Square)
Castel Sant' Angelo
Mausoleo di Augusto
Piazza di Spagna (Spanish Steps)
Trinità dei Monti
Palazzo di Giustizia
Fontana di Trevi (Trevi Fountain)
Pantheon
Piazza Navona
Palazzo Venezia
Colonna Traiano (Trajan's Column)
Mon. a Vittorio Emanuele II
Campo d. Fiori
Palazzo Farnese
Palazzo Corsini
Parco Gianicolense
Children's Hospital
Stazione di S. Pietro
Teatro di Marcello
Piazza d. Campidoglio
Foro Romano (Roman Forum)
Monte Palatino
Arco di Costantino (Arch of Constantine)
Colosseo (Colosseum)
Circo Massimo
Circus Maximus (Archaeological Site)
Parco del Celio
S. Cecilia
S. Pancrazio
S. Maria in Trastevere
S. Pietro in Montorio
Mon. a G. Garibaldi
Pontifical Urban University
Pontifical North American College
Ospedale S. Spirito
CORSO VITTORIO EMANUELE II
VIA DEL PLEBISCITO
VIA NAZIONALE
VIA CAVOUR
LUNGOTEVERE
SAN FRANCISCO, CALIF.
1 0 1 km 2 3 4 5
1 0 miles 1 2 3
A
B
C
1
2
3
Tiburon
Marin City
Belvedere
Angel Island State Park
Berkeley
Marin Peninsula
Sausalito
Blunt Point
Golden Gate National Rec. Area
MARIN CO.
San Francisco Bay
Emeryville
Treasure Island
Golden Gate Bridge
Alcatraz I.
Golden Gate
Fort Point Nat. Historic Site
Fort Mason Center
San Francisco Maritime National Historic Park
Oakland
Marine Sanctuary Visitor Center
Fisherman's Wharf
Yerba Buena I.
Golden Gate National Rec. Area
Palace of Fine Arts
Coit Tower
Transamerica Pyramid
Presidio
Pacific Hts.
Point Lobos
Lincoln Park
Legion of Honor
Western Addition
Japan Center
Grace Cath.
San Francisco-Oakland Bay Bridge
Alameda Point
Richmond
China Basin
AT&T Park San Francisco Giants
Alameda
California Academy of Sciences
Haight Ashbury
City Hall
Golden Gate Park
Mission S.F. De Asis
Potrero Point
Sunset
Univ. of California at San Francisco
Castro
Mission
Potrero Hill
Alameda Mem. State Beach Park
Twin Peaks
Mission Dolores Park
PACIFIC OCEAN
SAN FRANCISCO
Forest Hill
Bayview
Mt. Davidson
Parkside
Bernal Heights
Stonestown Galleria
L. Merced
San Francisco State Univ.
West of Twin Peaks
John McLaren Park
Visitacion Valley
Hunters Point
Outer Mission
Cow Palace
Daly City
Bayshore
SAN FRANCISCO CO.
SAN MATEO CO.
Westlake
Bayshore Fwy.
Broadmoor
Sterling Park
San Bruno Mountain State Park
Brisbane
San Francisco Bay
San Francisco
Colma
Serramonte Center
Serramonte
South San Francisco
Point San Bruno
Edgemar
Pacifica
Pacific Manor
TO SAN FRANCISCO (INTL.) (SFO)
West from Greenwich
CENTRAL SAN FRANCISCO
0 km 0.25
0 miles 0.125
a
b
c
1
2
3
S. S. Jeremiah O'Brien
U. S. S. Pampanito
Hyde Street Pier
Pier 39 Aquarium of the Bay
Bay Cruises
Fisherman's Wharf
Cruise Ship Terminal
San Francisco Bay
Fort Mason
National Maritime Museum
The Cannery
Ghirardelli Square
Telegraph Hill
Coit Tower
Pioneer Park
Exploratorium
Russian Hill
North Beach
St. Peter & St. Paul
THE EMBARCADERO
Ferry Terminal
Trans-Bay Tube (BART)
Broadway Tunnel
Chinatown
Transamerica Pyramid
Justin Herman Plaza
Haas-Lilienthal House
Cable Car Museum
Embarcadero Center
Nob Hill
Grace Cathedral
Financial District
Lafayette Park
Transbay Terminal
Willie L. Brown San Francisco-Oakland Bay Bridge
California Historical Society
SFMOMA
Union Square
Japan Center
Contemporary Jewish Museum
Yerba Buena Gardens
Yerba Buena Center for the Arts
Powell St. Cable Car Turntable
Moscone Center
St. Mary's Cath.
Jefferson Square
Civic Center
Children's Creativity Museum
South of Market
South Beach Harbor
S.F. War Memorial & Performing Arts Center
Opera Ho.
Asian Art Museum
City Hall
Main Library
Symphony Hall
Oracle Park
China Basin
Hall of Justice
Caltrain Depot
Mission Creek Marina
VAN NESS AVENUE
MARKET
Interstate route numbers
U.S. route numbers
State route numbers
Cable Car route

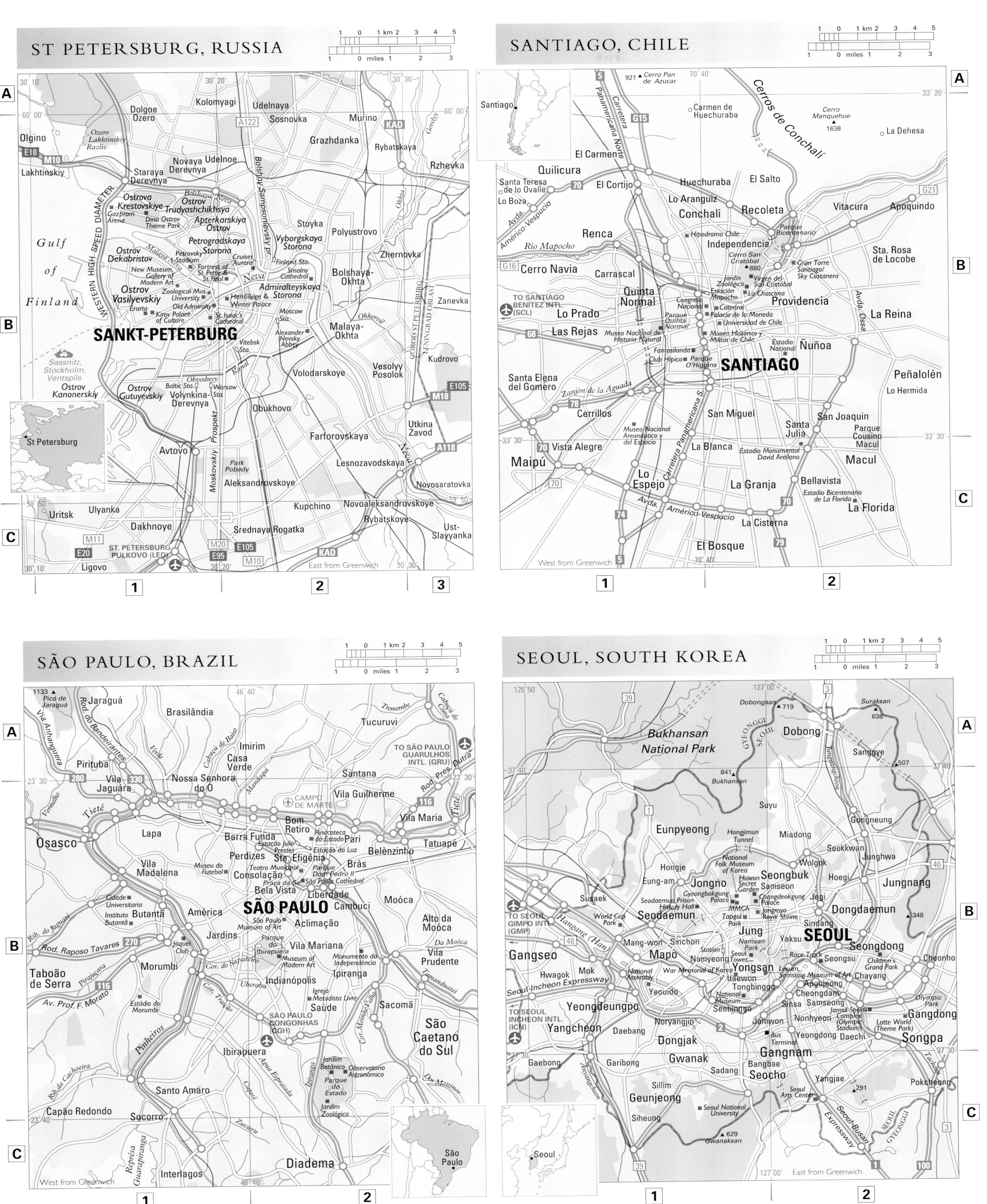
ST PETERSBURG, RUSSIA
SANKT-PETERBURG
Gulf of Finland
Kolomyagi
Udelnaya
Sosnovka
Murino
Grazhdanka
Rybatskaya
Rzhevka
Olgino
Lakhtinskiy
Novaya Derevnya
Udelnoe
Staraya Derevnya
Polyustrovo
Zhernovka
Bolshaya-Okhta
Malaya-Okhta
Zanevka
Kudrovo
Volodarskoye
Vesolyy Posolok
Obukhovo
Farforovskaya
Utkina Zavod
Avtovo
Lesnozavodskaya
Aleksandrovskoye
Novosaratovka
Uritsk
Ulyanka
Dakhnoye
Kupchino
Novoaleksandrovskoye
Rybatskoye
Ust-Slavyanka
Srednaya Rogatka
Ligovo
ST. PETERSBURG PULKOVO (LED)
East from Greenwich
St Petersburg
SANTIAGO, CHILE
SANTIAGO
Cerros de Conchalí
Carmen de Huechuraba
Cerro Manquehue 1638
La Dehesa
El Carmen
Quilicura
El Cortijo
Huechuraba
El Salto
Santa Teresa de lo Ovalle
Lo Boza
Lo Aranguiz
Conchalí
Recoleta
Vitacura
Apoquindo
Renca
Independencia
Cerro Navia
Carrascal
Quinta Normal
Providencia
Sta. Rosa de Locobe
La Reina
TO SANTIAGO BENITEZ INTL. (SCL)
Lo Prado
Las Rejas
Ñuñoa
Santa Elena del Gomero
Peñalolén
Lo Hermida
Cerrillos
San Miguel
San Joaquin
Santa Julia
Vista Alegre
Maipú
La Blanca
Macul
Lo Espejo
La Granja
Bellavista
La Florida
La Cisterna
El Bosque
West from Greenwich
Santiago
SÃO PAULO, BRAZIL
SÃO PAULO
Jaraguá
Brasilândia
Tucuruvi
Imirim
Casa Verde
TO SÃO PAULO GUARULHOS INTL. (GRU)
Pirituba
Vila Jaguara
Nossa Senhora do O
Santana
Vila Guilherme
Vila Maria
Osasco
Lapa
Bom Retiro
Barra Funda
Pari
Belènzinho
Tatuapé
Perdizes
Sta. Efigênia
Brás
Vila Madalena
Consolação
Bela Vista
Liberdade
Cambuci
Moóca
Butantã
América
Aclimação
Alto da Moóca
Jardins
Vila Mariana
Vila Prudente
Taboão de Serra
Morumbi
Indianópolis
Ipiranga
Sacomã
Saúde
São Caetano do Sul
SÃO PAULO CONGONHAS (CGH)
Ibirapuera
Santo Amaro
Capão Redondo
Socorro
Diadema
Interlagos
West from Greenwich
São Paulo
SEOUL, SOUTH KOREA
SEOUL
Bukhansan National Park
Dobong
Sanggye
Suyu
Gongneung
Eunpyeong
Miadong
Seokkwan
Junghwa
Jongno
Seongbuk
Jungnang
Dongdaemun
Seodaemun
Jung
Seongdong
Gangseo
Mapo
Yongsan
Cheonho
Yeongdeungpo
Gangdong
Yangcheon
Dongjak
Songpa
Gaebong
Garibong
Gwanak
Gangnam
Seocho
Yangjae
Pokcheong
Geunjeong
Siheung
TO SEOUL GIMPO INTL (GMP)
TO SEOUL INCHEON INTL. (ICN)
East from Greenwich
Seoul

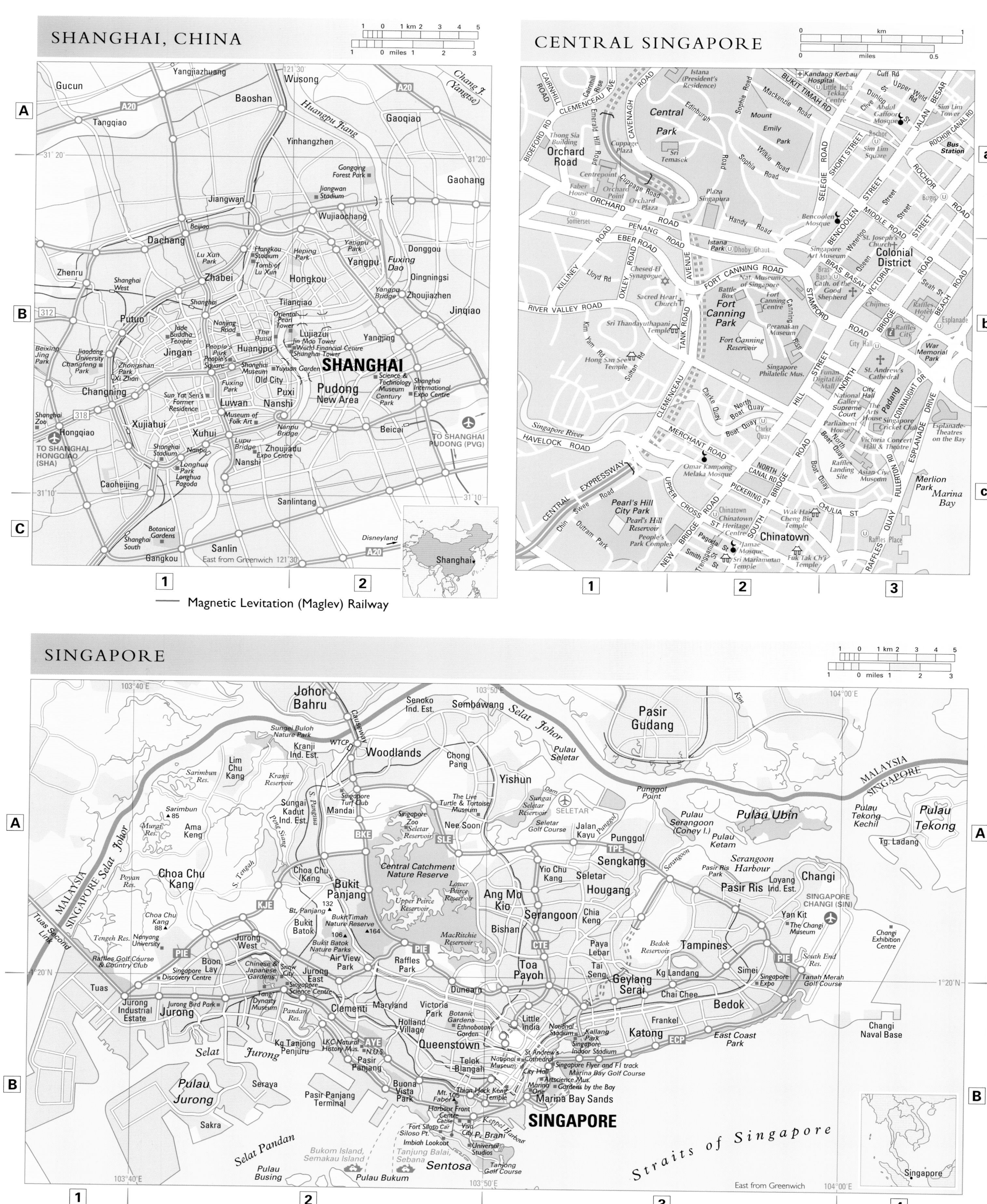
SHANGHAI, CHINA
Magnetic Levitation (Maglev) Railway
Yangjiazhuang
Wusong
Chang J. (Yangtse)
Gucun
Baoshan
Tangqiao
Gaoqiao
Huangpu Jiang
Yinhangzhen
Gongqing Forest Park
Gaohang
Jiangwan
Jiangwan Stadium
Wujiaochang
Beijiao
Dachang
Hongkou Stadium
Heping Park
Yangpu Park
Donggou
Lu Xun Park
Tomb of Lu Xun
Yangpu
Fuxing Dao
Zhenru
Shanghai West
Zhabei
Hongkou
Oingningsi
Yangpu Bridge
Zhoujiazhen
Tilanqiao
Putuo
Jinqiao
Oriental Pearl Tower
Jade Buddha Temple
Nanjing Road
The Bund
Lujiazui
Jin Mao Tower
World Financial Centre
Shanghai Tower
Yangjing
Beixing Jing Park
Jiaodong University
Changfeng Park
Jingan
People's Park
People's Square
Huangpu
SHANGHAI
Zhongshan Park
Xi Zhan
Shanghai Museum
Yuyuan Garden
Science & Technology Museum
Century Park
Shanghai International Expo Centre
Changning
Fuxing Park
Old City
Pudong New Area
Sun Yat Sen's Former Residence
Luwan
Nanshi
Puxi
Shanghai Zoo
Hongqiao
Xujiahui
Museum of Folk Art
Xuhui
Nanpu Bridge
Beicai
TO SHANGHAI HONGQIAO (SHA)
TO SHANGHAI PUDONG (PVG)
Shanghai Stadium
Lupu Bridge
Zhoujiadu
Expo Centre
Longhua Park
Longhua Pagoda
Nanshi
Caoheijing
Sanlintang
Botanical Gardens
Shanghai South
Disneyland
Sanlin
Gangkou
East from Greenwich
Shanghai
CENTRAL SINGAPORE
Istana (President's Residence)
Kandang Kerbau Hospital
Little India
Tekka Centre
Central Park
Orchard Road
Fort Canning Park
Colonial District
Singapore Art Museum
Nat. Museum of Singapore
Raffles Hotel
Raffles City
Chijmes
Esplanade
War Memorial Park
St. Andrew's Cathedral
Padang
Singapore Cricket Club
Esplanade-Theatres on the Bay
Victoria Concert Hall & Theatre
Asian Civ. Museum
Raffles Landing Site
Singapore River
Boat Quay
Clarke Quay
Chinatown
Chinatown Heritage Centre
Jamae Mosque
Sri Mariamman Temple
Fuk Tak Ch'i Temple
Wak Hai Cheng Bio Temple
Raffles Place
Merlion Park
Marina Bay
Pearl's Hill City Park
Pearl's Hill Reservoir
People's Park Complex
Omar Kampong Melaka Mosque
Singapore Philatelic Mus.
Peranakan Museum
Sri Thandayuthapani Temple
Hong San See Temple
Sacred Heart Church
Chesed-El Synagogue
Bencoolen Mosque
Abdul Gaffoor Mosque
Sim Lim Tower
Sim Lim Square
Bus Station
Plaza Singapura
Dhoby Ghaut
Somerset
Centrepoint
Orchard Point
Orchard Plaza
Cuppage Plaza
Thong Sia Building
Faber House
Sri Temasek
Mount Emily Park
Istana Park
Cath. of the Good Shepherd
Funan DigitaLife Mall
National Gallery
Supreme Court
Parliament House
The Arts House
City Hall
SINGAPORE
Johor Bahru
Senoko Ind. Est.
Sembawang
Selat Johor
Pasir Gudang
Sungei Buloh Nature Park
Kranji Ind. Est.
WTCP
Causeway
Woodlands
Chong Pang
Pulau Seletar
Yishun
Lim Chu Kang
Sarimbun Res.
Kranji Reservoir
Singapore Turf Club
Mandai
The Live Turtle & Tortoise Museum
Sungai Seletar Reservoir
SELETAR
Punggol Point
Pulau Serangoon (Coney I.)
Pulau Ubin
Pulau Tekong Kechil
Pulau Tekong
MALAYSIA SINGAPORE
Sungai Kadut Ind. Est.
Singapore Zoo
Seletar Reservoir
Nee Soon
Seletar Golf Course
Jalan Kayu
Punggol
Pulau Ketam
Tg. Ladang
Ama Keng
Murai Res.
Central Catchment Nature Reserve
Sengkang
Serangoon Harbour
Changi
Choa Chu Kang
Bukit Panjang
Upper Peirce Reservoir
Lower Peirce Reservoir
Ang Mo Kio
Yio Chu Kang
Seletar
Hougang
Pasir Ris
Pasir Ris Park
Loyang Ind. Est.
SINGAPORE CHANGI (SIN)
Yan Kit
The Changi Museum
Changi Exhibition Centre
Poyan Res.
Tengeh Res.
Nanyang University
Bt. Panjang
Bukit Timah Nature Reserve
Bukit Batok
Bukit Batok Nature Parks
MacRitchie Reservoir
Bishan
Serangoon
Chia Keng
Bedok Reservoir
Tampines
Tuas Second Link
Raffles Golf Course & Country Club
Singapore Discovery Centre
Boon Lay
Jurong West
Chinese & Japanese Gardens
Snow City
Singapore Science Centre
Jurong East
Air View Park
Raffles Park
Toa Payoh
Paya Lebar
Tai Seng
Geylang Serai
Kg Landang
Simei
South End Res.
Tanah Merah Golf Course
Singapore Expo
Tuas
Jurong Industrial Estate
Jurong
Jurong Bird Park
Tang Dynasty Museum
Pandan Res.
Clementi
Maryland
Victoria Park
Botanic Gardens
Ethnobotany Garden
Dunearn
Little India
National Stadium
Kallang Park
Singapore Indoor Stadium
Chai Chee
Bedok
Frankel
Katong
East Coast Park
Changi Naval Base
Holland Village
Queenstown
Kg Tanjong Penjuru
LKC Natural History Mus.
N.U.S.
Selat Jurong
Pasir Panjang
Telok Blangah
National Museum
St Andrew's Cathedral
City Hall
Singapore Flyer and F1 track
Marina Bay Golf Course
Artscience Mus.
Marina One
Gardens by the Bay
Marina Bay Sands
Pulau Jurong
Seraya
Buona Vista Park
Pasir Panjang Terminal
Mt. Faber
Thian Hock Keng Temple
Harbour Front Centre
Keppel Harbour
Sakra
Fort Siloso
Siloso Pt.
Cable Car
Vivo City
P. Brani
Imbiah Lookout
Universal Studios
Tanjong Golf Course
Selat Pandan
Bukom Island, Semakau Island
Tanjong Balai, Sebana
Sentosa
Pulau Busing
Pulau Bukum
Straits of Singapore
East from Greenwich
Singapore

STOCKHOLM, SWEDEN

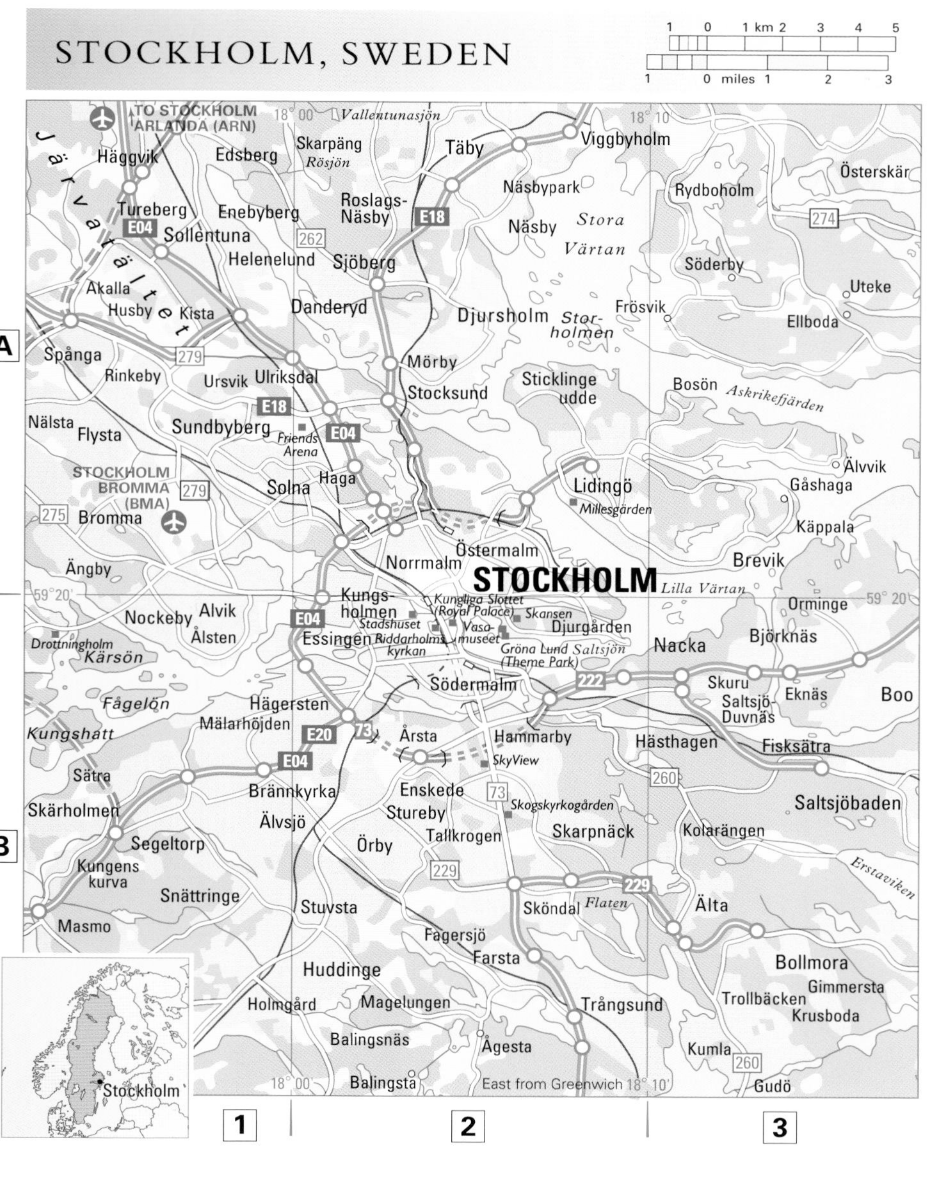

CENTRAL STOCKHOLM

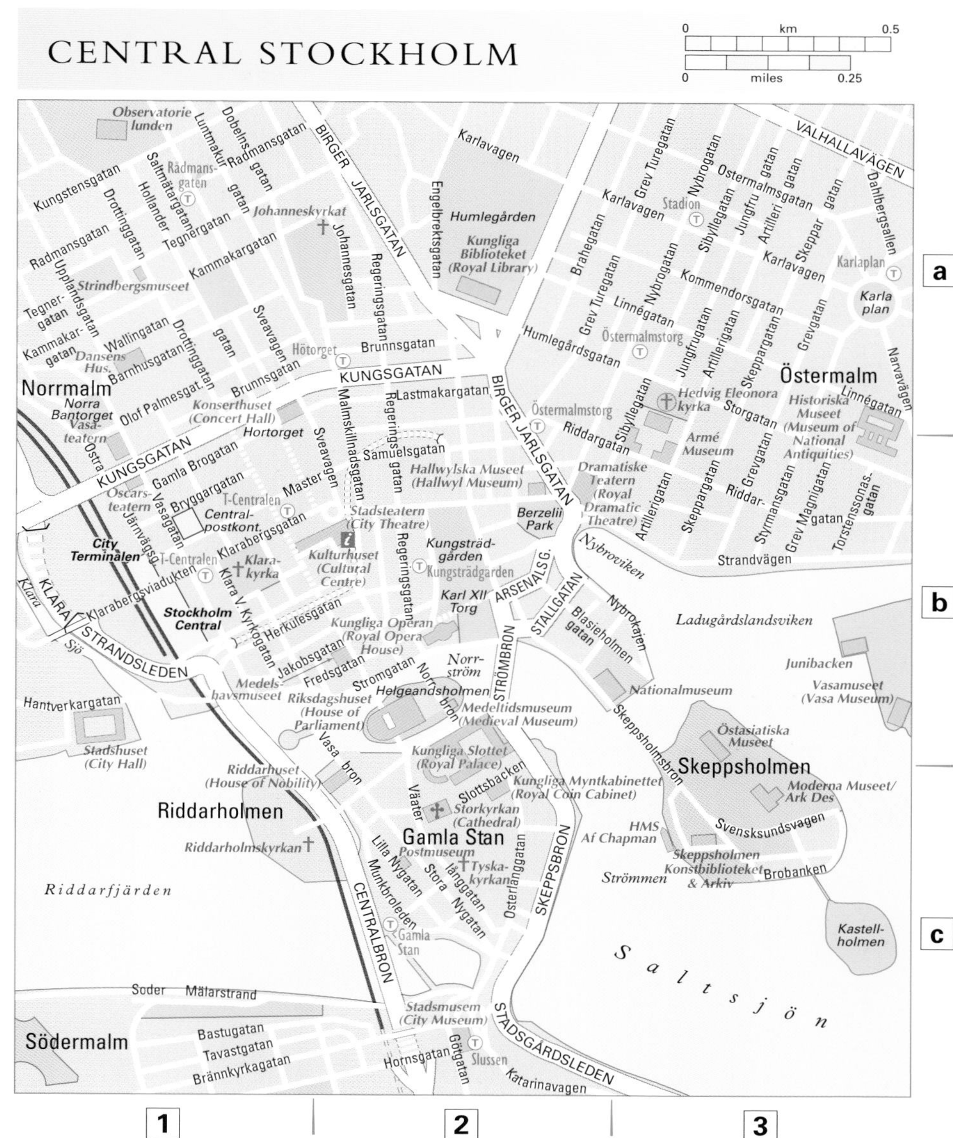

SYDNEY, AUSTRALIA

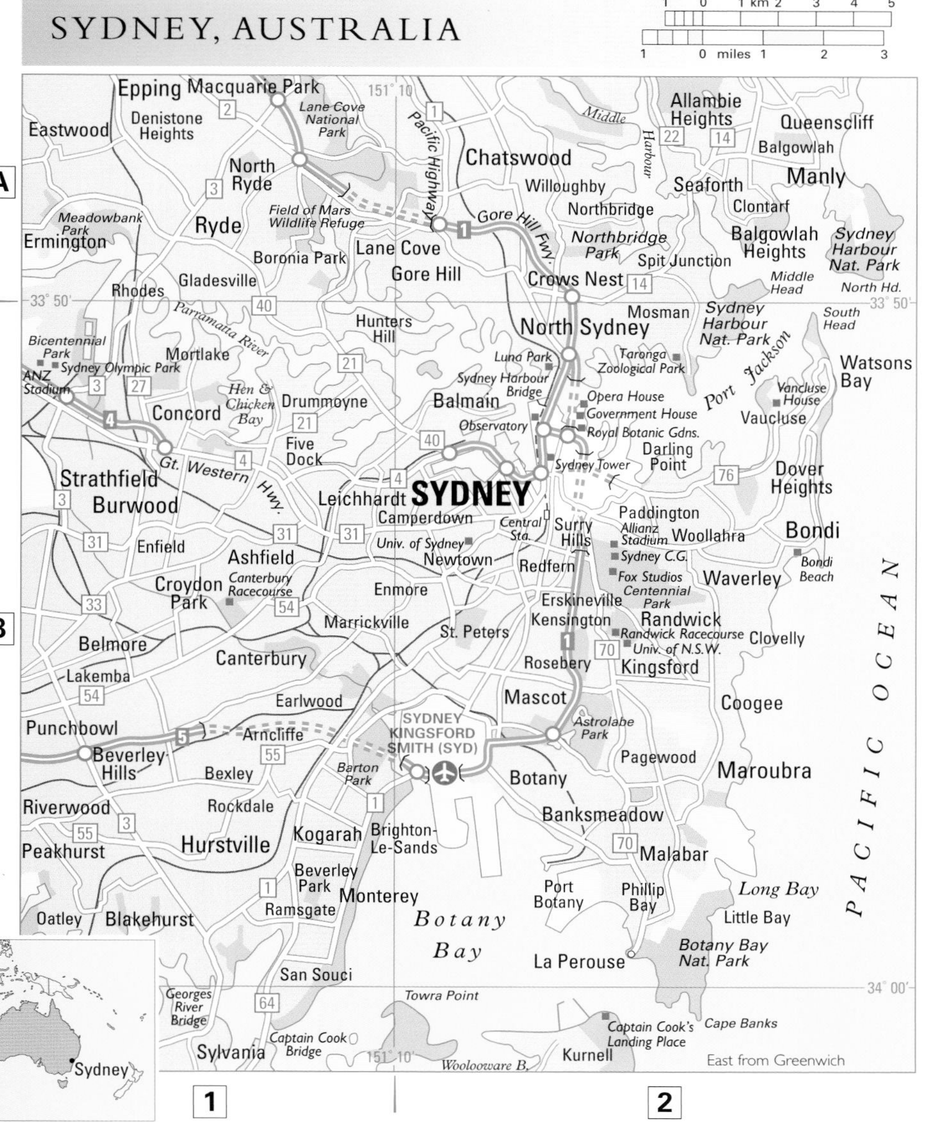

CENTRAL SYDNEY

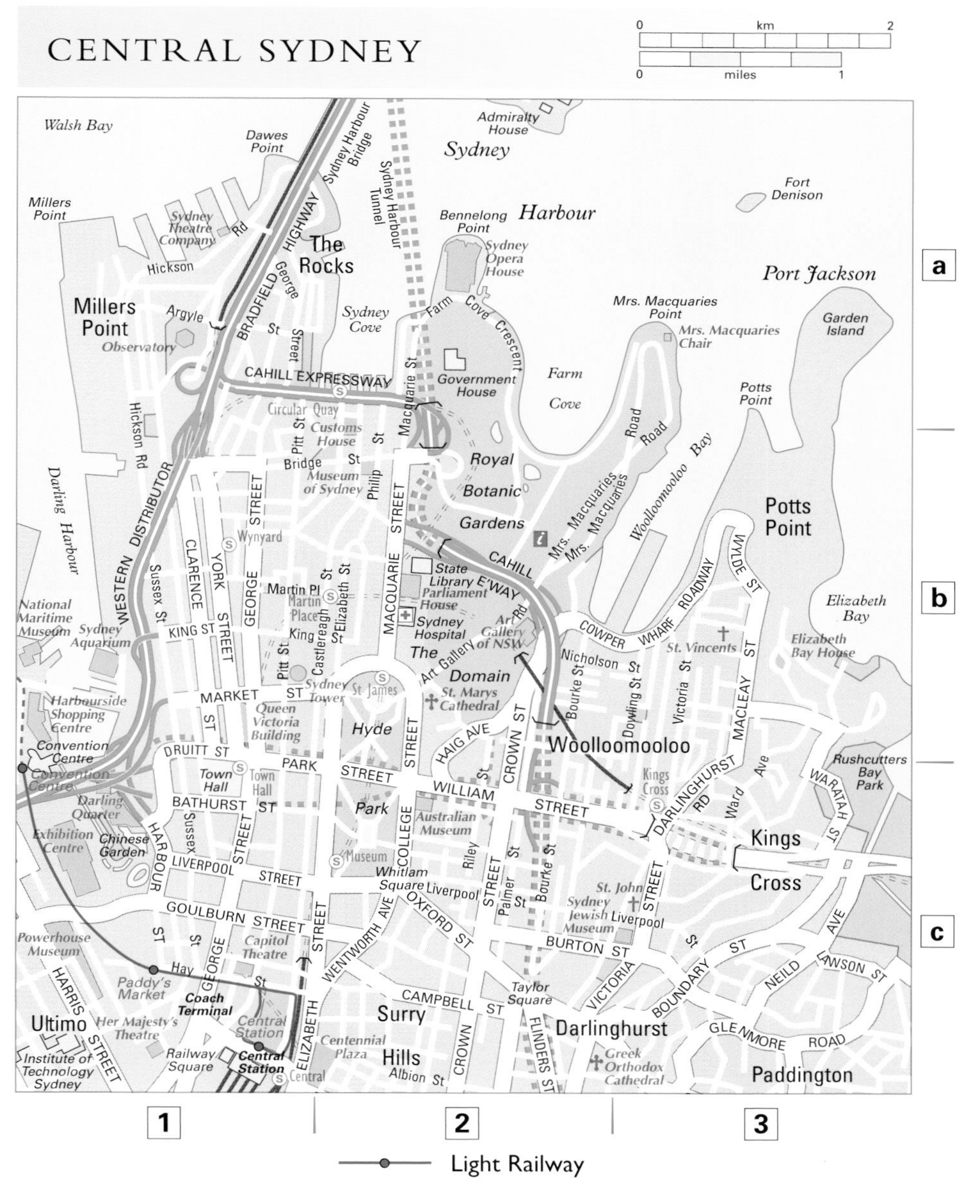

TOKYO, JAPAN

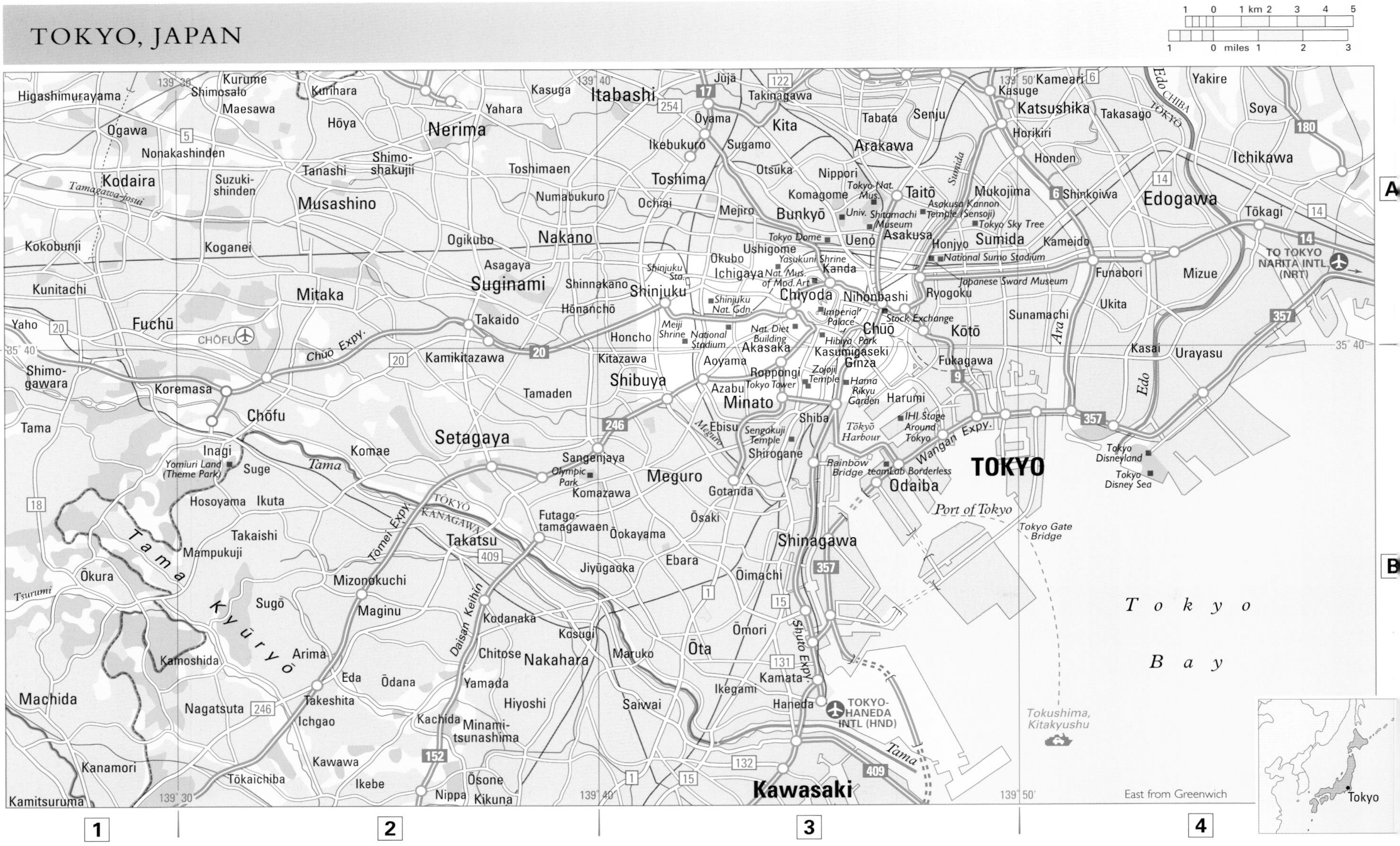

CENTRAL TOKYO

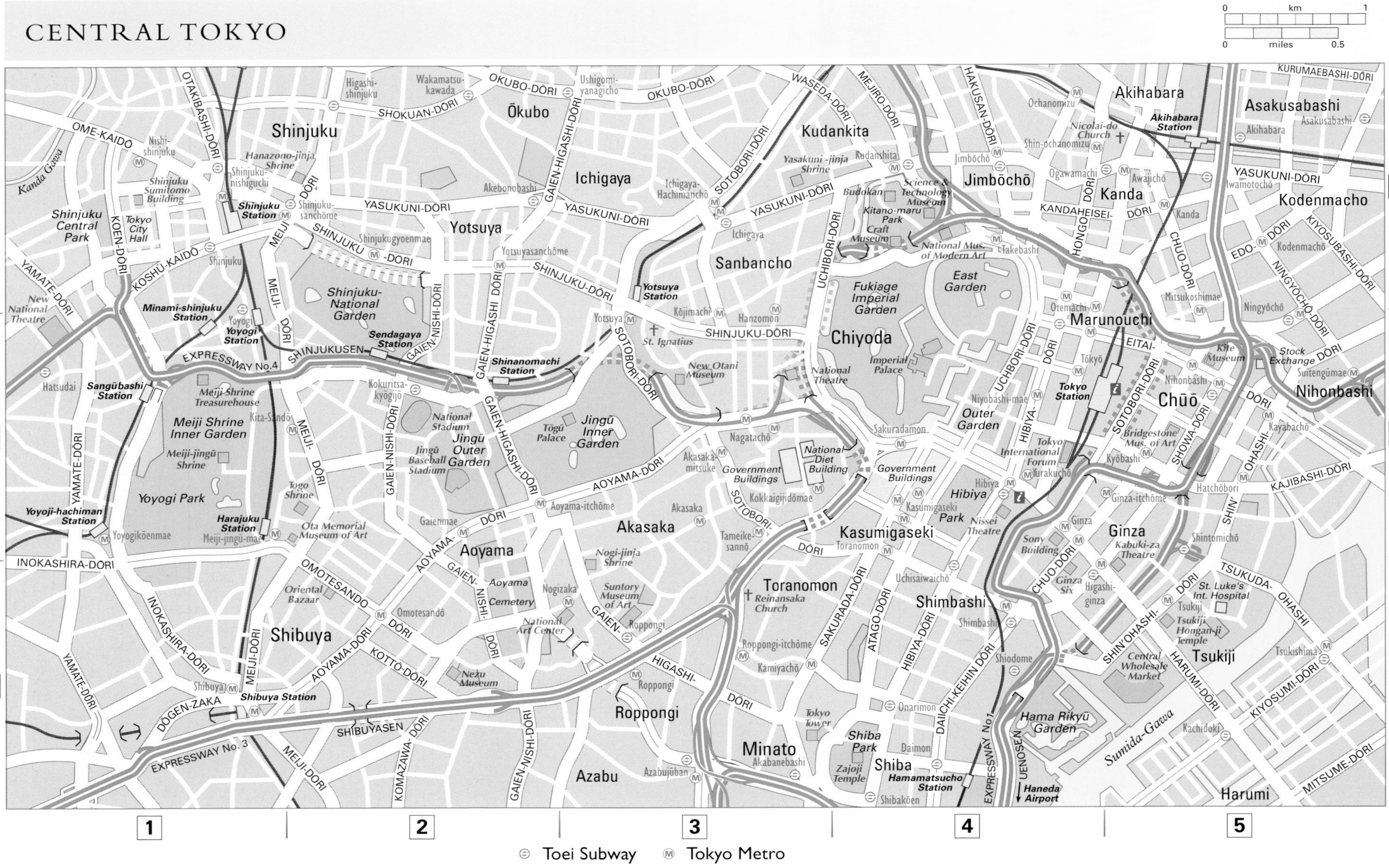

Toei Subway   Tokyo Metro

TEHRAN, IRAN
Reshteh-ye Kūhhā-ye Alborz (Elburz Mts.)
Tehrān
Darakeh
Darband
Nīāvarān
Nīāvarān Palace
Sa'dabad Palace
Towchāl Cable Car
Evin
Tajrīsh
Emāmzādeh Saleh
Sowhānak
Tehrān International Exhibition
Hesārak
Sa'ādatābād
Pārk-e Mellat
Lavīzān
Qolhak
Darrūs
Shahrak-e Qods (Gharb)
Pūnak
Vanak
Dāvūdīyeh
Qāsemābād
Hasanābād
Bāgh-e Feyz
Pardisān Nature Park
Milad Tower
Reza Abbasi Museum
Tehrān Pārs
Yūsofābād
Amīrābād
Nārmak
Karaj Expwy.
Tehran Museum of Contemporary Art
Carpet Mus.
Laleh Park
Jamshīdīyeh
Tehrān Now
Tehran West Bus Terminal
University
TEHRAN MEHRĀBĀD (THR)
Azadi Tower
City Theatre
Museum of Glass and Ceramics
TEHRĀN
Farahābād
Jey
National Mus. of Iran
Golestan Palace (Ethnographical Mus.)
Akbarābād
Shah Mosque
Razi Park
Bāzār
Dūlāb
Qasr-e Fīrūzeh
Tehran Station
Vasfenārd
Javādīyeh
Tehran South Bus Terminal
Afsarīyeh
Yaftābād
Qal'eh Morghī
N'ematābād
Dowlatābād
Pārk-e Azādegān
Shahrak-e Golshahr
Azadegān Expwy.
Shahr-e Rey (Rey)
TO TEHRAN IMAM KHOMEINI INTL. (IKA)
Qom Expwy.
Mesgarābād
East from Greenwich
CENTRAL TORONTO
University of Toronto
Toronto General Hospital
Ryerson University
Hospital for Sick Children
Coach Terminal
St Michael's Cathedral
Moss Park
The Art Gallery of Ontario
China Town
Toronto Eaton Centre
Nathan Philips Square
City Hall
Old City Hall
Downtown
Osgoode Hall
St James Cathedral
St James Park
Bank of Canada
Toronto Stock Exchange
Scotia Plaza
Royal Alexandra Theatre
Roy Thomson Hall
TD Gallery of Inuit Art
Hockey Hall of Fame
St Lawrence Market
Sony Centre for the Performing Arts
Canada Trust Tower
Metro Hall
Simcoe Park
CBC Broadcast Centre & Mus.
Union Station
Bus Terminal
Clarence Square Park
Metro Toronto Conv. Cen. (Nth)
Convention Centre (Sth)
Scotiabank Arena
Isabella Valancy Crawford Park
Rogers Centre (Sky Dome)
CN Tower
Roundhouse Park
City Core Golf & Driving Range
Police Station
Harbour Square Park
Toronto Island Ferry Terminal
Redpath Sugar Museum
Harbourfront Park
Queen's Quay Terminal
GARDINER EXPRESSWAY
LAKE SHORE BOULEVARD WEST
Lake Ontario
TORONTO, CANADA
Vaughan
Markham
Thornhill
Concord
Pine Grove
Woodbridge
Edgeley
Newtonbrook
Willowdale
Agincourt
Malvern
Brown
Toronto Zoo
Rouge Hill
Fairport
West Rouge
Port Union
Highland Creek
Boyd Conservation Area
Fisherville
York University
Black Creek Pioneer Village
Humber Summit
North York
Lansing
Northmount
Fairview Mall
Bendale
Woburn
West Hill
Beaumonte Heights
Armour Heights
York Mills
Victoria Village
Wexford
Scarborough
Guildwood
Thistletown
Downsview Park
Edwards Gardens & the Toronto Botanical Garden
Don Mills
Cliffside
Malton
Humberwood Park
Kipling Heights
Rexdale
Downsview
Humberlea
Lawrence Heights
Wilket Creek Park
Ontario Science Centre
Danforth
Woodbine Racetrack
Weston
Forest Hill
Thorncliffe
Leaside
Scarborough Junction
Bluffers Park
TORONTO PEARSON INTL. (YYZ)
Cedarvale Park
York
Casa Loma
East York
Dentonia Park
Birch Cliff
Scarborough Bluffs
Humber Valley Village
Mount Dennis
Royal Ontario Museum
Riverdale Park
Kew Gardens
Macdonald-Cartier Frwy.
Etobicoke
Lambton Mills
Swansea
University of Toronto
Ontario Legislative Building
Ashbridge's Bay Park
Hanlon
Islington
Kingsway
High Park
Old City Hall
CN Tower & Rogers Centre
Union Sta.
Lower Don Lands
TORONTO
Markland Wood
Humber Bay
Parkdale
Exhibition Place
BILLY BISHOP TORONTO CITY (YTZ)
Toronto Harbour
Tommy Thompson Park
Burnhamthorpe
Ontario Place
Toronto Islands
Island Park
Summerville
Humber Bay Park
Alderwood
Mimico
Gibraltar Point
LAKE ONTARIO
New Toronto
Square One
Dixie Mall
Humber College
Samuel Smith Park
Cooksville
Mississauga
Long Branch
West from Greenwich
Toronto
Provincial route numbers

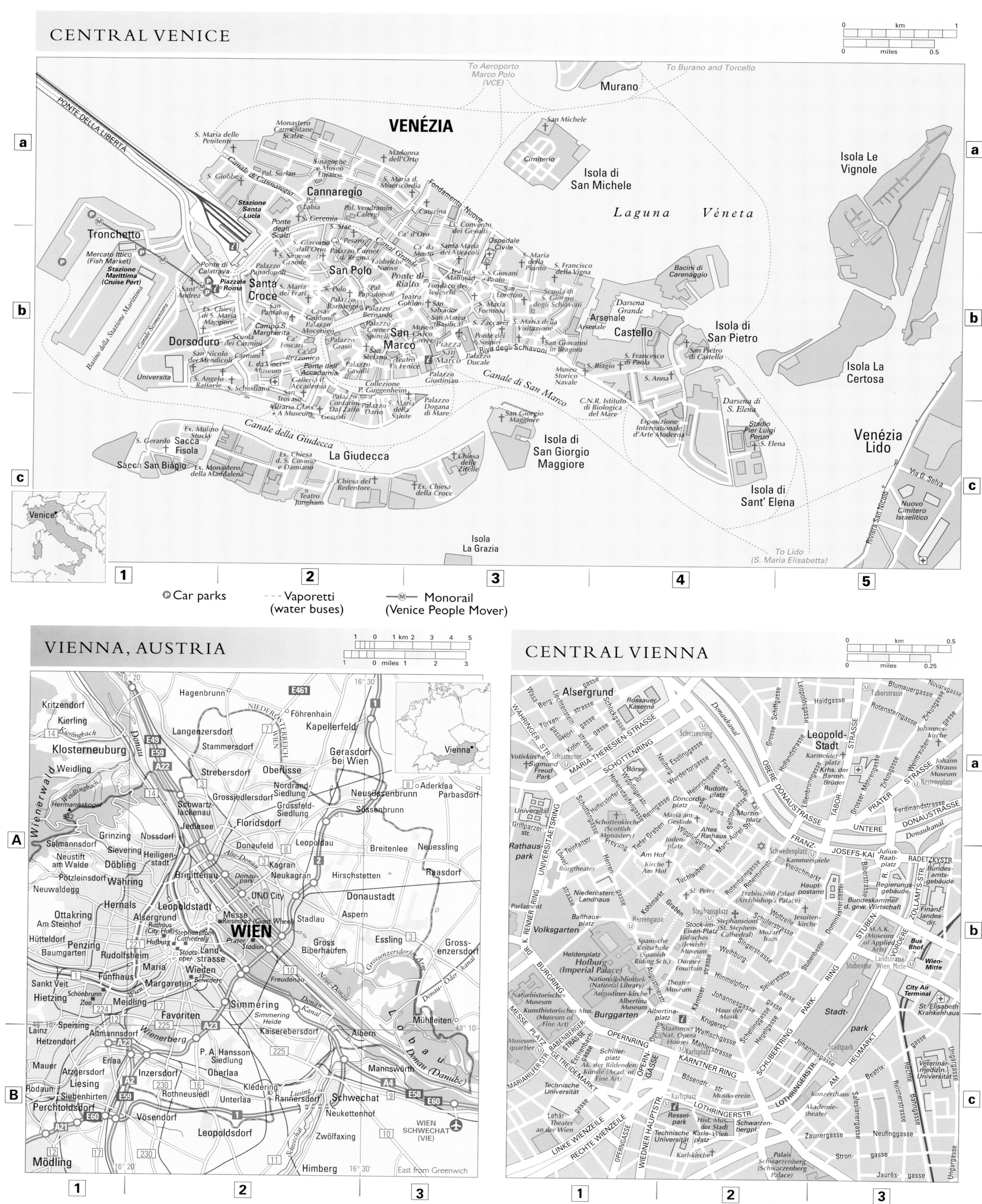

CENTRAL VENICE
0 km 1
0 miles 0.5
To Aeroporto Marco Polo (VCE)
To Burano and Torcello
Murano
VENÉZIA
Isola di San Michele
Cimitero
San Michele
Laguna Véneta
Isola Le Vignole
Tronchetto
Mercato Ittico (Fish Market)
Stazione Marittima (Cruise Port)
Basino della Stazione Marittima
PONTE DELLA LIBERTÀ
Stazione Santa Lucia
Canale di Cannaregio
Cannaregio
Fondamenta Nuove
Canal Grande
Piazzale Roma
Santa Croce
San Polo
Dorsoduro
San Marco
Castello
Arsenale
Isola di San Pietro
Isola La Certosa
Canale di San Marco
Canale della Giudecca
La Giudecca
Sacca Fisola
Sacca San Biagio
Isola di San Giorgio Maggiore
Isola di Sant' Elena
Venézia Lido
Nuovo Cimitero Israelitico
Isola La Grazia
To Lido (S. Maria Elisabetta)
Venice
Car parks
Vaporetti (water buses)
Monorail (Venice People Mover)
VIENNA, AUSTRIA
WIEN
Klosterneuburg
Wienerwald
Donau
Leopoldstadt
Simmering
Favoriten
Schwechat
WIEN SCHWECHAT (VIE)
Mödling
Perchtoldsdorf
East from Greenwich
Vienna
CENTRAL VIENNA
Alsergrund
Leopold-Stadt
Donaukanal
Rathaus-park
Volksgarten
Hofburg (Imperial Palace)
Burggarten
Stephansdom (St. Stephens Cathedral)
Staatsoper (Nat. Opera House)
Stadtpark
Karlsplatz
Karlskirche
Palais Schwarzenberg (Schwarzenberg Palace)
Wien Mitte
City Air Terminal

WARSAW, POLAND

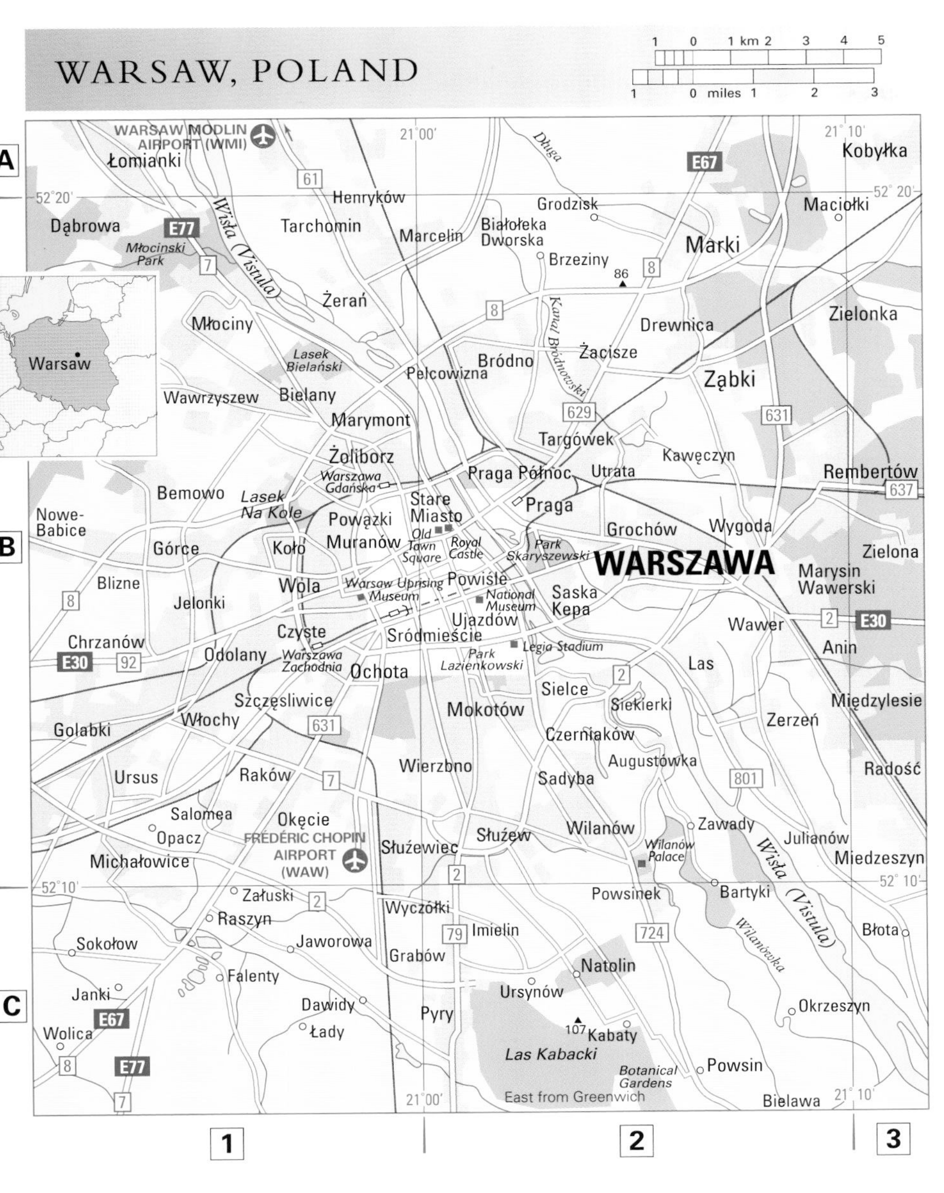

CENTRAL WARSAW

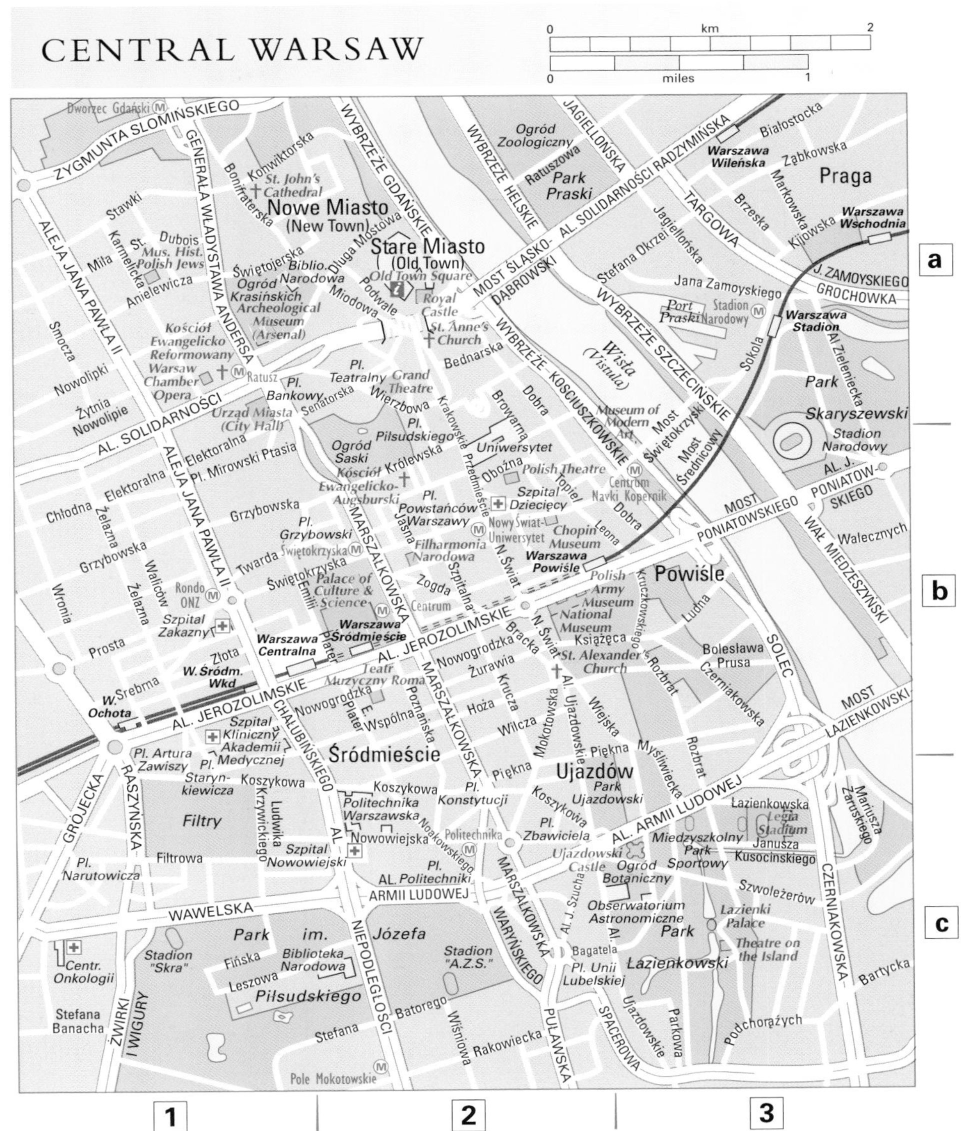

WASHINGTON D.C.

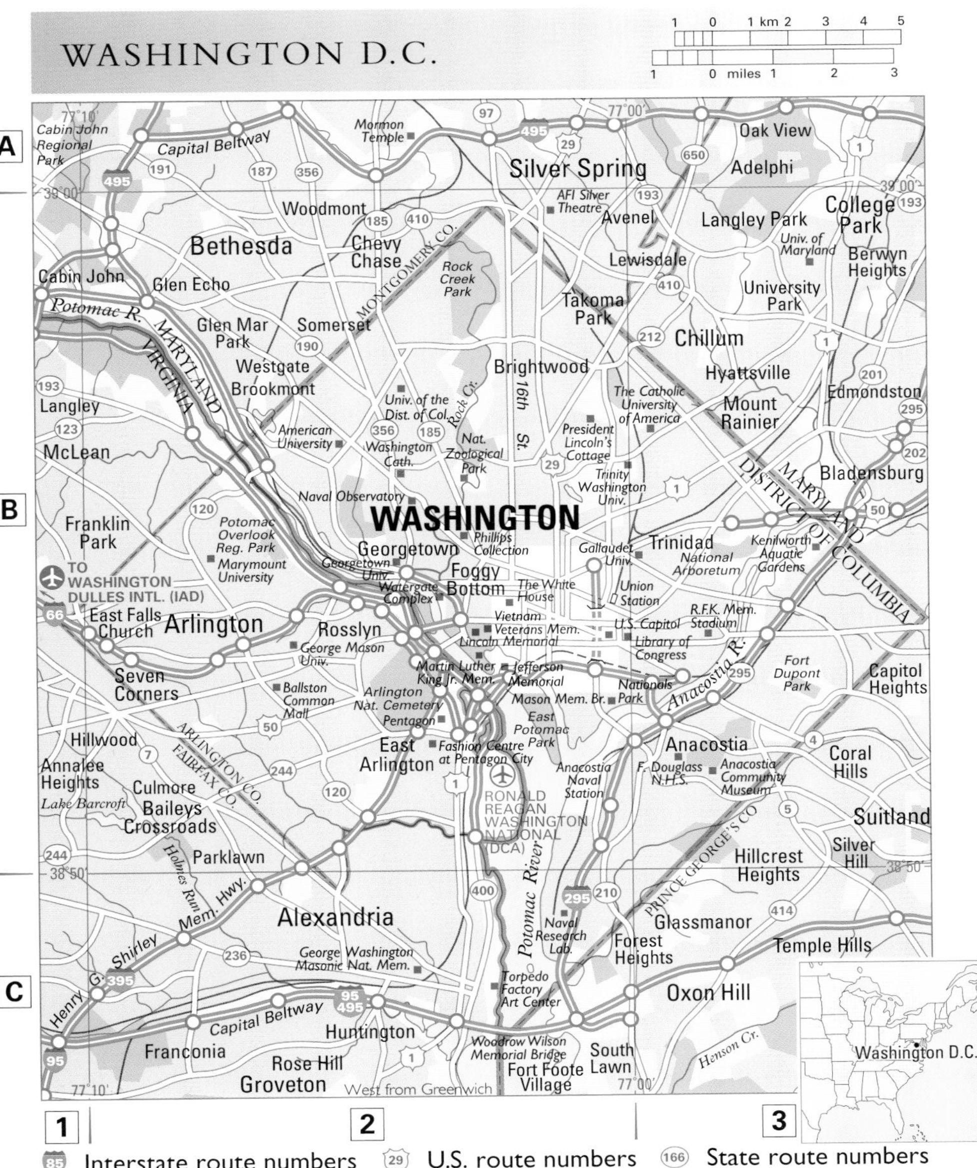

CENTRAL WASHINGTON

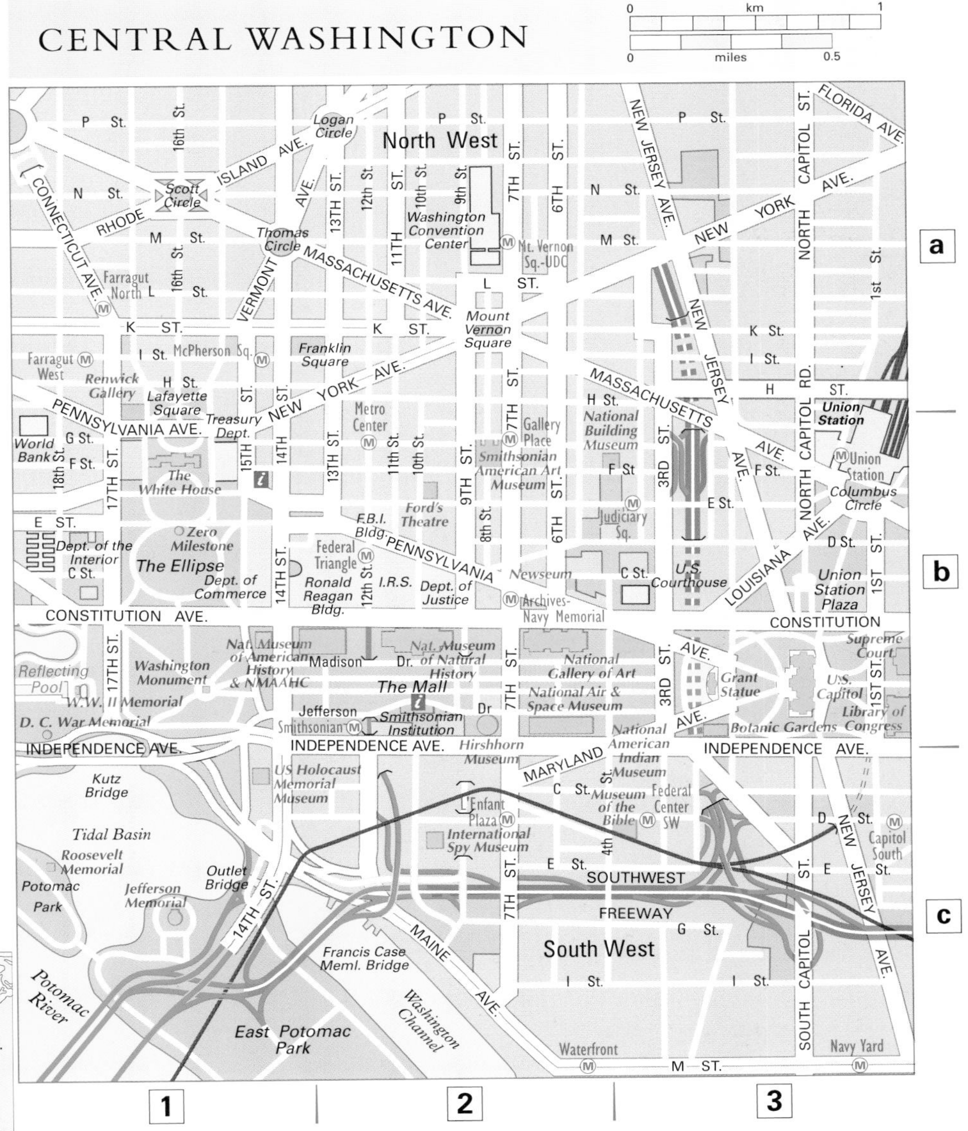

Interstate route numbers U.S. route numbers State route numbers

WORLD
MAPS

Equatorial Scale 1:76 000 000

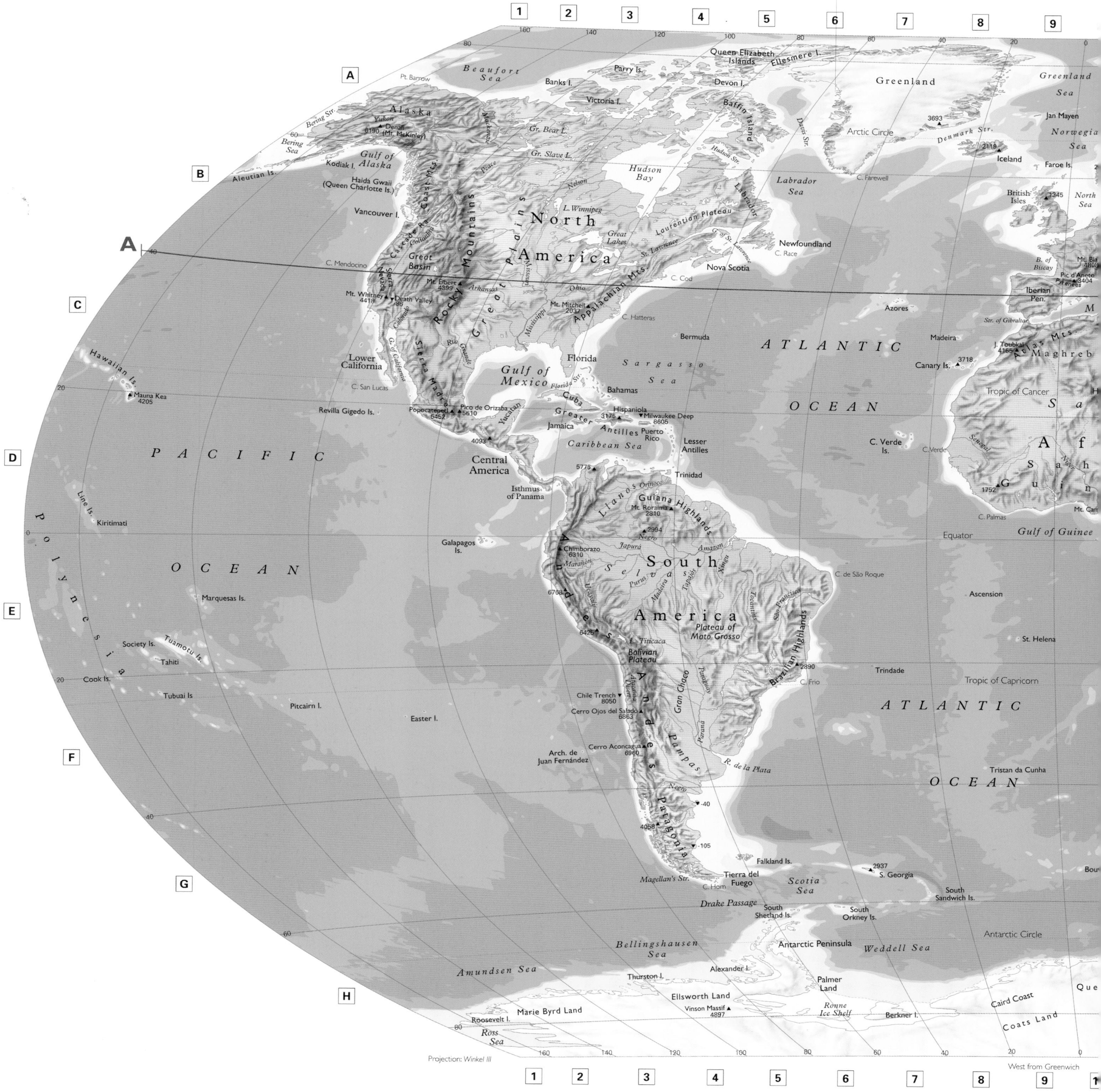

Projection: Winkel III

West from Greenwich

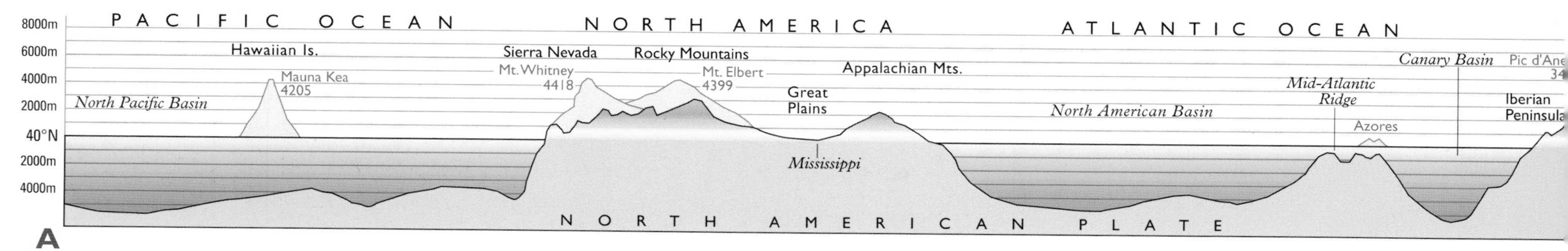

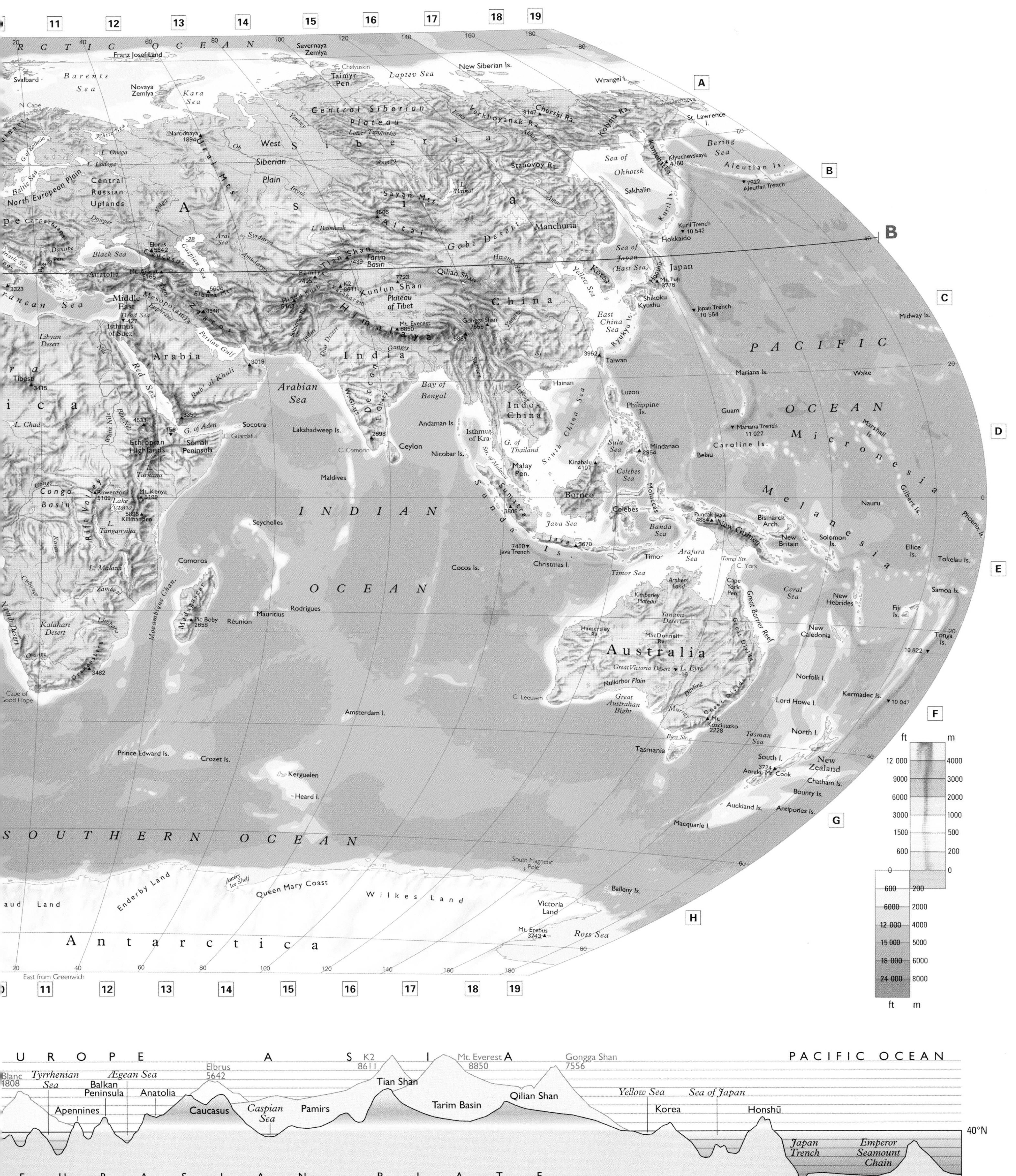
PACIFIC OCEAN
INDIAN OCEAN
SOUTHERN OCEAN
Australia
Antarctica
EURASIAN PLATE
40°N
COPYRIGHT PHILIP'S

Equatorial Scale 1:76 000 000

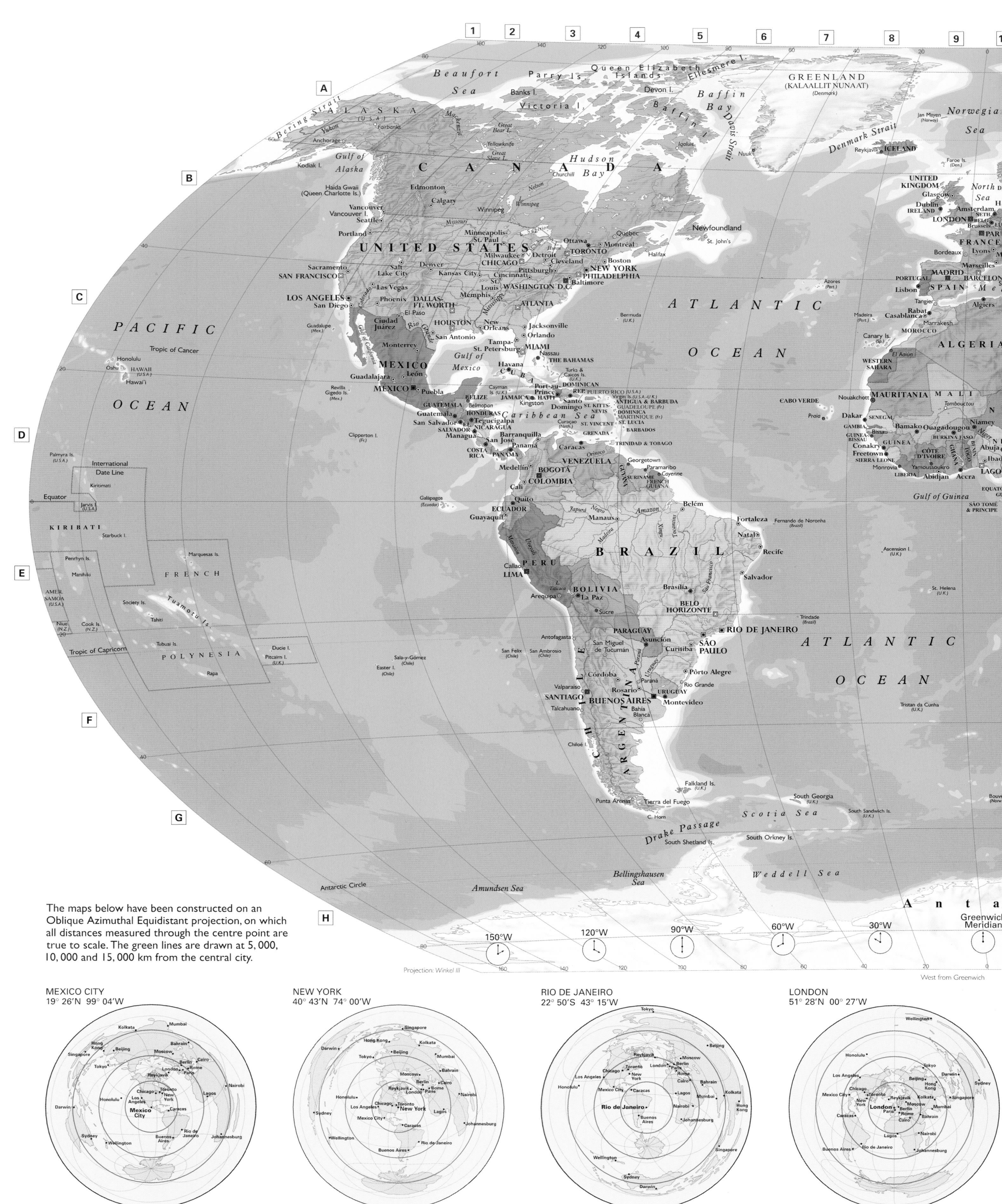

The maps below have been constructed on an Oblique Azimuthal Equidistant projection, on which all distances measured through the centre point are true to scale. The green lines are drawn at 5,000, 10,000 and 15,000 km from the central city.

MEXICO CITY
19° 26'N 99° 04'W

NEW YORK
40° 43'N 74° 00'W

RIO DE JANEIRO
22° 50'S 43° 15'W

LONDON
51° 28'N 00° 27'W

CAPE TOWN
33° 55′S 18° 35′E

DELHI
28° 39′N 77° 13′E

TOKYO
35° 33′N 139° 46′E

SYDNEY
33° 56′ S 151° 10′E

100 0 200 400 600 800 1000 1200 1400 km

1:28 000 000

100 0 200 400 600 800 1000 miles

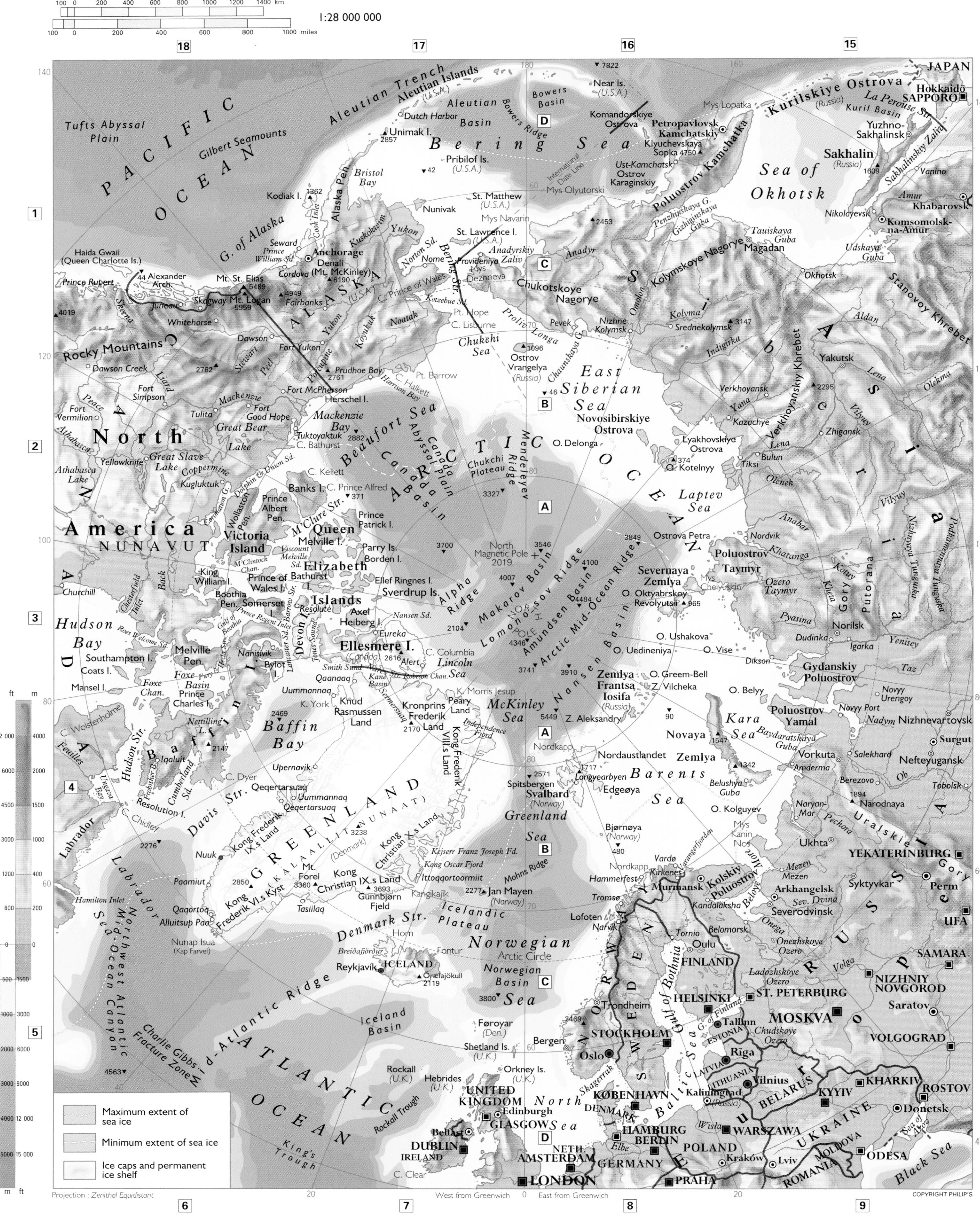

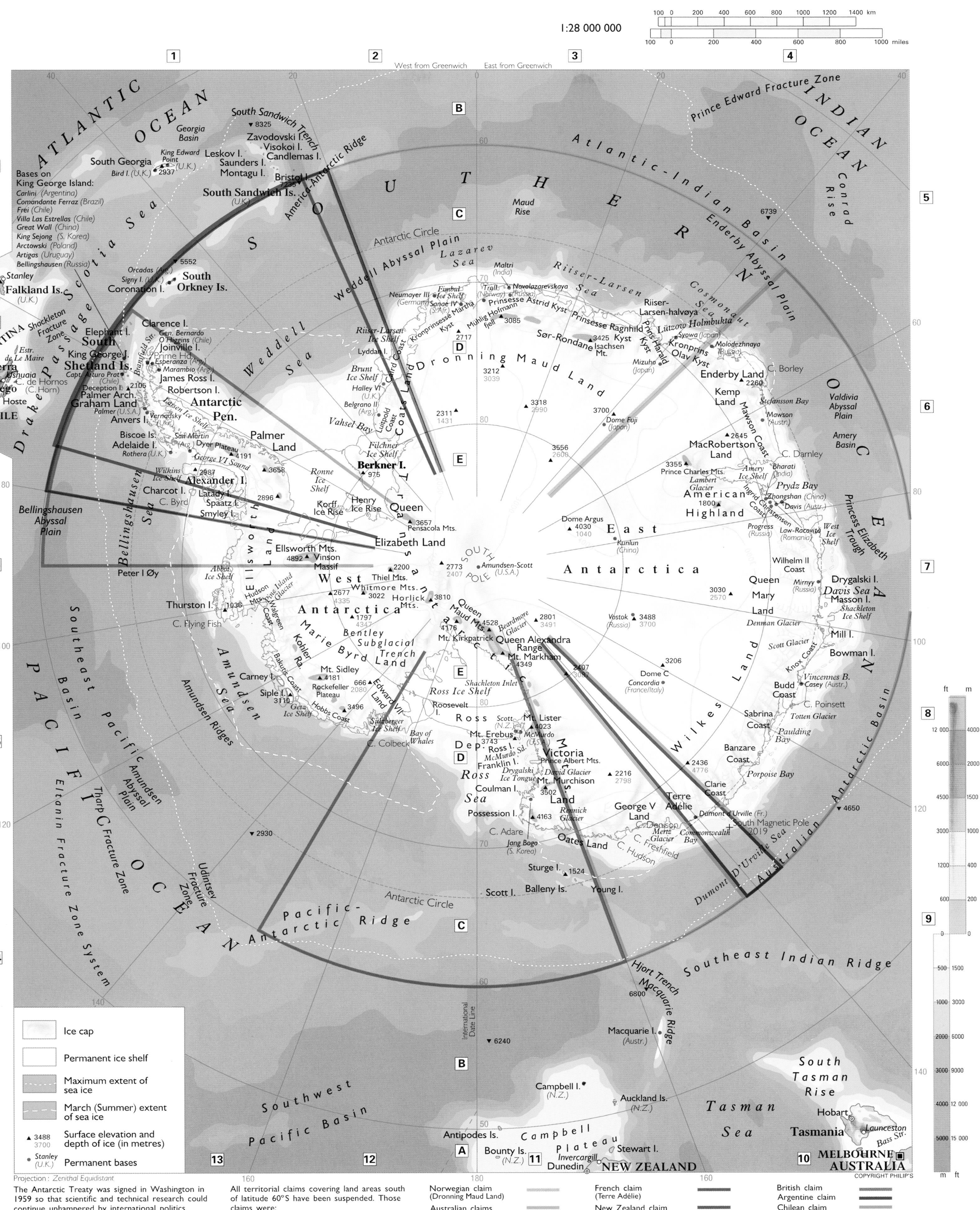

The Antarctic Treaty was signed in Washington in 1959 so that scientific and technical research could continue unhampered by international politics.

All territorial claims covering land areas south of latitude 60°S have been suspended. Those claims were:

- Norwegian claim (Dronning Maud Land)
- Australian claims
- French claim (Terre Adélie)
- New Zealand claim (Ross Dependency)
- British claim
- Argentine claim
- Chilean claim

Equatorial Scale 1:41 000 000

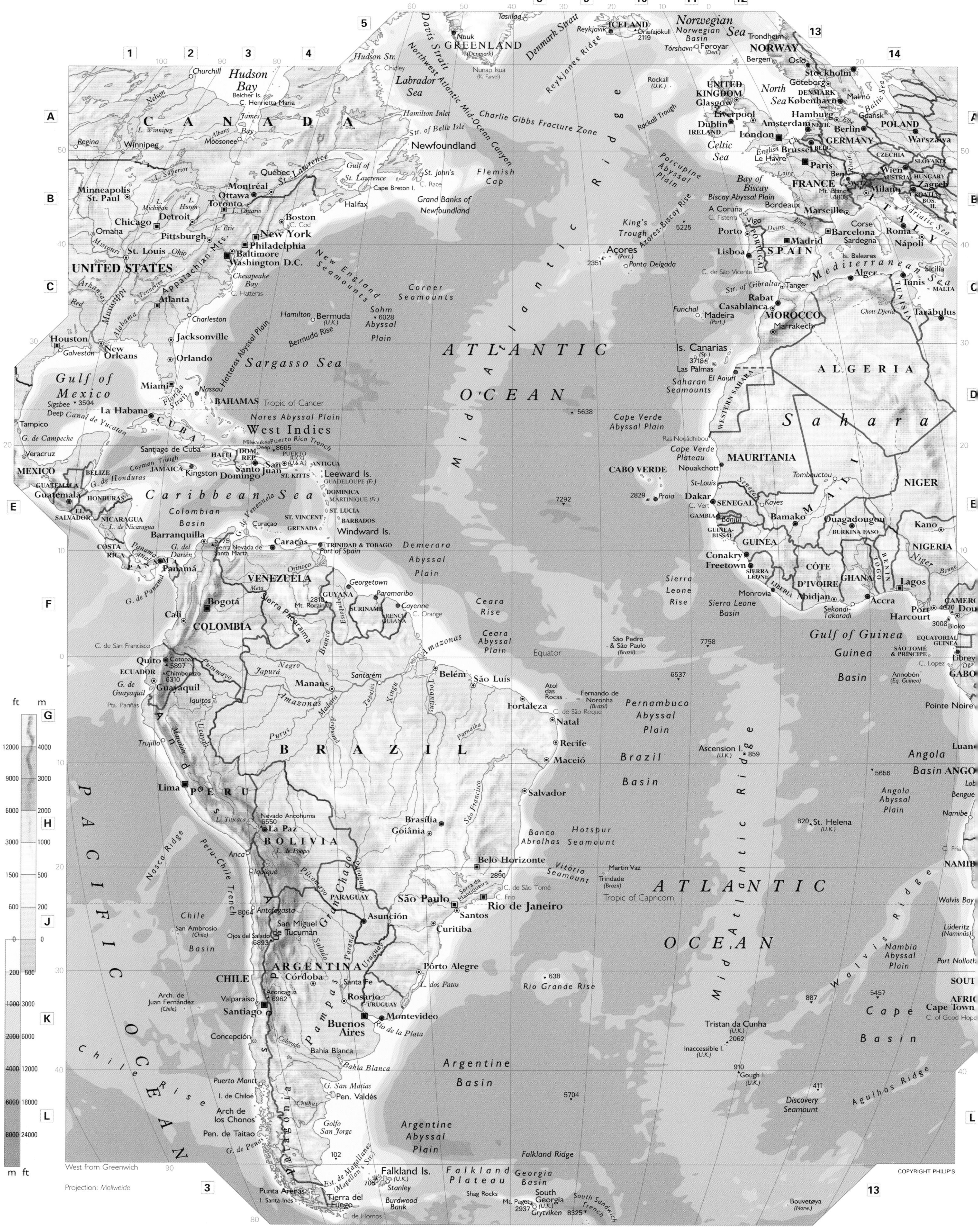

ATLANTIC OCEAN

PACIFIC OCEAN

Hudson Bay
CANADA
GREENLAND (Denmark)
Labrador Sea
Davis Strait
Denmark Strait
ICELAND
Norwegian Sea
Norwegian Basin
North Sea
Celtic Sea
Bay of Biscay
Mediterranean Sea
Baltic Sea
Adriatic Sea
UNITED STATES
Gulf of Mexico
Caribbean Sea
Sargasso Sea
West Indies
BAHAMAS
CUBA
HAITI
DOM. REP.
JAMAICA
PUERTO RICO (U.S.A.)
Leeward Is.
Windward Is.
TRINIDAD & TOBAGO
MEXICO
BELIZE
GUATEMALA
HONDURAS
EL SALVADOR
NICARAGUA
COSTA RICA
PANAMA
VENEZUELA
GUYANA
SURINAME
FRENCH GUIANA
COLOMBIA
ECUADOR
PERU
BOLIVIA
BRAZIL
PARAGUAY
CHILE
ARGENTINA
URUGUAY
Falkland Is. (U.K.)
South Georgia (U.K.)
UNITED KINGDOM
IRELAND
NORWAY
DENMARK
GERMANY
POLAND
FRANCE
SPAIN
PORTUGAL
ITALY
MOROCCO
ALGERIA
TUNISIA
WESTERN SAHARA
MAURITANIA
MALI
NIGER
SENEGAL
GAMBIA
GUINEA-BISSAU
GUINEA
SIERRA LEONE
LIBERIA
CÔTE D'IVOIRE
BURKINA FASO
GHANA
TOGO
BENIN
NIGERIA
CABO VERDE
Sahara
Açores (Port.)
Madeira (Port.)
Is. Canarias (Sp.)
Ascension I. (U.K.)
St. Helena (U.K.)
Tristan da Cunha (U.K.)
Gough I. (U.K.)
Bouvetøya (Norw.)
Gulf of Guinea
Guinea Basin
Angola Basin
Angola Abyssal Plain
Cape Basin
Walvis Ridge
Agulhas Ridge
Mid-Atlantic Ridge
Reykjanes Ridge
Charlie Gibbs Fracture Zone
Northwest Atlantic Mid-Ocean Canyon
Flemish Cap
Grand Banks of Newfoundland
New England Seamounts
Corner Seamounts
Sohm Abyssal Plain
Hatteras Abyssal Plain
Nares Abyssal Plain
Puerto Rico Trench
Porcupine Abyssal Plain
Rockall Trough
Biscay Abyssal Plain
King's Trough
Azores-Biscay Rise
Saharan Seamounts
Cape Verde Abyssal Plain
Cape Verde Plateau
Demerara Abyssal Plain
Ceara Rise
Ceara Abyssal Plain
Sierra Leone Rise
Sierra Leone Basin
Pernambuco Abyssal Plain
Brazil Basin
Hotspur Seamount
Vitória Seamount
Rio Grande Rise
Argentine Basin
Argentine Abyssal Plain
Falkland Ridge
Falkland Plateau
Georgia Basin
South Sandwich Trench
Discovery Seamount
Nasca Ridge
Peru-Chile Trench
Chile Basin
Chile Rise
Colombian Basin
Cayman Trough
Tropic of Cancer
Equator
Tropic of Capricorn

ft m
12000 4000
9000 3000
6000 2000
3000 1000
1500 500
600 200
0 0
200 600
1000 3000
2000 6000
4000 12000
6000 18000
8000 24000
m ft

West from Greenwich
Projection: Mollweide
COPYRIGHT PHILIP'S

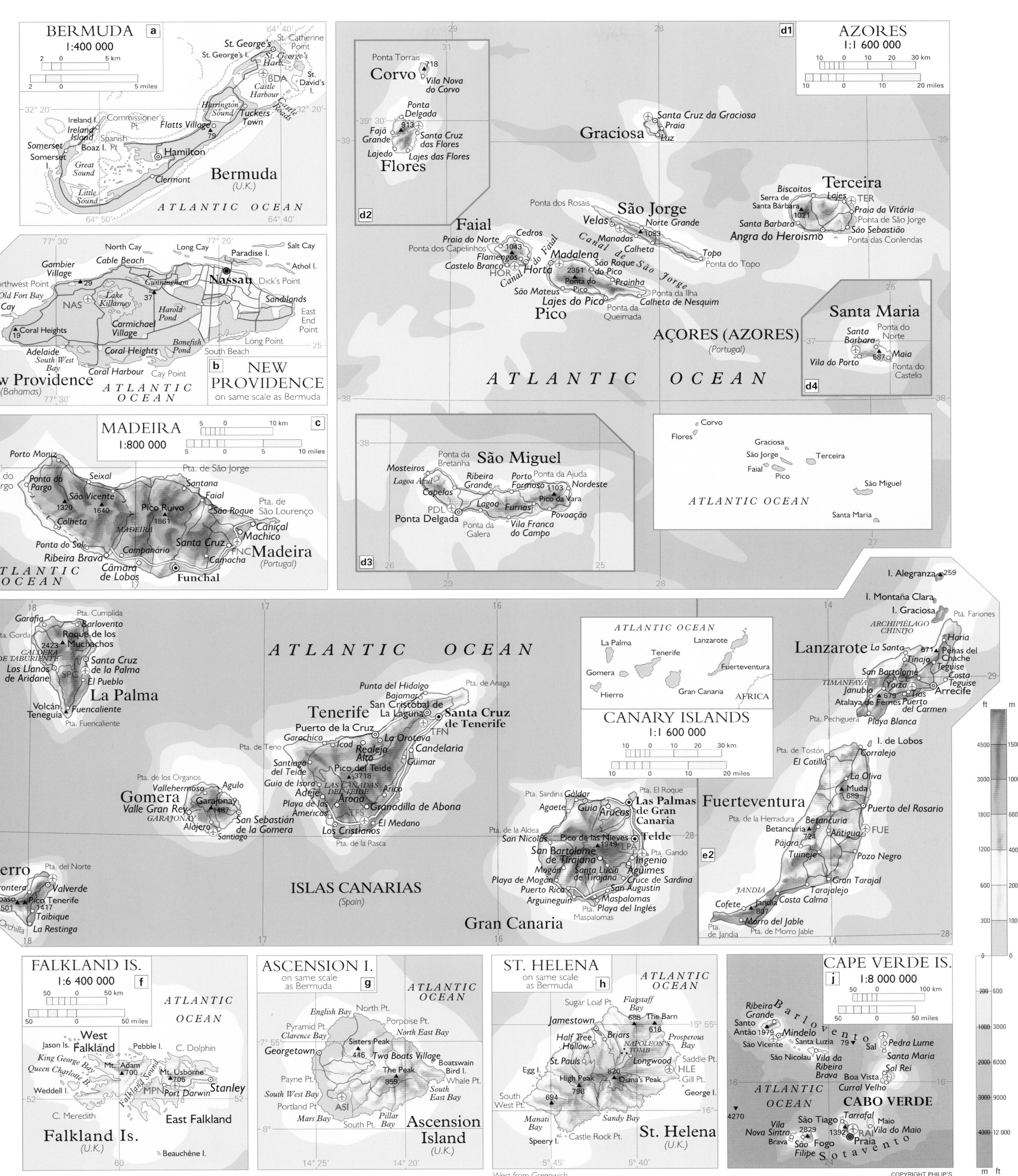
BERMUDA a
1:400 000
St. George's
St. George's I.
St. Catherine Point
St. George's Harb.
BDA
St. David's I.
Castle Harbour
Castle Roads
Harrington Sound
Tuckers Town
Ireland I.
Ireland Island
Commissioner's Pt.
Flatts Village
Spanish Pt.
Somerset
Somerset I.
Boaz I.
Hamilton
Great Sound
Little Sound
Clermont
Bermuda
(U.K.)
ATLANTIC OCEAN
North Cay
Long Cay
Salt Cay
Paradise I.
Athol I.
Gambier Village
Cable Beach
Nassau
Dick's Point
Lake Cunningham
Lake Killarney
NAS
Harold Pond
Sandilands
Old Fort Bay
Cay
Carmichael Village
East End Point
Coral Heights
Long Point
Adelaide
South West Bay
Coral Harbour
Bonefish Pond
South Beach
Cay Point
b
NEW PROVIDENCE
on same scale as Bermuda
(Bahamas)
ATLANTIC OCEAN
MADEIRA c
1:800 000
Porto Moniz
Pta. de São Jorge
Seixal
Ponta do Pargo
São Vicente
Santana
Faial
Pta. de São Lourenço
São Roque
Pico Ruivo
1861
1640
1320
Calheta
Caniçal
Machico
MADEIRA
Ponta do Sol
Santa Cruz
FNC
Campanário
Madeira
(Portugal)
Ribeira Brava
Camacha
Câmara de Lobos
Funchal
ATLANTIC OCEAN
d1
AZORES
1:1 600 000
Ponta Torrais
Corvo
718
Vila Nova do Corvo
Ponta Delgada
913
Fajã Grande
Santa Cruz das Flores
Lajedo
Lajes das Flores
Flores
d2
Santa Cruz da Graciosa
Praia
Graciosa
Luz
Terceira
Biscoitos
Serra de Santa Bárbara
1021
Lajes
TER
Praia da Vitória
Ponta de São Jorge
Santa Barbara
São Sebastião
Angra do Heroísmo
Ponta das Contendas
Ponta dos Rosais
Velas
São Jorge
Norte Grande
1083
Manadas
Calheta
Topo
Ponta do Topo
Faial
Cedros
Praia do Norte
Ponta dos Capelinhos
1043
Flamengos
Castelo Branco
HOR
Horta
Madalena
Canal do Faial
Canal de São Jorge
São Roque do Pico
2351
Ponta do Pico
Prainha
Ponta da Ilha
São Mateus
Lajes do Pico
Calheta de Nesquim
Pico
Ponta da Queimada
AÇORES (AZORES)
(Portugal)
ATLANTIC OCEAN
Santa Maria
Santa Barbara
Ponta do Norte
587
Maia
Vila do Porto
Ponta do Castelo
d4
Ponta da Bretanha
São Miguel
Mosteiros
Lagoa Azul
Ribeira Grande
Porto Formoso
Ponta da Ajuda
1103
Nordeste
Capelas
Pico da Vara
PDL
Lagoa
Furnas
Povoação
Ponta Delgada
Ponta da Galera
Vila Franca do Campo
d3
Corvo
Flores
Graciosa
São Jorge
Terceira
Faial
Pico
São Miguel
ATLANTIC OCEAN
Santa Maria
I. Alegranza
259
I. Montaña Clara
I. Graciosa
Pta. Fariones
ARCHIPIÉLAGO CHINIJO
Lanzarote
La Santa
671
Haría
Peñas del Chache
Tinajo
Teguise
San Bartolomé
Costa Teguise
TIMANFAYA
Janubio
Yaiza
679
Tías
Arrecife
Atalaya de Femes
Puerto del Carmen
Pta. Pechiguera
Playa Blanca
I. de Lobos
Corralejo
Pta. de Tostón
El Cotillo
La Oliva
Muda
689
Fuerteventura
Puerto del Rosario
Pta. de la Herradura
Betancuria
724
Antigua
FUE
Pájara
Tuineje
Pozo Negro
Gran Tarajal
JANDIA
Tarajalejo
Costa Calma
Cofete
Jandía
807
Morro del Jable
Pta. de Jandía
Pta. de Morro Jable
e2
Garafía
Pta. Cumplida
Barlovento
Pta. Gorda
Roque de los Muchachos
2423
CALDERA DE TABURIENTE
Santa Cruz de la Palma
Los Llanos de Aridane
SPC
El Pueblo
La Palma
Volcán Teneguía
Fuencaliente
Pta. Fuencaliente
ATLANTIC OCEAN
Punta del Hidalgo
Bajamar
Pta. de Anaga
Tenerife
San Cristóbal de La Laguna
Santa Cruz de Tenerife
TFN
Puerto de la Cruz
Garachico
Icod
La Orotava
Realejo Alto
Candelaria
Pta. de Teno
Santiago del Teide
Pico del Teide
3718
Güímar
Guía de Isora
LAS CAÑADAS DEL TEIDE
Arico
Adeje
Arona
Playa de las Américas
Granadilla de Abona
TFS
El Médano
Los Cristianos
Pta. de la Rasca
Pta. de los Organos
Vallehermoso
Agulo
Gomera
Garajonay
1487
Valle Gran Rey
GARAJONAY
San Sebastián de la Gomera
Alajeró
Santiago
ATLANTIC OCEAN
Lanzarote
La Palma
Tenerife
Fuerteventura
Gomera
Hierro
Gran Canaria
AFRICA
CANARY ISLANDS
1:1 600 000
Pta. Sardina
Gáldar
Pta. El Roque
Agaete
Guía
Arucas
Las Palmas de Gran Canaria
Pta. de la Aldea
San Nicolás
Pico de las Nieves
1949
LPA
Telde
Pta. Gando
San Bartolomé de Tirajana
Ingenio
Mogán
Santa Lucía de Tirajana
Agüimes
Playa de Mogán
Cruce de Sardina
Puerto Rico
San Augustín
Arguineguín
Maspalomas
Playa del Inglés
Pta. Maspalomas
Gran Canaria
ISLAS CANARIAS
(Spain)
Pta. del Norte
Valverde
Pico Tenerife
1417
1501
Taibique
La Restinga
FALKLAND IS. f
1:6 400 000
ATLANTIC OCEAN
Jason Is.
West Falkland
Pebble I.
C. Dolphin
King George Bay
Queen Charlotte B.
Mt. Adam
700
Falkland Sound
Mt. Usborne
705
Weddell I.
MPN
Port Darwin
Stanley
C. Meredith
East Falkland
Falkland Is.
(U.K.)
Beauchêne I.
ASCENSION I. g
on same scale as Bermuda
ATLANTIC OCEAN
English Bay
North Pt.
Porpoise Pt.
Pyramid Pt.
Clarence Bay
North East Bay
Georgetown
Sisters Peak
446
Two Boats Village
Boatswain Bird I.
The Peak
859
Whale Pt.
Payne Pt.
South West Bay
South East Bay
Portland Pt.
ASI
Mars Bay
South Pt.
Pillar Bay
Ascension Island
(U.K.)
ST. HELENA h
on same scale as Bermuda
ATLANTIC OCEAN
Sugar Loaf Pt.
Flagstaff Bay
Jamestown
688
The Barn
616
Half Tree Hollow
Briars
NAPOLEON'S TOMB
Prosperous Bay
St. Pauls
Longwood
Saddle Pt.
Egg I.
High Peak
798
820
Diana's Peak
HLE
Gill Pt.
George I.
694
South West Pt.
Sandy Bay
Manati Bay
Speery I.
Castle Rock Pt.
St. Helena
(U.K.)
West from Greenwich
CAPE VERDE IS. j
1:8 000 000
Ribeira Grande
Barlavento
Santo Antão
1979
Mindelo
São Vicente
Santa Luzia
79
Sal
Pedra Lume
São Nicolau
Vila da Ribeira Brava
Santa Maria
Sal Rei
Boa Vista
ATLANTIC OCEAN
Curral Velho
CABO VERDE
4270
Tarrafal
São Tiago
Maio
Vila Nova Sintra
2829
1392
RAI
Vila do Maio
Brava
São Filipe
Fogo
Praia
Sotavento
COPYRIGHT PHILIP'S

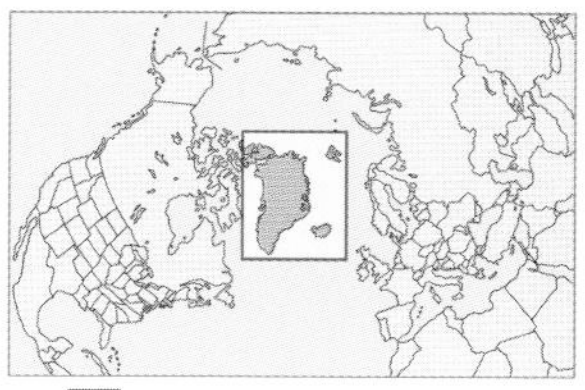

100 0 100 200 300 400 500 km

100 0 50 100 150 200 250 300 350 miles

1:10 000 000

150

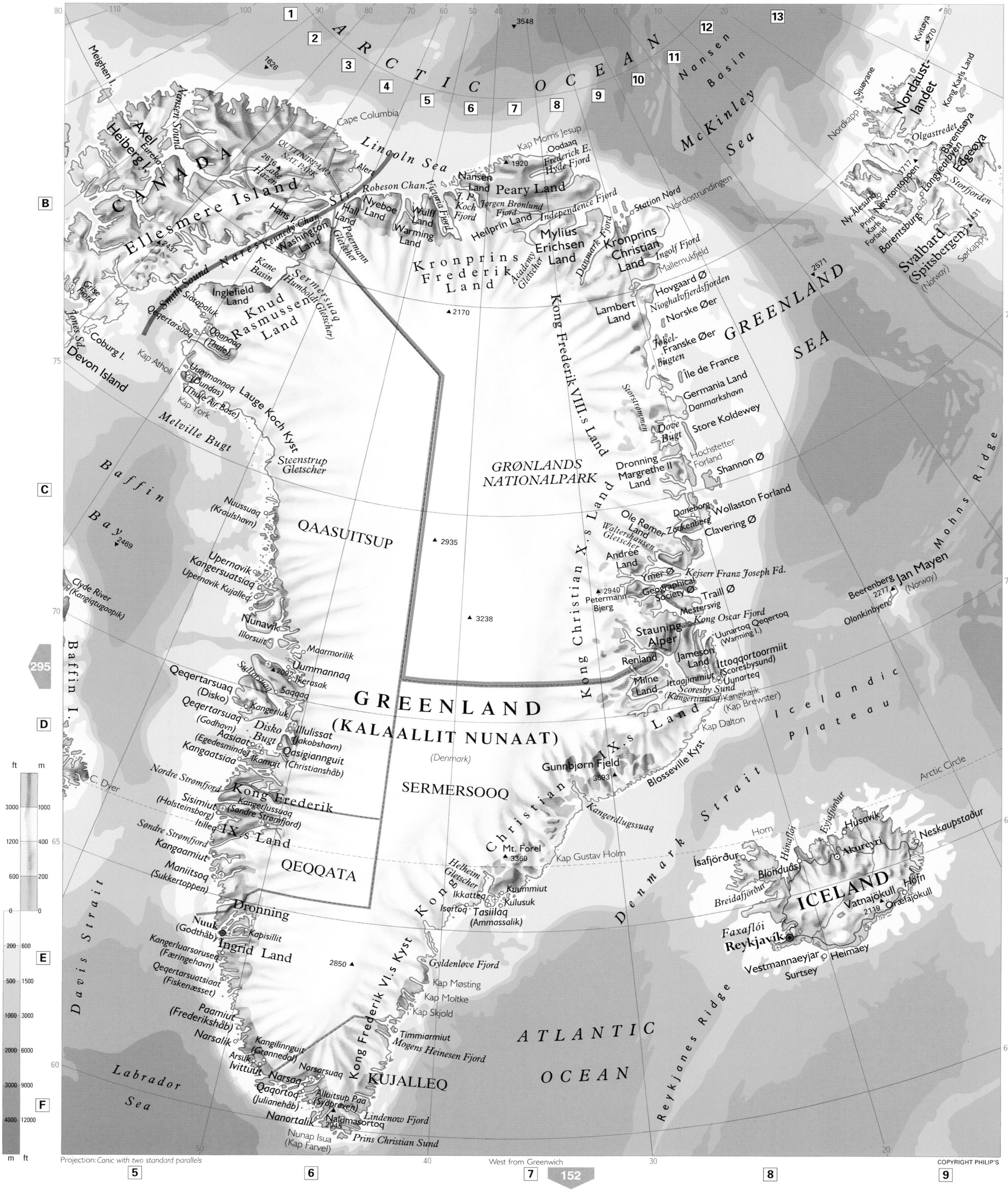

ARCTIC OCEAN

Nansen Basin

McKinley Sea

Lincoln Sea

Cape Columbia

Kap Morris Jesup

Oodaaq

Frederick E. Hyde Fjord

Nansen Land

Peary Land

J.P. Koch Fjord

Jørgen Brønlund Fjord

Independence Fjord

Heilprin Land

Station Nord

Nordostrundingen

Mylius Erichsen Land

Kronprins Christian Land

Ingolf Fjord

Mallemukfjeld

Danmark Fjord

Academy Gletscher

Kronprins Frederik Land

Warming Land

Wulff Land

Victoria Fjord

Nyeboe Land

Hall Land

Petermann Gletscher

Washington Land

Robeson Chan.

Alert

QUTTINIRPAAQ NAT. PARK

Lake Hazen

Eureka

Axel Heiberg I.

Meighen I.

Nansen Sound

CANADA

Ellesmere Island

Hans I.

Kennedy Chan.

Nares Str.

Smith Sound

Kane Basin

Humboldt Gletscher

Sermersuaq

Inglefield Land

Knud Rasmussen Land

Siorapaluk

Qeqertarsuaq

Qaanaaq (Thule)

Grise Fiord

Jones Sd.

Coburg I.

Devon Island

Kap Atholl

Uummannaq (Dundas) (Thule Air Base)

Kap York

Lauge Koch Kyst

Melville Bugt

Steenstrup Gletscher

Baffin Bay

Nuussuaq (Kraulshavn)

QAASUITSUP

Upernavik

Kangersuatsiaq

Upernavik Kujalleq

Clyde River (Kangiqtugaapik)

Nunavik

Illorsuit

Maarmorilik

Uummannaq

Ikerasak

Saqqaq

Sullorsuaq

Qeqertarsuaq (Disko)

Kangerluk

Qeqertarsuaq (Godhavn)

Disko Bugt

Ilulissat (Jakobshavn)

Aasiaat (Egedesminde)

Qasigiannguit (Christianshåb)

Kangaatsiaq

Ikamiut

Baffin I.

C. Dyer

Nordre Strømfjord

Sisimiut (Holsteinsborg)

Kangerlussuaq (Søndre Strømfjord)

Itilleq

Kong Frederik IX.s Land

Søndre Strømfjord

Kangaamiut

Maniitsoq (Sukkertoppen)

QEQQATA

Davis Strait

Nuuk (Godthåb)

Kapisillit

Dronning Ingrid Land

Kangerluarsoruseq (Færingehavn)

Qeqertarsuatsiaat (Fiskenæsset)

Paamiut (Frederikshåb)

Narsalik

Kangilinnguit (Grønnedal)

Arsuk

Ivittuut

Narsaq

Narsarsuaq

Qaqortoq (Julianehåb)

Alluitsup Paa (Sydprøven)

Nanortalik

Nalumasortoq

Lindenow Fjord

Nunap Isua (Kap Farvel)

Prins Christian Sund

Labrador Sea

KUJALLEQ

Kong Frederik VI.s Kyst

Timmiarmiut

Mogens Heinesen Fjord

Kap Skjold

Kap Moltke

Kap Møsting

Gyldenløve Fjord

GREENLAND (KALAALLIT NUNAAT)

(Denmark)

SERMERSOOQ

GRØNLANDS NATIONALPARK

Kong Frederik VIII.s Land

Kong Christian X.s Land

Kong Christian IX.s Land

Lambert Land

Hovgaard Ø

Nioghalvfjerdsfjorden

Norske Øer

Jøkel-bugten

Franske Øer

Île de France

Germania Land

Danmarkshavn

Storstrømmen

Dove Bugt

Store Koldewey

Hochstetter Forland

Shannon Ø

Dronning Margrethe II Land

Daneborg

Zackenberg

Wollaston Forland

Clavering Ø

Ole Rømer Land

Waltershausen Gletscher

Andrée Land

Ymer Ø

Kejserr Franz Joseph Fd.

Geographical Society Ø

Traill Ø

Petermann Bjerg

Mestersvig

Kong Oscar Fjord

Stauning Alper

Uunartoq Qeqertoq (Warming I.)

Renland

Jameson Land

Ittoqqortoormiit (Scoresbysund)

Uunarteq

Milne Land

Ittaajimmiut

Scoresby Sund (Kangertittivaq)

Kangikajik (Kap Brewster)

Kap Dalton

Gunnbjørn Fjeld

Blosseville Kyst

Kangerdlugssuaq

Mt. Forel

Kap Gustav Holm

Helheim Gletscher

Kuummiut

Ikkatteq

Kulusuk

Isortoq

Tasiilaq (Ammassalik)

Denmark Strait

Icelandic Plateau

Arctic Circle

GREENLAND SEA

Mohns Ridge

Jan Mayen (Norway)

Beerenberg

Olonkinbyen

ATLANTIC OCEAN

Reykjanes Ridge

ICELAND

Horn

Ísafjörður

Húnaflói

Eyjafjörður

Húsavík

Akureyri

Neskaupstaður

Blönduós

Breiðafjörður

Faxaflói

Reykjavík

Vatnajökull

Höfn

Öræfajökull

Vestmannaeyjar

Heimaey

Surtsey

Svalbard (Spitsbergen) (Norway)

Nordaust-landet

Kvitøya

Kong Karls Land

Sjuøyane

Nordkapp

Olgastredet

Barentsøya

Edgeøya

Newtontoppen

Longyearbyen

Ny-Ålesund

Prins Karls Forland

Barentsburg

Storfjorden

Sørkapp

Projection: Conic with two standard parallels

West from Greenwich

152

295

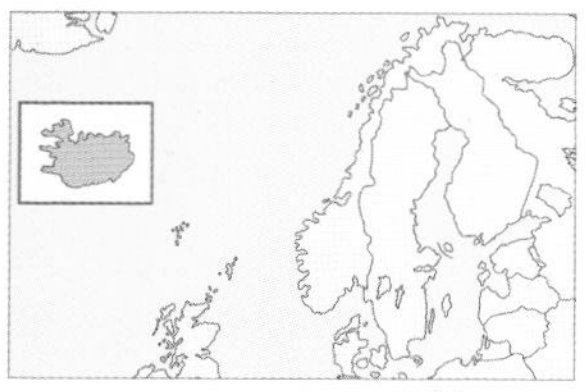

1:2 000 000

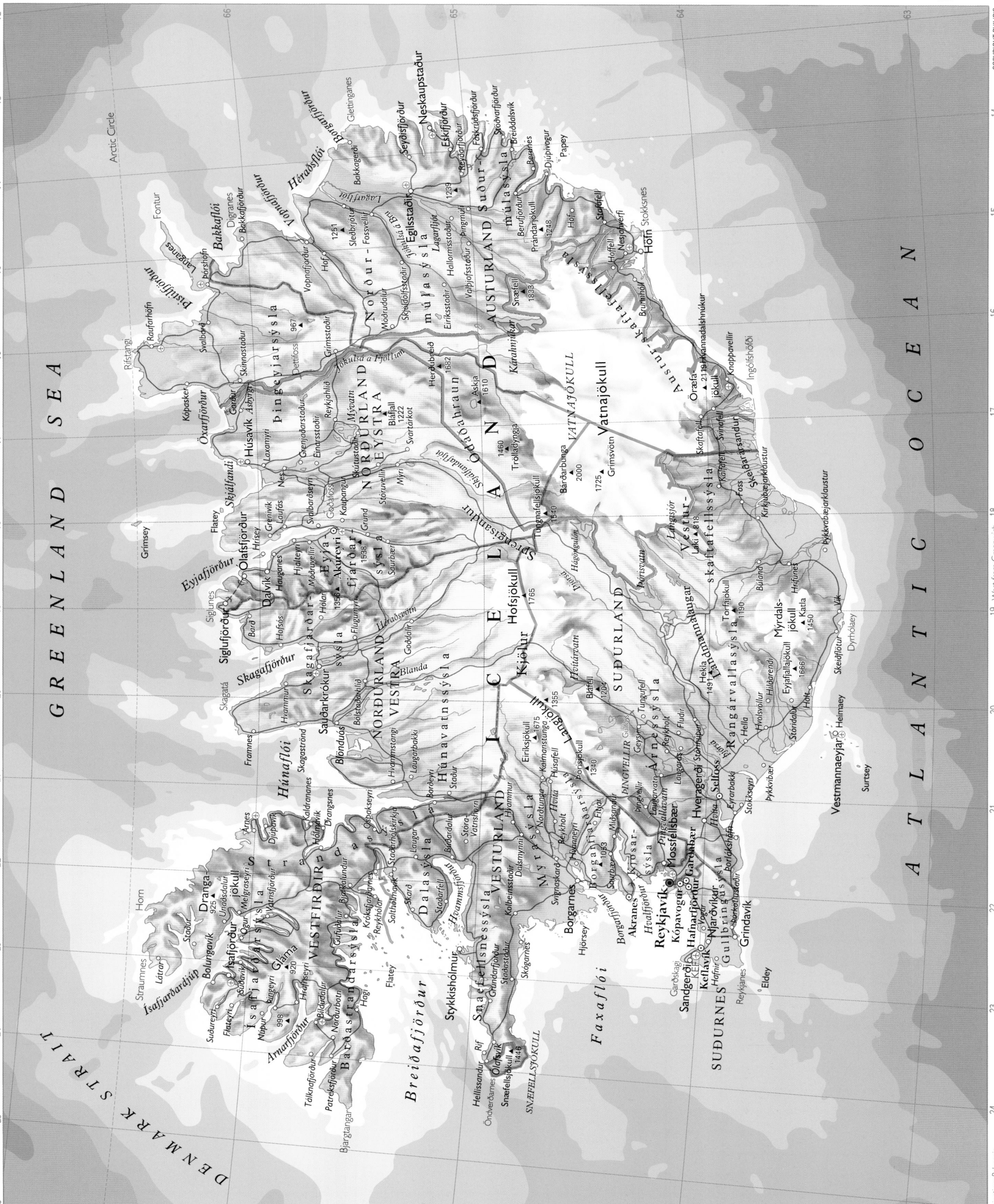

0 10 20 30 40 50 60 70 80 100 km

0 10 20 30 40 50 60 miles

GREENLAND SEA

DENMARK STRAIT

ATLANTIC OCEAN

ICELAND

Breiðafjörður

Faxaflói

Húnaflói

Skagafjörður

Eyjafjörður

Vatnajökull

Hofsjökull

Langjökull

Mýrdalsjökull

Reykjavík

Akureyri

VESTFIRÐIR

NORÐURLAND VESTRA

NORÐURLAND EYSTRA

AUSTURLAND

SUÐURLAND

VESTURLAND

SUÐURNES

Vestmannaeyjar

Arctic Circle

West from Greenwich

Projection: Polyconic

m ft

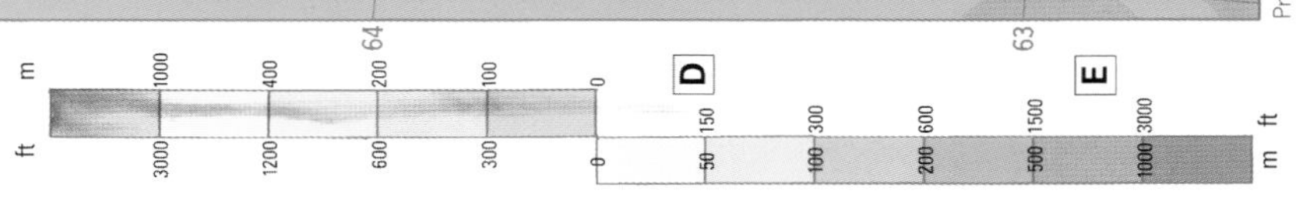

EUROPE

1:16 000 000

100 0 100 200 300 400 500 600 700 800 km
100 0 100 200 300 400 500 miles
Sea areas named in weather forecasts
Norwegian Sea
Barents Sea
White Sea
North Sea
Baltic Sea
G. of Bothnia
G. of Finland
ATLANTIC OCEAN
Bay of Biscay
English Channel
Celtic Sea
Irish Sea
Mediterranean Sea
Tyrrhenian Sea
Adriatic Sea
Ionian Sea
Ligurian Sea
Black Sea
Sea of Azov
Caspian Sea
Caspian Depression
Iceland
British Isles
Great Britain
Ireland
Scandinavia
Lapland
Finland
Kola Pen.
North European Plain
Central Russian Uplands
Ukraine
Volga Hts.
Northern Uvals
Timan Ridge
Ural Mountains
West Siberian Lowlands
Kirgiziya Steppe
Caucasus
Carpathians
Alps
Pyrenees
Apennines
Balkans
Rhodope
Pindus
Dinaric Alps
Iberian Peninsula
Sierra Morena
Sierra Nevada
Cantabrian Mts.
Massif Central
Plain of Hungary
Anatolia (Asia Minor)
Taurus Mts.
Pontine Mts.
Kurdistan
Mesopotamia
Plateau of the Shotts
Africa
Sicily
Sardinia
Corsica
Crete
Cyprus
Balearic Is.
Faroe Is.
Shetland Is.
Orkney Is.
Projection: Bonne
West from Greenwich
East from Greenwich
COPYRIGHT PHILIP'S
m ft
5000 15 000
4000 12 000
2000 6000
1000 3000
400 1200
200 600
0 0

1:16 000 000
100 0 100 200 300 400 500 600 700 800 km
100 0 100 200 300 400 500 miles
Norwegian Sea
ATLANTIC OCEAN
North Sea
Baltic Sea
G. of Bothnia
White Sea
Black Sea
Caspian Sea
Mediterranean Sea
Adriatic Sea
Tyrrhenian Sea
Ionian Sea
Aegean Sea
Bay of Biscay
English Channel
Skagerrak
Kattegat
Africa
Arctic Circle
ICELAND
Reykjavík
Faroe Is. (Den.)
Tórshavn
Shetland Is.
Lerwick
Orkney Is.
Kirkwall
Hebrides
Stornoway
UNITED KINGDOM
SCOTLAND
Aberdeen
Dundee
Glasgow
Edinburgh
N. IRELAND
Belfast
IRELAND
Dublin
Cork
Newcastle-upon-Tyne
Leeds
Manchester
Liverpool
Sheffield
WALES
ENGLAND
Birmingham
Cardiff
Bristol
Plymouth
Southampton
LONDON
NORWAY
Bergen
Stavanger
Trondheim
Oslo
Tromsø
Hammerfest
Narvik
SWEDEN
Kiruna
Luleå
Gävle
Uppsala
Örebro
Stockholm
Vänern
Vättern
Jönköping
Gothenburg
Malmö
Öland
Gotland
FINLAND
Vaasa
Tampere
Turku
Helsinki
Åland
DENMARK
Aalborg
Aarhus
Copenhagen
ESTONIA
Tallinn
Saaremaa
L. Chudskoye
LATVIA
Riga
LITHUANIA
Kaunas
Vilnius
Kaliningrad (Russia)
BELARUS
Minsk
Vitebsk
Mahilyow
Gomel
Brest
Pripet
W. Dvina
POLAND
Gdańsk
Szczecin
Bydgoszcz
Białystok
Poznań
Warsaw
Łódź
Wrocław
Lublin
Katowice
Kraków
Vistula
Oder
GERMANY
Kiel
Hamburg
Bremen
Hannover
Berlin
Magdeburg
Essen
Dortmund
Cologne
Bonn
Halle
Leipzig
Dresden
Chemnitz
Frankfurt am Main
Nuremberg
Stuttgart
Munich
Elbe
Rhine
NETHERLANDS
Amsterdam
The Hague
Rotterdam
BELGIUM
Antwerp
Brussels
LUX.
Luxembourg
FRANCE
PARIS
Lille
Le Havre
Rouen
Channel Is.
Brest
Nantes
Loire
Seine
Meuse
Strasbourg
Dijon
Limoges
Lyons
St-Étienne
Bordeaux
Gironde
Garonne
Toulouse
Marseilles
Toulon
Nice
Grenoble
Rhône
MONACO
Monte-Carlo
Corsica
Ajaccio
SWITZERLAND
Zürich
Bern
Geneva
LIECH.
Vaduz
AUSTRIA
Vienna
Linz
Salzburg
Innsbruck
Graz
CZECHIA
Prague
Ostrava
SLOVAKIA
Bratislava
Miskolc
HUNGARY
Budapest
Debrecen
SLOVENIA
Ljubljana
Trieste
CROATIA
Zagreb
Split
BOSNIA-HERZ.
Sarajevo
SERBIA
Belgrade
Niš
KOSOVO
Priština
MONTENEGRO
Podgorica
NORTH MACEDONIA
Skopje
ALBANIA
Tirana
GREECE
Corfu
Thessaloniki
Patra
Athens
Lesbos
Khíos
Crete
Rhodes
BULGARIA
Sofia
Plovdiv
Varna
ROMANIA
Cluj-Napoca
Timişoara
Braşov
Ploieşti
Bucharest
Galaţi
Constanţa
Danube
MOLDOVA
Kishinev
UKRAINE
Lvov
Zhytomyr
Kiev
Chernihiv
Kharkov
Dnipro
Donetsk
Zaporozhye
Krivoy Rog
Kherson
Nikolayev
Odessa
Dnieper
Dniester
Bug
CRIMEA (under Russian control)
Sevastopol
RUSSIA
MOSCOW
St. Petersburg
Vyborg
L. Ladoga
L. Onega
KARELIA
Murmansk
Arkhangelsk
N. Dvina
Kotlas
KOMI
Vologda
Rybinsk Res.
Yaroslavl
Kostroma
Ivanovo
Nizhniy Novgorod
MARI EL
CHUVASHIA
Kazan
TATARSTAN
UDMURTIA
Kirov
Perm
Nizhniy Tagil
Yekaterinburg
Chelyabinsk
Ufa
BASHKORTOSTAN
Magnitogorsk
Orenburg
Samara
Ulyanovsk
MORDVINIA
Penza
Saratov
Volga
Tula
Orel
Tambov
Voronezh
Kursk
Smolensk
Volgograd
Don
Taganrog
Rostov
Krasnodar
ADYGEA
KALMYKIA
Astrakhan
Stavropol
KARACHAY-CHERKESSIA
KABARDINO-BALKARIA
NORTH OSSETIA-ALANIYA
INGUSHETIA
CHECHENIA
DAGESTAN
Makhachkala
Ob
KAZAKHSTAN
Uralsk
Ural
Atyraū
GEORGIA
Tbilisi
ARMENIA
Yerevan
AZERBAIJAN
Baku
Araks
TURKEY
İSTANBUL
Bosporus
Bursa
İzmir
Ankara
Samsun
Erzurum
Kayseri
Konya
Antalya
Adana
Gaziantep
Diyarbakir
CYPRUS
Nicosia
SYRIA
Aleppo
Homs
Euphrates
Tigris
IRAQ
Mosul
BAGHDĀD
IRAN
Tabrīz
Asia
ITALY
Milan
Turin
Genoa
Venice
Bologna
San Marino
SAN MARINO
Florence
Tiber
Rome
Naples
Bari
Taranto
Sardinia
Cagliari
Sicily
Palermo
Messina
Catania
Pantelleria (Italy)
MALTA
Valletta
SPAIN
MADRID
La Coruña
Vigo
Bilbao
Valladolid
Zaragoza
Ebro
BARCELONA
ANDORRA
Andorra-la-Vella
Valencia
Alicante
Murcia
Córdoba
Guadalquivir
Seville
Granada
Málaga
Cádiz
Gibraltar (U.K.)
Str. of Gibraltar
Balearic Is.
Minorca
Majorca
Palma
Ibiza
Tagus
Guadiana
Douro
PORTUGAL
Porto
Lisbon
MOROCCO
Rabat
Fès
Tangier
Ceuta
Melilla
ALGERIA
Algiers
Constantine
Annaba
TUNISIA
Tunis
■ LONDON Capital Cities
Projection: Bonne
West from Greenwich
East from Greenwich
COPYRIGHT PHILIP'S

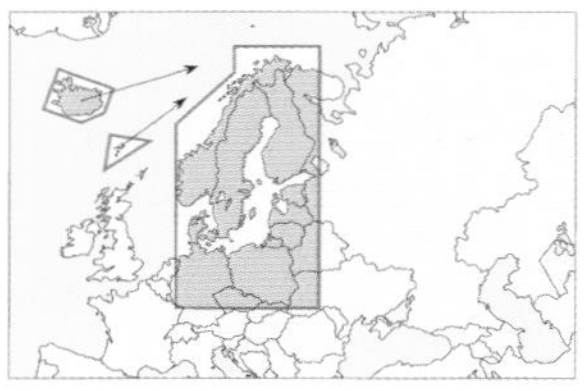

50 0 25 50 75 100 125 150 175 km

50 0 25 50 75 100 125 miles

1:4 800 000

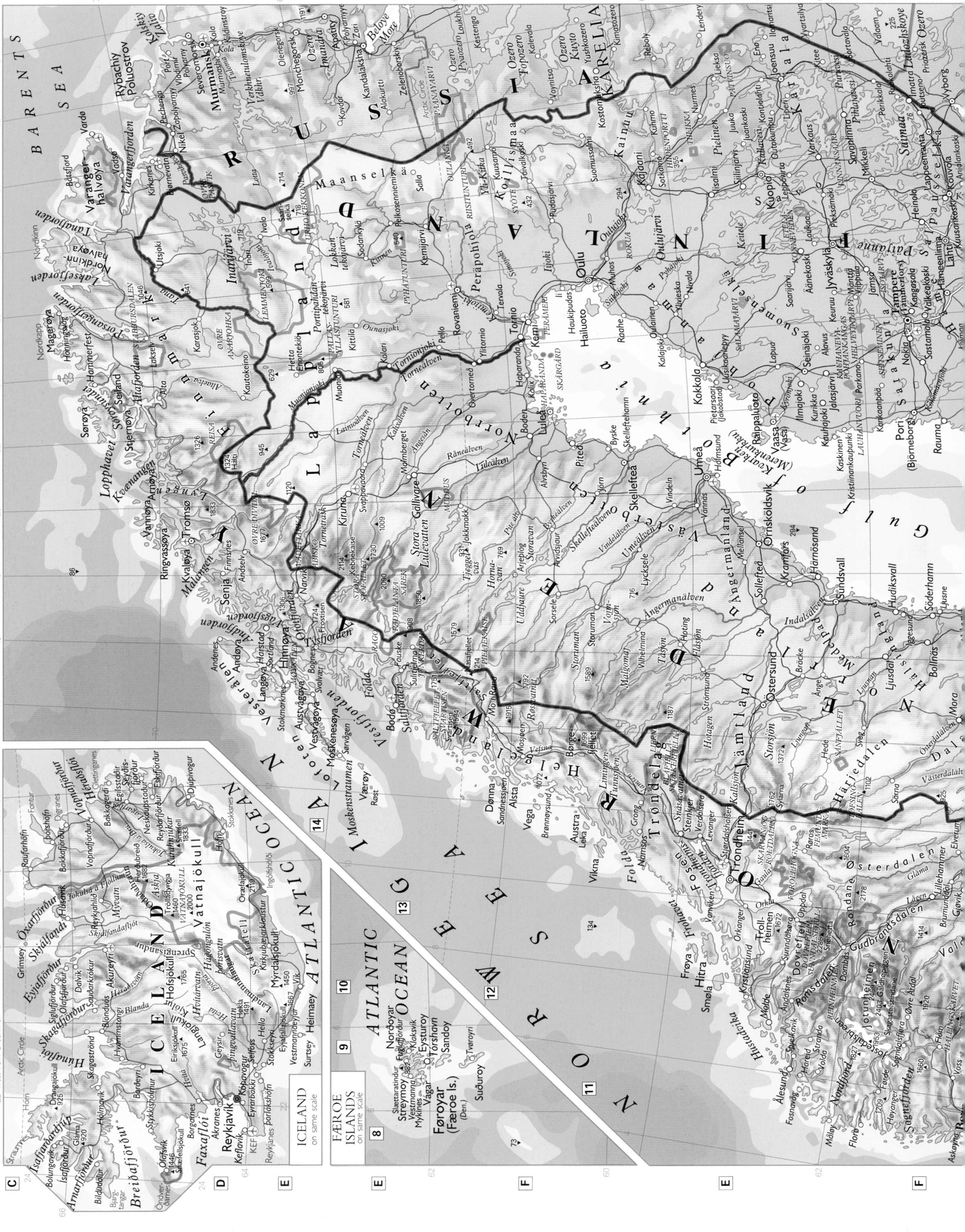
BARENTS SEA
NORWEGIAN SEA
ATLANTIC OCEAN
Gulf of Bothnia
RUSSIA
FINLAND
SWEDEN
NORWAY
ICELAND
ICELAND
on same scale
FÆROE
ISLANDS
on same scale
Føroyar
(Færoe Is.)
(Den.)

BALTIC SEA
NORTH SEA
Skagerrak
Kattegat
Gulf of Finland
Gulf of Riga
DENMARK
ESTONIA
LATVIA
LITHUANIA
KALININGRAD (Russia)
BELARUS
POLAND
GERMANY
CZECHIA
UKRAINE
OSLO
STOCKHOLM
KØBENHAVN (Copenhagen)
Tallinn
Riga
Vilnius
MINSK
WARSZAWA (Warsaw)
BERLIN
HAMBURG
PRAHA (Prague)
Gotland (Sweden)
Öland
Bornholm (Denmark)
Hiiumaa (Dagö)
Saaremaa (Ösel)
Rügen
Svealand
Götaland
Projection: Conical with two standard parallels
East from Greenwich
COPYRIGHT PHILIP'S

1:2 000 000
km
miles
Gulf of Bothnia
STOCKHOLM
Uppsala
Gävle
Sundsvall
Östersund
Trondheim
Oslo
Drammen
Karlstad
Örebro
Västerås
Falun
Borlänge
Lillehammer
Hamar
JÄMTLAND
HÄRJEDALEN
DALARNA
GÄVLEBORG
VÄSTERNORRLAND
VÄSTMANLAND
SÖDERMANLAND
VÄRMLAND
ÖREBRO
UPPSALA
HEDMARK
OPPLAND
BUSKERUD
AKERSHUS
ØSTFOLD
VESTFOLD
TELEMARK
SØR-TRØNDELAG
MØRE OG ROMSDAL
Jotunheimen
Dovrefjell
Rondane
Siljan
Mjøsa
Glomma
Klarälven
Västerdalälven
Österdalälven
Ljusnan
Indalsälven
Storsjön

161
160
164

BALTIC SEA
POLAND
GERMANY
DENMARK
Skagerrak
Kattegat
Småland
Skåne
Gotland (Sweden)
Öland (Sweden)
Bornholm (Denmark)
Anholt (Denmark)
Læsø (Denmark)
Göteborg
Malmö
KØBENHAVN
Århus
Aalborg
Odense
Jönköping
Norrköping
Linköping
Kalmar
Karlskrona
Helsingborg
Halmstad
Växjö
Visby
Flensburg
Kiel
Esbjerg
Sjælland
Fyn
Lolland
Falster
Jylland
Vättern
Store Bælt
Lille Bælt
Fehmarn Belt
Hanöbukten
Kalmarsund
Projection: Lambert's Conformal Conic
East from Greenwich
COPYRIGHT PHILIP'S
178
184

10 0 10 20 30 40 50 60 70 80 90 km

1:2 000 000

10 0 10 20 30 40 50 60 miles

160

NORWEGIAN SEA

Norskerenna

Skagerrak

NORWAY

SWEDEN

SØR-TRØNDELAG

MØRE OG ROMSDAL

SOGN OG FJORDANE

HORDALAND

ROGALAND

VEST-AGDER

AUST-AGDER

TELEMARK

BUSKERUD

OPPLAND

HEDMARK

AKERSHUS

VESTFOLD

ØSTFOLD

Trondheim

Kristiansund

Molde

Ålesund

Bergen

Haugesund

Stavanger

Kristiansand

Arendal

Oslo

Drammen

Lillehammer

Hamar

Fredrikstad

Dovrefjell

Jotunheimen

Jostedalsbreen

Hardangervidda

Sognefjorden

Hardangerfjorden

Mjøsa

ft m

6000 2000

4500 1500

3000 1000

1500 500

600 200

0 0

50 150

100 300

200 600

500 1500

1000 3000

m ft

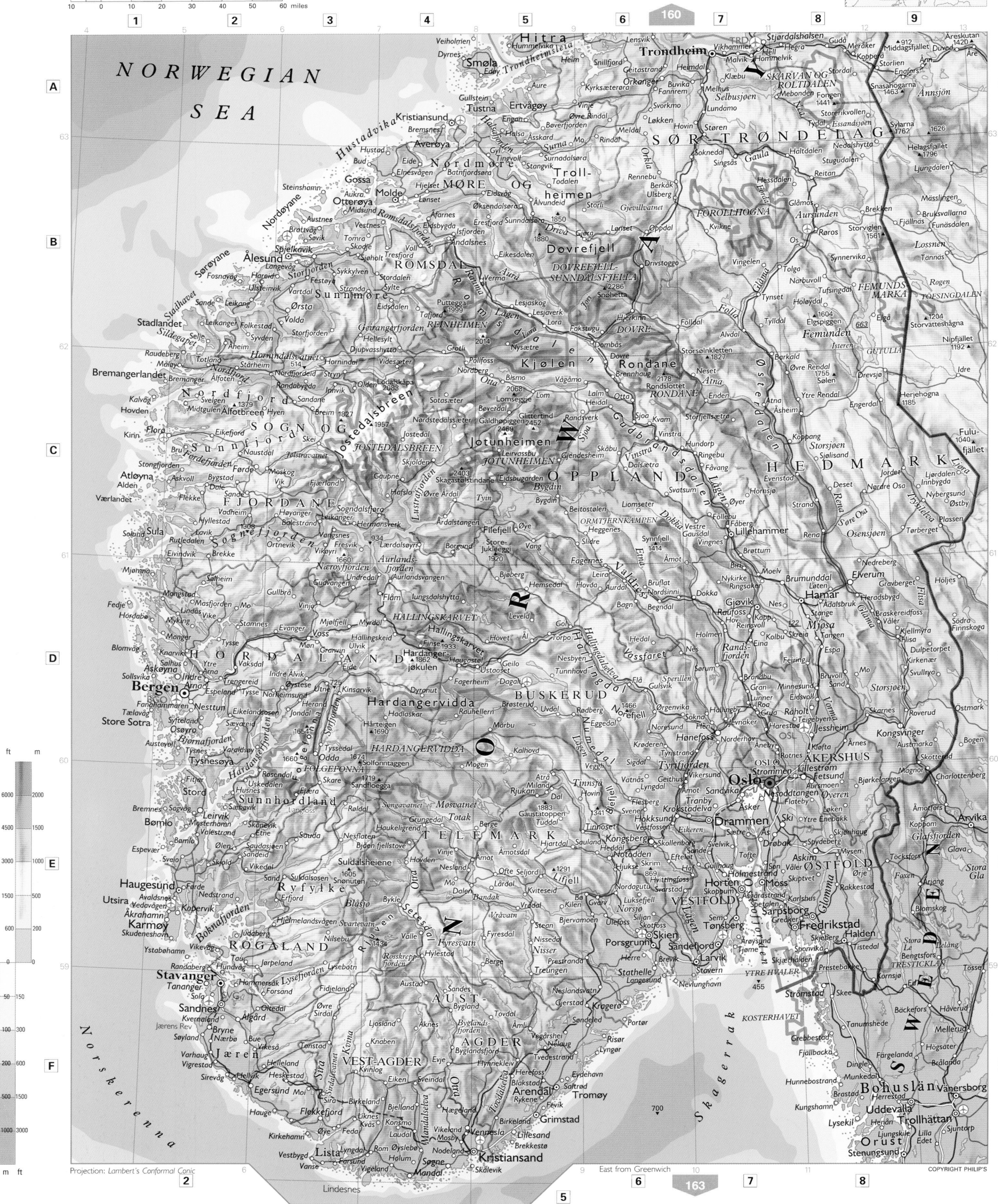

Projection: *Lambert's Conformal Conic*

East from Greenwich

163

1:4 000 000
km
miles
ATLANTIC OCEAN
NORTH SEA
IRISH SEA
CELTIC SEA
English Channel
St. George's Channel
Bristol Channel
North Channel
North Minch
Sea of the Hebrides
Pentland Firth
Moray Firth
Firth of Clyde
Cardigan Bay
Str. of Dover
UNITED KINGDOM
IRELAND
SCOTLAND
ENGLAND
WALES
NORTHERN IRELAND
NORWAY
NETHERLANDS
BELGIUM
FRANCE
Shetland Is. (U.K.)
Yell
Unst
Fetlar
Mainland
Lerwick
Foula
Fair Isle
Orkney Is.
Westray
Sanday
Stronsay
Kirkwall
Hoy
South Ronaldsay
North Rona
C. Wrath
Thurso
Wick
Helmsdale
Outer Hebrides
Inner Hebrides
Flannan Is.
Stornoway
Lewis
Harris
St. Kilda (U.K.)
North Uist
Benbecula
South Uist
Barra
Skye
Portree
Rum
Eigg
Coll
Tiree
Mull
Iona
Colonsay
Jura
Islay
Arran
North West Highlands
Grampian Mts.
CAIRNGORMS
Southern Uplands
Ullapool
Lairg
Golspie
Tain
Invergordon
Dingwall
Inverness
Nairn
Elgin
Buckie
Banff
Fraserburgh
Peterhead
Huntly
Inverurie
Aberdeen
Stonehaven
Ballater
Aviemore
Glen Mor
L. Ness
Mallaig
Fort William
Ben Nevis
Tobermory
Oban
L. Awe
L. Fyne
L. Lomond
Perth
Forfar
Montrose
Arbroath
Dundee
St. Andrews
Glenrothes
Kirkcaldy
Stirling
Dunfermline
Dunbar
Dumbarton
Greenock
GLASGOW
Paisley
Cumbernauld
Edinburgh
East Kilbride
Hamilton
Irvine
Kilmarnock
Ayr
Campbeltown
Girvan
Galashiels
Jedburgh
Hawick
Berwick-upon-Tweed
Alnwick
Cheviot Hills
Dumfries
Kirkcudbright
Stranraer
Mull of Galloway
Malin Hd.
Tory I.
Arranmore
Letterkenny
Buncrana
Coleraine
Derry/Londonderry
Ballymena
Larne
Lough Neagh
Antrim
Bangor
Belfast
Lisburn
Omagh
Craigavon
Armagh
Newry
Donegal
Bundoran
Lower L. Erne
Enniskillen
Clones
Sligo
Ballina
Achill I.
Castlebar
Westport
L. Conn
Leitrim
Cavan
Castleblaney
Dundalk
Drogheda
Kells
Lough Mask
Connemara
Roscommon
Longford
Lough Ree
Mullingar
Athlone
Lough Corrib
Galway
Galway B.
Aran Is.
Ballinasloe
Tullamore
Liffey
DUBLIN
Dun Laoghaire
Bray
Wicklow Mts.
Arklow
Lough Derg
Ennis
Portlaoise
Athy
Carlow
Limerick
Nenagh
Thurles
Kilkenny
Kilrush
Shannon
Listowel
Tipperary
Tralee
Clonmel
Carrick-on-Suir
Wexford
Rosslare
Waterford
Dingle
Killarney
Carrauntoohill
Macgillycuddy's Reeks
Mallow
Blackwater
Dungarvan
Cork
Youghal
Cobh
Bandon
Kinsale
Bantry
C. Clear
Workington
Whitehaven
Carlisle
Cumbrian Mts.
LAKE DISTRICT
Barrow-in-Furness
Douglas
I. of Man
Pennines
Newcastle-upon-Tyne
South Shields
Sunderland
Gateshead
Durham
Hartlepool
Redcar
Darlington
Middlesbrough
Stockton-on-Tees
N. YORK MOORS
Scarborough
YORKSHIRE DALES
Lancaster
Harrogate
York
Bridlington
Blackpool
Preston
Blackburn
Burnley
Keighley
Leeds
Bradford
Halifax
Huddersfield
Beverley
Kingston upon Hull
Scunthorpe
Humber
Grimsby
Bolton
MANCHESTER
Oldham
Barnsley
Doncaster
LIVERPOOL
Warrington
Stockport
Rotherham
Sheffield
Anglesey
Holyhead
Bangor
Colwyn Bay
Chester
Crewe
Chesterfield
PEAK DISTRICT
Mansfield
Lincoln
Louth
Skegness
Snowdon
SNOWDONIA
Wrexham
Stoke-on-Trent
Stafford
Derby
Nottingham
Trent
Grantham
Boston
The Wash
King's Lynn
Cromer
Norwich
THE BROADS
Great Yarmouth
Lowestoft
Pwllheli
Shrewsbury
Welshpool
Telford
Leicester
Nuneaton
Peterborough
Wolverhampton
BIRMINGHAM
Coventry
Rugby
Corby
Thetford
Aberystwyth
Cambrian Mts.
Redditch
Worcester
Royal Leamington Spa
Northampton
Bury St. Edmunds
Ely
Cambridge
Ipswich
Felixstowe
Hereford
Bedford
Milton Keynes
Stevenage
Harwich
Fishguard
Carmarthen
BRECON BEACONS
Brecon
Cheltenham
Cotswold Hills
Hemel Hempstead
Luton
Harlow
Colchester
Chelmsford
Haverfordwest
Milford Haven
Pembroke
PEMBROKESHIRE COAST
Merthyr Tydfil
Llanelli
Neath
Swansea
Port Talbot
Rhondda
Cwmbran
Newport
Cardiff
Barry
Gloucester
Oxford
High Wycombe
Watford
Basildon
Southend-on-Sea
Slough
LONDON
Thames
Bristol
Bath
Swindon
Newbury
Reading
Chatham
Margate
Canterbury
Dover
Maidstone
Ashford
Folkestone
Reigate
Guildford
Crawley
Basingstoke
Winchester
Salisbury
SOUTH DOWNS
Hastings
Weston-super-Mare
Exmoor
EXMOOR
Barnstaple
Taunton
Yeovil
Southampton
Fareham
Havant
Brighton
Worthing
Eastbourne
Portsmouth
NEW FOREST
Bournemouth
Poole
Newport
Isle of Wight
Weymouth
Bude
Exeter
Exmouth
Torbay
Dartmoor
DARTMOOR
Newquay
Truro
St. Austell
Plymouth
Falmouth
Penzance
Land's End
Isles of Scilly
Alderney
C. de la Hague
Pte. de Barfleur
Cherbourg-Octeville
Valognes
Cotentin
Guernsey
St. Peter Port
Sark
Jersey
St. Helier
Channel Is. (U.K.)
Bayeux
Caen
Trouville-sur-Mer
Lisieux
Le Havre
Bolbec
Seine
Elbeuf
Rouen
Fécamp
Pays de Caux
Dieppe
Le Tréport
Abbeville
Amiens
Somme
Picardie
St.-Quentin
Laon
Cambrai
Valenciennes
Bruay-la-Buissière
Lens
Béthune
St.-Omer
LILLE
Tourcoing
Villeneuve-d'Ascq
Tournai
Le Touquet-Paris-Plage
Boulogne-sur-Mer
C. Gris-Nez
Calais
Dunkerque
Vlaanderen
Brugge
Oostende
Zeebrugge
Gent
Antwerpen
Mechelen
BRUSSEL (Bruxelles)
Vlissingen
Zeeland
ROTTERDAM
Dordrecht
Hoek van Holland
's-Gravenhage (Den Haag)
Haarlem
Alkmaar
Den Helder
Texel
Askøyna
Bergen
Osøyro
Stord
Bømlo
Leirvik
Haugesund
Kopervik
Åkrahamn
Boknafjorden
Stavanger
Sandnes
Bryne
Nærbø
Projection: Conical with two standard parallels
West from Greenwich
East from Greenwich
COPYRIGHT PHILIP'S

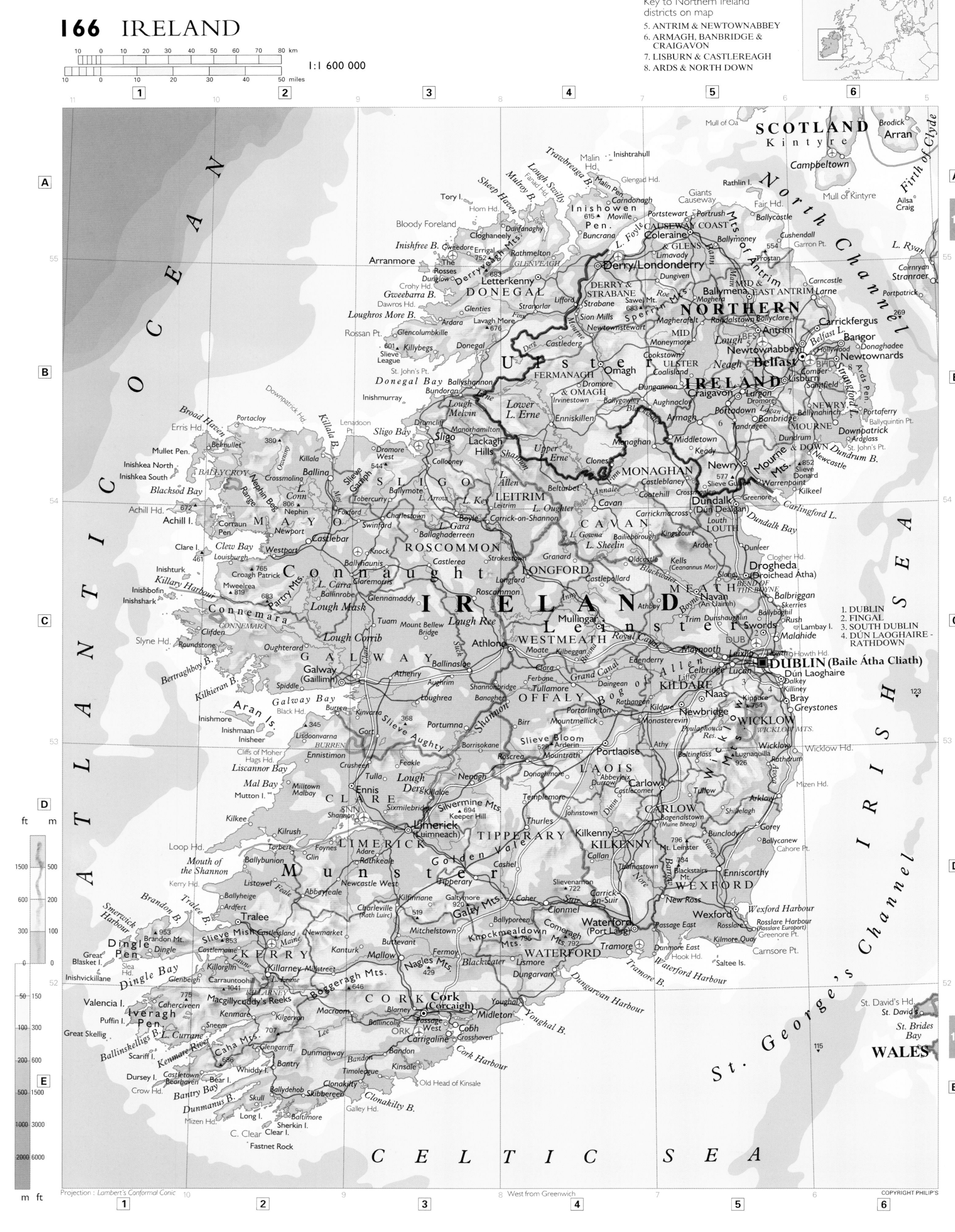
1:1 600 000
Key to Northern Ireland districts on map
5. ANTRIM & NEWTOWNABBEY
6. ARMAGH, BANBRIDGE & CRAIGAVON
7. LISBURN & CASTLEREAGH
8. ARDS & NORTH DOWN
1. DUBLIN
2. FINGAL
3. SOUTH DUBLIN
4. DÚN LAOGHAIRE - RATHDOWN
ATLANTIC OCEAN
CELTIC SEA
IRISH SEA
St. George's Channel
North Channel
IRELAND
NORTHERN IRELAND
SCOTLAND
WALES
Connaught
Leinster
Munster
Ulster
DUBLIN (Baile Átha Cliath)
Belfast
Cork (Corcaigh)
Galway (Gaillimh)
Limerick (Luimneach)
Waterford (Port Láirge)
Derry/Londonderry
Projection : Lambert's Conformal Conic
West from Greenwich
COPYRIGHT PHILIP'S

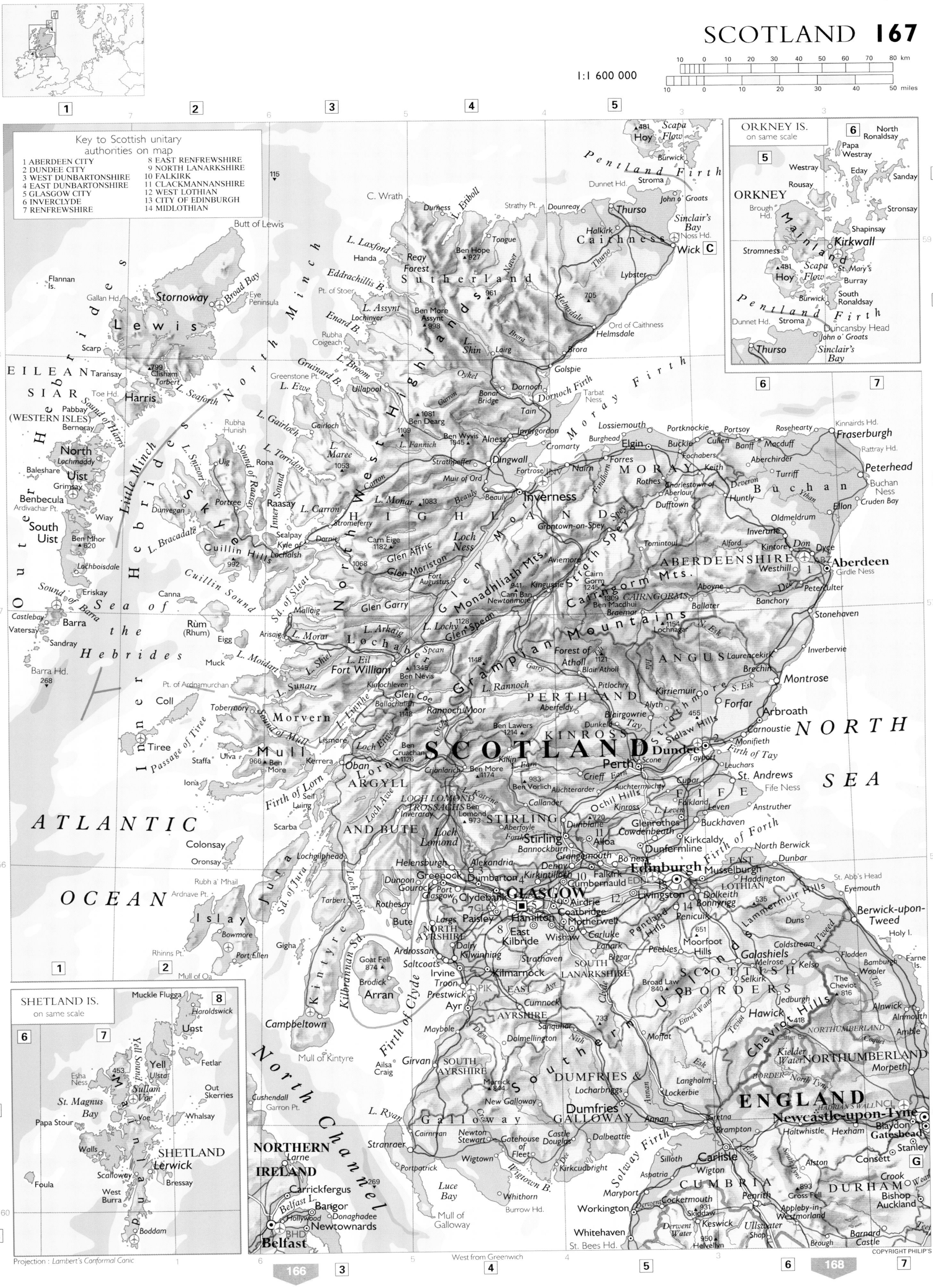

1:1 600 000

10 0 10 20 30 40 50 60 70 80 km

10 0 10 20 30 40 50 miles

Key to Scottish unitary authorities on map

1 ABERDEEN CITY
2 DUNDEE CITY
3 WEST DUNBARTONSHIRE
4 EAST DUNBARTONSHIRE
5 GLASGOW CITY
6 INVERCLYDE
7 RENFREWSHIRE
8 EAST RENFREWSHIRE
9 NORTH LANARKSHIRE
10 FALKIRK
11 CLACKMANNANSHIRE
12 WEST LOTHIAN
13 CITY OF EDINBURGH
14 MIDLOTHIAN

ORKNEY IS.
on same scale

SHETLAND IS.
on same scale

SCOTLAND

ATLANTIC OCEAN

NORTH SEA

North Channel

NORTHERN IRELAND

ENGLAND

EILEAN SIAR (WESTERN ISLES)

Outer Hebrides

Inner Hebrides

Sea of the Hebrides

North West Highlands

Grampian Mountains

Cairngorm Mts.

Southern Uplands

Pentland Firth

Moray Firth

Firth of Forth

Firth of Clyde

Solway Firth

ft m

3000 1000

1500 500

600 200

300 100

0 0

50 150

100 300

200 600

500 1500

1000 3000

Projection : Lambert's Conformal Conic

West from Greenwich

166

168

1:1 600 000

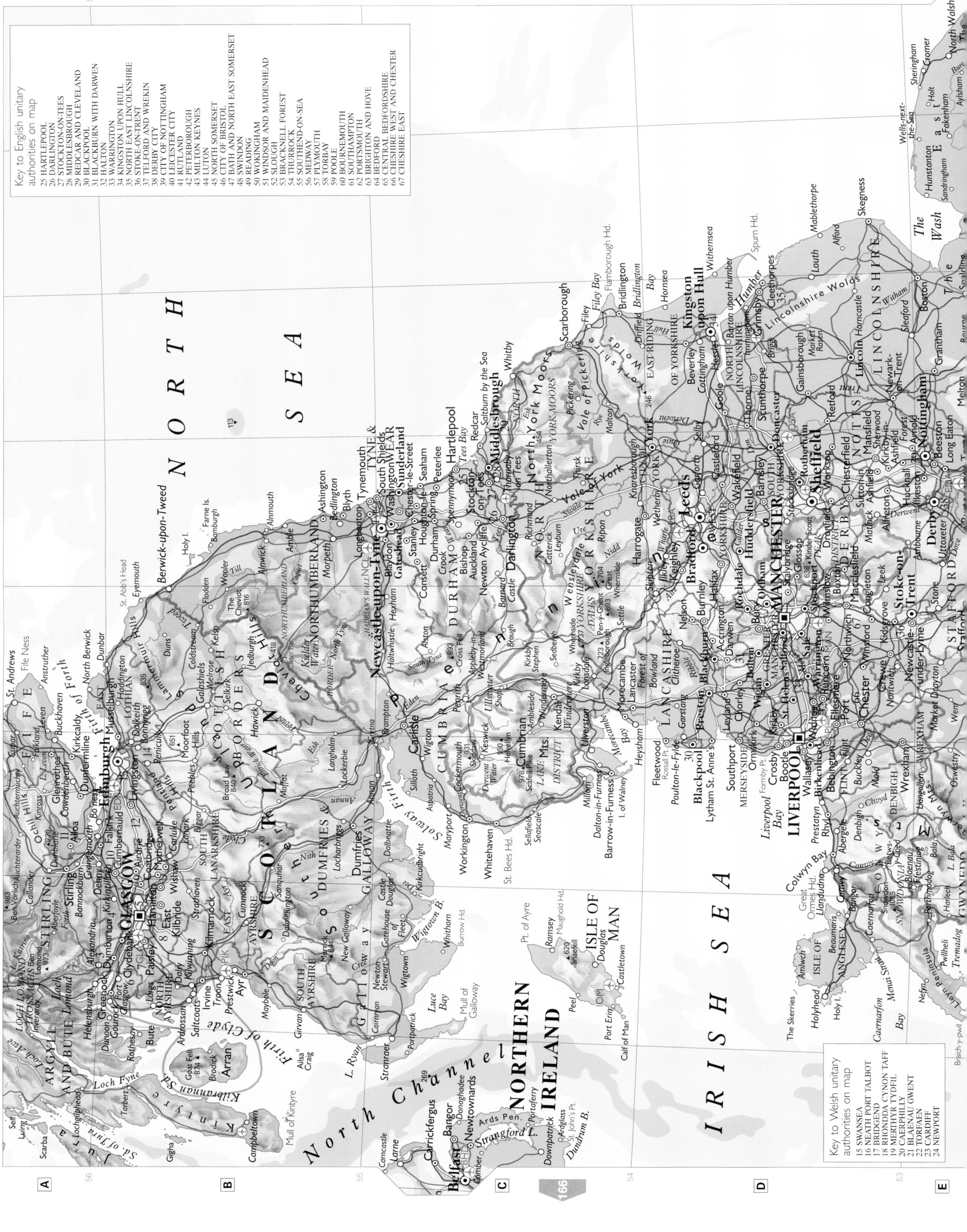
Key to English unitary authorities on map
25 HARTLEPOOL
26 DARLINGTON
27 STOCKTON-ON-TEES
28 MIDDLESBROUGH
29 REDCAR AND CLEVELAND
30 BLACKPOOL
31 BLACKBURN WITH DARWEN
32 HALTON
33 WARRINGTON
34 KINGSTON UPON HULL
35 NORTH EAST LINCOLNSHIRE
36 STOKE-ON-TRENT
37 TELFORD AND WREKIN
38 DERBY CITY
39 CITY OF NOTTINGHAM
40 LEICESTER CITY
41 RUTLAND
42 PETERBOROUGH
43 MILTON KEYNES
44 LUTON
45 NORTH SOMERSET
46 CITY OF BRISTOL
47 BATH AND NORTH EAST SOMERSET
48 SWINDON
49 READING
50 WOKINGHAM
51 WINDSOR AND MAIDENHEAD
52 SLOUGH
53 BRACKNELL FOREST
54 THURROCK
55 SOUTHEND-ON-SEA
56 MEDWAY
57 PLYMOUTH
58 TORBAY
59 POOLE
60 BOURNEMOUTH
61 SOUTHAMPTON
62 PORTSMOUTH
63 BRIGHTON AND HOVE
64 BEDFORD
65 CENTRAL BEDFORDSHIRE
66 CHESHIRE WEST AND CHESTER
67 CHESHIRE EAST
Key to Welsh unitary authorities on map
15 SWANSEA
16 NEATH PORT TALBOT
17 BRIDGEND
18 RHONDDA CYNON TAFF
19 MERTHYR TYDFIL
20 CAERPHILLY
21 BLAENAU GWENT
22 TORFAEN
23 CARDIFF
24 NEWPORT
NORTH SEA
IRISH SEA
North Channel
NORTHERN IRELAND
ISLE OF MAN
SCOTLAND
NORTHUMBERLAND
CUMBRIA
DURHAM
LANCASHIRE
LINCOLNSHIRE
LIVERPOOL
MANCHESTER
GLASGOW
Edinburgh
Newcastle-upon-Tyne
Leeds
Sheffield
Nottingham
Kingston upon Hull
167
166

ENGLISH CHANNEL
Bristol Channel
Strait of Dover
FRANCE
NORMANDIE
ENGLAND
WALES
CHANNEL ISLANDS (U.K.)
Baie de la Seine
Baie de la Somme
Lyme Bay
Cardigan Bay
ISLES OF SCILLY on same scale
LONDON
BIRMINGHAM
Bristol
Cardiff
Plymouth
Southampton
Portsmouth
Brighton
Bournemouth
Le Havre
Rouen
Cherbourg-Octeville
Caen
Dieppe
Calais
Boulogne-sur-Mer
Jersey
Guernsey
Alderney
Sark
Projection : Lambert's Conformal Conic
COPYRIGHT PHILIP'S
East from Greenwich
West from Greenwich

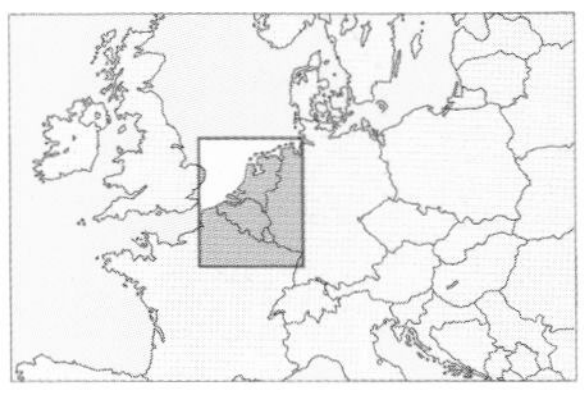

1:2 000 000

Underlined towns give their name to the administrative area in which they stand.

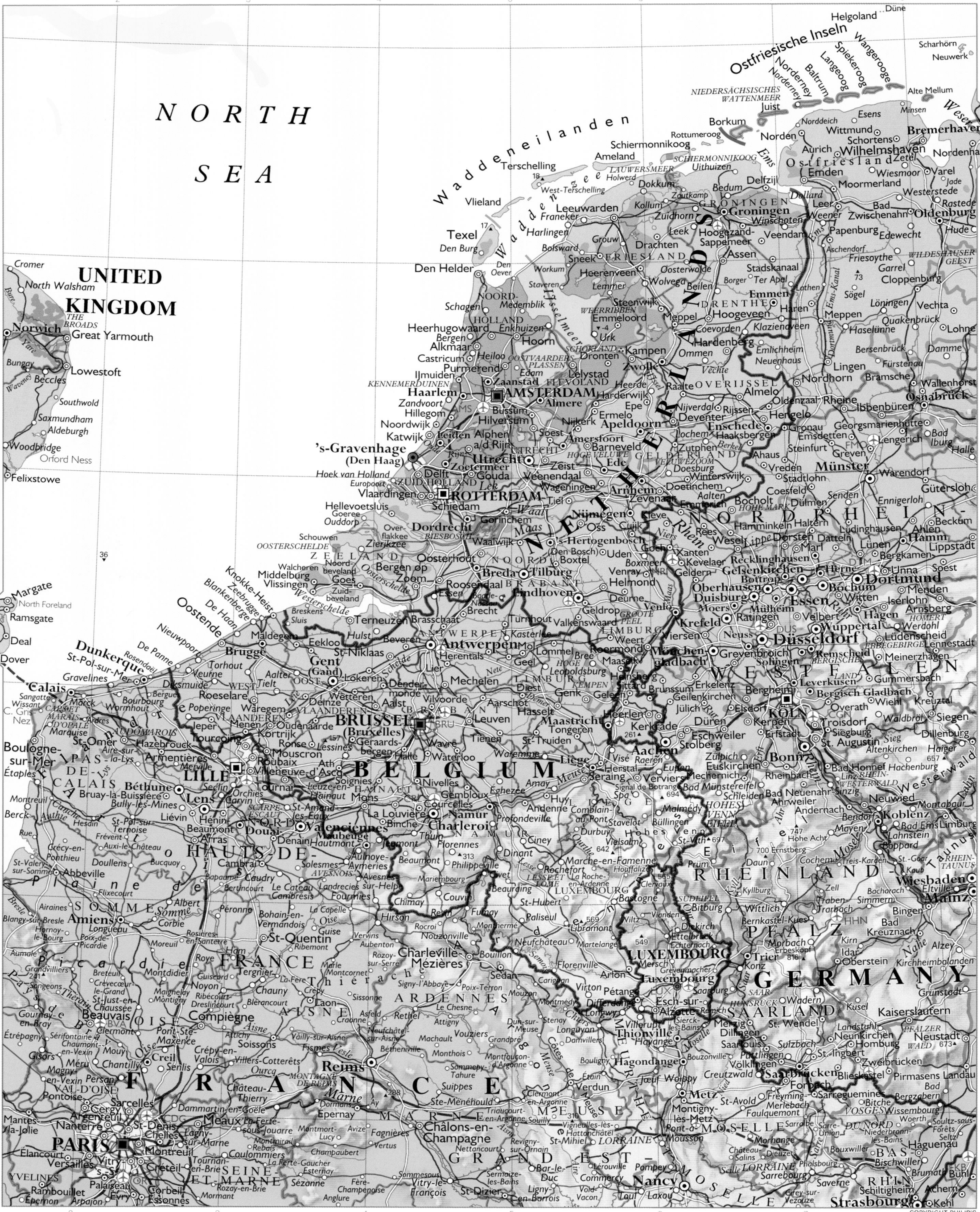

169
173
171

1:4 000 000

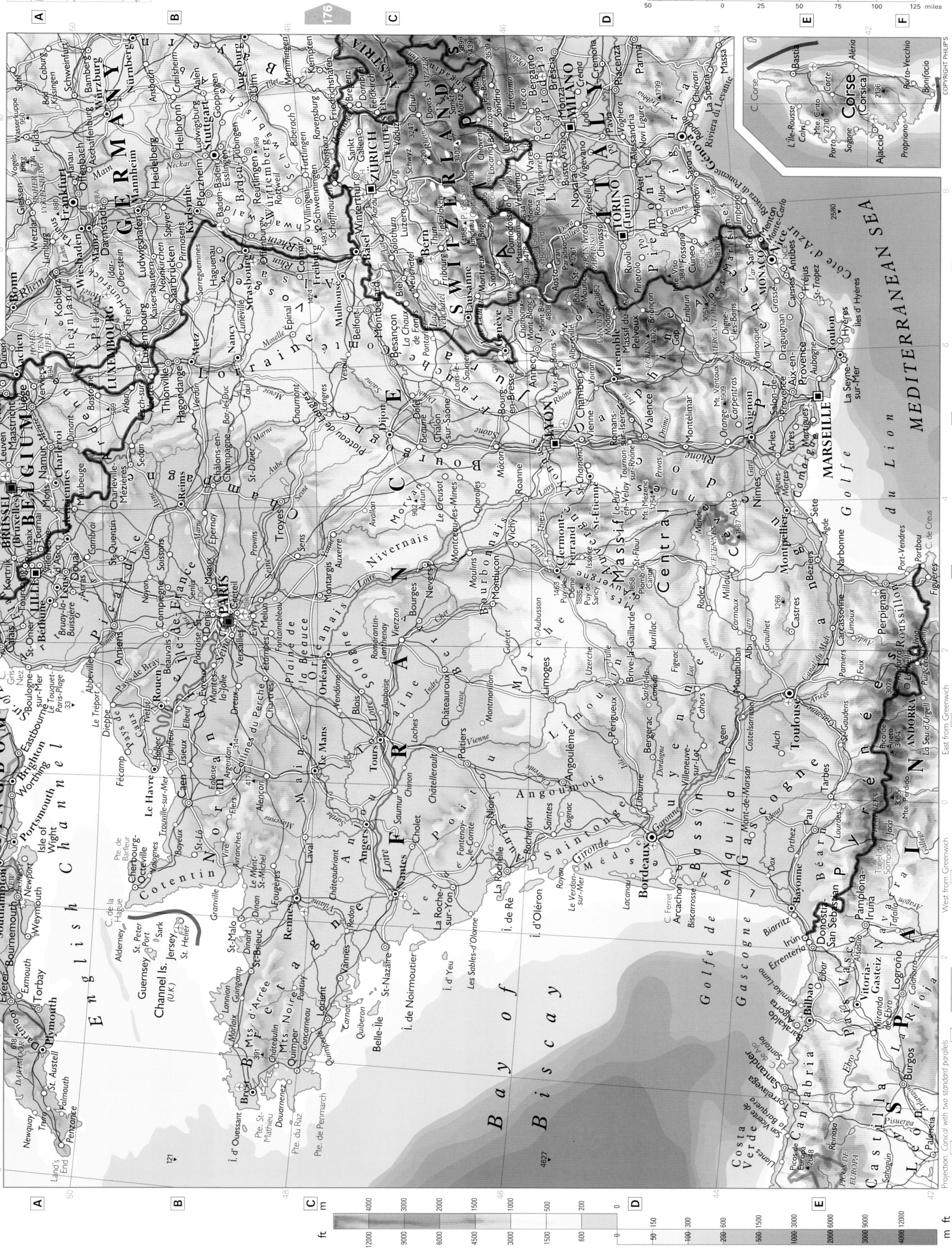

50 0 25 50 75 100 125 150 175 km

50 0 25 50 75 100 125 miles

Projection: Conical with two standard parallels

West from Greenwich | East from Greenwich

m ft

4000 12000

3000 9000

2000 6000

1500 4500

1000 3000

500 1500

200 600

100 300

50 150

0

176

192

1:2 000 000

169
174

DÉPARTEMENTS IN THE PARIS AREA
1 Ville de Paris 2 Seine-St-Denis 3 Val-de-Marne 4 Hauts-de-Seine

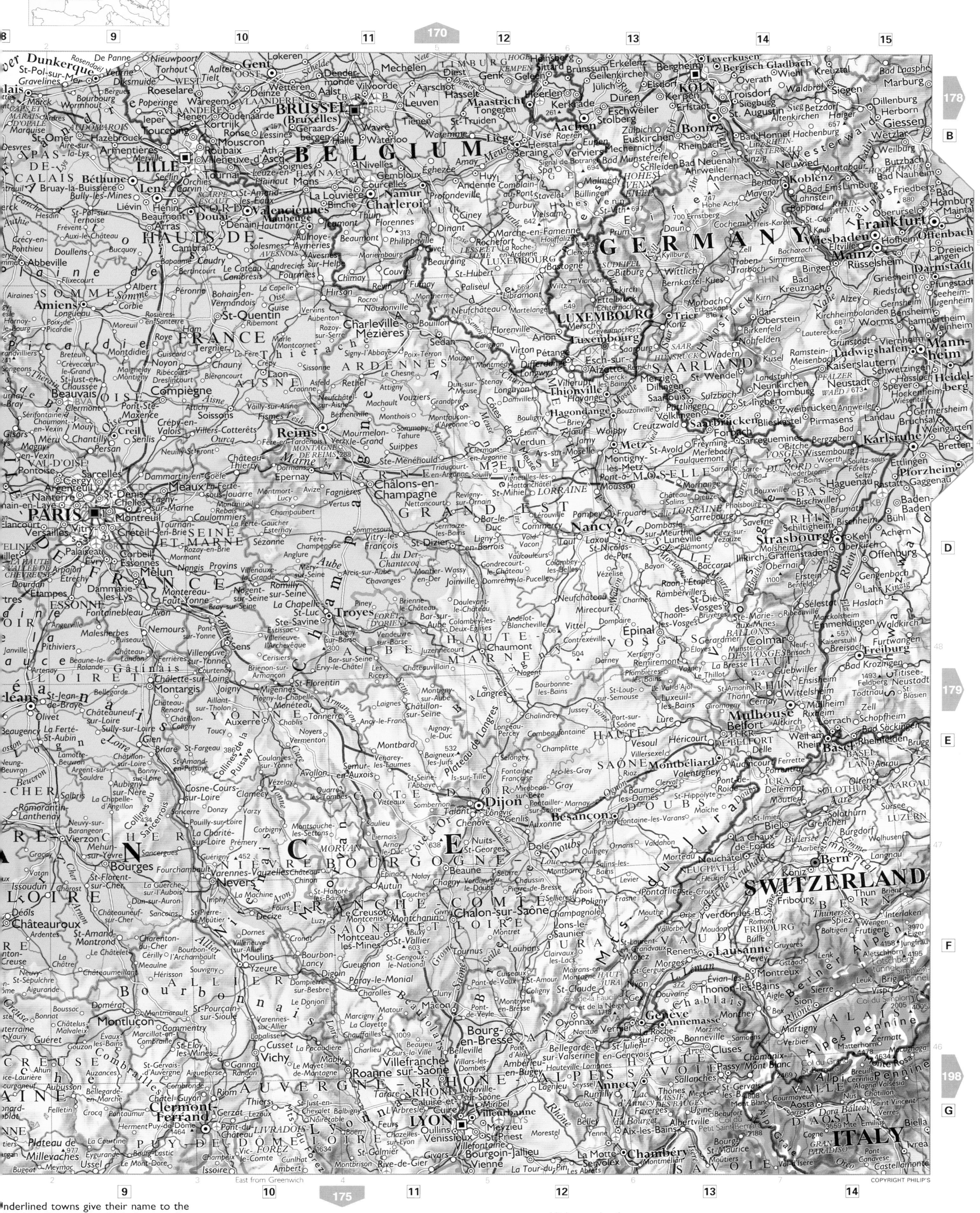

Underlined towns give their name to the administrative area in which they stand.

High-speed rail routes

1:2 000 000
km
miles
172
196
ATLANTIC OCEAN
Golfe de Gascogne
NOUVELLE-AQUITAINE
OCCITANIE
FRANCE
SPAIN
ANDORRA
NAVARRA
CATALUÑA
ARAGON
DEUX-SÈVRES
VENDÉE
VIENNE
CHARENTE
CHARENTE-MARITIME
HAUTE-VIENNE
CORRÈZE
CREUSE
INDRE
ALLIER
PUY-DE-DÔME
CANTAL
DORDOGNE
GIRONDE
LANDES
LOT-ET-GARONNE
LOT
AVEYRON
TARN-ET-GARONNE
GERS
HAUTE-GARONNE
PYRÉNÉES-ATLANTIQUES
HAUTES-PYRÉNÉES
ARIÈGE
AUDE
PYRÉNÉES-ORIENTALES
HUESCA
LLEIDA
GIRONA
BARCELONA
ZARAGOZA
Massif Central
Pyrénées
Limousin
Périgord
Quercy
Rouergue
Roussillon
Béarn
Bigorre
Pays Basque
Landes de Gascogne
Côte d'Argent
Côte Basque
Côte Vermeille
Costa Brava
Île d'Yeu
Île de Ré
Île d'Oléron
Cholet
Poitiers
Niort
La Rochelle
Rochefort
Angoulême
Limoges
Bourges
Châteauroux
Montluçon
Vichy
Clermont-Ferrand
Nevers
Moulins
Périgueux
Brive-la-Gaillarde
Bordeaux
Arcachon
Bergerac
Agen
Montauban
Toulouse
Albi
Rodez
Millau
Cahors
Aurillac
Mont-de-Marsan
Dax
Bayonne
Biarritz
Pau
Tarbes
Lourdes
Carcassonne
Narbonne
Béziers
Perpignan
Donostia-San Sebastián
Pamplona-Iruña
Huesca
Zaragoza
Lleida (Lérida)
Andorra la Vella
Girona
Figueres
Terrassa
Sabadell
Badalona
BARCELONA
Projection: Lambert's Conformal Conic
West from Greenwich
East from Greenwich

173
198
SWITZERLAND
ITALY
LIGURIAN SEA
MEDITERRANEAN SEA
Golfo di Génova
Riviera di Ponente
Riviera di Levante
Côte d'Azur
PROVENCE-ALPES-CÔTE D'AZUR
PIEMONTE
LOMBARDIA
VALLE D'AOSTA
LIGURIA
CORSE
HAUTE-CORSE
CORSE-DU-SUD
RHÔNE-ALPES
SAVOIE
HAUTE-SAVOIE
DRÔME
VAUCLUSE
ALPES-MARITIMES
BOUCHES-DU-RHÔNE
ALPES-DE-HAUTE-PROVENCE
HAUTES-ALPES
MONACO
Alpes Pennine
Alpi Lepontine
Berner Alpen
Mts. du Jura
Lyon
St-Etienne
Grenoble
Valence
Avignon
Marseille
Toulon
Aix-en-Provence
Nice
Cannes
Genève
Lausanne
Bern
Annecy
Chambéry
Torino
Milano
Génova
Savona
La Spezia
Livorno
Pisa
Lucca
Ajaccio
Bastia
Elba
Arcipelago Toscano
Montecristo
Capraia
Gorgona
Is. d'Hyères
Bouches de Bonifacio
Maddalena
Caprera
High-speed rail routes
PHILIP'S

50 0 25 50 75 100 125 150 175 km

50 0 25 50 75 100 125 miles

1:4 000 000

5 6

1 2 3 4 7 8

161

165

171

B C D E F G

ft	m
12000	4000
9000	3000
6000	2000
4500	1500
3000	1000
1500	500
600	200
0	0
50	150
100	300
200	600
500	1500
1000	3000
2000	6000
m	ft

Projection: *Conical with two standard parallels*

3 4 5 6 7 8

192

9 10 11 12 161 13 14 15 188 16

189

9 10 11 12 13 193 14 15

1:2 000 000
km
miles
184
170
163
NORTH SEA
BALTIC SEA
DENMARK
POLAND
NETHERLANDS
GERMANY
SCHLESWIG-HOLSTEIN
MECKLENBURG-VORPOMMERN
BRANDENBURG
NIEDERSACHSEN
SACHSEN-ANHALT
SACHSEN
THÜRINGEN
NORDRHEIN-WESTFALEN
HAMBURG
BREMEN
BERLIN
Kiel
Lübeck
Rostock
Stralsund
Rügen
Szczecin
Hannover
Magdeburg
Braunschweig
Bielefeld
Osnabrück
Münster
Dortmund
Essen
Düsseldorf
Köln
Bonn
Aachen
Leipzig
Dresden
Chemnitz
Halle
Erfurt
Kassel
Frankfurt
Cottbus
Potsdam
Schwerin
Groningen
Flensburg
Wilhelmshaven
Bremerhaven
Cuxhaven
Emden
Helgoland
Fehmarn
Kieler Bucht
Mecklenburger Bucht
Lübecker Bucht
Deutsche Bucht
Ostfriesische Inseln
Nordfriesische Inseln
Elbe
Weser
Ems
Rhein
Oder

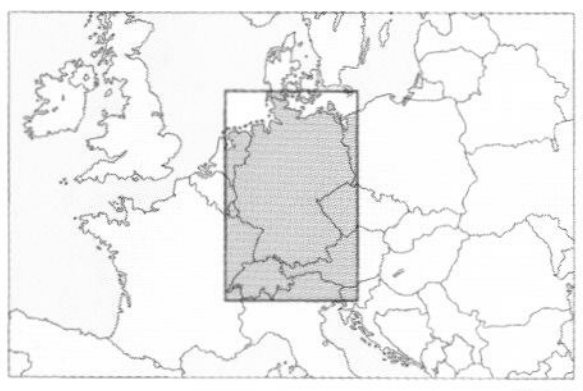

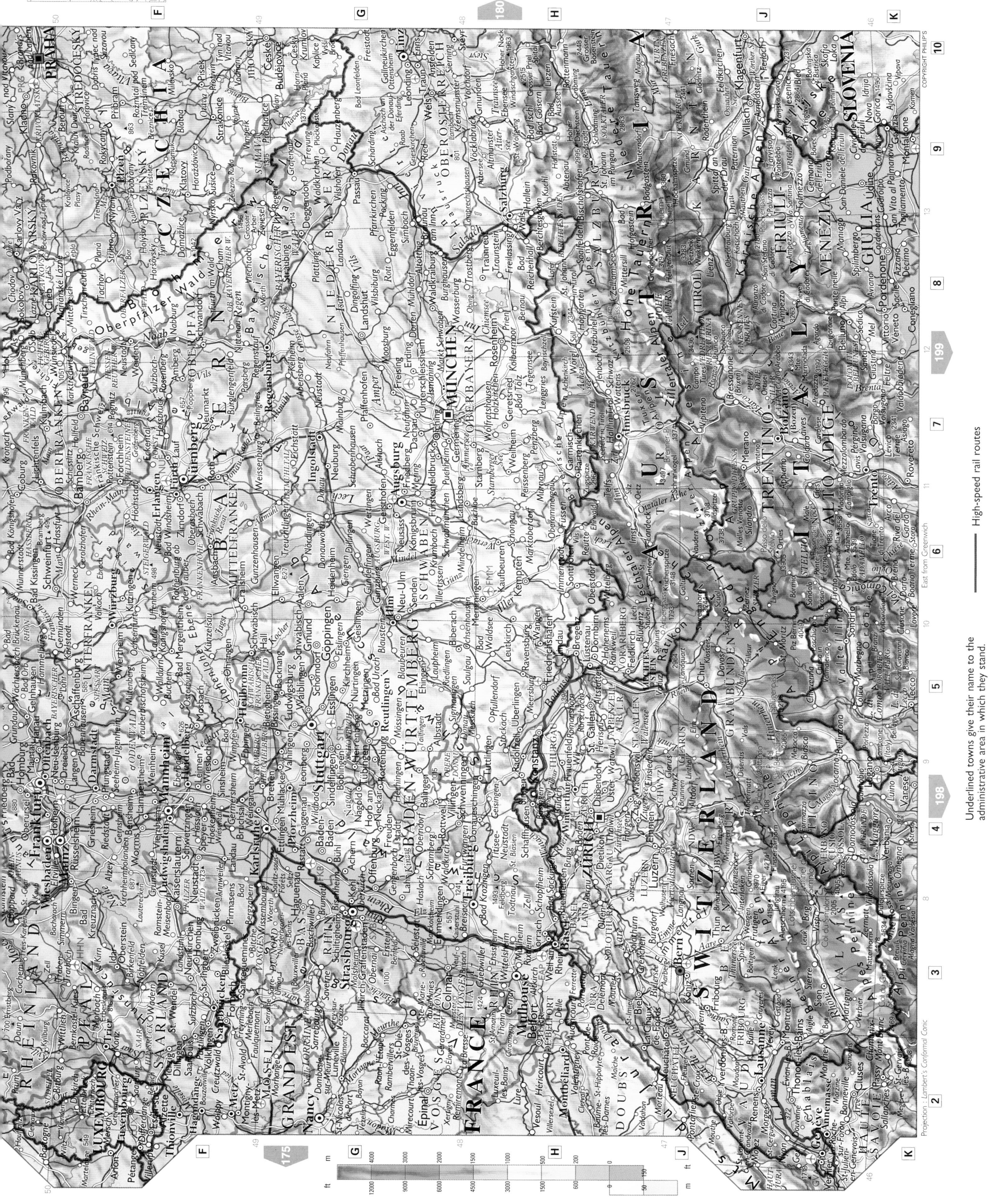
GERMANY
SWITZERLAND
CZECHIA
AUSTRIA
ITALY
FRANCE
SLOVENIA
LUXEMBOURG
BAYERN
BADEN-WÜRTTEMBERG
RHEINLAND-PFALZ
SAARLAND
GRAND EST
TRENTINO-ALTO ADIGE
FRIULI-VENEZIA GIULIA
PRAHA
München
Stuttgart
Frankfurt
Nürnberg
Zürich
Bern
Strasbourg
Salzburg
Innsbruck
Mannheim
Augsburg
Regensburg
Freiburg
Basel
Luxembourg
Lausanne
Genève
Bolzano
Trento
Plzeň
Linz
Klagenfurt
180
175
198
199
Underlined towns give their name to the administrative area in which they stand.
High-speed rail routes
Projection: Lambert's Conformal Conic
East from Greenwich
COPYRIGHT PHILIP'S

1:2 000 000
km
miles
178
179
198
Projection : Lambert's Conformal Conic
GERMANY
CZECH
AUSTRIA
SWITZERLAND
ITALY
SLOVENIA
THÜRINGEN
BAYERN
SCHWABEN
OBERBAYERN
NIEDERBAYERN
OBERPFALZ
OBERFRANKEN
UNTERFRANKEN
MITTELFRANKEN
KARLOVARSKÝ
PLZEŇSKÝ
STŘEDOČESKÝ
JIHOČESKÝ
VYSOČINA
LIBERECKÝ
ÚSTECKÝ
KRÁLOVÉHRADECKÝ
OBERÖSTERREICH
NIEDERÖSTERREICH
SALZBURG
STEIERMARK
KÄRNTEN
TIROL
VORARLBERG
TRENTINO-ALTO ADIGE
FRIULI-VENEZIA GIULIA
VENETO
LOMBARDIA
PRAHA
MÜNCHEN
Dresden
Chemnitz
Erfurt
Nürnberg
Augsburg
Stuttgart
Regensburg
Würzburg
Linz
Salzburg
Innsbruck
Graz
Klagenfurt
Ljubljana
Trieste
Venézia
Bolzano (Bozen)
Trento
Vicenza
Brescia
Plzeň
České Budějovice
Golfo di Venézia
Donau
Vltava
Hohe Tauern
Zillertaler Alpen
Karawanken
Bayerischer Wald
Böhmer Wald
Erzgebirge

185

187
183
182

Underlined towns give their name to the administrative area in which they stand.

1:2 000 000

Administrative divisions in Croatia:

1 Brodsko-Posavska
2 Koprivničko-Križevačka
4 Međimurska
5 Osječko-Baranjska
6 Požeško-Slavonska
8 Virovitičko-Podravska
9 Vukovarsko-Srijemska

180 199 189 202

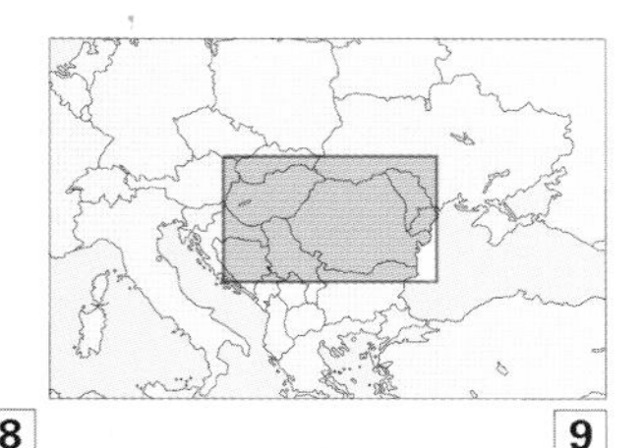

189

203

Underlined towns give their name to the administrative area in which they stand.

10 0 10 20 30 40 50 60 70 80 90 km

1:2 000 000

10 0 10 20 30 40 50 60 miles

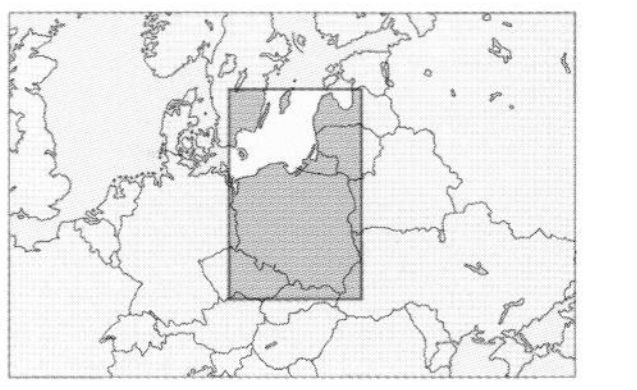

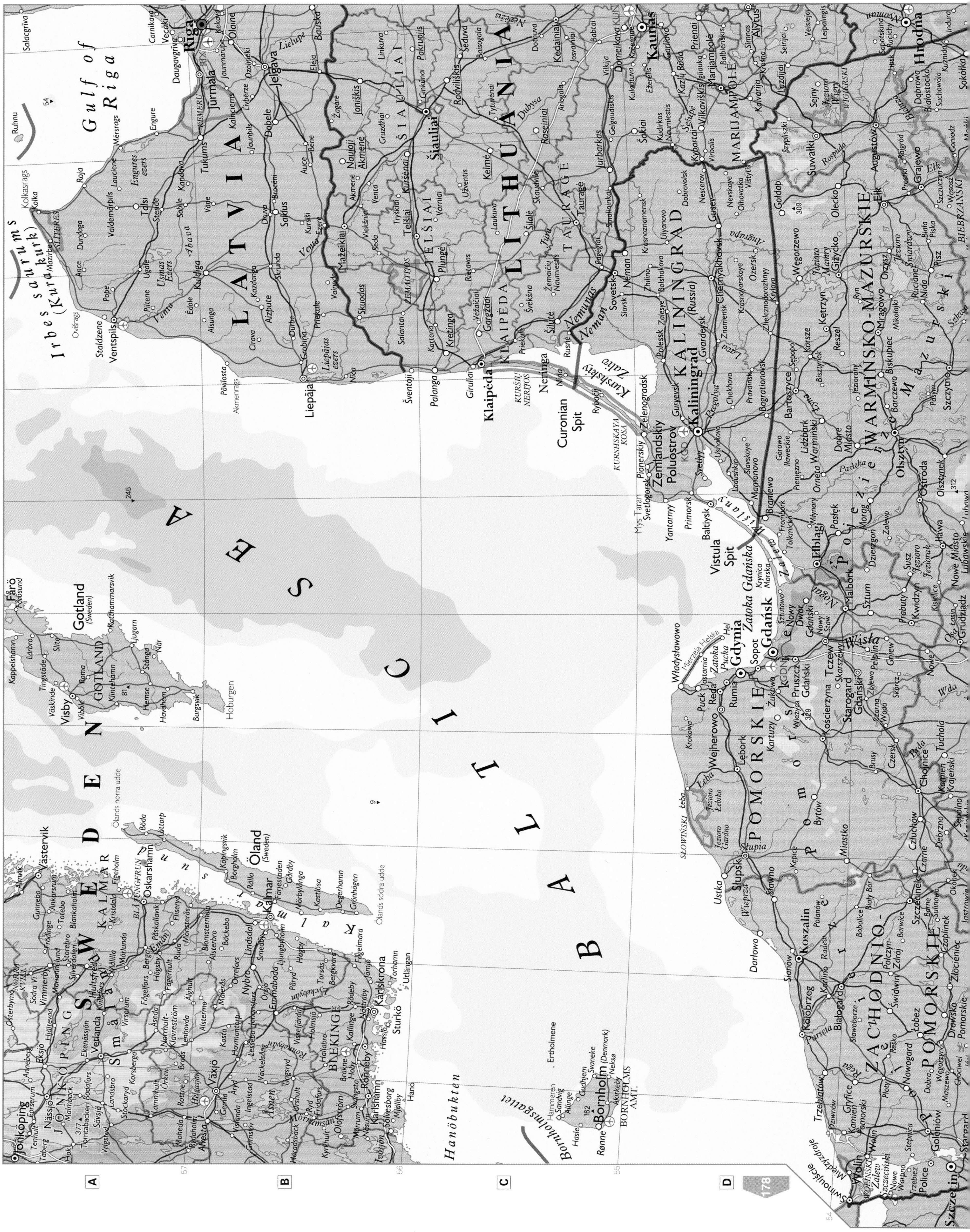

Underlined towns give their name to the administrative area in which they stand.

Projection: Lambert's Conformal Conic

East from Greenwich

m ft
6000 2000
4500 1500
3000 1000
1500 500
600 200
0 0
50–150
100–300
200–600

1:8 000 000

50 0 100 200 300 400 km
50 0 50 100 150 200 250 miles
214
A B C D
1 2 3 4 5 6 7 8 9 10 11 12
BARENTS SEA
Beloye More (White Sea)
BALTIC SEA
Gulf of Finland
Gulf of Bothnia
Gulf of Riga
Pechorskaya Guba
Cheshskaya Guba
Onezhskaya Guba
Dvinskaya Guba
Kandalakshskiy Zaliv
Ostrov Kolguyev
Ostrov Morzhovets
Poluostrov Kanin
Kolskiy Poluostrov
Ladozhskoye Ozero
Onezhskoye Ozero
Uralskie Gory
Timanskiy Kryazh
Severnyye Uvaly
Lapland
KOMI
KARELIA
UDMURTIA
TATARSTAN
BASHKORTOSTAN
CHUVASHIA
MARI EL
MORDVINIA
RUSSIA
FINLAND
SWEDEN
NORWAY
ESTONIA
LATVIA
LITHUANIA
BELARUS
POLAND
Kaliningrad (Russia)
MOSKVA (Moscow)
SANKT-PETERBURG
HELSINKI
Tallinn
Riga
Vilnius
MINSK
WARSZAWA (Warsaw)
KAZAN
UFA
SAMARA
NIZHNIY NOVGOROD
Arkhangelsk
Murmansk
Perm
Izhevsk
Kirov
Syktyvkar
Vologda
Yaroslavl
Kostroma
Ivanovo
Vladimir
Ryazan
Tula
Kaluga
Smolensk
Tver
Pskov
Velikiy Novgorod
Petrozavodsk
Oulu
Tampere
Turku
Kuopio
Ukhta
Vorkuta
Pechora
Orenburg
Penza
Saransk
Ulyanovsk
Togliatti
Cheboksary
Yoshkar Ola
Naberezhnyye Chelny
Sterlitamak
Magnitogorsk
Zlatoust
Nizhniy Tagil
Kotlas
Severodvinsk
Cherepovets
Rybinsk
Homyel
Mahilyow
Hrodna
Brest
Kaunas
Daugavpils
Tartu
Narva

BLACK SEA
CASPIAN SEA
Sea of Azov
MEDITERRANEAN SEA
KAZAKHSTAN
UKRAINE
ROMANIA
BULGARIA
MOLDOVA
GEORGIA
ARMENIA
AZERBAIJAN
TURKEY
SYRIA
IRAQ
IRAN
CYPRUS
LEBANON
TURKMENISTAN
Caucasus Mountains
CRIMEA (under Russian control)
KYIV (Kiev)
ODESA
KHARKIV
DNIPRO
VOLGOGRAD
ROSTOV
Astrakhan
TBILISI
YEREVAN
BAKI (Baku)
TEHRAN
ANKARA
ISTANBUL
BUCUREŞTI (Bucharest)
Chişinău
Projection: Conical with two standard parallels
East from Greenwich
COPYRIGHT PHILIP'S
216
246
193

1:4 000 000

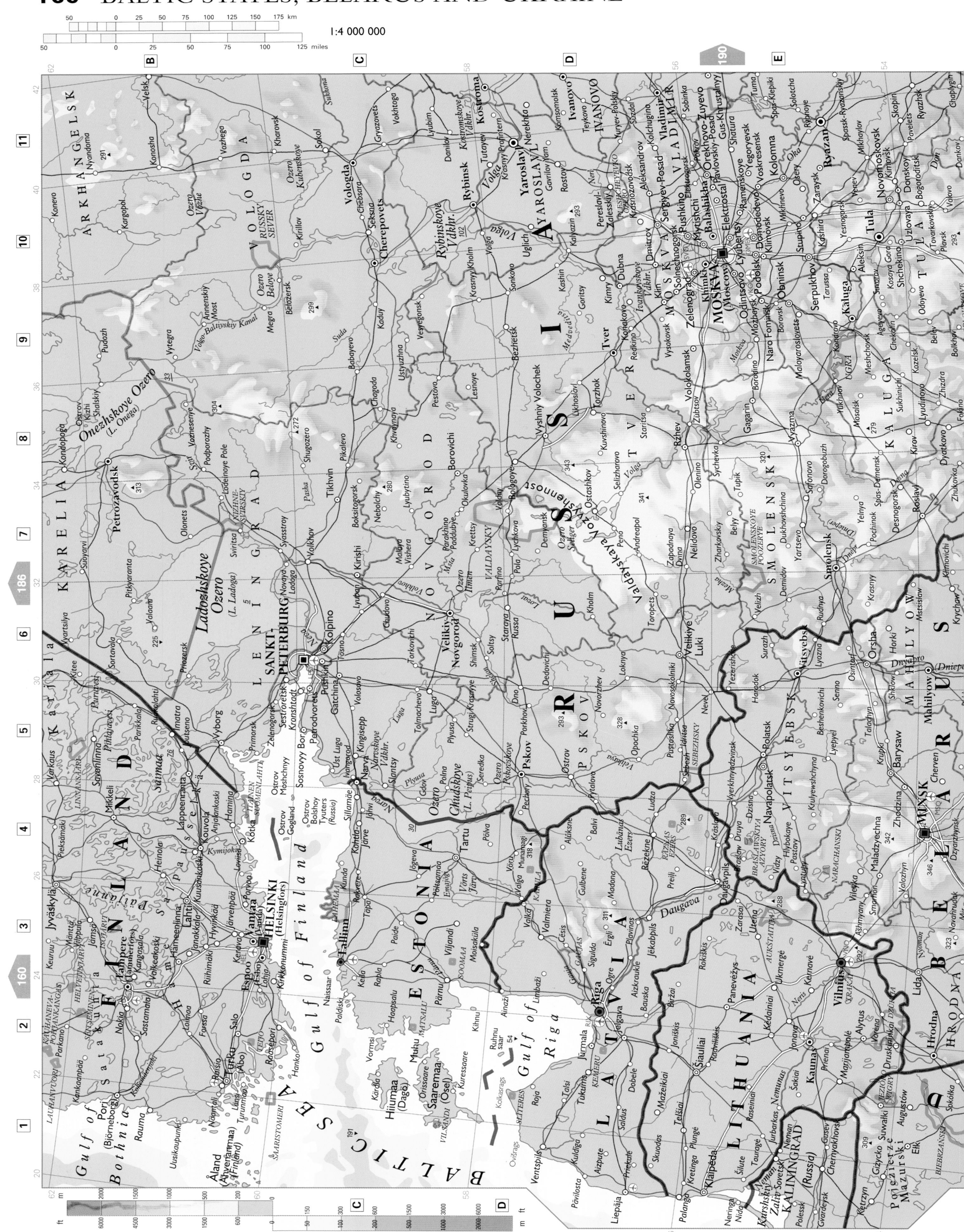

km
miles
FINLAND
ESTONIA
LATVIA
LITHUANIA
BELARUS
RUSSIA
BALTIC SEA
Gulf of Finland
Gulf of Riga
Gulf of Bothnia
HELSINKI (Helsingfors)
Tallinn
Riga
Vilnius
MINSK
SANKT-PETERBURG
MOSKVA (Moscow)
KALININGRAD (Russia)
Ladozhskoye Ozero (L. Ladoga)
Onezhskoye Ozero (L. Onega)
Ozero Chudskoye (L. Peipus)
Daugava
Volga

UKRAINE
BLACK SEA
Sea of Azov
MOLDOVA
ROMANIA
BULGARIA
HUNGARY
SLOVAKIA
KYIV (Kiev)
KHARKIV (Kharkov)
DNIPRO (Dnipropetrovsk)
ODESA
ROSTOV
BUCUREŞTI (Bucharest)
Chişinău (Kishinev)
CRIMEA (under Russian control)
Taganrogskiy Zaliv
Karkinitska Zatoka
Projection: Conical with two standard parallels
East from Greenwich
COPYRIGHT PHILIP'S

1:4 000 000
50 0 25 50 75 100 125 150 175 km
50 0 25 50 75 100 125 miles
B
C
D
E
216
214
188
UDMURTIA
TATARSTAN
MARI EL
CHUVASHIA
KIROV
KOSTROMA
NIZHNIY NOVGOROD
IVANOVO
YAROSLAVL
VLADIMIR
MOSKVA
TVER
SMOLENSK
KALUGA
TULA
RYAZAN
MORDVINIA
ULYANOVSK
SAMARA
PENZA
TAMBOV
LIPETSK
ORYOL
KURSK
BELGOROD
VORONEZH
SARATOV
VOLGOGRAD
BRYANSK
SUMY
RUSSIA
UKRAINE
BATYS QAZAQSTAN
KAZAN
SAMARA
MOSKVA (Moscow)
Nizhniy Novgorod
Saratov
Voronezh
Yaroslavl
Kostroma
Ivanovo
Vladimir
Ryazan
Tula
Kaluga
Tver
Orel (Oryol)
Kursk
Belgorod
Lipetsk
Tambov
Penza
Saransk
Ulyanovsk (Simbirsk)
Cheboksary
Yoshkar Ola
Togliatti
Syzran
Engels
Balakovo
Dzerzhinsk
Kineshma
Kharkiv (Kharkov)
Sumy
Poltava
Oral
Naberezhnyye Chelny
Almetyevsk
Volga
Oka
Don
Sura
Kuybyshevskoye Vdkhr.
Saratovskoye Vdkhr.
Volgogradskoye Vdkhr.
Rybinskoye Vdkhr.
Gorkovskoye Vdkhr.

1:8 000 000
km
miles
ATLANTIC OCEAN
Bay of Biscay
Golfe de Gascogne
English Channel
Str. of Dover
Isles of Scilly
Channel Is. (U.K.)
U.K.
LONDON
Bristol
Southampton
Portsmouth
Plymouth
Exeter
Brighton
Dover
Folkestone
NETHERLANDS
AMSTERDAM
's-Gravenhage
ROTTERDAM
Haarlem
BELGIUM
BRUSSEL
Antwerpen
Gent
LUXEMBOURG
GERMANY
KÖLN
Düsseldorf
Dortmund
Essen
Frankfurt
Stuttgart
MÜNCHEN
Hannover
FRANCE
PARIS
Lille
Calais
Dunkerque
Rouen
Le Havre
Cherbourg-Octeville
Caen
Brest
Rennes
St-Brieuc
Quimper
Lorient
Vannes
Nantes
St-Nazaire
Angers
Le Mans
Tours
Orléans
Reims
Metz
Nancy
Strasbourg
Dijon
Besançon
Mulhouse
La Rochelle
Rochefort
Poitiers
Limoges
Bordeaux
Massif Central
Clermont-Ferrand
LYON
St-Étienne
Grenoble
Valence
Avignon
Nîmes
Montpellier
Toulouse
Montauban
Bayonne
Pau
Perpignan
Narbonne
Béziers
Sète
MARSEILLE
Toulon
Aix-en-Provence
Nice
Cannes
MONACO
Golfe du Lion
Corse (France)
Ajaccio
Bastia
SWITZERLAND
Bern
ZÜRICH
Basel
Genève
Lausanne
LIECHTENSTEIN
AUSTRIA
Innsbruck
ITALY
MILANO
TORINO
Génova
Bologna
Firenze
Pisa
Livorno
ROMA
NÁPOLI
Verona
Venézia
Padova
Trento
Bolzano
SAN MARINO
Sardegna (Italy)
Cágliari
Sássari
Olbia
LIGURIAN SEA
TYRRHENIAN SEA
SPAIN
MADRID
BARCELONA
Valencia
Zaragoza
Sevilla
Málaga
Granada
Córdoba
Murcia
Cartagena
Alicante (Alacant)
Bilbao
Santander
Oviedo
Gijón (Xixón)
A Coruña (La Coruña)
Santiago de Compostela
Vigo
Valladolid
Salamanca
Burgos
León
Pamplona-Iruña
Vitoria-Gasteiz
Donostia-San Sebastián
Logroño
Tarragona
Castelló de la Plana
Albacete
Toledo
Badajoz
Cáceres
Huelva
Cádiz
Jerez de la Frontera
Almería
Gibraltar (U.K.)
Str. of Gibraltar
Islas Baleares (Spain)
Mallorca
Palma de Mallorca
Menorca
Eivissa
Formentera
Cordillera Cantábrica
Sierra Morena
Sierra Nevada
Pyrénées
ANDORRA
PORTUGAL
LISBOA
PORTO
Coimbra
Braga
Faro
MEDITERRANEAN SEA
MOROCCO
RABAT
FÈS
Meknès
Tanger
Tétouan
Ceuta (Sp.)
Melilla (Sp.)
Oujda
Moyen Atlas
Haut Atlas
Er Rachidia
ALGERIA
ALGER (Algiers)
Oran
Constantine
Annaba
Sétif
Blida
Tlemcen
Biskra
Batna
Djelfa
Laghouat
Ghardaïa
Ouargla
Touggourt
El Oued
Béchar
Hauts Plateaux
Atlas Saharien
Grand Erg Occidental
Grand Erg Oriental
Sahara
TUNISIA
TUNIS
Bizerte
Sousse
Sfax
Kairouan
Gabès
Djerba
Golfe de Hammamet
Golfe de Gabès
Chott Djerid
Sicilia
Trápani
Pantelleria (Italy)
Lampedusa (Italy)
TARĀBULUS (Tripoli)
Tarābulus (Tripolitania)
Projection : Conical with two standard parallels
West from Greenwich
East from Greenwich

261
258
260

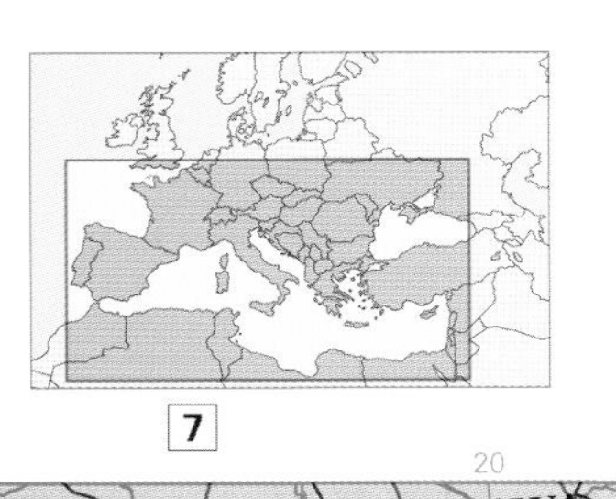

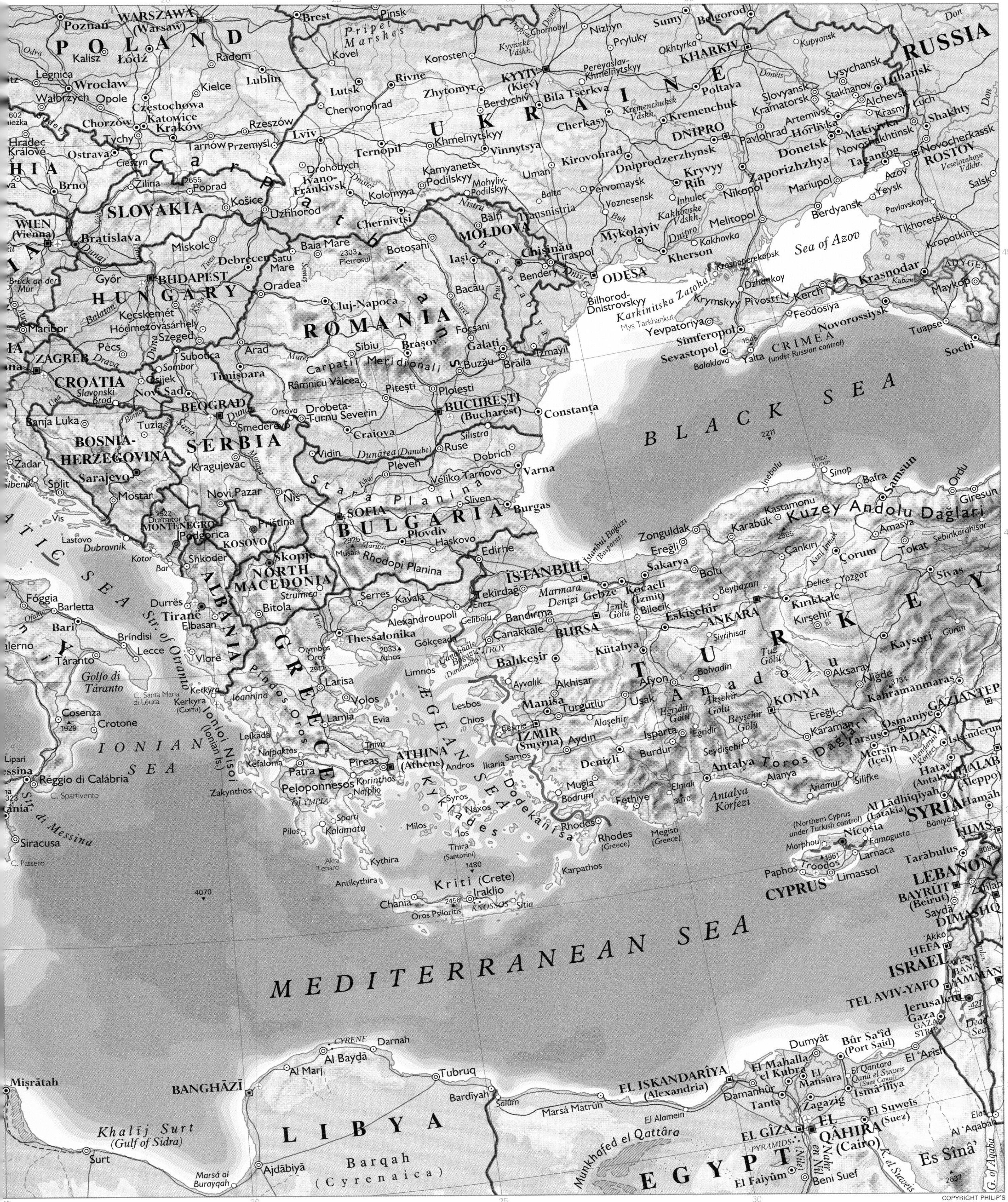

186

7 8 9 10 11 12

POLAND
WARSZAWA (Warsaw)
Poznań
Kalisz
Łódź
Radom
Lublin
Kielce
Wrocław
Legnica
Wałbrzych
Opole
Częstochowa
Katowice
Kraków
Chorzów
Tychy
Rzeszów
Tarnów
Przemyśl
Hradec Králové
Ostrava
Cieszyn
Brno
Žilina
Poprad
2655
Košice
Uzhhorod
SLOVAKIA
Carpathians
WIEN (Vienna)
Bratislava
Dunaj
Miskolc
Debrecen
Satu Mare
Baia Mare
2303 Pietrosul
Botoşani
Győr
BUDAPEST
HUNGARY
Bruck an der Mur
Balaton
Kecskemét
Hódmezővásárhely
Szeged
Maribor
Pécs
Oradea
Cluj-Napoca
ROMANIA
Arad
Timişoara
Sibiu
Braşov
Bacău
Iaşi
Focşani
Galaţi
Brăila
Buzău
Carpaţii Meridionali
Râmnicu Vâlcea
Piteşti
Ploieşti
BUCUREŞTI (Bucharest)
Constanţa
Drobeta-Turnu Severin
Orşova
Craiova
Vidin
Dunărea (Danube)
Ruse
Silistra
Dobrich
Varna
ZAGREB
Drava
CROATIA
Osijek
Sombor
Subotica
Novi Sad
Slavonski Brod
BEOGRAD
Smederevo
Banja Luka
Tuzla
Bosna
Sava
BOSNIA-HERZEGOVINA
SERBIA
Kragujevac
Sarajevo
Mostar
Zadar
Šibenik
Split
Novi Pazar
Niš
Priština
KOSOVO
2522 Durmitor
MONTENEGRO
Podgorica
Vis
Lastovo
Dubrovnik
Kotor
Bar
Shkodër
Skopje
NORTH MACEDONIA
Bitola
Strumica
ALBANIA
Durrës
Tiranë
Elbasan
Vlorë
SOFIA
BULGARIA
Pleven
Veliko Tarnovo
Sliven
Burgas
Stara Planina
Iskar
Plovdiv
Haskovo
2925 Musala
Maritsa
Rhodopi Planina
Edirne
Pinsk
Brest
Pripet Marshes
Kovel
Lutsk
Rivne
Korosten
Zhytomyr
Chervonohrad
Lviv
Ternopil
Khmelnytskyy
Vinnytsya
Drohobych
Ivano-Frankivsk
Kolomyya
Kamyanets-Podilskyy
Mohyliv-Podilskyy
Dnister
Chernivtsi
Bălţi
MOLDOVA
Nistru
Bessarabia
Chişinău
Tiraspol
Bendery
Transnistria
Prut
Siret
Izmayil
UKRAINE
KYYIV (Kiev)
Berdychiv
Bila Tserkva
Chornobyl
Kyyivske Vdskh.
Nizhyn
Pryluky
Sumy
Belgorod
Okhtyrka
KHARKIV
Kupyansk
Pereyaslav-Khmelnytskyy
Cherkasy
Kremenchuk
Kremenchutske Vdskh.
Poltava
DNIPRO
Dniprodzerzhynsk
Kirovohrad
Uman
Pervomaysk
Voznesensk
Kryvyy Rih
Inhulec
Nikopol
Zaporizhzhya
Kakhovske Vdskh.
Kakhovka
Melitopol
Mykolayiv
Kherson
ODESA
Bilhorod-Dnistrovskyy
Karkinitska Zatoka
Mys Tarkhankut
Yevpatoriya
Simferopol
Sevastopol
Balaklava
Yalta
1545
CRIMEA (under Russian control)
Krasnoperekopsk
Dzhankoy
Krymskyy Pivostriv
Kerch
Feodosiya
Sea of Azov
Berdyansk
Mariupol
Donetsk
Horlivka
Makiyivka
Artemivsk
Slovyansk
Kramatorsk
Pavlohrad
Lysychansk
Stakhanov
Alchevsk
Krasnyy Luch
Luhansk
Donets
Novoshakhtinsk
Shakhty
Novocherkassk
ROSTOV
Veselovskoye Vdkhr.
Taganrog
Azov
Yeysk
Salsk
Pavlovskaya
Tikhoretsk
Kropotkin
Krasnodar
Kuban
ADYGEA
Maykop
Novorossiysk
Tuapse
Sochi
RUSSIA
Don
BLACK SEA
2211
Ince Burun
Sinop
İnebolu
Bafra
Samsun
Ordu
Giresun
Kastamonu
Kuzey Andolu Dağlari
Karabük
Zonguldak
Ereğli
2565
Çankırı
Amasya
Şebinkarahisar
Tokat
Çorum
Kizil Irmak
Sakarya
Bolu
İstanbul Boğazı (Bosporus)
İSTANBUL
Tekirdağ
Marmara Denizi
Gebze
Kocaeli (İzmit)
İznik Gölü
Bilecik
Eskişehir
Beypazarı
ANKARA
Kırıkkale
Delice
Yozgat
Sivas
Kırşehir
TURKEY
Sivrihisar
Kayseri
Gürün
Tuz Gölü
Anadolu
Aksaray
Niğde
3734
Kahramanmaraş
GAZIANTEP
Bolvadin
Afyon
Uşak
Kütahya
Bursa
BURSA
Bandırma
Çanakkale
Çanakkale Boğazı (Dardanelles)
TROY
Gelibolu
Enez
Alexandroupoli
Kavala
Serres
Thessaloniki
Gökçeada
Olympos Oros 2917
2033 Athos
Balıkesir
Ayvalık
Akhisar
Manisa
Turgutlu
İZMIR (Smyrna)
Çeşme
Alaşehir
Aydın
Denizli
Eğirdir Gölü
Akşehir Gölü
Beyşehir Gölü
KONYA
Isparta
Eğirdir
Seydişehir
Burdur
Ereğli
Karaman
Toros Dağlari
Tarsus
Osmaniye
ADANA
Mersin (İçel)
Silifke
Anamur
Alanya
Antalya
Antalya Körfezi
Elmalı
3070
Fethiye
Muğla
Bodrum
Rhodes
Rhodes (Greece)
Megisti (Greece)
İskenderun
İskenderun Körfezi
Hatay (Antakya)
HALAB (Aleppo)
Al Lādhiqīyah (Latakia)
Bāniyās
Hamāh
SYRIA
HIMS
Tarābulus
3088
LEBANON
BAYRŪT (Beirut)
Zahlah
Saydā
DIMASHQ
'Akko
HEFA
ISRAEL
WEST BANK
'AMMAN
TEL AVIV-YAFO
Jerusalem
427
Gaza
GAZA STRIP
Dead Sea
(Northern Cyprus under Turkish control)
Nicosia
Famagusta
Morphou
1951 Troodos
Larnaca
Paphos
Limassol
CYPRUS
GREECE
Pindos Oros
Kerkyra
Kerkyra (Corfu)
Ioannina
Ionioi Nisoi (Ionian Is.)
Larisa
Volos
Limnos
Lesbos
Chios
Lamia
Evia
Thiva
Lefkada
Nafpaktos
Kefalonia
Patra
Pireas
ATHINA (Athens)
Andros
Ikaria
Samos
AEGEAN SEA
Zakynthos
Peloponnesos
Korinthos
Nafplio
OLYMPIA
Syros
Naxos
Kyklades
Dodekanisa
Sparti
Kalamata
Milos
Ios
Thira (Santorini)
Pilos
Akra Tenaro
Kythira
Antikythira
1480
Kriti (Crete)
Iraklio
Chania
2456
Oros Psiloritis
KNOSSOS
Sitia
Karpathos
ADRIATIC SEA
ITALY
Fóggia
Barletta
Ofanto
Bari
Bríndisi
Lecce
Táranto
Golfo di Táranto
C. Santa Maria di Leuca
Str. of Otranto
Salerno
Cosenza
1929
Crotone
IONIAN SEA
Lípari
Messina
Réggio di Calábria
C. Spartivento
Str. di Messina
Siracusa
C. Passero
4070
MEDITERRANEAN SEA
CYRENE
Darnah
Al Baydā
Al Marj
Tubruq
BANGHĀZĪ
Bardīyah
Salûm
Marsá Matrûh
El Alamein
Mişrātah
Khalīj Surt (Gulf of Sidra)
Surt
Marsá al Burayqah
Ajdābiyā
LIBYA
Barqah (Cyrenaica)
EL ISKANDARÎYA (Alexandria)
Damanhûr
Dumyât
El Mahalla el Kubra
El Mansûra
Bûr Sa'îd (Port Said)
El Qantara
Qanâ el Suweis (Suez Canal)
Ismâ'iliya
El 'Arîsh
Tanta
Zagazig
El Suweis (Suez)
EL GÎZA
EL QÂHIRA (Cairo)
PYRAMIDS
Nîl
Bahr en Nîl
Munkhafed el Qattâra
EGYPT
El Faiyûm
Beni Suef
Es Sînâ'
2637
Elat
Al 'Aqabah
G. of Aqaba

B C D E F

187
246

7 8 9 10

256

1:2 000 000
km
miles
196
Bay of Biscay
Costa Verde
Donostia-San Sebastián
Bilbao
Santander
Gijón (Xixón)
Oviedo
Avilés
A Coruña (La Coruña)
Ferrol
Lugo
Santiago de Compostela
Pontevedra
Vigo
Ourense (Orense)
Ponferrada
León
Burgos
Logroño
Vitoria-Gasteiz
Palencia
Valladolid
Zamora
Salamanca
Segovia
Ávila
Madrid
Guadalajara
Toledo
Plasencia
Talavera de la Reina
Bragança
Braga
Porto
Vila Nova de Gaia
Aveiro
Viseu
Guarda
Coimbra
Castelo Branco
Leiria
Figueira da Foz
GALICIA
ASTURIAS
CANTABRIA
PAÍS VASCO
LA RIOJA
CASTILLA Y LEÓN
MADRID
SPAIN
PORTUGAL
Picos de Europa
Cordillera Cantábrica
Sierra de Guadarrama
Sierra de Gredos
Duero
Douro
Tajo
Miño

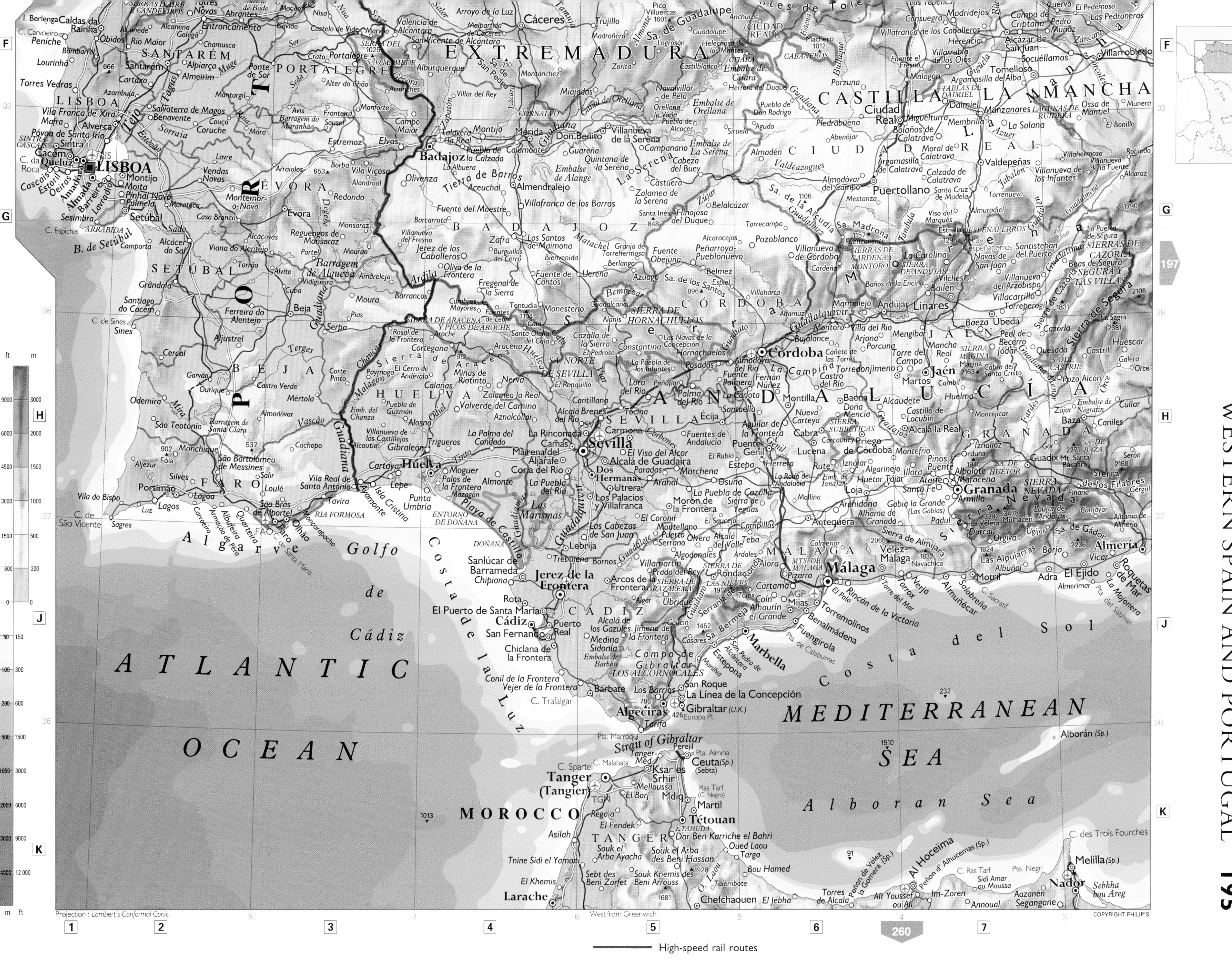
ATLANTIC
OCEAN
MEDITERRANEAN
SEA
Alboran Sea
Golfo de Cádiz
Costa de la Luz
Costa del Sol
Strait of Gibraltar
MOROCCO
EXTREMADURA
CASTILLA-LA MANCHA
ANDALUCÍA
LISBOA
SANTARÉM
PORTALEGRE
ÉVORA
SETÚBAL
BEJA
FARO
Algarve
BADAJOZ
SEVILLA
HUELVA
CÁDIZ
MÁLAGA
GRANADA
JAÉN
CÓRDOBA
CIUDAD REAL
TANGER
LISBOA
Setúbal
Sevilla
Córdoba
Granada
Málaga
Cádiz
Huelva
Badajoz
Cáceres
Almería
Jaén
Faro
Gibraltar (U.K.)
Tanger (Tangier)
Tétouan
Ceuta (Sp.)
Melilla (Sp.)
Sierra Nevada
Guadiana
Guadalquivir
Tejo
Projection : Lambert's Conformal Conic
West from Greenwich
COPYRIGHT PHILIP'S
High-speed rail routes
197
260

10 0 10 20 30 40 50 60 70 80 90 km

10 0 10 20 30 40 50 60 miles

1:2 000 000

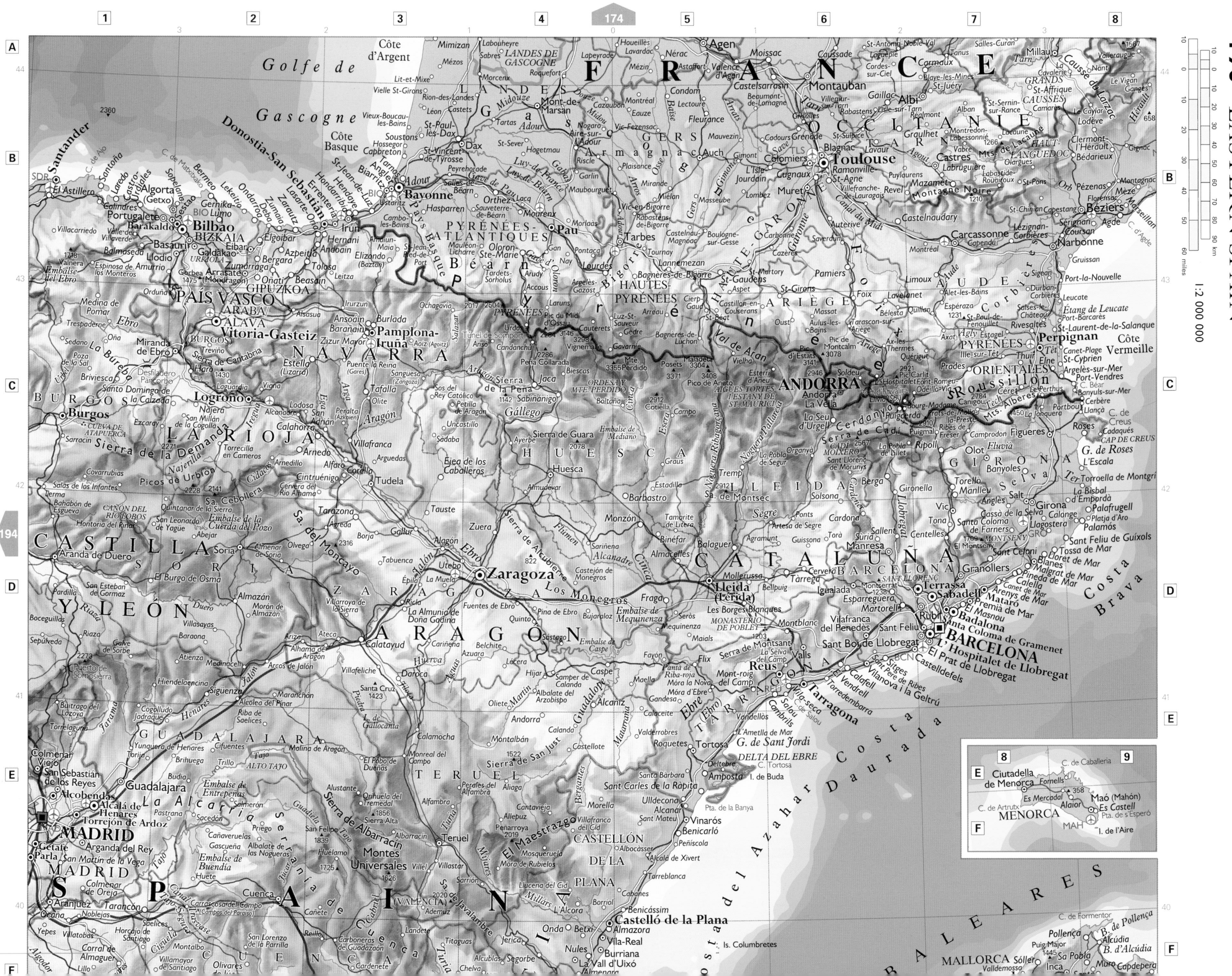

174

194

MEDITERRANEAN SEA
Golfo de Valencia
Costa Blanca
Costa Cálida
Costa del Sol
CASTILLA-LA MANCHA
CIUDAD REAL
ALBACETE
VALENCIA
ALICANTE
MURCIA
GRANADA
ALMERÍA
JAÉN
Valencia
Alicante (Alacant)
Murcia
Cartagena
Albacete
Granada
Almería
Elche (Elx)
Torrevieja
Lorca
Mar Menor
EIVISSA (IBIZA)
Formentera
Cabrera
Palma
ALGER (Algiers)
Oran (Ouahran)
Blida
Médéa
Mostaganem
Relizane
Tiaret
Mascara
Sidi-bel-Abbès
Ech Chéliff
Melilla (Sp.)
Nador
Alborán (Sp.)
ALGERIA
Golfe d'Arzew
Projection : Lambert's Conformal Conic
West from Greenwich
East from Greenwich
COPYRIGHT PHILIP'S
High-speed rail routes
195
260
261

10 0 10 20 30 40 50 60 70 80 90 km

10 0 10 20 30 40 50 60 miles

1:2 000 000

179

174

200

Projection : Lambert's Conformal Conic

East from Greenwich

m	4000	3000	2000	1500	1000	500	200	0
ft	12 000	9000	6000	4500	3000	1500	600	

ft	150	300	600	1500	3000	6000
m	0	50	100	200	500	1000	2000

Underlined towns give their name to administrative area in which they star

Administrative divisions in Croatia:

1 Brodsko-Posavska
2 Koprivničko-Križevačka
3 Krapinsko-Zagorska
4 Medimurska
6 Požeško-Slavonska
7 Varaždinska
8 Virovitičko-Podravska
10 Zagrebačka

High-speed rail routes

1:2 000 000

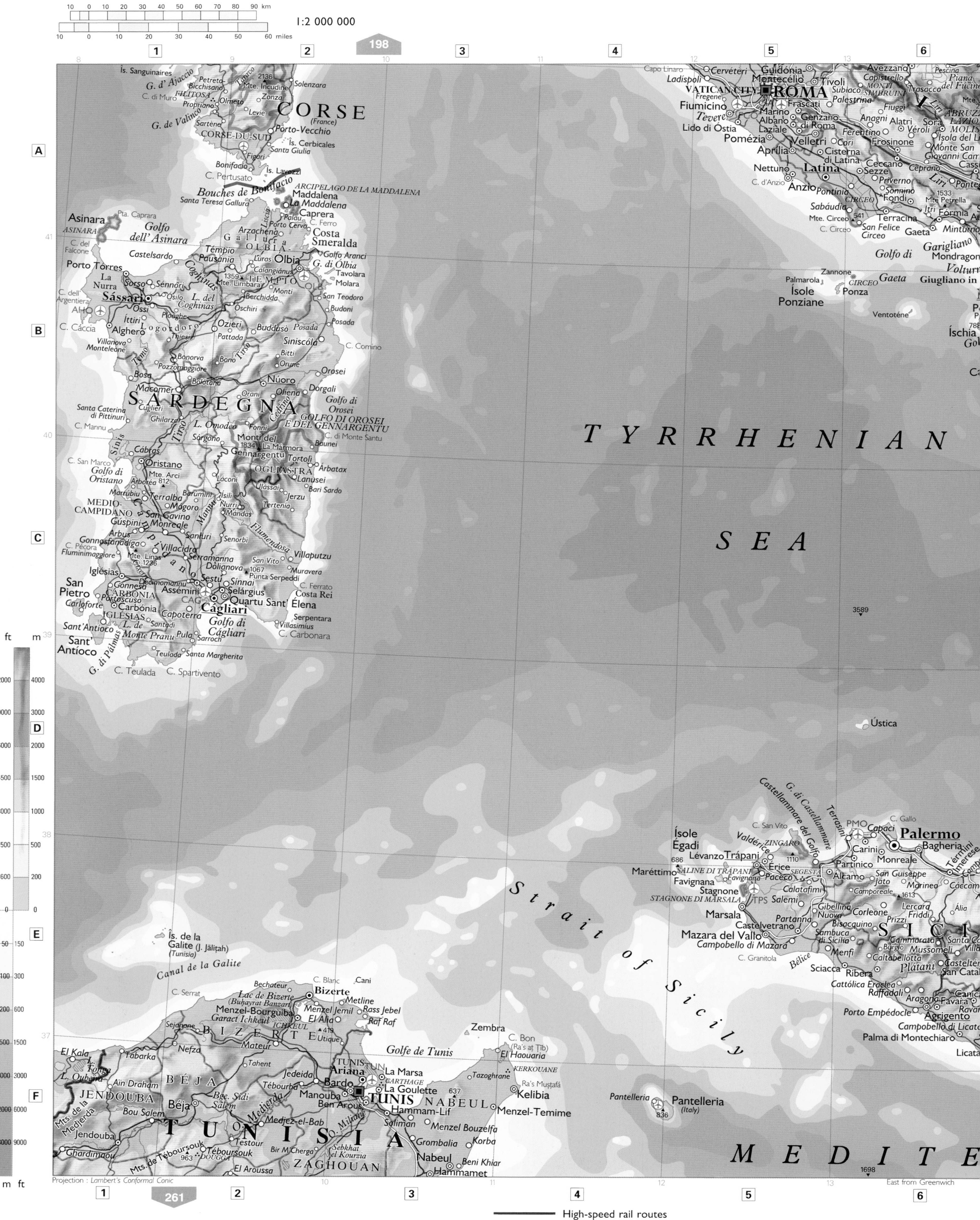

ft m
12000 4000
9000 3000
6000 2000
4500 1500
3000 1000
1500 500
600 200
0 0
50 150
100 300
200 600
500 1500
1000 3000
2000 6000
3000 9000
m ft

Projection : Lambert's Conformal Conic

East from Greenwich

High-speed rail routes

Underlined towns give their name to the administrative area in which they stand.

1:2 000 000
km
miles
ADRIATIC SEA
Strait of Otranto
ITALY
CROATIA
BOSNIA-HERZEGOVINA
REPUBLIKA SRPSKA
FEDERACIJA BOSNA I HERCEGOVINA
MONTENEGRO
SERBIA
VOJVODINA
KOSOVO
ALBANIA
NORTH MACEDONIA
GREECE
KENTRIKI MAKEDONIA
DYTIKI MAKEDONIA
BEOGRAD (Belgrade)
Novi Sad
Sarajevo
Podgorica
Prishtinë (Priština)
Skopje
Tiranë
SOFIA
Thessaloniki (Salonica)
Craiova
Niš
Kragujevac
Durrës
Shkodër
Bitola
Kerkyra (Corfu)
Brindisi
Lecce
Otranto
Dubrovnik
Mostar
Tuzla
Zenica
Novi Pazar
Peje
Prizren
Tetovo
Ohrid
Elbasan
Vlorë
Korçë
Kozani
Katerini
Thermaïkos Kolpos
Dunărea
Sava
Drina
Morava
Prokletije
Šar Planina
Projection : Lambert's Conformal Conic
East from Greenwich

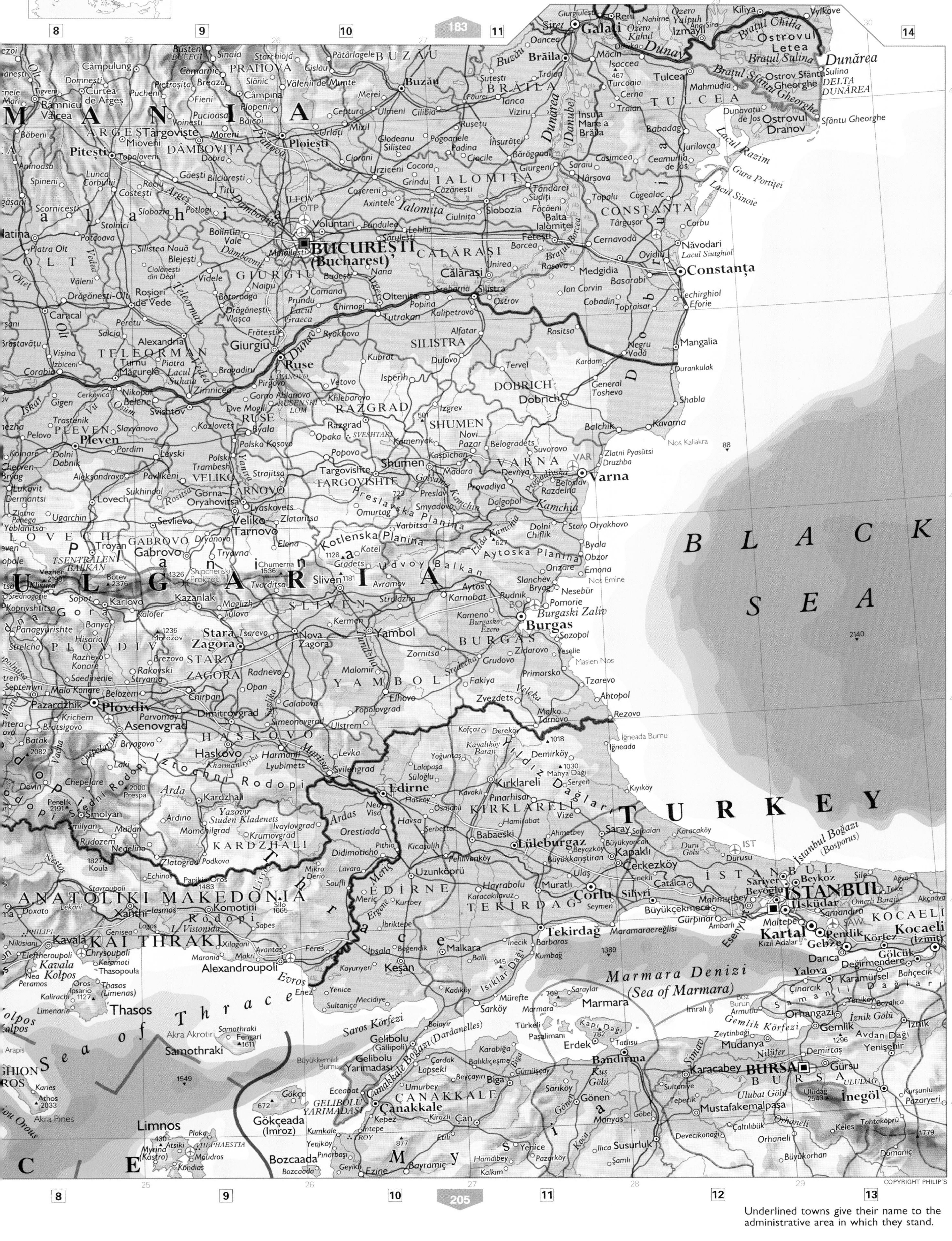

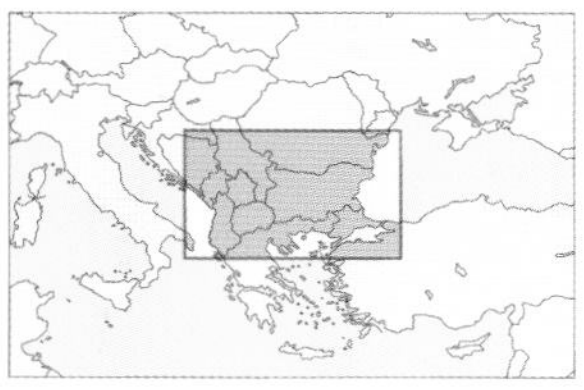

BLACK SEA

TURKEY

Marmara Denizi (Sea of Marmara)

Sea of Thrace

Underlined towns give their name to the administrative area in which they stand.

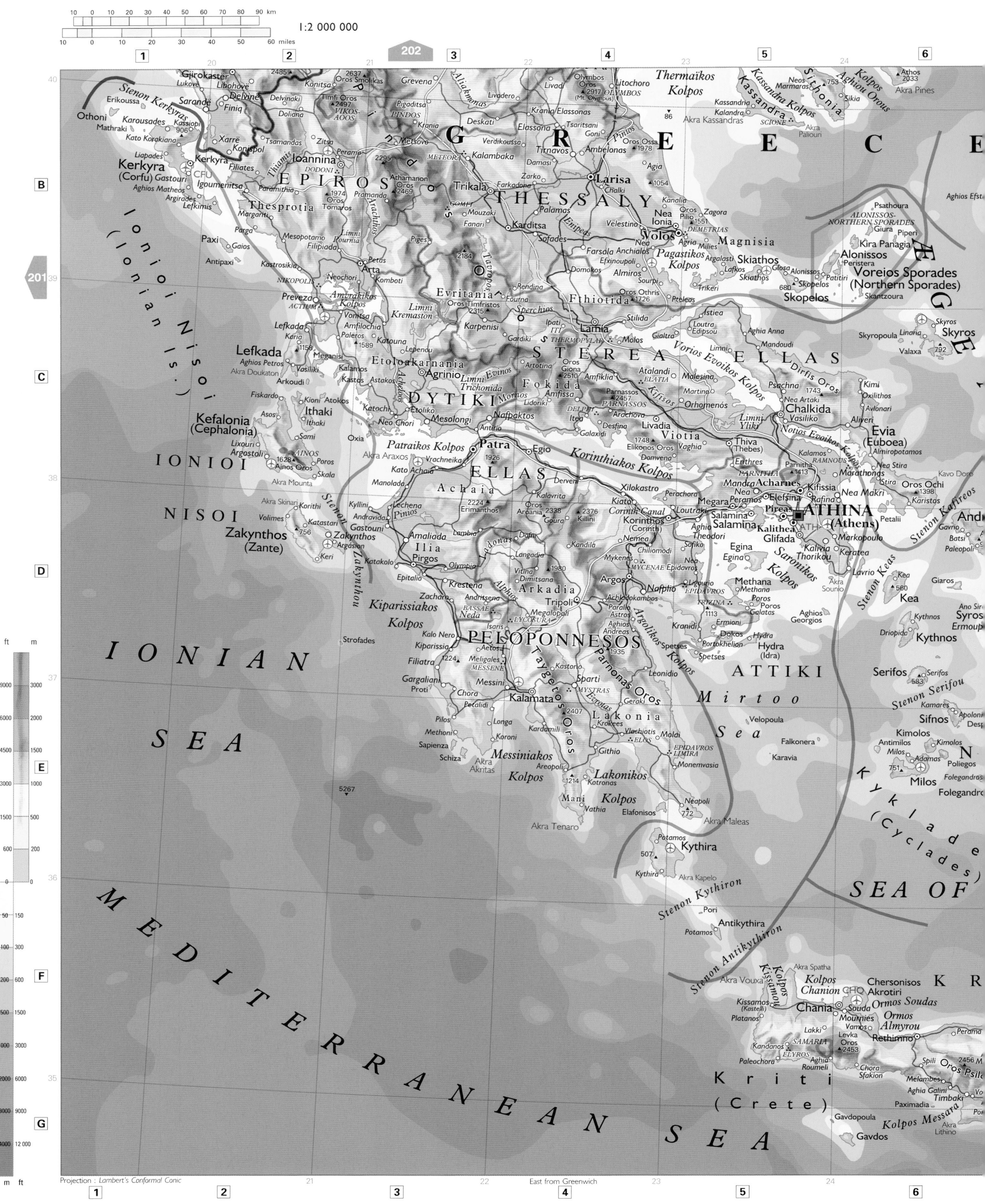
1:2 000 000
GREECE
IONIAN SEA
MEDITERRANEAN SEA
SEA OF
PELOPONNESOS
STEREA ELLAS
THESSALY
EPIROS
ATTIKI
IONIOI NISOI
Ionioi Nisoi (Ionian Is.)
Kykladeς (Cyclades)
Kriti (Crete)
ATHINA (Athens)
Patra
Larisa
Lamia
Volos
Ioannina
Kerkyra (Corfu)
Lefkada
Kefalonia (Cephalonia)
Zakynthos (Zante)
Ithaki
Kalamata
Tripoli
Korinthos (Corinth)
Chalkida
Evia (Euboea)
Voreios Sporades (Northern Sporades)
Skopelos
Skiathos
Alonissos
Skyros
Kythira
Antikythira
Chania
Rethimno
Gavdos
Milos
Kea
Serifos
Sifnos
Kimolos
Hydra (Idra)
Egina
Salamina
Patraikos Kolpos
Korinthiakos Kolpos
Saronikos Kolpos
Argolikos Kolpos
Lakonikos Kolpos
Messiniakos Kolpos
Kiparissiakos Kolpos
Thermaikos Kolpos
Pagastikos Kolpos
Mirtoo Sea
Stenon Kythiron
Stenon Antikythiron
Projection : Lambert's Conformal Conic
East from Greenwich

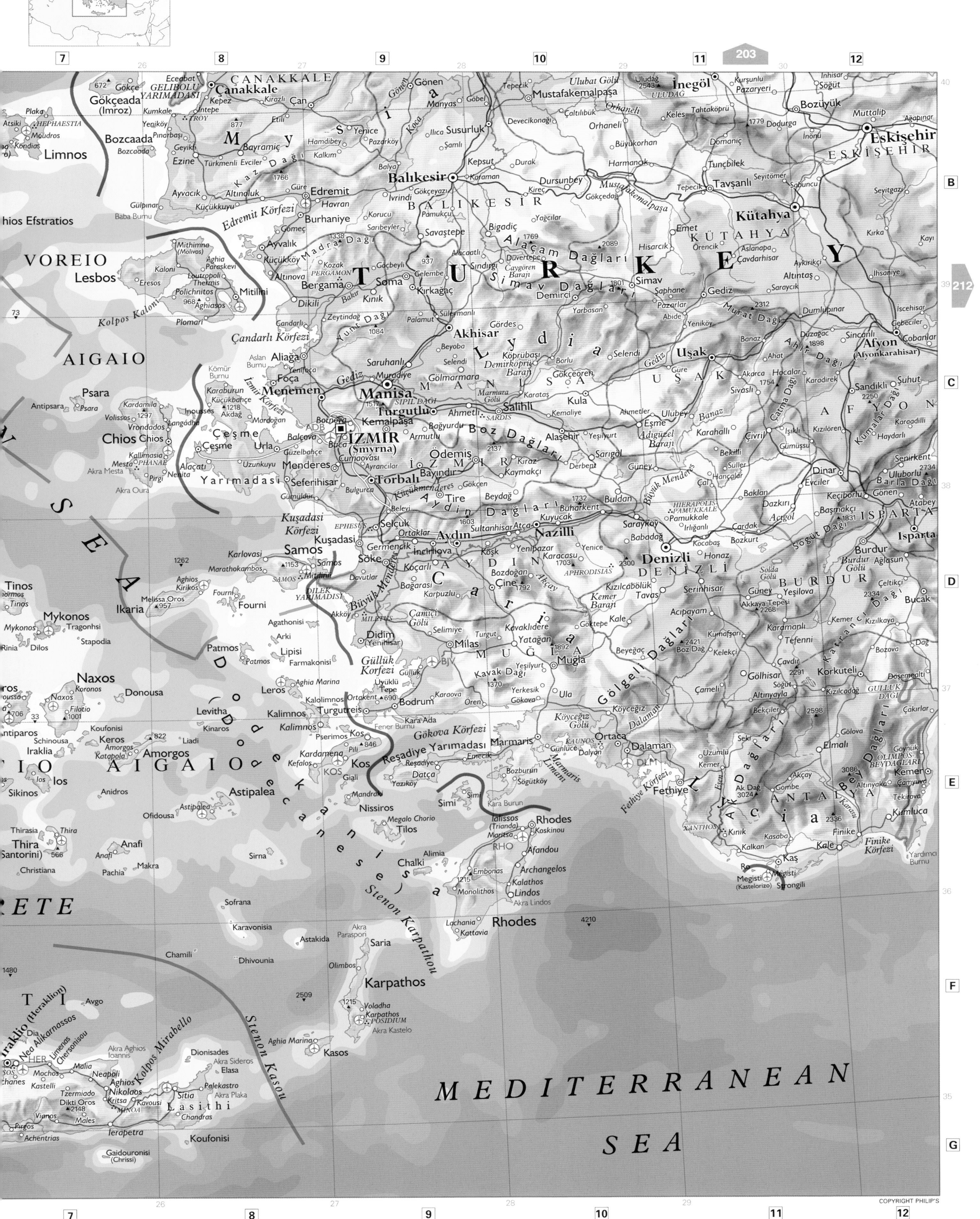

7
8
9
10
11
203
12
212
B
C
D
E
F
G
Çanakkale
Gökçeada (Imroz)
Bozcaada
Limnos
Ezine
Çan
Gönen
Manyas
Susurluk
Mustafakemalpaşa
Ulubat Gölü
İnegöl
Bozüyük
Eskişehir
Balıkesir
Edremit
Edremit Körfezi
Havran
Burhaniye
Ayvalık
Kaz Dağı
Madra Dağı
Bergama
Soma
Kırkağaç
Dikili
Akhisar
Tavşanlı
Kütahya
Simav
Simav Dağları
Gediz
Murat Dağı
Uşak
Afyon (Afyonkarahisar)
TURKEY
Lesbos
Mitilini
Plomari
Kolpos Kalloni
Çandarlı Körfezi
Aliağa
Foça
Menemen
Manisa
Turgutlu
Salihli
Kula
Alaşehir
İZMİR (Smyrna)
Kemalpaşa
İzmir Körfezi
Çeşme
Urla
Karaburun
Chios
Psara
Antipsara
Ödemiş
Torbalı
Menderes
Seferihisar
Boz Dağları
Tire
Kuşadası
Kuşadası Körfezi
Selçuk
EPHESUS
Aydın
Nazilli
Aydın Dağları
Denizli
Pamukkale
HIERAPOLIS
Buldan
Sarayköy
Dinar
Isparta
Burdur
Samos
Karlovasi
Söke
Büyük Menderes
Ikaria
Fourni
Patmos
Leros
Kalimnos
Kos
Didim
Milas
Yatağan
Muğla
Güllük Körfezi
Bodrum
Gökova Körfezi
Marmaris
Datça
Köyceğiz
Dalaman
Fethiye
Fethiye Körfezi
Kaş
Kale
Finike
Kemer
Elmalı
Gölhisar
Tefenni
Simi
Tilos
Nissiros
Chalki
Rhodes
Lindos
Kattavia
Karpathos
Saria
Kasos
Stenon Karpathou
Stenon Kasou
Dodecanese
Astipalea
Amorgos
Naxos
Mykonos
Tinos
Ios
Thira
Anafi
Sikinos
Kolpos Mirabello
Iraklio (Heraklion)
Agios Nikolaos
Ierapetra
Sitia
Lasithi
Koufonisi
Gaidouronisi (Chrissi)
AIGAIO
VOREIO
AEGEAN SEA
CRETE
MEDITERRANEAN SEA

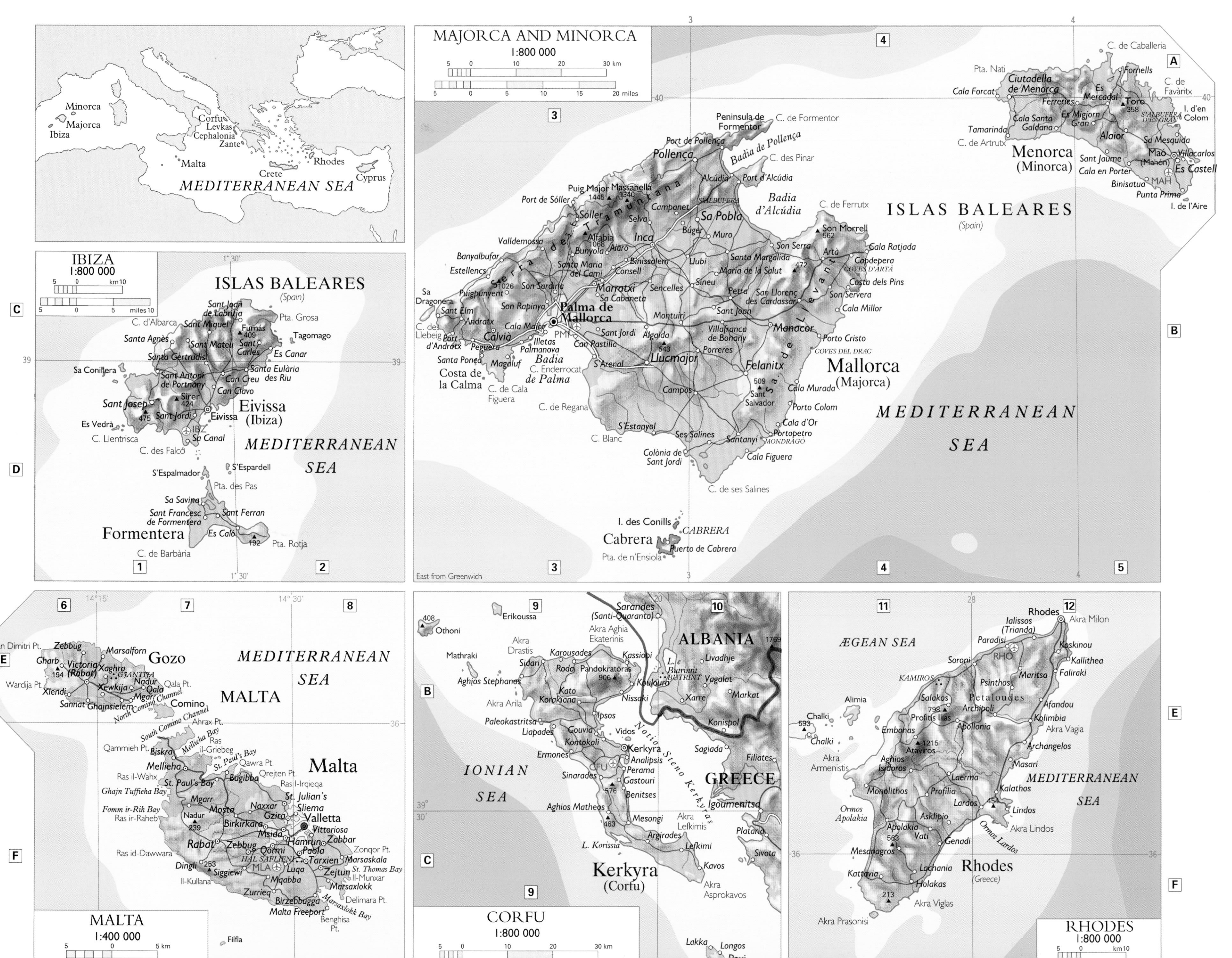
Minorca
Majorca
Ibiza
Corfu
Levkas
Cephalonia
Zante
Malta
Crete
Rhodes
Cyprus
MEDITERRANEAN SEA
MAJORCA AND MINORCA
1:800 000
ISLAS BALEARES
(Spain)
Menorca
(Minorca)
Ciutadella de Menorca
Maó (Mahón)
Mallorca
(Majorca)
Palma de Mallorca
Cabrera
MEDITERRANEAN
SEA
East from Greenwich
IBIZA
1:800 000
ISLAS BALEARES
(Spain)
Eivissa
(Ibiza)
Formentera
MEDITERRANEAN
SEA
MEDITERRANEAN
SEA
MALTA
Gozo
Comino
Malta
Valletta
MALTA
1:400 000
ALBANIA
GREECE
IONIAN
SEA
Kerkyra
(Corfu)
CORFU
1:800 000
ÆGEAN SEA
MEDITERRANEAN
SEA
Rhodes
(Greece)
RHODES
1:800 000

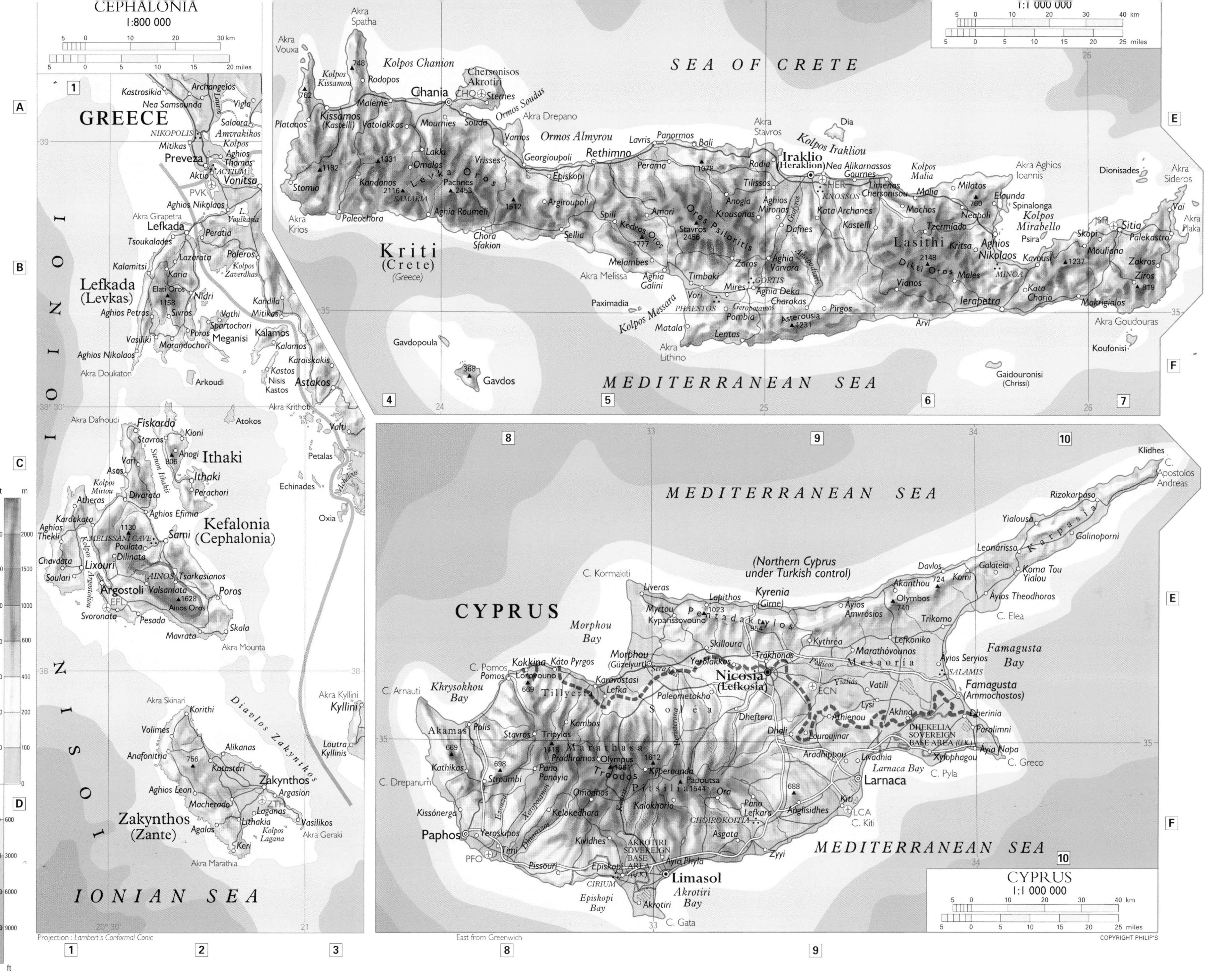
CEPHALONIA
1:800 000
GREECE
Lefkada (Levkas)
Ithaki
Kefalonia (Cephalonia)
Zakynthos (Zante)
Preveza
Vonitsa
Argostoli
Lixouri
IONIAN SEA
IONIOI NISOI
Kriti (Crete) (Greece)
SEA OF CRETE
MEDITERRANEAN SEA
Chania
Rethimno
Iraklio (Heraklion)
Agios Nikolaos
Sitia
Ierapetra
Gavdos
CYPRUS
(Northern Cyprus under Turkish control)
Nicosia (Lefkosia)
Famagusta (Ammochostos)
Larnaca
Limasol
Paphos
Kyrenia (Girne)
Morphou (Güzelyurt)
Troodos
Olympus
MEDITERRANEAN SEA
CYPRUS
1:1 000 000
Projection : Lambert's Conformal Conic
East from Greenwich
COPYRIGHT PHILIP'S

ASIA

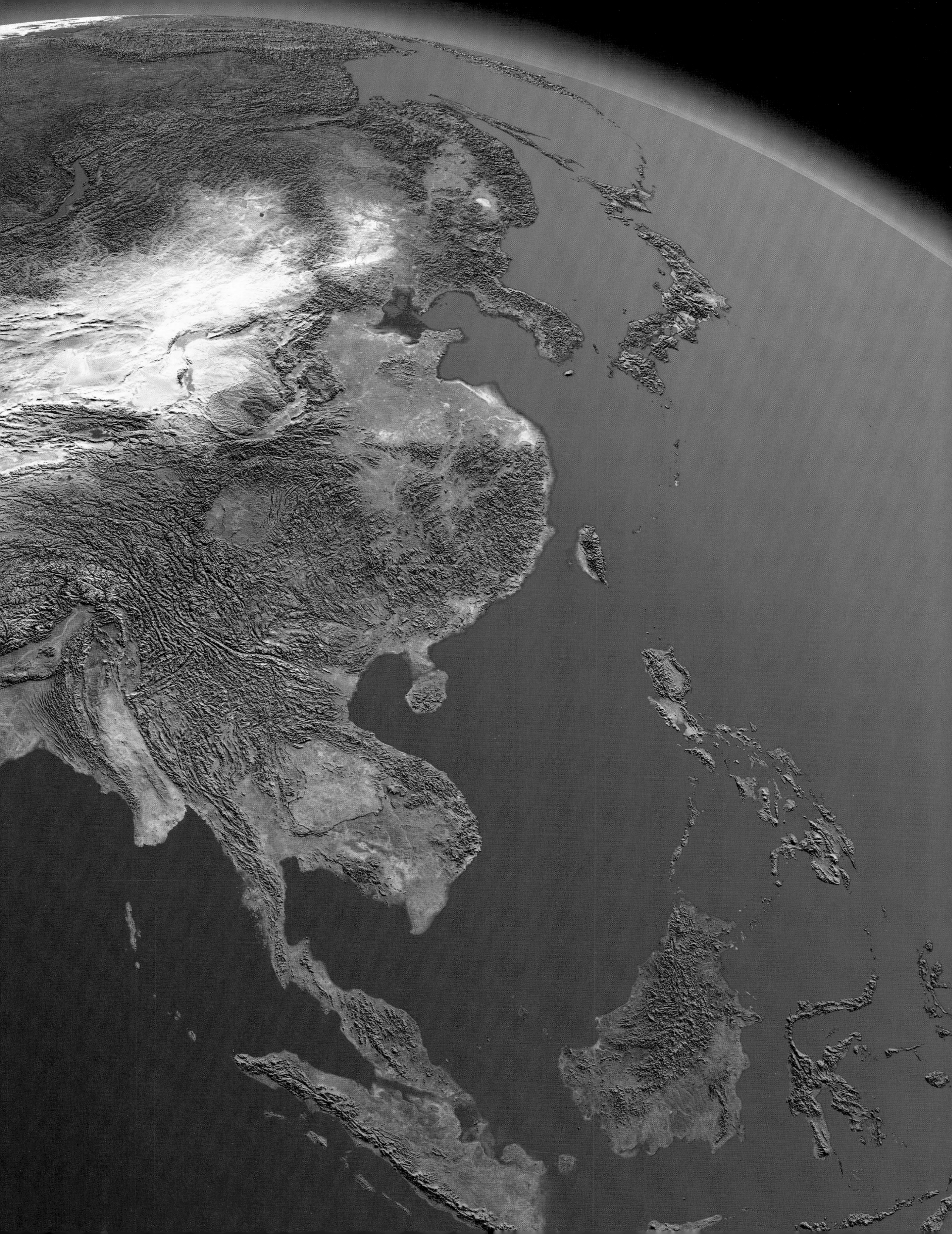

1:40 000 000

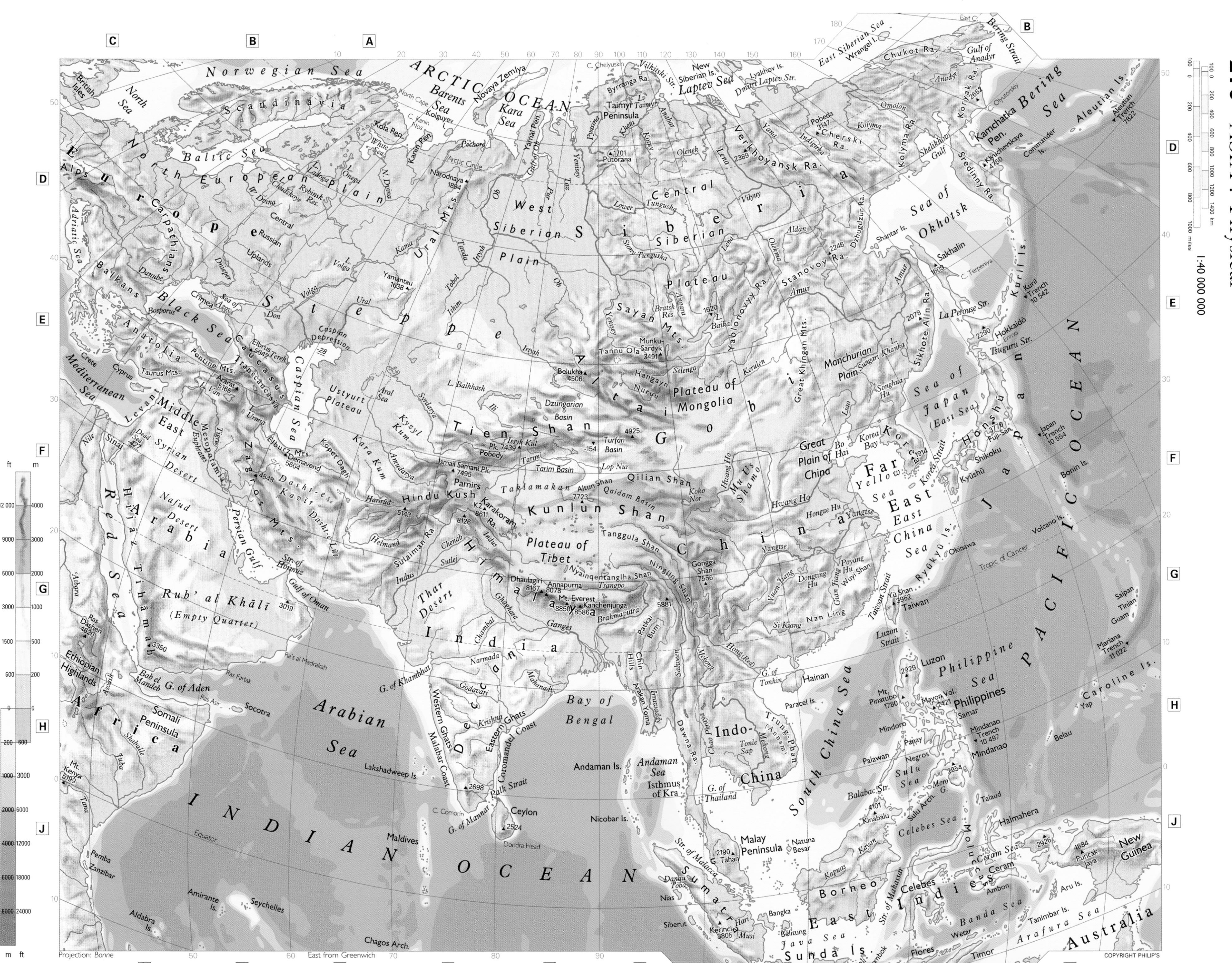
ARCTIC OCEAN
PACIFIC OCEAN
INDIAN OCEAN
Norwegian Sea
North Sea
Baltic Sea
Barents Sea
Kara Sea
Laptev Sea
East Siberian Sea
Bering Sea
Sea of Okhotsk
Sea of Japan (East Sea)
Yellow Sea
East China Sea
South China Sea
Philippine Sea
Sulu Sea
Celebes Sea
Java Sea
Banda Sea
Arafura Sea
Arabian Sea
Bay of Bengal
Andaman Sea
Caspian Sea
Black Sea
Mediterranean Sea
Red Sea
Persian Gulf
Gulf of Oman
G. of Aden
Europe
Scandinavia
North European Plain
Central Russian Uplands
Carpathians
Alps
Balkans
Caucasus
Ural Mts.
Steppe
Siberia
West Siberian Plain
Central Siberian Plateau
Verkhoyansk Ra.
Cherski Ra.
Kolyma Ra.
Stanovoy Ra.
Yablonovyy Ra.
Sayan Mts.
Altai
Gobi
Plateau of Mongolia
Tien Shan
Taklamakan
Tarim Basin
Kunlun Shan
Plateau of Tibet
Himalaya
Karakoram
Hindu Kush
Pamirs
Mt. Everest 8850
K2 8611
China
Far East
Manchurian Plain
Great Plain of China
Korea
Japan
Honshu
Hokkaido
Kyūshū
Shikoku
Sakhalin
Kamchatka Pen.
Taiwan
Hainan
Middle East
Anatolia
Mesopotamia
Zagros Mts.
Syrian Desert
Arabia
Rub' al Khālī (Empty Quarter)
Thar Desert
India
Deccan
Western Ghats
Eastern Ghats
Ceylon
Indo-China
Malay Peninsula
Sumatra
Borneo
Celebes
Philippines
East Indies
Sunda Is.
New Guinea
Australia
Africa
Ethiopian Highlands
Somali Peninsula
Projection: Bonne
East from Greenwich
COPYRIGHT PHILIP'S

1:40 000 000

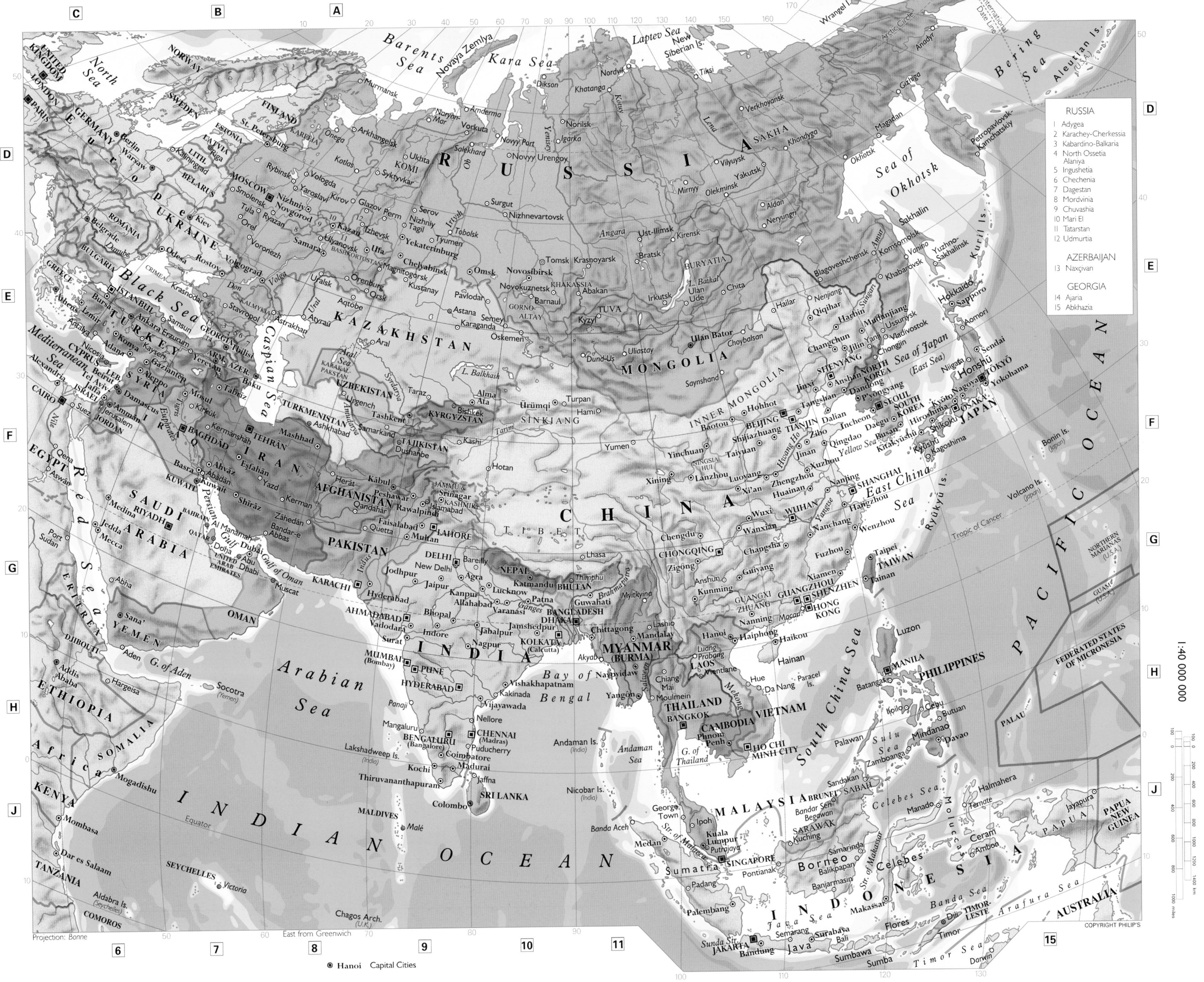
RUSSIA
1 Adygea
2 Karachey-Cherkessia
3 Kabardino-Balkaria
4 North Ossetia Alaniya
5 Ingushetia
6 Chechenia
7 Dagestan
8 Mordvinia
9 Chuvashia
10 Mari El
11 Tatarstan
12 Udmurtia
AZERBAIJAN
13 Naxçivan
GEORGIA
14 Ajaria
15 Abkhazia
Hanoi Capital Cities
East from Greenwich
Projection: Bonne
COPYRIGHT PHILIP'S
R U S S I A
C H I N A
I N D I A
M O N G O L I A
K A Z A K H S T A N
I N D O N E S I A
P A C I F I C O C E A N
I N D I A N O C E A N
Arabian Sea
Bay of Bengal
South China Sea
East China Sea
Sea of Okhotsk
Caspian Sea
Black Sea
Red Sea
Barents Sea
Kara Sea
Laptev Sea
Bering Sea
International Date Line
Tropic of Cancer
Equator

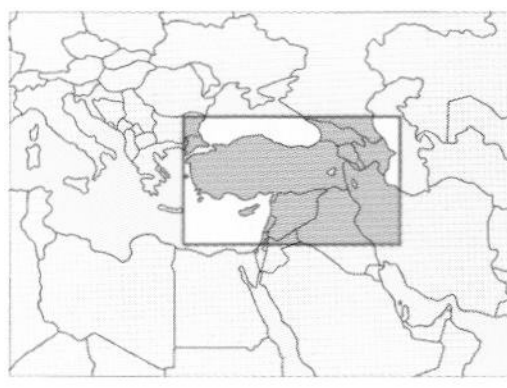

50 0 25 50 75 100 125 150 175 km

50 0 25 50 75 100 125 miles

1: 4 000 000

189

203

204

256

BULGARIA

BLACK SEA

TURKEY

GREECE

CYPRUS

(Northern Cyprus under Turkish control)

LEBANON

ISRAEL

WEST BANK

MEDITERRANEAN SEA

Anadolu

İSTANBUL

İstanbul Boğazi (Bosporus)

Marmara Denizi (Sea of Marmara)

ANKARA

BURSA

İZMIR (Smyrna)

KONYA

ADANA

GAZİANTEP (Antep)

Kayseri

Sivas

Samsun

Eskişehir

Antalya

Antalya Körfezi

Toros Dağlari

Küre Dağlari

Köroğlu Dağlari

Nicosia

Limassol

Larnaca

Famagusta

HALAB (Aleppo)

HIMS (Homs)

Ḥamāh

Al Lādhiqīyah (Latakia)

Ṭarābulus (Tripoli)

BAYRŪT (Beirut)

DIMASHQ (Damascus)

HEFA (Haifa)

TEL AVIV-YAFO

Jerusalem

'AMMĀN

Rhodes

Lesbos

Chios

Samos

Kos

Karpathos

Projection: Conical with two standard parallels

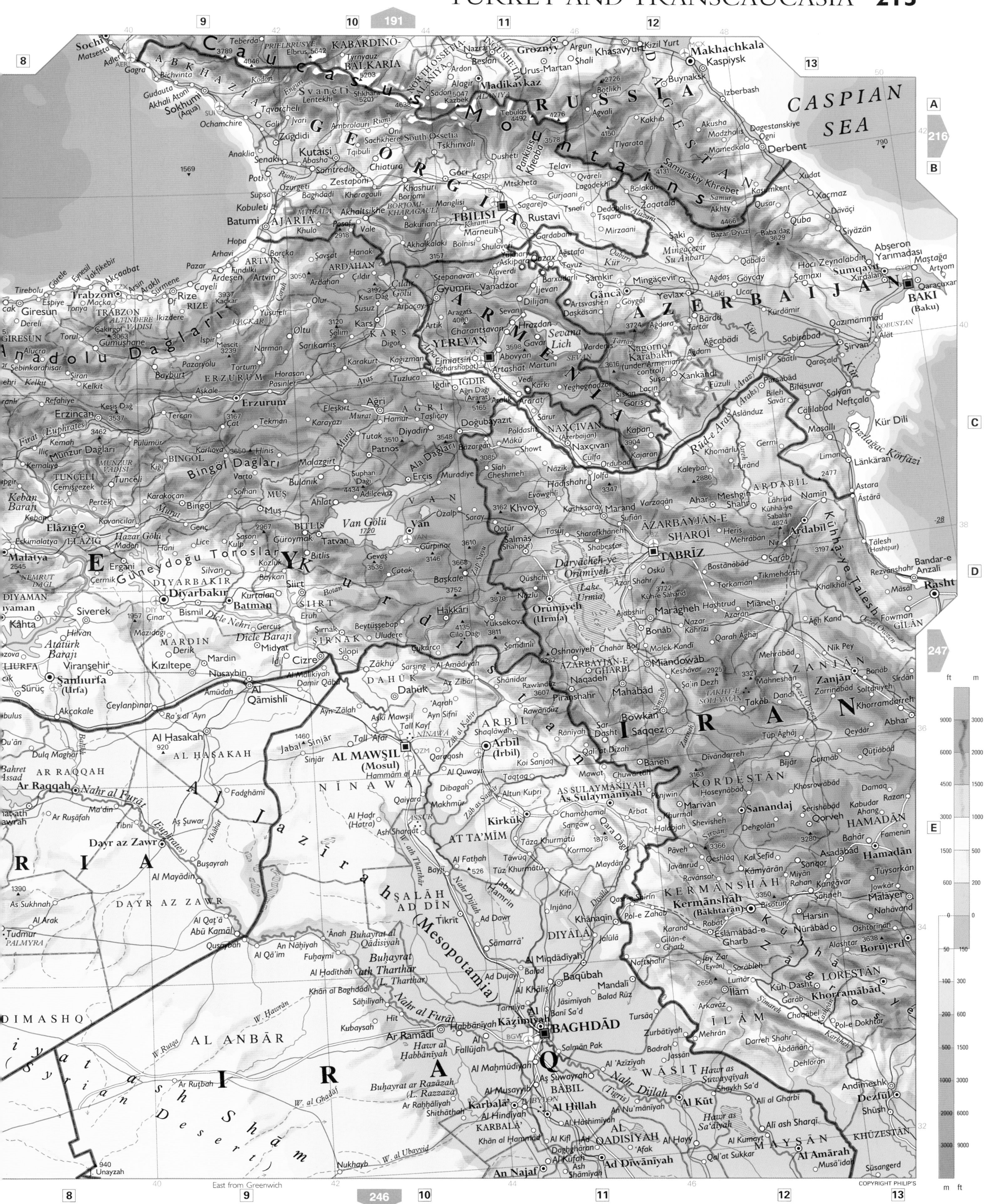

Underlined towns give their name to the administrative area in which they stand

100 0 100 200 300 400 500 600 700 800 km
1:16 000 000
100 0 100 200 300 400 500 miles
RUSSIA
1 Adygea
2 Karachey-Cherkessia
3 Kabardino-Balkaria
4 North Ossetia-Alaniya
5 Ingushetia
6 Chechenia
7 Dagestan
8 Mordvinia
9 Chuvashia
10 Mari El
11 Tatarstan
12 Udmurtia
13 Khakassia
AZERBAIJAN
14 Naxçivan
GEORGIA
15 Ajaria
16 Abkhazia
Norwegian Sea
Barents Sea
Kara Sea
Baltic Sea
North Sea
Gulf of Bothnia
Black Sea
Caspian Sea
Sea of Azov
Aral Sea
Zemlya Frantsa Iosifa
Novaya Zemlya
NORWAY
SWEDEN
FINLAND
ESTONIA
LATVIA
LITHUANIA
BELARUS
POLAND
UKRAINE
MOLDOVA
ROMANIA
GERMANY
DENMARK
RUSSIA
KAZAKHSTAN
UZBEKISTAN
TURKMENISTAN
KYRGYZSTAN
TAJIKISTAN
AFGHANISTAN
IRAN
IRAQ
TURKEY
GEORGIA
ARMENIA
AZERBAIJAN
MOSKVA
SANKT-PETERBURG
STOCKHOLM
HELSINKI
KYIV
MINSK
ASTANA
ALMATY
TASHKENT
BISHKEK
DUSHANBE
TEHRAN
BAKI (Baku)
YEREVAN
TBILISI
ASHGABAT
NOVOSIBIRSK
OMSK
YEKATERINBURG
CHELYABINSK
ÜRÜMQI
Ft m
12 000 4000
9000 3000
6000 2000
3000 1000
1200 400
600 200
0 0
200 600
2000 6000
4000 12 000
m ft
Projection: Conical Orthomorphic with two standard parallels
East from Greenwich

150

218

219

1:8 000 000
50 0 100 200 300 400 km
50 0 50 100 150 200 250 miles
191
214
187
247
ft m
18 000 6000
12 000 4000
9000 3000
6000 2000
4500 1500
3000 1000
1500 500
600 200
0 0
100 300
200 600
500 1500
m ft
Projection : Modified Miller oblated stereographic
RUSSIA
KAZAKHSTAN
UZBEKISTAN
TURKMENISTAN
AZERBAIJAN
ARMENIA
GEORGIA
TURKEY
IRAQ
IRAN
UKRAINE
CASPIAN SEA
Caspian Depression
Kirgiziya Steppe
Ustyurt Plateau
Caucasus Mountains
Privolzhskaya Vozvyshennost
Ergeni Vozvyshennost
Naryn Qum
Mughalzhar Taūy
Uralskie Gory
Garagum
Kopet Dagh
Reshteh-ye Kūhhā-ye Alborz (Elburz Mts)
Kūhhā-ye Zagros
Dasht-e Kavīr
Aral Sea
Northern Aral Sea
Southern Aral Sea
Garabogazköl Aylagy
Black Sea
Volga
Ural
Don
Emba
Orenburg
Oral
Aqtöbe
Atyraū
Astrakhan
Volgograd
Saratov
Samara
Togliatti
Ufa
Chelyabinsk
Magnitogorsk
Orsk
Qostanay
Rostov
Makhachkala
Grozny
Tbilisi
Yerevan
Baki (Baku)
Sumqayıt
Aqtaū
Türkmenbashi
Balkanabat (Nebitdag)
Ashgabat (Ashkhabad)
Nukus
Daşoguz
Urganch
Buxoro (Bukhara)
Türkmenabat (Chardzhou)
Mary
Mashhad
Tehrān
Qom
Tabrīz
Rasht
Kāshān
Hamadān
Baghdād
Al Mawşil
Herāt
Aral
Beyneu
Qulsary
Shalqar
Bayqonyr (Baikonur)

Underlined towns give their name to the administrative area in which they stand.

1:12 000 000

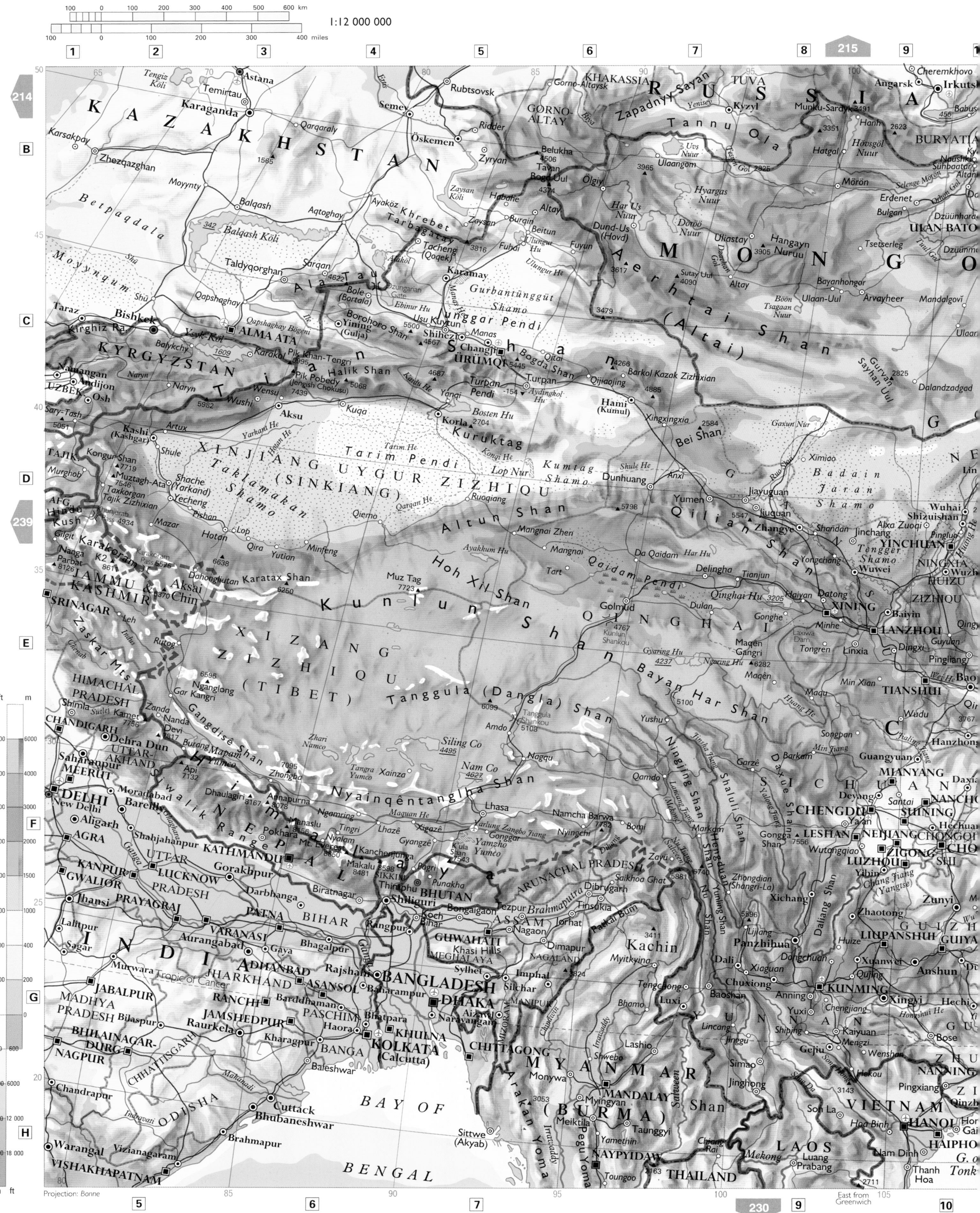
KAZAKHSTAN
RUSSIA
MONGOLIA
KYRGYZSTAN
XINJIANG UYGUR ZIZHIQU (SINKIANG)
XIZANG ZIZHIQU (TIBET)
QINGHAI
NEPAL
BHUTAN
BANGLADESH
INDIA
MYANMAR (BURMA)
LAOS
THAILAND
VIETNAM
BAY OF BENGAL
Tarim Pendi
Taklamakan Shamo
Kunlun Shan
Tian Shan
Himalaya
Tanggula (Dangla) Shan
Nyainqêntanglha Shan
Qilian Shan
Aerhtai Shan (Altai)
Junggar Pendi
Qaidam Pendi
Bayan Har Shan
ÜRÜMQI
ALMA ATA
Bishkek
Astana
Karaganda
KATHMANDU
DHAKA
KOLKATA (Calcutta)
DELHI
New Delhi
MANDALAY
NAYPYIDAW
KUNMING
CHENGDU
LANZHOU
XINING
YINCHUAN
HANOI
Lhasa
Mt. Everest 8850
K2 8611
Projection: Bonne
East from Greenwich

RUSSIA
NORTH KOREA
SOUTH KOREA
JAPAN
TAIWAN
PHILIPPINES
SEA OF JAPAN (EAST SEA)
YELLOW SEA
EAST CHINA SEA
SOUTH CHINA SEA
PACIFIC OCEAN
HEILONGJIANG
NEI MONGOL ZIZHIQU (INNER MONGOLIA)
Manchuria
Sakhalin
Hokkaidō
Honshū
Shikoku
Kyūshū
Hainan Dao
BEIJING
TIANJIN
SHANGHAI
HARBIN
SHENYANG
CHANGCHUN
P'YŎNGYANG
SEOUL
BUSAN
TŌKYŌ
ŌSAKA
NAGOYA
WUHAN
NANJING
GUANGZHOU (Canton)
SHENZHEN
HONG KONG (Xianggang)
T'AIPEI
Vladivostok
Khabarovsk
Korea Strait
Taiwan Strait
Tropic of Cancer
La Perouse Str.
Ryūkyū-Rettō
HONG KONG, MACAU AND SHENZHEN
1:800 000
Macau (Aomen)
Lantau Island (Tai Yue Shan)
Victoria
Kowloon (Jiulong)
GUANGDONG
Lingding Yang
COPYRIGHT PHILIP'S
232

1:4 000 000
km
miles
SEA OF OKHOTSK
SEA OF JAPAN
(EAST SEA)
Sakhalin
(Russia)
La Perouse Strait
(Sōya-Kaikyō)
HOKKAIDŌ
Hokkaidō
SAPPORO
Asahikawa
Kushiro
Obihiro
Hakodate
Otaru
Muroran
Wakkanai
Abashiri
Nemuro
Tsugaru-Kaikyō
Honshū
TŌHOKU
Aomori
SENDAI
Akita
Morioka
Niigata
Sado
Yamato Rise
RUSSIA
PRIMORSKIY KRAY
Khrebet Sikhote-Alin
Vladivostok
Nakhodka
Ussuriysk
Lake Khanka
Zaliv Petra Velikogo
CHINA
HEILONGJIANG
JILIN
Dongbei (Manchuria)
NORTH KOREA
Ch'ŏngjin
Najin
Hunchun
Tumen
JIXI
Hulin
Fujin
Hegang
JIAMUSI
Shuangyashan
219
227

SEA OF JAPAN
PACIFIC OCEAN
SOUTH KOREA
Korea Strait
CHŪGOKU
SHIKOKU
KYŪSHŪ
KINKI
KANTŌ
TŌKYŌ
YOKOHAMA
KAWASAKI
NAGOYA
HAMAMATSU
KYŌTO
KŌBE
ŌSAKA
HIROSHIMA
KITAKYŪSHŪ
FUKUOKA
Izu-Shotō
Oki-Shotō
Tsushima (Japan)
Ulleungdo (S. Korea)
Liancourt Rocks (Dokdo, Takeshima)
Kii-Suidō
Bungo-Suidō
Tosa-Wan
Wakasa-Wan
Toyama-Wan
Suruga-Wan
Ise-Wan
Ōsumi-Kaikyō
Tokara-Kaikyō
Tanegashima-Kaikyō
Tokara-Rettō
Ōsumi-Shotō
Satsunan-Shotō
RYUKYU ISLANDS
on same scale
EAST CHINA SEA
Ryūkyū-Shotō (Ryukyu Is.)
Okinawa-Guntō
Amami-Guntō
Sakishima-Guntō
Yaeyama-Rettō
Miyako-Rettō
Senkaku-Shotō
Okinawa-Jima
Naha
Amami-Ō-Shima
Projection: Conical with two standard parallels
East from Greenwich
COPYRIGHT PHILIP'S

1:2 000 000
km
miles
SEA OF JAPAN
(EAST SEA)
Yeongdeok
Heunghae
224
Pohang
SOUTH KOREA
Oki-Shotō
Daimanji-San
Dōgo
608
Saigō
Dōzen
DAISEN-OKI
Honshu
SANIN-KAIGAN
Shimane-Hantō
Jizō-Zaki
DAISEN-OKI
Matsue
Hirata
Shinji-Ko
Sakaiminato
Yonago
Hi-no-Misaki
Taisha
Shinji
Yasugi
Izumo
Daitō
Kisuki
TOTTORI
Iwami
Tottori
Kasumi
Toyooka
Hidaka
Kurayoshi
Dai-Sen
1729
Suga-no-Sen
1510
Wadayama
Wakasa
Chizu
DAISEN-OKI
CHŪGOKU-DISTRICT
Korea Strait
Ōda
IWAMI GINZAN
Sanbe-San
1126
Yunotsu
Gōtsu
Gō-Gawa
Dōgo-San
1269
Chūgoku-Sanchi
Katsuyama
Ochiai
Tsuyama
Ikuno
HYŌGO
Yamasaki
Nishiwaki
Hamada
SHIMANE
Bingo-Ochiai
Niimi
Tōjō
OKAYAMA
Yanahara
Sayo
Kasai
Tatsuno
Himeji
Aioi
Takasago
Kakogawa
Akashi
Kara-Saki
Kamiagata
Kamitsushima
Mi-Shima
Shōbara
Takahashi
Wake
Miyoshi
Masuda
HIROSHIMA
Akiōta
Yoshida
Okayama
Sōja
Bizen
Akō
Saidaiji
Ieshima-Shotō
Harima-Nada
Tsushima
Fuchū
Ibara
Yakage
Kurashiki
Kannabe
Kojima
Tamano
Shōdo-Shima
Tonoshō
Higashi-Hiroshima
Fukuyama
Kasaoka
Mihara
Onomichi
Awaji-Shima
Ōta-Gawa
Ōmi-Shima
Hagi
Aono-Yama
908
Kanmuri-Yama
1339
Tsuno-Shima
Atō
HIROSHIMA
Hatsukaichi
ITSUKUSHIMA SHRINE
Kaita
Takehara
Kure
In'noshima
Sakaide
Takamatsu
Sanuki
Sumoto
Mitsushima
Izuhara
649
Kō-Saki
Hibiki-Nada
Nagato
YAMAGUCHI
Yamaguchi
Ōtake
Hiroshima-Wan
Marugame
Higashi-kagawa
Naruto-Kaikyō
Toyoura
Mine
Ōgōri
Iwakuni
Ondo
Kurahashi-Jima
Ōmi-Shima
Tadotsu
Zentsūji
KAGAWA
Kotohira
Naruto
Minami-awaji
Higashi-Suidō
Genkai-Nada
San'yō
Hōfu
Tokuji
Shin-Nan'yō
Shūnan
Aki-Nada
Imabari
Hiuchi-Nada
Kan'onji
Onohara
Sanyuki-Sammyaku
Itano
Yoshino-gawa
Tokushima
Mima
Katsumoto
Iki
Gō-no-ura
Iki-Kaikyō
Ō-Shima
Munakata
Shimonoseki
Onoda
Ube
Kudamatsu
Yanai
Hikari
Niihama
Shikokuchūō
Hōjō
SETO NAIKAI
Ikeda
Komatsushima
Nakama
KITAKYŪSHŪ
Suō-Nada
Naga-Shima
Yashiro-Jima
Matsuyama
Toyo
Saijō
Iyo-Mishima
TOKUSHIMA
Anan
Fukuma
Koga
Nōgata
Iwai-Jima
Heigun-Tō
Iyo
Ishizuchi-Yama
1981
Shikoku-Sanchi
Ōtoyo
Tsurugi-San
1955
Gamoda-Saki
FUKUOKA
Miyata
Yukuhashi
Hime-Jima
Ō-Shima
Yobuko
Maebaru
Iizuka
Tagawa
Nakatsu
Futago-Yama
721
Nagahama
KŌCHI
1423
Ikitsuki-Shima
Karatsu
Kasuga
Dazaifu
Kama
Buzen
Kunisaki
Iyo-Nada
Kuma
EHIME
Mugi
Hirado
FUKUOKA
Tsukushi-Sanchi
Sefuri-San
1055
Chikushino
1200
Usa
Bungotakada
Sada-Misaki-Hantō
Hogo-Kaikyō
Ōzu
Uchiko
1562
Nankoku
Kami
Noichi
514
Matsuura
SAGA
Tosu
Ogōri
Amagi
Kitsuki
Yawatahama
Ino
Kōchi
Sakawa
Aki
Tōyō
Hirado-Shima
SAIKAI
Imari
Taku
Ogi
Kurume
Hita
Hiji
Sada-Misaki
Tosa
Saza
Takeo
Saga
Chikugo
Yufu-Dake
1584
Beppu-Wan
Uwa
Susaki
Tosa-Wan
Sasebo
Arita
Ōkawa
Yame
Kurogi
Kusu
Beppu
Tsurusaki
Saganoseki
Uwajima
Kihoku
Muroto
Yanagawa
Kashima
Ureshino
1076
Ariake-Tara
ASO-KUJŪ
1787
ŌITA
Ōita
Usuki
Shimanto
Muroto-Misaki
Shikoku
SHIKOKU-DISTRICT
NAGASAKI
Ōmura-Wan
Tara-Dake
Ariake-Kai
Ōmuta
Yamaga
Oguni
Kujū-San
Bungo-Suidō
Tsushima
Nishi-Tosa
Saga
Ōmura
Arao
Kikuchi
Aso
Tsukumi
Mie
Nishi-Sonogi-Hantō
Isahaya
Nagayo
Tamana
Kumamoto
Kōshi
Ichinomiya
Taketa
Mishō
Shimanto
Unzen-Dake
1360
Ōzu
Mashiki
Aso-Zan
1592
Sobo-Yama
1758
Saiki
Tsurumi-Saki
Sukumo
Nagasaki
Shimabara
KUMAMOTO
Kamae
ASHIZURI-UWAKAI
865
Tosa-Shimizu
Tachibana-Wan
Obama
UNZEN-AMAKUSA
Uto
Takachiho
Nomo-Zaki
Kuchinotsu
Misumi
Matsubase
Hinokage
Oki-no-Shima
Ashizuri-Zaki
Amakusa-Nada
Hondo
Matsushima
Kunimi-Dake
1739
Nobeoka
Amakusa-Shotō
Kami-Jima
UNZEN-AMAKUSA
Yatsushiro
Shiiba
Shimo-Jima
Yatsushiro-Kai
Itsuki
Hyūga
Taragi
MIYAZAKI
Kyūshū-Sanchi
Ushibuka
Hitoyoshi
Kyūshū
Minamata
Naga-Shima
Izumi
Tamana
Saito
Takanabe
KYŪSHŪ-DISTRICT
Akune
Ōkuchi
Ebino
Kami-Koshiki-Jima
Miyanojō
Yoshimatsu
1700
Kobayashi
Sadowara
Kurino
Kirishima-Yama
KIRISHIMA YAKU
Miyazaki
Satsuma-Sendai
Kyūshū-Palau Ridge
Koshiki-Rettō
604
Kushikino
Aira
Kirishima
Hayato
Miyakonojō
Shimo-Koshiki-Jima
Kagoshima
On-Take
Sakurajima
1118
Ijūin
Sōo
Nichinan
Koshiki-Kaikyō
KAGOSHIMA
Fukiage
Tarumizu
Shibushi
Aburatsu
Noma-Saki
Kaseda
Satsuma-Hantō
Kagoshima-Wan
Kanoya
Kushima
Kawanabe
Osaki
Shibushi-Wan
Kiire
Makurazaki
Bō-no-Misaki
Ibusuki
Kōyama
968
Kaimon-Dake
924
Yamagawa
Ōsumi-Hantō
KIRISHIMA YAKU
Sata-Misaki
Kyūshū Trench
5737
Projection: Lambert's Conformal Conic
Shinkansen lines

7
8
9
10
220
11
12
A
B
C
D
E
CHŪBU-DISTRICT
KANTŌ-DISTRICT
KINKI-DISTRICT
TOYAMA
ISHIKAWA
FUKUI
GIFU
NAGANO
GUNMA
TOCHIGI
IBARAKI
SAITAMA
CHIBA
YAMANASHI
KANAGAWA
SHIZUOKA
AICHI
MIE
SHIGA
KYŌTO
NARA
WAKAYAMA
TŌKYŌ
YOKOHAMA
KAWASAKI
NAGOYA
KYŌTO
ŌSAKA
Higashiōsaka
Sakai
Hamamatsu
Shizuoka
Saitama
Chiba
Utsunomiya
Maebashi
Takasaki
Nagano
Matsumoto
Kōfu
Toyama
Kanazawa
Fukui
Gifu
Tsu
Himi
Takaoka
Imizu
Uozu
Hitachi
Kashima
Mito
Tsukuba
Hachiōji
Sagamihara
Odawara
Atami
Numazu
Fuji
Mishima
Gotemba
Toyohashi
Okazaki
Toyota
Tokai
Ōtsu
Kusatsu
Hikone
Yokkaichi
Suzuka
Matsusaka
Ise
Toba
Shingū
Tanabe
Kushimoto
Wakayama
Hida-Sammyaku
Kiso-Sammyaku
Akaishi-Sammyaku
Kantō-Sanchi
Kii-Hantō
Izu-Hantō
Bōsō-Hantō
Shima-Hantō
Ise-Wan
Suruga-Wan
Sagami-Wan
Tōkyō-Wan
Wakasa-Wan
Enshū-Nada
Kumano-Nada
Sagami-Nada
Kashima-Nada
Izu-Shotō
Nampō-Shotō
Ō-Shima
To-Shima
Nii-Jima
Shikine-Jima
Kōzu-Shima
Miyake-Jima
Mikura-Jima
Hachijō-Jima
Aoga-Shima
Beyoneisu Retsugun
Sumisu-Jima
PACIFIC OCEAN
Omae-Zaki
Irō-Zaki
Shio-no-Misaki
Daiō-Misaki
Irago-Zaki
Nojima-Zaki
Inubō-Zaki
Echizen-Misaki
Kyō-ga-Saki
East from Greenwich
136
137
138
139
140
141
32
33
34
35
36
ft
m
9000
6000
4500
3000
1200
600
0
3000
2000
1500
1000
400
200
200
1000
2000
3000
4000
5000
600
3000
6000
9000
12 000
15 000
COPYRIGHT PHILIP'S

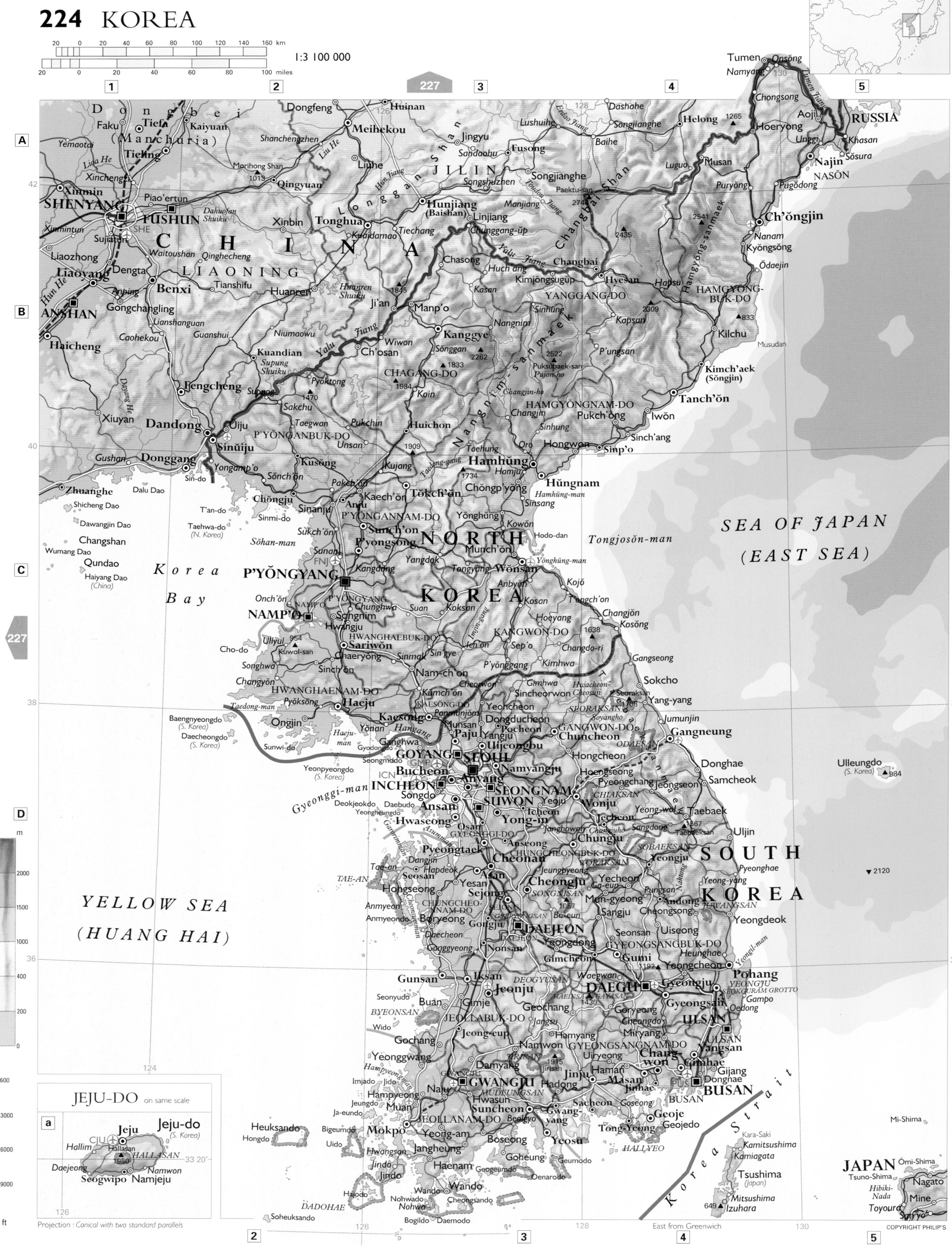
1:3 100 000
km
miles
227
Dongbei (Manchuria)
CHINA
JILIN
LIAONING
Changbai Shan
Longgang Shan
SHENYANG
FUSHUN
Tieling
Faku
Tiefa
Kaiyuan
Xinmin
Liaoyang
ANSHAN
Benxi
Haicheng
Fengcheng
Dandong
Donggang
Zhuanghe
Meihekou
Huinan
Dongfeng
Tonghua
Hunjiang (Baishan)
Ji'an
Changbai
Tumen
Namyang
Onsŏng
RUSSIA
Khasan
Najin
NASŎN
Ch'ŏngjin
Hoeryong
Musan
Paektu-san
2744
Hyesan
Kimjŏngsugŭp
YANGGANG-DO
HAMGYŎNG-BUK-DO
Hamgyŏng-sanmaek
Kilchu
Kimch'aek (Sŏngjin)
Tanch'ŏn
Kanggye
CHAGANG-DO
Manp'o
Yalu Jiang
Sinŭiju
P'YŎNGANBUK-DO
HAMGYŎNGNAM-DO
Nangnim-sanmaek
Hamhŭng
Hŭngnam
Sinp'o
NORTH KOREA
P'YŎNGYANG
NAMP'O
P'YŎNGANNAM-DO
Wŏnsan
Korea Bay
KANGWON-DO
HWANGHAEBUK-DO
HWANGHAENAM-DO
Sariwŏn
Haeju
Kaesŏng
Panmunjŏm
Baengnyeongdo (S. Korea)
SEA OF JAPAN (EAST SEA)
Tongjosŏn-man
SEOUL
INCHEON
GOYANG
Bucheon
SEONGNAM
SUWON
Anyang
Ansan
Uijeongbu
Chuncheon
GANGWON-DO
Gangneung
Donghae
Samcheok
Ulleungdo (S. Korea)
984
Gyeonggi-man
GYEONGGI-DO
Pyeongtaek
Cheonan
Cheongju
CHUNGCHEONGBUK-DO
CHUNGCHEONGNAM-DO
Chungju
Wonju
Jecheon
Taebaek
Uljin
SOUTH KOREA
DAEJEON
Andong
Yeongdeok
Pohang
Gyeongju
GYEONGSANGBUK-DO
DAEGU
Gumi
ULSAN
BUSAN
Gimhae
Changwon
Masan
Jinju
GYEONGSANGNAM-DO
JEOLLABUK-DO
Jeonju
Iksan
Gunsan
Jeong-eup
GWANGJU
JEOLLANAM-DO
Mokpo
Suncheon
Yeosu
Geoje
Tong-Yeong
Korea Strait
Tsushima (Japan)
Izuhara
JAPAN
Mi-Shima
YELLOW SEA (HUANG HAI)
JEJU-DO on same scale
Jeju
Jeju-do (S. Korea)
Hallasan
1950
Seogwipo
Namjeju
33 20'
Projection: Conical with two standard parallels
East from Greenwich
COPYRIGHT PHILIP'S
ft
m
High-speed rail routes

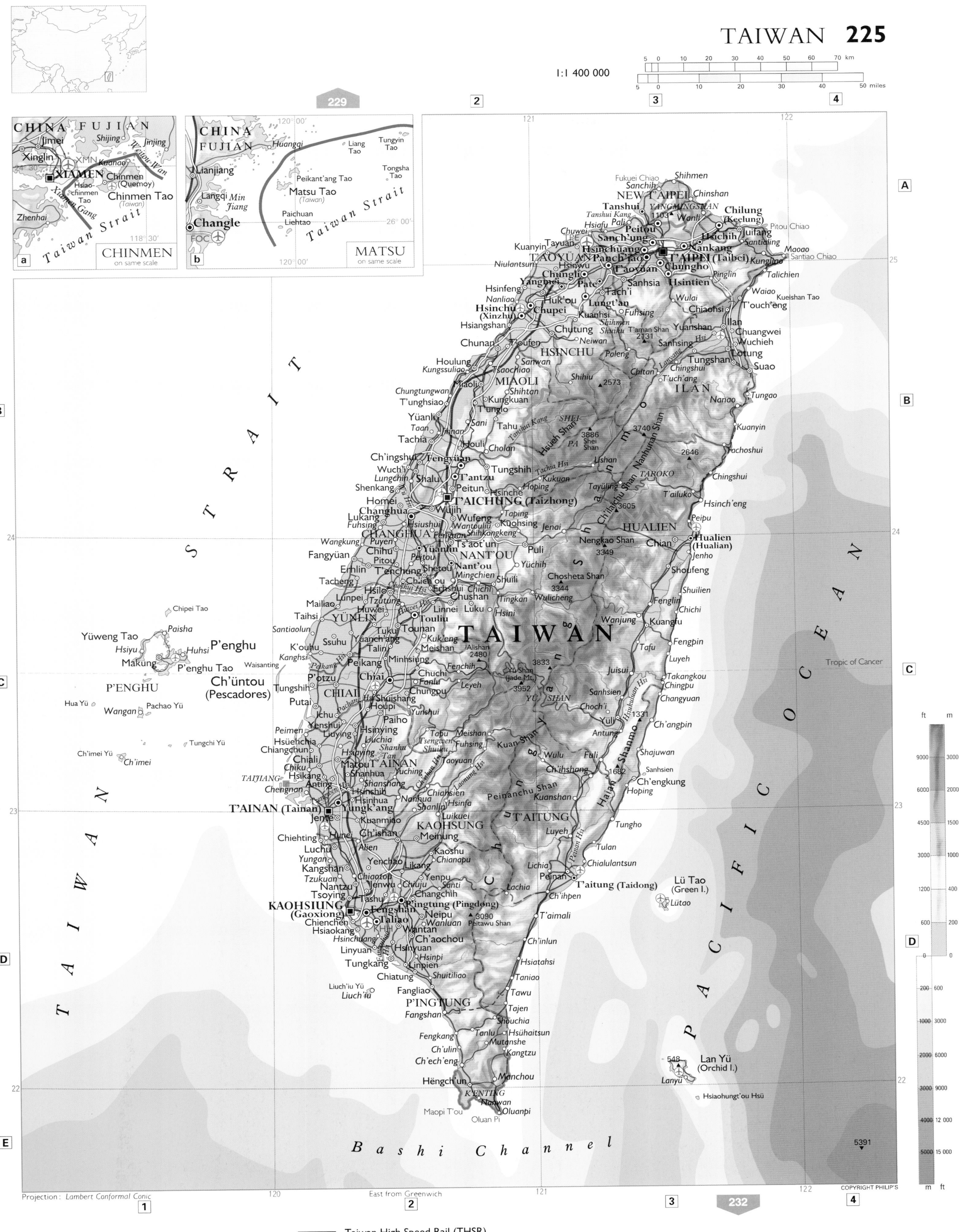
1:1 400 000
km
miles
229
232
CHINA FUJIAN
Jimei
Shijing
Jinjing
Xinglin
XMN
Kuanao
XIAMEN
Weitou Wan
Chinmen (Quemoy)
Hsiao-chinmen Tao
Chinmen Tao (Taiwan)
Xiamen Gang
Zhenhai
Taiwan Strait
CHINMEN
on same scale
CHINA FUJIAN
Huangqi
Liang Tao
Tungyin Tao
Tongsha Tao
Lianjiang
Peikant'ang Tao
Matsu Tao (Taiwan)
Langqi
Min Jiang
Paichuan Liehtao
Changle
FOC
Taiwan Strait
MATSU
on same scale
TAIWAN STRAIT
PACIFIC OCEAN
Bashi Channel
TAIWAN
Fukuei Chiao
Shihmen
Sanchih
NEW T'AIPEI
Chinshan
Tanshui
YANGMINGSHAN
Chilung (Keelung)
Tanshui Kang
Pitou Chiao
Peitou
Hsichih
Juifang
T'AIPEI (Taibei)
Chungho
Sanchung
Hsinchuang
Panch'iao
Kuanyin
Tayuan
TAOYUAN
T'aoyuan
Niulantsun
Chungli
Yangmei
Hsintien
Sanhsia
Santiao Chiao
Talichien
Waiao
Kueishan Tao
T'ouch'eng
Hsinfeng
Nanliao
Hsinchu (Xinzhu)
Chupei
Hsiangshan
Chutung
Wulai
Chiaohsi
Yuanshan
Ilan
Chuangwei
Wuchieh
Lotung
Suao
Chunan
Toufen
HSINCHU
Neiwan
Houlung
Kungssuliao
Miaoli
MIAOLI
Tungshan
ILAN
Nanao
Tungao
Chungtungwan
T'unghsiao
Yüanli
Tachia
Hsüeh Shan
3886
3740
2646
Kuanyin
Tachoshui
Ch'ingshui
Fengyüan
T'antzu
Tungshih
Shenkang
Shalu
T'AICHUNG (Taizhong)
TAROKO
Chingshui
Hsinch'eng
Homei
Changhua
Lukang
Fuhsing
CHANGHUA
Wujih
Wufeng
3605
Peifu
Hualien (Hualian)
Jenho
HUALIEN
Chian
Wangkung
Puyen
Yüanlin
NANT'OU
Nant'ou
Puli
Nengkao Shan 3349
Fangyüan
Erhlin
Tacheng
Chosheta Shan 3344
Shoufeng
Shuilien
Mailiao
YÜNLIN
Touliu
Fenglin
Chichi
Chipei Tao
Paisha
Yüweng Tao
Hsiyu
Huhsi
P'enghu
Makung
P'enghu Tao
P'ENGHU
Ch'üntou (Pescadores)
Hua Yü
Wangan
Pachao Yü
Tungchi Yü
Ch'imei Yü
Ch'imei
Taihsi
Santiaolun
Tuku
Tounan
Kuangfu
Tafu
Fengpin
Alishan 2480
Yü Shan (Jade Mt.) 3952
YÜ SHAN
Tropic of Cancer
Chiai
CHIAI
Putai
Tungshih
Chingpu
Takangkou
Changyuan
Yüli
1331
Ch'angpin
Shajuwan
Sanhsien
Ch'engkung
T'AINAN (Tainan)
Jente
T'AINAN
Kuan Shan
T'AITUNG
Tungho
KAOHSUNG
Chiehting
Luchu
Kangshan
Tsoying
KAOHSIUNG (Gaoxiong)
Fengshan
KHH
Pingtung (Pingdong)
3090
Peitawu Shan
Tulan
Chialulantsun
Peinan
T'aitung (Taidong)
Lü Tao (Green I.)
Lütao
Ch'ihpen
T'aimali
Ch'inlun
Hsiatahsi
Taniao
Tawu
Tajen
Linyuan
Tungkang
Liuch'iu Yü
Liuch'iu
Fangliao
P'INGTUNG
Fangshan
Shouchia
Fengkang
Hsühaitsun
Mutanshe
Kangtzu
Ch'ech'eng
Hengch'un
Manchou
KENTING
Nanwan
Maopi T'ou
Oluanpi
Oluan Pi
Lan Yü (Orchid I.)
548
Lanyu
Hsiaohungt'ou Hsü
5391
ft
m
Projection: Lambert Conformal Conic
East from Greenwich
COPYRIGHT PHILIP'S
Taiwan High Speed Rail (THSR)

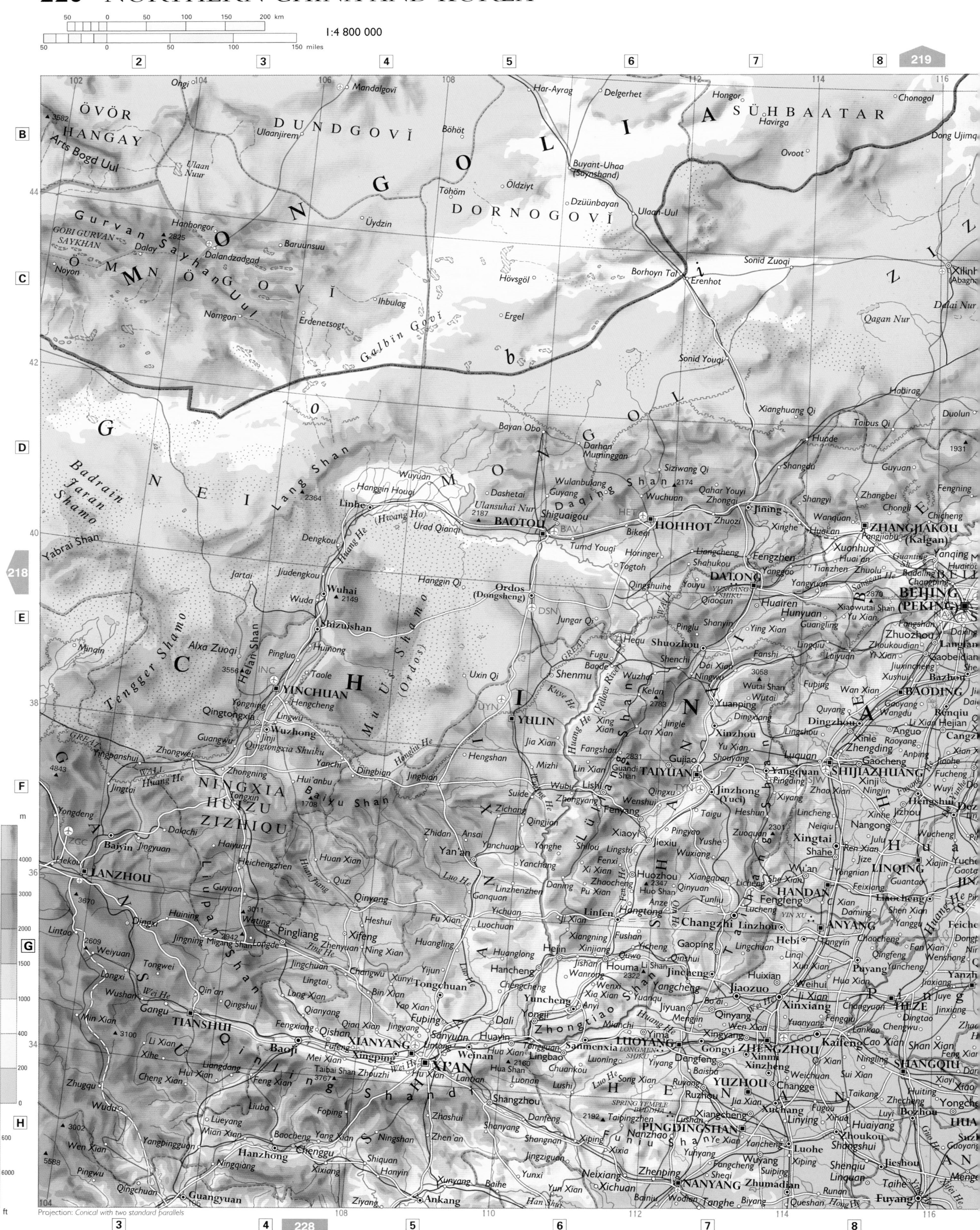

1:4 800 000
50 0 50 100 150 200 km
50 0 50 100 150 miles
ÖVÖR HANGAY
DUNDGOVĬ
DORNOGOVĬ
SÜHBAATAR
ÖMNÖGOVĬ
MONGOLIA
Gobi
NEI MONGOL
CHINA
NINGXIA HUIZU ZIZHIQU
GANSU
SHAANXI
SHANXI
HEBEI
HENAN
Mandalgovĭ
Ulaanjirem
Böhöt
Har-Ayrag
Delgerhet
Hongor
Havirga
Chonogol
Ovoot
Dong Ujimqin Qi
Arts Bogd Uul
Ulaan Nuur
Buyant-Uhaa (Saynshand)
Töhöm
Öldziyt
Dzüünbayan
Ulaan-Uul
Üydzin
Hanhongor
Gurvan Sayhan Uul
Dalay
Dalandzadgad
Baruunsuu
Noyon
Hövsgöl
Borhoyn Tal
Erenhot
Sonid Zuoqi
Xilinhot
Ihbulag
Nomgon
Erdenetsogt
Galbïn Govĭ
Ergel
Dalai Nur
Qagan Nur
Sonid Youqi
Xianghuang Qi
Duolun
Taibus Qi
Huade
Bayan Obo
Darhan Muminggan
Badrain Jaran Shamo
Lang Shan
Yabrai Shan
Wuyuan
Hanggin Houqi
Linhe
Dashetai
Ulansuhai Nur
Guyang
Daqing Shan
Wuchuan
Siziwang Qi
Qahar Youyi Zhongqi
Jining
Shangdu
Guyuan
Fengning
Zhangbei
Chongli
Chicheng
Shangyi
BAOTOU
HOHHOT
Shiguaigou
Urad Qianqi
Bikeqi
Zhuozi
Xinghe
Wanquan
ZHANGJIAKOU (Kalgan)
Huai'an
Xuanhua
Yanqing
Dengkou
Huang He (Hwang Ho)
Tumd Youqi
Horinger
Togtoh
Liangcheng
Shahukou
Fengzhen
Yanggao
Tianzhen
Zhuolu
Jartai
Jiudengkou
Wuhai
Wuda
Hanggin Qi
Ordos (Dongsheng)
Qingshuihe
Youyu
DATONG
Huairen
Hunyuan
Yangyuan
BEIJING (PEKING)
Shizuishan
Mu Us Shamo (Ordos)
Jungar Qi
Pinglu
Shanyin
Ying Xian
Guangling
Laiyuan
Zhuozhou
Alxa Zuoqi
Tengger Shamo
Helan Shan
Minqin
Huinong
Pingluo
Taole
YINCHUAN
Uxin Qi
Fugu
Baode
Hequ
Shuozhou
Shenchi
Dai Xian
Ningwu
Wutai Shan
Fuping
Wan Xian
BAODING
Yongning
Qingtongxia
Lingwu
Wuzhong
Shenmu
Wuzhai
Kelan
Yuanping
Dingxiang
Dingzhou
YULIN
Jia Xian
Xing Xian
Lan Xian
Jingle
Xinzhou
Guangwu
Zhongwei
Jinji
Qingtongxia Shuiku
Yanchi
Dingbian
Jingbian
Hengshan
Mizhi
Lin Xian
Fangshan
Gujiao
TAIYUAN
Shouyang
Yangquan
SHIJIAZHUANG
Xinji
Jingtai
Zhongning
Hui'anbu
Baiyu Shan
Suide
Wubu
Lishi
Zhongyang
Jinzhong (Yuci)
Wenshui
Fenyang
Qingxu
Taigu
Xiyang
Heshun
Hengshui
Yongdeng
Dalachi
Baiyin
Jingyuan
Haiyuan
Zichang
Qingjian
Xiaoyi
Jiexiu
Pingyao
Yushe
Zuoquan
Xingtai
Nangong
Zhidan
Ansai
Yan'an
Yanchuan
Yonghe
Shilou
Lingshi
Wuxiang
Shahe
LANZHOU
Hekou
Huan Xian
Heichengzhen
Liupan Shan
Yanchang
Fenxi
Xi Xian
Huozhou
Huo Shan
Qinyuan
Linzhenzhen
Daning
Pu Xian
Zhaocheng
HANDAN
LINQING
Guyuan
Quzi
Ganquan
Yichuan
Qinyang
Anze
Tunliu
Licheng
Fengfeng
Changzhi
Linzhou
ANYANG
Dingxi
Huining
Wating
Pingliang
Xifeng
Heshui
Fu Xian
Luochuan
Linfen
Hongtong
Jingning
Migang Shan
Longde
Zhenyuan
Ning Xian
Huangling
Xiangning
Xinjiang
Fushan
Yicheng
Gaoping
Hebi
Lintao
Weiyuan
Tongwei
Jingchuan
Changwu
Xunyi
Yijun
Huanglong
Hejin
Houma
Jincheng
Qinshui
Puyang
Longxi
Wushan
Gangu
Lingtai
Long Xian
Bin Xian
Tongchuan
Hancheng
Wanrong
Wenxi
Xia Xian
Yangcheng
Jiaozuo
Xinxiang
Huixian
Ji Xian
HEZE
Qin'an
Qingshui
Qianyang
Yao Xian
Yuncheng
Anyi
Zhongtiao Shan
Yuanqu
Jiyuan
Mengjin
Qinyang
Wei He
Min Xian
TIANSHUI
Fengxiang
Qishan
Qian Xian
Jingyang
Fuping
Sanyuan
Dali
Yongji
Mianchi
Yima
Wen Xian
Xingyang
Fengqiu
Kaifeng
Cao Xian
Li Xian
Xihe
Baoji
XIANYANG
Fufeng
Xingping
Mei Xian
Zhouzhi
XI'AN
Weinan
Huayin
Hua Xian
Hua Shan
Tongguan
Sanmenxia
Lingbao
Luoning
LUOYANG
Longmen Shiku
Gongyi
ZHENGZHOU
Xinmi
Xinzheng
SHANGQIU
Cheng Xian
Hui Xian
Liangdang
Feng Xian
Taibai Shan
Qinling Shandi
Lantian
Luonan
Lushi
Song Xian
Yiyang
Dengfeng
Baisha
YUZHOU
Ruyang
Ruzhou
Weichuan
Changge
Zhugqu
Wudu
Liuba
Foping
Zhashui
Shangzhou
Danfeng
Spring Temple Buddha
Xiangcheng
Xuchang
Jia Xian
Linying
Zhecheng
Bozhou
Lueyang
Mian Xian
Baocheng
Yang Xian
Ningshan
Zhen'an
Shanyang
Shangnan
Taipingzhen
PINGDINGSHAN
Funiu Shan
Ye Xian
Yancheng
Luohe
Zhoukou
Huaiyang
Shangshui
Wen Xian
Pingwu
Yangpingguan
Hanzhong
Chenggu
Xixiang
Ningqiang
Shiquan
Hanyin
Jingziguan
Yunxi
Xiping
Xixia
Neixiang
Xichuan
Zhenping
Wuyang
Fangcheng
Sheqi
Suiping
Xiping
Shenqiu
Linquan
Jieshou
Qingchuan
Guangyuan
Ankang
Xunyang
Baihe
Ziyang
Yun Xian
Han Shui
Bainiu
Wodian
NANYANG
Tanghe
Biyang
Zhumadian
Runan
Queshan
Taihe
Fuyang
Projection: Conical with two standard parallels

219
218
228

HARBIN
CHANGCHUN
SHENYANG
DALIAN
P'YŎNGYANG
SEOUL
INCHEON
BUSAN
DAEGU
NORTH KOREA
SOUTH KOREA
SEA OF JAPAN (EAST SEA)
YELLOW SEA (HUANG HAI)
BO HAI
Korea Bay
Korea Strait
JAPAN
RUSSIA
Vladivostok
TIANJIN
QINGDAO
YANTAI
Shandong Bandao
Liaodong Wan
East from Greenwich
COPYRIGHT PHILIP'S

1:4 800 000

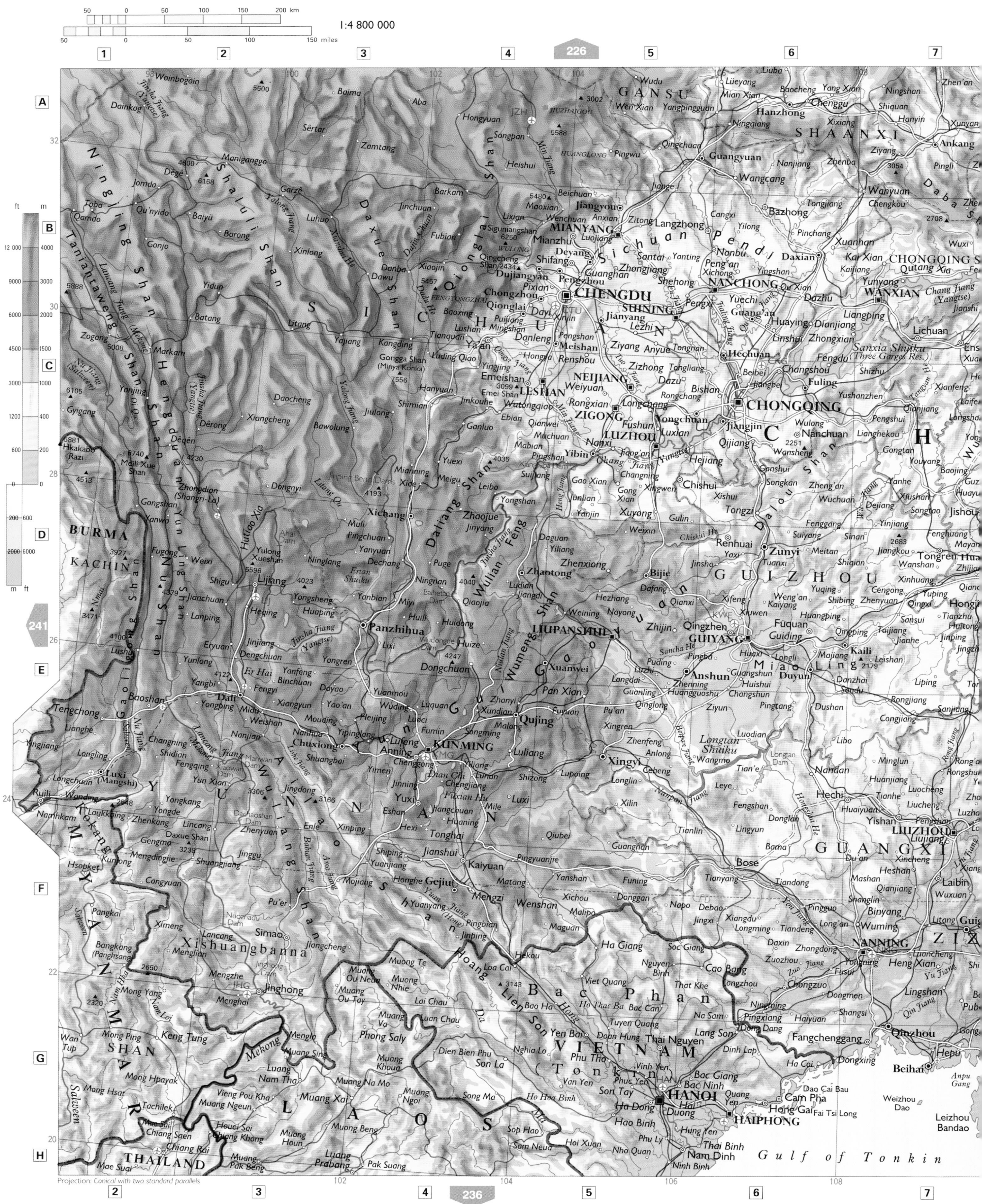

50 0 50 100 150 200 km
50 0 50 100 150 miles
226
236
241
GANSU
SHAANXI
SICHUAN
Sichuan Pendi
GUIZHOU
GUANGXI
YUNNAN
BURMA
KACHIN
MYANMAR
SHAN
LAOS
THAILAND
VIETNAM
(Tonkin)
Bac Phan
Xishuangbanna
Gulf of Tonkin
CHENGDU
CHONGQING
KUNMING
GUIYANG
NANNING
HANOI
HAIPHONG
MIANYANG
NANCHONG
SUINING
NEIJIANG
ZIGONG
LUZHOU
LESHAN
WANXIAN
LIUPANSHUI
LIUZHOU
Panzhihua
Xichang
Lijiang
Dali
Zunyi
Qujing
Anshun
Kaili
Baoshan
Jinghong
Simao
Gejiu
Kangding
Batang
Litang
Hanzhong
Ankang
Guangyuan
Bose
Qinzhou
Beihai
Luang Prabang
Dien Bien Phu
Nam Dinh
Sanxia Shuiku (Three Gorges Res.)
Longtan Shuiku
Gongga Shan (Minya Konka)
Daxue Shan
Qionglai Shan
Shaluli Shan
Ningjing Shan
Taniantaweng Shan
Hengduan Shan
Yun Ling Shan
Nu Shan
Gaoligong Shan
Daliang Shan
Wuliang Shan
Ailao Shan
Hoang Lien Son
Dalou Shan
Miao Ling
Daba Shan
Wumeng Shan
Jinsha Jiang (Yangtze)
Lancang Jiang (Mekong)
Nu Jiang (Salween)
Yalong Jiang
Min Jiang
Jialing Jiang
Hongshui He
Nanpan Jiang
Yuan Jiang (Hong)
Mekong
Salween
Er Hai
Dian Chi
Fuxian Hu
Projection: Conical with two standard parallels

227
HENAN
ANHUI
JIANGSU
HUNAN
JIANGXI
ZHEJIANG
FUJIAN
GUANGDONG
TAIWAN
SHANGHAI SHI
SHANGHAI
NANJING
WUHAN
CHANGSHA
NANCHANG
HANGZHOU
FUZHOU
GUANGZHOU (CANTON)
SHENZHEN
DONGGUAN
HONG KONG (XIANGGANG)
XIAMEN (Amoy)
SHANTOU
T'AIPEI
KAOHSIUNG
T'AICHUNG
T'AINAN
WENZHOU
NINGBO
HEFEI
CHANGZHOU
SUZHOU
WUXI
XINYANG
XIANGFAN
YUEYANG
HENGYANG
ZHUHAI
ZHANJIANG
Chang Jiang (Yangtse)
Poyang Hu
Dongting Hu
Tai Hu
Taiwan Strait
Luzon Strait
SOUTH CHINA SEA
Gulf of Tonkin
HAINAN
Hainan Dao
HAIKOU
VIETNAM
CHINA
Tropic of Cancer
East from Greenwich
HAINAN on same scale
COPYRIGHT PHILIP'S

1:10 000 000
Projection: Mercator
East from Greenwich
MYANMAR
YANGON (Rangoon)
THAILAND
BANGKOK (Krung Thep)
LAOS
VIETNAM
CAMBODIA
PHNOM PENH
THANH PHO HO CHI MINH (Saigon)
Vientiane (Viangchan)
Da Nang
Hue
CAN THO
Gulf of Thailand
ANDAMAN SEA
SOUTH CHINA SEA
Paracel Islands
Spratly Islands
Macclesfield Bank
Malay Peninsula
MALAYSIA
KUALA LUMPUR
SINGAPORE
Johor Bahru
BRUNEI
Bandar Seri Begawan
Kota Kinabalu
SABAH
SARAWAK
Kuching
Straits of Malacca
MEDAN
Padang
Pekanbaru
PALEMBANG
Jambi
INDONESIA
Greater Sunda Islands
JAVA SEA
JAKARTA
BANDUNG
Semarang
SURABAYA
Denpasar
Jawa (Java)
Java Trench
INDIAN OCEAN
Kepulauan Mentawai
Kepulauan Natuna
Kepulauan Anambas
Bangka
Belitung
Banjarmasin
Pontianak
Kalimantan (Borneo)
Bandar Lampung
Bengkulu
Phuket
George Town
Banda Aceh

JAVA AND MADURA
1:6 000 000
BALI
1:1 600 000
JAKARTA
Bogor
BANDUNG
Cirebon
Tegal
Semarang
Yogyakarta
Surakarta
Madura
SURABAYA
Malang
Jember
Banyuwangi
Bali
Denpasar
Singaraja
Lombok
Mataram
Jawa
BALI SEA
INDIAN OCEAN
Luzon
MANILA
Quezon City
Mindoro
Samar
Panay
Cebu
Negros
Mindanao
DAVAO
Zamboanga
General Santos
SULU SEA
CELEBES SEA
Sulawesi (Celebes)
Manado
Gorontalo
Halmahera
Ternate
MOLUCCA SEA
PACIFIC OCEAN
Equator
IRIAN JAYA BARAT
PAPUA
Pegunungan Maoke
Jayapura
PAPUA NEW GUINEA
Seram (Ceram)
Ambon
Buru
MALUKU
BANDA SEA
Kepulauan Aru
Kepulauan Tanimbar
ARAFURA SEA
Flores
Sumba
Sawu Sea
Timor
Dili
TIMOR-LESTE
NUSA TENGGARA TIMUR
Kupang
Lesser Sunda Is.
COPYRIGHT PHILIP'S

1:3 200 000

20 0 20 40 60 80 100 120 140 160 km
20 0 20 40 60 80 100 miles
continuation northwards on same scale
225
PHILIPPINE SEA
PACIFIC OCEAN
SOUTH CHINA SEA
Luzon Strait
Balintang Channel
Babuyan Channel
Babuyan Islands
Batan Islands
BATANES
CAGAYAN
Luzon
MANILA
Quezon City
Mindoro
Mindoro Strait
Sibuyan
Mindanao Trench
Benham Seamount
Scarborough Shoal
Lingayen Gulf
Lamon Bay
Lagonoy Gulf
Ragay G.
Polillo Islands
Catanduanes Island
CALABARZON
BICOL
ft
m

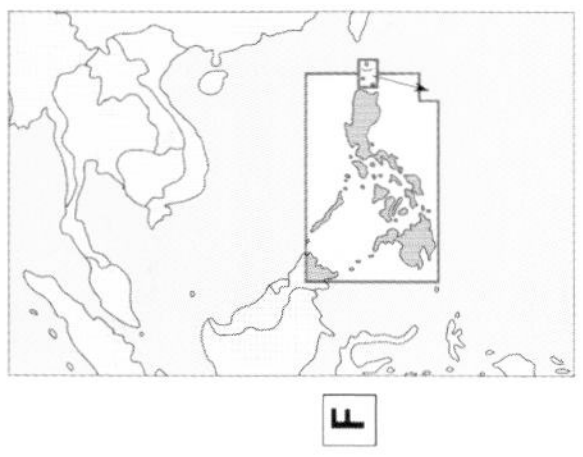

Projection: Lambert Conformal Conic

East from Greenwich

MIMAROPA
Palawan
Palawan Passage
Cuyo West Pass.
Cuyo East Pass.
Panay
Negros
VISAYAS
Sulu Sea
Mindanao
Celebes Sea
Moro Gulf
Sulu Archipelago
Bohol Sea
Camotes Sea
Leyte Gulf
Visayan Sea
Illana Bay
Davao Gulf
CARAGA
BANGSAMORO
SOCCSKSARGEN
MALAYSIA
SABAH
Borneo
Zamboanga
Cebu
Iloilo
Bacolod
Davao
Cagayan de Oro
Puerto Princesa
Tacloban
General Santos
Cotabato
Surigao
Butuan
Sandakan
Pulau Miangas (Indonesia)

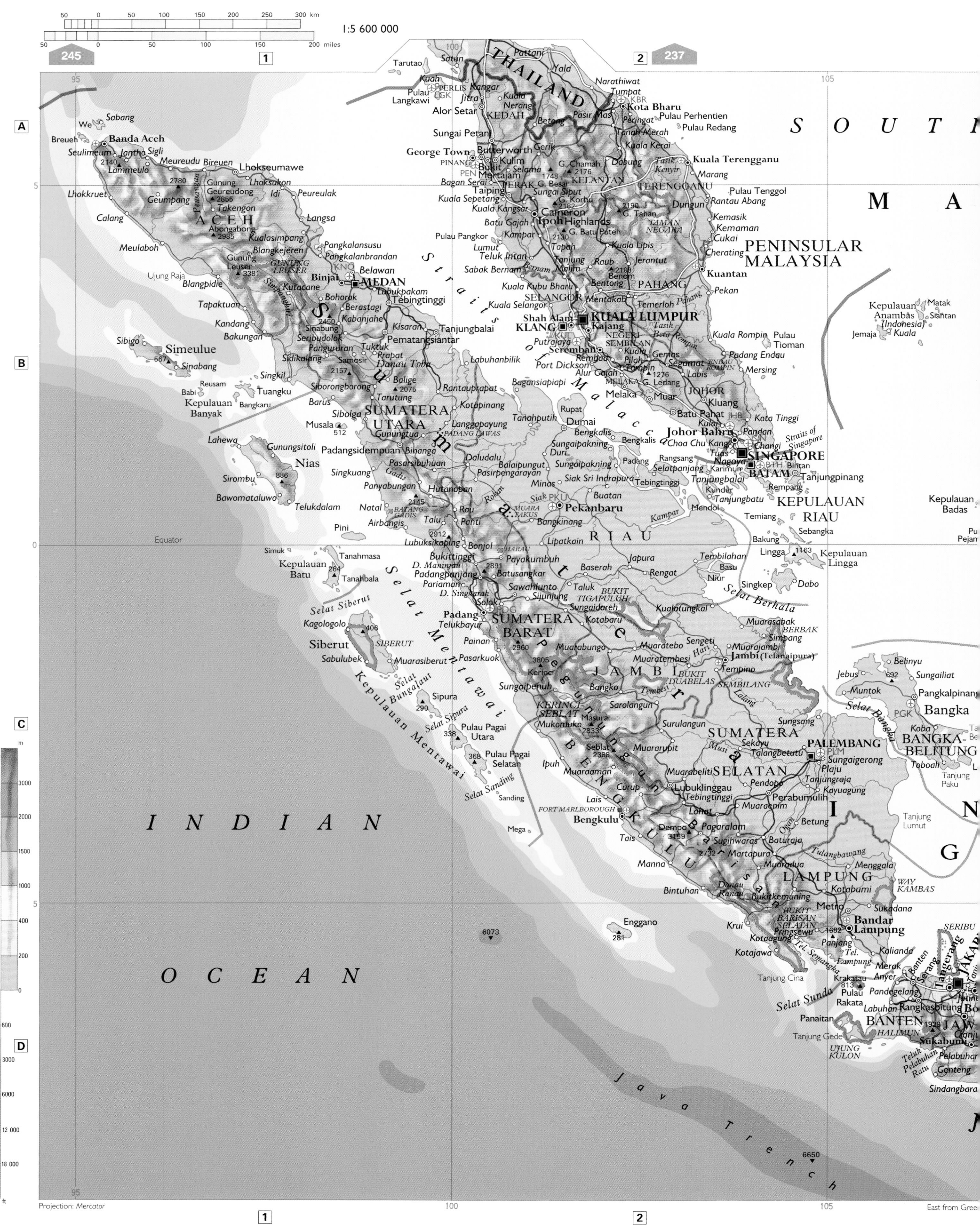
1:5 600 000
km
miles
245
237
SOUTH
MA
THAILAND
PENINSULAR MALAYSIA
KEDAH
PERAK
KELANTAN
TERENGGANU
PAHANG
SELANGOR
NEGERI SEMBILAN
MELAKA
JOHOR
ACEH
SUMATERA UTARA
SUMATERA BARAT
RIAU
JAMBI
BENGKULU
SUMATERA SELATAN
LAMPUNG
BANTEN
KEPULAUAN RIAU
BANGKA-BELITUNG
Sumatera
Straits of Malacca
Selat Mentawai
Kepulauan Mentawai
Pegunungan Barisan
INDIAN OCEAN
Java Trench
Equator
SINGAPORE
KUALA LUMPUR
MEDAN
PALEMBANG
Banda Aceh
Sabang
Lhokseumawe
Binjai
Belawan
Tebingtinggi
Pematangsiantar
Tanjungbalai
Sibolga
Padangsidempuan
Nias
Simeulue
Pekanbaru
Dumai
Bukittinggi
Padang
Siberut
Jambi
Bengkulu
Enggano
Bandar Lampung
George Town
Butterworth
Ipoh
Cameron Highlands
Kota Bharu
Kuala Terengganu
Kuantan
Klang
Seremban
Melaka
Johor Bahru
Batam
Tanjungpinang
Bangka
Pangkalpinang
Singkep
Lingga
Kepulauan Lingga
Kepulauan Anambas (Indonesia)
Pulau Tioman
Pulau Langkawi
Alor Setar
Sungai Petani
Taiping
Kepulauan Batu
Kepulauan Banyak
Pulau Pagai Utara
Pulau Pagai Selatan
Selat Sunda
Selat Bangka
Selat Berhala
Danau Toba
Krakatau
6073
6650
Projection: Mercator
East from Greenwich

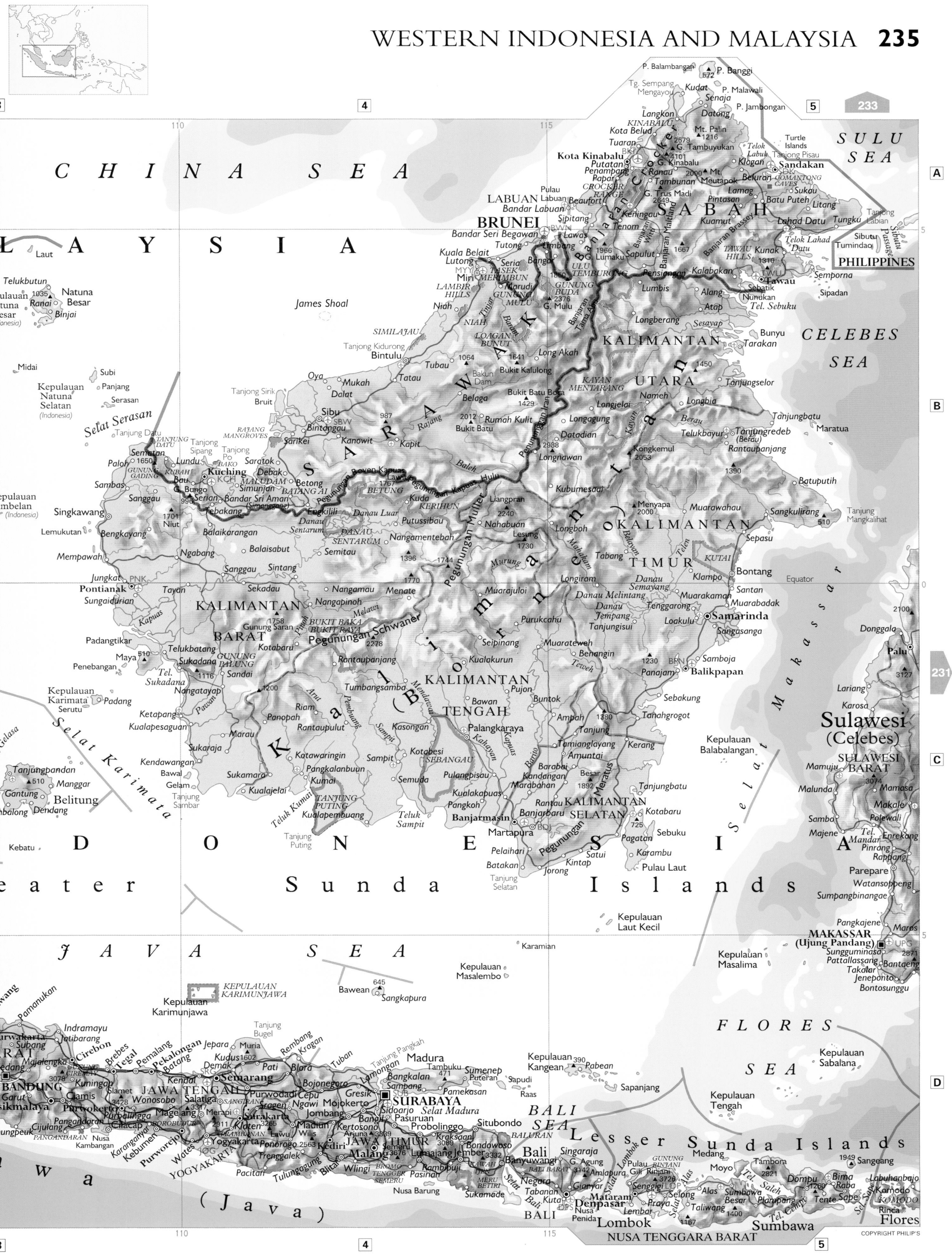

CHINA SEA
SULU SEA
CELEBES SEA
JAVA SEA
FLORES SEA
BALI SEA
MALAYSIA
INDONESIA
Greater Sunda Islands
Lesser Sunda Islands
Jawa (Java)
Kalimantan (Borneo)
Sulawesi (Celebes)
SULAWESI BARAT
SABAH
SARAWAK
BRUNEI
LABUAN
PHILIPPINES
KALIMANTAN UTARA
KALIMANTAN TIMUR
KALIMANTAN BARAT
KALIMANTAN TENGAH
KALIMANTAN SELATAN
JAWA TENGAH
JAWA TIMUR
YOGYAKARTA
BALI
NUSA TENGGARA BARAT
Selat Makasar
Selat Karimata
Selat Serasan
Selat Madura
Equator
James Shoal
Natuna Besar
Kepulauan Natuna Selatan (Indonesia)
Kepulauan Karimata
Belitung
Kepulauan Karimunjawa
Bawean
Madura
Kepulauan Masalembo
Kepulauan Laut Kecil
Kepulauan Masalima
Kepulauan Kangean
Kepulauan Sabalana
Kepulauan Tengah
Kepulauan Balabalangan
Pulau Laut
Bali
Lombok
Sumbawa
Flores
Nusa Penida
Kota Kinabalu
Sandakan
Tawau
Bandar Seri Begawan
Miri
Bintulu
Sibu
Kuching
Pontianak
Singkawang
Tarakan
Bontang
Samarinda
Balikpapan
Palangkaraya
Banjarmasin
Martapura
Palu
MAKASSAR (Ujung Pandang)
Surabaya
Semarang
Bandung
Cirebon
Yogyakarta
Surakarta
Malang
Denpasar
Mataram
Pegunungan Schwaner
Pegunungan Müller
Pegunungan Meratus
Pegunungan Iran
Banjaran Crocker
Mt. Kinabalu
Gunung Mulu
Mahakam
Kapuas
Barito
Kayan
Rajang
Turtle Islands
Sipadan
Tumindao
Sibutu Passage
233
231
4
5
A
B
C
D
110
115

1:4 800 000

50 0 50 100 150 200 km

50 0 50 100 150 miles

Gulf of Thailand
SOUTH CHINA SEA
MALAYSIA
PENINSULAR MALAYSIA
INDONESIA
Straits of Malacca
Kho Khot Kra (Isthmus of Kra)
Myeik Kyunzu (Mergui Archipelago)
PHNOM PENH
THANH PHO HO CHI MINH (Saigon)
CAN THO
KUALA LUMPUR
SINGAPORE
MEDAN
SUMATERA UTARA
ACEH
RIAU
KEDAH
PERAK
KELANTAN
TERENGGANU
PAHANG
SELANGOR
JOHOR
MELAKA
PERLIS
PINANG
1:800 000
KO PHUKET
1:800 000
Ko Phuket
ANDAMAN SEA
KO SAMUI
1:800 000
Gulf of Thailand
Ko Samui
PINANG
1:800 000
Pulau Pinang
SINGAPORE
1:800 000
Straits of Singapore
Projection: Conical with two standard parallels
104 East from Greenwich
238
COPYRIGHT PHILIP'S

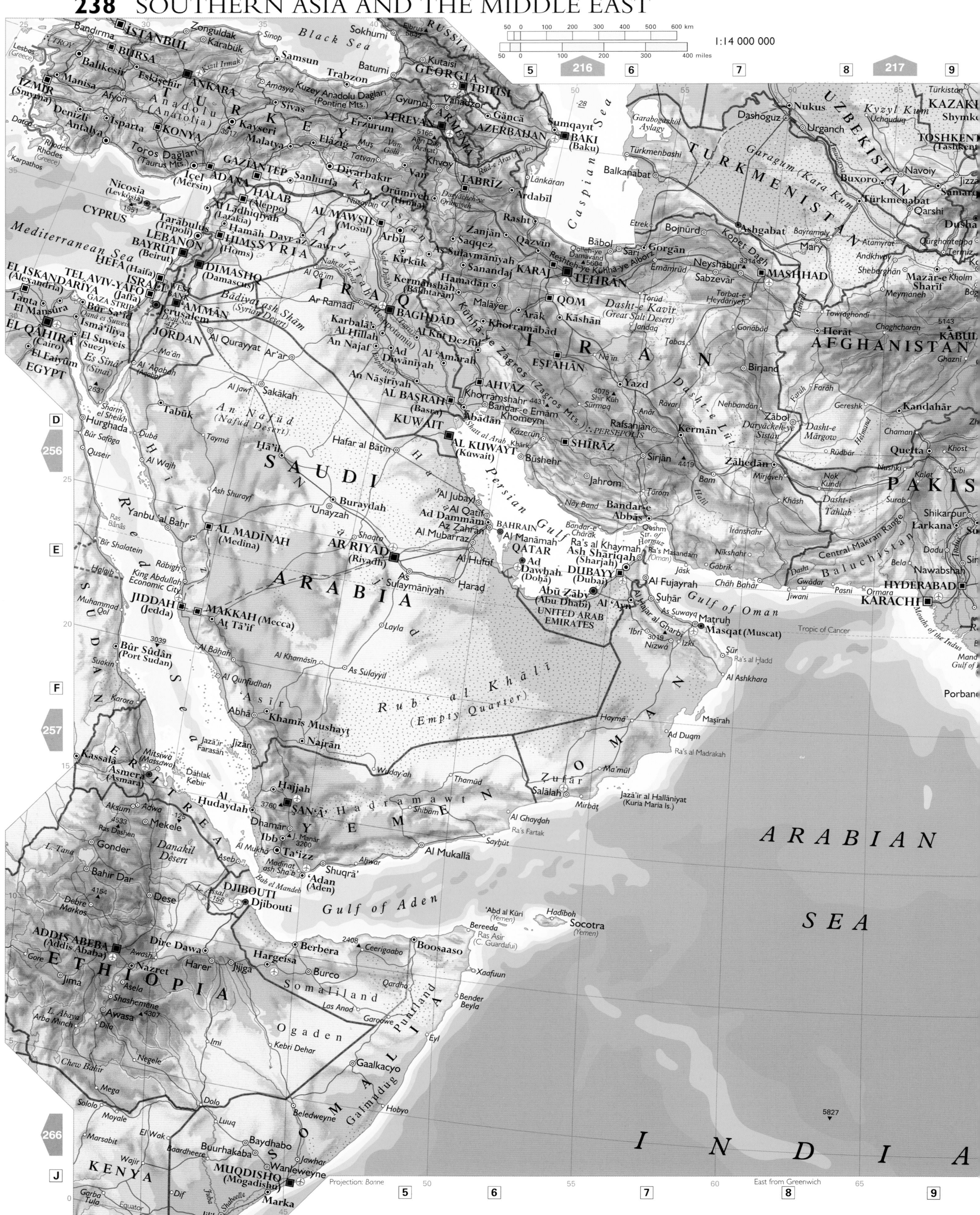

1:14 000 000
Projection: Bonne
East from Greenwich
Tropic of Cancer
Black Sea
Caspian Sea
Mediterranean Sea
Red Sea
Persian Gulf
Gulf of Oman
Gulf of Aden
ARABIAN SEA
INDIA
RUSSIA
GEORGIA
ARMENIA
AZERBAIJAN
TURKEY
CYPRUS
SYRIA
LEBANON
ISRAEL
JORDAN
IRAQ
IRAN
KUWAIT
BAHRAIN
QATAR
UNITED ARAB EMIRATES
SAUDI ARABIA
OMAN
YEMEN
ERITREA
DJIBOUTI
ETHIOPIA
SOMALIA
KENYA
EGYPT
TURKMENISTAN
UZBEKISTAN
AFGHANISTAN
İSTANBUL
ANKARA
BURSA
İZMIR (Smyrna)
KONYA
ADANA
GAZİANTEP
TBILISI
YEREVAN
BAKI (Baku)
TEHRĀN
MASHHAD
QOM
EṢFAHĀN
SHĪRĀZ
TABRĪZ
KARAJ
AHVĀZ
BAGHDĀD
AL BAṢRAH (Basra)
AL MAWṢIL (Mosul)
HALAB (Aleppo)
DIMASHQ (Damascus)
BAYRŪT (Beirut)
ḤIMṢ (Homs)
TEL AVIV-YAFO (Jaffa)
Jerusalem
'AMMĀN
EL ISKANDARĪYA (Alexandria)
EL QĀHIRA (Cairo)
AL KUWAYT (Kuwait)
AR RIYĀḌ (Riyadh)
AL MADĪNAH (Medina)
MAKKAH (Mecca)
JIDDAH (Jedda)
Ad Dawḥah (Doha)
Al Manāmah
DUBAYY (Dubai)
Abū Ẓaby (Abu Dhabi)
Masqaṭ (Muscat)
ṢAN'Ā'
'Adan (Aden)
Djibouti
ADDIS ABEBA (Addis Ababa)
MUQDISHO (Mogadishu)
HYDERABAD
KARACHI
KĀBUL
TOSHKENT (Tashkent)
Ashgabat
An Nafūd (Nafud Desert)
Rub' al Khālī (Empty Quarter)
Dasht-e Kavīr (Great Salt Desert)
Dasht-e Lūt
Bādiyat ash Shām (Syrian Desert)
Garagum (Kara Kum)
Kyzyl Kum
Kūhhā-ye Zāgros (Zagros Mts.)
Toros Dağları (Taurus Mts.)
Ḥaḍramawt
Socotra (Yemen)
Ogaden
Somaliland
Puntland

KYRGYZSTAN
Bishkek
Taraz
Balykchy
Karakol
Naryn
Namangan
Andijon
Osh
Farg'ona
Kashi
Artux
Yengisar
Shache
Yecheng
Hotan
Yutian
Mazar
Aksu
Wensu
Kuqa
Korla
Kuruktag
Yanqi
Bosten Hu
Lop Nur
Dunhuang
Anxi
Yumen
Jiayuguan
Zhangye
Shandan
Jinchang
Alxa Zuoqi
Shizuishan
YINCHUAN
Wuzhong
YULIN
NEI MONGOL ZIZHIQU
(INNER MONGOLIA)
NINGXIA HUIZU ZIZHIQU
Quintongzia
Wuwei
Baiyin
LANZHOU
XINING
Gonghe
Qinghai Hu
(Koko Nor)
Dingxi
Linxia
Pingliang
Tongchuan
XIANYANG
XI'AN
TIANSHUI
Baoji
Hanzhong
Wudu
Guangyuan
Jiangyou
Daxian
MIANYANG
NANCHONG
CHENGDU
SUINING
CHONGQING
LESHAN
ZIGONG
NEIJIANG
Yibin
Xichang
Zhaotong
GUIZHOU
LIUPANSHUI
Anshun
Qujing
Panzhihua
Dali
Baoshan
KUNMING
Kaiyuan
Gejiu
Y U N N A N
S I C H U A N
Yan'an
Qingyang
Dulan
Golmud
Da Qaidam
Tianjun
Mangnai
Ruoqiang
Qiemo
Qaidam Pendi
Tarim Pendi
(Tarim Basin)
Taklamakan Shamo
XINJIANG UYGUR ZIZHIQU
(SINKIANG)
Qilian Shan
Har Hu
Altun Shan
Ayakkum Hu
Hoh Xil Shan
Muz Tag
Kunlun Shan
Q I N G H A I
Gyaring Hu
Ngoring Hu
Huang He
Bayan Har Shan
C H I N A
Yushu
Hongyuan
Songpan
Tanggula Shankou
Tanggula Shan
(Dangla Range)
Amdo
Nagqu
XIZANG ZIZHIQU
(TIBET)
Siling Co
Nam Co
Nganglong Kangri
Rutog
Gar
Mapam Yumco
Xainza
Nyainqentanglha Shan
Lhasa
Xigazê
Yamzho Yumco
Yarlung Zangbo Jiang
Namcha Barwa
Qamdo
Ningjing Shan
Shaluli Shan
Garze
Jinsha Jiang
Lancang Jiang
Markam
Bomi
Zayü
Nu Jiang
Zhongdian
Yulong Jiang
Gongga Shan
Shimian
Chang Jiang
Maquan He
Zhongba
Lhazê
Ngamring
Himalaya
Mt. Everest
Dhaulagiri
Annapurna
Pokhara
NEPAL
KATHMANDU
Biratnagar
SIKKIM
BHUTAN
Thimphu
Darjiling
Shiliguri
ARUNACHAL PRADESH
Saikhoa Ghat
Dibrugarh
Sivasagar
Brahmaputra
ASSAM
NAGALAND
Tezpur
GUWAHATI
MEGHALAYA
MANIPUR
Imphal
Sylhet
Silchar
TRIPURA
MIZORAM
Patkai Bum
Kachin
Myitkyina
Putao
Hkakabo Razi
Chindwin
Tengchong
Luxi
Katha
Lashio
MYANMAR
(BURMA)
Shwebo
MANDALAY
Monywa
Myingyan
Kyaukse
Meiktila
Taunggyi
Yamethin
Magway
NAYPYIDAW
Minbu
Pyinmana
Toungoo
Pye
Pegu Yoma
Arakan Yoma
Sittwe
(Akyab)
Ramree I.
Cheduba I.
Hinthada
Pathein
(Bassein)
Insein
YANGON
(Rangoon)
Bago
Maubin
Pyapon
G. of Mottama
Mawlamyine
Ye
Dawei
Mergui
Tenasserim
Myeik Kyunzu
(Mergui Arch.)
Salween
Shan
Mong Ping
Jinghong
Simao
Jinggu
Wenshan
VIETNAM
Son La
Muang Xai
Luang Prabang
Mekong
LAOS
Vientiane
(Viangchan)
Nong Khai
Udon Thani
Khon Kaen
THAILAND
Chiang Mai
Chiang Rai
Mae Hong Son
Lampang
Uttaradit
Tak
Nakhon Sawan
Nakhon Ratchasima
Saraburi
BANGKOK
SAMUT PRAKAN
Rayong
Trat
CAMBODIA
Hua Hin
Gulf of Thailand
Chumphon
Kho Khot Kra
(Isthmus of Kra)
Ranong
Surat Thani
Nakhon Si Thammarat
Malay Pen.
Phuket
Songkla
Hat Yai
Kota Bharu
Kuala Terengganu
George Town
Ipoh
MALAYSIA
Kuantan
KLANG
KUALA LUMPUR
Putrajaya
Johor Bharu
SINGAPORE
BATAM
INDONESIA
MEDAN
Tanjungbalai
Pematangsiantar
Belawan
Aceh
Banda Aceh
Meulaboh
Sinkil
Simeulue
Straits of Malacca
Great Channel
Nicobar Is.
(India)
Great Nicobar
Car Nicobar
Ten Degree Channel
Andaman Is.
(India)
North Andaman
Middle Andaman
South Andaman
Port Blair
Little Andaman
Andaman Sea
Coco Is.
Preparis Is.
Maudin Sun
Bay of Bengal
INDIAN OCEAN
BANGLADESH
DHAKA
(Dacca)
Rajshahi
KHULNA
Barisal
CHITTAGONG
Sundarbans
KOLKATA
(Calcutta)
Haora
Kharagpur
PASCHIM BANGA
ASANSOL
DHANBAD
JHARKHAND
RANCHI
JAMSHEDPUR
Bhagalpur
Gaya
Aurangabad
PATNA
Ara
Chhapra
Darbhanga
BIHAR
Purnia
Gorakhpur
VARANASI
Mirzapur
Jaunpur
PRAYAGRAJ
LUCKNOW
UTTAR PRADESH
KANPUR
Etawah
Sitapur
Shahjahanpur
Bareilly
Moradabad
Aligarh
AGRA
Mathura
FARIDABAD
New Delhi
DELHI
GHAZIABAD
MEERUT
Saharanpur
Haridwar
Dehra Dun
UTTARAKHAND
Ambala
CHANDIGARH
Patiala
LUDHIANA
Jalandhar
AMRITSAR
PUNJAB
HIMACHAL PRADESH
HARYANA
Bahawalpur
MULTAN
Sahiwal
LAHORE
GUJRANWALA
Sialkot
Sargodha
Jhelum
Jammu
RAWALPINDI
Islamabad
SRINAGAR
JAMMU & KASHMIR
Leh
Aksai Chin
Karakoram Ra.
Gilgit
Nanga Parbat
Chitral
Khyber Pakhtunkhwa
Mardan
Khunjerab Pass
Pamir
Indus
Sutlej
Thar Desert
Bikaner
Rahimyar Khan
JAIPUR
RAJASTHAN
Ajmer
Beawar
Jodhpur
Udaipur
Palanpur
Mandsaur
Chambal
KOTA
Gwalior
Jhansi
Lalitpur
Guna
Sagar
Rewa
Son
MADHYA PRADESH
BHOPAL
JABALPUR
Ujjain
INDORE
Vindhya Range
Satpura Range
Narmada
Chhindwara
AHMADABAD
Godhra
VADODARA
RAJKOT
Bharuch
SURAT
G. of Khambhat
Dhule
Jalgaon
Akola
Amravati
Wardha
NAGPUR
RAIPUR
BHILAINAGAR-DURG
CHHATTISGARH
Bilaspur
Raurkela
ODISHA
Cuttack
Bhubaneshwar
Puri
Brahmapur
(Berhampur)
Mahanadi
Titlagarh
Indravati
Jagdalpur
Eastern Ghats
VISHAKHAPATNAM
Rajahmahendravaram
Kakinada
Eluru
VIJAYAWADA
Guntur
ANDHRA PRADESH
Nellore
CHENNAI
(Madras)
Coromandel Coast
Puducherry
(Pondicherry)
Kumbakonam
TIRUCHCHIRAPPALLI
MADURAI
Palk Strait
Rameswaram
Tuticorin
Tirunelveli
G. of Mannar
Nagercoil
Kanyakumari
(C. Comorin)
THIRUVANANTHAPURAM
Kollam
Alappuzha
Mattancheri
KOCHI
(Cochin)
KERALA
Palakkad
Anai Mudi
COIMBATORE
TAMIL NADU
Salem
KOZHIKODE
(Calicut)
Mysuru
BENGALURU
(Bangalore)
Kolar
KARNATAKA
Mangaluru
Udupi
Shivamogga
Davangere
Hindupur
Anantapur
Ballari
Hubballi
Dharwad
Gadag
Adoni
Kurnool
Belagavi
GOA
Panaji
Kolhapur
Sangli
Krishna
Kalaburagi
Vijayapura
SOLAPUR
HYDERABAD
TELANGANA
Warangal
Kottagudem
Nizamabad
Nanded
Adilabad
Chandrapur
Godavari
Ahmadnagar
AURANGABAD
Jalna
NASIK
MAHARASHTRA
Thane
MUMBAI
(Bombay)
PUNE
(Poona)
Bhima
Western Ghats
Malabar Coast
Lakshadweep Is.
Minicoy I.
(India)
MALDIVES
Malé
SRI LANKA
Jaffna
Mannar
Trincomalee
Batticaloa
Puttalam
Kandy
Pidurutalagala
COLOMBO
Dehiwala
Moratuwa
Galle
Dondra Head

50 0 50 100 150 200 250 300 km

50 0 50 100 150 200 miles

1:5 600 000

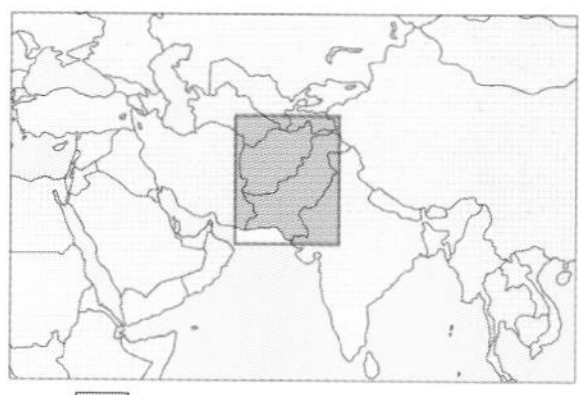

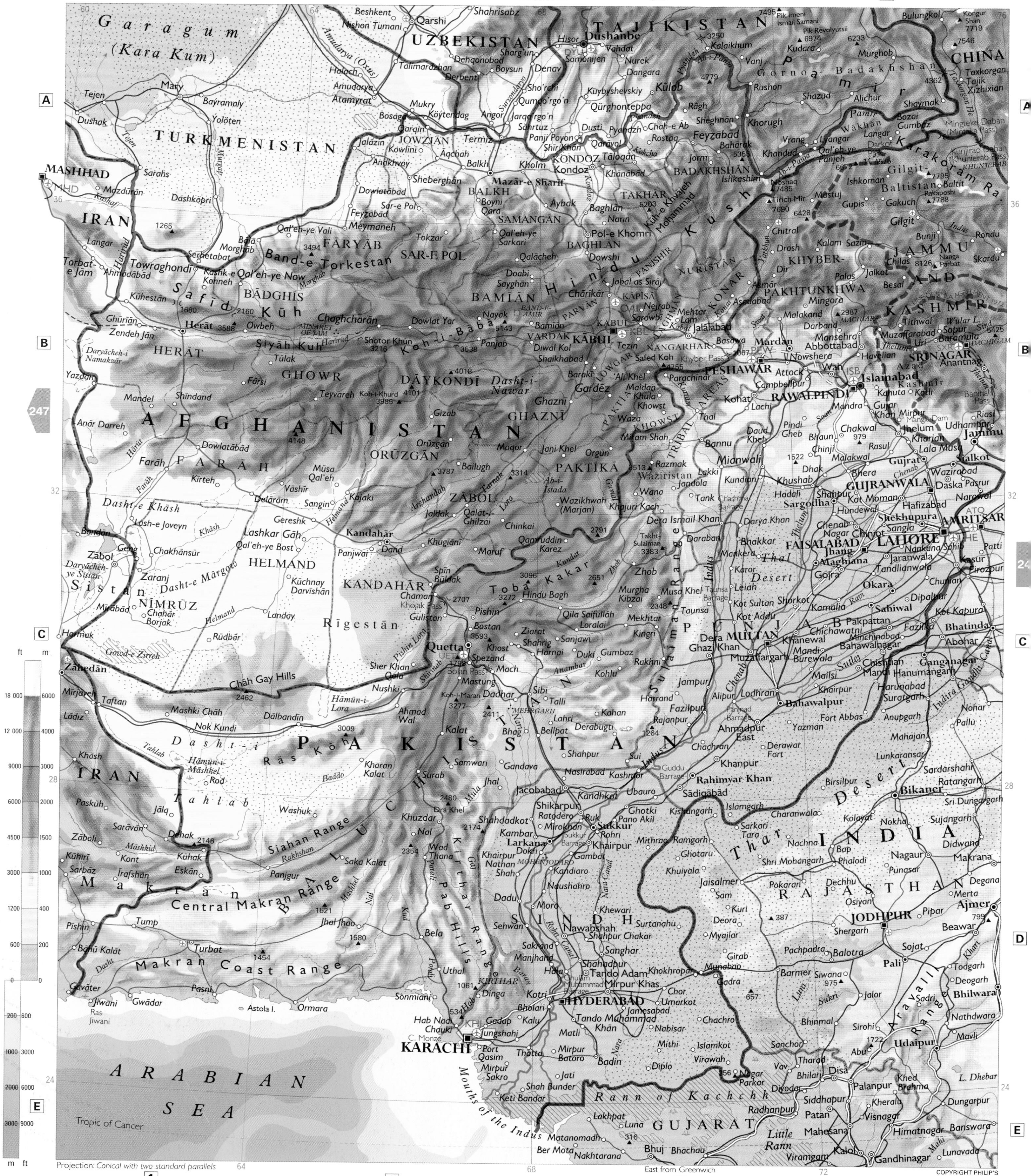

1 2 217 3 4

A B C D E

247

Projection: Conical with two standard parallels

East from Greenwich

1 2 3 4

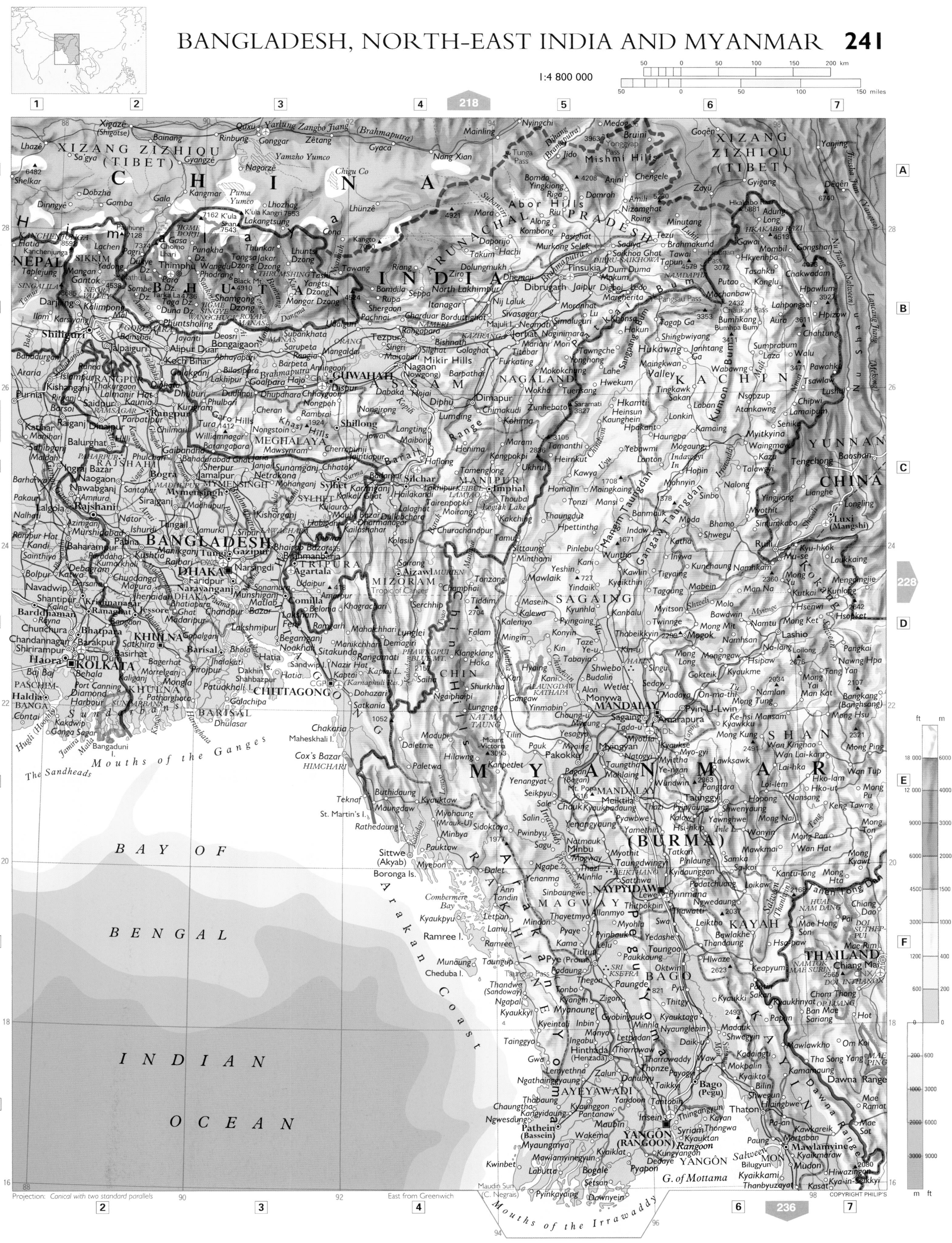
1:4 800 000
km
miles
218
228
236
XIZANG ZIZHIQU (TIBET)
CHINA
NEPAL
BHUTAN
INDIA
ARUNACHAL PRADESH
ASSAM
MEGHALAYA
NAGALAND
MANIPUR
MIZORAM
TRIPURA
BANGLADESH
DHAKA
RAJSHAHI
KHULNA
BARISAL
CHITTAGONG
KOLKATA
PASCHIM-BANGA
SYLHET
MYMENSINGH
RANGPUR
MYANMAR (BURMA)
KACHIN
SAGAING
CHIN
MANDALAY
MAGWAY
RAKHINE
BAGO
KAYAH
KAYIN
SHAN
AYEYAWADI
YANGON
MON
NAYPYIDAW
YANGON (RANGOON)
YUNNAN
THAILAND
BAY OF BENGAL
INDIAN OCEAN
Mouths of the Ganges
Mouths of the Irrawaddy
Arakan Coast
G. of Mottama
Tropic of Cancer
Projection: Conical with two standard parallels
East from Greenwich
COPYRIGHT PHILIP'S

50 0 50 100 150 200 km

50 0 50 100 150 miles

1:4 800 000

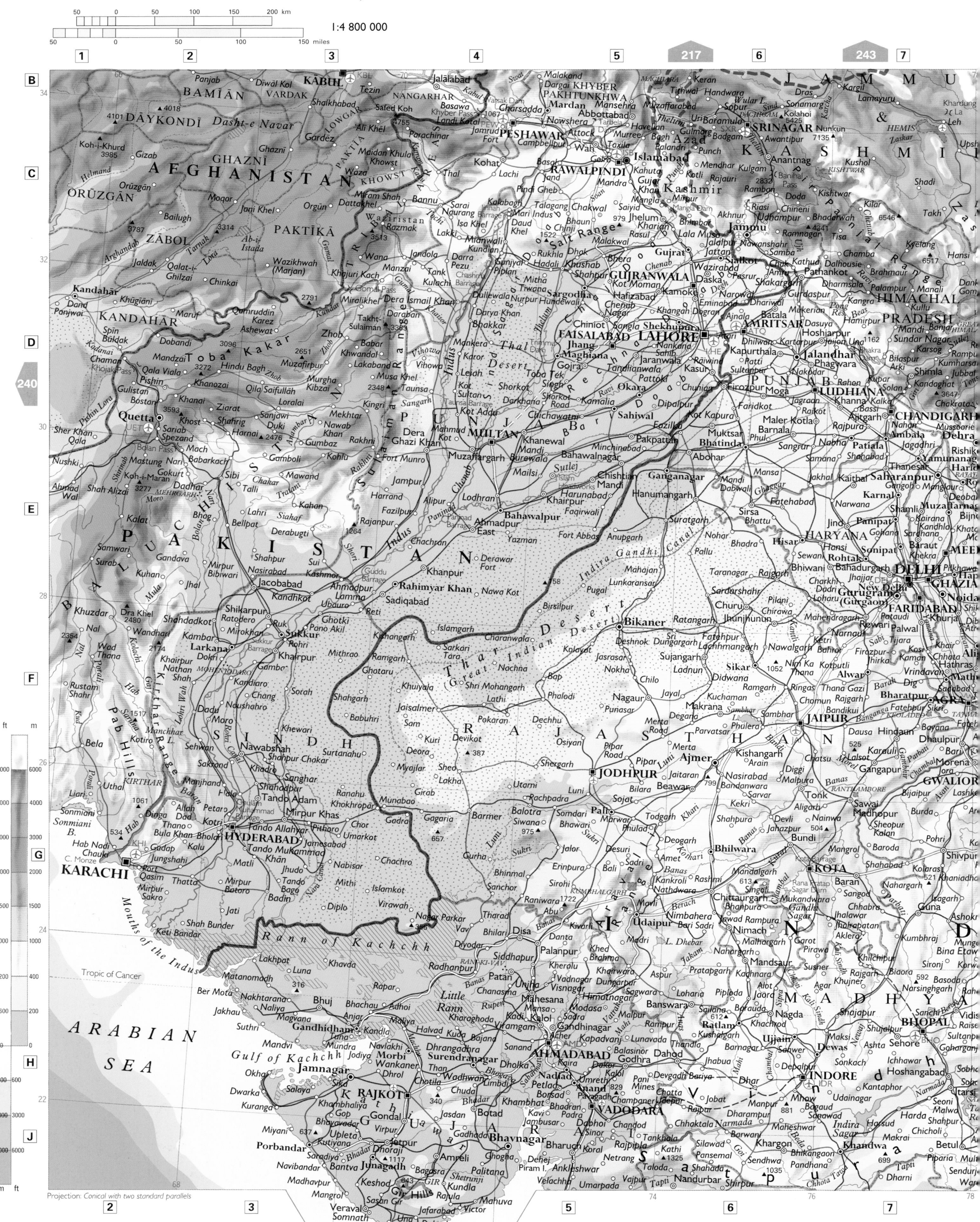

Projection: Conical with two standard parallels

JAMMU AND KASHMIR
on same scale
AFGHANISTAN
XINJIANG UYGUR ZIZHIQU (SINKIANG)
CHINA
XIZANG ZIZHIQU (TIBET)
KHYBER PAKHTUNKHWA (N.W. FRONTIER)
Gilgit-Baltistan (Northern Areas)
Hindu Kush
Karakoram Pass
Kunlun Shan
K2
Gasherbrum
Siachen Glacier
Aksai Chin
Soda Plains
Deosai Mts.
Ladakh Range
Zaskar Mountains
JAMMU & KASHMIR
SRINAGAR
Islamabad
RAWALPINDI
PUNJAB
Kashmir
Jammu
Sialkot
Gujrat
HIMACHAL PRADESH
Bangong Co
Gangdisê Shan
UTTARAKHAND
Nanda Devi
NEPAL
KATHMANDU
Annapurna
Dhaulagiri
Mt. Everest (Chomolungma or Sagarmatha)
Kanchenjunga
Makalu
Himalaya
Yarlung Zangbo Jiang (Brahmaputra)
Xigazê (Shigatse)
SIKKIM
Gangtok
Thimphu
BHUTAN
ASSAM
BANGLADESH
DHAKA
Rajshahi
KHULNA
Jessore
Barisal
UTTAR PRADESH
LUCKNOW
KANPUR
Bareilly
Moradabad
Gorakhpur
Faizabad
PRAYAGRAJ (Allahabad)
VARANASI
Mirzapur
BIHAR
PATNA
Muzaffarpur
Darbhanga
Gaya
Bhagalpur
Purnia
Shiliguri
JHARKHAND
RANCHI
JAMSHEDPUR
DHANBAD
ASANSOL
Bokaro
PASCHIM BANGA
KOLKATA
Haora
Durgapur
Barddhaman
Mouths of the Ganges
The Sandheads
Sundarbans
MADHYA PRADESH
JABALPUR
Satna
Rewa
Kaimur Hills
Maikala Ra.
CHHATTISGARH
Bilaspur
Korba
ODISHA
Sambalpur
Raurkela
Baleshwar
East from Greenwich
COPYRIGHT PHILIP'S

1:4 800 000

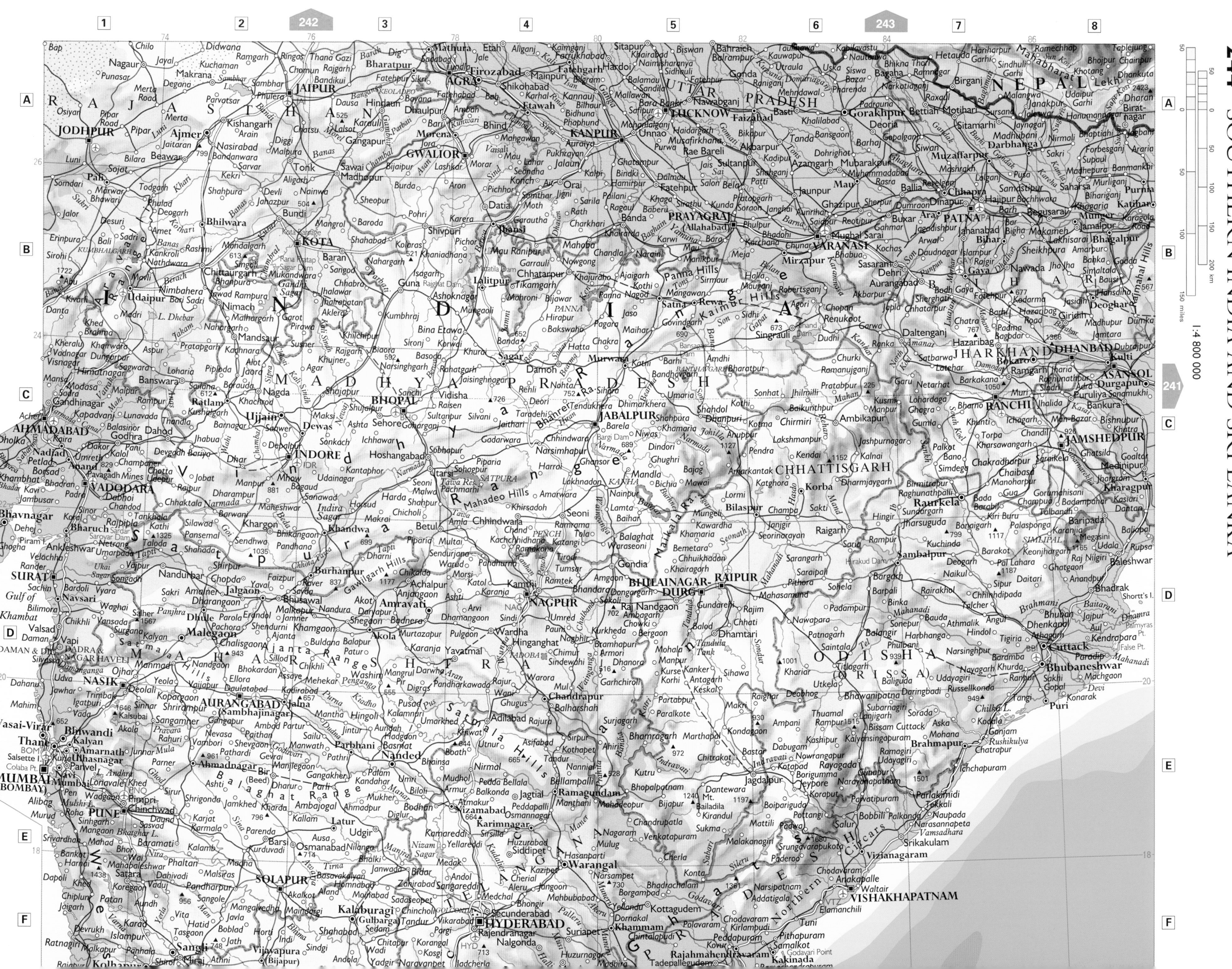
50 0 50 100 150 200 km
50 0 50 100 150 miles
NEPAL
UTTAR PRADESH
MADHYA PRADESH
CHHATTISGARH
JHARKHAND
ODISHA (ORISSA)
MAHARASHTRA
RAJASTHAN
INDIA
LUCKNOW
KANPUR
PATNA
VARANASI
PRAYAGRAJ (Allahabad)
BHOPAL
INDORE
JABALPUR
RAIPUR
BHILAINAGAR-DURG
NAGPUR
HYDERABAD
AHMADABAD
VADODARA
SURAT
MUMBAI (BOMBAY)
PUNE
NASIK
AURANGABAD (Sambhajinagar)
SOLAPUR
JAIPUR
JODHPUR
KOTA
GWALIOR
AGRA
RANCHI
DHANBAD
JAMSHEDPUR
ASANSOL
VISHAKHAPATNAM
Gulf of Khambat
Satpura Range
Vindhya Range
Ajanta Range
Balaghat Range
Northern Circars
241
242
243

BAY OF BENGAL
ANDAMAN SEA
Andaman Islands
ANDAMAN AND NICOBAR ISLANDS
(India)
Nicobar Islands
INDIAN OCEAN
ANDAMAN AND NICOBAR ISLANDS
on same scale
Ten Degree Channel
ANDRA PRADESH
KARNATAKA
KERALA
TAMIL NADU
SRI LANKA
(CEYLON)
CHENNAI (MADRAS)
BENGALURU (BANGALORE)
COLOMBO
Coromandel Coast
Malabar Coast
Gulf of Mannar
ARABIAN SEA
INDIAN OCEAN
LAKSHADWEEP ISLANDS
on same scale
LAKSHADWEEP
(India)
Nine Degree Channel
East from Greenwich
Projection: Conical with two standard parallels
COPYRIGHT PHILIP'S

1:5 600 000

50 0 50 100 150 200 250 300 km

50 0 50 100 150 200 miles

213

212

256

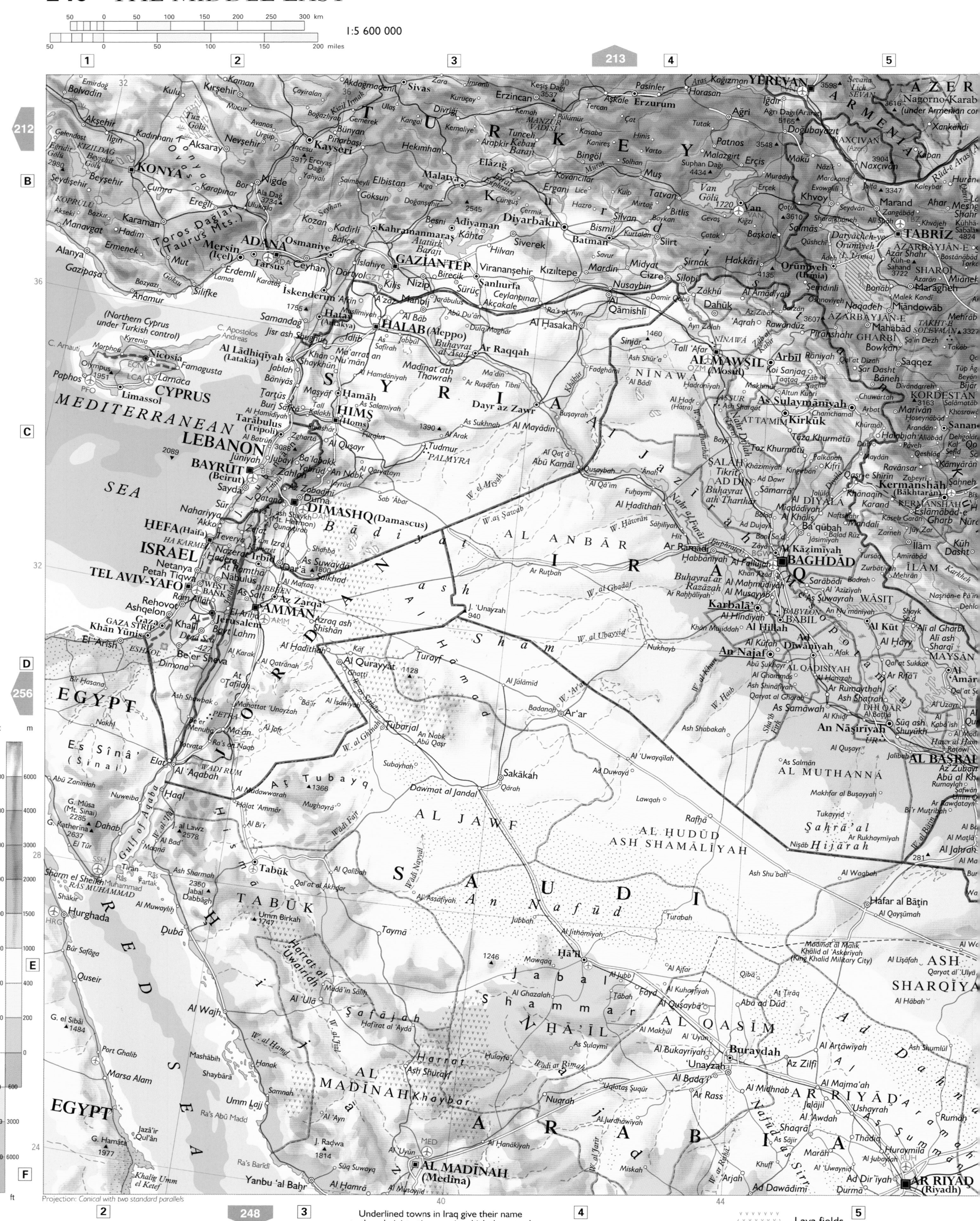

Projection: Conical with two standard parallels

Underlined towns in Iraq give their name to the administrative area in which they stand

Lava fields

248

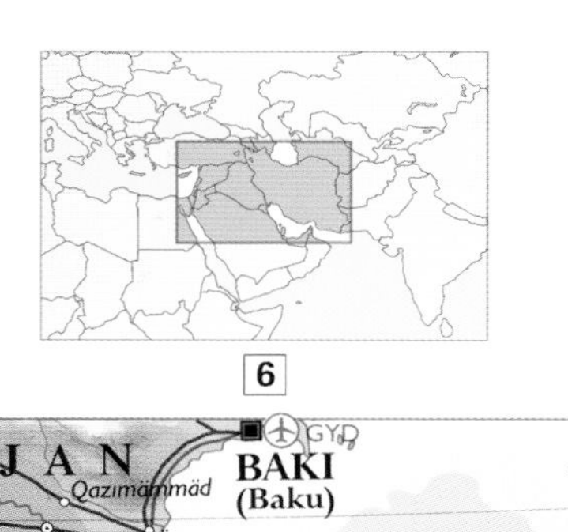

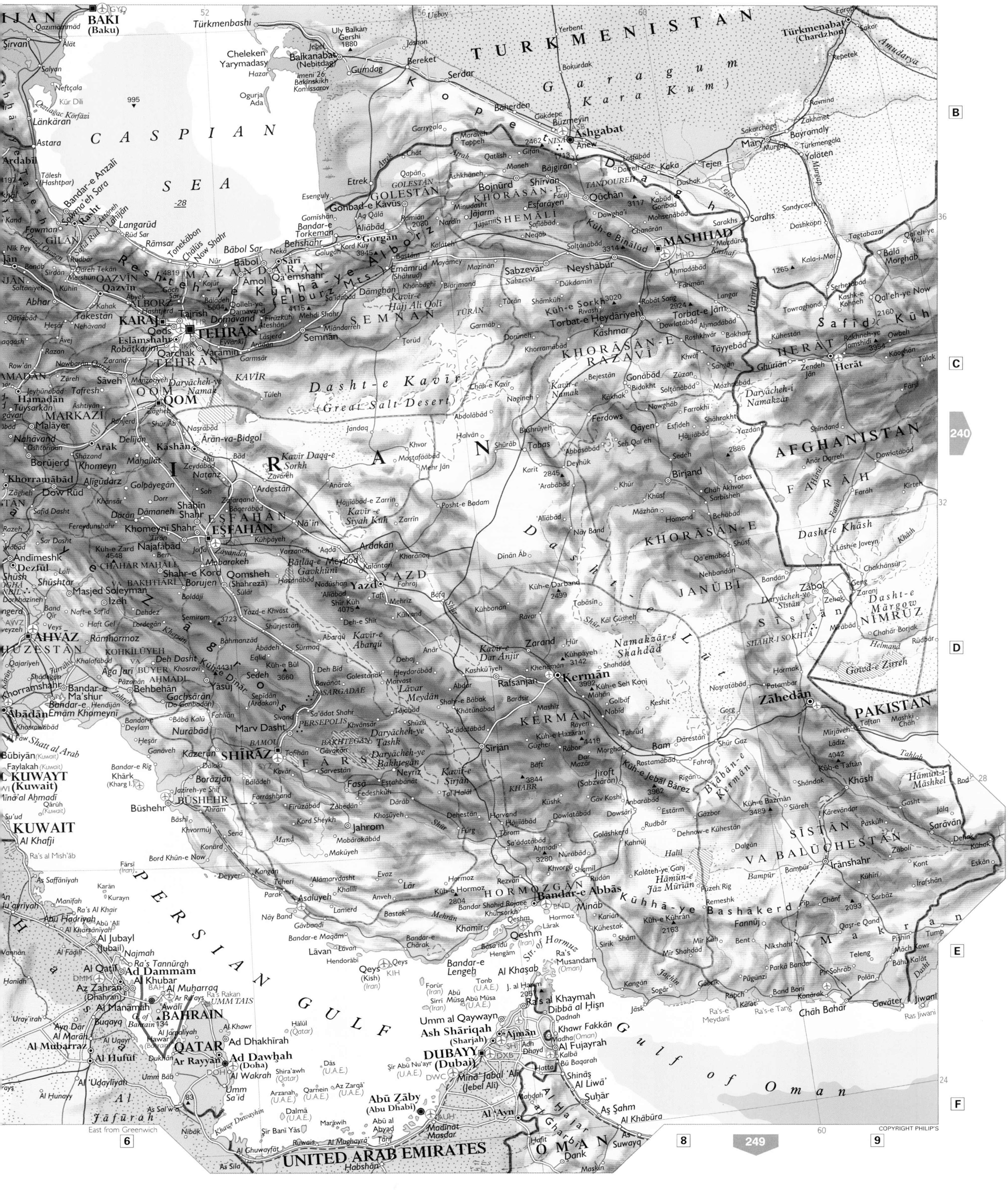

216
240
249

6 7 8 9 10

B C D E F

TURKMENISTAN

Garagum (Kara Kum)

Kopet Dag

CASPIAN SEA

BAKI (Baku)

Türkmenbashi

Balkanabat (Nebitdag)

Ashgabat

Mary

Türkmenabat (Chardzhou)

Amudarya

TEHRĀN

Reshteh-ye Kūhhā-ye Alborz (Elburz Mts.)

Dasht-e Kavīr (Great Salt Desert)

IRAN

MASHHAD

KHORĀSĀN-E RAZAVĪ

KHORĀSĀN-E JANŪBĪ

KHORĀSĀN-E SHEMĀLĪ

GOLESTĀN

MĀZANDARĀN

SEMNĀN

QOM

ESFAHĀN

YAZD

KERMĀN

FĀRS

HORMOZGĀN

SĪSTĀN VA BALŪCHESTĀN

KHŪZESTĀN

BŪSHEHR

Dasht-e Lūt

Kūhhā-ye Zāgros

Kūhhā-ye Bashākerd

AFGHANISTAN

HERĀT

FARĀH

NĪMRŪZ

Safīd Kūh

PAKISTAN

Makran

Zāhedān

Kermān

Shīrāz

Eşfahān

Yazd

Qom

Ahvāz

Ābādān

Bandar-e Abbās

Chāh Bahār

KUWAYT (Kuwait)

KUWAIT

BAHRAIN

QATAR

Ad Dawhah (Doha)

PERSIAN GULF

Str. of Hormuz

Gulf of Oman

Ash Shāriqah (Sharjah)

DUBAYY (Dubai)

Abū Ẓaby (Abu Dhabi)

UNITED ARAB EMIRATES

OMAN

Ad Dammām

Al Hufūf

East from Greenwich

50 0 50 100 150 200 250 300 km
50 0 50 100 150 200 miles
1:5 600 000

246

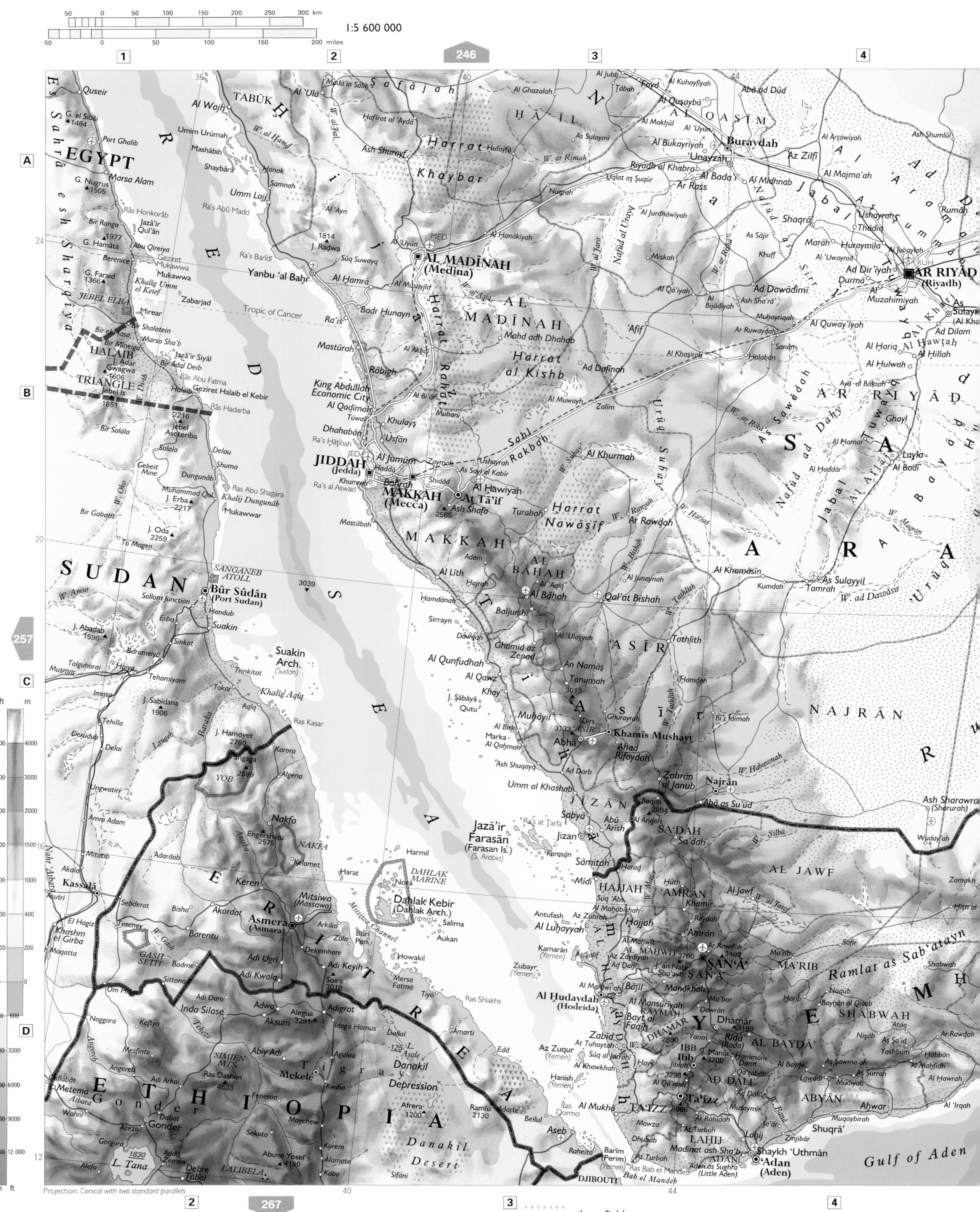

Projection: Conical with two standard parallels

257
267

Lava fields

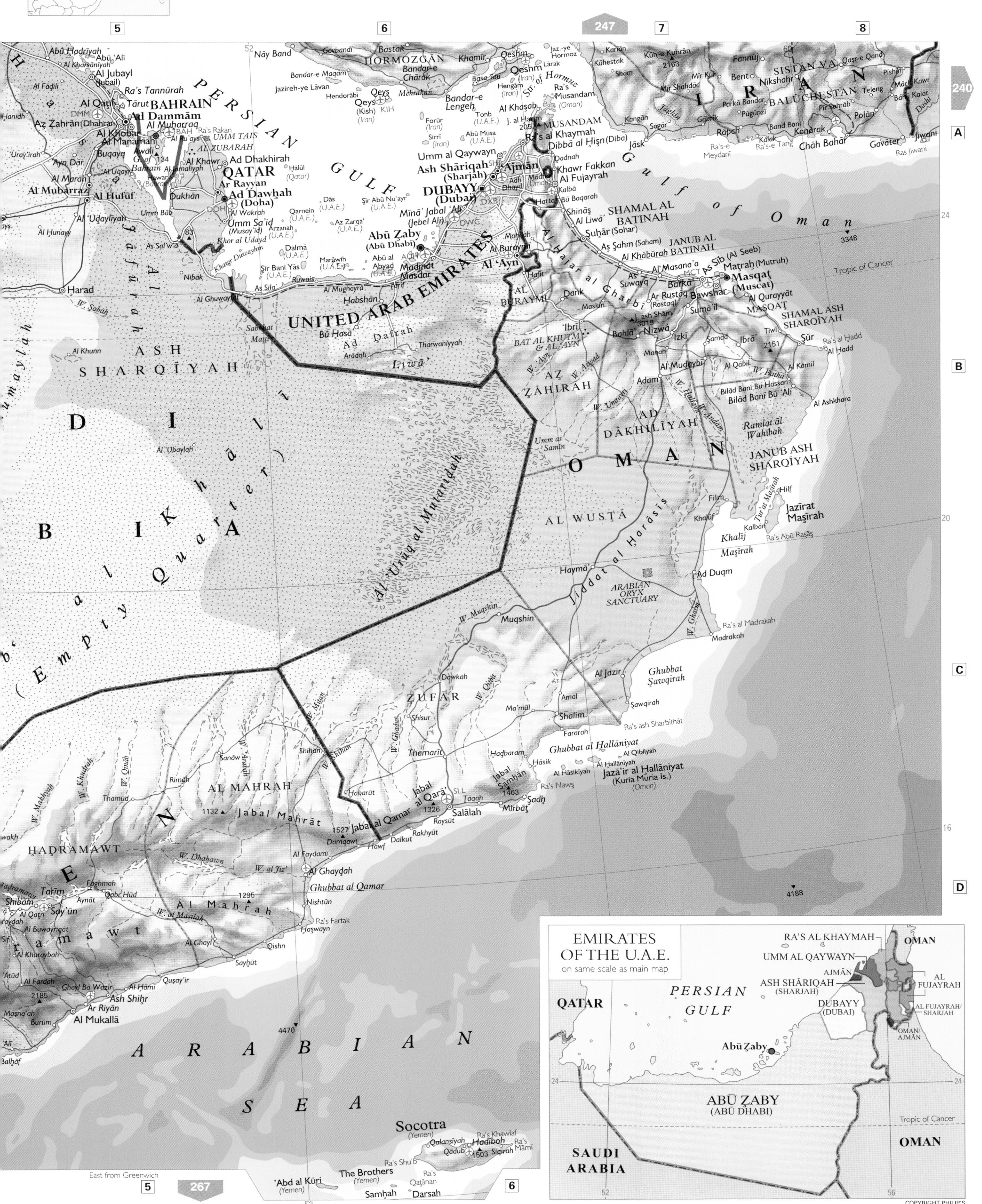

5
6
247
7
8
240
A
B
C
D
PERSIAN GULF
Gulf of Oman
ARABIAN SEA
Tropic of Cancer
BAHRAIN
Al Manamah
QATAR
Ad Dawhah (Doha)
Ar Rayyan
Dukhān
Umm Sa'id (Musay'id)
Al Khawr
Al Jubayl (Jubail)
Ra's Tannūrah
Al Qaţīf
Ad Dammām
Az Zahrān (Dhahran)
Al Khobar
Al Hufūf
Al Mubarraz
Harad
UNITED ARAB EMIRATES
Abū Zaby (Abū Dhabi)
DUBAYY (Dubai)
Ash Shāriqah (Sharjah)
Ajmān
Umm al Qaywayn
Ra's al Khaymah
Al Fujayrah
Khawr Fakkan
Al 'Ayn
Al Buraymī
Madīnat Masdar
Mīnā' Jabal 'Alī (Jebel Ali)
Liwā'
Ad Dafrah
MUSANDAM
Ra's Musandam
Str. of Hormuz
Qeshm
Bandar-e Lengeh
HORMOZGĀN
SISTĀN VA BALŪCHESTĀN
IRAN
Jāsk
Chāh Bahār
Gavater
Jiwani
OMAN
Masqaţ (Muscat)
Maţraḩ (Mutruh)
As Sīb (Al Seeb)
Şuḩār (Sohar)
Nizwá
Bahlā'
'Ibrī
Şūr
Ra's al Ḩadd
Al Hajar al Gharbī
JANUB AL BATINAH
SHAMAL AL BATINAH
AD DĀKHILĪYAH
AZ ZĀHIRAH
AL WUSŢÁ
JANUB ASH SHARQĪYAH
SHAMAL ASH SHARQĪYAH
Ramlat al Wahībah
Jazīrat Maşīrah
Khalīj Maşīrah
Haymā'
Ad Duqm
Jiddat al Ḩarāsīs
ARABIAN ORYX SANCTUARY
Ghubbat Şawqirah
Ra's al Madrakah
Muqshin
ZUFAR
Thamarīt
Şalālah
Mirbāţ
Jabal al Qarā'
Jabal Samḩān
Ghubbat al Ḩallāniyat
Jazā'ir al Ḩallāniyat (Kuria Muria Is.)
AL MAHRAH
Jabal Mahrāt
Al Ghayḑah
Ghubbat al Qamar
Ra's Fartak
Nishtūn
Sayḩūt
ḨADRAMAWT
YEMEN
Tarīm
Shibām
Say'ūn
Ash Shiḩr
Al Mukallā
ASH SHARQĪYAH
Ar Rub' al Khālī (Empty Quarter)
SAUDI ARABIA
Al 'Uruq al Mu'tariḑah
Socotra (Yemen)
Ḩadībūh
'Abd al Kūrī (Yemen)
The Brothers (Yemen)
Samḩah
Darsah
East from Greenwich
267
EMIRATES OF THE U.A.E.
on same scale as main map
RA'S AL KHAYMAH
UMM AL QAYWAYN
AJMĀN
ASH SHĀRIQAH (SHARJAH)
DUBAYY (DUBAI)
AL FUJAYRAH
AL FUJAYRAH/SHARJAH
OMAN/AJMĀN
ABŪ ZABY (ABŪ DHABI)
Abū Zaby
QATAR
SAUDI ARABIA
OMAN
PERSIAN GULF
Tropic of Cancer

1:2 000 000

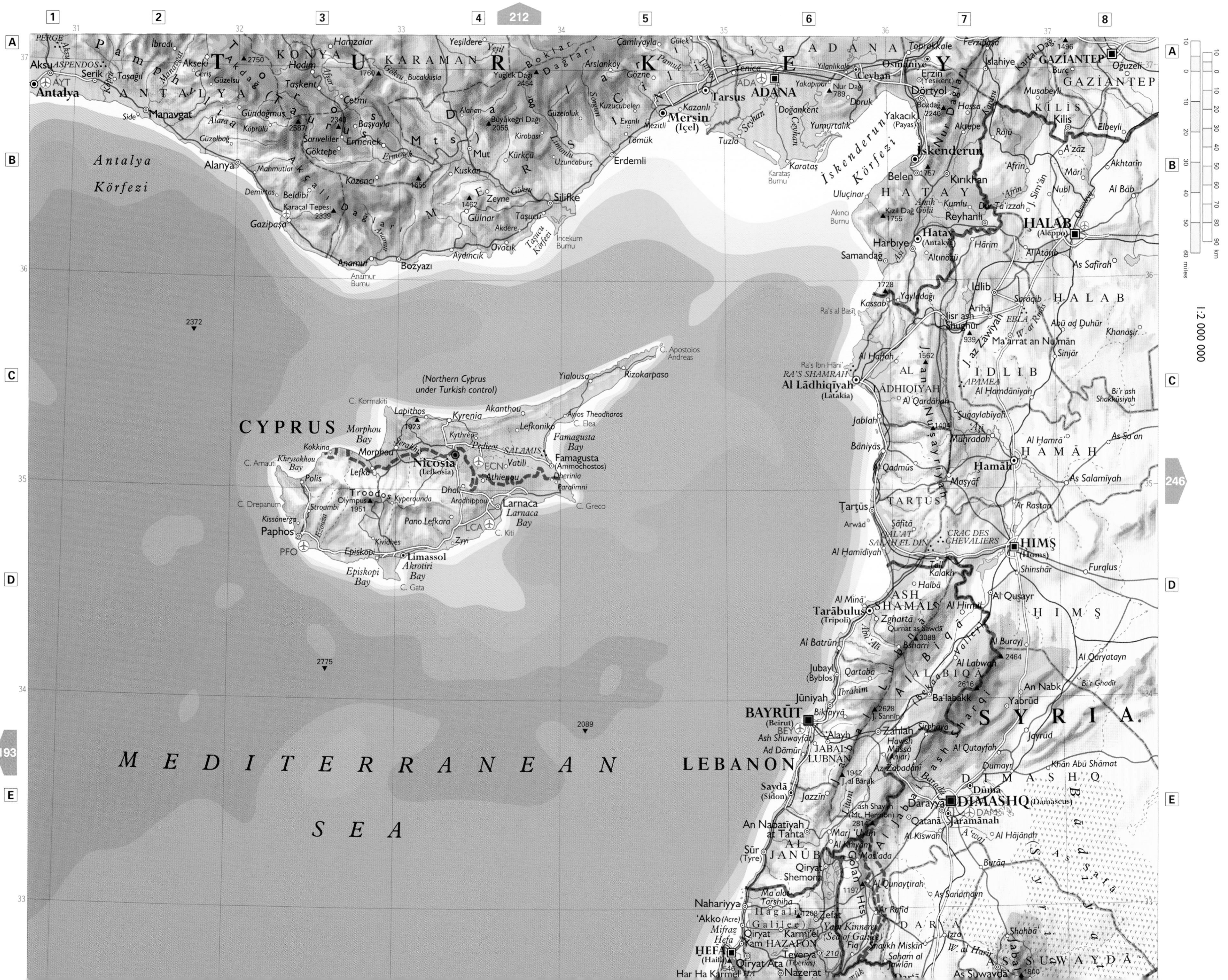
10 0 10 20 30 40 50 60 70 80 90 km
10 0 10 20 30 40 50 60 miles
212
246
193
MEDITERRANEAN
SEA
CYPRUS
(Northern Cyprus under Turkish control)
LEBANON
SYRIA
TURKEY
Antalya Körfezi
İskenderun Körfezi
Nicosia
(Lefkosia)
Kyrenia
Famagusta
(Ammochostos)
Larnaca
Larnaca Bay
Limassol
Akrotiri Bay
Episkopi Bay
Paphos
Morphou Bay
Famagusta Bay
C. Apostolos Andreas
C. Greco
C. Gata
C. Kormakiti
C. Arnauti
C. Drepanum
Troodos
Antalya
Alanya
Manavgat
Gazipaşa
Anamur
Bozyazı
Silifke
Erdemli
Mersin
(İçel)
Tarsus
ADANA
Ceyhan
İskenderun
Hatay
(Antakya)
Samandağ
GAZİANTEP
Kilis
HALAB
(Aleppo)
Idlib
Hamāh
HIMS
(Homs)
Al Lādhiqīyah
(Latakia)
Jablah
Bāniyās
Ţarţūs
Ţarābulus
(Tripoli)
BAYRŪT
(Beirut)
Şaydā
(Sidon)
Şūr
(Tyre)
DIMASHQ
(Damascus)
Golan Hts.
HEFA
(Haifa)
2372
2775
2089

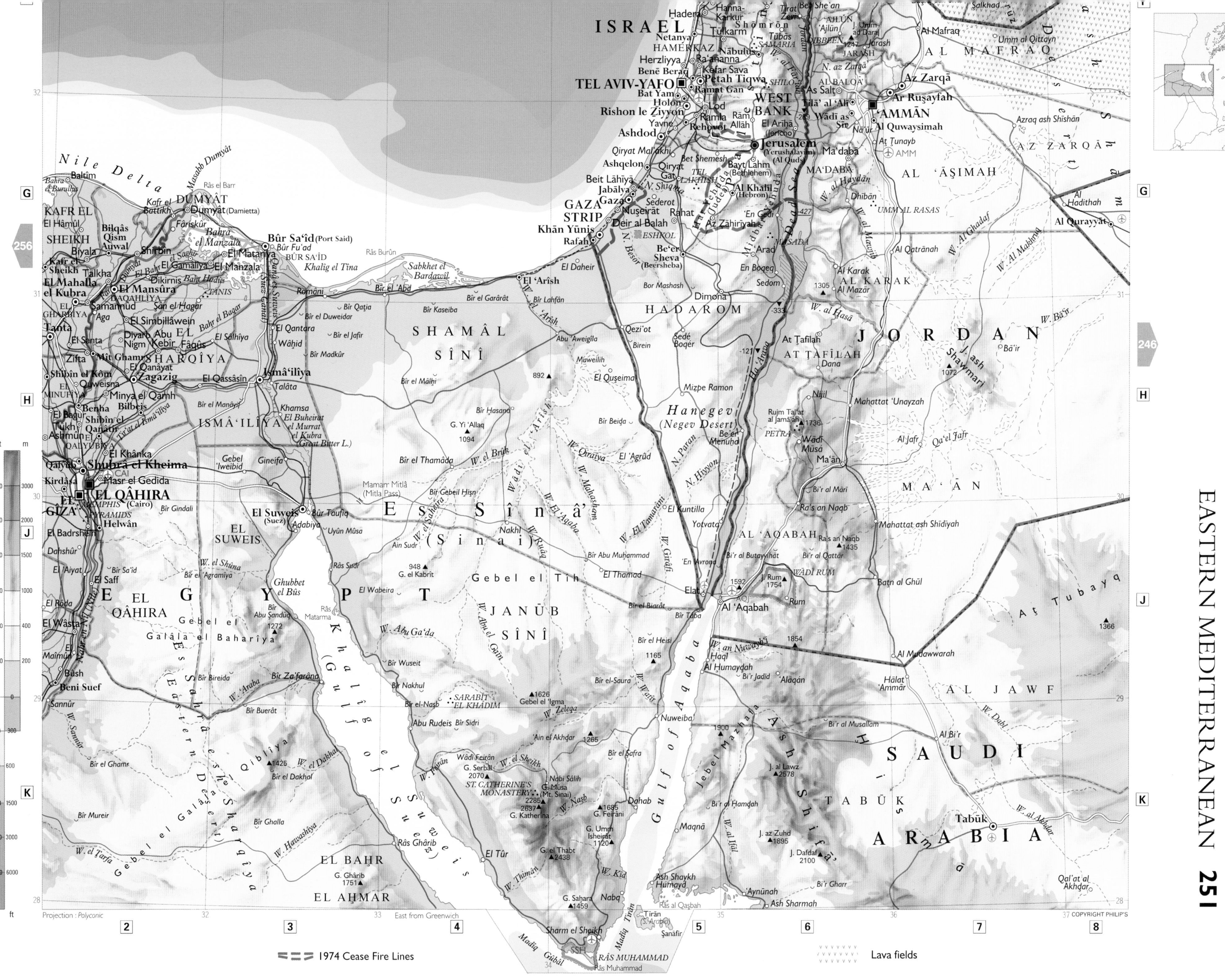
ISRAEL
JORDAN
SAUDI
ARABIA
E G Y P T
GAZA STRIP
WEST BANK
TEL AVIV-YAFO
Jerusalem
'AMMĀN
Gulf of Aqaba
Khalîg el Suweis (Gulf of Suez)
Nile Delta
EL QÂHIRA
Bûr Sa'îd (Port Said)
El Suweis (Suez)
Es Sînâ' (Sinai)
Hanegev (Negev Desert)
Lava fields
1974 Cease Fire Lines
Projection : Polyconic
East from Greenwich
COPYRIGHT PHILIP'S

AFRICA

1:33 600 000

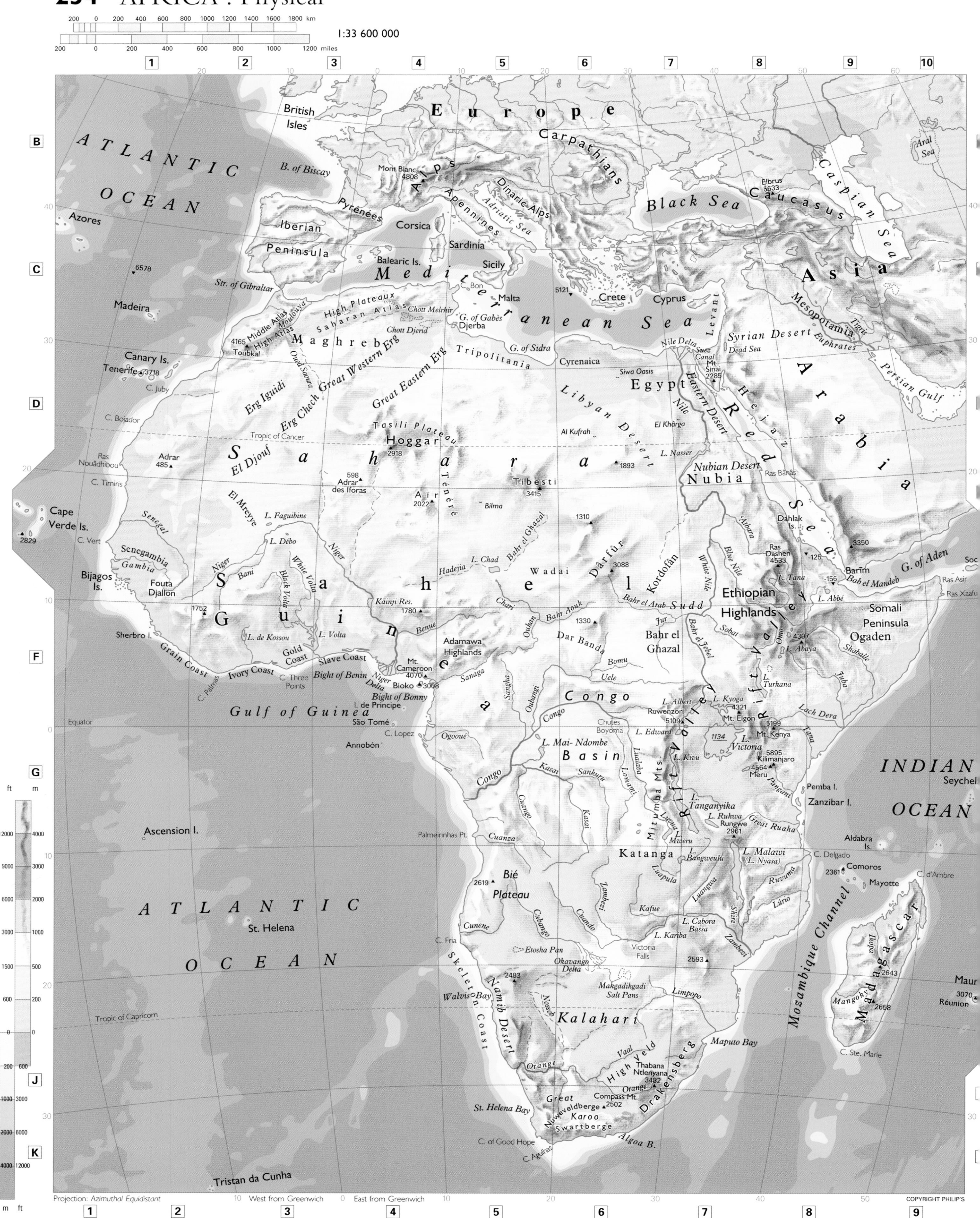

Projection: *Azimuthal Equidistant* West from Greenwich East from Greenwich

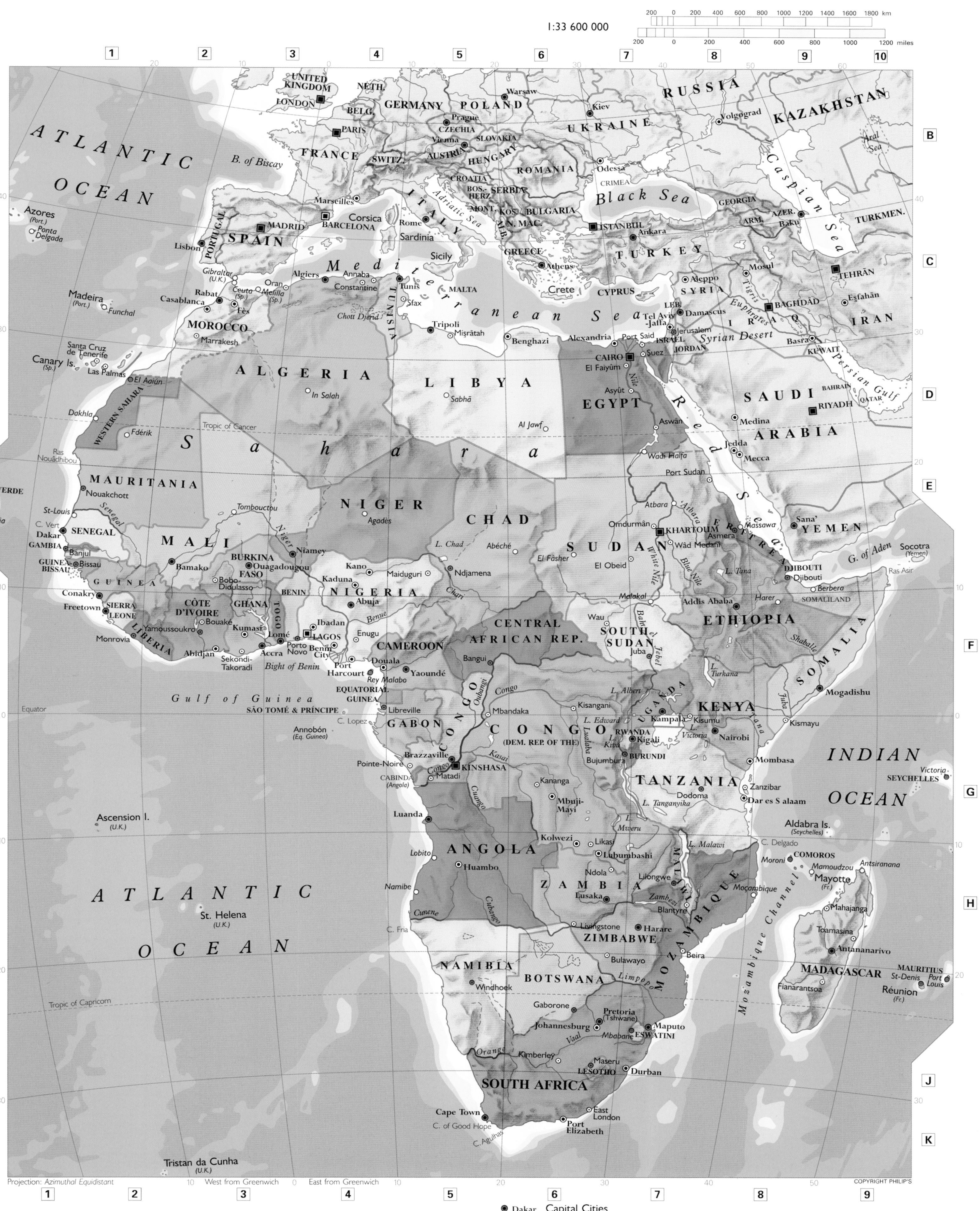
1:33 600 000
200 0 200 400 600 800 1000 1200 1400 1600 1800 km
200 0 200 400 600 800 1000 1200 miles
1 2 3 4 5 6 7 8 9 10
B C D E F G H J K
UNITED KINGDOM
LONDON
NETH.
BELG.
GERMANY
POLAND
Warsaw
RUSSIA
KAZAKHSTAN
Prague
CZECHIA
PARIS
Kiev
UKRAINE
Volgograd
Aral Sea
ATLANTIC OCEAN
B. of Biscay
FRANCE
SWITZ.
Vienna
SLOVAKIA
AUSTRIA
HUNGARY
ROMANIA
Odessa
CRIMEA
Caspian Sea
CROATIA
BOS.-HERZ.
SERBIA
Black Sea
Marseilles
Adriatic Sea
ITALY
MONT.
KOS.
BULGARIA
GEORGIA
AZER.
ARM.
Baku
TURKMEN.
Azores (Port.)
Ponta Delgada
PORTUGAL
SPAIN
MADRID
BARCELONA
Corsica
Rome
Sardinia
ALB.
N. MAC.
ISTANBUL
Ankara
TURKEY
Lisbon
GREECE
Athens
Sicily
Gibraltar (U.K.)
Rabat
Ceuta (Sp.)
Oran
Melilla (Sp.)
Algiers
Annaba
Constantine
Mediterranean Sea
Tunis
Sfax
MALTA
Crete
CYPRUS
Aleppo
SYRIA
Mosul
TEHRĀN
Eşfahān
IRAN
Madeira (Port.)
Funchal
Casablanca
Fès
MOROCCO
Marrakesh
Chott Djerid
TUNISIA
Tripoli
Mişrātah
Benghazi
Alexandria
Port Said
LEB.
Tel Aviv-Jaffa
Damascus
Jerusalem
ISRAEL
JORDAN
Syrian Desert
IRAQ
BAGHDĀD
Euphrates
Tigris
Basra
KUWAIT
Persian Gulf
Santa Cruz de Tenerife
Canary Is. (Sp.)
Las Palmas
El Aaiún
WESTERN SAHARA
ALGERIA
In Salah
LIBYA
Sabhā
CAIRO
El Faiyûm
Suez
Asyût
Nile
EGYPT
SAUDI ARABIA
BAHRAIN
QATAR
RIYADH
Medina
Dakhla
Tropic of Cancer
Fdérik
Sahara
Al Jawf
Aswân
Red Sea
Jedda
Mecca
Ras Nouâdhibou
Wadi Halfa
Port Sudan
MAURITANIA
Nouakchott
NIGER
Agadès
CHAD
Atbara
Omdurmân
KHARTOUM
ERITREA
Asmera
Massawa
Sana'
YEMEN
VERDE
St-Louis
Senegal
Tombouctou
C. Vert
Dakar
SENEGAL
GAMBIA
Banjul
GUINEA-BISSAU
Bissau
MALI
Niger
Niamey
L. Chad
Abéché
SUDAN
Wâd Medani
White Nile
Blue Nile
G. of Aden
Socotra (Yemen)
BURKINA FASO
Ouagadougou
Bamako
Kano
Maiduguri
Ndjamena
El Fasher
El Obeid
L. Tana
DJIBOUTI
Djibouti
Ras Asir
GUINEA
Bobo-Dioulasso
Kaduna
NIGERIA
BENIN
Berbera
SOMALILAND
Conakry
Freetown
SIERRA LEONE
CÔTE D'IVOIRE
GHANA
TOGO
Abuja
Chari
Malakal
Addis Ababa
Harer
ETHIOPIA
Bouaké
Yamoussoukro
Kumasi
Ibadan
LAGOS
Benue
CENTRAL AFRICAN REP.
Wau
SOUTH SUDAN
Bahr el Jebel
Monrovia
LIBERIA
Abidjan
Sekondi-Takoradi
Accra
Lomé
Porto Novo
Enugu
Benin City
CAMEROON
Juba
Shabeelle
SOMALIA
Port Harcourt
Bight of Benin
Douala
Rey Malabo
Yaoundé
Bangui
L. Turkana
Gulf of Guinea
EQUATORIAL GUINEA
Oubangui
Congo
L. Albert
UGANDA
Mogadishu
Equator
SÃO TOMÉ & PRÍNCIPE
Libreville
Mbandaka
Kisangani
KENYA
Juba
C. Lopez
GABON
CONGO
Kampala
Kisumu
Kismayu
Annobón (Eq. Guinea)
CONGO (DEM. REP. OF THE)
L. Edward
Lualaba
L. Kivu
RWANDA
Kigali
L. Victoria
Nairobi
Tana
BURUNDI
Bujumbura
Brazzaville
Kasai
INDIAN OCEAN
Pointe-Noire
KINSHASA
Matadi
Mombasa
Victoria
SEYCHELLES
CABINDA (Angola)
Kananga
TANZANIA
Zanzibar
Cuango
Mbuji-Mayi
Dodoma
Dar es Salaam
Ascension I. (U.K.)
Luanda
L. Tanganyika
L. Mweru
Aldabra Is. (Seychelles)
Kolwezi
Likasi
Lubumbashi
L. Malawi
C. Delgado
Lobito
ANGOLA
COMOROS
Moroni
Mamoudzou
Antsiranana
Huambo
Ndola
MALAWI
Mayotte (Fr.)
Namibe
ATLANTIC OCEAN
ZAMBIA
Lilongwe
Moçambique
Mozambique Channel
Lusaka
Zambezi
Mahajanga
Cubango
Cunene
St. Helena (U.K.)
Blantyre
C. Fria
Livingstone
Harare
ZIMBABWE
Toamasina
Antananarivo
MOZAMBIQUE
Beira
Bulawayo
NAMIBIA
BOTSWANA
MADAGASCAR
MAURITIUS
Port Louis
St-Denis
Réunion (Fr.)
Windhoek
Limpopo
Fianarantsoa
Tropic of Capricorn
Gaborone
Pretoria (Tshwane)
Johannesburg
Maputo
Mbabane
ESWATINI
Vaal
Orange
Kimberley
Maseru
LESOTHO
Durban
SOUTH AFRICA
Cape Town
C. of Good Hope
East London
Port Elizabeth
C. Agulhas
Tristan da Cunha (U.K.)
Projection: Azimuthal Equidistant
West from Greenwich
East from Greenwich
COPYRIGHT PHILIP'S
Dakar Capital Cities

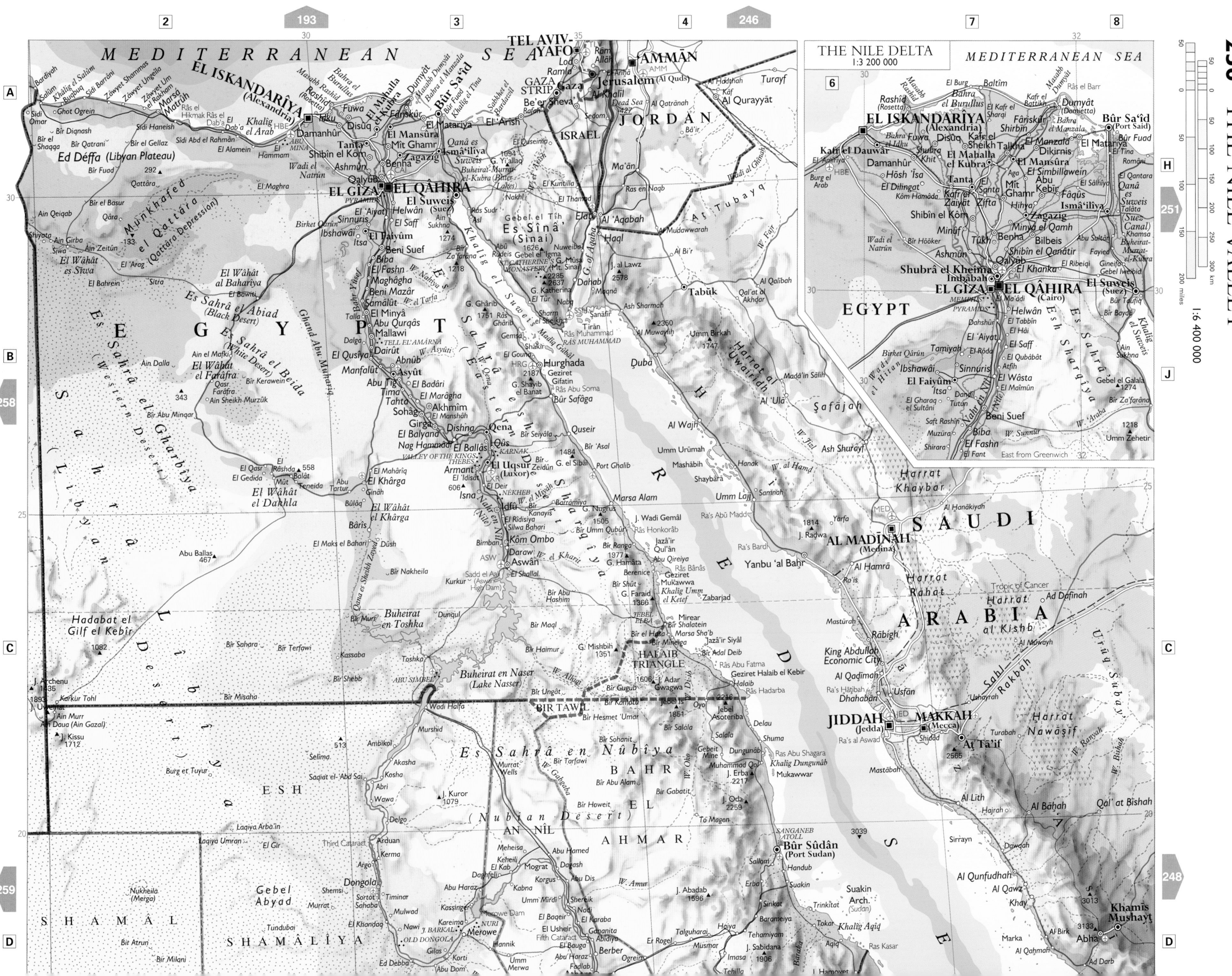
50 0 50 100 150 200 250 300 km
1:6 400 000
50 0 50 100 150 200 miles
THE NILE DELTA
1:3 200 000
MEDITERRANEAN SEA
EGYPT
EL ISKANDARÎYA (Alexandria)
EL QÂHIRA (Cairo)
EL GÎZA
Bûr Sa'îd (Port Said)
Dumyât (Damietta)
Rashîd (Rosetta)
Shubrâ el Kheima
El Mansûra
Tanta
Zagazig
Ismâ'ilîya
El Suweis (Suez)
Es Sahrâ Esh Sharqîya
East from Greenwich
JORDAN
ISRAEL
GAZA STRIP
'AMMÂN
Jerusalem (Al Quds)
TEL AVIV-YAFO
Es Sînâ' (Sinai)
Khalîg el Suweis
G. of Aqaba
SAUDI ARABIA
AL MADÎNAH (Medina)
MAKKAH (Mecca)
JIDDAH (Jedda)
Aţ Ţâ'if
Khamîs Mushayţ
Tabûk
Yanbu 'al Bahr
RED SEA
Hurghada
Qena
El Uqsur (Luxor)
Aswân
Asyût
El Minyâ
Beni Suef
El Faiyûm
Sohâg
Buheirat en Naser (Lake Nasser)
Wadi Halfa
HALAIB TRIANGLE
BIR TAWIL
Bûr Sûdân (Port Sudan)
Suakin
Dongola
Merowe
Es Sahrâ el Gharbîya (Western Desert)
Sahrâ Lîbîya (Libyan Desert)
Es Sahrâ en Nûbîya (Nubian Desert)
Es Sahrâ el Beida (White Desert)
Es Sahrâ el Abiad (Black Desert)
Munkhafed el Qattâra (Qattara Depression)
Ed Déffa (Libyan Plateau)
Hadabat el Gilf el Kebîr
El Wâhât el Khârga
El Wâhât el Dakhla
El Wâhât el Farâfra
El Wâhât al Bahariya
Sîwa
Marsâ Matrûh
ESH SHAMÂLÎYA
BAHR EL AHMAR
Tropic of Cancer

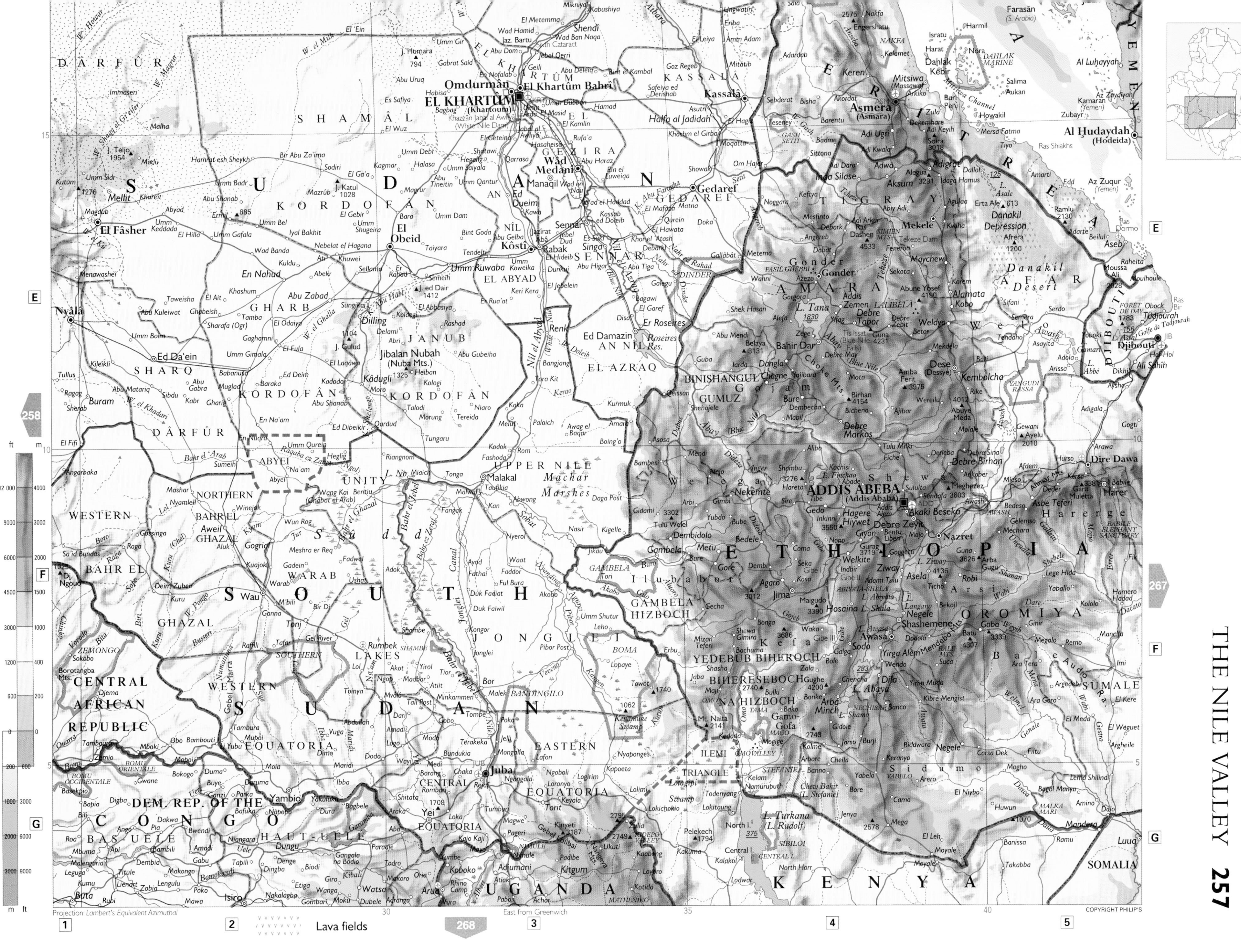
YEMEN
ERITREA
ETHIOPIA
SUDAN
SOUTH SUDAN
KENYA
UGANDA
SOMALIA
DJIBOUTI
CENTRAL AFRICAN REPUBLIC
DEM. REP. OF THE CONGO
ADDIS ABEBA (Addis Ababa)
EL KHARTÛM (Khartoum)
Omdurmân
El Khartûm Bahri
Asmera (Asmara)
Juba
Djibouti
Mitsiwa (Massawa)
Al Hudaydah (Hodeida)
Gonder
Dire Dawa
Harer
Dese (Dessye)
Nazret
Jima
Kassalâ
Gedaref
Kôstî
Wad Medani
El Obeid
Nyâlâ
El Fâsher
Wau
Malakal
Ed Damazin
Er Roseires
Sennar
L. Tana
L. Turkana (L. Rudolf)
Danakil Desert
Dankil Depression
ILEMI TRIANGLE
ABYEI
Projection: Lambert's Equivalent Azimuthal
East from Greenwich
COPYRIGHT PHILIP'S
Lava fields
258
267
268
m
ft

1:6 400 000

192
193
256
261

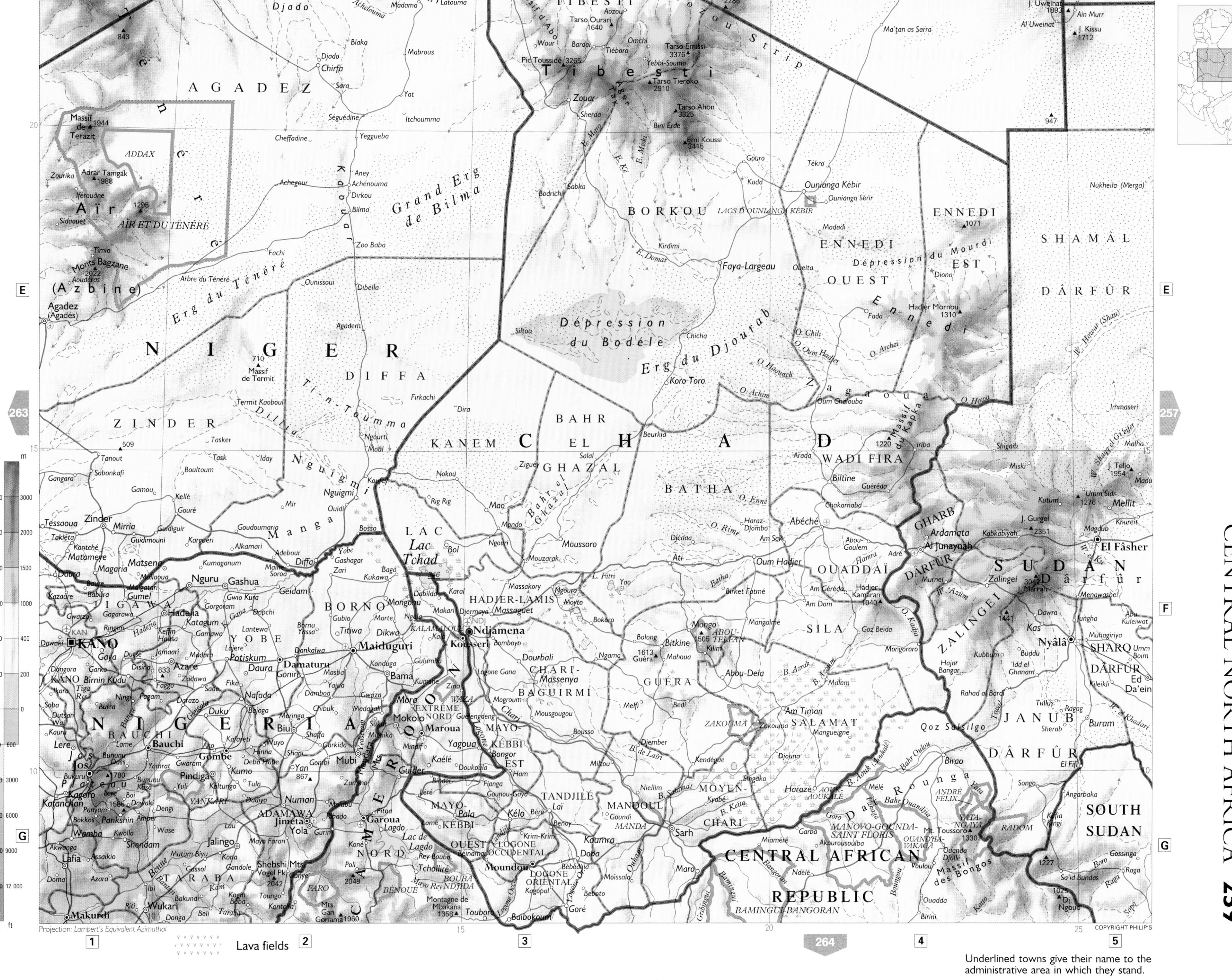
AGADEZ
NIGER
DIFFA
ZINDER
CHAD
KANEM
LAC
Lac Tchad
BAHR EL GHAZAL
BORKOU
ENNEDI OUEST
ENNEDI EST
BATHA
WADI FIRA
OUADDAÏ
SILA
SALAMAT
GUÉRA
HADJER-LAMIS
CHARI-BAGUIRMI
MAYO-KEBBI EST
MAYO-KEBBI OUEST
TANDJILÉ
LOGONE OCCIDENTAL
LOGONE ORIENTAL
MANDOUL
MOYEN-CHARI
SUDAN
SHAMÂL DÂRFÛR
GHARB DÂRFÛR
JANUB DÂRFÛR
SHARQ DÂRFÛR
ZALINGEI
SOUTH SUDAN
CENTRAL AFRICAN REPUBLIC
NIGERIA
CAMEROON
BORNO
YOBE
KANO
JIGAWA
BAUCHI
ADAMAWA
TARABA
EXTRÊME-NORD
NORD
Tibesti
Aïr
Grand Erg de Bilma
Erg du Djourab
Dépression du Bodélé
Erg du Ténéré
Ndjamena
Maiduguri
Kano
Zinder
Agadez (Agadès)
El Fâsher
Nyâlâ
Abéché
Moundou
Sarh
Garoua
Maroua
Faya-Largeau
Bilma
Jos
Bauchi
Yola
263
257
264
Projection: Lambert's Equivalent Azimuthal
Lava fields
COPYRIGHT PHILIP'S
Underlined towns give their name to the administrative area in which they stand.

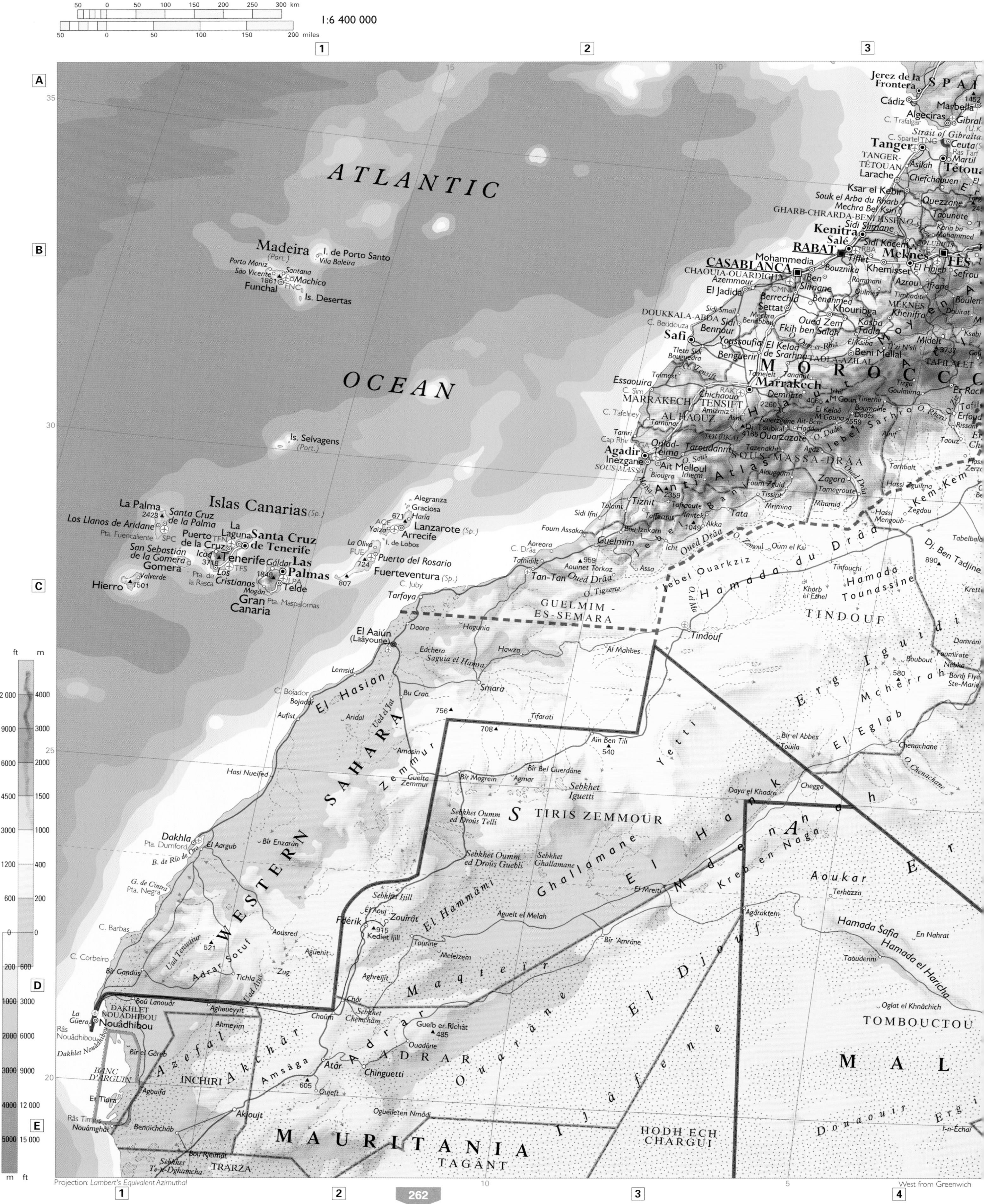

Projection: Lambert's Equivalent Azimuthal

West from Greenwich

262

Underlined towns give their name to the administrative area in which they stand

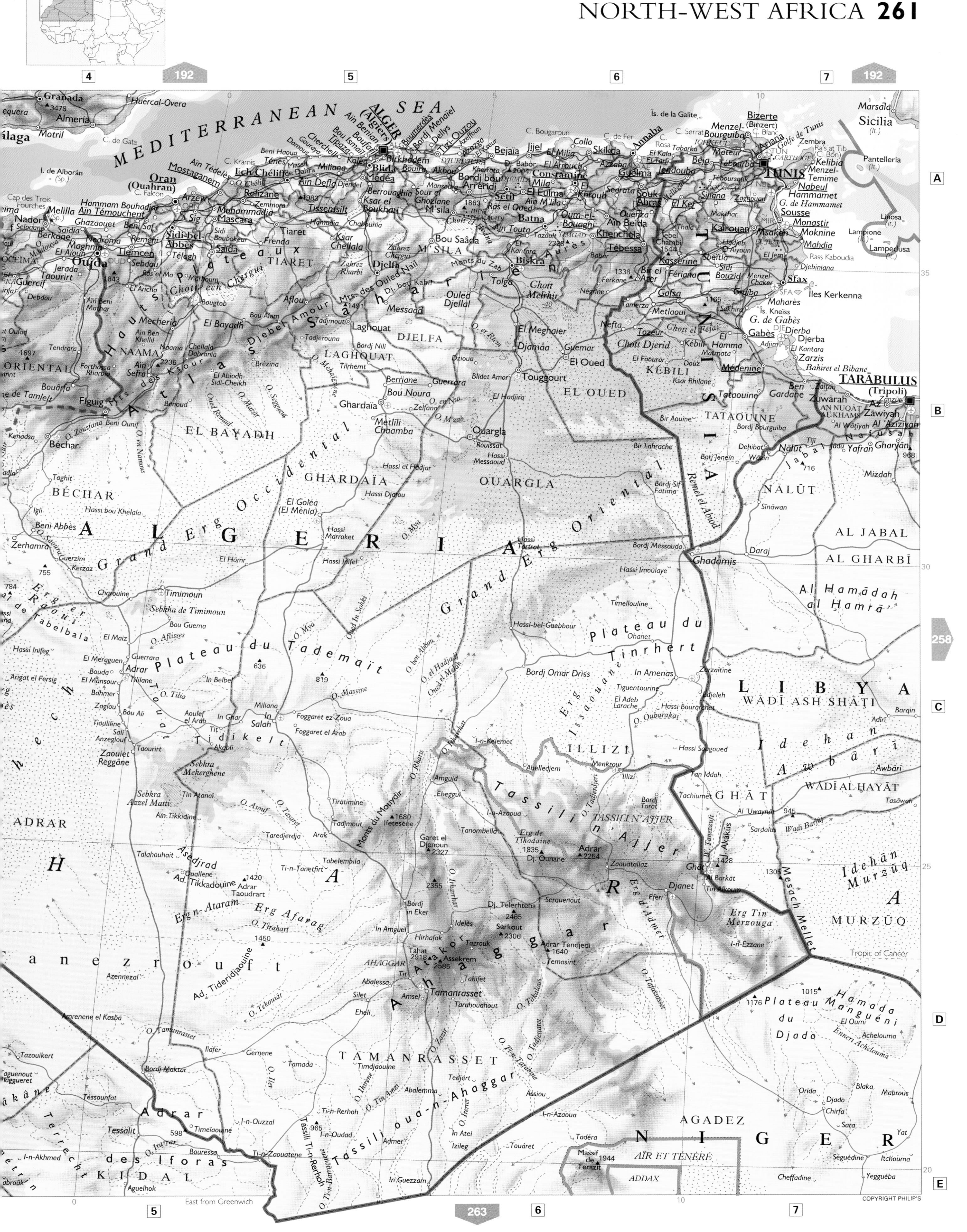
4
192
5
6
7
192
MEDITERRANEAN SEA
ALGER (Algiers)
Oran (Ouahran)
Mostaganem
Ech Chéliff
Tlemcen
Oujda
Sidi-bel-Abbès
Mascara
Tiaret
Saïda
Blida
Médéa
Boumerdès
Tizi-Ouzou
Bejaïa
Jijel
Skikda
Annaba
Constantine
Sétif
Batna
Biskra
Tébessa
Guelma
Bizerte (Binzert)
TUNIS
Sousse
Kairouan
Sfax
Gabès
Djerba
Gafsa
Tozeur
Nefta
Kasserine
Îles Kerkenna
Sicilia (It.)
Pantelleria (It.)
Lampedusa (It.)
Linosa (It.)
Lampione (It.)
TARĀBULUS (Tripoli)
Zuwārah
Nālūt
Ghadāmis
Granada
Almería
Málaga
I. de Alborán (Sp.)
Melilla (Sp.)
Nador
Béchar
Figuig
Laghouat
Djelfa
Ghardaïa
Ouargla
Touggourt
El Oued
Hassi Messaoud
El Goléa (El Ménia)
Timimoun
Adrar
In Salah
Illizi
Djanet
Tamanrasset
In Amenas
Bordj Omar Driss
Ghat
Hauts Plateaux
Atlas Saharien
Grand Erg Occidental
Grand Erg Oriental
Chott Melrhir
Chott el Djerid
Plateau du Tademaït
Plateau du Tinrhert
Tassili n' Ajjer
Ahaggar
Atakor
Tanezrouft
Adrar des Iforas
Tassili oua-n-Ahaggar
Erg Chech
Tidikelt
Assekrem 2585
Tahat 2918
A L G E R I A
T U N I S I A
L I B Y A
N I G E R
Al Ḩamādah al Ḩamrā'
Idehan Awbārī
Idehān Murzūq
Plateau du Manguéni
Hamada Manguéni
Plateau du Djado
Massif de Terazit 1944
AÏR ET TÉNÉRÉ
ADDAX
Tropic of Cancer
A
B
C
D
E
258
East from Greenwich
5
263
6
7
COPYRIGHT PHILIP'S

Underlined towns give their name to the administrative area in which they stand.

Administrative division in Côte d'Ivoire:
1 Sassandra-Marahoué

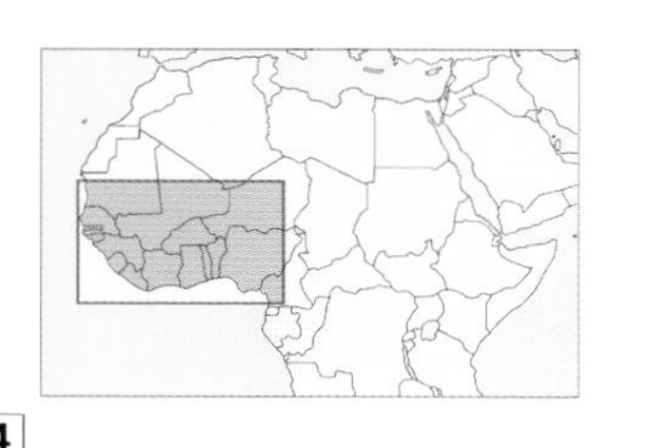

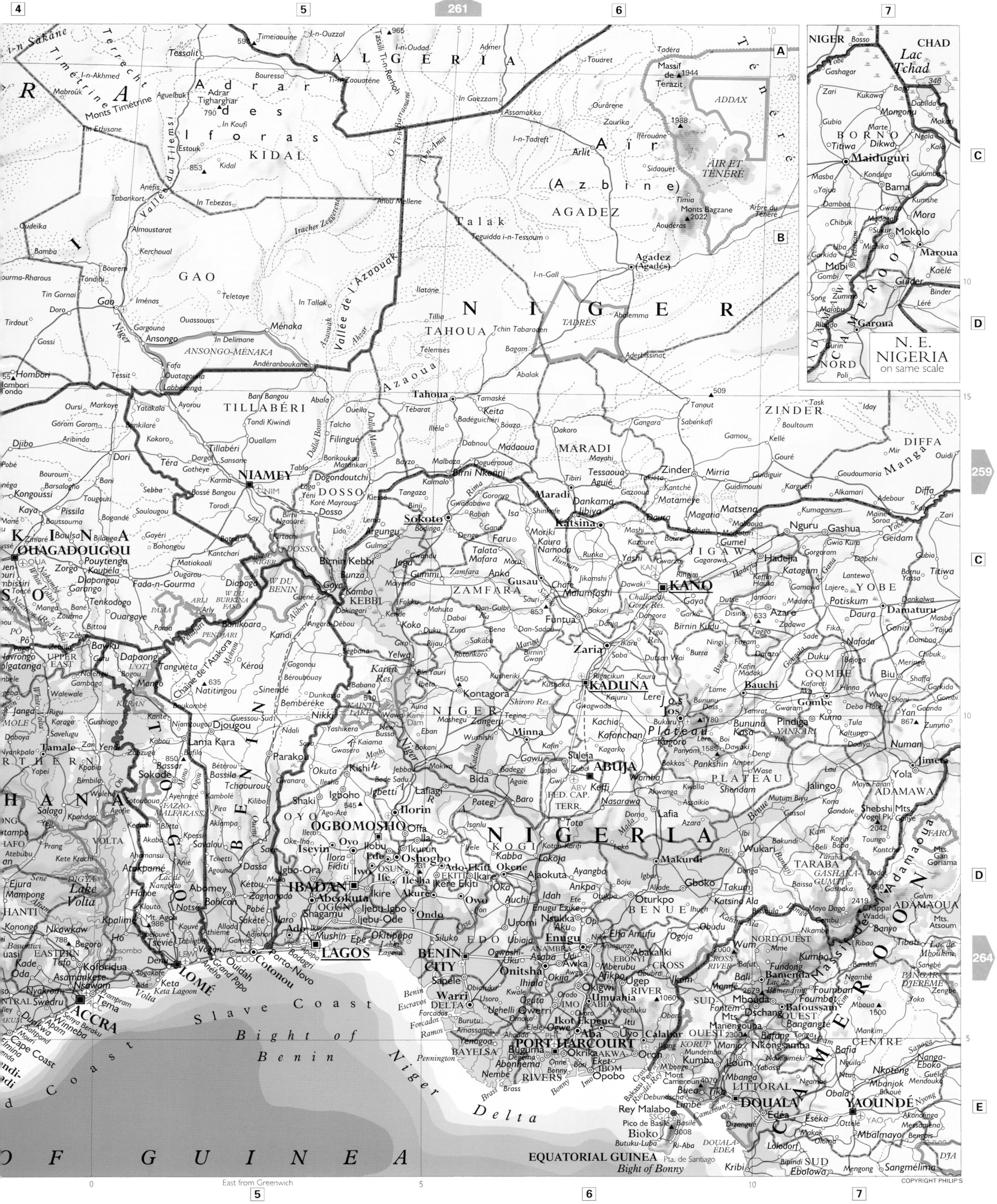

261
259
264

ALGERIA
NIGER
NIGERIA
CAMEROON
CHAD
GHANA
TOGO
BENIN
EQUATORIAL GUINEA
GULF OF GUINEA
Bight of Benin
Bight of Bonny
Slave Coast
Niger Delta
Adrar des Iforas
Aïr (Azbine)
Ténéré
KIDAL
GAO
TILLABÉRI
TAHOUA
AGADEZ
MARADI
ZINDER
DIFFA
DOSSO
NIAMEY
OUAGADOUGOU
ACCRA
LOMÉ
Porto-Novo
LAGOS
IBADAN
ABUJA
KADUNA
KANO
YAOUNDÉ
DOUALA
PORT HARCOURT
N. E. NIGERIA on same scale
East from Greenwich

1:6 400 000

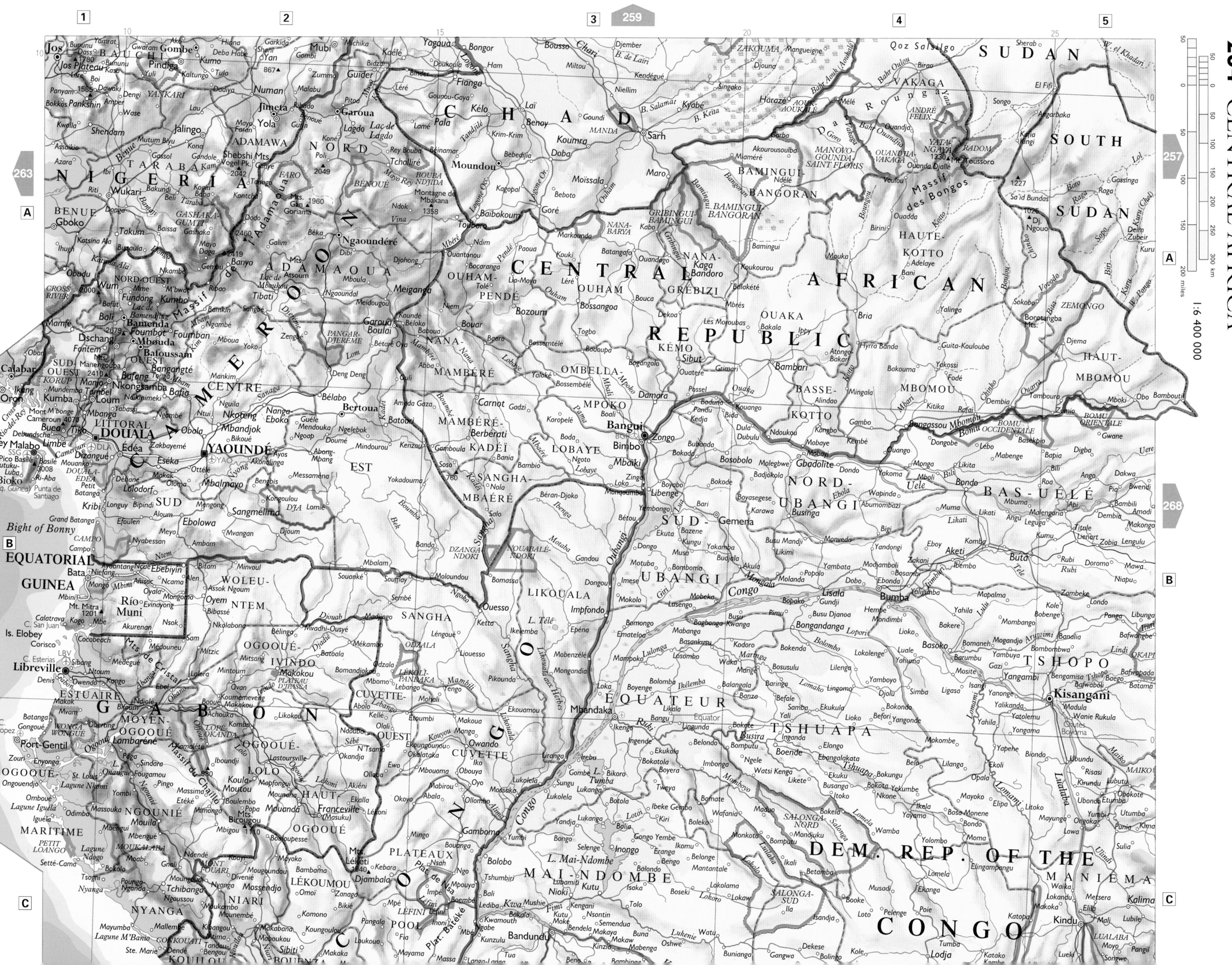
50 0 50 100 150 200 250 300 km
50 0 50 100 150 200 miles
257
268
259
263
A
B
C
1
2
3
4
5
SUDAN
SOUTH SUDAN
CHAD
CENTRAL AFRICAN REPUBLIC
NIGERIA
CAMEROON
EQUATORIAL GUINEA
GABON
CONGO
DEM. REP. OF THE CONGO
Bight of Bonny
Bangui
Yaoundé
Douala
Libreville
Kisangani
Mbandaka
Bandundu
Port-Gentil
Malabo
Bioko
Sarh
Moundou
Ngaoundéré
Garoua
Berbérati
Bossangoa
Bambari
Bria
Ouesso
Impfondo
Gemena
Lisala
Bumba
Kindu
Franceville
Lambaréné
Oyem
Bata
Río Muni
Congo
Oubangui
Sangha
Lualaba

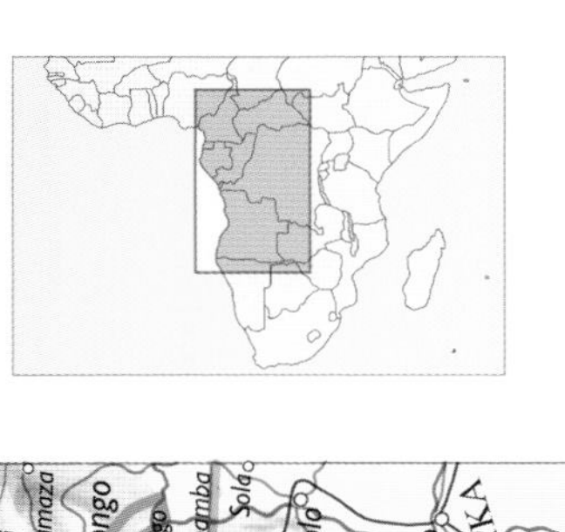

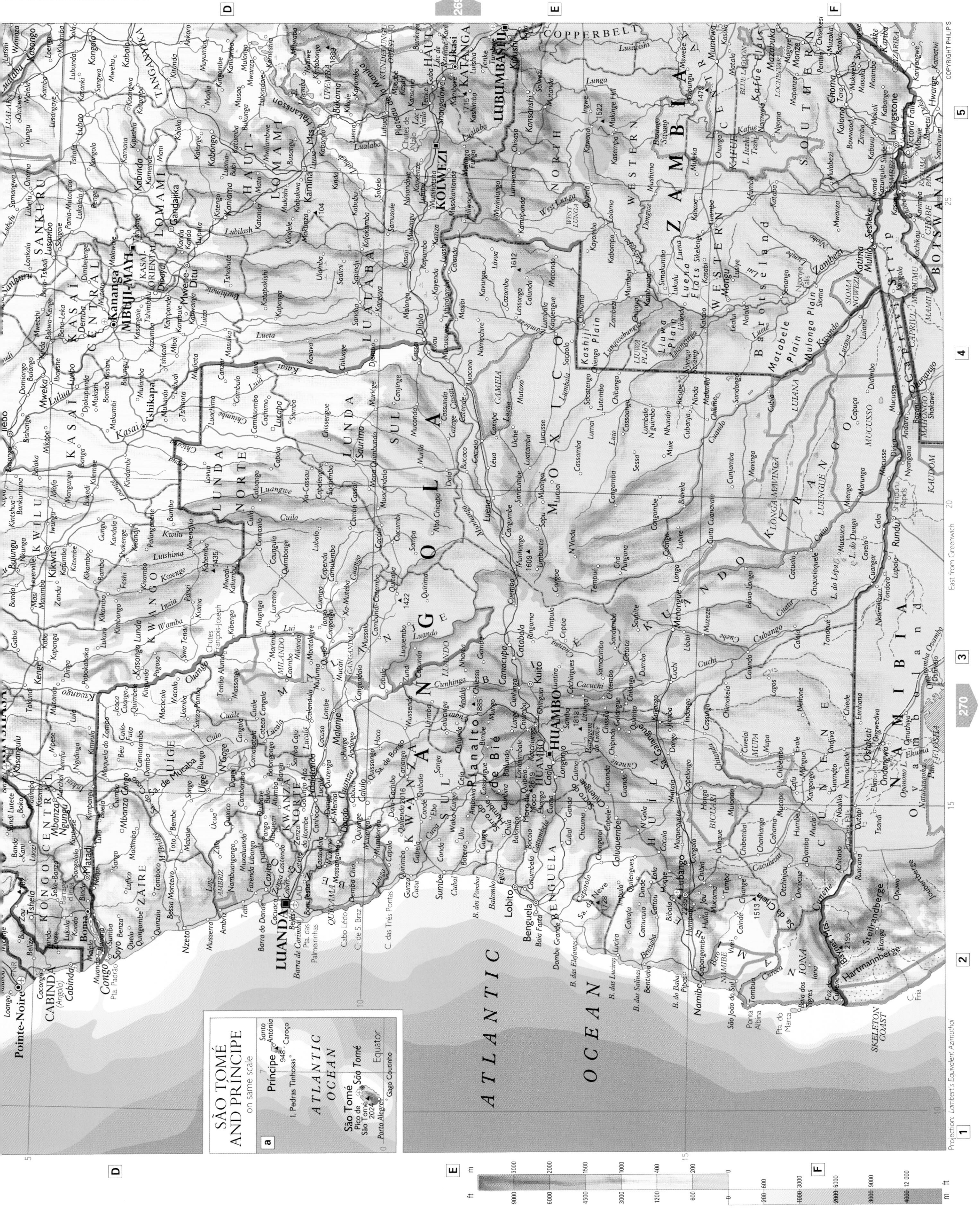

ATLANTIC OCEAN
ANGOLA
ZAMBIA
NAMIBIA
BOTSWANA
LUANDA
HUAMBO
LUBUMBASHI
KOLWEZI
SÃO TOMÉ AND PRÍNCIPE
on same scale
Equator
Projection: Lambert's Equivalent Azimuthal
East from Greenwich
COPYRIGHT PHILIP'S

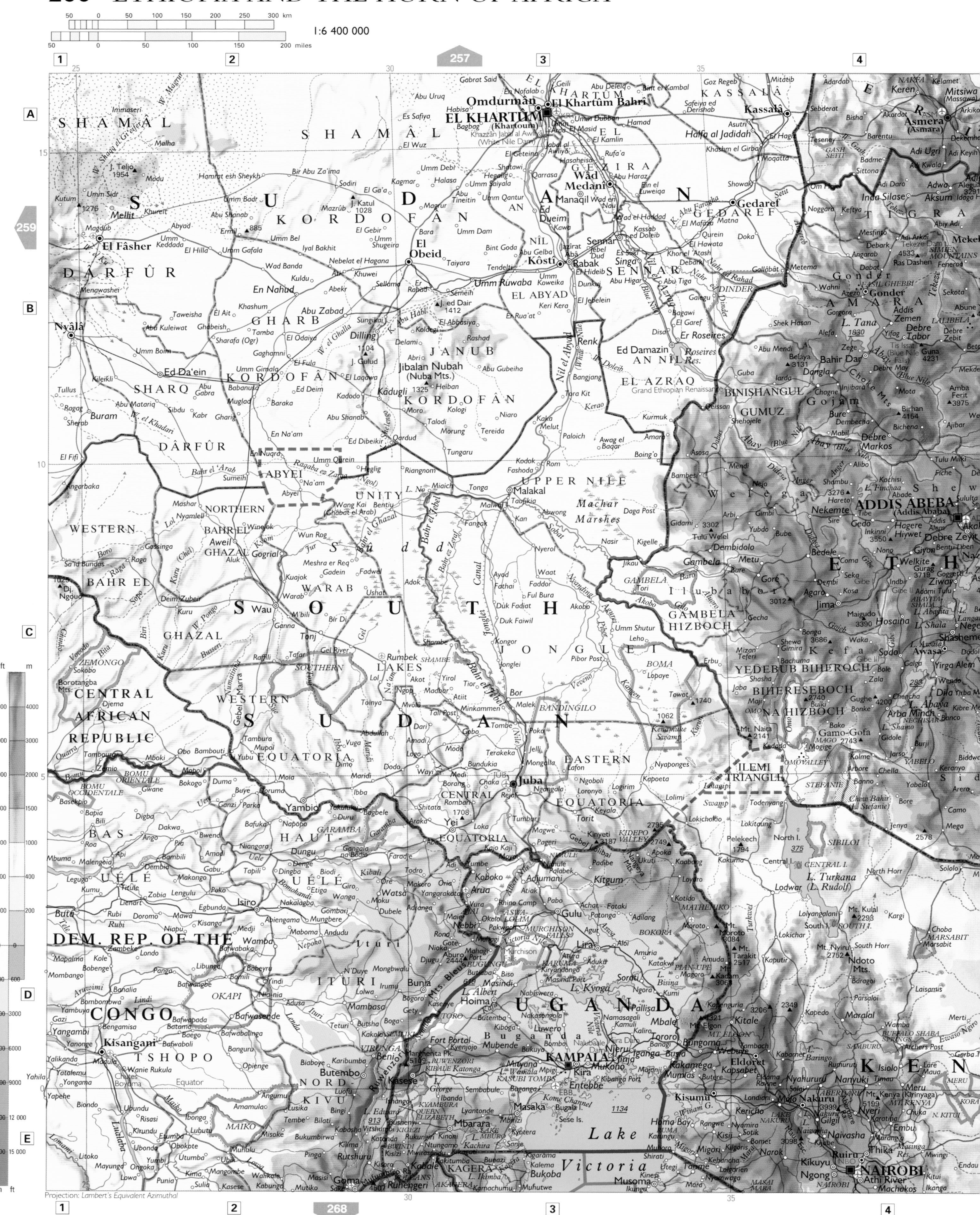

Projection: Lambert's Equivalent Azimuthal

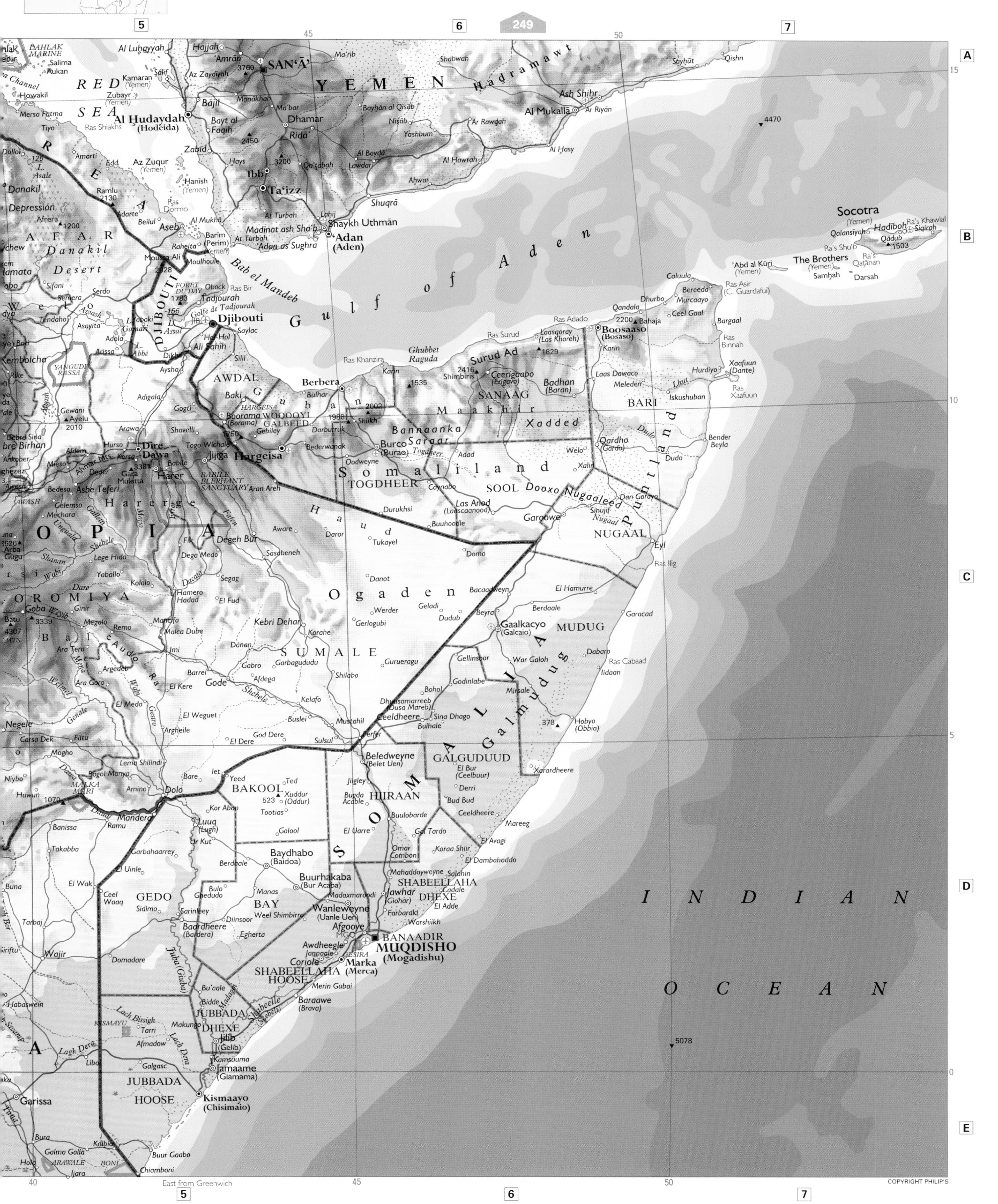

249
RED SEA
YEMEN
SAN'Ā'
Al Hudaydah (Hodeida)
Dhamar
Ta'izz
Ibb
Ḥadramawt
Ash Shihr
Al Mukalla
Shaykh Uthmān
Adan (Aden)
Gulf of Aden
Bab el Mandeb
Socotra (Yemen)
Hadiboh
The Brothers (Yemen)
'Abd al Kūri (Yemen)
Ras Asir (C. Guardafui)
DJIBOUTI
Djibouti
Tadjourah
Obock
Danakil Depression
AFAR
Danakil Desert
Aseb
AWDAL
Berbera
Hargeisa
Boorama (Borama)
Burco (Burao)
Somaliland
TOGDHEER
SANAAG
Ceerigaabo (Erigavo)
Boosaaso (Bosaso)
BARI
Puntland
SOOL
Las Anod (Laascaanood)
Garoowe
NUGAAL
Eyl
Dire Dawa
Harer
Jijiga
Hararge
OROMIYA
Ogaden
SUMALE
Gode
Kebri Dehar
Degeh Bur
Galkacyo (Galcaio)
MUDUG
Hobyo (Obbia)
GALGUDUUD
Beledweyne (Belet Uen)
HIIRAAN
BAKOOL
Baydhabo (Baidoa)
BAY
GEDO
SOMALIA
Jawhar (Giohar)
SHABEELLAHA DHEXE
BANAADIR
MUQDISHO (Mogadishu)
Marka (Merca)
SHABEELLAHA HOOSE
Baraawe (Brava)
JUBBADA DHEXE
Jilib (Gelib)
Jamaame (Giamama)
JUBBADA HOOSE
Kismaayo (Chisimaio)
Garissa
Mandera
Dolo
Negele
INDIAN OCEAN
5078
4470
East from Greenwich
COPYRIGHT PHILIP'S

1:6 400 000

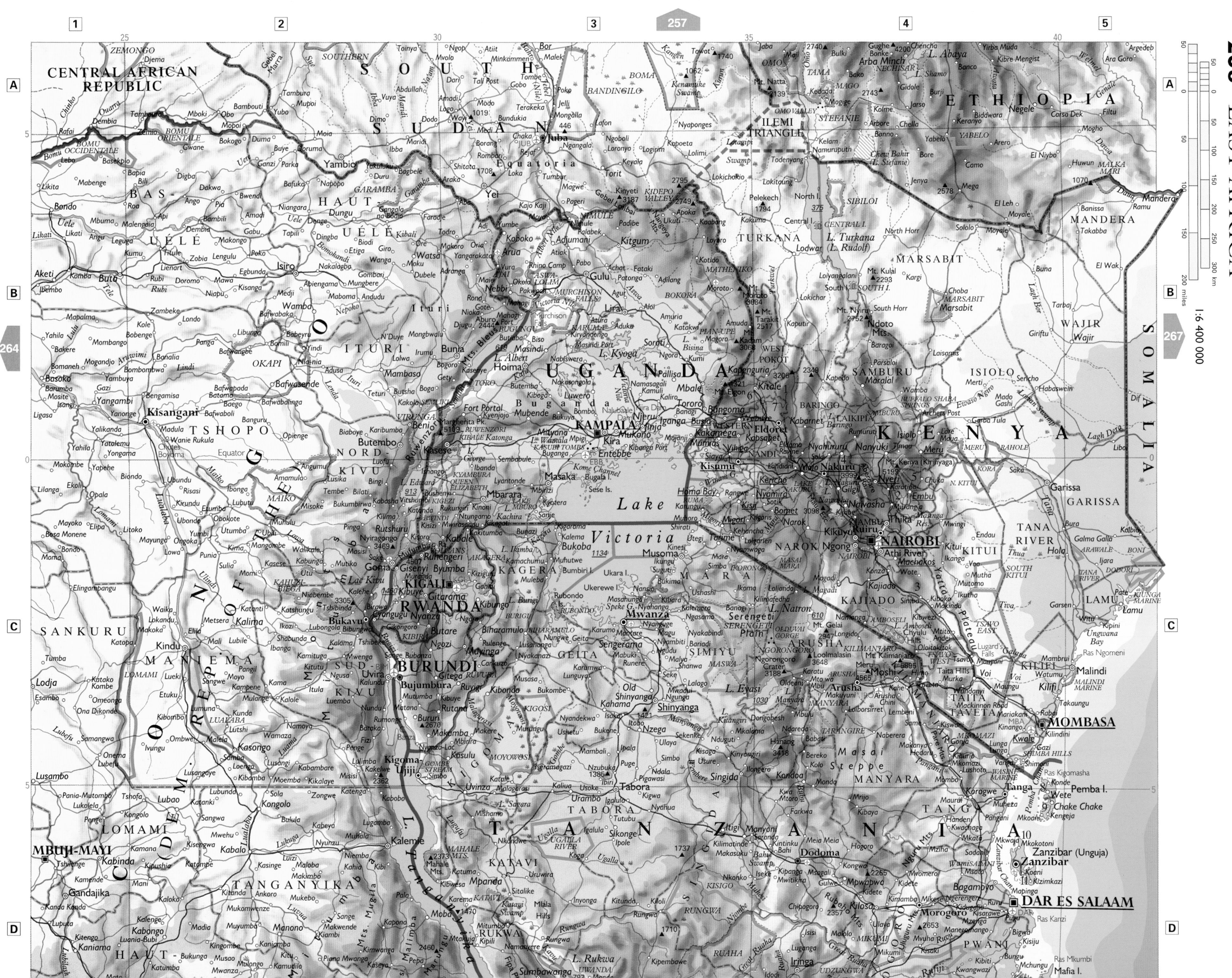
50 0 50 100 150 200 250 300 km
50 0 50 100 150 200 miles
257
264
267
CENTRAL AFRICAN REPUBLIC
SOUTH SUDAN
ETHIOPIA
SOMALIA
KENYA
UGANDA
RWANDA
BURUNDI
TANZANIA
ILEMI TRIANGLE
NAIROBI
MOMBASA
DAR ES SALAAM
KAMPALA
KIGALI
Juba
Lake Victoria
L. Turkana (L. Rudolf)
Kisangani
Mwanza
Dodoma
Zanzibar
Bujumbura
Kigoma
Tabora
Arusha
Entebbe
Malindi
MBUJI-MAYI
Kisumu
Eldoret
Garissa
Marsabit
Mandera
Lamu
Tanga
Morogoro
Kalemie
Bukavu
Goma
Gulu
Yei
Yambio
Isiro
Bunia
Kindu

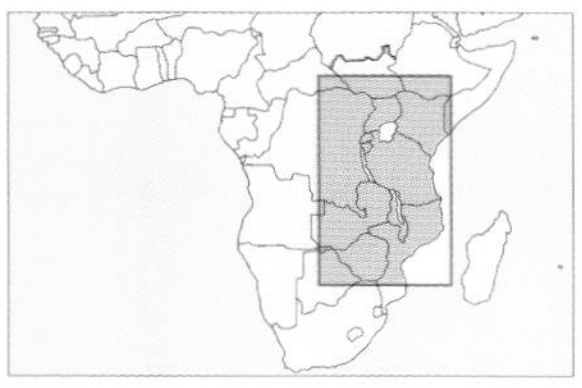

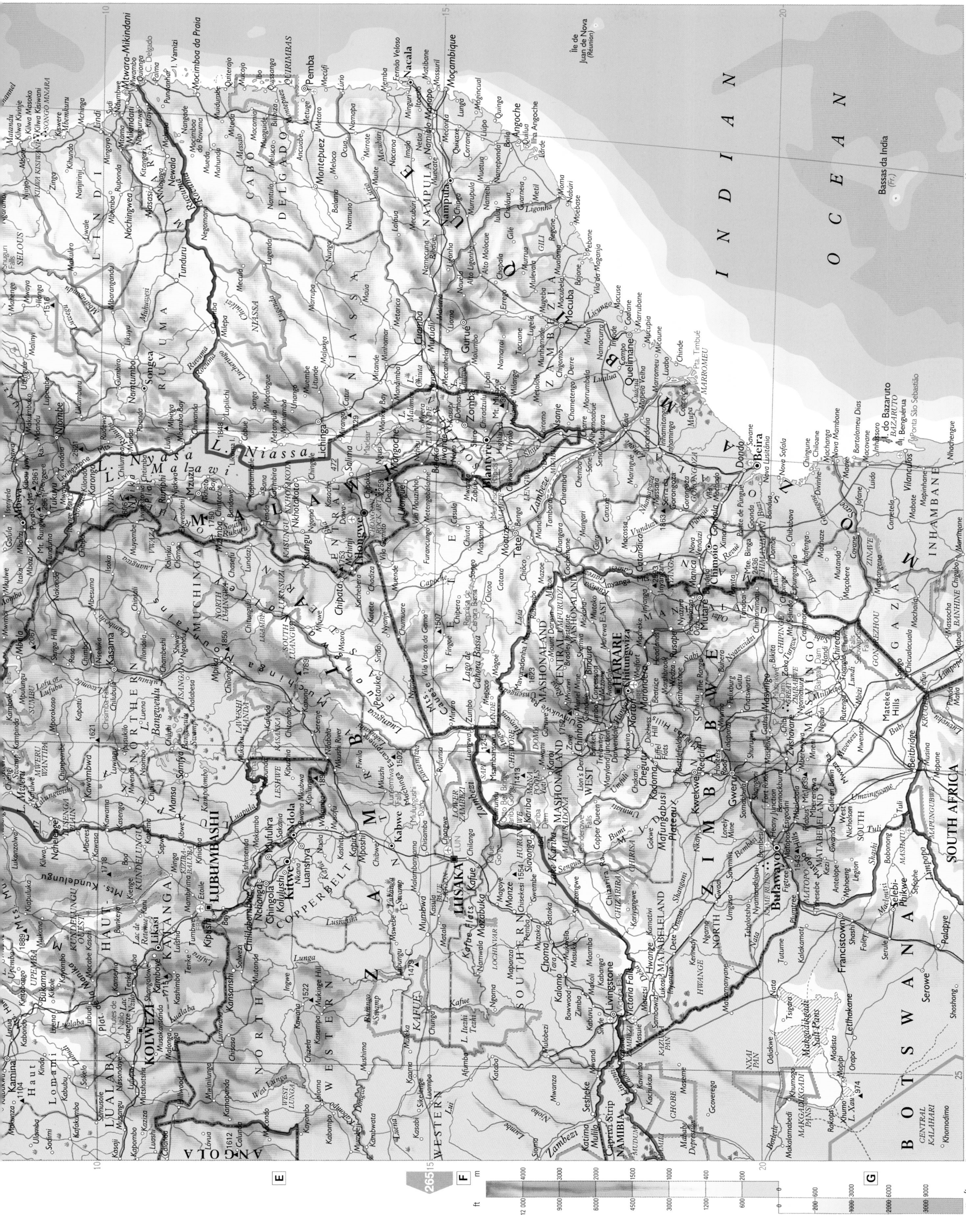
Administrative divisions in Kenya:
1 Elgeyo-Marakwet 2 Kirinyaga 3 Makueni 4 Nyandarua 5 Tharaka Nithi 6 Trans-Nzoia 7 Uasin Gishu
Administrative divisions in Tanzania:
8 North Pemba 9 South Pemba 10 North Zanzibar 11 South Zanzibar
Underlined towns give their name to the administrative area in which they stand.
INDIAN OCEAN
ZAMBIA
ZIMBABWE
MOZAMBIQUE
MALAWI
BOTSWANA
SOUTH AFRICA
NAMIBIA
ANGOLA
L. Nyasa
L. Niassa
Lago de Cahora Bassa
LUSAKA
HARARE
Lilongwe
Blantyre
Beira
Bulawayo
Projection: Lambert's Equivalent Azimuthal
East from Greenwich
COPYRIGHT PHILIP'S
270
271
272
265
m ft
4000 12 000
3000 9000
2000 6000
1500 4500
1000 3000
400 1200
200 600

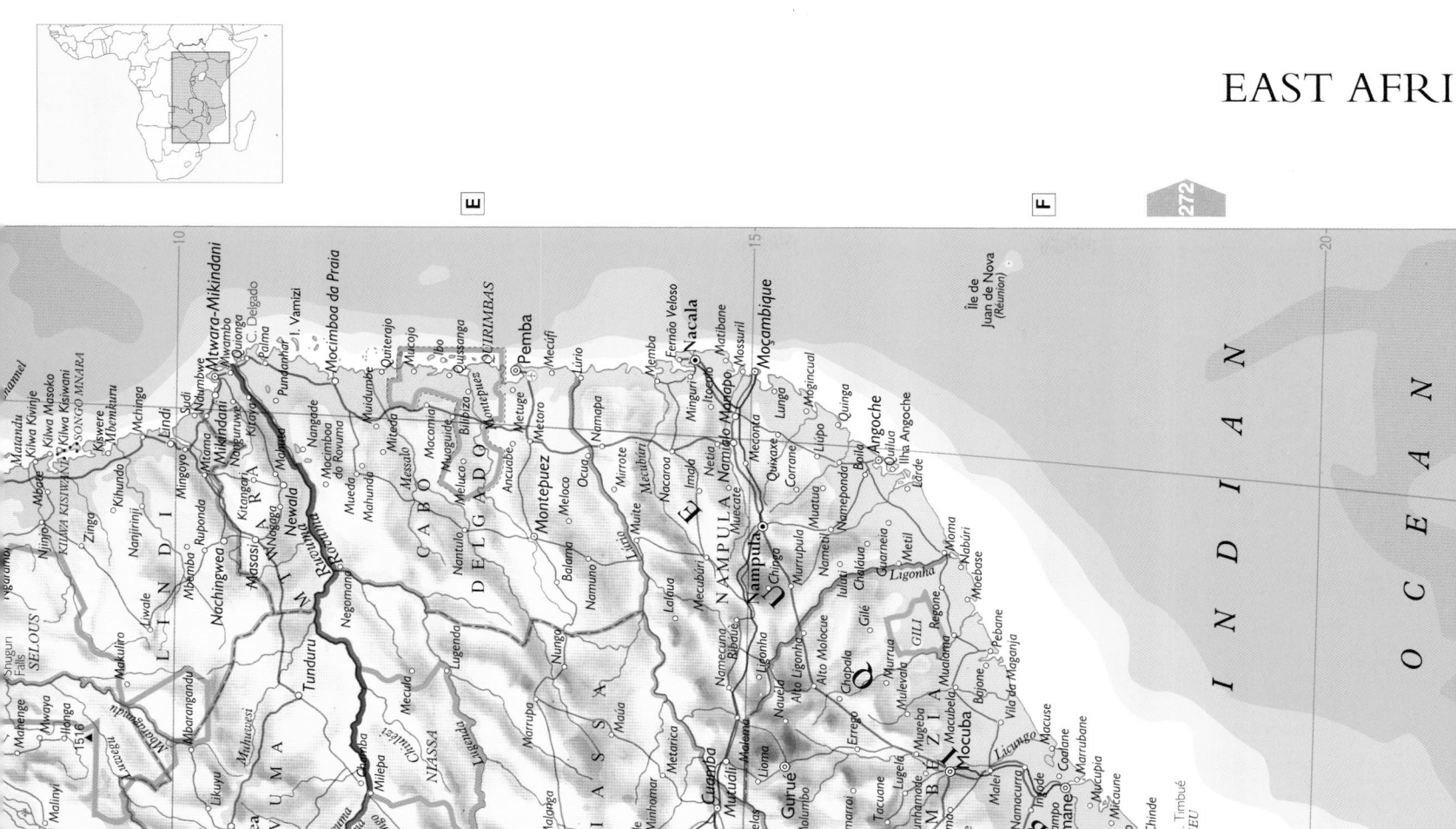

1:6 400 000

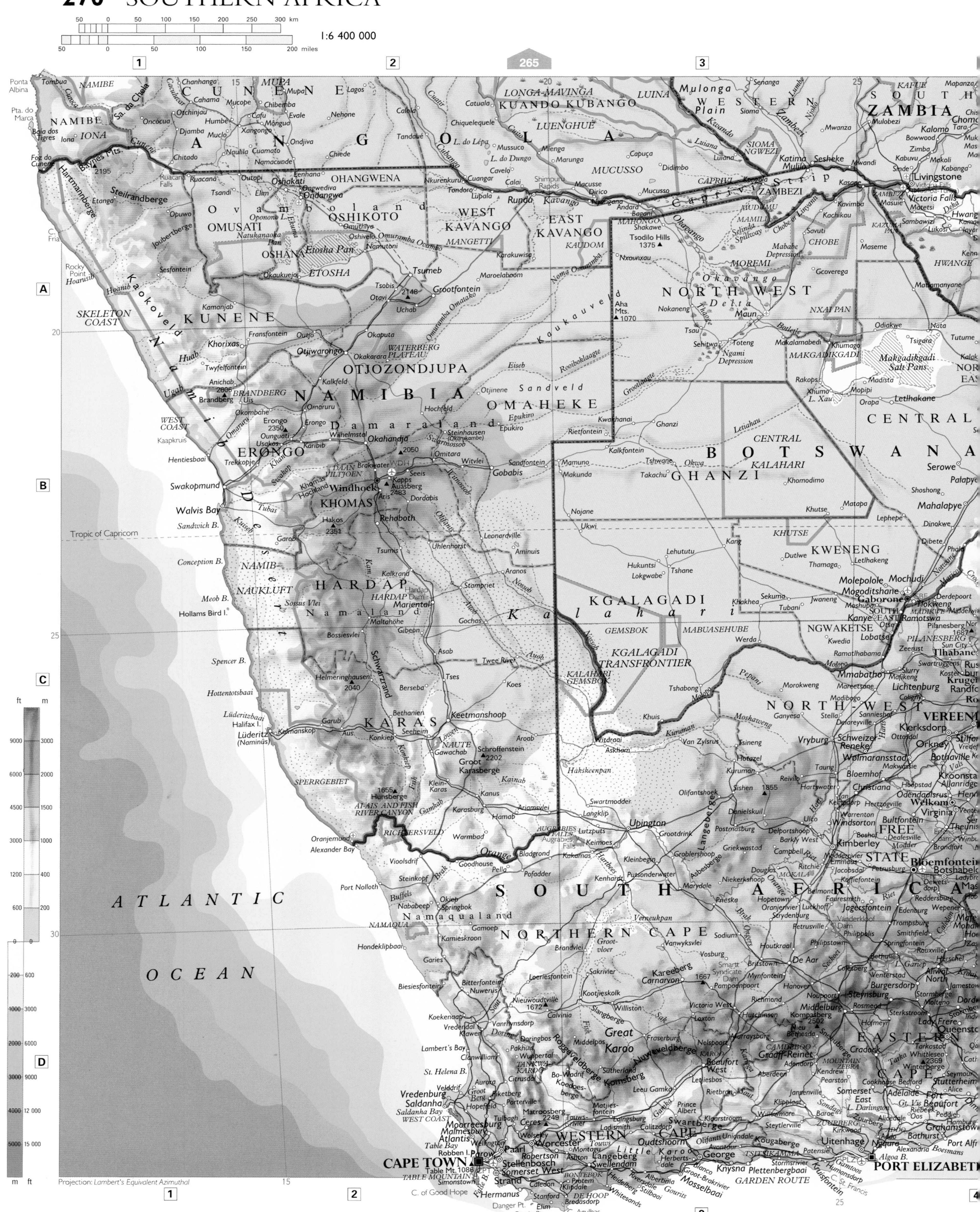

ZAMBIA
NAMIBIA
BOTSWANA
SOUTH AFRICA
ATLANTIC OCEAN
Windhoek
Gaborone
CAPE TOWN
PORT ELIZABETH
Kimberley
Bloemfontein
Walvis Bay
Swakopmund
Lüderitz
Keetmanshoop
Upington
Maun
Livingstone
Tropic of Capricorn
Kalahari
Namib Desert
Great Karoo
NORTHERN CAPE
WESTERN CAPE
EASTERN CAPE
FREE STATE
NORTH-WEST
Projection: Lambert's Equivalent Azimuthal

269
272
5
6
7
A
B
C
D
20
25
30
35
40
East from Greenwich
MALAWI
ZAMBEZIA
Z I M B A B W E
MASHONALAND CENTRAL
MASHONALAND WEST
MASHONALAND EAST
MANICA
SOFALA
MOZAMBIQUE
INHAMBANE
GAZA
MAPUTO
MASVINGO
MIDLANDS
MATABELELAND SOUTH
LIMPOPO
MPUMALANGA
ESWATINI
KWAZULU-NATAL
HARARE
Chitungwiza
Mutare
Chimoio
Beira
Dondo
Quelimane
Mocuba
Gweru
Bulawayo
Masvingo
Kadoma
Marondera
Chinhoyi
Kariba
Lago de Cahora Bassa
L. Kariba
Tete
Angoche
I. Angoche
Île de Júan de Nova (Fr.)
MOZAMBIQUE CHANNEL
Bassas da India (Fr.)
Île Europa (Fr.)
Tropic of Capricorn
I. do Bazaruto
Vilanculos
Inhambane
Maxixe
Chibuto
Chokwé
Xai-Xai
Maputo
Matola
Mbabane
Manzini
PRETORIA (Tshwane)
JOHANNESBURG
Benoni
Springs
Polokwane
Phalaborwa
Mbombela (Nelspruit)
Middelburg
Newcastle
Richards Bay
Empangeni
Pietermaritzburg
DURBAN
Umlazi
Port Shepstone
Margate
Mthatha
Ladysmith
L. St. Lucia
Beitbridge
Musina
Louis Trichardt (Makhado)
INDIAN OCEAN
COPYRIGHT PHILIP'S

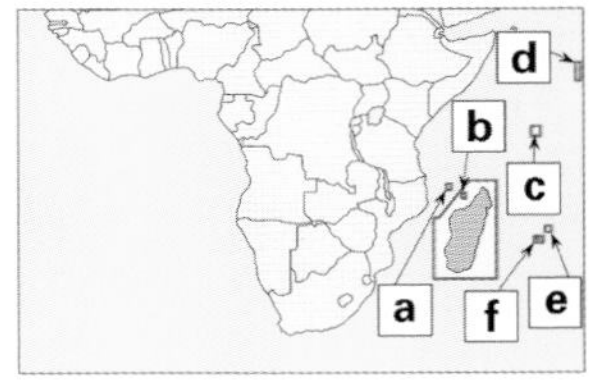

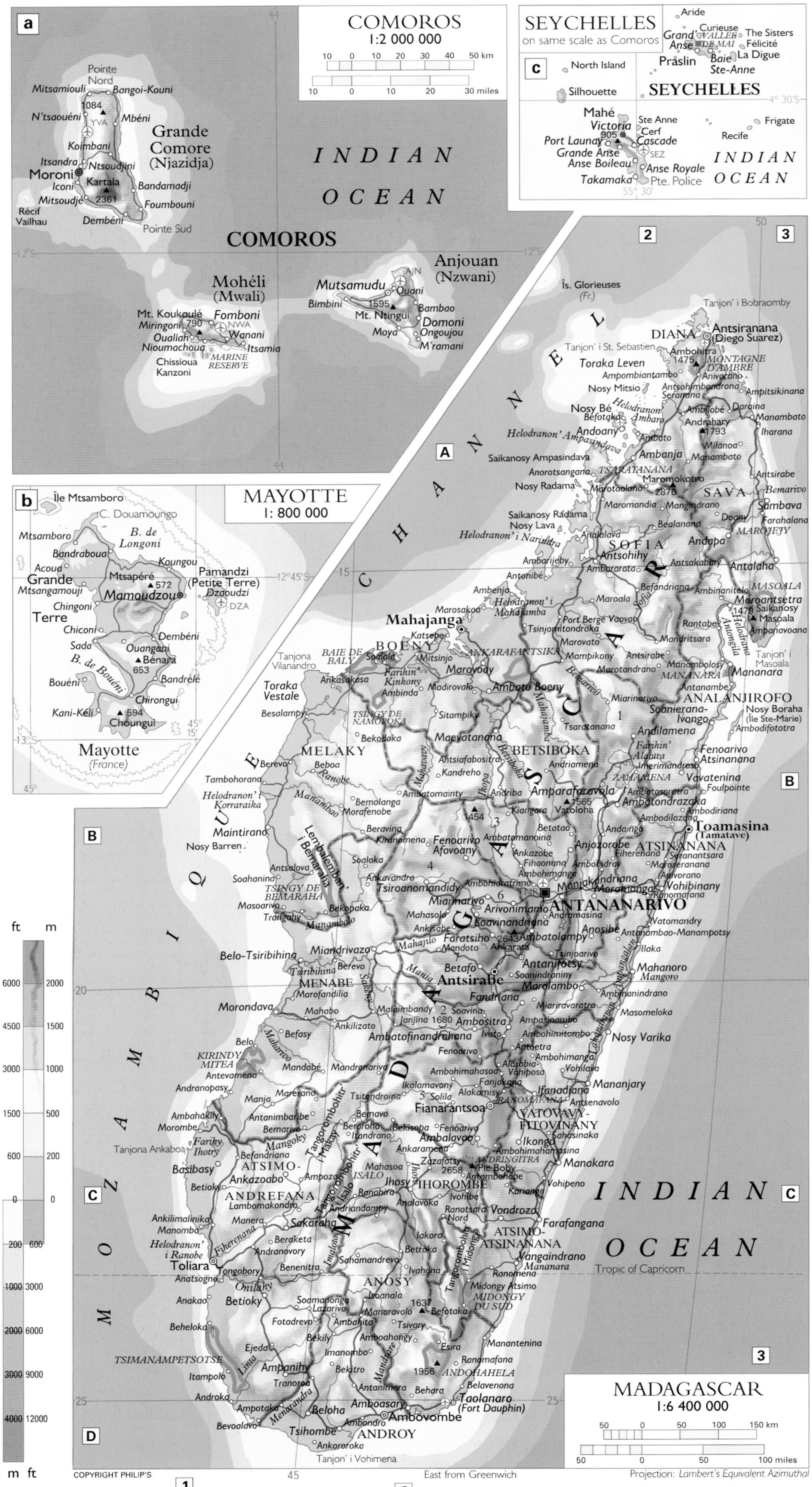

a COMOROS
1:2 000 000

10 0 10 20 30 40 50 km
10 0 10 20 30 miles

b MAYOTTE
1: 800 000

c SEYCHELLES
on same scale as Comoros

d MALDIVES
on same scale as Madagascar

e MAURITIUS
1: 800 000

f RÉUNION
1: 800 000

5 0 10 20 30 40 km
5 0 5 10 15 20 25 miles
1:800 000

MADAGASCAR
1:6 400 000

50 0 50 100 150 km
50 0 50 100 miles

ft m
6000 2000
4500 1500
3000 1000
1500 500
600 200
0 0
200 600
1000 3000
2000 6000
3000 9000
4000 12000
m ft

East from Greenwich

Projection: *Lambert's Equivalent Azimuthal*

Administrative divisions in Madagascar:
1 Alaotra-Mangoro 2 Amoron'i Mania 3 Analamanga 4 Bongolava 5 Haute Matsiatra 6 Itasy 7 Vakinankaratra

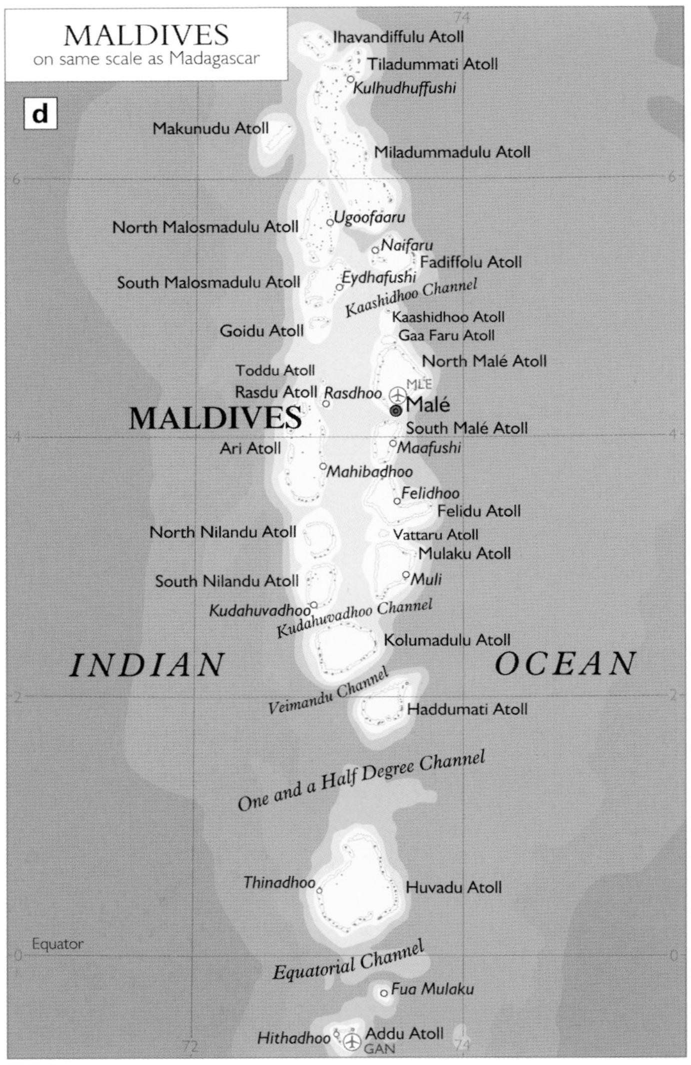

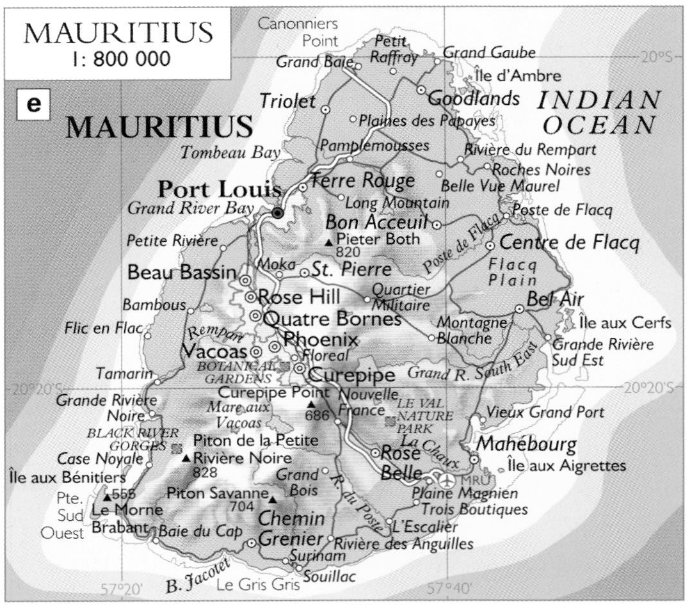

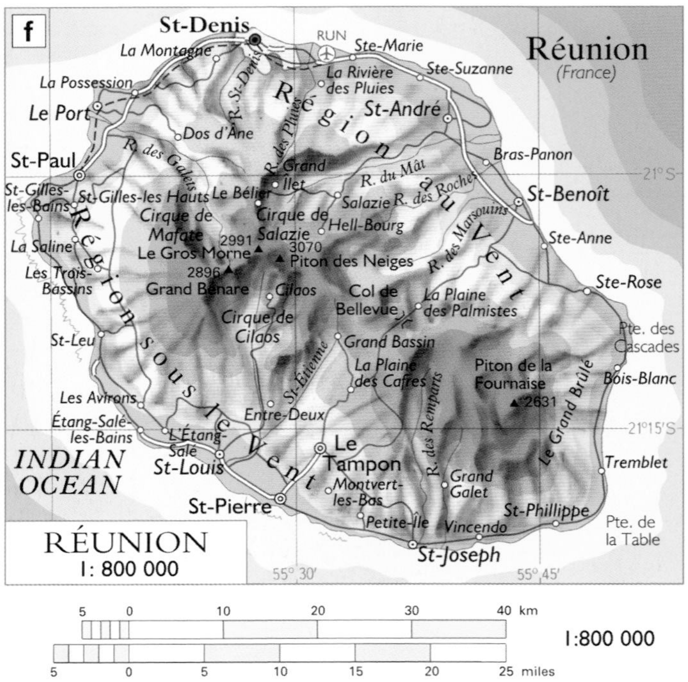

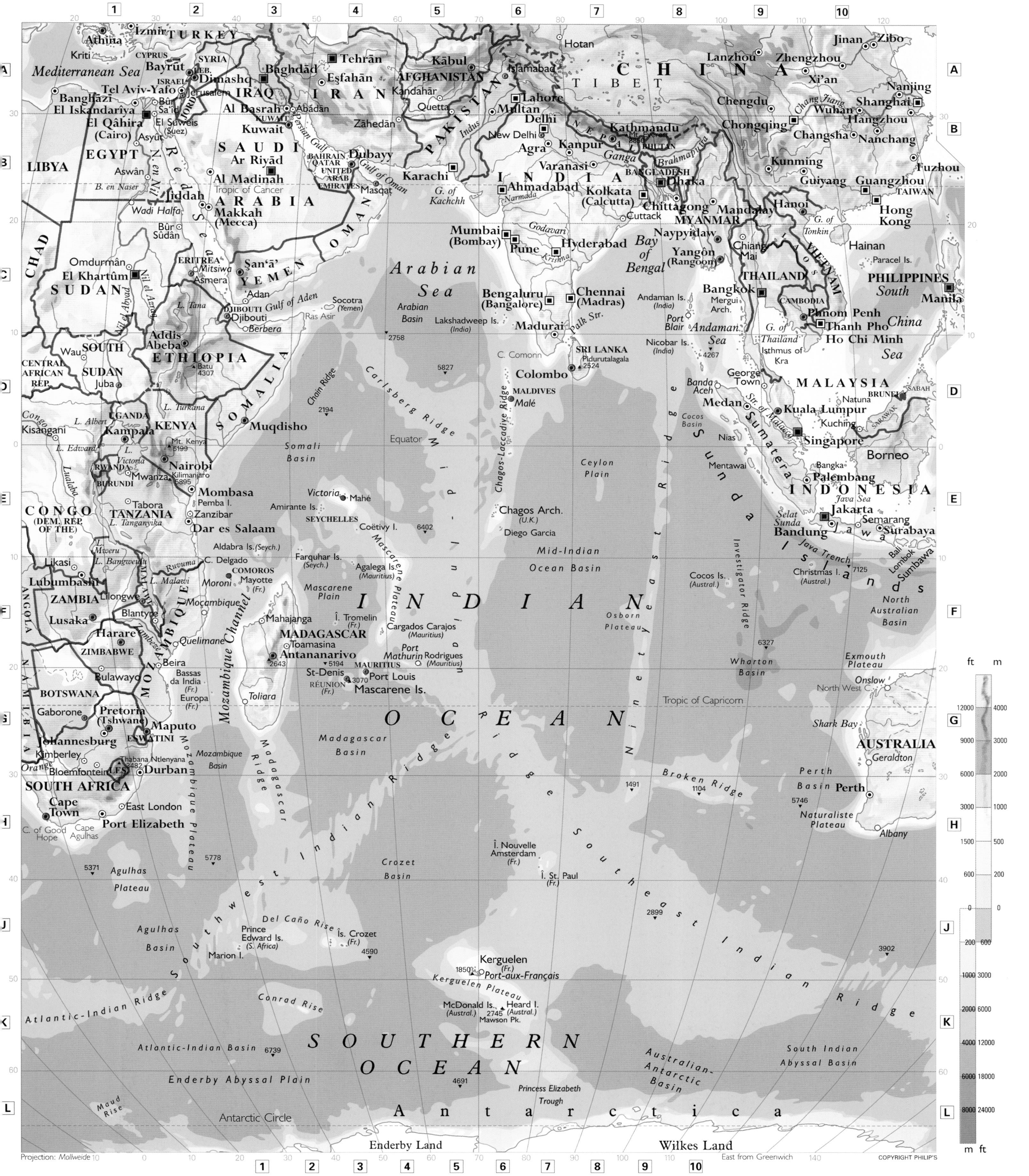

TURKEY
Athína
İzmir
Kriti
CYPRUS
SYRIA
LEB.
Bayrūt
Dimashq
ISRAEL
Tel Aviv-Yafo
Jerusalem
JORDAN
Mediterranean Sea
Banghāzī
El Iskandarîya
El Qâhira (Cairo)
Bûr Sa'îd
El Suweis (Suez)
Asyût
LIBYA
EGYPT
Aswân
B. en Naser
Wadi Halfa
Bûr Sûdân
Red Sea
N. en Nil
IRAQ
Baghdād
Al Basrah
Ābādān
KUWAIT
Kuwait
Tehrān
Eşfahān
IRAN
Zāhedān
SAUDI ARABIA
Ar Riyād
Al Madīnah
Jiddah
Makkah (Mecca)
Tropic of Cancer
Persian Gulf
BAHRAIN
QATAR
UNITED ARAB EMIRATES
Dubayy
Gulf of Oman
Masqat
OMAN
Kābul
AFGHANISTAN
Kandahār
Quetta
Islamabad
PAKISTAN
Indus
Lahore
Multan
Karachi
G. of Kachchh
Hotan
TIBET
CHINA
Delhi
New Delhi
Agra
Kanpur
Varanasi
NEPAL
Kathmandu
Mt. Everest 8848
BHUTAN
Ganga
Brahmaputra
BANGLADESH
Dhaka
INDIA
Ahmadabad
Narmada
Kolkata (Calcutta)
Chittagong
Cuttack
Mumbai (Bombay)
Pune
Godavari
Hyderabad
Krishna
Bay of Bengal
Bengaluru (Bangalore)
Chennai (Madras)
Madurai
Palk Str.
C. Comorin
SRI LANKA
Pidurutalagala 2524
Colombo
Lanzhou
Zhengzhou
Xi'an
Jinan
Zibo
Nanjing
Chengdu
Chang Jiang
Wuhan
Shanghai
Hangzhou
Chongqing
Changsha
Nanchang
Kunming
Fuzhou
Guiyang
Guangzhou
TAIWAN
Hong Kong
Hanoi
G. of Tonkin
Hainan
Paracel Is.
MYANMAR
Mandalay
Naypyidaw
Yangôn (Rangoon)
Chiang Mai
LAOS
VIETNAM
THAILAND
Bangkok
Mergui Arch.
CAMBODIA
Phnom Penh
Thanh Pho Ho Chi Minh
G. of Thailand
Isthmus of Kra
PHILIPPINES
Manila
South China Sea
Andaman Is. (India)
Port Blair
Andaman Sea
Nicobar Is. (India)
4267
CHAD
SUDAN
Omdurmân
El Khartûm
Nil el Abyad
Nil el Azraq
ERITREA
Mitsiwa
Asmera
Şan'ā'
YEMEN
'Adan
Gulf of Aden
DJIBOUTI
Djibouti
Berbera
Socotra (Yemen)
Ras Asir
L. Tana
Addis Abeba
ETHIOPIA
Batu 4307
SOUTH SUDAN
Wau
Juba
CENTRAL AFRICAN REP.
SOMALIA
L. Turkana
Muqdisho
Congo
Kisangani
L. Albert
UGANDA
Kampala
KENYA
Mt. Kenya 5199
L. Edward
L. Victoria
Nairobi
RWANDA
BURUNDI
Mwanza
Kilimanjaro 5895
Mombasa
Lualaba
Tabora
TANZANIA
Pemba I.
Zanzibar
Dar es Salaam
CONGO (DEM. REP. OF THE)
L. Tanganyika
L. Mweru
Likasi
L. Bangweulu
Lubumbashi
ZAMBIA
Lusaka
ANGOLA
Rovuma
L. Malawi
MALAWI
Lilongwe
Blantyre
Zambeze
Harare
ZIMBABWE
MOZAMBIQUE
Moçambique
Quelimane
Beira
Bulawayo
NAMIBIA
BOTSWANA
Gaborone
Pretoria (Tshwane)
Maputo
ESWATINI
Johannesburg
Kimberley
Orange
Bloemfontein
LESOTHO
Thabana Ntlenyana 3482
Durban
SOUTH AFRICA
Cape Town
C. of Good Hope
Cape Agulhas
East London
Port Elizabeth
Arabian Sea
Arabian Basin
2758
Lakshadweep Is. (India)
5827
Carlsberg Ridge
Chain Ridge
2194
MALDIVES
Malé
Chagos-Laccadive Ridge
Equator
Somali Basin
Mid-Indian Ridge
Victoria
Mahé
Amirante Is.
SEYCHELLES
Coëtivy I.
6402
Chagos Arch. (U.K.)
Diego Garcia
Ceylon Plain
Aldabra Is. (Seych.)
C. Delgado
COMOROS
Moroni
Mayotte (Fr.)
Farquhar Is. (Seych.)
Agalega Is. (Mauritius)
Mascarene Plain
Mascarene Plateau
Mid-Indian Ocean Basin
Mozambique Channel
Mahajanga
MADAGASCAR
Î. Tromelin (Fr.)
Cargados Carajos (Mauritius)
Toamasina
Antananarivo
2643
Port Mathurin
Rodrigues (Mauritius)
5194
MAURITIUS
St-Denis
RÉUNION (Fr.)
3070
Port Louis
Mascarene Is.
Bassas da India (Fr.)
Europa (Fr.)
Toliara
INDIAN OCEAN
Ninetyeast Ridge
Osborn Plateau
Madagascar Basin
Mozambique Basin
Mozambique Plateau
Madagascar Ridge
Southwest Indian Ridge
Southeast Indian Ridge
1491
Broken Ridge
1104
Cocos Basin
Sunda Islands
Sumatera
Banda Aceh
Medan
Nias
George Town
Str. of Malacca
MALAYSIA
Kuala Lumpur
Natuna
BRUNEI
SABAH
SARAWAK
Kuching
Singapore
Borneo
Mentawai
Bangka
Palembang
INDONESIA
Java Sea
Selat Sunda
Jakarta
Semarang
Bandung
Jawa
Surabaya
Bali
Lombok
Sumbawa
Java Trench
7125
Christmas I. (Austral.)
Cocos Is. (Austral.)
Investigator Ridge
North Australian Basin
6327
Wharton Basin
Exmouth Plateau
Onslow
North West C.
Tropic of Capricorn
Shark Bay
AUSTRALIA
Geraldton
Perth Basin
Perth
5746
Naturaliste Plateau
Albany
Î. Nouvelle Amsterdam (Fr.)
Î. St. Paul (Fr.)
Crozet Basin
5778
5371
Agulhas Plateau
Agulhas Basin
Del Caño Rise
Prince Edward Is. (S. Africa)
Marion I.
Îs. Crozet (Fr.)
4590
2899
3902
Kerguelen (Fr.)
1850
Port-aux-Français
Kerguelen Plateau
Conrad Rise
McDonald Is. (Austral.)
2745
Heard I. (Austral.)
Mawson Pk.
Atlantic-Indian Ridge
Atlantic-Indian Basin
6739
SOUTHERN OCEAN
Australian-Antarctic Basin
South Indian Abyssal Basin
Enderby Abyssal Plain
4691
Princess Elizabeth Trough
Maud Rise
Antarctic Circle
Antarctica
Enderby Land
Wilkes Land
Projection: Mollweide
East from Greenwich
ft m
12000 4000
9000 3000
6000 2000
3000 1000
1500 500
600 200
0 0
200 600
1000 3000
2000 6000
4000 12000
6000 18000
8000 24000
m ft

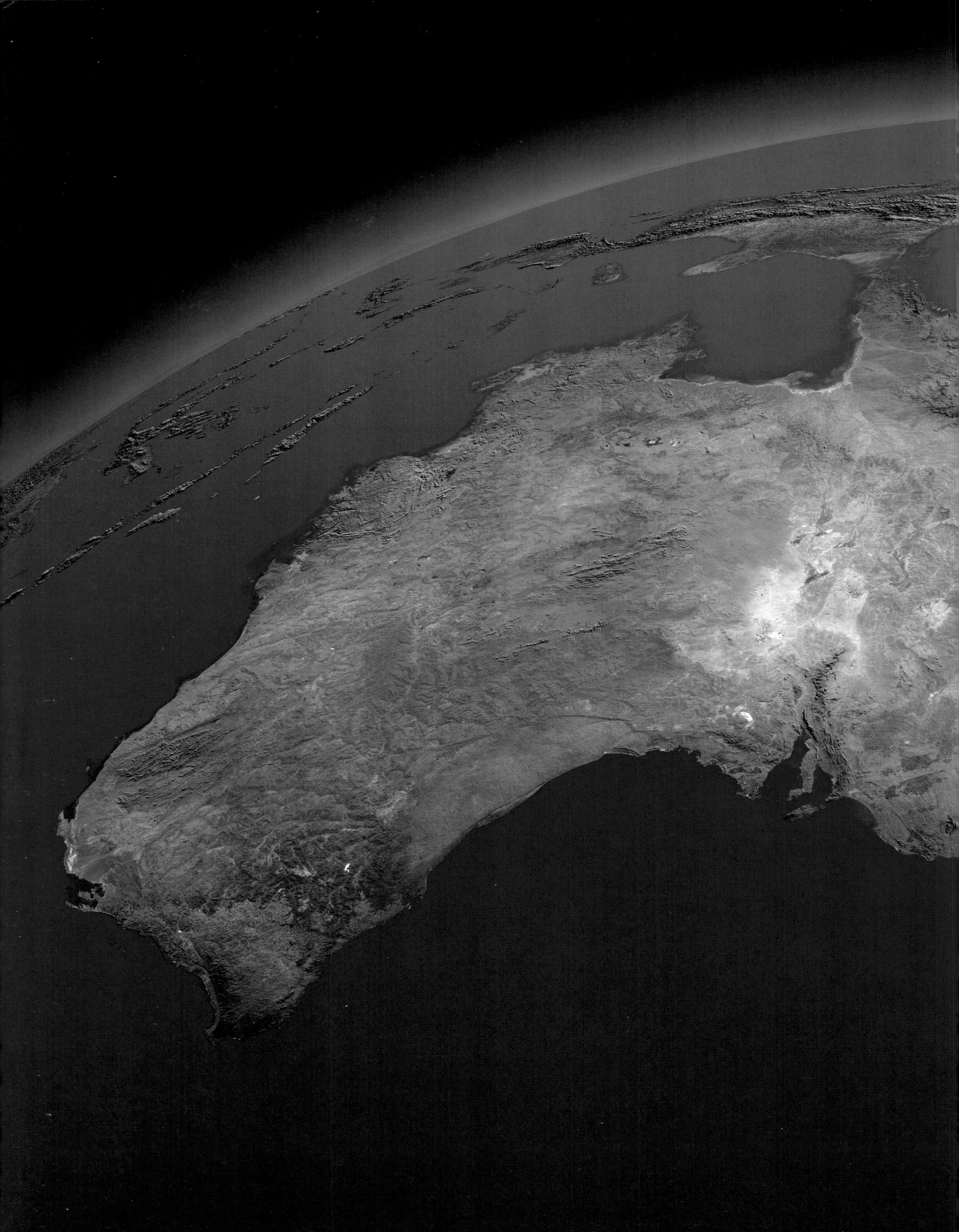

AUSTRALIA AND OCEANIA

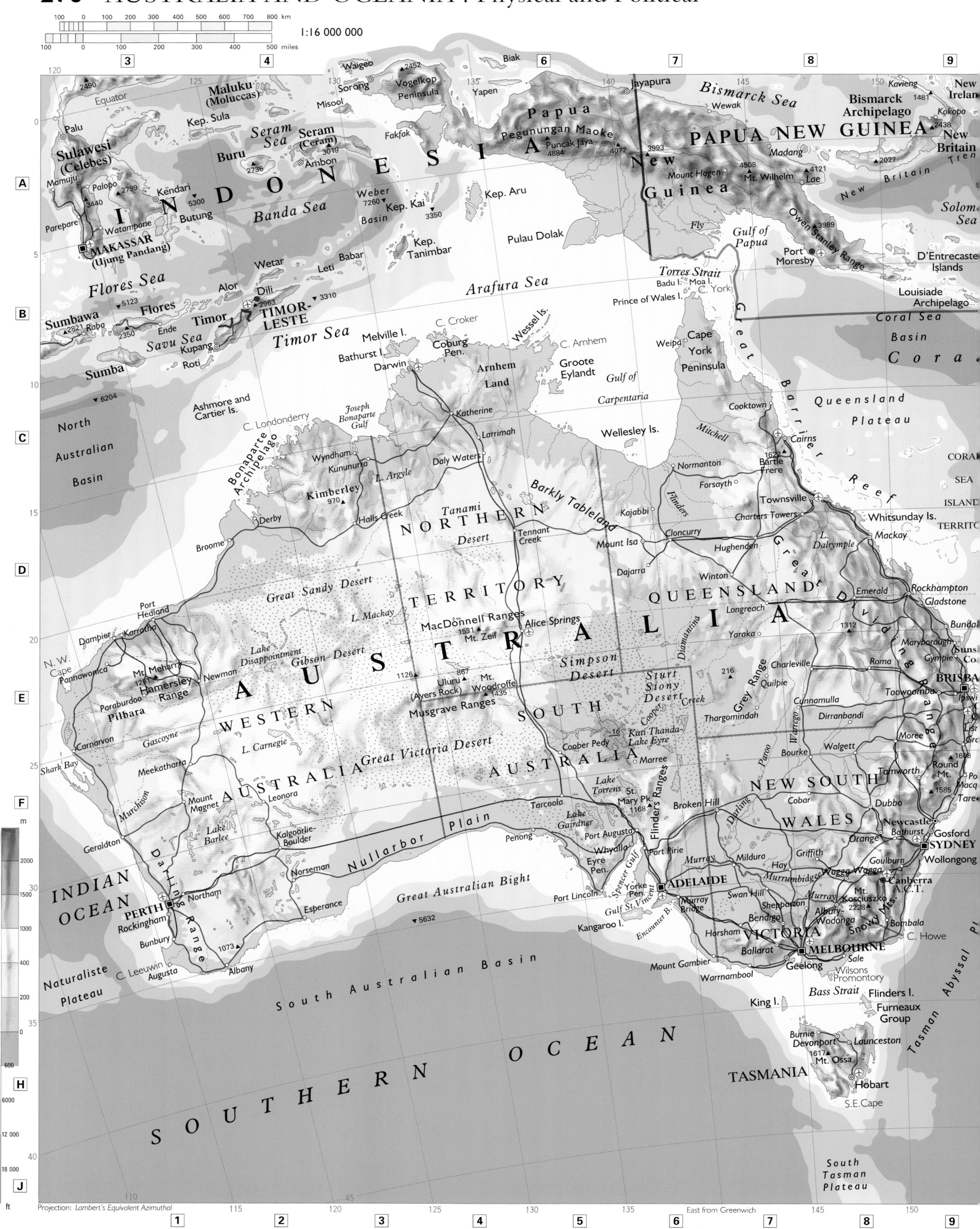
1:16 000 000
Projection: Lambert's Equivalent Azimuthal
East from Greenwich
INDONESIA
PAPUA NEW GUINEA
AUSTRALIA
WESTERN AUSTRALIA
NORTHERN TERRITORY
SOUTH AUSTRALIA
QUEENSLAND
NEW SOUTH WALES
VICTORIA
TASMANIA
A.C.T.
TIMOR-LESTE
INDIAN OCEAN
SOUTHERN OCEAN
Arafura Sea
Timor Sea
Banda Sea
Flores Sea
Savu Sea
Seram Sea
Bismarck Sea
Coral Sea
Gulf of Carpentaria
Great Australian Bight
Bass Strait
Torres Strait
Great Barrier Reef
Great Dividing Range
Great Sandy Desert
Gibson Desert
Great Victoria Desert
Tanami Desert
Simpson Desert
Sturt Stony Desert
Nullarbor Plain
Barkly Tableland
MacDonnell Ranges
Musgrave Ranges
Hamersley Range
Darling Range
Flinders Ranges
Kimberley
Arnhem Land
Cape York Peninsula
Kati Thanda-Lake Eyre
Lake Torrens
Uluru (Ayers Rock)
PERTH
ADELAIDE
MELBOURNE
SYDNEY
Canberra
Darwin
Alice Springs
Hobart
MAKASSAR (Ujung Pandang)
Port Moresby
South Australian Basin
North Australian Basin
Naturaliste Plateau
Queensland Plateau
South Tasman Plateau

Ontong Java Plateau
Solomon Rise
Melanesia
Bougainville
Choiseul
SOLOMON ISLANDS
Santa Isabel
New Georgia Is.
Vangunu
Russell Is.
Florida Is.
Malaita
Honiara
Guadalcanal
Makira (San Cristóbal)
South Solomon Trench
Pocklington Reef
Bellona
Rennell
Reef Is.
Duff Is.
Nendo
Santa Cruz Is.
Vanikoro
Fataka
Tikopia
Vitiaz Trench
Is. Torres
Vanua Lava
Is. Banks
Gaua
Espíritu Santo
VANUATU (New Hebrides)
Malakula
Epi
Shepherd Is.
Port Vila
Efate
Erromango
Tanna
Aneityum
Îles D'Entrecasteaux
Îles Chesterfield
Îles Bélep
New Caledonia (Fr.)
La Foa
Nouméa
Yaté
Î. Lifou
Î. Maré
Îles Loyauté
Î. des Pins
South New Hebrides Trench
Î. Matthew
Ceve-i-Ra
West Fiji Basin
Rotuma
Vanua Levu
Viti Levu
Taveuni
Suva
FIJI
Kadavu
Lau Group
Lau Ridge
Lau Basin
Tabiteuea
Beru
Nikunau
Onotoa
Tamana
Gilbert Is.
Arorae
KIRIBATI
Baker I. (U.S.A.)
Equator
International Date Line
Winslow Reef
McKean
Abariringa
Enderbury
Birnie
Nikumaroro
Phoenix Is.
Orona
Rawaki
Manra
Carondelet Reef
Namumea
Nanumanga
Niutao
Nui
Vaitupu
TUVALU (Ellice Is.)
Funafuti
Fongafale
Nukulaelae
Niulakita
Atafu
Nukunonu
Tokelau Is. (N.Z.)
Fakaofo
Mata-Utu
Uvea
Wallis & Futuna (Fr.)
Horn
Alofi
SAMOA
Savai'i
Apia
'Upolu
Pago Pago
Tutuila
American Samoa (U.S.A.)
Niuafo'ou
Niua Group
Niuatoputapu
Vava'u Group
Late
Ha'apai Group
TONGA
Nuku'alofa
Tongatapu Group
Eua
Ata
Alofi
Niue (N.Z.)
Tonga Trench
PACIFIC OCEAN
Tropic of Capricorn
South Fiji Basin
Lord Howe Seamount Chain
New Caledonia Trough
Norfolk Ridge
Norfolk I. (Austral.)
Norfolk Basin
Lord Howe I. (Austral.)
Lord Howe Rise
Raoul I.
Kermadec Is. (N.Z.)
Macauley I.
Curtis I.
Colville Ridge
Kermadec Trench
Southwest Pacific Basin
Tasman Sea
North C.
Kaitaia
Whangarei
AUCKLAND
North Island
Bay of Plenty
Tauranga
Hamilton
Challenger Plateau
New Plymouth
Rotorua
Ruapehu
Gisborne
NEW ZEALAND
Wanganui
Napier
Palmerston North
Masterton
Nelson
Blenheim
Cook Strait
Wellington
Greymouth
South Island
Southern Alps
Aoraki Mt. Cook
Christchurch
Chatham Rise
Queenstown
Timaru
Dunedin
Invercargill
Stewart I.
Chatham I.
Chatham Is. (N.Z.)
Pitt I.
West from Greenwich
COPYRIGHT PHILIP'S

1:6 400 000

50 0 50 100 150 200 250 300 km
50 0 50 100 150 200 miles
INDONESIA
TIMOR SEA
INDIAN OCEAN
Java Trench
6204
North Australian Basin
Sawu Sea
Joseph Bonaparte Gulf
Bonaparte Archipelago
Kimberley
King Leopold Ranges
Durack Range
Great Sandy Desert
Gibson Desert
Tanami Desert
NORTHERN TERRITORY
Hamersley Range
Chichester Ra.
Pilbara
Eighty Mile Beach
Darwin
Palmerston
Katherine
Kununurra
Wyndham
Halls Creek
Fitzroy Crossing
Derby
Broome
Port Hedland
Karratha
Dampier
Tom Price
Newman
Onslow
Exmouth
Exmouth Gulf
Barrow I.
Montebello Is.
Dampier Archipelago
Rowley Shoals
Ashmore and Cartier Is. (Australia)
Scott Reef
Browse I.
Adele I.
Melville I.
Bathurst I.
Van Diemen Gulf
Kupang
Timor
Roti
Sawu
Sumba
Waingapu
Sumbawa
Lombok
Bali
Buccaneer Archipelago
Lacepede Is.
KAKADU
LITCHFIELD
GREGORY
Victoria River
L. Argyle
Lake Gregory
Lake Mackay
CENTRAL DESERT
CENTRAL AUSTRALIA
Tropic of Capricorn
Mt. Ord 937
Mt. Hann 776
Mt. Wells 970
Mt. Bruce 1235
Mt. Meharry 1251
235
231
280
A
B
C
D
2
3
4
5
10
15
20
120
125
130

WESTERN AUSTRALIA
SOUTH AUSTRALIA
INDIAN OCEAN
SOUTHERN OCEAN
Great Australian Bight
Great Victoria Desert
Nullarbor Plain
Hampton Tableland
PERTH
Fremantle
Kwinana
Rockingham
Mandurah
Bunbury
Busselton
Albany
Esperance
Geraldton
Kalgoorlie-Boulder
Coolgardie
Kambalda
Southern Cross
Merredin
Northam
Norseman
Laverton
Leonora
Leinster
Meekatharra
Mount Magnet
Carnarvon
Denham
Kalbarri
Dongara
Moora
Wanneroo
Armadale
Midland
Collie
Katanning
Narrogin
Hopetoun
Ravensthorpe
Eucla
Nullarbor
Penong
Cook
Maralinga
Ooldea
Petermann Ranges
Musgrave Ranges
Mann Ranges
Everard Ranges
Robinson Ra.
Barr Smith Ra.
Carnarvon Ra.
Kennedy Ra.
Shark Bay
Dirk Hartog I.
Houtman Abrolhos
Rottnest I.
Archipelago of the Recherche
NORTHWEST COASTAL HWY
GREAT NORTHERN HWY
GREAT EASTERN HWY
EYRE HWY
TRANS AUSTRALIAN RWY
Aboriginal lands
Projection: Bonne
East from Greenwich
COPYRIGHT PHILIP'S
1. NGALIIWURRU / NUNGALI
2. WANIMIYN
3. WAMBARDI
4. LTALALTUMA
5. RODNA
6. NTARIA
7. ROULPMAULPMA
8. URUNA

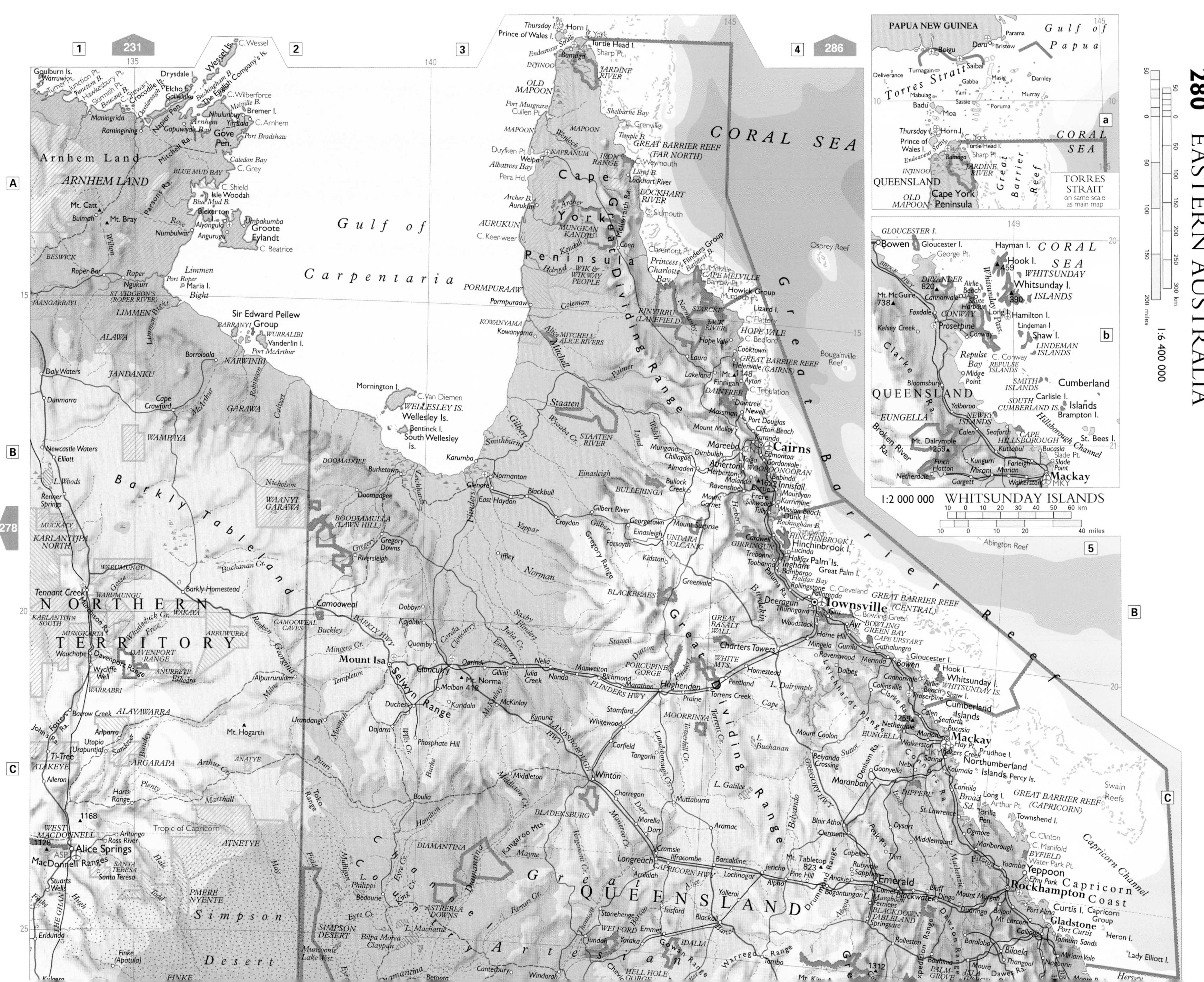
1:6 400 000
0 50 100 150 200 250 300 km
0 50 100 150 200 miles
CORAL SEA
Great Barrier Reef
Gulf of Carpentaria
Cape York Peninsula
Great Dividing Range
QUEENSLAND
NORTHERN TERRITORY
Barkly Tableland
Simpson Desert
Great Artesian Basin
Channel Country
Arnhem Land
ARNHEM LAND
Townsville
Cairns
Mackay
Rockhampton
Gladstone
Mount Isa
Alice Springs
Tennant Creek
Longreach
Winton
Emerald
Charters Towers
Cloncurry
Hughenden
Normanton
Bowen
Ingham
Innisfail
Groote Eylandt
Sir Edward Pellew Group
Wellesley Is.
Mornington I.
Thursday I.
Torres Strait
PAPUA NEW GUINEA
Gulf of Papua
TORRES STRAIT on same scale as main map
1:2 000 000 WHITSUNDAY ISLANDS
Tropic of Capricorn
Capricorn Channel
Capricorn Coast
Whitsunday I.
Hinchinbrook I.
Cumberland Islands
Northumberland Islands
Selwyn Range
Gregory Range
MacDonnell Ranges
231
286
278

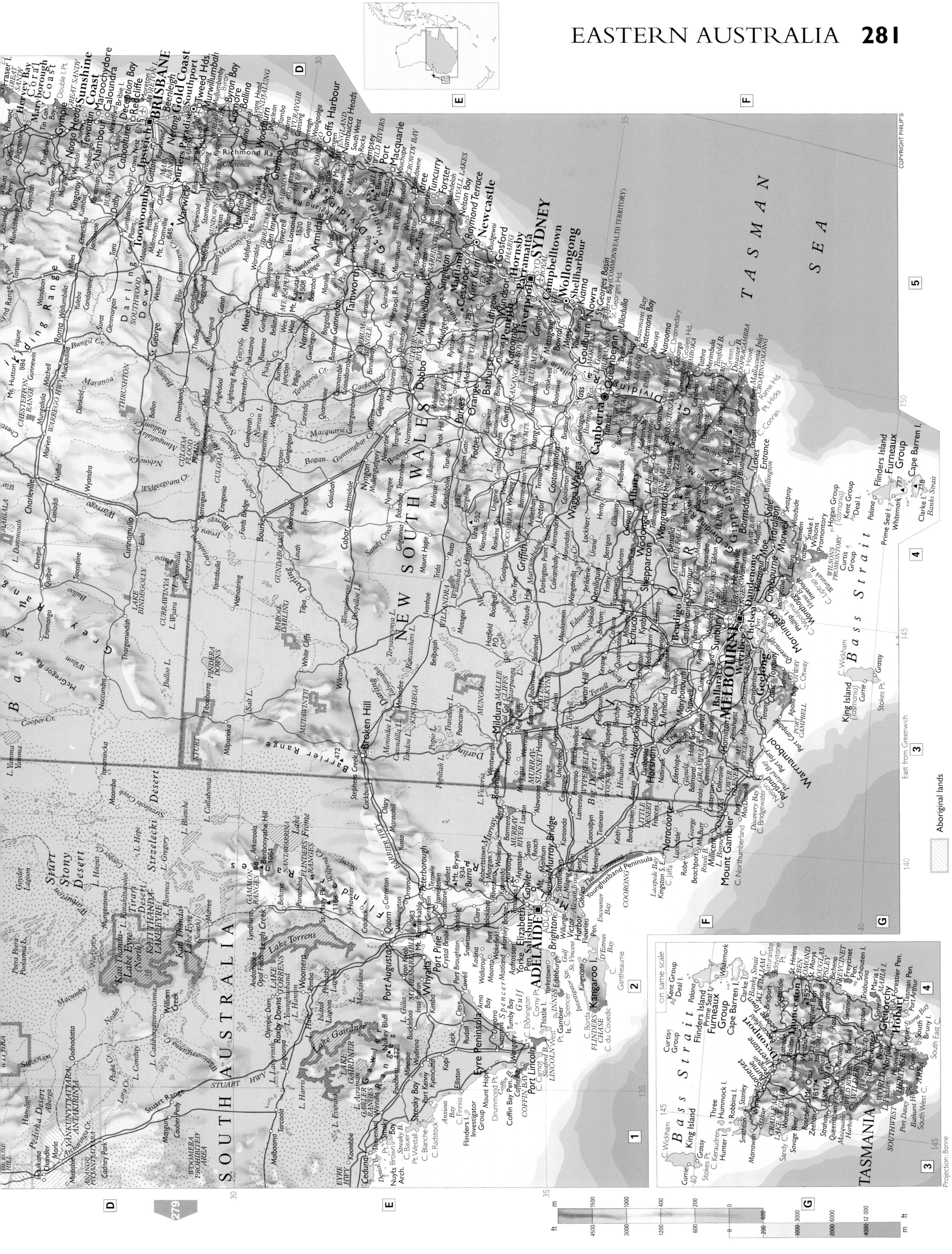

NEW SOUTH WALES

SOUTH AUSTRALIA

TASMANIA

TASMAN SEA

Bass Strait

SYDNEY

MELBOURNE

ADELAIDE

BRISBANE

Canberra

Aboriginal lands

on same scale

East from Greenwich

Projection: Bonne

279

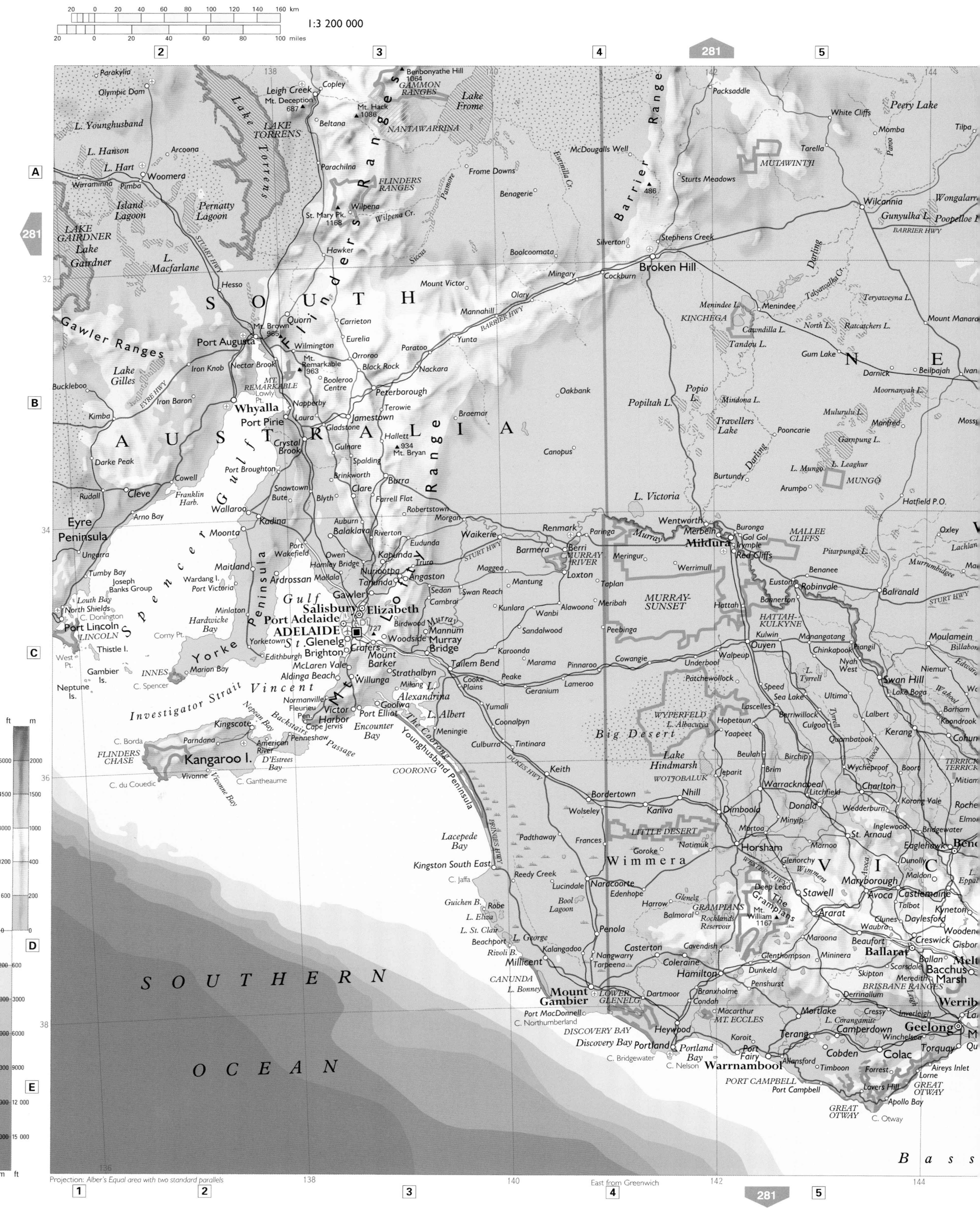

1:3 200 000
km
miles
281
SOUTH AUSTRALIA
NEW SOUTH WALES
VIC
Parakylia
Olympic Dam
L. Younghusband
L. Hanson
Arcoona
L. Hart
Woomera
Wirraminna
Pimba
Island Lagoon
Pernatty Lagoon
LAKE GAIRDNER
Lake Gairdner
L. Macfarlane
STUART HWY
Hesso
Lake Torrens
LAKE TORRENS
Leigh Creek
Copley
Mt. Deception 687
Beltana
Benbonyathe Hill 1064
GAMMON RANGES
Mt. Hack 1086
NANTAWARRINA
Lake Frome
Parachilna
FLINDERS RANGES
Flinders Ranges
Wilpena
St. Mary Pk. 1168
Wilpena Cr.
Hawker
Siccus
Pasmore
Frome Downs
Benagerie
McDougalls Well
Eurinilla Cr.
Barrier Range
486
Packsaddle
White Cliffs
Peery Lake
Momba
Paroo
Tilpa
Tarella
MUTAWINTJI
Sturts Meadows
Wilcannia
Wongalarra
Gunyulka L.
Poopelloe L.
BARRIER HWY
Silverton
Stephens Creek
Broken Hill
Boolcoomata
Mingary
Cockburn
Mount Victor
Olary
Mannahill
BARRIER HWY
Yunta
Darling
Menindee L.
Menindee
Talyawalka Cr.
Teryaweyna L.
KINCHEGA
Cawndilla L.
Tandou L.
North L.
Ratcatchers L.
Mount Manara
Gum Lake
Darnick
Beilpajah
Ivanhoe
Gawler Ranges
Quorn
Mt. Brown 965
Carrieton
Eurelia
Port Augusta
Wilmington
Orroroo
Paratoo
Nackara
Black Rock
Mt. Remarkable 963
MT. REMARKABLE
Booleroo Centre
Lowly Pt.
Iron Knob
Nectar Brook
Lake Gilles
EYRE HWY
Iron Baron
Buckleboo
Kimba
Whyalla
Port Pirie
Napperby
Laura
Peterborough
Terowie
Jamestown
Gladstone
Braemar
Oakbank
Popiltah L.
Popio L.
Mindona L.
Moornanyah L.
Mossgiel
Mulurulu L.
Manfred
Garnpung L.
Travellers Lake
Pooncarie
Hallett
Mt. Bryan 934
Crystal Brook
Gulnare
Spalding
Canopus
L. Mungo
L. Leaghur
MUNGO
Arumpo
Burtundy
Darke Peak
Cowell
Port Broughton
Brinkworth
Burra
Range
Cleve
Rudall
Franklin Harb.
Snowtown
Bute
Blyth
Clare
Farrell Flat
Robertstown
Morgan
L. Victoria
Hatfield P.O.
Eyre Peninsula
Arno Bay
Wallaroo
Kadina
Moonta
Auburn
Balaklava
Riverton
Eudunda
Waikerie
Renmark
Paringa
Murray
Wentworth
Merbein
Mildura
Buronga
Gol Gol
Irymple
Red Cliffs
MALLEE CLIFFS
Oxley
Lachlan
Pitarpunga L.
Ungarra
Spencer Gulf
Port Wakefield
Owen
Hamley Bridge
Kapunda
Truro
Barmera
Berri
MURRAY RIVER
Meringur
Werrimull
Murrumbidgee
Tumby Bay
Joseph Banks Group
Wardang I.
Port Victoria
Maitland
Yorke Peninsula
Ardrossan
Mallala
Nuriootpa
Tanunda
Angaston
Sedan
Maggea
Mantung
Loxton
Taplan
Benanee
Euston
Robinvale
Balranald
STURT HWY
Louth Bay
North Shields
C. Donington
Port Lincoln
LINCOLN
Minlaton
Hardwicke Bay
Gulf St Vincent
Gawler
Salisbury
Elizabeth
Port Adelaide
ADELAIDE
Glenelg
Brighton
Cambrai
Swan Reach
Kunlara
Wanbi
Alawoona
Meribah
MURRAY-SUNSET
Hattah
Bannerton
HATTAH-KULKYNE
Mount Lofty Ranges
Birdwood
Mannum
Murray Bridge
Woodside
727
Crafers
Mount Barker
Sandalwood
Peebinga
Kulwin
Ouyen
Manangatang
Chinkapook
Piangil
Moulamein
Billabong
Corny Pt.
Thistle I.
Yorketown
Edithburgh
McLaren Vale
Aldinga Beach
Strathalbyn
Tailem Bend
Karoonda
Marama
Pinnaroo
Cowangie
Underbool
Walpeup
West Pt.
Gambier Is.
INNES
Marion Bay
C. Spencer
Neptune Is.
Willunga
Milang
L. Alexandrina
Cooke Plains
Peake
Geranium
Lameroo
Patchewollock
Speed
Sea Lake
L. Tyrrell
Ultima
Nyah West
Swan Hill
Lake Boga
Niemur
Edward
Wakool
Barham
Koondrook
Investigator Strait
Nepean Bay
Backstairs Passage
Normanville
Fleurieu Pen.
Victor Harbor
Goolwa
Port Elliot
Cape Jervis
Encounter Bay
L. Albert
Meningie
The Coorong
Yumali
Coonalpyn
Tintinara
Culburra
WYPERFELD
L. Albacutya
Big Desert
Lascelles
Hopetoun
Yaapeet
Berriwillock
Culgoa
Tyrrell
Lalbert
Quambatook
Kerang
Cohuna
Kingscote
C. Borda
Parndana
American River
Penneshaw
FLINDERS CHASE
Kangaroo I.
D'Estrees Bay
C. du Couedic
Vivonne
Vivonne Bay
C. Gantheaume
Younghusband Peninsula
COORONG
DUKES HWY
Keith
Lake Hindmarsh
Beulah
Birchip
WOTJOBALUK
Jeparit
Brim
Avoca
Wycheproof
Boort
Warracknabeal
Charlton
Bordertown
Wolseley
Kaniva
Nhill
Dimboola
Donald
Litchfield
Korong Vale
Wedderburn
Inglewood
Bridgewater
St. Arnaud
Eaglehawk
Bendigo
Minyip
Murtoa
Marnoo
Padthaway
Frances
LITTLE DESERT
Goroke
Natimuk
Horsham
Wimmera
Lacepede Bay
BRIGES HWY
Kingston South East
C. Jaffa
Reedy Creek
Lucindale
Naracoorte
Edenhope
WESTERN HWY
Deep Lead
Glenorchy
Stawell
Dunolly
Maryborough
Avoca
Maldon
Castlemaine
Talbot
Kyneton
Guichen B.
Robe
L. Eliza
L. St. Clair
Beachport
Rivoli B.
L. George
Bool Lagoon
Penola
Harrow
Glenelg
Balmoral
GRAMPIANS
Rocklands Reservoir
The Grampians
Mt. William 1167
Ararat
Clunes
Daylesford
Waubra
Creswick
Woodend
Gisborne
Kalangadoo
Millicent
CANUNDA
L. Bonney
Mount Gambier
Nangwarry
Tarpeena
Casterton
Coleraine
Cavendish
Hamilton
Maroona
Glenthompson
Mininera
Beaufort
Ballarat
Ballan
Bacchus Marsh
Melton
Dunkeld
Skipton
Scarsdale
Meredith
BRISBANE RANGES
Leigh
Penshurst
Derrinallum
LOWER GLENELG
Dartmoor
Branxholme
Condah
Port MacDonnell
C. Northumberland
DISCOVERY BAY
Discovery Bay
Heywood
Portland
Macarthur
MT. ECCLES
Mortlake
L. Corangamite
Cressy
Inverleigh
Werribee
Geelong
Camperdown
Winchelsea
Terang
Koroit
Port Fairy
Portland Bay
C. Bridgewater
C. Nelson
Warrnambool
Allansford
Cobden
Colac
Timboon
Forrest
Torquay
Aireys Inlet
Lorne
PORT CAMPBELL
Port Campbell
Lavers Hill
GREAT OTWAY
Apollo Bay
C. Otway
SOUTHERN OCEAN
Bass
ft
m
Projection: Alber's Equal area with two standard parallels
East from Greenwich

Aboriginal lands

10 0 20 40 60 80 100 120 140 km

10 0 20 40 60 80 100 miles

1:2 800 000

1 2 3 4 5 6 7 8

A B C D E F G H

173 174 175 176 177 178 179

35 36 37 38 39 40 41

PACIFIC OCEAN

NORTH ISLAND
(Te Ika-a-Māui)

TASMAN SEA

C. Reinga
North C.
C. Maria van Diemen
Waitiki Landing
Parengarenga Harbour
Ninety Mile Beach
Rangaunu B.
Houhora Heads
C. Karikari
Doubtless B.
Whangaroa Harb.
Awanui
Mangonui
Cavalli Is.
Ahipara B.
Kaitaia
Kaeo
NORTHLAND
Waitangi
B. of Islands
C. Brett
Herekino
744
Kerikeri
Russell
Okaihau
Raihia
Opua
Whangaruru Harb.
Kohukohu
Rawene
Kaikohe
Kawakawa
Moerewa
Poor Knights Is.
Hokianga Harbour
781
Omapere
Hikurangi
Waipoua Forest
Donnelly's Crossing
Wairoa
Whangarei
Aranga
Kamo
Onerahi
Whangarei Harb.
Bream Hd.
Kirikopuni
Marsden Point
Bream B.
Hen & Chickens Is.
Dargaville
Waikiekie
Paparoa
Waipu
Bream Tail
Te Kopuru
Maungaturoto
Needles Pt.
Cradock Chan.
Port Fitzroy
Ruawai
Little Barrier I.
722
627
Great Barrier I.
Wellsford
C. Rodney
Tryphena
Kaipara Harbour
Matakana
C. Barrier
Kawau I.
Colville Chan.
Snells Beach
Cuvier I.
Warkworth
C. Colville
892
Port Charles
Hauraki G.
Helensville
Whangaparaoa Pen.
Mercury Is.
AUCKLAND
Takapuna
Ostend
Coromandel
Waiheke I.
Mercury B.
AUCKLAND
Mount Wellington
Whitianga
Muriwai Beach
AKL
Howick
Coromandel Pen.
Piha
Onehunga
Otahuhu
Firth of Thames
Tairua
Papatoetoe
846
Pauanui
Manukau Harbour
Papakura
Manukau
Pukekohe
Thames
Whangamata
Waiuku
Tuakau
Mercer
Turua
Mayor I.
Waikato
Te Kauwhata
L. Waikare
Waihi
Waihi Beach
BAY OF PLENTY
Paeroa
Katikati
Tauranga Harb.
Whakaari (White I.)
WAIKATO
Te Aroha
Huntly
Waitoa
Matakana I.
C. Runaway
Hicks Bay
Glen Afton
Ngaruawahia
Motiti I.
Glen Massey
Morrinsville
Mount Maunganui
Te Araroa
Tauranga
Bay of Plenty
East C.
Raglan Harbour
Raglan
Hamilton
Waharoa
Matamata
Te Puke
Te Kaha
Cambridge
Paengaroa
Edgecumbe
Whakatane
1067
Ohaupo
Karapiro
L. Rotoiti
Matata
Ohiwa Harbour
Hikurangi
1753
Ruatoria
Aotea Harbour
Leamington
Tirau
L. Rotorua
L. Rotoma
Te Awamutu
Arapuni
Putaruru
Te Teko
Opotiki
Raukumara Ra.
Waipiro Bay
Kawhia Harbour
Kawhia
Kihikihi
Mamaku
Ngongotaha
Kawerau
Taneatua
Albatross Pt.
Otorohanga
L. Tarawera
Tokomaru Bay
Tokoroa
Rotorua
Mt. Tarawera
1111
Waitomo Caves
Kinleith
Tirua Pt.
Te Kuiti
Rangitoto Ra.
Mangakino
Waiotapu
Galatea
GISBORNE
Tolaga Bay
Herangi Ra.
Atiamuri
TE UREWERA
Matawai
Puha
Te Karaka
1165
Whakamaru
Murupara
Aria
Mokai
Ngatapa
Ormond
Wairakei
Manuoha
Gisborne
Mokau
Ongarue
Taupo
1392
L. Waikareiti
Patutahi
Tuaheni Pt.
North Taranaki Bight
Kahukura
Hauhungaroa Ra.
369
L. Taupo
Waikaremoana
Poverty B.
Huiarau Ra.
Ohura
Taumarunui
Rangitaiki
Tuai
Waitara
Pukearuhe
Manunui
Tokaanu
Turangi
1383
Frasertown
Tahora
Owhango
L. Rotoaira
Ahimanawa Ra.
Mohaka
Nuhaka
New Plymouth
Whangamomona
Mt. Tongariro
1968
Tarawera
Waikokopu
Table C.
TARANAKI
Okato
Inglewood
Mt. Ngauruhoe
2287
1726
Putorino
Wairoa
403
Mahia Pen.
Mt. Taranaki or Mt. Egmont
Huiroa
TONGARIRO
Ruapehu
Kaweka Ra.
Portland I.
C. Egmont
2518
Midhirst
WHANGANUI
2797
Rahotu
EGMONT
Stratford
746
Ohakune
Rangataua
Kaimanawa Mts.
Hawke Bay
Opunake
Kapònga
Eltham
Pipiriki
Raetihi
Waiouru
Bay View
Kapuni
Normanby
Napier
Manaia
Hawera
Taradale
Clive
South Taranaki Bight
C. Kidnappers
Hastings
Havelock North
Patea
Waverley
Maxwell
Taihape
Opapa
Waitotara
Mangaweka
HAWKE'S BAY
Wanganui
Hunterville
1733
Otane
Castlecliff
Mangaweka
Waipawa
Apiti
Waipukurau
Turakina
Norsewood
Takapau
Marton
Halcombe
Ruahine Ra.
Wanstead
MANAWATU-WANGANUI
Bulls
Feilding
Ormondville
Rangitikei
Bunnythorpe
Dannevirke
Rongotea
Ashurst
Porangahau
Palmerston North
Woodville
Weber
Manawatu
Longburn
Puketoi Ra.
112
Foxton
Pahiatua
803
C. Turnagain
Herbertville
Levin
Shannon
Eketahuna
C. Farewell
Farewell Spit
C. Stephens
Stephens I.
Golden Bay
Rangitoto ke te tonga (D'Urville I.)
Otaki
Alfredton
Collingwood
Separation Pt.
Tararua Ra.
Mauriceville
Kahurangi Pt.
Takaka
ABEL TASMAN
Kapiti I.
1571
Mt. Mitre
Tinui
Tasman Bay
French Pass
Forsyth I.
Paraparaumu
Castlepoint
Devil River Pk.
Pelorus Sd.
Cook Strait
Paekakariki
Lower Hutt
Upper Hutt
Masterton
1780
Riwaka
1203
Porirua
Carterton
Tasman Mts.
Motueka
Greytown
KAHURANGI
NELSON
Johnsonville
Karamea
Nelson
Pelorus
Queen Charlotte Sd.
Arapawa I.
Petone
Featherston
WELLINGTON
Karamea
L. Wairarapa
Martinborough
Brightwater
Stoke
Havelock
Picton
Terawhiti
Wellington
Wainuiomata
Flat Pt.
Wakefield
Mt. Richmond
Tuamarina
665
Richmond
Port Nicholson
L. Onoke
Tadmor
Cloudy B.
Eastbourne
Aorangi Mts.
3122
Mt. Owen
Belgrove
1756
Richmond Ra.
Turakirae Hd.
Ruamahanga
Palliser B.
981
Mokihinui
Wairau
Renwick
Blenheim
1875
Glenhope
Seddon
C. Palliser
Buller
TASMAN
NELSON LAKES
2120
C. Campbell
Lyell
L. Rotoiti
1780
Awatere
Ward
Murchison
1320

ft m
9000 3000
6000 2000
3000 1000
1200 400
600 200
0 0
200 600
1000 3000
1500 4500
3000 9000
m ft

Projection: *Conical with two standard parallels*

East from Greenwich

285

1:2 800 000

10 0 20 40 60 80 100 120 140 km

10 0 20 40 60 80 100 miles

284

TASMAN SEA

SOUTH ISLAND
(Te Waipounamu)

Westland Bight

Karamea Bight

Golden Bay

Tasman Bay

Cloudy B.

Pegasus Bay

Canterbury Bight

Canterbury Plains

Southern Alps

WEST COAST

CANTERBURY

OTAGO

SOUTHLAND

FIORDLAND

NELSON

MARLBOROUGH

TASMAN

Christchurch

Dunedin

Invercargill

Nelson

Blenheim

Greymouth

Hokitika

Westport

Timaru

Oamaru

Ashburton

Queenstown

Gore

Kaikoura

Aoraki/Mount Cook 3724

Foveaux Str.

Stewart I. (Rakiura)

Solander I.

Codfish I.

Ruapuke I.

Banks Pen.

Otago Pen.

PACIFIC OCEAN

CHATHAM ISLANDS
on same scale

a

PACIFIC OCEAN

Chatham Islands
(Wharekauri)

The Sisters

C. Young

Munning Pt.

Chatham I.
(Rekohu)

Western Reef

Te One

Waitangi

The Forty Fours

Owenga

C. Fournier

The Horns

Pitt Strait

Star Keys

Mangere I.

Pitt I.

Rangatira I.

The Pyramid

West from Greenwich

Projection: Conical with two standard parallels

East from Greenwich

50 0 50 100 150 200 km

1:5 200 000

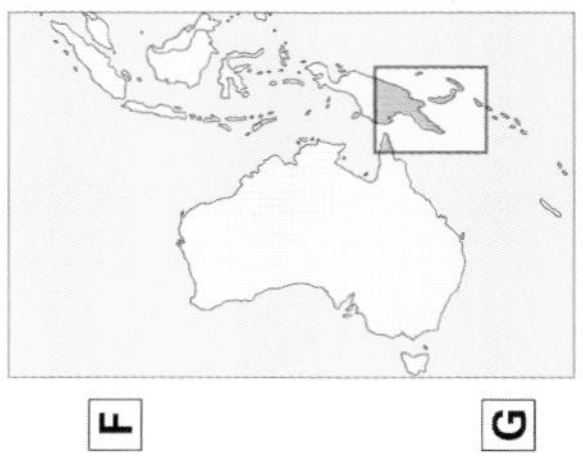

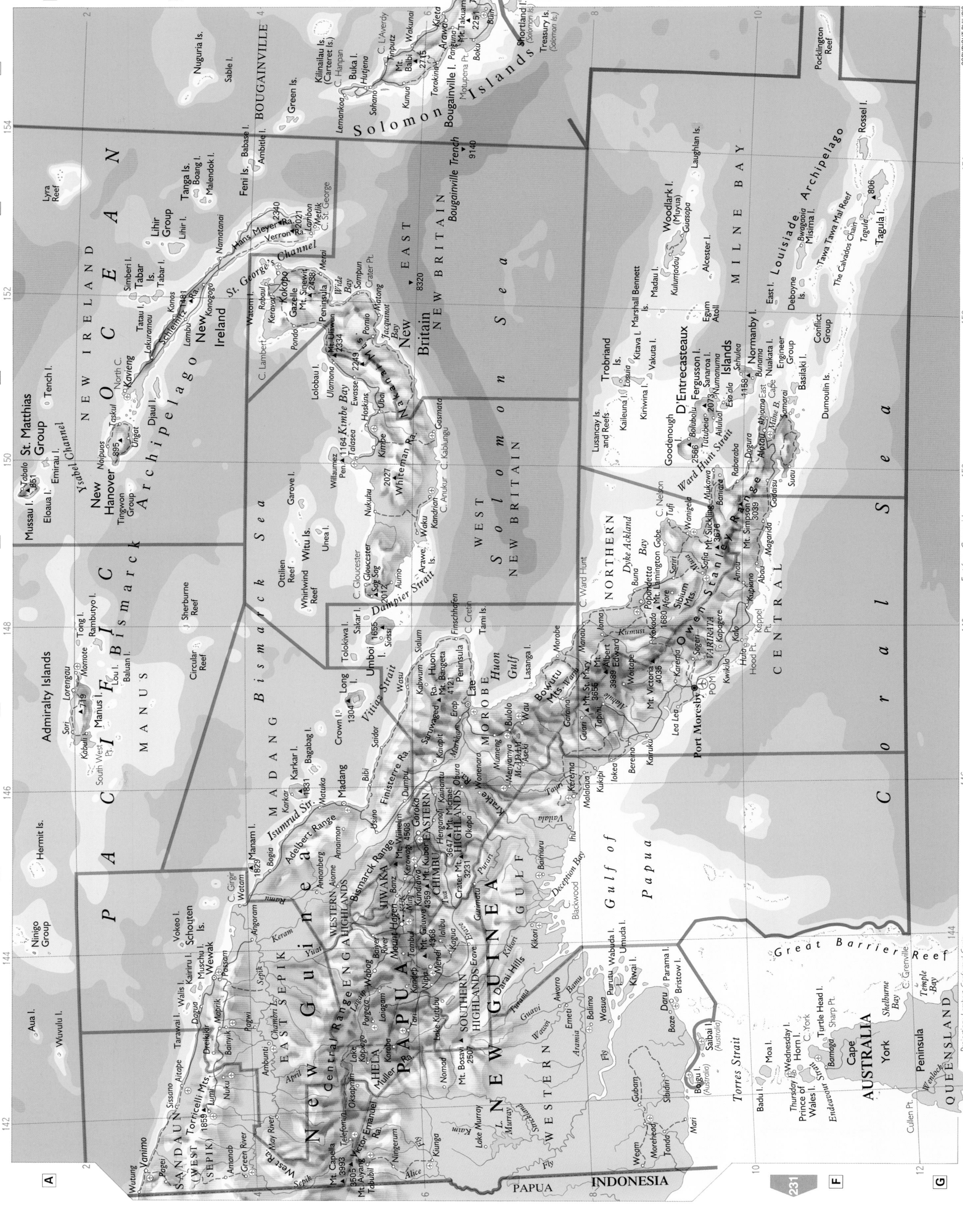

50 0 50 100 150 miles

m 6000 4000 2000 1000 400 200 0

ft 18 000 12 000 6000 3000 1200 600 0

m 0 200 600 1000 3000 6000 12 000

ft 0 600 2000 3000 6000 12 000 18 000

PACIFIC OCEAN

Bismarck Archipelago

Bismarck Sea

Solomon Sea

Coral Sea

Gulf of Papua

Solomon Islands

New Guinea

PAPUA NEW GUINEA

MANUS

NEW IRELAND

BOUGAINVILLE

EAST NEW BRITAIN

WEST NEW BRITAIN

MADANG

MOROBE

NORTHERN

MILNE BAY

CENTRAL

GULF

WESTERN

SOUTHERN HIGHLANDS

HELA

ENGA

WESTERN HIGHLANDS

JIWAKA

CHIMBU

EASTERN HIGHLANDS

EAST SEPIK

SANDAUN (WEST SEPIK)

PAPUA

INDONESIA

AUSTRALIA

QUEENSLAND

Cape York Peninsula

Torres Strait

Great Barrier Reef

Louisiade Archipelago

D'Entrecasteaux Islands

Trobriand Is.

Admiralty Islands

St. Matthias Group

New Hanover

New Ireland

New Britain

Bougainville I.

Port Moresby

Lae

Madang

Wewak

Rabaul

Kokopo

Kavieng

Alotau

Owen Stanley Range

Bismarck Range

Central Range

Mt. Wilhelm 4508

Mt. Giluwe 4368

Mt. Victoria 4035

Bougainville Trench 9140

Projection: Lambert Conformal Conic

East from Greenwich

287

231

280

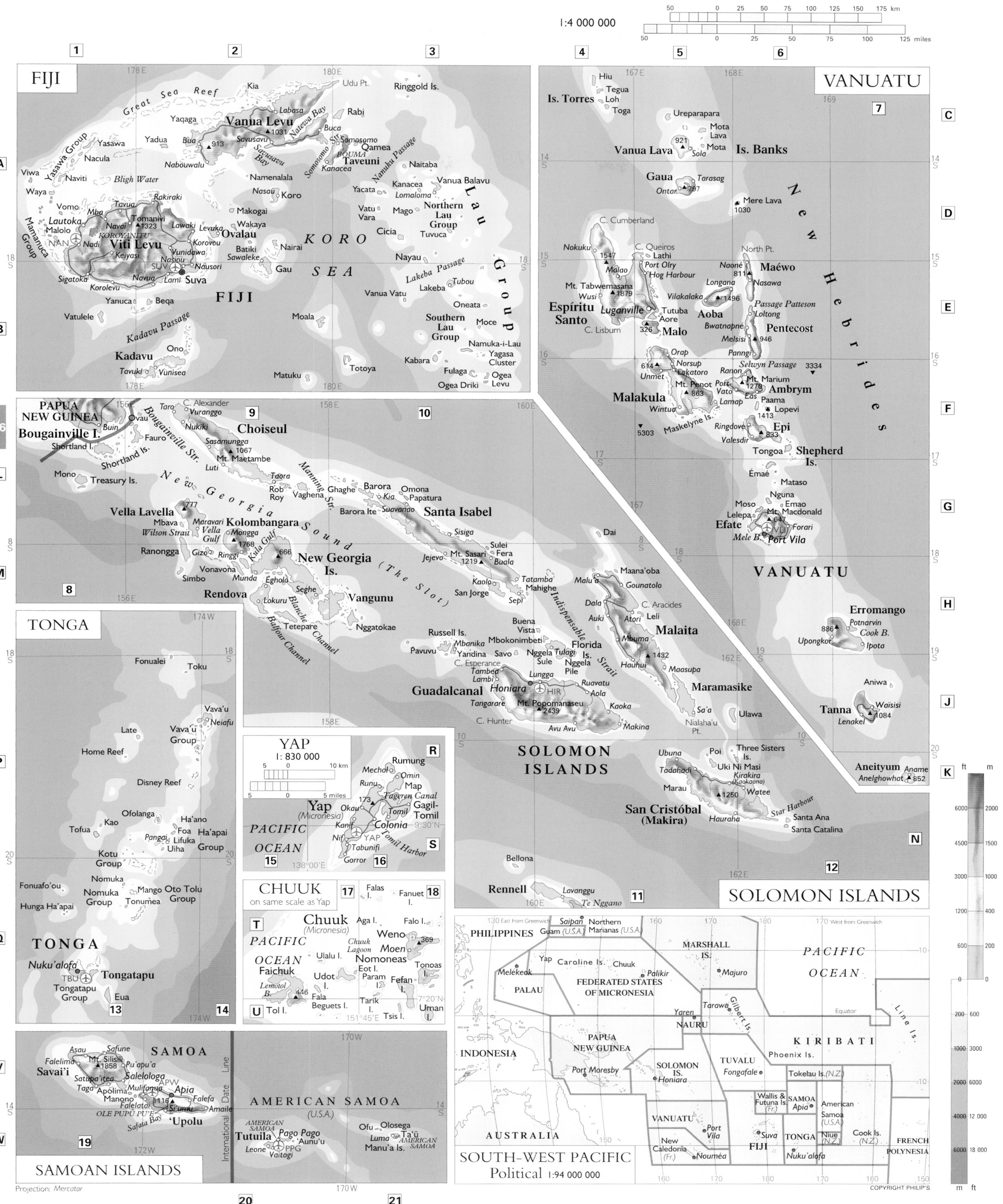
1:4 000 000
FIJI
Great Sea Reef
Kia
Udu Pt.
Ringgold Is.
Labasa
Vanua Levu
Natewa Bay
Rabi
Yaqaga
Yadua
Bua
Savusavu
1031
913
Buca
Somosomo
Somosomo Str.
Qamea
BOUMA
Taveuni
Kanacea
Yasawa
Yasawa Group
Nacula
Nabouwalu
Savusavu Bay
Nanuku Passage
Naitaba
Viwa
Naviti
Bligh Water
Namenalala
Koro
Vanua Balavu
Waya
Nasau
Yacata
Kanacea
Lomaloma
Vomo
Tavua
Rakiraki
Makogai
Vatu Vara
Mago
Northern Lau Group
Lau Group
Lautoka
Mba
Tomanivi
Lawaki
Wakaya
Cicia
Tuvuca
Malolo
Navai
1323
Levuka
Ovalau
KOROYANITU
NAN
Nadi
Viti Levu
Korovou
K O R O
Mamanuca Group
Keiyasi
Batiki
Nairai
Nayau
Sawaleke
Nasinu
Vunidawa
SUV
Nausori
Gau
S E A
Lakeba Passage
Sigatoka
Navua
Lami
Suva
Tubou
Korolevu
Lakeba
Vanua Vatu
Yanuca
Beqa
FIJI
Oneata
Vatulele
Moala
Southern Lau Group
Moce
Kadavu Passage
Namuka-i-Lau
Ono
Yagasa Cluster
Kadavu
Kabara
Totoya
Tavuki
Vunisea
Matuku
Fulaga
Ogea
Ogea Driki
Ogea Levu
VANUATU
Hiu
Tegua
Is. Torres
Loh
Toga
Ureparapara
Mota Lava
Mota
921
Sola
Vanua Lava
Is. Banks
Gaua
Tarasag
Ontar
797
Mere Lava
1030
New Hebrides
C. Cumberland
C. Queiros
Nokuku
1547
Lathi
North Pt.
Port Olry
Naoné
Hog Harbour
811
Maéwo
Malao
Nasawa
Mt. Tabwemasana
1879
Longana
Wusi
Vilakalaka
1496
Espíritu Santo
Luganville
Tutuba
Passage Patteson
Aore
Aoba
Loltong
C. Lisburn
326
Malo
Bwatnapne
Pentecost
Melsisi
946
Orap
Pangi
614
Norsup
Selwyn Passage
3334
Lakatoro
Ranon
Unmet
Mt. Marium
Mt. Penot
Port Vato
1270
863
Ambrym
Malakula
Eas
Paama
Wintua
Lamap
Lopevi
1413
Maskelyne Is.
Ringdové
5303
Epi
Valesdir
833
Tongoa
Shepherd Is.
Émaé
Mataso
Nguna
Moso
Emao
Lelepa
Mt. Macdonald
647
Efate
Forari
Mele B.
VLI
Port Vila
VANUATU
Erromango
Potnarvin
886
Cook B.
Upongkor
Ipota
Aniwa
Tanna
Waisisi
1084
Lenakel
Aneityum
Aname
Anelghowhat
852
PAPUA NEW GUINEA
Bougainville I.
Buin
Ovau
Shortland I.
Fauro
Taro
C. Alexander
Vuranggo
Nukiki
Choiseul
Bougainville Str.
Sasamungga
1067
Mt. Maetambe
Shortland Is.
Luti
Mono
Treasury Is.
New Georgia Sound
Manning Str.
Taora
Rob Roy
Ghaghe
Barora
Omona
Vaghena
Papatura
Kia
Barora Ite
Suavanao
Santa Isabel
Vella Lavella
777
Mbava
Maravari
Vella Gulf
Kolombangara
Wilson Strait
Mongga
1768
Sisiga
Gizo
Ringgi
Kula Gulf
666
Sulei
Ranongga
New Georgia Is.
Jejevo
Mt. Sasari
1219
Fera
Buala
(The Slot)
Vonavona
Simbo
Munda
Egholo
Kaolo
Tatamba
Mahighe
Rendova
Seghe
Vangunu
San Jorge
Sepi
Lokuru
Blanche Channel
Tetepare
Nggatokae
Balfour Channel
Indispensable Strait
Dai
Maana'oba
Malu'a
Gounatolo
Dala
C. Aracides
Auki
Atori
Leli
Malaita
Mbuma
1432
Hauhui
Maasupa
Buena Vista
Russell Is.
Pavuvu
Mbanika
Yandina
Mbokonimbeti
Savo
Nggela Sule
Tulagi
Nggela Pile
Florida Is.
C. Esperance
Tambea
Lambi
Lungga
Ruavatu
Guadalcanal
Honiara
HIR
Aola
Maramasike
Tangarare
Mt. Popomanaseu
2439
Kaoka
Sa'a
C. Hunter
Avu Avu
Makina
Nialaha'u Pt.
Ulawa
SOLOMON ISLANDS
Ubuna
Poi
Three Sisters Is.
Uki Ni Masi
Tadahadi
Kirakira (Kaokaona)
Marau
1250
Wate
Star Harbour
San Cristóbal (Makira)
Hauraha
Santa Ana
Santa Catalina
Bellona
Rennell
Lavanggu
Te Nggano
SOLOMON ISLANDS
TONGA
Fonualei
Toku
Vava'u
Neiafu
Late
Vava'u Group
Home Reef
Disney Reef
Ofolanga
Ha'ano
Tofua
Kao
Foa
Ha'apai
Pangai
Lifuka
Uiha
Ha'apai Group
Kotu Group
Nomuka
Fonuafo'ou
Nomuka Group
Mango
Oto Tolu Group
Hunga Ha'apai
Tonumea
TONGA
Nuku'alofa
TBU
Tongatapu
Tongatapu Group
Eua
YAP
1: 830 000
Rumung
Mechol
Omin
Map
Runu
Fageren Canal
Gagil-Tomil
173
Yap (Micronesia)
Okau
Tomil
Kanif
Colonia
PACIFIC OCEAN
YAP
Nif
Tabunifi
Tomil Harbor
Gorror
CHUUK
on same scale as Yap
Falas I.
Fanuet I.
Chuuk (Micronesia)
Aga I.
Falo I.
Weno
Chuuk Lagoon
Moen
369
PACIFIC OCEAN
Ulalu I.
Nomoneas
Faichuk
Eot I.
Tonoas
Udot I.
Param I.
Fefan I.
Lemotol B.
446
Fala Beguets I.
Tarik I.
Tol I.
Tsis I.
Uman I.
SAMOA
Asau
Safune
Falelima
Mt. Silisili
1858
Pu'apu'a
Savai'i
Satupa'itea
Salelologa
APW
Taga
Apolima
Mulifanua
Apia
Manono
Falelatai
1116
Falefa
OLE PUPU PU'E
Si'umu
Amaile
Safata Bay
'Upolu
International Date Line
AMERICAN SAMOA
(U.S.A.)
AMERICAN SAMOA
Tutuila
Pago Pago
'Aunu'u
Leone
PPG
Vaitogi
Ofu
Olosega
Luma
Ta'u
Manu'a Is.
SAMOAN ISLANDS
PHILIPPINES
Saipan
Guam (U.S.A.)
Northern Marianas (U.S.A.)
MARSHALL IS.
Yap
Caroline Is.
Chuuk
Palikir
Melekeok
Majuro
FEDERATED STATES OF MICRONESIA
PALAU
PACIFIC OCEAN
Tarawa
Gilbert Is.
Yaren
NAURU
Equator
Line Is.
PAPUA NEW GUINEA
KIRIBATI
INDONESIA
Port Moresby
Phoenix Is.
SOLOMON IS.
Honiara
TUVALU
Fongafale
Tokelau Is. (N.Z.)
Wallis & Futuna Is. (Fr.)
SAMOA
Apia
American Samoa (U.S.A.)
VANUATU
Port Vila
Suva
FIJI
TONGA
Niue (N.Z.)
Cook Is. (N.Z.)
AUSTRALIA
New Caledonia (Fr.)
Nouméa
Nuku'alofa
FRENCH POLYNESIA
SOUTH-WEST PACIFIC
Political 1:94 000 000
Projection: Mercator
COPYRIGHT PHILIP'S

Equatorial Scale 1:43 200 000
OKINAWA
on same scale as Palau
a
Hedo-misaki
Hedo
Okinawa
(Japan)
Kunigami
Ie-shima
Kouri-shima
Yagaji-shima
503
Yonaha-Dake
Seseko-shima
Nakijin
Minna-shima
Motobu
EAST CHINA SEA
Nago
Arume-wan
Nago-wan
Banno-saki
Onna
Oura-wan
Ishikawa
Kin-wan
Ikei-shima
Kadena
Uruma
Okinawa (Koza)
Takabanare-shima
Henna
Ginowan
Heanza-shima
Urasoe
Tsuken-jima
Naha
Nakagusuku-wan
OKA
Shuri
Kudaka-shima
PACIFIC OCEAN
Rukan-sho
Gushikami
Itoman
Kyan-zaki
128° E
IWO-JIMA
1:200 000
b
Kangoku Iwa
Kitano Hana
COAST GUARD STATION
Iwo-Jima
(Japan)
Hanare Iwa
108
Kama Iwa
IWO JIMA AIRFIELD
PACIFIC OCEAN
Suribachi Yama
167
Fatatsu Ne
Tobiishi Hana
141° 20' E
PALAU
c
Ngaregur
Konrei
Ngardmau Bay
Ngardmau
218
Babelthuap I.
Namai Bay
Melekeok
Komebail Lagoon
Koror
ROR
Garusuun
Malakal Harbor
Garreru
Koror I.
Aulong
Apurashokoru
Urukthapel I.
Ngobasangel
Sar Passage
Orukuizui
Eil Malk I. (Mecherchar)
Shonian Harbor
Ngeregong
Barnum Bay
Ngergoi
Ngesebus I.
Kongauru I.
Ngardololok
PACIFIC OCEAN
Peleliu I.
Angaur I.
134° 30' E
1:1 550 000
10 0 10 20 30 km
10 0 10 20 miles
RUSSIA
Lena
Irkutsk
Oz. Baykal
Chita
Okhotsk
Sea of Okhotsk
Poluostrov Kamchatka
Shirshov Ridge
Aleutian Basin
Bering Sea
Komandorskiye Ostrova
(Russia)
Near Is.
(U.S.A.)
Andreanof
Petropavlovsk-Kamchatskiy
7822
Aleutian Is.
Aleutian Trench
Amur
Sakhalin
Blagoveshchensk
Khabarovsk
Ulaanbaatar
Harbin
La Perouse Str.
Kurilskiye Ostrova
(Russia)
Kuril-Kamchatka Trench
10,542
Emperor Trough
Chinook Trough
Ürümqi
MONGOLIA
Changchun
Sapporo
Hokkaidō
Hakodate
Shenyang
Vladivostok
Sea of Japan
Northwest Pacific Basin
Emperor Seamount Chain
Beijing
Tianjin
NORTH KOREA
Honshū
Taiyuan
Dalian
Seoul
SOUTH KOREA
Sendai
CHINA
Huang He
Fuji-San 3776
Tōkyō
Nagoya
Kyōto
Yokohama
Lanzhou
Qingdao
Shatsky Rise
Kunlun Shan
Xi'an
Kitakyūshū
Ōsaka
JAPAN
XIZANG
Nanjing
Yellow Sea
Shikoku
Tamu Massif
1980
Chengdu
Wuhan
Shanghai
Kyūshū
10,554
Japan Trench
Chongqing
Lhasa
Chang Jiang
Hangzhou
East China Sea
Midway Is.
(U.S.A.)
Brahmaputra
Changsha
Okinawa
Iwo-Jima (Japan)
Ogasawara Gunto (Japan)
Kyushu-Palau Ridge
Shichito-Iwojima Ridge
Fuzhou
Taipei
Ryūkyū-rettō (Japan)
Kazan-Rettō (Japan)
Minami-Tori-Shima (Japan)
Lisianski I.
(U.S.A.)
Dhaka
Irrawaddy
Kunming
Taiwan Str.
Guangzhou
TAIWAN
Mandalay
Hong Kong
Macau
MYANMAR
LAOS
Hanoi
Philippine Sea
Mid-Pacific Seamounts
Salween
Wake I. (U.S.A.)
Hainan
C. Engano
West Mariana Basin
NORTHERN MARIANAS (U.S.A.)
International Date Line
Yangôn
Luzon
Philippine Basin
Paracel Is.
THAILAND
Mekong
Manila
Tinian
Saipan
East Mariana Basin
Bangkok
PHILIPPINES
GUAM (U.S.A.)
MARSHALL IS.
CAMBODIA
VIETNAM
Mindoro
Challenger Deep
11,022
Mariana Trench
Bikini Atoll
Phnom Penh
South China Sea
Samar
Enewetak Atoll
Ratak Chain
G. of Thailand
Thanh Pho Ho Chi Minh
Palawan
10,497
Micronesia
Ralik Chain
Kwajalein
SRI LANKA
Nicobar Is. (India)
Yap
Caroline Is.
Chuuk
Majuro
Colombo
Sulu Sea
Mindanao
Philippine Trench
Melekeok
FED. STATES OF MICRONESIA
Pohnpei
Palikir
Jaluit I.
MALAYSIA
4161
Davao
BRUNEI
SABAH
PALAU
East Caroline Basin
Kuala Lumpur
PEN. MALAYSIA
SARAWAK
Celebes Sea
West Caroline Basin
Melanesia
Solomon Rise
Butaritari
Maluku
Eauripik Rise
Melanesian Basin
Tarawa
Howland I. (U.S.A.)
Baker I.
Singapore
Gilbert Is.
Sumatera
Borneo
Halmahera
PAPUA NEW GUINEA
Yaren
NAURU
Banaba
Phoenix Is.
Abariringa
Enderbury
Sunda Islands
INDONESIA
Sulawesi
Seram
Admiralty Is.
Bismarck Arch.
Palembang
Buru
Puncak Jaya 4884
PAPUA
New Ireland
Makassar
New Guinea
Kokopo
8940
Ninetyeast Ridge
Java Sea
Banda Sea
Bougainville
Jakarta
Flores Sea
7440
Lae
New Britain
SOLOMON IS.
Fongafale
TUVALU
Tokelau (N.Z.)
Selat Sunda
Jawa
Surabaya
Flores
Dili
TIMOR-LESTE
Sunda Trench (Java Trench)
Bali
Sumbawa
Sumba
Arafura Sea
Port Moresby
Honiara
Guadalcanal
Torres Strait
C. York
Louisiade Arch.
Santa Cruz Is.
Christmas I. (Austral.)
C. Arnhem
9165
Cocos Is. (Austral.)
North Australian Basin
Darwin
Gulf of Carpentaria
Coral Sea Basin
Rotuma
Is. Wallis & Futuna (Fr.)
SAMOA
Apia
INDIAN OCEAN
Great Barrier Reef
Coral Sea
VANUATU
Espiritu Santo
Vanua Levu
Port Vila
West Fiji Basin
Viti Levu
Suva
FIJI
Cairns
Exmouth Plateau
Broome
Townsville
Îs. Chesterfield
7570
Wharton Basin
North West C.
Mount Isa
NEW CALEDONIA (Fr.)
Îs. Loyauté
Nuku'alofa
TONGA
Tonga Trench
AUSTRALIA
Nouméa
Rockhampton
10,822
OCEAN
Alice Springs
Great Dividing Ra.
Middleton Basin
Lord Howe Rise
New Caledonia Trough
Norfolk Ridge
South Fiji Basin
Brisbane
Kati Thanda-L. Eyre
Darling
Norfolk I. (Austral.)
Geraldton
Kermadec Is. (N.Z.)
Broken Ridge
Perth Basin
Lord Howe I. (Austral.)
Kermadec Trench
10,047
Perth
Sydney
Naturaliste Plateau
Great Australian Bight
Canberra
NEW ZEALAND
Albany
Adelaide
Murray
Mt. Kosciuszko 2228
Tasman Sea
Auckland
South Australian Basin
Melbourne
Cook Strait
Bass Str.
Wellington
Tasmania
Hobart
East Tasman Plateau
Aoraki Mt. Cook 3724
Christchurch
Chatham Rise
Chatham Is. (N.Z.)
Tasman Basin
South Tasman Rise
Dunedin
Bounty Trough
Invercargill
Bounty Is. (N.Z.)
Antipodes Is. (N.Z.)
Campbell Plateau
Auckland Is. (N.Z.)
Campbell I. (N.Z.)
SOUTHERN OCEAN
Macquarie I. (Austral.)
Projection: Mollweide's Homolographic
East from Greenwich
110
120
130
140
150
160
170
180
NEW CALEDONIA
1:5 750 000
50 0 50 100 km
50 0 50 miles
d
Îles Belep
Récif de Cook
Île Art
Récif de l'Astrolabe
Île Balabio
Nouvelle-Calédonie
(France)
Poum
Ouégoa
Pouébo
Mt. Panié
1628
Île Ouvéa
Hienghène
Koumac
Kaala-Gomén
Fayaoué
Chépénéhé
C. Escarpé
Wé
7570
Poindimié
Voh
Îles Loyauté
Ponérihouen
Kone
Île Lifou
Mou
Île Tiga
Houailou
C. de Flotte
Poya
La Roche
3566
Canala
Bourail
Thio
Tadine
C. Boyer
CORAL SEA
La Foa
Île Maré
1618
Mt. Humbolt
Boulouparis
2212
Païta
Dumbea
Yaté
Nouméa
Mont Dore
GEA
C. Ndoua
Grand Récif Sud
Ile des Pins
Vao
164°E
165°E
166°E
167°E
168°E
20°S
21°S
22°S

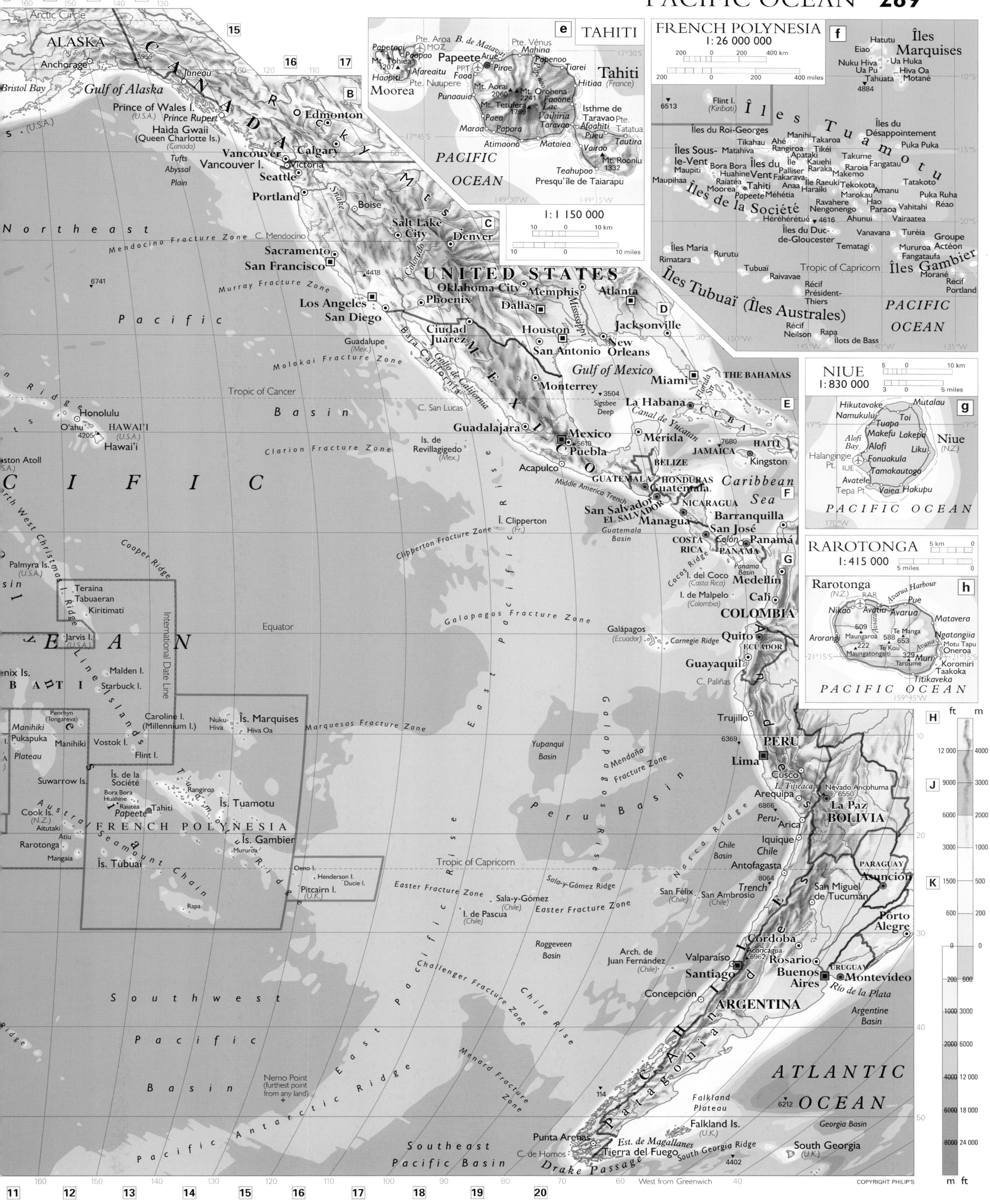

TAHITI 1: 1 150 000

FRENCH POLYNESIA 1: 26 000 000

NIUE 1: 830 000

RAROTONGA 1: 415 000

NORTH
AMERICA

1:28 000 000

ARCTIC OCEAN
Beaufort Sea
Chukchi Sea
Bering Sea
Lincoln Sea
Greenland
Iceland
Baffin Bay
Baffin Island
Queen Elizabeth Is.
Victoria I.
Hudson Bay
Hudson Strait
Labrador Sea
Canadian Shield
Alaska Range
Brooks Ra.
Mackenzie Mts.
Rocky Mountains
Great Plains
Great Lakes
Great Basin
Appalachian Mts.
Gulf of Alaska
Gulf of Mexico
Gulf of California
Western Sierra Madre
Eastern Sierra Madre
Mexican Plateau
Yucatán Peninsula
Caribbean Sea
West Indies
Central America
PACIFIC OCEAN
ATLANTIC OCEAN
Sargasso Sea
Projection: Bonne
West from Greenwich
COPYRIGHT PHILIP'S

1:28 000 000
100 0 200 400 600 800 1000 1200 1400 km
100 0 200 400 600 800 1000 miles
RUSSIA
Asia
International Date Line
ARCTIC OCEAN
Beaufort Sea
St. Lawrence I.
Bering Strait
Bering Sea
Yukon
ALASKA (U.S.A.)
Porcupine
Fairbanks
Anchorage
Kodiak I.
Gulf of Alaska
Queen Elizabeth Is.
Ellesmere I.
GREENLAND (Denmark)
Denmark Strait
ICELAND
Reykjavík
Baffin Bay
Davis Strait
Nuuk
Victoria I.
Baffin Island
NUNAVUT
Iqaluit
Hudson Strait
NORTHWEST TERRITORIES
Arctic Circle
Mackenzie
Great Bear L.
Back
YUKON
Whitehorse
Yellowknife
Great Slave L.
Dubawnt
Liard
Juneau
Hudson Bay
CANADA
NEWFOUNDLAND & LABRADOR
St John's
BRITISH COLUMBIA
Skeena
Peace
Athabasca
L. Athabasca
Churchill
Nelson
ALBERTA
Edmonton
MANITOBA
SASKATCHEWAN
Saskatchewan
Calgary
Regina
L. Winnipeg
Winnipeg
ONTARIO
QUÉBEC
Eastmain
St. Lawrence
PRINCE EDWARD I.
Charlottetown
St-Pierre et Miquelon (Fr.)
NEW BRUNSWICK
NOVA SCOTIA
Halifax
Fredericton
Québec
Fraser
Victoria
Vancouver
WASHINGTON
Olympia
Seattle
Portland
Salem
Columbia
OREGON
IDAHO
Boise
Snake
MONTANA
Missouri
Helena
NORTH DAKOTA
Bismarck
SOUTH DAKOTA
MINNESOTA
Minneapolis-St. Paul
L. Superior
WYOMING
WISCONSIN
Madison
Milwaukee
L. Michigan
MICHIGAN
Lansing
L. Huron
Detroit
Toledo
L. Erie
L. Ontario
TORONTO
Ottawa
Montréal
MAINE
Augusta
VT.
N.H.
Concord
Boston
MASS.
Providence
Hartford
NEW YORK
Buffalo
Cleveland
PA.
Pittsburgh
PHILADELPHIA
N.J.
Baltimore
DE.
MD.
WASHINGTON D.C.
Richmond
UNITED STATES
IOWA
CHICAGO
NEBRASKA
Lincoln
ILLINOIS
INDIANA
OHIO
Columbus
Indianapolis
Cincinnati
Sacramento
SAN FRANCISCO
San Jose
Carson City
NEVADA
UTAH
Salt Lake City
Denver
COLORADO
Kansas City
Topeka
KANSAS
Springfield
St. Louis
MISSOURI
W.V.
VIRGINIA
Raleigh
KENTUCKY
Nashville
TENNESSEE
NORTH CAROLINA
Charlotte
Columbia
SOUTH CAROLINA
Charleston
CALIFORNIA
Las Vegas
LOS ANGELES
San Diego
Tijuana
Mexicali
Colorado
ARIZONA
Phoenix
Tucson
NEW MEXICO
Santa Fe
Albuquerque
OKLAHOMA
Oklahoma City
ARKANSAS
Little Rock
Memphis
Mississippi
MISSISSIPPI
Jackson
Birmingham
ATLANTA
GEORGIA
ALABAMA
Montgomery
Tallahassee
Jacksonville
FLORIDA
Orlando
Tampa-St. Petersburg
MIAMI
DALLAS-FT. WORTH
TEXAS
El Paso
Ciudad Juárez
Austin
HOUSTON
Baton Rouge
LOUISIANA
New Orleans
San Antonio
Rio Grande
Bermuda (U.K.)
ATLANTIC OCEAN
PACIFIC OCEAN
Guadalupe (Mex.)
Hermosillo
Tropic of Cancer
MEXICO
Culiacán
Torreón
Monterrey
San Luis Potosí
León
Querétaro
Guadalajara
MÉXICO
Toluca
Puebla
Acapulco
Revilla Gigedo Is. (Mex.)
Gulf of Mexico
Mérida
THE BAHAMAS
Nassau
Florida Str.
Turks & Caicos Is. (U.K.)
Havana
CUBA
DOMINICAN REP.
HAITI
Port-au-Prince
Santo Domingo
San Juan
PUERTO RICO (U.S.A.)
Cayman Is. (U.K.)
JAMAICA
Kingston
Caribbean Sea
Belmopan
BELIZE
GUATEMALA
Guatemala
HONDURAS
Tegucigalpa
San Salvador
EL SALVADOR
NICARAGUA
Managua
L. Nicaragua
COSTA RICA
San José
PANAMA
Panamá
Barranquilla
Maracaibo
VENEZUELA
COLOMBIA
Medellín
South America
Projection: Bonne
West from Greenwich
MÉXICO Capital Cities
COPYRIGHT PHILIP'S

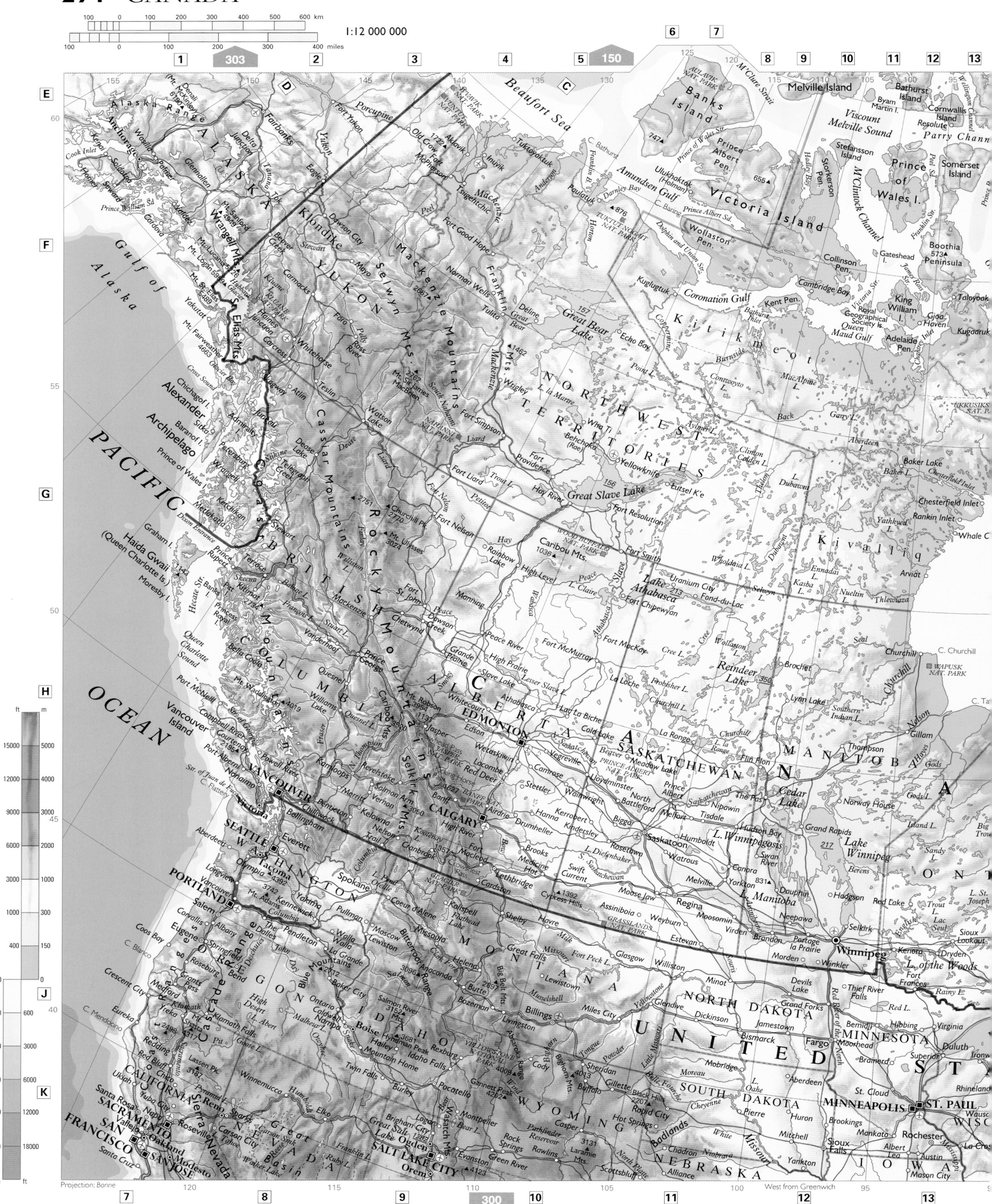
1:12 000 000
km
miles
Projection: Bonne
West from Greenwich
303
150
300
Beaufort Sea
Banks Island
Melville Island
Victoria Island
Prince of Wales I.
Amundsen Gulf
Coronation Gulf
Viscount Melville Sound
M'Clintock Channel
Boothia Peninsula
King William I.
Queen Maud Gulf
Kitikmeot
Kivalliq
NORTHWEST TERRITORIES
Great Bear Lake
Great Slave Lake
Yellowknife
Lake Athabasca
YUKON
Klondike
Dawson City
Whitehorse
Mackenzie Mountains
Selwyn Mts.
ALASKA
Alaska Range
Fairbanks
Anchorage
Gulf of Alaska
Wrangell Mts.
St. Elias Mts.
Juneau
Alexander Archipelago
PACIFIC OCEAN
Haida Gwaii (Queen Charlotte Is.)
Coast Mountains
Cassiar Mountains
Rocky Mountains
BRITISH COLUMBIA
Columbia Mountains
Vancouver Island
VANCOUVER
Victoria
Prince George
Prince Rupert
Kamloops
Kelowna
ALBERTA
EDMONTON
CALGARY
Red Deer
Lethbridge
Fort McMurray
Grande Prairie
SASKATCHEWAN
Saskatoon
Regina
Prince Albert
MANITOBA
Winnipeg
Lake Winnipeg
L. Winnipegosis
L. Manitoba
Churchill
Reindeer Lake
Baker Lake
Rankin Inlet
Chesterfield Inlet
Arviat
ON
UNITED STATES
WASHINGTON
SEATTLE
Tacoma
Olympia
Spokane
OREGON
PORTLAND
Salem
Eugene
IDAHO
Boise
MONTANA
Helena
Great Falls
Billings
Butte
WYOMING
Yellowstone National Park
Casper
NORTH DAKOTA
Bismarck
Fargo
SOUTH DAKOTA
Pierre
Rapid City
MINNESOTA
MINNEAPOLIS
ST. PAUL
Duluth
NEBRASKA
IOWA
UTAH
SALT LAKE CITY
Great Salt Lake
NEVADA
Reno
Great Basin
CALIFORNIA
SACRAMENTO
SAN FRANCISCO
SAN JOSE
Sierra Nevada
Cascade Range
Blue Mountains
L. of the Woods

NORTHERN CANADA
continuation northwards on same scale as main map
150
154
301
ARCTIC OCEAN
GREENLAND (KALAALLIT NUNAAT)
(Denmark)
Kronprins Frederik Land
Lincoln Sea
Alert
C. Columbia
Ellesmere Island
Axel Heiberg Island
Sverdrup Islands
Ellef Ringnes Island
Amund Ringnes I.
Borden Island
Prince Patrick Island
Queen Elizabeth Islands
Parry Islands
Melville Island
Bathurst Island
Cornwallis Island
Resolute
Devon Island
Grise Fiord
Jones Sound
Lancaster Sound
Prince of Wales I.
Somerset Island
Parry Channel
Viscount Melville Sound
Knud Rasmussen Land
Qaanaaq (Thule)
Lauge Koch Kyst
Melville Bugt
Baffin Bay
Davis Strait
NUNAVUT
N.W.T.
Baffin Island (Qikiqtaaluk)
Pond Inlet
Clyde River
Qikiqtarjuaq
Pangnirtung
Cumberland Peninsula
Cumberland Sd.
Iqaluit
Frobisher Bay
Foxe Basin
Foxe Channel
Melville Peninsula
Southampton I.
Hudson Strait
Hudson Bay
Labrador Sea
ATLANTIC OCEAN
Ungava Bay
Péninsule d'Ungava
Nunavik
Kuujjuaq
Nain
Hopedale
Labrador
NEWFOUNDLAND & LABRADOR
Happy Valley-Goose Bay
Churchill Falls
Labrador City
Smallwood Res.
James Bay
ONTARIO
QUÉBEC
Chibougamau
Sept-Îles
Î. d'Anticosti
Gulf of St. Lawrence
Cabot Strait
Newfoundland
St. John's
Gander
Corner Brook
NEW BRUNSWICK
PRINCE EDWARD I.
NOVA SCOTIA
Halifax
Sydney
Cape Breton I.
Charlottetown
Moncton
Saint John
Fredericton
Québec
MONTRÉAL
OTTAWA
TORONTO
Hamilton
L. Ontario
L. Huron
L. Erie
L. Michigan
Lake Superior
Sault Ste. Marie
Greater Sudbury
Thunder Bay
DETROIT
BUFFALO
ROCHESTER
CLEVELAND
BOSTON
PROVIDENCE
HARTFORD
MAINE
VERMONT
NEW HAMPSHIRE
NEW YORK
PENNSYLVANIA
MICHIGAN
MASS.
CONN.
R.I.

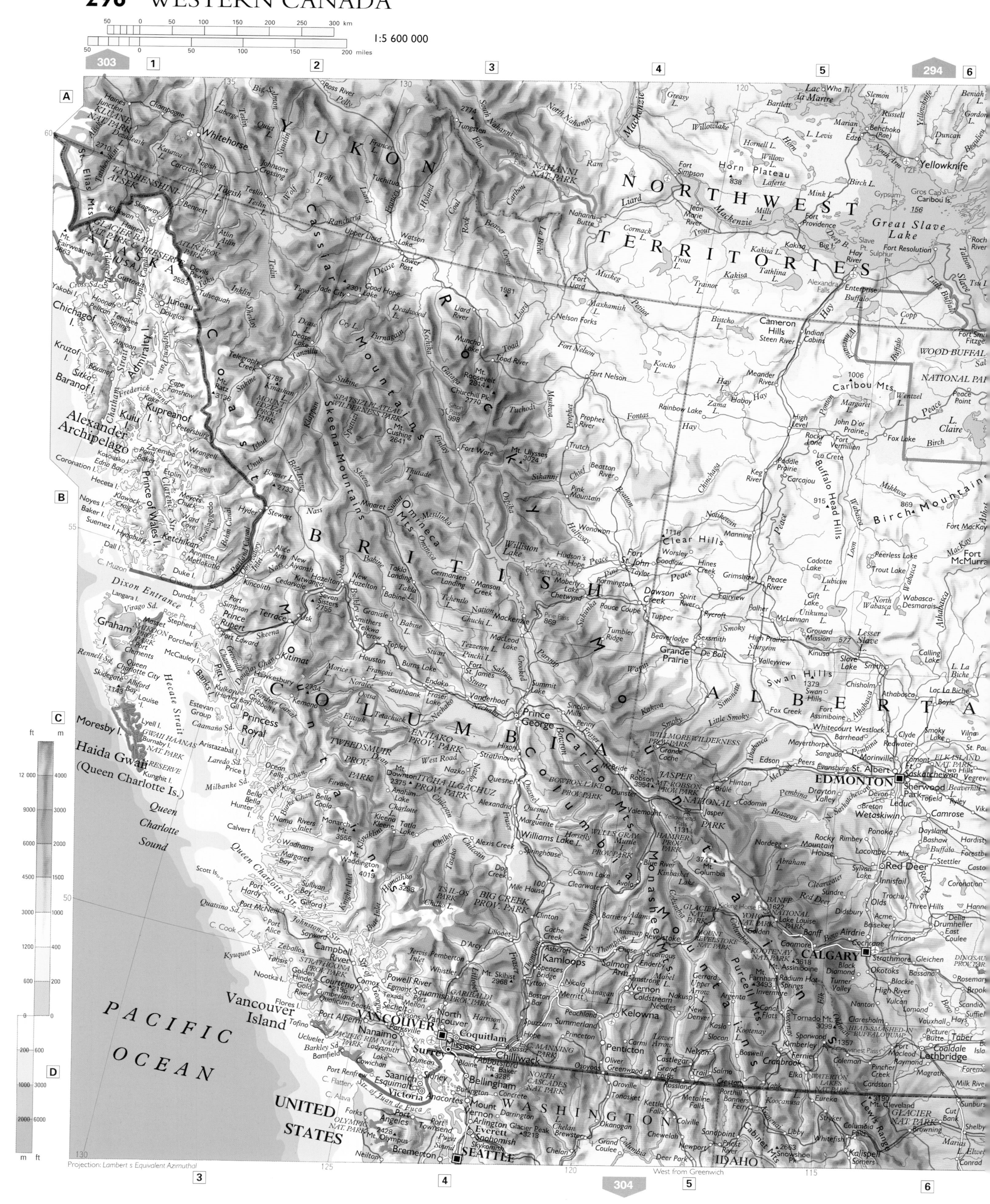
1:5 600 000
km
miles
303
294
304
YUKON
NORTHWEST TERRITORIES
BRITISH COLUMBIA
ALBERTA
ALASKA (USA)
WASHINGTON
IDAHO
UNITED STATES
PACIFIC OCEAN
Whitehorse
Yellowknife
EDMONTON
CALGARY
VANCOUVER
Victoria
SEATTLE
Prince George
Prince Rupert
Kamloops
Kelowna
Red Deer
Lethbridge
Fort Nelson
Fort St. John
Dawson Creek
Grande Prairie
Juneau
Great Slave Lake
Haida Gwaii (Queen Charlotte Is.)
Queen Charlotte Sound
Vancouver Island
Alexander Archipelago
Cassiar Mountains
Skeena Mountains
Coast Mountains
Rocky Mountains
Cariboo Mts.
Columbia Mts.
Monashee Mts.
Purcell Mts.
Selkirk Mts.
Caribou Mts.
Birch Mountains
Swan Hills
Clear Hills
Horn Plateau
Mackenzie
Liard
Peace
Fraser
Nahanni Nat. Park
Wood Buffalo National Park
Jasper National Park
Banff National Park
Glacier Nat. Park
Strathcona Prov. Park
Tweedsmuir Prov. Park
Projection: Lambert's Equivalent Azimuthal
West from Greenwich

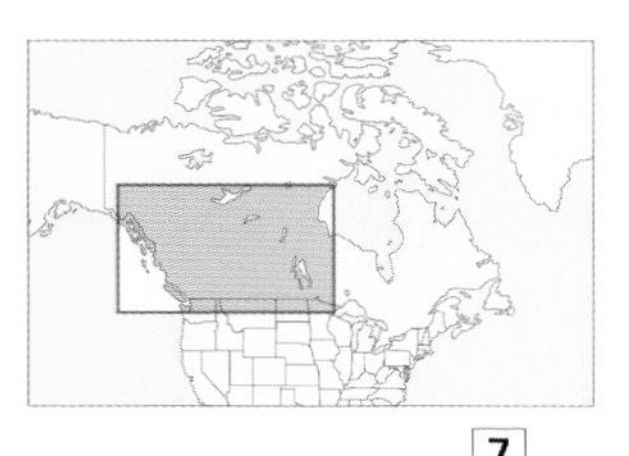

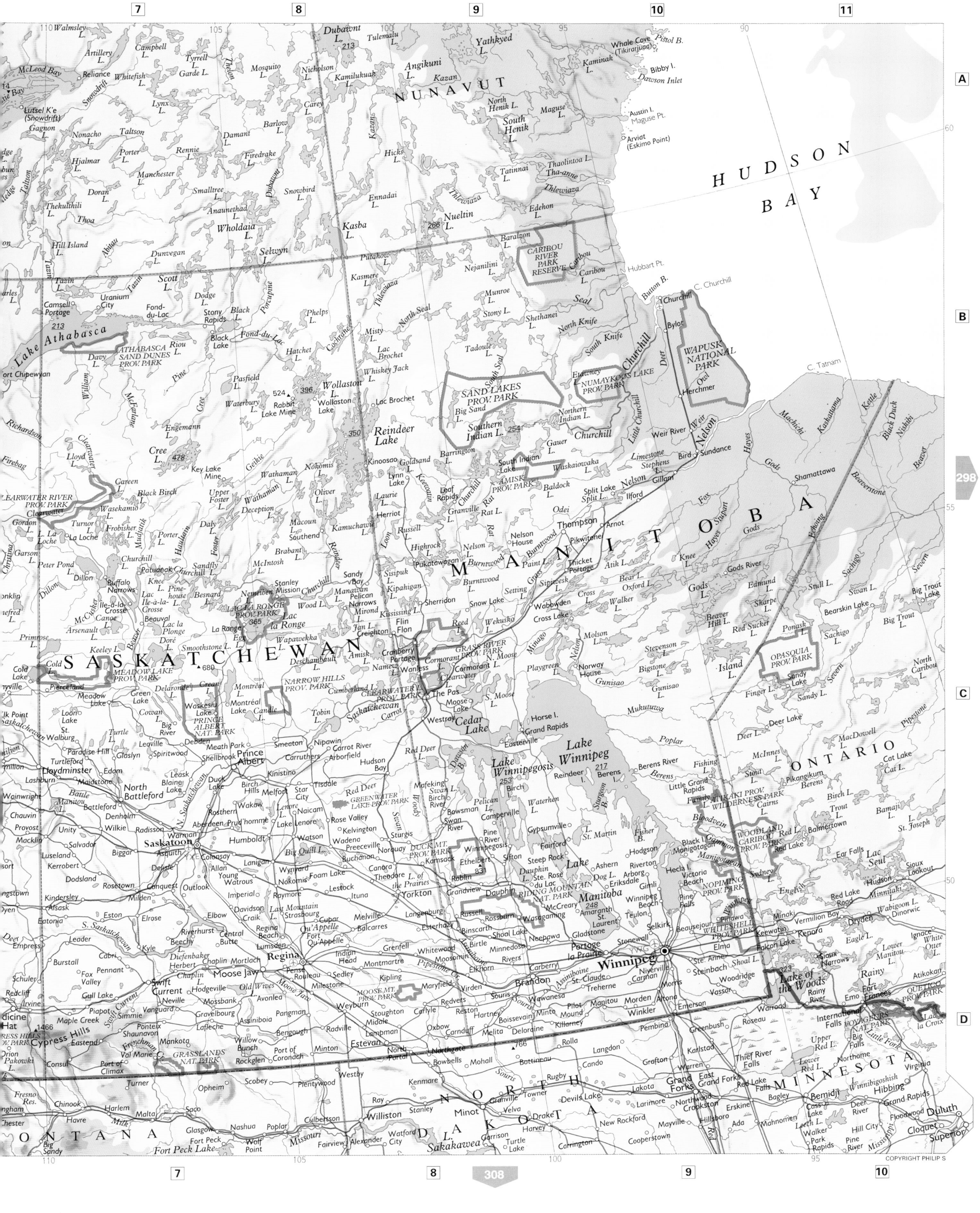

298
308

COPYRIGHT PHILIP S

1:5 600 000

50 0 50 100 150 200 250 300 km
50 0 50 100 150 200 miles
1 2 3 4 5
A B C D
297
308
MANITOBA
ONTARIO
HUDSON BAY
JAMES BAY
NUNAVUT
Belcher Islands
Akimiski I.
POLAR BEAR PROV. PARK
OPASQUIA PROV. PARK
WABAKIMI PROV. PARK
QUETICO PROV. PARK
ISLE ROYALE NAT. PARK
PUKASKWA NAT. PARK
LAKE SUPERIOR PROV. PARK
ALGONQUIN PROV. PARK
KILLARNEY PROV. PARK
FATHOM FIVE NAT. MARINE PARK
BRUCE PEN. NAT. PARK
GEORGIAN BAY IS. NAT. PARK
PT. PELEE NAT. PARK
PARC NATIONAL DE LA MAURICIE
PARC R.CR. DU MONT-TREMBLANT
ADIRONDACK PARK
L. Nipigon
Lac Seul
Thunder Bay
LAKE SUPERIOR
LAKE MICHIGAN
LAKE HURON
LAKE ONTARIO
LAKE ERIE
Georgian Bay
Green Bay
Saginaw Bay
L. Nipissing
Lac Mistassini
Rés. La Grande 4
Rés. La Grande 3
Rés. Robert Bourassa
Rés Eastmain
Rés. Gouin
Réservoir Cabonga
Lac Bienville
MICHIGAN
WISCONSIN
ILLINOIS
INDIANA
OHIO
NEW YORK
Moosonee
Timmins
Kapuskasing
Hearst
Sault Ste. Marie
Greater Sudbury
North Bay
Rouyn-Noranda
Val-d'Or
Chibougamau
Duluth
Superior
Marquette
Green Bay
MILWAUKEE
CHICAGO
Grand Rapids
Lansing
Flint
DETROIT
Windsor
Toledo
CLEVELAND
London
Sarnia
TORONTO
Hamilton
Kitchener
Niagara Falls
BUFFALO
ROCHESTER
Syracuse
Utica
Albany
Kingston
OTTAWA
Gatineau
MONTREAL
Laval
Peterborough
Barrie
Owen Sound
Trois-Rivières
Schenectady
Madison
Rockford
South Bend
Kalamazoo
Projection: Lambert's Equivalent Azimuthal

295

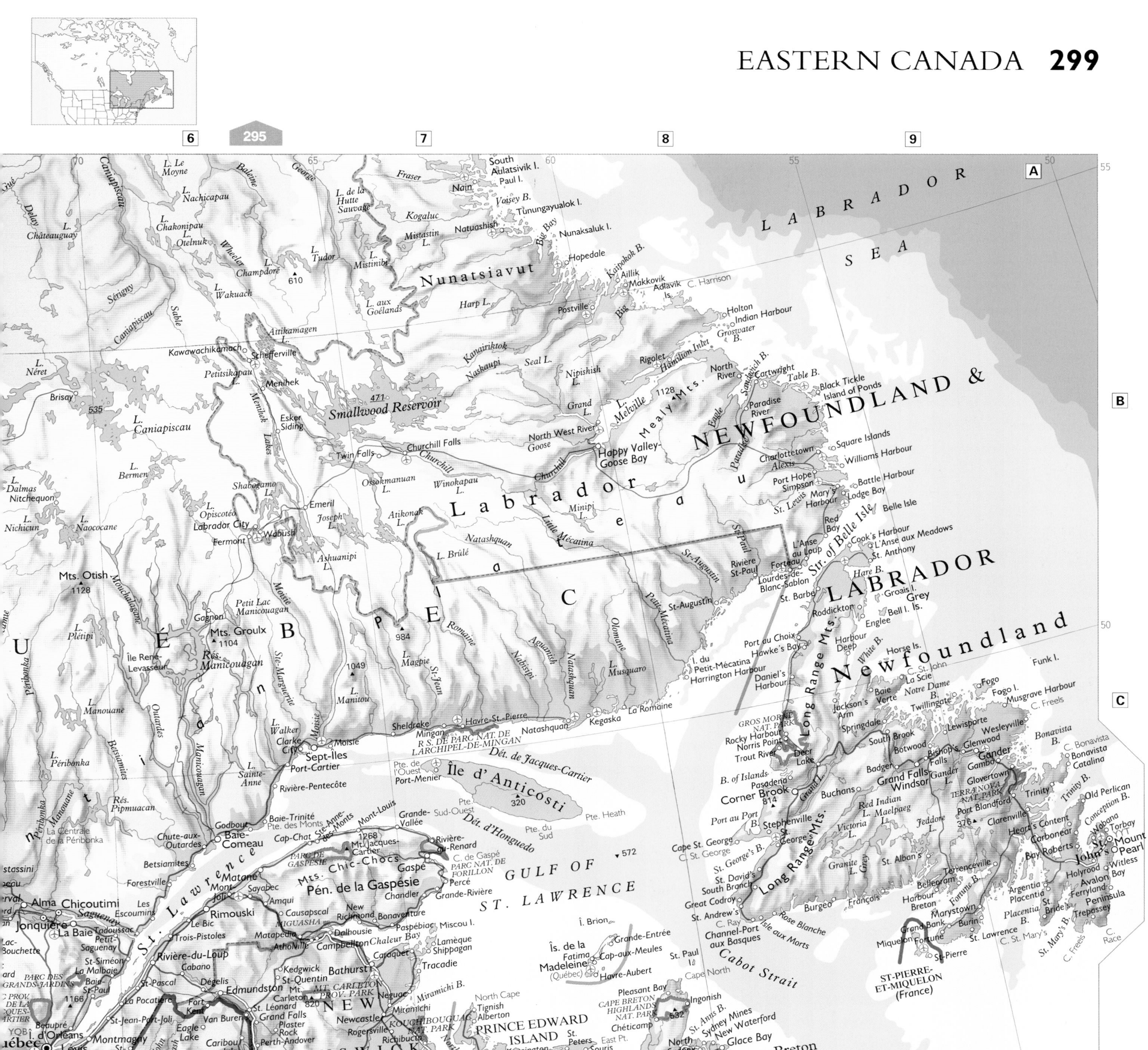
LABRADOR SEA
NEWFOUNDLAND & LABRADOR
Labrador
Newfoundland
Nunatsiavut
Smallwood Reservoir
Happy Valley-Goose Bay
Mealy Mts.
Long Range Mts.
Île d'Anticosti
GULF OF ST. LAWRENCE
St. Lawrence
Cabot Strait
Mts. Chic-Chocs
Pén. de la Gaspésie
NEW BRUNSWICK
PRINCE EDWARD ISLAND
Charlottetown
Cape Breton Island
NOVA SCOTIA
Halifax
Dartmouth
Bay of Fundy
Sable I. (Nova Scotia)
ATLANTIC OCEAN
ST-PIERRE-ET-MIQUELON (France)
Îs. de la Madeleine (Québec)
MAINE
UNITED STATES
BOSTON
Portland
Bangor
Saint John
Fredericton
Moncton
Sept-Îles
Baie-Comeau
Rimouski
Gaspé
Chicoutimi
Québec
Sherbrooke
Gander
St. John's
Corner Brook
Labrador City
Schefferville
Mts. Otish
Mts. Groulx
Rés. Manicouagan
COPYRIGHT PHILIP'S

1:12 000 000
km
miles
294
Anchorage
Washington D.C.
San Francisco
Honolulu
3363 miles
5412 km
2010 miles
3234 km
2438 miles
3923 km
2785 miles
4482 km
2395 miles
3854 km
Tropic of Cancer
PACIFIC OCEAN
West from Greenwich
BRITISH COLUMBIA
VANCOUVER
Victoria
SEATTLE
Tacoma
Olympia
Spokane
WASHINGTON
PORTLAND
Salem
Eugene
OREGON
IDAHO
Boise
MONTANA
Great Falls
Helena
Missoula
WYOMING
SALT LAKE CITY
Ogden
Provo
UTAH
NEVADA
Reno
Carson City
Las Vegas
SACRAMENTO
SAN FRANCISCO
Oakland
SAN JOSE
Stockton
Modesto
Fresno
Bakersfield
Santa Barbara
LOS ANGELES
Long Beach
Anaheim
SAN BERNARDINO
Riverside
SAN DIEGO
TIJUANA
Mexicali
ARIZONA
PHOENIX
Mesa
Tucson
Flagstaff
Colorado Plateau
Mojave Desert
Great Basin
Sierra Nevada
Coast Ranges
SONORA
ALASKA
on same scale
RUSSIA
Koryakskoye Nagorye
Chukotskoye Nagorye
Anadyrskiy Zaliv
CHUKCHI SEA
ARCTIC OCEAN
Bering Strait
Seward Peninsula
North Slope
Brooks Range
ALASKA
U.S.A.
Yukon Flats
Fairbanks
Denali (Mt. McKinley) 6190
Alaska Range
Kuskokwim Mountains
Anchorage
Chugach Mts.
Wrangell Mts.
Yukon Delta
Nunivak I.
St. Lawrence I. (U.S.A.)
St. Matthew I.
Pribilof Is.
BERING SEA
Bristol Bay
Alaska Peninsula
Kodiak I.
Gulf of Alaska
Aleutian Islands
Near Islands
Rat Islands
Andreanof Islands
Fox Islands
International Date Line
YUKON
Klondike
Alexander Arch
Projection: Albers' Equal Area with two standard parallels

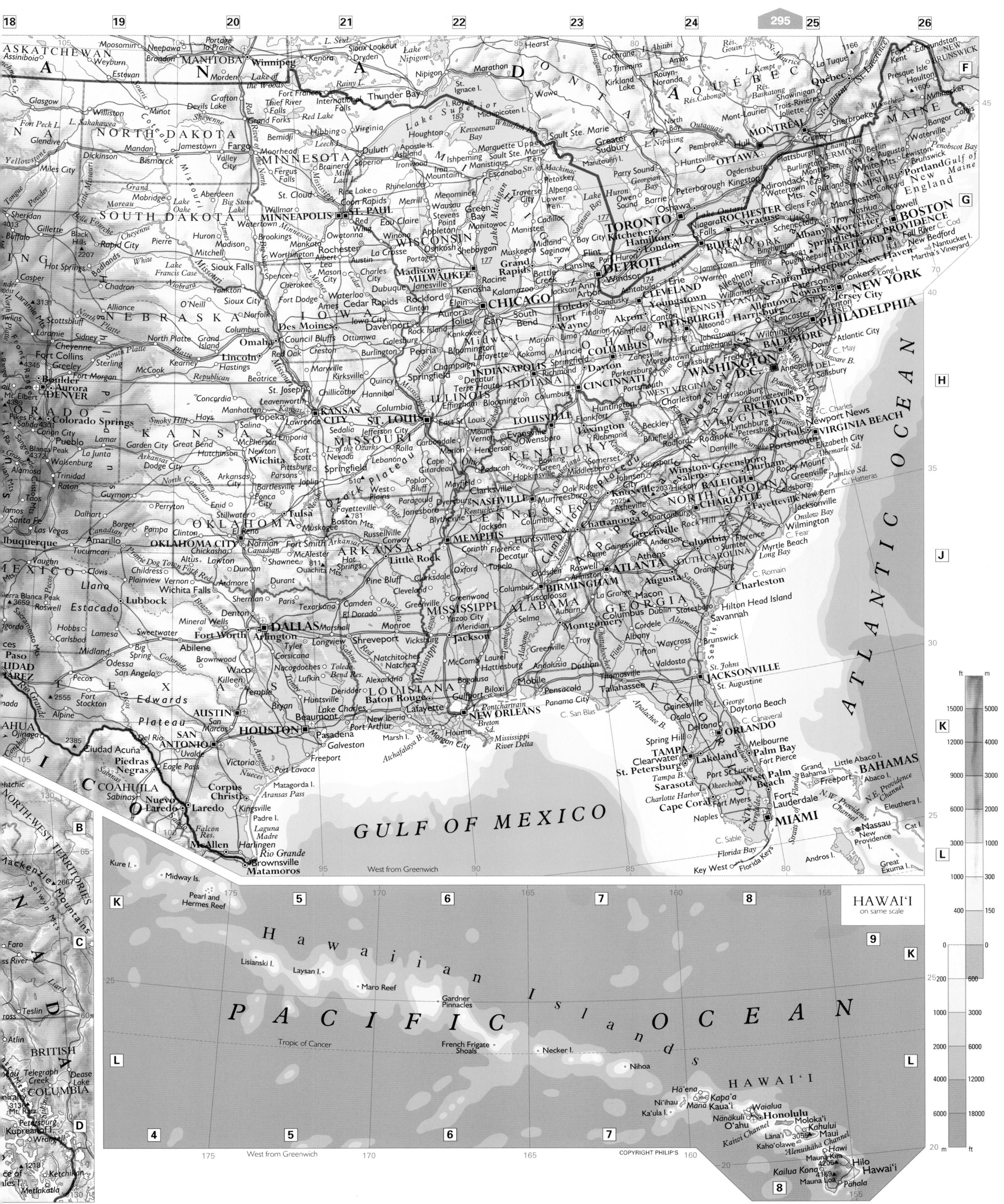

295
NORTH DAKOTA
SOUTH DAKOTA
NEBRASKA
KANSAS
OKLAHOMA
MINNESOTA
IOWA
MISSOURI
ARKANSAS
LOUISIANA
MISSISSIPPI
ALABAMA
GEORGIA
TENNESSEE
KENTUCKY
ILLINOIS
INDIANA
OHIO
WISCONSIN
MICHIGAN
NORTH CAROLINA
SOUTH CAROLINA
VIRGINIA
WEST VIRGINIA
PENNSYLVANIA
NEW YORK
MAINE
TEXAS
ONTARIO
QUÉBEC
MANITOBA
BAHAMAS
NEW BRUNSWICK
New England
Midwest
ATLANTIC OCEAN
GULF OF MEXICO
Lake Superior
Lake Michigan
Lake Huron
Lake Erie
Lake Ontario
Ozark Plateau
Llano Estacado
Edwards Plateau
Mississippi River Delta
CHICAGO
DETROIT
TORONTO
MONTREAL
OTTAWA
NEW YORK
PHILADELPHIA
BOSTON
BALTIMORE
WASHINGTON D.C.
PITTSBURGH
CLEVELAND
COLUMBUS
CINCINNATI
INDIANAPOLIS
LOUISVILLE
NASHVILLE
MEMPHIS
ATLANTA
BIRMINGHAM
CHARLOTTE
RICHMOND
VIRGINIA BEACH
ST. LOUIS
KANSAS CITY
MINNEAPOLIS
ST. PAUL
MILWAUKEE
OKLAHOMA CITY
DALLAS
HOUSTON
SAN ANTONIO
AUSTIN
NEW ORLEANS
JACKSONVILLE
ORLANDO
TAMPA
MIAMI
DENVER
West from Greenwich
COPYRIGHT PHILIP'S
HAWAI'I
on same scale
PACIFIC OCEAN
Hawaiian Islands
Tropic of Cancer
Kure I.
Midway Is.
Pearl and Hermes Reef
Lisianski I.
Laysan I.
Maro Reef
Gardner Pinnacles
French Frigate Shoals
Necker I.
Nihoa
Ni'ihau
Kaua'i
O'ahu
Honolulu
Moloka'i
Lana'i
Maui
Kaho'olawe
Hawai'i
Hilo
Kailua Kona
Mauna Kea
Mauna Loa
NORTH-WEST TERRITORIES
BRITISH COLUMBIA
Mackenzie Mountains
ft
m

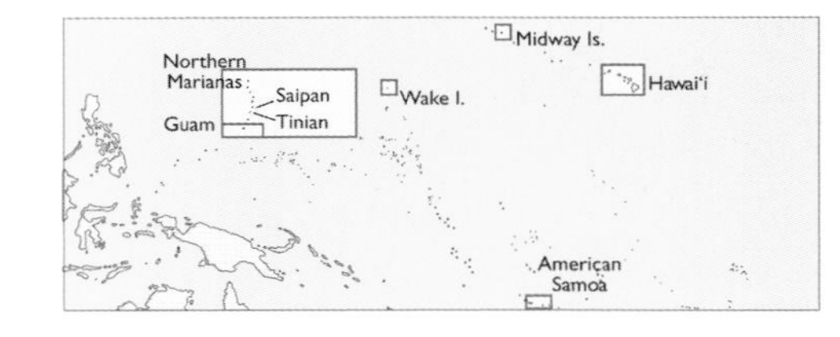

Midway Is.
Northern Marianas
Saipan
Tinian
Guam
Wake I.
Hawaiʻi
American Samoa

HAWAIʻI
1: 2 500 000
Kauaʻi
Niʻihau
Oʻahu
Molokaʻi
Lānaʻi
Maui
Kahoʻolawe
Hawaiʻi
Honolulu
Kauai Channel
Kaiwi Channel
ʻAlenuihāhā Channel
PACIFIC OCEAN
HAWAIIAN ISLANDS
1:21 000 000
Hawaiian Islands
PAPAHĀNAUMOKUĀKEA MARINE NAT. MONUMENT
Tropic of Cancer
OʻAHU
1: 500 000
Projection: Lambert's Conformal Conic
Projection: Albers Equal Area
West from Greenwich
NORTHERN MARIANAS
1: 17 500 000
Northern Marianas (U.S.A.)
Mariana Islands
Mariana Trench
WAKE I.
1:200 000
Wake I. (U.S.A.)
MIDWAY IS.
1:200 000
Midway Islands (U.S.A.)
GUAM
1: 800 000
Guam (Guåhån) (U.S.A.)
SAIPAN & TINIAN
1: 800 000
Saipan (U.S.A.)
Tinian (U.S.A.)
TUTUILA (AMER. SAMOA)
1: 640 000
Tutuila (U.S.A.)
MANUʻA IS. (AMER. SAMOA)
1: 640 000
Manuʻa Islands
COPYRIGHT PHILIP'S
1: 17 500 000
1: 800 000
1: 200 000
1: 640 000

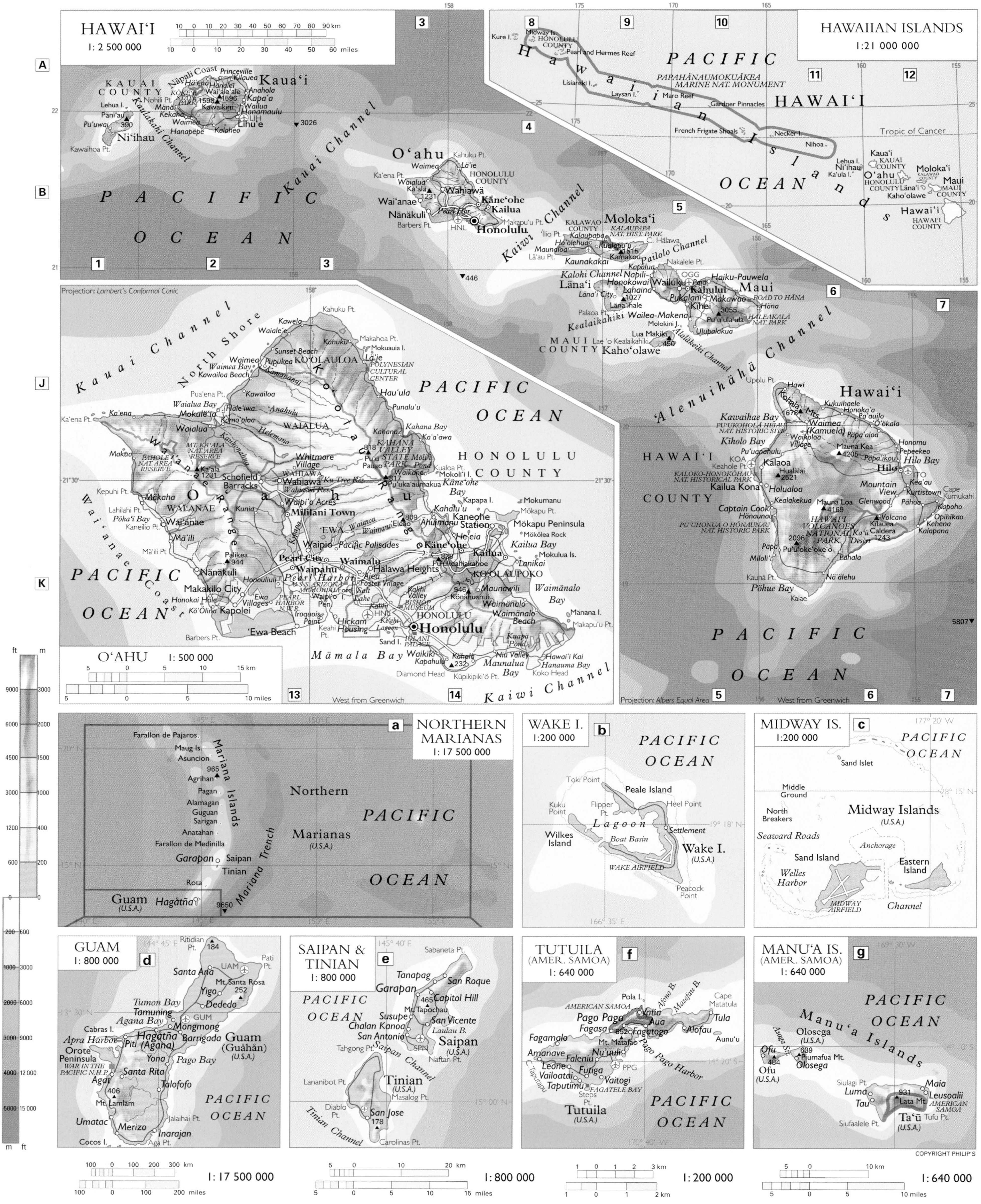

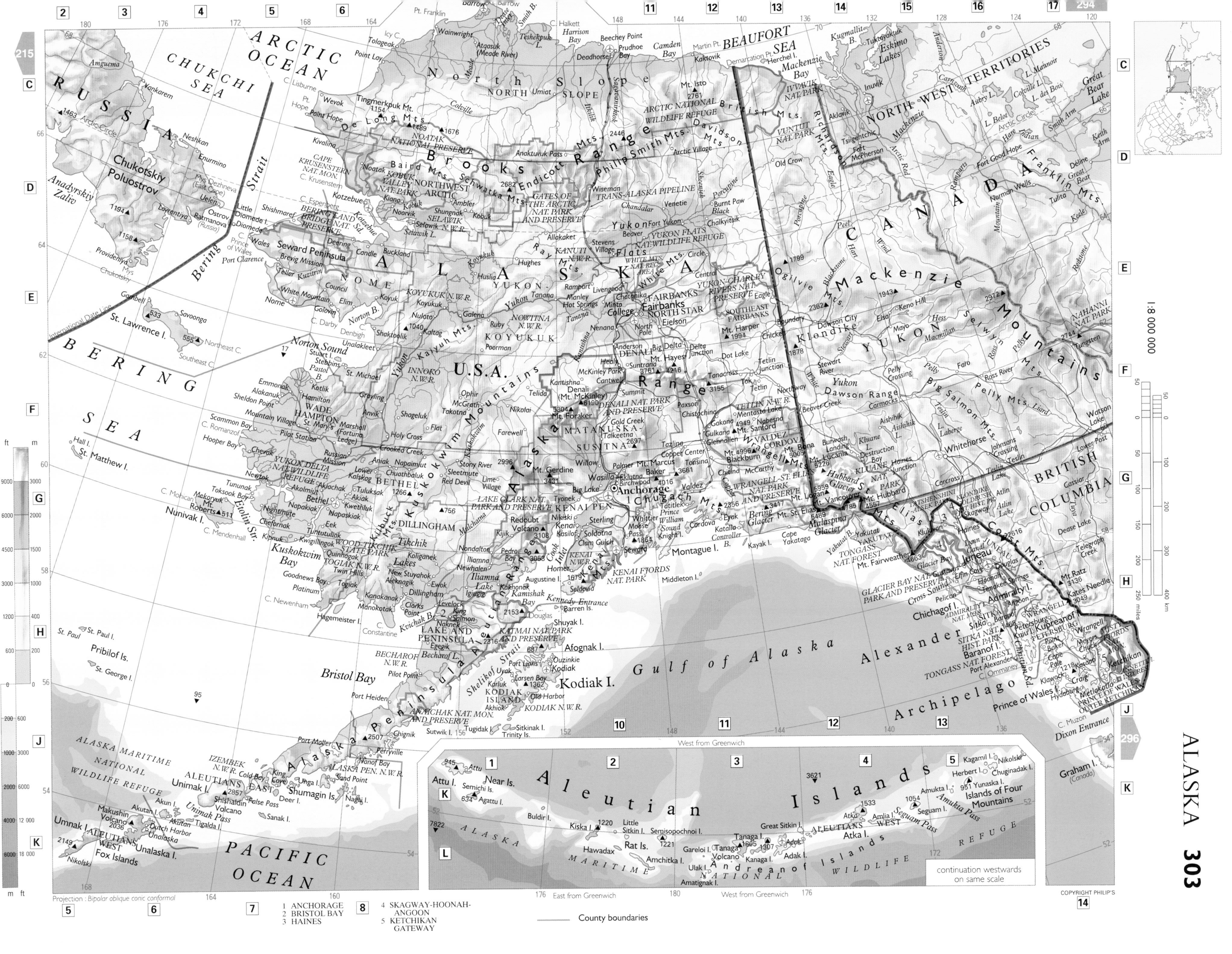
1:8 000 000
km
miles
ARCTIC OCEAN
CHUKCHI SEA
BEAUFORT SEA
BERING SEA
PACIFIC OCEAN
Gulf of Alaska
RUSSIA
CANADA
U.S.A.
ALASKA
YUKON
NORTH WEST TERRITORIES
BRITISH COLUMBIA
Brooks Range
Alaska Range
Mackenzie Mountains
Aleutian Islands
Alexander Archipelago
Bristol Bay
Norton Sound
Anchorage
Fairbanks
Juneau
Kodiak I.
St. Lawrence I.
Nunivak I.
Unalaska I.
continuation westwards on same scale
County boundaries
1 ANCHORAGE
2 BRISTOL BAY
3 HAINES
4 SKAGWAY-HOONAH-ANGOON
5 KETCHIKAN GATEWAY
Projection: Bipolar oblique conic conformal
COPYRIGHT PHILIP'S

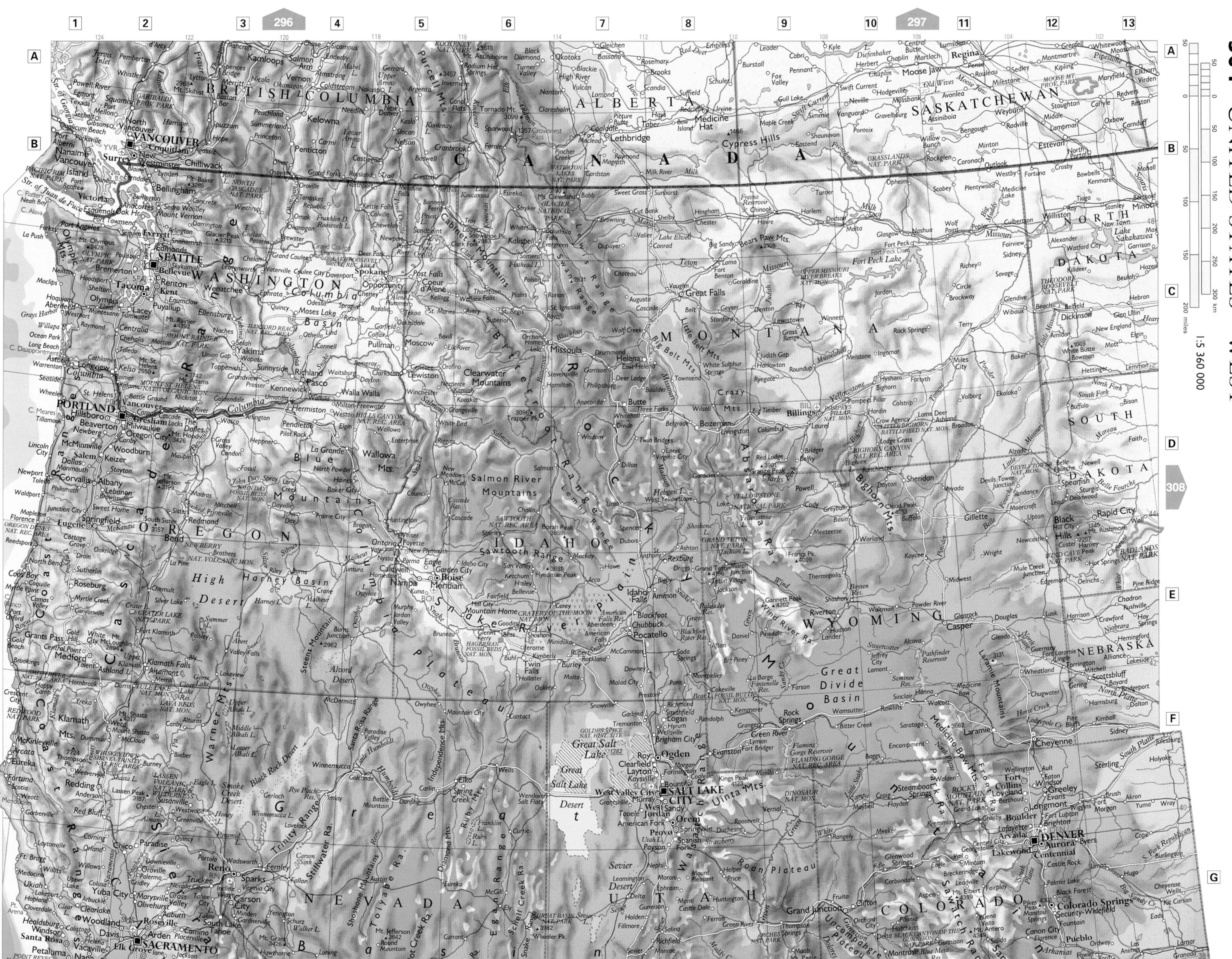
1:5 360 000
296
297
308
CANADA
BRITISH COLUMBIA
ALBERTA
SASKATCHEWAN
WASHINGTON
OREGON
IDAHO
MONTANA
WYOMING
NORTH DAKOTA
SOUTH DAKOTA
NEBRASKA
NEVADA
UTAH
COLORADO
VANCOUVER
SEATTLE
PORTLAND
SACRAMENTO
SALT LAKE CITY
DENVER
Great Salt Lake
Great Divide Basin
Salmon River Mountains
Blue Mountains
Clearwater Mountains
Bighorn Mts.
Wind River Ra.
Uinta Mts.
Laramie Mountains
Medicine Bow Mts.
Sawtooth Range
Snake River Plain
High Desert
Cypress Hills

PACIFIC
OCEAN
NEVADA
CALIFORNIA
ARIZONA
NEW MEXICO
TEXAS
SONORA
CHIHUAHUA
BAJA CALIFORNIA
BAJA CALIFORNIA SUR
MEXICO
Golfo de California
Colorado Plateau
Mojave Desert
Sonoran Desert
Llano Estacado
SAN FRANCISCO
SAN JOSE
LOS ANGELES
SAN BERNARDINO
SAN DIEGO
TIJUANA
PHOENIX
LAS VEGAS
CIUDAD JUÁREZ
El Paso
Tucson
Albuquerque
Santa Fe
Hermosillo
Chihuahua
Cedros Trench
Isla Guadalupe (Mexico)
Lava fields
West from Greenwich
Projection: Albers' Equal Area with two standard parallels
COPYRIGHT PHILIP'S

1:2 000 000
10 0 10 20 30 40 50 60 70 80 90 km
10 0 10 20 30 40 50 60 miles
304
305
296
WESTERN WASHINGTON REGION
on same scale
A
B
C
D
E
F
G
H
J
K
BRITISH COLUMBIA
CANADA
Vancouver Island
Strait of Georgia
Strait of Juan de Fuca
PACIFIC OCEAN
WASHINGTON
OREGON
Olympic Mountains
OLYMPIC NATIONAL PARK
PACIFIC RIM NATIONAL PARK RESERVE
MT. RAINIER NAT. PARK
MT. ST. HELENS NAT. VOLCANIC MONUMENT
VANCOUVER
Victoria
SEATTLE
Tacoma
Olympia
Bellingham
Everett
PORTLAND
Vancouver
Mt. Rainier 4392
Mt. St. Helens 2550
Mt. Adams 3742
Mt. Olympus 2428
Columbia
Pahute Mesa
Sierra Nevada
Lake Tahoe
Reno
Sparks
Carson City
YOSEMITE NATIONAL PARK
KINGS CANYON NATIONAL PARK
SEQUOIA NATIONAL PARK
Mt. Whitney 4418
White Mts.
Inyo Mts.
Mono Lake
SACRAMENTO
Stockton
Modesto
Merced
Fresno
Visalia
Sacramento Valley
San Joaquin Valley
Diablo Range
Coast Ranges
SAN FRANCISCO
Oakland
SAN JOSE
Santa Clara Valley
Salinas Valley
Santa Lucia Range
Monterey
Monterey Bay
Santa Cruz
Paso Robles
POINT REYES NATIONAL SEASHORE
PINNACLES NATIONAL PARK

N E V A D A
A R I Z O N A
M E X I C O
BAJA CALIFORNIA
P A C I F I C
O C E A N
Mojave Desert
Channel Islands
LAS VEGAS
Henderson
North Las Vegas
Spring Valley
Lake Mead
Boulder City
Bullhead City
Kingman
Lake Havasu City
Needles
Parker
Blythe
Yuma
Amargosa Range
Death Valley
Spring Mts.
Providence Mts.
Avawatz Mts.
Chocolate Mts.
Algodones Dunes
Salton Sea
Imperial Valley
El Centro
Calexico
Mexicali
Coachella
Indio
Palm Springs
San Bernardino Mts.
SAN BERNARDINO
Barstow
Victorville
Hesperia
Apple Valley
Ridgecrest
Lancaster
Palmdale
Bakersfield
Tehachapi Mts.
Santa Clarita
LOS ANGELES
Long Beach
Riverside
Temecula
Escondido
SAN DIEGO
TIJUANA
Chula Vista
Oceanside
Santa Barbara
Ventura
Oxnard
Santa Maria
Lompoc
San Pedro Channel
Santa Barbara Channel
Santa Catalina I.
San Clemente I.
San Nicolas I.
Santa Cruz I.
Santa Rosa I.
San Miguel I.
Gulf of Santa Catalina
Lava fields
Projection: Bonne
West from Greenwich
COPYRIGHT PHILIP'S
318

1:5 360 000
50 0 50 100 150 200 250 300 km
50 0 50 100 150 200 miles
297
298
304
314
NORTH DAKOTA
SOUTH DAKOTA
NEBRASKA
KANSAS
OKLAHOMA
TEXAS
MINNESOTA
IOWA
MISSOURI
ARKANSAS
WISCONSIN
ILLINOIS
MISSISSIPPI
ALABAMA
LAKE SUPERIOR
Sand Hills
Smoky Hills
Badlands
Black Hills
Ozark Plateau
Ouachita Mts.
Boston Mts.
Coteau des Prairies
MINNEAPOLIS
ST. PAUL
MILWAUKEE
CHICAGO
KANSAS CITY
ST. LOUIS
OKLAHOMA CITY
MEMPHIS
NASHVILLE
INDIANAPOLIS
Bismarck
Pierre
Lincoln
Omaha
Des Moines
Topeka
Wichita
Tulsa
Little Rock
Jefferson City
Springfield
Madison
Duluth
Fargo
Sioux Falls
Rapid City
Projection: Albers' Equal Area with two standard parallels
West from Greenwich

1:2 000 000

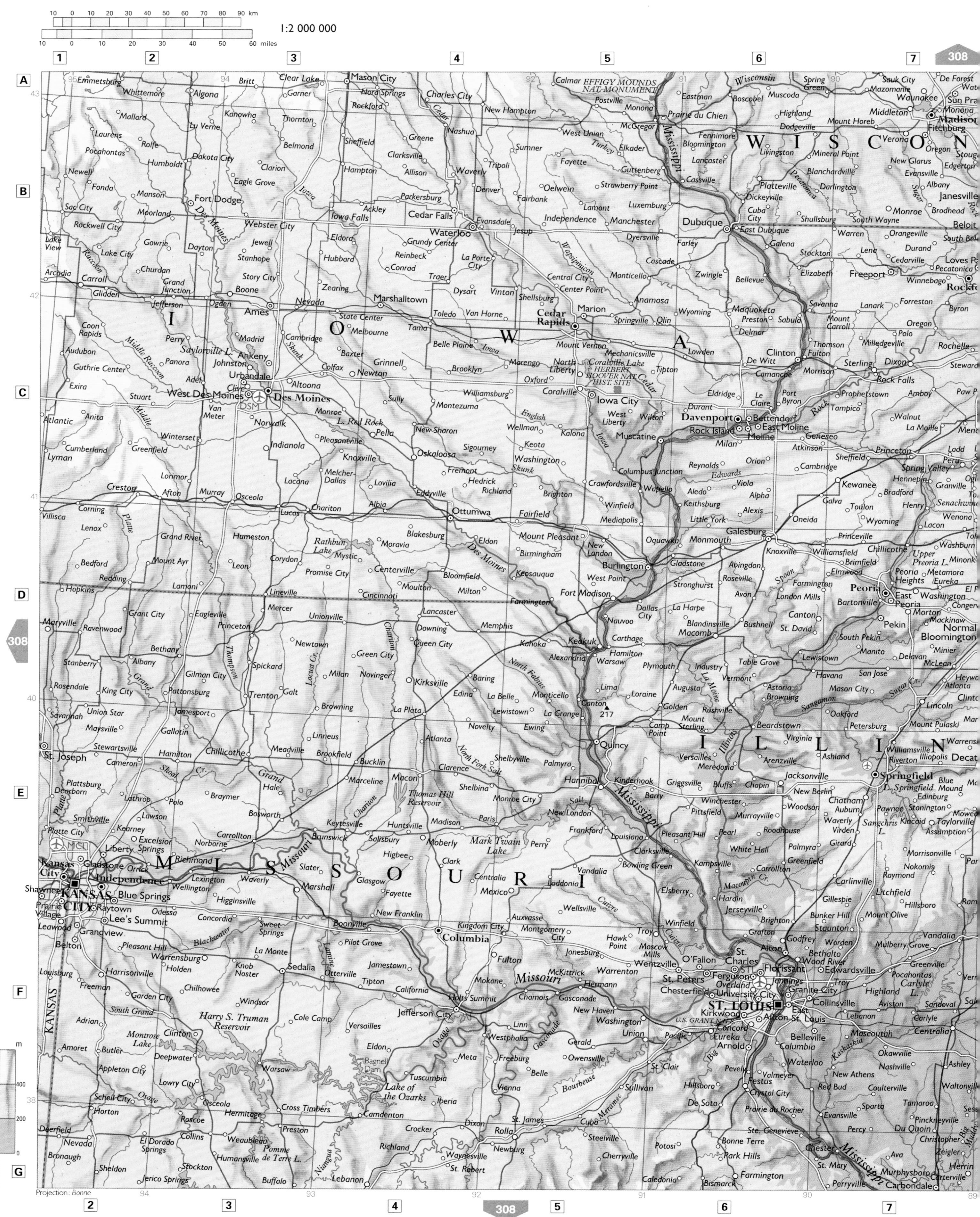

308
I O W A
W I S C O N
I L L I N
M I S S O U R I
KANSAS
Emmetsburg
Whittemore
Algona
Britt
Clear Lake
Mason City
Charles City
Calmar
EFFIGY MOUNDS NAT. MONUMENT
Wisconsin
Spring Green
Sauk City
Madison
Fitchburg
Mazomanie
Waunakee
Sun Prairie
Monona
Middleton
Mount Horeb
Verona
Oregon
Stoughton
Edgerton
Evansville
New Glarus
Albany
Janesville
Brodhead
Beloit
South Beloit
Mallard
Kanowha
Garner
Nora Springs
Rockford
New Hampton
Postville
Monona
McGregor
Prairie du Chien
Eastman
Boscobel
Muscoda
Highland
Dodgeville
Fennimore
Bloomington
Livingston
Mineral Point
Lancaster
Cassville
Blanchardville
Platteville
Darlington
Dickeyville
Cuba City
Shullsburg
South Wayne
Monroe
Laurens
Rolfe
Lu Verne
Thornton
Sheffield
Greene
Nashua
Sumner
West Union
Turkey
Elkader
Guttenberg
Pocahontas
Humboldt
Dakota City
Belmond
Clarksville
Allison
Tripoli
Fayette
Strawberry Point
Newell
Clarion
Hampton
Waverly
Fonda
Eagle Grove
Denver
Oelwein
Manson
Fort Dodge
Parkersburg
Fairbank
Lamont
Luxemburg
Sac City
Moorland
Ackley
Cedar Falls
Independence
Manchester
Dubuque
East Dubuque
Galena
Warren
Orangeville
Rockwell City
Webster City
Iowa Falls
Evansdale
Waterloo
Jesup
Dyersville
Farley
Lena
Durand
Lake View
Gowrie
Jewell
Eldora
Grundy Center
Reinbeck
La Porte City
Cascade
Stockton
Cedarville
Loves Park
Lake City
Dayton
Stanhope
Hubbard
Conrad
Traer
Monticello
Zwingle
Bellevue
Elizabeth
Freeport
Winnebago
Pecatonica
Rockford
Churdan
Story City
Central City
Center Point
Arcadia
Carroll
Grand Junction
Boone
Zearing
Dysart
Vinton
Shellsburg
Anamosa
Wyoming
Maquoketa
Savanna
Lanark
Forreston
Byron
Glidden
Jefferson
Ogden
Ames
Nevada
Marshalltown
Toledo
Van Horne
Cedar Rapids
Marion
Springville
Olin
Preston
Sabula
Mount Carroll
Oregon
State Center
Tama
Coon Rapids
Perry
Madrid
Cambridge
Melbourne
Polo
Saylorville L.
Ankeny
Baxter
Belle Plaine
Mount Vernon
Mechanicsville
Lowden
Delmar
Thomson
Fulton
Milledgeville
Rochelle
Audubon
Panora
Johnston
Urbandale
Grinnell
Clinton
Middle Raccoon
Newton
Colfax
Brooklyn
Marengo
North Liberty
Coralville Lake
HERBERT HOOVER NAT. HIST. SITE
Tipton
De Witt
Camanche
Morrison
Sterling
Dixon
Guthrie Center
Adel
Altoona
Oxford
Coralville
Iowa City
Eldridge
Le Claire
Port Byron
Prophetstown
Rock Falls
Amboy
Exira
Stuart
West Des Moines
Clive
Des Moines
DSM
Sully
Williamsburg
Montezuma
Durant
Davenport
Bettendorf
East Moline
Moline
Rock Island
Milan
Tampico
Walnut
La Moille
Atlantic
Anita
Van Meter
Norwalk
Monroe
L. Red Rock
Pella
New Sharon
Wellman
English
Kalona
West Liberty
Wilton
Muscatine
Geneseo
Cumberland
Winterset
Indianola
Pleasantville
Knoxville
Oskaloosa
Sigourney
Keota
Washington
Atkinson
Sheffield
Princeton
Ladd
Lyman
Greenfield
Melcher-Dallas
Fremont
Hedrick
Richland
Brighton
Columbus Junction
Reynolds
Edwards
Orion
Cambridge
Spring Valley
Peru
Lorimor
Lacona
Lovilia
Eddyville
Crawfordsville
Wapello
Aledo
Viola
Kewanee
Hennepin
Granville
Creston
Afton
Murray
Osceola
Albia
Ottumwa
Fairfield
Winfield
Keithsburg
Alpha
Galva
Bradford
Toulon
Henry
Corning
Lucas
Chariton
Mediapolis
Little York
Alexis
Oneida
Wyoming
Wenona
Villisca
Lenox
Grand River
Humeston
Rathbun Lake
Moravia
Blakesburg
Eldon
Mount Pleasant
New London
Oquawka
Monmouth
Galesburg
Knoxville
Princeville
Chillicothe
Lacon
Washburn
Bedford
Mount Ayr
Leon
Corydon
Mystic
Birmingham
Burlington
Gladstone
Williamsfield
Brimfield
Upper Peoria L.
Minonk
Redding
Promise City
Centerville
Bloomfield
Keosauqua
West Point
Abingdon
Elmwood
Peoria Heights
Metamora
Eureka
Hopkins
Lamoni
Lineville
Cincinnati
Moulton
Milton
Farmington
Fort Madison
Stronghurst
Roseville
Farmington
Peoria
East Peoria
Washington
Grant City
Eagleville
Mercer
Unionville
Lancaster
Dallas City
La Harpe
Avon
London Mills
Bartonville
Maryville
Princeton
Downing
Memphis
Nauvoo
Blandinsville
Canton
Morton
Mackinaw
Ravenwood
Newtown
Queen City
Kahoka
Keokuk
Carthage
Macomb
Bushnell
St. David
Pekin
Normal
Bloomington
Bethany
Green City
Alexandria
Hamilton
South Pekin
Stanberry
Albany
Spickard
Novinger
Kirksville
Baring
Warsaw
Plymouth
Industry
Table Grove
Lewistown
Manito
Delavan
McLean
Minier
Gilman City
Milan
North Fabius
Vermont
Havana
San Jose
Rosendale
King City
Pattonsburg
Trenton
Galt
Edina
La Belle
Monticello
Lima
Loraine
Augusta
La Moine
Astoria
Mason City
Atlanta
Union Star
Jamesport
Browning
La Plata
Lewistown
La Grange
Canton
217
Golden
Rushville
Browning
Sangamon
Lincoln
Savannah
Maysville
Gallatin
Novelty
Ewing
Camp Point
Mount Sterling
Beardstown
Oakford
Petersburg
Mount Pulaski
Stewartsville
Linneus
Meadville
Brookfield
Atlanta
Quincy
Illinois
Virginia
Williamsville
Riverton
Illiopolis
St. Joseph
Cameron
Hamilton
Chillicothe
Bucklin
Shelbyville
Palmyra
Versailles
Meredosia
Arenzville
Ashland
Springfield
Plattsburg
Dearborn
Shoal Cr.
Grand
Hale
Marceline
Macon
Clarence
North Fork Salt
Shelbina
Hannibal
Kinderhook
Barry
Griggsville
Bluffs
Chapin
Jacksonville
New Berlin
L. Springfield
Blue Mound
Edinburg
Platte
Lathrop
Polo
Braymer
Bosworth
Thomas Hill Reservoir
Monroe City
Salt
New London
Winchester
Pittsfield
Murrayville
Woodson
Chatham
Auburn
Pawnee
Stonington
Smithville
Lawson
Keytesville
Huntsville
Madison
Paris
Frankford
Pleasant Hill
Pearl
Roodhouse
Virden
Sangchris L.
Kincaid
Taylorville
Assumption
Platte City
Kearney
Carrollton
Brunswick
Salisbury
Moberly
Mark Twain Lake
Perry
Louisiana
Mississippi
Waverly
Girard
Excelsior Springs
Liberty
Norborne
Higbee
White Hall
Palmyra
Greenfield
Morrisonville
MCI
Kansas City
Gladstone
Richmond
Missouri
Slater
Clark
Clarksville
Bowling Green
Kampsville
Carrollton
Nokomis
Raymond
Orrick
Lexington
Waverly
Glasgow
Centralia
Vandalia
Laddonia
Macoupin Cr.
Carlinville
Litchfield
Independence
Wellington
Marshall
Fayette
Mexico
Cuivre
Elsberry
Hardin
Gillespie
Shawnee
KANSAS CITY
Blue Springs
Higginsville
Jerseyville
Hillsboro
Prairie Village
Raytown
Odessa
Concordia
New Franklin
Wellsville
Brighton
Bunker Hill
Mount Olive
Leawood
Lee's Summit
Sweet Springs
Boonville
Kingdom City
Auxvasse
Montgomery City
Troy
Winfield
Grafton
Staunton
Vandalia
Grandview
Blackwater
Columbia
Hawk Point
Moscow Mills
St. Charles
Alton
Godfrey
Bethalto
Worden
Mulberry Grove
Belton
Pleasant Hill
Pilot Grove
Fulton
Jonesburg
Wentzville
O'Fallon
Florissant
Wood River
Edwardsville
Greenville
Warrensburg
La Monte
Jamestown
Warrenton
St. Peters
Ferguson
Jennings
Pocahontas
Louisburg
Harrisonville
Holden
Knob Noster
Sedalia
Otterville
Tipton
Mokane
McKittrick
Hermann
Chesterfield
Overland
University City
Granite City
Troy
Highland
Carlyle L.
Freeman
Garden City
Chilhowee
Windsor
California
Holts Summit
Chamois
Gasconade
St. Louis
Collinsville
Aviston
Sandoval
South Grand
Cole Camp
Jefferson City
New Haven
Washington
Kirkwood
Affton
East St. Louis
Lebanon
Carlyle
Adrian
Harry S. Truman Reservoir
Versailles
Osage
Linn
Union
U.S. GRANT N.H.S.
Pacific
Concord
Eureka
Arnold
Belleville
Mascoutah
Centralia
Montrose Lake
Clinton
Eldon
Westphalia
Gerald
Columbia
Amoret
Butler
Deepwater
Bagnell Dam
Meta
Freeburg
Owensville
Big
Waterloo
Kaskaskia
Okawville
Nashville
Ashley
Appleton City
Warsaw
Tuscumbia
Belle
Bourbeuse
St. Clair
Pevely
Valmeyer
Festus
New Athens
Lowry City
Lake of the Ozarks
Vienna
Sullivan
Hillsboro
Crystal City
Red Bud
Coulterville
Waltonville
Schell City
Osceola
Iberia
De Soto
Prairie du Rocher
Sparta
Tamaroa
Horton
Roscoe
Hermitage
Cross Timbers
Camdenton
Meramec
Evansville
Pinckneyville
Preston
Crocker
Dixon
Rolla
St. James
Cuba
Ste. Genevieve
Percy
Du Quoin
Deerfield
Nevada
El Dorado Springs
Collins
Weaubleau
Pomme de Terre L.
Richland
Newburg
Steelville
Potosi
Bonne Terre
Chester
Christopher
Zeigler
Bronaugh
Humansville
Niangua
Waynesville
St. Robert
Cherryville
Park Hills
St. Mary
Ava
Herrin
Sheldon
Stockton
Jerico Springs
Buffalo
Lebanon
Caledonia
Bismarck
Farmington
Perryville
Murphysboro
Carterville
Carbondale
Projection: Bonne

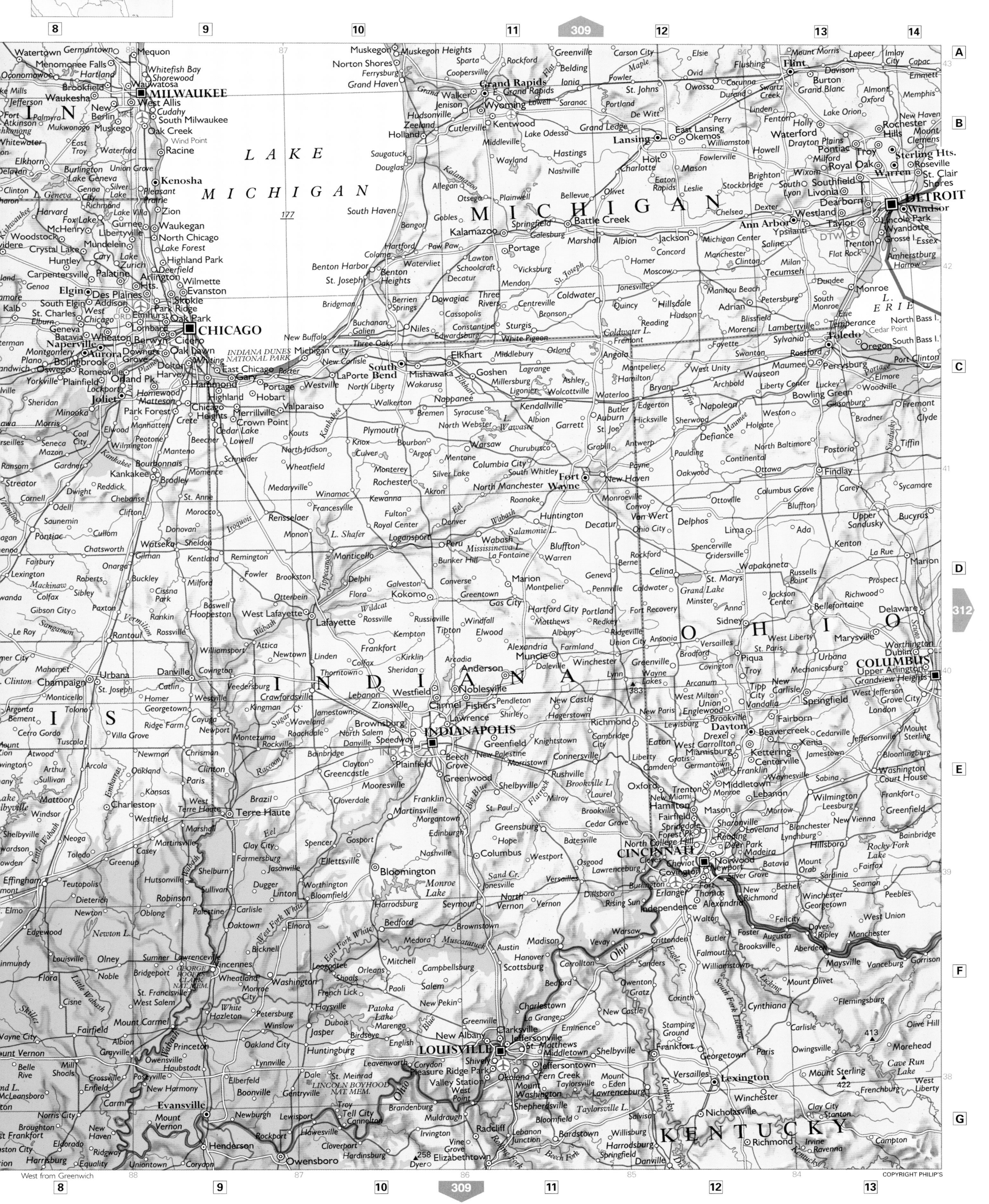
8
9
10
11
309
12
13
14
A
B
C
D
E
F
G
312
LAKE MICHIGAN
MICHIGAN
INDIANA
OHIO
KENTUCKY
LAKE ERIE
MILWAUKEE
CHICAGO
DETROIT
Windsor
Toledo
INDIANAPOLIS
CINCINNATI
COLUMBUS
LOUISVILLE
Lansing
Grand Rapids
Kalamazoo
Battle Creek
Ann Arbor
Flint
South Bend
Fort Wayne
Gary
Hammond
Joliet
Elgin
Naperville
Aurora
Kenosha
Racine
Waukegan
Evanston
Champaign
Urbana
Danville
Lafayette
West Lafayette
Kokomo
Muncie
Anderson
Terre Haute
Bloomington
Evansville
Owensboro
Henderson
Lexington
Frankfort
Dayton
Springfield
Hamilton
Lima
Findlay
Elkhart
Mishawaka
Valparaiso
Richmond
Columbus
Vincennes
New Albany
Jeffersonville
INDIANA DUNES NATIONAL PARK
GEORGE ROGERS CLARK NAT. MEM.
LINCOLN BOYHOOD NAT. MEM.
West from Greenwich
88
87
86
85
84
43
42
41
40
39
38
COPYRIGHT PHILIP'S

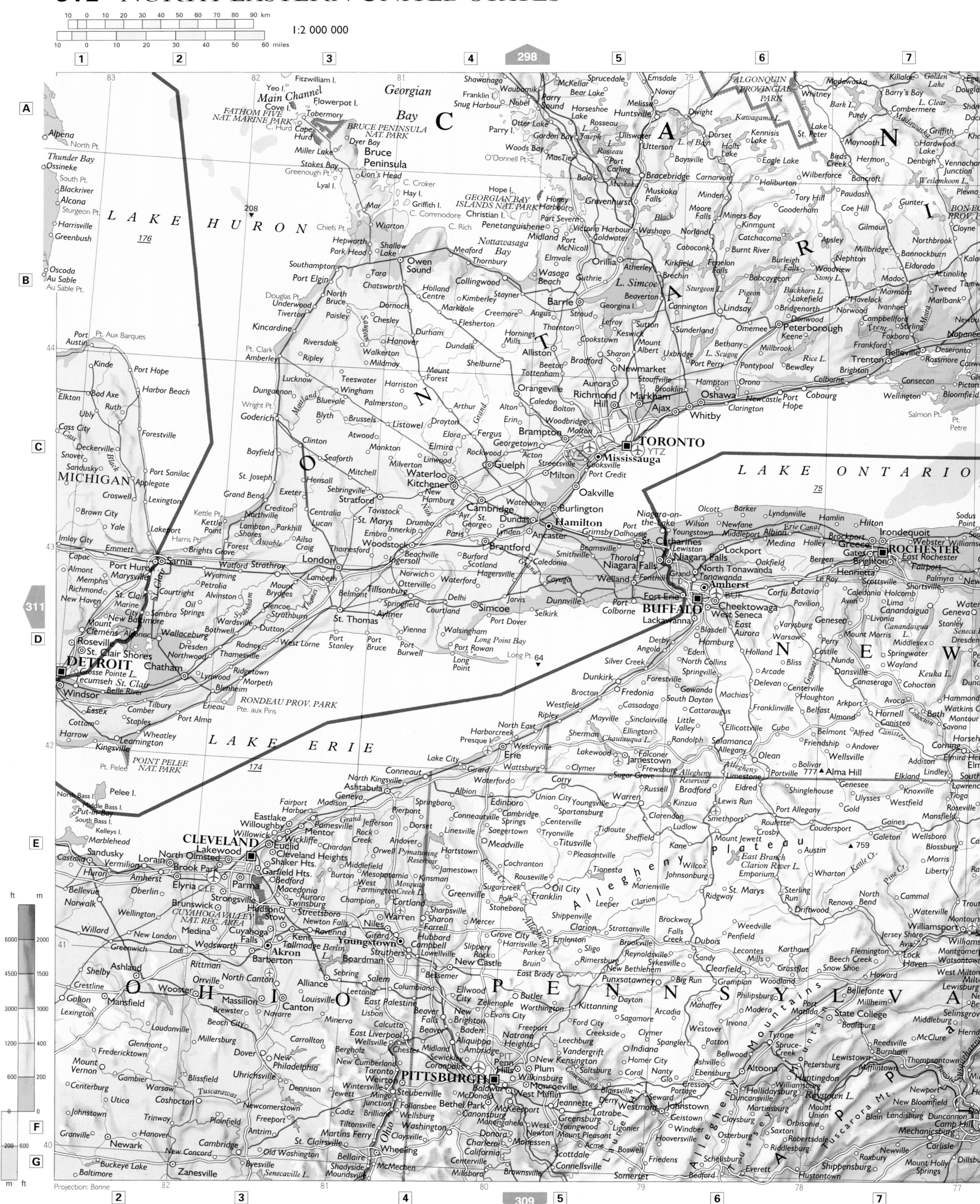
1:2 000 000
km
miles
298
309
311
LAKE HURON
LAKE ONTARIO
LAKE ERIE
Georgian Bay
Nottawasaga Bay
Bruce Peninsula
FATHOM FIVE NAT. MARINE PARK
BRUCE PENINSULA NAT. PARK
GEORGIAN BAY ISLANDS NAT. PARK
ALGONQUIN PROVINCIAL PARK
POINT PELEE NAT. PARK
RONDEAU PROV. PARK
CUYAHOGA VALLEY NAT. REC. AREA
C A N A D A
O N T A R I O
MICHIGAN
O H I O
P E N N S Y L V A N I A
N E W
TORONTO
Mississauga
Hamilton
BUFFALO
ROCHESTER
DETROIT
CLEVELAND
PITTSBURGH
Akron
Youngstown
Erie
Windsor
London
Kitchener
Waterloo
Guelph
Oshawa
Peterborough
Barrie
Niagara Falls
St. Catharines
Sarnia
Port Huron
Allegheny Plateau
Allegheny Mountains
Tuscarora Mt.
Projection: Bonne

298

8 9 10 11 12 13 14
A B C D E F G
MONTRÉAL
OTTAWA
QUÉBEC
MAINE
NEW HAMPSHIRE
VERMONT
MASSACHUSETTS
CONNECTICUT
RHODE ISLAND
NEW JERSEY
NEW YORK
BOSTON
PROVIDENCE
HARTFORD
PHILADELPHIA
Albany
Syracuse
Springfield
Worcester
Manchester
Concord
Montpelier
Burlington
Lake Champlain
ADIRONDACK PARK
Adirondack Mountains
Green Mountains
White Mountains
Catskill Mts.
Long Island
Long Island Sound
Block Island Sound
Martha's Vineyard
ATLANTIC OCEAN
Mt. Washington 1917
Mt. Marcy 1629

309

309

1:5 360 000
km
miles
308
305
318
NEBRASKA
IOWA
COLORADO
KANSAS
MISSOURI
OKLAHOMA
ARKANSAS
NEW MEXICO
TEXAS
LOUISIANA
MEXICO
COAHUILA
CHIHUAHUA
NUEVO LEÓN
GULF
Rocky Mts
Sangre de Cristo Mts.
San Juan Mts.
Sawatch Range
Smoky Hills
Llano Estacado
Edwards Plateau
Stockton Plateau
Balcones Escarpment
Ouachita Mts.
Boston Mts.
Bolsón de Mapimí
DENVER
Colorado Springs
Pueblo
Lincoln
Topeka
KANSAS CITY
Independence
St. Joseph
Wichita
Springfield
Tulsa
OKLAHOMA CITY
Norman
Lawton
Albuquerque
Santa Fe
Roswell
Lubbock
Amarillo
El Paso
Midland
Odessa
San Angelo
Abilene
Wichita Falls
Fort Worth
DALLAS
Arlington
Waco
AUSTIN
SAN ANTONIO
HOUSTON
Pasadena
Galveston
Beaumont
Port Arthur
Corpus Christi
Laredo
Nuevo Laredo
Brownsville
Matamoros
McAllen
Reynosa
MONTERREY
Saltillo
Monclova
Piedras Negras
Ciudad Acuña
Del Rio
TORREÓN
Gómez Palacio
Ciudad Lerdo
Little Rock
North Little Rock
Fort Smith
Fayetteville
Texarkana
Shreveport
Monroe
Alexandria
Lake Charles
Lafayette
Baton Rouge
Tyler
Longview
Bryan
College Station
Sherman
Denison
Joplin
Rio Grande
Red
Arkansas
Canadian
Pecos
Brazos
Colorado
Cimarron
Republican
Projection: Albers' Equal Area with two standard parallels
West from Greenwich

309
320
ILLINOIS
INDIANA
OHIO
PENNSYLVANIA
MARYLAND
DELAWARE
WEST VIRGINIA
VIRGINIA
KENTUCKY
TENNESSEE
NORTH CAROLINA
SOUTH CAROLINA
GEORGIA
ALABAMA
MISSISSIPPI
FLORIDA
THE BAHAMAS
ATLANTIC OCEAN
OF MEXICO
Cumberland Plateau
Appalachian Mts.
Sea Islands
PITTSBURGH
PHILADELPHIA
BALTIMORE
WASHINGTON D.C.
INDIANAPOLIS
COLUMBUS
CINCINNATI
LOUISVILLE
RICHMOND
VIRGINIA BEACH
NASHVILLE
MEMPHIS
RALEIGH
CHARLOTTE
ATLANTA
BIRMINGHAM
NEW ORLEANS
JACKSONVILLE
ORLANDO
TAMPA
MIAMI
ST. LOUIS
Lexington
Knoxville
Chattanooga
Greensboro
Columbia
Charleston
Savannah
Montgomery
Tallahassee
Pensacola
Mobile
Jackson
Norfolk
Wilmington
St. Petersburg
Fort Lauderdale
West Palm Beach
Key West
Florida Keys
Str. of Florida
Florida Bay
Mississippi River Delta
Pamlico Sound
Albemarle Sd.
C. Hatteras
C. Lookout
C. Fear
C. Canaveral
Lake Okeechobee
The Everglades
Freeport
Nassau
New Providence
Andros I.
Grand Bahama
Abaco I.
Northwest Providence Channel
Northeast Providence Channel
DRY TORTUGAS NAT. PARK
EVERGLADES NAT. PARK
BISCAYNE NAT. PARK
BIG CYPRESS NAT. PRESERVE
GREAT SMOKY MTS. NAT. PARK
MAMMOTH CAVE NATIONAL PARK
SHENANDOAH NAT. PARK
GULF ISLANDS NAT. SEASHORE
CAPE HATTERAS NAT. SEASHORE
CAPE LOOKOUT NAT. SEASHORE
CANAVERAL NAT. SEASHORE
CUMBERLAND ISLAND NAT. SEASHORE
ASSATEAGUE ISLAND NAT. SEASHORE
OKEFENOKEE NAT. WILDLIFE RESERVE
Okefenokee Swamp
Chesapeake Bay
Delaware Bay
9
10
11
12
13
14
15
16
17
B
C
D
E
F
G
H
J
COPYRIGHT PHILIP'S

1:2 000 000
km
miles
SOUTH CAROLINA
GEORGIA
ALABAMA
ATLANTIC OCEAN
Sea Islands
ATLANTA
Columbia
Charleston
Savannah
Augusta
Macon
Columbus
Montgomery
Tallahassee
JACKSONVILLE
Athens
Albany
Valdosta
Dothan
Okefenokee Swamp
Savannah
Chattahoochee
Ocmulgee
Oconee
Altamaha
St. Marys
Flint
Apalachicola
Dog I.
315

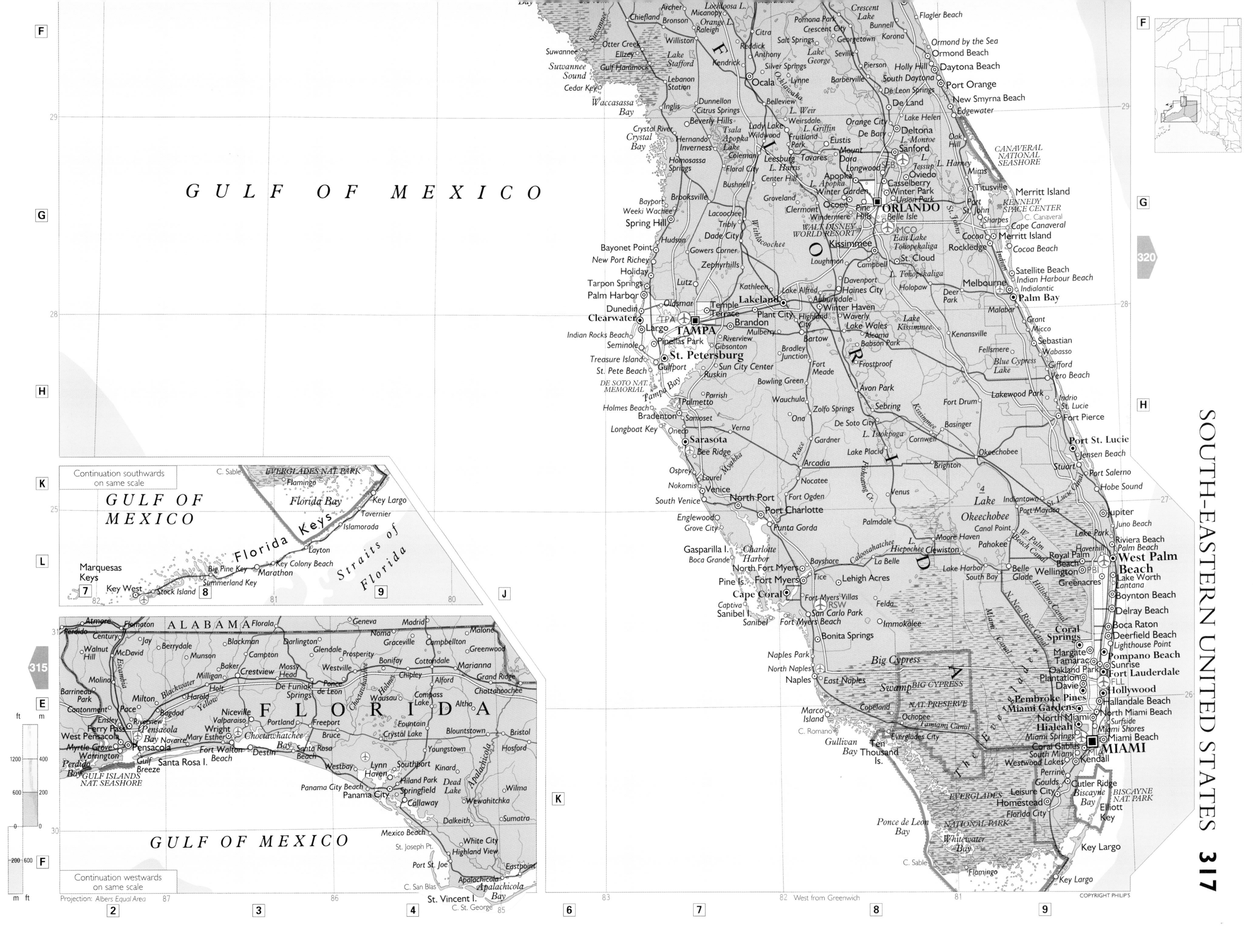
GULF OF MEXICO
FLORIDA
ALABAMA
ORLANDO
TAMPA
MIAMI
St. Petersburg
Clearwater
Lakeland
Sarasota
Fort Myers
Cape Coral
Naples
West Palm Beach
Fort Lauderdale
Hollywood
Hialeah
Daytona Beach
Ocala
Kissimmee
Melbourne
Port St. Lucie
Fort Pierce
Lake Okeechobee
Big Cypress Swamp
EVERGLADES NATIONAL PARK
BISCAYNE NAT. PARK
CANAVERAL NATIONAL SEASHORE
KENNEDY SPACE CENTER
WALT DISNEY WORLD RESORT
Florida Keys
Straits of Florida
Florida Bay
Key West
Key Largo
Marathon
Pensacola
Panama City
Fort Walton Beach
Apalachicola Bay
GULF ISLANDS NAT. SEASHORE
Continuation southwards on same scale
Continuation westwards on same scale
Projection: Albers Equal Area
West from Greenwich
COPYRIGHT PHILIP'S

1:6 400 000

Projection: *Bi-polar oblique Conical Orthomorphic*

West from Greenwich

State names in Central Mexico

1 DISTRITO FEDERAL	3 GUANAJUATO	5 MÉXICO	7 QUERÉTARO
2 AGUASCALIENTES	4 HIDALGO	6 MORELOS	8 TLAXCALA

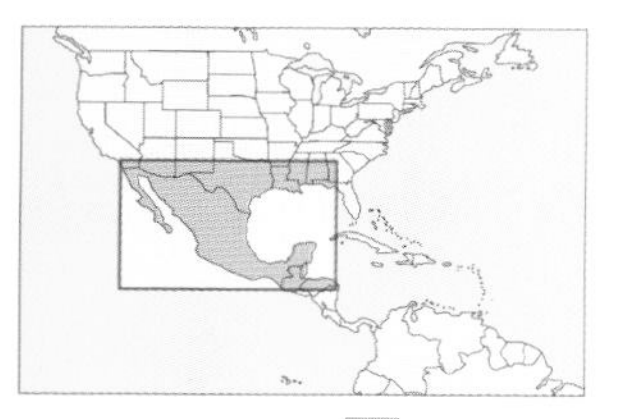

5 6 7 8 315

A B C D E

320

GULF OF MEXICO

Golfo de Campeche

Sigsbee Deep

Banco Campeche

Canal de Yucatán

Yucatan Basin

Golfo de Honduras

Golfo de Tehuantepec

UNITED STATES

TEXAS

ARKANSAS

MISSISSIPPI

ALABAMA

GEORGIA

LOUISIANA

FLORIDA

TAMAULIPAS

VERACRUZ

PUEBLA

OAXACA

GUERRERO

TABASCO

CHIAPAS

CAMPECHE

YUCATÁN

QUINTANA ROO

BELIZE

GUATEMALA

HONDURAS

CUBA

Wichita Falls

Denison

Sherman

Paris

Texarkana

Camden

El Dorado

Greenville

Tuscaloosa

Opelika

Columbus

Phenix City

Denton

Greenville

Fort Worth

DALLAS

Marshall

Monroe

Vicksburg

Jackson

Meridian

Selma

Montgomery

Americus

Cordele

Longview

Tyler

Shreveport

Tallulah

Troy

Albany

Tifton

Waycross

Cleburne

Corsicana

Natchez

Laurel

Hattiesburg

Dothan

Brewton

Valdosta

Tallahassee

Hillsboro

Palestine

Nacogdoches

Alexandria

McComb

Bogalusa

Lake City

Brownwood

Waco

Lufkin

Sam Rayburn Reservoir

Toledo Bend Res.

Temple

Baton Rouge

Hammond

Biloxi

Mobile

Pensacola

Panama City

Apalachee Bay

Huntsville

Bryan

College Station

Lake Charles

Lafayette

L. Pontchartrain

NEW ORLEANS

Gulfport

Mobile Bay

C. San Blas

Suwannee

AUSTIN

Navasota

Beaumont

Port Arthur

Breton Sd.

HOUSTON

SAN ANTONIO

Rosenberg

Galveston

Atchafalaya Bay

Terrebonne Bay

Mississippi River Delta

Clearwater

Victoria

Dilley

Nueces

Alice

Kingsville

Corpus Christi

Laredo

Nuevo Laredo

Zapata

PADRE ISLAND NAT. SEASHORE

Laguna Madre

Nueva Ciudad Guerrero

McAllen

Harlingen

Brownsville

Camargo

Reynosa

Río Bravo

Matamoros

China

Valle Hermoso

Santa Teresa

Laguna Madre

Villa de Méndez

Linares

San Fernando

Villagrán

Villa Hidalgo

Santander Jiménez

La Pesca

Soto la Marina

Ciudad Victoria

Soto la Marina

Sierra de Tamaulipas

Aldama

Pta. Jerez

González

Ciudad Mante

Altamira

Ciudad Madero

Tampico

Ebano

Ciudad Valles

Pánuco

L. de Tamiahua

Ozuluama

Naranjos

Tempoal de Sánchez

Tantoyuca

C. Rojo

Tamazunchale

Chicontepec

Tuxpan

Zimapán

Zacualtipán

Poza Rica

Papantla

Nautla

Juan del Río

Huichapan

Pachuca

Huauchinango

Tulancingo

Misantla

Zumpango

Teziutlán

Xalapa

Apizaco

Coatepec

Veracruz

Tlaxcala

PUEBLA

Pico de Orizaba 5610

Boca del Río

Alvarado

Amecameca

Popocatépetl 5452

Córdoba

Orizaba

Tlacotalpan

Cuernavaca

Tehuacán

Cosamaloapan

San Andrés Tuxtla

Izúcar de Matamoros

Tierra Blanca

Tres Valles

Coatzacoalcos

Minatitlán

Iguala

Chiautla

Acatlán

Tuxtepec

Acayucan

Huajuapan de León

Nochixtlán

Istmo de Tehuantepec

Chilapa

Chilpancingo

Tlaxiaco

Oaxaca

Tlacolula

Tehuantepec

Ayutla de los Libres

Ometepec

San Jerónimo Taviche

Ixtepec

Acapulco

Pinotepa Nacional

Juchitán de Zaragoza

Salina Cruz

Puerto Escondido

Puerto Ángel

San Pedro Pochutla

Miahuatlán

Paraíso

Frontera

Comalcalco

Ciudad del Carmen

L. de Términos

Palizada

Villahermosa

Macuspana

Cárdenas

Palenque

Teapa

Ocosingo

Tenosique

Copainalá

Simojovel

Chiapa de Corzo

Tuxtla Gutiérrez

San Cristóbal de las Casas

La Independencia

Comitán de Domínguez

La Concordia

Tonalá

Arriaga

Pijijiapan

Mapastepec

Motozintla de Mendoza

Huixtla

Tapachula

Puerto Madero

Campeche

Champotón

Escárcega

CALAKMUL

Progreso

MÉRIDA

Motul

Izamal

Tizimín

Río Lagartos

Cancún

Isla Mujeres

C. Catoche

Puerto Morelos

Playa del Carmen

Isla Cozumel

Cozumel

Valladolid

Espita

Temax

Maxcanú

Ticul

Peto

Tekax

Tenabo

Hopelchén

Felipe Carrillo Puerto

B. de la Ascensión

SIAN KA'AN

B. del Espíritu Santo

Costa Maya

Banco Chinchorro

Chetumal

Bacalar

Corozal

Orange Walk

Ambergris Cay

Belize City

Belmopan

Dangriga

Turneffe Is.

Barrier Reef

Benque Viejo

Victoria Pk. 1120

Maya Mts.

San Luis

Flores

La Libertad

Uaxactún

Monkey River

Puerto Barrios

Livingston

Is. de la Bahía

Guanaja

Roatán

Utila

La Ceiba

Tela

Trujillo

Puerto Castilla

Puerto Cortés

San Pedro Sula

El Progreso

Olanchito

Cobán

L. de Izabal

Huehuetenango

Quiché

Totonicapán

Sololá

Antigua

GUATEMALA

Mazatenango

Retalhuleu

Jalapa

Chiquimula

Santa Rosa de Copán

Siguatepeque

Comayagua

TEGUCIGALPA

Juticalpa

Catacamas

Yoro

La Paz

Santa Bárbara

Villanueva

Zacapa

Gualán

Isla

Guane

La Fé

C. San Antonio

C. Corrientes

La Esperanza

I. Desterrada

I. Pérez (Mexico)

Tropic of Cancer

32

35

82

3750

75

47

316

JAMAICA
CARIBBEAN SEA
JAMAICA
1:1 600 000
a
Montego Bay
Falmouth
Runaway Bay
St. Ann's Bay
Ocho Rios
Oracabessa
Port Maria
Lucea
Negril
Grange Hill
Savanna-la-Mar
CORNWALL
MIDDLESEX
SURREY
Black River
Santa Cruz
Mandeville
Christiana
Brown's Town
Linstead
Bog Walk
Spanish Town
May Pen
Old Harbour
Portmore
Kingston
Port Antonio
Annotto Bay
Highgate
Morant Bay
Yallahs
Hayes
Porus
Chapelton
Ewarton
Half Way Tree
West from Greenwich
FLORIDA
U. S. A.
West Palm Beach
Cape Coral
Fort Myers
Boca Raton
Fort Lauderdale
Naples
Hialeah
MIAMI
EVERGLADES NAT. PARK
Florida Bay
Florida Keys
Key West
Dry Tortugas (U.S.A.)
Straits of Florida
Freeport
Grand Bahama
Little Abaco
Hope Town
Marsh Harbour
Abaco
Northwest Providence Channel
Northeast Providence Channel
Bimini
Berry Is.
Nicolls Town
Nassau
New Providence
Eleuthera
Andros Town
Andros
Great Bahama Bank
Great Guana Cay
Great Exuma
Exuma Sound
Cay Sal Bank
Santaren Channel
Canal Nicholas
Canal Viejo de Bahama
A
LA HABANA (Havana)
Matanzas
Cárdenas
Arch. de Sabana
Sagua la Grande
Pinar del Río
Bahía Honda
Guanajay
San Antonio de los Baños
Batabanó
Güines
Jovellanos
Colón
Jagüey Grande
Pen. de Zapata
Cienfuegos
Santa Clara
Caibarién
Placetas
Arch. de Camagüey
Cayo Coco
Cayo Romano
Morón
Ciego de Avila
Florida
Camagüey
Nuevitas
Las Tunas
Trinidad
Sancti Spíritus
Júcaro
CUBA
Nueva Gerona
I. de la Juventud
Arch. de los Canarreos
Cayo Largo
Golfo de Guacanayabo
Bayamo
Manzanillo
Sierra Maestra
Holguín
Arch. de Jardines de la Reina
Cayman Islands (U.K.)
Cayman Brac
Little Cayman
George Town
Grand Cayman
Cayman Trench
Greater Antilles
Yucatan Basin
Misteriosa Bank
Canal de Yucatán
Gulf of Mexico
B
Progreso
MÉRIDA
YUCATÁN
Motul
Izamal
Tizimín
Valladolid
Cancún
Isla Mujeres
Puerto Morelos
Playa del Carmen
Cozumel
Isla Cozumel
Campeche
Champotón
Ciudad del Carmen
Escárcega
CAMPECHE
MEXICO
QUINTANA ROO
Felipe Carrillo Puerto
Chetumal
Bacalar
Corozal
Orange Walk
Ambergris Cay
San Pedro
Belize City
Belmopan
San Ignacio
BELIZE
Turneffe Is.
Dangriga
Punta Gorda
Maya Mts.
Flores
La Libertad
Cobán
GUATEMALA
Huehuetenango
Quetzaltenango
Totonicapán
Sololá
Antigua
GUATEMALA
Escuintla
Livingston
Puerto Barrios
Puerto Cortés
San Pedro Sula
Choloma
Tela
La Ceiba
Trujillo
El Progreso
HONDURAS
Santa Rosa de Copán
Comayagua
Juticalpa
Catacamas
TEGUCIGALPA
Mosquitia
Puerto Lempira
Laguna de Caratasca
C. Gracias a Dios
Is. de la Bahía
Roatán
Utila
Guanaja
Golfo de Honduras
Santa Ana
Ahuachapán
SAN SALVADOR
EL SALVADOR
San Miguel
Usulután
La Unión
Choluteca
Golfo de Fonseca
C
D
NICARAGUA
Chinandega
León
MANAGUA
Masaya
Granada
Jinotega
Matagalpa
Estelí
Lago de Nicaragua
Puerto Cabezas
Bluefields
Costa de Mosquitos
Cayos Miskitos (Nicaragua)
I. de Providencia (Colombia)
I. de San Andrés (Colombia)
Is. del Maíz (Nicaragua)
San Juan del Norte
COSTA RICA
SAN JOSÉ
Cartago
Alajuela
Puntarenas
Limón
Liberia
G. de Papagayo
G. de Nicoya
PACIFIC OCEAN
Guatemala Trench
Pedro Bank
Rosalind Bank
Serranilla Bank
Banco Gorda
Bajo Nuevo (Colombia)
Is. Santanilla (Swan Islands) (Honduras)
Cayos Roncador (Colombia)
CARIBBEAN
Isthmus of Panama
PANAMÁ
Colón
Bocas del Toro
David
Santiago
Chitré
Pen. de Azuero
Golfo de Panamá
Golfo del Darién
Archipiélago de San Blas
Arch. de las Perlas
La Chorrera
Serranía del Darién
G. de Chiriquí
I. de Coiba
E
1
2
3
4
CARIBBEAN SEA
PANAMA
Colón
Cristobal
Gatún
Lago Gatún
Gamboa
Chilibre
Paraíso
L. Miraflores
San Miguelito
Balboa
PANAMA
PACIFIC OCEAN
La Chorrera
Arraiján
Escobal
L. Alajuela
PANAMA CANAL
1:800 000
c
Projection: Conical with two standard parallels
Place of interest
1:6 400 000

319

328

5

PUERTO RICO AND THE VIRGIN IS.

b 1:1 600 000

10 0 10 20 30 40 50 60 70 km

10 0 10 20 30 40 50 miles

ATLANTIC OCEAN

CARIBBEAN SEA

PUERTO RICO (U.S.A.)

SAN JUAN
Carolina
Bayamón
Caguas
Ponce
Mayagüez
Arecibo
Aguadilla
Fajardo
Humacao
Guayama
Cordillera Central
Mts. de Uroyan
Cerro de Punta 1338
I. Caja de Muertos
Culebra
Vieques
Sonda de Vieques
Virgin Passage

VIRGIN ISLANDS (U.K.)
Anegada
Tortola
Road Town
Virgin Gorda
Spanish Town
Jost Van Dyke I.
Guana I.
Great Camanoe
Beef I.
Peter I.

VIRGIN ISLANDS (U.S.A.)
Charlotte Amalie
St. Thomas I.
St. John I.
Cruz Bay
VIRGIN IS. NAT. PARK
St. Croix I. (U.S.A.)
Christiansted
Frederiksted
Mt. Eagle 353

West from Greenwich

6 7

B C D E

BAHAMAS
New Bight
Cat I.
San Salvador
Conception I.
Rum Cay
Long I.
Tropic of Cancer
Clarence Town
Samana Cay
Crooked I. Passage
Crooked I.
Plana Cays
Albert Town
Snug Corner
Acklins
Mayaguana Passage
Mayaguana I.
Mira por vos Cay
Caicos Passage
Turks & Caicos Is. (U.K.)
Providenciales
Caicos Is.
Cockburn Town
Turks Is.
Turks Island Passage
Hogsty Reef
Little Inagua
Great Inagua
Matthew Town
Lake Rosa
Mouchoir Bank
Silver Bank
Silver Bank Passage
Navidad Bank

Puerto Rico Trench
Milwaukee Deep 8605

Baracoa
Guantánamo
Maisí
Paso de los Vientos (Windward Passage)
Î. de la Tortue
Cap-Haïtien
Port-de-Paix
Jean Rabel
Gonaïves
Hinche
St-Marc
HAITI
PORT-AU-PRINCE
Jérémie
Dame Marie
Massif de la Hotte
Les Cayes
Jacmel
Pointe-à-Gravois
Î. à Vache
Î. de la Gonâve

DOMINICAN REP.
SANTO DOMINGO
Santiago de los Caballeros
San Francisco de Macorís
Puerto Plata
La Vega
Pico Duarte 3175
Cord. Central
Nagua
Samana
Sánchez
Hato Mayor
Higüey
San Pedro de Macorís
La Romana
San Juan
L. Enriquillo
Barahona
Azua de Compostela
Baní
San Cristóbal
Pedernales
I. Saona
C. Engaño
I. Beata
C. Beata

Hispaniola
Antilles
Muertas Trough
Beata Ridge
Aguadilla
Mona Passage
Isla Mona (U.S.A.)
Anegada Passage
Sombrero (U.K.)
Anguilla (U.K.)
St.-Martin (Fr.)
St. Maarten (Neth.)
St.-Barthélemy (Fr.)
Saba (Neth.)
St. Eustatius (Neth.)
Barbuda
ANTIGUA & BARBUDA
St. John's
ST. KITTS & NEVIS
Basseterre
Nevis
Redonda
Montserrat (U.K.)
Guadeloupe Passage
GUADELOUPE (Fr.)
Pointe-à-Pitre
Basse-Terre
Marie-Galante (Fr.)
La Désirade
Dominica Passage
DOMINICA
Roseau
Martinique Passage
MARTINIQUE (Fr.)
Fort-de-France
St. Lucia Channel
ST. LUCIA
Castries
St. Vincent Passage
St. Vincent
Kingstown
BARBADOS
Bridgetown
ST. VINCENT & THE GRENADINES
GRENADA
St. George's
Leeward Islands
Lesser Antilles
Windward Islands
I. de Aves (Venezuela)
Aves Ridge
Grenada Basin
Tobago Basin

Venezuelan Basin
CARIBBEAN SEA
Colombian Basin

ABC Islands
Lesser Antilles
Aruba (Neth.)
Oranjestad
Curaçao (Neth.)
Willemstad
Bonaire (Neth.)
Is. Las Aves (Ven.)
Is. Los Roques (Ven.)
I. Orchila (Ven.)
I. Blanquilla (Ven.)
Is. Los Hermanos (Ven.)
Is. Los Testigos (Ven.)
I. de Margarita
NUEVA ESPARTA
La Asunción
Porlamar
I. La Tortuga (Ven.)

COLOMBIA
GUAJIRA
Pen. de la Guajira
Ríohacha
Santa Marta
Ciénaga
Barranquilla
Soledad
Valledupar
CÉSAR
MAGDALENA
El Banco
Ocaña
Cúcuta
NORTE DE SANTANDER
BOLÍVAR

VENEZUELA
Pen. de Paraguaná
Punto Fijo
Coro
FALCÓN
Golfo de Venezuela
MARACAIBO
Lago de Maracaibo
ZULIA
Cabimas
Ciudad Ojeda
BARQUISIMETO
LARA
VALENCIA
MARACAY
CARACAS
Puerto Cabello
Los Teques
Barcelona
Cumaná
Carúpano
SUCRE
Maturín
MONAGAS
ANZOÁTEGUI
GUÁRICO
Calabozo
BARINAS
Barinas
Mérida
Pico Bolívar 4981
TRUJILLO
PORTUGUESA
COJEDES
San Fernando de Apure
Ciudad Guayana
Ciudad Bolívar
DELTA AMACURO
Tucupita
Orinoco

TRINIDAD & TOBAGO
Port of Spain
Tobago
Scarborough
San Fernando
Dragon's Mouths
Serpent's Mouth
G. de Paria

West from Greenwich

4000 3000 2000 1500 1000 400 200 0 600 3000 6000 12 000 18 000 24 000 ft

12 000 9000 6000 4500 3000 1200 600 0 200 1000 2000 4000 6000 8000 m

328

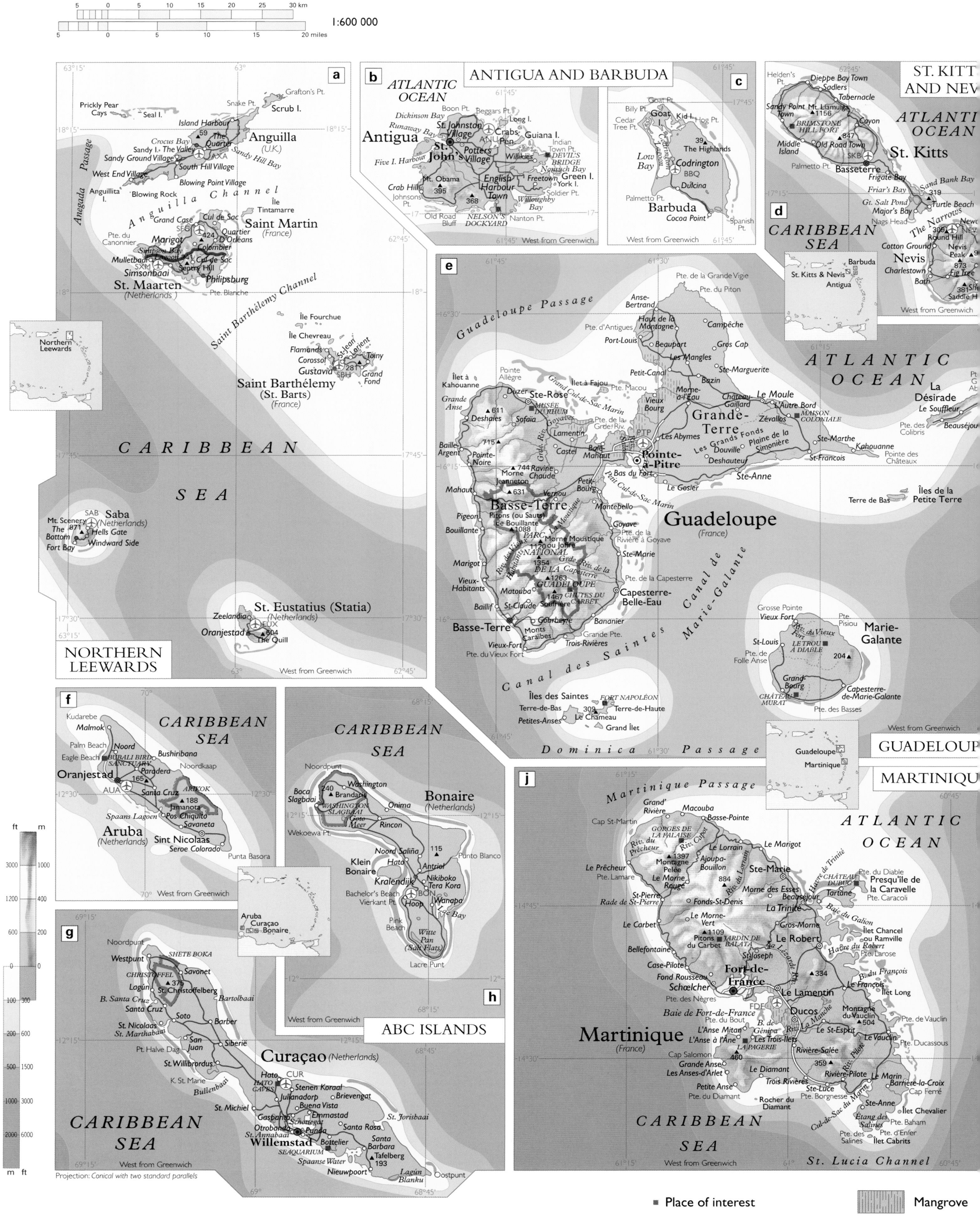

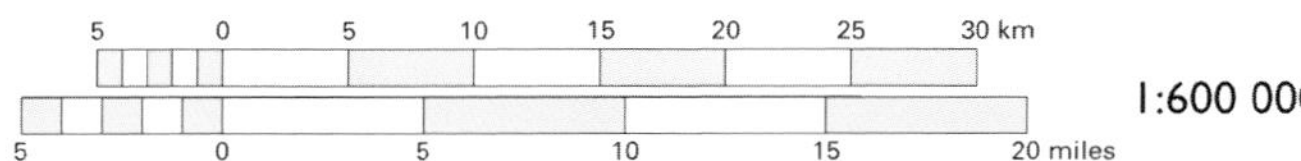

1:600 000

a NORTHERN LEEWARDS

b ANTIGUA AND BARBUDA

c

d ST. KITTS AND NEVIS

e GUADELOUPE

f

g

h ABC ISLANDS

j MARTINIQUE

West from Greenwich

Projection: Conical with two standard parallels

■ Place of interest

Mangrove

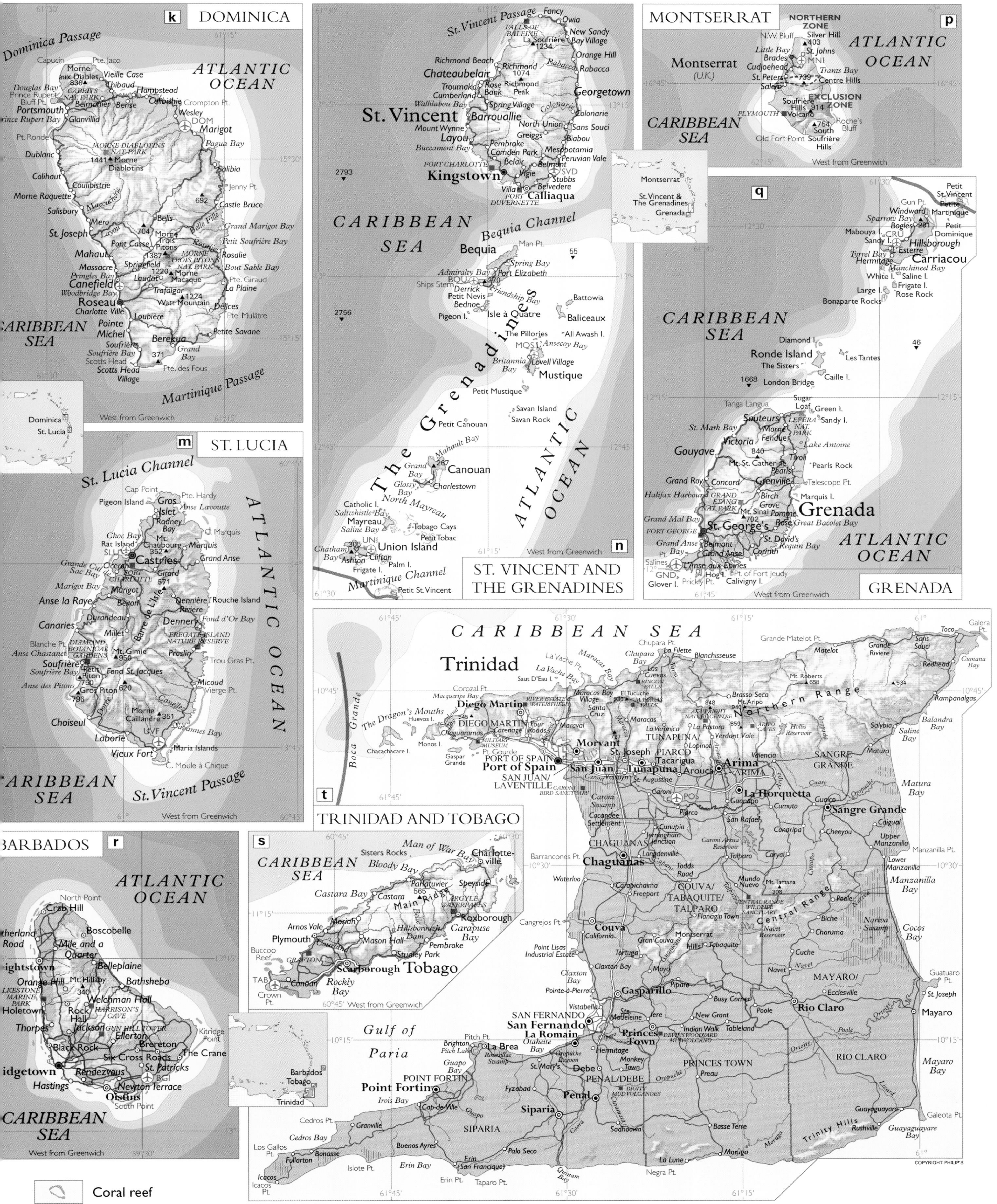
k
DOMINICA
Dominica Passage
ATLANTIC OCEAN
CARIBBEAN SEA
Martinique Passage
Portsmouth
Marigot
Morne Diablotins
Castle Bruce
St. Joseph
Mahaut
Canefield
Roseau
Pointe Michel
Soufrière
Scotts Head Village
Grand Bay
MORNE DIABLOTINS NAT. PARK
MORNE TROIS PITONS NAT. PARK
West from Greenwich
Dominica
St. Lucia
m
ST. LUCIA
St. Lucia Channel
ATLANTIC OCEAN
CARIBBEAN SEA
St. Vincent Passage
Gros Islet
Castries
Marigot
Anse la Raye
Canaries
Soufrière
Dennery
Micoud
Choiseul
Laborie
Vieux Fort
Maria Islands
West from Greenwich
St. Vincent Passage
St. Vincent
Kingstown
Calliaqua
Georgetown
Chateaubelair
Barrouallie
Layou
La Soufrière 1234
CARIBBEAN SEA
Bequia Channel
Bequia
Port Elizabeth
The Grenadines
Mustique
Baliceaux
Battowia
Isle à Quatre
Canouan
Charlestown
Mayreau
Tobago Cays
Union Island
Clifton
Palm I.
Petit St. Vincent
ATLANTIC OCEAN
Martinique Channel
n
ST. VINCENT AND THE GRENADINES
West from Greenwich
Montserrat
St. Vincent & The Grenadines
Grenada
MONTSERRAT
p
NORTHERN ZONE
EXCLUSION ZONE
Montserrat (U.K.)
ATLANTIC OCEAN
CARIBBEAN SEA
St. Johns
Brades
Plymouth
Soufrière Hills
West from Greenwich
q
Petit St. Vincent
Petite Martinique
Windward
Hillsborough
Carriacou
Petit Dominique
CARIBBEAN SEA
Ronde Island
Diamond I.
Les Tantes
Caille I.
London Bridge
Sauteurs
Victoria
Gouyave
Grenville
Grenada
St. George's
ATLANTIC OCEAN
GRENADA
West from Greenwich
t
CARIBBEAN SEA
Trinidad
Northern Range
The Dragon's Mouths
Boca Grande
Diego Martin
Port of Spain
San Juan
Tunapuna
Arima
Sangre Grande
Chaguanas
Couva
Central Range
Gulf of Paria
San Fernando
La Romain
Princes Town
Point Fortin
Penal
Siparia
Rio Claro
Mayaro
Matura Bay
Manzanilla Bay
Cocos Bay
Galeota Pt.
Icacos Pt.
Trinity Hills
COPYRIGHT PHILIP'S
TRINIDAD AND TOBAGO
s
CARIBBEAN SEA
Man of War Bay
Charlotteville
Speyside
Roxborough
Tobago
Scarborough
Plymouth
Crown Pt.
West from Greenwich
BARBADOS
r
ATLANTIC OCEAN
CARIBBEAN SEA
North Point
Speightstown
Holetown
Bridgetown
Bathsheba
Mt. Hillaby 340
The Crane
Oistins
South Point
West from Greenwich
Barbados
Tobago
Trinidad
Coral reef

SOUTH
AMERICA

1:28 000 000

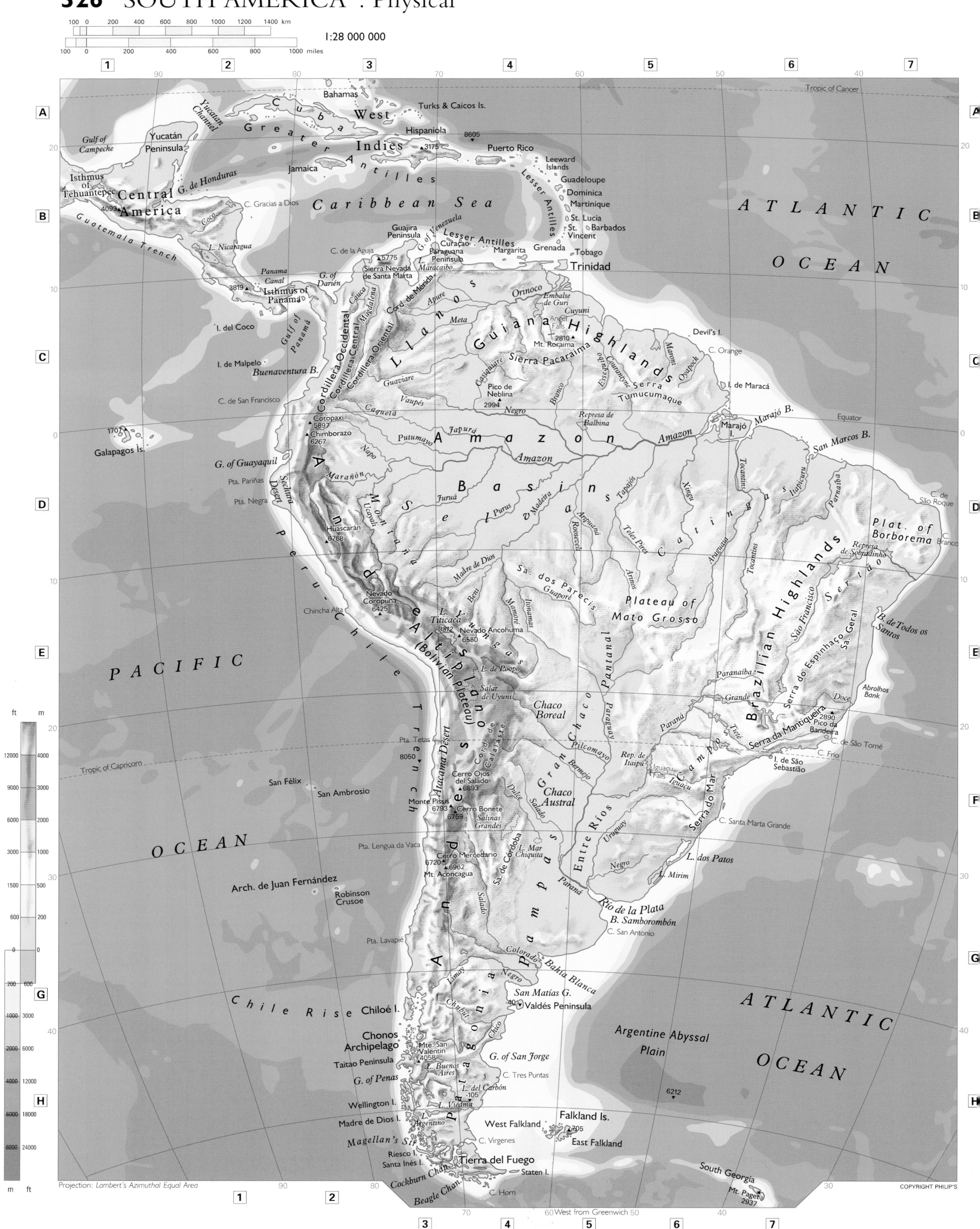

ATLANTIC OCEAN
PACIFIC OCEAN
Caribbean Sea
Amazon Basin
Guiana Highlands
Brazilian Highlands
Andes
Llanos
Pampas
Patagonia
Gran Chaco
Plateau of Mato Grosso
Caatinga
Altiplano (Bolivian Plateau)
Atacama Desert
Sechura Desert
Central America
Greater Antilles
Lesser Antilles
West Indies
Falkland Is.
Tierra del Fuego
Galapagos Is.
Argentine Abyssal Plain
Peru-Chile Trench
Chile Rise
Tropic of Cancer
Equator
Tropic of Capricorn
Projection: Lambert's Azimuthal Equal Area
West from Greenwich

1:28 000 000
100 0 200 400 600 800 1000 1200 1400 km
100 0 200 400 600 800 1000 miles
Tropic of Cancer
Havana
CUBA
THE BAHAMAS
Turks & Caicos Is. (U.K.)
Cayman Is. (U.K.)
JAMAICA
Kingston
HAITI
Port-au-Prince
DOMINICAN REP.
Santo Domingo
San Juan
PUERTO RICO (U.S.A.)
Virgin Is. (U.S.A. - U.K.)
Anguilla (U.K.)
St. Martin (Fr. - Neth.)
ST. KITTS & NEVIS
ANTIGUA & BARBUDA
Basse-Terre
GUADELOUPE (Fr.)
DOMINICA
Fort-de-France
MARTINIQUE (Fr.)
Castries
ST. LUCIA
ST. VINCENT
Kingstown
BARBADOS
Bridgetown
GRENADA
St. George's
Port of Spain
TRINIDAD & TOBAGO
ARUBA (Neth.)
CURAÇAO (Neth.)
Oranjestad
Willemstad
MEXICO
BELIZE
GUATEMALA
Guatemala
HONDURAS
Tegucigalpa
San Salvador
EL SALVADOR
NICARAGUA
Managua
COSTA RICA
San José
Panamá
PANAMA
Caribbean Sea
ATLANTIC OCEAN
Barranquilla
Cartagena
Maracaibo
Barquisimeto
Caracas
Valencia
G. of Darién
Cúcuta
San Cristóbal
Bucaramanga
Medellín
VENEZUELA
Orinoco
Ciudad Guayana
Georgetown
GUYANA
Paramaribo
SURINAME
Cayenne
C. Orange
FRENCH GUIANA
I. del Coco (Costa Rica)
Gulf of Panamá
BOGOTÁ
Magdalena
Cali
I. de Malpelo (Colombia)
COLOMBIA
Boa Vista
RORAIMA
Branco
Essequibo
AMAPÁ
Macapá
Equator
Marajó I.
Belém
Galapagos Is. (Ecuador)
Quito
ECUADOR
Putumayo
Japurá
Napo
Guayaquil
G. of Guayaquil
Amazon
Manaus
Santarém
São Luís
Fortaleza
Iquitos
Marañón
AMAZONAS
PARÁ
Xingu
Tapajós
Tocantins
MARANHÃO
Teresina
CEARÁ
Juruá
Madeira
Purus
Imperatriz
RIO G. DO NORTE
Natal
PARAÍBA
João Pessoa
Chiclayo
Ucayali
Trujillo
Chimbote
ACRE
Rio Branco
Pôrto Velho
Parnaíba
PIAUÍ
Campina Grande
PERNAMBUCO
Recife
Palmas
TOCANTINS
Araguaia
ALAGOAS
Maceió
SERGIPE
Aracaju
PERU
RONDÔNIA
BRAZIL
Madre de Dios
Callao
LIMA
Cusco
MATO GROSSO
BAHIA
Salvador
Mamoré
L. Titicaca
GOIÁS
Cuiabá
Brasília
DIS. FED.
São Francisco
Arequipa
La Paz
BOLIVIA
Goiânia
Cochabamba
Santa Cruz
PACIFIC OCEAN
Sucre
Paraguay
MINAS GERAIS
MATO GROSSO DO SUL
BELO HORIZONTE
ESPÍRITO SANTO
Iquique
Ribeirão Prêto
Campo Grande
Paraná
Juiz de Fora
Vitória
SÃO PAULO
PARAGUAY
Campinas
R. DE J.
Campos
Pilcomayo
SÃO PAULO
Niterói
RIO DE JANEIRO
Santos
Antofagasta
Salta
PARANÁ
Asunción
Curitiba
Tropic of Capricorn
San Félix (Chile)
San Ambrosio (Chile)
San Miguel de Tucumán
Resistencia
Corrientes
SANTA CATARINA
Florianópolis
Uruguay
Salado
RIO GRANDE DO SUL
Pôrto Alegre
Córdoba
Santa Fé
San Juan
Paraná
Pelotas
Viña del Mar
Valparaíso
Mendoza
Rosario
URUGUAY
SANTIAGO
BUENOS AIRES
Montevideo
Arch. de Juan Fernández (Chile)
Robinson Crusoe
La Plata
Río de la Plata
Talca
Concepción
Bahía Blanca
Mar del Plata
Neuquén
Colorado
Valdivia
Negro
Viedma
Puerto Montt
CHILE
ARGENTINA
Chubut
Comodoro Rivadavia
Gulf of San Jorge
Gulf of Penas
West Falkland
FALKLAND IS. (U.K.)
Stanley
East Falkland
Magellan's Str.
Punta Arenas
Tierra del Fuego
C. Horn
South Georgia (U.K.)
Projection: Lambert's Azimuthal Equal Area
West from Greenwich
LIMA Capital Cities

50 0 50 100 150 200 250 300 km

1:6 400 000

50 0 50 100 150 200 miles

321 320 330

MARGARITA
1:600 000
0 5 10 15 km
0 5 10 miles
CARIBBEAN SEA
NUEVA ESPARTA
Isla de Margarita
(Venezuela)
Isla Cubagua
Isla Coche
Peninsula de Macanao
La Asunción
Porlamar
Juangriego
Pampatar
Isla Los Frailes
West from Greenwich
ATLANTIC OCEAN
GRENADA
St. George's
The Grenadines
Tobago
TRINIDAD AND TOBAGO
Port of Spain
Scarborough
San Fernando
Trinidad
I. de Margarita
Cumaná
Barcelona
Maturín
Delta del Orinoco
Ciudad Guayana
Ciudad Bolívar
Embalse de Guri
GUYANA
Georgetown
New Amsterdam
Linden
Pakaraima Mts.
SURINAME
Paramaribo
Nieuw Nickerie
Nieuw Amsterdam
Wilhelmina Geb.
FRENCH GUIANA
Cayenne
St-Laurent-du-Maroni
Kourou
Iles du Salut
Serra Tumucumaque
MONTANHAS DO TUMUCUMAQUE
AMAPÁ
Macapá
Equator
Ilha de Marajó
RORAIMA
Boa Vista
Serra Pacaraima
Serra Parima
Represa de Balbina
BRAZIL
Amazonas
Negro
MANAUS
Santarém
Óbidos
Parintins
Itacoatiara
Altamira
Xingu
PARÁ
AMAZONAS
Madeira
COPYRIGHT PHILIP'S
331
332
Administrative divisions in Guyana
1 POMEROON-SUPENAAM
2 ESSEQUIBO ISLANDS - WEST DEMERARA
3 DEMERARA-MAHAICA
4 MAHAICA-BERBICE
5 EAST BERBICE - CORENTYNE

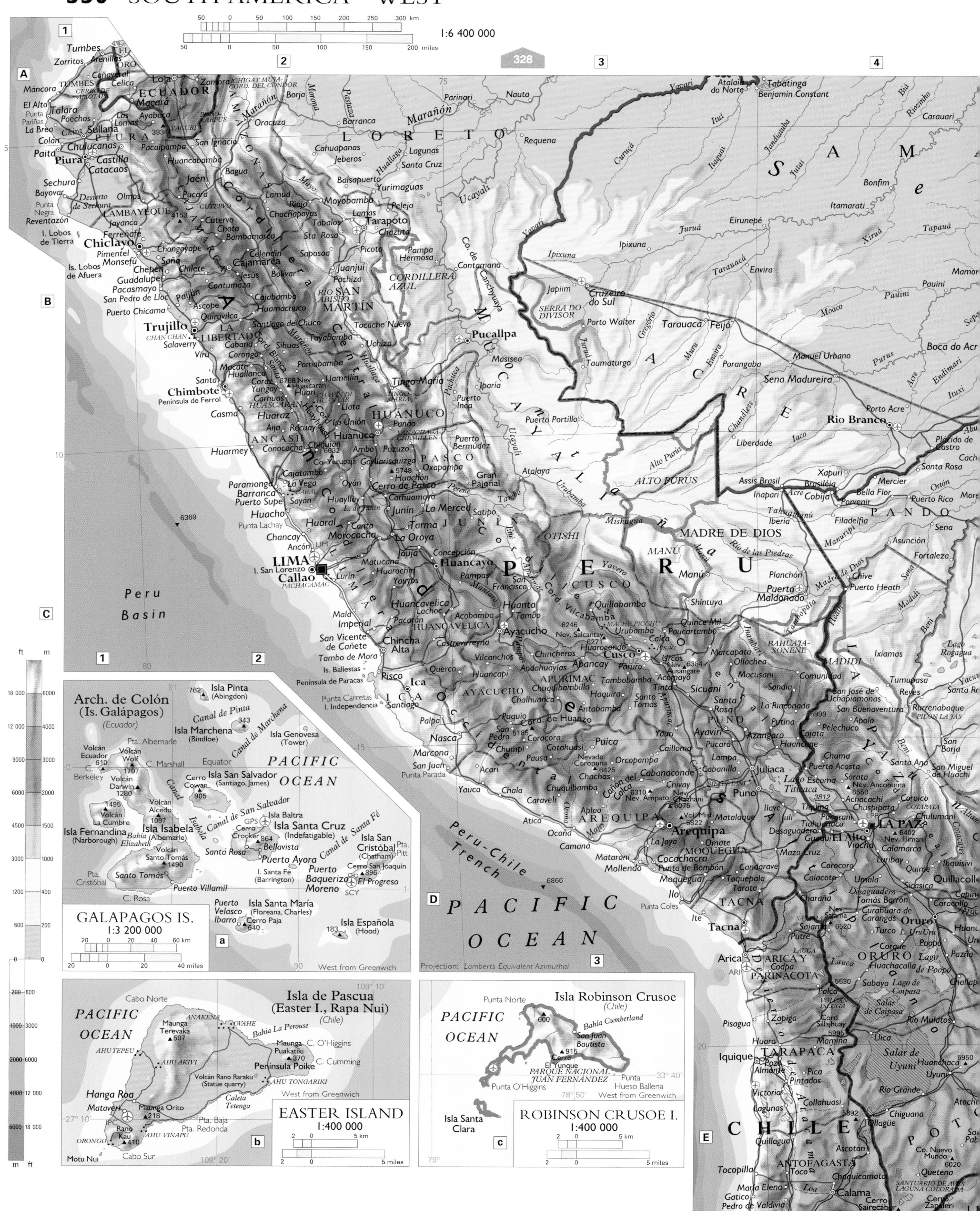
1:6 400 000
328
ECUADOR
LORETO
PERU
LIMA
Callao
Trujillo
Chiclayo
Chimbote
Arequipa
Cusco
Huancayo
Ayacucho
Pucallpa
Iquitos
Tacna
Arica
Iquique
Antofagasta
Calama
LA PAZ
El Alto
Oruro
Rio Branco
Lago Titicaca
Salar de Uyuni
CHILE
Peru Basin
Peru-Chile Trench
PACIFIC OCEAN
Cordillera Central
Cordillera Occidental
Cordillera Azul
Arch. de Colón (Is. Galápagos)
(Ecuador)
GALAPAGOS IS.
1:3 200 000
West from Greenwich
Isla de Pascua (Easter I., Rapa Nui)
(Chile)
EASTER ISLAND
1:400 000
Isla Robinson Crusoe
(Chile)
ROBINSON CRUSOE I.
1:400 000
Projection: Lamberts Equivalent Azimuthal

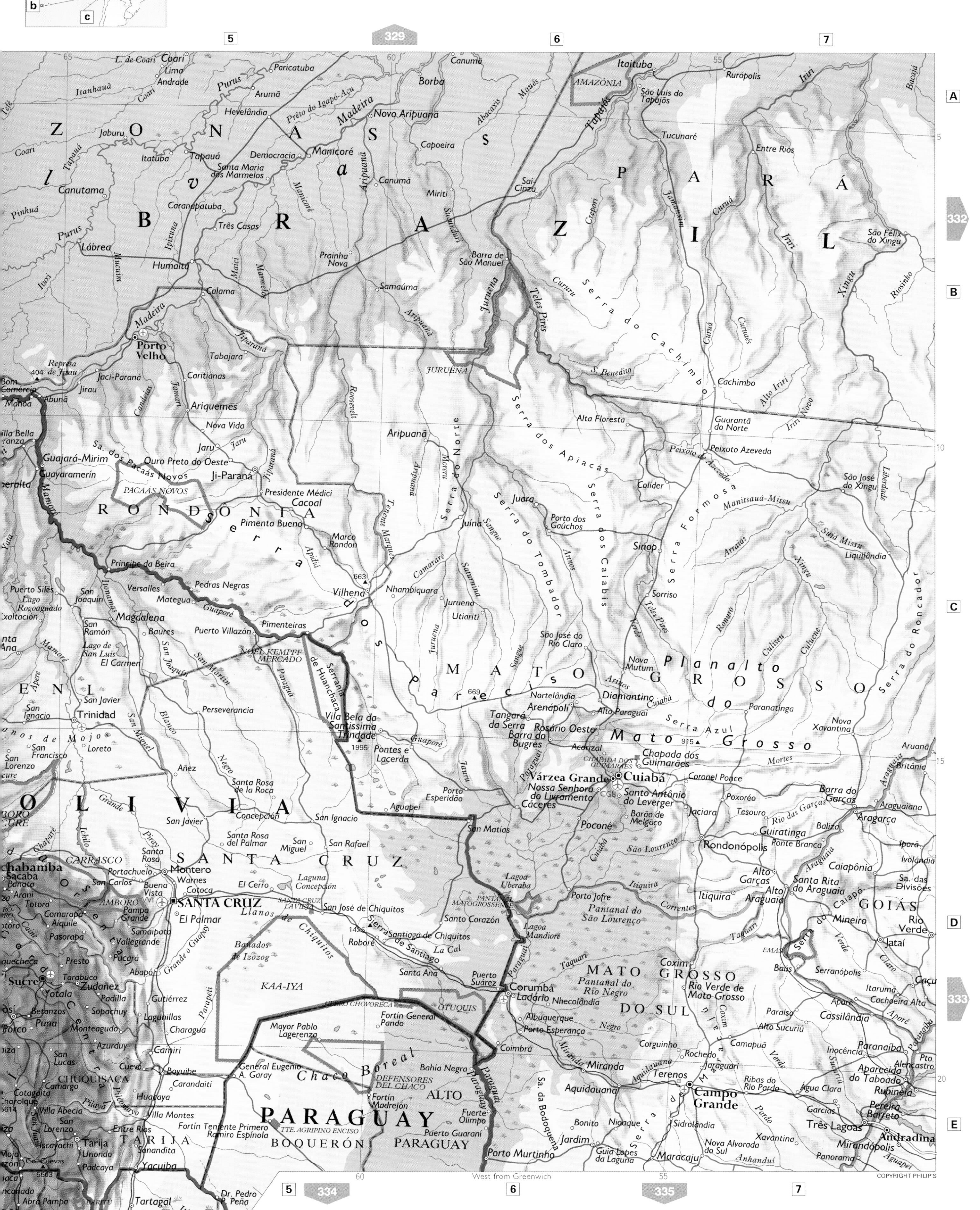

329
332
333
334
335
5
6
7
A
B
C
D
E
BRAZIL
AMAZONAS
PARÁ
RONDÔNIA
MATO GROSSO
MATO GROSSO DO SUL
GOIÁS
BOLIVIA
SANTA CRUZ
CHUQUISACA
TARIJA
PARAGUAY
ALTO PARAGUAY
BOQUERÓN
SALTA
Coari
L. de Coari
Lima
Andrade
Paricatuba
Canumã
Borba
Itaituba
Rurópolis
Iriri
Bacajá
Itanhauã
Purus
Arumã
Maués
AMAZÔNIA
São Luís do Tapajós
Tapajós
Hevelândia
Prêto do Igapó-Açu
Madeira
Novo Aripuanã
Abacaxis
Jaburu
Tucunaré
Entre Rios
Capoeira
Itatuba
Tapauá
Democracia
Manicoré
Santa Maria dos Marmelos
Canutama
Aripuanã
Canumã
Sai-Cinza
Cururu
Crepori
Jamanxim
Curuá
Caranapatuba
Mirití
Pinhuá
Ipixuna
Três Casas
Sucunduri
São Félix do Xingu
Lábrea
Prainha Nova
Barra de São Manuel
Humaitá
Mucuim
Maici
Marmelos
Samaúma
Juruena
Teles Pires
Xingu
Riozinho
Inuxi
Calama
Serra do Cachimbo
Curuaés
Porto Velho
Tabajara
Jiparaná
JURUENA
S. Benedito
Represa de Jirau
404
Jaci-Paraná
Caritianas
Cachimbo
Alto Iriri
Bom Comércio
Jirau
Candeias
Jamari
Roosevelt
Iriri Novo
Manoa
Abunã
Ariquemes
Alta Floresta
Guarantã do Norte
Nova Vida
Aripuanã
Serra do Norte
Serra dos Apiacás
Vila Bella
Jaru
Peixoto de Azevedo
Peixoto Azevedo
Guajará-Mirim
Sa. dos Pacaás Novos
Ouro Preto do Oeste
Guayaramerín
Ji-Paraná
Colíder
São José do Xingu
Liberdade
PACAÁS NOVOS
Presidente Médici
Cacoal
Juara
Serra Formosa
Manitsauá-Missu
Mamoré
Pimenta Bueno
Serra dos Parecis
Serra do Tombador
Serra dos Caiabis
Porto dos Gaúchos
Marco Rondon
Tenente Marques
Juína
Sangue
Arinos
Sinop
Suiá Missu
Liquilândia
Yata
Príncipe da Beira
663
Camararé
Saturnina
Arraias
Puerto Siles
Versalles
Pedras Negras
Nhambiquara
Sorriso
Serra do Roncador
San Joaquín
Mategua
Guaporé
Vilhena
Juruena
Lago Rogoaguado
Exaltación
Magdalena
Utiariti
Teles Pires
Romuro
San Ramón
Baures
Puerto Villazón
Pimenteiras
Verde
Culiseu
Culuene
Lago de San Luis
El Carmen
NOEL KEMPFF MERCADO
São José do Rio Claro
Nova Mutum
Planalto do Mato Grosso
Serrania de Huanchaca
San Martín
Paraguá
Apere
San Joaquín
Diamantino
Cuiabá
Nortelândia
669
Arenápolis
Alto Paraguai
Paranatinga
San Javier
Perseverancia
Trinidad
San Ignacio
Vila Bela da Santíssima Trindade
Tangará da Serra
Rosário Oeste
Serra Azul
Nova Xavantina
Llanos de Mojos
San Francisco
Loreto
San Miguel
Blanco
1995
Pontes e Lacerda
Guaporé
Barra do Bugres
Acorizal
915
Chapada dos Guimarães
CHAPADA DOS GUIMARÃES
Aruanã
Britânia
San Lorenzo
Mortes
Araguaia
Añez
Negro
Jauru
Várzea Grande
Cuiabá
Coronel Ponce
Santa Rosa de la Roca
Porto Esperidião
Nossa Senhora do Livramento
CGB
Santo Antônio do Leverger
Poxoréo
Barra do Garças
Grande
Aguapeí
Cáceres
Jaciara
Tesouro
Rio das Garças
Araguaiana
Ichilo
San Javier
Concepción
San Ignacio
Barão de Melgaço
Aragarças
Chaparé
San Matías
Poconé
Baliza
Piray
Santa Rosa del Palmar
San Miguel
San Rafael
Guiratinga
Rondonópolis
Ponte Branca
Iporá
Ivolândia
Santa Rosa
CARRASCO
São Lourenço
Cochabamba
Sacaba
Portachuelo
Montero
Warnes
Laguna Concepción
Caiapônia
Punata
San Carlos
Buena Vista
El Cerro
Lagoa Uberaba
Itiquira
Alto Garças
Santa Rita do Araguaia
Sa. das Divisões
Arani
Totora
AMBORO
Cotoca
SANTA CRUZ
SANTA CRUZ LA VIEJA
PANTANAL MATOGROSSENSE
Porto Jofre
Itiquira
Alto Araguaia
Caiapó
Comarapa
Aiquile
Pampa Grande
El Palmar
Llanos de Chiquitos
San José de Chiquitos
Correntes
Pantanal do São Lourenço
Mineiro
Rio Verde
Pasorapa
Samaipata
Vallegrande
1425
Sierra de Santiago
Santiago de Chiquitos
Santo Corazón
Lagoa Mandioré
Taquari
Serra do Caiapó
EMAS
Jataí
Grande o Guapay
Roboré
La Cal
Bañados de Izozog
Presto
Pucará
Abapó
Santa Ana
Puerto Suárez
Paraguai
Coxim
Baús
Serranópolis
Sucre
Tarabuco
Zudañez
Corumbá
Ladário
Pantanal do Rio Negro
Rio Verde de Mato Grosso
Itarumã
Caçu
Yotala
Padilla
KAA-IYA
Parapeti
Gutiérrez
Nhecolândia
Aporé
Cachoeira Alta
Betanzos
Sopachuy
CERRO CHOVORECA
Fortín General Pando
OTUQUIS
Albuquerque
Paraíso
Cassilândia
Puna
Lagunillas
Porto Esperança
Negro
Alto Sucuriú
Monteagudo
Mayor Pablo Lagerenza
Charagua
Azurduy
Camiri
Coimbra
Corguinho
Camapuã
Paranaíba
San Lucas
Chaco Boreal
Cuevo
Miranda
Rochedo
Inocência
Pto. Alencastro
Boyuibe
General Eugenio A. Garay
Bahía Negra
Aquidauana
Jaraguari
Sucuriú
Aparecida do Taboado
Carandaiti
DEFENSORES DEL CHACO
Terenos
Camargo
Cotagaita
Huacaya
Pilcomayo
Pilaya
Fortín Madrejón
Campo Grande
Ribas do Rio Pardo
Água Clara
Rubinéia
Villa Abecia
Villa Montes
Fuerte Olimpo
Sa. da Bodoquena
Pardo
Garcias
Pereira Barreto
San Lorenzo
Fortín Teniente Primero Ramiro Espínola
TTE. AGRIPINO ENCISO
Entre Ríos
Bonito
Nioaque
Sidrolândia
Xavantina
Três Lagoas
Andradina
Tarija
Uriondo
Iscayachi
San Juan
Sanandita
Puerto Guaraní
Jardim
Nova Alvorada do Sul
Mirandópolis
Padcaya
Guia Lopes da Laguna
Maracaju
Anhanduí
Panorama
Aguapeí
Yacuiba
Porto Murtinho
5603
Abra Pampa
BARITÚ
Tartagal
Itiyuro
Dr. Pedro P. Peña
65
60
55
10
15
20
West from Greenwich
COPYRIGHT PHILIP'S

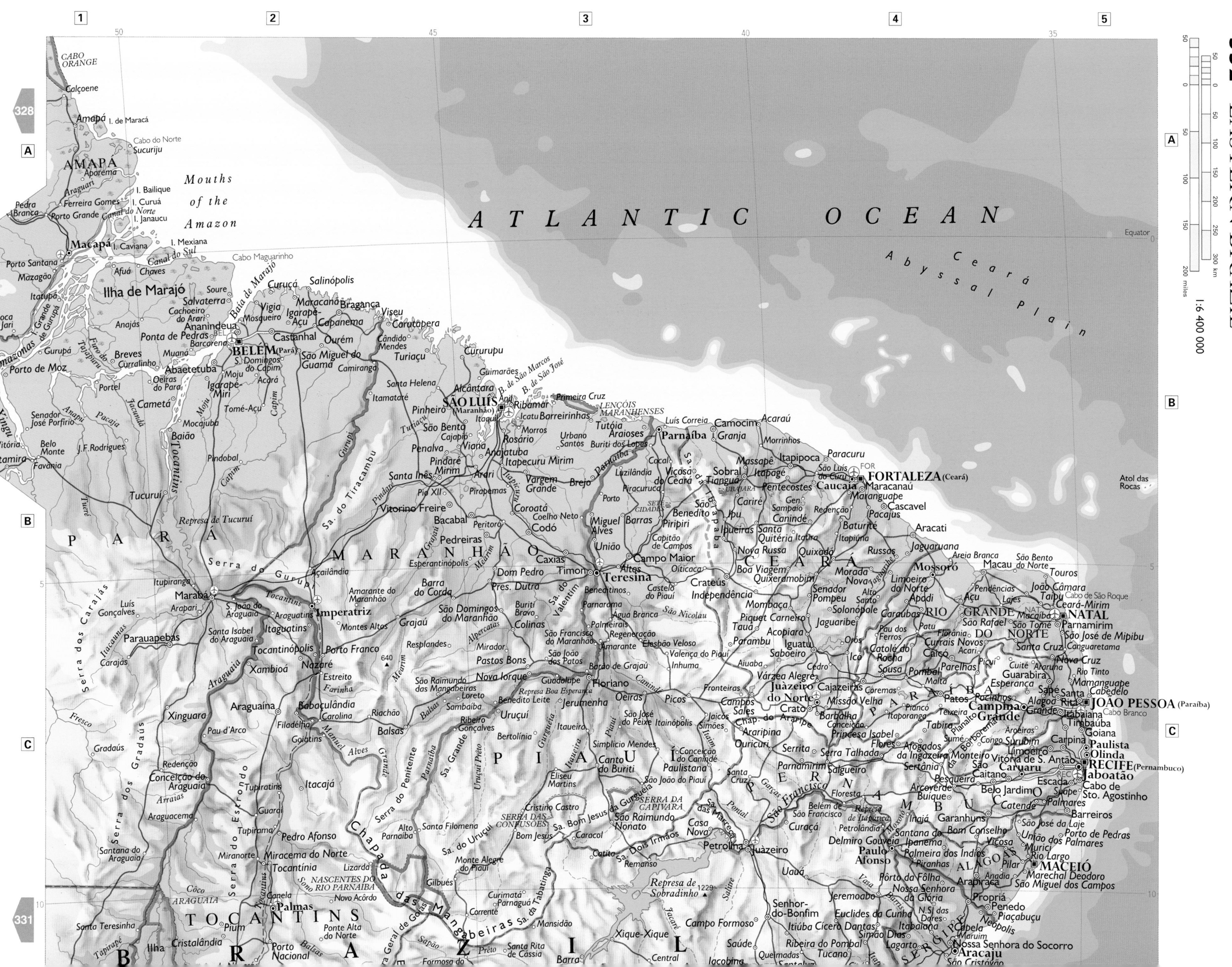

50 0 50 100 150 200 250 300 km
50 0 50 100 150 200 miles
1:6 400 000
A
B
C
1
2
3
4
5
ATLANTIC OCEAN
Ceará Abyssal Plain
Equator
Atol das Rocas
Mouths of the Amazon
Ilha de Marajó
Baía de Marajó
AMAPÁ
Macapá
BELÉM (Pará)
SÃO LUÍS (Maranhão)
FORTALEZA (Ceará)
NATAL
JOÃO PESSOA (Paraíba)
RECIFE (Pernambuco)
MACEIÓ
Aracaju
Teresina
Imperatriz
Marabá
Palmas
Campina Grande
Juàzeiro do Norte
Petrolina
Juazeiro
Mossoró
Parnaíba
Tocantins
Xingu
CABO ORANGE
Cabo do Norte
Cabo Maguarinho
Cabo Branco
Cabo de São Roque
PARÁ
MARANHÃO
PIAUÍ
CEARÁ
RIO GRANDE DO NORTE
PARAÍBA
PERNAMBUCO
ALAGOAS
SERGIPE
TOCANTINS
BRAZIL
Serra dos Carajás
Serra do Gurupi
Sa. do Tiracambu
Chapada das Mangabeiras
Serra do Penitente
Represa de Tucuruí
Represa de Sobradinho
LENÇÓIS MARANHENSES
328
331

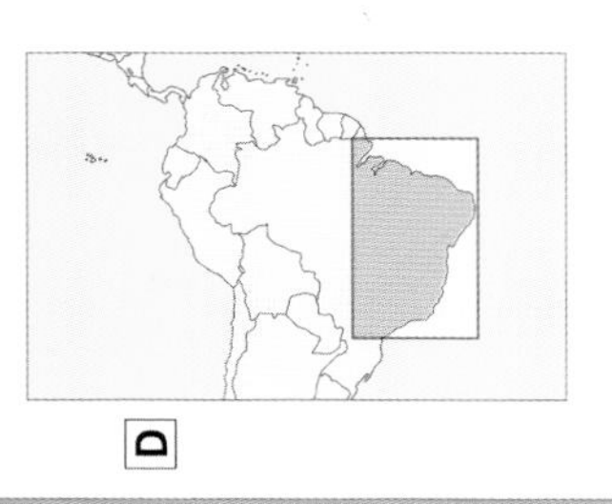

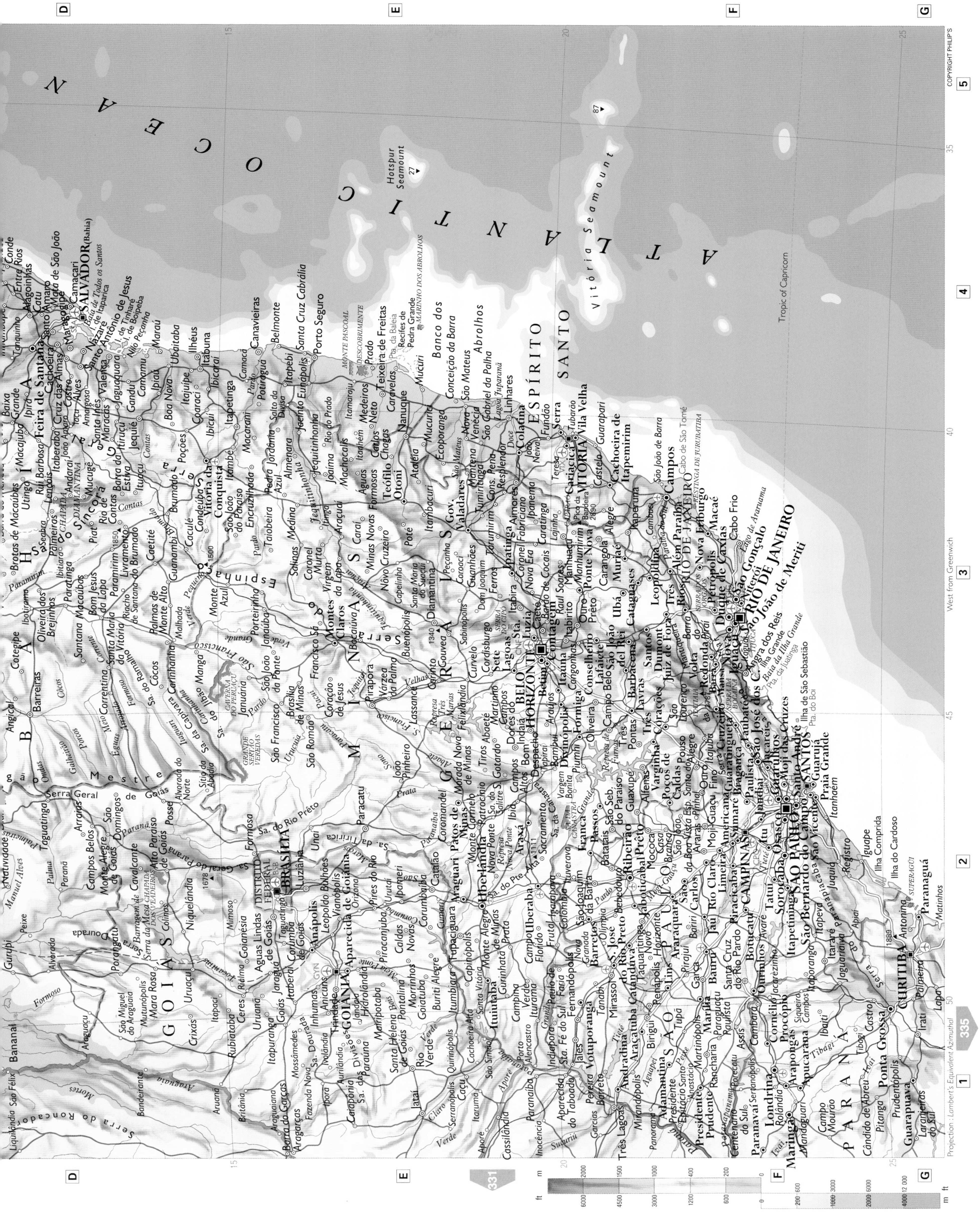

D E F G

1 2 3 4 5

West from Greenwich

Projection : Lambert's Equivalent Azimuthal

331

335

m	ft
2000	6000
1500	4500
1000	3000
400	1200
200	600
0	0
200	600
1000	3000
2000	6000
4000	12 000

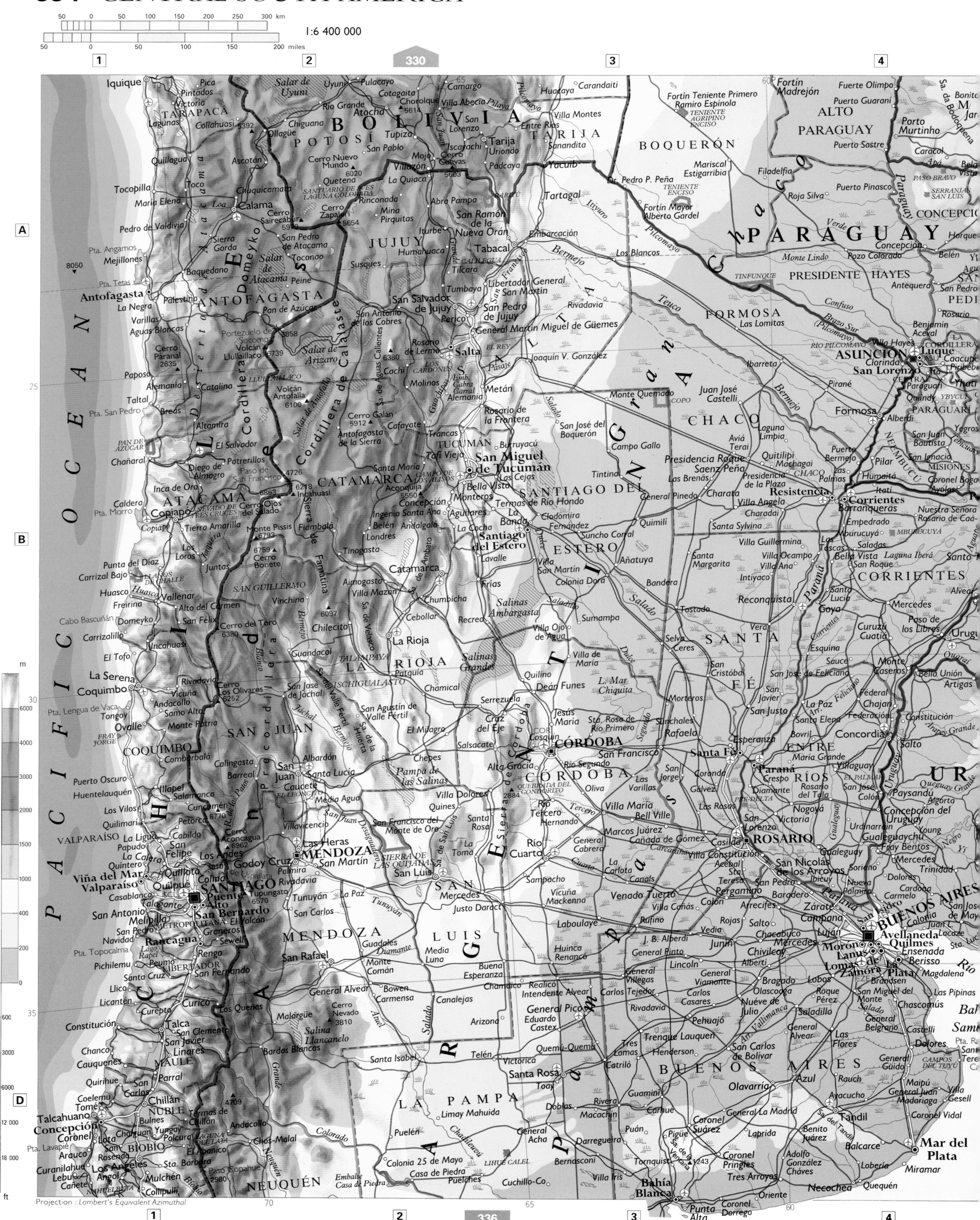

1:6 400 000
km
miles
330
336
PACIFIC OCEAN
BOLIVIA
PARAGUAY
ARGENTINA
CHILE
Gran Chaco
Cordillera Domeyko
Desierto de Atacama
Cordillera de Calalaste
Cordillera de San Buenaventura
Sierra de Famatina
Precordillera
Pampas
TARAPACÁ
ANTOFAGASTA
ATACAMA
COQUIMBO
VALPARAÍSO
METROPOLITANA
LIBERTADOR
MAULE
BIOBÍO
POTOSÍ
TARIJA
BOQUERÓN
ALTO PARAGUAY
PRESIDENTE HAYES
JUJUY
SALTA
FORMOSA
CHACO
CATAMARCA
TUCUMÁN
SANTIAGO DEL ESTERO
LA RIOJA
SAN JUAN
CÓRDOBA
SANTA FÉ
CORRIENTES
ENTRE RÍOS
MENDOZA
SAN LUIS
LA PAMPA
NEUQUÉN
BUENOS AIRES
ASUNCIÓN
SANTIAGO
BUENOS AIRES
Iquique
Calama
Antofagasta
Copiapó
La Serena
Coquimbo
Valparaíso
Viña del Mar
Rancagua
Talca
Concepción
Los Angeles
Salta
San Salvador de Jujuy
San Miguel de Tucumán
Santiago del Estero
Catamarca
La Rioja
San Juan
MENDOZA
CÓRDOBA
San Luis
Santa Fe
Paraná
ROSARIO
Resistencia
Corrientes
Formosa
Santa Rosa
Bahía Blanca
Mar del Plata
La Plata
Tandil
Projection : Lambert's Equivalent Azimuthal

ATLANTIC
OCEAN
BRAZIL
PARANÁ
SANTA CATARINA
RIO GRANDE DO SUL
SÃO PAULO
RIO DE JANEIRO
BELO HORIZONTE
VITÓRIA
SÃO PAULO
RIO DE JANEIRO
CAMPINAS
SANTOS
CURITIBA
JOINVILLE
FLORIANÓPOLIS
PORTO ALEGRE
MONTEVIDEO
Tropic of Capricorn
West from Greenwich
333
5
6
7
A
B
C
D
55
50
45
40
25
30
35
5304

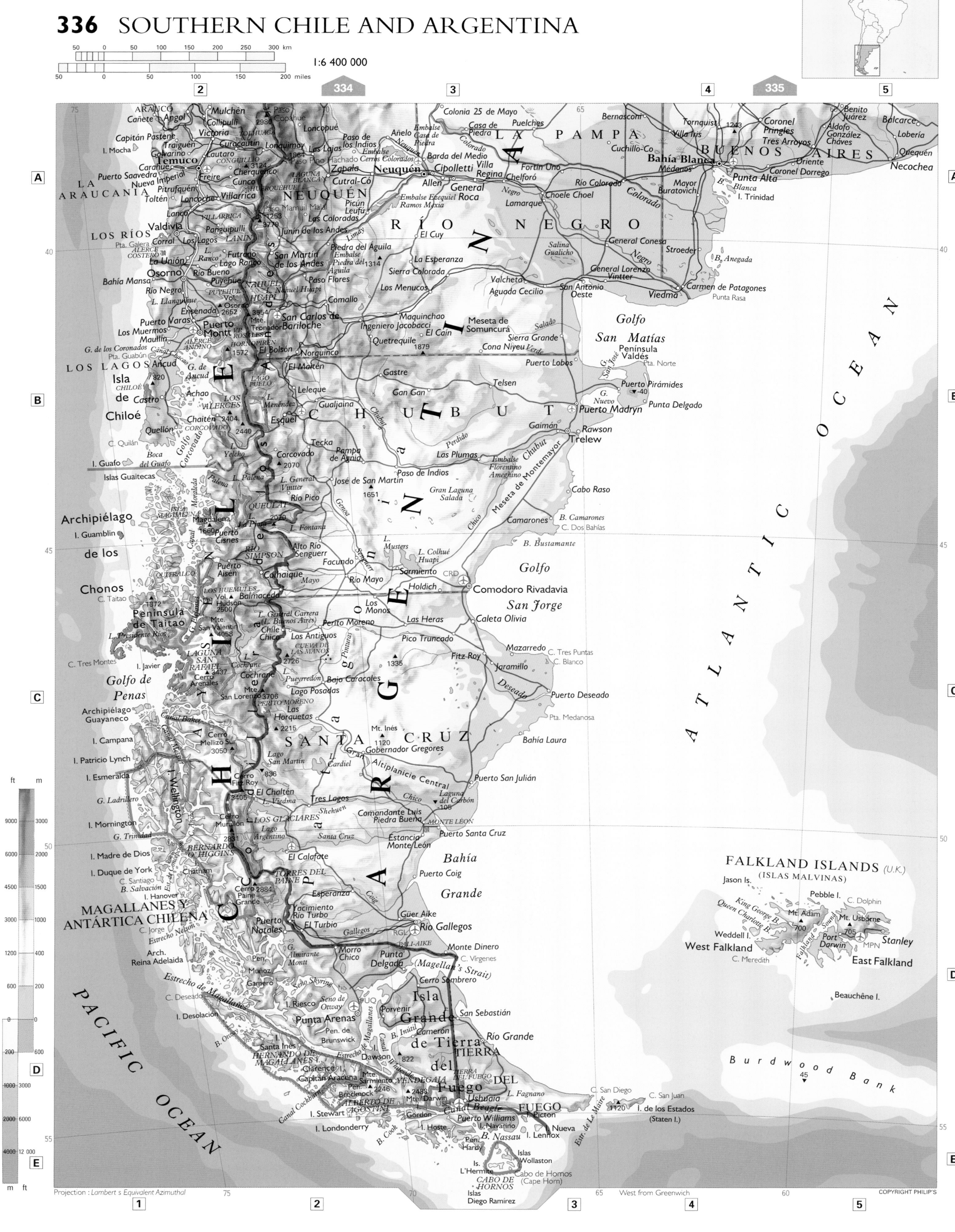
1:6 400 000
km
miles
334
335
LA PAMPA
BUENOS AIRES
NEUQUÉN
RÍO NEGRO
CHUBUT
SANTA CRUZ
TIERRA DEL FUEGO
LA ARAUCANIA
LOS RÍOS
LOS LAGOS
MAGALLANES Y ANTÁRTICA CHILENA
ARGENTINA
CHILE
Patagonia
ATLANTIC OCEAN
PACIFIC OCEAN
FALKLAND ISLANDS (U.K.)
(ISLAS MALVINAS)
West Falkland
East Falkland
Stanley
Burdwood Bank
Golfo San Matías
Golfo San Jorge
Bahía Grande
Golfo de Penas
Estrecho de Magallanes
(Magellan's Strait)
Isla Grande de Tierra del Fuego
Isla de Chiloé
Archipiélago de los Chonos
Península de Taitao
Península Valdés
Temuco
Valdivia
Osorno
Puerto Montt
Neuquén
Cipolletti
Bahía Blanca
Viedma
Carmen de Patagones
San Carlos de Bariloche
Esquel
Puerto Madryn
Trelew
Rawson
Comodoro Rivadavia
Caleta Olivia
Coihaique
Puerto Aisén
Puerto Deseado
Puerto San Julián
Puerto Santa Cruz
Río Gallegos
Puerto Natales
Punta Arenas
Porvenir
Río Grande
Ushuaia
Puerto Williams
Cabo de Hornos
(Cape Horn)
I. de los Estados
(Staten I.)
Projection : Lambert's Equivalent Azimuthal
West from Greenwich
COPYRIGHT PHILIP'S

GEOGRAPHICAL GLOSSARY

This is a list of the geographical terms from various foreign languages that are found in the place names on the maps and in the index. Each is followed by the language and its English meaning.

Afr. Afrikaans
Alb. Albanian
Amh. Amharic
Ar. Arabic
Belo. Belorussian
Berb. Berber
Bulg. Bulgarian
Burm. Burmese
Cam. Cambodian
Cat. Catalan
Chin. Chinese
Czec. Czech
Dan. Danish
Dut. Dutch
Est. Estonian
Fin. Finnish
Fr. French
Gae. Gaelic
Ger. German
Gr. Greek
Heb. Hebrew
Hin. Hindi
Hung. Hungarian
I.-C. Indo-Chinese
Ice. Icelandic
It. Italian
Indo. Indonesian
Jap. Japanese
Kaz. Kazakh
Kor. Korean
Kyrg. Kyrgyz
Lapp. Lapp (Sami)
Lat. Latvian
Lith. Lithuanian
Malag. Malagasy
Mong. Mongolian
Nor. Norway
Pash. Pashto
Per. Persian
Pol. Polish
Port. Portuguese
Rom. Romanian
Russ. Russian
Sin. Sinhalese
Ser.-Cr. Serbo-Croat
Slov. Slovene
Som. Somali
Span. Spanish
Swe. Swedish
Tib. Tibetan
Turk. Turkish
Ukr. Ukrainian
Viet. Vietnamese

-á *Ice.* river
-å *Dan., Nor., Swe.* stream
-abad *Farsi, Russ.* town
Abyaḍ *Ar.* white mountain
Ada, Adasi *Turk.* island
Addis *Amh.* new
Adrar *Ar., Berb.* mountains
Aiguille *Fr.* peak
Aïn, Aîn (A.) *Ar.* spring
Ákra *Gr.* cape, point
Akrotíri *Gr.* cape, point
Alb *Ger.* mountains
Albufera *Span.* lagoon
-ålen *Nor.* islands
Alpen *Ger.* mountain ranges
Alpes *Fr.* mountains
Alpi *It.* mountains
Alt *Ger.* old
Alta, Alto *Port.* high, upper
Altos *Span.* mountains
-älv, -älven *Swe.* stream, river
Amtskommune (Amt.) *Dan.* first-order administrative division
-ån *Swe.* river
Anse *Fr.* bay
Ao *Thai* bay
Appennino *It.* mountain range
Archipel *Fr.* archipelago
Archipiélago (Arch.) *Span.* archipelago
Arcipélago *It.* archipelago
Arquipélago (Arq.) *Port.* archipelago
Arrecife *Span.* reef
Arroyo (Arr.) *Span.* stream
-ås, -åsen *Nor., Swe.* hill
Ayios *Gr.* island
Ayn *Ar.* well, waterhole

Baai, -baai *Afr., Dut.* bay
Bāb *Ar.* gate, strait
Bäck, -bäcken *Swe.* stream
Back, -backen, *Swe.* hill
Bad, -baden *Ger.* spa
Badia *Cat.* bay
Bādiyah, Bādiyat *Ar.* desert
Bæk *Dan.* stream
Bælt *Dan.* strait
Baharu *Malay* new
Bahia (B.) *Span.* bay
Bahiret *Ar.* lagoon
Bahr *Ar.* sea, lake, river
Bahra Bahrat *Ar.* lake
Baia (B.) *Port.* bay
Baie (B.) *Fr.* bay
Baixa, Baixo *Port.* lower
Baja, Bajo *Span.* lower
Bakke *Nor.* hill
Bala *Farsi* upper
Ballon *Fr.* dome
Baltă *Rom.* marsh, lake
Ban *Lao, Thai* village
-Bana *Jap.* cape
Banc *Fr.* bank
Banco *Span.* bank
Bandao *Chin.* peninsula
Bandar *Ar., Malay* port, harbour
Bandar *Farsi* bay
Banja *Ser.-Cr.* spa, resort
Banjaran *Malay* mountain range
Baraji *Turk.* dam
Barat *Indo., Malay* western
Barrage (Barr.) *Fr.* dam
Barragem (Barr.) *Port.* dam, reservoir
Bas, basse *Fr.* lower
Bassin *Fr.* basin
-batang *Indo.* river
Baṭlaq *Farsi* marsh
Batu *Malay* mountain
Bayt *Heb.* house, village
Bazar *Hin.* market, bazaar
-beek *Afr., Dut.* river
Be'er *Heb.* well
Bei *Chin.* north, northern
Beinn, Ben *Gae.* mountain
Beit *Heb.* village
Belaya, Belo, Beloye, Belyy *Russ.* white
Belogorye *Russ.* hills, mountain range
Bender *Som.* harbour
Berg(e), -berg(e) *Afr., Ger.* mountain(s)
-berg, -en, -et *Nor., Swe.* hill, mountain, rock
Besar *Indo., Malay* big
Bet *Heb.* house, village
Bir, Bîr, Bi'r *Ar.* well
Birkat, Birket *Ar.* lake, marsh, well
Bishti *Alb.* cape
-bjerg *Dan.* hill, point
Blaenau *Welsh* upland
-bo *Chin.* lake
Boca *Port., Span.* river mouth, inlet
Bodden *Ger.* bay, inlet
Bogaz, Boğazı *Turk.* channel, strait
Bogd *Mong.* mountain range
Bois *Fr.* woods
Boka *Ser.-Cr.* gulf, inlet
Bolshoi, Bolshaya, Bolshoye (Bol.) *Russ.* great, large
Bordj (Bj.) *Ar.* fort
-borg *Dan., Nor., Swe.* castle, fort
Bory *Pol.* woods
Bosque *Span.* woods
-botn *Nor.* valley floor
Bouche(s) *Fr.* mouth(s)
Braṭul *Rom.* distributary stream, branch
-bre, -breen *Nor.* glacier
Bredning *Dan.* bay
Brücke *Ger.* bridge
-brug *Dut.* bridge
-brunn *Swe.* well, spring
Bucht *Ger.* bay
Bugt *Dan.* bay
-bugten *Dan.* bay
Buheirat *Ar.* lake, reservoir
Bukit *Malay* hill
-bukt, -a *Nor.* bay
-bukten *Swe.* bay
-bulag *Mong.* spring
Bulag *Chin.* lake
Bulu *Malay* mountain
Bum *Burm.* mountain
Bûr *Ar.* port
Burg. *Ar.* fort
Burg, -burg *Ger.* castle
Burnu, Burun *Turk.* cape
Butt *Gae.* promontory
Büyük *Turk.* big
-by *Dan., Nor., Swe.* town
-byen *Nor., Swe.* town

Cabeza *Span.* peak, hill
Cabo (C.) *Port., Span.* headland, cape
Cachoeira *Port.* waterfall
Cala Cat. *It.* bay
Camp Port. *Span.* land, field
Câmpia *Rom.* plain
Campo *It., Port., Span.* plain
Campos *Span.* upland
Canal (Can.) *Fr., Port., Span.* canal, channel
Canale (Can.) *It.* channel
Canalul (Can.) *Ser.-Cr.* canal
Cao Nguyen *Thai* plateau, tableland
Cap (C.) *Cat., Fr.* cape
Capo (C) *It.* cape
Carn *Gae.* hill
Carse *Gae.* valley
Catarata *Port., Span.* cataract
Cauce *Span.* intermittent stream
Causse *Fr.* limestone plateau
Cay, Cayi, -cay, -cayi *Turk.* river
Cayo(s) *Span.* rock(s), islet(s)
Cefn *Welsh* hill
Cerro *Span.* hill, peak
Česká, Český, České *Czec.* Czech
Chaco *Span.* jungle
Chaîne(s) *Fr.* mountain range(s)
Chang *Chin.* mountain
Chapa *Span.* hills, upland
Chapada *Port.* hills, upland
Chaung *Burm.* stream, river
Chi *Chin.* salt lake
-ch'ŏn *Kor.* river
-chŏsuji *Kor.* reservoir
Chott *Ar.* salt lake, depression
Chu *Tib.* river
Chute *Fr.* waterfall
Città *It.* city
Ciudad *Span.* city
Co *Tib.* lake
Cochilla (Coch.) *Port.* hills
Col *Fr., It.* pass
Colina(s) *Span.* hill(s)
Colle *It.* pass
Colline(s) *Fr.* hill(s)
Conca *It.* plain, basin
Cordillera (Cord.) *Span.* mountain range
Costa *It., Port., Span.* coast
Côte *Fr.* coast, slope, hill
Coteaux *Fr.* hills
Cuchilla *Span.* hills
Cuenca *Span.* river basin
Cu-Lao *Viet.* island

Da *Chin.* big
Da *Viet.* river
Daban *Mong.* pass
Dağ(ı) *Turk.* mountain(s)
Dāgh *Farsi* mountain
Dağları *Turk.* mountain range
-dai, -daichi *Jap.* plateau
-Dake *Jap.* mountain
-dal, -e *Dan., Swe.* valley
-dal, -en *Swe., Nor.* valley, stream
Dalay Mong. large lake
-ðalir, -ðalur *Ice.* valley
-damm, -en *Swe.* lake
Danau *Malay* lake
Dao *Chin., Viet.* island
Dar *Ar.* region
Darya *Russ.* river
Daryācheh *Farsi* marshy lake, lake
Dasht *Farsi* desert, steppe
Daung *Burm.* mountain, hill
Dayr *Ar.* monastery
Debre *Amh.* hill
Deli *Ser.-Cr.* mountain
Deniz, -i *Turk.* sea
Département (Dépt.) *Fr.* first-order administrative division
Dere *Turk.* stream
Desierto (Des.) *Span.* desert
Détroit *Fr.* strait
Dhar *Ar.* region, mountain range
Diep *Dut.* channel
Dijk *Dut.* dyke
Ding *Chin.* mountain
Dingzi *Chin.* hill, mountain
Djebel (Dj.) *Ar.* mountain
-djúp *Ice.* fjord
-djupet *Swe.* channel, sound
-Do *Jap., Kor.* island
Dolina *Russ.* valley
Dolna, Dolni *Bulg.* lower
Dolna, Dolne, Dolny *Russ.* lower
Dolni *Czec.* lower
Dolok (D.) *Malay* mountain
-dong *Kor.* village, town
Dong *Chin.* east, eastern
Donja, Donji *Ser.-Cr.* lower
-dorf *Ger.* village
-dorp *Afr.* village
-drif *Afr.* ford
-dybet *Dan.* marine channel
Dzong *Tib.* town, settlement
Dzüün *Mong.* east, eastern

-egga *Nor.* peak
-eiland, -en (eil.) *Afr., Dut.* island(s)
Eilean *Gae.* island
-elv, -a *Nor.* river
Embalse *Span.* reservoir
'Emeq *Heb.* plain, valley
Ensenada *Span.* bay
Erg *Ar.* sand desert
Estero *Span.* estuary
Estrada *Span.* bay
Estrecho *Span.* strait
Estuaire *Fr.* estuary
Estuario *Span.* estuary
Étang *Fr.* lagoon, lake
-ey, -jar *Ice.* island(s)
-ežeras *Lith.* lake
-ezers *Lat.* lake

Falaise *Fr.* cliff
-fallet *Swe.* waterfall
Farihy *Malag.* lake
Faro *Span.* lighthouse
-feld *Ger.* field
-fell *Ice.* mountain, hill
Feng *Chin.* mountain range
Fiume (F.) *It.* river
-fjäll, -en, -et *Swe.* hill(s), mountain(s), ridge
-fjärden *Swe.* fjord
Fjeld *Dan.* mountain
-fjell, -et *Nor.* mountain range
-fjord, -en *Dan., Nor., Swe.* fjord
-fjorður *Ice.* fjord, bay, inlet
Fleuve (Fl.) *Fr.* river
-flói *Ice.* bay, marshy country
Fluss (F.) *Ger.* river
Foce, Foci *It.* mouth(s)
Folyó (F.) *Hung.* river
-fonn *Nor.* glacier
-fontein *Afr.* fountain, spring
Forêt *Fr.* forest
-fors, -en *Swe.* waterfall, rapids
-foss, -en *Ice., Nor.* waterfall
Forst *Ger.* forest
Foum *Ar.* pass
Fuente *Span.* source
-furt *Ger.* ford
Fylke *Nor.* first-order administrative division

-gang *Chin.* bay, harbour
-gang *Kor.* river
Ganga *Hin., Sin.* river
Gangri *Tib.* mountain
Gaoyuan *Chin.* plateau
-gat *Dan.* sound
-Gata *Jap.* lake
-gau *Ger.* district
-Gawa *Jap.* river
Gebel (G.) *Ar.* mountain
Gebirge (Geb.) *Ger.* hills, mountains
Gezirat, Geziret *Ar.* island
Ghat *Hin.* range of hills
Ghiol *Rom.* lake
Ghubbat *Ar.* bay, inlet
Gjiri *Alb.* bay
Gjol *Alb.* lagoon, lake
Glava (Gl.) *Ser.-Cr.* mountain, peak
Glen *Gae.* valley
Gletscher (Gl.) *Ger.* glacier
Gobi *Mong.* desert
Gol *Mong.* river
Göl *Azeri, Turk.* lake
Golfe (G.) *Fr.* gulf
Golfo (G.) *It., Span.* gulf
Gölü *Turk.* lake
Gomba *Tib.* settlement
Gora, Góra *Bulg., Russ., Ser.-Cr., Pol.* mountain
Gorje *Ser.-Cr.* hills, mountains
Gorno *Russ.* mountainous
-gorod *Russ.* small town
Gory, Góry *Pol., Russ.* mountain
-grad *Bulg. Russ., Ser.-Cr.* town, city
-grada *Russ.* ridge
Gran *It., Span.* big, great
Grand, -e *Fr.* big, great
Groot (Gt.) *Afr., Dut.* big, great
Gross, -e, -en, -er *Ger.* big, great(er)
Grupo *Span.* group
Gruppo *It.* group
Guan *Chin.* pass
Guba (G.) *Russ.* bay
-Guntō *Jap.* island group
Gunong, Gunung (G.) *Indo., Malay* mountain
Gurā *Rom.* passage

Hadabat *Ar.* plateau
Hadjer *Ar.* mountain
-hafen *Ger.* harbour, port
Haff *Ger.* bay, lagoon
Hai *Chin.* lake, sea
Haixia *Chin.* channel, strait
Halbinsel *Ger.* peninsula
Halvø *Dan.* peninsula
Halvøya *Nor.* peninsula
Hāmad, Hamada, Hammādah, Hammādat *Ar.* stony desert, plateau
-hamn *Swe., Nor.* harbour, anchorage
Hāmūn *Farsi* marsh, lake
-Hantō *Jap.* peninsula
Har(e) *Heb.* hill(s), mountain(s)
Hassi (Hi.) *Ar.* well
-haug *Nor.* hill
Hav, Havet *Nor., Swe.* sea
-havn *Dan., Nor.* bay, harbour
Havre *Fr.* harbour
Hawd *Ar.* oasis
Hawr *Ar.* lake, marsh
He *Chin.* river
-hegység *Hung.* hills, forest
Heide *Ger.* heath, moor
Helodranon' *Malag.* bay
Higashi *Jap.* east, eastern
-ho *Kor.* lake
-hø *Nor.* peak
Hoch *Ger.* high
Hochland *Afr.* highland
Hoek, -hoek *Afr., Dut.* cape, point
-höfn *Ice.* harbour, port
-hög, -en, -högar, -högarna *Swe.* hill(s), peak, mountain
Höhe *Ger.* height
Hohen *Ger.* high, upper
-hoi *Chin.* bay
-høj, -e *Dan.* hills
-holm, -holme, -holmen *Dan., Nor., Swe.* island
Hon *Viet.* island
Hoog *Dut.* high
Hora *Czec., Ukr.* mountain
-horn *Ger.* peak
Hory *Czec.* mountains, hills
-hot *Mong.* town
-hoved *Dan.* point, headland, peninsula
-hrad *Czec.* town
Hráun *Ice.* lava
-hsi *Chin.* river
-hsia *Chin.* gorge, strait
-hsien *Chin.* district
Hu *Chin.* lake, reservoir
Huk *Dan., Ger.* cape
-huk *Swe.* cape
Huken *Nor.* cape

Idd *Ar.* well
Idehan *Ar., Berb.* sandy plain, dunes
-ike *Jap.* lake
Île(s) (I(s).) *Fr.* island(s)
Ilha(s) (I(s).) *Port.* island(s)
imeni *Russ.* 'in the name of'
Inish *Gae.* island
Insel(n) (I.) *Ger.* island(s)
Irmak *Turk.* river
'Irq *Ar.* dunes
Isla(s) (I(s).) *Span.* island(s)
Iso *Fin.* big, great
Isol, -a, -e (I.) *It.* island(s)
Isthme *Fr.* isthmus
Istmo *Span.* isthmus
-iwa *Jap.* island

Jabal *Ar.* mountain range
Järv *Est.* lake
järvi *Fin.* lake, bay, pond
-jaur, -javre *Lapp.* lake
Jazā'ir *Ar.* islands
Jazīra, jazīrat *Ar.* island
Jazireh *Farsi* island
Jebel *Ar.* mountain
Jezero *Ser.-Cr.* lake
Jezioro *Pol.* lake
Jiang *Chin.* river
Jiao *Chin.* cape
-Jima *Jap.* island
Jøkulen *Nor.* glacier, ice cap
-joki *Fin.* river
-jökull *Ice.* glacier, ice cap
Jūras Līcis *Lat.* bay, gulf

Kaap (K.) *Afr.* cape
-kai *Jap.* bay, channel, sea
-kaikyō *Jap.* strait
-kaise *Lapp.* mountain
kalnas *Lith.* hill
Kamennyy *Russ.* stony
Kampong *Cam.* village
Kampung *Malay* village
-kanaal *Dut.* canal
Kanal *Dan.* channel, gulf
Kanal *Ger., Swe.* canal
-kanal *Ser.-Cr.* channel, canal
Kanava *Fin.* canal
Kang *Kor.* river, bay
Kap (K.) *Dan., Ger.* cape, point
-kapp *Nor.* cape, point
-kaupstaður *Ice.* market town
-kaupunki *Fin.* town
Kavīr *Farsi* salt desert
Kébir *Ar.* great
Kecil *Malay* lesser, little
Kefar *Heb.* village, hamlet
-Ken *Jap.* first-order administrative division
Kep, -i (K.) *Alb.* cape
Kepulauan (Kep.) *Indo., Malay* archipelago
Keski- *Fin.* middle, central
Khalīg, Khalīj *Ar.* gulf
-khamba *Tib.* source, spring
Khawr *Ar.* bay, channel, wadi
Khlong *Thai* river
Kho Khot *Thai* isthmus
Khōr *Farsi* bay, estuary
Khrebet *Russ.* mountain range
Kita- *Jap.* north
Klein,-e, -er *Ger.* small
-klint *Dan.* cliff
Klintar *Swe.* hills
-kloof *Afr.* gorge, pass
Knude *Dan.* point
-Ko *Jap.* lake
Ko *Thai* island
-kōchi *Jap.* mountainous region
-kōgen *Jap.* plateau
Kohi *Pash.* mountains
Kol *Kaz., Kyrg.* lake
Kólpos *Gr., Turk.* gulf, bay
Kolymskoye *Russ.* mountain range
Kompong *Malay* landing place
-kop *Afr.* hill
-kopf *Ger.* hill
-köping *Swe.* market town
Körfäzi *Azeri* gulf
Körfezi *Turk.* gulf
Kosa *Russ., Ukr.* spit
-koski *Fin.* rapids
-kraal *Afr.* native village
-kraj *Czec., Pol., Ser.-Cr.* region
Krasnyy *Russ.* red
Kryazh *Russ.* ridge, hills
Kuala *Malay* bay
-kuan *Chin.* pass
Kūh(ha) *Farsi* mountain(s)
Kul *Russ.* lake
-kulle *Swe.* hill
Kum *Russ.* sandy desert
Kumpu *Fin.* hill
Kwe *Burm.* bay, gulf
-kylä *Fin.* village
Kyst, -en *Dan., Nor.* coast
Kyun(zu) *Burm.* island(s)

La *Tib.* pass
-laagte *Afr.* watercourse

Lääni *Fin.* first-order administrative division
Lac (L.) *Fr.* lake
Lacul (L.) *Rom.* lake, lagoon
Lago (L.) *It., Port., Span.* lake, lagoon
Lagoa (L.) *Port.* lagoon
Lagos *Port., Span.* lakes
Laguna (L.) *It., Span.* lagoon, lake
Lagune (L.) *Fr.* lake
-laht *Est.* bay
Lahti *Fin.* bay, gulf, cove
Lakhti *Russ.* bay, gulf
Lam *Thai* river
Lampi *Fin.* lake
Län *Swe.* first-order administrative division
Land *Ger.* first-order administrative division
-land *Dan.* region
-land *Afr., Nor.* land, province
Lande *Fr.* heath
Laut *Indo.* sea
Law *Gae.* hill, mountain
Līcis *Lat.* gulf
Lido *It.* beach, shore
Liedao *Chin.* islands
Lilla *Swe.* small
Lille *Dan., Nor.* small
Liman *Russ.* bay, gulf
Límni (L.) *Gr.* lake
Ling *Chin.* mountain range
-linna *Fin.* fort
Llano *Span.* prairie, plain
Llyn *Welsh* lake
Loch (L.) *Gae.* lake, inlet
Lough (L.) *Gae.* lake, inlet
Lum *Alb.* river
Lund *Dan.* forest
-lund, -en *Swe.* wood(s)
-luoto *Fin.* island

-maa *Est.* island
Madīnat *Ar.* town, city
Madiq *Ar.* strait
Maja *Alb.* mountains
-mäki *Fin.* hill, hillside
Mal *Alb.* mountain
Maloye, Malyy, Malyya *Russ.* little, small
Mala, Mali, Malo *Ser.-Cr.* little, small
Malaya *Belo.* small
Malé *Czec., Slovak* small
Mali *Alb.* mountain
-man *Kor.* bay
Mar *Span.* lagoon, sea
Marais *Fr.* marsh
Mare *It.* sea
Mare *Rom.* great
Marisma *Span.* marsh
-mark *Dan., Nor.* land
Marsâ *Ar.* anchorage, bay, inlet
Masabb *Ar.* river mouth, estuary
Massif *Fr.* upland, mountains
Mato *Port.* forest
Mazar *Farsi* shrine, tomb
Meer, -meer *Afr., Dut., Ger.* lake, sea
-men *Chin.* bay, gorge, channel
Mesto *Ser.-Cr., Czec.* town
Mezzo *It.* middle
Midbar *Heb.* wilderness
Mierzeja *Pol.* spit
Mifraz *Heb.* bay
Mina *Ar.* port
Minami *Jap.* south, southern
-misaki *Jap.* cape, point
Mittel *Ger.* central, middle
-mo *Nor., Swe.* heath, island
-mon *Swe.* heath
Mong *Burm.* town
Mont(s) (Mt(s).) *Fr.* hill(s), mountain(s)
Montagna (Mt.) *It.* mountain
Montagne(s) (Mt(s).) *Fr.* hill(s), mountain(s)
Montaña(s) (Mt(s).) *Span.* mountain(s)
Montanyes *Cat.* mountains
Monte(s) (Mte(s).) *It., Port., Span.* mountain(s)
Monti (Mti.) *It.* mountains
More *Russ.* sea
Mörön *Mong.* river
Moyen *Fr.* central, middle
Muang *Malay* town
Mui *Viet.* cape
Mull *Gae.* promontory
Mund, -mund *Afr.* mouth
Munkhafed *Ar.* depression
Munte (Mte.) *Rom.* mount
Munți(i) (Mti.) *Rom.* mountain(s)
Muong *Malay* village
Myit *Burm.* river
Myitwanya *Burm.* mouths of river
Mynydd *Welsh* mountain
-myr *Nor., Swe.* swamp
-mýri *Ice.* swamp
Mys (M.) *Russ.* cape

-Nada *Jap.* bay, gulf
-næs *Dan.* point, cape
Nafūd *Ar.* sandy desert
Nagorye *Russ.* hills, mountains
Nagy *Hung.* big
Nahal (N.) *Heb.* river
Nahr (N.) *Ar.* river, stream
Najd *Ar.* plateau, pass
Nakhon *Thai* town
Nam *Kor., Viet.* river
-nam *Kor.* south
Namakzār *Per.* salt flat
Nan *Chin.* south, southern
-nao *Chin.* lake
-näs *Swe.* cape
Neder *Dut.* lower
Nedre *Nor.* lower
Nei *Chin.* inner
Nek *Afr.* pass
-nes *Ice., Nor.* cape
Ness, -ness *Gae.* promontory, cape
Nevada, Nevado *Span.* snow-capped mountain
Nez *Fr.* cape
Nieder *Ger.* lower
-niemi *Fin.* cape, point, peninsula, island
Nieuw, -e *Dut.* new
Nishi *Jap.* west, western
Nisos, Nisoi *Gr.* island(s)
Nizhneye, Nizhniy *Russ.* lower
Nizina *Belo., Pol.* lowland
Nizmennost *Russ.* plain, lowland
Nízní *Czec.* lower
Noord *Dut.* north, northern
Nord *Fr.* north, northern
Norra *Swe.* north, northern
Nørre *Dan.* north, northern
Norte *Port., Span.* north, northern
Nos *Bulg., Russ.* cape, point
Nosy *Malag.* island
Nouveau, Nouvelle *Fr.* new
Nova, Novi *Bulg., Port., Serb.-Cr.* new
Novaya, Novo, Novoye, Novyy *Russ.* new
Nové, Novy *Czec., Slovak* new
Novo *Port.* new
Nowa, Nowe, Nowy *Pol.* new
Nudo *Span.* mountain
Nueva, Nuevo *Span.* new
Nur *Chin.* lake
Nur *Tib.* peak
Nuruu *Mong.* mountain range
Nusa *Indo.* island
Nuur *Mong.* lake
Ny *Dan., Nor., Swe.* new

-ø *Dan., Nor.* island
-ö *Swe.* island,
-öar, -na *Swe.* islands
Ober *Ger., Ukr.* upper
Oblast *Russ.* administrative division
Öbor *Mong.* inner
Occidental *Fr., Span.* western
-odde *Dan., Nor.* point, peninsula, cape
Oeste *Span.* west, western
Oglat *Ar.* well
Oji *Alb.* bay
Ojo *Span.* spring
-Oki *Jap.* bay
-ön *Swe.* island
Ondör *Mong.* upper
Oost(er) *Dut.* east(ern)
Orașu *Rom.* city
Ord *Gae.* point
Óri *Gr.* mountains
Oriental, -e *Fr., Span.* east, eastern
Órmos *Gr.* bay
Óros *Gr.* mountain(s)
Ort *Ger.* point, cape
Ost *Ger.* east
Øst(er) *Den., Nor.* east(ern)
Öst(ra) *Swe.* east(ern)
Ostriv *Ukr.* island
Ostrov(a) *Russ.* island(s)
Otok(i) *Ser.-Cr.* island(s)
Ouabi, Ouadi (O.) *Ar.* dry watercourse, wadi
Oud, -e *Dut.* old
Oued, -i (O.) *Ar.* watercourse
Ouest *Fr.* west, western
Ouzan *Farsi* river
Ova, -si *Turk.* plains, lowlands
Over- *Dan., Dut.* upper
Över-, Övre *Nor., Swe.* upper
-øy, -a *Nor.* island(s)
Oya *Hin.* point
Oya *Sin.* river
Ozero, Ozera (Oz.) *Russ., Ukr.* lake(s)

-pää *Fin.* hill(s), mountain
Pahta *Lapp.* hill
Pampa(s) *Span.* plain(s)
Pantanal *Port.* marsh
Pantano *Span.* reservoir
Pantao *Chin.* peninsula
Parbat *Urdu* mountain
Pas *Fr.* strait
Paso (P.) *Span.* pass
Passage *Fr.* channel
Passe *Fr.* channel
Passo (P.) *It.* pass
Pasul (P.) *Rom.* pass
Patam *Hin.* small village
Patna, -patnam *Hin.* small village
Pegunungan *Indo., Malay* mountain range
Pei, -pei *Chin.* north
Pélagos *Gr.* sea
Pen *Welsh* hill
Peña *Span.* rock, peak
Pendi *Chin.* basin, depression
Péninsule *Fr.* peninsula
Penisola (Pen.) *It.* peninsula
Pereval (Per.) *Russ.* pass
Pervo-, Pervyy- *Russ.* first
Pertuis *Fr.* channel, strait
Peski *Russ.* sand desert
Petit, -e *Fr.* small
Phanom *Thai* mountain
Phnum *Cam.* mountain
Phou *Lao.* mountain
Phu *Thai, Viet.* mountain
Piano *It.* plain
Pic *Cat., Fr.* peak
Pico(s) *Span.* peak(s)
-piggen *Dan.* peak
Pik *Russ.* peak
Pingyuan *Chin.* plain
Pique *Fr.* peak
Piton *Fr.* peak
Pivostriv *Ukr.* peninsula
Piz, Pizzo *It.* peak
Plage *Fr.* beach
Plaine *Fr.* plain
Planalto *Port.* plateau
Planina (Pl.) *Bulg., Ser.-Cr.* mountain range
Plato *Russ., Bulg.* plateau
Playa *Span.* beach
-po *Chin.* lake, wetland
Pointe (Pte.) *Fr.* point, cape
Pojezierze *Pol.* lakes
Polder *Dut.* reclaimed farmland
-pólis *Gr.* city, town
Poluostrov (Pov.) *Russ.* peninsula
Półwysep *Pol.* peninsula
Pont *Fr.* bridge
Ponta (Pta.) *Port.* point, cape
Ponte *Port.* bridge
Poort *Afr.* passage, gate
-poort *Dut.* port
Porta *Port.* pass
Porțile *Rom.* gate
Portillo *Span.* pass
Porto *It., Port., Span.* port
Potámi, Potamós *Gr.* river
Pradesh *Hin.* state
Praia *Port.* beach, shore
Presa *Span.* reservoir
Presqu'île *Fr.* peninsula
Prokhod *Bulg.* pass
Proliv *Russ.* strait
Promontorio *Span.* promontory
Průsmyk (Pr.) *Czec.* pass
Pueblo *Span.* village
Puerto (Pto.) *Span.* port
Puig *Cat.* peak
Pulau (P.) *Indo., Malay* island
Puna *Span.* desert plateau
Puncak *Indo.* peak
Punta (Pta.) *It., Span.* point, peak
Puy *Fr.* peak

Qal'at *Ar.* fort
Qanat *Ar.* canal
Qasr *Ar.* fort
Qiryat *Heb.* town
Qiuling *Chin.* plateau
Qolleh *Farsi* mountain
-qundao *Chin.* islands

Rach *Viet.* river
Rags *Lat.* cape
Rambla *Cat.* river
Ramlat *Ar.* sandy desert
Rão (R.) *Port.* river
Rann *Hin.* swampy region
Rao *I.-C.* river
Ras *Amh., Ar., Farsi* cape, point
Récif(s) *Fr.* reef(s)
Recife(s) *Port.* reef(s)
Reka *Bulg.* river
Repede *Rom.* rapids
Reprêsa *Port.* reservoir
Reshteh *Farsi* mountain range
-rettō *Jap.* group of islands, chain
Ria *Port., Span.* estuary, bay
Ribeirão (R.) *Port.* river
Ribera (R.) *Span.* river bank
Rijeka *Ser.-Cr.* river
Rio (R.) *Port., Span.* river
Rivier (R.) *Afr., Dut.* river
Riviera *It.* coastal plain, coast
Rivière (R.) *Fr.* river
Roca *Span.* rock
Rocca *It.* rock, peak
Roche *Fr.* rock
Rt *Ser.-Cr.* cape, point
Rubh', Rubha *Gae.* cape, point
-rück *Ger.* ridge
Rūd *Farsi* stream, river
Rudohorie *Slovak* mountains
Rzeka (R.) *Pol.* river

-saar *Est.* island
-saari *Fin.* island
Sabkhat, Sabkhet *Ar.* salt flats
Sadd *Ar.* dam
Sagar,-a *Hin., Urdu* lake
Sahrâ *Ar.* desert
-Saki *Jap.* cape, point
Salar *Span.* salt flat
Salina(s) *Span.* salt marsh(es)
-salmi *Fin.* strait, sound, lake, channel
Saltsjöbad *Swe.* resort
-Sammyaku *Jap.* mountain range
Samut *Thai* gulf
San (S.) *It., Port., Span.* saint
-San *Jap., Kor.* hill, mountain
-Sanchi *Jap.* mountain range
Sankt (St.) *Ger., Russ.* saint
-sanmaek *Kor.* mountain range
-sanmyaku *Jap.* mountain range
Santa (Sta.) *It., Port., Span.* saint
Santo (Sto.) *It. Port., Span.* saint
São (S.) *Port.* saint
Sarīr *Ar.* desert
Sasso *It.* mountain
Satu *Rom.* village
Saurums *Lat.* strait
Sebkha, Sebkhet *Ar.* salt flat
See, -see *Ger.* lake
-şehir *Turk.* town
Selat *Indo., Malay* strait
Selatan *Indo.* southern
-selkä *Fin.* bay, lake, ridge, hills
Selo *Ser.-Cr., Russ.* village
Selva *Port., Span.* forest, wood
Seno *Span.* bay, sound
Serir *Ar.* stony desert
Serra (Sa.) *Cat., Port.* range of hills
Serranía *Span.* mountain ridge
Severo, Severnaya, Severnoye, Severnyy (Sev.) *Russ.* north, northern
Sfântu *Rom.* saint
Shahr, -shahr *Farsi* city, town
Shamo *Chin.* desert
Shan *Chin.* hills, mountains
Shankou *Chin.* pass
Shanmo *Chin.* mountain range
Sharm *Ar.* bay
Shatt *Ar.* river mouth, estuary
-Shima *Jap.* island
Shimāli *Ar.* northern
-Shotō *Jap.* group of islands
-shui *Chin.* river
-shuiku *Chin.* reservoir
Sierra (Sa.) *Span.* mountain range
-sjö, -sjön, -sjø *Swe., Nor.* lake
-sjøen *Dan.* sea
-sjór *Ice.* lake
-sker *Ice.* island
-skär *Swe.* island, rock, cape
-skog, -skogen *Nor., Swe.* wood(s)
-skov *Dan.* forest
Slieve *Gae.* hill, mountain
Sø *Dan., Nor.* lake
Söder, Södra *Swe.* south, southern
Sør *Nor.* south, southern
Solonchak *Russ.* salt lake, marsh
Sønder, Søndra *Dan.* south, southern
Song *Viet.* river
Souk *Ar.* market
-spitze *Ger.* peak, mountain
-spruit *Afr.* stream
Sredna, Sredno *Bulg.* middle, central
Sredne, Sredneye *Russ.* middle, central
Srednja *Ser.-Cr.* middle, central
-stad *Afr., Nor., Swe.* town
-stadt *Ger.* town
-staður *Ice.* town
Stara, Stari *Ser.-Cr.* old
Stará, Staré, Stary *Czec.* old
Staraya, Staroye, Staryy *Russ.* old
Stare, Staro, Stary *Ukr.* old
Stausee *Ger.* reservoir
Stenón *Gr.* strait, pass
Step *Russ.* steppe
Stor, -a *Swe.* big
Store *Dan.* big
-strand *Dan., Ger., Nor., Swe.* beach
-strede *Nor.* straits
Strelka *Russ.* spit
-strete *Nor.* straits
Stretto (Str.) *It.* strait
Strædet (Str.) *Dan.* strait
-ström, -strömmen *Swe.* stream(s)
-stroom *Afr.* large river
Sud *Fr.* south, southern
Süd, -er *Ger.* south, southern
Suid *Afr.* south, southern
-Suidō *Jap.* strait, channel
Sul *Port.* south, southern
Sûn *Burm.* cape
-sund, -et *Swe., Nor.* sound, estuary, inlet
Sungai *Indo., Malay* river
Sur *Span.* south, southern
Sveti *Bulg.* saint
Syd *Dan., Swe.* south, southern
Sýsla *Ice.* first-order administrative division

-tag *Uighur* mountain
Tai -tai *Chin.* tower
-Take *Jap.* mountain
Tal *Mong.* plain, steppe
-tal *Ger.* valley
Tall *Ar.* hills
Tanjona *Malag.* cape, point
Tanjung, Tanjong (Tg.) *Indo., Malay.* cape, point
Tao *Chin.* island
Tasik *Malay* lake
Tassili *Ar.* rocky plateau
Tau *Russ.* mountain range
Taung *Burm.* mountain
Taungdan. *Burm.* mountain range
Taunggya *Burm.* pass
-tekojärvi *Fin.* reservoir
Teluk *Indo., Malay* bay, gulf
Ténéré *Berb.* desert
Tengah *Indo.* middle, central
-thal *Ger.* valley
Thok *Tib.* town
Tien *Chin.* lake, marsh
Tierra *Span.* land, country
Timur *Indo.* eastern
-tind *Nor.* peak
-ting *Chin.* mountain
Tjärn, -en, -et *Swe.* lake
-Tō *Jap.* island
Tong *Kor.* village, town
Tong *Burm., Thai, Kor.* mountain range
Tonlé *Cam.* lake
Top *Dut.* peak
-topp, -en *Nor.* peak
-träsk *Swe.* lake, swamp
Tsangpo *Tib.* large river
Tso *Tib.* lake
Tsu *Jap.* entrance, bay
Tsui *Chin.* cape, point
Tulur *Ar.* hill
-tunturi *Fin.* hill(s), mountain(s), ridge

Uad *Ar.* dry watercourse, wadi
Über *Ger.* upper
-udde, -udden *Swe.* point, cape
Uebi *Som.* river
Ujung *Indo., Malay* cape
Unter- *Ger.* lower
Us *Mong.* water
Ust, Ustye *Russ.* river mouth
Utara *Indo.* north, northern
Uttar *Hin.* north, northern
Uul *Mong., Russ.* mountain range

-vaara *Fin.* hill, mountain ridge, peak
Vaart *Dut.* canal
-våg *Nor.* bay
Val *Fr., Port., Span.* valley
Valea *Rom.* valley
-vall, -en *Swe.* mountain
Valle *It., Span.* valley
Vallée *Fr.* valley
Valli *It.* lake, lagoon
-város *Hung.* town
-varre *Nor.* mountain
Väst, Västra *Swe.* west, western
-vatn *Ice., Nor.* lake
-vatnet *Nor.* lake
-vatten, vattnet *Swe.* lake
-vecchio *It.* old
Vechi *Rom.* old
-ved, -veden *Swe.* hills
Veld, -veld *Afr.* field
Velha, Velho *Port.* old
Velika, Velike, Veliki, Veliko *Ser.-Cr., Slov.* big, large
Velikaya, Velikiy *Russ.* big, large
Velká, Velké, Velký *Czec.* big, large
Verkhne, Verkhniy *Russ.* upper
-vesi *Fin.* water, lake, bay, sound, strait
Vest, Vester, Vestre *Dan., Nor.* west, western
-vidda *Nor.* plateau
Vieille, Vieux *Fr.* old
Vieja, Vejo *Span.* old
Vig *Dan.* bay, inlet, cove, lagoon, lake
-vik *Ice.* bay
-vik, -a, -en *Nor., Swe.* bay, gulf, inlet, lake
Vila *Port.* small town
Villa *Span.* town
Ville *Fr.* town
Vinh *Viet.* bay
Vîrful (Vf.) *Rom.* peak, mountain
-viz *Hung.* river
-víztároló *Hung.* reservoir
-vlei *Afr.* lake, salt pan
-vliet *Dut.* canal
-vloer *Afr.* salt pan
Vodokhranilishche (Vdkhr.) *Russ.* reservoir
Vodoskovyshche (Vdskh.) *Ukr.* reservoir
Volcán (Vol.) *Span.* volcano, mountain
Vorota *Russ.* pass, channel, strait
Vostochno, Vostochnyy *Russ.* east, eastern
-vötn *Ice.* lakes
Vozvyshennost *Russ.* heights, uplands
Vozyera *Belo.* lake
Vrata *Bulg.* gate, pass
Vrchovina *Czec.* mountainous country
Vrch(y) *Czec.* mountain (range)
Vung *Viet.* bay, gulf
-vuori *Fin.* mountain, hill
Vychodné *Slovak* east, eastern
Vysochyna *Ukr.* upland

-waard *Dut.* polder
Wadi (W.) *Ar.* dry watercourse
Wâhât *Ar.* oasis
Wald *Ger.* forest, mountains
-Wan *Chin., Jap.* bay, harbour
Wāw *Ar.* well
Webi *Amh.* river
Wes *Afr.* west, western
Wielka, Wielki, Wielko *Pol.* big, large
Woestyn *Afr.* desert
Wysoka, Wysoki *Pol.* upper
Wyżyna *Pol.* plateau

Xi *Chin.* river
Xia *Chin.* gorge, strait
Xiao *Chin.* small

Yam *Heb.* sea
-Yama *Jap.* mountain
-yan *Chin.* gorge, island
Yang *Chin.* bay, sea, sound
Yangi *Russ.* new
Yazovir *Bulg.* reservoir
Yeni *Turk.* new
Yli *Fin.* upper
Ynys *Welsh* island
Yoma *Burm.* mountain range
Ytre-, Ytter- *Nor., Swe.* outer
-yuan *Chin.* stream
Yugo- *Ser.-Cr.* south, southern
Yunhe *Chin.* canal
Yuzhni, Yuzhno *Russ.* south, southern

-Zaki *Jap.* point
Zalew *Pol.* lagoon, swamp
Zaliv *Russ.* bay, gulf
-Zan *Jap.* mountain
Zangbo *Tib.* stream, river
Zapadnaya, Zapadno, Zapadnyi (Zap.) *Russ.* west, western
Zatoka *Pol., Ukr.* bay, gulf
-zee *Dut.* lake, sea
Zemlya *Russ.* land, island(s)
Zhang *Chin.* mountain
-zhou *Chin.* island
Zhong *Chin.* middle, central
Zhou *Chin.* island
Zizhiqu *Chin.* autonomous region
Zuid, Zuider *Dut.* south, southern

INDEX TO WORLD MAPS

HOW TO USE THE INDEX

The index contains the names of all the principal places and features shown on the World and City Maps. Each name is followed by an additional entry in italics giving the country or region within which it is located. The alphabetical order of names composed of two or more words is governed primarily by the first word, then by the second, and then by the country or region name that follows. This is an example of the rule:

Mir *Niger* 14°5N 11°59E **259** F2
Mīr Kūh *Iran* 26°22N 58°55E **247** E8
Mīr Shahdād *Iran* 26°15N 58°29E **247** E8
Mira *Italy* 45°26N 12°8E **199** C9

Physical features composed of a proper name (Erie) and a description (Lake) are positioned alphabetically by the proper name. The description is positioned after the proper name and is usually abbreviated:

Erie, L. *N. Amer.* 42°15N 81°0W **312** D4

Where a description forms part of a settlement or administrative name, however, it is always written in full and put in its true alphabetical position:

Mount Olive *U.S.A.* 39°4N 89°44W **310** E7

Names beginning with M' and Mc are indexed as if they were spelled Mac. Names beginning St. are alphabetized under Saint, but Sankt, Sint, Sant', Santa and San are all spelt in full and are alphabetized accordingly. If the same place name occurs two or more times in the index and all are in the same country, each is followed by the name of the administrative subdivision in which it is located.

The geographical co-ordinates which follow each name in the index give the latitude and longitude of each place. The first co-ordinate indicates latitude – the distance north or south of the Equator. The second co-ordinate indicates longitude – the distance east or west of the Greenwich Meridian. Both latitude and longitude are measured in degrees and minutes (there are 60 minutes in a degree). Latitude and longitude references are not used on the Central Area City Maps.

The latitude is followed by N(orth) or S(outh) and the longitude by E(ast) or W(est).

The number in bold type which follows the geographical co-ordinates refers to the number of the map page where that feature or place will be found. This is usually the largest scale at which the place or feature appears.

The letter and figure that are immediately after the page number give the grid square on the map page, within which the feature is situated. The letter represents the latitude and the figure the longitude. A lower-case letter immediately after the page number refers to an inset map on that page.

In some cases the feature itself may fall within the specified square, while the name is outside. This is usually the case only with features that are larger than a grid square.

Rivers are indexed to their mouths or confluences, and carry the symbol → after their names. The following symbols are also used in the index: ■ country, ◪ overseas territory or dependency, □ first-order administrative area, ☆ U.S. county, △ national park, ⌓ other park (provincial park, nature reserve or game reserve), ☼ Australian aboriginal land, ⋏ U.S. Indian reservation, ✈ (LHR) principal airport (and location identifier).

HOW TO PRONOUNCE PLACE NAMES

English-speaking people usually have no difficulty in reading and pronouncing correctly English place names. However, foreign place name pronunciations may present many problems. Such problems can be minimized by following some simple rules. However, these rules cannot be applied to all situations, and there will be many exceptions.

1. In general, stress each syllable equally, unless your experience suggests otherwise.
2. Pronounce the letter 'a' as a broad 'a' as in 'arm'.
3. Pronounce the letter 'e' as a short 'e' as in 'elm'.
4. Pronounce the letter 'i' as a cross between a short 'i' and long 'e', as the two 'i's in 'California'.
5. Pronounce the letter 'o' as an intermediate 'o' as in 'soft'.
6. Pronounce the letter 'u' as an intermediate 'u' as in 'sure'.
7. Pronounce consonants hard, except in the Romance-language areas where 'g's are likely to be pronounced softly like 'j' in 'jam'; 'j' itself may be pronounced as 'y'; and 'x's may be pronounced as 'h'.
8. For names in mainland China, pronounce 'q' like the 'ch' in 'chin', 'x' like the 'sh' in 'she', 'zh' like the 'j' in 'jam', and 'z' as if it were spelled 'dz'. In general, pronounce 'a' as in 'father', 'e' as in 'but', 'i' as in 'keep', 'o' as in 'or', and 'u' as in 'rule'.

Moreover, English has no diacritical marks (accent and pronunciation signs), although some languages do. The following is a brief and general guide to the pronunciation of those most frequently used in the principal Western European languages.

		Pronunciation as in
French	é	day and shows that the 'e' is to be pronounced; e.g. Orléans.
	è	mare
	î	used over any vowel and does not affect pronunciation; shows contraction of the name, usually omission of 's' following a vowel.
	ç	's' before 'a', 'o' and 'u'.
	ë, ï, ü	over 'e', 'i' and 'u' when they are used with another vowel and shows that each is to be pronounced.
German	ä	fate
	ö	fur
	ü	no English equivalent; like French 'tu'.
Italian	à, é	over vowels and indicates stress.
Portuguese	ã, õ	vowels pronounced nasally.
	ç	boss
	á	shows stress.
	ô	shows that a vowel has an 'i' or 'u' sound combined with it.
Spanish	ñ	canyon
	ü	pronounced as 'w' and separately from adjoining vowels.
	á	usually indicates that this is a stressed vowel.

ABBREVIATIONS

A.C.T. – Australian Capital Territory
A.R. – Autonomous Region
Afghan. – Afghanistan
Afr. – Africa
Ala. – Alabama
Alta. – Alberta
Amer. – America(n)
Ant. – Antilles
Arch. – Archipelago
Ariz. – Arizona
Ark. – Arkansas
Atl. Oc. – Atlantic Ocean
B. – Baie, Bahía, Bay, Bucht, Bugt
B.C. – British Columbia
Bangla. – Bangladesh
Barr. – Barrage
Bos.-H. – Bosnia-Herzegovina
C. – Cabo, Cap, Cape, Coast
C.A.R. – Central African Republic
C. Prov. – Cape Province
Calif. – California
Cat. – Catarata
Cent. – Central
Chan. – Channel
Colo. – Colorado
Conn. – Connecticut
Cord. – Cordillera
Cr. – Creek
D.C. – District of Columbia
Del. – Delaware
Dem. – Democratic
Dep. – Dependency
Des. – Desert
Dét. – Détroit
Dist. – District
Dj. – Djebel
Dom. Rep. – Dominican Republic
E. – East
El Salv. – El Salvador
Eq. Guin. – Equatorial Guinea
Est. – Estrecho
Falk. Is. – Falkland Is.
Fd. – Fjord
Fla. – Florida
Fr. – French
G. – Golfe, Golfo, Gulf, Guba, Gebel
Ga. – Georgia
Gt. – Great, Greater
Guinea-Biss. – Guinea-Bissau
H.K. – Hong Kong
H.P. – Himachal Pradesh
Hants. – Hampshire
Harb. – Harbor, Harbour
Hd. – Head
Hts. – Heights
I.(s). – Île, Ilha, Insel, Isla, Island, Isle
Ill. – Illinois
Ind. – Indiana
Ind. Oc. – Indian Ocean
J. – Jabal, Jebel
Jaz. – Jazīrah
Junc. – Junction
K. – Kap, Kapp
Kans. – Kansas
Kep. – Kepulauan
Ky. – Kentucky
L. – Lac, Lacul, Lago, Lagoa, Lake, Limni, Loch, Lough
La. – Louisiana
Ld. – Land
Liech. – Liechtenstein
Lux. – Luxembourg
Mad. P. – Madhya Pradesh
Madag. – Madagascar
Man. – Manitoba
Mass. – Massachusetts
Md. – Maryland
Me. – Maine
Medit. S. – Mediterranean Sea
Mich. – Michigan
Minn. – Minnesota
Miss. – Mississippi
Mo. – Missouri
Mont. – Montana
Mozam. – Mozambique
Mt.(s) – Mont, Montaña, Mountain
Mte. – Monte
Mti. – Monti
N. – Nord, Norte, North, Northern, Nouveau, Nahal, Nahr
N.B. – New Brunswick
N.C. – North Carolina
N. Cal. – New Caledonia
N. Dak. – North Dakota
N.H. – New Hampshire
N.I. – North Island
N.J. – New Jersey
N. Mex. – New Mexico
N.S. – Nova Scotia
N.S.W. – New South Wales
N.W.T. – North West Territory
N.Y. – New York
N.Z. – New Zealand
Nac. – Nacional
Nat. – National
Nebr. – Nebraska
Neths. – Netherlands
Nev. – Nevada
Nfld. & L. – Newfoundland and Labrador
Nic. – Nicaragua
O. – Oued, Ouadi
Occ. – Occidentale
Okla. – Oklahoma
Ont. – Ontario
Or. – Orientale
Oreg. – Oregon
Os. – Ostrov
Oz. – Ozero
P. – Pass, Passo, Pasul, Pulau
P.E.I. – Prince Edward Island
Pa. – Pennsylvania
Pac. Oc. – Pacific Ocean
Papua N.G. – Papua New Guinea
Pass. – Passage
Peg. – Pegunungan
Pen. – Peninsula, Péninsule
Phil. – Philippines
Pk. – Peak
Plat. – Plateau
Prov. – Province, Provincial
Pt. – Point
Pta. – Ponta, Punta
Pte. – Pointe
Qué. – Québec
Queens. – Queensland
R. – Rio, River
R.I. – Rhode Island
Ra. – Range
Raj. – Rajasthan
Recr. – Recreational, Récréatif
Reg. – Region
Rep. – Republic
Res. – Reserve, Reservoir
Rhld-Pfz. – Rheinland-Pfalz
S. – South, Southern, Sur
Si. Arabia – Saudi Arabia
S.C. – South Carolina
S. Dak. – South Dakota
S.I. – South Island
S. Leone – Sierra Leone
Sa. – Serra, Sierra
Sask. – Saskatchewan
Scot. – Scotland
Sd. – Sound
Sev. – Severnaya
Sib. – Siberia
Sprs. – Springs
St. – Saint
Sta. – Santa
Ste. – Sainte
Sto. – Santo
Str. – Strait, Stretto
Switz. – Switzerland
Tas. – Tasmania
Tenn. – Tennessee
Terr. – Territory, Territoire
Tex. – Texas
Tg. – Tanjung
Trin. & Tob. – Trinidad & Tobago
U.A.E. – United Arab Emirates
U.K. – United Kingdom
U.S.A. – United States of America
Univ. – University, Université, Universidad
Ut. P. – Uttar Pradesh
Va. – Virginia
Vdkhr. – Vodokhranilishche
Vdskh. – Vodoskhovyshche
Vf. – Vîrful
Vic. – Victoria
Vol. – Volcano
Vt. – Vermont
W. – Wadi, West
W. Va. – West Virginia
Wall. & F. Is. – Wallis and Futuna Is.
Wash. – Washington
Wis. – Wisconsin
Wlkp. – Wielkopolski
Wyo. – Wyoming
Yorks. – Yorkshire

A

B

D

D.C. War Memorial
Washington, D.C., U.S.A. 143 b1
D.H.A. Phase VIII *Pakistan* 24°47N 67°2E 123 B2
Da ➝ *Vietnam* 21°15N 105°20E 228 G5
Da Hinggan Ling *China* 48°0N 121°0E 219 B13
Da Lat *Vietnam* 11°56N 108°25E 237 G7
Da Moóca ➝ *Brazil* 23°35S 46°35W 137 B2
Da Nang *Vietnam* 16°4N 108°13E 236 C6
Da Qaidam *China* 37°50N 95°15E 218 D8
Da Yunhe ➝ *Hopei, China* 39°10N 117°10E 227 E9
Da Yunhe ➝ *Jiangsu, China* 34°25N 120°5E 227 H10
Da'an *China* 45°30N 124°7E 227 B13
Daan Viljoen ⌂ *Namibia* 22°2S 16°45E 270 B2
Daanbantayan *Phil.* 11°17N 124°2E 233 F5
Dab'a, Ras el *Egypt* 31°3N 28°31E 256 H6
Daba Shan *China* 32°0N 109°0E 228 B7
Dabai *Nigeria* 11°25N 5°15E 263 C6
Dabajuro *Venezuela* 11°2N 70°40W 328 A3
Dabakala *Côte d'Ivoire* 8°15N 4°20W 262 D4
Dabaka *India* 26°7N 92°52E 241 B4
Dabaro *Somalia* 6°21N 48°43E 267 C6
Dabas *Hungary* 47°11N 19°19E 182 C4
Dabat *Ethiopia* 12°58N 37°41E 257 E4
Dabbagh, Jabal *Si. Arabia* 27°52N 35°45E 246 E2
Dabeiba *Colombia* 7°1N 76°16W 328 B2
Daber = Dobra *Poland* 53°34N 15°20E 184 E2
Dabhoi *India* 22°10N 73°20E 242 H5
Dąbie *Poland* 52°5N 18°50E 185 F5
Dabie Shan *China* 31°20N 115°20E 229 B10
Dabilda *Cameroon* 12°45N 14°35E 259 F2
Dabl, W. ➝ *Si. Arabia* 29°5N 36°16E 251 J7
Dąblice *Czechia* 50°8N 14°29E 135 B2
Dabnou *Niger* 14°10N 5°22E 263 C6
Dabo *Indonesia* 0°30S 104°33E 234 C2
Dabola *Guinea* 10°50N 11°5W 262 C2
Dabou *Côte d'Ivoire* 5°20N 4°23W 262 D4
Daboya *Ghana* 9°30N 1°20W 263 D4
Dabravolya *Belarus* 52°55N 23°59E 185 F10
Dąbrowa *Poland* 52°19N 20°52E 143 B1
Dąbrowa Białostocka *Poland* 53°40N 23°21E 184 E10
Dąbrowa Górnicza *Poland* 50°15N 19°10E 185 H6
Dąbrowa Tarnowska *Poland* 50°10N 20°59E 185 H7
Dabu *China* 24°22N 116°41E 229 E11
Dabugam *India* 19°27N 82°26E 244 E6
Dabung *Malaysia* 5°23N 102°1E 237 K4
Dabus ➝ *Ethiopia* 10°48N 35°10E 257 E4
Dacato ➝ *Ethiopia* 7°25N 42°40E 257 F5
Dacca = Dhaka *Bangla.* 23°43N 90°26E 241 D3
Dachang *Jiangsu, China* 32°13N 118°45E 229 A12
Dachang *Shanghai, China* 31°17N 121°24E 138 B1
Dachang ✈ *China* 31°18N 121°25E 138 B1
Dachaoshan Dam *China* 24°1N 100°22E 228 E3
Dachau *Germany* 48°15N 11°26E 131 A1
Dachau-Ost *Germany* 48°15N 11°27E 131 A1
Dachauer Moos *Germany* 48°13N 11°27E 131 A1
Dacheng = Tacheng *Taiwan* 23°51N 120°19E 225 C2
Dachigam △ *India* 34°10N 75°0E 242 B6
Dachstein, Hoher *Austria* 47°28N 13°35E 180 D6
Dačice *Czechia* 49°5N 15°26E 180 B8
Dacre *Canada* 45°22N 76°57W 312 A8
Dacula *U.S.A.* 33°59N 83°54W 316 B6
Dadanawa *Guyana* 2°50N 59°30W 329 C6
Dadar *India* 19°0N 72°49E 130 A1
Daday *Turkey* 41°28N 33°27E 212 B5
Dade City *U.S.A.* 28°22N 82°11W 317 G7
Dadès, Oued ➝ *Morocco* 30°58N 6°44W 260 B3
Dadeville *U.S.A.* 32°50N 85°46W 316 C4
Dadhar *Pakistan* 29°28N 67°39E 242 E2
Dadiya *Nigeria* 9°35N 11°24E 263 D7
Ḍadnah *U.A.E.* 25°32N 56°22E 247 E8
Dadohae △ *S. Korea* 34°0N 126°0E 224 E3
Dadra = Achalpur *India* 21°22N 77°32E 244 D3
Dadra & Nagar Haveli □ *India* 20°5N 73°0E 244 D1
Dadri = Charkhi Dadri *India* 28°37N 76°17E 242 E7
Dadu *Pakistan* 26°45N 67°45E 242 F2
Dadu He ➝ *China* 29°31N 103°46E 228 C4
Daebang *S. Korea* 37°30N 126°55E 137 B1
Daebudo *S. Korea* 37°14N 126°35E 224 D3
Daecheongdo *S. Korea* 37°49N 124°42E 224 D2
Daechi *S. Korea* 37°30N 127°2E 137 B2
Daegu *S. Korea* 35°50N 128°37E 224 E4
Daejeon *S. Korea* 36°20N 127°28E 224 D3
Daejeon □ *S. Korea* 36°20N 127°25E 224 D3
Daejeong *S. Korea* 33°8N 126°17E 224 a
Daemodo *S. Korea* 34°11N 126°45E 224 E3
Daet *Phil.* 14°2N 122°55E 232 D4
Daeyeonpyeong = Yeonpyeongdo *S. Korea* 37°40N 125°45E 224 D2
Dafang *China* 27°9N 105°39E 228 D5
Dafdaf, J. *Si. Arabia* 28°16N 35°35E 251 K6
Dafeng *China* 33°3N 120°45E 227 H11
Dafnes *Greece* 35°13N 25°3E 207 E6
Dafni *Athina, Greece* 37°55N 23°44E 112 B2
Dafni *Peloponnese, Greece* 37°48N 22°1E 204 D4
Dafnoudi, Akra *Greece* 38°28N 20°32E 207 C2
Dağ *Turkey* 37°12N 30°31E 205 D12
Daga Post *South Sudan* 9°13N 33°58E 266 C3
Dagali *Norway* 60°25N 8°28E 164 D5
Dagana *Senegal* 16°30N 15°35W 262 B1
Dagash *Sudan* 19°19N 33°25E 256 D3
Dagenham *U.K.* 51°32N 0°8E 125 A4
Dagestan □ *Russia* 42°30N 47°0E 191 J8
Dagestanskiye Ogni *Russia* 42°6N 48°12E 191 J9
Dagg Sd. *N.Z.* 45°23S 166°45E 285 F1
Daggett *U.S.A.* 34°52N 116°52W 307 L10
Daghestan Republic = Dagestan □ *Russia* 42°30N 47°0E 191 J8
Daghfeli *Sudan* 19°18N 32°40E 256 D3
Daglfing *Germany* 48°8N 11°39E 131 B2
Dağlıq Qarabağ = Nagorno-Karabakh □ *Azerbaijan* 39°55N 46°45E 213 C12
Dagö = Hiiumaa *Estonia* 58°50N 22°45E 188 C2
Dagu *China* 38°59N 117°40E 227 E9
Dagua *Papua N. G.* 3°27S 143°20E 286 B2
Daguan *China* 27°43N 103°56E 228 D4
D'Aguilar Pen. *Hong Kong, China* 22°13N 114°5E 122 B2
Dagupan *Phil.* 16°3N 120°20E 232 C3
Daguragu *Australia* 17°33S 130°30E 278 C5
Daguragu ◎ *Australia* 17°24S 130°48E 278 C5
Dahab *Egypt* 28°31N 34°31E 251 K5
Dahab, Gezîret el *Egypt* 29°59N 31°13E 117 B2
Dahanu *India* 19°58N 72°44E 244 E1
Daheisha *West Bank* 31°42N 35°11E 123 B2
Dahivadi *India* 17°43N 74°33E 244 F2
Dahlak Kebir *Eritrea* 15°50N 40°10E 257 D5
Dahlak Marine △ *Eritrea* 15°35N 40°15E 257 D5
Dahlem *Germany* 52°27N 13°16E 115 B2
Dahlenburg *Germany* 53°11N 10°44E 178 B6
Dahlonega *U.S.A.* 34°32N 83°59W 315 D13
Dahlwitz-Hoppegarten *Germany* 52°30N 13°41E 115 A5
Dahme *Germany* 51°52N 13°25E 178 D9
Dahod *India* 22°50N 74°15E 242 H6
Dahomey = Benin ■ *Africa* 10°0N 2°0E 263 D5
Dahong Shan *China* 31°25N 113°0E 229 B9
Dahongliutan *China* 35°45N 79°20E 243 B8
Dahongmen *China* 39°48N 116°21E 114 C2
Dahra *Libya* 29°30N 17°50E 258 C3
Dahra *Senegal* 15°22N 15°30W 262 B1
Dahra, Massif de *Algeria* 36°7N 1°21E 261 A5
Dahshûr *Egypt* 29°45N 31°14E 256 J7
Dahu = Tahu *Taiwan* 24°26N 120°52E 225 B2
Dahūk *Iraq* 36°50N 43°1E 213 D10
Dahūk □ *Iraq* 36°50N 42°50E 213 D10
Dahuofan Shuiku *China* 41°52N 124°12E 224 B2
Dahy, Nafūd ad *Si. Arabia* 22°0N 45°25E 248 B4
Dai *Solomon Is.* 7°54S 160°40E 287 L11
Dai Hao *Vietnam* 18°1N 106°25E 236 C6
Dai-Sen *Japan* 35°22N 133°32E 222 B5
Dai Shan *China* 30°25N 122°10E 229 B14
Dai Xian *China* 39°4N 112°58E 226 E7
Daiba = Odaiba *Japan* 35°38N 139°47E 140 B3
Daicheng *China* 38°42N 116°38E 226 E9
Daigo *Japan* 36°46N 140°21E 223 A12
Daik-u *Myanmar* 17°47N 96°40E 241 G6
Daikondi = Dāykondī □ *Afghan.* 34°0N 66°0E 240 B2
Dailekh *Nepal* 28°50N 81°44E 243 E9
Daimanji-San *Japan* 36°14N 133°20E 222 A5
Daimiel *Spain* 39°5N 3°35W 195 F7
Daingean *Ireland* 53°18N 7°17W 166 C4
Daingean, An = Dingle *Ireland* 52°9N 10°17W 166 D1
Daingean, An = Dingle ...
Dainkog *China* 32°30N 97°58E 228 A1
Daintree *Australia* 16°20S 145°20E 280 B4
Daintree △ *Australia* 16°8S 145°2E 280 B4
Daiō-Misaki *Japan* 34°15N 136°45E 223 C8
Dair, J. ed *Sudan* 12°27N 30°42E 257 E3
Dairen = Dalian *China* 38°50N 121°40E 227 E11
Dairût *Egypt* 27°34N 30°43E 256 B3
Daisen *Japan* 39°27N 140°29E 220 E10
Daisen-Oki △ *Japan* 35°23N 133°34E 222 B5
Daisetsu-Zan *Japan* 43°30N 142°57E 220 C11
Daisetsu-Zan △ *Japan* 43°30N 142°55E 220 C11
Daitari *India* 21°10N 85°46E 244 D7
Daitō *Japan* 35°19N 132°58E 222 B4
Daiyun Shan *China* 25°50N 118°15E 229 E12
Dajarra *Australia* 21°42S 139°30E 280 C2
Dajia = Tachia *Taiwan* 24°25N 120°28E 225 B2
Dajiaoting *China* 39°51N 116°27E 114 B2
Dajiawa *China* 37°9N 119°0E 227 F10
Dajin Chuan ➝ *China* 31°16N 101°59E 228 B3
Dajti △ *Albania* 41°22N 19°56E 202 E3
Dak Dam *Cambodia* 12°20N 107°21E 236 F6
Dak Nhe *Vietnam* 15°28N 107°48E 236 E6
Dak Pek *Vietnam* 15°4N 107°44E 236 E6
Dak Song *Vietnam* 12°19N 107°35E 237 F6
Dak Sui *Vietnam* 14°55N 107°43E 236 E6
Dakar *Senegal* 14°34N 17°29W 262 C1
Dakar □ *Senegal* 14°45N 17°20W 262 C1
Dakhal, W. el ➝ *Egypt* 28°48N 32°47E 251 K3
Dakhin Shahbazpur = Dakhin *Bangla.* 22°30N 90°45E 241 D3
Dakhla *W. Sahara* 23°50N 15°53W 260 D1
Dakhla, El Wâhât el *Egypt* 25°30N 28°50E 256 B2
Dakhnoye *Russia* 59°49N 30°15E 137 C1
Dakingari *Nigeria* 11°37N 4°1E 263 C5
Dakoank *India* 7°2N 93°43E 245 L11
Dakor *India* 22°45N 73°11E 242 H5
Dakoro *Niger* 14°31N 6°46E 263 C6
Dakota City *Iowa, U.S.A.* 42°43N 94°12W 310 B2
Dakota City *Nebr., U.S.A.* 42°25N 96°25W 308 D5
Đakovica = Gjakovë *Kosovo* 42°22N 20°26E 202 D4
Đakovo *Croatia* 45°19N 18°24E 182 E3
Dal *Norway* 59°53N 8°40E 164 E5
Dala *Lunda Sul, Angola* 11°3S 20°17E 265 E4
Dala *Uíge, Angola* 8°5S 15°49E 265 D3
Dala *Solomon Is.* 8°30S 160°41E 287 M11
Dala-Cachibo *Angola* 10°30S 14°41E 265 E2
Dala-Järna *Sweden* 60°33N 14°22E 162 D8
Dalaba *Guinea* 10°47N 12°12W 262 C2
Dalachi *China* 36°48N 105°0E 226 F3
Dalagan = San Antonio *Phil.* 14°57N 120°5E 232 D3
Dalaguete *Phil.* 9°46N 123°32E 233 G4
Dalai Nur *China* 43°20N 116°45E 226 C9
Dālakī *Iran* 29°26N 51°17E 247 D6
Dalälven ➝ *Sweden* 60°12N 16°43E 162 D10
Dalaman *Turkey* 36°48N 28°47E 205 E10
Dalaman ➝ *Turkey* 36°41N 28°43E 205 E10
Dalandzadgad *Mongolia* 43°27N 104°30E 226 C3
Dalanganem Is. *Phil.* 10°40N 120°17E 233 F3
Dalap-Uliga-Darrit = Majuro *Marshall Is.* 7°9N 171°12E 288 G9
Dalarna *Sweden* 61°0N 14°0E 162 D8
Dalarna □ *Sweden* 61°0N 14°15E 162 C8
Dalasýsla *Iceland* 65°15N 22°0W 155 B4
Dalat *Malaysia* 2°44N 111°56E 235 B4
Dālbandīn *Pakistan* 29°0N 64°23E 240 C2
Dalbeattie *U.K.* 54°56N 3°50W 167 G5
Dalbeg *Australia* 20°16S 147°18E 280 C4
Dalbosjön *Sweden* 58°40N 12°45E 163 F6
Dalby *Queens., Australia* 27°10S 151°17E 281 D5
Dalby *Skåne, Sweden* 55°40N 13°22E 163 J7
Dalby Söderskog △ *Sweden* 55°41N 13°21E 163 J7
Dale *Sogn og Fjordane, Norway* 61°22N 5°23E 164 C2
Dale *Ind., U.S.A.* 38°10N 86°59W 311 F10
Dale City *U.S.A.* 38°38N 77°19W 309 F15
Dale Hollow L. *U.S.A.* 36°32N 85°27W 315 C12
Dalejský potok ➝ *Czechia* 50°2N 14°24E 135 B2
Dalen *Norway* 59°26N 8°0E 164 E4
Dalet *Myanmar* 19°59N 93°51E 241 F4
Daletme *Myanmar* 21°36N 92°46E 241 E4
Daleville *Ala., U.S.A.* 31°19N 85°43W 316 D4
Daleville *Ind., U.S.A.* 40°7N 85°33W 311 D11
Dalga *Egypt* 27°39N 30°41E 256 B3
Dalgān *Iran* 27°31N 59°19E 247 E8
Dalgety Bay *U.K.* 56°2N 3°20W 121 A1
Dalgopol *Bulgaria* 43°3N 27°22E 203 C11
Dalhart *U.S.A.* 36°4N 102°31W 314 C3
Dalhousie *N.B., Canada* 48°5N 66°26W 299 C6
Dalhousie *India* 32°38N 75°58E 242 C6
Dali *Shaanxi, China* 34°48N 109°58E 226 G5
Dali *Yunnan, China* 25°40N 100°10E 228 E3
Dalian *China* 38°50N 121°40E 227 E11
Daliang Shan *China* 28°0N 102°45E 228 D4
Daliao = Taliao *Taiwan* 22°36N 120°23E 225 C2
Dalin = Talin *Taiwan* 23°36N 120°27E 225 C2
Daling He ➝ *China* 40°55N 121°40E 227 D11
Dalj *Croatia* 45°29N 18°59E 182 E3
Dalkeith *Midloth., U.K.* 55°54N 3°4W 121 B3
Dalkeith *Fla., U.S.A.* 30°0N 85°9W 316 E4
Dalkey *Ireland* 53°16N 6°6W 166 C5
Dallas *Ga., U.S.A.* 33°55N 84°51W 316 B5
Dallas *Oreg., U.S.A.* 44°55N 123°19W 306 D2
Dallas *Tex., U.S.A.* 32°47N 96°48W 120 B4
Dallas City *U.S.A.* 40°38N 91°10W 310 D5
Dallas-Fort Worth Int. ✈ (DFW) *U.S.A.* 32°54N 97°2W 314 E6
Dallas-Fort Worth Int. ✈ (DFW) *Tex., U.S.A.* 32°53N 97°2W 120 A3
Dallas-Fort Worth Meacham Int. ✈ (FTW) *U.S.A.* 32°49N 97°21W 120 B1
Dalle = Yirga Alem *Ethiopia* 6°48N 38°22E 257 F4
Dalles, The *U.S.A.* 45°36N 121°10W 304 D3
Dallgow *Germany* 52°32N 13°5E 115 A1
Dallol *Ethiopia* 14°14N 40°17E 257 E5
Dalmā *U.A.E.* 24°30N 52°20E 247 E7
Dalmacija *Croatia* 43°20N 17°0E 199 E13
Dalmas, L. *Canada* 53°30N 71°50W 299 B5
Dalmatia = Dalmacija *Croatia* 43°20N 17°0E 199 E13
Dalmau *India* 26°4N 81°2E 243 F9
Dalmellington *U.K.* 55°19N 4°23W 167 F4
Dalmeny *N.S.W., Australia* 36°10S 150°8E 283 D9
Dalmeny *Edinburgh, U.K.* 55°59N 3°22W 121 B1
Dalnegorsk *Russia* 44°32N 135°33E 220 B7
Dalnerechensk *Russia* 45°50N 133°40E 220 B6
Dalnevostochnyy □ *Russia* 67°0N 140°0E 215 C14
Dalny = Dalian *China* 38°50N 121°40E 227 E11
Daloa *Côte d'Ivoire* 7°0N 6°30W 262 D3
Dalou Shan *China* 28°15N 107°0E 228 C6
Dalry *U.K.* 55°42N 4°43W 167 F4
Dalrymple, L. *Australia* 20°40S 147°0E 280 C4
Dalrymple, Mt. *Australia* 21°1S 148°39E 280 b
Dals Långed *Sweden* 58°56N 12°18E 163 F6
Dalsætra *Norway* 61°28N 9°26E 164 C6
Dalsjöfors *Sweden* 57°46N 13°5E 163 G7
Dalsland *Sweden* 58°50N 12°15E 163 F6
Dalsmynni *Iceland* 64°48N 21°29W 155 C5
Dalston *U.K.* 51°32N 0°4W 125 A3
Daltenganj *India* 24°0N 84°4E 243 H11
Dalton *Ga., U.S.A.* 34°46N 84°58W 315 D12
Dalton *Mass., U.S.A.* 42°28N 73°11W 313 D11
Dalton *Nebr., U.S.A.* 41°25N 102°58W 308 E2
Dalton, Kap *Greenland* 69°25N 24°3W 154 D8
Dalton-in-Furness *U.K.* 54°10N 3°11W 168 C4
Daludalu *Indonesia* 1°4N 100°15E 234 B2
Dalupiri I. *Cagayan, Phil.* 19°5N 121°12E 232 B3
Dalupiri I. *N. Samar, Phil.* 12°25N 124°16E 232 E5
Dalvík *Iceland* 65°58N 18°32W 155 B8
Dálvvadis = Jokkmokk *Sweden* 66°35N 19°50E 160 C18
Dalwallinu *Australia* 30°17S 116°40E 279 F2
Dalworthington Gardens *U.S.A.* 32°42N 97°9W 120 B3
Daly ➝ *Australia* 13°35S 130°19E 278 B5
Daly City *U.S.A.* 37°42N 122°27W 136 B2
Daly L. *Canada* 56°32N 105°39W 297 B7
Daly River *Australia* 13°46S 130°42E 278 B5
Daly River-Port Keats ◎ *Australia* 14°13S 129°36E 278 B4
Daly Waters *Australia* 16°15S 133°24E 280 B1
Dalyan *Turkey* 36°50N 28°39E 205 E10
Dam *Amsterdam, Neths.* 112 a2
Dam Doi *Vietnam* 8°50N 105°12E 237 H5
Dam Ha *Vietnam* 21°21N 107°36E 236 B6
Damachova *Belarus* 51°45N 23°36E 185 G10
Damaia *Portugal* 38°44N 9°12W 126 A1
Daman *India* 20°25N 72°57E 244 D1
Daman & Diu □ *India* 20°25N 72°58E 244 D1
Dāmaneh *Iran* 33°1N 50°29E 247 C6
Damanganga ➝ *India* 20°25N 72°56E 244 D1
Damanhûr *Egypt* 31°0N 30°30E 256 H7
Damant L. *Canada* 61°45N 105°5W 297 A7
Damaq *Iran* 35°25N 48°49E 213 E13
Damar *Indonesia* 7°7S 128°40E 231 F7
Damara *C.A.R.* 4°58N 18°42E 264 B3
Damaraland *Namibia* 20°0S 15°0E 270 B2
Damascus = Dimashq *Syria* 33°30N 36°18E 250 E7
Damascus *U.S.A.* 31°18N 84°43W 316 D5
Damasi *Greece* 39°43N 22°11E 204 B4
Damaturu *Nigeria* 11°45N 11°55E 263 C7
Damāvand *Iran* 35°57N 52°7E 247 C7
Damāvand, Qolleh-ye *Iran* 35°57N 52°7E 247 C7
Damba *Angola* 6°44S 15°20E 265 D3
Damboa *Nigeria* 11°15N 12°55E 259 F2
Dâmbovița □ *Romania* 45°0N 25°30E 183 F10
Dâmbovița ➝ *Romania* 44°12N 26°26E 183 F11
Dâmbovnic ➝ *Romania* 44°28N 25°18E 183 F10
Dambrowica = Dubrovytsya *Ukraine* 51°31N 26°35E 177 C14
Dambulla *Sri Lanka* 7°51N 80°39E 245 L5
Dame Marie *Haiti* 18°34N 74°26W 321 C5
Dämeritzsee *Germany* 52°34N 13°43E 115 B5
Dāmghān *Iran* 36°10N 54°17E 247 B7
Dămienesti *Romania* 46°44N 26°59E 183 D11
Damietta = Dumyât *Egypt* 31°24N 31°48E 251 G2
Daming *China* 36°15N 115°6E 226 F8
Damīr Qābū *Syria* 36°58N 41°51E 246 B4
Dammai I. *Phil.* 5°47N 120°25E 233 J3
Dammam = Ad Dammām *Si. Arabia* 26°20N 50°5E 247 E6
Dammarie-les-Lys *France* 48°31N 2°39E 173 D9
Dammartin-en-Goële *France* 49°3N 2°41E 173 C9
Damme *Germany* 52°32N 8°11E 178 C4
Damodar ➝ *India* 23°17N 87°35E 243 H12
Damoh *India* 23°50N 79°28E 243 H8
Damous *Algeria* 36°31N 1°42E 261 A5
Dampier *Australia* 20°41S 116°42E 278 D2
Dampier, Selat *Indonesia* 0°40S 131°0E 231 E8
Dampier Arch. *Australia* 20°38S 116°32E 278 D2
Dampier Str. *Papua N. G.* 5°50S 148°0E 286 C5
Damqawt *Yemen* 16°34N 52°50E 249 D6
Damrak *Amsterdam, Neths.* 112 a2
Damrani *Algeria* 27°45N 2°56W 260 C4
Damrei, Chuor Phnum *Cambodia* 11°30N 103°0E 237 G4
Damroh *India* 28°26N 95°14E 241 A5
Damvillers *France* 49°20N 5°21E 173 C12
Damyang *S. Korea* 35°19N 126°59E 224 E3
Dan Gorayo *Somalia* 8°43N 49°20E 267 C6
Dan-Gulbi *Nigeria* 11°40N 6°15E 263 C6
Dan Ryan Woods *U.S.A.* 41°44N 87°40W 119 C2
Dan-Sadau *Nigeria* 11°17N 6°29E 263 C6
Dana *Indonesia* 11°0S 121°15E 231 F6
Dana *Jordan* 30°41N 35°37E 251 H6
Dana *Nepal* 28°32N 83°37E 243 E10
Dana, L. *Canada* 50°53N 77°20W 298 B4
Dana, Mt. *U.S.A.* 37°54N 119°12W 306 H7
Danakil Depression *Ethiopia* 13°0N 41°0E 267 B5
Danakil Desert *Ethiopia* 12°45N 41°0E 257 E5
Danan *Ethiopia* 6°31N 43°30E 267 C5
Danané *Côte d'Ivoire* 7°16N 8°9W 262 D3
Danao *Phil.* 10°31N 124°1E 233 F5
Danau Sentarum △ *Indonesia* 0°51N 112°6E 235 B4
Danba *China* 30°54N 101°48E 228 B3
Danbury *U.S.A.* 41°24N 73°28W 313 E11
Danby L. *U.S.A.* 34°13N 115°5W 307 L11
Dand *Afghan.* 31°28N 65°32E 242 D1
Dande ➝ *Angola* 8°28S 13°21E 265 D2
Dande ⌂ *Zimbabwe* 15°56S 30°16E 269 F3
Dandeldhura *Nepal* 29°20N 80°35E 243 E9
Dandeli *India* 15°5N 74°30E 245 G2
Dandenong *Australia* 38°0S 145°15E 283 E6
Danderhall *U.K.* 55°55N 3°7W 121 B3
Danderyd *Sweden* 59°24N 18°1E 139 A2
Dandī *Iran* 36°32N 47°37E 213 D12
Dandīl *Egypt* 29°10N 31°2E 256 J7
Dandong *China* 40°10N 124°20E 224 B2
Daneborg *Greenland* 74°18N 20°14W 154 C8
Danfeng *China* 33°45N 110°25E 226 H6
Danforth *Canada* 43°43N 79°16W 141 A3
Dangan Liedao *China* 22°2N 114°8E 229 F10
Dangcagan *Phil.* 7°36N 125°0E 233 H5
Dange *Angola* 7°56S 15°3E 265 D3
Dangé-St-Romain *France* 46°56N 0°36E 174 B4
Dângeni *Romania* 47°51N 26°58E 183 C11
Danger Is. = Pukapuka *Cook Is.* 10°53S 165°49W 289 J11
Danger Pt. *S. Africa* 34°40S 19°17E 270 D2
Dangjin *S. Korea* 36°53N 126°37E 224 D3
Dangla *Ethiopia* 11°18N 36°56E 257 E4
Dangla Shan = Tanggula Shan *China* 32°40N 92°10E 218 E7
Dangora *Nigeria* 11°30N 8°7E 263 C6
Dangouadougou *Burkina Faso* 10°9N 4°56W 262 D4
Dangrek, Mts. = Dangrek, Phnom *Thailand* 14°20N 104°0E 236 E5
Dangrek, Phnom *Thailand* 14°20N 104°0E 236 E5
Dangriga *Belize* 17°0N 88°13W 320 C2
Dangshan *China* 34°27N 116°22E 226 G9
Dangtu *China* 31°32N 118°25E 229 B12
Dangyang *China* 30°52N 111°44E 229 B8
Dania Beach *U.S.A.* 26°3N 80°9W 129 B3
Daniel *U.S.A.* 42°52N 110°4W 304 E8
Daniel's Harbour *Canada* 50°13N 57°35W 299 B8
Danielskuil *S. Africa* 28°11S 23°33E 270 C3
Danielson *U.S.A.* 41°48N 71°53W 313 E13
Danielsville *U.S.A.* 34°8N 83°13W 316 A6
Danilov *Russia* 58°16N 40°13E 188 C11
Danilovgrad *Montenegro* 42°38N 19°4E 202 D3
Danilovka *Russia* 50°25N 44°12E 190 E7
Daning *China* 36°28N 110°45E 226 F6
Danish West Indies = Virgin Is. (U.S.) ☒ *W. Indies* 18°20N 65°0W 321 C7
Danissa *Kenya* 3°17N 40°59E 267 D5
Danja *Nigeria* 11°21N 7°30E 263 C6
Danje-la-Menha *Angola* 9°32S 14°39E 265 D2
Danjiangkou *China* 32°31N 111°30E 229 A8
Danjiangkou Shuiku *China* 32°37N 111°30E 229 A8
Dank *Oman* 23°33N 56°16E 247 F8
Dankalwa *Nigeria* 11°52N 12°12E 263 C7
Dankama *Nigeria* 13°20N 7°44E 263 C6
Dankhar Gompa *India* 32°10N 78°10E 242 C8
Dankov *Russia* 53°20N 39°5E 188 F10
Danleng *China* 30°1N 103°31E 228 B4
Danlí *Honduras* 14°4N 86°35W 320 D2
Danmark = Denmark ■ *Europe* 55°45N 10°0E 163 J3
Danmark Fjord *Greenland* 81°30N 22°0W 154 A8
Danmarkshavn *Greenland* 76°45N 18°50W 154 B9
Dannemora *U.S.A.* 44°43N 73°44W 313 B11
Dannenberg *Germany* 53°6N 11°5E 178 B7
Dannevirke *N.Z.* 40°12S 176°8E 284 G5
Dannhauser *S. Africa* 28°0S 30°3E 271 C5
Danot *Ethiopia* 7°33N 45°17E 267 C6
Dansalan = Marawi City *Phil.* 8°0N 124°21E 233 G5
Danshuei = Tanshui *Taiwan* 25°10N 121°28E 225 A3
Dansville *U.S.A.* 42°34N 77°42W 312 D7
Danta *India* 24°11N 72°46E 242 G5
Dantan *India* 21°57N 87°20E 243 J12
Dante = Xaafuun *Somalia* 10°25N 51°16E 267 B7
Dantewara *India* 18°54N 81°21E 244 E5
Danube = Dunărea ➝ *Europe* 45°20N 29°40E 183 E14
Danubyu *Myanmar* 17°15N 95°35E 241 G5
Danvers *U.S.A.* 42°34N 70°56W 313 D14
Danville *Ga., U.S.A.* 32°37N 83°15W 316 C6
Danville *Ill., U.S.A.* 40°8N 87°37W 311 D9
Danville *Ind., U.S.A.* 39°46N 86°32W 311 E10
Danville *Ky., U.S.A.* 37°39N 84°46W 311 G12
Danville *Pa., U.S.A.* 40°58N 76°37W 313 F8
Danville *Va., U.S.A.* 36°36N 79°23W 309 G14
Danville *Vt., U.S.A.* 44°25N 72°9W 313 B12
Danyang *China* 32°0N 119°31E 229 B12
Danzhai *China* 26°11N 107°48E 228 D6
Danzhou *China* 19°31N 109°33E 229 a
Danzig = Gdańsk *Poland* 54°22N 18°40E 184 D5
Dao *Antique, Phil.* 10°30N 121°57E 233 F3
Dao *Capiz, Phil.* 11°24N 122°41E 233 F4
Dão ➝ *Portugal* 40°20N 8°11W 194 E2
Dao Xian *China* 25°36N 111°31E 229 E8
Daocheng *China* 29°0N 100°10E 228 C3
Daora *W. Sahara* 27°5N 12°59W 260 C2
Daoud = Aïn Beïda *Algeria* 35°50N 7°29E 261 A6
Daoukro *Côte d'Ivoire* 7°10N 3°58W 262 D4
Dapa *Phil.* 9°46N 126°3E 233 G6
Dapaong *Togo* 10°55N 0°16E 263 C5
Dapchi *Nigeria* 12°32N 11°31E 263 C7
Dapiak, Mt. *Phil.* 8°15N 123°28E 233 G4
Dapitan *Phil.* 8°39N 123°25E 233 G4
Dapoli *India* 17°46N 73°11E 244 F1
Daporijo *India* 27°59N 94°13E 241 B5
Daqahlîya □ *Egypt* 30°55N 31°30E 251 H2
Daqing *China* 46°35N 125°0E 219 B13
Daqing Shan *China* 40°40N 111°0E 226 D6
Daqq-e Sorkh, Kavīr *Iran* 33°45N 52°50E 247 C7
Daqu Shan *China* 30°25N 122°20E 229 B14
Dar Banda *Africa* 8°0N 23°0E 254 F6
Dar el Beida = Casablanca *Morocco* 33°36N 7°36W 260 B3
Dar es Salaam *Tanzania* 6°50S 39°12E 268 D4
Dar Mazār *Iran* 29°14N 57°20E 247 D8
Dar Rounga *C.A.R.* 0°45N 22°20E 264 A4
Dār Ta'izzah *Syria* 36°20N 36°52E 250 B7
Dar'ā *Syria* 32°36N 36°7E 250 F7
Dar'ā □ *Syria* 32°55N 36°10E 250 F7
Dara Dere = Zlatograd *Bulgaria* 41°22N 25°7E 203 E9
Dārāb *Iran* 28°50N 54°30E 247 D7
Daraban *Pakistan* 31°44N 70°20E 242 D4
Darabani *Romania* 48°10N 26°39E 183 B11
Darai Hills *Papua N. G.* 7°8S 143°33E 286 D2
Daraina *Madag.* 13°12S 49°40E 272 A2
Daraj *Libya* 30°10N 10°28E 258 B2
Darakeh *Iran* 35°49N 51°22E 141 A2
Daram *Phil.* 11°38N 124°48E 233 F5
Dārān *Iran* 32°59N 50°24E 247 C6
Đaravica = Gjeravicë *Kosovo* 42°32N 20°8E 202 D4
Daraw *Egypt* 24°22N 32°51E 256 C3
Dārayyā *Syria* 33°28N 36°15E 250 E7
Darazo *Nigeria* 11°1N 10°24E 263 C7
Darband *Tehrān, Iran* 35°49N 51°27E 141 A2
Darband *Pakistan* 34°20N 72°50E 242 B5
Darband, Kūh-e *Iran* 31°34N 57°8E 247 D8
Darbhanga *India* 26°15N 85°55E 243 F11
Darburruk *Somalia* 9°44N 44°31E 267 C5
Darby, C. *U.S.A.* 64°19N 162°47W 303 D7
D'Arcy *Canada* 50°33N 122°29W 296 C4
Darda *Croatia* 45°40N 18°41E 182 E3
Darđanë *Kosovo* 42°35N 21°35E 202 D5
Dardanelle *Ark., U.S.A.* 35°13N 93°9W 314 D8
Dardanelle *Calif., U.S.A.* 38°20N 119°50W 306 G7
Dardanelles = Çanakkale Boğazı *Turkey* 40°17N 26°32E 203 F10
Dare ➝ *Ethiopia* 7°20N 42°11E 257 F5
Darende *Turkey* 38°31N 37°30E 212 C7
Dārestān *Iran* 29°9N 58°42E 247 D8
Darfield *N.Z.* 43°29S 172°7E 285 D7
Darfo-Boario Terme *Italy* 45°53N 10°11E 196 C7
Dārfūr *Sudan* 13°40N 24°0E 259 F4
Dargai *Pakistan* 34°25N 71°55E 242 B4
Dargaville *N.Z.* 35°57S 173°52E 284 B2
Dargol *Niger* 13°54N 1°22E 263 C5
Darhan *Mongolia* 49°37N 106°21E 218 B10
Darhan Muminggan Lianheqi *China* 41°40N 110°28E 226 D6
Dari *South Sudan* 5°48N 30°26E 257 F3
Darıca *Turkey* 40°45N 29°23E 212 B3
Darien *U.S.A.* 31°23N 81°26W 316 D8
Darién, G. del *Caribbean* 9°0N 77°0W 320 E4
Darién, Serranía del *Cent. Amer.* 8°30N 77°30W 320 E4
Darién △ *Panama* 7°36N 77°57W 320 E4
Dariganga = Ovoot *Mongolia* 45°21N 113°45E 226 B7
Daringbadi *India* 19°54N 84°8E 244 E7
Dario, Palazzo *Venice, Italy* 142 c2
Darjeeling = Darjiling *India* 27°3N 88°18E 241 B2
Darjiling *India* 27°3N 88°18E 241 B2
Darkan *Australia* 33°20S 116°43E 279 F2
Darke Peak *Australia* 33°27S 136°12E 282 B2
Darkhana *Pakistan* 30°39N 72°11E 242 D5
Darkhazīneh *Iran* 31°54N 48°39E 247 D6
Darkot Pass *Pakistan* 36°45N 73°26E 243 A5
Darling ➝ *Australia* 34°4S 141°54E 282 C4
Darling Downs *Australia* 27°30S 150°30E 281 D5
Darling Harbour *Sydney, Australia* 139 b1
Darling Point *Australia* 33°52S 151°15E 139 B2
Darling Ra. *Australia* 32°30S 116°20E 279 F2
Darlington *Durham, U.K.* 54°32N 1°33W 168 C6
Darlington *Fla., U.S.A.* 30°57N 86°3W 316 E3
Darlington *S.C., U.S.A.* 34°18N 79°52W 315 D15
Darlington *Wis., U.S.A.* 42°41N 90°7W 310 B6
Darlington □ *U.K.* 54°32N 1°33W 168 C6
Darlington, L. *S. Africa* 33°10S 25°9E 270 D4
Darlington Point *Australia* 34°37S 146°1E 283 C7
Darlot, L. *Australia* 27°48S 121°35E 279 E3
Darłowo *Poland* 54°25N 16°25E 184 D3
Dărmănești *Bacău, Romania* 46°21N 26°33E 183 D11
Dărmănești *Suceava, Romania* 47°44N 26°9E 183 C11
Darmstadt *Germany* 49°51N 8°39E 179 F4
Darnah *Libya* 32°45N 22°45E 258 B4
Darnah □ *Libya* 31°0N 23°40E 258 B4
Darnall *S. Africa* 29°23S 31°18E 271 C5
Darney *France* 48°5N 6°2E 173 D13
Darnick *Australia* 32°48S 143°38E 282 B5
Darnley *Australia* 9°35S 143°46E 280 a
Darnley, C. *Antarctica* 68°0S 69°0E 151 C6
Darnley B. *Canada* 69°30N 123°30W 294 D7
Daroca *Spain* 41°9N 1°25W 196 D3
Daror *Ethiopia* 8°14N 44°42E 267 C5
Darou-Mousti *Senegal* 15°3N 16°3W 262 B1
Darr ➝ *Australia* 23°39S 143°50E 280 C3
Darra Pezu *Pakistan* 32°19N 70°44E 242 C4
Darran Mts. *N.Z.* 44°37S 167°59E 285 E2
Darreh Shahr *Iran* 33°7N 47°22E 213 F12
Darrequeira *Argentina* 37°42S 63°10W 334 D3
Darrington *U.S.A.* 48°15N 121°36W 304 B3
Darrūs *Iran* 35°46N 51°27E 141 A2
Darsah *Yemen* 12°56N 53°16E 249 D6
Darsana *Bangla.* 23°35N 88°48E 241 D2
Darsi *India* 15°46N 79°44E 245 G4
Darsser Ort *Germany* 54°28N 12°32E 178 A8
Dart ➝ *U.K.* 50°24N 3°39W 169 G4
Dartford *U.K.* 51°26N 0°13E 125 B5
Dartmoor *Vic., Australia* 37°56S 141°19E 282 D4
Dartmoor *Devon, U.K.* 50°38N 3°57W 169 G4
Dartmoor △ *U.K.* 50°37N 3°59W 169 G4
Dartmouth *N.S., Canada* 44°40N 63°30W 299 D7
Dartmouth *Devon, U.K.* 50°21N 3°36W 169 G4
Dartmouth, L. *Queens., Australia* 26°4S 145°18E 281 D4
Dartmouth, L. *Vic., Australia* 36°34S 147°32E 283 D7
Dartuch, C. = Artrutx, C. de *Spain* 39°55N 3°49E 206 B4
Daru *Papua N. G.* 9°3S 143°13E 286 E2
Daruvar *Croatia* 45°35N 17°14E 182 E2
Darvaza = Içoguz *Turkmenistan* 40°11N 58°24E 216 D5
Darvel, Teluk = Lahad Datu, Telok *Malaysia* 4°50N 118°20E 235 B5
Darvi *Mongolia* 46°27N 94°7E 217 C12
Darwen *U.K.* 53°42N 2°29W 168 D5
Darwendale *Zimbabwe* 17°41S 30°33E 271 A5
Darwha *India* 20°15N 77°45E 244 D3
Darwin *N. Terr., Australia* 12°25S 130°51E 278 B5
Darwin *Calif., U.S.A.* 36°15N 117°35W 307 J9
Darwin, Mt. *Chile* 54°47S 69°55W 336 D3
Darwin, Volcán *Ecuador* 0°10S 91°18W 330 a
Darya Ganj *Delhi, India* 120 a3
Darya Khan *Pakistan* 31°48N 71°6E 242 D4
Daryapur *India* 20°55N 77°20E 244 D3
Daryoi Amu = Amudarya ➝ *Uzbekistan* 43°58N 59°34E 216 D5
Dās *U.A.E.* 25°20N 53°30E 247 E7
Dashahe *China* 42°44N 128°10E 224 A4
Dashen, Ras *Ethiopia* 13°8N 38°26E 257 E4
Dasher *U.S.A.* 30°45N 83°13W 316 E6
Dashetai *China* 41°0N 109°5E 226 D5
Dashi *China* 23°1N 113°17E 121 B2
Dashiqiao *China* 40°38N 122°30E 227 D12
Dashkesan = Daşkäsän *Azerbaijan* 40°25N 46°0E 191 K7
Dashköpri *Turkmenistan* 36°16N 62°8E 247 B9
Dasht ➝ *Pakistan* 25°10N 61°40E 240 D1
Dasht-i-Tahlab *Pakistan* 28°40N 62°25E 240 C1
Dashu = Tashu *Taiwan* 22°41N 120°25E 225 D2
Daska *Pakistan* 32°20N 74°20E 242 C6
Daşkäsän *Azerbaijan* 40°25N 46°0E 191 K7
Dasmariñas *Phil.* 14°20N 120°56E 232 D3
Daşoguz *Turkmenistan* 41°49N 59°58E 216 D5
Dasol B. *Phil.* 15°52N 119°50E 232 D2
Dassa *Benin* 7°46N 2°14E 263 D5
Dasuya *India* 31°49N 75°38E 242 D6
Datadian *Indonesia* 2°1N 115°13E 235 B5
Datansha *China* 23°8N 113°12E 121 B2
Datça *Turkey* 36°46N 27°40E 205 E9
Date *Japan* 42°28N 140°52E 220 C10
Datia *India* 25°39N 78°27E 243 G8
Datian *China* 25°40N 117°50E 229 E11
Datong *Anhui, China* 30°48N 117°44E 229 B11
Datong *Qinghai, China* 36°20N 102°50E 218 D9
Datong *Shanxi, China* 40°6N 113°18E 226 D7
Datong He ➝ *China* 32°54N 69°46E 242 C3
Dattakhel *Pakistan*
Dattapur = Dhamangaon *India* 20°48N 78°9E 244 D4
Datteln *Germany* 51°39N 7°21E 178 D3
Datu, Tanjung *Indonesia* 2°5N 109°39E 235 B3
Datu Piang *Phil.* 7°2N 124°30E 233 H5
Datuk, Tanjong = Datu, Tanjung *Indonesia* 2°5N 109°39E 235 B3
Datun *China* 40°0N 116°23E 114 B2
Daua = Dawa ➝ *Africa* 4°11N 42°6E 257 G5
Daud Khel *Pakistan* 32°53N 71°34E 242 C4
Daudnagar *India* 25°2N 84°24E 243 G11
Daugava ➝ *Latvia* 57°4N 24°3E 188 D3
Daugavpils *Latvia* 55°53N 26°32E 188 E4
Daulatabad *India* 19°57N 75°15E 244 E2
Daulatpur *India* 28°44N 77°6E 120 a1
Daule *Ecuador* 1°56S 79°56W 328 D2
Daule ➝ *Ecuador* 2°10S 79°52W 328 D2
Daule-Peripa, Presa *Ecuador* 1°0S 79°30W 328 D2
Daulpur *India* 26°45N 77°59E 242 F7
Daun *Germany* 50°11N 6°49E 179 E2
Daund *India* 18°26N 74°40E 244 E2
Daung Kyun *Myanmar* 12°13N 98°4E 237 F2
Dauphin *Man., Canada* 51°9N 100°5W 297 C8
Dauphin *Pa., U.S.A.* 40°22N 76°56W 312 F8
Dauphin L. *Canada* 51°20N 99°45W 297 C9
Dauphiné *France* 45°15N 5°25E 175 C9
Daura *Borno, Nigeria* 11°31N 11°24E 263 C7
Daura *Katsina, Nigeria* 13°2N 8°21E 263 C6
Daurada, Costa *Spain* 41°12N 1°15E 196 D6
Dausa *India* 26°52N 76°20E 242 F7
Däväçi *Azerbaijan* 41°15N 48°57E 191 K9
Davangere *India* 14°25N 75°55E 245 G2
Davao *Phil.* 7°0N 125°40E 233 H5
Davao □ *Phil.* 7°50N 125°55E 233 H5
Davao del Sur □ *Phil.* 7°0N 125°30E 233 H5
Davao G. *Phil.* 6°30N 125°48E 233 H5
Davao Occidental □ *Phil.* 6°0N 125°30E 233 H5
Davao Oriental □ *Phil.* 7°10N 126°30E 233 H6
Dāvar Panāh = Sarāvān *Iran* 27°25N 62°15E 247 E9
Davenport *Calif., U.S.A.* 37°1N 122°12W 306 H4
Davenport *Fla., U.S.A.* 28°10N 81°36W 317 G8
Davenport *Iowa, U.S.A.* 41°32N 90°35W 310 C6
Davenport *Wash., U.S.A.* 47°39N 118°9W 304 C4
Davenport Ra. *Australia* 20°28S 134°0E 280 C1
Davenport Range △ *Australia* 20°36S 134°22E 280 C1
Daventry *U.K.* 52°16N 1°10W 169 E6
David *Panama* 8°30N 82°30W 320 E3
David City *U.S.A.* 41°15N 97°8W 308 E5
David Glacier *Antarctica* 75°20S 162°0E 151 D11
David Gorodok = Davyd Haradok *Belarus* 52°4N 27°8E 177 B14
David's Citadel *Jerusalem* 123 b3
David's Tomb *Jerusalem* 123 b3
Davidson *Canada* 51°16N 105°59W 297 C7
Davidson, Mt. *U.S.A.* 37°44N 122°27W 136 B2
Davidson Mts. *U.S.A.* 68°41N 142°22W 303 B12
Davidson's Mains *U.K.* 55°58N 3°16W 121 B2
Davie *U.S.A.* 26°3N 80°14W 129 B2
Davis *Antarctica* 68°34S 77°55E 151 C6
Davis *Calif., U.S.A.* 38°33N 121°44W 306 G5
Davis Dam *U.S.A.* 35°12N 114°34W 307 K12
Davis Mts. *U.S.A.* 30°50N 103°55W 314 F3
Davis Sea *Antarctica* 66°0S 92°0E 151 C7
Davis Str. *N. Amer.* 65°0N 58°0W 295 D19
Davisboro *U.S.A.* 32°59N 82°36W 316 C7
Davison *U.S.A.* 43°2N 83°31W 311 A13
Davlos *Cyprus* 35°25N 33°54E 207 E9
Davo ➝ *Côte d'Ivoire* 5°0N 6°10W 262 D3
Davos *Switz.* 46°48N 9°49E 179 J5
Dāvūdiyeh *Iran* 35°45N 51°25E 141 A2
Davutlar *Turkey* 37°43N 27°17E 205 D9
Davy L. *Canada* 58°53N 108°18W 297 B7
Davyd Haradok *Belarus* 52°4N 27°8E 177 B14
Davydkovo *Russia* 55°43N 37°29E 129 B1
Dawa ➝ *Africa* 4°11N 42°6E 257 G5
Dawaki *Bauchi, Nigeria* 9°25N 9°33E 263 D6
Dawaki *Kano, Nigeria* 12°5N 8°23E 263 C6
Dawei *Myanmar* 14°2N 98°12E 236 E2
Dawes Ra. *Australia* 24°40S 150°40E 280 C5
Dawidy *Poland* 52°8N 20°58E 143 C1
Dawkah *Oman* 18°39N 54°5E 249 C6
Dawley = Telford *U.K.* 52°40N 2°27W 169 E5
Dawlish *U.K.* 50°35N 3°28W 169 G4
Dawmat al Jandal *Si. Arabia* 29°55N 39°40E 246 D3
Dawna Ra. *Myanmar* 16°30N 98°30E 236 D2
Dawnyein *Myanmar* 15°54N 95°36E 241 G5
Dawqah *Si. Arabia* 19°36N 40°54E 248 C3
Dawrān *Yemen* 14°45N 44°12E 248 D4
Dawros Hd. *Ireland* 54°50N 8°33W 166 B3
Dawson *U.S.A.* 31°46N 84°27W 316 D5
Dawson, I. *Chile* 53°50S 70°50W 336 D2
Dawson B. *Canada* 52°53N 100°49W 297 C8
Dawson City *Canada* 64°10N 139°30W 294 E4
Dawson Creek *Canada* 55°45N 120°15W 296 B4
Dawson Inlet *Canada* 61°50N 93°25W 297 A10
Dawson Ra. *Australia* 24°30S 149°48E 280 C4
Dawu *Hubei, China* 31°34N 114°7E 229 B10
Dawu *Sichuan, China* 30°55N 101°10E 228 B3
Dawwah *Oman* 20°38N 58°48E 249 B7
Dawwara, Ras id- *Malta* 35°52N 14°21E 206 F7
Dax *France* 43°44N 1°3W 174 E2
Daxi = Tach'i *Taiwan* 24°53N 121°17E 225 B3
Daxian *China* 31°15N 107°23E 228 B6
Daxin *China* 22°50N 107°11E 228 F6
Daxindian *China* 37°30N 120°50E 227 F11
Daxing *China* 39°47N 116°24E 114 C2
Daxinggou *China* 43°25N 129°40E 227 C15
Daxue Shan *Sichuan, China* 30°30N 101°30E 228 B3
Daxue Shan *Yunnan, China* 23°42N 99°48E 228 F2
Day *U.S.A.* 30°12N 83°17W 316 E6
Daya el Khadra *Mauritania* 25°14N 6°2W 260 C3
Dayang He ➝ *China* 39°51N 123°38E 224 C1
Dayao *China* 25°43N 101°20E 228 E3
Daye *China* 30°6N 114°58E 229 B10
Dayet en Naharat *Mali* 17°39N 3°10W 262 B4
Dayi *China* 30°41N 103°29E 228 B4
Dāykondī □ *Afghan.* 34°0N 66°0E 240 B2
Daylesford *Australia* 37°21S 144°9E 282 D6
Dayong = Zhangjiajie *China* 29°11N 110°30E 229 C8
Dayr az Zawr *Syria* 35°20N 40°5E 213 E9
Dayr az Zawr □ *Syria* 34°50N 40°0E 213 E9
Daysland *Canada* 52°50N 112°20W 296 C6
Dayton *Iowa, U.S.A.* 42°16N 94°4W 310 B2
Dayton *Nev., U.S.A.* 39°14N 119°36W 306 F7
Dayton *Ohio, U.S.A.* 39°45N 84°12W 311 E12
Dayton *Pa., U.S.A.* 40°53N 79°15W 312 F5
Dayton *Tenn., U.S.A.* 35°30N 85°1W 315 D12
Dayton *Wash., U.S.A.* 46°19N 117°59W 304 C5
Dayton *Wyo., U.S.A.* 44°53N 107°16W 304 D10
Daytona Beach *U.S.A.* 29°13N 81°1W 317 F8
Dayu *China* 25°24N 114°22E 229 E10
Dayuan = Tayuan *Taiwan* 25°3N 121°11E 225 A3
Dayville *U.S.A.* 44°28N 119°32W 304 D4
Dazaifu *Japan* 33°32N 130°32E 222 D2
Dazhu *China* 30°41N 107°15E 228 B6
Dazkırı *Turkey* 37°57N 29°52E 205 D11
Dazu *China* 29°40N 105°42E 228 C5
De Aar *S. Africa* 30°39S 24°0E 270 D3
De Armanville *U.S.A.* 33°38N 85°45W 316 B4
De Bary *U.S.A.* 28°54N 81°18W 317 G8
De Forest *U.S.A.* 43°15N 89°20W 310 A7
De Funiak Springs *U.S.A.* 30°43N 86°7W 316 E3
De Grey ➝ *Australia* 20°12S 119°13E 278 D2
De Haan *Belgium* 51°16N 3°2E 170 C3
De Hoop △ *S. Africa* 34°30S 20°28E 270 D3
De Kalb Junction *U.S.A.* 44°30N 75°16W 313 B9
De Land *U.S.A.* 29°2N 81°18W 317 F8
De Leon *U.S.A.* 32°7N 98°32W 314 E5
De Leon Springs *U.S.A.* 29°7N 81°21W 317 F8
De Long Mts. *U.S.A.* 68°10N 163°30W 303 B7
De Panne *Belgium* 51°6N 2°34E 170 C2
De Pere *U.S.A.* 44°27N 88°4W 308 C9
De Queen *U.S.A.* 34°2N 94°21W 314 D7
De Quincy *U.S.A.* 30°27N 93°26W 314 F8
De Ruyters *U.S.A.* 42°45N 75°53W 313 D9
De Smet *U.S.A.* 44°23N 97°33W 308 C5
De Soto *Mo., U.S.A.* 38°8N 90°34W 310 F6
De Soto *Tex., U.S.A.* 32°35N 96°51W 120 C5
De Soto City *U.S.A.* 27°27N 81°24W 317 H8
De Tour Village *U.S.A.* 46°0N 83°56W 309 B12
De Witt *Ark., U.S.A.* 34°18N 91°20W 314 D9
De Witt *Iowa, U.S.A.* 41°49N 90°33W 310 C6
De Witt *Mich., U.S.A.* 42°51N 84°34W 311 B12
Dead L. *U.S.A.* 30°10N 85°10W 316 E4
Dead Sea *Asia* 31°30N 35°30E 251 G6
Deadhorse *U.S.A.* 70°11N 148°27W 303 A10
Deadman B. *U.S.A.* 29°30N 83°30W 317 F6
Deadwood *U.S.A.* 44°23N 103°44W 308 C2
Deadwood L. *Canada* 59°10N 128°30W 296 B3
Deal *U.K.* 51°13N 1°25E 169 F9
Deal I. *Australia* 39°30S 147°20E 281 F4
Dealesville *S. Africa* 28°41S 25°44E 270 C4
De'an *China* 29°21N 115°46E 229 C10
Dean ➝ *Canada* 52°49N 126°58W 296 C3
Dean, Forest of *U.K.* 51°45N 2°33W 169 F5
Dean Chan. *Canada* 52°30N 127°15W 296 C3
Deán Funes *Argentina* 30°20S 64°20W 334 C3
Dearborn *Mich., U.S.A.* 42°19N 83°10W 311 B13

E

F

H

J

K

Kisigo ⌓ Tanzania 6°27S 34°17E 268 D3
Kisii Kenya 0°40S 34°45E 268 C3
Kisiju Tanzania 7°23S 39°19E 268 D4
Kısıklı Turkey 41°1N 29°2E 122 B2
Kisir Turkey 41°0N 43°5E 213 B10
Kisizi Uganda 1°0S 29°58E 268 C2
Kiska I. U.S.A. 51°59N 177°30E 303 L2
Kiskomárom = Zalakomár Hungary 46°33N 17°10E 182 D2
Kiskörei-víztároló Hungary 47°31N 20°36E 182 C5
Kiskőrös Hungary 46°37N 19°20E 182 D4
Kiskundorozsma Hungary 46°16N 20°5E 182 D5
Kiskunfélegyháza Hungary 46°42N 19°53E 182 D4
Kiskunhalas Hungary 46°28N 19°37E 182 D4
Kiskunmajsa Hungary 46°30N 19°48E 182 D4
Kiskunsági △ Hungary 46°39N 19°30E 182 D4
Kislovodsk Russia 43°50N 42°45E 191 J6
Kismaayo Somalia 0°22S 42°32E 267 E5
Kismayu △ Somalia 1°25N 41°30E 267 D5
Kiso-Gawa → Japan 35°20N 136°45E 223 B8
Kiso-Sammyaku Japan 35°45N 137°45E 223 B9
Kisofukushima Japan 35°52N 137°43E 223 B9
Kisoro Uganda 1°17S 29°48E 268 C2
Kispest Hungary 47°27N 19°8E 117 B2
Kissamos Greece 35°29N 23°38E 207 E4
Kissamou, Kolpos Greece 35°30N 23°38E 207 E4
Kissidougou Guinea 9°5N 10°5W 262 D2
Kissimmee U.S.A. 28°18N 81°24W 317 G8
Kissimmee → U.S.A. 27°9N 80°52W 317 H8
Kissimmee, L. U.S.A. 27°55N 81°17W 317 H8
Kississing L. Canada 55°10N 101°20W 297 B8
Kissónerga Cyprus 34°49N 32°24E 207 F8
Kissu, J. Sudan 21°37N 25°10E 256 C2
Kista Sweden 59°24N 17°57E 139 A1
Kistanje Croatia 43°58N 15°55E 199 E12
Kistna = Krishna → India 15°57N 80°59E 245 G5
Kisújszállás Hungary 47°12N 20°50E 182 C5
Kisuki Japan 35°17N 132°54E 222 B4
Kisumu Kenya 0°3S 34°45E 268 C3
Kisvárda Hungary 48°14N 22°4E 182 B7
Kiswani Tanzania 4°5S 37°57E 268 C4
Kiswere Tanzania 9°27S 39°30E 269 D4
Kit Carson U.S.A. 38°46N 102°48W 304 G12
Kita Ōsaka, Japan 34°41N 135°30E 133 A2
Kita Tōkyō, Japan 35°44N 139°44E 140 A3
Kita Mali 13°5N 9°25W 262 C3
Kita-Ura Japan 36°0N 140°34E 223 B12
Kitaibaraki Japan 36°50N 140°45E 221 F10
Kitakami Japan 39°20N 141°10E 220 E10
Kitakami-Gawa → Japan 38°25N 141°19E 220 E10
Kitakami-Sammyaku Japan 39°30N 141°30E 220 E10
Kitakata Japan 37°39N 139°52E 220 F9
Kitakyūshū Japan 33°50N 130°50E 222 D2
Kitale Kenya 1°0N 35°0E 268 B4
Kitami Japan 43°48N 143°54E 220 C11
Kitami-Sammyaku Japan 44°22N 142°43E 220 B11
Kitangiri, L. Tanzania 4°5S 34°20E 268 C3
Kitanglad △ Phil. 8°57N 124°21E 233 G5
Kitano Hana Iwo Jima 24°49N 141°20E 288 b
Kitano-Kaikyō Japan 34°17N 134°58E 222 C6
Kitaotao Phil. 7°40N 125°1E 233 H5
Kitava I. Papua N. G. 8°40S 151°20E 286 E6
Kitaya Tanzania 10°38S 40°8E 269 E5
Kitazawa Japan 35°39N 139°40E 140 B3
Kitcharao Phil. 9°27N 125°36E 233 G5
Kitchener Canada 43°27N 80°29W 312 C4
Kitee Finland 62°5N 30°8E 188 A6
Kitega = Gitega Burundi 3°26S 29°56E 268 C2
Kitengo Dem. Rep. of the Congo 7°26S 24°8E 265 D4
Kitgum Uganda 3°17N 32°52E 268 B3
Kíthira = Kythira Greece 36°8N 23°0E 204 E5
Kíthnos = Kythnos Greece 37°26N 24°27E 204 D6
Kiti Cyprus 34°50N 33°34E 207 F9
Kiti, C. Cyprus 34°48N 33°36E 207 F9
Kitikmeot Canada 67°0N 110°0W 294 D9
Kitimat Canada 54°3N 128°38W 296 C3
Kitinen → Finland 67°14N 27°27E 160 C22
Kitiyab Sudan 17°13N 33°35E 257 D3
Kitombe Dem. Rep. of the Congo 5°22S 18°59E 265 D3
Kitridge Pt. Barbados 13°9N 59°25W 323 r
Kitros Greece 40°22N 22°34E 202 F6
Kitsman Ukraine 48°26N 25°46E 183 B10
Kitsuki Japan 33°25N 131°37E 222 D3
Kittakittaooloo, L. Australia 28°3S 138°14E 281 D2
Kittanning U.S.A. 40°49N 79°31W 312 F5
Kittatinny Mt. U.S.A. 41°19N 74°39W 313 F10
Kittery U.S.A. 43°5N 70°45W 313 C14
Kittilä Finland 67°40N 24°51E 160 C21
Kitui Kenya 1°17S 38°0E 268 C4
Kitui □ Kenya 1°30S 38°25E 268 C4
Kitwanga Canada 55°6N 128°4W 296 B3
Kitwe Zambia 12°54S 28°13E 269 E2
Kityang = Jieyang China 23°35N 116°21E 229 F11
Kitzbühel Austria 47°27N 12°24E 180 D5
Kitzbühler Alpen Austria 47°20N 12°20E 180 D5
Kitzingen Germany 49°44N 10°9E 179 F6
Kiukiang = Jiujiang China 29°42N 115°58E 229 C10
Kiunga Papua N. G. 6°7S 141°18E 286 D1
Kiunga Marine ⌓ Kenya 2°1S 41°14E 268 C5
Kivalina U.S.A. 67°44N 164°33W 303 C6
Kivalliq Canada 62°0N 97°30W 294 E12
Kivarli India 24°33N 72°46E 242 G5
Kivertsi Ukraine 50°50N 25°28E 177 C13
Kividhes Cyprus 34°46N 32°51E 207 F8
Kivik Sweden 55°41N 14°13E 163 J8
Kivistö Finland 60°18N 24°50E 121 B2
Kivotos Greece 40°13N 21°26E 202 F5
Kivu, L. Dem. Rep. of the Congo 1°48S 29°0E 268 C2
Kiwai I. Papua N. G. 8°35S 143°30E 286 E2
Kiwirrkurra Australia 22°49S 127°45E 278 D4
Kiwirrkurra ✿ Australia 22°49S 127°45E 278 D4
Kiyev = Kyyiv Ukraine 50°30N 30°28E 177 C16
Kiyevskoye Vdkhr. = Kyyivske Vdskh. Ukraine 51°0N 30°25E 177 C16
Kıyıköy Turkey 41°38N 28°5E 203 E12
Kiza → Japan 34°37N 135°27E 133 B1
Kizel Russia 59°3N 57°40E 186 C10
Kizhi, Ostrov Russia 62°4N 35°13E 188 B8
Kiziba-Baluba ⌓ Dem. Rep. of the Congo 11°50S 28°0E 269 E2
Kiziguru Rwanda 1°46S 30°23E 268 C3
Kızıl Adalar Turkey 40°52N 29°5E 203 F13
Kızıl Dağ Turkey 36°19N 35°57E 250 B6
Kızıl Irmak → Turkey 41°44N 35°58E 212 B6
Kizil Jilga China 35°26N 78°50E 243 B8
Kizil Yurt Russia 43°13N 46°54E 191 J8
Kızılcabölük Turkey 37°37N 29°1E 205 D11
Kızılcadağ Turkey 37°1N 29°58E 205 D11
Kızılcahamam Turkey 40°30N 32°30E 212 B5
Kızıldağ △ Turkey 38°5N 31°20E 246 B1
Kızılhisar Turkey 37°32N 29°17E 212 D3
Kızılırmak Turkey 40°21N 33°59E 212 B5
Kızılkaya Turkey 37°18N 30°27E 205 D12
Kızılören Turkey 38°15N 30°10E 205 C12
Kızıltepe Turkey 37°12N 40°35E 213 D9
Kızıltoprak Turkey 40°58N 29°3E 122 C2
Kizimkazi Tanzania 6°28S 39°30E 268 D4
Kizlyar Russia 43°51N 46°40E 191 J8
Kizuri Japan 34°38N 135°34E 133 B2
Kizyl-Arvat = Serdar Turkmenistan 39°4N 56°23E 247 B8
Kjellerup Denmark 56°17N 9°25E 163 H3
Kjellmyra Norway 60°39N 12°1E 164 D9
Kjelsås Norway 59°57N 10°47E 133 A3
Kjølen Norway 62°3N 8°45E 164 C5
Kjölur Iceland 64°50N 19°25W 155 C7
Kjósarsýsla Iceland 64°15N 21°30W 155 C5
Kladanj Bos.-H. 44°14N 18°42E 182 F3
Kladnica Serbia 43°23N 20°2E 202 C4
Kladno Czechia 50°10N 14°7E 180 A7
Kladovo Serbia 44°36N 22°33E 202 B6
Kladow Germany 52°27N 13°9E 115 B1
Klæbu Norway 63°18N 10°29E 164 A7
Klaeng Thailand 12°47N 101°39E 236 F3
Klagan Malaysia 5°58N 117°27E 235 A5
Klagenfurt Austria 46°38N 14°20E 180 E7
Klaipėda Lithuania 55°43N 21°10E 184 C8
Klaipėda □ Lithuania 55°43N 21°7E 184 C8
Klaksvík Færoe Is. 62°14N 6°35W 160 E9
Klamath → U.S.A. 41°33N 124°5W 304 F1
Klamath Falls U.S.A. 42°13N 121°46W 304 E3
Klamath Mts. U.S.A. 41°50N 123°20W 304 F2
Klamono Indonesia 1°8S 131°30E 231 E8
Klampenborg Denmark 55°46N 12°35E 118 A3
Klampo Indonesia 0°7N 116°58E 235 B5
Klang Malaysia 3°2N 101°26E 237 L3
Klangklang Myanmar 22°41N 93°26E 241 D4
Klanjec Croatia 46°3N 15°45E 199 B12
Klappan → Canada 58°0N 129°43W 296 B3
Klara = Trysilelva → Norway 61°2N 12°35E 164 C9
Klarälven → Sweden 59°23N 13°32E 162 E7
Klässbol Sweden 59°33N 12°45E 162 E6
Klaten Indonesia 7°43S 110°36E 235 D4
Klatovy Czechia 49°23N 13°18E 180 B6
Klausenburg = Cluj-Napoca Romania 46°47N 23°38E 183 D8
Klawer S. Africa 31°44S 18°36E 270 D2
Klawock U.S.A. 55°33N 133°6W 303 J14
Klazienaveen Neths. 52°44N 7°0E 170 B6
Klé Mali 12°0N 6°28W 262 C3
Klečany Czechia 50°10N 14°24E 135 A2
Klecko Poland 52°38N 17°25E 185 F4
Kleczew Poland 52°22N 18°9E 185 F5
Kledering Austria 48°8N 16°26E 142 B2
Kleena Kleene Canada 52°0N 124°59W 296 C4
Klein Bonaire Bonaire 12°9N 68°18W 322 h
Klein Jukskei → S. Africa 26°6S 27°57E 123 A1
Klein-Karas Namibia 27°33S 18°7E 270 C2
Klein-Schlatten = Zlatna Romania 46°8N 23°11E 183 D8
Kleinbegin S. Africa 28°54S 21°40E 270 C3
Kleinmachnow Germany 52°24N 13°14E 115 B2
Kleinschönebeck Germany 52°29N 13°42E 115 B5
Klekovača Bos.-H. 44°25N 16°32E 199 D13
Klembivka Ukraine 48°23N 28°25E 183 B13
Klemetsrud Norway 59°50N 10°51E 133 A4
Klender Indonesia 6°12S 106°54E 122 A2
Klenoec N. Macedonia 41°32N 20°49E 202 E4
Klenovec Slovakia 48°36N 19°54E 181 C12
Klerksdorp S. Africa 26°53S 26°38E 270 C4
Kleszczele Poland 52°35N 23°19E 185 F10
Kletnya Russia 53°23N 33°12E 188 F7
Kletsk = Klyetsk Belarus 53°5N 26°45E 177 B14
Kletskiy Russia 49°16N 43°11E 191 F6
Kleve Germany 51°47N 6°7E 178 D2
Kličany Czechia 50°11N 14°25E 135 A2
Klickitat U.S.A. 45°49N 121°9W 304 D3
Klickitat → U.S.A. 45°42N 121°17W 306 E5
Klidhes Cyprus 35°42N 34°36E 207 E10
Klimovichi Belarus 53°36N 32°0E 188 F6
Klimovsk Russia 55°21N 37°28E 188 E9
Klin Russia 56°20N 36°48E 188 D9
Klinaklini → Canada 51°21N 125°40W 296 C3
Klinë Kosovo 42°37N 20°35E 202 D4
Klintehamn Sweden 57°24N 18°12E 163 G12
Klintsy Russia 52°50N 32°10E 189 F7
Klip → S. Africa 27°3S 29°3E 271 C4
Klipdale S. Africa 34°19S 19°57E 270 D2
Klippan Sweden 56°8N 13°10E 163 H7
Klipplaat S. Africa 33°1S 24°22E 270 D3
Klipriviersberg Nature Reserve ⌓ S. Africa 26°16S 28°2E 123 B2
Klishkivtsi Ukraine 48°26N 26°16E 183 B11
Klisura Bulgaria 42°40N 24°28E 203 D8
Kljajićevo Serbia 45°45N 19°17E 182 E4
Ključ Bos.-H. 44°32N 16°48E 199 D13
Kłobuck Poland 50°55N 18°55E 185 H5
Klockestrand Sweden 62°53N 17°55E 162 B11
Kłodawa Poland 52°15N 18°55E 185 F5
Kłodzko Poland 50°28N 16°38E 185 H3
Kløfta Norway 60°4N 11°10E 164 D8
Klondike Canada 64°0N 139°26W 294 E4
Klondike Goldrush ⌓ U.S.A. 59°27N 135°19W 303 G14
Klong Wang Chao △ Thailand 16°20N 99°9E 236 D2
Klos Albania 41°28N 20°10E 202 E4
Klosterneuburg Austria 48°18N 16°19E 142 A1
Klosters Switz. 46°52N 9°52E 179 J5
Klötze Germany 52°37N 11°10E 178 C7
Klouto Togo 6°57N 0°44E 263 D5
Klövsjö Sweden 62°32N 14°11E 162 B8
Kluane △ Canada 60°45N 139°30W 296 A1
Kluane L. Canada 61°15N 138°40W 294 E4
Kluang Malaysia 2°3N 103°18E 237 L4
Kluczbork Poland 50°58N 18°12E 185 H5
Klukhori = Karachayevsk Russia 43°50N 41°55E 191 J5
Klukwan U.S.A. 59°24N 135°54W 296 B1
Klungkung Indonesia 8°32S 115°24E 231 K18
Klyetsk Belarus 53°5N 26°45E 177 B14
Klyuchevskaya, Sopka Russia 55°50N 160°30E 215 D17
Klyuchi Russia 56°18N 160°51E 215 D17
Knaben Norway 58°40N 7°4E 164 F4
Knappavellir Iceland 63°54N 16°36W 155 D10
Knäred Sweden 56°31N 13°19E 163 H7
Knaresborough U.K. 54°1N 1°28W 168 C6
Knarvik Norway 60°32N 5°19E 164 D2
Knee L. Man., Canada 55°3N 94°45W 298 A1
Knee L. Sask., Canada 55°51N 107°0W 297 B7
Kneïss, Îs. Tunisia 34°22N 10°18E 258 B2
Knesset Jerusalem 123 b1
Knezha Bulgaria 43°30N 24°5E 203 C8
Knight I. U.S.A. 60°21N 147°45W 303 F11
Knight Inlet Canada 50°45N 125°40W 296 C3
Knighton U.K. 52°21N 3°3W 169 E4
Knights Ferry U.S.A. 37°50N 120°40W 306 H6
Knights Landing U.S.A. 38°48N 121°43W 306 G5
Knightsbridge London, U.K. 125 c2
Knightstown U.S.A. 39°48N 85°32W 311 E11
Knin Croatia 44°3N 16°17E 199 D13
Knislinge Sweden 56°12N 14°5E 163 H8
Knittelfeld Austria 47°13N 14°51E 180 D7
Knivsta Sweden 59°43N 17°48E 162 E11
Knjaževac Serbia 43°35N 22°18E 202 C6
Knob, C. Australia 34°32S 119°16E 279 F2
Knob Lake = Kawawachikamach Canada 54°48N 66°50W 299 B6
Knob Noster U.S.A. 38°46N 93°33W 310 F3
Knock Ireland 53°48N 8°55W 166 C3
Knockmealdown Mts. Ireland 52°14N 7°56W 166 D4
Knokke-Heist Belgium 51°21N 3°17E 170 C3
Knossos Greece 35°16N 25°10E 207 E6
Knowlton Canada 45°13N 72°31W 313 A12
Knox U.S.A. 41°18N 86°37W 311 C10
Knox Coast Antarctica 66°30S 108°0E 151 C8
Knoxville Ga., U.S.A. 32°47N 83°59W 316 C6
Knoxville Ill., U.S.A. 40°55N 90°17W 310 D6
Knoxville Iowa, U.S.A. 41°19N 93°6W 310 C4
Knoxville Pa., U.S.A. 41°57N 77°27W 312 E7
Knoxville Tenn., U.S.A. 35°58N 83°55W 315 D13
Knud Rasmussen Land Greenland 78°0N 60°0W 154 B4
Knysna S. Africa 34°2S 23°2E 270 D3
Knyszyn Poland 53°20N 22°56E 184 E9
Ko Kha Thailand 18°11N 99°24E 236 C2
Kō-Saki Japan 34°5N 129°13E 222 C1
Ko Tarutao △ Thailand 6°31N 99°26E 237 J2
Ko Yao Thailand 8°7N 98°35E 237 a
Koani Tanzania 6°8S 39°17E 268 D4
Koartac = Quaqtaq Canada 60°55N 69°40W 295 E18
Koba Aru, Indonesia 6°37S 134°37E 231 F8
Koba Bangka, Indonesia 2°26S 106°14E 234 C3
Köbánya Hungary 47°28N 19°9E 117 B2
Kobarid Slovenia 46°15N 13°30E 199 B10
Kobayashi Japan 31°56N 130°59E 222 F2
Kobbegem Belgium 50°55N 4°15E 116 A1
Kobdo = Hovd □ Mongolia 48°2N 91°37E 217 C12
Kōbe Japan 34°41N 135°13E 223 C7
Kobelyaky Ukraine 49°11N 34°9E 189 H8
København Denmark 55°40N 12°26E 118 A2
København ✕ (CPH) Denmark 55°37N 12°39E 118 B3
Kobenni Mauritania 15°58N 9°24W 262 B3
Kōbi-Sho E. China Sea 25°56N 123°41E 221 M1
Koblenz Germany 50°21N 7°36E 179 E3
Kobo Dem. Rep. of the Congo 4°54S 17°9E 265 C3
Kobo Ethiopia 12°2N 39°56E 257 E4
Kobryn Belarus 52°15N 24°22E 177 B13
Kobuchizawa Japan 35°52N 138°19E 223 B10
Kobuk U.S.A. 66°55N 156°52W 303 C8
Kobuk → U.S.A. 66°54N 160°38W 303 C7
Kobuk Valley △ U.S.A. 67°0N 160°0W 303 C7
Kobuleti Georgia 41°55N 41°45E 191 K5
Kobyletska Polyana Ukraine 48°3N 24°4E 183 B9
Kobylin Poland 51°43N 17°12E 185 G4
Kobylisy Czechia 50°7N 14°26E 135 B2
Kobyłka Poland 52°20N 21°10E 143 A3
Kobylkino Russia 54°8N 43°56E 190 C6
Koca → Turkey 40°8N 27°57E 203 F11
Kocabaş Turkey 37°49N 29°20E 205 D11
Kocaeli Turkey 40°45N 29°50E 203 F13
Kocaeli □ Turkey 40°45N 29°55E 203 F13
Kočane Serbia 43°12N 21°52E 202 C5
Kočani N. Macedonia 41°55N 22°25E 202 E6
Koçarlı Turkey 37°45N 27°43E 205 D9
Koceljevo Serbia 44°28N 19°50E 202 B3
Kočevje Slovenia 45°39N 14°50E 199 C11
Kocgiri = Zara Turkey 39°58N 37°43E 212 C7
Koch Bihar India 26°22N 89°29E 241 B2
Kochas India 25°15N 83°56E 243 G10
Kocher → Germany 49°13N 9°12E 179 F5
Kochi India 9°58N 76°20E 245 K3
Kōchi Japan 33°30N 133°35E 222 D5
Kōchi □ Japan 33°40N 133°30E 222 D5
Kochiu = Gejiu China 23°20N 103°10E 228 F4
Kochkor Kyrgyzstan 42°13N 75°46E 217 D9
Kochubey Russia 44°23N 46°32E 191 H8
Kock Poland 51°38N 22°27E 185 G9
Kodaira Japan 35°43N 139°28E 140 A1
Kodala India 19°38N 84°57E 244 E7
Kodanaka Japan 35°34N 139°37E 140 B2
Kodarma India 24°28N 85°36E 243 G11
Koddiyar B. Sri Lanka 8°33N 81°15E 245 K5
Kode Sweden 57°57N 11°51E 163 G5
Kodenmacho Tokyo, Japan 140 a5
Kodi Dem. Rep. of the Congo 3°34S 22°12E 264 C4
Kodiak U.S.A. 57°47N 152°24W 303 H9
Kodiak I. U.S.A. 57°30N 152°45W 303 H9
Kodikkarai = Point Calimere India 10°17N 79°49E 245 J4
Kodinar India 20°46N 70°46E 242 J4
Kodinsk Russia 58°40N 99°10E 215 D10
Kodlipet India 12°48N 75°53E 245 H2
Kodok South Sudan 9°53N 32°7E 257 F3
Kodori → Georgia 42°47N 41°10E 191 J5
Kodoro Dem. Rep. of the Congo 1°16N 20°6E 264 B4
Kodungallur = Cranganore India 10°13N 76°13E 245 J3
Kodyma Ukraine 48°6N 29°7E 183 B14
Koedoesberge S. Africa 32°40S 20°11E 270 D3
Koekelberg Belgium 50°52N 4°20E 116 A1
Koes Namibia 26°0S 19°15E 270 C2
Kofarnihon Tajikistan 38°33N 69°1E 217 E7
Kofçaz Turkey 41°58N 27°12E 203 E11
Koffiefontein S. Africa 29°30S 25°0E 270 C4
Kofiau Indonesia 1°11S 129°50E 231 E7
Köflach Austria 47°4N 15°5E 180 D8
Koforidua Ghana 6°3N 0°17W 263 D4
Kōfu Japan 35°40N 138°30E 223 B10
Koga Fukuoka, Japan 33°45N 130°25E 222 D2
Koga Ibaraki, Japan 36°11N 139°43E 223 A11
Kogaluc → Canada 56°12N 61°44W 299 A7
Koganei Japan 35°42N 139°31E 140 A2
Kogarah Australia 33°57S 151°8E 139 B1
Køge Denmark 55°27N 12°11E 163 J6
Køge Bugt Denmark 55°34N 12°24E 163 J6
Kogi □ Nigeria 7°45N 6°45E 263 D6
Kogin Baba Nigeria 7°55N 11°35E 263 D7
Kogo Eq. Guin. 1°5N 9°42E 264 B1
Kogon Uzbekistan 39°43N 64°33E 216 E6
Koh-i-Khurd Afghan. 33°30N 65°59E 242 C1
Koh-i-Maran Pakistan 29°18N 66°50E 242 E2
Koh Ker Cambodia 13°47N 104°32E 236 F5
Koh Wai Thailand 11°54N 102°25E 237 H4
Kohala Mts. U.S.A. 20°5N 155°45W 302 C6
Kohat Pakistan 33°40N 71°29E 242 C4
Kohima India 25°35N 94°10E 241 C5
Kohkīlūyeh va Būyer Aḥmadi □ Iran 31°30N 50°30E 247 D6
Kohler Ra. Antarctica 77°0S 110°0W 151 D15
Kohlfurt = Węgliniec Poland 51°18N 15°10E 185 G2
Kohlu Pakistan 29°54N 69°15E 242 E3
Kohtla-Järve Estonia 59°20N 27°20E 188 C4
Kohukohu N.Z. 35°22S 173°38E 284 B2
Kohylnyk → Ukraine 45°49N 29°40E 183 E14
Koi Sanjaq Iraq 36°5N 44°38E 213 D11
Koidu S. Leone 8°38N 10°59W 262 D2
Koihoa India 8°12N 93°29E 245 K11
Koilkuntla India 15°14N 78°19E 245 G4
Koillismaa Finland 65°44N 28°36E 160 D23
Koimbani Comoros Is. 11°37S 43°21E 272 a
Koin N. Korea 40°28N 126°18E 224 B3
Koinare Bulgaria 43°21N 24°8E 203 C8
Koindu S. Leone 8°26N 10°19W 262 D2
Koivisto = Primorsk Russia 60°22N 28°37E 188 B5
Koivupää Finland 60°18N 24°53E 121 B2
Koja Indonesia 6°8S 106°52E 122 A2
Koja Utara Indonesia 6°5S 106°53E 122 A2
Kojetín Czechia 49°21N 17°20E 181 B10
Kojŏ N. Korea 38°58N 127°58E 224 C3
Kojonup Australia 33°48S 117°10E 279 F2
Kojūr Iran 36°23N 51°43E 247 B6
Kokand = Qo'qon Uzbekistan 40°31N 70°56E 217 D8
Kokang Myanmar 23°45N 98°30E 228 F2
Kokas Indonesia 2°42S 132°26E 231 E8
Kokava Slovakia 48°35N 19°50E 181 C12
Kokcha → Afghan. 37°9N 69°24E 240 A3
Kokchetav = Kökshetaū Kazakhstan 53°20N 69°25E 217 B7
Kōke'e State Park ⌓ U.S.A. 22°6N 159°40W 302 A2
Kokemäenjoki → Finland 61°32N 21°44E 188 B1
Kokerite Guyana 7°12N 59°35W 329 B6
Kokhav Ya'akov West Bank 31°53N 35°14E 123 A2
Kokhma Russia 56°57N 41°8E 190 B5
Koki Senegal 15°30N 15°59W 262 B1
Kokiu = Gejiu China 23°20N 103°10E 228 F4
Kokkilai Sri Lanka 9°0N 80°57E 245 K5
Kokkina Cyprus 35°11N 32°36E 207 E8
Kokkola Finland 63°50N 23°8E 160 E20
Koko Nigeria 11°28N 4°29E 263 C5
Koko Head U.S.A. 21°16N 157°43W 302 K14
Koko Kyunzu Myanmar 14°7N 93°22E 245 G11
Koko Nur = Qinghai Hu China 36°40N 100°10E 218 D9
Kokobunji Japan 35°42N 139°27E 140 A1
Kokobunji-Temple Japan 35°44N 139°55E 140 A4
Kokoda Papua N. G. 8°54S 147°47E 286 E4
Kokologo Burkina Faso 12°11N 1°53W 262 C4
Kokolopozo Côte d'Ivoire 5°8N 6°5W 262 D3
Kokomo U.S.A. 40°29N 86°8W 311 D10
Kokopo Papua N. G. 4°22S 152°19E 286 C7
Kokoro Niger 14°12N 0°55E 263 C5
Koksan N. Korea 38°46N 126°40E 224 C3
Kökshetaū Kazakhstan 53°20N 69°25E 217 B7
Koksoak → Canada 58°30N 68°10W 295 F18
Kokstad S. Africa 30°32S 29°29E 271 D4
Köktal Kazakhstan 44°8N 79°48E 217 D9
Kokubu = Kirishima Japan 31°44N 130°46E 222 F2
Kokyar China 37°23N 77°10E 217 E9
Kola Indonesia 5°35S 134°30E 231 F8
Kola Russia 68°45N 33°8E 160 B25
Kola Pen. = Kolskiy Poluostrov Russia 67°30N 38°0E 186 A6
Kolachel India 8°10N 77°15E 245 K3
Kolachi → Pakistan 27°8N 67°2E 242 F2
Kolahoi India 34°12N 75°22E 243 B6
Kolahun Liberia 8°15N 10°4W 262 D2
Kolaka Indonesia 4°3S 121°46E 231 E6
Kolar India 13°12N 78°15E 245 H4
Kolar Gold Fields India 12°58N 78°16E 245 H4
Kolarängen Sweden 59°16N 18°10E 139 B3
Kolaras India 25°14N 77°36E 242 G6
Kolari Finland 67°20N 23°48E 160 C20
Kolarovgrad = Shumen Bulgaria 43°18N 26°55E 203 C10
Kolárovo Slovakia 47°54N 18°0E 181 D10
Kolasib India 24°15N 92°45E 241 C4
Kolašin Montenegro 42°50N 19°31E 202 D3
Kolayat India 27°50N 72°50E 242 F5
Kolbäck Sweden 59°34N 16°15E 162 E10
Kolbäcksån → Sweden 59°36N 16°16E 162 E10
Kolbeinsstaðir Iceland 64°59N 22°16W 155 C4
Kolberg = Kołobrzeg Poland 54°10N 15°35E 184 D2
Kolbermoor Germany 47°51N 12°4E 179 H8
Kolbio Kenya 1°8S 41°12E 267 E5
Kolbotn Norway 59°48N 10°48E 133 B3
Kolbu Norway 60°39N 10°45E 164 D7
Kolbuszowa Poland 50°15N 21°46E 185 H8
Kolchugino = Leninsk-Kuznetskiy Russia 54°44N 86°10E 217 B11
Kolchugino Russia 56°17N 39°22E 188 D10
Kolda Senegal 12°55N 14°57W 262 C2
Kolda □ Senegal 13°5N 14°50W 262 C2
Koldegi Sudan 12°3N 30°16E 257 E3
Kolding Denmark 55°30N 9°29E 163 J3
Kole Dem. Rep. of the Congo 3°16S 22°42E 264 C4
Koléa Algeria 36°38N 2°46E 261 A5
Kolepom = Dolak, Pulau Indonesia 8°0S 138°30E 231 F9
Kolguyev, Ostrov Russia 69°20N 48°30E 186 A8
Kolhapur India 16°43N 74°15E 244 F2
Kolia Côte d'Ivoire 9°46N 6°28W 262 D3
Koliganek U.S.A. 59°48N 157°25W 303 G8
Kolimbia Greece 36°15N 28°10E 206 E12
Kolín Czechia 50°2N 15°9E 180 A8
Kolind Denmark 56°21N 10°34E 163 H4
Kolkas rags Latvia 57°46N 22°37E 184 A9
Kolkata India 22°34N 88°21E 124 B2
Kolkata Maidan India 22°33N 88°21E 124 B1
Kolkata Netaji Subhash Chandra Bose Int. ✕ (CCU) India 22°38N 88°26E 124 B2
Kollam India 8°50N 76°38E 245 K3
Kölleda Germany 51°11N 11°15E 178 D7
Kollegal India 12°9N 77°9E 245 H3
Kolleru L. India 16°40N 81°10E 244 F5
Kollum Neths. 53°17N 6°10E 170 A6
Kolmanskop Namibia 26°45S 15°14E 270 C2
Köln Germany 50°56N 6°57E 178 E2
Kolno Poland 53°25N 21°56E 184 E8
Koło Warszawa, Poland 52°14N 20°56E 143 B1
Koło Wielkopolskie, Poland 52°14N 18°40E 185 F5
Kołobrzeg Poland 54°10N 15°35E 184 D2
Kolochava Ukraine 48°26N 23°41E 183 B8
Kologi Sudan 10°51N 30°58E 257 E3
Kolokani Mali 13°35N 7°45W 262 C3
Kolokinthou Greece 38°0N 23°42E 112 B2
Koloko Burkina Faso 11°5N 5°19W 262 C3
Kololo Ethiopia 7°29N 41°58E 257 F5
Kolombangara Solomon Is. 8°0S 157°5E 287 M9
Kolomna Russia 55°8N 38°45E 188 E10
Kolomyagi Russia 60°0N 30°19E 137 A1
Kolomyya Ukraine 48°31N 25°2E 183 B10
Kolondiéba Mali 11°5N 6°54W 262 C3
Kolonodale Indonesia 2°0S 121°19E 231 E6
Kolonos Greece 37°59N 23°43E 112 B2
Kolonowskie Poland 50°39N 18°22E 185 H5
Kolpashevo Russia 58°20N 83°5E 214 D9
Kolpino Russia 59°44N 30°39E 188 C6
Kolpny Russia 52°17N 37°1E 189 F9
Kolsås Norway 59°55N 10°30E 133 A2
Kolskiy Poluostrov Russia 67°30N 38°0E 186 A6
Kolskiy Zaliv Russia 69°23N 34°0E 160 B26
Kolsva Sweden 59°36N 15°51E 162 E9
Kolubara → Serbia 44°35N 20°15E 202 B4
Kolumadulu Atoll Maldives 2°22N 73°7E 272 d
Koluszki Poland 51°45N 19°46E 185 G6
Kolwezi Dem. Rep. of the Congo 10°40S 25°25E 269 E2
Kolyma → Russia 69°30N 161°0E 215 C17
Kolymskoye Nagorye Russia 63°0N 157°0E 215 C16
Kôm Hamâda Egypt 30°46N 30°41E 256 H7
Kôm Ombo Egypt 24°25N 32°52E 256 C3
Koma Tou Yialou Cyprus 35°25N 34°8E 207 E10
Komadugu Gana → Nigeria 13°5N 12°24E 263 C7
Komae Japan 35°37N 139°34E 140 B2
Komagane Japan 35°44N 137°58E 223 B9
Komagome Japan 35°43N 139°45E 140 A3
Komaki Japan 35°17N 136°55E 223 B8
Komandorskiye Is. = Komandorskiye Ostrova Russia 55°0N 167°0E 215 D17
Komandorskiye Ostrova Russia 55°0N 167°0E 215 D17
Komárno Slovakia 47°49N 18°5E 181 D11
Komarnyky Ukraine 48°59N 23°3E 182 B8
Komárom Hungary 47°43N 18°7E 182 C3
Komárom-Esztergom □ Hungary 47°35N 18°20E 182 C3
Komáromújváros = Komárom Hungary 47°43N 18°7E 182 C3
Komatipoort S. Africa 25°25S 31°55E 271 C5
Komatsu Japan 36°25N 136°30E 223 A8
Komatsushima Japan 34°0N 134°35E 222 D6
Komavangard = Sobinka Russia 56°0N 40°0E 188 E11
Komazawa Japan 35°37N 139°40E 140 B3
Komba Dem. Rep. of the Congo 2°52N 24°3E 264 B4
Kombissiri Burkina Faso 12°4N 1°20W 263 C4
Kombo Gabon 0°20S 12°22E 264 C2
Kombong India 28°7N 94°51E 241 A5
Kombori Burkina Faso 13°26N 3°56W 262 C4
Komboti Greece 39°6N 21°5E 204 B3
Kome Channel Uganda 0°10S 32°35E 268 C3
Komebail Lagoon Palau 7°25N 134°25E 288 c
Komen Slovenia 45°49N 13°45E 199 C10
Komenda Ghana 5°4N 1°28W 263 D4
Komi Cyprus 35°24N 34°0E 207 E9
Komi □ Russia 64°0N 55°0E 186 B10
Kominter = Novoshakhtinsk Russia 47°46N 39°58E 189 J10
Komintern = Marhanets Ukraine 47°40N 34°40E 189 J8
Komiža Croatia 43°3N 16°11E 199 E13
Komló Hungary 46°15N 18°16E 182 D3
Kommamur Canal India 16°0N 80°25E 245 G5
Kommunarsk = Alchevsk Ukraine 48°30N 38°45E 189 H10
Kommunizma, Pik = imeni Ismail Samani, Pik Tajikistan 39°0N 72°2E 217 E8
Komodo Indonesia 8°37S 119°20E 235 D5
Komodo △ Indonesia 8°36S 119°34E 235 D5
Komono Congo 3°10S 13°20E 264 C2
Komoran, Pulau Indonesia 8°18S 138°45E 231 F9
Komoro Japan 36°19N 138°26E 223 A10
Komotau = Chomutov Czechia 50°28N 13°23E 180 A6
Komotini Greece 41°9N 25°26E 203 E9
Komovi Montenegro 42°41N 19°39E 202 D3
Kompasberg S. Africa 31°45S 24°32E 270 D3
Kompong Chhnang = Kampong Chhnang Cambodia 12°20N 104°35E 237 F5
Kompong Chikreng Cambodia 13°5N 104°18E 236 F5
Kompong Kleang Cambodia 13°6N 104°8E 236 F5
Kompong Luong Cambodia 11°49N 104°48E 237 G5
Kompong Pranak Cambodia 13°35N 104°55E 236 F5
Kompong Som = Kampong Saom Cambodia 10°38N 103°30E 237 G4
Kompong Som, Chhung = Kampong Saom, Chaak Cambodia 10°50N 103°32E 237 G4
Kompong Speu Cambodia 11°26N 104°32E 237 G5
Kompong Sralau Cambodia 14°5N 105°46E 236 E5
Kompong Thom Cambodia 12°35N 104°51E 236 F5
Kompong Trabeck Cambodia 13°6N 105°14E 236 F5
Kompong Trach Cambodia 11°25N 105°48E 237 G5
Kompong Tralach Cambodia 11°54N 104°47E 237 G5
Komrat = Comrat Moldova 46°18N 28°40E 183 D13
Komsberg S. Africa 32°40S 20°45E 270 D3
Komsomolets = Qarabalyq Kazakhstan 53°45N 62°2E 216 B6
Komsomolets, Ostrov Russia 80°30N 95°0E 215 A10
Komsomolsk Ivanovo, Russia 57°2N 40°20E 188 D11
Komsomolsk Ukraine 49°1N 33°38E 189 H7
Komsomolsk-na-Amur Russia 50°30N 137°0E 219 A16
Komsomolskiy Russia 54°27N 45°33E 190 C7
Komsomolskoe Kazakhstan 50°25N 60°5E 216 B6
Komsomolsky = Chirchiq Uzbekistan 41°29N 69°35E 217 D7
Kömür Burnu Turkey 38°39N 26°12E 205 C8
Kon Ka Kinh △ Vietnam 14°19N 107°23E 236 E6
Kon Tum Vietnam 14°24N 108°0E 236 E7
Kon Tum, Plateau du Vietnam 14°30N 108°30E 236 E7
Kona Paschimbanga, India 22°37N 88°18E 124 B1
Kona Mali 14°57N 3°53W 262 C4
Kona Nigeria 8°57N 11°21E 263 D7
Kona ✕ (KOA) U.S.A. 19°44N 156°3W 302 D5
Kōnāhuanui U.S.A. 21°21N 157°47W 302 K14
Konakovo Russia 56°40N 36°51E 188 D9
Konala Finland 60°14N 24°52E 121 B2
Konar □ Afghan. 34°30N 71°3E 240 B3
Konarak India 19°54N 86°7E 244 E8
Konārak Iran 25°21N 60°23E 247 E9
Konārī Iran 28°13N 51°36E 247 D6
Konch India 26°0N 79°10E 243 G8
Kondagaon India 19°35N 81°35E 244 E5
Konde Tanzania 4°57S 39°45E 268 C4
Kondias Greece 39°49N 25°10E 205 B7
Kondinin Australia 32°34S 118°8E 279 F2
Kondli India 28°36N 77°19E 120 B2
Kondo Dem. Rep. of the Congo 5°35S 13°0E 265 D2
Kondoa Tanzania 4°55S 35°50E 268 C4
Kondopoga Russia 62°12N 34°17E 188 A8
Kondoz Afghan. 36°50N 68°50E 240 A3
Kondoz → Afghan. 37°0N 68°16E 240 A3
Kondratyevo Russia 57°22N 98°15E 215 D10
Kondrovo Russia 54°48N 35°56E 188 E8
Konduga Nigeria 11°35N 13°26E 263 C7
Kondukur India 15°12N 79°57E 245 G4
Kondūz □ Afghan. 36°50N 68°50E 240 A3
Koné Cameroon 8°50N 13°17E 259 G2
Koné N. Cal. 21°4S 164°52E 288 d
Köneürgench Turkmenistan 42°19N 59°10E 216 D5
Konevo Russia 62°8N 39°20E 188 A10
Kong = Khong → Cambodia 13°32N 105°58E 236 F5
Kong Côte d'Ivoire 8°54N 4°36W 262 D4
Kong, Koh Cambodia 11°20N 103°0E 237 G4
Kong Christian IX.s Land Greenland 68°0N 36°0W 154 D7
Kong Christian X.s Land Greenland 74°0N 29°0W 154 C8
Kong Frederik IX.s Land Greenland 67°0N 52°0W 154 D5
Kong Frederik VI.s Kyst Greenland 63°0N 43°0W 154 E6
Kong Frederik VIII.s Land Greenland 78°30N 26°0W 154 B8
Kong Karls Land Svalbard 79°0N 28°0E 154 B13
Kong Oscar Fjord Greenland 72°20N 24°0W 154 C8
Kongauru I. Palau 7°3N 134°16E 288 c
Kongbo C.A.R. 4°44N 21°23E 264 B4
Kongeå → Denmark 55°23N 8°39E 163 J2
Kongelunden Denmark 55°34N 12°34E 118 B3
Kongens Lyngby Denmark 55°46N 12°30E 118 A3
Kongernes Nordsjælland △ Denmark 56°5N 12°15E 163 H6
Kongerslev Denmark 56°54N 10°6E 163 H4
Kongkemul Indonesia 1°52N 116°10E 235 B5
Konglu Myanmar 27°13N 97°57E 241 B6
Kongmoon = Jiangmen China 22°32N 113°0E 229 F9
Kongo Helsinki, Finland 60°20N 24°47E 121 A1
Kongo Liberia 7°20N 11°6W 262 D2
Kongo Central □ Dem. Rep. of the Congo 5°0S 15°0E 265 D2
Kongola Namibia 17°45S 23°20E 270 A3
Kongolo Kasai-Or., Dem. Rep. of the Congo 5°26S 24°49E 265 D4
Kongolo Katanga, Dem. Rep. of the Congo 5°22S 27°0E 268 D2
Kongor South Sudan 7°1N 31°27E 257 F3
Kongossambougou ⌓ Mali 14°0N 8°30W 262 C3
Kongoulou Cameroon 2°59N 11°7E 264 B2
Kongoussi Burkina Faso 13°19N 1°32W 263 C4
Kongsberg Norway 59°39N 9°39E 164 E6
Kongsvinger Norway 60°12N 12°2E 164 D9
Kongur Shan China 38°34N 75°18E 217 E9
Kongwa Tanzania 6°11S 36°26E 268 D4
Koni Dem. Rep. of the Congo 10°40S 27°11E 269 E2
Koniakari Mali 14°35N 10°50W 262 C2
Koniecpol Poland 50°46N 19°40E 185 H6
Königgrätz = Hradec Králové Czechia 50°15N 15°50E 180 A8
Königs Wusterhausen Germany 52°19N 13°38E 178 C9
Königsberg = Chojna Poland 52°58N 14°25E 185 F1
Königsberg = Kaliningrad Russia 54°42N 20°32E 184 D7
Königsbrunn Germany 48°16N 10°54E 179 G6
Königshütte = Chorzów Poland 50°18N 18°57E 185 H5
Königslutter Germany 52°15N 10°49E 178 C6
Konin Poland 52°12N 18°15E 185 F5
Köninginhof an der Elbe = Dvůr Králové nad Labem Czechia 50°27N 15°50E 180 A8
Koninklijk Paleis Amsterdam, Neths. 112 a2
Konispol Albania 39°42N 20°10E 206 B10
Konitsa Greece 40°5N 20°48E 204 A2
Köniz Switz. 46°56N 7°25E 179 J3
Konjic Bos.-H. 43°42N 17°58E 182 G2
Konkiep Namibia 26°49S 17°15E 270 C2
Konkō Japan 34°33N 133°36E 222 C4
Konkouré → Guinea 9°50N 13°42W 262 D2
Konnagar India 22°42N 88°21E 124 A2
Könnern Germany 51°41N 11°47E 178 D7
Konnur India 16°14N 74°49E 245 F2
Kono S. Leone 8°30N 11°5W 262 D2
Konogogo Papua N. G. 3°29S 152°10E 286 B7
Konohana Japan 34°40N 135°26E 133 A1
Konongo Ghana 6°40N 1°15W 263 D4
Konos Papua N. G. 3°10S 151°44E 286 B6
Konosha Russia 61°0N 40°5E 188 B11
Kōnosu Japan 36°3N 139°31E 223 A11
Konotop Ukraine 51°12N 33°7E 189 G7
Konqi He → China 40°45N 90°10E 217 D11
Konradshof = Skawina Poland 49°59N 19°50E 185 J6
Konradshöhe Germany 52°35N 13°13E 115 A2
Konrei Palau 7°43N 134°36E 288 c
Konsankoro Guinea 9°2N 9°0W 262 D3
Końskie Poland 51°15N 20°23E 185 G7
Konsmo Norway 58°16N 7°23E 164 F4
Konstadt = Wołczyn Poland 51°1N 18°3E 185 G5
Konstancin-Jeziorna Poland 52°5N 21°7E 185 F8
Konstantinograd = Krasnohrad Ukraine 49°27N 35°27E 189 H8
Konstantinovka = Kostyantynivka Ukraine 48°32N 37°39E 189 H9
Konstantinovsk Russia 47°33N 41°10E 191 G5
Konstantynów Łódźki Poland 51°45N 19°20E 185 G6
Konstanz Germany 47°40N 9°10E 179 H5
Kont Iran 26°55N 61°50E 247 E9
Konta India 17°48N 81°23E 244 F5
Kontagora Nigeria 10°23N 5°27E 263 C6
Kontcha Cameroon 7°59N 12°15E 263 D7
Kontiolahti Finland 62°46N 29°50E 160 E23
Kontokali Greece 39°38N 19°51E 206 B9
Konya Turkey 37°52N 32°35E 212 D5
Konya □ Turkey 37°46N 32°20E 212 D5
Konya Ovası Turkey 38°9N 33°5E 212 C5
Konyin Myanmar 22°58N 94°42E 241 D5
Konz Germany 49°42N 6°34E 179 F2
Konza Kenya 1°45S 37°7E 268 C4
Koo-wee-rup Australia 38°13S 145°28E 283 E6
Koocanusa, L. Canada 49°20N 115°15W 304 B6
Kookynie Australia 29°17S 121°22E 279 E3
Ko'olau Range U.S.A. 21°35N 157°50W 302 J14
Ko'olauloa District U.S.A. 21°35N 157°55W 302 J14
Ko'olaupoko District U.S.A. 21°25N 157°50W 302 K14
Kō'Ōlina U.S.A. 21°19N 158°7W 302 K13
Koolyanobbing Australia 30°48S 119°36E 279 F2
Koondrook Australia 35°33S 144°8E 282 C6
Koonibba Australia 31°54S 133°25E 281 E1
Koorawatha Australia 34°2S 148°33E 283 C8
Koorda Australia 30°48S 117°35E 279 F2
Kooskia U.S.A. 46°9N 115°59W 304 C6
Kootenay → U.S.A. 49°19N 117°39W 296 D5
Kootenay △ Canada 51°0N 116°0W 296 C5
Kootenay L. Canada 49°45N 116°50W 304 B5
Kootingal Australia 31°3S 151°4E 283 A9
Kootjieskolk S. Africa 31°15S 20°21E 270 D3
Kopanina Czechia 50°3N 14°17E 135 B1
Kopanovka Russia 47°28N 46°50E 191 G8
Kopaonik Serbia 43°10N 20°50E 202 C4
Kopaonik △ Serbia 43°20N 20°50E 202 C4
Kopargaon India 19°51N 74°28E 244 E2
Koparkhairna India 19°6N 72°59E 130 A2
Kópasker Iceland 66°18N 16°27W 155 A10
Kópavogur Iceland 64°6N 21°55W 155 C5
Kopayhorod Ukraine 48°52N 27°53E 183 B12
Köpenick Germany 52°26N 13°35E 115 B4
Koper Slovenia 45°31N 13°44E 199 C10
Kopervik Norway 59°17N 5°17E 164 E2
Kopet Dagh Asia 38°0N 58°0E 247 B8
Kopeysk Russia 55°7N 61°37E 216 A6
Kopi Australia 33°24S 135°40E 281 E2
Köping Sweden 59°31N 16°3E 162 E10
Köpingsvik Sweden 56°53N 16°43E 163 H10
Kopište Croatia 42°48N 16°42E 199 F13
Koplik Albania 42°15N 19°25E 202 D3
Köpmanholmen Sweden 63°10N 18°35E 162 A12
Koppa India 13°33N 75°21E 245 H2
Koppal India 15°23N 76°5E 245 G3
Koppang Norway 61°34N 11°3E 164 C8
Kopparberg Sweden 59°52N 15°0E 162 E9
Koppeh Dāgh = Kopet Dagh Asia 38°0N 58°0E 247 B8
Kopperå Norway 63°24N 11°50E 164 A8
Koppies S. Africa 27°20S 27°30E 271 C4
Koppom Sweden 59°43N 12°10E 162 E6
Koprivlen Bulgaria 41°31N 23°53E 202 E7
Koprivnica Croatia 46°12N 16°45E 199 B13
Kopřivnice Czechia 49°36N 18°9E 181 B11
Koprivshtitsa Bulgaria 42°40N 24°19E 203 D8
Köprü → Turkey 36°48N 31°11E 250 B2
Köprübaşı Turkey 38°43N 28°23E 205 C10
Köprülü Turkey 36°43N 32°10E 250 B3
Köprülü △ Turkey 37°20N 31°5E 246 B1
Kopychyntsi Ukraine 49°7N 25°58E 177 D13
Kor Aban Somalia 3°58N 42°44E 267 D5
Kora △ Kenya 0°14S 38°44E 268 C4
Koraa Shiir Somalia 3°16N 46°16E 267 D6
Korab N. Macedonia 41°44N 20°40E 202 E4
Korahe Ethiopia 6°39N 44°5E 267 C5
Koral India 21°50N 73°12E 242 J5
Korangal India 17°6N 77°38E 244 E3

L

M

O

P

T

U

V

X

Y

Z